# The Palgrave Handbook of Religion, Peacebuilding, and Development in Africa

Susan M. Kilonzo • Ezra Chitando
Joram Tarusarira
Editors

# The Palgrave Handbook of Religion, Peacebuilding, and Development in Africa

*Editors*
Susan M. Kilonzo
Maseno University
Maseno, Kenya

Ezra Chitando ⓘ
University of Zimbabwe
Mount Pleasant, Zimbabwe

Joram Tarusarira
University of Groningen
Groningen, The Netherlands

ISBN 978-3-031-36828-8     ISBN 978-3-031-36829-5  (eBook)
https://doi.org/10.1007/978-3-031-36829-5

© The Editor(s) (if applicable) and The Author(s), under exclusive licence to Springer Nature Switzerland AG 2023
This work is subject to copyright. All rights are solely and exclusively licensed by the Publisher, whether the whole or part of the material is concerned, specifically the rights of translation, reprinting, reuse of illustrations, recitation, broadcasting, reproduction on microfilms or in any other physical way, and transmission or information storage and retrieval, electronic adaptation, computer software, or by similar or dissimilar methodology now known or hereafter developed.
The use of general descriptive names, registered names, trademarks, service marks, etc. in this publication does not imply, even in the absence of a specific statement, that such names are exempt from the relevant protective laws and regulations and therefore free for general use.
The publisher, the authors, and the editors are safe to assume that the advice and information in this book are believed to be true and accurate at the date of publication. Neither the publisher nor the authors or the editors give a warranty, expressed or implied, with respect to the material contained herein or for any errors or omissions that may have been made. The publisher remains neutral with regard to jurisdictional claims in published maps and institutional affiliations.

Cover credit: spooh/Getty Images

This Palgrave Macmillan imprint is published by the registered company Springer Nature Switzerland AG.
The registered company address is: Gewerbestrasse 11, 6330 Cham, Switzerland

Paper in this product is recyclable.

# Foreword

I warmly welcome this very timely and strategic resource on religion, peacebuilding and Sustainable Development Goal (SDG) 16 in Africa. Interrogating the contribution of religious actors to peacebuilding and sustainable development in Africa, it is extremely relevant to religious leaders, theological institutions, governments, non-governmental organisations, development practitioners and others. I am particularly impressed by how African scholars from diverse regions of the continent have taken their time to deploy their intellectual acumen to reflect on how the continent can achieve sustainable peace, security and development. This will ensure that Africa regains its dignity and take its rightful player as a major player in global affairs.

The experience of the All Africa Conference of Churches (AACCC) is that religious actors in Africa are playing a critical role in promoting peace, justice and development. While the cynics and critics might point to the number of violent conflicts in Africa as evidence of the challenges of peacebuilding in Africa, the harsh reality is that the situation would have been even much worse if the religious actors were not involved. Despite the numerous challenges, including threats to life, religious actors in Africa continue to be advocates of peace. As the Bible enjoins, "Blessed are the peacemakers, for they shall be called children of God" (Matthew 5: 9; New Revised Standard Version Updated Edition). This handbook is a compendium of the experiences, exploits and challenges of African peacemakers.

The idea of bringing together academics, peace activists, development practitioners, ecumenical leaders and other experts to share reflections on religion, peacebuilding and sustainable development in Africa has proven to be a truly inspired one. This handbook confirms the urgency of the mantra of finding "African solutions to African problems," while working with other members of the human family. It brings together insights from diverse fields to confirm the value of multidisciplinary approaches to peacebuilding and development in Africa.

As the AACC, we recognise the value of interfaith approaches to peacebuilding and development and have been actively involved in the struggles for peace in the continent. Our central value is, "Churches in Africa together for life, peace, justice and dignity." Violent conflicts and wars blight Africa's opportunities to live up to these values. We are firmly committed to our young people thriving in Africa, hence our solidarity with them through the slogan, "Africa My Home! Africa My Future!" This vision can best be realised through peace, security and development in Africa. Then, we can achieve the "Africa We Want" as envisaged by the African Union's Agenda 2063. In pursuit of clarifying the theological implications of this continental development blueprint, the AACC continues to offer platforms for dialogue and enrichment.

A peaceful and prosperous Africa is desirable and possible. As this handbook demonstrates, religious actors are well placed to contribute towards the attainment of this vision. In informative and challenging ways, the authors have brought the focus back on religious peacebuilding in Africa. I would like to call upon the readers to engage with the proposals raised in this volume so that, collectively, we can enhance the chances of having an Africa that is peaceful, proud of itself and, with God's help, enables all the people of God to enjoy life in abundance.

All Africa Conference of Churches (AACC), Nairobi, Kenya

May 2023                                                         Fidon Mwombeki

# Contents

1 Religion, Peacebuilding and Development in Africa: An Introduction 1
Susan M. Kilonzo and Ezra Chitando

Part I Contextualising Religion, Peacebuilding and Development in Africa 17

2 Religion, Peacebuilding, and Development in Africa: A Critical Appreciation 19
Susan M. Kilonzo

3 Religion and Peacebuilding in African Religious Studies and Theology: An Overview and Preliminary Evaluation 39
Ezra Chitando

4 Religion, Peacebuilding and Development in Africa: Challenges 63
Molly Manyonganise

5 The Bible, Peace Building and Sustainable Development in Africa 79
Lovemore Togarasei and Clemence Makamure

6 Teaching About Religion, Peacebuilding and Development in Africa 93
Johan Strijdom

7   Intersectionalities: Whiteness, Religion, Peacebuilding and
    Development in Africa                                              105
    Masiiwa Ragies Gunda

8   Climate Security and Religion in Africa: Towards Sustainable
    Development Goals                                                  125
    Joram Tarusarira

Part II   Country Case Studies on Religion, Peacebuilding and
          Development in Africa                                        143

9   Religion, Conflict and Peacebuilding in Rwanda                     145
    Ezechiel Sentama

10  Building Resilience and Everyday Peace at the Micro-Levels
    in South Sudan                                                     163
    Patrick Karanja Mbugua and Abraham K. Nyuon

11  Developing Transformatively: Religion and Peace Mediation
    in Nigeria                                                         181
    Sokfa F. John

12  Ethnic and Political Conflicts Resolution in Burundi: The
    Contribution of Religious Organisations                            199
    Elias Sentamba

13  Reclaiming Everyday Peace in the Micro-Spaces in Burundi           217
    Patrick Karanja Mbugua

14  Religion and Peacebuilding in Tanzania: Institutionalisation
    of Interfaith Peace Committee                                      235
    Alexander Makulilo and Rodrick Henry

15  Religion and Peacebuilding in the Democratic Republic of the
    Congo (DRC)                                                        251
    Donatien M. Cicura

16  Religion, Peacebuilding, and Development in Uganda                 271
    David Andrew Omona

17  Indigenous Spirituality, Peacebuilding, and Development in
    Eswatini                                                                287
    Sonene Nyawo

Part III  Diverse Religions in Africa, Peacebuilding and
          Development                                                      305

18  The Role of Traditional Authorities in the Promotion of
    Electoral Justice and Peacebuilding in Ghana                           307
    Christopher Appiah-Thompson and Jim Jose

19  Rastafari Insights into Peace-building and Sustainable
    Development                                                            327
    Fortune Sibanda

20  Islamophobic Agenda: An Analysis of Media Representation
    of Radicalization and Terrorism in Kenya Since 2000                    341
    Suleiman A. Chembea

21  Islam, Conflict, Peace and Security in Africa                          363
    Mohamed Suleiman Mraja

22  Apostolic Churches and Youth Response to Social Challenges
    Post-Violence in Zimbabwe                                              381
    Obadiah Dodo

Part IV  Actors in Religion, Peacebuilding and Development                 399

23  African Traditions in the Study of Religion, Peacebuilding
    and Development in Africa: Engaging with Emmanuel
    Katongole                                                              401
    Ezra Chitando

24  Traditional Leaders and the Quest for Sustainable Peace in
    Kenya                                                                  419
    Shamsia Ramadhan

25  Decolonising Peacebuilding for Development in South Africa:
    African Traditional Spiritual Leaders as Critical Assets               435
    Beatrice Dube and Sinenhlanhla S. Chisale

26  Religious Peacebuilding's Response to Violent Extremism in Informal Settlements in Egypt  455
Patrick Karanja Mbugua and Nahed Talaat Ayoub

27  Peace, Justice, and Strong Institutions: The Role of Church Leaders During Political Electioneering Periods in Kenya  475
Simon Omare and Eunice Kamaara

28  Religion, Conflict Transformation, Peacebuilding, and Development in Ghana: The Role of the National Peace Council  493
Edmond Akwasi Agyeman

29  The All Africa Conference of Churches (AACC): Youth, Peacebuilding, and Development in Africa  513
Brian Muyunga

Part V  Interfaith Networks, Peacebuilding and Development in Africa  529

30  Interfaith Networks, Peacebuilding and Development in Africa: Analysis of the Contribution of the Fellowship of Christian Councils and Churches to Peacebuilding  531
Elias Opongo

31  Interfaith Dialogue, Peacebuilding, and Sustainable Development in Nigeria: A Case of the Nigeria Inter-Religious Council (NIREC)  553
Dodeye Uduak Williams

32  Xenophobia, Interfaith Networks, Peace Building and Development in Botswana  569
Tshenolo J. Madigele and Elizabeth P. Motswapong

33  Role of Islamic Networks in Peacebuilding and Development in Kenya, and the War on Terror  587
Newton Kahumbi

34  Re-building Muslim-Christian Relations and Everyday Peace in West Nile, Uganda  607
Patrick Karanja Mbugua

## Part VI  Gender, Religion, Peacebuilding and Development in Africa — 625

**35** Gender, Religion, Peacebuilding, and Development in Zimbabwe — 627
Lindiwe Princess Maseko and Sophia Chirongoma

**36** Religion, Feminist Peace, and Security in Nigeria and Uganda — 643
Helen Kezie-Nwoha

**37** Gender, Religion, Peacebuilding, and Development in Zambia: Doreen Mazuba Malambo's Trajectory in Peacekeeping Missions — 661
Nelly Mwale, Joseph Chita, and Habeenzu Mulunda

**38** Disability and Migration: Religious and Traditional Disability Beliefs as Causes of Migration of Zimbabwean Mothers of Children with Disabilities to South Africa — 683
Willson Tarusarira and Joram Tarusarira

**39** Gender, SDG 16, Peacebuilding and Development in Kenya — 701
Loreen Maseno

**40** The Role of Women Church Leaders in Peacebuilding and Social Economic Transformation in Post-Conflict Uganda — 717
Alice Wabule

## Part VII  Topical Issues in Religion, Peacebuilding and Development in Africa — 735

**41** Ubuntu, Peacebuilding, and Development in Africa: Reflections on the Promises and Challenges of a Popular Concept — 737
Ezra Chitando and Susan M. Kilonzo

**42** Shaping the Instruments of Peace: Religion in Digital Peacebuilding in Africa — 753
Sokfa F. John

43  Religion and Agriculture for Peacebuilding in Rwanda:
    Analysing the Role of Christian Faith-Based Organisations in
    the Post-genocide Agrarian Change                                   771
    Fortunée Bayisenge

44  Arts, Religion, Peacebuilding and Development in
    Post-conflict Northern Uganda                                       789
    Viola Karungi

Part VIII    Conclusion                                                 807

45  Imagining the Future of Religion, Peacebuilding and
    Development in Africa                                               809
    Susan M. Kilonzo and Ezra Chitando

Index                                                                   825

# Notes on Contributors

**Edmond Akwasi Agyeman** is Associate Professor in African Studies at the University of Education, Winneba, Ghana. He was a visiting lecturer at Hamburg University in 2022 and a postdoctoral research fellow at Tohoku University in 2012/2013. His research interest focuses on African migration, post-coloniality, religion, culture and development.

**Christopher Appiah-Thompson** is a Research Fellow with the Electoral Integrity Project (EIP) and a Sessional Academic at the University of Newcastle, Australia. His doctoral degree is from Australia's University of Newcastle with a thesis titled "Ghana's Disputed Elections of 1992 and 2012: The Significance of Political Culture." His research interests include political culture, electoral governance and peace and conflict studies in Africa.

**Nahed Talaat Ayoub** is a consultant for the UN agencies in Cairo, Egypt. Her research and publications interests include gender-based violence, peace and tolerance, women and peacebuilding and community peacebuilding.

**Fortunée Bayisenge** is Lecturer of policy, gender and development at the Protestant Institute of Arts and Social Sciences, Rwanda. Her research and publication interests include agrarian policy and development, gender and development, religion and development, post-war peacebuilding and development, and other related fields.

**Suleiman A. Chembea** is Lecturer of Islamic Studies at Bomet University College, a Constituent College of Moi University, Kenya. His research and publication interests include religion and social welfare practices, security, Muslim-Christian relations, religious knowledge production and dissemination dynamics, Islamic popular culture and others.

**Sophia Chirongoma** is a senior lecturer in the Religious Studies Department at Midlands State University, Zimbabwe. She is also a research fellow at the Research Institute for Theology and Religion (RITR) at the University of

South Africa. Her research interests and publications focus on the interface between culture, ecology, religion, health and gender justice.

**Sinenhlanhla S. Chisale** is a Zimbabwean and the executive director for the Ecumenical Church Leaders Forum (ECLF) in Zimbabwe. Chisale holds a Doctor of Theology in Practical Theology from University of South Africa; Master of Arts–Sociology (Cumulaude) from University of South Africa; Master of Theology and Development from University of Kwa-Zulu Natal. She is a research fellow at the University of Pretoria, Department of Practical Theology and Mission Studies. Her research focuses on pastoral care, gender, disability, gender-based violence, Ubuntu, ecology, migration and sexuality.

**Joseph Chita** is a lecturer in the Department of Religious Studies at the University of Zambia. His research and publication interests are in religion and society, comparative religion, gender, migration, education and development.

**Ezra Chitando** serves as Professor of History and Phenomenology of Religion at the University of Zimbabwe. He is also an extraordinary professor at the Desmond Tutu Centre for Religion and Social Justice at the University of the Western Cape, South Africa. He has diverse research and publication interests. These include peacebuilding, violence, masculinities, women's rights, climate change, politics and others.

**Donatien M. Cicura** is Associate Professor of Philosophy and Religion at Georgia Gwinnett College. His research focuses on Philosophy of History, African philosophy, Sub-Saharan African Identity, Philosophy of law, the influence of religion on war and peace, and the metamorphoses of religious language in the postmodern age.

**Obadiah Dodo** is Associate Professor of Conflictology. He has been with Bindura University, Zimbabwe, for over ten years before joining an international research institution beginning 2023. Obadiah's research interests cover youth violence, youth in politics, endogenous conflict resolution and society and conflict.

**Beatrice Dube** is a senior lecturer in the Department of Development Studies at the University of South Africa. Her research and publication interests include water and development, decolonial discourses, gender and water, sustainable livelihoods, rural development and others. Her most recent publications are on deficit thinking in water allocation discourses and the complexities of equity in water allocation reform.

**Masiiwa Ragies Gunda** is a programme executive of the World Council of Churches coordinating work on overcoming racism, xenophobia and related discriminations. He also serves as an adjunct professor at the Ecumenical Institute of Bossey, Switzerland. His research interests lie on the intersections of the Bible and contemporary socio-theological challenges ranging from human sexuality, gender imbalances, human relations (racism, xenophobia and Casteism).

**Mulunda Habeenzu** is a communication officer for the University of Zambia and a graduate of Peace and Conflict Studies from the Copperbelt University with a specialisation in Environment, Sustainable Development and Peace. His areas of interest include environmental peace, gender war and peace, religion, diplomacy, media and others.

**Rodrick Henry** holds a PhD in Political Science. He teaches politics at the University of Dar es Salaam. His research and publication interests include democratization, elections, conflict, peace, religion, gender, inclusive politics, traditional governance and political dialogue.

**Jim Jose** is Emeritus Professor of Politics and International Relations in the Newcastle Business School, The University of Newcastle, Australia. He has published in various areas of political theory, governance and public policy, gender politics and African political development. Further details can be found at: www.newcastle.edu.au/profile/jim-jose.

**Newton Kahumbi** is a senior lecturer, Department of Philosophy & Religious Studies, Kenyatta University, Nairobi. His research interest is Islamic Studies, Christian-Muslim Relations, Gender and Culture. His latest publications are on family planning, Shirazi civilization, freedom of religion and history of Christian–Muslim relations.

**Eunice Kamaara**, Professor of African Christian Ethics at Moi University, Eldoret, Kenya, has over 20 years' experience in holistic health research. She passionately translates this into practical development through policy influence and community engagement. She has distinguished strengths in mainstreaming gender and values in teaching/learning, research and service.

**Viola Karungi** teaches Drama and Film at the College of Humanities and Social Sciences, Makerere University, Uganda. Her research focuses on how arts, culture and media apply in Conflict analysis, prevention, management, and resolution. Her legal training in International Criminal Law and Transitional Justice enhances her research.

**Helen Kezie-Nwoha** is the executive director of the Women's International Peace Centre, a regional organization that promotes women's participation in peace building. Her research and publication interests include feminist peace building, women, peace and security in Africa, feminist foreign policies and conflict related sexual violence.

**Susan M. Kilonzo** is Associate Professor of Sociology of Religion at Maseno University, Kenya. Her research centers on the place of religion in contemporary socio-economic and political issues such as conflicts and peacebuilding, elections and electoral processes, health, gender, social (in)equalities, climate change and environmental sustainability, and public policy.

**Tshenolo J. Madigele** is Theology Lecturer at the University of Botswana. Her research interest includes human sexuality, pastoral care and counselling to The LGBTIQ+ community, gerontology, Botho pastoral care and counselling as well as health, spirituality and healing.

**Clemence Makamure** is chairperson and a senior lecturer in the Department of Religious Studies and Philosophy at Zimbabwe Open University. He holds a PhD in Religion and Social Transformation from the University of KwaZulu Natal (South Africa). He has research interests in African Christianity, with special focus on African Independent Churches and their leadership system, religion and politics, religion and development, religion and disability, human sexuality, human rights, religion and environment and leadership and ethics.

**Alexander Makulilo** is Professor of Political Science at the University of Dar es Salaam. His research focuses on governance, democracy, gender, public opinion, constitutionalism, peace and security, development, political dialogue and comparative politics.

**Molly Manyonganise** is a senior lecturer at the Zimbabwe Open University and a research associate of the Department of Religion Studies, Faculty of Theology and Religion, University of Pretoria. Her research interests comprise religion and politics, gender and religion, religion and sexuality, African Indigenous Religion(s) as well as African Christianity.

**Lindiwe Princess Maseko** is a PhD student in Gender and Religion at the University of KwaZulu Natal. Her areas of research interest are reproductive health and rights, reproductive justice and African woman's identity.

**Loreen Maseno** is a research fellow, Faculty of Theology, University of Pretoria, and a senior lecturer, Department of Religion, Theology and Philosophy, Maseno University, Kenya. She is an Ambassador Scientist for the Alexander von Humboldt Foundation. Her research interests include gender and theology, ecofeminism, Pentecostalism and development, among others.

**Patrick Karanja Mbugua** is a Nairobi-based Peace & Conflict Studies academic and consultant on peacebuilding, conflict transformation and preventive diplomacy. His research and publication interests include peacebuilding, conflict transformation, preventive diplomacy, peace processes, international humanitarianism and the interphase between armed conflicts and climate change.

**Elizabeth P. Motswapong** is Senior Lecturer in Comparative Religions in the Department of Theology and Religious Studies at University of Botswana. Her research interest is in Gender Studies and other aspects across religions.

**Mohamed Suleiman Mraja** is Senior Lecturer in Islamic Studies at Bomet University College (a Constituent College of Moi University). His research and publication interests include religion and marriage, family law, Islamic education, environment, health, radicalization, and Muslim personalities.

**Brian Muyunga** is a student of Theology at St Paul's University, Kenya. He is the executive secretary for youth at the All Africa Conference of Churches (AACC) and a member of the World Council of Churches (WCC) Executive and Central committees. His research and publication interests include religion and public health, gender, among others.

**Nelly Mwale** is a senior lecturer in the Department of Religious Studies at the University of Zambia. Her research interests are religion in the public sphere, religion and education, religion and development, religion and environment, church history and African Indigenous Religions.

**Sonene Nyawo** is a senior lecturer in the Department of Theology and Religious Studies at the University of Eswatini. She has published widely in the following areas of her research interests: new religious movements in Africa, traditional ritualization, women's fertility, climate change, religion and gender, women and peacebuilding.

**Abraham K. Nyuon** is Assistant Professor of Political Science and dean of the School of Social and Economic Studies at the University of Juba. His research and publication interests include international politics, foreign policy, political economy, strategic planning, peace and security.

**Simon Omare** is Senior Lecturer of Sociology of Religion at Moi University, Kenya. His research interests are on religion and society. His latest publication is on "The African Worldview on Corruption" in *Corruption and Society* Bangura A. and J. T. Gire. Rowman & Littlefield (2023).

**David Andrew Omona** holds a PhD in Political Studies with a focus on international relations. Besides, he holds other qualifications in various fields of academia. Currently, he is Associate Professor of Ethics and International Relations and dean of School of Social Sciences at the Uganda Christian University. He has carried out research and published several journal articles and book chapters.

**Elias Opongo** is a senior lecturer at Hekima Institute of Peace Studies and International Relations (HIPSIR), Hekima University College-Kenya, and the director of the Centre for Research, Training and Publications (CRTP) at the same university. He is a peace and conflict researcher and practitioner.

**Shamsia Ramadhan** is a peace practitioner with over 15 years of peacebuilding work at various levels. She is currently a PhD candidate at the Institute of Social Transformation, Tangaza University College, specializing in peace and security. Her research interests include inter-religious peacebuilding, gender-responsive peacebuilding, prevention of violent extremism, religious and traditional peacemaking, and mediation.

**Ezechiel Sentama** holds a PhD in Peace and Development Research. With more than twenty years of academic experience in Rwanda and Sweden, his research interests focus on peacebuilding, peace education, transitional justice and reconciliation. Sentama is currently employed as an assistant professor at Coventry University, Institute for Peace and Security.

**Elias Sentamba** is Professor of Political Science and History at University of Burundi and Consultant on Political Governance and Public Policy analysis. His research and lecturing focus on public policy analysis, ethno-political conflict management, religion, gender, civil society, security and so on.

**Fortune Sibanda** is Professor of Religious Studies, Department of Theology and Religious Studies, University of Eswatini and a research fellow in the Research Institute for Theology and Religion, UNISA. His research interests include religion and peace-building, health, climate change, law, gender, human rights, among others.

**John F. Sokfa** is a research fellow and deputy director of the Centre for Mediation in Africa (CMA), University of Pretoria. His research and practice interests are in ethnoreligious and digital conflict/peacebuilding and peace mediation.

**Johan Strijdom** is Professor in Religious Studies at the University of South Africa. His research and publication interests include African indigenous religions and human rights, religious nationalism and violence, and material religion, informed by critical theories of religion (comparative and historical, colonial and post-colonial, sociological and anthropological).

**Joram Tarusarira** is Assistant Professor of Religion, Conflict and Peacebuilding at the University of Groningen, the Netherlands. His research interests include religion, conflict, peacebuilding, and climate peace and security.

**Willson Tarusarira** is a PHD candidate in Health and Rehabilitation Sciences at Stellenbosch University. His research and publication interests include disability, migration and development.

**Lovemore Togarasei** is Professor and Programme Leader at Zimbabwe Open University in the Department of Religious Studies and Philosophy. He teaches courses in Biblical Studies and has published widely in the area of the Bible and social transformation in Africa. He is the co-editor (together with Ezra Chitando) of *Lobola (Bride price) in Contemporary Southern Africa*, Cham: Palgrave Macmillan. 2021.

**Alice Wabule** is a senior lecturer, Faculty of Socioeconomic Sciences, Cavendish University Uganda. She has rich experience of NGOs and has contributed to capacity building for grassroots communities. Her research and publication interests include ethics and good governance, diversity and social inclusions, community empowerment, human rights, peace and conflict.

**Dodeye Uduak Williams** is Associate Professor of Political Science at the University of Calabar, Nigeria, and a Research Fellow at the Institute for Gender Studies, UNISA. Her research and publication interests include politics and religion, peace and conflict, security, gender, terrorism/counterterrorism/violent extremism in Africa, and others.

# LIST OF FIGURES

| | | |
|---|---|---|
| Fig. 12.1 | Religions in Burundi percentage: prepared by the author on the basis of ISTEEBU data (ISTEEBU, 2008) | 205 |
| Fig. 25.1 | Lederach's peacebuilding pyramid (Lederach, 1997, p. 39) | 441 |
| Fig. 25.2 | Gogo Dineo Tweet with responses | 446 |
| Fig. 25.3 | Centring Ubuntu for justice and healing in peacebuilding. (Source: Adapted from Lederach and Mansfield (2010)) | 448 |
| Fig. 42.1 | Four interfaces of peacebuilding and digital technologies. (Source: Author, with reference to Schirch, 2020) | 758 |

# List of Tables

| | | |
|---|---|---|
| Table 22.1 | Zimbabwe National Elections | 382 |
| Table 38.1 | Refugee and asylum-seeking mothers of disabled children in the Western Cape Province (PASSOP database per country; accessed February 2017, February 2020, & February 2022) | 688 |

CHAPTER 1

# Religion, Peacebuilding and Development in Africa: An Introduction

*Susan M. Kilonzo and Ezra Chitando*

## INTRODUCTION

While the violence associated with religion (often understating the real causes) tends to grab the headlines globally, the quiet peacebuilding work done by religious actors often gets overlooked. When religious actors get acknowledged, it is mostly when some distinguished leaders would have accomplished the momentous feat of bringing the belligerents to the negotiating table and secured peace. In order to contribute towards changing this unsatisfactory state of affairs, this handbook seeks to present, amplify, critique and sharpen the religious contribution to peacebuilding and development in Africa. Contributors to this handbook explore whether, and the extent to which, religion in Africa meets the aspirations of the United Nations (UN) Sustainable Development Goal (SDG) Number 16, namely, to "[P]romote peaceful and

S. M. Kilonzo (✉)
Department of Religion, Theology & Philosophy, Maseno University, Maseno, Kenya

E. Chitando
Department of Philosophy, Religion and Ethics, University of Zimbabwe, Harare, Zimbabwe

© The Author(s), under exclusive license to Springer Nature Switzerland AG 2023
S. M. Kilonzo et al. (eds.), *The Palgrave Handbook of Religion, Peacebuilding, and Development in Africa*,
https://doi.org/10.1007/978-3-031-36829-5_1

inclusive societies for sustainable development, provide access to justice for all and build effective, accountable and inclusive institutions at all levels."[1]

Scholars and practitioners from different fields, methodological standpoints, institutions and countries approach diverse religions and themes in an effort to clarify how religion interfaces with peacebuilding and development in Africa. Acutely aware of Africa's need to "run while others walk" (Mkandawire, 2011) in terms of both knowledge production and socio-economic development, the contributors to this volume have sought to interrogate how religious actors (individual (lay), leaders, faith-based organizations (FBOs), institutions, networks, etc.) are contributing to peacebuilding and sustainable development in Africa. They have sought to explore the different forms of conflict being experienced in Africa, the numerous strategies that faith actors are deploying to address them, as well as how this relates to development. Overall, the handbook bears testimony to the often understated and overlooked initiatives by African religious peacebuilders at multiple levels. It also confirms the need to continue to invest in bringing together African scholars on religion and peace activists to reflect on the continent's struggle for peace, security and sustainable development.

In order to put this handbook into its proper perspective, the first section of this introductory chapter grapples with the theme of Africa's conflicts. Without subscribing to the Afro-pessimistic view of Africa as the land of misery, violent conflict and cheap deaths (see e.g. Michira, 2002), (although there are some positive development amidst the persistence of neo-colonial images of Africa (see e.g. Ezeru, 2022)), it remains necessary to concede that the continent has its (un)fair share of conflicts. In order to appreciate the urgency of peacebuilding in Africa, the section below provides an overview of the different conflicts that afflict the continent. However, as the war between Russia and Ukraine confirms, violent conflicts are not a monopoly of Africa

The section on Africa's conflicts is followed by a summary on religion and religious peacebuilding. While the focus on violent extremism associated with religion is gaining momentum (see e.g. Gurski, 2019), it remains helpful to review the contribution of religion to peacebuilding (Brewer et al., 2010). Such an approach seeks to balance the equation, as the danger is real that policy makers will tend to dismiss religion as the "ultimate enemy of progress and development." The section also reviews the social capital (see e.g. Steen-Johnsen, 2021) that religious leaders bring to the African peacebuilding arena. Given the ubiquitous nature of religion in Africa, it is logical that religious peacebuilding is an integral part of the peacebuilding architecture of the continent. The same section also pays attention to the knotty question of defining religion.

The section on religion, peacebuilding and SDG 16 reflects on the intractable relationship across the three concepts. If the end goal is Africa's sustainable development (see e.g. Odusola, 2017), then religion might be regarded as

[1] https://sdgs.un.org/goals/goal16

a resource to secure peace. The peaceful environment then becomes a platform or launchpad for development. In this interpretive paradigm, development is dependent on peace, while peace needs religion. This would be the most straightforward (and popular) reading. However, the situation is more complex than this. Religion on its own can enable development, while development can facilitate peace, and development can enable religion to flourish, and so on. Thus, there is a complex entanglement of these concepts. The central idea, however, is that religious leaders are strategically placed to facilitate peacebuilding and development in Africa. Thus:

> the resources religious actors can offer the peace process and their various roles as advocates, observers, educators, mediators, and institution builders must be valued. Strategic and thoughtful religious leaders, faith-based organizations, and development practitioners can capitalize upon these skills, networks, and cultural assets to work to prevent conflict and promote peace. (Flanigan, 2013: 265).

## Overview of Africa's Conflicts

Africa is a resource-rich continent. It is also widely varied, with diverse ethnic groups within each country, and subsequently, diverse cultures, ethnic groups, languages, and religions. Politically, Africa seems to largely borrow from its former colonial oppressors (Guyo, 2017; Karari, 2018; O'Connell, 2010) and subsequently, use of leadership styles that are colonial. The rich resources in the continent, are not only exploited by the West (and now, East) (Anderson, 2005; Campell, 2007; Haustein, 2017; Sen, 1999), but also mismanaged by some African leaders (Iliffe, 2007; Karari, 2018). This partly explains the resultant effect, namely, the recurrence of poverty and conflicts (Mazrui, 2008; O'Connell, 2010). Conflicts also arise for different reasons, as this introductory chapter and others in the handbook will show.

While analysing the trends of conflicts in Africa, Palik et al. (2022) show that, in 2021, within the continent, 25 state-based[2] conflicts were recorded, compared to 30 in 2020, and 27 in 2019. The study records that in 2021, twelve (12) African countries had to engage external actors in their domestic conflicts, with increased Islamic State activity as a factor in these conflicts, which also drew in countries that had not previously featured on conflict data sets, such as Tanzania. Further, trends show an increase in non-state conflicts in the continent, which are dominated by communal conflicts, as seen in Nigeria, South Sudan (Palik et al., 2022: 9), Ethiopia, Central Africa Republic (CAR), Burundi and the Democratic Republic of Congo (DRC). In 2021, as Palik et al. (2022) observe, the governments of Burundi, Cameroon, Central African Republic, Democratic Republic of Congo (DRC), Eritrea, eSwatini,

---

[2] The term is used to refer to "contested incompatibility over government and/or territory, with at least one party being a state, and involving the use of armed force." Non-state conflict is the use of armed force between organized groups, none of which is the government of a state (Palik et al., 2022:7).

Ethiopia, Mali, Mozambique, South Sudan, and Sudan[3] engaged in one sided-violence by use of organized groups or the state/government itself against civilians. Non-state conflicts, which take the form of formally organized groups, informally organized groups and informally organized identity groups (with religious, ethnic, clan or tribal identities) are quite common in the continent and cause considerable human suffering (Palik et al., 2022).

Juma (2002: 1-2) takes a broad perspective of categorizing conflicts within the continent, using regional dynamics, by noting that:

> In West Africa, four issues stand out: the Charles Taylor factor; the Franco-Nigerian rivalry; the link between the exploitation of natural resources and war; and the proliferation of small arms and light weapons. Southern Africa's security architecture is defined to a large extent by the legacy of apartheid and the fear of South Africa's economic and political dominance in the post apartheid era, as well as by the fragility of democratization throughout the subregion. In Central Africa, three broad factors define conflicts and responses to them: ethnicity and governance; the scramble for resources; and the prevalent, sometimes conflicting interests of regional and international actors. Finally, in the Horn of Africa, the nature and dynamics of conflicts are determined by the legacy of superpower rivalry and the weakening, sometimes fragmentation of the state; proliferation of small arms and light weapons; and (involuntary) human migration.

While this might not be a complete picture of conflicts in the continent, the scenario implies a diversity of causes of conflicts, but also the need to understand that the occurrence of any of these factors within a country may be detrimental. Other efforts to categorize conflicts in the continent can be found in the work of Zeleza (2008), with examples of irredentist wars as seen in Somalia and Eritrea— wars caused by devolution like in the case of Sudan, wars of regime change like in the case of Uganda, social banditry wars as seen in Sierra Leone and Central Africa Republic, inter-communal and inter-state wars and terror wars. Gilpin (2016) also provides a typology of wars in the continent, while focusing on geopolitics and statist politics. More recently, Nshimbi (2020) summarizes Africa's current theatres of conflicts to include civil wars; those resulting from separatist Anglophones as seen in the case of Cameroon; regional conflicts in the Sahel; and, wars resulting from terror groups. Sandy (2020), in line with Nshimbi (2020) and Aall (2015), explains that the main causes to Africa's conflicts are contested political transitions, especially related to elections, amendments or revisions of constitutions, prolonged years in a political office, closure of civic spaces, passing or restrictive laws, intimidatory state tactics and use of undue force. All these provide a rich typology that may be a fair image of the causes and nature of conflicts in the continent.

The diversity of the conflicts is complicated by various influential factors within each individual country, including the richness of identities—including

---

[3] The majority of the countries (6/11) cited here are in East Africa, hence accounting for the preponderance of countries from this region among the case studies in this volume.

ethnicities, languages, cultures, religion, among others; governance issues and, by extension, resource allocation; and external influence. The resultant effects of conflict in any of the African countries are far-reaching and require concerted efforts to rebuild the nation. Juma (2002), Zeleza (2008) and Gilpin (2016) articulate the effects of these conflicts as costly and in the end robbing the development potential of the countries. Further, the road to reconstruction and search for solutions to peace becomes very demanding, complicated and convoluted, despite the regional, sub-regional, national and community infrastructures for peacebuilding. This is seen in the cases of South Africa's Apartheid, Rwanda's genocide, Nigeria's fundamentalism wars, Central Africa Republic's ethnic and religious conflicts (Zeleza 2008), the DRC's State and Inter-State involvement conflicts (Palik et al., 2022), among other examples. Significant in Africa's conflicts is the fact that most of these wars trace their origin to colonial histories (Musisi, 2002, Mazrui, 2008, Zeleza 2008, Kastfelt, 2005, Gilpin, 2016, Haustein, 2017, and Karari, 2018, among others). Besides the colonial roots, Zeleza (2008) argues that the wars also need to be understood from the post-colonial and neo-liberal globalization perspectives that involve national, regional and international actors, as well as networks.

The diverse range of causes and effects of these wars means that conflict resolution and peacebuilding processes take a similar trajectory of diversity. Aall (2015) explains that the creation of regional organizations with robust mandates in the peace and security arena includes a basis for strong continental and sub-regional organizations, but still, the availability of such outstrips the demand, with most of these conflicts, such as those resulting from the activities of terror groups, social banditry and political resistance groups, making international headlines for their violence and hostilities towards their governments and societies (Aall, 2015).

The effects of conflict call for concerted efforts from communities, states, inter-governmental cooperation and the African Union (AU) in the peacebuilding processes if sustainable peace is to be achieved (African Union, 2019). The fourth aspiration of Agenda 2063, which is the AU strategic Framework for socio-economic transformation of the continent over the next four decades, highlights the need for dialogue-centred conflict prevention. It involves taking into account the political history of the continent, marred by the effects of colonization, slavery and unpaid extraction and exploitation of natural resources that creates a huge burden for African and its people (Lusaka Roadmap, 2016). This process as Zondi (2017) shows, is a peacebuilding road that hinges on continued decolonization of the African state and transformation to maintain decolonial peace—meaning, pursuit of peace in a way that deals with the colonial continuities in the nature of the inherited state, which underlies war and violence, and the colonial political economy (see also Zeleza 2008). Zondi (2017) explains that peace efforts undertaken by the AU and regional economic communities have a fundamental weakness arising from the fact that they envisage peace without a clear place for underlying logics of coloniality and its support for perpetual and repeated violence. Subsequently, for Zondi, peace efforts that are not decolonialized register progress in peacebuilding that is reversible and fragile because the heritage of structural violence remains in place under neo-colonial arrangements set in place by independence. Thus, decolonial peace, is same as detoxing the body while applying measures to heal the diseases that nest in the toxic conditions (Zondi, 2017: 107).

While this handbook may not consistently focus on the decoloniality of peacebuilding by making direct references to this process, the histories of the various cases studies presented examine peacebuilding processes that highlight some of the causes that emanate from the colonial legacies and challenges of independence in African countries, to show what is, and what is not, working for religious peacebuilding efforts. The handbook takes a unique orientation to focus not just on the peacebuilding efforts, but to also show, through the various case studies, how these efforts from religious actors, align to the global peace agenda. As Tadevosyan (2022) argues, the global proliferation of the peace agenda allows for different actors to take part in the national (international peace agendas). Although the place of non-state actors has always been restricted by the authoritarianism of the state, there is still a place for them, especially in the developing world where there are challenges of poverty and inequality. This is the same approach that the global peacebuilding agenda by United Nations, through the Sustainable Development Goal (SDG) 16.

## Religion and Religious Peacebuilding: An Overview

There is overwhelming evidence that religion can play a double role in conflicts. Religion has been blamed for inciting and fuelling conflicts, but it has also been useful in resolving conflicts and decreasing tensions (Appleby, 1996, 2000, Abu-Nimer, 2001, Bouta et al., 2005, Coward & Smith, 2004, Sampson, 2007, Basedau et al., 2011). On fueling conflicts, Basedau et al. (2011) argue that religious demography in Africa is diverse and often considered a risk, since the institutions have the ability to contest on political, social and economic issues. Further, certain religious structures in the continent, such as parallel ethnic affiliations which come with language and cultural identities are prone to mobilization in politics and violent religious conflicts. In their study examining religious factors as influencers of onset of armed conflicts, Basedau et al. (2011) use an inventory from all sub-Saharan African countries in the period between 1990-2008, that focus on actual politicization of religion on factors such as interreligious tensions, resource discrimination and incitement of religious leaders. Their results show that religion plays a significant role in African armed conflicts. As we shall see in some of the case studies in this handbook, in States where religion overlaps with ethnic identities as well as religious dominance, conflicts tend to occur more frequently. However, it is also true that religion does not only incite conflict but also contributes to peace and peacebuilding (Appleby, 2000). It, therefore, implies that when discussing religious peacebuilding, a lot depends on how religious actors manage key non-religious factors (including historical, political, ethnic, regional, socio-economic and others).

This terminology, *religion*, has been defined variedly. Simply conceived, religion is the belief in the supernatural. The belief means that adherents of a given religion have to subscribe to certain sacred practices that through faith, connects them to the supernatural. In this handbook, we however extend this simple definition to note that, religion may not just be about religious ideas. In Africa, almost all aspects of life are imbued with the Sacred (Magesa, 2013). Religion is further understood from demographic structures, organization and related behaviour of actors (Basedau et al., 2011). These facets are important in religious peacebuilding, because under demographics, religious identities are special in connecting to particular religious ideals and structures that influence the behaviour and shared values within these structures (Harowitz 2009). This then influences the response of actors to incite and fuel conflicts, or resolve them, and engage in peacebuilding. For the avoidance of doubt, each contributor was allowed to work with their tentative or operational definition of religion. However, as the different chapters particularly in Part III confirm, there is a general appreciation of phenomena categorized as religion in Africa (and beyond).

*Religious peacebuilding*, according to Coward and Smith (2004: 5) is the range of activities performed by religious actors and institutions for the purpose of resolving and transforming conflicts. The transformation bit of peacebuilding means that peacebuilding is not a one-off activity, but a process that requires concerted efforts from various stakeholders, with conflicting communities at the centre of the activities. The goal of religious peacebuilding, therefore, is to build social relations, community and political institutions characterized by ethos of tolerance and non-violence. This however does not imply that absence of violence implies peace. As Galtung (1996) has shown, there is positive and negative peace. Positive peace implies the need to address the root causes of conflicts and build structures that contribute to social justice.

There are individual actors, religious institutions as well as non-governmental organizations that are faith-based, that have used religion as a tool for conflict reconstruction and continued peacebuilding. All these are the different faces of religious peacebuilding that this handbook engages. If anything, in the recent past, as Hayward (2012) shows, the field of religion and peacebuilding has begun to move closer to the mainstream of conflict resolution practice and theory. In fact, Hayward explains that although we see the efforts of religious peacebuilding in places such as the USA emerging after September 11 2001, in Africa, religion and religious groups seem to have longer experience in peacebuilding. While examining methodological approaches and tools for measuring change and the results for working with religion and religious actors for peace and reconciliation in East Africa, Lagho and Bonaya (2016) evidence that faith-based actors enjoy unmatched legitimacy with faith communities compared to civil society organizations (CSOs). This may be attributed to the fact that communities see faith-based communities as non-partisan, and as such, in times of conflict, they seek refuge in religious spaces where they are also provided with humanitarian aid, as well as space and environment for peace talks/dialogue, healing and reconciliation (see Kilonzo 2020, 2022 and Hughes, 2022).

This trust of religious actors, therefore, implies the need for unique resources that empower the religious institutions and actors to resolve conflicts and contribute to peacebuilding processes. Appleby (2000), Coward and Smith (2004), and Sampson (2007), explain that these resources include, but are not limited to, inner inspiration and transformation; scriptural and theological resources; religious rituals; established networks and hierarchies for enhancing advocacy; empowerment and equality; mobilization of practical and financial resources; humility on part of the peacebuilders; and, wisdom. It also calls for building on religious values that are shared within the different religions and that which can contribute to peaceful co-existence. These however cannot be achieved without engaging with and working hand in hand with the affected communities. If anything, Ayindo et al. (2001) explain that peacebuilders have to walk the rough road, not just by breaking their silence on their experiences, but engaging communities to tell their stories, challenges and how they come to terms with these challenges. The work of faith-based actors in peacebuilding, therefore, according to Bouta et al. (2005), is to provide emotional and spiritual support to the affected communities, mobilize communities for peace, mediate between conflicting parties, promote reconciliation, dialogue, disarmament, demobilization and reintegration, as some of the cases will show in this handbook.

Further, for sustainable peace, the handbook reckons that the religious actors cannot work in isolation, and besides interreligious networks for peacebuilding that different authors exemplify, there is need, as a number of chapters recommend, for a useful culture of collaboration to be developed that encourages peacebuilding work between religious and non-religious actors, including CSOs in order to enhance the capacity of the stakeholders (Lagho & Bonaya, 2016) in addressing issues of justice, peaceful and inclusive societies, as desired in SDG 16.

## Religion, Peacebuilding and SDG 16

The SDG 16 is tailored towards promoting peaceful and inclusive societies for sustainable development, providing access to justice for all and building effective, accountable and inclusive institutions at all levels (https://sdg-tracker.org/peace-justice). The inclusive aspect in peacebuilding remains important because in the past, religion and religious actors have been involved in peacebuilding efforts, but were hardly included in the mainstream and/or state peacebuilding processes. Bouta et al. (2005) explain this challenge and note that part of the reason is lack of institutionalization of religious/faith-based peacebuilding work, that then goes unaccounted for. Nevertheless, the evidence available shows that religious peacebuilding has succeeded variously contributing to positive accounts in situations of conflicts. Cox (2014) shows that, where religious peacebuilding is institutionalized with autonomous structures embedded within religious communities, these can be leveraged to build social cohesion. The opposite is also true, that these structures can be used to escalate violence.

Subsequently, the active role of religion in peacebuilding and structures within which they source their strength, including local communities, religious leaders, civil society organizations (CSOs), non-governmental organizations, and the government, to engage with local or international peacebuilding processes, can be argued to contribute to the national, regional, continental and global peacebuilding architecture. An example would be the vision of the AU's peacebuilding architecture, and specifically the AU Transitional Justice Policy (AUTJP, 2019), which encourages support and respect for community accountability mechanisms that promote communal dispute settlement. It also encourages exploration of alternative and non-formal dispute resolution that tap from positive African traditional practices and customs as well as norms. These practices have characterized religious peacebuilding, as some cases in this handbook will show. The said mechanisms also centre on dialogue, forgiveness, retribution and reconciliation (Kilonzo 2022), which cannot be realized without engaging local leadership and local ownership. These are the dimensions of inclusivity, equity and non-discrimination in peacebuilding, as stipulated under SDG 16. Some cases in this handbook will show that religious peacebuilding processes may fall short of certain stipulations of SDG 16, such as due regard to gender and generational dimensions. These are some of the loopholes that religious peacebuilders will need to reflect on, and as shown in the handbook, they remain to be a focus of continental peacebuilding architecture as seen in AUTJP (2019).

Religious peacebuilding is likely to benefit not just from the communities within which the religion in question is located, but also from the national and international stakeholders. This implies their ability not just to provide timely interventions that are effectively coordinated from where the conflicts emanate, but also their potential to coordinate peacebuilding and development activities that speak to the needs resulting from the conflicts. They also have the potential to encourage and enhance social cohesion, by building bridges across ethnic, cultural and religious divides (Khadiagala 2002, Ntale, 2012, Kilonzo and Onkware 2022, Kilonzo 2022). On this, the need is to understand the role of interfaith work in peacebuilding and development, and is articulated in different case studies from the continent. In a different Palgrave volume, edited by Ezra Chitando and Ishanesu Gusha (2022) on *Interfaith Networks and Development*, in the introductory section, Chitando shows that there are some ecumenical bodies that do not limit their development work to those of their faith but collaborate with others. He gives examples of the World Council of Churches (WCC) and the All Africa Conference of Churches (AACC), which have promoted interfaith dialogue and development in the continent and beyond (Chitando, 2022:8). Such are efforts seem, in this handbook, not just from organizational perspective, but also from different religions, as they work towards peacebuilding within communities in the continent.

## CHAPTERS IN THIS HANDBOOK

This handbook is divided into seven main parts and a conclusion. Part I is entitled, "Contextualizing Religion, Peacebuilding and Development in Africa." It provides the theoretical framing of this handbook, paying close attention to conceptualizing religion, peacebuilding and development in Africa and to how communities, governments and practitioners understand the place of religion in peacebuilding and development in the continent. The section explores the interrelatedness and the interphase of the three—religion, peacebuilding and development processes. The section focuses on key specific tools such as morality, scholarship, the Bible, strategies for teaching, intersectionalities, as well as highlights topical issues such as climate change, to show how these variously speak to Africa's context. It reflects how religion is interwoven within these aspects to contribute, positively or negatively, to the peacebuilding and development processes. Further, the section looks at the challenges faced by these institutions in this endeavour, which to a great extent is meant to help suggest recommendations that religious and institutions involved in policy-making may take up to strengthen the positive contributions of SDG 16.

After introduction, in Chap. 2, Susan M. Kilonzo provides critical reflections on religion, peacebuilding and development in Africa, while in Chap. 3 Ezra Chitando undertakes a review of African scholarship on religion and peacebuilding in African theology and religious studies. Molly Manyonganise tackles the theme of the challenges relating to religion, peacebuilding and development in Africa in Chap. 4, while Lovemore Togarasei reviews the interface between the Bible and peacebuilding in Africa in Chap. 5. Johan Strijdom, in Chap. 6, focuses on strategies for teaching religion, peacebuilding and development in Africa. Masiiwa R. Gunda analyses intersectionalities relating to religion and peacebuilding in Africa, paying special attention to the dynamics of race and racism, in Chap. 7. Joram Tarusarira concludes this Part, in Chap. 8, with a current debate on a topical issue, "Climate Security and Religion in Africa", in the context of Sustainable Development Goals.

Part II is, "Country Case Studies on Religion, Peacebuilding and Development in Africa." It presents the dynamics of religion, peacebuilding and development in selected African countries. These have been selected to cover the sub-Saharan Africa in the Eastern, Western, Southern and Central regions. The aim of the country-specific cases is to provide detailed accounts of the efforts of various religious bodies in resolving conflicts and contributing to the bigger picture of peacebuilding processes. This part opens with Chap. 9, where Ezechiel Sentama examines the case of Rwanda. In Chap. 10, Patrick Karanja Mbugua & Abraham K. Nyuon uses the concept of everyday peace to reflect on religion and peacebuilding in South Sudan. This is followed by Chap. 11 by John Sokfa where he analyses the situation in Nigeria. In Chap. 12,

Elias Sentamba pursues the theme of how religious organizations have sought to respond to ethnic and political conflicts in Burundi. The focus on Burundi is discussed in Chap. 13 by Mbugua. Alexander Makulilo & Henry Rodrick, in Chap. 14, concentrate on Tanzania's case, presenting the role of the Interfaith Peace Committee. In Chap. 15, Donatien M. Cicura engages in an analysis of religion and peacebuilding in the Democratic Republic of Congo (DRC), with David Andrew Omona reviewing religion, peacebuilding and development in Uganda in Chap. 16. The Part closes with Sonene Nyawo's reflections on Eswatini in Chap. 17, with special reference to the role of indigenous spirituality. The predominance of East African countries in this Part is not accidental: with some parts of West Africa, the region has experienced some long running violent conflicts.

"Diverse Religions in Africa, Peacebuilding and Development," constitutes Part III. This part focuses on how different religions have been appropriated and deployed to contribute towards peacebuilding and development in Africa. It pays attention to specific religiosities, that is, diverse denominations and actors in these religions as a way of detailing how, beyond the bigger umbrella of religion in specific countries, different religions are engaged in conflict situations and peacebuilding efforts. A sample of religious bodies across the Eastern, Western and Southern regions, is represented. In Chap. 18, Christopher Appiah-Thompson and Jim Jose analyse the contribution of traditional institutions to the resolution of electoral conflicts in Ghana. Fortune Sibanda distils insights on peacebuilding from Rastafari in Chap. 19. In Chap. 20. Suleiman A. Chembea interrogates Islamophobia and the role of media, in the case of Kenya, while Chap. 21 presents Mraja's perspective on Islam, conflict, peace and security in Africa. Obadiah Dodo shifts focus to the role of Apostolic (African Independent/Indigenous/Initiated) Churches and youth in Zimbabwe, to close this section of diverse religions and peacebuilding with Chap. 22.

There are key religious actors whose contributions have been prominent in peacebuilding processes and worth documenting. Part IV is on, "Actors in Religion, Peacebuilding and Development in Africa," and subsequently focuses on these actors both at State and community levels. The actors are either documented as individuals or leaders and activists within certain religious institutions. The section presents and assesses various categories of actors in the field of religious peacebuilding and development in Africa. In Chap. 23, Chitando engages with the work of Emmanuel Katongole, while in Chap. 24, Shamsia Ramadhan evaluates the contribution of traditional leaders to peacebuilding in Kenya. Beatrice Dube & Sinenhlanhla S. Chisale apply decolonial perspectives to appreciate the contribution of traditional leaders to peacebuilding in South Africa in Chap. 25. Patrick Mbugua and Nahed Ayoub, in Chap. 26 analyse religious peacebuilding in informal settlements in Egypt. Simon Omare and Eunice Kamaara explore the ambivalent role of church leaders in peacebuilding relating to Kenyan elections in Chap. 27. Edmond A. Agyeman focuses on the National Peace Council in Ghana in Chap. 28, and in final chapter of this section, Chap. 29, Brian Muyunga analyses the contribution of the All Africa Conference of Churches (AACC) to peacebuilding in Africa, paying particular attention to the role of the youth.

The monolithic focus of religious traditions in peacebuilding and development efforts may not be enough to illustrate a true picture of the continent's efforts in enhancing peaceful and inclusive societies for sustainable development (SDG) 16. Interfaith networks have emerged as strategic resources in promoting peace and development in Africa. They are the focus of Part V, "Interfaith Networks, Peacebuilding and Development in Africa." The section is specific to trajectories around interreligious dialogue and interfaith networks that unite Africans of diverse faiths for peacebuilding course. It opens with Chap. 30 by Elias Opongo on the contribution of the Fellowship of Christian Councils and Churches to peacebuilding. This is followed by Dodeye U. Williams' assessment of the Nigeria Inter-Religious Council in Chap. 31. Jennifer T. Madigele tackles the theme of xenophobia, interfaith networks and peacebuilding in Botswana in Chap. 32, while Newton Kahumbi surveys the role of Islamic interfaith networks in peacebuilding in Kenya under the shadow of the War on Terror in Chap. 33. The Part closes with Patrick Mbugua's Chap. 34, which assesses the re-building of Christian-Muslim relations in West Nile, Uganda.

Since SDG 16 focuses on "inclusive societies for sustainable development and providing access to justice for all", Part VI, of the Handbook aims at exploring how religious institutions have dealt with the agency of gender and gender mainstreaming. It is entitled, "Gender, Religion, Peacebuilding and Development in Africa." The chapters in this section interrogate the efforts of the various religious groups and actors towards inclusive peacebuilding processes. Such processes are assumed to centrally take into account the needs and input of men, women, youth, the physically challenged, immigrants, children, and vulnerable populations in general, in peacebuilding and development processes. Lindiwe P. Maseko and Sophia Chirongoma focus on the theme with special reference to Zimbabwe in Chap. 35, with Helen Kezie-Nwoha engaging the feminist perspective to examine the role of religion in Nigeria and Uganda in Chap. 36. As Nelly Mwale, Joseph Chita & Mulunda Habeenzu show in Chap. 37, many actors in spaces that would be considered secular in Africa are motivated by religion. These three authors utilize the case of Doreen Malambo to discuss gender, religion, peacebuilding and development in Zambia. A rarely discussed vulnerability among immigrants and disability is presented in Willson Tarusarira's and Joram Tarusarira's Chap. 38. They examine the impact of traditional disability beliefs in Zimbabwe and their impact on mothers of children with disability who migrate to South Africa. In Chap. 39, Loreen Maseno reflects on the theme of religion, gender and peacebuilding within the Kenyan context, while in Chap. 40, Alice Webule analyses the role of women church leaders in peacebuilding and social transformation in Uganda.

There are quite a number of topical issues that influence actors in religious peacebuilding process. Part VII of this handbook is therefore dedicated to,

"Religion, Peacebuilding and Other Topical Issues in Africa." In Chap. 41, Ezra Chitando and Susan Kilonzo explore the concept Ubuntu, and its application in peacebuilding processes, paying close attention to ways in which Ubuntu can be revitalized in situations of varied conflicts in Africa. In Chap. 42, John Sokfa examines religion and digital peacebuilding. Fortunée Bayisenge addresses the theme of religion and agriculture for peacebuilding in Rwanda in Chap. 43, while paying attention to the models used by the State and how these delimit farmers and religious actors. In Chap. 44, the final in this section, Viola Karungi centres on the role of the arts in the discourse on religion, peacebuilding and development in post-conflict Northern Uganda. She uses drama to show how art can be applied with humour and sarcasm to communicate messages that would be otherwise challenging to pass in other forms.

In the concluding chapter, Susan Kilonzo and Ezra Chitando strive to synthesize the themes have emerged from the chapters in this handbook. They call for ongoing investment as scholars, activists and practitioners seek to understand and implement activities relating to religion, peacebuilding and development in Africa more effectively.

## Conclusion

Religion remains a significant reality in Africa. Initiatives to promote peace and sustainable development in Africa must, therefore, budget for the impact of religion. Although the overwhelming majority of the contributors in this handbook have focused on the positive role of religion, a few show and explain ways in which religion has been used for violence and underdevelopment. The handbook therefore readily concedes that religion has been deployed by conflict entrepreneurs to widen cleavages and inflame tense situations in Africa. The task, as we see it, lies in resolutely multiplying the positive role of religious actors in promoting peace, security and development, while systematically subtracting the negative role of the same. The voices of those involved in religious peacebuilding processes need to be heard more and more. The African continent, long associated with violent conflict and de-development, can utilize the opportunities granted by religion to achieve collective peace, security, inclusion and development, in line with the vision of SDG 16.

## References

Aall, P. (2015). Conflict in Africa: Diagnosis and Response. CIGI Papers. No. 71. Centre for International Governance and Innovation. Waterloo. Ontario.

Abu-Nimer, M. (2001). Conflict Resolution, Culture, and Religion: Toward a Training Model of Interreligious Peacebuilding. *Journal of Peace Research, 38*(6), 685–704.

African Union. (2019). *Transitional Justice Policy: An integrated, prosperous and peaceful Africa.* AU.

Anderson, D. (2005). *Histories of the Hanged: The Dirty War in Kenya and the End of Empire.* Weidenfeld & Nicolson.

Appleby, S. R. (1996). Religion as an Agent of Conflict Transformation and Peacebuilding. In C. A. Crocker, F. O. Hampson, & P. Aall (Eds.), *The Challenges of Managing International Conflict* (pp. 821–840). United States Institute of Peace Press.

Appleby, S. (2000). *The Ambivalence of the Sacred: Religion, Violence, and Reconciliation.* Rowman & Littlefield.

Ayindo, B., Doe, S., & Jenner, J. (2001). *When You Are the Peacebuilder: Stories and Reflections on Peacebuilding from Africa.* Conflict Transformation Program: Eastern Mennonite University.

Basedau, M., Strüver, G., Vüllers, J., & Wegenast, T. (2011). Do Religious Factors Impact Armed Conflict? Empirical Evidence from Sub-Saharan Africa, GIGA Working Papers, No. 168, German Institute of Global and Area Studies (GIGA), Hamburg.

Bouta, T., Kadayifci-Orellana, A., & Abu-Nimer, M. (2005). *Faith-based peacebuilding: mapping and analysis of Christian Muslim & multi-faith actors.* Netherlands Institute of International Relations.

Brewer, J., Higgins, G., & Teeney, F. (2010). Religion and peacemaking: A Conceptualization. *Sociology, 44*(6), 1019–1037.

Campell, C. (2007). *Race and Empire: Eugenics in Colonial Kenya.* Manchester University Press.

Chitando, E. (2022). Interfaith Networks and Development. In E. Chitando & I. Gusha (Eds.), *Interfaith Networks and Development: Case Studies from Africa* (pp. 3–26). Palgrave Macmillan.

Coward, H., & Smith, G. (Eds.). (2004). *Religion and Peacebuilding.* SUNY Press.

Ezeru, C. W. W. (2022). Africa's Global Media Image in a Digital World as an Exclusive Western Preserve? *The International Communication Gazette, 84*(5), 379–400.

Flanigan, S. T. (2013). Religion, Conflict and Peacebuilding in Development. In M. Clarke (Ed.), *Handbook of Research on Development and Religion* (pp. 252–267). Edward Elgar Publishing Inc..

Gilpin, R. (2016). Understanding the Nature and Origins of Violent Conflict in Africa. In P. Pamela Aall & C. Crocker (Eds.), *Minding the Gap: African Conflict Management in a Time of Change* (pp. 21–32). CIGI Publications.

Gurski, P. (2019). *When Religion Kills: How Extremists Justify Violence through Faith.* Lynne Reiner Publishers.

Guyo, F. (2017). Colonial and Post-colonial Changes and Impact on Pastoral Women's Roles and Status. *Pastoralism Research. Policy & Practice, 7*(13), 1. https://doi.org/10.1186/S13570-017-0076-2

Haustein, J. (2017). Strategic Tangles: Slavery, Colonial Policy, and Religion in German East Africa, 1885–1918. *Atlantic Studies, 14*(4), 497–518.

Hughes, C. (2022). Peacebuilding, Governance and Development. In W. Hout & J. Hutchi (Eds.), *Handbook on Governance and Development: Political Science and Public Policy* (pp. 308–321). Elgar Handbooks in Development. https://doi.org/10.4337/9781789908756

Iliffe, J. (2007). *Africans: The History of a Continent.* Cambridge University Press.

Juma, M. (2002). *The Infrastructure of Peace in Africa. Assessing the Peacebuilding Capacity of African Institutions. A Report submitted by the Africa Program of the International Peace Academy to the Ford Foundation.* International Peace Academy.

Karari, P. (2018). Modus Operandi of Oppressing the 'savages': The Kenya British Colonial Experience. *Peace and Conflict Studies, 25*, 1. Article 2. Available at: https://nsuworks.nova.edu/pcs/vol25/iss1/2.

Kastfelt, N. (Ed.). (2005). *Religion and African Civil Wars*. Palgrave Macmillan.

Lagho, W., & Bonaya, A. (2016). *Religion and Peace in East Africa: Pilot Study on Methodological Approaches and Tools for Measuring Change and the Results for Working with Religion and Religious Actors for Peace and Reconciliation*. DANMISSION.

Lusaka Master Roadmap. (2016). African Union Master Roadmap of Practical Steps to Silence The Guns in Africa by Year 2020. Retrieved December 21, 2022, from https://au.int/sites/default/files/documents/37996-doc-au_roadmap_silencing_guns_2020.pdf.en_.pdf.

Magesa, L. (2013). *What Is Not Sacred? African Spirituality*. Orbis Books.

Mazrui, A. (2008). Conflicts in Africa: An overview. In A. Nhema & P. Zeleza (Eds.), *The Roots of Africa Conflicts: The Causes and Costs*. Ohio University Press.

Michira, J. (2002). Images of Africa in the Western Media.. http://www.teachingliterature.org/teachingliterature/pdf/multi/images_of_africa_michira

Mkandawire, T. (2011). Running While Others Walk: Knowledge and the Challenge of Africa's Development. *Africa Development, 36*(2), 1–36.

Musisi, N. (2002). The Politics of Perception or Perception of Politics? Colonial and Missionary Representation of Baganda Women. In S. Geiger, N. Musisi, & M. Allman (Eds.), *Women in African Colonial Histories: An Introduction* (pp. 1900–1945). Indiana University Press.

Nshimbi, C. (2020). 'Why the African Union has Failed to "Silence the Guns". And Some Solutions'. Retrieved January 17, 2023, from https://africacenter.org/spotlight/the-emergence-of-violent-extremism-in-northern-mozambique/.

Ntale, F. (2012). Religious Actors and the Agenda for Peace in Northern Uganda. *The Journal of Social, Political and Economic Studies, 37*(3), 322–346.

O'Connell, S. (2010). Colonial Economic Structures in Africa: Their Purpose and Legacy. Unpublished paper, Swarthmore College.

Odusola, A. (2017). Achieving the Sustainable Development Goals in Africa in the Context of Complex Global Development Cooperation. CESDEV Issue Paper No. 2017/2. Ibadan: Centre for Sustainable Development University of Ibadan, Nigeria.

Palik, J., Obermeier, A., & Rustad, S. (2022). *Conflict Trends in Africa, 1989-2021*. Peace Research Institute Oslo.

Sampson, C. (2007). Religion and Peacebuilding. In W. Zartman (Ed.), *Peacemaking in International Conflict* (pp. 273–323). United States Institute of Peace.

Sen, A. (1999). *Development as Freedom*. Oxford University Press.

Steen-Johnsen, T. (2021). A Social Capital Perspective on the Peace Work of Religious Women. *Journal of Ecumenical Studies, 56*(1), 55–75.

Tadevosyan, M. (2022). Peacebuilding in Politically Challenging Environments: How Do Local Peacebuilders Navigate Muddy Waters in the South Caucasus?, *International Negotiation* (published online ahead of print 2022). doi: https://doi.org/10.1163/15718069-bja10084.

Zondi, S. (2017). Africa Union Approaches to Peacebuilding: Efforts at Shifting the Continent Towards Decolonial Peace. *African Journal on Conflict Resolution, 17*(1), 105–131.

PART I

# Contextualising Religion, Peacebuilding and Development in Africa

CHAPTER 2

# Religion, Peacebuilding, and Development in Africa: A Critical Appreciation

*Susan M. Kilonzo*

## INTRODUCTION

Ideally, peace should be every human's concern, given the need for humans to flourish, and lead holistic lives. Africa, being a resource-rich continent, should be flourishing and peaceful. However, a number of factors have rendered the continent poor, and also unable to sustain peaceful populations. Although this could be said of other continents, Africa is particularly food, peace and jobs-starving. Food, jobs, and peace are interconnected in Africa. The availability of food is essential for the sustenance of individuals and the growth of the economy. The production of food in Africa requires labour, and therefore, jobs are created in the agriculture sector. In Africa, the agriculture sector employs about 60% of the labour force and contributes significantly to the continent's economic growth (Lowder et al., 2016). However, agriculture productivity in Africa remains low due to limited access to land, water, and inputs, among other challenges (Lowder et al., 2016). Therefore, the sector's potential to create jobs and contribute to food security remains untapped. The food poverty and lack of jobs are a contributing factor to violence. The youth, especially the idle lot that is without jobs, and which forms the majority of Africa's population is a factor that is weaponized for political violence. On religion, Pew Research Centre (2015) ranks Africa notably as a continent whose population practices almost all world religions. It is a "religious" continent, and as Pew Research Centre (2015) projects, the sub-Saharan Africa Christian religion is projected

S. M. Kilonzo (✉)
Department of Religion, Theology & Philosophy, Maseno University, Maseno, Kenya

© The Author(s), under exclusive license to Springer Nature Switzerland AG 2023
S. M. Kilonzo et al. (eds.), *The Palgrave Handbook of Religion, Peacebuilding, and Development in Africa*,
https://doi.org/10.1007/978-3-031-36829-5_2

to double from 517 million in 2010, to 1.1 billion in 2050. Observably, indigenous religions are still widely practised (Pew Forum on Religion and Public Life, 2020), and as Tarusarira (2017) argues, African religious beliefs are a prime source of guidance and support for most people in the continent. In fact, as Pew Forum on Religion and public Life (2020) shows, many of those who practise Christianity and Islam, are deeply committed to their indigenous beliefs and practices: with many consulting African traditional healers; believing in protective power of charms and amulets; keeping sacred objects and animals, and consulting and participating ceremonies to honour their ancestors, among other beliefs and practices.

One would therefore assume that, with such practices, and holding all the other factors constant, religion would, through the tenets that advocate for peace, largely unite people and avert conflicts and war in the continent. But there is also the other side of religion, in which case, it is seems as though it is a tool for propagating violence (see Appleby, 2000; Bouta et al., 2005). Some of the conflicts and wars that still greatly characterize everyday life in most African countries with diverse nature and magnitude, have religious roots, but others do not. Regardless of the origin, they rob the affected countries, and the continent in general, of the development potential because they are not just costly, but also present daunting challenges when solutions for the same are sought (Zeleza, 2008). This said, the role of religion and religious institutions has clearly been instrumental in solutions, whether short- or long- term, to the challenge of conflicts in Africa. Religion has been useful in resolving conflicts in different contexts, building and maintaining peace, as the chapter will show.

Subsequently, religion, in the context of war and conflicts in Africa and beyond, can be described as a double-edged sword. It can play both roles: contributing to violence, and providing solutions for conflicts. Religion, in and of itself, may not be the cause of conflict. In fact, in most situations of conflicts where religion and religious actors are implicated, there is always an underlying issue that is a key contributory factor to the conflict. However, when religious actors or groups take sides, or one religious group fronts itself as an aggrieved faction, as seen in the case of Central Africa Republic in this chapter, the conflict takes religious overtones. The same may be said of religious peacebuilding. Although the actors in search of solutions to the conflicts may be from one or different religious groups, as seen in the case of Kenya and Uganda in this chapter, their solutions may not be religious in nature, but secular, aimed at resolving either the religious wars or the root causes of conflicts that are not in themselves religious.

This chapter is an appraisal of case studies that speak to the two sides of religion and religious institutions. It is written from a theoretical approach, but also from the author's observations and past field research experiences. The case studies from three different African countries emphasize the need to understand religion as an influential resource whose potential to influence spread of conflicts and war, or resolve conflicts and contribute to the peacebuilding processes, is entirely in the hands and minds of various actors in the communities. Importantly, religious actors, and specifically the leaders of different religions, are shown to have power and moral authority that may change the perspectives of either the communities or political leaders, and other stakeholders involved in the conflicts. This is because as members of the communities affected by the conflicts, the religious leaders are familiar with the contexts, local circumstances that lead to conflicts, the actors in the conflicts; and, they are more often than not non-partisan. They are also in many ways affected by the conflicts. In most cases, since as religious leaders, they are in positions of moral authority and command respect from the community members, their voices can turn around situations of conflicts. They also employ an inclusive approach that speaks to communal and religious orientation at the local level. Further, some of these leaders are aware of the global designs of peacebuilding, and specifically the United Nations Sustainable Development Goals (SDGs) and the Africa Union's (AU) Peacebuilding Architecture, that speaks to the need for grassroots approaches, whether formal or non-formal (AU, Transitional Justice Policy [AUTJP], 2019).

The chapter is therefore written within the lens of SDG 16, and the various targets thereof. SDG 16 aims at promoting peaceful and inclusive societies for sustainable development, providing access to justice for all and building effective, accountable, and inclusive institutions at all levels (https://sdgs.un.org/goals/goal16, accessed 3 January 2023). Besides the global development models, the continent of Africa has also put in place certain policies and by extension models, that speak to the continent's context but also the global peacebuilding agenda. The AUTJP (2019), for instance, has been contextualized within the continent in a way that it encourages not just peaceful but inclusive societies for sustainable peace and development, but also enhances effective and accountable institutions. Achieving these goals can only be evidenced through various milestones, as well as the efforts of individuals, communities, and institutions. This chapter focuses on religious institutions, and how they play roles in conflicts to either move towards the realization of peaceful and inclusive societies that are effective and accountable, or how their involvement in the conflicts disenfranchises the realization of sustainable peace and development.

## Operational Definitions

*Peace*, as most of the arguments in this handbook will show, in the context of violent conflicts, can be understood as a mere lack of violent conflicts, which amounts to negative peace; or, a situation where the root causes of violent conflicts are targeted to contribute to social justice for all, with an aim of enhancing accountability on the part of perpetrators, governments, and other actors, for sustainable development (see Galtung, 1996, for deeper analysis of positive and negative peace). The cases highlighted in this chapter will not only be used to show the relevance of religion in conflict resolution, but their strengths and weaknesses in strengthening inclusivity and accountability as a way of promoting social justice for sustained peace and development.

*Development*, in the words of Tarusarira (2017, p. 402), "has come to be understood as a multidimensional concept, that is people centred." It aims to better the human conditions while maximizing the potential of all members of the society through social and economic policies (see Gunda, 2020; Chitando et al., 2021). Development in the African context refers to the process of socio-economic transformation aimed at improving the living standards of people on the continent (Asongu, 2017; Nkwi, 2016). According to UNDP (2018), development in Africa involves expanding access to basic social services such as education, healthcare, and water supply, enhancing infrastructure development, increasing agricultural productivity, promoting industrialization, creating employment opportunities, and fostering inclusive economic growth. The African Union (2020) defines development as a multi-dimensional process that entails the pursuit of economic, social, and political objectives aimed at eradicating poverty, reducing inequality, and promoting sustainable development. In African societies, development is not viewed solely as an economic process, but rather as a holistic approach to addressing the challenges facing communities. Scholars such as Amartya Sen have emphasized the importance of human development, which encompass access to education, healthcare, and other basic needs (Sen, 1999). Development in Africa is also viewed as a process of empowerment that involves giving people the knowledge, skills, and resources they need to take control of their own lives and make decisions that affect their well-being (United Nations Economic Commission for Africa, 2015).

*Sustainable development*, one would argue, therefore, employs mechanisms that target the root causes of human and environmental injustices, with an aim of resolving these for a better world that minds the present but also the future generations (Tarusarira, 2017). This, in the context of this handbook on religion, peacebuilding, and development in Africa, implies the need to understand not just the mechanisms employed by the various religions and religious institutions in conflict resolution and peacebuilding processes, but also the efforts of these actors to understand the causes, depths, and vastness of the conflicts as well as systemic challenges. Such an approach would help them gauge their solutions for sustainable peacebuilding endeavours.

*Peacebuilding* is a continuous process that is not achieved through short-term goals. It takes a while for positive peace to be realized. The process of peacebuilding may therefore include a wide range of approaches, actors, and strategic planning. For *religious peacebuilding*, deeper reflections on what it means and what its aims and approaches are is key. Coward and Smith (2004, p. 5) define religious peacebuilding as "the range of activities performed by religious actors and institutions for the purpose of resolving and transforming deadly conflicts, with a goal of building social relations and political institutions characterized by ethos of tolerance and non-violence." This seems a comprehensive definition, only that one needs to realize that in the case of

Africa's conflicts, peacebuilding processes may be complicated, especially as a result of colonial history. Religious peacebuilding therefore may not be able to comprehensively address the historical root causes of violent conflicts. While evidencing this challenge, Kilonzo (2022) explains that the efforts of religious institutions to transition conflicting communities in Kenya's ethnic conflicts are limited when it comes to resolving issues revolving resources such as land. These require political will and reforms, which is hard to come by, since politicians use such issues to pit one ethnic group against the other. With such historical squabbles, a religious peacebuilding process that is all-round, tolerant, transformative, and sustainable remains out of reach for many religious actors in the field of peacebuilding. Defining religious peacebuilding within the realities of the experiences of conflicts in the continent of Africa, therefore, implies the need to examine the experiences, outcomes, and continued efforts of religious actors. It also invites approaches that target communities over time, with the need to document what has worked and what has not. This will allow a re-evaluation of the mechanisms of peacebuilding for improved efforts as informed not just by religious resources at hand, but also global perspectives, such as UN's and AU's objectives for peacebuilding.

Religious resources, as Owen and King (2013), Appleby (2000) and Sampson (2007) explain, include inner spiritual inspiration and transformation, scriptural and theological resources; religious rituals, established networks and hierarchies for enhancing advocacy, empowerment and equality, and mobilization of practical and financial resources, among others. A closer look at these, one would think of religious peacebuilding as an integrated approach that borrows from within religious and secular spaces for a comprehensive redress of violent conflicts. Subsequently, for one to claim to be a religious peacebuilder or actor in peacebuilding, their roles are not just open to playing religious leadership roles, but a non-partisan who can prophesy, observe, evaluate, negotiate, mediate, facilitate, educate, advocate, and sometimes sacrifice for conflicts to be resolved and peacebuilding to take course. As Owen and King (2013) argue, a religious peacebuilder should also encourage an inductive approach that aims at evaluation of scenarios, listening to the warring parties, and understanding of the religious (as well as cultural) ideas and values of those involved.

In this chapter, religious peacebuilding is considered as the efforts and activities of religious groups and actors to engage in conflict resolution and peacebuilding processes of communities experiencing violent conflicts of various nature. Their efforts may or may not be aimed at addressing the root causes of conflicts, for this may not be within their reach, but are efforts targeted at restoring human dignity after a difficult time of violent conflicts or war. The chapter, through this definition, will allow for the interrogation of various case studies in the continent, and raise the question whether these efforts are contributing towards the realization of SDG 16 and targets thereof. The chapter raises fundamental concerns that may be useful to stakeholders in this area, to further rethink their efforts, frameworks, and models for peacebuilding as they reflect on long-lasting solutions to conflicts in Africa. This is important because as scholars have pointed out, the field of religion and peacebuilding is moving closer to the mainstream of conflict resolution practice and theory (Hayward, 2012), and, faith-based organizations and actors seem to enjoy unmatched legitimacy within faith communities when compared to other actors such as civil society organizations (Lagho & Bonaya, 2016). This should give the religious actors an upper hand in moving towards sustainable peacebuilding processes that are inclusive and just, which in turn contribute to sustainable development.

The section below, in view of the role that religious peacebuilding espouses, interrogates both positive and negative contributions to the process. By highlighting three case studies in different African countries, this section shows that religious peacebuilding is varied. It may rely on one key actor as in the case of Kenya, but also interreligious approaches as in the cases of Central Africa Republic and Uganda. The reader needs to know that these cases are summarized, and there are details that one may need to refer to full analysis of the cases as presented in various literature, including those cited herein. The cases deploy diverse models that are valuable windows into the character and significance of religious peacebuilding in Africa.

## CASE STUDIES FOR RELIGIOUS CONFLICTS AND RELIGIOUS PEACEBUILDING

### *Bishop Cornelius Korir and the Amani Mashinani Model in Uasin Gishu, Kenya*

The late Cornelius Korir worked as a Bishop of the Diocese of Eldoret from 1992, until his death in October 30, 2017. His peacebuilding efforts begun in earnest in 1997 when he witnessed ethnic clashes, that were now a characteristic of every electioneering period, in various areas in the country, and specifically to his concern, in the North Rift. In his book, "*Amani Mashinani*, lit. Peace at the grassroots: experiences of community peacebuilding in the North Rift Region of Kenya," Korir (2009, p. 1) observes:

> It was in 1997 and my Diocese was engulfed in the ferocious turmoil surrounding the second multiparty elections after many years of dictatorial single party rule. Political authorities were sowing seeds of discord, dividing citizens along tribal lines and instigating terrible communal violence. At the same time, battles between Pokot and Marakwet warriors, instigated by cattle rustling, raged in the Kerio Valley.

Korir had an experience in the same year, 1997, where a shoot-out between Pokot and Marakwet[1] gunmen broke out as he was returning from a visit in West Pokot. He had to take shelter at a parish house in Chesongoch until the fights settled. He then returned to Eldoret but was informed that the gunmen saw his vehicle and let him pass, before they shot at the District Commissioner's vehicle that was just a few minutes behind Bishop's car. He notes:

> [O]ne of the Pokot commanders told the Sisters [at Chesongoch] that they had discussed whether to shoot at my vehicle. The warriors had wanted to, but had eventually decided against it, because I was a Bishop and because the Diocese had provided their villages with food during a recent famine. (2009, p. 2)

It is then that the Bishop realized that the Church needed to do more stewardship work by working together with communities for sustainable peace and development. When the Bishop asked the elders how the Church would be of help to them, the elders from the warring communities, through the leadership of Catholic Justice and Peace Commission—CJPC—indicated that they needed help with mediation, that would facilitate dialogue amongst the elders, as a starting point to conflict resolution. At the start, they held meetings at hotels but realized the real peace talks were needed more at *mashinani* (grassroots), as a way of reaching out to perpetrators, for sustainable peacebuilding efforts to take root (Korir, 2009; Kilonzo & Onkware, 2022). The late Bishop notes that bringing the warring communities together was not easy, but for grassroots peacebuilding, it was important. His argument was that wisdom was called for, on the part of religious leaders during the meetings. Although the initial meetings held were between the chiefs as representatives of the two communities and the Bishop, they latter knew there would be a lot of finger-pointing, accusations, and almost fights. This, however, was the only way, for peace to be realized. This inductive approach that allows for conflicting parties to tell their stories, experiences, grievances, and what they understood to be the best way of resolving conflicts within their own contexts (Owen & King, 2013; Kilonzo, 2022).

Part of the initiatives in the North Rift, especially among the pastoralists, was to establish communal projects for the fighting parties, as a way of starting dialogue. A school for children who had been affected by the never-ending war was built along the border of the two communities. To cure their animals of diseases that ravaged the stocks, they also, through the help of the Bishop, and the Catholic Church, built a cattle dip along the border, at a neutral place that is accessible to both communities (Korir, 2009, p. 4). Kilonzo and Onkware (2022) while evaluating the usefulness of such border projects, indicate that, as part of the peacebuilding process, dialogue is inevitable, and therefore, meeting

---

[1] The Pokot and Marakwet are two ethnic groups found in two neighbouring counties in the NorthRift, West Pokot and Elgeyo Marakwet counties. For many years, the two have been rivals, especially because they are both pastoralists. The rivalry is as a result of limited resources, pasture and water, for their cattle. Cattle rustling is therefore common in this area.

points, even for treating animals, or school parents' meetings, are spaces for dialogue. Kilonzo and Onkware (2022, p. 193) indicate that the Amani Mashinani model *"is based on a contact theory of change. That is, if conflicting communities continuously interact, there is a strong likelihood of reaching harmony between them."* The twelve steps of the model—which include analysis of the situation; protection, sanctuary, and relief; one-on-one meetings; small-group to small-group meetings; sharing food; intra-ethnic meetings; airing of grievances; preparation of the agenda and inter-ethnic meetings; reporting back and caucusing with communities; peace connector projects; social contract; and, monitoring and ongoing development of the agenda (for details on these stages see Korir, 2009; and for elaborate examples and analysis of the model, see Kilonzo & Onkware, 2022)—are all meant to ensure community dialogue throughout the conflict resolution and peacebuilding processes. A few examples below, to show how a number of these steps have worked out.

To strengthen the dialogue, the community mobilization through the peace committees—formed and coordinated by the communities—at the grassroots level, for purpose of conflict resolution, is therefore key. In 2007/2008, for instance, the post-election violence, mainly instigated by politicians, and largely pitting the Kalenjin against the Kikuyu in the North Rift, stretched the Churches' capabilities beyond limits. Over 10,000 internally displaced persons flocked into the Sacred Heart Cathedral, the headquarters of the Eldoret Diocese. This meant need for humanitarian assistance in healthcare, food, and trauma healing. Korir (2009) explains that their experience in working with communities in West Pokot and Elgeyo Marakwet were useful in helping him and the Church to address the crisis of 2007/2008. The steps of handling conflicts developed in the previous conflicts among the Pokots and the Marakwets proved useful in the conflicts, mainly among the Kikuyu and the Kalenjin in Uasin Gishu County. The Bishop, just as he did in 1997 and way before in 1992 during ethnic clashes, tried not just to initiate a conversation, but also interrupt the conflict. He remembered that in 1992 he had tried to drive from Eldoret to Turbo Town, which is about 34 km away, to check on the safety of Sisters who lived in a Parish in the Turbo. He had been warned that the place was inaccessible and that warriors had barricaded the roads and overwhelmed the police, but he decided to drive anyway. In a scary instance, he notes:

> As the Kalenjin youth sent about 20 men forward to draw fire and force the police to use up their ammunition, I stepped between them and the police, putting my hands above my head and shouting "Don't shoot! Don't shoot!" I do not know where I got the courage and doubt, I could do that again. After a tense standoff, the youth agreed to retreat if I would escort them, to ensure they were not shot in the back by the police. I did so and as we walked away, I overheard them complaining to each other, saying, "We should have gone earlier, before the pastor arrived." (p. 10)

He further gives examples of places where he negotiated for release of Kikuyus who had been cornered by Kalenjins in a village in Ol'Lessos, and surrounded as they awaited to be executed, but he negotiated for their release (Korir, 2009, p. 10). From these experiences, he knew non-violent interruption of armed violence, through the moral authority of a clergy in cassock and collar, gives the warring groups time to think, and as they do so, there is an opportunity to devise a strategy. In the 2007/2008 post-election violence, the Bishop would always meet up with the youth, men and women, involved in the conflicts and would urge them, since it was a planting season, to plant and get back to war. Of course, he knew by the time they finished planting, most probably, the talks that he had already started with the elders, would be advanced to allow for dialogue, and other steps for conflict resolution and peacebuilding.

The idea behind the one-on-one meetings is to allow for an understanding of the need to end violence, and begin dialogue that is aimed at addressing the root causes of conflicts. The Bishop reasoned that it is easier to control and help make sense of the situation, with a small group before rolling the process out to the communities, by use of the few individuals. The Bishop's role therefore, becomes that of a facilitator or a mediator, who was suited to do so because of his neutral and non-partisan position. Further, the model also benefited from the experience that dealing with small intra-group meetings helps understand their struggles without fracas because they speak of the same challenges. By listening and talking with them, they know what to expect in the inter-ethnic meetings, and importantly, how to articulate their grievances.

In the inter-ethnic meetings, as Korir (2009, p. 16) observes, the mediator should not rush the process, for there is need to listen to each side of the group. He notes that food brings communities together, and in order to show good faith, the conflicting parties should share in a meal. This speaks to inculturation, in which case the Church borrows from cultural practices that can be useful in peace processes. This is a way of cementing an agreement that despite their differences and grievances, they agree to forge forward peacefully until the conflicts are resolved. It is in the sharing of meals that the groups then agree to come up with a list of issues they accuse the other of, then the lists are later read out in a joint meeting so that the whole group can forge an agenda for peacebuilding engagement, including development projects and social contracts (for details on how these steps work, see Korir, 2009, and for more examples see Kilonzo & Onkware, 2020).

Development projects resulting from this model of peacebuilding were evidenced in construction of connector bridges, schools, and cattle dips, as well as milk cooling plants, table banking activities and agricultural activities in various localities in the North Rift. While some of these activities were financially supported by the Catholic Church through help from Catholic Relief Services (CRS), most of them were initiated by community members as a means to continue with dialogue, healing, and reconciliation. A number of them continue up to the time of writing (for details see Kilonzo, 2022).

This case illustrates how a religious actor bears vision for those in need of peace and development, and how this vision may help bring to an end the vicious cycle of violence, as spelt out under SDG 16, target 16.1, but also engage various actors with an aim of developing effective, accountable, and transparent grassroots institutions and communities (SDG 16.6), for sustainable peace and development. The model adopted by Bishop Korir and the Catholic Church extensively aims at responsive, inclusive, and participatory approaches to peacebuilding, that target not just local leaders and community members, young and old, in the decision-making process as seen in target 16.7. To this end, the top-down approach, mostly used by many government institutions, is replaced by the need for communities to make their own decisions, grow these decisions into action, and own the processes of peacebuilding for sustained peace and development as advocated for in SDG 16.6.

The development projects are not just meant to provide economic support for individuals and families but act as a basis for continued healing and reconciliation without a focus on people's religious or ethnic affiliations. They are meeting avenues for community members and their leaders. For this model, therefore, the idea is to forge forward and create grassroots institutions that serve people better through cooperation with those of other tribes, as well as connections to local and international bodies that can help them transition to peaceful co-existence and prevent future violence as SDG target 16.a encourages. This case therefore argues for transformative development that then leads to peace. One way in which development can promote peace in Africa is by reducing poverty and inequality, which are often underlying causes of conflict (UNDP, 2018). By promoting economic growth and social development, development can help address these root causes and reduce the risk of conflict. Further, development can promote social cohesion and build strong institutions that are essential for maintaining peace and stability. This includes investing in education and healthcare, improving access to justice and human rights, and promoting participatory governance and democracy (UNECA, 2021; UNEP, 2019). In the case of *Amani Mashinani* model, the projects established are clearly, a source of social cohesion.

From the use of a model that is already well articulated to help communities build peace, we now move to a door-to-door interreligious approach that is led by leaders of Christian churches and their Islamic counterparts. Whereas the case above speaks to a model that is led by an individual through community leaders and members, the Central Africa Republic approach differs in the sense of general public appeal for ending conflicts.

### *Christian–Muslim Joint Efforts in Central Africa Republic*

Central African Republic (CAR) has suffered extreme violent conflicts for a while (Gerlach, 2010), often referred to as the "forgotten" conflict (Marcucci, 2018), to become a very fragile state (WEA, 2014). Isaacs-Martin (2016, p. 26), shows that, since 1960, CAR has experienced wars resulting from "competitors attempting to usurp or maintain political leadership and power, and the constant scourge of rebel armies, militias, armed youths, bandits, and civilian criminality." She further argues that "CAR experienced violence, extrajudicial executions, torture, arbitrary arrest and detention, and rampant state corruption," albeit the presence of multiple state and non-state actors. More recently, although the 2013–2014 conflict is often understood as a religious confrontation that did not only pit government troops against militia but also resulted into civil and community confrontations, the real cause of violent conflicts is political leadership, and wrangles over the same (Isaacs-Martin, 2016). This observation below explains the political squabbles:

> Although Ange-Félix Patasse was elected democratically in 1993, he was ousted by François Bozizé in 2003. Bozizé in turn was ousted by Michel Djotodia who proclaimed himself president in 2013. Current president Faustin Touadera was elected democratically, after the caretaker interim government of Catherine Samba-Panza, although his rival Anicet Dologuele claimed there were irregularities. (Isaacs-Martin, 2016, p. 26)

Marcucci (2018, p. 2) indicates that President François Bozizé failed to implement "the disarmament, demobilization and reintegration programme in the northeast, investigate rebel and government crimes that had occurred since 2005, when Bozizé was officially elected, and for the general lack of governance in the region." Out of this political instability "a coalition of four mainly Muslim rebel groups, referred to as Seleka, led by Michel Djotodia, started their aggressive march towards Bangui, making steady gains in the northern and central regions of the country" (WEA, 2014, p. 5). From the end of 2012 to the beginning of 2013, the Seleka coalition, composed of armed groups from the Northeastern CAR, strongly opposed President François Bozizé (Marcucci, 2018). WEA (2014, p. 6) explains that "on 24 March 2013, the rebels were able to take over Bangui. Subsequently, Bozizé fled the country, and Michel Djotodia declared himself President, becoming the first Muslim President of the country (Siradag, 2016). He subsequently repealed the constitution and dissolved the national assembly." He also, in September 2013, officially called for the dissolution of the Seleka coalition (Marcucci, 2018). Although Djotodia took over leadership of the country. This did not last for long for he could not control the rebel movement and the armed forces. The Muslim rebels continued to terrorize the population, leading to the rise of other militia groups, mainly Christian and Animist self-defence groups called anti-Balaka, which means "anti-machete" in the Gbaya language (Marcucci, 2018; WEA, 2014). The anti-Balaka militia attacks targeted the Seleka members and the Muslim families, while the Seleka group targeted Christians, leading to a vicious violence (WEA, 2014).

It is in this context that the efforts of various religious groups and actors must be seen. In March 2013, CAR Christians issued a joint appeal to the international community to help stop bloodshed, through a declaration drafted by Church leaders that bore witness to 1.6 million internally displaced people (IDPs), 480,000 victims of malnutrition and 3500 children recruited into armed groups (WEA, 2014). Another declaration was issued on 4 February 2014 in which the Church leaders condemned the violence, and denounced unjust execution of Muslims carried out by mobs, calling on peace and reconciliation processes to begin (WEA, 2014).

Further, religious peacebuilding efforts are seen in the efforts of the collaboration of Protestant, Catholic, and Muslim communities in resolving the conflicts and starting a peacebuilding process, as exemplified by the leadership of Archbishop Dieudonné Nzapalainga, Pastor Guerekoyane-Gbangou and Imam Oumar Kobine Layama. The three travelled throughout the country to initiate interreligious dialogue among the communities divided by hatred and fear, albeit the death threats issued to some of these leaders. Imam Kobine, for instance suffered personal loss when his house was looted and burned down; and, death threats sent to him and his family (WEA, 2014). He had to take refuge in Archbishop Nzapalainga's residence. The archbishop and the pastor shielded the Imam form various attacks and called him their brother. The calls of these religious leaders at the community level, and in the media through the local radio stations or reconciliation were fearless efforts to reconcile the warring groups. They became the representatives of National Interfaith Peace Platform, setting up more than twenty peace committees in Bangui and outside the capital to promote dialogue in the villages. They used local church leaders as a way of dissuading mobs from heinous crimes, and encouraging dialogue through interreligious meetings (WEA, 2014).

Their efforts therefore attracted a lot of attention internationally, and they sought to, or were invited to meet high-level panels and leaders all over the globe to table the case for CAR. They met the then President of France, the UN Secretary General Ban Ki-moon, and were invited to the World Evangelical Alliance in Geneva to meet several dignitaries. In this latter meeting, they underscored the possibility of a split of CAR into North Eastern Muslim and Southern Christian sections if international help was not accorded. This would later happen in July 2014, "the ex-Seleka factions and anti-Balaka representatives signed a ceasefire agreement in Brazzaville leading, by the end of the year, to a de facto territorial partition of CAR with the Seleka controlling the north and anti-Balaka militias the south" (Marcucci, 2018, p. 3). The religious leaders, still in the Geneva meeting, further appealed for financial support for the Interim President at the time, Catherine Samba-Panza, whom they explained was not able to pay her staff. Through their grassroots efforts, they expected reconciliation to extend to higher levels of society and political spheres (WEA, 2014). When the general elections were held in December 2015, former prime minister Faustin-Archange Touadéra was elected President, and took office in February 2016, marking return to constitutional order (Marcucci, 2018, p. 3).

On 19 June 2017, through the Roman Catholic Church peace group Sant'Egidio, an "immediate ceasefire" deal was signed in Rome between the CAR government and 14 armed groups. However, the killings continued after the signing of the deal, with the UN giving warning of early signs of genocide, between the Fulani of Islam orientation and Christians (Marcucci, 2018). As the fights continued, in July 2017, the leader of Christian Revolution and Justice, Clément Bélanga, was killed by members of the National Movement for the Liberation, backed by Fulani fighters from Chad, leading to eruption of more violence (Marcucci, 2018, p. 4). This is an indication of the danger that religious leaders face in situations of conflicts.

This case illustrates the double-edge character of religion. First as a tool that can be appropriated within the political inadequacies to terrorize and maim citizens, and dislodge peace. From the case we see how religion can undermine the very principles of love and peace for all that it espouses, and wage war against those perceived as "others," going against most of what is espoused under SDG targets 16.1, 16.2, 16.5, 16.6, 16.7 and 16.a. This leads to discord, war, revenge, and unimaginable suffering as seen in the case of CAR. However, religion is also seen to play a useful role in encouraging ending of all forms of violence (SDG 16.1), fighting for end of abuse and violence against children (SDG 16.2), forging for stoppage of bribery and corruption towards the rebels (SDG 16.5); and through dialogue, both at national and international levels, moving towards transparency of individuals and institutions (SDG 16.6; 16.7), by enhancing open discussions among those fighting as well as interreligious dialogue; and, encouraging engagement of both national and international institutions in the peacebuilding processes (SDG 16.a). Although these three religious leaders might not have fully been able to help CAR achieve positive peace, their dedication, sacrifice, and commitment to the people of CAR is evidenced by their initiative, not just at the local level, but also engagement with the local leaders and international community. They might not have been able to achieve the targets set out by UN, but their contributions cannot be ignored.

This case study from Cetnral Africa Republic becomes useful in advancing the discourse that, even when there are no formal models for rallying for peaceful co-existence, the presence of religious leaders, and their action, remains important in calling for end to war. The successes, albeit with a number of challenges, cannot be under-estimated. The final case below applies an interreligious approach as well, although there seems to be a well outlined structure for use in the peace processes.

### *Catholic–Pentecostal–Muslim Joint Mission in Northern Uganda*

Northern Uganda has suffered civil conflicts for a long period. In fact, today, the one question that a researcher and a conflict analyst should seek to answer is whether the Northern Uganda is still at peace or is it at a phase of latent conflict that waits for an opportune time for conflicts to flare (ACCS, 2013). Khadiagala (2001) explains that civil conflicts in Northern Uganda had for a long time pit the Lord's Resistance Army (LRA) led by Joseph Kony against the government of President Yoweri Museveni after his victory over Tito

Okello, who had taken over from Milton Obote. After he assented to power, Museveni captured Gulu and Kitgum, and this led to a seed of dissent by the local opposition forces who had been dealt with violently (Okello, 2002, p. 5). Subsequently, the Okello's loyalists moved to Southern Sudan to form Uganda People's Democratic Army (UPDA) and began insurgency against government in Acholiland, also called Northern Uganda (Okello, 2002). In such a state of lawlessness Alice Auma Lakwena, claiming to cleanse the Acholi people, formed a new rebel movement, the Holy Spirit Movement (Okello, 2002). Lakwena claimed to have been inspired by the Holy Spirit. The movement attracted civilian following and put Museveni's government at a threat. The continued government push defeated Lakwena's movement in 1987 (Okello, 2002), and she fled to Kenya. Factions of dissatisfied Holy Spirit Movement, as (Okello, 2002) shows, continued their struggle, and were joined by others like Uganda People's Democratic Army, who had been defeated by Museveni government, to form the Lord's Resistance Army (LRA), led by Lakwena's cousin Joseph Kony (Khadiagala, 2001).

Several efforts were in place then, including brokered deals that were unsuccessful, both from within and outside Uganda. However, grassroots Church initiatives bore some fruit in restoring peace. For instance, a mediation by the Catholic Bishop of Gulu, Cypriano Kihangire between UPDA leaders and the government, which resulted into incorporation of the rebel leaders into the government, leaving the LRA guerrillas as the peripheral source of northern insurgency in Acholiland. The government created isolation camps as a way of isolating civilians from rebels. This marked the start of deterioration of relations between the Acholi and the government (Khadiagala, 2001). As the situation worsened, the government tried negotiations using the local leaders but this was not successful. Instead, the LRA received support from Sudanese government, especially finances from Islamic government in Khartoum, to strengthen LRAs operations. Sudanese involvement was in retaliation for Yoweri Museveni's involvement in supporting the rebel Sudan People's Liberation Army (SPLA). This kind of war made it difficult for actors to broker peace. A lot of atrocities were committed, including abduction of children (Yousuf, 2015), who were either trained as soldiers or acted as sex slaves (Khadiagala, 2001).

Part of religious peacebuilding efforts, as Khadiagala (2001) shows, involved the Acholi Religious Leaders Peace Initiative (ARLPI), who included Anglican Bishop of Northern Uganda Rev. Nelson Onono-Onweng, Catholic Archbishop of Gulu Diocese Most Rev. John Baptist Odama, the Anglican Bishop of Kitgum Diocese Rev. Macleod Baker Ochola, the Muslim chief Kadhi of Gulu Sheikh Suleiman Wadriff and Muslim Chief Kadhi of Gulu Sheikh Musa Khalil. Their interventions sought to draw from their moral and religious power, as well as the extensive organizational anchor of churches, parishes, and mosques. Since the Acholi belong to one or other of these religions, they became a basis for mobilization and interventions for both community members, local and national leaders; NGOs and international actors for mediated solutions to the conflicts. Their aim was to coordinate efforts for reconciliation and promote dialogue (Khadiagala, 2001; Latigo, 2008).

Their initial peace talks at Kitgum in the months of June and August 1997 resulted into a Joint-Justice and Peace organization as a result of prayers that were held jointly by Christians and Muslims (Khadiagala, 2001; Ntale, 2012). They condemned the establishment of protected camps by the government, and in place, called for peaceful approaches to the conflicts (Ntale, 2012; Khadiagala, 2001). They further sought help with the United Nations Development Programme (UNDP) office through Bishop Onono-Onweng, who acted as a liaison person as they had access to national and international networks (Latigo, 2008; Yousuf, 2015). By 1998, these peace initiatives had spread to Gulu. The leaders encouraged forgiveness, reconciliation, active community participation in healing, restoration, and development (Latigo, 2008). Through the help of UNDP, the leaders held workshops, meetings, and travelled to establish contacts with LRA and its allies. They had a structured approach to understand causes of insurgency, causes of its persistence, its impact on Acholiland and measures that all parties needed to take (Khadiagala, 2001; Latigo, 2008; Ntale, 2012). They also held meetings with local leaders such as District Commissioners, Local Council Chairs and Members of Parliament from Gulu and Kitgum. This made tabling of their findings easy at Uganda's Parliament. In November 1999, according to Khadiagala (2001, p. 8), "The Ugandan Parliament passed an Amnesty Act, reversing the previous resolution to use military force with the LRA, with the President indicating that he would accept ceasefire with the rebels." The advocacy for dialogue, non-use of military force as gestures for peaceful reconciliation had finally afforded ARLPI a win.

ARLPI, according to Khadiagala (2001, p. 9), embarked on sensitization campaigns that mostly happened in places of worship and within communities. By August 2002, ARLPI had trained sixty (60) Volunteer Peace Animators (VPAs) that corresponded to the 60 sub-counties in Gulu and Kitgum. These were local actors who understood the community well and were the "bedrock for sub-county peace committees ... that resolved individual and group conflicts, fostered gender relations, and promoted collaborative action in peacebuilding." ARLPI also became the buffer zone between rebels, abducted children and the government authorities.

Overall, as Khadiagala (2001) shows, ARLPI altered the behaviour of the government and its organs, including the military and the security forces in relation with the society as a whole. Museveni's apology in June 2000—" I am sorry about the continuing problems of insecurity... I have completely subdued my anger on Kony with his LRA soldiers in the interest of Ugandans and signed the Amnesty Bill"—is seen as an invite for those aggrieved to join forces and start working towards peace. It also was a starting point for reducing the perception of government marginalization of the North and the siege mentality that had characterized the Acholi community (Khadiagala, 2001, p. 11; Yousuf, 2015).

The offshoots of these peace efforts by the ARLPI included the creation of important institutions such as the Kitgum Joint Peace Forum (KJPF) and the District Reconciliation and Peace Team (DRPT) in Gulu, both aimed at spearheading joint peace initiatives (Ntale, 2012; Khadiagala, 2001). Further peace efforts by the ARLPI are seen in their negotiations for return of rebels that were a breakaway from LRA, and who had taken refuge in Kenya. The rebels trusted ARLPI to negotiate and assure them of safety on their return, hence an Amnesty Bill (Yousuf, 2015, p. 9).

Here again is a case that depicts religion negatively and positively in the peacebuilding environment. Alice Lakwena's movement can easily be faulted for her interest in encouraging rebellion against the government, and in fact, it is the movement from where LRA is seen to have its roots. However, the important role of religion is seen in the efforts of the various religious leaders to form a peace initiative—ARLPI. The moral authority of the religious leaders, their knowledge of the community, and overall command, seem to have earned them respect, not just within the community, but also with local government leaders, the rebels and the state leadership. They advocated zero use of military force, which might have in the end contributed towards SDG 16.4 that speaks to reduction of illicit financial and arms flows. This significantly reduced all forms of violence (SDG 16.1), and to a great extent ended abuse of children (SDG 16.2) who would has always been abducted to serve as soldiers and sex slaves. As the case illustrates, the religious leaders were able to alter the behaviour of the government and its organs, leading to State apology, that engaged the need for rule of law (SDG 16.3—see the three indicators in this target). This approach also encouraged dialogue, healing from trauma and through volunteer peace animators, engaged communities in decision-making processes (SDG 16.6 and 16.7), while tapping from the strengths of the government and international cooperation, especially through UNDP (SDG 16.a). These are achievements that would have not come by from without a well-thought-out approach to ending the violence.

Nevertheless, it might not be the case that Northern Uganda region claims to be in a state of positive peace. In fact, ACCS (2013) shows that inadequately addressed legacies of the war with LRA, especially the grievances of marginalization, are keeping the communities in Northern Uganda in a state of latent conflict, where any triggers can escalate violence of a high magnitude. This therefore calls for concerted efforts and continued thought-processes by religious leaders, actors, and other stakeholders to evaluate the situation in Northern Uganda and diagnose what aspects still require serious redress for sustainable peace. Although Yousuf (2015) explains that ARLPI conducts trauma-healing therapy for those affected by violence, and has mediated localized conflicts such as land disputes, there are still challenges since the mediation, especially on land can only be resolved fully by state actors.

## Towards a Conclusion

The conflicts exemplified in this chapter are Kenya's ethnic atrocities, CAR's political with religious overtones, and Northern Uganda's insurgency and civil unrests resulting from marginalization. These three summarized cases exemplify diversified ways in which religious leaders can engage in peacebuilding processes within the various forms of conflicts. There is evidence that religious peacebuilding is a contributory factor to peace, albeit with myriad challenges. Some of the challenges are noted in the inability of religious actors to make certain decisions that only require political will and push to resolve the underlying causes of conflicts, like in the case of Kenya and CAR. The case of Northern Uganda brings forth an ideal approach where the religious leaders, from the very beginning involve local leaders and parliamentarians in the peace talks. This then encourages swift uptake of the recommendations of the peacebuilding meetings and workshops, leading to enactment of legislations and Bills that influence the overall outcome.

In all the cases, a visible gap is noted on the role of women, and their leadership potential. Although they may be relegated other duties, all the three cases seem not to mainstream gender in key leadership. The marginalization of women and youth is a challenge noted of interfaith collaborations in development activities, by Chitando (2022), and which requires attention, if the inclusivity that is encouraged in SDG 16 is to be realized.

The chapter therefore concludes that for religious peacebuilding to succeed, and contribute to sustainable peace and development in the continent, there is need to pursue peacebuilding approaches that are participatory in nature, multi-layered with relevant stakeholders from the community, civil society organizations, local and international communities, as well as the decision-makers and legislators in the government. Further, religious peacebuilding should be led by leaders with moral authority, and respectable individuals, who the various stakeholders can engage. There is need for wisdom, humility, and vision for communities involved. The team must, as Owen and King (2013) explain, be ready to listen and learn from the experiences of the communities they are working with.

The chapter further concludes that these case studies on peacebuilding in Africa offer insights to the global scholarly communities on the complex relationship between religion and development. We see the relevance of religious institutions and actors in the role in promoting sustainable development. Importantly, the religious institutions are often deeply rooted in local communities, making them well-positioned to address development challenges such as poverty, inequality, and social exclusion.

The chapter also concludes that, there is need to take stock of the contributions of religious actors, since most of their efforts go unrecognized. This is so especially because, in order for the contributions to count towards the indicators of SDG 16, evaluation of the peacebuilding processes should be documented with accuracy and accompanying narratives listened to. There is so much peacebuilding activity, especially from the work of women and youth, which has religious inclination, but this is hardly documented. How and when will these efforts speak to the targets and indicators of SDG 16?

## References

ACCS. (2013). *Northern Uganda Conflict Analysis*. ACCS. Retrieved January 10, 2023, from https://www.files.ethz.ch/isn/170822/accs%2D%2D-northern-uganda-conflict-analysis-report.pdf

African Union. (2019). *Transitional Justice Policy: An Integrated, Prosperous and Peaceful Africa*. AU.

African Union. (2020). Silencing the Guns: Creating Conducive Conditions for Africa's Development. https://au.int/sites/default/files/documents/38615-doc-silencing_the_guns_2020_eng.pdf

Appleby, S. (2000). *The Ambivalence of the Sacred: Religion, Violence, and Reconciliation*. Rowman & Littlefield.

Asongu, J. J. (2017). *African Development: Theories, Policies and Practices*. Springer International Publishing.

Bouta, T., Kadayifci-Orellana, A., & Abu-Nimer, M. (2005). *Faith-based Peacebuilding: Mapping and Analysis of Christian Muslim & Multi-faith Actors*. Netherlands Institute of International Relations.

Chitando, E. (2022). Interfaith Networks and Development. In E. Chitando & I. Gusha (Eds.), *Interfaith Networks and Development: Case Studies from Africa* (pp. 3–26). Palgrave Macmillan.

Chitando, E., Gunda, M., & Togarasei, L. (2021). *Religion and Development in Africa*. University of Bamberg Press.

Coward, H., & Smith, G. (Eds.). (2004). *Religion and Peacebuilding*. SUNY Press.

Galtung, J. (1996). *Peace by Peaceful Means*. Sage.

Gerlach, C. (2010). *Extremely Violent Societies: Mass Violence in the Twentieth Century World*. New York: Cambridge University Press.

Gunda, M. R. (2020). Rethinking Development in Africa and the Role of Religion. In E. Chitando, M. Gunda, & L. Togarasei (Eds.), *Religion and Development in Africa* (pp. 37–57). University of Bamberg.

Hayward, S. (2012). Religion and Peacebuilding Reflections on Current Challenges and Future Prospects. Special Report 313. USIP.

Isaacs-Martin, W. (2016). Political and Ethnic Identity in Violent Conflict: The Case of Central African Republic. *International Journal of Conflict and Violence*, 10(1), 26–39.

Khadiagala, G. M. (2001). The Role of Acholi Religious Leaders in Peace Initiatives and Peace Building in Northern Uganda (USAID). The Full Report Can Be Found at: http://www.usaid.gov/regions/afr/conflictweb/pbp_report.pdf

Kilonzo, S. (2022). Transitional Justice and the Mitigation of Electoral Violence through *Amani mashinani* Model in UASIN Gishu County, Kenya. In E. Opongo & T. Murithi (Eds.), *Elections, Violence and Transitional Justice in Africa* (pp. 136–159). Routledge.

Kilonzo, S., & Onkware, K. (2020). Gendered Conflict Resolution: The Role of Women in Amani Mashinani's Peacebuiding Processes in UASIN Gishu County, Kenya. *The Journal of Social Encounters*, 4(1), 44–56.

Kilonzo, S., & Onkware, K. (2022). The Adaptability of the Catholic Church's *Amani Mashinani* Model in Kenya's North Rift Conflicts. *International Bulletin of Mission Research, 46*(2), 190–199.

Korir, C. (2009). *"Amani Mashinani" (Peace at the grassroots): Experiences of Community Peacebuilding in the North Rift Region of Kenya*. Catholic Diocese of Eldoret, Eldoret, Kenya.

Lagho, W., & Bonaya, A. (2016). Religion and Peace in East Africa: Pilot Study on Methodological Approaches and Tools for Measuring Change and the Results for Working with Religion and Religious Actors for Peace and Reconciliation. DANMISSION.

Latigo, J. (2008). Northern Uganda: Tradition-based Practices in the Acholi Region. In L. Huyse & M. Salter (Eds.), *Traditional Justice and Reconciliation after Violent Conflict Learning from African Experiences*. IDEA.

Lowder, S. K., Skoet, J., & Raney, T. (2016). The Number, Size, and Distribution of Farms, Smallholder Farms, and Family Farms Worldwide. *World Development, 87*, 16–29.

Marcucci, G. (2018). Central African Republic: Sectarian and Inter-communal Violence Continues. The War Report. Geneva Academy. https://www.geneva-academy.ch/joomlatools-files/docman-files/Central%20African%20Republic%20Sectarian%20And%20InterCommunal%20Violence%20Continues.pdf

Nkwi, P. N. (2016). African Development and Governance Strategies in the 21st Century. *International Journal of African Development, 3*(1), 5–21.

Ntale, F. (2012). Religious Actors and the Agenda for Peace in Northern Uganda. *The Journal of Social, Political and Economic Studies, 37*(3), 322–346.

Okello, L. (2002). *Protracted Conflicts, Elusive Peace: Initiative to End the Violence in Northern Uganda*. ACCORD.

Owen, M., & King, A. (2013). *Religious Peacebuilding and Development in Nepal. Winchester Centre of Religions for Reconciliation and Peace*. UK.

Pew Forum on Religion and Public Life. (2020). *Tolerance and Tension: Islam and Christianity UIN Sub-Saharan Africa*. Pew Research Centre.

Pew Research Centre. (2015). *The Future of World Religions: Population Growth Projections, 2010–2050. Pew-Templeton Global Religious Futures Project*. Pew Research Centre. https://assets.pewresearch.org/wpcontent/uploads/sites/11/2015/03/PF_15.04.02_ProjectionsFullReport.pdf

Sampson, C. (2007). Religion and Peacebuilding. In W. Zartman (Ed.), *Peacemaking in International Conflict* (pp. 273–323). United States Institute of Peace.

Sen, A. (1999). *Development as Freedom*. Anchor Books.

Siradag, A. (2016). Explaining the Conflict in Central African Republic: Causes and Dynamics. *Epiphany: Journal of Transdisciplinary Studies, 9*(3), 86–103.

Tarusarira, J. (2017). African Religion, Climate Change and Knowledge Systems. *The Ecumenical Review, 69*(3), 398–410.

UNDP. (2018). Africa Human Development Report 2016: Advancing Gender Equality and Women's Empowerment in Africa. Retrieved from https://www.undp.org/content/undp/en/home/librarypage/hdr/2016-africa-human-development-report.html

UNECA. (2015). The Structural Transformation Imperative in Africa. https://www.uneca.org/sites/default/files/PublicationFiles/sti-africa-2015-report_0.pdf

UNECA. (2021). Building Strong Institutions for Sustainable Development in Africa. https://www.uneca.org/sites/default/files/PublicationFiles/eca_policy_brief_-_building_strong_institutions_for_sustainable_development_in_africa.pdf

UNEP. (2019). From Conflict to Peacebuilding: The Role of Natural Resources and the Environment. https://www.unep.org/resources/report/conflict-peacebuilding-role-natural-resources-and-environment

WEA. (2014). *The Contribution of the Interfaith Platform to the Reconciliation Process I the Central Africa Republic*. Geneva: Switzerland, Geneva Liaison Office of World Evangelical Alliance.

Yousuf, Z. (2015). Accord Insight: In the Midst of Violence: Local Engagement with Armed Groups. In S. Haspeslagh & Z. Yousuf (Eds.) (pp. 6–9). Accord. https://rc-services-assets.s3.euwest1.amazonaws.com/s3fspublic/Local_engagement_with_armed_groups_in_the_midst_of_violence_Accord_Insight_2.pdf

Zeleza, P. T. (2008). Introduction: The Causes & Costs of War in Africa: From Liberation Struggles to the "War on Terror". In A. Nhema & T. Zeleza (Eds.), *The Roots of Africa Conflicts*. OSSREA and James Curry.

CHAPTER 3

# Religion and Peacebuilding in African Religious Studies and Theology: An Overview and Preliminary Evaluation

*Ezra Chitando*

## Introduction

The field of religion and peacebuilding has gradually taken shape (see e.g. Shannahan & Payne, 2016), with scholars from within religious and peace studies, as well as from other disciplines, making significant contributions. As the probing review by Omer (2012) confirms, there are diverse approaches and standpoints within the field. However, apart from a few references to reflections from South Africa, the reader of Omer's article would be forgiven for imagining that there is very little material on religion and peacebuilding that is emerging from Africa. To say this is not to blame Omer, but to acknowledge the absence of publications that present the literature on religion and peacebuilding in Africa in a more coherent and systematic way (for a contribution from an earlier period, see e.g. Carney, 2010).

As this chapter will attempt to demonstrate, there is a sizeable body of literature that has emerged (and continues to be generated) on religion and peacebuilding in Africa by African scholars. The situation where African scholars were condemned to taking up the role of only being reviewers of books on religion and peacebuilding in Africa published by scholars from the global North has changed, with a number of African scholars and practitioners

---

E. Chitando (✉)
Department of Philosophy, Religion and Ethics, University of Zimbabwe, Harare, Zimbabwe

© The Author(s), under exclusive license to Springer Nature Switzerland AG 2023
S. M. Kilonzo et al. (eds.), *The Palgrave Handbook of Religion, Peacebuilding, and Development in Africa*,
https://doi.org/10.1007/978-3-031-36829-5_3

publishing full-length books on religion and peacebuilding in Africa. These have been accompanied by the now numerous articles in refereed journals, chapters in books and other publication platforms on the theme.

This chapter seeks to summarise and evaluate publications on religion and peacebuilding in Africa by African scholars. It is envisaged that the evaluation shall be utilised to spur further reflections on how the field can achieve the objectives of the United Nations Sustainable Development Goal Number 16, focusing on "promoting peaceful and inclusive societies". In this regard, therefore, this chapter itself does not engage with SDG 16 at length, but seeks to provide a platform to enable reviews of the extent to which African scholars of religion and theologians are contributing towards understanding the role of religion in meeting the objective of SDG 16 (see e.g. Flaningan, 2013 for a review of religion, peacebuilding and development). *The Bulletin of Ecumenical Theology* (Volume 25, 2013) anticipated the SDGs by focusing on "Peacebuilding, Social Transformation and Religion in Africa."

From the onset, I must underscore the point that the chapter does not claim to be exhaustive or to be the definitive guide: only a larger study can attempt to do justice to the significant body of literature on religion and peacebuilding in Africa that has been produced and continues to be generated by African scholars. In the Section, "Contextual Factors Relevant for Understanding the Growth of Scholarship on Religion and Peacebuilding in Africa", the chapter outlines the context in which research and publication on religion and peacebuilding in Africa is being undertaken. In the Section, "Religion and Peacebuilding in Africa: Summarising Emerging Themes from Within African Religious Studies and Theology", the chapter summarises some of the key areas of focus/dominant themes emerging from the field. In the Section, "African Scholarship on Religion and Peacebuilding in Africa: A Critical Appreciation", the chapter analyses some areas for further strengthening the African scholars' engagement with religion and peacebuilding in Africa. In conclusion, the chapter acknowledges the significant contribution that African scholars are making to this very strategic field.

## Contextual Factors Relevant for Understanding the Growth of Scholarship on Religion and Peacebuilding in Africa

In order to put the remarkable growth in the number of publications on religion and peacebuilding in Africa, particularly since the early 2000s in its proper context, it is necessary to highlight some factors that have contributed to this development. If religion in Africa (and elsewhere) must be understood in society (Bourdillon, 1991), it is equally helpful to appreciate the context in which publications on religion and peacebuilding in Africa have emerged. While such an engagement might appear to be a form of postponing the discussion of the core issues, such an interpretation would be unfortunate. It would emerge from the wrong assumption that scholars of religion operate outside the material conditions that influence their teaching, research, publication and activist interests (see e.g. Ensign and Karegere, 2020). Indeed, there is a challenge when African scholars of religion and theologians are not located in their specific/definite life settings and the focus is overwhelmingly on the supposedly disembodied content of their courses (see e.g. Amanze, 2012). As is the case with other academics, scholars of religion and theologians are located in space and time and their teaching, research, publication and community engagement activities are influenced by their contexts. Further, being aware of issues that are preoccupying researchers in other fields within African Studies in Africa serves to de-marginalise African religious studies and theology and relate it more closely to other areas of study. Below, I outline some of the factors that have contributed to the growing interest in religion and peacebuilding in Africa (including themes generated by scholars from outside the continent).

### *Growing Interest in Conflict and Violence, and Peacebuilding in Africa, Including Violence Against Women*

Africa has experienced (and continues to experience) a disproportionate number of violent conflicts, with those given to theorising conflicts stampeding to provide explanatory frameworks. In particular, the genocide in Rwanda in 1994, the Truth and Reconciliation Commission (TRC) in South Africa (1995–2002, responding to Apartheid), the First Civil War in Liberia (1989–1996), the contemporary violent extremism in various parts of the continent, coups, violence against women and girls and other factors have precipitated growing interest in conflict and peacebuilding in Africa. For example, Aremu (2010) summarises the causes of violence in Africa as including arbitrary borders by colonial powers, tensions due to heterogeneous ethnic populations, inept leadership, corruption and poverty. Other African scholars from diverse disciplines have sought to account for Africa's seeming covenant with conflict and violence. Alao (2007) reviewed the role of resources in African conflicts. Nhema and Zeleza (2008) edited the volume, *The Roots of African Conflicts: The Cause and Costs*, and the contributors seek to explain the dynamics of conflicts in Africa. Similarly, Chingono (2016) seeks to account for violent conflicts on the continent and makes the following submission:

> [T]he paper advances four interrelated propositions. First, violent conflicts in Africa have many causal and escalation factors, and these include: psychological, political, economic, and social conditions; the nature of the protagonists and key actors; the relations between conflict parties; the conditioning contexts which structure the conflict (economic, ethnic and religious); and external forces. Second, depending on circumstances, any of the many causes of conflict may assume primacy, while other equally important causes may be overlooked, often with serious implications for post-war peace building. Third, underlying the many apparent causes of conflicts in Africa is the undying desire for happiness, a desire

which has been frustrated by our inadequate political, economic and social systems. Finally, changes in key actors and of the external environment can lead to a redefinition of the goals of the conflict … individual personalities, social processes, systems and institutions, historical coincidences, and local and global forces have all contributed to shaping the goals, dynamics and consequences of violent conflicts in Africa. (Chingono, 2016, p. 200)

The reality of conflict and violence in Africa that Chingono draws attention to in the foregoing citation has spurred an accompanying interest in reconciliation, healing, conflict transformation and peacebuilding. Thus, interest in human security in Africa has increased among scholars. For example, Adedeji's (1999) edited volume, *Comprehending and Mastering African Conflicts: The Search for Sustainable Peace and Good Governance*, represents such a quest. Juma (2002) undertook an informative evaluation of African institutions in relation to peacebuilding capacity and potential. Significantly, however, religious institutions did not feature in the review. As I illustrate below, this overlooks the role of religious institutions in contributing to peace in Africa.

The shift from state-centric interpretations of security (see e.g. Aall and Crocker, 2017) to human security has seen investments in describing human security in Africa (see e.g. Asaka & Oluoko-Odingo, 2022). The ongoing commitment towards unpacking peacebuilding in Africa (see e.g. Mawere & Marongwe, 2016; Karbo & Virk, 2018; Kalu & Kieh, 2021 and, Charbonneau & Ricard, 2022) has put the theme firmly on the agenda of African Studies in Africa and beyond. Similarly, Spiegel et al.'s (2022) massive volume, *Peace Studies for Sustainable Development in Africa: Conflicts and Peace Orientated Conflict Resolution*, provides insights into this strategic area of study. The extent to which traditional justice mechanisms can be applied after violent conflict in Africa has been explored in an informative way in Huyse and Salter's (2008) edited volume, *Traditional Justice and Reconciliation after Violent Conflict: Learning from African Experiences*. However, Boege's (2011) "Potential and Limits of Traditional Approaches in Peacebuilding" seeks to proffer a more balanced perspective. Reviews of individual leadership qualities that predispose one towards reconciliation-oriented leadership, as in Nelson Mandela (Lieberfeld, 2014), have also contributed towards understanding peacebuilding in Africa.

It is in the same context of seeking to address violence that there has been a growing commitment towards tackling violence against women in war times, as well as in intimate relationships. Literature on violence against women in Africa is increasing (see e.g. Onditi & Odera, 2021), with various contributors demonstrating its widespread nature. Other scholars have highlighted the vulnerability of women to violence in conflict situations, as acknowledged by the United Nations Security Council Resolution 1325 of 2000 (see e.g. the chapters in Section IV, "African Women in Conflict and Peace," in Yacob-Haliso & Falola, 2021). The volume, *Feminist Solutions for Ending War* (MacKenzie & Wegner, 2021), offers helpful insights into women's agency in ending war. On her part, Onyegbula (2018) analyses the contribution of women to peacebuilding in Northern Nigeria. Some reflections on women and violence have also included re-examining the role of men and masculinities in violent conflicts in Africa. This relates to their role as both perpetrators and victims or survivors of violence.

African scholars of religion from diverse fields could not remain uninfluenced by the growing interest in the themes of conflict and peacebuilding in Africa. It is in this environment where contributors from other fields of study have been raising questions about the causes of violent conflicts, as well as seeking how to contribute towards effective peacebuilding in Africa that African scholars on religion must be located. Debates on the relationship between peace and justice (see e.g. African Union Panel of the Wise, 2013), transitional justice (see e.g. Wachira et al., 2014) and the role of regional economic communities and peacebuilding (Murithi, 2019; Adetula et al., 2021) show the willingness of African scholars to engage with challenging issues. Like their counterparts in the different regions of the continent and beyond, they seek to contribute towards the African Union's vision of a peaceful and prosperous Africa, as articulated in Agenda 2063: The Africa We Want (https://au.int/en/agenda2063/overview).

## *Significant Investment in Peacebuilding by Funders and Organisations*

One major factor enabling the growing scholarship on violence and peacebuilding in Africa is that there has been a consistent commitment towards funding research in these areas by different funders (but mostly from the US). For example, the Harry Frank Guggenheim Foundation has been running a number of research grants that have attracted many African scholars. These include the Harry Frank Guggenheim African Fellows (formerly Harry Frank Guggenheim Young African Scholars), where young African scholars in the Social Sciences and Humanities, including some from religious studies and theology, have undertaken research and publication in violence and peacebuilding in Africa.

Other funders in the field include the African Peacebuilding Network (APN), supported by the Social Science Research Council (SSRC). The APN has facilitated the emergence of younger African academics who are providing valuable reflections on violence and peacebuilding in Africa. For example, Festus K. Aubyn (2018), one of their alumni, has generated this chapter's operational definition of peacebuilding. Thus:

> peacebuilding is today understood to encompass the full array of processes, approaches, and stages needed to transform conflict situations toward more sustainable peaceful relationships, and development before and after conflicts. ... The expansion of the term has been accompanied by a growing body of literature from diverse geographic, disciplinary, and intellectual backgrounds and traditions

that have attempted to make sense of peacebuilding activities and their consequences. (Aubyn, 2018, p. 1)

Equally significant are continental and regional social science organisations such as the Council for the Development of Social Science Research in Africa (CODESRIA) and the Organization for Social Science Research in Eastern and Southern Africa (OSSREA). They have supported scholarship on violence and peacebuilding in Africa. More directly relevant to the funding of research on religion and peacebuilding in Africa is the Nagel Institute, based at Calvin University in the US. They have been supporting diverse projects, including those focusing on religion and peacebuilding in Africa.

### *Notable Increase in the Number of Church-Related, Public and Private Universities Offering Peace Studies*

While the challenge of securing African epistemic decolonisation continues in African universities (see e.g. Ndlovu-Gatsheni, 2017), it is worth noting that the number of universities in Africa continues to increase significantly. With Africa's youthful population demanding access to higher education, governments and the private sector have been motivated to increase the number of universities. In particular, there has been notable expansion in the number of church-related universities in Africa (Carpenter, 2017). In the different regions of the continent, many theological institutions have transitioned to become Christian universities (see e.g. Mulatu, 2017). Significantly, this includes African Pentecostal institutions. In those African countries where Pentecostalism is gaining momentum, including Nigeria, Ghana, Kenya, Zimbabwe and others, Pentecostal churches are establishing competitive universities. Many of the church-related universities (as well as the new public and private universities) have programmes and courses that focus on peacebuilding or related content. Reviewing these, however, requires a separate study.

The increase in the number of Christian universities in Africa has seen a corresponding rise in the number of participants in African theology and religious studies. This expansion of the sector has also led to the diversity of themes, including younger researchers who have explored the theme of religion and peacebuilding. They have sought to challenge the emerging emphasis on religion and violence by highlighting religion's peacebuilding capacities. As the chapter highlights below, scholars in African theology and religious studies have approached the theme from diverse angles, consistent with the diversity that now characterises the field.

# Religion and Peacebuilding in Africa: Summarising Emerging Themes from Within African Religious Studies and Theology

Having explored some of the key factors influencing the notable output on religion and peacebuilding in Africa by scholars in African religious studies and theology in the foregoing sections, in this section I seek to summarise some of the major themes that are emerging in this field. The thematic approach adopted implies that no exhaustive discussion of the contributions is possible and that the publications cited under a specific theme are representative, rather than being deemed as definitive. Further, the non-inclusion of particular publications is not indicative of my perception of their quality, but confirms the impact of space constraints or lack of access to such literature on my part. I must also readily concede that other narratives on the same theme might organise the material differently and present a different picture.

In terms of coverage, while Wijsen (2007, p. 32) includes European scholars who specialise in African studies within the ambit of his definition of an African scholar, I am operating with a more restricted definition of the same. Thus, I am focusing mostly on the work of black African scholars who have been born on the continent and trace their ancestral heritage to Africa. This is not to reject the contribution of Africanists (white scholars writing on Africa), but to privilege the voices and amplify the presence of African scholars, who are mostly silenced and invisibilised due to power differentials in the study of Africa (see e.g. Olukoshi, 2007, p. 10). For the avoidance of doubt, the works of white African scholars on religion/theology/the Bible and peacebuilding in Africa are included in this review.

## *Multiple Approaches to Religion and Peacebuilding in Africa*

One striking fact about publications on religion and peacebuilding in Africa is that they emerge from various sub-fields within and beyond African religious studies and theology and began to appear with greater frequency from the early 2000s (but gaining momentum from the late 1990s, probably due to the increase in publishing opportunities and the expansion of higher education in Africa). This inter/trans/multi-disciplinarity has ensured that the field is very rich and diverse. I should hasten to add, however, that there are considerable overlaps across the categories that I have utilised to filter the publications on religion and peacebuilding in Africa. The main focus was on works that focus on how religion (broadly defined) serves as a resource for peacebuilding in Africa. Therefore, one needs to approach them with a high degree of flexibility, avoiding methodological puritanism and absolutism. This implies that there should be no contradiction between, for example, biblical studies approaches and women's studies approaches to religion and peacebuilding, if, for example (as has happened and is happening), some African women scholars have utilised the Bible in their reflections on religion and peacebuilding in Africa.

To begin with, some scholars have employed insights from social scientific approaches to the study of religion to outline the complexities of religion and violence in Africa. For example, Joram Tarusarira's (2016) *Reconciliation and Religio-political Non-Conformism in Zimbabwe* uses the historical-critical approach to examine how religious movements on the margins approach the themes of reconciliation and political engagement. Tesfai's (2010) *Holy Warriors, Infidels, and Peacemakers in Africa* provides an overview of religion and violence in the different regions of the continent and some examples of religious peacebuilding in Africa. On the other hand, Sewe (2018) explores the teachings on peace in the different religions and proceeds to analyse how religious women in Liberia contributed to peacebuilding, as does Kumah (2021) with reference to Uganda and Sierra Leone. Nigerian scholars of religion feature prominently among those who have been consistent in grappling with the role of religion in peacebuilding. Some of them have sought to provide the platform for taking up analyses of religious peacebuilding by presenting historical accounts of religion and violence in Nigeria. These include reflections by Sulaiman (2016) and Alao (2022). These studies confirm the need for systematic analysis of religion in society. There is an accompanying call for students of religion to be accorded a strategic place in society and to increase appreciation of the role of religious literacy/education in facilitating peace (see e.g. Ushe, 2015). Thus:

> [t]he way out of dysfunctional character of religion in human society is rigorous study of religion[,] especially in institutions of learning. The aim would be to understand religion as such: its meaning and content, the basic differences and similarities with the determination to play down the differences and emphasize the similarities … a rigorous study of Religion is important for sustainable development in Nigeria, a pluralistic country of varied cultures, ethnic groups, political affiliations and consequently religious groups. The focus is on how to resolve the conflicts that often greet pluralism to the destruction of sustainable development. (Ibeifuna & Uzoigwe, 2012, pp. 133–134)

The insights from social scientific approaches have been supplemented by publications that embrace diverse approaches. This includes Girma's (2018) *The Healing of Memories: African Christian Responses to Politically Induced Trauma*, Nel et al.'s (2020) *Reconciliation, Forgiveness and Violence in Africa: Biblical, Pastoral and Ethical Perspectives* and Kanu and Ndubisi's (2020) *Religion and Peacebuilding in Africa*. Here, it is important to acknowledge the role of scholars from within African biblical studies, such as Loba (-) Mkole and Mugambi's (2020) *Peace-Building in Africa: Biblical Insights* (see also e.g. Adamo, 1997, Zulu, 1998, Agbiji & Etukamana, 2018 and Chamburuka, 2020). It is also possible to regard Gerald West's work on Contextual Bible Study, particularly as it relates to addressing sexual and gender-based violence in Africa, as expressions of peacebuilding and development. He elaborates as follows:

> The knowledge of the poor is vital to any project of social transformation. Development cannot be done without the presence of the poor themselves. They are the agents of their own development and they have assets; among these assets is religion. … Faith, and faith-based resources like the Bible, are potential assets which the poor (and other marginalised sectors) can deploy in projects of social transformation. By engaging with gender-based violence, it is the presence and participation and knowledge of the habitual victims of gender-based violence—women—which provides the starting point of social transformation. Their epistemology is fundamental to an analysis of gender-based violence and their epistemology provides the necessary 'logic' for the forms of action which they might choose to take as part of a transformative project. (West, 2019, pp. 156–157)

What these publications confirm is that religion and peacebuilding is a broad theme that can (and must?) be approached from multiple angles. Thus, contributors utilise multiple approaches to the study of religion, including historical and phenomenological, psychological, philosophical and feminist approaches, as well as biblical studies, to showcase how religion is contributing to peacebuilding in Africa.

## *The Dominance of Perspectives from Within Christianity*

Consistent with Christianity's dominance and influence in African religious studies and theology, the bulk of the literature on religion and peacebuilding in Africa utilises perspectives from within Christianity. To this extent, one might argue that for many contributors to the discourse, "religion" is almost synonymous with "Christianity." Some of the leading contributors—such as Desmond Tutu (see e.g. 1999; for a more detailed engagement with Tutu's approach, see e.g. Nadar et al., 2021), Michael Lapsley (2012) and Emmanuel Katongole (see e.g. 2017)—write from within African Christian theology (though they also appropriate indigenous concepts). Scholars in this category seek to apply insights from Christian theology to interpret the role of the churches in peacebuilding in Africa (see also Phiri et al., 1996; Getui & Kanyandago, 2003). Similarly, although edited by scholars who are from outside Africa (but in solidarity with the continent), the volume, *Seeking Peace in Africa: Stories from African Peacemakers* (Miller et al., 2007), provides space to African Christian peace activists. They explore the mandate of church leaders and lay members in countering cultures of violence by embracing and putting into action teachings on peace and justice from within the Christian tradition. In an informative review of the turn towards reconciliation in African theology, Carney (2010) makes the following submission, which I cite at considerable length due to the insights it avails:

> Reconciliation not only has deep Christian roots, but like all successful theology it speaks to the current context. If reconstruction emerged from the ephemeral hopes of the second wave of African democratization, reconciliation grew out of

the enduring pain of ethnic and political conflict in places like Northern Uganda, Nigeria, and Burundi. … Philosophically, the paradigm recognizes post-modern difference while moving beyond the paralysis of post-modern parochialism to a critical synthesis of Christian revelation, African tradition, and Western modernity. Politically, reconciliation theology has had great influence, most famously in South Africa's Truth and Reconciliation Commission but also in post-conflict resolution efforts in countries ranging from Sierra Leone to Rwanda to Mozambique. Ecclesially, reconciliation has emerged as a dominant missional theme for Christian groups as diverse as the Lausanne Evangelicals and the Roman Catholic Church. … The paradigm responds to the post-colonial critique of otherworldly missionary theology without losing sight of the graced horizon. In short, reconciliation seems to be basking in a unique *kairos* moment. (Carney, 2010, p. 553)

It is strategic to single out the impact of contributions from within the Catholic Church to peacebuilding in Africa. Due to space considerations, I shall summarise two main issues (a separate review of the contribution of Catholic scholars to peacebuilding in Africa is required). First, there is a consistent commitment to reflect on the role of Catholic leaders to peacebuilding in Africa. For example, the volume, *Catholic Church Leadership in Peace Building in Africa* (Opongo & Kaulemu, 2014), offers valuable insights into the activities of leaders of the Catholic Church in Africa in relation to peacebuilding. It details how Catholic Church leaders in diverse African settings are undertaking effective peacebuilding work. Reflecting on the many assets and gifts that the institutional church possesses, African Catholic theologians have sought to challenge the Church to be more effective in peacebuilding in Africa (see, among others, Orobator, 2011; Katongole, 2017).

Second, the Catholic Church in Africa has given rise to activist-scholars such as Bishop Matthew Hassan Kukah in Nigeria and Fr Fidelis Mukonori in Zimbabwe. Kukah has been an exceptionally courageous, perceptive (see e.g. Kukah, 1993) and consistent peacebuilder in Nigeria. Operating with a broader concept of human security as human flourishing and addressing the daily challenges of the average Nigerian, Kukah brings forth an amplified reading of and approach to peacebuilding. As Bishop of the Catholic Diocese of Sokoto, Kukah delivered a blistering 2020 Christmas message that spoke truth to power and redefined peace as guaranteeing the health, well-being and flourishing of the regular citizen.[1] Thus, alongside the Kukah Centre and chairing Committees on Interreligious Dialogue in Nigeria and West Africa for the Bishops' Conferences, Kukah has gravitated towards recognising peacebuilding as affirming justice, dignity as well as liveable and fulfilling lives for all. On the other hand, Mukonori (see e.g. 2017) has been actively involved in peacebuilding in Zimbabwe, starting from the 1970s' war of liberation and through the early 1980s' Gukurahundi massacres. Perhaps his finest hour was in November

---

[1] See https://saharareporters.com/2020/12/30/full-text-bishop-kukahs-christmas-message-sparked-reactions, accessed 9 January 2023.

2017 when he was instrumental in persuading former President Robert Mugabe to step down and avoid a bloodbath during the military action that led to regime change in the country. As noted above, Kukah and Mukonori can be read as activist-scholars in the discourse on religion and peacebuilding in Africa.

While more space is required in order to try and do justice to the contribution of Catholic scholars and activist-scholars to peacebuilding in Africa, one might draw attention to the impact of rigorous training in philosophy and theology/religious studies, exposure to different settings, supportive/enabling systems and participating in a long tradition of commitment to and activism for justice and peace. African Catholic scholars and activist-scholars tend to possess high academic qualifications, have experienced life in other settings in Africa and elsewhere, remain active in academic and intellectual reflections and often can count on the Catholic Church's global networks for support. Further, Catholic universities in Africa have remained vibrant, benefitting from contextual theological reflection and effective leadership (see e.g. Ilo, 2018 for a discussion on Catholic education in Africa).

There is less literature on the contribution of African Initiated/Indigenous Churches (AICs) and Pentecostal churches to peacebuilding in Africa. However, one can envisage more publications on the contributions of Pentecostalism, as it is playing a significant role in the politics of a sizeable number of African countries (see e.g. Kaunda, 2018; Obadare, 2018). For a discussion in relation to Pentecostalism, politics and development, see for example Burgess (2020). While Pentecostalism's generally militant approach towards some aspects of African culture might generate tension and conflict (see e.g. Machingura et al., 2018), this does not exclude its potential to promote peace, integration and harmony within communities. The increase in the number of Pentecostal universities in Africa that I referred to in an earlier section suggests that more African Pentecostal scholars are likely to be highlighting the positive role of Pentecostalism to peacebuilding in Africa in the immediate future.

### *Reflections on Islam, and Interfaith Contributions to Peacebuilding in Africa*

AlongsideChristianity, Islamenjoys a significant following on the African spiritual market. As studies of Islam in Africa continue to grow, as confirmed by, for example, *The Palgrave Handbook of Islam in Africa* (Ngom et al., 2020) and the *Routledge Handbook of Islam in Africa* (Østebø, 2022), there has been an accompanying interest in the role of Islam in peacebuilding in Africa. This is particularly the case given the extent to which Christianity and Islam are often projected as being locked in mortal combat (though in reality Christians and Muslim have been able to get along very well in the past, in the present and, most likely, in the future). Given the extent to which Islamophobia, whereby Islam is often presented by the Western media as a violent religion harbouring terrorists, focusing on Islam's contribution to peacebuilding might be regarded as integral to the role of the scholar of religion. This is in relation to the scholar of religion's task of being balanced and contributing to social transformation (see e.g. Van Klinken, 2020).

Since it is not possible to provide an exhaustive review of scholarship on Islam and peacebuilding in Africa in the scope of this chapter, I shall draw attention to two notable trends. First, there is interest in how specific Muslim groups seek to make their contributions to peacebuilding in local contexts. Thus, Kilonzo (2011), confirming the importance of engaging local leaders (see e.g. Ruppel & Leib, 2022), has analysed the contribution of the Ahmadiyya Muslims in Kisumu, Kenya. Second, some researchers adopt country-wide approaches. This is the case with Zagoon-Sayeed (2018)'s focus on Islam and peacebuilding in Ghana, and Omar's (2022) focus on Islam, peace and development in Somalia. Similarly, Baderin (2020) seeks to apply Islamic precepts for peace, security and socioeconomic development in Nigeria. Equally informative is Ludovic's (2021) reference to Islamic social and humanitarian services in Africa (see also Weiss, 2020).

Due to the strategic contribution of interfaith initiatives and networks to peacebuilding (and development, see e.g. Chitando and Gusha, 2022) in Africa, many scholars have sought to discuss how these operate in different settings. In most instances, these interfaith networks are dominated by Christians and Muslims, hence the decision to address the theme in this section. The focus on interfaith networks in the extant literature is understandable, given the fact that in many African contexts they provide the institutional setting in which formal dialogue takes place between the two religions/their representatives. These national interreligious councils are strategic in preventing electoral violence in Africa (Nakabiito, 2022). Prominent examples include the Inter-Religious Council of Sierra Leone, which has been actively involved in brokering peace and responding to health emergencies such as Ebola (see e.g. Conteh, 2015). Other scholars analyse interfaith dialogue as a resource for peace (see e.g. Iweze, 2021), as well as Christian-Muslim relations after the genocide in Rwanda (see e.g. Kubai, 2007). Omotosho (2014) discusses the interreligious mediation peace strategy in Nigeria, while Ludovic (2021) gives examples of interfaith peacebuilding from Côte d'Ivoire and the Central African Republic.

## *Indigenous Approaches to Peacebuilding in Africa*

With calls for the indigenisation and Africanisation of approaches to peacebuilding in Africa gaining momentum, there has been a notable increase in the number of publications that privilege indigenous knowledge systems (IKS) or specific indigenous concepts and practices in peacebuilding in Africa. Here, the dominant ideological conviction running through the scholarship on this theme is that there must be a more deliberate and conscious effort to decolonise peacebuilding in Africa. This calls for recognising that Africans had and have effective peacebuilding strategies that predate colonisation and the advent of missionary religions. Africans who have converted to missionary are invited to respect their cultural heritage and have the intellectual courage to utilise indigenous peacebuilding concepts and strategies. Thus:

> [t]he greatest challenge African people face may be that of identity. In the interplay of African traditions, Westernisation, Islam and Christianity, the African finds the question of identity a delicate one. It would seem that colonisation has left indelible marks. It is not uncommon to meet Africans who do not want to look at the past, who feel their traditions have nothing to offer in the modern world, or who view their traditions and culture as irrelevant. Yet peacebuilding must be rooted in our traditions and culture. No one will build peace for us. We must do it ourselves. We must develop the confidence to do so. (Ayindo et al., 2001, p. 14)

One concept that continues to enjoy a lot of currency is Ubuntu (summarised as, "I am because you are"). Ubuntu has been prescribed as a powerful resource for conflict transformation, reconciliation and peacebuilding in Africa (see also the chapter by Chitando and Kilonzo in this volume). It features prominently in reflections by, among many, Tutu (1999; see e.g. Chasi, 2018 for an elaboration), Murithi (2006), Villa-Vicencio (2009), Akinola and Uzodike (2018), Arthur (2015) and others. Ubuntu places emphasis on communal solidarity, forgiveness and commitment towards cooperation and mutual growth. Maphosa (2009) presents a very informative study on the Centre Ubuntu in Burundi, which applies Ubuntu principles to achieve peacebuilding from below. Ubuntu is sometimes offered as a uniquely African peacebuilding concept or is sometimes prescribed to supplement insights from Christianity and Islam. If there are some critics who wonder if Africa can offer anything new/creative to the discourse on peacebuilding, some scholars from within African philosophy, theology, religious studies and related areas of study maintain that Ubuntu does represent one such unique concept or Africa's very own free gift to a hurting world.

However, it would be misleading to consider Ubuntu as the only indigenous concept that has been put forward in efforts to have contextually relevant approaches to peacebuilding in Africa (see e.g. Dodo, 2015). The *Handbook of Research on the Impact of Culture in Conflict Prevention and Peacebuilding* (Essien, 2020), while restricted to the Nigerian context, remains quite informative in this regard. In the same vein, some scholars have called for the recognition of African Traditional Religions in peacebuilding in Africa (see e.g. Kasomo, 2010; Kagema, 2015; Akano & Bamigbose, 2019), charging that the dominance of Christian approaches perpetuates colonising approaches in the field. Other contributors also recommend the application of effective and relevant local concepts and practices (see particularly Dama, 2021 for the call for African Christians and Muslims to take these seriously). Overall, this insistence on the integrity of traditional/indigenous approaches to peacebuilding in Africa is consistent with the Africanist/Afri/o/centric stance that characterises some perspectives within the field.

## African Women, Religion and Peacebuilding

There is a growing concern with the role of women in peacebuilding, globally and in Africa. The volume, *Women's Leadership in Peace Building: Conflict, Community and Care* (Van Reisen, 2015), has many chapters that describe African women's active and meaningful contribution to peacebuilding in Africa, using indigenous concepts and practices. When discussing the now established concern with violence in Africa, I drew attention to the prominence that is now given to the theme of violence against women. This theme has been taken up by the Circle of Concerned African Women Theologians (the Circle). In various publications (see e.g. Hinga et al., 2008), the Circle has exposed and explored the contours of violence against women in Africa, paying attention to the impact of the religion, culture and gender socialisation (Maluleke & Nadar, 2002). Circle activists might rightly be regarded as peace activists since their work seeks to attain a ceasefire in the wars fought on African women's bodies and Mother Earth. The Circle is, therefore, an interfaith peacebuilding movement that has expanded the scope of African theology and religious studies (the change in nomenclature here is deliberate due to the dominance of theology in the work of the Circle) in a decisive way.

The interface between religious peacebuilding and African women receives attention in the work of some African women scholars. This includes reflections by Anne Kubai, who has emerged as one of the leading African scholar-practitioners in the field, with special interest in the genocide in Rwanda and women's experiences of the same (see e.g. 2014, p. 118). Musa W. Dube (see e.g. 1996, 2018) has provided valuable perspectives on women, healing and development from within biblical and women's studies, while Susan Kilonzo (see e.g. 2021) has dubbed women the "silent peacemakers" with special reference to their peacebuilding work in Kenya's North Rift conflicts. Rose Nyirimana (2012) provides a gripping account of the role of women in the genocide in Rwanda through the frame of the Fourth Gospel. Rukia Bakari (2021) analyses how women in Casamance, Senegal, deploy traditional methods of conflict resolution to achieve peace. Ayesha Imam et al. (2020) discuss religious women's participation in peacebuilding in Africa, while Merab Ochieng (2019) approaches the same theme from the perspective of the Catholic Church. Although I have focused on the African women scholars of religion and theologians' engagement with women and peacebuilding, it would, however, be misleading to conclude that all their writings on peacebuilding are about women's roles. They do address other themes, as can be confirmed by some references in this essay and in their other works.

While more space is required to discuss African women scholars' contribution to peacebuilding in Africa, one can already acknowledge the commitment towards ensuring that African women are seen and heard in matters that affect them directly. Further, one can also appreciate the creative insights that they bring to both the discourse and practice of peacebuilding by bringing women's bodies and Mother Earth to the centre.

## African Scholarship on Religion and Peacebuilding in Africa: A Critical Appreciation

As the preceding sections confirm clearly, African scholars in religious studies and theology are making a significant contribution to the study and practice of religion and peacebuilding in Africa. They are addressing most of the key issues that their counterparts in the Humanities and Social Sciences are grappling with, including identifying the root causes of violent conflicts in Africa and exploring the role of religion/religious actors in dousing the flames and building sustainable peace. They also pursue how religious actors can contribute to the struggle against sexual and gender-based violence and achieve gender justice. In this regard, they have done very well to ensure that the study of religion in Africa is undertaken in conversation with other disciplines in the academy in Africa. Crucially, by addressing the existential issue of violence and peacebuilding, they have gone a long way towards responding to the critique that the study of religion in Africa does not contribute towards social transformation/development (see e.g. Chitando, 2010; Amanze, 2012).

It is also noteworthy that many of the publications adopt rigorous social scientific methods of research and even the theological formulations are helpful to the quest to achieve SDG 16 ("peace and strong institutions"), as well as the African Union's Agenda 2063 vision of a peaceful and prosperous Africa, namely, one that proudly takes its rightful place in global platforms. Viewed collectively, the publications demonstrate the importance of multiple approaches to the study of religion and peacebuilding. The insights drawn from African Christianity and African Islam's engagement with peacebuilding demonstrate their unique offerings to the global quest for healing, integration, reconciliation and peacebuilding. When one adds the broadening of the peacebuilding canvass facilitated by the appeals to Ubuntu, IKS and African women's distinctive approaches, one can further appreciate the strategic contribution of African scholars to the field of religion and peacebuilding. There is ongoing innovation and the recent shift towards religion and climate change-induced conflicts in Africa promises to bring fresh perspectives to the global discourse on religion and peacebuilding (see e.g. Tarusarira, 2022).

Whereas the contribution of African scholars to the field of religion and peacebuilding in Africa and globally is noteworthy, there are a number of areas that require further attention. Space considerations mean that I cannot debate each of these areas at length. First, the field continues to rely on global North scholarship for its theoretical foundations. Thus, most of the African scholars appear to endorse the 'canonical' status of the dominant theoretical formulations by scholars from the global North. There is limited willingness to critique or review how the African context might call for variations of these theoretical foundations. Second, although (hopefully) this chapter might go some way in confirming that African scholars of religion and theologians are making a contribution to the study of religion and peacebuilding in Africa, it must be conceded that the field is still rather amorphous. Only a few scholars have published and continue to publish consistently on the theme. These include Tutu (now late), Katongole, Kubai, Kilonzo, Elias Opongo, Tarusarira and a few others. It would appear the theme of Ubuntu and peacebuilding is attracting more scholars, but there is scope for more rigorous engagement with the concept of Ubuntu. In order for the field to take a more definite shape, it is critical for more contributors to come on board, as well as for internal appreciation/critique and conversation to increase. Whereas scholars in the field from the global North cite each other frequently, African scholars of religion and peacebuilding tend to cite the same global North scholars regularly, at the expense of engaging their fellow African researchers (including other African scholars on violence and peacebuilding from within African Studies).

Third, there is a need for scholars from the different African regions and countries to become more visible in the field. Perhaps in keeping with the development of African religious studies and theology, it is scholars from countries that use English as the official language of business who dominate. Even then, they tend to be from Nigeria, South Africa, Kenya and Ghana and, to a less extent, Zimbabwe, Botswana, Rwanda, Uganda and Tanzania. Fourth, a religionist ethos is discernible throughout the literature. This is mostly due to the fact that most scholars of religion and theologians in Africa are ideologically committed to religion as a positive social fact (or force). Thus, the descriptions of religion's role in peacebuilding tend to be overwhelmingly positive. However, this results in an intriguing paradox that is not always resolved. The argument runs like this: "Religion is a very dangerous phenomenon that has contributed to serious conflicts and violence in society. Thankfully, we have religion (religious actors) doing fantastic work to overcome conflicts and violence in African society."

Fifth, while the Catholic scholars' commitment to justice and peace results in greater willingness to confront global and national oppressive political, economic and ideological systems, most of the contributors do not probe structural injustices that sponsor violent conflict in Africa. Thus, there needs to be greater investment in unravelling the drivers of the different violences that afflict Africa so that the interventions by religious actors will be more effective and sustainable. Sixth, the extant literature sustains the myth of the "three religions of Africa" (African Traditional Religions, Christianity and Islam). Thus, there must be greater coverage of the multiple religions of Africa in their complexity and their interface with peacebuilding in Africa. Seventh, but by no means less crucial, more male African scholars of religion and theologians need to join the Circle in analysing and contributing towards addressing violence against women. The prevailing situation seems to suggest that violence against women in Africa is a women's issue (or any issue for women to address by themselves). Yet, violence against women in Africa (and everywhere else) is a human issue and everyone must play their part in eliminating this serious violation of women's rights and dignity. Studying how peaceful masculinities contribute to human flourishing in everyday African settings is promising in this regard (see e.g. Drery et al., 2022). Finally, more effective linkages with policymakers need to be nurtured so that the engagement can become more transformative and contribute towards the achievement of the peaceful and inclusive societies for sustainable development, as envisaged by SDG 16.

## Conclusion

African scholars of religion and theology are not bystanders in the field of religion and peacebuilding in Africa. They have been making significant contributions to the field by exploring, using different disciplinary and methodological angles, the interface between religion and peacebuilding in Africa. They have moved from the periphery to the centre and their commitment towards justice, peace and sustainable development (as envisaged in SDG 16) is noteworthy. Effectively contesting the image of their continent as hopeless, violent and insignificant, they are rewriting the narrative by highlighting the courageous acts by peace activists inspired by religion. One can, therefore, confidently declare that the story of, and commentary on, religious peacebuilding in Africa is an African story (see e.g. Kalu, 2005) told by Africans themselves (with valuable additions by dedicated allies from beyond the continent).

## References

Aall, P., & Crocker, C. A. (Eds.). (2017). *The Fabric of Peace in Africa: Looking beyond the State*. Centre for International Governance Innovation.

Adamo, D. T. (1997). Peace in the Old Testament and in the African Heritage. In H. W. Kinoti & J. M. Waliggo (Eds.), *The Bible in African Christianity: Essays in Biblical Theology* (pp. 99–111). Acton.

Adedeji, A. (Ed.). (1999). *Comprehending and Mastering African Conflicts: The Search for Sustainable Peace and Good Governance*. Zed Books.

Adetula, V., Bereketeab, R., & Obi, C. (Eds.). (2021). *Regional Economic Communities and Peacebuilding in Africa Lessons from ECOWAS and IGAD*. Routledge.

African Union Panel of the Wise. (2013, February). *Peace, Justice, and Reconciliation in Africa: Opportunities and Challenges in the Fight Against Impunity*. The African Union Series, New York: International Peace Institute.

Agbiji, O. M., & Etukamana, G. (2018). Leadership, Violent Conflict and Reconciliation in Africa: The Theological-sociocultural Engagement of Luke's Gospel in Social Transformation. *Stellenbosch Theological Journal, 4*(1), 11–37.

Akano, E. K., & Bamigbose, J. O. (2019). The Role of African Traditional Religion in Conflict Management in Nigeria. *Journal of Living Together, 6*(1), 246–258.

Akinola, A. O., & Uzodike, U. O. (2018). *Ubuntu* and the Quest for Conflict Resolution in Africa. *Journal of Black Studies, 49*(2), 91–113.

Alao, A. (2007). *Natural Resources and Conflict in Africa: The Tragedy of Endowment*. University of Rochester Press.

Alao, A. (2022). *Rage and Carnage in the Name of God: Religious Violence in Nigeria*. Duke University Press.

Amanze, J. N. (2012). The Voicelessness of Theology and Religious Studies in Contemporary Africa: Who Is to Blame and What Is to Be Done? Setting a New Agenda. *Missionalia, 40*(3), 189–204.

Aremu. (2010). Conflicts in Africa: Meaning, Causes, Impact and Solution. *African Research Review, 4*(4), 549–560.

Arthur, D. D. (2015). An Analysis of the Influence of Ubuntu Principle on the South Africa Peace Building Process. *Journal of Global Peace and Conflict, 3*(2), 633–677.

Asaka, J., & Oluoko-Odingo, A. A. (Eds.). (2022). *Human Security and Sustainable Development in East Africa*. Routledge.

Aubyn, F. K. (2018). *An Overview of Recent Trends in African Scholarly Writing on Peacebuilding*. African Peacebuilding Network, APN Working Papers No. 21. Retrieved January 6, 2023, from https://s3.amazonaws.com/ssrc-cdn1/crmuploads/new_publication_3/%7BF599C121-36AF-E811-A969-000D3A34A0AA%7D.pdf

Ayindo, B., Doe, S. G., Jenner, J. M., & Abdi, N. A. (2001). *When You Are the Peacebuilder: Stories and Reflections on Peacebuilding from Africa*. Conflict Transformation Program, Eastern Mennonite University.

Baderin, M. (2020). Advocating Islamic Precepts for Peace, Security and Socioeconomic Development in Nigeria. In Y. O. Imam et al. (Eds.), *Religion, Peace Building and National Integration: Festschrift in Honour of Professor Muibi Omolayo Opeloye* (pp. 2–17). Obafemi Awolowo University.

Bakari, R. (2021). *Women and Peacebuilding: The Use of Traditional Methods of Conflict Resolution by Women from Casamance, Senegal*. Doctoral thesis submitted to Der Fakultät für Geschichte, Kunst- und Regionalwissenschaften, der Universität Leipzig. Retrieved January 11, 2023, from https://ul.qucosa.de/api/qucosa%3A74203/attachment/ATT-0/

Boege, V. (2011). Potential and Limits of Traditional Approaches to Peacebuilding. In B. Austin, et al. (Eds.), *Advancing Conflict Transformation* (pp. 431–457). The Berghof Handbook II. Barbara Budrich Publishers. Online at www.berghof-handbook.net

Bourdillon, M. F. C. (1991). *Religion and Society: A Text for Africa*. Mambo Press.

*Bulletin of Ecumenical Theology*. (2013). Volume 25. "Peacebuilding, Social Transformation and Religion in Africa: Contextual Theological Reflection.

Burgess, R. (2020). *Nigerian Pentecostalism and Development: Spirit, Power, and Transformation*. Routledge.

Carney, J. J. (2010). Roads to Reconciliation: An Emerging Paradigm of African Theology. *Modern Theology, 26*(4), 549–569.

Carpenter, J. (2017). Christian Universities are Growing Rapidly in Africa. *University World News*. Retrieved January 6, 2023, from https://www.universityworldnews.com/post.php?story=20170131142300487

Chamburuka, S. W. (2020). Matthean Jesus and Peacebuilding in Zimbabwe 2018-2019. *HTS Teologiese Studies/Theological Studies, 76*(4), a6106. https://doi.org/10.4102/hts.v76i4.6106

Charbonneau, B., & Ricard, M. (Eds.). (2022). *Routledge Handbook of African Peacebuilding*. Routledge.

Chasi, C. T. (2018). Tutuist Ubuntu and Just War. *Politicon: South African Journal of Political Studies, 45*(2), 232–244.

Chingono, M. (2016). Violent Conflicts in Africa: Towards a Holistic Understanding. *World Journal of Social Science Research, 3*(2), 199–218.

Chitando, E. (2010). Equipped and Ready to Serve? Transforming Theology and Religious Studies in Africa. *Missionalia, 38*(2), 197–210.

Chitando, E., & Gusha, I. S. (Eds.). (2022). *Interfaith Networks and Development: Case Studies from Africa*. Palgrave Macmillan.

Conteh, A. B. (2015). *The Inter Religious Response to the Ebola Outbreak in Sierra Leone*. Retrieved January 12, 2023, from https://jliflc.com/wp-content/uploads/2015/07/Final-Inter-religious.pdf

Dama, D. (2021). The African Epistemic Logic of Peacemaking: A Model for Reconciling the Sub-Saharan African Christians and Muslims. *Transformation, 38*(1), 46–62.

Dodo, O. (2015). *Endogenous Conflict Resolution Approaches: The Zezuru Perspective*. IDA Publishers.

Drery, I., Baataar, C., & Khan, A. R. (2022). Everyday Peacebuilding Among Ghanaian Men: Ambiguities, Resistances and Possibilities. *Journal of the British Academy, 10*(s1), 35–53.

Dube, M. W. (1996). 'Woman, What Have I to do With You?' A Post-colonial Feminist Theological Reflection on the Role of Christianity in Development, Peace and Reconstruction in Africa. In I. Phiri et al. (Eds.), *The Role of Christianity in Development, Peace and Reconstruction* (pp. 244–258). All Africa Conference of Churches.

Dube, M. W. (2018). The Cry of Rachel: African Women's Reading of the Bible for Healing. In M. Girma (Ed.), *The Healing of Memories: African Christian Responses to Politically Induced Trauma* (pp. 115–135). Lexington Books.

Ensign, M., & Karegere, J.-P. (Eds.). (2020). *Religion in War and Peace in Africa*. Routledge.

Essien, E. (Ed.). (2020). *Handbook of Research on the Impact of Culture in Conflict Prevention and Peacebuilding*. IGI Global.

Flaningan, S. T. (2013). Religion, Conflict and Peacebuilding in Development. In M. Clark (Ed.), *Handbook of Research on Development and Religion* (pp. 252–267). Edward Elgar.

Getui, M., & Kanyandago, P. (Eds.). (2003). *From Violence to Peace: A Challenge for African Christianity* (2nd ed.). Acton.

Girma, M. (Ed.). (2018). *The Healing of Memories: African Christian Responses to Politically Motivated Trauma*. Lexington Books.

Hinga, Telesia, A.N Kubai, P. Mwaura, H. Ayanga 2008. Religion and HIV/AIDS in Africa: Responding to Ethical and Theological Challenges. : Cluster.

Huyse, L., & Salter, M. (Eds.). (2008). *Traditional Justice and Reconciliation after Violent Conflict Learning from African Experiences*. Uppsala.

Ibeifuna, B., & Uzoigwe, A. (2012). Studying Religion for Sustainable Development in Nigeria. *UJAH: Unizik Journal of Arts and Humanities, 13*(1), 132–159.

Ilo, S. C. (2018). The Future of Catholic Education in Africa: Narrating and Documenting Our Own Stories. *Bulletin of Ecumenical Theology, 30*, 6–338.

Imam, A., Biu, H., & Yahi, M. (2020). *Women's Informal Peacebuilding in North East Nigeria*. CMI Brief No. 2020: 09. Chr. Michelsen Institute. Retrieved January 9, 2023, from https://www.cmi.no/publications/7296-womens-informal-peacebuilding-in-north-east-nigeria

Iweze, D. O. (2021). Boko Haram Insurgency, Interfaith Dialogue, and Peacebuilding in Kano: Examining the Kano Covenant. *African Conflict and Peacebuilding Review, 11*(1), 32–54.

Juma, M. (2002). *The Infrastructure of Peace in Africa Assessing the Peacebuilding Capacity of African Institutions: A Report submitted by the Africa Program of the International Peace Academy to the Ford Foundation*. Retrieved January 3, 2023, from https://www.ipinst.org/wp-content/uploads/publications/ford.pdf

Kagema, D. N. (2015). The Role of the African Traditional Religion in the Promotion of Justice, Reconciliation and Peace in Africa in the Twenty-first Century: A Kenyan Experience. *International Journal of African and Asian Studies, 15*, 1–9.

Kalu, K. A., & Kieh, G. K. (Eds.). (2021). *Peacebuilding in Africa: The Post-Conflict State and its Multidimensional Crises*. Lexington Books.

Kalu, O. U. (Ed.). (2005). *African Christianity: An African Story*. Department of Church History, University of Pretoria.

Kanu, I. A., & Ndubisi, E. J. O. (Eds.). (2020, June 10–11). *Religion and Peacebuilding in Africa: Proceedings of the International Conference of the Association for the Promotion of African Studies on African Ideologies, Human Security and Peace Building*. APSA. Retrieved January 12, 2023, from https://www.researchgate.net/publication/344264473_RELIGION_AND_PEACE_BUILDING_IN_AFRICA

Karbo, T., & Virk, K. (Eds.). (2018). *The Palgrave Handbook of Peacebuilding in Africa*. Palgrave Macmillan.

Kasomo, D. (2010). The Position of African Traditional Religion in Conflict Prevention. *International Journal of Sociology and Anthropology, 2*(2), 23–28.

Katongole, E. (2017). *The Journey of Reconciliation: Groaning for a New Creation in Africa*. Orbis.

Kaunda, C. (2018). *The Nation That Fears God Prospers: A Critique of Zambian Pentecostal Theopolitical Imaginations*. Augsburg Fortress Press.

Kilonzo, S. M. (2011). The Ahmadiyya Muslim Community and Peacebuilding in Kisumu District. *Kenya. Journal of Peacebuilding and Development, 6*(1), 80–85.

Kilonzo, S. M. (2021). Silent Peacemakers: Grass-roots Transitional Justice and Peacebuilding by Women in Kenya's North Rift Conflicts. *Journal of the British Academy, 9*(s2), 53–74.

Kubai, A. (2007). Walking a Tightrope: Christians and Muslims in Post-Genocide Rwanda. *Islam and Christian-Muslims Relations, 18*(2), 219–235.

Kubai, A. (2014). Conducting Fieldwork in Rwanda: Listening to Silence and Processing Experiences of Genocide. In I. Maĉek (Ed.), *Engaging Violence: Trauma, Memory and Representation* (pp. 111–126). Routledge.

Kukah, M. H. (1993). *Religion, Politics and Power in Northern Nigeria*. Spectrum in association with Safari Books.

Kumah, S. A. (2021). *The Use of Religion in Violent Conflict, Conflict Resolution, and Peacebuilding: Cases from Uganda and Sierra Leone*. FIU Electronic Theses and Dissertations. 4630. https://digitalcommons.fiu.edu/etd/4630

Lapsley, M. (2012). *Redeeming the Past: My Journey from Freedom Fighter to Healer*. Orbis Books.

Lieberfeld, D. (2014). Nelson Mandela: Personal Characteristics and Reconciliation-Oriented Leadership. In B. G. Jallow (Ed.), *Leadership in Postcolonial Africa: Trends Transformed by Independence* (pp. 143–167). Palgrave Macmillan.

Loba (-) Mkole, J.-C., & Mugambi, J. N. K. (Eds.). (2020). *Peace-Building in Africa: Biblical Insights*. Acton.

Ludovic, L. T. (2021). Religion and Peacebuilding in Sub-Saharan Africa. In T. McNamee & M. Muyangwa (Eds.), *The State of Peacebuilding in Africa: Lessons Learned for Policy Makers and Practitioners* (pp. 47–64). Palgrave Macmillan.

Machingura, F., Togarasei, L., & Chitando, E. (Eds.). 2018. *Pentecostalism and Human Rights in Contemporary Zimbabwe*. Cambridge Scholars Publishing.

MacKenzie, M., & Wegner, N. (Eds.). (2021). *Feminist Solutions for Ending War*. Pluto Press.

Maluleke, T. S., & Nadar, S. (2002). Breaking the Covenant of Violence against Women. *Journal of Theology for Southern Africa, 114*, 5–17.

Maphosa, S. B. (2009). Building Peace from Below: The Centre Ubuntu in Burundi. *Africa Peace and Conflict Journal, 2*(2), 58–71.

Mawere, M., & Marongwe, N. (Eds.). (2016). *Violence, Politics and Conflict Management in Africa: Envisioning Transformation, Peace and Unity in the Twenty-First Century*. Langaa RPCIG.

Miller, D. E., Holland, S., Johnson, D., & Fendall, L. (2007). *Seeking Peace in Africa: Stories from African Peacemakers*. World Council of Churches.

Mukonori, F. (2017). *Man in the Middle: A Memoir*. The House of Books.

Mulatu, S. (2017). *Transitioning from a Theological College to a Christian University: A Multi-Case Study in the East African Context*. ICETE Series. Langham Global Library.

Murithi, T. (2019). *Regional Reconciliation in Africa: The Elusive Dimension of Peace and Security*. Claude Ake Memorial Lecture No. 10. The Nordic Africa Institute and Uppsala University. http://nai.diva-portal.org/smash/get/diva2:1290131/FULLTEXT01.pdf

Murithi, T. (2006). Practical Peacemaking Wisdom from Africa: Reflections on Ubuntu. *The Journal of Pan African Studies, 1*(4), 25–34.

Nadar, S., Sarojini, N., Tinyiko, M., Dietrich, W., Vicentia, K., & Rudolf, H. (2021). *Ecumenical Encounters with Desmond Mpilo Tutu*. Regnum.

Nakabiito, J. G. (2022). *National Inter-Religious Councils and Electoral Violence Restraint in Africa*. Masters Thesis, Department of Peace and Conflict Research, Uppsala University. Retrieved January 12, 2023, from https://www.diva-portal.org/smash/get/diva2:1701595/FULLTEXT02

Ndlovu-Gatsheni, S. J. (2017). The Emergence and Trajectories of Struggles for an 'African University': The Case of Unfinished Business of African Epistemic Decolonisation. *Kronos, 53*, 51–77.

Nel, M. J., Forster, D. A., & Thesnaar, C. H. (Eds.). (2020). *Reconciliation, Forgiveness and Violence in Africa: Biblical, Pastoral and Ethical Perspectives*. African Sun Media.

Ngom, F., Kurfi, M. H., & Falola, T. (Eds.). (2020). *The Palgrave Handbook of Islam in Africa*. Palgrave Macmillan.

Nhema, A., & Zeleza, P. T. (Eds.). (2008). *The Roots of African Conflicts: The Causes and Costs*. Ohio University Press.

Nyirimana, R. M. (2012). *Women and Peace Building: A Contextual Approach to the Fourth Gospel and its Challenge to Women in Post Genocide Rwanda*. A Doctoral Thesis Submitted to the School of Religion and Theology, University of KwaZulu-Natal. Retrieved January 12, 2023, from https://researchspace.ukzn.ac.za/bitstream/handle/10413/8439/Nyirimana_Rose_Mukansengimana_2012.pdf

Obadare, E. (2018). *Pentecostal Republic: Religion and the Struggle for State Power in Nigeria*. Zed Books.

Ochieng, M. (2019). Role of Women in Peacebuilding and Post-Conflict Transformation Africa: A Catholic Church Perspective. *International Journal of Arts, Humanities and Social Sciences, 1*(2), 1–12.

Olukoshi, A. (2007). African Scholars and African Studies. In H. Melber (Ed.), *On Africa: Scholars and African Studies: Essays in Honour of Lennart Wolgemuth* (pp. 7–22). Nordic Africa Institute.

Omar, Y. S. (2022). The Role of Islam in Peace and Development in Somalia (Continuity and Change). *Religions, 13*, 1074. https://doi.org/10.3390/rel13111074

Omer, A. (2012). Religious Peacebuilding: The Exotic, the Good, and the Theatrical. *Practical Matters, 5*, 1–31.

Omotosho, M. (2014). Managing Religious Conflicts in Nigeria: The Inter-Religious Mediation Peace Strategy. *African Development, 39*(2), 133–151.

Onditi, F., & Odera, J. (Eds.). (2021). *Understanding Violence Against Women in Africa An Interdisciplinary Approach*. Palgrave Macmillan.

Onyegbula, R. I. (2018). *Women's Experiences in Peace Building Processes: A Phenomenological Study of Undeterred Female Leaders in Northern Nigeria*. Doctoral Dissertation. Nova Southeastern University. Retrieved from NSUWorks, College of Arts, Humanities and Social Sciences—Department of Conflict Resolution Studies. (110) https://nsuworks.nova.edu/shss_dcar_etd/110

Opongo, E. O., & Kaulemu, D. (Eds.). (2014). *Catholic Church Leadership in Peace Building in Africa*. Paulines Publications Africa.

Orobator, A. E. (2011). *Reconciliation, Justice, and Peace: The Second African Synod*. Orbis Books.

Østebø, T. (Ed.). (2022). *The Routledge Handbook of Islam in Africa*. Routledge.

Phiri, I., Ross, K. R., & Cox, J. L. (Eds.). (1996). *The Role of Christianity in Development, Peace and Reconstruction*. All Africa Conference of Churches.

Ruppel, S., & Leib, J. (2022). Same but Different: The Role of Local Leaders in the Peace Processes in Liberia and Sierra Leone. *Peacebuilding*. https://doi.org/10.1080/21647259.2022.2027152

Sewe, L. J. (2018). The Contribution of Religion to Social Reconciliation: A Case Study of Liberia. *Journal of Global Peace and Conflict, 6*(2), 1–9.

Shannahan, C., & Payne, L. (2016). *Faith-based Interventions in Peace, Conflict and Violence: A Scoping Study*. Joint Learning Initiative on Faith & Local Communities. Retrieved January 3, 2023, from https://jliflc.com/wp-content/uploads/2016/05/JLI-Peace-Conflict-Scoping-Paper-May-2016.pdf

Spiegel, E., George, M., Cheng, L., & Lester, R. K. (Eds). (2022). *Peace Studies for Sustainable Development in Africa: Conflicts and Peace Oriented Conflict Resolution*. Palgrave Macmillan.

Sulaiman, K.-d. O. (2016). Religious Violence in Contemporary Nigeria: Implications and Options for Peace and Stability Order. *Journal for the Study of Religion, 29*(1), 85–103.

Tarusarira, J. (2016). *Reconciliation and Religio-Political Non-conformism in Zimbabwe*. Routledge.

Tarusarira, J. (2022). Religious Environmental Sensemaking in Climate-Induced Conflicts. *Religions, 13*, 204. https://doi.org/10.3390/rel13030204

Tesfai, Y. (2010). *Holy Warriors, Infidels, and Peacemakers in Africa*. Palgrave Macmillan.

Tutu, D. (1999). *No Future Without Forgiveness*. Doubleday.

Ushe, M. U. (2015). Religious Conflicts and Education in Nigeria: Implications for National Security. *Journal of Education and Practice, 6*(2), 117–129.

Van Klinken, A. (2020). Studying Religion in the Pluriversity: Decolonial Perspectives. *Religion, 50*(10, 148–155.

Van Reisen, M. (2015). *Women's Leadership in Peace Building: Conflict, Community and Care International Colloquium on Women in Peace-building From Monrovia (2009) to Harare (2014)*. Africa World Press.

Villa-Vicencio, C. (2009). *Walk with Us and Listen: Political Reconciliation in Africa*. Georgetown University Press.

Wachira, G., Kamungi, P., & Sillah, K. (2014). *Stretching the Truth: The Uncertain Promise of TRCs in Africa's Transitional Justice*. Nairobi Peace Initiatives-Africa (NPI-A) and the West African Network for Peacebuilding (WANEP).

Weiss, H. (Ed.). (2020). *Muslim Faith-Based Organizations and Social Welfare in Africa*. Palgrave Macmillan.

West, G. O. (2019). Recovering the Biblical Story of Tamar: Training for Transformation, Doing Development. In R. Odén & T. Samuelsson (Eds.), *For Better or Worse: The Role of Religion in Development Cooperation* (Second revised and expanded ed., pp. 155–167). SMC-faith in Development.

Wijsen, F. (2007). Seeds of Conflict in a Haven of Peace: From Religious Studies to Interreligious Studies in Africa. In *Studies in World Christianity and Interreligious Relations*. Rodopi.

Yacob-Haliso, O., & Falola, T. (Eds.). (2021). *The Palgrave Handbook of African Women's Studies*. Palgrave Macmillan.

Zagoon-Sayeed, H. (2018, February). *Islam and Peacebuilding in the Context of the Muslim Community in Ghana*. A Thesis Submitted to the University of Birmingham for the degree of DOCTOR OF PHILOSOPHY, Department of Theology and Religion School of Philosophy, Theology and Religion College of Arts and Law University of Birmingham. Retrieved January 9, 2023, from https://core.ac.uk/download/pdf/200371146.pdf

Zulu, E. (1998). Reconciliation from an African Perspective: An Alternative View. *Old Testament Essays, 11*(1), 182–194.

CHAPTER 4

# Religion, Peacebuilding and Development in Africa: Challenges

*Molly Manyonganise*

## Introduction

The pervasiveness of religion in discourses on peacebuilding and development is evidence of its centrality in critical fields that shape humanity's existence. Religion plays an ambivalent role in shaping the concepts of peacebuilding and development. While on the one hand, it can be disruptive, it can also be constructive on the other. In my 2021 publication, "Development as a Factor in the Religion and Human Security Nexus in Africa" (Manyonganise, 2021) I examined the intersections of religion, human security and development. This chapter builds on this publication by redirecting the focus to the intersections of religion, peacebuilding and development in Africa. Since the study is largely a desktop one, I engage with published literature in order to make sense of the various ways in which the three concepts are intertwined. The aim of this analysis is to bring out the challenges that emerge at the point of the intersection of religion, peacebuilding and development. In order to put this study into its proper context, it is imperative that the definitions of the key terms making up this chapter be provided.

M. Manyonganise (✉)
Department of Religious Studies and Philosophy, Zimbabwe Open University, Harare, Zimbabwe

Department of Religion Studies, Faculty of Theology and Religion, University of Pretoria, South Africa

## Definition of Key Terms

Religion is a complex phenomenon which is difficult to define. For a long time, scholars of religion have been preoccupied with the need to define and to understand the concept of religion (Molendijk, 1999, p. 3). The greatest challenge in this endeavour has been in identifying what constitutes a religion and what does not. Sibanda, Muyambo and Chitando (2022, p. 2) argue that the term "religion" is "fluid and at times associated with misleading connotations because it is binding and confessional." Neville (2018, p. 3) avers that religion means different things to different people. He argues among other things that

> For some people, religion means a spiritual path. For some people, religion means a community of practice and belief within which members live out a spiritual path. For some people, religion means a set of beliefs about ultimate things, whatever "ultimate" is construed to be. For some people, religion means belief in supernatural beings, whether or not they are ultimate. For some people, religion means a tradition of beliefs and practices with a special vocabulary and a history of development and definition over against other traditions. For some people, religion means a rich evolving culture whose images and institutions prompt great literature, music, dance, architecture and art.

These varied meanings of religion have led other scholars to argue that defining religion may not be necessary. Molendijk (1999, p. 3) calls for the reconsideration of the concept of religion as a way of trying to come to grips with societal developments and how to deal with the transformations of religion(s) in (late) modernity. In relation to defining religion, Platvoet (1999) opines that the challenges encountered by scholars are a result of the fact that religions are many and different. To this, he poses a pertinent question, "Are not the religions of men so diverse, and are they not each such poly-morphic, poly-semantic and poly-functional phenomena, that it is an illusion to conceive that they will ever collectively or singly, be adequately reflected in a definition acceptable to all scholars of religion, let alone one that is unambiguously accepted as universally valid for the whole of human religious history in the full diachronic depth of at least 100000 years and its worldwide synchronic diversity?" (Platvoet, 1999, p. 247). In his analysis, it is not possible to come up with such a definition that is universally acceptable. He, therefore, questions whether it is even necessary to define religion. He argues that if it remains necessary to define religion, such definitions need to be de-Westernised so that they can serve as useful 'operational definitions' for descriptive and comparative research into religions. In his opinion, this would safeguard the peculiarities of the different religious traditions. For Platvoet (1999, p. 255), an 'operational definition' would, among other things, adapt religion to the specific traits and marks of a particular other religion, or several other religions as can be allowed by the Western concept of religion [so that] it may fruitfully serve the heuristic, analytical and explanatory research purposes in the study of that religion or those similar religions for which it has been developed. The challenge with

Platvoet's argument is that he wants an 'operational definition' of religion to fit within the Western concept of religion. He does not explain the implications of his argument in the event that non-Western scholars come up with such definitions that are outside of the West's concept of religion. Would such definitions be disregarded because they do not fit the Western conceptualisation of what religion ought to be?

Schilderman (2014, p. 176) views the definition of religion and the empirical exploration of its beliefs, texts, practices as representing a complex problem in the study of religion. For him, the problem lies in the fact that the phenomenological landscape of religion change rapidly, as do institutions and disciplines in which religion is studied. He, therefore, provides three dependencies from which the concept of religion can be discussed within the Humanities. He argues that (i) it can be maintained that any conceptualisation of religious beliefs and practices is tributary to the intended forms of meaning, which represent the obvious cultural assumptions without which any interpretation would remain futile (ii) the humanities' study of religion is subjected to the power formations, in which a religion has its habitat; and that implicitly or explicitly filter or enforce certain interpretations as more valid, authentic or reliable as compared to others. In his analysis, this challenge has been raised throughout the history of the study of religion; (iii) the study of religion is bound to deal with issues of truth, fairness, taste and other standards of practical reason, without which any aim of interpretation would lack motive or aim. Schilderman (2014, p. 180) opines that the third dependency remains a controversial one in the study of religion because it "runs the risks of reintroducing the ideological claims of the studied religion, requires integration of a philosophical competence in religious studies that attunes only with great difficulty to the empirical grassroots' expertise of anthropological research traditions."

Hence, Wilfred Cantwell Smith (1991) suggests that the concept of religion has to be abolished altogether since it does not exist as an intelligible entity in itself. In place of religion, he suggests the adoption of the concept of faith because it is the "noun by which a religious situation may always be identified" (Asad, 2001, p. 209). In the same vein, Fitzgerald argues that religion is an ideologically motivated social construct (Schilbrack, 2012, p. 97) implying that there is, therefore, "no coherent non-theological theoretical basis for the study of religion as a separate academic discipline" (Fitzgerald, 2000, p. 3). He avers that, "the concept of religion is non-existent, since it cannot be found as a distinctive cross-cultural reality" (Schilderman, 2014, p. 183). For Fitzgerald, religious studies block a clear view of what happens in other cultures. He, therefore, suggests that focus should be "on how the beliefs and practices that are commonly referred to as religious become expressed and how religious forms of meaning come to be understood as such" (Schilderman, 2014, p. 183). Hence, instead of the nomenclature 'religious studies', he proposes the use of 'cultural studies' which points to the study of the institutions and the institutionalised values of specific societies, and the relation between those institutionalised values and the legitimation of power (Stone, 2001, p. 243).

However, Schilbrack (2012, p. 98) contests Fitzgerald's argument for the non-existence of religion and argues that 'religion' "is descriptively and analytically useful, and it is useful because there really are religions that exist 'out there' in the world." In concurrence with Schilbrack (2012), this study adopts Neville's (2018, p. 1) definition of religion in which it is viewed as "the human engagement of ultimacy, which requires harmonising semiotic cultural systems, aesthetic achievements, social institutions with their own dynamics, and psychological structures, along with intentional relations with what is ultimate." I contend that this definition is closer to the general understanding of religion in African societies where it pervades almost every facet of life. This pervasiveness, as shall be shown later, may pose challenges for peacebuilding and development processes when actors in both fields fail to respect the religiosity of certain African beliefs and practices. Albert cited in Curtis (2012, p. 16) argues that the underpinnings of peace in Africa need to be located in the commitment to cultural values, beliefs, and norms as well as in societal role expectations.

Moving on to peacebuilding, Goetze (2017, p. 1) argues that peacebuilding has no proper definition as the term summarises many different activities conducted in countries and societies riddled by violent conflict, including humanitarian assistance, demilitarisation and demobilisation, human rights education, police force training, administration, and rights. Focusing specifically on Africa, Africa (2020, n.d) notes that given the ambiguity of violence in Africa, peacebuilding processes tend to be complex, multifaceted and messy, with several processes overlapping or running concurrently. Goetze (2017) opines that the term is often used as a synonym for state-building, democratisation, humanitarian intervention or peace-making. In her analysis, peacebuilding is "a notoriously unbounded phenomenon that takes very different practical and visible forms in various environments" (2017, p. 2). Hence, its meaning is contextual and depends on who is defining it. In the same vein, Schirch (2008, p. 2) opines that peacebuilding is most often used as an 'umbrella term' or 'meta-term' to encompass other terms such as conflict resolution, management, mitigation, prevention, or transformation. In this analysis, the term peacebuilding is utilised by those who focus on the larger goals of peace and security rather than on the problem of conflict. Boutros-Ghali (1992, p. 11) defines peacebuilding as action to identify and support structures which would tend to strengthen and solidify peace in order to avoid relapse into conflict. In this case, "peacebuilding may take the form of concrete cooperative projects which link two or more countries in a mutually beneficial undertaking that cannot only contribute to economic and social development but also enhance the confidence that is so fundamental to peace" (Boutros-Ghali, 1992, p. 36). Peacebuilding is aimed at preventing a recurrence of conflict. Murithi (2009) is of the view that peacebuilding includes processes of rebuilding the political security, social and economic dimensions of society emerging from conflict. For him, building peace entails the promotion of social and economic justice as well as the establishment or reform of political structures of governance and the rule of law (2009, p. 3). For Murithi (2009,

p. 3), the aim of peacebuilding is to bring about the healing of a war-torn community through reconciliation. In his opinion, reconciliation is not sustainable without socio-economic reconstruction, both of which require enormous resources. He therefore categorises peace into negative and positive peace. From his point of view, negative peace is a condition in which peace is based on the absence of violence while positive peace promotes reconciliation and co-existence on the basis of human rights and social, economic and political justice (Murithi, 2009, p. 4). The diverse understandings of peacebuilding are crucial for this chapter. As argued by Curtis (2012, p. 3) "highlighting the diverse expressions and contexts of peacebuilding helps us understand the intended and unintended consequences and limitations of peacebuilding programmes in Africa." In his analysis, the trajectories of peacebuilding programmes and initiatives in Africa tend to be messy and multifaceted. It, therefore, becomes obvious that in such cases, challenges in building permanent peace are bound to emerge.

Like the above terms, development is also difficult to define. Hopper (2012, p. 11) notes that conceptualising development is complicated by the fact that its nature and meaning have changed over time. While initial definitions focused mainly on economic growth, current definitions have shifted to focus on the quality of human life thereby attaching greater emphasis on the political freedom and social welfare targets. Hopper (2012) indicates that from the 1980s, the United Nations Development Programme (UNDP) began to employ the Human Development Index (HDI) as an alternative measurement of development. Manyonganise (2021) engages with the UNDP's understanding of development as centred on people. For example, in 1991, the UNDP Human Development Report explained that

> The basic objective of human development is to enlarge the range of people's choices to make development more democratic and participatory. The choices should include access to income and employment opportunities, education and health, and a clean and safe physical environment. Each individual should also have the opportunity to participate fully in community decisions and to enjoy human, economic and political freedoms.

This is a total departure from the historical definitions of development which associated development with wealth, where the Gross Domestic Product (GDP) and Gross National Income (GDI) defined a nation's wealth (Trebilcock & Prado, 2014, p. 3). In this case, the UNDP criticised the sole focus on income in earlier definitions of development as wrong. It argued that men, women and children must be the centre of attention. For the UNDP (1991), development should be woven around people and not people around development. As such, the UNDP's HDI focuses on three aspects, that is, "longevity, as measured by life expectancy at birth; knowledge, as measured by a weighted average of adult literacy and mean years of schooling; and standard of living, as measured by per capita income" (Trebilcock & Prado, 2014, p. 9).

Hence, the focus is on human well-being through the factoring in of "issues to do with participation in the life of the community, human security and empowerment" (Hopper, 2012, p. 11). In its 2021/2022 Human Development Report, the UNDP expanded its understanding of development as one that goes beyond well-being achievements to include agency and freedoms (UNDP, 2021/2022, p. 11). For the UNDP, the uncertainty prevailing globally due to the impact of climate change, COVID-19 and the eruption of wars such as the Russia-Ukraine war, have a great impact on agency since it has the power to disempower people. The resultant factor has been the drop of the HDI from 2020. The focus of the UN currently is on 'sustainable development' which has become the buzz word in development discourse (Mensah, 2019). Sustainable development has been regarded as a very broad concept of development which has resulted in various definitions depending on context. Despite the many proffered definitions, the most acceptable and widely used definition is the one given by Schaefer and Crane (2005) taking from the Brundtland Commission Report, who define sustainable development as development that meets the needs of the current generation without compromising the ability of future generations to meet their own needs (Mensah, 2019). The focus of sustainable development is on intergenerational equity. The Brundtland Commission Report described sustainable development not as a "fixed state of harmony, but rather a process of change in which the exploitation of resources, the direction of investments, the orientation of technological development, and institutional change are made consistent with the future as well as present needs" (UN, 1987, p. 15). The contestations over the meaning and interpretation of development as a concept speaks to its success and failure in the African context. Ake cited in Curtis (2012, p. 16) bemoans the fact that development practices have elevated European experiences while ignoring the specificities of African experiences.

In light of the above challenges in defining the terms, the study notes all the working definitions put forward and moves on to examine how the three concepts relate more specifically.

## Religion and Peacebuilding

Scholarship on peacebuilding and conflict resolution/management has emphasised the critical role that religion plays in the field (Appleby, 2015; Abu-Nimer, 2013; Silvestri & Mayall, 2015; Manyonganise, 2020; Ludovic, 2021). Abu-Nimer (2013, p. 69) notes that peacebuilding scholars and practitioners have been advocating for a more central role for religious peacebuilding interventions. He premises his argument on the fact that religious identity is a key influence on protracted conflict dynamics, especially in areas in which political parties have managed to manipulate their community's identity in ways that place their religious differences at the core or centre of the conflict. Silvestri and Mayall (2015, p. 28) aver that religious beliefs or values, religious leaders and faith-based organisations have huge potential in promoting peace in any society as well as in the international sphere. In their analysis, religion can assist in building trust between and among social groups. In cases of conflict, mediation by religious actors is seen as an important contributor to peace (Silvestri & Mayall, 2015, p. 34).

Philpott (2013) puts more emphasis on religious freedom as a crucial component of peacebuilding. He argues that the absence of religious freedom in any society may be the genesis of violence. Hence, he calls for the theorisation of religious freedom within discourses of peacebuilding. In his opinion, religious freedom is important to societies in two ways namely: (i). through institutional independence, that is, through the autonomy of religious actors (ii). through it being embodied in the doctrine of religious and political actors whose behaviour influences peace or violence. As a result, Philpott (2013, p. 31) opines that non-governmental organisations and scholars need to integrate religious freedom into their best practices and methodologies as well.

Focusing specifically on Africa, Ludovic (2021) argues that the role of religion in peacebuilding in Africa has to be located within the wider framework of the role of religion in the public space in Africa. He notes that discourses of peace, justice and reconciliation feature prominently among the religious expectations of African believers. From his perspective, people in Africa resort to religion for resources to avoid conflicts or to bring back peace as well as promote violence (see Chitando & Tarusarira, 2017). In his analysis, religious organisations in Africa have been involved in the three dimensions of peacebuilding, that is, preventing violence, managing conflict and transforming conflicts (Ludovic, 2021, p. 49). He further notes the many ways in which religious diplomacy succeeded in restoring peace in contexts where state and international actors had failed. A good example is the Catholic lay movement of Sant'Egidio in Mozambique which was instrumental in brokering peace between Resistencia Nacional Mozambicana (RENAMO) and Frente de Libertacao de Mozambique (FRELIMO). Desmond Tutu is also a good example of how religious leaders, churches and religious organisations have committed to peace on the African continent. Tutu played a critical role in the Truth and Reconciliation Commission (TRC) in post-apartheid South Africa. Ludovic recognises the role of interfaith peacebuilding initiatives by the following groups: African Council of Religious Leaders (ACRL), Religions for Peace, the Interfaith Action for Peace in Africa (IFAPA), the Programme for Christian-Muslim Relations in Africa (PROCMURA) and the Religious Council of Sierra Leone (IRCSL). Commenting on the Sierra Leonean case, Religions for Peace (2018, p. 13) notes that from the beginning of the crisis, the IRCSL successfully facilitated communication among various rebel factions, contributing to the rebels' ability to serve as viable parties to the peace process. In his analysis, the IRCSL represented a "unified voice of collaboration among the nation's religious communities, which led directly to the conflict's resolution and helped keep society from fracturing" (2018, p. 13). Within Zimbabwe, Kraybill (1994) explains how the Catholic Commission for Justice and Peace (CCJP) along with other religious agencies such as the Quackers mounted a global campaign to get the parties to the negotiating table in order to end the war for independence. As a result, Ludovic (2021, p. 51) argues that multi-faith associations in peacebuilding have the potential to neutralise attempts to divide communities along religious lines. In concurrence, Abu-Nimer (2013, p. 70) is of the view that "interfaith dialogue and religious peacebuilding can be a key factor in unlocking the deep-rooted conflicts in many of the above identity – based conflict areas." He notes that in most cases, warring parties may use sacred texts to justify the conflict. Therefore, he argues that "conflict dynamics that rely on religious affiliation require that peacebuilding practitioners and activists learn how to engage with their local communities through their faiths rather than through humanist or secular sets of peacebuilding values and methods" (Abu-Nimer, 2013, p. 70).

## Religion and Development

Scholarship on religion and development has noted the historical absence of religion in most literature focusing on development. This is despite religious institutions having participated in development projects within the contexts they exist. Clarke (2011, p. 1) notes that religious belief has long been ignored in mainstream development paradigms and by development practitioners, resulting in less than optimal development outcomes. Buijs (2004, p. 104) had noted this challenge earlier when he argued that "in the practice and theory of development cooperation very often the role of religions and religious sentiments and religious experiences of meaning is played down." In his analysis, the result is a mismatch between development intentions and development results. However, Chitando, Gunda and Togarasei (2020, p. 14) argue that despite many years of religion being 'exiled' from development discourse, it has found its way back forcefully. Part of the reason, particularly in Africa, is that religion continues to be actively involved in the public sphere defying secularist views which had projected the death of religion as societies modernise. From Gunda's (2020, p. 44) analysis, such secularist thinking led to the marginalisation of religion in development discourses. However, religion has shocked the 'prophets of doom' by its increasing influence in public life. Gunda (2020, p. 44) is of the view that ignoring religion by secular development agencies led to their failure in Africa. Tomalin, Haustein and Kidy (2019, p. 107) view religion as critical to development and they argue that "unless development policy and practice takes religion seriously, both in terms of how religious traditions still prevail across much of the world, as well as the significant contribution that faith actors make to the development and humanitarian field, then efforts are likely to be met with limited success." Hence, Narayanan (2013, p. 132) argues that, "religion's role in humanitarian work, as well as militancy, makes development's engagement with religion mandatory." In her analysis, religion contributes to development in three ways, that is, through some important values that religion can offer, through its potential for activism and finally, in the more personal realm of self-development (2013, p. 132).

A critical analysis of the history of development in Africa shows that religion was central to the whole process. In pre-colonial Africa, sacred practitioners played pivotal roles in the socio-economic, religio-political as well as health and well-being of the African people. The introduction of colonialism saw missionaries playing pivotal roles in education and health through the building of schools and hospitals. Hence, Appleby (2015) avers that religious development actors develop and sustain schools, colleges, seminaries universities among others as well as maintaining health centres. As public health institutions continue to be dilapidated, Zimbabweans, for example, have found relief in mission hospitals. In this case, Gunda (2020, p. 47) argues that religion has always been part of development and that any attempt to isolate if would result in resistance by believers. Werner (2019, p. 40) explains clearly the above point on religion and development. I quote him at length. He argues that

> It is not by chance that in a majority of countries in sub-Saharan Africa, more than half of the national educational and the health care systems were originally brought up and supported by Christian churches. In several settings, Christian churches and their diakonia systems are still the major health care providers. They reach out to even the remotest local areas. Christian mission history provides a vast panorama of examples of the intersection of evangelism and diakonia, as it belongs to the essence of the Christian faith that it becomes active and concrete in personal and institutionalized forms of charity, social care, relief work and educational efforts.

Religious organisations such as Christian Care, Catholic Relief Services (CRS) and World Vision have been instrumental in carrying out development work in sub-Saharan Africa. The work they do has gone a long way in alleviating poverty as well as promoting justice and human rights. Tomalin, Haustein and Kidy (2019, p. 102) note that with religion being increasingly recognised as a human resource rather than an impediment to development, greater portion of development aid is currently being channelled through faith-based organisations (FBOs). It has now been established that religious leaders in particular have the respect of their communities more than foreign development actors and they can easily convince their members on accepting development projects. Hence, SDGs' success depends largely on local actors such as religious leaders. From the perspective of Tomalin, Haustein and Kidy (2019, p. 103)

> The SDGs seek to ensure a more grassroots and locally owned type of development based on the recognition that "local people" are better placed to both understand and respond to development challenges. Since local societies in development aid recipients countries are often centred around faith communities, the engagement and role played by them becomes even more critical to the discussion on sustainable development.

What makes religious actors important in development practice is that they have a longer if not permanent presence within communities well after the departure of development actors.

## RELIGION, PEACEBUILDING AND DEVELOPMENT: THE CHALLENGES

Although 'religion', 'peacebuilding' and 'development' are contested terms with multiple meanings (Appleby, 2015, p. 183), they interface in various ways. The discussion above has shown the pervasiveness of religion in both peacebuilding and development. For example, Appleby (2015, p. 185) avers that development has expanded to include a host of practices that overlap, replicate and coincide with some of the practices of peacebuilders and religious actors. In fact, development is subsumed in the grammar of peacebuilding. However, a number of challenges are noticeable as the three concepts intersect. In this section, I seek to highlight some of these challenges.

The emphasis of religious peacebuilding on reconciliation and forgiveness (which terms are deeply rooted in religion) may overlook the need for truth-telling, reparation and accountability by the perpetrators of violence and the state. This may lead to temporary peace which is detrimental for development. The religious leaders' apparent willingness to prioritise forgiveness and reconciliation over imprisonment and other forms of retributive justice mandated by state law is often a source of scandal in some secular-religious spaces (Appleby, 2015, p. 198). For example, the South African case where the Truth and Reconciliation Commission traded justice for truth-telling left many victims unsatisfied. In Zimbabwe, a one-man pronunciation of peace and reconciliation [1] without truth and justice has historically been viewed as a cover-up of the war and the Gukurahundi [2] atrocities. Manyonganise (2016) critiques the culture of impunity that characterises the Zimbabwean political space and highlights the way it has kept the wounds of victims festering beneath false notions of peace and reconciliation. Hence, Africa (2020, n.d) observes that "where there have been gross violation of human rights and perpetrators have not been brought to book, the failure to effect transitional justice hangs a cloud over the affected societies or countries."

In the name of peacebuilding and promotion of development, religious freedom may be suppressed or certain religious values may be broken, leading to resentment by members of that specific religion and this may be the genesis of conflict. Svensson (2016, p. 12) notes that the suppression of religious rights can create underlying grievances that spark political violence and civil wars. This is exacerbated if political leaders in a particular context, in their bid to

---

[1] In 1980, Robert Mugabe single-handedly pronounced peace and reconciliation in his victory speech after election victory that ended white minority rule.

[2] Gukurahundi is an ethnic genocide that was perpetrated on the Ndebele ethnic group from 1983 by the ZANU PF led government in Zimbabwe.

regulate religion, show favouritism to certain religious institutions within society. Svensson (2016, p. 13) argues that it has been established through research that there exists a connection between the occurrence of religious terrorism and the lack of religious freedom. For example, Seul (2019, p. 17) is of the view that "where political and military power are tightly aligned with dominant religion and its dominant institutions, religion may influence the conflict pervasively, and in ways that may be rather hidden in plain sight to some stakeholders and observers." In Zimbabwe, as the country prepares to go for elections in 2023, there has emerged a worrying development where a certain Christian tradition, the African Independent Churches (AICs), have begun a Mapositori4ED campaign in support of the incumbent president. Historically, the leadership of political parties have always graced AICs' meetings when it is election time to drum up support for their campaigns (see Chitando, 2020; Manyonganise, 2014, 2022; Vengeyi, 2011). However, there has never been a movement created to campaign for a specific presidential candidate by AICs in Zimbabwe, though some of the leaders have publicly declared their presidential choices. In a case alluded to above, the AICs [3] of the Johane Masowe sect have deviated from the norm by creating a group that sees itself as critical in campaigning for the incumbent president, Emmerson Dambudzo Munangagwa who is often referred to as ED (derived from the first and second names respectively), hence the name "Mapositori4ED". This has the danger of infusing religion within an already volatile political environment which not only endangers peace but development processes as well. Beyond Africa, in Myanmar, Buddhism aligns itself against the Muslim and Hindu Rohingya people. Hence, most secular organisations approach the terrain of FBOs with caution (Kaunda & Sokfa, 2020, p. 60).

Abu-Nimer and Nelson (2021) note that policy makers and religious agencies often speak different languages and have in some ways opposing operational frameworks to assess their contribution to solving problems. They note that "policy makers tend to rely on written results that are evidence-driven and action oriented while the subculture of religion and interreligious peacebuilding tends to be oral, anecdotal, and relationship oriented" (2021, p. 3). As a result, FBOs and religious actors in peacebuilding find it difficult to communicate their significance in the field to policymakers.

In the field of development, Appleby (2015, p. 185) notes that some development theorists continue to view religion as an impediment to progress. This is often a result of viewing religion in sacred terms and development in secular terms. Hence, most often, religion is treated as a subordinated partner in development discourse. Appleby (2015, p. 186) further notes that the sacral elements of religion display the pre-eminence of spiritual and otherworldly actors and interests which pose enormous challenges to the collaboration of religion with secular development actors. In such cases, development actors may choose to ignore religion in their projects which may result in development

---

[3] AICs in Zimbabwe are also referred to as Mapositori (the term is derived from 'Apostolic').

programmes igniting or deepening conflict thereby hindering peacebuilding efforts. Gunda (2020, p. 47) opines that it is important that "religion becomes more than merely an invited guest to becoming a policy developer and an integral insider in the development agenda setting and execution."

In both peacebuilding and development processes, religious actors may deviate from course to engage in proselytism (Omer, 2015; Appleby, 2015). In development, Appleby (2015, p. 197) argues that religious groups bent on conversion and on using development as an advantage for proselytism can complicate efforts to provide comprehensive development. Since peacebuilding is closely tied to development, the same issue arises in this field where religious actors elevate their religious beliefs above those of communities within which they intend to restore peace. Appleby also makes a critical observation that the notion of what accounts for development may differ between religious and development actors. For example, they may clash on issues pertaining to human rights, more specifically women's rights. In this case, powerful elements in Islam and Christianity may deviate from the liberal consensus on women's rights, reproductive practices, scientific research and other matters touching the hierarchy of human values (Appleby, 2015, p. 197). Hence, while religion can be a powerful development force, it can derail development processes. This is worsened by the suspicions held by believing communities against development actors and about how they can impact their religious beliefs and practices. For instance, some religious institutions such as the Johane Marange African Apostolic Church (JMAAC) in Zimbabwe continue to practice child marriages, while others still stigmatise and discriminate against those living with HIV. Such practices go against important dimensions of development. Garred and Abu-Nimer (2018, p. 10) note that in peacebuilding, religion can lead to exclusion. They argue

> Where religious hierarchies are involved, they tend to shape who gets involved in peacebuilding and in what types and roles. This sometimes results in exclusion, such that people belonging to marginalized groups may find it difficult to take up prominent roles in religious institutional peacebuilding.

For example, most religions have remained largely patriarchal (Manyonganise, 2021). As such, women are often excluded from leadership positions, which minimises their recognition as critical players in both peacebuilding and development processes in African societies. For example, most Christian traditions on the African continent have used biblical texts to subordinate, marginalise and bar women from ordination. As such, Chitando, Gunda and Togarasei (2020, p. 24) argue that religion has not always been good to people on the margins. Hence, when it comes to regulating gender relations, religion can oppose development. It is, therefore, instructive to note that religion plays an ambivalent role in both peacebuilding and development. In *The Ambivalence of the Sacred*, Appleby (2000) sought to show both the positive and negative role of religion in building peace in society. Narayanan (2013, p. 132) also notes that religion's presence and absence may present both possibilities and problems in development.

The other challenge with the nexus of religion, peacebuilding and development is the time taken to restore peace in post-conflict zones. Abu-Nimer and Nelson (2021, p. 9) argue that, "Dialogue and interreligious peacebuilding are not rapid processes. Since interreligious peacebuilding primarily relies on attitudinal and behavioural changes that the macro-level societal change- will take years to achieve or be observed."

This obviously affects development processes that depend on the prevalence of peace. There are certain risks that are noted within the field of peacebuilding such as compartmentalisation of religion to a certain sphere of peacebuilding separate from greater peacebuilding processes (Garred & Abu-Nimer, 2018, p. 15). Tomalin, Haustein and Kidy (2019, p. 108) indicate that complaints from FBOs have come through to the effect that their "resources and social capital have been instrumentalised by global development institutions to achieve a secular development model rather than one that is more human-centred and takes the human relationship with the divine seriously." Abu-Nimer and Nelson (2021, p. 12) further note that at times, NGOs and government agencies organise activities under the pretext of interreligious dialogue and interreligious peacebuilding, yet their programmes do not have any relation to interreligious peacebuilding or to religion and religious traditions. They argue that while participants may be from different religious backgrounds, the programmes, their design and processes tend to be devoid of religion or spirituality. In certain cases, religious peacebuilding runs the risk of over-emphasising religion thereby losing focus of the root causes of conflict such as power, politics, environment, ethnic and socio-economic dynamics, resources and so on (Abu-Nimer & Nelson, 2021, p. 13). This has implications for sustainable development as there are dangers of conflict recurring. Africa (2020) notes that a worrying challenge of peacebuilding is that in most fragile post-conflict countries, the prospect of a relapse into violence often looms. Mozambique provides a good example where failure to respond to socio-economic injustices has led to conflict recurring not only between FRELIMO and RENAMO, but also among Islamic militants rising against the Mozambican government as well.

Negative perception about religion in the fields of peacebuilding and development is another great challenge. Kulska (2015, p. 4) notes that this challenge stems from a lack of balance in the perception of religion among a wider audience shaped in its views on religion by the violent and tragic pictures of atrocities committed in the name of God. In this case, religion is presented in a misleading way with much of the attention paid to those who kill in the name of religion and not to those who heal in the same name (Kulska, 2015, p. 4). Kulska further notes that knowledge of religion being the solution to problems in global politics instead of the source of the problem is limited. For example, in non-Muslim contexts, Islam is associated with fundamentalism, militants and bombs to an extent that the peacebuilding and development work that is done by Muslim agencies is overlooked. Within Africa, the activities of Boko Haram and Al Shabab are sometimes valorised in ways that negate the peacebuilding efforts of Muslim organisations.

## Conclusion

The intention of this chapter was to examine the challenges that emerge at the intersection among religion, peacebuilding and development. The greatest challenge noted is in bringing three independent concepts, but which overlap in various ways, together. In this regard, the chapter engaged with the definitions of the concepts showing how all of meanings attached to them are contestable. The interface of religion and peacebuilding, as well as religion and development, was analysed as a way of bringing out the utility of religion in both peacebuilding and development discourses. The chapter then noted the challenges that are noticeable as religion, peacebuilding and development interact. Despite the various challenges noted, it is instructive to note that the study established that religion is very much present in the public sphere, particularly in Africa. As such, both peacebuilding and development actors may immensely benefit by treating religion with the seriousness it deserves. However, the study also showed the ambivalence of religion in peacebuilding and development. Hence, it is important for sustainable development as well as peacebuilding actors to negotiate carefully the terrain of religion so that its positive aspects for both concepts are utilised in ways that maintain peace and promote development

## References

Abu-Nimer, M. (2013). Religion and Peacebuilding. In R. MacGinty (Ed.), *Routledge Handbook of Peacebuilding* (pp. 69–80). Routledge.

Africa, S. (2020). Challenges of Peacebuilding in Africa. ACCORD, *Conflict and Resilience Monitor*, 3, n.d.

Appleby, R. S. (2015). The New Name for Peace? Religion and Development as Partners in Strategic Peacebuilding. In A. Omer, S. Appleby, & D. Little (Eds.), *The Oxford Handbook of Religion, Conflict and Peacebuilding* (pp. 183–211). Oxford University Press.

Asad, T. (2001). Reading a Modern Classic: W.C. Smith's "The Meaning and End of Religion". *History of Religions, 40*(3), 205–222.

Boutros-Ghali, B. (1992). *An Agenda for Peace: Preventive Diplomacy, Peacemaking and Peace-keeping*. United Nations.

Chitando, E. (2020). Introduction. In E. Chitando (Ed.), *Politics and Religion in Zimbabwe: The Deification of Robert G. Mugabe* (pp. 1–16). Routledge.

Chitando, E., & Tarusarira, J. (2017). The Deployment of a 'Sacred Song' in Violence in Zimbabwe: The Case of the Song *'Zimbabwe Ndeye Ropa Ramadzibaba'* (Zimbabwe was/is Born of the Blood of the Father/Ancestors) in Zimbabwean Politics. *Journal for the Study of Religion, 30*(1), 5–25.

Chitando, E., Gunda, M. R., & Togarasei, L. (2020). Introduction: Religion and Development in Africa. In E. Chitando, M. R. Gunda, & L. Togarasei (Eds.), *Religion and Development in Africa* (pp. 13–35). University of Bamberg Press.

Curtis, D. (2012). Introduction: The Contested Politics of Peacebuilding in Africa. In D. Curtis & G. A. Dyinesa (Eds.), *Peacebuilding, Power and Politics in Africa* (pp. 1–28). Ohio University Press.

Fitzgerald, T. (2000). *The Ideology of Religious Studies*. Oxford University Press.

Garred, M., & Abu-Nimer, M. (2018). Introduction. In M. Garred & M. Abu-Nimer (Eds.), *Making Peace with Faith: The Challenges of Religion and Peacebuilding* (pp. 1–26). Rowman & Littlefield.

Goetze, C. (2017). *The Distinction of Peace: A Social Analysis of Peacebuilding*. University of Michigan Press.

Gunda, M. R. (2020). Rethinking Development in Africa and the Role of Religion. In E. Chitando, M. R. Gunda, & L. Togarasei (Eds.), *Religion and Development in Africa* (pp. 37–57). University of Bamberg Press.

Hopper, P. (2012). *Understanding Development: Issues and Debates*. Polity Press.

Kaunda, C. J., & Sokfa, F. J. (2020). Religion and Development in Africa: A Critical Analysis. In E. Chitando, M. R. Gunda, & L. Togarasei (Eds.), *Religion and Development in Africa* (pp. 59–74). Bamberg; University of Bamberg Press.

Kraybill, R. (1994). Transition from Rhodesia to Zimbabwe: The Role of Religious Actors. In D. Johnston & C. Sampson (Eds.), *Religion, The Missing Dimension of Statecraft* (pp. 208–257). Oxford University Press.

Kulska, J. (2015). *A balanced perception of religion in International Relations*. Retrieved November 29, 2022, from https://www.e-ir.info/2015.

Ludovic, L. T. (2021). Religion and Peacebuilding in Sub-Saharan Africa. In T. McNamee & M. Muyangwa (Eds.), *The State of Peacebuilding in Africa: Lessons Learned for Policymakers and Practitioners* (pp. 47–64). Springer.

Manyonganise, M. (2014). African Independent Churches: The Dynamics of their Political Participation in Zimbabwe. In E. Chitando, M. R. Gunda, & J. Kuegler (Eds.), *Multiplying in the Spirit: African Initiated Churches in Zimbabwe* (pp. 162–174). University of Bamberg Press.

Manyonganise, M. (2016). The Church, National Healing and Reconciliation: A Womanist Perspective on Churches in Manicaland (CiM). [Unpublished Doctoral Thesis]. University of Pretoria.

Manyonganise, M. (2021). Development as a Factor in the Religion and Human Security Nexus. In J. Tarusarira & E. Chitando (Eds.), *Themes in Religion and Human Security in Africa* (pp. 134–151). Routledge.

Manyonganise, M. (2022). The March Is not Ended: Church Confronting the State Over the Zimbabwean Crisis. *Religions, 13*, 107. https://doi.org/10.3390/rel13020107

Mensah, J. (2019). Sustainable Development: Meaning, History, Principles, Pillars and Implications for Human Action: Literature Review. *Cogent Social Sciences, 5*(1), 1653531. https://doi.org/10.1080/23311886.1653531

Molendijk, A. L. (1999). In Defence of Pragmatism. In J. G. Platvoet & A. L. Molendijk (Eds.), *The Pragmatics of Defining Religion: Contexts, Concepts and Contests* (pp. 3–22). Brill.

Murithi, T. (2009). *The Ethics of Peacebuilding*. Edinburgh University Press.

Narayan, N. (2013). Religion and Sustainable Development: Analysing the Connections. *Sustainable Development, 21*, 131–139.

Neville, R. C. (2018). *Defining Religion: Essays in Philosophy of Religion*. State University of New York.

Philpott, D. (2013). Religious Freedom and Peacebuilding: May I introduce you two? *The Review of Faith and International Affairs, 11*(1), 31–37.

Platvoet, J. G. (1999). To Define or not to Define: The Problem of the Definition of Religion. In J. G. Platvoet & A. L. Molendijk (Eds.), *The Pragmatics of Defining Religion: Contexts, Concepts and Contests* (pp. 245–265). Brill.

Religions for Peace. (2018). *Caring for Our Common Future through Preventing and Transforming Conflicts, including War and Terrorism*. RfP.

Schaefer, A., & Crane, A. (2005). Addressing Sustainability and Consumption. *Journal of Macromarketing, 25*(1), 79–92.

Schilbrack, K. (2012). The Social Construction of 'Religion' and its Limits: A Critical Reading of Timothy Fitzgerald. *Method and Theory in the Study of Religion, 24*, 97–117.

Schilderman, H. (2014). Defining Religion: A Humanities Perspective. In H. Schilderman (Ed.), *The Concept of Religion: Defining and Measuring Contemporary Beliefs and Practices* (pp. 176–197). Brill.

Schirch, L. (2008). Strategic Peacebuilding: State of the Field. Peace Prints. *South Asian Journal of Peacebuilding, 1*(1), 1–17.

Seul, J. R. (2019). Inclusion of Religious Actors in Peace and National Dialogue Processes. *Journal of Interreligious Studies, 27*, 5–34.

Sibanda, F., Muyambo, T., & Chitando, E. (2022). Introduction: Religion and Public Health in the Shadow of COVID-19 Pandemic in Southern Africa. In F. Sibanda, T. Muyambo, & E. Chitando (Eds.), *Religion and the COVID-19 Pandemic in Southern Africa* (pp. 1–24). Routledge.

Silvestri, G., & Mayall, J. (2015). *The Role of Religion in Conflict and Peacebuilding*. The British Academy.

Smith, W. C. (1991). *The Meaning and End of Religion*. Fortress Press.

Stone, J. (2001). Review: The Ideology of Religious Studies by Timothy Fitzgerald. *Religious Studies, 37*(2), 242–246.

Svensson, I. (2016). Conflict and Peace. In D. Yamane (Ed.), *Handbook of Religion and Society* (pp. 467–484). Springer.

Tomalin, E., Haustein, J., & Kidy, S. (2019). Religion and the Sustainable Development Goals. *Review of Faith and International Affairs, 17*(2), 102–118.

Trebilcock, M. J., & Prado, M. M. (2014). *Advanced Introduction to Law and Development*. Edward Elgar Publishing Limited.

UNDP. (1991). *Human Development Report*. Oxford University Press.

United Nations. (1987). *Our Common Future: Report on the World Commission on Environment and Development*. United Nations.

Vengeyi, O. (2011). Mapositori Churches and Politics in Zimbabwe: Political Drama to Win Support of Mapositori Churches. *Exchange*, 351–368.

Werner, D. (2019). New Trends in the Global Discourse on Religion and Development. In J. Amanze, M. Masango, E. Chitando, & L. Siwila (Eds.), *Religion and Development in Southern Africa, Volume 1* (pp. 24–52). Mzuni Press.

CHAPTER 5

# The Bible, Peace Building and Sustainable Development in Africa

*Lovemore Togarasei and Clemence Makamure*

## INTRODUCTION

That sustainable development can only take place in contexts of peace and security cannot be disputed by anyone. Peace and security can therefore be described as building blocks for sustainable development. No wonder the 2015 General Assembly of the United Nations identified peace and security as prerequisites for achieving sustainable development by 2030 (Zannier, 2015). In addition, Goal 16 of the Sustainable Development Goals is about promoting peaceful and inclusive societies, providing access to justice for all and building effective, accountable and inclusive institutions at all levels. Despite this reality, peace in the world remains elusive and its achievement, a pipe dream. Even the several initiatives undertaken by different organizations such as the UNESCO, through its Week for Peace and Sustainable Development (UNESCO, 2017), have not yet achieved total peace in the world. Africa, for example, remains a hotbed of conflicts as we outline below. As we write this chapter, Africa is experiencing an outburst of conflict in Sudan which has seen nations scrambling to repatriate their citizens as all developmental infrastructure is under attack. These conflicts present devastating consequences to all developmental efforts. For this reason, the search for peace for sustainable development needs to be a multisectoral one. No sector should lag behind. Writing in 1996, White and

L. Togarasei (✉) • C. Makamure
Department of Religious Studies and Philosophy, Zimbabwe Open University, Harare, Zimbabwe
e-mail: makamurec@zou.ac.zw

© The Author(s), under exclusive license to Springer Nature Switzerland AG 2023
S. M. Kilonzo et al. (eds.), *The Palgrave Handbook of Religion, Peacebuilding, and Development in Africa*,
https://doi.org/10.1007/978-3-031-36829-5_5

Tiongco would ask whether theology had a voice in the area of development, "Theology seems too abstract, too removed more concerned with the hereafter than the here and now" (1996: 11). But as they concluded, theology indeed has a role in development. They wrote, "Theology can provide vision and motivation. ... It can also help discern and identify guidelines on how to put the dreams and visions into operation" (White & Tiongco, 1996: 28). It is in this spirit of combined effort in the search for peace and security that this chapter reflects on the role that the Bible can and should play in peace building for sustainable development in Africa. We call upon the engagement of the Bible on the basis that it remains important in shaping values and attitudes among a significant population, especially in Christian communities. Basing on the theoretical argument by Coward and Gordon (2004) that the Bible is a vital source for social togetherness, we therefore seek to explore the teaching of the Bible (selected New Testament [NT] texts) on peace and peace building and propose ways by which Christian communities can engage this teaching in contribution to SDGs' call for inclusive communities for peace and resultant sustainable development. Data for the chapter is derived from document analysis, personal observations and historical narratives. The chapter is divided into four sections. We open it by exploring conflicts in Africa to justify the need for peace building. In section "Peace Building and Sustainable Development: Some Theoretical and Methodological Approaches" we explore theoretical and methodological approaches to peace building and sustainable development. Section "The Bible on Peace and Peace Building: A Study of Selected New Testament Texts" then studies selected New Testament texts to establish some teaching of the Bible on peace and peace building. Section "The Bible and Peace Building: Some Suggested Approaches" then proposes some approaches for using the Bible for promoting peace to enable sustainable development. Concluding remarks wrap up the chapter.

## THE NEED FOR PEACE BUILDING IN AFRICA

Africa as a continent has been vulnerable to intra and inter-state wars and conflicts from time immemorial. This has impelled the intimation that Africa is the home of wars, poverty and instability. Most wretched about these conflagrations is that they have defied any meaningful solution and their negative impacts have stunted progress and sustainable development in Africa. Worse to the situation is the contention that the end to these devious scenarios seems to be obscure. Armed conflicts in Africa throughout the twentieth century have caused massive loss of human life, the downfall of socio-economic systems, and the squalor of health and education services across the continent. Rather, twentieth-century conflicts exposed civilians to penetrating physical and psychological trauma that deleteriously impacted sustainable development throughout many African nations. To understand the magnitude and scope of inflicted trauma, this section of the chapter presents a synopsis of wars and conflicts in selected countries in Africa as we seek to demonstrate the need to seek solutions for peace building in Africa.

In 1991, Mohamed Siad Barre, the then President of the Somali Democratic Republic, was ousted by a coup. This shift in the balance of power sparked a civil war that killed and exposed many lives to violence, famine and diseases. Subsequent to the removal of Barre from supremacy, the Somali Democratic Republic was divided into two opposing parties, that is the Somali National Movement in the north and the United Somali Congress in the southern part of the nation. This separation exacerbated the conflicts between the contesting factions because no one ruling entity was recognized by all Somalis (Girard, 2019). This implies that those from the north were not ready to legitimize and recognize the authority of those in the southern faction. At the same time, the southerners were opposed to the leadership of the northern Somalis. As a way of trying to find remedy to the mess, the United Nations and the United States became involved in the conflict from 1992 to 1995 by sending military forces and humanitarian aid to the country. However, due to the lack of imaginable resolution in ending the conflicts and financial costs, the United States legitimately ended its involvement in Somalia in 1994, leaving the nation with no optimism of grace. The Somali Civil War led to large death tolls and protracted conflicts which deterred sustainable development because the heavy fighting between the warlords obstructed timeous relief and peace efforts (Mukand & Rodrik, 2016).

Upon achieving independence from Britain in 1960, Nigeria was divided into ethnically defined regions. This saw the Igbo people occupying the southeast, the Yoruba were pushed to the southwest, while the Hausa and Fulani occupied the northern region. Tensions broke up as the nation's military usurped power following the attainment of independence and fighting ensued among the regions (Haas, 2014). It is estimated that the conflict resulted in the massacre of 30,000 Igbos by the Yoruba. Colonel Emeka Ojukwu on 30 May 1967 seceded the Igbo territory and declared it to be the Republic of Biafra. With the help of Great Britain, the Nigerian federal government reacted quickly, gaining control of the oil-rich southeast coast and blockading supplies to the region, causing severe famine and leading to the deaths of 2 million civilians and 100,000 military personnel. Ojukwu tendered over control of the Biafran government to Major General Philip Effiong of the Biafran Army in 1970 and fled the country with his family. Effiong subsequently surrendered to Nigerian military head of state, General Yakubu Gowon, thereby immediately ending the thirty months civil war (Haas, 2014). So, the Nigerian Civil War resulted in different ethnic factions fighting one another, creating chaos and leading to a massive crisis, including the deaths of countless civilians as well as the political redrawing of West Africa. When the conflict ended, the Nigerian government declared to the Igbo that there was "no victor, no vanquished," but historians say the war did and still does affect national politics and policy-making in the region. This in turn is affecting sustainable development in Nigeria today.

In Rwanda the ethnic group called Hutus that comprised approximately fifteen per cent of the nation's population murdered Juvenal Habyarimana, the Rwandan President in 1994. This event invigorated the methodical and vicious genocide of roughly 800,000 Tutsis (Union, 2017). The genocide had a span of hundred days of ruthless massacres which made neighbours pitting against each other. Surprisingly, in some instances, Hutu husbands were forced to mercilessly kill their wives. The situation was worsened by the fact that Rwandan identification cards name a person's ethnic classification, and this made it impossible for Tutsis to escape the persecution and butchery. The massacre ended on 4 July 1994 when the Rwandan Patriotic Front (RFP), through the support of the Ugandan army, invaded the capital city of Kigali and defeated the Hutus (Amin, 2019). It is only after peace was restored that economic and social development began in the country.

Another case of conflicts in Africa is the two-year war between Eritrea and Ethiopia, which began in 1998 triggered over a border dispute. The conflict claimed approximately 80,000 lives. The war opened when military and police from both countries exchanged fire in a rural area near the disputed border. It ended in the year 2000 after a negotiated cease-fire agreement called the Algiers Peace Treaty (Union, 2017). This war was classified as a border war and the parties who negotiated the treaty took a purely legal stance at resolving the conflict, which left both sides unsatisfied and failed to ease tensions between the countries.

These tracks of wars and conflict in most African countries show that after gaining independence from colonial masters, Africa had to face another demise as the nature of conflicts the world over took another dimension in the contemporary politics (Schmitter & Karl, 1991). There was a sharp increase in sponsored insurgency, terrorism, disputes due to diversity and differences on ethnicity and religion leading to political clashes or in some cases civil wars. Whilst colonialism and liberation struggles were the first episodes of conflicts in Africa, ethnicity and religion had dominated the contemporary problems of Africa (Mukand & Rodrik, 2016). The case in point was the emergence of insurgency and terrorism that had its highest magnitude registered, as noted above, in the Somalia Civil War, the Rwanda genocide, and recently the Ethiopia Tigray war and the Mozambique Islamic insurgency. Union (2017) said that Africa has accounted for more of multifaceted armed conflicts than any other continent.

## Peace Building and Sustainable Development: Some Theoretical and Methodological Approaches

Although Ndeche and Iroye (2022) say there is no overarching theoretical framework for conflict resolution and peace building, there are peace-making frameworks that have been in use for peace building and for ending conflicts in Africa. Here we discuss a few of them as we set the stage for advocating for peace building using the Bible. The first theory we discuss is that liberal democratic practices promote peace. This theory is in line with Rawls' (1971) moral theory of justice based on equity and fairness in the distribution of goods for a well-ordered society and argues that peace is conditioned and regulated by a shared public conception of justice (Ndeche & Iroye, 2022). Liberal democracy is the combination of a liberal political ideology that operates under a representative democratic form of government. Liberal democracy contains the provision of civil rights—the non-discrimination in the provision of public goods such as justice, security, education and health—in addition to political rights—the guarantee of free and fair electoral contests (Doomen, 2014). Liberal democracy is characterized by elections between multiple distinct political parties, a separation of powers into different branches of government, the rule of law in everyday life as part of an open society, a market economy with private property, and the equal protection of human rights, civil rights, civil liberties and political freedoms for all people (Adams, 2001). Liberal democracies often draw upon a constitution, either codified or uncodified, to delineate the powers of government and enshrine the social contract. After a period of expansion in the second half of the twentieth century, liberal democracy became a prevalent political system in the world (Lührmann et al., 2020). Advocates of this theory believe that peace is easier to achieve where there is liberal democracy. They see the absence of liberal democracy as the seedbed for conflicts and wars.

The need for liberal democracy has been the most common approach to trying to build peace in Africa, especially through the work of the African Union (AU). Ensuring lasting peace, prosperity and stability in Africa is a major objective of the AU. The organization's support for strengthening democratic institutions, promoting the rule of law and protecting human rights helps to nurture sustainable development (International Food Policy Research Institute (IFPRI), 2016). The AU has also developed specific tools and programmes tailor-made to help governments address the root causes of intolerance and discrimination and continues to promote inclusive societies, tolerance for diversity and integration. Recognizing the crucial importance of the free flow of information in maintaining peace, advancing democracy and ensuring sustainable development, the AU continues its support for free and pluralistic media in all its participating states (Addis Ababa Action Agenda, 2015).

The second theory, related to the first in some way, is that multi-party systems promote peace. As the name suggests, this is a system that consists of various political parties that stand across the political spectrum in the normal course of the electoral process (Gilens & Page, 2014). These parties may exclusively win a majority or may form a coalition government which is contingent upon the public support it receives through the vote. The party system is broadly divided into three categories which any democracy may choose to follow: One-party system, Two-party system and Multi-party system. In order to create a conducive environment for peace and national development, this theory says a multi-party system is universally preferred (Gilens & Page, 2014).

Third is the theory that peace is built upon a free-market economy system. This theory has been advocated for to enforce peace in Africa (Morlino, 2004). The system implies that prices for goods and services are set by the open market and not by a centralized government or authority. In this system the prices of goods and services are transparent, and goods can be bought or sold by any individual or firm at their fixed prices or negotiated ones. This is believed to create a peaceful environment. A free-market economy operates in line with the supply and demand which reflects the needs as well as the available resources for the production of goods and services (Morlino, 2004).

In terms of methodology, broadly two approaches are mainly used for peace building and conflict resolution: diplomatic mediation and informal dialogue. While a full definition and analysis of these approaches is necessary for peace and conflict studies (see Lederach, 1995), in this chapter we provide just brief explanations of these approaches. The diplomatic mediation approach is the most common approach to peace building and conflict resolution. It involves the intervention of a third party to mediate between conflict parties. The whole process is usually formalized and, at national or international levels, includes the signing of peace agreements. This can be done by individuals or institutions such as non-governmental organizations. Informa dialogue, on the other hand, is not formalized and may take place at lower levels such as among individuals.

It appears the theories and methodologies discussed above have informed peace building efforts in Africa. However, this has not seen the achievement of the desired peace. Cases of conflicts and wars continue to escalate. It is for this reason therefore that we suggest other approaches to peace building such as the use of the Bible in Christian communities.

## THE BIBLE ON PEACE AND PEACE BUILDING: A STUDY OF SELECTED NEW TESTAMENT TEXTS

While it would be prudent among Christian communities if a simplified position on the Bible, peace and peace building could be given, this is practically impossible given the fact that the Bible is not a single book but a real library containing several books that address different issues. And while texts and themes on peace and peace building can be identified, the fact remains that there is no unified position of the different biblical books on this subject. What this section of this chapter intends to do, therefore, is to glean some teachings of the Bible on peace and peace building by limiting itself to the New Testament. But even as we try to delimit ourselves to the New Testament, we need to admit again that the New Testament itself has several texts that can be addressed in the context of the search for peace and peace building. What we do then in this section is to select a few texts to build a case and demonstrate that the Bible is a strong tool for promoting peace for sustainable development among Christian communities in Africa. We acknowledge that this attempt has already been made by other scholars and that we are building upon this as we amplify the call for using biblical views for peace, peace building and sustainable development in Africa. For example Rose Mukansengimana-Nyirimana and Jonathan A. Draper (2012: 299–318) argued for the peace-making role of the New Testament by focusing on the Johannine story of the Samaritan woman (John 4:1–42). Responding to the Rwandan genocide of 1994, the two scholars interpreted the story of the Samaritan woman from a literary narrative critical approach to argue that the Samaritan woman and Jesus acted as bridges to connect the ever-warring Jews and Samaritans. In the same way, they further argued, Rwandan women (we believe they had Rwandan Christian women in mind) can play the same role of bridging a situation of discrimination and ethnic conflict that led to the Rwandan genocide (Mukansengimana-Nyirimana and Draper 2012: 299).

The word peace (Greek: *Eirene* and Hebrew: *Shalom*) appears several times in the Bible. In the NT alone it appears more than a hundred times. The table below contains some of the New Testament texts on peace. Note that the emphasis on peace is ours.

- Finally, brothers and sisters, rejoice! Strive for full restoration, encourage one another, be of one mind, **live in peace**. And the God of love and **peace** will be with you (1 Cor. 13:11).
- They must turn from evil and do good; they must **seek peace** and pursue it (1 Peter 3:11).
- And **the peace of God**, which transcends all understanding, will guard your hearts and your minds in Christ Jesus (Philippians 4:7).
- Now may **the Lord of peace** himself **give you peace** at all times and in every way. The Lord be with all of you (2 Thess. 3:16).
- Whatever you have learned or received or heard from me, or seen in me—put it into practice. And **the God of peace** will be with you (Philippians 4:9).
- But the fruit of the Spirit is love, joy, **peace**, forbearance, kindness, goodness, faithfulness (Gal. 5:22).
- Let **the peace of Christ** rule in your hearts, since as members of one body **you were called to peace**. And be thankful (Col. 3:15).
- Therefore, since we have been justified through faith, **we have peace with God** through our Lord Jesus Christ (Rom. 5:1).
- The mind governed by the flesh is death, but the mind governed by the Spirit is life and **peace** (Rom. 8:6).
- **Blessed are the peacemakers**, for they will be called children of God (Mat. 5:9).
- **Peace I leave with you; my peace I give you**. I do not give to you as the world gives. Do not let your hearts be troubled and do not be afraid (John 14:27).
- Make every effort to **live in peace** with everyone and to be holy; without holiness no one will see the Lord (Heb. 12:14).
- May God himself, **the God of peace**, sanctify you through and through (1 Thess. 5).
- **Peacemakers who sow in peace** reap a harvest of righteousness (James 3:18).
- If it is possible, as far as it depends on you, **live at peace** with everyone (Rom. 12:18).
- Let us therefore make every effort **to do what leads to peace** and to mutual edification (Rom. 14:19).
- For God is not a God of disorder **but of peace**—as in all the congregations of the Lord's people (1 Cor. 14:33).

From the above NT texts, we can pick up several insights on peace and peace building as these relate to believers:

- That God is the God of peace (1 Cor. 13:11, 2 Thess. 3:16, Philippians 4:9, etc.)
- That peace belongs to God (Philippians 4:7) and to Christ (Col. 3:15)
- That peace should be sought after (1 Peter 3:11)
- That peace is given by God (2 Thess. 3:16) and by Christ (John 14:27)
- That peace is a fruit of the Spirit (Gal. 5:22)
- That Christians should be peacemakers (Mat. 5:9, Rom. 14:19, James 3:18)
- That Christians should live at peace with everyone (1 Cor. 13:11, Rom 12:18)
- That Christians should actively seek/pursue peace (Gal. 5:22, Eph. 6:15)

Although generally the word peace means the tranquillity or the absence of war among individuals, groups and nations, the sum total of its use in the New Testament passages analysed above shows that the word means well-being. It was used as an expression of greeting both when people met and when they parted. Paul used it as an opening address in his letters (Gal 1:13). This well-being according to the NT comes from God, who is peace. Through Jesus Christ, this peace of God should be extended to believers. Believers then have peace through their connection with God, with the connection with God having to be extended to other human beings. According to Oke (2022), this peace gives humanity, "freedom from fear, anxiety and worry, freedom from conflict and violence, freedom from depression and sadness, freedom from oppression and injustice ..." These are indeed prerequisites for sustainable development. No wonder then, referring to the Hebrew word translated peace (*shalom*), Maddocks (1981: 10) says the well-being brought by peace can be manifested in prosperity, bodily health, contentedness, good relations between nations and between humanity, salvation, and so on. The Bible therefore mandates Christians to live in, and to promote, peace.

Whilst the Bible calls believers to seek and promote peace, some NT texts we have noted above assure believers that since God is peace itself, believers should live with the assurance of God's peace even in the midst of challenges. Breisinger et al., (2014) calls this kind of peace "inner peace" and says it is not earned but received as a gift from God. It is the kind of peace that carries one through even in times of turmoil and hostility. Harries says it is the peace that carried Jesus through even as he faced persecution (Luke 23:34). The Bible does not therefore promise that all will be well. As John 14:27 states, even as they face challenges, the hearts of believers should not be troubled.

With these lessons on peace in the NT, how then can the Bible be used for peace building for sustainable development in Africa? We turn to address this in the next section.

## THE BIBLE AND PEACE BUILDING: SOME SUGGESTED APPROACHES

In section "Peace Building and Sustainable Development: Some Theoretical and Methodological Approaches" of this chapter, we considered some of the models and theories that have been put forward to build peace. Common among them is the diplomatic approach to peace building whereby peace brokers (who are often the powerful individuals or nations) broker peace between the warring parties. This often involves meetings and signing of peace agreements. For a long time in Africa, the church has also played this role guided by the biblical teaching on love and peaceful coexistence of people. P. H. Gundani (1996), for example, looks at the role played by the Catholic Commission for Justice and Peace in Zimbabwe, and S. Chamango (1996) looks at the role of the church during periods of conflict in Mozambique. Whilst we do acknowledge the importance of these approaches, we do hereby argue that the Bible provides other approaches to peace building and promotion of peaceful coexistence in Christian communities. The Bible's holistic teaching on peace means we do not need to wait until conflicts arise that we then start peace negotiations. Rather, the Bible's approach is to promote peace every day. This is the point this chapter underlines: sustainable peace for development needs to be built in the day-to-day activities of every member of the community. The church's teaching on love promotes peace and, this way, it stands a good chance of contributing to the achievement of SDG Goal 16 of promoting peaceful and inclusive societies. As we have seen in section "The Bible on Peace and Peace Building: A Study of Selected New Testament Texts" where we looked at NT texts on peace, God is the God of peace and peace itself. Thus, to believe in God is to believe in peace. When we recall Jesus' greatest commandment that one should love God and neighbour (Matt 22:37–39), it becomes apparent that at the centre of Christian teaching is peaceful coexistence of the individual with God and fellow human beings. 1 John 4:20 states this plainly, "If anyone says, 'I love God' and hates his brother, he is a liar, for he who does not love his brother and sister, whom he has seen, cannot love God, whom he has not seen." The New Testament (NT) therefore calls on all Christians to live in peace.

Secondly, New Testament texts also show that besides living in peace, believers have to actively make peace. Jesus referred to peacemakers as the children of God (Matthew 5:9), the greatest honour that one can have in the kingdom of God. Considering that Jesus also taught his followers to be the salt of the earth (Matthew 5:13) and the light of the world (Matthew 5:14), it is clear that believers have to play an active role in peace building. This biblical approach to peace building multiplies the number of peace brokers as it makes every believer a peace broker. If this approach was to be applied in its letter, it would mean that conflicts are resolved at very lower (individual) levels rather than when they have escalated to higher (societal/national/regional) levels.

Thirdly, NT texts give believers the responsibility to reconcile the world (2 Cor. 5:18–20). While believers have to live in peace, the NT texts show that this will not always be the case. When conflicts arise, then believers have the responsibility of calling for reconciliation. 2 Cor 5:18–20 gives believers a ministry of reconciliation, "All this is from God, who through Christ reconciled us to himself and gave us the ministry of reconciliation, that is, in Christ God was reconciling the world to himself, not counting their trespasses against them, and entrusting to us the message of reconciliation."

Fourth, one cannot provide peace when they do not have peace in themselves (Onwu, 1996: 31). Using the NT, the church in Africa needs to cultivate this individual inner peace. The NT shows that individual inner peace is essential for development both at individual and societal levels. It is a kind of peace to be promoted for human development. In Phil. 4, Paul identifies seven principles of inner peace which are important for sustainable development (Onwu, 1996: 35). These principles are: standing firm in the Lord (4:1); rejoicing in the Lord (4:4); not being anxious about anything (4:6); living a moral life with emphasis on truth, honesty, justice, holiness, love, striving for excellence (4:8–9); being content with what one has (moderation, not being greedy) (4:11); paying attention to the word of God (4:9) and being generous (4:14–19). Considering the selfishness expressed in practices like corruption and attendant conflicts caused by human greed, individualism, injustice, hate and dishonesty in African societies, these principles speak to what Africa needs for peace and sustainable development.

"Lastly, the NT texts analysed above and indeed the greater teaching of the Bible show that God is the source, custodian and guarantor of all forms of peace" (Mugambi, 2003: 79). Peace can therefore be guaranteed if more people seek the peace of God, that is the union of the divine and human will (Breisinger et al., 2014: 98). As succinctly summarized by Mugambi (2003: 79), "Human effort at mediation, though important and essential, cannot succeed unless they are undertaken through and by divine support, which makes possible the meeting of conflicting minds and wills." It is important then that as human beings seek peace and take efforts to mediate those in conflict, they appeal for divine intervention for lasting peace. It is possibly in light of this realization that we find organizations like Tearfund (Blackman, 2003) bringing in the Bible in the search for lasting peace whether at community or at international levels.

As we call for biblical and Christian approaches to peace and peace building, we do so fully aware of the fact that Christianity has in the past been involved in political entanglements that militate against the search for peace. Especially African missionary Christianity, as it was introduced by the missionaries, did more harm than good to the recipients especially in the areas of African identify and pride through its denunciation of everything African. Using examples from Congo and Rwanda, Namakula Mayanja (2020) highlights how African Christians are giants in making war but pygmies in making peace. As a result, writers like Musa Dube (1996) see Christianity as also responsible for the current developmental problems in Africa. Others, like Lovemore Togarasei (2007), find the divisive nature of Christianity especially as expressed in denominationalism, as stimulating conflicts that are detrimental to sustainable development. It is important then to highlight that Christians need unity and introspection if they are to promote peace for sustainable development.

## Concluding Remarks

The Hebrew word *shalom* summaries the biblical concept of peace. We highlight Harries' (1995: 91–92) definition of *shalom* as

> peace which envelopes the whole of human life. It is not just the peace of solitary individuals but the peace of the whole community. It is not only an inward state but an outward condition. It embraces life in its totality, inward and outward; personal, social, political, economic and environmental. The root meaning of the word Shalom is 'whole' and it indicates well-being in its fullness, spiritual harmony and physical health; material spirituality untouched by violence or misfortune.

This meaning of *shalom* means there can never be development where there is no peace. *Shalom* provides a wide scope of peace, not only individual peace. As we write this chapter, we are aware of developments in Sudan where the fighting has resulted in people fleeing from their homes, water and electricity infrastructure being destroyed and development being stalled. Development can never take place where there is no peace. If we make peace in our families, societies and nations, only then can it be possible to develop our countries. Lastly, development can only be sustainable where there is peace; otherwise, the outbreak of wars and all other forms of instability destroys even that we have developed. It is for this reason that this chapter proposed biblical peace as an addition to other approaches for peace building for sustainable development. It is a direct contribution to SDG 16's quest for peaceful and inclusive societies by 2030 through its call for Christian communities to adopt the biblical concept of peace. The chapter has underlined the need to build peace at individual level as opposed to institutional level that has been emphasized before. With N. Mayanja (2020: 382) we can conclude that the church in Africa must transit from a statistical church to a church with quality believers who promote peace in their daily lives. It is only through peaceful individual believers that we can achieve the goal of peaceful and inclusive societies by 2030.

## References

Adams, W. M. (2001). *Green Development: Environment and Sustainability in the Third World* (2nd ed., pp. 1–2). Abingdon-on-Thames: Routledge.

Addis Ababa Action Agenda. (2015). *Addis Ababa Action Agenda of the Third International Conference on Financing for Development*. Addis Ababa, Ethiopia, 13–16 July (New York: United Nations). Retrieved January 20, 2023, from http://www.un.org/esa/ffd/wp-content/uploads/2015/08/AAAA_Outcome.pdf

Amin, A. (2019). Preface. In *Violence and Democracy*. The British Academy. Retrieved January 22, 2023, from https://www.thebritishacademy.ac.uk/documents/242/Violence-and-Democracy.pdf

Blackman, R. (2003). *Peace-building Within Our Communities*. Tearfund.

Breisinger, C., et al. (2014). *Building Resilience to Conflict Through Food-Security Policies and Programs: An Overview*. 2020 Conference Brief 3, 15–17 May, Addis Ababa, Ethiopia (Washington, DC, International Food Policy Research Institute [IFPRI]). http://www.ifpri.org/publication/building-resilience-conflict-through-food-security-policies-and-programs-overview

Coward, H., & Gordon, S. Smith (eds.). (2004). *Religion and Peacebuilding*. Albany: State University of New York Press.

Chamango, S. (1996). The Role of Christianity in Development, Peace and Reconstruction: The Case of Mozambique. In I. Phiri, K. Ross, & J. Cox (Eds.), *The Role of Christianity in Development, Peace and Reconstruction* (pp. 156–164). AACC.

Doomen, J. (2014). *Freedom and Equality in a Liberal Democratic State*. Bruylant.

Dube, M. (1996). "Woman, What Have I To Do With You?": A Post-Colonial Feminist Theological Reflection on the Role of Christianity in Development, Peace and Reconstruction. In I. Phiri, K. Ross, & J. Cox (Eds.), *The Role of Christianity in Development, Peace and Reconstruction* (pp. 244–258). AACC.

Gilens, M., & Page, B. (2014). Testing Theories of American Politics: Elites, Interest Groups, and Average Citizens. *Perspectives on Politics, 12*(3), 564–581.

Girard, R. (2019). *Yascha Mounk, The People vs. Democracy: Why Our Freedom Is in Danger and How to Save It*. Harvard University Press.

Gundani, P. H. (1996). The Catholic Justice and Peace Commission, 1972–1980: Implications for Peace and Development. In I. Phiri, K. Ross, & J. Cox (Eds.), *The Role of Christianity in Development, Peace and Reconstruction* (pp. 120–139). AACC.

Haas, M. (2014). *Deconstructing the "Democratic Peace": How a Research Agenda Boomeranged*. Publishing House for Scholars.

International Food Policy Research Institute (IFPRI), Report. (2016). Washington, DC.

Lederach, J. P. (1995). *Preparing for Peace: Conflict Transformation Across Cultures*. Syracuse University Press.

Lührmann, A. S., Maerz, F., Grahn, S., Alizada, N., Gastaldi, L., Hellmeier, S., Hindle, G., & Lindberg, S. I. (2020). *Autocratization Surges—Resistance Grows*. Democracy Report 2020, Varieties of Democracy Institute (V-Dem).

Maddocks, M. (1981). *The Christian Healing Ministry*. SPCK.

Mayanja, N. E. B. (2020). Theology and Peacemaking in Africa. In E. K. Bongmba (Ed.), *The Routledge Handbook of African Theology* (pp. 381–398). Routledge.

Morlino, L. (2004). What Is a 'Good' Democracy? *Democratization, 11*(5), 10–32. https://doi.org/10.1080/13510340412331304589

Mugambi, J. N. K. (2003). The Christian Ideal of Peace and Political Reality in Africa. In M. N. Getui & P. Kanyandago (Eds.), *From Violence to Peace: A Challenge for African Christianity* (pp. 70–96). Acton Publishers.

Mukand, S. W., & Rodrik, D. (2016). The Political Economy of Liberal Democracy. *The Economic Journal, 130*(627), 765–792.

Mukansengimana-Nyirimana, R., & Draper, J. A. (2012). The Peace-making Role of the Samaritan Woman in John 4:1–42: A Mirror and Challenge for Rwandan Women. *Neotestamentica: Journal of the New Testament Society of South Africa, 46*(2), 299–318.

Ndeche, O., & Iroye, S. O. (2022). Key Theories in Peace and Conflict Studies and Their Impact on the Study and Practice. *Noun International Journal of Peace Studies and Conflict Resolution, 2*(2), 20–34.

Oke, M. 2022. Peace in the New Testament. Retrieved January 23, 2023, from https://churchgists.com/peace-in-the-new-testament/#:~:text=In%20the%20new%20testament%2C%20peace%20is%20defined%20as,that%20he%20has%20come%20to%20give%20us%20peace

Onwu, N. (1996). Biblical Perspectives for Peace, Development and Reconstruction: Its Socio-religious Implications for the Churches in Africa. In I. Phiri, K. Ross, & J. Cox (Eds.), *The Role of Christianity in Development, Peace and Reconstruction* (pp. 30–47). AACC.

Rawls, J. (1971). *A Theory of Justice*. Cambridge, Massachusetts: The Belknap Press of Harvard University Press.

Schmitter, P. C., & Karl, T. L. (1991). What Democracy Is ... and Is Not. *Journal of Democracy, 2*(3), 75–88. https://doi.org/10.1353/jod.1991.0033

Togarasei, L. (2007). Being a Church in a World of Disunity: Reflections from 1 Corinthians 1–4. *Scriptura, 94*(1), 65–72.

UNESCO. (2017). UNESCO Week for Peace and Sustainable Development: The Role of Education. Retrieved February 15, 2023, from https://en.unesco.org/esd-gced-week

Union, A. (2017). Main Successes of the AU in Peace and Security, Challenges and Mitigation Measures in Place. *Addis Ababa, 22*.

White, S., & Tiongco, R. (1996). What has Theology to do with Development, Peace and Reconstruction. In I. Phiri, K. Ross, & J. Cox (Eds.), *The Role of Christianity in Development, Peace and Reconstruction* (pp. 10–29). AACC.

Zannier, L. (2015). *Fostering Peace and Sustainable Development*. Implementing the 2030 Agenda: The Challenge of Conflict, No. 4(LII), United Nations. Retrieved November 1, 2022, from https://www.un.org/en/chronicle/article/fostering-peace-and-sustainable-development

CHAPTER 6

# Teaching About Religion, Peacebuilding and Development in Africa

*Johan Strijdom*

### INTRODUCTION

In his "Foreword" to *Religion and Development: Ways of Transforming the World*, James Wolfensohn (2011, p. xviii), during whose presidency of the World Bank (1995–2005) the Millennium Development Goals were formulated, emphatically states: "If development is to succeed, development policies must truly be integral in scope. Religion, therefore, cannot be excluded from the debate." In her introduction to this particular volume, the editor and Professor of Religion and Development at the International Institute of Social Studies in The Hague, Gerrie ter Haar (2011, p. 5) explains that whereas development theorists used to consider development a secular matter and religion "an obstacle to progress," the "new debate" of "integral development" has come to realize that religion "can help build human societies rather than contribute to their destruction"—even if suspicions "may be (understandable) in some respects."

This positive appraisal of the role that religion can play in transforming society for improving the quality of people's lives has indeed not led these authors to overlook the fact that religion can also have the opposite effect. If development policies are to include not only economic issues but also "non-economic factors that affect the quality of life in developing countries, … [such as] issues

J. Strijdom (✉)
Department of Religious Studies and Arabic, University of South Africa, Pretoria, South Africa
e-mail: strijjm@unisa.ac.za

of governance generally, the regulation of markets, management of the natural development, attention to both inherited and living culture, and a host of social factors" and if "[r]eligion has an effect on many peoples' attitudes to everything, including ... economic decisions ... [and] areas we had come to see as vital for successful development, like schooling, gender equality, and approaches to health care," we need to realize that "religion could be an important driver of change, even as it could be a brake to progress" (Wolfensohn, 2011, p. xvii). Gerrie ter Haar (2007) has for her part in fact made an important contribution to the analysis of the problem of witchcraft accusations in South Africa and has argued for possible interventions, as we will see in more detail below.

The United Nations General Assembly's Development Agenda "Transforming Our World: The 2030 Agenda for Sustainable Development" (2015), in taking the Millennium Development Goals further, adopted seventeen Sustainable Development Goals (SDGs). Sustainable Development Goal 16 "Peace, Justice and Strong Institutions" (2015), which provides the context of the focus of this *Palgrave Handbook on Religion, Peacebuilding and Development in Africa*, aims to "promote peaceful and inclusive societies for sustainable development, provide access to justice for all and build effective, accountable and inclusive institutions at all levels."

Although higher education features in several SDGs, Milton (2021, p. 90) has recently reviewed the literature and argued that the role that higher education can play in the promotion of SDG 16 "in fragile and conflict-affected contexts ... towards the building of peaceful, just, and inclusive societies" needs further analysis. In addition to research, explicit mission statements and plans by universities, and cooperation between northern and southern universities, Milton (2021) also insists that the wide-ranging and interconnected targets of SDG 16 should feature in the curricula of multiple disciplines at university level.

It will be the purpose of this chapter to show how teaching about religion and religions in the academic field of Religious Studies may contribute to this aim. Three examples of critical importance to conflict and violence, as well as peace and development within the African context that I have developed and taught in Religious Studies at the University of South Africa (Unisa), will be discussed to illustrate the argument. In these examples, students are not only taught about the ideals of peacebuilding and development but importantly guided to critically analyse debates on the interplay between religion, on the one hand, and exclusionary collectivities and asymmetrical power relations of gender, class and ethnicity, on the other hand.

As working definition of religion, Emile Durkheim's sociological definition is adapted, according to which "religion" refers to beliefs (i.e. myths and doctrines) and practices (i.e. rituals and festivals) relative to the sacred that serve to unite adherents, with the "sacred" understood as anything "set apart" from the ordinary (Durkheim, 1915, p. 47). This functional definition is then adapted by foregrounding systemic power relations of inclusion and exclusion, and conflict concerning gender, class and ethnicity—an approach that follows on Chidester's plea for a "critical phenomenology" rather than a traditional phenomenology of religion that tended to overlook such power relations (Chidester, 1994).

Conceptualizing the singular "religion" in the above sense as a generic term and the plural "religions" as referring to species or examples of the genus (Chidester, 1987, p. 3), African indigenous religions are considered a species of the genus. Considering African indigenous religions not as pure and fixed but as subject to historical change within new contexts, the critical issues from African indigenous religions in this chapter concern gender and ethnic relations as taught in Religious Studies at Unisa during the past decade.

The first problem requires students to weigh arguments of cultural relativists and human rights activists on rituals of female circumcision/female genital mutilation. Students compare the argument of Martha Nussbaum on capabilities with the argument of a selection of anthropologists who support the relativist view so that students may formulate their own position.

The second problem deals with witchcraft accusations, mostly of marginalized elderly women, and human rights interventions as part of development programmes. The focus here is the development project led by Gerrie ter Haar with a number of anthropologists and intellectuals from the Netherlands and South Africa. Students are again to consider this analysis of a problem and the proposed solutions in order to argue their own stance.

Lastly, students need to engage with the problem of exclusionary collectivities by reading Peter Geschiere's nuanced historical and critical analysis of the changing role of funerary rituals in postcolonial Cameroon, and considering his comparison of the problem of exclusionary nationalist and ethnic groups in the Netherlands and France, the Ivory Coast and Botswana, and xenophobic outbursts in South Africa (Geschiere, 2009). Students need to reflect on and argue a position on the extent to which inclusive cultural, ethnic and national collectivities in human rights discourses and policies might assist in addressing this problem of hierarchies and exclusions.

At issue is a rethinking of interventions in university curricula to promote peace through justice, inclusive institutions and societies, and human development in contexts of conflict—issues that are illustrated by means of examples from the teaching of Religious Studies at a university in South Africa that may contribute to the United Nations' Sustainable Development Goal 16 and its targets.

## Three Problems

### *The First Problem: Female Genital Mutilation/Female Circumcision*

The first target of SDG 16 (2015) is to "significantly reduce all forms of violence ... everywhere" and takes as an indicator the "proportion of population subjected to ... physical violence ... in the previous 12 months," whereas the second target aims specifically to "end … all forms of violence against children." Under the interconnected SDG 5 (2015) that aims to "achieve gender equality and empower all women and girls," female genital mutilation as a form of violence is listed for particular attention: "At least 200 million girls and women today have been subjected to female genital mutilation, mainly in 31 countries." It takes as indicator the "proportion of girls and women aged 15–49 years who have undergone female genital mutilation/cutting, by age," and envisages the "promotion of laws, policies, budgets and institutions that advance gender equality" as "not only a fundamental human right, but a necessary foundation for a peaceful, prosperous and sustainable world."

Universities as important institutions can, as indicated above, make a contribution to these interconnected SDGs by analysing forms of systemic violence against women, such as female genital mutilation, and considering solutions to promote the well-being of women as a matter of social development. A study unit taught in Religious Studies at Unisa may serve as example (Strijdom, 2021).

Students are required to compare and weigh arguments of cultural relativists and human rights activists on rituals of female circumcision/female genital mutilation. The selected readings include publications by feminist philosopher and development theorist Martha Nussbaum on capabilities (developed with Amartya Sen as part of a UN project on measuring the quality of life of nations) and by cultural anthropologists who support the relativist view and an African indigenous scholar (Magesa, 1997; Nussbaum, 1999; Nussbaum & Sen, 1993; Salmon, 1997; Skinner, 1988; Welsch & Endicoff, 2003).

As point of departure students need to distinguish between and describe different types of female circumcision as a rite of passage and understand the difference in terminology between "female circumcision" (preferred by cultural anthropologists and indigenous authors) and "female genital mutilation" (preferred by human rights activists). They are introduced to Nussbaum's argument that there are basic human rights that all women in the world should enjoy that would make it possible for them to live a fulfilled life, that there are clear cases where religions have violated such rights, as well as her proposal to address this dilemma.

In answer to cultural relativists who maintain that human rights are a western imposition, Nussbaum (1999) holds that it is possible to make a rational argument for and list capabilities (more specific than a vague notion of human rights) that should be available to all women and make it possible for them to live a life worthy of a human being. She, furthermore, insists that cultures are diverse and that a nuanced, historical study of any culture would uncover voices that are in line with universal human rights—voices that need to be highlighted in the interest of women within their local contexts.

One issue that she addresses specifically is female genital mutilation as a violation of a woman's basic right to bodily integrity. Her proposal is that this be addressed by means of liberal national constitutions, as well as the education of liberal citizens. Where religions are involved in the practice, gentle pressure from democratic state constitutions and public education institutions can serve as agents to persuade such religions to change their practices for the betterment of the lives of women.

Moving from arguments by a philosopher to those of cultural anthropologists, students need to engage with the contrasting views of two anthropologists on female circumcision (Salmon, 1997; Skinner, 1988; Welsch & Endicoff, 2003). They are then in a position to assess Laurenti Magesa's presentation of female circumcision as the most intense part of initiation rituals in some African indigenous religions, during which initiates learn about their roles in society, particularly their sexual duty to get married and have children, thus confirming African indigenous religions' communal ethics of "vital force." The "purpose behind inflicting pain" during circumcision, Magesa holds, is *inter alia* to "[celebrate] courage" and to unite the group of boys or girls as an "age-group": "By mingling and sharing their blood by way of the initiation knife, or because they shed it at the same time, they become true brothers or sisters and must be ready to defend one another. ... the initiation operation leaves an indelible mark on the part of the body not easily ignored that reminds a young person of his or her place, responsibility and rights in society" (Magesa, 1997, pp. 92–101).

To broaden the perspective of students, they finally listen to the Ghanaian-American philosopher Kwame Anthony Appiah's interview with the Egyptian doctor and feminist activist Nawal El-Saadawi (2009) on female genital mutilation and Islam within her context.

Having been introduced to these voices and perspectives in the debate, students are expected to formulate their own argued position in an essay. They have been guided in this way to move from a phenomenological description of types of female circumcision/female genital mutilation to critical assessments defending and opposing the ritual practice, and finally to taking an informed and argued stance of their own. In my view this intervention cultivates thinking citizens, who become sensitive to a debate at the heart of development goals as formulated in SDG 16 and the related SDG 5.

### *The Second Problem: Witchcraft Accusations*

If the first target of SDG 16 (2015) has as its general aim to "significantly reduce all forms of violence ... everywhere," a subsequent resolution in recalling SDGs 16 and 5 condemns specifically witchcraft accusations and ritual attacks that violate the human rights of primarily women, children and people with albinism in parts of Africa, and urges States to do everything possible to eliminate violent attacks resulting from witchcraft accusations and protect such victims in vulnerable situations (Human Rights Council, 2021).

A study unit on witchcraft accusations and human rights taught in Religious Studies at Unisa may illustrate the contribution that a higher education institution can make through its curriculum towards this development goal (Strijdom, 2019b). The focus here is the development project led by Gerrie ter Haar

(2007) with a number of anthropologists and intellectuals from the Netherlands and South Africa.

Students begin with a working definition of the term "witchcraft" as referring to the belief that some people are inherently evil and are able to do harm to other people. Once identified as the cause of evil in a group, action is to be taken against such a person which can be quite violent. Although belief in witchcraft does not necessarily lead to witch hunts, the link between beliefs and deeds should not be understated.

In using this working definition to analyse contemporary manifestations of the problem, the problematic history of the term is emphasized to better understand the current problem. Nineteenth-century European evolutionary theorists, colonists and missionaries not only generally considered African indigenous religions at the bottom and Christianity at the top of the scale but also demonized the whole of "primitive religion" by superimposing their own recent experience of witchcraft onto the whole of African indigenous religions. The traditionally "neutral" African spirit realm, that could do either good or cause harm, was transformed in the process into an evil realm. To acknowledge this history is important, since it clarifies that the working definition used here does not condemn African indigenous religion *in toto*, but only practices in it that are harmful to people.

Considering a proper methodology to interpret the phenomenon, students begin with a careful description of the phenomenon and a limited comparison of cases, before they study assessments of it and argue their own views. Taking seriously the thesis that by means of a nuanced comparison of contextualized cases, the cases may shed light on each other and help us understand the phenomenon itself in a new light (Smith, 2004, pp. 29-30, 197-198), students compare, with the help of Ellis (2007), witchcraft in early modern Europe and contemporary Africa. In the case of Europe it is, according to Ellis (2007), clear that it was not the discontinuation of the belief in witchcraft during the Enlightenment that stopped the persecution of witches but rather the fact that the modern state stopped prosecuting witches in civil courts. In the case of Africa, however, it was mistakenly assumed that colonial legislation to suppress witchcraft would end witchcraft practices. The accusation and violent victimization of mostly older women, and recently children in certain parts of Africa, therefore call for urgent intervention.

In the project led by Ter Haar (2007) the phenomenon of witchcraft accusations in Africa is not only described from an emic perspective, explained within its African context from an etic perspective, and compared with the phenomenon in early modern Europe, but also addressed as an ethical matter that requires researchers to propose interventions. Taking the United Nations' Declaration of Human Rights as norm, the victimization and killing of alleged witches is seen as a violation of the most basic right to life. The problem in the view of Ter Haar and her group is that although international agreements and national constitutions may protect the right to life, the ideal has often not been implemented in the case of witchcraft accusations in many African countries.

Not denying the importance of such policy and legal interventions, they argue that education which critically engages with African traditions from a human rights and development perspective is crucial, as well as NGOs and religious organizations that act in the interest of the victims of witchcraft accusations. It is, however, important to caution against Pentecostal churches that may "strengthen fear of witchcraft rather than [help] to reduce them" (Ter Haar, 2007, p. 26).

As a final exercise, students are expected to write a critical response to Magesa's presentation of witchcraft in Africa. According to Magesa (1997) African religion is in essence moral in that it promotes communal life through its sacred stories and rituals, and that witchcraft is its main enemy. Witches, often women who are unsociable and non-conformist, are seen as a major cause of evil in the world (notably illness, death and misery). They are to be identified by diviners, and action needs to be taken against them to restore communal harmony and solidarity. Magesa (1997, 171–172) states: "Witchcraft is intolerable for any society that values ethical principles and life itself … we can clearly see the role of witchcraft as sanction against immoral behaviour." The consequences for someone convicted of witchcraft, Magesa (1997, 172) continues, "are invariably grave. The Lamba of Zambia spear a witch to death. The Akamba of Kenya execute proven witches by arrows. Some African communities kill witches by beating or strangling them to death, or by burning them alive. Another form of punishment is banishment from the community, which, in the African conception of human life, is the equivalent of death."

Having been introduced to a working definition of the term "witchcraft" with its problematic history, a description, nuanced comparison and contextualized interpretation of the phenomenon, as well as assessments of it from indigenous and human rights perspectives, students are in a position to argue their own stance. By means of this intervention students become sensitive to a debate closely related to SDG 16 (2015) and the subsequent, recent resolution on witchcraft accusations of the United Nations' Human Rights Council (2021).

### *The Third Problem: Exclusionary Collectivities*

Building inclusive societies and institutions for peace and sustainable development is a key objective of SDG 16 (2015): "Goal 16 is about promoting peaceful and inclusive societies, providing access to justice for all and building effective, accountable and inclusive institutions at all levels." An accompanying document, "Peace, Justice, and Strong Institutions: Why they Matter" (2020), explains further that "people everywhere need to be free of fear from all forms of violence and feel safe as they go about their lives whatever their ethnicity, faith or sexual orientation," and proposes that "governments, civil society and communities must work together to implement lasting solutions to reduce violence, deliver justice, combat corruption and ensure inclusive participation at all times." The inclusion of people of different ethnic origins in decision-making processes "to improve the conditions for a life of dignity for all" is an important aspect of SDG 16 (2015) that needs further attention.

A study unit in which students in Religious Studies at Unisa need to analyse problems caused by the construction of rigid, exclusionary group boundaries may serve as a final example of a curricular intervention of importance to SDG 16 (Strijdom, 2019a). As case study, students are required to engage with the problem of exclusionary collectivities by reading the cultural anthropologist Peter Geschiere's nuanced historical and critical analysis of the changing role of funerary rituals in postcolonial Cameroon, and considering his comparison of the problem of exclusionary ethnic and nationalist collectivities within the Netherlands and France, the Ivory Coast and Botswana, and xenophobic outbursts in South Africa (Geschiere, 2009). Students need to reflect on and argue a position on the extent to which inclusive cultural, ethnic and national collectivities in human rights discourses and policies might assist in addressing this problem of hierarchies and exclusions.

To analyse the dangers of exclusionary collectivities, Geschiere (2009) uses "autochthony" as key term. Derived from Greek *autos* ("self") and *chthon* ("earth") and applied in the classical Athenian debate between those who claimed to be authentic "children of the soil" (e.g. Plato) and historians (notably Thucydides), the term *autochthon* may be understood as a synonym for "indigenous." The opposite term, *allochthons* (from Greek *allos* "other" and *chthon* "earth"), refers to those who originated from elsewhere, that is they are those who are labelled by indigenists as "strangers" who do not belong to the territory of the *autochthons*.

Geschiere's argument is that autochthonous discourses and policies tend to be exclusionary and harmful to society, which can be seen in the changing role and use of funerary rituals in postcolonial Cameroon. Although an analysis that focuses on historical change may challenge essentialisms, the persistence of exclusionary indigenist claims and their powerful hold on people's emotions and political consequences need to be critically analysed.

It is instructive to compare Geschiere's distinction between autochthonous and historical approaches with David Chidester's map of approaches in postcolonial studies of religion (Chidester, 2000, pp. 432–436). On the one hand are those who emphasize "indigeneity," claiming that indigenous religions have essentially remained the same "since time immemorial." On the other side of the spectrum are those scholars who focus on diversity, mixture and change of cultural and religious traditions. Although Chidester himself follows the latter approach, he is sympathetic to the strategic use of essentializing, indigenist discourses for the sake of the recovery of traditions that were suppressed and humiliated under colonialism and its aftermath, and does not problematize essentialist discourses and practices to the extent that Geschiere does.

In analysing the changing role and use of funerary rituals in postcolonial Cameroon, Geschiere (2009) contextualizes the phenomenon within its changing political context. He argues that these rituals changed in form and function in post-independence Cameroon. Under Ahmadou Ahidjo (from the

Muslim North of the country) independent Cameroon quickly turned into a dictatorship that enforced nationalist rituals to unify the nation and suppressed local ethnic rituals that would divide the nation. When Ahidjo unexpectedly stepped down in 1982, he chose Paul Biya (from the Christian South and belonging to the ethnic Béti group) as his successor.

Biya continued Ahidjo's dictatorial policy against ethnic dissidents and their rituals until 1990, when due to international political and economic pressure (particularly from development organizations like the World Bank and the International Monetary Fund) he was forced to introduce multiparty elections. It was during this period after 1990 that Biya started to use funerary rituals, emotionally more intense than rigid nationalist ones, in an exclusionary way to divide opposition parties along ethnic lines (traditional funerary rituals, equally intense, used to be more inclusive, mediating fluid boundaries between insiders and outsiders, according to Geschiere). Proving to which village one's ancestors belonged on the basis of the location of their graves now became the qualifying factor in determining one's ethnic belonging.

Although the main political parties had their regional and associated ethnic strongholds, there were internal ethnic divisions within each area that Biya exploited with his autochthonous discourses and policies in order to stay in power. Biya's support was in the Centre, South and East Provinces, with the Béti ethnic group as the majority. The supporters of the opposition led by John Fri Ndi were in the anglophone North-West and South-West Provinces as well as francophone West Province, with the Bamileke as its major ethnic group. The main party in the northern provinces belonged primarily to the Fulbe group and were Muslims who had converted to Islam in the nineteenth century. In order to divide the North, Biya supported the Kirdi, who had not converted to Islam and who sought liberation from the Fulbe. In Ndi's western stronghold, Biya exploited not only tensions between anglophones and francophones but also amongst francophones themselves by siding with coastal minorities of Bakwera and Doula who complained about being swamped by northern highlanders migrating to the coast for job opportunities. It is within this context that Biya used funerals from one's village of origin as ultimate test of belonging with tragic consequences of xenophobic violence.

To enable students to better understand the potential of autochthonous discourses to exclude and enhance intolerance to the point of violence, they are expected to consider Geschiere's instructive comparison of the problem within the context of other African states (Ivory Coast, Botswana, South Africa) and Europe (Netherlands and France).

Having been guided to define, describe and critically analyse the problem of exclusionary ethnic collectivities that are created and maintained by essentialist political discourses and enacted in ritual practices, students are in a position to argue their own stance. A consideration of human rights and development arguments and interventions, formulated in SDG 16 and related inclusive initiatives, needs to necessarily feature in students' analyses and assessments.

In general, students have taken up the challenge and have intensely engaged with these controversial issues. The success is in my view due to the essay format in which students must weigh arguments on both sides in order to develop their own views. This dialogical or dialectical pedagogical method has been followed with some success in Religious Studies courses at Unisa, not only in the above case studies that I have selected from African indigenous religions but also in case studies that I have taken from Christianity and Islam in Africa, where there is a conflict between human rights and religious practices, and where there are exclusions and hierarchies of race (e.g. Afrikaner nationalist religion in apartheid South Africa), economic class (e.g. Pentecostal-charismatic prosperity movements) or gender (e.g. LGBTQI+ victimizations and responses in African Christianity and Islam). The cumulative effect of these case studies is to create amongst students a deep awareness that Religious Studies as an academic field does not simply aim to identify and describe controversial issues but also by cultivating critical citizens aims to contribute to constructive changes in society. Since critique presupposes an individual and systemic ethical framework, students need to give content to such a normative framework in debate with scholars from southern Africa, such as Prozesky (2007) and Chitando (e.g. Van Klinken & Chitando, 2021; Chitando et al., 2022), and global discourses and initiatives of human rights, capabilities and Sustainable Development Goals.

## Conclusion

The central tenet of this chapter has been that teaching about peace, justice and inclusive collectivities at universities constitutes an important intervention to engage with SDG 16 and related development initiatives. Three examples from the curriculum in Religious Studies at the University of South Africa were discussed to illustrate the argument. The examples deal specifically with entanglements of religion with violence against women and children in rituals of female genital mutilation/female circumcision, witchcraft accusations and exclusionary communities—issues that feature in the indicators and targets of SDG 16, its related SDG 5 and subsequent UN discussions and resolutions.

Following from this discussion, I would like to make *three recommendations* that need attention in teaching about these development goals.

First, students should not only be taught about the ideals of justice, peace and inclusive communities but also be guided to analyse the opposite realities of violence, injustice, and exclusionary collectivities as contexts that call for development interventions.

Secondly, students need to think about the relationship between universal and local values. This means that they need to engage with ways in which these fundamental concepts have been theorized, thought about and practised by universalists, critical theorists, cultural relativists and indigenous participants.

Thirdly, and related to the above, students need to engage with a diversity of current and historical voices and perspectives, which will enable them to compare views in a nuanced way and argue their own point of view. This will require from them not to be content with a phenomenological description of the issues at hand but importantly to get a clear comparative understanding of exclusionary and hierarchical power relations of gender, ethnicity and class at work, and finally to argue a stance of their own on theoretical and practical interventions regarding fundamental issues that impact on people's quality of life.

## REFERENCES

Chidester, D. (1987). *Patterns of Action: Religion and Ethics in a Comparative Perspective.* Wadsworth.

Chidester, D. (1994). The Poetics and Politics of Sacred Space: Towards a Critical Phenomenology of Religion. In A. T. Tymieniecka (Ed.), *From the Sacred to the Divine: A New Phenomenological Approach* (Analecta Husserliana: The Yearbook of Phenomenological Research) (Vol. XLIII, pp. 211–231). Kluwer.

Chidester, D. (2000). Colonialism. In W. Braun & R. McCutcheon (Eds.), *Guide to the Study of Religion* (pp. 423–437). Cassell.

Chitando, E., et al. (2022). *Women and Religion in Zimbabwe: Strides and Struggles.* Rowman & Littlefield.

Durkheim, E. (1915). *The Elementary Forms of the Religious Life* (J. W. Swain, Trans.). Allen & Unwin. https://www.gutenberg.org/files/41360/41360-h/41360-h.htm

Ellis, S. (2007). Witching Times: A Theme in the Histories of Africa and Europe. In G. ter Haar (Ed.), *Imagining Evil: Witchcraft Beliefs and Accusations in Contemporary Africa.* Africa World Press.

El-Saadawi, N., & Appiah, K. A. (2009). *Arthur Miller Freedom to Write Lecture.* PEN World Voices. https://www.youtube.com/watch?v=jue04c1_wkY

Geschiere, P. (2009). *The Perils of Belonging: Autochthony, Citizenship, and Exclusion in Africa and Europe.* University of Chicago Press.

Human Rights Council. (2021). Resolution Adopted by the Human Rights Council on 12 July 2021: 47/8. Elimination of Harmful Practices Related to Witchcraft and Ritual Attacks. United Nations. https://ap.ohchr.org/documents/dpage_e.aspx?si=A/HRC/47/L.9

Magesa, L. (1997). *African Religion: The Moral Traditions of Abundant Life.* Orbis Books.

Milton, S. (2021). Higher Education and Sustainable Development Goal 16 in Fragile and Conflict-Affected Contexts. *Higher Education, 81*, 89–108. https://doi.org/10.1007/s10734-020-00617-z

Nussbaum, M. (1999). Religion and Women's Human Rights. In M. Nussbaum (Ed.), *Sex and Social Justice.* Oxford University Press.

Nussbaum, M., & Sen, A. (Eds.). (1993). *The Quality of Life* (UNU-WIDER Studies in Development Economics). Oxford University Press.

Peace, Justice, and Strong Institutions: Why They Matter. (2020). United Nations. https://www.un.org/sustainabledevelopment/wp-content/uploads/2019/07/16_Why-It-Matters-2020.pdf

Prozesky, M. (2007). *Conscience: Ethical Intelligence for Global Well-Being.* University of KwaZulu-Natal Press.

Salmon, M. (1997). Ethical Considerations in Anthropology and Archaeology, or Relativism and Justice for All? *Journal of Anthropological Research*, 53(1), 47–63.

Skinner, E. (1988). Female Circumcision in Africa: The Dialectics of Equality. In R. Randolph, D. Schneider, & M. Diaz (Eds.), *Dialectics and Gender: Anthropological Approaches* (pp. 194–210). Routledge.

Smith, J. Z. (2004). *Relating Religion: Essays in the Study of Religion*. University of Chicago Press.

Strijdom, J. (2019a). The Political Use of Funerary Rituals: Struggles Over Belonging in Postcolonial Cameroon. In J. Strijdom (Ed.), *Problematising Africa's Religious Heritage and World Religions: Study Guide for RST3711*. University of South Africa.

Strijdom, J. (2019b). Witchcraft Accusations and Human Rights. In J. Strijdom (Ed.), *Problematising Africa's Religious Heritage and World Religions: Study Guide for RST3711*. University of South Africa.

Strijdom, J. (2021). Universal and Relative Values: The Case of Female Circumcision of Female Genital Mutilation. In J. Strijdom (Ed.), *Analysing the Social Functions of Religion: Study Guide for RST3709*. University of South Africa.

Sustainable Development Goal 16: Peace, Justice and Strong Institutions. (2015). United Nations. https://www.un.org/ruleoflaw/sdg-16/

Sustainable Development Goal 5: Achieve Gender Equality and Empower All Women and Girls. (2015). United Nations. https://sdgs.un.org/goals/goal5 and https://www.un.org/sustainabledevelopment/gender-equality/

Ter Haar, G. (2007). The Evil Called Witchcraft. In G. Ter Haar (Ed.), *Imagining Evil: Witchcraft Beliefs and Accusations in Contemporary Africa*. Africa World Press.

Ter Haar, G. (Ed.). (2011). *Religion and Development: Ways of Transforming the World*. Hurst & Company.

United Nations General Assembly's Development Agenda. (2015). *Transforming Our World: The 2030 Agenda for Sustainable Development*. https://sdgs.un.org/2030agenda

van Klinken, A., & Chitando, E. (2021). *Reimagining Christianity and Sexual Diversity in Africa*. Hurst & Company.

Welsch, R., & Endicoff, K. (2003). Issue 16: Should Anthropologists Work to Eliminate the Practice of Female Genital Mutilation? In R. Welsch & K. Endicoff (Eds.), *Taking Sides: Clashing Views on Controversial Issues in Cultural Anthropology*. McGraw-Hill.

Wolfensohn, J. (2011). Foreword. In G. Ter Haar (Ed.), *Religion and Development. Ways of Transforming the World* (pp. xvii–xviii). Hurst & Company.

CHAPTER 7

# Intersectionalities: Whiteness, Religion, Peacebuilding and Development in Africa

*Masiiwa Ragies Gunda*

## INTRODUCTION

That Africa is reeling under a seemingly unending wave of conflicts is a fact. A cursory survey of Africa shows conflict in South Sudan, Ethiopia, Nigeria, Cameroon, Mali, Democratic Republic of Congo, Chad, Central African Republic, Somalia, Zimbabwe, and Mozambique. All these conflicts are different but also related in some ways, not always obvious. Even in many other countries that are not named here, there are also conflicts brewing or cooking. Why is conflict finding a comfortable home in Africa? Alternatively, why does Africa find peace in conflict? Battling these conflicts means Africa is far from being on track to realise Sustainable Development Goal (SDG) 16 by 2030. This chapter hypothesises that African conflicts are legacies of the colonial era where seeds were sown, seeds of intolerance, supremacism and violence that continue to germinate in post-colonial African countries and communities. In sowing of these seeds, not only political colonisers but also religious missionaries actively planted these seeds, thereby giving rise to the second hypothesis of this chapter, that is even secular looking conflicts when unpacked fully may betray a religious connection. This is particularly important because at a time when some western scholars were predicting the end and removal of religion "from the sphere of politics, economic development, warfare, and education" (Little & Appleby, 2004, p. 1), the opposite actually happened and religion continues

M. R. Gunda (✉)
World Council of Churches & Ecumenical Institute of Bossey, Geneva, Switzerland

to be alive and even more entrenched in the areas where it was expected to vanish from.

When it comes to conflict and peacebuilding, religion is paradoxical, promoting both, sometimes simultaneously. According to Scott Appleby, a leading voice in research on religion and peacemaking, "religion is a source not only of intolerance, human rights violations, and extremist violence, but also of non-violent conflict transformation, the defence of human rights, integrity in government, and reconciliation and stability in divided societies" (Appleby, 1996, p. 821). That religion is needed in transformation of conflicts in Africa, peacebuilding efforts and sustaining peaceful conflict resolutions across Africa is a given. This chapter will focus on the intersectionalities of whiteness, Christianity and colonisation of Africa, the Sustainable Development Goal number 16 and its threats in Africa.

While there are various approaches to the impact and intent of Christian missions in Africa, this chapter deliberately focuses on the contributions of Christian missions in the imposition of white supremacist ideology and the culture of whiteness that solidified fluid identities in Africa into supposed qualitative and defining traits for separation of the people of God.

## Agenda 2030: Realising SDG 16

The persistence of conflict across the African continent is not only a threat to the lives and livelihoods of persons that are trapped in these conflict zones, but conflict is a threat to the general wellbeing of all people in Africa; it increases the vulnerability of Africans to expanding conflict zones, poverty and general insecurity. Conflict is forcing Africans to flee their countries in search of stable and safe spaces, which increases their vulnerability to human trafficking, modern slavery, xenophobic violence, racial discrimination and death related to unsafe means of transportation. It must be noted that conflict is not limited to Africa, but it is being experienced across the whole world. The United Nations made the promotion of peace and inclusive societies one of its goals in its Sustainable Development Goals in the Agenda 2030 because of the global nature of conflict. In the preamble of Resolution A/RES/70/1, the United Nations states that it "seeks to strengthen universal peace" (United Nations, 2015, p. 1). They went on to pronounce:

> We are determined to foster peaceful, just and inclusive societies which are free from fear and violence. There can be no sustainable development without peace and no peace without sustainable development.

In these words, the United Nations highlights the intersectionalities that exist between peace, justice and sustainable development. Therefore, conflicts stand for everything that undermines these aspirations. According to the resolution, this is only possible if all forms of violence and avoidable deaths are reduced or brought to an end. In general, SDG 16 seeks to end all conflicts as a prerequisite to driving societies, the world over, towards sustainable development. Conflicts are by nature draining: draining of resources both human and material, draining of tolerance and solidarity among human beings, draining of the worth and value of human life, which is seen as expendable in conflict situations (United Nations, 2015, pp. 25–26). In this regard, Sustainable Development Goal 16 is described as a quest to

> Promote peaceful and inclusive societies for sustainable development, provide access to justice for all and build effective, accountable and inclusive institutions at all levels. (United Nations, 2015, p. 25)

In target 16.4 of the SDG 16, the United Nations commit to "significantly reduce illicit financial and arms flows, strengthen the recovery and return of stolen assets and combat all forms of organized crime," while in 16.5 it commits to "substantially reduce corruption and bribery in all their forms" (United Nations, 2015, pp. 25–26). Implied in this SDG is the need for peacebuilding, peacemaking and conflict resolution because without such efforts, conflict will derail the Agenda 2030. The urgent need for peacebuilding cannot be overstated because at the time of writing, eight years before the lapse of Agenda 2030, Africa is far away from being on track to achieve these goals. It is no longer time to experiment with sidelining religion from these efforts, hence the need for inclusion, in a substantive and intentional way, of faith leaders in order to make use of their religious and social capital in resolving conflicts. Other than this, it is critical that the invisible hands fanning conflicts in Africa be exposed.

In a previous contribution on religion and development in Africa, I have suggested that "common among all these dimensions of development is the desire to eliminate poverty and the marginalizations that come with being poor, meaning development begins and ends with the situation of the human being" (Gunda, 2020, p. 50). Development is by nature not outside the aspirations of religious communities, making the SDG 16 and its targets legitimate goals for faith communities.

## Religious Views and Beliefs Matter, Especially in Africa!

The idea that conflicts among people that are "notoriously religious" (Mbiti, 1969, p. 1), whether the conflict itself is religious, ethnic, economic or political, can be sustainably resolved by sidelining religion is illogical. Evidence-based researches affirm that "Africans are generally much more religious than the Europeans, perhaps even than Americans—both in the sense of believing in 'an invisible world' and of actually practicing religion" (Møller, 2006, p. 10). This dominance of religion and religious practice in all conflict hotspots across Africa suggests that religious interventions in peacemaking and peacebuilding are not only a possibility but also a necessity. While these views apply to all the religions found in Africa, Christianity is in focus in this chapter. While the interventions of outsiders have always been extolled yet "[i]n recent years, a growing chorus of activists and organisations have been pushing for the 'localisation' of development, humanitarian aid and peacebuilding efforts" (Fellow & Paige, 2020, p. 8). If peacebuilding is to be localised effectively, it entails making use of local resources and religion is one such resource.

The religious landscape of Africa is fundamentally different from the European context; hence, peacebuilding in Africa needs to acknowledge the role of religion in Africa.

> In contemporary Western societies there is a tendency to disregard religious beliefs, which are seen as mere opinions, or even as superstitions—in contrast to empirically based knowledge—which is regarded as factual. Such a distinction veils the fact that both positions appear as 'true' and 'factual' to the individual who holds them. Disregarding the intensity and sincerity of religious beliefs—to the believers—has often proven counterproductive to conflict resolution. Relatedly, there is also a tendency to see strong religious convictions primarily as a negative force that feeds conflicts, undermines political and economic development, and prevents rational dialogue and conflict resolution. (Harpviken & Røislien, 2005, p. 7)

Since strong religious beliefs are held across Africa and are not negotiable, a peacebuilding approach that seeks to undermine or disrespect such religiosity will radicalise the religious views and risk inflaming conflict instead of making peace. It is important to grasp the different ways in which religion affects communities, especially the social dimensions of religion are important when searching for instruments for peacebuilding because religions provide a personal-communal identity and self-understanding that affects social relationships. Since most religions have teachings that are considered normative by believers, it is important to construct alternative and peacebuilding counter-narratives in conflict situations that build on existing normativity that is likely going to be accepted by believers (Harpviken & Røislien, 2005, p. 8).

Faith leaders possess religious and social capital that takes them into all areas of wider society including in conflict zones. Such leaders do not operate as islands unto themselves but rather through well-established, formal and non-formal organisations that have access to all including non-members. Such religious organisations can also provide strong platforms from which peacebuilding efforts are driven and sustained by not only the leadership but also the grassroots. Central to the involvement of faith communities is the acceptance that religious views and beliefs matter in peacebuilding because religions have strong injunctions on the sanctity of life and healthy relationships among all people of God. There is a strong affirmation of the dignity and Image of God in all human beings in Christianity (Genesis 1: 26–27) and that can become a strong launch pad for Christian peacebuilding efforts. Abu-Nimer (2001, p. 2) argues that religion can "bring social, moral and spiritual resources to the peacebuilding process."

While western and western-influenced educators, researchers, and policy makers have tended to focus on the negative effects and influences of religion in conflict situations, this chapter proposes a cautious resistance to blanket dismissal of religions in peacebuilding efforts. Besides the toxicity of religions, there are "multiple dimensions of religion in its publicness," including "the genius of religiously inspired social welfare and peacemaking activism," thereby giving rise to "the ambivalence of the sacred" which provides the entry point to counter-narratives for peacebuilding. Religion promotes "tolerance of the strongest type—the willingness to live with, explore, and honour difference" (Little & Appleby, 2004, p. 2). These elements of religious views, beliefs, practices and norms are critical for peacebuilding, especially in Africa where the majority of people involved in conflicts are religious.

Religious views and beliefs, especially as they relate to the understanding of humanity, human relations, and the relationship between God and humanity, are critical in peacebuilding. Where religious views are cited as promoting conflict, alternative religious views will offer a firm counter-narrative that could undermine the religious basis for conflict. Religious resources such as sacred writings can play a central role not only in challenging toxic narratives but in constructing transformative and peaceful counter-narratives. According to Kwamboka (2014, p. 21),

> The basis of Christian peacebuilding is informed by the Bible's teachings on peace and peacemakers; "blessed are the peacemakers, they shall be called children of God" (Matt. 5:9 NIV). The Bible also teaches of love: "love your neighbour as yourself" (Matt. 22:37–39 NIV) and non-violence; Jesus, the founder of the faith asserts that the proof of discipleship lies in the ability to "love one's enemies". (Luke 6:27)

The realisation of SDG 16 in Africa and the world over demands the inclusion of religious peacebuilding in the multi-pronged approaches to peacemaking that will result in just and inclusive peaceful societies that will enhance the opportunities to thrive for all human beings.

## Conflict in Africa: Some Findings from Existing Literature

Understanding conflicts in Africa requires a journey into the past because most of the conflicts are legacies from the past. According to Amnesty International (2021),

> [t]he COVID-19 pandemic has exposed the terrible legacy of deliberately divisive and destructive policies that have perpetuated inequality, discrimination, and oppression across Sub-Saharan Africa …

This is a particularly important observation for this chapter, and the legacies of colonisation and evangelisation of Africa will be interrogated. In fact, "[a] growing number of groups are increasingly discriminating others because of differences of origin, race, ethnicity, gender and physical ability" (UNESCO, African Union and Angola, 2021, p. 1).

That there is a possible connection between contemporary manifestations of conflicts in Africa and the colonial past, raises another dimension that needs to be interrogated, especially in sub-Saharan Africa, that is the role of Christianity. "Christianity did indeed come to the continent as a companion of the successive waves of colonisation" (Møller, 2006, p. 25), thereby suggesting there might be some evangelisation legacy to conflicts in Africa. While acknowledging the companionship between evangelisation and colonisation, it must be acknowledged that the earliest attempts at evangelisation in Africa preceded the colonisation waves referred to above. Attempts were made in East, West, Central and Southern Africa around the fifteenth century (Fatokun, 2005). However, these early, pre-colonial attempts largely failed. This chapter will take a particular interest in unpacking the Christian contributions to the sowing of seeds that are germinating as conflicts today.

There has been suspicion and negative assessment of the contributions of religions to peacebuilding efforts. Scholars and activists have largely "viewed religion either as being an instigator of conflict or dismissed it altogether, because religious issues involved in conflict cannot be addressed from an empirical or positivist perspective" (Githigaro, 2012, pp. 96–97). The fact that some religious leaders have been quoted as supporting and promoting conflict has been used as if it were exhaustive of the ways in which religion contributes to conflict, that is instigating or resolving conflict; hence, the World Council of Churches proclaimed:

> However, the task of building peace in a violent world has often failed to be seen as an important step in the pursuit of Christian unity. Churches have always stood divided and continue to do so on issues of war and peace, exposing the complexity of considerations that churches have to make in such situations. This is exacerbated by different ways in which churches are associated with 'the state' or 'political powers' which varied from overt support to total indifference as well as critical engagement. Relationships based on such attitudes continue to determine the role of the churches in witnessing to peace in situations of war and violence. (WCC Faith and Order Team, 2001, p. 1)

Christian-generated ideas have enjoyed wide circulation in Africa because they were considered normative not only by believers in churches but by believers in other professional spheres, including in media. Wide circulating media such as printed newspapers, television and radio embraced Christian ideas and helped disseminate them, sometimes in a negative way. While considering the role of media in conflicts in Africa, Nyamnjoh (2010, p. 62) writes,

In 2005 I published *Africa's Media: Democracy and the Politics of Belonging*. One of the main findings of that study was that the media have assumed a partisan, highly politicised, militant role in Africa. They have done so by dividing citizens into the righteous and the wicked, depending on their political party, ideological, regional, cultural or ethnic belonging.

The media has also built on Christian foundations that divide people into a duality of righteous and wicked, light and darkness, white and black, and so on. This duality, also present in Islam using somewhat different terminologies, is consistently present in all conflicts, with accusations flying between the feuding parties.

An element about contemporary conflicts in Africa that is receiving little to no attention at all from scholars is the role that colonial and missionary racist ideology of white supremacism and the attendant culture of whiteness plays, which may also explain the difficulties encountered in conflict resolution and peacebuilding efforts. Abu-Nimer (2001, p. 2) posits that since the end of the Cold War, many scholars have argued that most conflicts are driven from "clashes of communal identity based on race, ethnicity, or religious affiliations." According to Nyamnjoh (2010, p. 58),

> Racism and ethnicity become issues of concern for media when tracing belonging and identity through exclusion becomes obsessive and problematic—forcing upon others exclusion when they expect inclusion, and seeking to justify such exclusion with porous arguments, stereotypes, stigmatisation and scapegoating. Xenophobia (whether racially or ethnically inspired) is indicative of such problematic and obsessive tendencies to define and confine belonging and identity in terms of cultural differences, with little regard to the reality of interconnections and ongoing relationships forged across communities by individuals as navigators and negotiators of various identity margins.

In short, racism, in its post-colonial manifestations, is central to understanding conflicts in Africa, with conflict antagonists claiming for themselves the position of superiority in terms of knowledge, morality and spirituality, thereby justifying the use of any necessary means to dominate, and even exterminate, the other. A white supremacist ideology was super-imposed as an organising principle in colonised communities, where colonisers inflamed existing tribal and ethnic lines into qualitative markers that were used to rank indigenous groups into superior and inferior. Stereotypes were generalised for ethnic groups creating evident different levels of civility and quality among the groups, thereby sowing seeds of mistrust among indigenous groups. The Belgian policy in Rwanda that favoured Tutsis over Hutus has been cited as partly to blame for the Rwandan genocide of 1994. Groups that embraced the culture of whiteness were extolled, while those that resisted whiteness were regarded as backward and uncivilised. These deliberate moves became fault lines that continue to fuel conflicts in Africa (Bethke, 2012).

If race is used to categorise people into different groups, what then is the meaning of racism? In simple terms, racism refers to the belief that the diversities observable among human beings speak to inherent qualitative differences between entire groups of people, in which some groups are considered to be inherently better than others. Racism in this case refers to "the belief that race is the primary determinant of human traits and capacities and that racial differences produce an inherent superiority of a particular race" (Farfan-Vallespin & Bonick, 2016, p. 4). The effect of racism was to create in Europeans the belief that Europeans were superior to all other people in all the parts of the world; this self-belief became the basis of racial discrimination and practice driving not only colonisation but also the enslavement of Africans by Europeans. With Europeans describing themselves as white, racism gave rise to "white supremacist ideology" and "whiteness" as the culture of Europeans that considered everything European to be superior and normal while everything else was considered inferior and backward. Individual differences within groups of people were considered inconsequential because every individual was as good as their assigned "race."

What the conflicts in Africa are doing is play on the categories that were planted via slavery, colonisation and Christianisation of the continent by western slave traders, colonisers and missionaries who were mostly Christians. Everything in Africa was considered black and continues to be understood as such, even in the present. This blackening of everything African was building on aspects of European thinking that can already be observed in ancient Greek thought but was popularised and globally propagated when it became part of Christian thought.

> The words black/blackness and their various cognates and connotations function semantically in the abstract in ways that synonymously signal and invoke a host of negative characteristics and conditions. Every standard English dictionary, for example, defines black as *impure, dirty, ugly, guilty, evil* in juxtaposition to white as *pure, clean, beautiful, innocent, holy*. How did this dichotomy develop? Through what knowledge-making processes did these terms come to be defined in asymmetrical opposition to each other? Asymmetry aptly describes their relationship because the valence of white/whiteness clearly outweighs black/blackness in terms of social value, status, and power. But how did black acquire its negative meaning compared to white? And where and when did these ideas take root? (Chenault, 2022, p. 6)

The last key observation from existing literature is the belief that even as conflicts drain resources and cost lives, there are profits being made by some. Hence, there are attempts to follow the money in research on conflict profits. "Real leverage for peace and human rights will come when the people who benefit from war will pay a price for the damage they cause … the objective is to follow the money and deny those war profiteers the proceeds from their crimes" (eNCA, 2015).

A survey of existing literature raises a few critical areas of focus; this chapter seeks to interrogate further the association of contemporary conflicts in Africa with historic deprivations, discriminations that have been suffered by Africans. Of particular importance are the intersectionalities between white supremacist ideology, whiteness, colonisation, Christianisation and conflicts in Africa. In the next section, we focus on the intersectionalities between the triple or quad Cs and white supremacy, whiteness and violence in Africa.

## Colonisation, Civilisation, Commerce and Christianity: White Supremacy, Whiteness and Violence

As conflicts continue to afflict Africa, it is pertinent that we ask the question: What is the legacy of the past in the present? How is that legacy threatening SDG 16? This chapter is problematising the legacy of racist colonial and Christianisation ideologies in the conflicts that continue to afflict Africa and Africans. This section analyses the legacy of the triple C (Commerce, Christianity and Civilisation) approach used by the colonial settlers and missionaries. The focus is on the legacy and persistence of the white supremacist ideology and the culture of whiteness in contemporary conflicts in Africa. The ideology and culture were central to the success of the colonial and evangelisation projects by European states and churches. Central to the colonisation and evangelisation of Africa was the promotion of

> conceptual metaphors about Blackness on African people that depicted them as the exemplars of evil to teach Christian doctrine about sin and salvation. It connects these original antiblack discourses directly to the theo-political arguments Western European Christians used centuries later to justify African hereditary enslavement, western colonialism, and the ethos and polity of white supremacy. (Chenault, 2022, p. v)

The triple C approach emerged from the ideas and strategies adopted by David Livingstone as he sought to open up the African interior for Europeans. It is possible to expand triple C to a quad C by adding "colonisation" to the list of Cs. Livingstone's legacy remains contested. According to Fidelis Nkomazana (1998, p. 44),

> Livingstone's concept of missionary enterprise differed from most of his older colleagues among London Missionary Society (L.M.S.) missionaries. He saw mission centres not only for strictly evangelization purposes, but encompassing the whole spectrum of human activity. He divided this into three categories: commerce, Christianity, and civilization (meaning good government, education etc). Christian missions should be autonomous centres that provided for all the people's social, economic, political and spiritual needs.

Nkomazana does extol Livingstone for loving and caring for Africans; however, he does not explore how Livingstone came to the conclusion that Africans needed the triple C if not that he was convinced that they were the manifestations of evil for being black. The only justification for the triple C onslaught has to be found in white supremacist ideology and whiteness because commerce, religion and civilisation were in Africa before the arrival of Livingstone. However, European-controlled commerce, Christianity, and civilisation were absent, and it would be impossible for colonisation unless European control was imposed on the indigenous communities. There is neither love, care nor respect in Livingstone's triple C agenda. In fact, Nkomazana fails to acknowledge another critical fact, that is

> Africa was evangelized through colonial machinery. It is not an overstatement to say that colonialism aided missions in nineteenth century Africa. It is also correct to say that missionaries, traders and colonial administrators had a common interest in Africa. Africans throughout the continent are living under the pains and consequences of colonialism. Mission Christianity, which was imposed through colonial military power, has become the dominant religion with various strands and variegated manifestations. (Okon, 2014, p. 192)

Walter Rodney (1972, p. 277) contended that "missionaries were as much part of the colonizing forces as were the explorers, traders and soldiers … missionaries were agents of colonialism in the practical sense, whether or not they saw themselves in that light." The relationship between the colonial project and the evangelisation project was so intricate that it is impossible to untangle them. Metaphorically, Christianity was the software, targeting mental and ideological conquest, post Berlin Conference 1884–1885; Christian missionaries were expected and tasked with winning the hearts and minds of the colonised peoples (Møller, 2006, p. 26). Colonisation was the hardware thriving on physical force and military violence. Both missionaries and colonists subscribed to white supremacism, with both believing their own construction of Africans "as categorically intellectually, morally, and physiologically inferior?" (Chenault, 2022, p. 7). That some good came out of white supremacist-driven missionary projects must not minimise the impact of the Christian teachings on the mental health of Africans who were taught to hate themselves for being black and to aspire to be white.

Separating missionaries from colonists only on the basis that they set up schools, clinics and hospitals that helped indigenous peoples is to trivialise the underlying and foundational ideas behind these projects, that is white supremacist ideology and the culture of whiteness. White supremacism, as it emerged in Europe, divided human beings and everything else into two main categories, the normal and the other. In this construction, white life was the normal; it was the standard for life. Every other claim to life had to be measured against white life. Europeans described themselves as "white" and "People," thereby demanding that all others be qualified to African people, Asian people,

Indigenous people, etc. In Africa, notwithstanding the various shades of brown, Africans were classified simply as black in line with their Christian theological and philosophical understanding of blackness. Whiteness meant a culture of dominance, power, privilege and patterns of thinking associated with white people and not simply skin colour (Harris, 2018). The service provision offered by missionaries under the influence of white supremacism and whiteness had a place in the sustenance of the domination of Africans by Europeans, and Christianity was central:

> The ideologies promulgated by the missionaries included such as gave the subjects of the respective colonial empire an obligation to work hard, i.e. to "eat their food by the sweat of their brows" (Genesis, 3:19), to rest content themselves with merely a small part of the produce of their labour, thus "giving to Caesar what is Caesar's" (Matthew 22:21). Above all, however, they were to remain submissant. The colonial subject was thus urged to submit himself to the governing authorities, for there is no authority except that which God has established (Romans, 13:1). (Møller, 2006, p. 27)

Christian theological teachings, whether intentionally or unintentionally, helped in doctoring Africans to accept white supremacism as the only legitimate approach to understanding environmental diversities that exist among human beings. The teachings and the social realities that were being constructed all around them had the effect of reinforcing each other; that is white people were superior because God is white, Jesus is white, the Bible says all good things are white; therefore, it is true that Europeans are white and superior and we are black and inferior. The Christian Satan was black; evil thrived in darkness (=black) and many other examples of how God detests blackness. If this was explicitly or implicitly taught in church, going outside, Africans were met with European-controlled systems, the new medium of economic transactions (money) was European, Europeans gave jobs, Europeans ran schools and clinics. All their lives were now at the mercy of Europeans, making Europeans superior and they became inferior in their own land. This mutual reinforcement made Africans more vulnerable to evangelisation and conversion, as well as more vulnerable to exploitative employment from the profiteering colonists for them to be able to function in this new social reality. When Africans and African resources were being plundered, missionaries were preaching peace, forgiveness, good neighbourliness and heaven (Okon, 2014, p. 199). Rodney (1972, p. 278) writes,

> The church's role was primarily to preserve the social relations of colonialism … the Christian church stressed humility, docility and acceptance. Ever since the days of slavery in the West Indies, the church had been brought in on condition that it should not excite the African slaves with doctrine of equality before God.

While separating Europeans and Africans into the categories of white and black, the divisions did not end there. As it was impossible for Africans to become Europeans, at least, it was possible for "progressive Africans," meaning those that willingly submitted to European domination, to be elevated in the social structure. The Europeanised Christian schooled converts began to think and act within the framework of white supremacism and to live in accordance with whiteness. They considered themselves better and superior to their unEuropeanised non-Christian converts whom they began to look at as backward (Møller, 2006, p. 28). Africans have adopted and adapted Christian and colonial racist ideologies, keeping these ideologies in circulation long after the end of formal colonisation. Racism, manifesting as xenophobia, is a contemporary not just a historic problem in Africa today and might be central in conflict zones.

To conclude this section, it is pertinent to point out that the colonial and evangelisation projects on the African continent were driven by a white supremacist ideology and its culture of whiteness that cut across both aspects of the occupation of Africa by Europeans, whether missionaries or colonists. The Christianity that joined hands, literally and metaphorically, with the colonising empires and kingdoms theologically supported white violence to subdue blackness in Africa. The tacit approval of violence was inherent in some of the fundamental teachings and theological positions of this church; from atonement and Christological formulas, Western Christianity had successfully divorced "the death of Jesus" from the "life and teaching of Jesus," making it easy to be indifferent or in support of violence in the name of God.

> The abstract, ahistorical formulas, whether of atonement or christology, do not challenge violence, which means that they accommodate it for Christians. This accommodation applies both to overt violence (exercised in war and in capital punishment) and to systemic violence (such as racism, sexism, and poverty). In a sense, all other discussions of violence accommodation and modeling provide specific instances of this claim. (Weaver, 2001, p. 161)

The movement that started off as a peaceful transformative movement in Palestine grew to become one of the most violent or sponsors of violence against people "othered" by the European version of supremacism, that is white supremacist ideology and whiteness (Gopin, 2000, p. 11). Africa remains in the throes of a white supremacist framework and a culture of whiteness that threatens the realisation of SDG 16 in Africa, as it continues to fan conflict and violence.

## Dismantling White Supremacy and Whiteness for Peacebuilding and Development

This chapter has so far argued that Christianity was involved in the twin project of colonisation and evangelisation of Africa by playing the role of the intellectual vanguard, providing the instruments for distracting the African "mind and heart" from the plunder and exploitation. However, the same Christianity has an opportunity to contribute to ending the cycles of violence that were entrenched, sponsored and promoted by the frameworks of white supremacism and whiteness since the colonial days by once again providing the basis for liberating the African "mind and heart" from the destructive colonial-era teachings. Christianity acknowledges the human dignity of all people as bearers of the Image of God. Conflict undermines the commitment not only to Christian Unity but to the Unity of Humankind, hence a threat to peace and SDG 16's targets.

From its inception in Palestine, the Jesus' movement, which evolved to become the Christian movement and Christianity, sought the transformation of the world in words and understanding that may not be fundamentally different from the ideals expressed by the United Nations in Agenda 2030, including SDG 16. It sought that transformation through peaceful and non-violent ways; it sought to present an alternative to the violent unjust ways of the governing systems of the Romans (Weaver, 2001). Since Christianity is involved, directly or indirectly, in most of the conflict zones in sub-Saharan Africa, it is resourced to help resolve these conflicts and initiate sustainable peacebuilding. Christianity is implicated either because the conflicts are an extension of animosities that are the legacies of colonisation and evangelisation or because the antagonists in these conflicts are members of the faith community. Some of them even claim to act "for Christianity and God" such as the Lord's Resistance Movement and Army that was led by Joseph Kony and operated in northern Uganda for some time (Dolnik & Butime, 2016).

For Christians and Christianity to be effective in peacebuilding in conflict zones in Africa, there is need to promote a high degree of openness and inclusivity that is accompanied by brutally honest self-appraisal, especially regarding the legacies of the evangelisation era when European missionaries sought to convert Africans to the faith. The conflation of white supremacism and whiteness and the "good news of the Gospels and the scriptures" contaminated the process of evangelisation of the continent and helped in solidifying fluid diversities that existed before colonisation and evangelisation. This quest can be realised if the faith leaders and actors possess the critical competences not only to understand the public manifestation of the conflict but its underlying and invisible dimensions, some of which can be legacies of Christian evangelisation (Harris, 2018, p. 5).

Earlier, we noted that the Christian teachings around atonement and Christology could be regarded as condoning violence or at best as indifferent to violence. An alternative approach to Christian faith resources, especially the Bible, can lead us to different conclusions when it comes to Christian commitment to peaceful co-existence, tolerance of diversities and most importantly eradicating conflict in society. Throughout the New Testament, Jesus Christ is presented as Victorious in the battles between God and the forces that oppose God. Whereas, previously, especially after Christianity became state-religion around 325 CE, this victory was almost presented as one that could not be achieved without violence, yet according to Denny J. Weaver (2001, pp. 167–168),

The Gospels present the same story as that told in Revelation, but from a different standpoint. Revelation tells the story of Jesus from the perspective of the heavenly throne room and the future culmination of the reign of God. The Gospels narrate that same story from the earthly vantage point of the folks who got dust on their sandals as they walked along the roads of Palestine with Jesus. Both accounts locate the victory of the reign of God on earth and in history — narrative *Christus Victor*— and make quite clear that the triumph occurred not through the sword and military might but non-violently, through death and resurrection. The intrinsically nonviolent character of the victory eliminates what is usually called triumphalism of the church. As intrinsically nonviolent, its stance to the other or toward those who differ and are different can only be non-violent. To be otherwise is to cease to be a witness to the reign of God and to join the forces of evil who oppose the reign of God. At the same time, reading that story in the Gospels shows that Jesus was not a passive victim, whose purpose was to get himself killed in order to satisfy a big cosmic legal requirement. Rather, Jesus was an activist, whose mission was to make the rule of God visible. And his acts demonstrated what the reign of God looked like — defending poor people, raising the status of women, raising the status of Samaritans, performing healings and exorcisms, preaching the reign of God, and more. His mission was to make the reign of God present in the world in his person and in his teaching, and to invite people to experience the liberation it presented. And when Jesus made the reign of God visible and present in that way, it was so threatening that the assembled array of evil forces killed him. These forces include imperial Rome, which carried ultimate legal authority for his death, with some assistance from the religious authorities in Jerusalem, as well as Judas, Peter, and other disciples, who could not even watch with him, and the mob that howled for his death. Resurrection is the reign of God made victorious over all these forces of evil that killed Jesus.

What this entails is that Christianity needs to be intentionally anti-racist in its approach to peacebuilding across Africa because its racist legacy is a critical dimension to contemporary conflicts because different groups in Africa are seeking to achieve "whiteness," that is dominance, power, and privilege over and against their neighbours. Christianity has a duty and a responsibility to dismantle the racist white supremacist ideology and the culture of whiteness that it helped plant in Africa to achieve sustainable peace and justice. Christianity in its pristine form is anti-racist. According to Alex Carter (2021), antiracism is "the active process of identifying and eliminating racism by changing systems, organizational structures, policies and practices and attitudes, so that power is redistributed and shared equitably." Whereas colonisation and evangelisation had sought to divide people on the basis of external diversities, that is not compatible with some of the fundamental elements of the Christian faith. Christianity can gather people together, not scatter them.

Since there is a foreign element to most conflicts in Africa, Christianity can also play a significant role in triggering its global networks for a global response to the fanning of violence by some international groups, sometimes including foreign state actors. Once faith actors have established the identity of the invisible hands that are fanning and profiting from conflicts in Africa, they can invoke their social and faith capital to invoke a response from their networks globally to incapacitate the racist invisible hands that continue to finance and fan conflicts for profits at the expense of African lives. The historic and contemporary hand behind these conflicts needs to be exposed and countered with an alternative propagation of the self-understanding not only of the Christian in Africa but of all Africans, whether in Africa or in the diaspora. Christianity's stock has not waned at all (Owen & King, 2019, p. 5). This persistence and strengthening of religious influence suggest an even greater need for religious interventions in peacebuilding. Central to Christian peacebuilding efforts, and recognising the complicity of Christian theologians and missionaries in the entrenchment of racist Christian teachings in Africa, must be a reiteration of the Christian fundamental narrative:

> As sinners, in one way or another, we are all part of those sinful forces that killed Jesus. Jesus died making the reign of God present for us while we were still sinners. To acknowledge our human sinfulness is to become aware of our participation in the forces of evil that killed Jesus, including their present manifestations in such powers as militarism, nationalism, racism, sexism, heterosexism and poverty that still bind and oppress. And because God is a loving God, God invites us to join the rule of God in spite of the fact that we participated with and are captive to the powers that killed Jesus. God invites us to join the struggle of those seeking liberation from the forces that bind and oppress. This invitation envisions both those who are oppressed and their oppressors. When the oppressed accept God's invitation, they cease collaborating with the powers that oppressed and join the forces who represent the reign of God in making a visible witness against oppression. And when the oppressors accept God's invitation, they cease their collaboration with the powers of oppression, and join the forces who represent the reign of God in witnessing against oppression. Thus under the reign of God, former oppressed and former oppressors join together in witnessing to the reign of God. (Weaver, 2001, p. 168)

While it looks increasingly difficult to realise Agenda 2030, especially SDG 16 in Africa due to the multiple conflicts, Christianity has an opportunity to atone for its historic complicitous involvement in the solidification of diversities and thereby engendering violent conflicts among African groups.

Christianity and Christian institutions can pursue the following in the quest for just, peaceful and inclusive societies in Africa:

- Integrate an intentional critical appraisal of European strategies for evangelising sub-Saharan Africa in theological education.
- Adopt a decolonising and anti-racist approach to mission and biblical studies to equip faith leaders with critical competencies necessary for evaluating impact of Christian teaching, past and present.
- Promote grassroots ecumenism by encouraging greater cohesion in Christian activities bringing people together to act for the common good.

- Become advocates for inclusion, justice and the rule of law in wider societies.
- Embrace diakonia and public witnessing among victims and survivors of conflict as an integral element of Christian mission.

## Conclusion

In reflections on violence and peace, the World Council of Churches came to the position that public violence was a manifestation of internal violence within the self. Internalised violence is something that Africans struggle with as they were violated severally historically, especially, under white-supremacist-driven mass exploitation projects such as slavery, colonisation and evangelisation. While Christianity has also done a lot of good for Africans, it helped inflict mental violence on Africans. The call by the World Council of Churches on violence is, thus,

> Overcoming violence clearly involves undertaking first the hard work of overcoming violence within one's self, and then affirming human dignity, the rights of all peoples and the integrity of creation; confronting the violent powers with alternative ways of exercising power; and realising mutuality and interdependence in relationships. The insights gained from each of the above themes would be helpful in elaborating the theological bases for a vocation of peace, reconciliation and non-violent resistance. These affirmations pose several challenges to the churches to present themselves and also propose alternatives to all structures of relationships which turn oppressive and violent (WCC Faith and Order Team, 2001, p. 10)

Churches in Africa have a responsibility to engage with the violence that manifests itself in contemporary societies but whose roots might actually be thriving in the history of evangelisation of Africa. While the racist environment of the evangelisation period contaminated the gospel, time has come to challenge this contamination and promote the gospel that promotes justice, equality, equity and human dignity for all, that is SDG 16.

White supremacist ideology remains alive and functional in Africa, even without the presence of European people. However, the public absence of European people must also not be mistaken for the absence of European influence, dominance and agenda in contemporary conflicts in Africa. There is need for critical "follow the money" researches that can explore the paper trail or the trail of resources from conflict zones or weapons into the conflict zones and thus expose those profiting from the conflicts. There is a strong possibility that among those profiting are persons that either profess to be Christians or identify with the racist ideology of white supremacism that Christianity helped develop and entrench throughout the world. That conflicts are associated with low standard of living, unfair distribution of resources or unequal access to national resources are all legacies of the colonial-evangelisation onslaught in

Africa. These historical legacies need to be addressed for sustainable peacebuilding to yield peace and justice.

Christianity, having played the role of intellectual vanguard to the Europeanisation of Africans, must now seek to dismantle the instruments that allowed it to eradicate self-esteem and dignity among Africans because contemporary Africans are descendants of a people that was trained to hate the self and aspire to be "white." While the Bible speaks of the Image of God in every human being, Christianity contributed to the division of people of God that made Europeans see Africans as not equal to them before God and even led Africans not to see each other as brothers and sisters all created in the Image of God. Conflicts in Africa are a manifestation of the persistence of this indoctrination, which was presented as God's ordination for people, to be different and to dominate those you consider to be below yourself in the hierarchy of humanity.

Religious peacebuilding in Africa is not optional, but it is obligatory, not only because Africans are a religious people but because some of the fundamental and underlying factors triggering conflicts are steeped in the manner religions, especially foreign religious traditions, presented themselves and how they packaged themselves for maximum success on the continent. Christianity was central in setting up a racially motivated conflict-prone society and now can atone for that by stepping up to dismantle and replace that racially motivated society with a just and inclusive society in which diversity is celebrated as of God.

## References

Abu-Nimer, M. (2001). Conflict Resolution, Culture and Religion: Toward a Training Model of Inter-religious Peacebuilding. *Journal of Peace Research, 38*(6), 685–704.

Amnesty International. (2021, April 7). *Amnesty International: Sub-Saharan Africa: The Devastating Impact of Conflicts Compounded by COVID-19.* Retrieved December 12, 2022, from https://www.amnesty.org/en/latest/news/2021/04/subsaharan-africa-the-devastating-impact-of-conflicts-compounded/

Appleby, S. R. (1996). Religion as an Agent of Conflict Transformation and Peacebuilding. In C. A. Crocker, F. O. Hampson, & P. Aall (Eds.), *The Challenges of Managing International Conflict* (pp. 821–840). United States Institute of Peace Press.

Bethke, F. S. (2012). The Consequences of Divide-and-Rule Politics in Africa south of the Sahara. *Peace Economics, Peace Science and Public Policy, 18*(3), 1–13. https://doi.org/10.1515/peps-2012-0002

Carter, A. (2021, February 12). *Antiracism in Peace-Building and Conflict Resolution.* Columbia Law School Mediation Clinic. Retrieved December 1, 2022, from https://unitar.org/sites/default/files/media/file/Antiracism%20in%20Peace-Building%20and%20Conflict%20Resolution-compressed.pdf

Chenault, J. (2022). *Western Christianity and the Origins of Antiblackness, Eurocentrism, and White Supremacist Ideology.* Electronic Theses and Dissertations. Paper 3835 PhD Thesis, Louisville: ThinkIR: The Univ ThinkIR: The University of Louisville's

Institutional Repository. Retrieved December 12, 2022, from https://ir.library.louisville.edu/etd/3835/

Dolnik, A., & Butime, H. (2016). *Understanding the Lord's Resistance Army Insurgency.* World Scientific.

eNCA. (2015). *Who Funds Africa's Wars and Why? George Clooney's Money Will Reveal All.* News release, Pretoria: eNCA Dstv Channel 403. Retrieved December 16, 2022, from https://www.enca.com/africa/new-clooney-project-probe-financing-african-wars

Farfan-Vallespin, A., & Bonick, M. (2016). On the Origins and Consequences of Racism. *Beiträge zur Jahrestagung des Vereins für Socialpolitik 2016: Demographischer Wandel—Session: Development Economics II, No. D13-V3.* Kiel and Hamburg: Leibniz-Informationszentrum Wirtschaft. Retrieved November 28, 2022, from https://www.econstor.eu/handle/10419/145767

Fatokun, S. A. (2005). Christianity in Africa: A Historical Appraisal. *Verbum et Ecclesia*, 26(2), 357–368. Retrieved January 10, 2023, from https://www.researchgate.net/publication/269965860_Christianity_in_Africa_a_historical_appraisal/link/57e24ac308ae1f0b4d958c76/download

Fellow, S., & Paige, S. (2020). *Time to Decolonise Aid: Insights and Lessons from a Global Consultation.* Peace Direct.

Githigaro, J. M. (2012). Faith-Based Peacebuilding: A Case Study of the National Council of Churches of Kenya. *Peace and Conflict Studies*, 19(1), 93–120. https://doi.org/10.46743/1082-7307/2012.1135

Gopin, M. (2000). *Between Eden and Armageddon: The Future of World Religions, Violence, and Peacemaking.* Oxford University Press, Inc.

Gunda, M. R. (2020). Rethinking Development in Africa and the Role of Religion. In E. Chitando, M. R. Gunda, & L. Togarasei (Eds.), *Religion and Development in Africa—Exploring Religion in Africa 4* (pp. 37–57). University of Bamberg Press.

Harpviken, K. B, & Røislien, H. E. (2005). *Mapping the Terrain: The Role of Religion in Peacemaking—State of the Art Paper for the Norwegian Ministry of Foreign Affairs.* State of the Art Paper. Norwegian Ministry of Foreign Affairs. Retrieved November 22, 2022, from https://www.files.ethz.ch/isn/38134/2005_07_mapping_the_terrain_stateoftheartpaper__jul05_.pdf

Harris, M. (2018, June 10). Racism and White Defensiveness in Aotearoa: A Pākehā Perspective. *E-Tangata: Comment and Analysis.* Retrieved December 9, 2022, from https://e-tangata.co.nz/comment-and-analysis/racism-and-white-defensiveness-in-aotearoa-a-pakeha-perspective/

Kwamboka, O. K. (2014). *Religion, Gender and Peacebuilding in Africa: A case study of Kenya 2007/8.* Master of Arts Thesis. University of Nairobi: Institute of Diplomacy and International Relations.

Little, D., & Appleby, S. (2004). A Moment of Opportunity? The Promise of Religious Peacebuilding in an Era of Religious and Ethnic Conflict. In H. Coward & G. S. Smith (Eds.), *Religion and Peacebuilding* (pp. 1–23). State University of New York Press.

Mbiti, J. (1969). *African Religions and Philosophy.* Heinemann.

Møller, B. (2006). *Religion and Conflict in Africa: With a special focus on East Africa DIIS 2006:6.* Study Report. Danish Institute for International Studies, DIIS. Retrieved November 26, 2022, from www.diis.dk

Nkomazana, F. (1998). Livingstone's Ideas of Christianity, Commerce and Civilization *Pula: Botswana Journal of African Studies*, 12(1 & 2), 44–57. Retrieved December 15, 2022, from http://digital.lib.msu.edu/projects/africanjournals/

Nyamnjoh, F. B. (2010). *Africa Spectrum, 45*(1), 57–93. Retrieved December 1, 2022, from www.africa-spectrum.org

Okon, E. E. (2014). Christian Missions and Colonial Rule in Africa: Objective and Contemporary Analysis. *European Scientific Journal, 10*(17), 192–209. Retrieved December 15, 2022, from https://eujournal.org/index.php/esj/article/view/3557/3397

Owen, M., & King, A. (2019). Enhancing the Efficacy of Religious Peacebuilding Practice: An Exploratory Evidence-Based Framework for Assessing Dominant Risks in Religious Peacebuilding. *Religions, 10*(641), 1–19. https://doi.org/10.3390/rel10120641

Rodney, W. (1972). *How Europe Underdeveloped Africa*. L'ouverture.

UNESCO, African Union and Angola. (2021). *Theme 3: Africa in the Face of Conflicts, Crisis and Inequality—Biennale of Luanda: Pan African Forum for the Culture and Peace*. Concept Note. UNESCO. Retrieved November 28, 2022, from https://en.unesco.org/sites/default/files/concept_note_3_-_africa_in_the_face_of_conflicts_crisis_and_inequality.pdf

United Nations. (2015). *Transforming Our World: The 2030 Agenda for Sustainable Development A/RES/70/1*. Resolution. United Nations. Retrieved December 16, 2022, from https://www.un.org/en/development/desa/population/migration/generalassembly/docs/globalcompact/A_RES_70_1_E.pdf

WCC Faith and Order Team. (2001). *Nurturing Peace, Overcoming Violence: In the Way of Christ for the Sake of the World—An Invitation to a Process of Theological Study and Reflection on Peace, Justice and Reconciliation during the Decade to Overcome Violence: Churches Seeking Peace and R*. Study Document. World Council of Churches. Retrieved November 26, 2022, from https://www.oikoumene.org/resources/documents/nurturing-peace-overcoming-violence-in-the-way-of-christ-for-the-sake-of-the-world

Weaver, D. J. (2001). Violence in Christian Theology. *CrossCurrents, 51*(2), 150–176.

CHAPTER 8

# Climate Security and Religion in Africa: Towards Sustainable Development Goals

*Joram Tarusarira*

## Introduction

Climate impacts in Africa contribute to climate-related security risks—understood as climate change's significant ramifications for patterns of conflict, violence and instability—in numerous pathways. Cases in point include the worsening of livelihood conditions, which contribute to escalating grievances or competition and clashes over dwindling resources and the subsequent adaptation strategies; climate-induced mobility, which increases the risk of community-based violence and conflict when migrants come into confrontation with other groups; and armed groups' use of climate impacts by using the strain of the climate-related effects to boost recruitment (SIPRI, Savelli et al., 2022). The literature has a consensus that there is no direct link between climate change and conflict. Climate change does not cause conflict but multiplies the risk of climate-related risks in combination with other factors. The simplistic assertions such as 'resource scarcity leads to conflict', while resource abundance leads to peace, are implausible, unsustainable and untenable. The situation is much more complex than that because it is contextual and socially mediated. Because of this consensus, the discussion has begun to shift the focus of inquiry, language and register to talk about the relationship between climate and security from identifying

J. Tarusarira (✉)
Department of Comparative Study of Religion, University of Groningen, Groningen, The Netherlands

Alliance of Bioversity International and CIAT, Rome, Italy
e-mail: j.tarusarira@rug.nl

© The Author(s), under exclusive license to Springer Nature Switzerland AG 2023
S. M. Kilonzo et al. (eds.), *The Palgrave Handbook of Religion, Peacebuilding, and Development in Africa*,
https://doi.org/10.1007/978-3-031-36829-5_8

linear causal linkages to developing a more nuanced understanding of this relationship in general. With qualitative research, the narrative has shifted away from 'causes and drivers' towards 'multi-causality', 'threat multipliers' and 'tipping points' (Peters & Vivekananda, 2014; Burrows & Kinney, 2016; Schaar, 2018). Mediating and moderating factors, thus, explain how climate change promotes or undermines climate-related security risks. This chapter takes a focused analysis of religion as one hitherto absent variable in the climate security discourse. Religion is conspicuously absent despite the fact that most of the research on climate security has been carried out in Africa (Fjelde & von Uexkull, 2012), where the population is highly religious and, in some cases, treat natural resources as sacred. In addition, when climate-related conflicts ensue, groups may form alliances along religious lines of difference.

The chapter conceptualizes religion from the lived religion perspective (see, e.g. Knibbe & Kupari, 2020). Instead of looking for the best definition of religion, it suggests focusing on people's everyday practices rather than studying only official texts, organizations and experts. It, thus, includes attention to rituals, stories and spiritual experiences that may draw on official religious traditions but may extend beyond them. It analyses dynamics such as how and what people eat, how they dress and how they deal with birth and death, everyday sacralized spaces, and the physical and artistic things people do together, such as singing, dancing and other community traditions that enact a spiritual sense of solidarity and transcendence (Ammerman, 2016).

In foregrounding religion as a mediating factor in climate-related security risks, the chapter broadens the variables to be considered in the search for climate-proof peace and contributes to two sustainable development goals (SDGs), namely SDG 13, that is climate action: taking urgent action to combat climate change and its impacts; and SDG 16: promoting peaceful and inclusive societies for sustainable development, providing access to justice for all and build effective, accountable and inclusive institutions at all levels in Africa. In what follows, based on literature review, it discusses the impact of framing climate security for conceptualization and practice to pave the way to account for how religion is marginalized in the discourse. It then outlines the relationship between climate change, peace and security in Africa to set the context for the discussion. It does not claim to homogenize the entire African continent. However, it will reference and draw on examples from Africa. It proceeds to articulate the complexity of the climate security discourse to show how one discipline cannot analyse it and, subsequently, the need for multiple disciplines, including the critical study of religion, to understand it holistically and effectively. It then discusses the dominance of economic and techno-scientific explanations and solutions at the expense of non-technological and value-based ones, such as religion, in the climate security discourse. This is not meant to pit these approaches against each other, undermine the contributions of quantitative research or overlook the methodologically hybrid and collaborative work that has been undertaken by positivist and quantitative researchers and constructivist and qualitative ones. But to acknowledge the legacies of the dominance of the positivist and quantitative approaches, including the exclusion of themes, such as religion, that cannot be analysed using their instruments. Demonstrating the marginalization of religion dovetails with SDG 16's concern for inclusive societies. Religious practices and beliefs are an essential part of some communities, such that excluding them is an affront to the idea of inclusive societies. Having shown the marginalization of religion, the chapter presents concrete climate-related security risk examples which threaten peace and stability in Africa, in which religion can be a variable to show its presence and relevance and the need to integrate it into the climate security discourse. It concludes by arguing that the integration of religion into the security discourse in Africa is strategically positioned to contribute to the pursuit of peace in a context where climate change is threatening stability.

## Framing Climate Security

The climate crisis' epistemological and ontological framing has shaped responses to climate-related security in African contexts. Framing—how a situation is described and labelled—shapes institutional design and policy actions, what the problem is and how it can be addressed (Bremberg et al., 2022). Furthermore, it determines what is worth knowing and how it can be known. One of the hindrances to climate action is differences in values and worldviews, which are representations of frames (Romsdahl et al., 2018). In Africa, religion underwrites most of the values and worldviews and has a powerful role in constructing an unseen, meaningful world that structures life (Asma, 2018). Religion defines values, worldviews, norms, beliefs, knowledge and practices that impact the climate-conflict nexus. The current framings of climate change prioritize innovative technologies, statistical analysis and big data, which are predominant in the natural sciences. This technical framing prioritizes the enhancement of factors with positive impacts on the environment and new infrastructures that seek to create biophysical changes such as water control infrastructures to tree plantations or geoengineering for carbon sequestration (Nightingale et al., 2020), genetic diversity, endemic species richness or economic growth indicators to enhance adaptive capacities. They perceive new infrastructures as variables that determine the nature (magnitude and/or reversal) of the effect of climate change on security risks. This perspective implies that weak technological and adaptive capacities will increase and strengthen climate security risks. Non-technological phenomena such as religion have, thus, received fleeting attention. However, some contexts, inspired by religious beliefs, treat water as a living entity. This worldview means it cannot be divided into elements such as chemical composition, smell or colour associated with different degrees of importance for what is considered 'good quality'. The religious significance of water thus has significant implications for how actors position themselves in times of water scarcity, as we will see later in the example of the conflict between Muslims and Christians over water in Lamu in Kenya (see Schoderer & Ott, 2022).

Framing climate crises in physical, political and economic terms in Africa has, thus, directed attention to mitigation (efforts to reduce or prevent the emission of greenhouse gasses) and adaptation (the process of adjusting to the actual or expected effects of climate change), using positivist, secular, political, economic and technical approaches. The assumption of the framing and the subsequent economic and techno-scientific responses resonates with the argument that environmental changes may periodically put human well-being at risk, but humans will adapt to resource scarcities through market mechanisms, technological innovations, social institutions for resource allocation or any combination thereof (Lomborg, 2001). People will be able to respond to new environmental changes and challenges through technology and efficiency (Simon, 1996). This kind of thinking has led to privileging the knowledge of scientists, engineers and economists, and emphasizing incremental reforms such as market or technology-based responses (Blue, 2018), using a linear understanding of how systems change and a rational choice grounded on a technocratic conceptual interpretation of climate crises (Day & Hunt, 2022). Consequently, non-economic, non-political or non-physical dimensions of climate crises, such as religion, have been marginalized (Blue, 2018). However, climate security risks are not only physical, economic or political but also human and cultural. Their outcomes are emergent and non-linear but complex (see Ibid Blue, 2018).

## Previous Research: Climate Change and Security Nexus

The climate security discourse developed around the link between climate and conflict. In its inception, the discourse built on environmental security scholarship traceable to projects such as the Environmental Change and Acute Conflict Project at the University of Toronto Group led by Thomas Homer-Dixon in the early 1990s, which pioneered the study of the links between environmental stress and violent conflict (Homer-Dixon, 1994). Another notable project is the Environment and Conflicts Project (ENCOP) at ETH Zürich, led by Spillmann and Bächler (1995), which implemented large empirical studies that demonstrated the multifaceted and indirect links between resource scarcity and conflict. It must be noted to nuance the conclusions, Baechler (1998, 32) stated that whether conflict broke out depends upon socio-political factors rather than 'the degree of environmental degradation' as such. The resource scarcity theory emerged from such projects to explain the relationship between climate and conflict. The theory asserts that

> through its impacts on both short-term environmental shocks and long-term trends, climate change will exacerbate resource pressures and scarcities and, in turn, feed increased resource competition, economic and social vulnerability, migration and displacement, and civil and political conflict at multiple sites and scale – all aided and abetted by existing patterns of poverty and fragility (Selby et al., 2022: 3).

Building on the resource scarcity theory, some studies argued that there is evidence for a climate–civil war relationship in Africa (Burke et al., 2009; Hsiang et al., 2011). The 2003–05 Darfur war became the poster child of climate security thinking. Ban Ki-moon, then UN Secretary-General, in an Op-Ed for *The Washington Post,* stated that the crises in Darfur 'began as an ecological crisis, arising at least in part from climate change'. Darfur became known as the world's first climate change war. Various stakeholders, including political leaders, activists, think tanks and public intellectuals, agreed that carbon emissions significantly affected the region's troubles. The other case is the crisis of Lake Chad. After an attempt to suppress what would be known as Boko Haram, the region has become a deep security crisis, which has embroiled all four states around the Lake—Cameroon, Chad, Niger and Nigeria. There have been widespread casualties, displacements, and acute economic and food insecurity. Again, climate change was named as a significant contributing factor (Selby et al., 2022).

The robustness of the claims and the related research findings have been questioned (Buhaug, 2010; Gleditsch, 2012). Many large-N studies (Theisen et al., 2012) find little support that climate-induced environmental stress is associated with an increased risk of armed conflict in Africa. With respect to Darfur and Lake Chad, some scholars assert that there is little solid evidence that climate change and drought are sparking large-scale armed conflicts in this region. They blamed the conflicts on inadequate structures, systems and practices of drought adaptation (Selby et al., 2022). They draw attention to factors such as poverty, institutional weakness, economic marginalization and political exclusion mediating the translation of the climate change impacts to violent conflicts (Homer-Dixon, 1999; Kahl, 2006; Raleigh, 2010). They point towards political and economic forces and power relations as responsible for environmentally related insecurities, vulnerabilities and risks, and criticize the current climate security discourse as too positivist and dominated by a problematic ensemble of policy-led framings and assumptions (Selby et al., 2022). Abrahams (2020) calls for a consideration of spatiotemporal factors, considering that the relationship between climate change and conflict 'engages myriad stakeholders and processes that operate across diffuse spatial and temporal scales' because the spatial and temporal scales at which a particular topic or case is examined alter how that topic or case is understood. Where and when the climate-related conflict ensues might point towards the factors that significantly drive or undermine the conflict. While in some spaces the driving factors might be economical and political, in others, it might be religious beliefs, practices or identity.

Some scholars argue that one possible reason for the inconclusive results on the link between climate change and conflict is the almost exclusive focus on armed rebellion against the state in the large N-studies (Fjelde & von Uexkull, 2012). They further observe that much of the arguments within the former environmental security literature suggest that pressure on vital resources such as water or arable land tends to heighten inter-group tension and spur violence between groups rather than attacks against the state. This communal violence mobilizes actors along local cleavages based on ethnic or religious affiliations, kinship ties or livelihood (ibid). A case in point of these communal conflicts is those over land that frequently erupt between farmers and pastoralists in arid and semi-arid lands in Kenya (Medina et al., 2022). The conflicts between the two are often voiced in zero-sum terms. While religion is mentioned as a variable in the conflicts (Fjelde & von Uexkull, 2012), it is rarely foregrounded and analysed as an independent variable that can modulate the conflicts. Yet these communities sometimes treat the natural resources such as land, water or cattle, which they consider sacred, or build alliances along religious affiliations when conflicts involving natural resources ensue.

In contrast to the resource scarcity theory, scholars like Collier and Hoeffler (1998) argued that resource abundance in developing countries increases the amount of lootable income and the risks of conflict outbreaks. Furthermore, Raleigh and Kniveton (2012) also demonstrate the opposite of the traditional resource scarcity theory. They assert that extreme rains are more likely to lead to inter-communal conflict types, whereas anomalous dry periods are more likely to lead to conflict between rebel groups and the state (see Abrahams, 2020). Political ecologists have also argued that rather than absolute resources, relative abundance and scarcity are mediated by a host of social, economic and political factors and local institutions that affect conflict outcomes (Benjaminsen, 2016; Kahl, 2006; Klare, 2001).

## Religion and Climate Security in Africa

The link between climate change and conflict, thus, remains unsettled, and resource scarcity and resource abundance, founded on positivism, have failed to explain it fully. In the same way political ecologists would like to isolate economic and political factors, this chapter sets itself apart from the current literature by shining light on the 'religion' factor in the climate security discourse in Africa. It founds itself on constructivism—an approach that 'holds that the patterns in the social world' result from context-specific meaning at the 'personal or at a discursive level, reflecting norms and the dominant view on a topic at any time' and hence favouring 'contingent, context-dependent, and in-depth idiographic knowledge over-generalizations' (Beaumont & de Coning, 2022; Theisen, 2017). As already intimated, the African continent is highly religious and religious worldviews play a significant role in how some people structure their lives (see, e.g. Magesa, 1997). The chapter is alive to the criticism that in highly religious contexts, analysts want to explain resource conflicts, such as water conflicts, as products of cultural norms, values or ideas underpinned by religion, thereby expressing a culturalist and often pejorative proposition. It acknowledges that propositions involving religion should not be simplistic generalizations about communities, is attentive to the heterogeneity and local variability of attitudes and beliefs, does not ignore the fact that traditions are dynamic and constantly changing, and does not disregard the practical, material dimensions of culture, depicting it purely in ideational terms. It does not claim that people are imbued with the precepts of or are bound by traditional beliefs about natural resources (Selby, 2003). Neither does it charge religion with the agency to cause conflict. It seeks to acknowledge the moral makeup of human beings, which is also founded on religious beliefs and practices. It concurs with what political ecologists foreground as contributing to climate-related security risks: the legacies of colonial rule, the uneven development of capitalism, the distribution and control of economic and coercive resources, and the organizational and practical difficulty of maintaining control (and constructing effective and legitimate state institutions) in the face of long-historical and structural constraints, weak governments, which give opportunists such as armed groups the fertile ground to recruit people into their organizations (Selby, 2003, 2022). This does not mean, however, that we ignore that in some communities in Africa, religion, whichever way it is understood spatiotemporally, is mobilized to provide cognitive, emotional and moral meanings to some individuals' and communities' lives. The chapter does not treat religion pejoratively but as a phenomenon that those who practise it are proud of.

Many African nations face extreme weather conditions, undermining food security, contributing to population displacement, and driving unrest and instability. This has been acknowledged by the African Union in its Communique of the 1051th meeting of the AU Peace and Security Council (PSC) held on 26 November 2021 on the theme: Climate Change and Peace and Security: The need for an Informed Climate-Security-Development nexus for Africa: The Peace and Security Council: 'Expresses deep concern over the increasingly negative and disproportionate impact of climate change on the development gains in Africa as evidenced by extreme weather patterns manifesting as floods, droughts, heatwaves, forest fires, storms, cyclones, and slow-onset events such as the rise of sea levels and, changing and unpredictable rainfall patterns'; and 'Acknowledges the wide-ranging risks of climate change, as a threat multiplier, to the peace and security landscape in the continent including on food and water insecurity, loss of livelihoods, failure of management of natural resources, the scarcity of water resources, climate-induced displacements, and possibly aggravating existing vulnerabilities, tensions and conflicts' (AU, 2021).

Considering the hitherto absent analysis of religion in climate-related security debates resonates with the fact that climate crises do not only impact the economic and physical aspects in many African contexts. It involves losing access to territory, cultural heritage, and indigenous and local knowledge embedded in indigenous religions. The non-economic and non-physical dimension, such as the religious dimension of climate crises, requires as much attention as the physical, economic and political ones for a practical and holistic understanding and response. The focus on economic, political and physical dimensions of climate security and undermining of religion has been in part due to positivist literature's focus on using historical data and testing hypotheses (Selby, 2014). Positivism assumes that 'there are systematic regularities in the social world, and that these can be objectively sensed, recorded, and accumulated to build knowledge using tools that allow for generalizations' (Beaumont & de Coning, 2022). While it is open to qualitative analysis, it tends to accommodate it on the proviso that it realizes the goals of positivist and quantitative approaches such as making generalizations (Van Baalen & Mobjörk, 2018). Religion does not fit into the dominant positivist approaches because it cannot be quantified. The assumption has been that post-Enlightenment secularization forces were stamping out religion and spirituality (Farrell, 2015). The Indian historian and diplomat K. M. Panikkar argued that religion would decline in Africa following the end of western colonial rule. It was thought that it would decline because it was associated with colonialism and depended on mission school systems (Gifford, 1995: 2). This has not been the case in many African contexts. Moreover, communities most vulnerable to climate-induced conflicts often possess religious worldviews inspired by missionary religious traditions and indigenous religions or both, which they use to make sense of these conflicts and peace (Tarusarira, 2017).

Factoring religion into the discourse and practice of climate security might explain the nature and dynamics of some climate-related security risks. For instance, instead of only asserting that women in Africa suffer the most during climate-related insecurity since they have to fetch the fuel to feed their families and may not be able to move as an adaptation strategy because they may have to take care of the vulnerable members of the community like children and the elderly, the complex theory's interest in local culture and history (de Coning, 2020) also analyses how religion in Africa justifies and motivates these experiences. This is in order because, in some African communities, religion determines gender roles and assigns care duties to women. Okunade (2022) observes that in the African religion, women play important roles as mothers and caregivers. For example, in the myth of Ibibios in Nigeria, they are described mythologically as the 'mother of mankind, from whom all people originated'. The idea is to link human life directly to God through humans. Women, thus, do not just give birth to humans but care for and nurse them from birth to death. He further argues that women in almost all African societies are traditional medical practitioners and health practitioners in charge of children and other women's medical needs.

Some indigenous religions and spiritualities perceive land, rivers, water and cattle as social, cultural, spiritual (or religious) and ontological assets that structure the social identity and life of communities (Cabot, 2017), thus engendering 'action and notions of responsiveness towards what is regarded as sacred' (Knowles, 1992). For indigenous groups, whose identities rely on collective access to the land and waters traditionally occupied by their ancestors, migration as a climate adaptation strategy is the last resort. Underlying in-migration tensions between pastoral conflicts in Kenya among the Turkana people are prayers of blessing and protection for the cattle raiders and a strong connection between the elders and traditional religious leaders with the cattle raiders (Lines, 2009), making fighters fight with vigour and confidence under the pretext of defending their sacred natural resources. Before going on raids, Turkana elders and fortune tellers bless the pastoralists. The fortune tellers can even tell the warriors if they will be killed through the rituals they perform. They also inform the raiders of the routes to take. When the raiders return, they are cleansed before entering the homesteads; they will have killed so many people, so the elders cast out all the bad spirits and demons of those they have killed (Medina et al., 2022).

Cultural beliefs such as attachment to cattle, heroism, dowry payment, initiation rites and attachment to the land have shaped the conflicts that manifest themselves in cattle rustling, ethnic killings/murder and land conflicts (Chebunet et al., 2013). Islamic law and local water-management customs (*'urf*) are still at the heart of water management in Muslim societies (Daoudy, 2020) This makes the following questions legitimate: How do cultural and religious values influence their positions and positioning during climate-related insecurity? This question is legitimate and resonates with the observation of the Intergovernmental Science-Policy Platform on Biodiversity and Ecosystem Services (IPBES), which established that how nature is conceived of and valued has implications for different consumption and production choices that influence degradation.

The concern for the influence of religion in climate-related security risks is not restricted to indigenous religions. In line with the observation that during a conflict over natural resources, alliances are built along religious lines, a study analysing how the significant divide and tension between the Christian community living in Lamu and the Muslim majority relate to increasing water shortages in Lamu observed that water plays a major role in the purposes of cleansing and purification rituals associated with Islamic prayers. Islamic elders have a significant role in the management of water in Lamu. This is a potential trigger for water-related conflict because while Lamu is a predominantly Muslim region, it also comprises other religious groups and cultures. This means that earmarking local water for religious purposes would be to the detriment of other cultures and religions that do not follow the same practices. Secondly, preferentially supplying water to one group will make it harder for the other smaller groups in the region to find water. So as water scarcity persists, unequal distribution and access between the Christians and Muslims in the region could cause conflict. The whole situation is worsened by the fact that relations are already on edge in this region. Persistent water scarcity can thus escalate existing tensions (Maingay et al., 2022). The study concluded that religion is a factor that can heighten the potential for water-related conflict in the region. Hence must be urgently addressed and integrated into Lamu's water-management mechanism to avoid water-related conflicts.

The preceding religious imaginations are overlooked, yet they are central to decisions communities affected by climate change make. Conceptions and responses to climate-related security are framed as another environmental forcing, and the responses have been techno-scientific and economic. Ultimately, in contravention of the idea of inclusive societies (SDG 16), religion is muted, ignored or misunderstood, thus leaving the communities that practise religion behind. So are social sciences and humanities disciplines that can study the religious dimension and open new imaginaries. Thus, this chapter argues that religion's role should be taken more into account to address such a complex problem effectively and sustainably towards peaceful and inclusive societies.

## USHERING RELIGION INTO THE CLIMATE SECURITY DISCOURSE THROUGH THE COMPLEXITY THEORY

Climate security risks are multifaceted, highly context-specific, locally experienced and contested, hence perceived and experienced differently and disproportionately. They involve various stakeholders and processes that operate across diffuse spatial and temporal scales. An effective and holistic understanding of the climate-conflict relationships thus requires acknowledging how processes and people interact in particular contexts and across particular scales (Abrahams, 2020). Accordingly, multiple realities, experiences and knowledge about climate security risks exist. This discussion is pertinent for the context of Africa, whose knowledge systems have been marginalized. Understanding and addressing climate-related security risks, thus, requires foregrounding epistemological and ontological questions from the African contexts for relevant and impactful responses. A complex theory approach can thus help to analyse, address and localize such a multifaceted problem. The complexity theory argues for 'greater acceptance of the uncertainties and complexities of conflict settings, and proposal for modesty and realism when it comes to designing external interventions, and to understand how change takes place in conflict-affected settings' (Day & Hunt, 2022). The effectiveness and legitimacy of current legislation and policy development in the face of environmental, security and climate changes in many African contexts are currently questioned because they are perceived to reflect and reproduce an ensemble of Northern stereotypes, ideologies and policy agendas (Selby, 2014).

This chapter leverages the complexity theory to allow for the combination of perspectives from Africa and outside Africa, as well as positivist and non-positivist approaches, towards inclusive policy interventions, effectiveness and legitimacy regarding climate-induced conflicts. In that vein, without dislodging positivist epistemology and quantitative methods, it foregrounds the African indigenous people as experts whose epistemologies and ontologies, represented by religion, can contribute to compelling and legitimate legislation. This chapter thus deploys it to argue that the complexity of climate security risks requires more than the techno-scientific and economic valuation but also a critical consideration of religion, which is a critical constituent element of these risks, as we have seen above, but have received less attention. A complex system 'involves constituent elements interacting together to create effects different from what each element would produce on its own' (Day & Hunt, 2022).

Ignoring, excluding or marginalizing local religion-based values often leads to socio-environmental conflicts linked to value clashes (IPBES, 2022). And when religion becomes a factor in climate-related conflicts such as cattle rustling, the conflicts assume a different texture from ordinary conflicts. The conflict ceases to be about truth and falsity but about right or wrong, which are domains of religion. Such are climate security-related risks. The interaction of socio-economic, scientific, political and cultural variables such as religion produces conflicts whose texture is often unanticipated.

Climate security risks can thus be complex and not complicated (Beaumont & de Coning, 2022; Day & Hunt, 2022). A complicated system can be fully understood and predicted when sufficient information is provided. For instance, designing, building and launching a rocket into space is highly complicated, but once it is mastered, the same process can be repeated with a reasonable degree of certainty and predictability (Beaumont & de Coning, 2022; Day & Hunt, 2022). In contrast, complex systems are non-linear and dynamic. The interactions between constituent parts are dynamic and non-linear, displaying emergent, adaptive qualities rather than input-output trajectories (Day & Hunt, 2022). This is more so when some constituent elements are different, that is non-measurable, non-quantifiable and non-controllable, like religion, within a constellation of quantifiable and measurable elements. Thus, their outcomes are emergent such that it is impossible to find general laws with which to make predictions with certainty about the outcomes themselves and how particular societies or communities will react to changes in the environment (de Coning 2020, Cillier, 2002). Failure to understand complex systems is a matter of their essence and not a result of imperfect knowledge or lack of thorough scrutiny (Beaumont and de Coning 2022). The complexity of climate security risks should not be taken to suggest that efforts to understand them are in vain or futile. Rather, it should broach the need for inclusive research that integrates marginalized dimensions of climate-related security risks, such as religion in Africa. Furthermore, it affirms that no one discipline or perspective can address such a complex phenomenon that requires multidisciplinary expertise ranging from climate science, cultural and religious studies, and gender studies to peace and conflict studies. Despite that, much of the research on climate security has been conducted in Africa (Scheffran et al., 2019). Religions ranging from missionary to indigenous religions are rife and play a significant role in people's thinking about and reacting to reality. However, disciplines, such as the critical study of religion, have not been part of the climate security discourse since its inception two decades ago. Yet they might explain what lies behind climate security motivations and experiences.

Integrating religion as a variable resonates with the observation that for a peace process to become self-sustainable, it has to be founded on the local culture, history and socio-economic context (de Coning, 2020); and de Coning's proposal for adaptive peace practice in which he invites peacekeepers, together with the communities and people affected by the conflict, to actively engage in iterative processes of learning and adaptation towards peacebuilding and think through the ethical implications of both their macro theories for resolving conflict and sustaining peace and the specific choices and actions they make in any given context. This translates to being conscious of the knowledge claims and assumptions that inform their choices and their actions' potential consequences—intended and unintended. Thus, peace practitioners are impelled to develop interventions that do not interfere so much that they end up causing harm by inadvertently disrupting the feedback loops critical for self-organization to emerge and be sustained (de Coning, 2020). Such an approach, thus, must include the 'religion' factor, which intersects with knowledge claims and assumptions as well as ethics in Africa. Overlooking religion and preferring only techno-scientific solutions might lead to initiating or exacerbating existing conflicts or a lack of social acceptability, making it challenging to mobilize communities for participation.

While techno-scientific approaches are insightful, they cannot fully explain the dynamics of the conflicts (Haberman, 2021). They also produce diverging results which require contextualization and interpretation (Gleditsch, 2012, Boas et al., 2020). They can be absorbed with identifying threats and responding to impacts and slip insistently to technological measures, despite widespread acknowledgement of their pitfalls (Adger et al., 2009; Nightingale et al., 2020; O'Brien & Selboe, 2015). Consequently, they can assume that climate change is a stressor external to society, and society and the environment are two separate, interacting domains (Nightingale et al., 2020). Climate security impacts are thus separated from human and cultural factors such as religion. Yet, religion could shed critical theoretical and practical light on why climate-induced conflicts become intense, intractable or otherwise. This often-forgotten aspect could have fundamental implications for how successful societies address conflicts induced by climate change because of the differential ways it influences attitudes and behaviour (Chester, 2005). Techno-scientific approaches have the danger of assuming that data quantifying resource scarcity can help us predict engagement or action, overlooking the fact that there is no necessary connection between resource scarcity and conflict, nor between resource abundance and peace and security (Jägerskog et al., 2014, Delli Priscoli & Wolf, 2009, Abrahams, 2020). Other factors, which also determine how natural resources are valued, such as religion can be the mediating factor between resource scarcity and conflict, and not the data about the extent of the impact of climate change.

Dominating climate change debates with only ideas from positivist and quantitative methodology results in an epistemological homogeneity that narrows the range of viewpoints and understandings of solutions to the challenges of climate change. These approaches can represent epistemic power and hierarchy through which other knowledge systems, such as those influenced by or embedded in religion, are excluded and marginalized. They can also promote the illusion that technological progress can control, fully manage and solve our problems, thereby underestimating their human and cultural dimensions (Bergmann, 2009). In the encyclical letter Laudato Si, Pope Francis

(2015: 43) foregrounds the relevance of religion by asserting that the environmental crisis is a spiritual crisis. He challenges advocates of hyper-technical responses to climate as advancing 'the myth of progress' and telling us 'that ecological problems will solve themselves simply with the application of new technology'. Using the example of the indigenous communities, he asserts that 'many intensive forms of environmental exploitation and degradation exhaust the resources which provide local communities with their livelihood and undo the social structures which, for a long time, shaped cultural identity, and their sense of the meaning of life and community.' He, thus, recommends that it is essential to show special care for indigenous communities and their cultural traditions (LS145, LS146). The current epistemological challenge is that different disciplines, like the critical study of religion, are not accorded equal opportunities to contribute to thinking about climate change challenges. Resultantly, underlying non-standard drivers of climate security risks, such as religion and spirituality, are left unattended. The Intergovernmental Panel on Climate Change (IPCC) has received criticism for allegedly numerous biases, which include favouring the natural sciences over the social sciences and humanities and western science over religion, spirituality and indigenous knowledge (Chakraborty & Sherpa, 2021). This chapter does not aim to make a false dichotomy between the technical approaches in the West and non-technical ones in Africa because climate change challenges, including peace and security risks, do not fit into such binaries. Instead, it argues that other than good infrastructure and smart technology, marginalized religio-cultural meaning systems can shape conceptualization and responses to climate peace and security risks in Africa without displacing scientific and technical approaches.

## Integrating Techno-science and Religion

This chapter argues that religion influences consumption, production choices, actions and reactions when climate and environmental-related conflicts arise. Specifically, when security risks related to climate change ensue, religion influences the actors' positions and positioning. In building alliances during conflicts over natural resources, conflicting parties mobilize religious identity to build alliances. Yet, as already intimated, climate security has been perceived as an extension of the climate change discourse, which has been the domain of natural sciences, guided by positivist epistemology. This is evident in the numerous large-N studies conducted and the numerous technologies suggested in Africa in response to climate change impacts, including climate security (Scheffran et al., 2019). Consequently, the climate security discourse has also carried over positivist epistemology and quantitative methods, whose results are presented in numbers and graphs (Meirding, 2013; see Ide, 2017, Ide & Scheffran, 2014). Religion is better examined through the lenses of social sciences and humanities disciplines, such as religious studies, which are located at the bottom (the 'weakest' type of knowledge) (see Blue 2018) but strategically positioned to engage with the context-specific local variables of problems. Techno-optimistic responses, such as smart technologies and methodologies such as statistical analysis and big data, can override the political and epistemological assumptions behind and embedded in their instruments (boyd & Crawford, 2012; Gabrys, 2016). They can focus on 'expert' knowledge and are informed by the 'device paradigm'—a belief that human-made problems can be controlled and fully managed and solved by technological progress (see Bergmann, 2009)—at the expense of local religion, spirituality or indigenous knowledge systems (Haberman, 2021). They conceptualize the natural environment as a resource—an *unenchanted material good* for human survival, subject to empirical investigation and measurement. They consider nature a set of quantifiable, physicochemical phenomena (van Koppen, 2000). Policymakers, who need evidence to formulate policies in pursuit of specific agendas and interests, have propelled the positivist epistemology and quantitative approach to addressing climate change challenges. Numbers and graphs present the immediate and arguably most convincing results. This has compromised researchers' focus on the complexity of climate crises, thus not focusing on dynamics such as religion because they do not fit the linear, positivist epistemology and quantitative methods. Consequently, there has been the risk of unreflexively foregrounding some scientific and policy approaches at the expense of other approaches (Petersen, 2000). Victims of this scenario have been non-disciplinary, expert knowledge—for example from practitioners or indigenous knowledge holders and religious practitioners (ibid).

Religion and ecology scholars have concentrated on how norms and values of specific faith traditions have contributed to pro-or anti-environment beliefs and attitudes, with the view to analysing how they can contribute to climate change mitigation and adaptation. Despite the appreciation of the need for a nuanced approach to climate security risks, the social dimensions included in the discussions are those that satisfy positivist epistemology but not fully integrating complexity lenses. What still requires further investigation is how religion shapes conflict that ensues when climate change exceeds the adaptive capacities of communities. In the name of religion, conflicts can both be ensured and solved. Religion, thus, needs to be factored into discussions about the climate security nexus for holistic lenses and a framework for thinking and addressing complex climate change challenges.

## Conclusion

Using the case of climate-related security risks, this chapter has also shown that the pursuit of SDG 13—namely climate action: taking urgent action to combat climate change and its impacts—and SDG 16—promoting peaceful and inclusive societies for sustainable development, providing access to justice for all, and building effective, accountable and inclusive institutions at all levels in Africa—cannot be undertaken from one epistemological and methodological approaches. It has demonstrated that framing climate security influences how scholars, policymakers and practitioners conceptualize and respond to the crisis. A positivist framing invokes economic and techno-scientific responses, which are essential and indispensable because they provide up-to-date information on climatic changes. However, they are inadequate. Their positivist epistemology and quantitative methods cannot analyse non-quantifiable phenomena like religion, which gives cognitive, emotional and moral guidance to religious communities. It is, thus, necessary to understand the latter because most of the communities affected by climate change and climate-related security risks in Africa are highly religious. Hence, their religious worldview influences their conceptualization and responses to climate security. So beyond factoring in religion as an important theme, the chapter calls for a multidisciplinary approach which brings in disciplines which have not been part of the climate discourses, such as the critical study of religion, for a holistic, sustainable and effective understanding and responses to climate change challenge.

**Acknowledgments** This work was carried out with support from the CGIAR Initiative on Climate Resilience, ClimBeR, and the CGIAR Initiative on Fragility, Conflict, and Migration. We would like to thank all funders who supported this research through their contributions to the CGIAR Trust Fund: https://www.cgiar.org/funders/.

## REFERENCES

Abrahams, A. (2020). Conflict in Abundance and Peacebuilding in Scarcity: Challenges and Opportunities in Addressing Climate Change and Conflict. *World Development, 132*, 2020.

Adger, W. N., Lorenzoni, I., & O'Brien, K. L. (Eds.). (2009). *Adapting to Climate Change: Thresholds, Values, Governance*. Cambridge University Press.

African Union. (2021). Communique of the 1051st meeting of the AU Peace and Security Council (PSC) held on 26 November 2021 on the theme: Climate Change and Peace and Security: The need for an Informed Climate-Security-Development nexus for Africa.

Ammerman, N. T. (2016). Lived Religion as an Emerging Field: An Assessment of its Contours and Frontiers. *Nordic Journal of Religion and Society, 29*(2), 83–99. https://doi.org/10.18261/issn.1890-7008-2016-02-01

Baechler, G. (1998). Why Environmental Transformation Causes Violence: A Synthesis. *Environmental Change and Security Project Report, 4*(1), 24–44.

Beaumont, P., & de Coning, C. (2022). Coping with Complexity: Toward Epistemological Pluralism in Climate–Conflict Scholarship. *International Studies Review, 24*(4), viac055. https://doi.org/10.1093/isr/viac055

Benjaminsen, T. A. (2016). *Does Climate Change Lead to Conflicts in the Sahel? The End of Desertification?* (pp. 99–116). Springer. https://doi.org/10.1007/978-3-642-16014-1_4

Bergmann, S. (2009). Climate Change Changes Religion. *Studia Theologica - Nordic Journal of Theology, 63*(2), 98–118.

Boas, I., Dahm, R., & Wrathall, D. (2020). Grounding Big Data on Climate-Induced Human Mobility. *Geographical Review, 110*(1-2), 195–209. https://doi.org/10.1111/gere.12355

Boyd, D., & Crawford, K. (2012). Critical Questions for Big Data. *Information, Communication & Society, 15*(5), 662–679.

Bremberg, N., Mobjörk, M., & Krampe, F. (2022). Global Responses to Climate Security: Discourses, Institutions and Actions. *Journal of Peacebuilding & Development, 17*(3), 341–356. https://doi.org/10.1177/15423166221128180

Buhaug, H. (2010). Climate not to Blame for African Civil Wars, https://doi.org/10.1073/pnas.1005739107.

Burke, M. B., Miguel, E., Satyanath, S., Dykema, J. A., & Lobell, D. B. (2009). Warming Increases the Risk of Civil War in Africa. *Proceedings of the National Academy of Sciences, 106*(49), 20670–20674.

Cabot, C. (2017). Climate Change and Farmer-herder Conflicts in West Africa. In C. Cabot (Ed.), *Climate Change, Security Risks and Conflict Reduction in Africa* (pp. 11–44). Springer.

Chakraborty, R., & Sherpa, P. Y. (2021). From Climate Adaptation to Climate Justice: Critical Reflections on the IPCC and Himalayan Climate Knowledges. *Clim Change, 167*(3-4), 49. https://doi.org/10.1007/s10584-021-03158-1

Chebunet, P. K., et al. (2013). Cultural Beliefs as a Source of Ethnic Conflicts: A Study of the Turkana and Pokot Pastoralists of Kenya. *Journal of Global Peace and Conflict, 1*(1), 01–14.

Chester, D. K. (2005). Theology and Disaster Studies: The Need for Dialogue. *Journal of Volcanology and Geothermal Research, 146*(4), 319–328.

Cillier, P. (2002). Why We Cannot Know Complex Things Completely. *Emergence, 4*(1-2), 77–84.

Collier, P., & Hoeffler, A. (1998). On Economic Causes of Civil War. *Oxford Economic Papers, 50*(4), 563–573.

Daoudy, M. (2020). The Context: History, Geography, Security. In *The Origins of the Syrian Conflict: Climate Change and Human Security* (pp. 1–100). Cambridge University Press.

Adam, Day & Charles T. Hunt (2022). A Perturbed Peace: Applying Complexity Theory to UN Peacekeeping, International Peacekeeping, DOI: https://doi.org/10.1080/13533312.2022.2158457.

Farrell, J. (2015). *The Battle for Yellowstone: Morality and the Sacred Roots of Environmental Conflict*. Princeton University Press.

Fjelde, H., & von Uexkull, N. (2012). Climate Triggers: Rainfall Anomalies, Vulnerability and Communal Conflict in Sub-Saharan Africa. *Political Geography, 31*(7), 444–453.

Francis, Pope. (2015). *Laudato Si': On Care for Our Common Home* [Encyclical]., http://w2.vatican.va/content/francesco/en/encyclicals/documents/papa-francesco_20150524_enciclica-laudato-si.html.

Gabrys, J. (2016). *Program Earth: Environmental Sensing Technology and the Making of a Computational Planet*. University of Minnesota Press.

Gifford, P. (1995). Democratization and the churches. In P. Gifford (Ed.), *The Christian Churches and the Democratization of Africa*. Brill.

Gleditsch, N. P. (2012). Whither the Weather? Climate Change and Conflict. *Journal of Peace Research, 49*(1), 3–9.

Haberman. (2021). *Understanding Climate Change through Religious Lifeworlds*. Indiana University Press.

Homer-Dixon, T. F. (1994). Environmental Scarcities and Violent Conflict: Evidence from Cases. *International Security, 19*(1), 5–40.

Homer-Dixon, T. (1999). *Environment, scarcity and violence*. Princeton University Press.
Hsiang, S., Meng, K., & Cane, M. (2011). Civil Conflicts Are Associated with the Global Climate. *Nature, 476*, 438–441. https://doi.org/10.1038/nature10311
Ide, T. (2017). Research Methods for Exploring the Links Between Climate Change and Conflict, Wiley Interdiscip. *Rev. Clim. Change, 8*, 1–14.
Ide, T., & Scheffran, J. (2014). On Climate, Conflict and Cumulation: Suggestions for Integrative Cumulation of Knowledge in the Research on Climate Change and Violent Conflict. *Global Change, Peace & Security, 26*(3), 263–279.
IPBES. (2022). Methodological Assessment Report on the Diverse Values and Valuation of Nature of the Intergovernmental Science-Policy Platform on Biodiversity and Ecosystem Services. In P. Balvanera, U. Pascual, M. Christie, B. Baptiste, & D. González-Jiménez (Eds.), *IPBES secretariat*. https://doi.org/10.5281/zenodo.6522522
Kahl, C. (2006). *States, Scarcity, and Civil Strife in the Developing World*. Princeton University Press.
Knibbe, K., & Kupari, H. (2020). Theorizing Lived Religion: Introduction. *Journal of Contemporary Religion, 35*(2), 157–176. https://doi.org/10.1080/13537903.2020.1759897
Knowles, J. G. (1992). Geopiety, the Concept of Sacred Place: Reflections on an Outdoor Education Experience. *The Journal of Experiential Education, 15*, 6–12.
van Koppen, C. S. A. K. (2000). Resource, Arcadia, Lifeworld. Nature Concepts in Environmental Sociology. *Sociologia Ruralis, 40*(3), 300–318.
Lines, K. P. (2009). *Is Turkana Cattle Raiding a Part of Turkana Ethnicity? An Anti-Essentialist View of both Internal and External Factors for Ngingoroko*. Asbury Theological Seminary, Wilmore, KY.
Lomborg, B. (2001). *The Skeptical Environmentalist: Measuring the Real State of the World*. Cambridge University Press.
Magesa, L. (1997). *African Religion: The Moral Traditions of Abundant Life*. Orbis Books.
Maingay, Y., et al. (2022). The Impacts of Increasing Water Scarcity and the Potential for Water-related Conflict in Lamu, Kenya. *Water Supply, 22*(2), 1983–1994.
Medina, L., et al. (2022). *Towards a Common Vision of Climate Security in Kenya*. CGIAR Climate Security Focus.
Nightingale, A. J., et al. (2020). Beyond Technical Fixes: Climate Solutions and the Great Derangement. *Climate and Development, 12*(4), 343–352.
O'Brien, K., & Selboe, E. (2015). *The Adaptive Challenge of Climate Change*. Cambridge University Press.
Okunade, A. O. (2022). The Role of Women in African Traditional Religion. In I. S. Aderibigbe & T. Falola (Eds.), *The Palgrave Handbook of African Traditional Religion*. Palgrave Macmillan.
Peters, K., & Vivekananda, J. (2014). *Topic guide: conflict, climate and environment. Evidence on demand*. Department for International Development.
Petersen, A. C. (2000). Philosophy of climate science. *Bulletin of the American Meteorological Society, 81*(2), 265–271.
Raleigh, C. (2010). Political Marginalization, Climate Change and Conflict in African Sahel States. *International Studies Review, 12*(1), 69–86.
Raleigh, C., & Kniveton, D. (2012). Come Rain or Shine: An Analysis of Conflict and Climate Variability in East Africa. *Journal of Peace Research, 49*(1), 51–64.

Romsdahl, R., Blue, G., & Kirilenko, A. (2018). Action on Climate Change Requires Deliberative Framing at the Local Governance Level. *Climatic Change, 149*, 277–287.

Savelli A., Schapendonk F., Sarzana C., Dutta Gupta T., Caroli G., Duffy M., de Brauw A., Thornton P., Pacillo G., & Läderach P. (2022). The Climate Security-Mobility Nexus: Impact Pathways and Research Priorities. Position Paper No. 2022/2. CGIAR FOCUS Climate Security. Available at: https://cgspace.cgiar.org/handle/10568/117589.

Schaar, J. (2018). *The Relationship Between Climate Change and Violent Conflict*. Sida. (https://cdn.sida.se/app/uploads/2020/12/01105650/working-paper-climate-change-andconflict.pdf)

Scheffran, J., Link, M. P., & Schilling, K. (2019). 'Climate and Conflict in Africa', in Oxford Research Encyclopaedia of Climate Science, https://doi.org/10.1093/acrefore/9780190228620.013.557.

Schoderer, M., & Ott, M. (2022). Contested Water- and Miningscapes – Explaining the High Intensity of Water and Mining Conflicts in a Meta-study. *World Development, 154(C)*, 1.

Selby, J. (2003). *Water, Power and Politics in the Middle East: The Other Israeli–Palestinian Conflict*. I.B. Tauris & Co Ltd.

Selby, J. (2014). Positivist Climate Conflict Research: A Critique. *Geopolitics, 19*(4), 829–856.

Selby, J., Daoust, G., & Hoffman, C. (2022). *Divided Environments: An International Political Ecology of Climate Change*. Cambridge University Press.

Spillmann, K. R., & Bächler, B. (Eds.). (1995). *Environmental Crisis: Regional Conflicts and Ways of Cooperation*. Bern.

Tarusarira, J. (2017). African Religion, Climate Change and Knowledge Systems. *The Ecumenical Review, 69*(3), 398–410.

Theisen, O. M. (2017). Climate Change and Violence: Insights from Political Science. *Current Climate Change Reports, 3*(4), 210–221.

Theisen, O. M., Holtermann, H., & Buhaug, H. (2012). Climate Wars? Assessing the Claim that Drought Breeds Conflict. *International Security, 36*(3), 79–106.

Van Baalen, S., & Mobjörk, M. (2018). Climate Change and Violent Conflict in East Africa: Integrating Qualitative and Quantitative Research to Probe the Mechanisms. *International Studies Review, 20*(4), 547–575.

PART II

# Country Case Studies on Religion, Peacebuilding and Development in Africa

CHAPTER 9

# Religion, Conflict and Peacebuilding in Rwanda

*Ezechiel Sentama*

## Introduction

Rwanda has experienced a troubled history in the colonial and post-colonial periods, in which ethnicity and politics have always been wound tightly together. Power struggle, resentment and hatred between the Hutu and Tutsi identity groups (further discussed below) erupted in cyclical episodes of violence and a four-year-long deadly civil war (1990–1994) between the Hutu government of Juvénal Habyarimana and the Tutsi Rwandan Patriotic Front (RPF) rebel group led by Paul Kagame, which climaxed in one of the most brutal and devastating genocides in history, April–July 1994. The genocide targeted mainly the Tutsi who were living in the country but also the Hutu from the opposition, as well as those who opposed the genocide, refused to participate in the slaughter or protected the targeted Tutsi. It is estimated that around one million people were killed (NURC, 2009, 2015; Sentama, 2022).

Yet Rwandans, notably Hutu and Tutsi, had always been reputed to be religious and loyal to God for so long. Both Hutu and Tutsi were predominantly Christian, as over 90% of the Rwandan population claimed to be of the Christian faith (Longman, 2001; Haworth, 2018). This thus begs the question of *the role of religion, notably the Christian Church—both in its institutionalized forms as churches and in its intellectual forms as theology—in Rwanda's conflict history and the 1994 genocide.*

E. Sentama (✉)
Centre for Trust, Peace and Social Relations, Institute for Peace and Security, Coventry University, Coventry, UK
e-mail: ad3464@coventry.ac.uk

The 1994 genocide ended with the victory of the Tutsi-led RPF. The victory of the RPF and its seizing of power, in July 1994, had nothing to celebrate since the civil war and genocide had profoundly destroyed the socio-economic and political fabric of Rwanda. The civil war and genocide had left a deeply divided and traumatized society and a country that had acquired a status of a failed state. How to rebuild the fabric of such a devastated, divided and traumatized society became the pressing task of the post-genocide new government led by the RPF (NURC, 2009; Sentama, 2022). At the time of writing this chapter, twenty-eight years have now elapsed since Rwanda, headed by the RPF, embarked on the journey to recovery, the promotion of peace and justice, national unity and reconciliation, and socio-economic reconstruction to which state and non-state actors are called to contribute. This begs another question of the *role of religion, as one of these actors, in the post-genocide peacebuilding* mission of the new government led by the victorious RPF.

Although peacebuilding remains a complex concept that is difficult to define, this chapter understands it broadly as an umbrella that encompasses both long- and short-term transformative efforts, which point to the entire conflict cycle involving conflict escalation and de-escalation. In this encompassing and broad view, peacebuilding includes, among other things, early warning and response efforts, violence prevention, advocacy work, ceasefire agreements, humanitarian assistance, socio-economic development and reconciliation. This points to the work against both physical and structural/cultural violence towards peacebuilding at the personal (healing), relational, structural and cultural dimensions (Lederach, 1997; Lambourne, 2004; Ramsbotham et al., 2005). These strategies are indeed in line with the current Sustainable Development Goal 16, namely promoting peaceful and inclusive societies, which this chapter hopes to inform.

This chapter is guided by the above-highlighted two interrogations about the role of religion in Rwanda's conflict history and post-conflict peacebuilding, and aims to provide *a contextual analysis of Rwanda's experience with the nexus of religion, conflict and peacebuilding* by answering the following three questions:

1. What has been the role of religion in Rwanda's conflict history?
2. What has been the role of religion in Rwanda's peacebuilding processes during the civil war and genocide, and in their aftermath to the present?
3. How can we make sense of the nexus of religion and conflict and peacebuilding in Rwanda and what lessons can be learnt?

In addressing these three questions, a historical perspective is paramount. After a brief history of Rwanda's conflict, the first section discusses religion in relation to Rwanda's conflict history. It focuses on the periods before, during and after colonization, as well as during the period of the four-year-long civil war (1990–1994), and the 1994 genocide. The second section is about the contribution of religion to peacebuilding, both during the civil war and genocide, as well as in their aftermath to the present. The chapter shows the two faces of religion in Rwanda's history, namely as having both the potential for violent conflicts and peace, with the overall aim of advancing its institutional agenda. This is in agreement with Banyanga and Bjöekqvist (2017) whose study that focused solely on the genocide also depicted the dual role of religion, as both instigator and healer.

By discussing religion in Rwanda, this chapter will restrict its focus to Christian churches (often referred to as "the Church"), particularly the Roman Catholic Church for two reasons: firstly, over the years, the Christian Church (particularly the Roman Catholic) has always been the largest and strongest institution in Rwanda (Longman, 2001, 2010). Since the arrival of colonial Christian missionaries (the Roman Catholic in 1900 and Protestants in 1907), almost all Rwandans converted to Christianity. In post-colonial Rwanda, as it was in most of the independent African countries, the first generation of political leadership was Christian, commonly the product of Christian mission schools, and these pioneers were often active church members in their own right (Haworth, 2018). Consequently, before the 1990–1994 civil war and ensuing 1994 genocide, around 90% of the Rwandan population considered itself Christian, with 62.6% Roman Catholics and 27.2% Protestants. Muslims composed only 1.2% of the population (Grant, 2018, p. 38). Secondly, in the aftershock of the 1994 genocide, many questioned the role of Christian churches and attempted to fathom the association of Rwanda's Christian churches with the genocide. As a consequence, the Christian churches faced numerous criticisms from diverse fronts and have been repeatedly blamed for culpability in the violence that occurred during the genocide (Longman, 2010).

In terms of methodology, the chapter took a historical perspective. The process of data collection relied on document analysis, as well as the author's own research projects on peacebuilding since the end of the genocide. Besides the author's academic research projects, the chapter also relied on the author's various research projects carried out on behalf of the National Unity and Reconciliation Commission (NURC) and civil society organizations in Rwanda, particularly between 2010 and 2016. The document analysis process involved a careful examination of relevant documents on peacebuilding in Rwanda. Relevant materials included policy and legal documents, country programmes, strategies and annual reports, evaluation reports, as well as other research reports including peer-reviewed publications. The fact that the author is a native of Rwanda constituted an added value and was addressed in a way that refrained from using personal experience and identity to influence the study process.

## The Historical Context of the Conflict and Genocide in Rwanda

The history of Rwanda speaks much about centuries of a community commingling three identity groups of people in the pre-colonial period: the Hutu (85%), the Tutsi (14%) and the Twa (1%) (Uvin, 2003; Sentama, 2022). Before colonization, these identities were described in Rwanda as flexible social categories and occupational designations, rather than ethnic groups. Cow breeders were considered "Tutsi", farmers were called "Hutu", while the "Twa" were potters and hunter-gatherers (Sentama, 2022). Nevertheless, there was a form of stratification with a dominant ruling class (minority Tutsi) over a bonded labour class (majority Hutu) for centuries, under a monarchical system. The Twa group was marginalized by both Tutsi and Hutu and has, thus, never been part of the conflict and power struggle (King, 2014, p. 39).

At the Berlin Conference of 1884/1885, Rwanda and Burundi were allocated to Germany as part of German East Africa. Germany colonized Rwanda in 1885, but following World War I the colony became a trustee territory of Belgium. The colonialists and Christian missionaries coveted the idea of eventually bringing Rwanda under their colonial yoke and exploiting the already existing Hutu-Tutsi stratification. Colonial powers exacerbated the tension and polarization between the Hutu and Tutsi when they solidified the boundaries between the different social groups. Through indirect rule, this strategy employed a theory of superior and inferior races—the European *"Hamitic" Hypothesis*.[1] It hardened Hutu-Tutsi identities and racial distinction by viewing Tutsi as Hamitic, closest to the Europeans, intelligent and naturally superior to the Hutu. In the early colonial period, colonizers decisively characterized Tutsi as superior foreigners. In particular, the Belgian colonizers (1916–1962) created structural changes in the relationship between the Hutu and Tutsi that greatly enhanced the Tutsi dominance and the Hutu exploitation. Belgian authorities introduced a political reform and appointed almost exclusively Tutsi as district chiefs. While this policy already heightened the distinction between Hutu and Tutsi, the introduction of identity cards according to ethnic groups in the 1930s cemented it as it made them fixed racial/ethnic categories. The Belgian divide-and-rule policy was also institutionally implemented through Tutsi favouritism in both employment and education (Shyaka, 2002, p. 129; Obura, 2003, p. 103).

The situation changed in the 1950s when the Hutu rose to overthrow the Tutsi monarchy. Having observed the Hutu determination towards political change, coupled with the wave of movements claiming independence in Africa, the Belgian administration gave up on the Tutsi-ruling elite and, in a policy turnaround, supported the Hutu "majority". In 1959, the Hutu rebelled against the Tutsi monarchy through a "social revolution", which culminated in

---

[1] All about the "Hamitic Hypothesis", see Eltringham (2006), Berkeley (2001, p. 2581), Uvin (1998, pp. 30–31), Gourevitch (2000, pp. 50–53), Peterson (2000, pp. 258–59).

all the Tutsi elites who were in positions of power being pushed out of power. The Tutsi monarchy was abolished and a wave of Tutsi elites found their way into exile (Staub, 2003).

At the time of independence from colonial rule in 1962, Rwanda was an ethnically divided state (Haworth, 2018), this time under the Hutu leadership. The Hutu's successive two governments maintained the ethnic identity system instituted by the colonial administration and initiated a policy of discrimination against the minority Tutsi who had remained in the country in retaliation for the years of subjugation under colonial-Tutsi rule (Sentama, 2022).

On 1 October 1990, the exiled Tutsi and their descendants, who had formed the Rwandan Patriotic Front (RPF), invaded Rwanda from Uganda, which revived the Hutu memories of past periods of exploitation and subjugation under Tutsi domination and culminated in the three-month genocide, April–July 1994. The genocide claimed more than 1 million lives. The civil war ended with the victory of the RPF, a situation which also put an end to the genocide. The Tutsi-dominated RPF established a new government on 19 July 1994 and was leading the country, at the time of writing, under the presidency of Paul Kagame (Sentama, 2022).

The post-genocide new government was thus faced with the overall challenge of reconstructing the country's socio-economic and political fabric from scratch and bringing about peace, justice, national unity and reconciliation. On a national level, Rwanda's "National Unity and Reconciliation Commission" (NURC) was created in 1999 and policies, as well as projects for socio-economic recovery and sustainable development, were formulated. A law No 47/2001 of 18 December 2001 instituting the punishment for offences of discrimination and sectarianism was passed to ban the use of the ethnic descriptions "Tutsi", "Hutu", and "Twa". On the judicial level, Rwanda turned to its traditional judicial courts, Gacaca—an official form of the restorative and community-based justice system that aimed to reveal the truth about the genocide, speed up trials and reconcile Rwandans (NURC, 2010).

## Religion and Conflict in Rwanda

This section discusses the role of religion in Rwanda's conflict history, notably the Christian religion during and after the colonial period, in which the role of the Roman Catholic Church dominates the discussions as a strong and large institution. It is worth emphasizing that in pre-colonial Rwanda, traditional religion was practised, although there were neither temples nor communal cults for worship. Rwandans believed in the existence of a supreme, powerful, immaterial, benevolent, omnipotent and omnipresent being called "Imana" or God. Traditional religion was a unifying factor. The King was considered a national priest who links the spirit of ancestors and the divine world (Gatwa, 2014).

### Christian Religion and Conflict During the Colonial Period

Religion in Rwanda's colonial period (1900–1962) began with the process of seeking the eradication of traditional religious conceptions of God and Christianizing Rwanda. It is upon the arrival of *Le Pères Blancs* ("White Fathers")—the European French Catholic missionaries—in 1900 that this process of seeking the eradication of the traditional religion began (Haworth, 2018). Although the quest to eliminate completely traditional religion was not successful, it was heavily weakened and almost lost entirely its meaning and active practice.

When the first Catholic missionaries arrived in Rwanda in 1900, they determined to focus on converting the country's elite, believing that if the country's leaders converted to Catholicism, the rest of the population would follow. For example, when King Musinga resisted conversion, he was deposed and his son Mutara III Rudahigwa, a devout Catholic, was appointed as his successor. The masses eventually followed when their King, Rudahigwa, was baptized in 1943 (Grant, 2018, pp. 38–39). Cardinal Charles Martial Allemand-Lavigérie was the leader of this top-down vision of evangelization. Thus, "there was a perfect relationship between Church and State" (Katongole, 2005a).

Claiming to be "agents of Christian civilization" (Haworth, 2018), Catholic missionaries also interpreted power relations in Rwanda largely in ethnic terms, viewing the Tutsi minority as a racially superior group that naturally dominated the subservient Hutu majority and small Twa group, and they focused their conversion efforts on the Tutsi (Longman, 2018). In this strategy, the Catholic missionaries established the Church as a close ally of the colonial administration and the Tutsi-dominated royal court/elites. Ethnicity was a crucial factor in the Church's mission strategy in order to determine the elite and target them for conversion. The missionaries based their vision and activities on the concepts of nineteenth-century explorers and anthropologists, such as John Hanning Speke and James Augustus Grant, who racialized the Hutu-Tutsi-Twa distinction and stratification by helping propagate the previously discussed colonial "Hamitic" Hypothesis (Haworth, 2018; Mamdani, 2001). For example, in 1902, Monsignor Léon-Paul-Classe—the most important Catholic leader of his generation who served as Vicar Apostolic of Rwanda between 1922 and 1945—echoed Lavigérie's pedagogy of evangelization by stating that "the Batutsi are superb men, with straightforward and regular features, with something of the Aryan and Semitic type" (Gatwa, 2000, p. 6). Similarly, in 1948, Father Alexandre Arnoux, in his book, *Les Pères Blancs aux Sources du Nil* (The White Father at the Sources of the Nile), posited that "Obviously, the Batutsi who are related to the Abyssinians, arrived a long time ago after the other races. Those among them who descended from the nomadic root are recognizable by their Semitic features, height and other physical details" (Gatwa, 2000, p. 6). Here, "physical anthropology was called on to justify the [colonial] theories of difference" present in Church politics (Gatwa, 2000, p. 6).

The Church's implementation of the Hamitic Hypothesis is not only best expressed via the interwoven relationship between church and state but also through the institutionalization of mission schools (Carney, 2012a, 2012b; Gatwa, 2000; Longman, 2001; van't Spijker, 1997). Based on the "Hamitic" Hypothesis, both the colonialists and missionaries gave education and employment opportunities almost exclusively to the Tutsi. The Hutu-Tutsi stratification thus grew inside the Christian churches as church affiliation was oftentimes a way to achieve political power and socio-economic opportunities. This was most evident in the area of schooling, a pastoral priority that Monsignor Classe saw as essential to determining whether the leadership elite will be for (to the benefit of) the Church or not. A 1927 excerpt by Léon Classe, quoted by Carney, contends that: "The question is whether the ruling elite will be for or against us, whether the important places in native society will be in Catholic or non-Catholic hands; whether the Church will have through education, and its formation of youth, the preponderant influence in Rwanda" (Carney, 2012b, p. 85).

It was in the 1920s that Monsignor Léon Classe introduced a two-tiered educational system. Whereas Hutu and Tutsi had been educated together in the early years of Catholic missions, students were segregated by ethnic group, and Tutsi received a far more rigorous course than their Hutu colleagues (Carney, 2012b). This helped ensure that only Tutsi qualified for the most influential positions in the colonial administration. In Léon Classe's view, Hutu children should receive an education, but it should be an education suited to those who "would have places to take in mines and farming" (Carney, 2012b, pp. 179–180).

One of the research participants, in a study on *National Reconciliation in Rwanda: Experiences and Lessons Learnt* (Sentama, 2022), contended that being educated and possibly sponsored in a church school was often the only chance of gaining social status and escaping the spiral of poverty. The hierarchy within the Church was thus mirrored in society through the construction of hegemony. Much power was concentrated in the hands of a few deciding who would get hired and fired and receive financial or practical aid. Even when the churches' policy changed from privileging Tutsi to favouring Hutu after 1959, as discussed below, the underlying structures remained in place. With the Church being the main source of practical help and opportunities, dependants had little choice but to consent to its policies. This was a problem not only in the Catholic Church but also in Protestant denominations that had sprung up since 1907 and, later on, the Presbyterian Church (Schliesser, 2016; Longman, 2010).

After World War II, in the 1950s, as ideas of social justice and political independence spread across Africa, the unequal relations between Hutu and Tutsi came into question in Rwanda. Catholic clergy and laypeople were key to Hutu efforts to argue for greater rights and helped to inspire a 1959 uprising against Tutsi chiefs that led to a transfer of power (Longman, 2018). As Carney notes, "missionaries and indigenous Catholic journalists exhorted Catholics to join and shape Rwanda's evolving 'march for progress'" (Carney, 2012a, p. 184). For example, in 1957, Fathers Dejemeppe and Ernotte were the ones who guided the Hutu elite to write and publish "The Bahutu Manifesto", which demanded, "the retention of 'ethnic designation in official documents'" (Safari, 2010, p. 877). Riot recounts the educational practices propagated by the Church in its switch from Tutsi to Hutu political support. Riot states: "At the beginning of the 1950s, bishops in Rwanda made the decision to strengthen the structures of the Catholic movement", opting for the *Xaveri* Movement formula (Riot, 2015, p. 941). Riot suggests that this movement "played a key role in the social and cultural transformation of the educated [Hutu] youth", for it was "based on a culturalist and racial fantasy, essentializing socio-economic, cultural, and political structures which existed just before colonization" (Riot, 2015, pp. 943, 947).

### *Christian Religion in the Post-colonial Period (1962–1994)*

Although Rwandan politics and the structures of ethnic power were upended by the 1959 revolution, the churches were able to establish a close relationship with the post-colonial regime swiftly. At the time of independence in 1962, Rwanda was an institutionally and ethnically divided state (Mamdani, 2001). Grégoire Kayibanda, the president of the Republic between 1962 and 1973, "associated the church's civilizing mission with the Catholic obligation to protect the common good and defend Rwanda's status as a bulwark of African Christianity … 'baptising the structures and institutions' of Rwanda'" so as to provide a "basis for the further evolution of Rwandan society" (Mamdani, 2001, p. 104; Carney, 2012a, p. 183). This was the continuation of the secularization of religion, which had started in the 1950s, and with the arrival of the new post-World War II generation of missionaries in the 1940s (Haworth, 2018). President Kayibanda sought popular legitimacy as an advocate for the Hutu majority, and massacres of Tutsi took place in the first years of his rule. Rwanda's Christian churches remained silent in the face of these attacks on civilians (Longman, 2018).

When President Kayibanda was deposed in a 1973 coup by his Defence Minister Juvénal Habyarimana, churches were again swift to develop close ties with the new regime. Both Catholic and Anglican churches began to promote Hutu bishops from President Habyarimana's region in an effort to strengthen ties with the new leadership. To name but one notorious example of this intimacy between religious and political power, under the Habyarimana regime, Vincent Nsengiyumva, the archbishop of Kigali, was an active committee member of Habyarimana's ruling political party, the Mouvement Révolutionnaire National pour le Dévéloppement (MRND); translated as 'The National Revolutionary Movement for Development' (Schliesser, 2016).

In 1990, when the Tutsi Rwandese Patriotic Front (RPF) invaded Rwanda, the Church institution had not openly spoken out against the anti-Tutsi violence (between 1962 and 1993) and the growing propaganda being broadcast throughout the country. On the contrary, it displayed its own anti-Tutsi prejudices. Some leaders of the Church continued to call for support of the regime in a time of war, which was interpreted by the public as an endorsement of the anti-Tutsi message. Rwandan Christians came to believe that organizing to defend against potential Tutsi treachery was consistent with well-established Church practice (Longman, 2001, p. 180). When a series of small-scale massacres of Tutsi heightened ethnic polarization and normalized ethnic violence in the country, some church leaders played a role in promoting peace talks and called for all sides to show respect (as discussed later), but the Church as an institution failed to specifically call out human rights abuses, even when church personnel were targeted in attacks (Longman, 200).

### *Christian Religion During the 1994 Genocide*

During the 1994 genocide, some religious leaders and officials participated in the killings, and churches and parishes became "Rwanda's primary killing fields" (Longman, 2010, p. 4; Grant, 2018, p. 38). According to African Rights, "more Rwandese died in churches and parishes than anywhere else" during the 1994 genocide (African Rights in Haworth, 2018). Yet, as put previously, in 1994 it was estimated that 90% of the Rwandan population was Christian. Given the history of strong church support for the regime, the long-standing practice of ethnic discrimination in the churches and the failure of church leaders to condemn ethnic violence, both in the early independence era and since 1990, many Rwandans understood anti-Tutsi violence as something their churches tolerated (Longman, 2018).

Longman contends that "if churches became implicated in Rwanda's genocide, it was not simply because church leaders hoped to avoid opposing their governmental allies but because the ethnic conflict was an integral part of Christianity in Rwanda. Christians could kill without obvious qualms of conscience ... because Christianity as they had always known it had been a religion defined by struggles for power" (Longman, 2001, p. 164). National church leaders did not thus speak out against the violence while it was taking place, and instead, some officials and politicians claimed that the killings "met with God's favour" (Grant, 2018, p. 38).

### *Christian Religion in the Post-Genocide Period*

In the years immediately following the genocide, Rwanda's Christian churches were slow to take up the issue of peacebuilding. The churches were initially in a rebuilding mode, literally repairing their buildings while seeking as well to reconstruct congregations that had lost many members to death and many more to exile. The ranks of the clergy were devastated, as many pastors, priests, brothers and nuns were either killed in the genocide or in exile outside the country, some of them under the cloud of complicity in the genocide.

The Rwandan Patriotic Front (RPF), which had defeated the Hutu government and took power in July 1994, also regarded the mainline churches with suspicion and was particularly hostile towards the Christian churches, notably the Catholic Church, which it accused of colluding with the Hutu government (Grant, 2018, p. 39). Even the Catholic Church of Rwanda's recent apology in November 2016 for its members' involvement in the genocide did not produce approval from the Rwandan government. The current leadership, at the time of writing, under President Paul Kagame, as Vice President in 1994 and as President since 2000, questioned why the global Catholic Church has not apologized.

While the RPF's hostile stance towards the Catholic Church limited its role and power in the post-genocide period, it also created new possibilities for other Christian religious agents (Grant, 2018, p. 39). Following the RPF's seizing of power, hundreds of thousands of exiled Tutsi began returning to Rwanda from Uganda, Burundi, the Democratic Republic of Congo, Kenya and Tanzania. Amid this flood of Tutsi returnees were young "Pentecost" (*Abarokore*) pastors, who began founding new Christian churches and ministries. The arrival of these new churches in Rwanda has been described as an "explosion" and an "onslaught", attesting to the speed of their growth and their tendency to hold loud, often all-night prayer vigils.

In the post-genocide period, the new Pentecostal churches thus also quickly capitalized on this moment of relative openness to plant churches in the capital and elsewhere (Grant, 2018, pp. 39–40). While there have been substantial shifts within the institutionalized Christian faith, the overall adherence to Christianity has remained stable and strong at 90% of the population. As Anne Kubai points out, "religion has been and continues to be part of Rwanda's system of meaning-making and meaning-interpretation, and hence has contributed to shaping new values, demands of propriety and interpretations of old norms that have emerged after the genocide" (Kubai, 2016, p. 3). The RPF also realized the need for support from religious institutions in its peacebuilding strategies.

## Religion and Peacebuilding in Rwanda

Religion, particularly the Christian churches, has assumed a crucial role in all processes that affected and are still affecting Rwandan society. History records and accounts about the role of the Christian religion, notably the Christian Church, in peacebuilding in Rwanda indicate that it has generally been seldom during the colonial period. This thus accords them high significance, particularly in the country's peacebuilding process, since the 1990–1994 civil war and particularly in the aftermath of the 1994 genocide.

## Christian Religion and Peacebuilding After Rwanda's Independence Until 1990

Opposing the state's structural violence, although seldom, was one of the few peacebuilding initiatives of the Christian religion since Rwanda's accession to independence. For example, in 1966, the government of Kayibanda (1962–1973) nationalized all educational institutions in Rwanda under the condition that the state would be responsible for the "recruitment, promotion, and dismissal of students and staff, both lay and religious" (Safari, 2010, p. 879). Fearing the seizure of parochial schools, a secularized educational curriculum, the bishops of Rwanda issued an unequivocal condemnation of the government of Kayibanda and his party, stating: "If there are social problems to be resolved, and there is no lack of them, let those who are in charge, and not individuals and anonymous groups, do so by means of dialogue" (Safari, 2010, p. 879). In response to this statement, the government of Kayibanda "sacked the Tutsi Monsignor Matthieu from his position as Rector of the seminary of Nyundo and replaced him with a Hutu soldier, Major Alex Kanyarengwe" (Safari, 2010, p. 879). However, historical records do not indicate any role of religion in the thwarted 1993 Arusha Peace Accords/Agreements between the then government and the RPF rebel group.

## Religion and Peacebuilding During the 1990–1994 Civil War and 1994 Genocide

One prominent effort for de-escalation and peace was the Christian Church's ecumenical initiative, which was manifested through the creation of the so-called *Contact Committee* in the middle of the civil war, in 1991, with the aim of promoting peace and de-escalating violence. The Committee was created by ten Protestant and Catholic Church leaders even though "the collaboration between Protestants and Catholics was rather limited at the time" (van't Spijker, 1997, p. 244). It was meant to provide a platform for mediation between the different political parties, especially between the Hutu government and the Tutsi rebels of the RPF, encouraging democratization and political reconciliation (Gatwa, 2005, pp. 206–208).

The *Contact Committee* also supported the meeting of the All Africa Conference of Churches (AACC) in Mombasa, Kenya, in November 1993. Not only did South African Archbishop Desmond Tutu issue an urgent call for peace during this meeting, but it also provided a platform for talks between the Rwandan government and the RPF. While the *Contact Committee* could ultimately not prevent the 1994 genocide, it helped facilitate the transition to a multiparty system. On the eve of the genocide, on 1 January 1994, the *Contact Committee* organized a peace march for all Christians across denominations. Thousands of Christians marched and prayed for peace in Rwanda's capital, Kigali, and other cities throughout the country.

Next to these ecumenical endeavours, two particular church efforts for peace ought to be mentioned. In December 1991, Thaddée Nsengiyumva—Bishop of Kabgayi and President of the Rwandan Episcopal Conference—issued the pastoral letter *Convertissons-nous pour vivre ensemble dans la paix*, translated as "Let us convert to live together in peace". The pastoral letter was both a call for the Church to acknowledge its own responsibility in creating and sustaining ethnic divisions and a call for renewal within the Church. During the genocide, Bishop Nsengiyumva also supported the International Committee of the Red Cross (ICRC) in helping war displaced in his bishopric as he repeatedly made public appeals for the killings to stop. He was murdered on 5 June 1994 (NURC, 2015; Grant, 2018).

Another peace initiative was undertaken by the Presbyterian Church through their booklet *Ukuri kubaka igihugu* ("A Constructive Truth", translated literally as "Truth Builds a Country"), issued in February 1992. In the booklet, the Presbyterian Church called for a strong stance against the ethnic strife that was being experienced then. At the same time, the Church acknowledged its own failures in not speaking out clearly enough against the ethnic violence since 1959. The booklet called on all Christians to act responsibly and in accordance with the Gospel of Love with regard to issues such as human rights, ethnicity and refugee protection. Furthermore, one needs to mention that it was Pope John Paul II who, during a general audience on 27 April 1994, was the first to publicly call the ethnic violence in Rwanda a genocide and demand for it to stop (Grant, 2018). Other Christian laypeople have also been very active in human rights organizations, challenging political leaders, and organizing marches for peace at the beginning of 1994 (Gatwa, 2005).

### *Religion and Peacebuilding After the 1994 Genocide*

After the civil war and genocide in 1994, the joint efforts and cooperation of all were required if the country were to rise out of the ashes and reach out towards development and sustainable peace. The post-genocide new government, headed by the victorious Tutsi-led RPF, decreed a policy of national unity and reconciliation, which lies within the wider perspective of post-conflict reconstruction, the promotion of justice and peace. The churches were ultimately pushed to begin to focus on reconciliation and socio-economic recovery after the government adopted reconciliation and national unity as major priorities (Longman, 2018).

This policy coincided with the rise and mushrooming of the new Christian churches, notably the Pentecostal movement. Although the Catholic Church retains its dominant position, these Pentecostal churches attracted new members because they claimed to offer something "new". Since young returnees had started the vast majority of these new churches, they were viewed as less "tainted" than the mainline churches, and they capitalized on Rwandans' disillusionment with institutional religion. In a context of spiritual and political upheaval, the new Pentecostal churches offered converts an intimate relationship with God and the possibility of personal transformation/healing (Grant, 2018, pp. 40–42).

Building on the Christian tradition of confession, the churches played a major role in encouraging confession in the transitional justice processes, such as the Gacaca courts. Confession was particularly important among Pentecostals, who integrated Gacaca confessions into the process of spiritual rebirth required for conversion. As a number of scholars have documented (see, e.g. Schliesser, 2018; Grant, 2018; Katongole & Wilson-Hartgrove, 2009; Katongole, 2017; van't Spijker, 2017; Gatwa, 2005; Carney, 2015; van Butselaar, 2002), Rwanda's Christian churches—both old and new—have established a wide range of reconciliation programmes. For example, the Catholic Church established Peace and Justice Commissions. However, only in 2016 did the Rwandan Catholic Bishop Conference issue the "Announcement Which Closes the Jubilee Year of God's Mercy", asking for forgiveness for the role that some of its members had played during the 1994 genocide. The Bishop's Announcement refused, however, to address any institutional guilt but rather saw only individual members of the Church implicated. A few months later, in March 2017, Pope Francis surpassed the Bishop's Announcement by accepting both individual and institutional guilt as he asked for forgiveness for the sins and failings of the Church and its members (Grant, 2018).

Protestant churches have similarly developed numerous local-level reconciliation and peace initiatives but have lacked comprehensive national programmes. The two major Protestant ecumenical groups, the Protestant Council of Rwanda, whose members include most of the mainline churches, but also the Pentecost Church Associations, known under 'The Association Des Eglises de Pentêcote au Rwanda' (ADEPR), and the Evangelical Alliance of Rwanda (EAR) (an umbrella body for many of Rwanda's new churches), have each sponsored seminars and small-scale activities focused on reconciliation, as have most of the major denominations and international Protestant groups like World Vision and Church World Service. The EAR, for example, formed the Collective of Peace and Reconciliation Builders (CAPR), which has trained both pastors and lay leaders in peacemaking, but the scope of the programme remains modest. The Lutheran Church of Rwanda has organized its own reconciliation seminars, to create a safe space where, for example, a survivor and a released perpetrator may learn about Christian reconciliation together, and begin the process of rebuilding their relationships in an environment in which they feel comfortable, a church, as well as a prison ministry and other programmes, but again the scope of the programmes is limited. The Presbyterian Church of Rwanda (EPR) has a national commission for unity, reconciliation and genocide prevention (Nsengimana, 2015, p. 82). The EPR was in fact the first religious institution that issued the first official confession of guilt—the so-called Confession of Detmold of 1996 (Confession of Detmold), which is the theological and moral foundation of the EPR's engagement in the reconciliation process. This "theology of reconciliation" (see, e.g. Schliesser, "From a 'Theology of Genocide' to a 'Theology of Reconciliation'" 2018) consists of different theoretical and practical aspects, encompassing the dimensions of theology, institutions, relationships and remembrance. For twenty-eight years, it would remain the sole public confession of a church.

## Discussion: Learning from Rwanda's Conflict and Peacebuilding Experience

The above findings reveal two faces of the Christian religion in Rwanda's conflict history and as a political institution: on the one hand, the role of the Christian religion in driving the ethnopolitical conflict in Rwanda; on the other hand, the role of religion as an actor in peacebuilding processes. The findings are generally in agreement with Banyanga and Bjöekqvist (2017) whose study also concluded on the dual role of religion, as both instigator and healer although their study was restricted to the 1994 genocide.

This study's findings indicated that from Christianity's arrival in Rwanda, the religion was distinguished by two key principles: a cosy relationship between church and state, and a practice of playing ethnic politics. During and after the colonial period, the Christian religion in Rwanda contributed heavily to the conflict and antagonism between the Hutu and Tutsi identity groups. In agreement with Longman (2010), a fundamental role performed by the Christian missionaries in driving Rwanda's ethnopolitical conflict was to ally actively with the colonial and post-colonial states' ethnic and divisive policies and thus set the grounds for the racial framework within which the 1990–1994 deadly civil war and the 1994 genocide occurred. By openly supporting the political regime and legitimizing ethnic discrimination, the Church was crucial in rendering the action of the Tutsi monarchy during the colonial period and then of the Hutu governments after colonization morally justifiable. However, while it is true that the Catholic missionaries invoked Hamitic or tribalist language in describing Hutu and Tutsi identities and utilized the Hamitic language, they were far more concerned with protecting the Catholic institutional interests than instituting a racialist apartheid system within the Church or society.

In agreement with Katongole (2017), it appears that while the Church had failed to question the socially constructed identities (successively named races and ethnicities), during colonization, the Church equally failed to provide an alternative conception or imagination to the tribalism within post-colonial Rwanda. During the 1990–1994 civil war and the 1994 genocide, despite some commendable individual initiatives condemning violence and calling for peace, the Christian religion played a critical role in either motivating the top decision-makers, making their commands comprehensible or tolerable, legitimizing the government's actions and encouraging popular submission to the government authority or simply remaining silent and failing to condemn human rights abuses. Although the Christian churches alone could not have prevented the genocide from occurring, they represented the only institution within civil society in possession of enough autonomy and influence to attempt to change or deviate from the course of the events, oppose the divisive regime, and, at the same time, create awareness and put pressure on the international community. In agreement with Denis (2019), its reluctance and often outright refusal to do so have come to represent one of the heaviest failures of Christian ethics and of the institutions that profess and practise its commandments.

In view of the above, the Church's general failure can thus be reflected in both its attitude and actions. Attitude at both institutional and individual levels, in the sense of having been indifferent (silent and inactive) as it was interested much in conversions without real-life transformation. Actions in the sense of some members of the clergy and Church officials actively participating or being accomplices in violent conflicts and the 1994 genocide. It is worth mentioning that, peculiarly, in the context of Rwanda, religious convictions did not function as organizers of group identity (Longman, 2010). For example, the genocide was not pursued on the dividing lines between religious groups, as it happened in other theatres of violence such as Lebanon, India, Sudan, Sri Lanka or Northern Ireland. Nevertheless, Christianity and its proselytizers were essential in defining and crystalizing lines between ethnicities in a context where ethnic differentiation would have otherwise been negligible. Eventually, the genocide was pursued by the regime precisely on the base of this racialization of ethnicity. Churches could have played an important role in supporting those who resisted the genocide, informing the world about what was happening in Rwanda and making genocide more difficult to execute.

In the aftermath of the 1994 genocide, numerous peacebuilding initiatives that were engaged are commendable. Nevertheless, these peacebuilding initiatives have barely been emphasizing justice in their strategies. Despite this overall criticism, Christian reconciliation programmes have made important contributions to promoting peace and development in Rwanda.

## Conclusion

Rwanda is a unique and complex case where the genocide, the civil war and related horrendous crimes took place concurrently as a result of long histories of animosity and division between the Hutu and the Tutsi people with the blessing of religious institutions.

This chapter aimed to provide a contextual analysis of Rwanda's experience with the nexus of religion, conflict and peacebuilding. The overall lesson learnt from Rwanda's experience is that of the two faces or potential of religion, either as a contributor to conflict and/or as a potential for peace. On the one hand, the Christian religion, particularly the Catholic Church, played a particular role in Rwanda's conflict and antagonism between the Hutu and Tutsi people, which culminated in the 1990–1994 civil war and the 1994 genocide in Rwanda. On the other hand, religion has played an important role in working for peace, particularly during the 1994–1994 civil war and the 1994 genocide. This involved religious organizations, as institutions but also individual religious leaders and members of the clergy. This role was however found minimal or insufficiently exploited given the peace potential (theology), power and opportunity that religion has always had in Rwandan society throughout history.

In conclusion, this chapter argues that religion in Rwanda, particularly the Christian religion, has always been, and still is, a political institution. As found, politics matters more than ethnicity in Rwanda's religion as ethnicity was, and is still, used as a tool to access and maintain power in the Church and to be on good terms with the regime in place. The chapter highlighted some commendable religious peacebuilding initiatives, notably during the civil war and the genocide, particularly in the aftermath of the 1994 genocide. In the context of Sustainable Development Goal 16, on "promoting peaceful and inclusive societies", this study agrees with Schliesser (2016) that any long-term developmental success will depend on the sustainability of peace as brought about by reconciliation, it follows that development and reconciliation go together. As found and discussed above, this is where the Church has proven to be vital. However, in general, Christian religious institutions in Rwanda failed to detach from the state's evil policies or to specifically call out and oppose human rights abuses, even when church personnel were targeted in segregation and attacks. Up to the present, they continue to express a sense of weakness and/or complicity as their alliance with the state still fails to call out or oppose its human rights abuses. Hence, drawing on Rwanda's experience, the following interrelated lessons can be drawn as they appear to be useful for countries that have experienced massive violent conflicts (e.g. divided societies):

1. It is important to problematize the capacity of religious institutions to challenge the authoritarian state, particularly when the latter engages in human rights abuses and crimes.
2. Religious institutions have the potential and power to resist and challenge human rights abuses and crimes from occurring in both attitudes and actions.
3. Religious institutions have the potential and capacity to address the painful past, construct the present and build a peaceful future for individuals and communities that have experienced violent conflicts.
4. Religious institutions need to be apolitical, while at the same time questioning and delegitimizing the state's policies and actions and suggesting alternatives, to contribute to peace and sustainable development effectively.

## References

Banyanga, J., & Bjöekqvist. (2017). The Dual Role of Religion Regarding the Rwandan 1994 Genocide: Both Instigator and Healer. *Journal of African Studies and Development, 3*(1), 1–12.

Berkeley, B. (2001). *The Graves Are Not Yet Full: Race, Tribe and Power in the Heart of Africa*. Basic Books.

Carney, J. (2012a). Beyond Tribalism: The Hutu-Tutsi Question and Catholic Rhetoric in Colonial Rwanda. *Journal of Religion in Africa, 42*(2), 172–202. https://doi.org/10.1163/157006612X646178

Carney, J. (2012b). 'Far from having unity, we are tending towards total disunity': The Catholic Major Seminary in Rwanda, 1950-62. *Studies in World Christianity, 18*(1), 82–102. https://doi.org/10.3366/swc.2012.0007

Carney, J. J. (2015). A Generation After Genocide: Catholic Reconciliation in Rwanda. *Theological Studies, 76*(4), 785–812.

Denis, P. (2019). Christian Gacaca and Official Gacaca in Post-Genocide Rwanda. *Journal for the Study of Religion, 32*(1), 1–27.

Eltringham, N. (2006). 'Invaders who have stolen the country': The Hamitic Hypothesis, Race and the Rwandan Genocide. *Journal for the Study of Race, Nation and Culture, 12*(4), 425–446.

Gatwa, T. (2000). Mission and Belgian Colonial Anthropology in Rwanda. Why Churches Stood Accused in the 1994 Tragedy? What Next? *Studies in World Christianity, 6*(1), 1–20. https://doi.org/10.3366/swc.2000.6.1.1

Gatwa, T. (2005). *The Churches and Ethnic Ideology in the Rwanda Crisis 1900–1994*. Regnum Books.

Gatwa, T. (2014). God in the Public Domain: Life Giver, Protector, or Indifferent Sleeper during the Rwandan Tragedies. *Exchange, 43*(4), 313–338. https://doi.org/10.1163/1572543X-12341335

Gourevitch, P. (2000). *We wish to Inform You That Tomorrow We Will be Killed with Our Families: Stories from Rwanda*. Picador.

Grant, A. M. (2018). Noise and Silence in Rwanda's Postgenocide Religious Soundscape. *Journal of Religion in Africa, 48*, 35–64.

Haworth, M. T. (2018). *Church and State in Rwanda: Catholic Missiology and the 1994 Genocide Against the Tutsi*. https://digitalcollections.sit.edu/cgi/viewcontent.cgi?article=3854&context=isp_collection

Katongole, E. (2005a). Christianity, Tribalism, and the Rwandan Genocide: A Catholic Reassessment of Christian "Social Responsibility". *Logos: A Journal of Catholic Thought and Culture, 8*(3), 67–93. https://doi.org/10.1353/log.2005.0027

Katongole, E. (2005b). Violence and Social Imagination: Rethinking Theology and Politics in Africa. *Religion and Theology, 12*(2), 145–171. https://doi.org/10.1163/157430105X00031

Katongole, E. (2017). *The Journey to Reconciliation: Groaning for a New Creation in Africa*. Orbis Books.

Katongole, E., & Wilson-Hartgrove, J. (2009). *Mirror to the Church: Resurrecting Faith after Genocide in Rwanda*. Zondervan.

King, E. (2014). *From Classrooms to Conflict in Rwanda*. Cambridge University Press.

Kubai, A. (2016). 'Confession' and 'Forgiveness' as a Strategy for Development in Post-Genocide Rwanda. *HTS Theological Studies, 72*(4). https://doi.org/10.4102/hts.v76i4.6276

Lambourne, W. (2004). *Post-conflict Peacebuilding: Meeting Human Needs for Justice and Reconciliation, Peace, Conflict and Development*. Issue four.

Lederach, J. P. (1997). *Building Peace: Sustainable Reconciliation in Divided Societies*. United States Institute of Peace Press.

Longman, T. (2001). Church Politics and the Genocide in Rwanda. *Journal of Religion in Africa, 31*(2), 163–186. https://doi.org/10.1163/157006601X00112

Longman, T. (2010). *Christianity and Genocide in Rwanda*. Cambridge University Press.

Longman, T. (2018). Christian Churches in Post-Genocide Rwanda: Reconciliation and Its Limits. In M. Girma (Ed.), *The Healing of Memories: African Christian Responses To Politically Induced Trauma* (pp. 55–76). Lexington Books.

Mamdani, M. (2001). *When Victims Become Killers: Colonialism, Nativism, and the Genocide in Rwanda*. Princeton University Press.

Nsengimana, C. (2015). *Peacebuilding Initiatives of the Presbyterian Church in Post-Genocide Rwandan Society*. Globalethics.net, no. 24.

NURC. (2009). *15 Years of Unity and Reconciliation Process in Rwanda: The ground Covered to Date*.

NURC. (2010). *Rwanda Reconciliation Barometer*.

NURC. (2015). *Rwanda Reconciliation Barometer*.

Obura, A. (2003). *Never Again: Educational Reconstruction in Rwanda*. International Institute for Educational Planning: UNESCO.

Peterson, S. (2000). *Me Against My Brother: At War in Somalia, Sudan, and Rwanda*. Routledge.

Ramsbotham, O., Woodhouse, T., & Miall, H. (2005). *Contemporary Conflict Resolution* (2nd ed. fully revised and expanded). Polity Press.

Riot, T. (2015). A Roundabout Revolution: Rethinking the Decolonization of Rwanda by the Practices of the Catholic Scouting Movement, 1954–1964. *The International Journal of the History of Sport, 32*(7), 939–951. https://doi.org/10.1080/09523367.2015.1044299

Safari, P. (2010). Church, State, and the Rwandan Genocide. *Political Theology, 11*(6), 873–893. https://doi.org/10.1558/poth.v11i6.873

Schliesser, C. (2016). Contextualized Development in Post-Genocide Rwanda: Exploring the Roles of Christian Churches in Development and Reconciliation. In J. Koehrsen & A. Heuser (Eds.), *Faith-Based Organisations in Development Discourses* (pp. 39–161). Routledge.

Schliesser, C. (2018). From "a Theology of Genocide" to a "Theology of Reconciliation"? On the Role of Christian Churches in the Nexus of Religion and Genocide in Rwanda. *Religions, 9*, 34. https://mdpi-res.com/religions/religions-09-00034/article_deploy/religions-09-00034.pdf?version=1516724927

Sentama, E. (2022). *National Reconciliation in Rwanda: Experiences and Lessons Learnt*. Research Project Report. European University Institute.

Shyaka, A. (2002). La génèse des conflits dans les pays d'Afrique des Grands lacs: Rwanda, Burundi, DRC et l'Ouganda. In *Peuplement du Rwanda: enjeu et perspectives* (pp. 121–143). Cahier du Centre de Gestion des Conflits (No.5), Université Nationale du Rwanda.

Staub, E. (2003). *The Psychology of Good and Evil: Why Children, Adults, and Groups Help and Harm Others* (p. 437). Cambridge University Press.

Uvin, P. (1998). *Aiding Violence: The Development Enterprise in Rwanda*. Kumarian Press.

Uvin, P. (2003). The Gacaca Tribunals in Rwanda. In IDEA (Ed.), *Reconciliation after Violent Conflict*. International Institute for Democracy and Electoral Assistance (IDEA).

van Butselaar. (2002). Religion, Conflict and Reconciliation in Rwanda. In J. D. Gort, H. Hansen, & H. M. Vroom (Eds.), *Religion, Conflict and Reconciliation: Multifaith Ideals and Realities* (pp. 327–329). Rodopi B.Y.

van't Spijker, G. (1997). The Churches and Genocide in Rwanda. *Exchange, 26*(3), 233–255. https://doi.org/10.1163/157254397X00421

van't Spijker, G. (2017). Focused on Reconciliation: Rwandan Protestant Theology After the Genocide. *Transformation, 34*(1), 66–74.

CHAPTER 10

# Building Resilience and Everyday Peace at the Micro-Levels in South Sudan

*Patrick Karanja Mbugua and Abraham K. Nyuon*

INTRODUCTION

Academic and popular writings on the civil war in South Sudan have since 2018 paid extensive attention to the implementation of the Revitalised Agreement on the Resolution of the Conflict in the Republic of South Sudan (R-ARCSS) (ACCORD, 2019; ICG, 2019; Onapa, 2019; Onditi, 2019). However, the role of grassroots actors in promoting peaceful relations in micro-spaces has received less attention. While the civil war started at the top level of the country's leadership, it disrupted peaceful coexistence, altered inter-ethnic relations, destroyed livelihoods, and wrecked economic

---

P. K. Mbugua (✉)
Peace & Conflict Studies Academic and Consultant, Peacebuilding, Conflict Transformation, and Preventive Diplomacy, Nairobi, Kenya

A. K. Nyuon
School of Social and Economic Studies, University of Juba, Juba, South Sudan

© The Author(s), under exclusive license to Springer Nature Switzerland AG 2023
S. M. Kilonzo et al. (eds.), *The Palgrave Handbook of Religion, Peacebuilding, and Development in Africa*,
https://doi.org/10.1007/978-3-031-36829-5_10

production at lower levels.[1] Additionally, while the national leaders were stuck in internationally mediated peace negotiations and intransigent stances over the implementation of ARCSS, grassroots actors struggled to resolve inter-ethnic hostilities and to mitigate other consequences of the civil war in the micro-spaces. Among these grassroots actors were the Evangelical Alliance of South Sudan (EASS) and the Pan-African Christian Women's Alliance (PACWA). Between December 2018 and February 2020, EASS and PACWA implemented peacebuilding interventions, which employed a bottom-up approach that integrated technical peacebuilding aspects with Christian beliefs, values, and tools in three regions, namely Juba City, Bor Town, and Yei Town. This chapter uses the everyday peace concept of the bottom-up approach to analyse the impact of EASS/PACWA peacebuilding interventions.

The bottom-up approach and the notion of everyday peace have emerged in scholarship in the last two decades as ways of conceptualising and understanding lower-level interventions in contexts of protracted armed conflicts (Mac Ginty, 2016). Literature contrasts bottom-up peacebuilding with the liberal peace approach, also known as liberal peacebuilding, liberal interventionism, or liberal internationalism, which has been the dominant form of internationally supported peacebuilding (Paris, 2002, 2007, 2010; Richmond, 2006, 2007; Richmond & Franks, 2009). Based on International Studies democratic peace theory, liberal peacebuilding aims to create peace within states recovering from civil wars through the promotion of liberal democracy and free markets. In other words, liberal peacebuilding aims to align the domestic governance of countries transitioning from armed conflicts with the prevailing standards of the international system (Paris, 2010). However, the liberal peace approach has some limitations, including privileging global norms, emphasising the structural and institutional aspects of state-building, failing to consider local perspectives, ignoring local agency, and bypassing local ownership (Mac Ginty & Richmond, 2013; Ripsman, 2016; Ljungkvist & Jarstad, 2021). These limitations have led to the development of an alternative bottom-up peacebuilding approach.

The bottom-up peacebuilding approach privileges local perspectives and agency and emphasises local ownership (Gopin, 2009; Mac Ginty, 2010a, 2011, 2017, 2021; Mac Ginty & Richmond, 2013; Montville, 1990, 1993,

---

[1] Data on the South Sudanese population is very unreliable. However, various studies claim that there are at least 64 ethnic groups, although they differ on the classification of some of the ethnic groups into language families (e.g. whether to classify them as Niger-Congo or Ubangian language families and Central-Sudanic or Nilo-Saharan language families). The most populous group, Dinka, comprises 36% of the population followed by Nuer at 16%. Each of the other big groups (Azande, Bari, and Shilluk) has less than 5% of the population; none of the other 59 groups reach 2%. Most of the ethnic groups are very small; studies indicate that each of the 30 small ethnic groups has a population of less than 30,000, while each of the 13 groups at the bottom has a population of less than 10,000. Moreover, studies show that 35 of the ethnic groups are concentrated in the 3 Equatoria regions (18 in Eastern Equatoria, 11 in Central Equatoria, and 5 in Western Equatoria) and 18 ethnic groups are located in the Western Bahr el Ghazal State.

2009; Paffenholz, 2015; Randazzo, 2017; Richmond, 2001, 2009a, 2009b, 2011). According to Mac Ginty & Richmond (2013), the essence of bottom-up peacebuilding is emancipation and inclusion of local agency, as expressed through voices from below. Further, literature emphasises that attaining sustainable peace after a protracted civil war, especially in deeply divided societies, requires the involvement of all levels of society (Lederach, 1997). Involving lower-level agents is, therefore, critical because they experience daily hatred, prejudices, and hostilities (Lederach, 1997). Because of the particularity of everyday experience, a central component of bottom-up peacebuilding is the concept of everyday peace.

Literature conceptualises everyday peace as social practices that ordinary people perform as they conduct their daily lives in conflict contexts, or societies emerging from protracted conflicts, to minimise the effects of direct, structural, and cultural violence and strengthen peaceful relations (Ware et al., 2022; Mac Ginty, 2014, 2015, 2017, 2021; Mac Ginty & Firchow, 2016; Richmond & Mac Ginty, 2019). Therefore, everyday peace centres on the daily experiences, perspectives, and agency of ordinary people, implying that it is contingent, contextual, and temporal, and has no universal indicators. According to Mac Ginty (2014, p. 550), 'everyday' in this understanding refers to "the normal habitus for individuals and groups even if what passes as normal in a conflict-affected society would be abnormal elsewhere". Thus, individuals and groups in a particular context and at a specific time choose their indicators of everyday peace. This chapter applies the everyday peace concept to analyse the impacts of EASS and PACWA's interventions. It suggests that their peacebuilding interventions were targeted at fostering everyday peace in micro-spaces, and posits that the interventions implicitly align with UN's Sustainable Development Goal (SDG) 16, specifically target 16.1, which stipulates the reduction of all forms of violence at all levels, and indicators 16.1.2 and 16.1.3, which encourage the reduction of physical violence and conflict-related deaths. Another aim of the chapter is to contribute to the growing body of literature on everyday peace, which includes conceptual and theoretical arguments and country empirical studies.

Research for the study involved primary and secondary data collection. Primary research occurred from August to November 2021 and surveyed 92 respondents, who were categorised into 15 participants for the key informant interviews (KIIs), 50 participants for the focus group discussions, and 27 respondents for one-to-one telephone interviews. Respondents were evenly distributed across the three regions and between men and women, with 71 of them being young people below 40 years. Secondary research involved reviewing 20 EASS/PACWA documents, including a baseline survey that collected initial data from at least 100 respondents between January and May 2019. The following section will summarise the contextual issues that informed the two partners' bottom-up approach and their choice of everyday peace indicators; the subsequent section will analyse the empirical data; and the last section will conclude the chapter.

## Everyday Peace in the Context of a Stalled Peace Agreement

The Republic of South Sudan seceded from the Republic of Sudan in July 2011 following a prolonged 22-year civil war, which killed at least 2,000,000 people and displaced 6,000,000 others. In December 2013, the newly independent republic descended into a devastating civil war, which analysts attribute to several factors, including neo-patrimonial politics, weak state structures, heritage of the past governance by the old Sudan, and legacies of the previous civil wars (De Waal, 2014; Moro, 2022; Rolandsen, 2015; Wassara, 2015). From December 2013 to June 2016, the war was mostly fought in the northern regions, especially the Jonglei, Unity, Lakes, and Upper Nile States.[2] According to UNHCR (2016), 1,690,000 people were internally displaced and at least 1,000,000 fled to neighbouring countries as refugees during this phase of the war. A second phase of the civil war in July 2016 shifted the epicentre to the previously peaceful regions in Central and Western Equatoria States as the government forces, Sudan People's Liberation Army (SPLA), and their opponents, Sudan People's Liberation Army-In Opposition (SPLA-IO) and other armed groups,[3] fought in these locations (Associated Press, 2016; Kindersley & Rolandsen, 2017; ICG, 2019; Kuol, 2020; Wassara, 2022). According to Médecins Sans Frontières (MSF) (2021), the shift increased internally displaced peoples (IDPs) to 1,870,000 and refugees in neighbouring countries to 2,200,000. By September 2018, when the main parties signed the R-ARCSS, the war had reached a military stalemate (ICG, 2019).

Therefore, the country was in a state of no-war no-peace when EASS and PACWA planned their peacebuilding interventions in October 2018. Mac Ginty (2010b) refers to no-war no-peace cases as those that continue to be mired in insecurity, on-off armed conflicts at the lower levels, chronic poverty, and the persistence of the factors that sparked and sustained the civil war despite a ceasefire or peace agreement. While there was a peace agreement, the South Sudan countryside continued to experience persistent insecurity and war conditions at the micro-levels, such as recruitment of ethnic militias and on-off

---

[2] South Sudan in divided into ten states: Eastern Equatoria, Central Equatoria, Western Equatoria, Jonglei, Unity, Upper Nile, Lakes, Warrap, Western Bahr el Ghazal, and Northern Bahr el Ghazal.

[3] Among these groups were: *Arrow Boys* which emerged in the mid-2000s; *Revolutionary Movement for National Salvation (REMNASA)* that was formed in early 2015; *Alfred Futiyo* group that emerged in 2015; *South Sudan National Liberation Movement (SSNLM)* that was formed in 2015; and *National Salvation Front (NSF)* that emerged in March 2017. For a detailed study of these movements, see Koos, C. (2014). Why and How Civil Defense Militias Emerge: The Case of the Arrow Boys in South Sudan. *Studies in Conflict and Terrorism* 37(12): 1039–1057; Jok, M.J., Schomerus, M., Taban, C., Kuol, L.B.D., Breidlid, I.M., & Arensen, M.J. (2017). *Informal Armies: Community Defence Groups in South Sudan's Civil War*. London: Saferworld; International Crisis Group (ICG). 2021. South Sudan's Other War: Resolving the Insurgency in Equatoria. *ICG Report No. 169*. Brussels/Nairobi.

armed conflicts. For instance, Yei Town and its surrounding areas experienced on-off clashes between SPLA and the National Salvation Front (NSF) from 2017 to 2020 (HRW, 2017; ICG, 2019; Olouch, 2019). The consequences of widespread violence at lower levels are documented in various reports by UN agencies and international human rights organisations. For example, a UN report (May 2018) shows violations of International Humanitarian Law (IHL), including execution of civilians and gang-raping of women by armed militias; another report by Amnesty International (AI) (September 2018) documents killing of civilians and gang-raping of women by armed groups; and Amnesty International (AI) (July 2016) records the impacts of the war on survivors' mental health. Additionally, a **UNMISS report** (March 2021) claims that local leaders and traditional chiefs sustained armed violence at the lower levels by recruiting militias from their ethnic groups. The consequences of such widespread violence at the lower levels include displacement, gender-based violence, destroyed inter-ethnic relations, shattered communities and families, and ruined economic, social, and cultural institutions.

This is the context in which EASS and PACWA conceived bottom-up peacebuilding initiatives. Due to the nature of the challenges, the two partners emphasised a number of basic indicators of psycho-social healing, conciliation, and everyday peace. Specifically, the two partners chose three indicators of everyday peace: enhancing individual resilience, transforming individual perceptions of the ethnic 'other', and improving relations between individuals from different ethnic groups. As Christian organisations, they integrated technical aspects of peacebuilding, such as community dialogues, peace committees, and training on psycho-social support, with Christian beliefs, values, and tools.

That approach concurs with the arguments in the literature that religious peacebuilding integrates technical peacebuilding activities with religious values, tools, texts, narratives, and vocabulary to resolve conflicts and promote reconciliation and peaceful relations (Bercovitch & Kadayifci-Orellana, 2009; Dubois, 2008; Powers, 2010). Such incorporation of spiritual elements of culture into religious peacebuilding makes it community-based, relationship-centred, and participatory (Dubois, 2008). Thus, while religious-based actors implement the same activities as secular peacebuilders, they add religious tools, including spiritual guidance, prayers, and empathy in envisioning new possibilities. Similarly, peacebuilding literature recognises the religious origin of reconciliation concepts such as healing, forgiveness, and restorative justice, and asserts that all religions have language that describes ways of healing broken human relationships and acceptance that enables humans to pursue peaceful relations (Hamber, 2007; Peterson, 2001). The approach clearly agrees with Lederach's (2005) idea of moral imagination.

As it were, the two partners chose to pilot their interventions in Juba City, Bor Town, and Yei Town because they were among the locations that were most devastated by the civil war, while the no-peace no-war situation informed their choice of everyday peace indicators. The choice of enhancing individual resilience was particularly informative. Juncos and Joseph (2020) explain resilience as the ability of individuals, households, communities, or countries to withstand and recover from stresses and shocks. In the context of South Sudan, this implies the ability of individuals, families, communities, and ethnic groups to cope with, mitigate, recover from, and respond to the consequences of protracted and nested armed conflicts and displacement. This chapter argues that EASS and PACWA opted to build individual resilience and attain micro-level everyday peace for four reasons. First, there were uncertainties over the implementation of the R-ARCSS due to the national factions' previous failure to implement the ARCSS. Second, armed groups resorted to rent-seeking rebellion, violence as a bargaining method, and returning to war when they were stuck at the negotiation table. Third, it was grassroots actors that had to deal with the deadly consequences of intermittent armed conflicts at the lower levels. Fourth, building individual resilience was a necessary precondition for promoting everyday peace, which, in turn, was a necessary precondition for promoting group reconciliation. Since individuals are the foundation of local groups, EASS and PACWA viewed individual transformation as a prerequisite to the improvement of relations between different ethnic communities. Such changes were particularly necessary if the transformed individuals were to become change agents in South Sudan, where it is challenging to achieve institutional and group changes in a short period.

Thus, while conceiving individual resilience as the foundation, EASS/PACWA reasoned that enhanced individual resilience would lead to a change in perceptions of the ethnic 'other' and better relations between individuals from different ethnic groups. Relating with ethnic 'others' meant accepting them in their moral frames and physical neighbourhoods, tolerating their worldviews, sharing public spaces, emphasising commonalities, forming social networks, and performing collective activities in the micro-environments. Accordingly, these three indicators were some of the necessary preconditions for everyday peace. This approach was consistent with two findings of the baseline survey: 40% of Bor residents and 35% of Yei residents rarely engaged with neighbours from another ethnic group; and the majority of the population in Juba, Bor, and Yei prefers to live in mono-ethnic neighbourhoods and villages for safety reasons. One of the pointers of ethnic mistrust that PACWA cited was the refusal by Christians from the same denomination to share the same church service; Bari Catholics, for instance, could not share church services with Dinka Catholics. Such ethnic mistrust was a consequence of the cycles of killings that had characterised the civil war since 2013.

Therefore, EASS and PACWA developed an intervention strategy that started with training individuals on trauma healing, psycho-social support, and forgiveness. These individuals then became the focal points at the lower levels where their role was to organise citizen-to-citizen engagements, dialogue forums, and local peace committees. Each local peace committee acted as an early warning mechanism, built confidence, conducted dialogue forums, and encouraged conciliation between individuals from different ethnic groups.

Subsequently, EASS and PACWA presented on three radio stations—Spirit FM in Yei, Radio Bakhita in Juba, and Jonglei FM in Bor—which framed public discussions on everyday peace and privileged narratives of tolerance and peaceful relations at the lower levels. This was consistent with the baseline survey, which showed 88% of Juba residents, 94% of the Bor population, and 94% of Yei inhabitants relied on radio as the main source of news. The peak of their interventions was a peace concert that involved different Christian denominations.

These interventions created spaces of contact, promoted interactions, and encouraged mutual understanding. Importantly, the two partners integrated Christian beliefs, values, and tools into their activities, hoping that the approach would provide the language of empathy, forgiveness, and recovery. In other words, the Christian spirituality would give survivors of the civil war hope, provide meaning in life, and offer an alternative frame of healing. This concurs with arguments in the literature on religion and resilience that most cultures use religion and spirituality to cope with trauma, grief, and loss because believing in a higher power comforts survivors and assists them in their recovery (Boss, 2006). Neither EASS nor PACWA documents acknowledge the UN Sustainable Development Goals (SDGs). However, this chapter postulates that their approach implicitly addresses Goal 16, specifically target 16.1 that calls for reducing all forms of violence and deaths associated with them, and 16.1.2 and 16.1.3 that call for reducing conflict-related violence at both macro- and micro-levels.

## Enhancing Individual Resilience and Changing Perceptions

A baseline survey revealed three profound findings. First, 81% of Juba residents, 100% of Yei inhabitants, and 88% of the Bor population believed that ethnic violence was the most widespread form of violence in South Sudan. By ethnic violence, they meant direct violence perpetrated by informal armed groups or formal security forces recruited exclusively from specific ethnic groups against civilians of other ethnic identities. Examples include the widespread killings of Nuer civilians by Dinka SPLA soldiers in Juba City and the execution of Dinka civilians by a Nuer militia in Bor (HRW, 2017; Amnesty International, 2017). Second, 81% of Juba residents, 90% of the Yei population, and 88% of Bor inhabitants knew others, including close relatives, who had been displaced, injured, or killed by violence. Third, 75% of Yei dwellers, 63% of the Juba population, and 65% of Bor inhabitants believed that their ethnic groups had grievances which the South Sudan State had failed to address. Because an incessant fear of armed violence dominates everyday existence, EASS and PACWA opted to start with interventions that targeted individual resilience.

PACWA insisted on special attention to women because all the armed groups had used rape as a weapon of war. "Women were nursing multiple pains: loss of husbands and sons, the trauma of mass rape, destruction of our homes, shattering of our families, inter-ethnic killings, and challenges of survival in IDP and refugee camps," a PACWA leader explained. "We advised those in IDP and refugee camps to hold weekly prayer sessions to share their pain and help each other deal with trauma, grief, and loss." She emphasised that "healing trauma and building women's abilities to cope with the effects of the war was a prerequisite to rebuilding their lives". This evidence highlights three points: the need for individual and group resilience, the necessity for perception change, and the use of religious beliefs to empathise with survivors and envision a better future. PACWA's specific focus on women recognised that all ethnic groups in South Sudan held women as the foundation of society and carriers of an ethnic group's future. This agrees with an argument in South Sudan studies that the practice of mass killings and rapes was never a part of South Sudan's warfare practices until the second civil war in the 1980s (Jok & Hutchinson, 1999; Hutchinson, 2001). According to Hutchinson (2001), the practice emerged as an 'ideological' shift in the 1980s when elite competition within armed groups and the deployment of ethnic militias by the Islamist government in Khartoum created a devastating wave of massacres that the Nuer civilians viewed as 'a curse from God'. Therefore, enhancing individual resilience and transforming perceptions was central to PACWA's strategy.

Empirical evidence from a male in Bor supports EASS/PACWA's approach. "I am a pastor from Langbar. I survived the war that made our lives unbearable. I was reluctant to participate in EASS/PACWA activities at Malek School in Madingbor because I did not want to interact with other tribes." In short, after surviving the violence, he harboured extreme hatred for other ethnic identities. "I started to change towards my family and members of other tribes after attending the training sessions. I know other survivors who attended the same forums." It is probable that aggression towards his family members and hatred of ethnic 'others' were symptoms of trauma. However, the training sessions changed him as the use of Christian beliefs, values, and tools appealed to him as a pastor. "I improved relations in my family and between my community and other tribes," he affirmed. "Neighbours from all tribes came together after training and assisted each other when floods destroyed our village and armed bandits from the neighbouring Mading area attacked our neighbourhood." His decision to foster better relations with members of other ethnic groups and participate in collective activities indicates enhanced resilience and transformed perceptions. Such changes affirm some of EASS/PACWA's premises: Christian spirituality gives survivors of violence hope and offers an alternative frame of healing, and regular contact and continuous communication and joint collective activities lead to reduced hostility, improved relations, and tolerance for others.

A woman from Bor shared a similar experience. "I am a single mother who survived the cycles of killings in Bor. I have been psychologically unstable for a long time." Of course, witnessing cycles of killings traumatised her and she struggled to overcome her grief and loss. However, EASS and PACWA's use of Christian values and tools resonated with her. "I started changing after attending the training on trauma healing and reconciliation. After the first EASS/PACWA meeting, I participated in all the other activities." Then she joined the Bor peace committee and brought others to the training. "I am a member of the Bor peacebuilding committee and serve in a local church. I have become an advocate for tolerance and peace; I encourage all to live peacefully with each other." This evidence is illuminating because she demonstrates enhanced resilience and changed perceptions of ethnic 'others' by inviting 'others' to the forums, participating in the local peacebuilding committee, using church space to influence the views of 'others', forming cross-ethnic networks, and promoting everyday peace in her locality.

Similar changes are evident in Yei. "I narrowly escaped death when the fighters killed my husband and two sons and some of our neighbours. I was so shocked and did not know what to do. I started having nightmares and wild dreams; I could not sleep at night, so I turned to alcoholism," a female respondent narrated. Studies on the civil war highlight these as some of the widespread symptoms of Post-Traumatic Stress Disorder (PTSD) (Lauren et al., 2017; Pritchard et al., 2020). She probably suffered PTSD after witnessing the traumatic killing of her family and neighbours. Indeed, her evidence is consistent with media reports on the violence in Yei, which claim that SPLA soldiers and SPLA-IO combatants, who were mainly from Bahr el Ghazal and Upper Nile ethnic groups, targeted Yei's native population when renewed violence extended to the region in July 2016.[4] For example, the Associated Press (17 November 2016) reports: "Civilians in Yei began to suffer in August when the army came in to fight nearby rebels. The military, which residents and local government officials say are from the Dinka tribe, attacked other tribes who are natives of Yei and the surrounding Equatoria State on suspicion they supported the rebels, the locals said." The same report adds that: "In early November, 11 people traveling from Yei were rounded up by unidentified individuals, placed in a thatched hut, and burned alive, local government officials said. Their charred corpses were still there in mid-November when AP counted seven bodies, some with their arms bound behind their backs." **A UNMISS report** (February 2017) documents hundreds of such killings.

However, the issue for this chapter is EASS/PACWA's aim to build the resilience of individuals and transform their perceptions. In this case, the use of Christian beliefs gave her hope and a frame of healing. "One day, I was in a beer club when I received information that a group known as PACWA would train women in our area; a friend encouraged me to attend." While she liked

[4] South Sudan studies show that the native ethnic groups in Yei and its surrounding areas are Kakwa, Baka, Pojulu, Keliko, Mündü, Avukaya, Lugbara, and Bari. However, other ethnic groups from other regions of the country moved to Yei Town at different times due to displacement by the civil war.

the session on trauma healing and also attended the subsequent forums, PACWA used that opportunity to strengthen her resilience. Eventually, she joined the local peace committee. "I found it difficult to change because I had suffered so much; I just wanted revenge. But PACWA encouraged me to read the Holy Bible and gave me hope for the future." She found it very difficult to embrace forgiveness, however. "I will never forgive those who killed my husband and my sons, but I can stand in front of women from all tribes and testify about my pain. I openly talk about women and relations between neighbours and tribes in Yei." Public sharing of her story affirms a premise in the literature that open discussion of traumatic events makes them less overwhelming and helps survivors recognise commonalities (Koessler et al., 2010; Lauren et al., 2017). She probably viewed the killers of her family as representatives of their ethnic groups and possibly harboured murderous hostility towards everybody from those ethnic groups, but PACWA's approach gave her hope, purpose, and confidence to envision an alternative future. Sharing her story in a multi-ethnic women group reduced her bitterness and hostility towards the ethnic 'other' because it provided the space to interact with others and overcome prejudice and hostility.

Sharing a similar transformation, a young male from Yei testified: "The fighters in Yei killed my parents and relatives and burned our home and properties. I was displaced together with the majority of my neighbours. I saw them murder my parents and relatives; I have always wanted revenge." He probably suffered from PTSD because he witnessed the killing of his parents and relatives, but EASS/PACWA's approach addressed his grief and loss. "When I attended PACWA meetings, I could not talk about my experience because it was very painful. They supported and encouraged me until I acquired the confidence to speak about my pain in front of other people." Such open discussion of his trauma made it less overwhelming and helped him recognise others who had similar experiences. "They encouraged me to forgive and connected me with other orphaned young men. Yes, I am still nursing pain and bitterness, but I talk about my problems with others." This testimony interweaves the weighty issues of trauma, grief and loss, mental health in a conflict context, and war-induced transformation of worldview. It shows that EASS/PACWA's integration of trauma healing with Christian spirituality and envisioning an alternative future helped him cope with his grief and loss, and gave him a new life purpose. While he probably shared the prevailing prejudices against ethnic 'others' in his neighbourhood and viewed the killers of his family as representatives of those ethnic 'others', PACWA enhanced his resilience and changed his perceptions. Indicators of his transformation include improved relations, forgiveness and discarding thoughts of revenge, and joining a social network that gave him space to share his experience with others.

Another young male from Yei followed a similar path of transformation. "The fighters in Yei killed a lot of people and burned homes and properties. They killed some of my family members; those who survived and all my neighbours fled to Uganda and the DRC. I was so depressed that I used to cry every day." Since he witnessed traumatic events, that is killing of his relatives and neighbours, his depression and continuous crying were probably signs of PTSD. However, PACWA's approach gave him a second chance at life. "When PACWA invited me to their activity, they encouraged me to read the Bible. I started reading it after training sessions. I thank PACWA for changing the way I view those who killed my relatives and displaced my family; I have accepted my fate and want to move on with my life." Clearly, PACWA's interventions built his resilience by helping him cope with trauma, grief, and loss, and giving him hope and new meaning in life. The approach gave him space and opportunity to change his self-image and perceptions of others and embrace forgiveness.

Empirical evidence from Juba is no different. "After I survived the killings in Juba, I lived with shock and pain for four years. It is PACWA's training sessions and Bible reading that helped me cope with my grief and loss and turned me into a new person," a female explained. Such transformation is consistent with three premises in EASS/PACWA's model: incorporating religious beliefs and spirituality into activities would inject hope and provide a new meaning to life; believing in a higher power comforts survivors and assists them in their recovery; and the approach provides an alternative frame of healing. As the respondent affirms, "I have accepted that conflict is part of humanity, as illustrated in the Holy Bible through the sin of Adam. The Holy Book also says that I give you my peace and you pass it on to others. PACWA's training has taught me that the right way to live in this world is to live peacefully with each other." Thus, PACWA created the space for her to transform her perception of the ethnic 'other', reduce her prejudice and hostility, and re-humanise the ethnic 'other' at her micro-level.

Corroborating that evidence, another Juba resident declared: "I am an evangelist and a leader in Akel-Roho Church. The killings in Juba shocked us and displaced many people." After participating in all trauma healing sessions, local peace committee forums, and the peace concert, she admitted that they greatly assisted her transformation. "The concert was the most wonderful event that I have ever attended in Juba because it encouraged women from all ethnic groups in South Sudan to support each other and learn from each other." This evidence illuminates that EASS/PACWA's approach did not just address her psycho-social challenges but also helped her form new contacts, engage with others, reduce prejudice and hostilities, change enemy images, and re-humanise the ethnic 'other'. Ultimately, she participated in social networks and collective activities that promoted everyday peace in her micro-space.

Overall, the strategy of integrating technical peacebuilding with Christian spirituality resonated with many survivors of civil war in the Bor, Juba, and Yei Towns. While this chapter does not claim that the model appealed to all those who participated in EASS/PACWA activities, empirical evidence shows that the strategy appealed to the majority of participants. By enhancing individual resilience and transforming perceptions of the ethnic 'other', the approach contributed to tolerance and better relations between individuals from different ethnic groups at the micro-level. This impact aligns with SDG goal 16, sub-section 16.1 and articles 16.1.2 and 16.1.3.

## Improving Relations Between Individuals from Different Ethnic Groups

More empirical evidence illustrates that EASS and PACWA interventions fostered better relations between individuals from different ethnic groups. A young male from Bor explained: "I was deeply hurt when someone from the Murle militia killed my friend; I planned revenge." Just before he and members of his ethnic community could kill the Murle militiaman, EASS invited him to an awareness forum. "I was shocked to see many Murle young men at the forum. I saw them as enemies and I could not talk to them or sit next to them." This evidence is consistent with an argument in the literature that unsettled conflicts strain ethnic relations at the lower levels because they allow revenge cycles to become the only form of justice available to individuals and ethnic groups. In this case, however, the young man changed after participating in EASS/PACWA training. "I began to overcome my hatred and abandoned my revenge plans." Subsequently, he approached one of the Murle young men during one of the activities. "As we talked, I realised he was my age mate and we shared an interest in livestock. After some months of continuous talking, we became friends and discussed the sheep trade." Then they involved other young men in their group. "We have witnessed a reduction in revenge attacks in Bor."

This evidence is powerful because Bor was the epicentre of devastating battles between Dinka, Nuer, and Murle armed groups. Clearly, the killing of his friend intensified his hatred of the Murle as an ethnic group. As intended, EASS/PACWA activities provided him with space and opportunity to change his stereotypes and prejudices, engage young Murle men, transform his perceptions, improve his relations with them, and start attributing actions to individuals as opposed to ethnic groups. His change affirms the EASS/PACWA strategy that contact and continuous communication increase knowledge, reduce hostility, demystify prejudices, remove enemy images, and re-humanise the ethnic 'other'. Corroborating the transformation, another male shared: "I come from Malou in Bor. The first time I joined EASS training on trauma healing and reconciliation was in October 2019. The sessions stimulated my interest in EASS activities." He subsequently became one of the EASS/PACWA presenters on Radio Jonglei. "I presented on peace, tolerance, and peaceful relations; I have since then made friends from all ethnic groups in Bor: Dinka, Nuer, and Murle." He used the radio presentation to advocate better relations and more interaction in common spaces. "Our motto has become peaceful relations regardless of our ethnic groups."

In Juba, a pastor who appeared on Radio Bhakita stated that the "training and other peacebuilding forums opened my eyes. I realised that one cannot help others unless one respects their rights." The starting point should be "returning stolen property, apologising, or by forgiving and being forgiven." For him, forgiveness is the foundation of reconciliation. "I urge members of my ethnic group to return other people's properties, including land, which they grabbed during the conflict." In other words, he viewed micro-level restitution as the key to improving relations between individuals from different ethnic groups. Additional evidence from a PACWA leader, who presented on Radio Bhakita, showed that juxtaposing bottom-up peacebuilding with Christian beliefs, values, and tools improved individual relations because it helped them to see each other as survivors of the same armed conflict. "The fighting has stopped, especially in Yei. We tell youth from all tribes to see each other as one." Lastly, a Juba woman reinforced this argument. "PACWA activities have brought different churches and tribes together. All of us have war pain, but PACWA and EASS have encouraged us to support each other regardless of our tribes. I urge them to continue with the activities to bring peace to our neighbourhoods."

In summary, empirical evidence shows that EASS and PACWA interventions provided spaces and opportunities for grassroots actors to improve relations between individuals from different ethnic communities. Such improvement sought to reduce prejudice and hostility, re-humanise the ethnic 'other', and promote common humanity. In turn, improved relations would contribute to everyday peace at the micro-levels. Subsequently, many islands of peace at lower levels would decrease inter-ethnic violence, promote trust across ethnic groups, and break the cycles of violence in the regions. These aims align with the requirements of SDG 16, specifically target 16.1 that calls for reducing all forms of violence and deaths associated with them, as well as indicators 16.1.2 and 16.1.3 that call for the reduction of conflict-related violence at all levels.

## Conclusion

This chapter has examined the impact of the bottom-up peacebuilding activities that EASS and PACWA implemented from December 2018 to February 2020 in Juba City, Bor Town, and Yei Town. When the two partners planned their interventions, the country was in a no-war no-peace situation, at least 4,000,000 people were either in internally displaced people (IDP) or refugee camps, and the national leaders were striving to revive a stalled peace agreement. The reality of a no-war no-peace context prompted EASS and PACWA to develop an intervention strategy that integrated techniques of bottom-up peacebuilding with Christian beliefs, values, and tools. Aiming to enhance individual resilience, transform individual perceptions of the ethnic 'other', and improve relations between individuals from different ethnic groups, the strategy started with training sessions on trauma healing, psycho-social support, and forgiveness. Then participants in those forums became the focal persons to organise citizen-to-citizen engagements, dialogue forums, and local peace committees, which promoted conciliation and served as early warning mechanisms at the lower levels. Subsequently, EASS and PACWA supported these micro-level activities with radio presentations and a peace concert.

Adduced empirical evidence has revealed that there was rampant individual and group trauma and a widespread sense of grief and loss at lower levels. In such a context, enhancing individual resilience, transforming perceptions of the ethnic 'other', and improving relations between individuals from different ethnic groups were the necessary preconditions for the attainment of conciliation and everyday peace in micro-spaces. Evidence has shown that the model of integrating bottom-up peacebuilding with Christian beliefs, values, and tools helped individuals attain these three preconditions. EASS and PACWA hoped that many islands of everyday peace would promote inter-ethnic relations and be a building block for regional peace formation. Meanwhile, neither EASS nor PACWA acknowledged the UN SDGs, but their aim of ending ethnic violence and promoting peaceful relations at the lower levels aligns with SDG 16, specifically target 16.1, which stipulates reduction of all forms of violence, and indicators 16.1.2 and 16.1.3, which advocate reduction of armed conflicts.

## References

African Centre for the Constructive Resolution of Disputes (ACCORD). (2019, March 11). Reviving Peace in South Sudan Through the Revitalised Peace Agreement. *Conflict & Resilience Monitor*, 2018/4. https://www.accord.org.za/conflict-trends/reviving-peace-in-south-sudan-through-the-revitalised-peace-agreement/

Amnesty International. (2016, July 6). *South Sudan: "Our hearts have gone dark": The Mental Health Impact of South Sudan's Conflict*. Amnesty International Report. https://www.amnesty.org/en/documents/afr65/3203/2016/en/

Amnesty International. (2017, July 24). *South Sudan: "Do not remain silent": Survivors of Sexual Violence in South Sudan Call for Justice and Reparations*. Amnesty International Report. https://www.amnesty.org/en/documents/afr65/6469/2017/en/

Associated Press. (2016, November 17). Wave of Ethnic Killings in South Sudan Town 'could evolve into genocide,' UN Warns. *Associated Press News*. https://www.cbc.ca/news/world/south-sudan-yei-ethnic-killings-1.3856122

Bercovitch, J., & Kadayifci-Orellana, S. A. (2009). Religion and Mediation: The Role of Faith-Based Actors in International Conflict Resolution. *International Negotiation*, 14(1), 175–204.

Boss, P. (2006). *Loss, Trauma, and Resilience: Therapeutic Work with Ambiguous Loss*. WW Norton & Co.

De Waal, A. (2014). When Kleptocracy Becomes Insolvent: Brute Causes of the Civil War in South Sudan. *African Affairs*, 113(452), 347–369.

Dubois, H. (2008). Religion and Peacebuilding: An Ambivalent Yet Vital Relationship. *Journal of Religion, Conflict and Peace*, 1(2), 1–21.

Gopin, M. (2009). *To Make the Earth Whole: The Art of Citizen Diplomacy in an Age of Religious Militancy*. Rowman & Littlefield Publishers.

Hamber, B. (2007). Forgiveness and Reconciliation: Paradise Lost Or Pragmatism? *Peace and Conflict: Journal of Peace Psychology*, 13(1), 115–125.

Human Rights Watch (HRW). (2017, April 27). "Soldiers assume we are rebels": Escalating violence and abuses in South Sudan's Equatorias. *Human Rights Watch Report.* https://www.hrw.org/report/2017/08/01/soldiers-assume-we-are-rebels/escalating-violence-and-abuses-south-sudans

Hutchinson, S. (2001). A Curse from God? Religious and Political Dimensions of the post-1991 Rise of Ethnic Violence in South Sudan. *Journal of Modern African Studies, 39*(2), 307–331.

International Crisis Group. (2019, March 13). Salvaging South Sudan's Fragile Peace Deal. *International Crisis Group report No. 270.* Juba/Nairobi/Brussels.

Jok, M. J., & Hutchinson, S. E. (1999). Sudan's Prolonged Second Civil War and the Militarisation of Nuer and Dinka Ethnic Identities. *African Studies Review, 42*(2), 125–145.

Juncos, A. E., & Joseph, J. (2020). Resilient Peace: Exploring the Theory and Practice of Resilience in Peacebuilding Interventions. *Journal of Intervention and Statebuilding, 14*(3), 289–302.

Kindersley, N., & Rolandsen, O. H. (2017). Civil War on a Shoestring: Rebellion in South Sudan's Equatoria Region. *Civil Wars, 19*(3), 308–324.

Koessler, S., Wöhrmann, C., Zwissler, B., Pfeiffer, A., Ertl, V., & Kissler, J. (2010). Does Remembering Cause Forgetting in Chronically Stressed People? A Study of Ugandan Civil War Refugees with and Without PTSD. *Journal of Psychology, 218*(2), 71–79.

Kuol, L. B. D. (2020). South Sudan: The Elusive Quest for a Resilient Social Contract? *Journal of Intervention and Statebuilding, 14*(1), 64–83.

Lauren, C., López, N. G., Pritchard, M., & Deng, D. (2017). Post-traumatic Stress Disorder, Trauma, and Reconciliation in South Sudan. *Social Psychiatry and Psychiatric Epidemiology, 52*, 705–714.

Lederach, J. P. (1997). *Building Peace: Sustainable Reconciliation in Divided Societies.* United States Institute of Peace Press.

Lederach, J. P. (2005). *The Moral Imagination: The Art and Soul of Building Peace.* Oxford University Press.

Ljungkvist, K., & Jarstad, A. (2021). Revisiting the Local Turn in Peacebuilding Through the Emerging Urban Approach. *Third World Quarterly, 42*(10), 2209–2226.

Mac Ginty, R. (2010a). Hybrid Peace: Interaction Between Top-down and Bottom-up Peace. *Security Dialogue, 41*(4), 391–412.

Mac Ginty, R. (2010b). No War, No Peace: Why So Many Peace Processes Fail to Deliver Peace. *International Politics, 47*(2), 145–162.

Mac Ginty, R. (2011). *International Peacebuilding and Local Resistance: Hybrid Forms of Peace.* Palgrave Macmillan.

Mac Ginty, R. (2014). Everyday Peace: Bottom-up and Local Agency in Conflict-Affected Societies. *Security Dialogue, 45*(6), 548–564.

Mac Ginty, R. (2015). Where Is the Local? Critical Localism and Peacebuilding. *Third World Quarterly, 36*(5), 840–856.

Mac Ginty, R. (2016). *No War, No Peace: The Rejuvenation of Stalled Peace Processes and Peace Accords* (3rd ed.). Palgrave Macmillan.

Mac Ginty, R. (2017). Everyday Social Practices and Boundary-Making in Deeply Divided Societies. *Civil Wars, 19*(1), 4–25.

Mac Ginty, R. (2021). *Everyday Peace: How So-called Ordinary People Can Disrupt Violent Conflict.* Oxford University Press.

Mac Ginty, R., & Firchow, F. (2016). Top-down and Bottom-up Narratives of Peace and Conflict. *Politics, 36*(3), 308–323.

Mac Ginty, R., & Richmond, O. (2013). The Local Turn in Peace Building: A Critical Agenda for Peace. *Third World Quarterly, 34*(5), 763–783.

Médecins Sans Frontières. (2021). South Sudan at 10: An MSF Record of the Consequences of Violence. *Médecins Sans Frontières (MSF) Report*, July 2021. https://www.msf.org/sites/msf.org/files/2021-07/MSF-SS-Report-Web-SinglePages.pdf

Montville, J. (1990). The Arrow and the Olive Branch: A Case for Track Two Diplomacy. In D. V. Vamik et al. (Eds.), *The Psychodynamics of International Relationships* (pp. 161–175). Lexington Books.

Montville, J. (1993). The Healing Function in Political Conflict Resolution. In D. Sandole & H. van der Merwe (Eds.), *Conflict Resolution Theory and Practice: Integration and Application* (pp. 112–128). Manchester University Press.

Montville, J. (2009). Track Two Diplomacy: The Work of Healing History. *Journal of Diplomacy and International Relations, 7*(2), 15–25.

Moro, L. N. (2022). South Sudan After Secession: The Failure as a New State and the Outbreak of War Since 2013. In J. N. Bach (Ed.), *Routledge Handbook of the Horn of Africa* (pp. 55–63). Routledge.

Olouch, F. (2019). Fresh Fighting in South Sudan's Yei: Troika Warns of Looming Crisis. *The EastAfrican*, February 23. https://www.theeastafrican.co.ke/tea/news/east-africa/fresh-fighting-in-south-sudan-s-yei-troika-warns-of-looming-crisis-1412998

Onapa, S. A. (2019). South Sudan Power-Sharing Agreement R-ARCSS: The Same Thing Expecting Different Results. *Africa Security Review, 28*(2), 75–94.

Onditi, F. (2019). Introduction to the Special Issue: A Human Security Perspective to the 2018 Revitalised ARCSS and Beyond. *African Conflict & Peacebuilding Review, 11*(2), 1–16.

Paffenholz, T. (2015). Unpacking the Local Turn in Peacebuilding: A Critical Assessment Towards an Agenda for Future Research. *Third World Quarterly, 36*(5), 857–874.

Paris, R. (2002). International Peacebuilding and the 'mission civilisatrice'. *Review of International Studies, 28*(4), 637–657.

Paris, R. (2007). *At War's End: Building Peace After Civil Conflict*. Cambridge University Press.

Paris, R. (2010). Saving Liberal Peacebuilding. *Review of International Studies, 36*(2), 337–365.

Peterson, R. (2001). A Theology of Forgiveness. In R. Helmick & R. Petersen (Eds.), *Forgiveness and Reconciliation: Religion, Public Policy, and Conflict Transformation* (pp. 3–26). Templeton Foundation Press.

Powers, G. F. (2010). Religion and Peacebuilding. In D. Philpot & G. F. Powers (Eds.), *Strategies for Peace: Transforming Conflict in a Violent World* (pp. 317–352). Oxford University Press.

Pritchard, M. F., Deng, D. K., & Sharma, M. (2020). Trauma and Inter-communal Relations Among a Captive Population: Preliminary Findings from the Malakal Protection of Civilians Site, South Sudan. In G. Campbell & A. Stanziani (Eds.), *The Palgrave Handbook of Bondage and Human Rights in Africa and Asia* (pp. 327–345). Palgrave Macmillan.

Randazzo, E. (2017). *Beyond Liberal Peacebuilding: A Critical Exploration of the Local Turn*. Routledge.

Richmond, O. (2001). Rethinking Conflict Resolution: The Linkage Problematic Between "track I" and "track II". *Journal of Conflict Studies, 21*(2), 109–132.

Richmond, O. (2006). The Problem of Peace: Understanding the 'liberal peace'. *Conflict, Security & Development, 3*, 291–314.

Richmond, O. (2007). Emancipatory Forms of Human Security and Liberal Peacebuilding. *International Journal, 62*(3), 459–477.

Richmond, O. (2009a). A Post-liberal Peace: Eirenism and the Everyday. *Review of International Studies, 35*(3), 557–580.

Richmond, O. (2009b). Becoming Liberal, Unbecoming Liberalism: Liberal-Local Hybridity Via the Everyday as a Response to the Paradoxes of Liberal Peacebuilding. *Journal of Intervention and Statebuilding, 3*(3), 324–344.

Richmond, O. (2011). De-romanticising the Local, De-mystifying the International: Hybridity in Timor Leste and the Solomon Islands. *The Pacific Review, 24*(1), 115–136.

Richmond, O., & Franks, J. (2009). *Liberal Peace Transitions: Between Statebuilding and Peacebuilding*. Edinburgh University Press.

Richmond, O., & Mac Ginty, R. (2019). Mobilities and Peace. *Globalizations, 16)5)*, 606–624.

Ripsman, N. M. (2016). *Peace-Making from Above, Peace from Below: Ending Conflict Between Regional Rivals*. Cornell University Press.

Rolandsen, O. H. (2015). Another Civil War in South Sudan: The Failure of Guerrilla Government? *Journal of East African Studies, 9*(1), 163–174.

UNHCR. (2016). The Number of South Sudanese Refugees Reaches 1 Million Mark. *UNHCR Report*, September 16. https://www.unhcr.org/news/briefing/2016/9/57dbb5124/number-south-sudanese-refugees-reaches-1-million-mark.html

UNMISS. (2017, February). Human Rights Violations in Yei July 2016–January 2017. *United Nations Mission in South Sudan (UNMISS) Report*.

UNMISS. (2021, March). Armed Violence Involving Community-Based Militias in Greater Jonglei, *United Nations Mission in South Sudan (UNMISS) Report*. https://www.ohchr.org/Documents/Countries/SS/Jonglei-report.pdf

Ware, A., Ware, V.A., & Kelly, L. M. (2022). Strengthening Everyday Peace Formation After Ethnic Cleansing: Operationalising a Framework in Myanmar's Rohingya conflict. *Third World Quarterly, 43*(2), 289–308.

Wassara, S. S. (2015). South Sudan: State Sovereignty Challenged at Infancy. *Journal of East African Studies, 9*(4), 634–649.

Wassara, S. S. (2022). The Sudan People's Liberation Movement/Army: Between Separation and Unity. In J. N. Bach (Ed.), *Routledge Handbook of the Horn of Africa* (pp. 43–54). Routledge.

CHAPTER 11

# Developing Transformatively: Religion and Peace Mediation in Nigeria

*Sokfa F. John*

## Introduction

The term religion carries a vibrant connotation with reference to Nigeria. It is one of the most visible aspects of private and public life and has a troubling association with the persistent, constantly evolving, and shape-shifting violence and conflicts in the country. Irrespective of the source of a conflict, religion may manifest in the form of identity couched in various types of narratives, as a tool for mobilization or recruitment (Agbiboa, 2013; Osaghae & Suberu, 2005; USAID, 2009), or as a site for competition and contesting other issues, such as access to resources or indigeneity/citizenship (John, 2018). Religion is, therefore, an increasingly important consideration for peace and development work within and outside the framework of the Sustainable Development Goals (SDGs). SDG 16 aims to promote peaceful and inclusive societies, access to justice for all, and effective and accountable institutions at all levels. Religion has a salient role in the achievement of this goal. This chapter is interested in (a) targets 16.1: significantly reduce all forms of violence and related death rates everywhere, particularly, indicator 16.1.3: conflict-related deaths (war, conflict, and terrorism); and (b) target 16.3, the promotion of the rule of law and equal access to justice, particularly, indicator 16.3.3: increasing the population who have access to a formal or informal dispute resolution mechanism. The chapter will appraise the religious and interfaith peace

S. F. John (✉)
Centre for Mediation in Africa, University of Pretoria, Pretoria, South Africa

© The Author(s), under exclusive license to Springer Nature Switzerland AG 2023
S. M. Kilonzo et al. (eds.), *The Palgrave Handbook of Religion, Peacebuilding, and Development in Africa*,
https://doi.org/10.1007/978-3-031-36829-5_11

mediation and peacebuilding as central to sustainable development and peace in Nigeria.

Although rarely discussed, religion is central to Nigeria's peace, unity, and development efforts and architecture. Religious actors, institutions, and resources contribute immensely to peace and development at all levels, and beyond the ethnoreligious dimensions of conflicts. In outlining how religion impacts Nigeria's development priorities, Marshall (2020), for example, observed that religious dynamics are visible in peacebuilding and interfaith response to malaria and have a major potential for engagement with national priorities such as education, the fight against corruption, and conflict resolution. The active role that religion plays in mediation and peacebuilding in Nigeria will be briefly discussed in this chapter. I will then discuss, using secondary sources, the work of the Interfaith Mediation Centre (IMC, n.d.) as one of the most profound examples of religious and interfaith peacemaking and peacebuilding from a transformative perspective on conflict and peace. I argue that the work of the IMC is exemplary of transformative mediation and peacebuilding, which has a more positive view of conflicts as opportunities for change, and addresses conflicts in a way that does not only end violence but makes people and society better, and produces better relationships and structural-cultural changes that make future interactions less likely to be violent.

Thus, mediation, as I use it in this chapter, refers to much more than external intervention of neutral third parties to facilitate problem-solving. It is used analytically to include processes, communication, interaction, mobilization, and platforms that enable and empower communities and parties in conflict to understand their differences, recognize each other, find common ground, and work together to inclusively build better and sustainable relationships, commit to non-violent futures and transformation at the personal, structural, cultural, and social levels. The phrase "peace mediation" is, therefore, preferred to align with its increasing usage to refer to interventions that take a multi-track and inclusive approach, and include a broad range of activities that demonstrate how mediation contributes to peace at all levels—from grassroots peacebuilding to high-level diplomacy (Turner & Wählisch, 2021). Peace mediation also highlights the growing appeal of relationship-centred and transformative approaches amongst scholars, organizations, and practitioners. It is this transformative thinking on mediation and peacebuilding that will frame this chapter's appraisal and recommendations on the role of religion in Nigeria's search for sustainable peace.

## Transformative Perspectives on Conflict and Peace

Transformative approaches to peacebuilding, such as conflict transformation and transformative mediation, are often considered the most recently developed approaches. They have developed, and are advanced, as capable of addressing the limitations of the more prevalent problem-solving and interest-based approaches that, despite their recorded successes, have largely failed to build just, positive, lasting, and sustainable peace. Lederach (2015), Bush and Folger (2004), Burgess et al. (1997), and several others have extensively outlined the differences between transformative and other approaches to conflict and peace. According to Burgess et al. (1997) transformative approaches generally use the term "transformation" to denote fundamental change. Thus, scholars and practitioners believe that social conflict intervention should be an opportunity for broader change beyond problem-solving or ending immediate violence. As Lederach noted "You can solve a problem and not change anything. That happens all the time" (Tippet, 2012). Conflict is not necessarily negative or violent but can, in fact, be positive and an opportunity for broader change. Resolution is an opportunity for a change of behaviour and attitude at several levels—personal, structural, community, social, and more. It involves changing beliefs, perspectives, and the patterns of thoughts and action that reproduce and sustain violence, in order to move towards new and better relationships, reconciliation, and a more constructive, positive, and non-violent attitude and commitment towards future conflicts.

Transformative perspectives centralize the people involved and affected by conflicts. They recognize the actors' ownership of their disputes, the resolution process, and outcome; and empower them to transform the cultures and systems that encourage destructiveness during conflicts. Peace is also viewed as necessarily connected to social justice. Dominant conflict resolution and problem-solving approaches are viewed as usually leaving injustices unaddressed because of their focus on bringing parties to settlement without changing the conflict environment, cultures, and relationships (Galtung, 1990; Lederach & Maiese, 2009). Thus, transformative approaches aim to address the problem, the actors, and the dynamics of the conflict through a focus on the personal, relational, cultural, and structural levels of the conflict. It, however, can be time consuming, may require a lot of resources, a diversity of tools, and may not always be applicable depending on the situation. Nonetheless, transformative perspectives are arguably the most promising for just, positive, and sustainable peace and social transformation. Examples of transformative approaches include transformative mediation (Bush & Folger, 2004), conflict transformation (Lederach, 2003), dialogue, collaborative learning (Burgess et al., 1997), and several indigenous and local approaches found across Africa and other parts of the world which centralize factors such as relationship-building and renewal, healing, harmony, non-violence, and change.

Transformative approaches have a rich diversity of sources, including religious ones, such as the non-violent movement of Mahatma Gandhi, the US civil rights movement, the struggles against apartheid and the Truth and Reconciliation Commission in South Africa, indigenous peoples' movements around the world, and the liberation theology of South America (Martin, 2019). This does not mean that these processes themselves or their leaders necessarily achieved fundamental and lasting change in Society. In fact, criticisms of, for example, Gandhi, or the Truth and Reconciliation Commission in South Africa, exist that make it difficult to view these movements as transformative conflict resolution processes in the sense explained above (Lal, 2008; Nanda, 1998; Verwoerd, 1999). However, ideals, such as non-violent means to peace, or the desire to heal and rebuild community and relationships, among others, which were part of these efforts, contributed to thinking about transformative peacebuilding. Some of the most prominent conflict transformation figures developed their ideas using religious sources and/or were inspired by their personal religious commitment. Johan Galtung, for example, used principles and values from several of the world's major religions, and Lederach's work is deeply rooted in his Mennonite pacifist ethics (Martin, 2019).

This is an indication of the diverse ways that religious actors and sources contribute to conflict resolution, peace, and transformation. Religious values, teachings, worldviews have been powerful sources of peace and major social change. According to Bercovitch and Kadayifci-Orellana (2009, pp. 176–177), faith-based actors

> have an impact on changing behaviours, attitudes, and negative stereotypes; educating the parties; healing trauma and injuries; disseminating ideas such as democracy and human rights; drafting committed people to do work; challenging traditional structures that perpetuate structural violence; mediating between conflicting parties; reaching out to governments to incorporate elements of peace building in their policies; encouraging disarmament, reintegration of soldiers and developing a sustained interfaith dialogue.

In the section that follows, I map out religious peacebuilding work in Nigeria. The goal is to give a comprehensive picture of whom the actors are, the type of work they do, how Nigeria as a state approaches peacebuilding from a religious perspective, as well as the challenges and limitations of some of these efforts.

## Religious Peace Work in Nigeria

Nweke (2019, p. 441) rightly observes that religious actors and faith-based organizations are the "fulcrum of most peacebuilding activities in Nigeria" and that civil authorities usually depend on them to de-escalate conflicts and to build peace afterwards. Religious actors are tasked with promoting messages of peace, reconciliation, unity, and harmony in the country to prevent future violence and resolve existing conflicts. Nweke (2019) lists some of the practical ways that religious actors contribute towards peace in Nigeria, including, organizing dialogues, town hall meetings, peace education and training, establishing early warning teams and community peace enablers, election monitoring, electoral violence prevention initiatives, legal aid and support, micro-finance, mediation, implementation of peace agreements, monitoring, trauma healing, post-conflict peacebuilding, and more.

Dialogue is central to religious peace work in Nigeria. Interfaith dialogue became a prominent word in public discourse following the many instances of ethnoreligious violence over the past three decades. Several government and non-governmental organizations organized formal dialogue meetings, usually, as one of the immediate responses to occurrences of conflicts. These dialogues mostly involved religious leaders and heads of religious associations, academics, government officials, and sometimes civil society leaders. In the 2000s and 2010s, most of these dialogues appeared to have a lot of limitations. Some of them include taking formal academic and theological conference formats where Christians and Muslim presenters mostly recount scriptural messages and arguments to support their positions that their respective religions were peaceful and were against violence, without confronting the underlying role of their respective religions in the conflicts. These dialogues, especially those organized by governments, were also elitist, involving actors who did not have close proximity to the actuarial violence or were not directly affected, therefore, having little to no trickledown effect on the grassroots where most of the violence occurred. Thus, they were generally perceived as ineffective. Additionally, interfaith dialogue in Nigeria was mostly reactive. As Ojo and Lateju (2010) pointed out, most such initiatives did not address tensions in their early stages but only responded after such tensions had escalated into violence. Nonetheless, these efforts contributed to slowly building a national tradition, or at least, a certain consciousness, of dialogue as a better way to address differences and pursue group interests. It also encouraged responses at the grassroots as many became concerned about the gap between high-level dialogue and grassroots tensions.

Religious and interfaith peace work in Nigeria occurs at the local community, state, regional, national, and international levels, involving a broad range of local and international, government and non-governmental organizations and entities. International organizations such as the Centre for Humanitarian Dialogue (HD Centre), United States Institute of Peace (USIP), Peace Direct, United Nations Development Programme (UNDP), World Council of Churches (WCC), Catholic Relief Services (CRS), United States Agency for International Development (USAID), and KAICIID support faith-based peacebuilding in Nigeria, mainly as funders, but sometimes through other forms of engagement. Younger organizations like the International Centre for Ethnoreligious Mediation (ICERMediation), which has had longstanding interest in Nigeria, are also taking steps to establish interfaith peacebuilding work in Nigeria. ICERMediation, for example, is currently establishing an office in Nigeria and looking to establish its Living Together Movement (LTM) across Nigerian institutions of higher learning and communities as a proactive peacebuilding strategy, while also working with traditional leaders to promote ethnoreligious and cultural mediation and peacebuilding.

Nationally, the federal and state governments support the work of interreligious organizations and have also established their own interfaith bodies. The federal government supported the establishment of the Nigeria

Inter-Religious Council (NIREC) in 1999 as a voluntary association of representatives of Nigeria's two largest religions Islam and Christianity. Membership of the council initially constituted 50 seats equally divided between Christians and Muslims in 2019 was increased to 60 to increase youth and women participation (nirec.org.ng). The council's leadership includes prominent religious leaders such as the Sultan of Sokoto and chair of the Nigerian Supreme Council of Islamic Affairs, and leading Christian Bishops who were also presidents of the Christian Association of Nigeria (nirec.org.ng). NIREC engages in interfaith dialogue and collaborates with local and international organizations to promote peace, development, and well-being of Nigerians (Omotosho, 2014). It also advises the government on how to respond to ethnoreligious issues. NIREC enjoys public support and funding from the government, although it is established as an independent body. It has received criticism in recent years for being absent and unresponsive to the increasing polarizations and religion-related insecurities in the country (Sote, 2021).

The two umbrella religious bodies in Nigeria, the Christian Association of Nigeria (CAN) and the Jama'tu Nasril Islam (JNI), have been at the forefront of protecting and promoting the interests of their respective religions in the country, fighting for justice and equality for members of their religions. They have also played significant roles in promoting peace through their public declarations and activities, and interaction with one another. Other notable organizations in religious and interfaith peace work include the Kukah Centre (TKC), the Interfaith Action for Peace (IFAP), the Federation of Muslim Women's Associations in Nigeria (FOMWAN), International Peace Leave (IPL), the Conference of Religious Educators and Leaders (COREL), and the Women's Wing of the Christian Association of Nigeria (WOWICAN) (Isola, 2014).

The federal and state governments have in the past inaugurated commissions of inquiry immediately after violent incidents to identify root causes and perpetrators and make recommendations to improve accountability and prevent impunity. For example, this strategy was used by different governments in Plateau State to respond to ethnoreligious conflicts between 1994 and 2008 and in Kaduna State in previous and more recent tensions, such as the clash between the Shia sect, Islamic Movement in Nigeria (IMN), and the Nigerian army in 2015 (Shiklam & Somirin, 2016), and to establish the facts in killings in Kajuru, Kaduna, in 2019 (Agande, 2019). This approach has generally not achieved the expected benefits for the society and is considered ineffective. This is partly because such commissions tend to be entangled in state or federal politics, have competing interests, and fail to ultimately achieve the desired accountability as their recommendations are not implemented, especially when it negatively affects powerful people and politicians (Oosterom et al., 2021).

Middle Belt states like Kaduna and Plateau have in recent years decided to establish permanent peace agencies or commissions, beyond ad hoc incident-specific commissions of inquiry (Kew, 2021). The federal equivalent of this would be the Institute for Peace and Conflict Resolution, established in 2000, although it is a think tank, more focused on research, training, and policy. The Kaduna State Peace Commission (KSPC) was established in 2017, with a religious leader as its chair, and Plateau Peace Building Agencies (PPBA) was established in 2016 (Daily Post, 2016; Sesan, 2017). These entities engage in conflict prevention, peace advocacy, proactively build tolerance and peaceful co-existence, engage in conflict resolution and multi-track diplomacy and mediation, work with civil society organizations and grassroots entities, and so on. Given the role of religion and ethnicity in conflicts in these states, the work of these entities will significantly revolve around interfaith peacebuilding. According to Kew (2021), these entities are meant to bring conflict resolution closer to the communities and deal with conflicts at their sources in order to prevent them from growing and igniting larger ethnic, religious, or political tensions in the states. While these entities have successfully intervened in conflicts and have potential for immense impact, they are faced with challenges. Their identification with the governments that established them threatens their survival in future regimes, their independence and autonomy and being government entities reporting to the government, is questionable and ambiguous (Kew, 2021).

The religious and interfaith peacemaking and peacebuilding environment in Nigeria is evidently an active one at all levels. However, Nweke (2019) argues that the local community level is the "heartbeat" of religious peacebuilding in the country. It is at this level that the most important and most effective mobilization for conflict occurs, and it is this level that determines peace at the national level (Nweke, 2019). These accounts of peace work in Nigeria do not accommodate the many unknown or little-known individuals, preachers, students, petty traders, and other entities who, inspired by their faith and as a commitment to their religious values, engage in the dialogue of life and peacebuilding in their everyday interactions, behaviours, and decisions, sometimes risking their own well-being and security in the process. These are at the heart of everyday peace, healing, and reconciliation in Nigeria. They are the custodians of the cultures of peace and the extensive periods of peaceful co-existence and tolerance that Nigeria enjoys. It is also they who make it possible to return to peace following violent eruptions.

Religious and interfaith peace work in Nigeria faces several limitations and challenges. One such limitation is the fact that religion in Nigeria is often taken for granted to mean Christianity and Islam, and interfaith relations to mean Christian-Muslim relations. While some acknowledgement is made of indigenous religions, they are often treated as inferior and irrelevant in the country's priority concerns. The many non-Christian and non-Muslim religions and spiritualities, humanist expressions, and others in the country are often excluded in the analysis and framing of issues, in the assessment of those affected and stakeholders, and in designing policies and interventions. This shows that interfaith peacebuilding in Nigeria is concerned primarily with the religions with the larger numbers and which are most visible during conflicts.

Organizations such as the NIREC and other efforts appear not to have any meaningful interaction with other religions. Alozieuwa (2017) notes that interfaith dialogue in Nigeria has a doubtful viability because of its failure to include other religions, especially indigenous religions, despite their capacity to provide the environment for Christianity and Islam to peacefully coexist. As the human rights activist, Leo Igwe (2022), also criticized, restricting formal conversational spaces on issues that affect everyone in Nigeria to two faiths is problematic. This approach only worsens the problem it attempts to resolve, and all faith and no-faith traditions need to be included. For Igwe, the religious crisis in Nigeria is complicated and complex and cannot be reduced to an issue between Christians and Muslims. It has many dimensions. It is "a conflict within and without faith communities. The religious crisis is a conflict between Christians and Traditionalists, Muslims and Muslims, Christians and Humanists/Atheists, Muslims and Humanists/Atheists etc.", thus, the constitution and operations of bodies like the NIREC need to be revised (Igwe, 2022).

Nigeria's exclusivist approach to interfaith relations and peacebuilding is a missed opportunity for other religious actors to actively contribute to peacebuilding and the forging of common national values and identity. Religious actors that are neither Christian nor Muslim may sometimes be in a better position to mediate conflicts between Christians and Muslims if given the opportunity. Quakers, for example, were recommended for the important mediation role they played during the Nigerian civil war because of their unofficial religious status in Nigeria (Sampson, 1994, p. 93). Organizations like the World Council of Churches, despite its deep humanitarian and peacebuilding involvement during the civil had unresolved dilemmas that did not allow it to effectively mediate during the war (von Rütte, 2016). Other Christian and Muslim attempts were also viewed with suspicion because of the accusations of religious motives behind the war, but Quakers were accepted because they were considered trustworthy as an outside religious organization (Faseke, 2019).

Other challenges, according to Isola (2014), include the fact that some religious leaders only participate in interreligious mediation and peacebuilding as an opportunity for personal benefit, political power, and privilege, rather than a genuine commitment to peace and reconciliation. Also many of them do not have the required skills and education to effectively mediate and some religious actors and parties approach the process with rigid fundamentalist attitudes, while conflict entrepreneurs seek to undermine interfaith mediation efforts to maintain their financial gains from conflicts.

## The Interfaith Mediation Centre

The IMC belongs to the category of interfaith peacebuilding organizations that explicitly focus on interfaith mediation in addition to other activities. The remarkable stories of the co-directors of the IMC and their transformation from sworn enemies to friends and collaborative peace mediators and peacebuilders are always fresh in richness and lessons. Imam Muhammad Ashafa and Pastor James Wuye both grew up in Kaduna, which has a long history of ethnoreligious conflicts and other grievances rooted in colonial as well as pre-/post-colonial formations (John, 2018). It is also one of the states that have been heavily affected by activities of religious extremists, violence involving herdsmen, and the recent kidnapping economy.

During the Zango-Kataf violent conflict of 1992, both Wuye and Ashafa were leaders of Christian and Muslim groups, respectively, who engaged in violence against members of each other's religion. Wuye lost his right hand to Ashafa's boys, and Ashafa lost his mentor and two relatives to Wuye's boys during this conflict (Eteng, 2020). They remained bitter enemies hoping to kill each other someday until a friend urged them towards mutual forgiveness and to work for peace (Interfaith Mediation Centre, n.d.). This took some time and further encouragement from their own religious organizations and superiors, but they eventually forgave each other, laid the foundation for a new relationship, and became partners in peacebuilding (Eteng, 2020).

Ashafa and Wuye founded the IMC in 1995, initially, the Muslim-Christian Youth Dialogue Forum, as a faith-based, non-governmental, and non-profit organization to promote peace, resolve conflict, promote inclusive governance, and rural health in Nigeria (Interfaith Mediation Centre, n.d.). Based in Kaduna, the IMC works mostly in grassroots peacebuilding but also works at the state, national, and international levels. The IMC's website says that it is now an important player in human rights and conflict resolution with a focus on religion, social development, and good governance at a multi-track level. It has also successfully intervened in over 200 conflicts and worked in Nigeria, Sudan, Kenya, Chad, Libya, Sri Lanka, Iraq, and Ethiopia. Its work includes advocacy, mediation and conflict resolution capacity building for faith-based organizations, direct mediation, crisis response, relationship-building, interfaith dialogue, and early warning and response, amongst others (Interfaith Mediation Centre, n.d.).

The IMC has mediated Christian-Muslim conflicts in Nigeria and developed a community of peace activists including young people, traditional leaders, religious actors, women, and others. It has successfully brought Muslims and Christians together to collaborate and support each other to address damages due to conflict. It has also worked with young people and has established clubs in several institutions of higher learning in Nigeria. Some of the IMC's current projects involve faith-based approach to corruption; addressing farmer-herder conflicts in Taraba state, Nigeria, in collaboration with women organizations and others; health accountability and advocacy; combating violent extremism and promoting peaceful co-existence; training in dialogue, and strengthening early warning, including in six Nigerian states in preparation for the 2023 Nigerian general elections (Interfaith Mediation Centre, n.d.).

The IMC has several notable mediation achievements (Eteng, 2020; Harvard Divinity School, 2013; Isola, 2014). For example, its intervention during the Sharia conflict and post-conflict peacebuilding in 2000 and its facilitation of the Kaduna Peace Declaration between Christians and Muslims in 2002 in collaboration with the state government. A case worth recounting is the successful mediation of the Yelwa-Shendam conflict in Plateau State in 2004.

The tensions between the Christian and Muslim communities had built up for years with several government and non-governmental efforts failing to achieve a resolution. Thus, in 2004, a flare-up resulted in the deaths of over 1000 people, leading to the declaration of a state of emergency in Plateau State by the federal government (Sadiq, 2013). Ashafa and Wuye were invited by the interim administrator to mediate and were able to lead the parties to sign a peace affirmation in which the parties agreed to end violence, accommodate each other, and use dialogue instead of violence to address any future disputes. Ashafa and Wuye used several strategies, including a series of faith-based and interfaith workshops and training for groups such as youth, women, and community members and religious leaders (Eteng, 2020). These covered conflict resolution, trauma counselling, mediation, and reconciliation, and also resulted in the formation of a local interfaith working group to collaborate with government and civil society organizations to sustain peace in the area. During their meetings with religious leaders, they also used preaching and other conflict resolution techniques. The mediation was not a smooth process, and parties were confrontational in the first few days of the initial five-day meeting, but gradually recognized each other, agreed on the causes of the conflicts, took responsibility for their roles, apologized, sought forgiveness, agreed to work together towards resolution, and developed a peace agreement. The peace agreement prioritized local concerns and actions that community leaders and members could take, including addressing things such as disrespect of traditional authority, use of derogatory language, and the spread of inflammatory information and misinformation, amongst other things (Harvard Divinity School, 2013). The communities celebrated the agreement with thousands of attendees in 2005 and have remained peaceful for over 15 years since.

The primary strategies of the IMC is dialogue and mediation, using scriptural texts from the Bible and the Quran to facilitate forgiveness, reconciliation, love, peaceful co-existence, and trust. In their extensive peacebuilding work, they also provide trauma counselling, rehabilitation of former combatants, providing economic opportunities, including financial support for skills and business development, amongst other things.

From a transformative lens, Wuye and Ashafa, as well as the work of their organization, the IMC, offer many key lessons on conflict intervention to achieve the relevant targets of SDG 16. The personal transformation and reconciliation of Wuye and Ashafa represents an ideal goal of conflict transformation at a personal level. They did not only resolve to stop targeting each other or being violent towards each other, but they were personally changed and became different people. They developed a constructive, better, and more positive relationship, and the process also transformed them into highly impactful peacebuilders that are significantly bringing about change at the cultural, structural, and other relationship levels of society—addressing the fundamental issues and patterns, at the grassroots, that create conducive environments for violence. Their personal commitment to their faiths, while using religious resources to collaboratively promote peace and social change, is also exemplary of the powerful potential of religious resources and religious collaboration for peace and development.

Transformative approaches to conflict sometimes take time and resources, dealing with the complexity of the conflict and, as Lederach puts it with regard to conflict transformation, to "envision and respond to the ebb and flow of social conflict as life-giving opportunities for creating constructive change processes that reduce violence, increase justice in direct interaction and social structures, and respond to real-life problems in human relationships" (Lederach, 2003). The IMC's use of a combination of strategies that address conflicts and the parties holistically is responsive in this regard. For example, their use of trauma counselling, scriptures, workshops, dialogue, negotiation, and involvement of a broad range of affected stakeholders at the committee level during the Yelwa-Shendam mediation enabled them to address not only the immediate problem of violence but to address other social, psychological, material, and spiritual needs. They not only solved a problem but also changed relationships, changed people, attitudes, behaviours, sowed seeds for constructive conflicts in the future, both in getting the parties to see each other and conflicts differently and to commit to non-violent futures, and in their establishment of a local committee to continue the work they had started. Thus, the foundations they laid for transformation are likely to result in a more sustainable peace, significantly reduce the likelihood of violence, and encourage a culture of non-violence and collaboration.

The work of the IMC is also an important critique of the dominant problem-solving model of mediation which sees mediation as primarily an intervention by an outsider and neutral third party. As Kadayifci-Orellana and Maassarani (2021) in their recent USIP Religion and Mediation Action Guide, a more common practice in religious and traditional mediation, as well as other contexts, is the insider-multipartial model. The authors clarified with a comparison what they refer to as the problem-solving outsider-impartial model to further clarify. In the latter, parties are treated as individuals that interact in a confidential and private space; the mediator has no affiliation with the parties, and is an expert; participation is voluntary, although not participating could have legal consequences; it is a linear, problem-solving process, where mediators are primarily concerned with the process and indirectly influence the outcome; and explicit written agreements are the expected results. On the other hand, in religious or traditional insider-multipartial mediation, the parties are viewed as members of a community interacting in a public space; the mediator is a community member and has relationships with participants; voluntariness is implicit, and non-participation may carry social consequences for the participants; the process focuses on maintaining relationships and community, and is not linear; mediators may directly influence outcome and are not primarily focused on process; and the result can be explicit or implicit understanding (Kadayifci-Orellana & Maassarani, 2021). The IMC's intervention is an indication that other approaches to mediation do work and in some cases achieve better results than any rigid problem-solving or formal interest-based approach. It also offers an opportunity to re-examine values such as neutrality and their applicability in actual practice. The IMC works with religious communities in the context of religious conflicts and uses religious resources. As religious leaders and insiders, Wuye, Ashafa, and their colleagues enjoy legitimacy and trustworthiness that religiously neutral outsiders may never receive. As members of the ethnoreligious communities whose conflicts they mediate, they have proven to be highly effective, and as previous violent perpetrators and victims in similar situations, they are motivated, and their intervention is likely as personal as it is altruistic.

The IMC's focus on the local is key to its success (Harvard Divinity School, 2013). Religious peacebuilding has a good impact at the grassroots as religious leaders and institutions tend to be closer to the people. The IMC's multi-track connections and access also show that religious actors are well suited for multi-track intervention. The influence of religion and religious authorities often transcends any single sphere, cleavage, and identity group. Thus, religious leaders and organizations are able to reach the grassroots as much as they can reach national and international stakeholders. This is an important resource and leverage for multi-track peacebuilding and diplomacy.

## Concluding Reflections and Recommendations

Religion has much to offer to significantly reduce all forms of violence and deaths due to conflict, war, and terrorism, as envisioned in SDG 16.1. It can also help in promoting effective dispute resolution as in SDG 16.3. The extensive religious and interfaith peacebuilding work in Nigeria examined in this chapter attests to this. Taking advantage of the power of religion and religious entities in places like Nigeria requires a more extensive and genuine engagement with religious organizations, individuals, and resources. It also requires an equally extensive engagement with the role that religion already plays in creating and sustaining peace and conflicts. So much effort goes into understanding religious dimensions of conflicts, while an important step towards sustainable peace may lie more in actually understanding and expanding the role of religions in sustainable everyday peace.

An important aspect of the local turn in international peacebuilding (Leonardsson & Rudd, 2015; Mac Ginty & Richmond, 2013), which is crucial to any successful intervention, is that peace targets need to increasingly align with local conceptions of peace. In places like Nigeria, such local visions of peace often significantly include religious dimensions that are dear to people, and which are missed by exclusively liberal peace intervention targets. For example, a USIP study on what people in Bauchi, Kaduna, Nasarawa, and Plateau States define as or would consider to be indicators of peace was revealing. Most participants in all states saw peace as more than the absence of direct violence and insecurity, but as good relations with their neighbours and/or their communities, between different ethnic or religious communities, and harmony within families (Bukar et al., 2021). Over 80 per cent of the study's respondents in all states (nearly 9 in 10) ranked "freedom to practice my religion and/or conduct religious activities" as the "most important" indicator of peace; and 8 in 10 also ranked the occurrence of "people of different faiths socializing together" as the "most important" indicator of peace (Bukar et al., 2021). Other indicators that relate to fundamental needs and economic activities were also highly ranked, but this study suggests that religious and transformative/relational concerns are high on people's priorities and understanding of peace.

It is also important to develop an adequate and comprehensive understanding of religion in order to successfully and effectively engage religion for SDG 16, through peace mediation and other interventions. Due to the extreme difficulty in offering a universal definition of religion without essentializing with dangerous material impact, several analytical models exist for understanding religion and religious components, depending on one's purpose. In their guide for religion in mediation, Kadayifci-Orellana and Maassarani (2021) suggests Owen and Frazer's (2018) five interrelated dimensions of religion as useful for understanding the role of religion in conflict and peacebuilding. These include religion as a set of ideas: religion as community, religion as symbols and practices, and religion as spirituality (Owen & Frazer, 2018). Models like these and an extensive contextual understanding of religion in the specific context of intervention are invaluable to successful peace mediation and other interventions. This is especially important given how coloniality, orientalism, racism, and other power dynamics and knowledge regimes have shaped contemporary understanding of non-Western cultures and the current efforts towards decolonization. Thus, an application of the wrong model to understand religion can further alienate conflicting communities and dehumanize them under the guise of peacebuilding. The IMC's advantage is that it has both Muslim and Christian insider resources and commitment, and draws on these theological resources to engage people with the same spiritual commitments. Other contexts may present very different religious situations, and these need to be assessed carefully and thoroughly.

A rigorous understanding and responsiveness to the religious landscape of targeted intervention location is extremely crucial. In Nigeria, this can be confusing despite appearances and popular narratives. For example, it is very common to speak of religious tensions as existing between Christians and Muslims, and because of their ties to ethnic identities, religions easily become regional or ethnic identities. Yet, religious tensions in Nigeria could also refer to intra-religious tensions. The Muslim community, for example, may appear to be, and is sometimes represented by outsiders and Christians as being, strongly united, but there are complex divisions and sometimes fatal sectarianism internally within Nigeria's Islam (Mustapha, 2014; Mustapha & Bunza, 2014). Also, the uncritical and uninformed regionalism mindset of many Nigerians leads them to generalize and essentialize regions such as the North as Muslim or Hausa, and the South as Christian, but significant numbers of Christians exist in the North, and the Middle Belt axis predominantly constitutes Christian ethnic minorities, and there are a considerable number of Muslims in the east, including Igbos. Generalizations of Christian-Muslim conflicts also often overlook the exemplary interfaith integration in Western Nigeria and other places, where religious differences and identities are not as negatively important as other issues, and people do not only respect each other's religions but celebrate them. It has also been noted earlier that interfaith relations in Nigeria is a question bigger than Christianity and Islam. Continued exclusion or assimilation of other faith and no-faith expressions into these two categories is counterproductive. These dynamics may seem dismissible, but they matter to those affected because they are closely tied to their identities, everyday life, and related struggles. When it comes to religious identities and populations, the lack of quality and reliable statistics in Nigeria is another challenge, thus, decisions that impact religious constituencies can be a source of serious contestations. Therefore, a careful and nuanced analysis of the religious landscape of a conflict location can make a tremendous difference in whether interventions are positively or negatively impactful.

**Acknowledgement** The author wishes to acknowledge the National Institute for the Humanities and Social Sciences (NIHSS), South Africa, for its funding and support, through the Centre for Mediation in Africa, University of Pretoria.

## References

Agande, B. (2019, March 3). Kaduna to Establish Judicial Commission of Inquiry into Kajuru Killings. *Vanguard News.* https://www.vanguardngr.com/2019/03/kaduna-to-establish-judicial-commission-of-inquiry-into-kajuru-killings/

Agbiboa, D. E. (2013). Ethno-religious Conflicts and the Elusive Quest for National Identity in Nigeria. *Journal of Black Studies, 44*(1), 3–30.

Alozieuwa, S. H. O. (2017). The Troubled Relationship, Interfaith Dialogue and the Long Search for Peaceful Co-existence. *Ubuntu: Journal of Conflict and Social Transformation, 6*(2), 43–62. https://doi.org/10.10520/EJC-bcb509a4b

Bercovitch, J., & Kadayifci-Orellana, S. A. (2009). Religion and Mediation: The Role of Faith-based Actors in International Conflict Resolution. *International Negotiation, 14*(1), 175–204.

Bukar, Y., Kwaja, C., & Verjee, A. (2021). *Six Alternative Ways to Measure Peace in Nigeria.* United States Institute of Peace. https://www.usip.org/publications/2021/09/six-alternative-ways-measure-peace-nigeria

Burgess, H., Burgess, G., Glaser, T., & Yevsyukova, M. (1997). *Transformative Approaches to Conflict.* Conflict Research Consortium. Retrieved August 17, 2005, from Http://www.Colorado.Edu/Conflict/Transform/

Bush, R. A. B., & Folger, J. P. (2004). *The Promise of Mediation: The Transformative Approach to Conflict*. John Wiley & Sons.

Daily Post, S. (2016, August 22). Plateau Peace Building Agency was Created to Promote Mutual Trust Among Residents—DG. *Daily Post Nigeria*. https://dailypost.ng/2016/08/22/plateau-peace-building-agency-created-promote-mutual-trust-among-residents-dg/

Eteng, E. I. (2020). *Imam Ashafa and Pastor James Wuye: Bringing Peace to Warring Nigerian Communities*. Centre for Religion and Civic Culture. https://crcc.usc.edu/imam-ashafa-and-pastor-james-wuye-bringing-peace-to-warring-nigerian-communities/

Faseke, B. O. (2019). Quaker Mission in the Nigerian Civil War and Ephraim Isaac's Mediation in the Ethiopian Civil War: Lessons in Religious Peacebuilding. *Journal of Religion & Spirituality in Social Work: Social Thought, 38*(4), 350–367. https://doi.org/10.1080/15426432.2019.1674235

Galtung, J. (1990). Cultural Violence. *Journal of Peace Research, 27*(3), 291–305. https://doi.org/10.1177/0022343390027003005

Harvard Divinity School. (2013). *Case Study: Interfaith Peacebuilding*. Religion in Context. https://rpl.hds.harvard.edu/religion-context/country-profiles/nigeria/case-study-interfaith-peacebuilding

Igwe, L. (2022, December 7). A Humanist Perspective on Interfaith Dialogue in Nigeria. *Tribune Online*. https://tribuneonlineng.com/a-humanist-perspective-on-interfaith-dialogue-in-nigeria-2/

Interfaith Mediation Centre (IMC). (n.d.). History—Interfaith Mediation Centre. Retrieved December 27, 2022, from https://interfaithmediation.org/history/

Isola, O. O. (2014). *Interfaith Conflict Mediation Mechanisms and Peacebuilding in Nigeria—ICERMediation*. Annual International Conference. https://icermediation.org/interfaith-conflict-mediation-in-nigeria/

John, S. F. (2018). Genocide, Oppression, Ambivalence: Online Narratives of Identity and Religion in Postcolonial Nigeria. *Open Library of Humanities, 4*(2), 1–28. https://doi.org/10.16995/olh.284

Kadayifci-Orellana, S. A., & Maassarani, T. (2021). *Religion and Mediation Action Guide*. United States Institute of Peace. https://www.usip.org/programs/religious-peacebuilding-action-guides

Kew, D. (2021). *Nigeria's State Peacebuilding Institutions: Early Success and Continuing Challenges* (Special Report No. 496). United States Institute of Peace. https://www.usip.org/publications/2021/06/nigerias-state-peacebuilding-institutions-early-success-and-continuing

Lal, V. (2008). The Gandhi Everyone Loves to Hate. *Economic and Political Weekly, 43*(40), 55–64.

Lederach, J. (2003). *Little Book of Conflict Transformation: Clear Articulation of the Guiding Principles by a Pioneer in the Field*. Good Books.

Lederach, J. (2015). *Little Book of Conflict Transformation: Clear Articulation of the Guiding Principles by a Pioneer in the Field*. Good Books.

Lederach, J. P., & Maiese, M. (2009). Conflict Transformation: A Circular Journey with a Purpose. *New Routes, 14*(2), 7–11.

Leonardsson, H., & Rudd, G. (2015). The 'Local Turn' in Peacebuilding: A Literature Review of Effective and Emancipatory Local Peacebuilding. *Third World Quarterly, 36*(5), 825–839.

Mac Ginty, R., & Richmond, O. P. (2013). The Local Turn in Peace Building: A Critical Agenda for Peace. *Third World Quarterly, 34*(5), 763–783.

Marshall, K. (2020). *The Impact of Ethnic and Religious Diversity on Nigeria's Development Priorities*. World Faiths Development Dialogue; Berkley Centre for Religion, Peace and World Affairs. https://berkleycenter.georgetown.edu/publications/the-impact-of-ethnic-and-religious-diversity-on-nigeria-s-development-priorities

Martin, M. S. (2019, December 29). What Is Conflict Transformation? *Brave Talk Project*. https://bravetalkproject.com/what-is-conflict-transformation/

Mustapha, A. R. (2014). *Sects & Social Disorder: Muslim Identities & Conflict in Northern Nigeria* (Vol. 5). Boydell & Brewer Ltd.

Mustapha, A. R., & Bunza, M. U. (2014). Contemporary Islamic Sects and Groups in Northern Nigeria. In *Sects and Social Disorder: Muslim Identities and Conflict in Northern Nigeria* (pp. 54–97). James Currey.

Nanda, B. R. (1998). *Gandhi and His Critics*. Oxford University Press.

Nweke, P. C. (2019). Religious Peacebuilding in Nigeria. *Peace Review, 30*(4), 440–447.

Ojo, M. A., & Lateju, F. T. (2010). Christian–Muslim Conflicts and Interfaith Bridge-Building Efforts in Nigeria. *The Review of Faith & International Affairs, 8*(1), 31–38. https://doi.org/10.1080/15570271003707762

Omotosho, M. (2014). Managing Religious Conflicts in Nigeria: The Inter-religious Mediation Peace Strategy. *Africa Development, 39*(2), 133–151.

Oosterom, M., Sha, D. P., & Dowd, C. (2021). Commissions of Inquiry and Pathways to Accountability in Plateau State, Nigeria. *The Journal of Modern African Studies, 59*(4), 439–462. https://doi.org/10.1017/S0022278X21000252

Osaghae, E. E., & Suberu, R. T. (2005). *A History of Identities, Violence and Stability in Nigeria* (Vol. 6). Centre for Research on Inequality, Human Security and Ethnicity.

Owen, M., & Frazer, O. (2018). *Religion in Conflict and Peacebuilding*. https://www.usip.org/sites/default/files/USIP_Religion-in-Conflict-Peacebuilding_Analysis-Guide.pdf.

von Rütte, H. (2016, May 19). The Problem of How to Enact Diakonia: The World Council of Churches and the Nigerian Civil War, 1967–1970. *CIHA Blog*. https://www.cihablog.com/problem-enact-diakonia-world-council-churches-nigerian-civil-war-1967-1970/

Sadiq, L. (2013, September 7). Nigeria: Yelwa-Shendam—Rising from Ashes, Nine Years after Bloodbath. *Daily Trust*. https://allafrica.com/stories/201309070163.html

Sampson, C. (1994). 'To Make Real the Bond Between Us All': Quaker Conciliation during the Nigerian Civil War. In *Religion: The Missing Dimension of Statecraft* (pp. 88–118). Oxford University Press.

Sesan. (2017, November 2). S'Kaduna Crisis: El-Rufai Inaugurates Peace Commission. *Punch Newspapers*. https://punchng.com/skaduna-crisis-el-rufai-inaugurates-peace-commission/

Shiklam, J., & Somirin, Z. (2016). Kaduna Judicial Panel Recommends Prosecution of Soldiers, El-Zakzaky—THISDAYLIVE. *This Day*. https://www.thisdaylive.com/index.php/2016/08/02/kaduna-judicial-panel-recommends-prosecution-of-soldiers-el-zakzaky/

Sote, L. (2021, September 21). Whatever Happened to NIREC? *Punch Newspapers*. https://punchng.com/whatever-happened-to-nirec/

Tippet. (2012). *John Paul Lederach—The Art of Peace*. Retrieved December 31, 2022, from https://onbeing.org/programs/john-paul-lederach-the-art-of-peace/

Turner, C., & Wählisch, M. (2021). Rethinking Peace Mediation: Trends and Challenges. In *Rethinking Peace Mediation: Challenges of Contemporary Peacemaking Practice* (pp. 1–14). Bristol University Press. https://www.jstor.org/stable/j.ctv1d82h8q

USAID. (2009). *Religion, Conflict and Peacebuilding.* https://jliflc.com/resources/usaid-religion-conflict-peacebuilding/

Verwoerd, W. J. (1999). Toward the Truth about the TRC: A Response to Key Moral Criticisms of the South African Truth and Reconciliation Commission. *Religion and Theology, 6*(3), 303–324.

CHAPTER 12

# Ethnic and Political Conflicts Resolution in Burundi: The Contribution of Religious Organisations

*Elias Sentamba*

## INTRODUCTION

In spite of the current meanings, Hutu, Tutsi, Twa and Ganwa in Burundi cannot be defined as 'ethnic groups' as is the case in several African countries. The term 'ethnic group' implies a human grouping with a specific culture, language, territory and so on, in relation to the others. Here, all these 'segments' share these elements and had a social cohesion as a nation before the Belgian colonial intrusion. They only became 'ethnic components' in violent conflict as a result of political mismanagement since independence. The crises of 1965, 1972, 1993 and 2015 have finally inoculated Burundians with an ethno-political culture that is difficult to ward off. Even the Arusha Agreements (2017) have not decanted the ethno-political reflexes, since each electoral process is followed by violent conflicts, always on the ethno-political terrain.

It is in this context that religions are working, in line with the SDG 16 (Sustainable Development Goal) whose motto is "*Peace and governance (just, peaceful and inclusive societies)*" (République du Burundi, 2018). These are the main religions, namely Christianity and Islam. The former has many religious organisations: the Catholic Church on the one hand and several Protestant churches such as the Anglican, Pentecostal, Methodist and Adventist, to mention only the best known, on the other. As for the second, it has two main

E. Sentamba (✉)
Department of Political Science, University of Burundi, Bujumbura, Burundi

religious organisations, namely the Sunnis and the Shiites. It should be noted that these different religious organisations enjoy varying degrees of social rootedness. As the most deeply rooted of these have been able to carry out charitable works without the distinction of multiple affiliations, they have proved to be the most appropriate actors to resolve the ethno-political conflicts in Burundi. It should be noted that this chapter focuses on the two main religions, Christianity and Islam. Within the former, only the Catholic Church (62% of the Burundian population) and the Anglican and Pentecostal Churches (the most important Protestant organisations) are included. As for the second (Islam), it is retained without the distinction of religious organisations. Finally, the 'traditional religion' (k*ubandwa* cult) in which all the clans (*miryango*) met before colonisation and therefore before the introduction of the Christian and Islamic faiths remains alive even if the cult is practised rather discreetly, except in some regions such as Mwaro and the east of the country.

As human institutions, the selected religions necessarily have strengths and weaknesses. Strengths include ethno-political inclusiveness, as religious leaders are indiscriminately Hutu and Tutsi on the one hand, and the faithful come from all ethnic and political backgrounds on the other. Moreover, as their work (preaching and charity) benefits all segments of society, religious organisations try to build a 'universal brother/sisterhood' by bringing Burundians together in a large 'family of God' beyond multiple affiliations (ethno-political and religious). In doing so, these religions contribute to the construction of a peaceful society as stated in MDG 16.

As for the weaknesses, we can cite the tendency to 'over-politicise', which characterises electoral periods: in the absence of relevant social projects, political leaders know how to gain the confidence of voters, who are otherwise loyal to the said religious confessions, by manipulating the painful history of our country. The resentments inherent in badly healed wounds are not slow to reawaken. Ethno-political identity then supplants that of 'universal brother/sisterhood' and consequently opens the door to ethno-political violence by undermining the efforts hitherto invested by these religious organisations.

## Deadly Ethno-political Cleavages Since Independence

The social cleavages that Burundians have suffered so much from, and that need to be analysed in this section, are in fact of two kinds: ethnic and political. However, since we are analysing the role played by religious organisations (which are the subject of conflict elsewhere), I will say a word about them.

## Social Construction of Ethnic Identities with Deadly Consequences

When one hears about the Hutu, Tutsi and Twa ethnic groups in Burundi, one might think that they are groups with their own language, culture, geographical area and so on, as in many African countries. However, Hutu, Tutsi and Twa share the same language (*Kirundi*), have the same culture, practise (before colonisation) the same monotheistic religion by worshipping *Imana* (God) through the cult of *kubandwa*, live together on the same hills and so on. In short, Burundi was indeed a single ethnic group *stricto sensu*.

The Burundian population was simply made up of a multitude of *miryango* (i.e. clans) scattered throughout the country, some of which were more influential than others according to the roles they played at the royal court. It was from the Bajiji clan, for example, that the ritualists *(banyamabanga)* were recruited. Their role was to organise the *umuganuro* (i.e. the sowing festival). All the clans were involved in the life of the kingdom to varying degrees. In this way, the *mwami* demonstrated 'participatory governance' in which practically all segments of Burundian society were involved. In other words, all the clans were involved in the various services of the monarchy. Michel Bahenduzi's statement is more precise:

> The links between the populations and the power were first of all through the lineages and not by social categories (Hutu and Tutsi) as one would tend to believe. The informants interviewed during our surveys spontaneously answered that such and such a role belonged to the Bajiji, the Bavumu, the Bashubi, the Bahima, etc. It is only after thinking for a while that they establish the correspondence between the lineage they come from and the social category in which the clan or lineage usually classifies itself. (1991, p. 235)

On their arrival, the German (1898–1916) and Belgian (1916–1962) colonisers, inspired by the paradigm of the hierarchy of races that had prevailed in Europe, considered the Ganwa and Tutsi (whom they confused with each other) as the superior race, the Hutu as an intermediate race and the Twa as the inferior race. This is why the Belgian colonial administration restructured the Burundian nation:

1. Firstly, by removing key functions of the kingdom, notably the ritualistic roles controlled by the predominantly Hutu clans, such as the *Bajiji*.
2. Secondly, by restructuring the administration: not only were all Hutu chiefs systematically removed from their positions as chiefs, judges, and auxiliaries in important posts, but also an ideology that portrayed Ganwa and Tutsi as the 'superior race' on the one hand, and Hutu and especially Twa as the 'inferior race' on the other, was inculcated in the Burundian population.
3. Furthermore, by establishing the Groupe Scolaire d'Astrida (Rwanda) in 1925: while this school for the first elites welcomed Ganwa, Hutu and

Tutsi, the 'candidate chiefs' section was exclusively reserved for children whose fathers were serving chiefs. However, as the Hutus had been removed from office, their children could not be admitted to this section. This meant that the laureates of this section came to replace their fathers who were retiring. And it was they who enjoyed dazzling 'social success' (purchase of vehicles, construction of permanent houses, etc.).

This upheaval has led to a profound ethnicisation of society. It is therefore not surprising that around the 1960s, political parties mobilised the electoral campaign on the ethnic register. Similarly, many recurrent crises (1961, 1965, 1969, 1972, 1988, 1993, etc.) are part of this register:

1. The assassinations of elites at the top of the State: since the assassination of Prince Louis Rwagasore, the hero of independence, many Hutu personalities have been assassinated. Particularly in 1965 during the failed coup against King Mwambutsa. Several parliamentarians, officers and senior officials were eliminated for their ethnic identity. The macabre cycle was also observed in 1972 when, following a rebellion in the south of the country, all Hutu leaders were systematically killed throughout the country. The assassinations that took the life of President Melchior Ndadaye and several of his collaborators in 1993 are part of this cycle (Lemarchand, 1996).
2. The massacres of the humble peasants in the hills: in 1965, peasants in the centre of the country (Bugarama and Busanga) awoke to unspeakable violence. Tutsi peasants were massacred with machetes by their Hutu neighbours. Similarly, following the assassination of President Ndadaye, Tutsis (of all categories) were massacred by Hutus, this time throughout the country! In this way, ethnic violence raged on all the hills of the country, entering the hearts and minds of Burundians (Ngayimpenda, 2004).

In short, as Jean-Pierre Chrétien rightly writes, "the trap was closing on Burundi: following the crises of 1965 and 1972, the split between Hutu and Tutsi became as deep as in Rwanda. It is based on an omnipresent fear. What is it to be a Hutu or a Tutsi? [...] It is to remember who killed your relatives fifteen years ago or to wonder who will kill your child in ten years ahead" (2000, pp. 298-299).

## Political Cleavages with Recurrent Violence

In response to the spiral of ethnic violence that has marked the country's history, the stakeholders in the Burundian crisis, namely the government, the transitional parliament, the ten so-called "Tutsi" parties commonly known as the "G10" and the six so-called "Hutu" parties commonly known as the "G6", participated in the Arusha negotiation process. This resulted in the Arusha Agreements for peace and reconciliation in Burundi signed in 2000 under the mediation of the Tanzanian and South African presidents respectively. Once adopted by the National Assembly, these Arusha Agreements saw their pillars cast in the constitutions that Burundi has known so far: those of 2005 and 2018 (Buyoya, 2012).

The designers of the Agreements seem to have been inspired by the theory of consociational democracy developed by Arend Lipjhart (1999). In concrete terms, ethnic quotas were adopted as follows: 60% for Hutus and 40% for Tutsis as well as 30% for women in political institutions such as the Government and the National Assembly on the one hand, and 50% for Hutus and 50% for Tutsis with 30% women in the Senate, 50% for Hutus and 50% for Tutsis in the Army and the Police. And each time, the Twa are co-opted (Sentamba, 2008).

While these quota mechanisms have undoubtedly contributed to appeasing the ethnic reflex gradually, crises have become more political than ethnic. This has been observed over time, especially during sensitive periods such as electoral processes. For example, let us take the elections of 2005, 2010, 2015 and 2020.

1. The 2005 electoral process: after the transition period led by Pierre Buyoya (Tutsi) of UPRONA and Domitien Ndayizeye (Hutu) of FRODEBU, the 2005 elections did not see any major violence, as the fear of civil war was so great that the CNDD-FDD fighters, fresh from the bush rebellion, jealously guarded the terrain against any intrusion by another political party. For example, the FRODEBU parliamentarians who went to the east of the country (Ruyigi Province) almost lost their lives. This is because the two Hutu-dominated parties, CNDD-FDD and FRODEBU, were in reality hunting on the same Hutu electoral terrain.
2. The 2010 electoral process: with the victory of the CNDD-FDD in the communal elections, 11 opposition parties including FRODEBU, FNL, CNDD and MSD cried electoral fraud. They formed a coalition called *Democratic Alliance for Change* (ADC-Ikibiri) to reject the results of the communal elections. An arm-wrestling match was then engaged between the ADC-Ikibiri and the CNDD-FDD. As this coalition was qualified as illegal by the Ministry of the Interior, the electoral process was continued with the support of UPRONA (a party that is considered to be predominantly Tutsi, more wrongly than rightly), while the leaders of the member parties of the said coalition had to go into exile, fearing for their safety. This was followed by a series of targeted assassinations against militants of the opposition parties in general and FNL supporters in particular. Even the media and civil society organisations that dared to report on the situation were persecuted by the government. It should be noted that even some CNDD-FDD activists were assassinated for reasons of revenge, hence the spiral of appalling violence in the capital Bujumbura and the surrounding regions.
3. The 2015 electoral process: as soon as President Nkurunziza announced his intention to run for a third term, huge demonstrations took place in the capital Bujumbura in general and in the working-class neigh-

bourhoods that had won over the opposition in particular. Called by the opposition and some civil society organisations, the demonstrators denounced a mandate deemed to be contrary to the Arusha Agreements and the 2005 Constitution. As these demonstrations were qualified as illegal by the Ministry of Interior, the demonstrators were subjected to relentless police and military repression. Moreover, they were worsened by the failed coup d'état (13 May 2015) against President Nkurunziza: this gave the authorities the opportunity to lump the demonstrators and the coup plotters together and thus to carry out a ruthless repression against them: hundreds of young people from neighbourhoods such as Nyakabiga, Musaga, Ngagara and Mutakura were rounded up and reported missing. As these neighbourhoods are predominantly Tutsi, the wounds of ethnic violence quickly resurfaced, fuelling movements of exile in neighbouring countries such as Rwanda and Tanzania or even distant destinations such as Europe. At the same time, political violence hit activists irrespective of ethnicity: members of the CNDD-FDD opposed to Nkurunziza's third term in office (known as 'frondeurs') were also persecuted, and many had to go into exile abroad (Banshimiyubusa, 2022).
4. The 2020 electoral process: coming on the heels of the 2018 constitutional referendum marked by raw violence and hate speech against any 'no' campaigner, the 2020 electoral process took place in a climate of unspeakable fear. The main opposition party, the predominantly Hutu CNL (National Congress for Freedom), was largely targeted: its activists were intimidated, arrested and even murdered. To take just one example, a police commissioner in Mwaro Province publicly threatened to throw those who opposed the CNDD-FDD march into the Ruvyironza River, and lifeless bodies were indeed found in the same river a few days later. Lewis Mudge, Human Right Watch's Central Africa director, made this point poignantly in his June 2020 report.

In short, the leaders of the CNDD-FDD have used two main methods during the electoral process: the exploitation of the ethnic card and violence. In the first one, they awaken the resentments inherent in the crises the country suffered in the past to gain the confidence of the Hutu electoral majority. In the second, they blocked the way to the main challenger, the CNL, as soon as it was hunting on the same Hutu electoral ground. It is therefore not surprising that every election rhymes with violence, which makes many citizens living near the borders such as in the provinces of Rumonge or Makamba flee to neighbouring countries when the elections approach!

In such conditions, MDG 16 is difficult to implement. Without social cohesion, where Burundians see themselves as antagonistic sub-national identities and not as daughters and sons of the same nation, the ideals of peace and good governance struggle to take root. As a result, the various institutions lose legitimacy as soon as those in charge at all levels are perceived as having been appointed or elected only because of their ethnic or political affiliation and not as having proven competence.

## Possible Inter-religious Conflicts in Prospect?

Even before the German and Belgian colonial intrusion, Burundians had always believed in one God (*Imana*), whom they worshipped through the cult of *Kubandwa* (Gorju, 1938). Only with the takeover of the Belgian colonial administration was this traditional religion suppressed in favour of the Catholic religion. As the Belgian colonial power worked hand in hand with the Catholic Church (Mvuyekure, 2003), other religions such as Islam or organisations such as Protestants were not welcome.

The colonial administration relied on the Catholic Church to such an extent that it entrusted it with the management of the first primary and secondary schools accompanying the parishes and bishoprics. It is understandable that this religion has had a virtual monopoly on the training of almost all the elites from the colonial era until very recently. This favouritism also explains the fact that the chief towns of the first dioceses were built near the provincial capitals, while the dioceses of the Protestant churches were located on the 'periphery' and that the Catholic faith was established in practically all the hills of the country. However, apart from the areas where the Pentecostal denomination was first established, such as Kiremba (Bururi) and Matana (Bururi) for the Anglican denomination., the Protestant denominations only spread to all the provinces and communes of the country later on.

As for Islam, it has been confined to towns such as Rumonge, Bujumbura, Gitega and Muyinga, mainly (Castryck, 2019). This is how mosques have been established in the remote hills of deepest Burundi for only about ten years. This is naturally at the expense of previously powerful organisations such as Catholic, Anglican and Pentecostal. The following graph shows the demographic distribution of the different religions and denominations (Fig. 12.1).

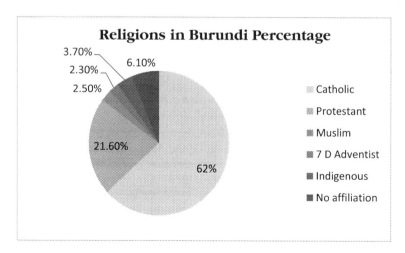

**Fig. 12.1** Religions in Burundi percentage: prepared by the author on the basis of ISTEEBU data (ISTEEBU, 2008)

This graph shows that Catholics constitute the majority of believers with 62% and that Protestants come in second place with 21.6%, the others being in a very small minority. It should be noted in passing that within the Protestants there are several variants, the main organisations of which are the Anglicans, Pentecostals and Methodists on the one hand, and a multitude of evangelical churches, some of which have no real social or regional base on the other. Similarly, Islam has two main faiths: Sunni and Shia. And COMIBU (Islamic Community of Muslims) includes all Muslim faiths. Although its headquarters is in Bujumbura, its scope of action covers the entire national territory. According to the IRCB, COMIBU's missions include (a) contributing to the peaceful propagation of Islam in Burundi by appropriate means, (b) promoting the education of Muslims in all areas and at all levels of the education system, (c) contributing to the improvement of the well-being of the members of the Community and Burundian society: education, health, the fight against HIV/AIDS and STIs, economic development and so on (IRCB, 2019, p. 12).

Finally, believers in traditional religions are difficult to identify since the cult of *kubandwa*, which brought people together during the pre-colonial period, seems to be very marginal today and is practised in secret… except perhaps in the province of Mwaro.

These religious organisations bring together all the ethnic components and the militants of all the political parties mentioned above. Apart from differences in confession, one cannot speak of conflicts among them: apart from a few stigmatisations such as the fact that drinking alcohol is prohibited among certain Protestant or Muslim confessions, whereas it does not pose a problem among Catholics and certain Protestants, there are no inter-religious conflicts, strictly speaking.

It is worth noting that the religious groups meet regularly through their platform (IRCB). Comprising the major religions (Catholic, Protestant and Muslim), the IRCB operates as a large non-profit association and has a philosophy that fits well with MDG 16 as stated in its strategic plan 2016–2023: IRCB "engages and fosters dialogue, cooperation and collaboration among religious communities for the transformation of conflicts, the promotion of just and harmonious societies, the building of democratic, equitable, peaceful and reconciled communities, the protection and promotion of human rights and gender, the fight against HIV/AIDS and the participation in the socioeconomic development of the country" (IRCB, 2019). And this is translated into action in two main directions. On the one hand, during the ecumenical prayers regularly organised throughout the country. To take just one example, the one organised on 26 January 2023 in the Catholic parish of Bukeye (Muramvya Province). The participation of many non-Catholic leaders (including Muslims) pleasantly surprised the population. It was unheard of between faiths and a novelty for the community members to see leaders of different religions walking together towards God!

The IRCB regularly organises development work in the field. This was the case in Mwaro Province on 21 May 2022 (cleaning of gutters on the

Kigutu-Gihinga road), where leaders from different religions worked in a 'family' atmosphere. This pleased both the leaders of the IRCB and the provincial authorities very much, according to the speeches of their respective representatives.

In sum, the different religions really do not have conflicts with each other, as the above-mentioned facts show. And while it is true that there was some suspicion between some religious organisations, the IRCB has succeeded in creating an interfaith cohesion that is increasingly perceptible on the ground. In doing so, it is undoubtedly working towards MDG 16.

## Religious Organisations as Relevant Actors in Resolving Ethno-political Conflicts

And this hierarchical dominance makes religious organisations the most appropriate actors to inculcate the principles of 'universal brotherhood' to the masses. In doing so, they contribute to the implementation of MDG 16 by advocating not only a just society but also a 'big family' of God.

## Religious Confessions, a Hierocracy at the Service of Social Cohesion

With Hutu, Tutsi, Twa and Ganwa on the one hand and militants of all the above-mentioned political parties on the other, different religious groups enjoy an unparalleled power over them: hierocratic domination, that is, an enormous power that they draw from registers of shared sacred beliefs. Through masses/cults or a variety of activities such as 'liturgical' feasts that follow one another throughout the year, on the one hand, and through all informal socialisation on the other, the leaders of religious organisations have the power to build/reinforce very strong religious identities. By drawing their teachings from the Holy Scriptures (Bible or Koran), they inculcate in their flock a behaviour that reinforces social cohesion beyond multiform allegiances.

After having exchanged with some religious leaders and notables of the different religious organisations, I can take as illustrations some themes developed by religious organisations with a view to consolidating peace:

1. Universal brother/sisterhood: by the prayer "*Our Father in Heaven*", which is very significant in all Christian denominations, for example, all believers are daughters and sons of the same Creator. Consequently, they would be brothers and sisters in God and would constitute by definition a large family/community or Umma for Muslims. Moreover, since Christ is a universal saviour, even believers of other religions are also children of God; hence the "universal brotherhood" that Pope Francis defends in his Encyclical "Fratelli Tutti". It should be noted that Pope Francis himself does not hesitate to interact with his brothers from other religions such as the Orthodox Church or Islam:

if I found inspiration in my brother Bartholomew, the Orthodox Patriarch who has promoted with great vigour the safeguarding of creation, in this case I felt particularly encouraged by the great Iman Ahmad Al-Tayyeb whom I met in Abu Dhabi to recall that God 'created all human beings equal in rights, duties, and dignity, and called them to coexist as brothers and sisters'. (Pope Francis, 2020)

2. The Fifth commandment, "*Thou shalt not kill*" (Exodus 20:13): We know the biblical case where Cain out of jealousy killed his brother Abel. Fearing revenge for such a crime, he wandered off and said to God, "*If anyone finds me, he will kill me*". And God put a sign on his forehead and warned against anyone who dared to kill Cain: "*If anyone kills Cain, he will be avenged seven times*". In other words, religious leaders keep explaining, God absolutely forbids humans to take the life that only God has given to humans and whose course only God can stop. Even in the case of murder, as in the case of Abel, no one can be allowed to kill in revenge!Applied to the spiral of civil wars that Burundi has experienced over time, it is clear that the victims of the above-mentioned assassinations or massacres would find it difficult to digest such messages, if they were delivered by civilian leaders and under normal circumstances. For, as Mamood Mamdani (2001) has shown in the case of genocidal violence in Africa's Great Lakes region, the victims' vengeance is not directed at the real perpetrators but at their innocent descendants! As a result, the victims become the executioners in their turn, hence the vicious circle that fuels interminable civil wars in our countries. On the other hand, religious leaders easily give the said teachings, and the faithful welcome them with fervour…? as long as the communication takes place in the rather sacred register.

3. Forgiveness: when his executioners were putting him to death, Jesus Christ prayed, "Father, forgive them, for they know not what they do" (Luke 23:34). Religious leaders keep explaining that even though he suffered horribly on the cross not for his own sins but for the sins of men, Jesus still asked his Father to forgive his killers, believing that they did not really know what they were doing, and therefore they were killing not only an innocent but also a Son of God sent to earth to save them from their darkness. The same is true, mutatis mutandis, in the Islamic religion, in which forgiveness occupies a considerable place: "O My servants who have committed excesses to your own detriment: do not despair of God's mercy, for He will forgive all sins" (Quran 39:53).

That said, Pope Francis makes it clear that forgiveness does not consist of turning the second cheek to the wrongdoer who has slapped the first. This would allow the evil to continue indefinitely. Instead, one must think of a way out of the impasse, so that the evil ceases both for the offender him/herself and for the victims: "Forgiving does not mean allowing him/her [the offender] to continue trampling on his/her own dignity and that of the other, or letting a criminal continue to do harm."

Applied to the spiral of civil wars that Burundi has been experiencing, many religious leaders have converged on the following idea: Burundian citizens should forgive each other without ignoring what really happened and without shying away from restorative justice for the victims where possible. This would be a better way to ward off evil. And in so doing, ensure that the victims of one crisis are not the perpetrators of subsequent crises, especially since those who are the object of revenge are rarely the actors of the facts underlying the revenge in question. And that in reality, this would be true forgiveness, a forgiveness that produces lasting reconciliation.

In short, unlike state leaders who are obliged to use physical coercion (cf. police, courts, etc.), religious leaders exercise sacred power over the masses, all social categories included, without the slightest physical coercion because recourse to God alone is more than enough. And the teachings of the Holy Scriptures are so persuasive that they are often preceded by songs with such fascinating content, music so enchanting that the hearts of the faithful are psychologically prepared. This is why religious groups seem to us to be the best actors to inculcate the ideals of peace in the masses for at least three reasons.

Firstly, the teachings are derived from the Holy Scriptures which no one would dare to dispute, so much so that the cognitive register is shared. Secondly, their leaders enjoy, for almost all of them, an unquestionable social legitimacy based on a better education (all Catholic priests have not only studied philosophy and theology, which constitute their basic training) but have also pursued master's and doctoral studies in the best universities in the world…? in various disciplines. The same is true, to a lesser extent, of the older Protestant churches such as the Anglican Church and the Pentecostal Church. Moreover, as they cover the entire national territory down to the remotest hills (at least for the major Christian denominations), the religious organisations supervise their followers more closely, in particular through the prayer movements which are practised within small groups of dwellings (streets in urban centres and "villages" in the rural areas). Finally, the religious organisations know how to make the most of demographic variables: young people and women. Knowing that the Burundian population is predominantly young (65.7% or two-thirds of the population are under 25 years old), all the religious organisations invest considerable efforts in the supervision of young people (Catholic action movements for the Catholic Church, Sunday Schools for the Protestant Churches, Koranic schools for Islam, etc., on the one hand, and a whole series of associative organisations in favour of young people for practically all religious organisations on the other). Similarly, different religions invest substantial efforts in the supervision of women: not only do they represent about 52% of the Burundian population, but they are also the ones who impart basic education to children. This is why all religious organisations make use of women's networks as much as possible.

## Scope of "Universal Brother/Sisterhood" Promotion

The contribution of religious organisations to peace-building in Burundi is a multi-dimensional process that we can measure in terms of a variety of facts and actions. In concrete terms, I will take facts that have a fairly considerable impact on society. I will therefore take the following three tracks:

1. For seemingly innocuous things such as public greetings: we can take the simple greetings that people give to the public when they speak: "*Tugire Kristu*" (Let us have Christ) to which everyone responds "*Ni aganze Kristu*" (i.e. "May Christ reign"), "*Yesu ashiimwe*" (Jesus be praised) to which everyone responds "*Amen*", "*As-salamu alay-kum wa rahmatu-l-lah*" ("May God's peace and mercy be upon you") to which everyone responds "*Amin*", depending on whether one is Catholic, Protestant and Muslim respectively. It should be noted that people are so used to this that the formulas pass without difficulty, except perhaps with regard to the Muslim greeting formulated in Arabic.

    It should be noted that these formulas replaced old formulas in use at national level, which paid tribute to the regimes in place, '*Tugire amahoro na Micomb.ero yayaduhaye*' (i.e. 'Let's have peace with President Micombero who gave it to us'), '*Tugire amahoro n'umugambwe w'abasasigana UPRONA*' (i.e. 'Let's have peace with the UPRONA party') and so on. It should be noted that many people only cited this greeting reluctantly since the ethno-political civil wars had already divided Burundians to the point that many Hutu did not fit in. It is undoubtedly this cognitive dissonance that the new religious greetings have come to appease. But it is still necessary to find one that is consensual beyond the religious organisations.

2. Charities: the charities that the different religious organisations undertake are important in peace-building. Three main areas of intervention can be cited: education, health and social assistance. Firstly, in the area of education, the main religious organisations have primary and secondary schools to which all children have access without ethnic, political or religious distinction. This work contributes to cohesion when young people are socialised together in several schools belonging to different religious organisations, with a good mix of religious training depending on the organisations. Secondly, in terms of health, the religious organisations have health centres and sometimes hospitals throughout the country that serve all Burundian citizens without the distinction of ethnic, political or religious affiliation. In addition, organisations assist the poor or victims of natural disasters. For example, through the Caritas project, the Catholic Church helped the population of Mugoboka and Kirundo Province (ODEDIM/CARITAS, 2021) for example, regardless of ethnic, political or religious affiliation. Finally, religious organisations build orphanages to take in children without parents or guardians: in view of

the painful history of our country, many orphans would not have had any assistance without these charitable souls.

As the parish priest of Mutanga-South explained to us, "it is through works of charity that religious organisations demonstrate that they are not mere associations but families of believers founded on Christ. Moreover, it is through works at the service of the great Family of God that universal fraternity is translated into action." Here we find the *Fratelli Tutti* of Pope Francis: by walking together and enjoying the same support according to the needs of each person and not according to ethnic, political or religious affiliation, the beneficiaries effectively become "brothers/sister in God", hence a more solid and quite lasting social cohesion.
3. Protection of victims of ethno-political crises: during the ethno-political crises that Burundi has experienced, some religious organisations have intervened to protect the lives of victims of violence. Two cases can serve as an illustration, the Catholic Church on the one hand and Islam on the other.

With regard to the Catholic Church, two cases can be mentioned. On the one hand, no seminary experienced violence between Hutu and Tutsi students during the 1993 crisis, unlike schools of the same level in the same region. For example, the seminary of Buta (Bururi Province) is located near the high schools of Kiremba (less than 2 km) and Bururi (about 5 km), both of which experienced shooting and throwing of grenades among students! Similarly, the seminaries of Mureke (16 km from Ngozi) and Burasira (32 km from Ngozi) did not experience any 'inter-student' violence, whereas the lycée of Burengo (near the provincial capital of Ngozi) was the object of violence that took human lives. This can be explained by a pedagogical framework (targeted recruitment for both pupils and staff members, who are, in principle, Catholic and of good morality) and a religious framework (masses, prayers, Catholic action movements, etc.) that develop a 'fraternal' cohesion over and above ethnic or political affiliations. This is not the case in secondary schools run by lay leaders: not only do the pupils and staff come from different religions, but also the supervision is not as tight as in seminaries. In other words, as soon as a socio-political crisis breaks out, the already fragile social cohesion easily gives way to the violence in the immediate environment. Moreover, the legitimacy enjoyed by the priest-managers of the seminaries allowed the leaders of the seminaries to contain the anger of the activists who were targeting the schools.

On the other hand, the seminary of Buta was the object of a heroic cohesion between young Hutu and Tutsi pupils in 1997: when the Hutu rebels attacked the school, they ordered the seminarians to split into two Hutu and Tutsi groups, which the teenagers refused. The latter were coldly shot with Kalashnikovs, hence the 40 martyrs of Buta (Bukuru, 2004).

As for Islam, two facts can also be cited for the 1993 crisis. On the one hand, the victims fleeing the atrocities from the hills above the town of Rumonge (on the shores of Lake Tanganyika). According to an Imam from the Rumonge mosque whom I interviewed in 2019, a crowd of children, women and men had taken refuge in the Rumonge mosque. The faithful of Islam took turns to help them, like brothers and sisters in Allah, without distinguishing between Hutu and Tutsi. These '*displaced persons*' spent several months there before their hills of origin found some calm. On the other hand, when the Tutsi militia "*Sans Echec*" chased the Hutu out of Bujumbura in 1993, they never entered the Islamic-dominated neighbourhood of Buyenzi. According to concordant witnesses of former members of the '*Sans Echec*' militia, it was formally forbidden to pursue anyone who found refuge there at the risk of facing 'evil spirits' (*amajini*). In reality, an old imam told us, a criminal who dared to enter the neighbourhood in pursuit of a fugitive would not come out: he was arrested and handed over to the gendarmerie (Faith to Action Network 2019).

In short, in both cases of protection among Catholics and Muslims, religious identity was able to override ethnic identity. In other words, the students of the different seminaries in general and those of the seminary of Buta in particular showed such a strong social cohesion that it dominated the Hutu and Tutsi ethnicities, while the teachers and other support staff were both Hutu and Tutsi. The same is true for the Muslims who protected the Hutu and Tutsi escapees: themselves composed of Hutu and Tutsi, their Muslim identity supplanted the ethnic identity. So they perceived them as creatures of God (Allah) rather than mere Hutu and Tutsi! And it is precisely here that the religious organisations translated peace-building into action. And if all Burundians had followed this model, the conditions of MDG 16 could undoubtedly have been met!

## LIMITATIONS OF PROMOTING SOCIAL COHESION

As I have shown above, religious organisations have undoubtedly invested incalculable efforts in peace-building through a variety of actions. But these efforts are set in a socio-historical context that has many variables that skew their impact on the expected peace. At least four elements should be mentioned.

1. With intense political mobilisation, ethnic identity takes precedence over religious identity: many political leaders seeking votes do not hesitate to mobilise their potential voters along ethnic lines. By insidiously manipulating Burundi's painful history, they know how to draw arguments from an ethnic register that is all the more shared because all Burundians have suffered from poorly healed wounds since independence. A well-documented example by Denis Banshimiyubusa (Banshimiyubusa, 2022) is revealing in this respect: the third mandate sought and won by the late Pierre Nkurunziza. In the face of fierce opposition to a third term deemed to be against both the Arusha Agreements and the Constitution, President Nkurunziza and those close to him distilled hateful speeches 'Tutsising' the rejection of the said term. However, the anti-third man-

date mobilisers came first from his own party (the 'frondeurs', the most numerous being the Hutu) and even more so from the Council of Elders (the supreme organ of the CNDD-FDD) such as the former President of the National Assembly and the former second Vice-President of the Republic. They then came from the parties of the opposition, the political parties and the government. They then came from the predominantly Hutu and Tutsi opposition parties. Finally, they came from certain civil society organisations naturally composed of all the social components of Burundian society.

However, these hateful and 'ethnicising' speeches ended up presenting the Tutsi as the main instigators of the demonstrations. This is how the so-called protesting neighbourhoods, coincidentally inhabited mainly by Tutsi (Musaga, Nyakabiga, Ngagara, Mutakura), were subjected to a repression that was as indiscriminate as it was deadly, and which targeted young people in particular (Carayol, 2016)! Under these conditions, ethnic identity could only resurface and take precedence over any other identity, including religious identity.

2. Religious leaders are also human beings: if I consider only those who were born during the two crises that engulfed the entire country and from which all Burundians suffered in one way or another (1972, 1993), they are now 40 and 29 years old, respectively. Knowing how young the Burundian population is (ISTEEBU, 2008) on the one hand and taking into account the generation of the parents of those who are now 40 years old on the other hand, one understands that the majority of religious leaders have personally experienced the atrocities, hence the resentment inherent in the above-mentioned wars. This explains the participation of some religious personnel either in certain massacres or in some political parties openly mobilising for massacres of this or that ethnic group.

3. Religious organisations doing more business than religious service, hence leadership conflicts: according to a workshop organised for religious organisations by the Ministry of Internal Affairs in March 2021, many "evangelical organisations" are not yet socially based. They do not have many followers, and many of their leaders seem to do more business than religious service. This is why internal rivalries between members of the leadership lead to scuffles during worship, and hence the intervention of the police, arrests of "pastors" in front of the faithful, arbitration by the Ministry of the Interior, legal proceedings in court and so on. Such cases are common in Burundian towns and urban centres. For example, let us read the minutes of a meeting held in Sororezo (Bujumbura) on 30 November 2021 for 40 religious organisations with internal disputes:

Ndirakobuca Gervais [Minister of the Interior] thus ordered that the activities of unauthorised churches be suspended, the legal representatives of churches who are foreigners or who live abroad be replaced in accordance with the law by Burundians living in the country, the judicial sentences handed down on conflicts within the churches be properly executed.

The role of such religious organisations in peace-building becomes unlikely as divisions are observed even among the faithful, resulting in an anti-model of a classical church or mosque. This is why the faithful are quick to realise that they have been manipulated by leaders of dubious morality. According to Professor Nicodème Bugwabari interviewed on this subject: "it is normal that within religious organisations there are conflicts that intensify in churches where the degree of institutionalisation is much lower. [...] these churches should activate socialisation and compromise, to the great joy of the millions of Burundians who suffer from their conflicts. If the church does not lead by example, who else will?"

4. Religious "sects" contributing to social disintegration: the "sect" of a then 36-year-old woman, Eusebie Ngendakumana, was followed by a crowd of followers. And as the 'prophetess' wanted to make Businde her sanctuary, the government prevented her from doing so. In a tussle between her followers and the Police in 2013, the Police fired into the crowd, taking the lives of 12 people. Since then, the crowd of followers wanders between Burundi, Rwanda and the Democratic Republic of Congo (Bukeyeneza, 2018).

The problem is that this "sect" snatches married people, who leave behind spouses and children (of whatever age). And the children who follow the harsh wandering naturally drop out of school. Similarly, care provided by official health facilities such as health centres and hospitals is prohibited by the Zebiya 'doctrine': the faithful then lead an unspeakable life through the Congolese forests, on interminable walks between the three countries, where they find themselves unwanted every time.

As a colleague explained to me, quoting Emile Durkheim (Durkheim, 1912), these practices contravene social integration, one of the main functions normally performed by religious organisations. Instead of reinforcing social cohesion at the micro level where it operates, the sect constructs a "counter-society" by preaching practices (prohibition to eat certain food products, to be treated in contemporary health centres, etc.) which are harmful to the normal functioning of society.

All in all, religious organisations are certainly better placed to resolve ethno-political conflicts in Burundi because of their ability to build 'universal brother/sisterhood'. But stubborn facts such as politicisation and weaknesses inherent in human nature from which religious leaders are not spared have constantly ruined this potential in times of political crisis. Let us take the example of youth: at each crisis, youth organisations affiliated to the parties in power have taken the lead in violence…? whereas religions had invested enormously in youth. This is why the implementation of MDG 16 is not easy if things do not change in the direction of peace-building.

## Conclusion

This chapter has taught us a few lessons. Firstly, the Belgian colonial administration left Burundians with a heavy ethnic heritage which they unfortunately appropriated by turning it into a weapon of self-destruction. In other words, the 'socially constructed ethnic groups', whereas Burundi has only one ethnic group, have continued to underpin the fratricidal wars that Burundi has experienced (1965, 1972, 1988, 1993, 2015). Even conflicts of a political nature have always been wrapped up in ethnicity.

It is in such an ethno-politically 'polluted' environment that the religious organisations have come to work. By enjoying their hierocratic authority and conducting a proximity supervision, the leaders of the main religious organisations were able to build considerable social cohesion. Already composed of all the social components of the population (Hutu, Tutsi, Twa, Ganwa) and addressing the faithful from all the 'ethnic groups' and all the political parties, the religious leaders managed to build a 'universal brother/sisterhood', that is, an identity supplanting the ethno-political affiliations, at least in times of peace.

Unfortunately, during sensitive periods such as electoral processes, 'over-politicisation' on an ethno-political basis awakens ethno-political consciences. For past resentments are used as an easy springboard to effortlessly gain the trust of the population. This opens the door to murderous violence that can sweep away the efforts invested by religious organisations. This explains the difficulty of bringing lasting peace to Burundian society and setting up institutions that are both legitimate and peaceful.

In this regard, some recommendations can be made: (1) all stakeholders in the resolution of ethno-political conflicts in general and religious organisations in particular should continue their commendable work during periods of peace and redouble their efforts in the run-up to sensitive periods such as electoral processes; (2) through IRCB the different religious organisations should institute common messages to promote social cohesion among the population before, during and after electoral processes; (3) through IRCB, religious organisations should invest as much effort as possible to ensure the emergence of a political leadership socialised to the ideal of 'universal brother/sisterhood' and therefore in line with MDG 16.

## References

Bahenduzi, M. (1991). *Le rituel du Muganuro dans l'histoire du Burundi des origines au XXe siècle*. Histoire Paris, Université de Paris 1—Panthéon-Sorbonne.

Banshimiyubusa, D. (2022). Crispations identitaires et "identités légitimatrices" pendant crise politique: un regard rétrospectif sur la crise du 3ème mandat au Burundi. IOB Discussion Papers 2022.01, Universiteit Antwerpen, Institute of Development Policy (IOB).

Bukeyeneza, G.-A. (2018). *Zebiya, la rebelle de Dieu*. Journal Iwacu.

Bukuru, Z. (2004). *Les quarante martyrs de Buta au Burundi (1997)*. Ed. Karthala.

Buyoya, P. (2012). *Les négociations inter-burundaises: la longue marche vers la paix.* L'Harmattan.
Carayol, R. (2016). *Torture au Burundi: l'enfer à côté de la maison de Dieu.* Jeune Afrique.
Castryck, G. (2019). Living Islam in Colonial Bujumbura_The Historical Translocality of Muslim Life Between East and Central Africa. *History in Africa, 46*, 263–298.
Chrétien, J. P. (2000). *L'Afrique des Grands Lacs: deux mille ans d'histoire.* Aubier.
Conseil Inter-Confessionnel au Burundi. (2019). *Rapport annuel*, p. 12.
Durkheim, E. (1912). *Formes élémentaires de la vie religieuse.* Ed. Félix Alcan.
Gorju, J. (1938). *Face au royaume hamite du Ruanda: Le royaume frère de l'Urundi: Essai de reconstitution historique. Mœurs pastorales.* Vromant et Cie.
ISTEEBU. (2008). *Recensement général de la population et de l'habitat.* Bujumbura.
Lemarchand, R. (1996). *Burundi: Ethnic Conflict and Genocide.* Woodrow Wilson Center/Cambridge University Press.
Lipjhart, A. (1999). *Patterns of Democracy.* Yale University Press.
Mamdani, M. (2001). *When Victims Become Killers, Colonialism, Nativism and the Genocide in Rwanda.* Princeton University.
Mvuyekure, A. (2003). *Le catholicisme au Burundi, 1922–1962: approche historique des conversions.* Kharthala.
Ngayimpenda, E. (2004). *Histoire du conflit politico-ethnique burundais: Les premières marches du calvaire (1960–1973).* Ed. de La Renaissance.
ODEDIM/CARITAS. (2021). *Rapport annuel, Diocèse de Muyinga.*
Pope Francis. (2020). Encyclical: 'Fratelli Tutti, l'appel pressant du pape François à la fraternité universelle'.
République du Burundi. (2018). *Plan National de Développement 2018–2027.*
Sahinguvu, L.-D., & Vircoulon, T. (2017). *Requiem pour l'Accord d'Arusha.* IFRI.
Sentamba, E. (2008). Burundi: un Processus de Négociation Entre le Gouvernement et le Palipehutu Fnl dans l'impasse. *Journal of African Conflicts and Peace Studies, 1*, 30–51.

CHAPTER 13

# Reclaiming Everyday Peace in the Micro-Spaces in Burundi

*Patrick Karanja Mbugua*

## INTRODUCTION

In the last decade, peacebuilding theory and practice has been framed around a debate between top-bottom liberal peacebuilding and bottom-top peacebuilding. Liberal peacebuilding, which is also known as liberal peace, liberal interventionism, or liberal internationalism, has been the dominant form of internationally supported peacebuilding (Paris, 2002, 2007, 2010; Richmond, 2006, 2007; Richmond & Franks, 2009). Linked to the broader liberal peace debate, which arises from the democratic peace theory in International Relations (IR), the liberal peacebuilding approach implies building peace within states emerging from civil wars based on liberal democracy and market economics. As Paris (2010) notes, post-war liberal peacebuilding seeks to align the domestic governance of war-shattered states with the prevailing standards of the international system. However, the limitations of the liberal peace approach, including interweaving peacebuilding interventions with liberal state-building, privileging global norms, and emphasising the structural and

---

The Communities Richer in Diversity (CRID) consortium published a simplified general readers' version of this study using parts of the evidence cited in this chapter as Case Study Series No. 4 in April 2022, which is available here: https://www.faithtoactionnetwork.org

P. K. Mbugua (✉)
Peace & Conflict Studies Academic and Consultant, Peacebuilding, Conflict Transformation, and Preventive Diplomacy, Nairobi, Kenya

institutional aspects of state-building, have led to the development of an alternative top-bottom peacebuilding approach.

Variously known as peacebuilding from below, grassroots peacebuilding, community peacebuilding, local peacebuilding, citizen-to-citizen peacebuilding, or Track II diplomacy, bottom-top peacebuilding asserts that attaining sustainable peace after a protracted civil war, especially in deeply divided societies, requires the involvement of all levels of society (Montville, 1990, 1993, 2009; Gopin, 2009; Mac Ginty, 2010, 2011, 2017, 2021; Mac Ginty & Richmond, 2013; Paffenholz, 2015; Randazzo, 2017, 2021; Richmond, 2001, 2009a, 2009b, 2011). A core component of bottom-up peacebuilding is the notion of everyday peace, which literature conceptualises as social practices that ordinary people perform as they conduct their daily lives in conflict contexts, or societies emerging from protracted conflicts, to minimise the effects of direct, structural, and cultural violence and to strengthen peaceful relations (Ware et al., 2022; Mac Ginty, 2014, 2015, 2017, 2021; Mac Ginty & Firchow, 2016; Richmond & Mac Ginty, 2019). Since everyday peace focuses on the daily experiences and perspectives of ordinary people, literature asserts that it has no universal indicators as it is contingent, contextual, and temporal. As Mac Ginty (2014, p. 550) explains, everyday within that understanding refers to "the normal *habitus* for individuals and groups even if what passes as normal in a conflict-affected society would be abnormal elsewhere". In other words, individuals and groups in a particular context and at a specific time determine their indicators of everyday peace.

This study employs the bottom-up peace approach and the notion of everyday peace to analyse the outcomes and impacts of peacebuilding interventions that the *Conseil Inter-Confessionnel du Burundi* (CICB) implemented from October 2018 to December 2019 as a response to the political-security crisis that erupted in 2014.[1] Subsequently, the situation deteriorated in May 2015 after an abortive military *coup d'état* led to the return of armed rebellion, reprisal killings, targeted assassinations, widespread violations and abuses of human rights, and forced displacement. Available data shows that there were 420,689 Burundi refugees and asylum seekers in neighbouring countries and 200,000 internally displaced persons (IDPs) by May 2017 (UNHRC, 2017b). Since

---

[1] A group of religious leaders, comprising Catholics, Methodists, Anglicans, the Evangelical Church of Burundi, Muslims, and Lutherans, founded CICB in June 2008 as an inter-religious organisation to implement peacebuilding programmes because the country had just emerged from a protracted 12-year civil war. With financial support from international funders, CICB has over the years implemented a wide range of peacebuilding interventions and programmes.

Burundi's recent history is marked by widespread political and ethnic[2] massacres in 1965, 1972, 1988, 1991, and 1993 (Malkki, 1995; Lemarchand, 1994, 2008a, 2008b; Nshimirimana, 2020; Bigirimana, 2021), the return of the pre-2005 civil war climate revived mass anxiety and memories of past killings. CICB was particularly concerned about the involvement of religious leaders in ethnic extremism and political violence, as well as the large number of young people who had joined violent militias. Such concerns aligned with the UN Strategic Development Goal (SDG) 16, target 16.1, which calls for reducing all forms of violence at all levels of society, as the climate of violence affected all sectors of Burundi society, and there was no macro-level peace process. Thus, CICB adopted a bottom-up peacebuilding strategy to reduce youth recruitment into violent militias, rebuild resilience, promote reconciliation, and restore everyday peace in the micro-spaces, beginning in the four provinces of Bujumbura Mairie, Bujumbura Rural, Muyinga, and Rumonge.

This study has two aims. First, it aims to document the achievements of the CICB's bottom-up approach and show how it aligns with UN's Sustainable Development Goal (SDG) 16, specifically target 16.1, which calls for the reduction of all forms of violence in macro-spaces and micro-spaces, and indicators 16.1.2 and 16.1.3, which encourage the reduction of conflict-related deaths and physical violence in all spheres. Second, it seeks to contribute to the expanding body of literature on everyday peace by adding Burundi to the list of several documented cases, including India (Williams, 2015), Bosnia and Herzegovina (Marijan, 2017), Northern Ireland (Marijan, 2017), Colombia (Berents, 2018), Iraq (O'Driscoll, 2021), South Korea (Kang, 2022), and Myanmar (Ware et al., 2022).

Empirical data was collected using two methods: primary data collection by interviewing 3 CICB staff and 31 project participants and beneficiaries between May and December 2021, and secondary data collection through a review of 23 CICB documents, namely 12 monthly reports, 4 quarterly reports, 1 annual report, 2 video documentaries, 2 conference papers, 1 baseline survey, and 1 endline survey. The baseline and endline surveys collected primary data from

---

[2] The way notions of ethnic, cultural, and 'tribal' identities are understood in Burundi and Rwanda is very different from the way they are understood in the other Eastern and Central African countries such as Tanzania, Uganda, Kenya, Democratic Republic of Congo (DRC), South Sudan, and Ethiopia. In Kenya, Uganda, Tanzania, DRC, Ethiopia, and South Sudan, the concepts 'tribal' identity and ethnic identity are synonymous and are widely understood to mean language-based cultural identity. Burundi and Rwanda are different. In the sense of anthropological language-based cultural identity, Burundi has only one ethnic group, Barundi, which has the same culture and the same language, Kirundi. However, colonial and post-colonial political and administrative practices divided the Barundi ethnic group into four 'tribal' identities: Baganwa, Tutsi, Hutu, and Twa. Scholarly studies show that the military regimes of the 1960s, 1970s, and 1980s forcefully assimilated Baganwa, the former ruling group from the pre-colonial Kingdom up to 1966, into the Tutsi category. Similarly, Rwanda has only one anthropological ethnic group, Banyarwanda, that has the same culture and the same language, Kinyarwanda, but political and administrative practices of the last 100 years divided the same ethnic group into three 'tribes': Tutsi, Hutu, and Twa.

more than 200 participants on different dates between October 2018 and March 2020. The subsequent sections will provide an overview of the contextual issues that informed CICB's interventions, the organisation's pathway for change, and the choice of everyday peace indicators. They will then discuss the empirical data and conclude the chapter.

## Religious Approach to Everyday Peace in a Context of Continuing Conflict

From 2014 to early 2020, Burundi experienced a political-security crisis characterised by a complex matrix of political violence, ethnic extremism, religious fragmentation, a stalled national reconciliation process, and a revival of narratives of the past massacres. The proximate cause of the crisis was a political dispute among the country's elite regarding the candidature of the late President, Pierre Nkurunziza, in the 2015 presidential elections. At the centre of the dispute were clashing interpretations of Article 7(3) of the Arusha Peace Agreement (APA) and Article 96 of the 2005 Constitution.[3] Article 7(3) of the APA states that the President of the Republic "shall be elected for a term of five years, renewable only once" and "no one may serve more than two presidential terms", while Article 96 of the 2005 Constitution stipulates that the "President of the Republic is elected by universal direct suffrage for a term of five years renewable one time". Arguing that the 2005 election was indirect since members of the National Assembly and the Senate elected the President, Mr. Nkurunziza's supporters insisted that Article 96 of the Constitution allowed him to run in the 2015 elections because the 2010 presidential election was the first one by universal suffrage. In contrast, his opponents declared that he was ineligible to run because Article 7(3) of the APA stipulated two terms. Underneath this legal dispute, however, lay deep-seated political, economic, and ethnic issues, which the Nkurunziza administration had not resolved since the end of the civil war in 2005.

As tensions mounted, the simmering conflict erupted into violent clashes between demonstrators opposed to Nkurunziza's candidacy and the security

---

[3] The Arusha peace process was based on four points of agreement.

1. A power-sharing formula, based on an agreed formula of ethnic quotas in politics.
2. Representation of all parties in the state bureaucracy
3. Constitutional restrictions to prevent any single party from becoming excessively powerful.
4. Pathways to integrate former rebels and minority groups in the Burundian armed forces.

The 2005 indirect presidential elections occurred on 19 August 2005, when Members of the National Assembly and Senate chose the new President of the Republic for a five-year term. The sole candidate, Pierre Nkurunziza of the Conseil National Pour la Défense de la Démocratie – Forces pour la Défense de la Démocratie (CNDD–FDD), attained 151 yes votes. While nine voted against him, one vote was invalid. He was sworn in on 26 August 2005. The election was held using multiple round systems. To win in the first round of voting, Nkurunziza was required to receive at least two-thirds of the vote (108 votes).

forces, who accused the demonstrators of mounting an insurrection. The violence was intense in Bujumbura Mairie, the capital city, in early 2015. According to Amnesty International (2015), security forces killed at least 58 protesters in April and May 2015. Then the situation deteriorated as a failed military *coup d'état* on 13 May 2015 was followed by targeted assassinations, armed rebellion,[4] violations and abuses of human rights by both state and non-state actors, and displacement unseen in the country since the end of the civil war in 2005 (AI, 2016, 2017; BBC, 2015, May 13; France 24, 2015, May 13; Guardian, 2015, May 15; UNHRC, 2017a). Much worse, the situation turned ominous as security forces framed the failed coup as an attempt to restore pre-2005 Tutsi hegemony over the Hutu majority. Such framing exacerbated the pre-existing challenges, including the stalled national reconciliation process, the political, economic, and cultural structures that make state-society relations overwhelmingly top-down, the persistent memories of past massacres, and the sedimented ethnic discourse, which was normalised in the popular imagination in micro-spaces by past violence and political practices, as Lemarchand notes (2008a, 1994).

As it were, the popular imagination regarded the abortive *coup d'état* as a harbinger of another ethnic bloodbath because past killings followed a similar pattern. Thus, the 1965 killings followed a failed *coup d'état*; the 1972 carnage followed an armed insurrection; the 1988 massacres followed a successful *coup d'état*; and the 1993 bloodbath followed an abortive *coup d'état* and the assassination of the democratically elected president. The return of violence therefore caused mass anxiety, as it revived memories of past killings and displacement (Daley & Popplewell, 2016; HRW, 2018, 2019). Evidently, the crisis profoundly affected Burundi society to the extent that it engendered the fragmentation of religious leaders between those who supported President Nkurunziza and those who wanted him to step down. Because the climate of mistrust, suspicion, and intolerance between religious leaders affected social relations at the grassroots (Hatcher, 2015, 4 August), it prompted CICB to plan peacebuilding interventions, which integrated the religious approach with technical aspects of bottom-up peacebuilding to restore everyday peace in the microspaces. The organisation chose to pilot its interventions in four provinces, Bujumbura Mairie, Bujumbura Rural, Muyinga, and Rumonge, because they were among the locations that were most devastated by violence after 2015.

---

[4] A report by the Commission of Inquiry on Burundi, which the UN Human Rights Council (UNHRC) appointed in September 2016, lists the armed groups as follows. *Forces Nationales pour la Libération* (FNL), which is a splinter group from the original PALIPEHUTU-FNL and is led by General Aloys Nzabampema; *Forces Républicaines du Burundi* (FOREBU), which emerged in 2015 and is led by General Godefroid Niyombare and other soldiers who led the May 2015 coup attempt; and *Résistance pour un Etat de Droit (RED-Tabara)* that emerged in January 2016. Other armed groups that emerged in December 2015, but there was no sufficient information about them during the field research, are *Mouvement de la Résistance Populaire* (MRP); *Union des Patriotes pour la Révolution* (UPR); *Force de Libération de la Démocratie au Burundi* (FLDB); *Mouvement Patriote Chrétien* (MPC); and *MALIBU-Front Patriotique du Salut* (MALIBU-FPS).

The approach speaks to the arguments in the literature that religious peacebuilding combines secular activities with religious values, rituals, traditions, texts, narratives, and vocabulary to resolve conflicts and promote peace, reconciliation, and peaceful coexistence (Bercovitch & Kadayifci-Orellana, 2009; Dubois, 2008; Powers, 2010). According to Dubois (2008), the employment of the spiritual elements of culture makes religious peacebuilding community-oriented, relationship-centred, and broadly participatory. Thus, while religious actors implement the same activities as secular interlocutors, they add unique religious tools, including spiritual guidance, prayers, meditation, and empathy in envisioning new possibilities. While recognising the religious origin of concepts such as healing, forgiveness, and restorative justice, peacebuilding literature asserts that all religions have language that describes ways of healing broken human relationships and acceptance that enables humans to pursue peaceful relations (Hamber, 2007; Peterson, 2001).

It is worth noting the broad categories of literature including those that theorise the relations between religion and peace (Omer, 2012, 2021; Mitchell et al., 2022) and those that study religious peacebuilding in broad terms, meaning they cover aspects such as theorising religious peacebuilding, analysing the role of faith-based actors in peacebuilding interventions, and evaluating case studies from different parts of the world (Brewer et al., 2010; Appleby, 2000; Little & Appleby, 2004; Kew & Kwaja, 2022; Gruchy, 2022; Qurtuby, 2022). While these categories of literature have made a significant contribution to the scholarship of religious peacebuilding, they do not explicitly acknowledge the debate between liberal peace and bottom-up peacebuilding or recognise, mention or utilise the concept of everyday peace as explained in the opening section of this chapter. Therefore, even though the author considers these categories of literature as fundamental contributions to studies of religious peacebuilding, their analysis is beyond the scope of this chapter.

In essence, CICB chose to pursue everyday peace in micro-spaces for three reasons. First, there was no national peace process; second, it was necessary to address persistent prejudices and memories and change the perceptions of youth; and third, Burundi fell into violence, killings, and armed insurrection in 2015, despite previous peacebuilding programmes by international NGOs. Accordingly, CICB identified three indicators of everyday peace that it wanted to attain in the micro-spaces: changing individual perceptions towards the 'other', improving group relations, and resolving conflicts. To achieve these changes, it empowered local religious leaders with conflict resolution skills and then deployed them so that they could use their moral authority, faith spaces, and religious instruments to lead community peace committees; conduct dialogue forums, citizen-to-citizen engagements, local-level mediation; and provide the communities with an alternative frame of healing, forgiveness, empathy, and tolerance. CICB then reinforced its messages of peaceful relations with activities such as peace marches, sports for peace, and traditional drumming performances. According to CICB end of the project report, the organisation directly reached 4151 participants, who cascaded the work into their localities.

Although CICB does not acknowledge the UN SDGs in its documents, a global reading of its interventions reveals that its approach addressed Goal 16, specifically target 16.1 that calls for reducing all forms of violence and deaths associated with them, as well as indicators 16.1.2 and 16.1.3 that call for reducing conflict-related violence in both macro- and micro-spaces.

## Changing Individual Perceptions and Transforming Group Relations

CICB understood the demographics of the country, the complexity of the conflict, the effects of post-2014 violence, and the persistent memories of the past ethnic massacres. Accordingly, it aimed to utilise the voices and moral authority of religious leaders and spaces of religious institutions to change individual perceptions towards the 'other' and improve relations between ethnic groups, political factions, religious formations, and grassroots neighbourhoods. As reconciliation literature espouses, attaining these changes required participants to build their resilience through healing, which means letting the last go, forgiving and re-humanising the 'other', developing empathy, and acknowledging that all Burundians share the same civic identity and humanity.

Empirical evidence from the four provinces shows that CICB contributed to changing individual perceptions towards the 'other'. For example, a young political activist in Bujumbura Mairie revealed that he "used to participate in political marches and perpetrate violence against others".[5] However, he changed after attending CICB forums. As he explained, "now I work with my former opponents in the other political factions, and we support each other. That is a real change for me, and I attribute it to the CICB dialogue sessions which I attended." Not only did the young man change, but he started changing others. As he narrated, "I am actively involved in facilitating dialogues between young men and women of the ruling party and the opposition parties. I did that during and after the 2020 elections." This piece of evidence is illuminating because it is from a respondent who admits perpetrating direct violence against perceived political enemies, and then he changed his perceptions and views towards the 'other'. Another young man from the Anglican Church, who resides in the Mutakura suburb in Bujumbura Mairie, admitted that the killings of 2015 changed his life. "I hated those who did not share my ethnicity and political preference. I desired to know how to use a gun so that I could avenge the atrocities they committed against my ethnic group. I wanted revenge." He was full of bitterness and hatred when CICB invited him to attend a training forum. However, the training sessions made him understand that not "all people from other political factions and ethnic groups are evil".

---

[5] Parts of this evidence and others cited in this chapter were in the CRID general readers' version produced as Case Study Series No. 4 in April 2022, which is available here: https://www.faithtoactionetwork.org/interfaith-peacebuilding-from-below-in-burundi-building-everyday-peace-in-the-lower-stratacrid-case-study-series-4/case-study-series-no-4/.Â

Thus, he changed his views towards members of the 'other ethnic group'. As he emphasised, "I decided to advocate peace in my area. For the country to have peace, I must be the first one to safeguard peace in my neighbourhood." In essence, changes by the two young men speak to the CICB's indicators of everyday peace in the micro-spaces. As they changed their perceptions, the two young men and their compatriots, who attended CICB sessions, accepted that all neighbours shared Burundi civic identity and common humanity. Therefore, they could tolerate each other and live peacefully in the same neighbourhoods in spite of their divergent political preferences and ethnic identities.

CICB recorded similar changes in Bujumbura Rural, which encircles Bujumbura Mairie, and is one of the locations where *Parti pour la Libération du Peuple Hutu—Forces Nationales de Libération*-(PALIPEHUTU-FNL), which has strong anti-Tutsi sentiments, has been active since 1980. Empirical evidence suggests that CICB's use of religious values, texts, narratives, and tools transformed individual perceptions and group relations. As a young woman from the Anglican Church reported, "I was not interested in ethnic issues before 2015. But the events of 2015 changed me. I started mistrusting those from the 'other' ethnic group and I wanted to avenge atrocities against my people." However, CICB's use of religious texts and narratives transformed her; it made her understand that ethnicity is a matter of perception. In her words, "God did not mention ethnicity during creation." Therefore, she started changing the views of her friends and improving interethnic relations in her neighbourhood.

Such use of religious texts and narratives also resonated with a male pastor from the region. "I participated in the CICB forums as a returnee. My parents fled to western Tanzania in 1972 when the army massacred our Hutu people. I was a child when my parents fled to Tanzania," he explained. "As I grew up in camps for Burundi refugees, I learned that we were not Tanzanians but Hutu refugees from Burundi; I learned that Tutsis made us refugees."[6] While he always dreamt of returning to his country, "it was not easy to settle when we finally returned home because the Tutsis had taken our land. I harboured murderous hatred against the Tutsis; I could not tolerate them or coexist with them. I saw them as selfish, greedy, and inhuman." This evidence is consistent with documented testimonies from survivors of the 1972 killings, which had elements of genocide, as some studies intimate (Greenland, 1976; Lemarchand, 1994, 1998; Malkki, 1995).

Using testimonies from Hutu refugees in the Mishamo refugee camp in western Tanzania, Lemarchand (1994) observes that the macabre ethnic cleansing left a devastated Burundi society where Tutsis were the only elites. Thus, the post-1972 system was an ethnocracy where only Tutsis were allowed

---

[6] Parts of this evidence and others cited in this chapter were in the CRID general readers' version produced as Case Study Series No. 4 in April 2022, which is available here: https://www.faithtoactionetwork.org/interfaith-peacebuilding-from-below-in-burundi-building-everyday-peace-in-the-lower-stratacrid-case-study-series-4/case-study-series-no-4/.Å

access to power, influence, and wealth for the next 15 years. According to studies (Lemarchand, 1994; Greenland, 1976), that access to power and wealth included the transfer of the properties owned by the killed and displaced Hutus into the hands of the Tutsis both at the national level and at the lower levels. As Greenland (1976) notes, one of the motivators for ordinary Tutsi participation in the 1972 violence against Hutus in the countryside was to seize their properties, including land and cattle. Moreover, several studies show that everyday interactions among Hutu refugees in Tanzania, and elsewhere in the region, were instrumental in sustaining memories of the 1972 killings and constructing a *mythico-historical* narrative of the Hutu people (Malkki, 1995). Blending historical facts with fiction arising from the struggles of everyday life in refugee camps, that *mythico-historical* narrative gave meaning to their life of displacement and envisioned a collective return to their homeland (Lemarchand, 1994; Malkki, 1995). In other words, the establishment of a Tutsi ethnocracy undergirded by military violence reconfigured the discursive structures upon which Hutu and Tutsi constructed identity boundaries. The pastor's testimony is therefore consistent with other testimonies, such as those documented by Malkki (1995).

In this case, however, the argument is that CICB transformed his worldview. "When I received an invitation to participate in a CICB activity, I could not sit next to a Tutsi," he explained. "Over time, as I participated in more dialogue forums, I started to overcome my hatred of Tutsis. It was not easy to change, but I changed and I now understand that Tutsis are normal people like us."[7] Since his worldview towards the Tutsi people was shaped by narratives of oppression, the pain of displacement, and memories of the past massacres committed against the Hutu people by an all-Tutsi army, bitterness and hatred towards Tutsis determined his relations with his neighbours after he returned to Bujumbura Rural. However, CICB's use of religious values, tools, and texts in its training and dialogue forums resonated with him as a trained pastor. The approach appealed to his Christian notions of healing, forgiveness, empathy, and re-humanisation of the 'other'. While his change was understandably slow, he ultimately overcame his anti-Tutsi narratives and intention for revenge, embraced his Tutsi neighbours in his moral sphere, and accepted that they all shared common humanity. Thus, he promoted tolerance and sought to improve Hutu-Tutsi relations as indicators of everyday peace in his micro-space.

A similar moment of transformation affected the late CICB Secretary-General. As a Tutsi from Rumonge, a former senior military officer, and a former government minister during the military rule in the 1980s, he had avoided visiting certain regions of Burundi, including Bujumbura Rural, since the onset of the civil war in 1993. However, as the CICB leader, he had to visit the

---

[7] Parts of this evidence and others cited in this chapter were in the CRIDâ€™s general readers' version produced as Case Study Series No. 4 in April 2022, which is available here: https://www.faithtoactionnetwork.org/interfaith-peacebuilding-from-below-in-burundi-building-everyday-peace-in-the-lower-stratacrid-case-study-series-4/case-study-series-no-4/.Â

province. "I did not want to go to Bujumbura Rural. I was very fearful and trembled in the car when we started the trip because I expected hostile reception," he explained. "However, I was surprised when the project beneficiaries accepted me. I could not believe my eyes when I saw neighbours interacting freely regardless of their 'tribes' and religious denominations. I was delighted to see how our project was transforming the participants." Such evidence shows that CICB's use of religious texts, including the Christian Bible and the Holy Qur'an, and tools, such as prayers and spiritual reflections, resonated with the population and promoted tolerance, peaceful relations, and everyday peace in the neighbourhoods.

Evidence from Muyinga, a province with the highest concentration of Muslims in Burundi, shows similar changes. Muyinga experienced mass killings in the pre-2005 civil war and an armed group, MALIBU-FPS, which was formed after 2015, was active in the area. A young Muslim cleric argued that the 2015 crisis shocked the province. "After the attempted coup in 2015 and the attack on a military camp in 2017, we expected continued violence; we thought the 2020 elections would be violent." However, he added, CICB introduced dialogues in 2018 which "changed young people and religious leaders. I believe that was why there was no violence in the 2020 elections." The turning point for him was mutual visits to each other's holy shrines. "We appreciate when we see young Muslims, while dressed in the long tunic and the prayer hat, entering Catholic or Protestant churches and when we see Christians entering mosques." In essence, CICB's use of religious tools and texts in dialogue sessions resonated with the values and beliefs of ordinary people and, thus, contributed to changing the perceptions of young participants towards members of different political factions, religions, and ethnicity. This study infers that mutual visits to holy shrines pointed to their willingness to embrace each other and attain everyday peace. Such change in individuals' views towards the 'other' was critical for tolerance and improved group relations in an area where memories of past killings influenced interpretations of current events.

In Rumonge, violent clashes between youth militias of the ruling party and the opposition occurred from 2015 to 2017. It was also the province where the 1972 ethnic killings started and experienced violence in the 1990s. A young Muslim woman, who was a member of the ruling party militia, *imbonerakure*, admitted her involvement in violence against 'others'. However, she changed her perspective after participating in CICB forums. "I am a member of the CNDD-FDD and I am active in *imbonerakure*," she explained. "I thank CICB for facilitating understanding between different ethnic groups and political parties. Before I joined CICB activities, I used to participate in fights between *imbonerakure* and the youth militias of the opposition CNL. The CICB became a bridge between us; now I have changed." Not only does the respondent admit her involvement in violence, but she explicitly articulates her change of views towards the 'other' and espouses tolerance between different ethnic and political groups. Further, she embraces improvement in group relations and accepts her political opponents as citizens of Burundi with whom she shares the same cultural heritage and a common humanity. As a Muslim, she also espouses interfaith coexistence. In her words, "I believed that a Catholic Christian could not marry someone belonging to another religion and vice versa before I joined the CICB inter-religious forums. I thank CICB for the training because I have changed. For example, I know a Muslim girl who has changed her religion to marry her Catholic fiancé." Such neighbourhood tolerance and acceptance of the 'other' is a pillar of improvement in group relations and attainment of everyday peace in micro-spaces.

Another piece of evidence from a female Anglican lay leader reinforces the change in group relations in Rumonge. "I am an Anglican and a woman leader in my church …. CICB has promoted dialogues between church representatives and this has strengthened relations between churches and neighbours," she affirms. "Before the project, neighbours were hostile to each to each other and had problems coexisting in the common spaces. In particular, the returnees experienced problems because others occupied their properties. The CICB project has changed those hostile relations and neighbours have started welcoming returnees." In addition to corroborating the claims of the pastor in Bujumbura Rural, this evidence confirms that CICB activities helped individuals change their views towards the 'other', reduce hostilities between neighbours, and improve relations between political factions, religious formations, and ethnic groups. Such changes underscore CICB's approach of using religious spaces, tools, and values to encourage participants to heal, forgive, tolerate, and embrace the 'other' and, thus, promote everyday peace.

This chapter does not imply that all those who participated in the CICB interventions shifted their views towards the 'other' and promoted improvement in group relations. However, the evidence suggests that the majority of the participants changed at a personal level. While some overcame hate narratives and memories of the past and started promoting intergroup relations, others changed their perceptions towards their political and ethnic adversaries and embraced them in their moral sphere. These changes were consistent with CICB's approach of transforming the worldview of individuals, who become change agents, and improving intergroup relations in micro-spaces. As the bottom-up and everyday peace approach postulates, such changes in many micro-spaces would cumulatively break the cycles of violence at the national level. It should be noted that there is no evidence that CICB's grassroots actors were aware of SDG 16 or its principles. Nonetheless, this study infers that they inadvertently contributed to the achievement of Goal 16 and its target 16.1 and indicators 16.1.2 and 16.1.3 through their practices of reducing violence, conflicts, and hostilities in their micro-spaces, embracing their neighbours, and restoring everyday peace. Indeed, improving relations between individuals and groups in the micro-spaces required resolving conflicts which contributed to the breakdown of those relations.

## Conflict Resolution in the Micro-Spaces

Empirical evidence shows CICB's contribution to the resolution of conflicts as one of its indicators of everyday peace. Although the political-security crisis was mainly at the national level, the organisation aimed to enhance the conflict resolution skills of grassroots religious leaders. Specifically, the pattern of post-2014 killings and the persistent memories of past ethnic massacres shaped the discursive construction of worldview and exclusion boundaries towards ethnic identities, tolerance, and reconciliation in the micro-spaces. Another problem that CICB identified was the hostile relations between returnees and those who remained during different phases of ethnic violence. The logic of CICB interventions was to empower religious leaders with basic conflict resolution skills so that they would utilise religious spaces, symbols, and moral authority to resolve conflicts at the micro-levels.

One of the trained leaders, a female from Rumonge, observed that religious leaders "have a great role to play in the processes of social cohesion and peace-building". Explaining that CICB trained them on "conflict resolution and peaceful coexistence", she elaborated how the training sessions "strengthened their capacities and enabled them build trust, harmony, and social cohesion". She applied the acquired skills by organising sessions in her community and sharing the knowledge with other members of local communities. She particularly advised them on the dangers of ethnic and political extremism and stressed the need for peaceful relations between neighbours. Such involvement of grassroots religious leaders and improvement of group relations align with the postulates of CICB's bottom-up peacebuilding approach and the notion of everyday peace. In essence, religious leaders used religious tools, texts, and narratives that resonated with the population to promote everyday peace.

Additional evidence from a male civil society activist from Rumonge corroborates the foregoing. In his words, "the CICB project helped us resolve many disputes between returnees and those who remained in the province. We held an awareness forum at Kigwena with several religious leaders, those who had just returned and those who had remained." Adding that they did not have a mechanism for resolving such disputes before the CICB interventions, he explained how CICB assisted them "develop a framework of engagement that we explained to them and later used to resolve land disputes between returnees and those who remained during the armed conflict. All of them accepted our framework, and they now live peacefully as neighbours." The bigger issue in this evidence is the legacy of forced migration and the challenges of post-conflict recovery.

A baseline survey at the start of CICB interventions found that land claims by returnees constituted one of the main causes of bitterness, hatred, and conflicts in the micro-spaces after the end of the civil war. Such conflicts often degenerated into direct violence and fed into the discursive construction of the pre-existing ethnic stereotypes and prejudices. Therefore, resolving them was central to improving group relations and attaining everyday peace. A young female Muslim participant from Muyinga affirmed this point, stating that CICB interventions provided "a bridge between the families of the returnees and those who remained in the country. We knew families who took other people's properties and plots of land after they fled. It became chaotic and violent when the owners of those lands and properties returned." Establishing mechanisms for resolving land disputes in the four provinces was therefore one of the ways of improving group relations, promoting tolerance, and cultivating everyday peace. Additional evidence from two women from Bujumbura Rural, a Lutheran and a Catholic, supports the argument that the empowered religious leaders became bridges of everyday peace.

In summary, this study holds that CICB employed a combination of technical peacebuilding approaches, such as training workshops and dialogue forums, and religious texts and tools, such as the Holy Bible, the Holy Quran, prayers and spiritual reflections, to change perceptions and resolve conflicts in the micro-spaces in Bujumbura Mairie, Bujumbura Rural, Muyinga and Rumonge provinces. This approach resonated with the grassroots actors, who were struggling with the effects of the post-2014 violence and the persistent narratives and memories of the past killings. By providing spaces, mechanisms, forums, and language (idioms, narratives, and symbols) for addressing pain and resolving conflicts, CICB explicitly contributed to the improvement of individual and group relations and the attainment of everyday peace and implicitly contributed to the achievement of SDG 16. Incorporating religious dimensions into secular peacebuilding approaches helped CICB tackle persistent subjects, such as narratives and memories of past killings, and promote everyday peace in micro-spaces. While the strategy encountered some conceptual, operational, and financial challenges, it offered a few universal lessons about bottom-up peacebuilding and the restoration of everyday peace.

## Challenges and Lessons

Since the practice of everyday peace emphasises tolerance and peaceful relations at micro-levels, the first challenge that CICB encountered was the national character of the political-security crisis and many underlying issues. Among these were grievances and memories of past ethnic massacres, which still shape worldviews towards tolerance, reconciliation, and everyday peace. Everyday peace interventions in such a context require conceptual clarity and an investment in time and resources. While the organisation possessed conceptual clarity and a clear understanding of the country's context, it lacked sufficient financial resources to make a long-term commitment. Therefore, it chose a model built upon small, practical steps involving grassroots-based religious leaders, hoping that they would cascade the work after the international funder terminated its funding.

A second challenge was that the armed conflict did not start at the bottom; it began at the top of the national government, and the combatants were national security forces, armed groups, and youth militias. Therefore, CICB opted for everyday peace in different micro-spaces, believing that attaining many islands of peaceful relations in different micro-spaces would build tolerance and peaceful coexistence at those levels, end the cycles of violence, and influence peace formation at the macro-level.

The third challenge related to the structure of CICB's model of utilising religious leaders. While such leaders used their religious institutions, legitimacy, moral power, and religious symbols, tools, and values to promote tolerance, improve group relations, and build everyday peace, CICB lacked resources and a mechanism for following their activities because they came from different religious denominations.

These challenges notwithstanding, the model offers a few lessons. First, Burundi studies argue that the country's political, economic, and cultural structures are such that the macro-level and the micro-spaces are mutually constituted and state-society relations are heavily top-down. The vertical relationships have led to a power imbalance between the two levels as personalised ties and the logic of hierarchy are stronger. In contrast, the logic of everyday peace in micro-spaces relies on horizontal linkages. Therefore, as much as the CICB interventions aim at everyday peace at micro-levels through religious leaders and institutions, long-term commitment requires engagement with state actors. Particularly significant would be involving state agents in the middle and lower tiers to buttress everyday peace in the micro-spaces.

Second, the CICB model of focusing on everyday peace in a case of political and ethnic violence is viable, and the logic of building islands of everyday peace, which contribute to ending cycles of violence, can be universalised.

Third, despite the challenges of implementing bottom-up peacebuilding interventions in a situation of on-going conflict, CICB activities achieved a quantifiable impact. As such, the lesson for the model is to increase the number of activities at each location and to add activities in other geopolitical zones.

Lastly, a notable point for the interveners was the recruitment of youth militias that relied on the sedimented discourse of essentialised ethnic identities that has been normalised in the popular imagination as a result of past massacres and political practices. The discourse challenges the formation of a civic identity that bounds all Burundians in a shared future. Therefore, the organisation's strategy of integrating bottom-up peacebuilding with religious tools and values provided a way of rupturing the discourse.

## Conclusion

From the argument made in this chapter, CICB understood the Burundi context, the consequences of the post-2014 political violence and armed insurrection, and the role of religious leaders in responding to those challenges. The organisation underpinned its bottom-up peacebuilding and everyday peace strategy on the understanding that religious leaders are persuasive agents of change as they employ religious institutions, moral legitimacy, power, spaces, and texts to advocate for tolerance, reconciliation, and everyday peace. It recognised that the post-2014 political-security crisis had divided religious leaders, revived memories of the past massacres, and the country faced the prospects of plunging into another phase of civil war. Therefore, CICB chose a religious approach that employed grassroots-based leaders as change agents. Adduced evidence shows that CICB's starting point was empowering religious leaders with basic conflict resolution skills. Then the trained leaders employed their legitimacy, moral power, and religious institutions, tools, and texts in micro-space activities, such as dialogue forums, peace committees, mediation sessions, and citizen-to-citizen outreaches. Such interventions sought to promote tolerance and conciliation and improve relations between ethnic groups, religious formations, and political factions. Subsequently, CICB organised public events that further reinforced its messages of peaceful relations in the micro-spaces.

Specifically, empirical evidence from the four provinces of Bujumbura Mairie, Bujumbura Rural, Muyinga, and Rumonge shows that CICB interventions changed the worldview of individuals and perceptions towards the 'other'; improved group relations; and encouraged tolerance, conciliation, healing, forgiveness, and empathy as the foundations of everyday peace in the micro-spaces. Overall, CICB intended that sufficient islands of everyday peace in different locations would encourage Burundians from all ethnicities, political factions, and religious formations to accept that they shared common humanity and civic identity. Such acceptance would ultimately contribute to breaking the cycles of violence and promote peaceful coexistence in the micro-spaces and the macro-level.

## References

Agencies in Bujumbura. (2015, May 15). Failed Burundi Coup Plotters Arrested as President Returns from Tanzania. *The Guardian*. https://www.theguardian.com/world/2015/may/15/burundi-army-dead-radio-station-battle-coup-leaders-arrested

Amnesty International. (2016). *Burundi Report 2015/16*. Amnesty International Annual Report. https://www.amnesty.org/en/latest/research/2016/02/annual-report-2015/16/

Amnesty International. (2017). *Conform or Flee: Repression and Insecurity Pushing Burundians into Exile*. Amnesty International Report, Index Number: AFR 16/7139/2017. https://www.amnesty.org/en/documents/afr16/7139/2017/en/

Appleby, R. S. (2000). *The Ambivalence of the Sacred: Religion, Violence, and Reconciliation*. Rowman & Littlefield Publishers.

BBC Reporter. (2015, May 13). Burundi President Nkurunziza Faces Attempted Coup. *BBC World News*. https://www.bbc.com/news/world-africa-32724083

Bercovitch, J., & Kadayifci-Orellana, S. A. (2009). Religion and Mediation: The Role of Faith-based Actors in International Conflict Resolution. *International Negotiation*, *14*(1), 175–204.

Berents, H. (2018). *Young People and Everyday Peace: Exclusion, Insecurity and Peacebuilding in Colombia.* Taylor & Francis.

Bigirimana, S. (2021). The Meaning of Violence and the Violence of Meaning: The Politics of Knowledge in Burundi. In B. Jones & U. Lühe (Eds.), *Knowledge for Peace: Transitional Justice and the Politics of Knowledge in Theory and Practice* (pp. 214–244). Warwick Interdisciplinary Research Centre for International Development (WICID).

Brewer, J. D., Higgins, G. L., & Teeney, F. (2010). Religion and Peacemaking: A Conceptualization. *Sociology, 44*(6), 1019–1036.

Burundi Crisis Deepens as General Claims President Ousted. (2015, May 13). *France 24 World News.* https://www.france24.com/en/20150513-live-burundi-coup-attempt-president-nkurunziza

Daley, P., & Popplewell, R. (2016). The Appeal of Third Termism and Militarism in Burundi. *Review of the African Political Economy, 43*(150), 648–657.

Dubois, H. (2008). Religion and Peacebuilding: An Ambivalent Yet Vital Relationship. *Journal of Religion, Conflict and Peace, 1*(2), 1–21.

Gopin, M. (2009). *To Make the Earth Whole: The Art of Citizen Diplomacy in an Age of Religious Militancy.* Rowman & Littlefield Publishers.

Greenland, J. (1976). Ethnic Discrimination in Rwanda and Burundi. In W. A. Veenhoven (Ed.), *Case Studies in Human Rights and Fundamental Freedoms: A World Survey* (Vol. 4, pp. 93–133). Martinus Nijhoff.

Gruchy, J. W. (2022). Reconciliation and Non-violent Transformation in South Africa: At the Interface of Theology and Secular Politics. In J. Mitchell, S. R. Millar, F. Po, & M. Percy (Eds.), *Religion and peace* (pp. 155–163). Blackwell Publishing Ltd.

Hamber, B. (2007). Forgiveness and Reconciliation: Paradise Lost or Pragmatism? *Peace and Conflict: Journal of Peace Psychology, 13*(1), 115–125.

Hatcher, J. (2015, August 4). Church vs State: A Worrying Dynamic for Burundi. *IRIN News.* http://www.irinnews.org/report/101824/church-v-state-worrying-dynamic-burundi

Human Rights Watch. (2018). *"We Will Beat You to Correct You": Abuses Ahead of Burundi's Constitutional Referendum.* Human Rights Watch Report. https://www.hrw.org/node/317989/printable/print

Human Rights Watch. (2019). *Burundi: 15 Years On, No Justice for Gatumba Massacre.* Human Rights Watch Report. https://www.hrw.org/news/2019/08/13/burundi-15-years-no-justice-gatumba-massacre

Kang, H. (2022). Enforced Silence or Mindful Non-violent Action? Everyday Peace and South Korean Victims of Civilian Massacres in the Korean War. *Peacebuilding, 10*(3), 297–312.

Kew, D., & Kwaja, C. M. A. (2022). Religion and Peacebuilding in Nigeria. In J. Mitchell, S. R. Millar, F. Po, & M. Percy (Eds.), *Religion and Peace* (pp. 143–154). Blackwell Publishing Ltd.

Lemarchand, R. (1994). *Burundi: Ethnic Conflict and Genocide.* Woodrow Wilson Centre.

Lemarchand, R. (1998). Genocide in the Great Lakes: Which Genocide? Whose Genocide? *African Studies Review, 41*(1), 3–16.

Lemarchand, R. (2008a). *The Dynamics of Violence in Central Africa.* University of Pennsylvania Press.

Lemarchand, R. (2008b, June 27). *The Burundi Killings of 1972: Mass Violence and Résistance*. [Online publication]. http://bo-k2s.sciences-po.fr/mass-violence-war-massacre-resistance/en/document/burundi-killings-1972, ISSN 1961-9898.

Little, D., & Appleby, S. (2004). A Moment of Opportunity? The Promise of Religious Peacebuilding in an Era of Religious and Ethnic Conflicts. In H. Coward & G. S. Smith (Eds.), *Religion and Peacebuilding* (pp. 69–92). State University of New York Press.

Mac Ginty, R. (2010). Hybrid Peace: Interaction between Top-down and Bottom-up Peace. *Security Dialogue, 41*(4), 391–412.

Mac Ginty, R. (2011). *International Peacebuilding and Local Resistance: Hybrid Forms of Peace*. Palgrave Macmillan.

Mac Ginty, R. (2014). Everyday Peace: Bottom-up and Local Agency in Conflict-Affected Societies. *Security Dialogue, 45*(6), 548–564.

Mac Ginty, R. (2015). Where Is the Local? Critical Localism and Peacebuilding. *Third World Quarterly, 36*(5), 840–856.

Mac Ginty, R. (2017). Everyday Social Practices and Boundary-Making in Deeply Divided Societies. *Civil Wars, 19*(1), 4–25.

Mac Ginty, R. (2021). *Everyday Peace: How So-called Ordinary People Can Disrupt Violent Conflict*. Oxford University Press.

Mac Ginty, R., & Firchow, F. (2016). Top-down and Bottom-up Narratives of Peace and Conflict. *Politics, 36*(3), 308–323.

Mac Ginty, R., & Richmond, O. (2013). The Local Turn in Peace Building: A Critical Agenda for Peace. *Third World Quarterly, 34*(5), 763–783.

Malkki, L. H. (1995). *Purity and Exile: Violence, Memory, and National Cosmology among Hutu Refugees in Tanzania*. University of Chicago Press.

Marijan, B. (2017). The Politics of Everyday Peace in Bosnia and Herzegovina and Northern Ireland. *Peacebuilding, 5*(1), 67–81.

Mitchell, J., Millar, S. R., Po, F., & Percy, M. (2022). *Religion and Peace*. Blackwell Publishing Ltd.

Montville, J. (1990). The Arrow and the Olive Branch: A Case for Track Two Diplomacy. In D. V. Vamik et al. (Eds.), *The Psychodynamics of International Relationships* (pp. 161–175). Lexington Books.

Montville, J. (1993). The Healing Function in Political Conflict Resolution. In D. Sandole & H. van der Merwe (Eds.), *Conflict Resolution Theory and Practice: Integration and Application* (pp. 112–128). Manchester University Press.

Montville, J. (2009). Track Two Diplomacy: The Work of Healing History. *The Whitehead Journal of Diplomacy and International Relations, 7*(2), 15–25.

Nshimirimana, F. (2020). Managing Ethnic Conflicts, Militarisation, and Democratic Failure in the Post-Arusha Burundi. *African Journal of Democracy and Governance, 7*(3/4), 151–172.

O'Driscoll, D. (2021). Everyday Peace and Conflict: (Un)privileged Interactions in Kirkuk, Iraq. *Third World Quarterly, 42*(10), 2227–2246.

Omer, A. (2012). Religious Peacebuilding: The Exotic, the Good, and the Theatrical. *Practical Matters Journal*. http://practicalmattersjournal.org/?p=241.

Omer, A. (2021). Religion and the Study of Peace: Practice without Reflection. *Religions, 12*(12), 1069. https://doi.org/10.3390/rel12121069. https://www.mdpi.com/2077-1444/12/12/1069

Paffenholz, T. (2015). Unpacking the Local Turn in Peacebuilding: A Critical Assessment Towards an Agenda for Future Research. *Third World Quarterly, 36*(5), 857–874.

Paris, R. (2002). International Peacebuilding and the 'Mission Civilisatrice'. *Review of International Studies*, 28(4), 637–657.
Paris, R. (2007). *At War's End: Building Peace after Civil Conflict*. Cambridge University Press.
Paris, R. (2010). Saving Liberal Peacebuilding. *Review of International Studies*, 36(2), 337–365.
Peterson, R. (2001). A Theology of Forgiveness. In R. Helmick & R. Petersen (Eds.), *Forgiveness and Reconciliation: Religion, Public Policy, and Conflict Transformation* (pp. 3–26). Templeton Foundation Press.
Powers, G. F. (2010). Religion and Peacebuilding. In D. Philpot & G. F. Powers (Eds.), *Strategies for Peace: Transforming Conflict in a Violent World* (pp. 317–352). Oxford University Press.
Qurtuby, S. (2022). Grassroots Peacebuilding in Contemporary Indonesia. In J. Mitchell, S. R. Millar, F. Po, & M. Percy (Eds.), *Religion and Peace* (pp. 112–123). Blackwell Publishing Ltd.
Randazzo, E. (2017). *Beyond Liberal Peacebuilding: A Critical Exploration of the Local Turn*. Routledge.
Randazzo, E. (2021). The Local, the 'Indigenous' and the Limits of Rethinking Peacebuilding. *Journal of Intervention and Statebuilding*, 15(2), 141–160.
Richmond, O. (2001). Rethinking Conflict Resolution: The Linkage Problematic between 'Track I' and 'Track II'. *Journal of Conflict Studies*, 21(2), 109–132.
Richmond, O. (2006). The Problem of Peace: Understanding the 'Liberal Peace'. In A. Swain, R. Amer, & J. Ojendal (Eds.), *Globalisation and Challenges to Building Peace* (pp. 17–38). Anthem Press.
Richmond, O. (2007). Emancipatory Forms of Human Security and Liberal Peacebuilding. *International Journal*, 62(3), 459–477.
Richmond, O. (2009a). A Post-Liberal Peace: Eirenism and the Everyday. *Review of International Studies*, 35(3), 557–580.
Richmond, O. (2009b). Becoming Liberal, Unbecoming Liberalism: Liberal-Local Hybridity via the Everyday as a Response to the Paradoxes of Liberal Peacebuilding. *Journal of Intervention and Statebuilding*, 3(3), 324–344.
Richmond, O. (2011). De-romanticising the Local, De-mystifying the International: Hybridity in Timor Leste and the Solomon Islands. *The Pacific Review*, 24(1), 115–136.
Richmond, O., & Franks, J. (2009). *Liberal Peace Transitions: Between Statebuilding and Peacebuilding*. Edinburgh University Press.
Richmond, O., & Mac Ginty, R. (2019). Mobilities and Peace. *Globalizations*, 16(5), 606–624.
UN Human Rights Council. (2017a). *Detailed Final Report of the Commission of Inquiry on Burundi*. UN Human Rights Council Report, September 2017. https://www.ohchr.org/en/hrbodies/hrc/coiburundi/pages/coiburundi.aspx
UN Human Rights Council. (2017b). Burundi Situation Report 2017. https://www.unhcr.org/59244aa77.pdf
Ware, A., Ware, V. A., & Kelly, L. M. (2022). Strengthening Everyday Peace Formation after Ethnic Cleansing: Operationalising a Framework in Myanmar's Rohingya Conflict. *Third World Quarterly*, 43(2), 289–308.
Williams, P. (2015). *Everyday Peace? Politics, Citizenship and Muslim Lives in India*. Wiley Blackwell.

CHAPTER 14

# Religion and Peacebuilding in Tanzania: Institutionalisation of Interfaith Peace Committee

*Alexander Makulilo and Rodrick Henry*

## INTRODUCTION

Historically, Tanzania is regarded as a peaceful country. Despite such a favourable profile, the country has experienced social, political and economic conflicts. Some of these conflicts required intervention to prevent them from escalating. Several mechanisms have been employed to resolve conflicts in Tanzania. These include government, non-governmental, legal and religious mechanisms. Tanzania's peace mechanisms are primarily based on a conflict prevention approach. The approach traces its origins from national building taken at the infancy stages of the nation. The then nation-building approach aimed to create an egalitarian society where everyone could live together without discrimination. Local authorities based on chieftaincy among tribes were abolished. They remained ceremonial, without real power to make decisions or enforce laws. Swahili was encouraged as the national language, and vernaculars could not be taught at school. The reforms were oriented towards attaining a unified nation in which the tribal, religious and social differences would play a minor role in the socioeconomic and political direction of the country.

A. Makulilo (✉) • R. Henry
Department of Political Science, University of Dar es Salaam, Dar es Salaam, Tanzania
e-mail: makulilo76@udsm.ac.tz

© The Author(s), under exclusive license to Springer Nature Switzerland AG 2023
S. M. Kilonzo et al. (eds.), *The Palgrave Handbook of Religion, Peacebuilding, and Development in Africa*,
https://doi.org/10.1007/978-3-031-36829-5_14

Similarly, the national-building project aimed to create a modernised society. In 1965 the country adopted a one-party system. President Nyerere justified one-party system by arguing that in Africa people sit under the big tree and discuss until they reach an agreement. Competitive politics were feared for being divisive. As post-colonial states were artificial creations, liberalised politics raised the danger of returning the state to pre-colonial periods where there was no such thing as Tanganyika, Kenya or Nigeria but tribes.

To effectively institute a one-party state, independent civil societies, media and alternative sources of views were also abolished. This period was officially known as an era of party supremacy. In 1967, Tanzania promulgated the Arusha Declaration, which adopted "Africa Socialism and Self Reliance" as the state's official ideology and policy. The declaration nationalised the major private import-export firms. It replaced them with State Trading Corporation. The banking sector was nationalised, and the National Bank of Commerce took over all finance activities. Also, buildings were expropriated through the Building and Acquisition Act of 1971 (Muganda, 2004). The government also promoted religious freedom as it insisted that religion was a private affair in which the government should never interfere. That was cemented by the constitutional provision, which pronounced freedom of religion among citizens (Westerlund, 1980). Therefore, the national-building project suppressed tribal, ethnic and political divisions among the people (Wijsen, 2004).

Tanzania is known as a very religious society. Religion remains a strong identity among its people. Tanzanians, just like other Africans, tend to identify themselves with religion more than other identities (Mukandala et al., 2006). Likewise, Tanzania exhibits tremendous confidence and respect for religious institutions and leaders. Religious institutions dominate Tanzanians' lives, including providing health and education services (Mukandala et al., 2006; Mhina, 2007). Paradoxically, the influence of religion and religious leaders in Tanzania has been a source of peace and conflict at different times (Wijsen, 2004). Religious institutions have been crucial in the national building processes in the post-independence period. The Catholic Church played a crucial role in campaigning for Ujamaa ideology (Westerlund, 1980). Similarly, the government once acquired the schools under religious institutions, mainly owned by the church, to facilitate education for all.

Similarly, the government created the Muslim Supreme Council of Tanzania (BAKWATA) in 1968. This was after the banning of the East African Muslim Welfare Society (EAMWS), created in 1945 to promote the welfare of Muslims. The ban on EAMWS and the creation of BAKWATA are attributed to the need of the post-colonial state to curtail Muslim political activism, which was seen as a threat to the regime and peace (Said, 1998; Njozi, 2003; Tambila, 2006). The ban was, however, not surprising, taking a similar move taken by the government in limiting political and social freedoms, which included the abolition of multipartism, independent trade unions and civil societies. During this period, the legal and institutional framework provided a little avenue for individuals and organisations, including religious institutions, to express different views from the state. As such, the two actors had fewer contestations on the perception of peace. In the two decades of independence, Tanzania experienced a peaceful and tolerant religious climate (Mesaki, 2011); however, that changed in the late 1980s and early 1990s due to political and economic liberalisation.

Tanzania instituted liberalisation in the late 1980s. After the departure of Nyerere from power in 1985, the new administration under President Mwinyi rolled economic liberalisation. It was followed by political liberalisation in 1992, which, among other things, expanded the freedom to organise and express. Under this new context, religious organisations could now challenge the actions and policies of the state if they were against religious and societal interests. Similarly, the newly adopted policies allowed some religious organisations to emerge. Consequently, in the late 1980s, radical and fundamental religious preachers rose from both Christian and Islam religions (Mesaki, 2011). The preachers flourished on the attacks against the other faiths. The attacks were based on conspiracies and hatred. These activities were concentrated in Dar es Salaam and some urban areas. Such activities culminated in an unprecedented lift between Muslims and Christians (Wijsen, 2004; Tambila, 2006).

In April 1993, Muslim fundamentalists stoned and demolished three pork butcheries in Dar es Salaam. Thirteen people were arrested because of the violence and another 13 when they tried marching to protest the arrest of their colleagues (Mesaki, 2011). However, the Muslim Council of Tanzania (BAKWATA) denounced these actions. Indeed, Chief Sheikh Hemed bin Juma bin Hemed and the head of BAKWATA supported and commended the government response by noting that Tanzania was a secular state. He further advised Muslims to maintain peace and stability. The government attributed the attacks to a group of externally financed persons (Britain-Tanzania Society, 1993; Wijsen, 2004).

In February 1998, riots erupted between a section of Muslims against the security apparatus. The events are popularly known as the Mwembechai incident. The incident commenced with the arrest of members of Khidmat Daawat Islamiya on February 10, 1998, and their leader was apprehended on February 12, 1998. Among those arrested was the prominent Islamic preacher Sheikh Mesaki (2011). The arrest drew reactions, in the form of protests, from his followers demanding his release. The protests drew many people and turned violent, even targeting the community, passers-by and their properties. As a result, 57 public and private vehicles were damaged, a car was wholly burnt, 525 crates and 40 cartons of beer were stolen and 14 civilians and 6 policemen were injured. Police attempt to calm the situation culminated in the use of tear gas and the arrests of 136 people. The next day, the riots resumed but with increased magnitude leaving 20 people injured, including 4 police officers, 2 people being shot dead and 6 injured by police bullets. The police force claimed that the use of live ammunition was in self-defence, which is allowed according to Police Force Regulations. Also, the riots damaged 35 vehicles, 5 police posts and the Ward Executives Officers' Office in the neighbourhood, while the office of the ruling party, Chama Cha Mapinduzi (CCM), a branch office, was vandalised. On February 16, 1998, 131 people were charged in court for participating in the riots (Mesaki, 2011).

The other interfaith conflict was the clashes on the slaughtering of livestock, which occurred in February 2013 in Buseresere. The clashes resulted from the decision by Christians, instigated by their leaders, to slaughter animals, a cow and two goats, and sell the meat at the local market (Makulilo, 2019; Terdiman, 2013). The clashes resulted in the beheading of Pastor Mathayo Kachili of the Tanzanian Assemblies of God Church and the injury of several others as well as significant property damage. A local pastor, Isaya Rutta, had slaughtered animals and his followers were arrested and charged with breaking health laws, inciting the public and causing the death of Pastor Kachili (Terdiman, 2013).

Besides religious conflicts, Tanzania has also experienced political, resource and land conflicts, which have endangered the country's peace. For example, the Zanzibar electoral conflict of 2001 resulted in the death of 23 people, according to government reports, and 60 people, according to Civic United Front (CUF) reports. The victims were killed while protesting the electoral results. Also, 2000 people fled the Isles to Kenya and became refugees (Bakari, 2012). Some other conflicts included the Kilosa farmer-headers conflict of 2000, the Loliondo land conflict in 2009, the Nyamongo violence of 2011 and the Mtwara violence on the gas pipeline of 2013. The surge of this violence in these conflicts threatened the peaceful nature of Tanzania (Heilman & Kaiser, 2002; LHRC, 2012, 2013).

In 2009 faith leaders from different religions met and affirmed their essential duty to peace in Tanzania. They expressly declared their intervention to maintain peace. This came against the background of increasing interfaith clashes and conflicts. The state of affairs threatened peaceful coexistence among different faiths, which Tanzania has experienced since independence. The intervention was based on trust and influence amongst the society in Tanzania. Religious leaders believed they could play an active role in conflict management and peacebuilding since many Tanzanians identify with a particular religion. These leaders thought their engagement would only be effective through an official mechanism. This resulted in the formation of the Interfaith Peace Committee (IPC). The committee was created for prevention, mediation, conflict resolution and peacebuilding through various activities. Over a decade has passed since these committees were established, and it is time to evaluate them. Against this background, this chapter studies the institutionalisation of the committees. The purpose of assessing institutionalisation is premised on the supposition that conflict and peace mechanisms need a certain level of institutionalisation to achieve their intended purpose.

## RELIGION AND PEACEBUILDING REVISITED

In his book *The Clash of Civilizations*, Samuel Huntington held that religion would be the leading player in the post-Cold War period (Huntington, 1996). Religion plays a vital role in peace and conflict management. This role has been, however, paradoxical. Boulding maintains that most religions have two distinct cultures: the "holy war" and the "peaceable kingdom." Religions present, to their believers, the doctrine of peace from worldly chaos facing humanity by psychologically and emotionally assured of being on the righteous, just and prosperous path, unlike the non-believers. Most religions teach peaceful coexistence and fraternity among believers. It includes condemnation of injustices and oppression (Appelby, 1999). The message forms a basis for a peaceful and orderly society among people of the same faith (Appelby, 1999; Fox, 2004). Also, most religions have teachings which stress tolerance and peaceful coexistence with non-believers. Nevertheless, within the same religions, non-believers are accorded a negative image and status for not being on the perfect path in life. This can fuel violence against non-believers or the secular state (Appelby, 1999; Haynes, 1996).

Religion may embrace or opt to be silent towards the institutions which perpetuate injustices, oppression and exploitation—the sources of conflicts. Appelby (1999) contends that there is an intimate relationship between the ability of religion to influence violence and its power as a tool of peace. As much as religion has brought peace, it has also been condoned as the source of violent conflicts in societies worldwide (Frost, 2015). It is this ambivalence of religion's role in peace which has raised the interest of researchers in the field of peace and conflict. Notwithstanding, most states confine religion's role to maintaining peace by guiding the believers to abide by the laws of the land and even support the government's policies. Going contrary to the government, even when there are justifications, is often viewed as a source to destabilise peace (Ahamed, 2014). To have religious institutions and agents support this version of maintaining peace, states have been providing them with rewards of various kinds. These are economic, social and even political. In Italy, Mussolini won the backing of the Roman Catholic Church after he offered to grant it its lost status. In 1929 following the Lateran Accords between the Holy See and Mussolini government, the Vatican City became a sovereign state owning fundamental properties in Rome. The government paid compensation amounting to $92 million to the church. Moreover, Catholicism became Italy's official religion. Mussolini gave these offers in exchange for the church's loyalty and support towards his government. This classic case of the church and state in Italy is still relevant today, even in states widely modelled as secular and democratic. Religion has been used to support or challenge the state in conflict. Thus, religion is an effective mobilisation agency to achieve both ends (Appelby, 1999; Basedau & de Juan, 2008).

Across the world, the instances under which religion challenges the state, thus contradicting peace, are fewer (Bakari & Ndumbaro, 2006). Enlightenment scholars such as Voltaire, Montesquieu and Rousseau condemned the church's complicity in maintaining the monarchies' absolutism. Voltaire's analysis of the pre-revolution French society found that the first estate (Clergy) had become very rich and parasitic. This made it a static force against the revolution. Enlightenment scholars argued that for the liberty of individuals, religion had to remain in the private domain, separated from the state. Karl Marx conceived religion as a tool used by the dominant class to legitimise their domination. For him, religious institutions and agents are not different from the state apparatus as they are both aimed at perpetuating exploitation, inequality and oppression of the dominant class over the population. Marx referred to religion as the opium of the mass, which pacifies them to accept exploitation. Nevertheless, unlike most Enlightenment thinkers, he called for eliminating religion (Marx, 1959). From these experiences, one can argue that religion plays a role in sustaining exploitative, inequality and unjust structures, which are inimical to peace as they attract conflicts.

Understanding religious institutions' role in promoting peace should start by systematically investigating which positive or negative roles they play now (Reychler, 1997). For this to be achieved, Reychler outlines four roles played by religion and religious organisations in peace which are conflicting parties, bystanders, peacebuilders and peacemakers. The fact that religions have followers makes them a valuable asset in conflict and peacemaking. The followers are the resources that can be deployed to wage conflict or be pursued to de-escalate violence (Behrend, 1999). Also, religious institutions promote peace by being vocal against moral decay and injustices in society. Appleby (1999, p. 213) believes that religious organisations and agents are active "as social critics calling government officials and political, military, and business elites to account for unjust and abusive policies." This role is essential as the structural theory of conflicts sees conflicts and violence as the result of inequalities and exploitation and breeds injustices. The argument is aligned with political economy theory, which is premised on the supposition that "conflicts derive from the clash between different socioeconomic forces. The causes and driving forces of conflict are inequality in the society; violence is the manifest of these struggles" (Jeong, 1999, p. 89). The role of religion in fighting injustices has been the subject of debate for a long time, as their perspective of peace often contradicts that of states.

Religious institutions, just like the government, must recognise the concerns and demands of their followers (Molner, 1988). Even when that is done, it can only last for a short time as it is counterproductive. Turning a blind eye towards society's socioeconomic and political demands can corrode the legitimacy of religious institutions and leaders from their followers and non-followers (Ratzinger, 2001). This state of affairs has three consequences. First, it can wither the role of religion in society. Second, it can weaken the influence of religious institutions and leaders over the people, thus diminishing their constituency. Third, related to the second but with massive impact, it limits the clout held by respective religious institutions and leaders over the state and political leadership.

The structural theory of conflict highlights the critical role of the state towards the infringement of social, economic and political rights as the primary sources of conflicts (Ramsbotham et al., 2011). Conflicts stemming from these sources have a high potential to threaten societal peace. The victims of these structures can mobilise through religion to call for reforms or actions to alleviate the injustices. Even after long hesitance, religious institutions, leaders or individual leaders tend to join these calls (Daniel & Napoo, 2013). This can be through voicing support or taking an active role.

Nevertheless, joining the people to challenge these structures means putting themselves on a conflicting path with the state or other authorities. This contradicts the notion of religious engagement in peace from the state's perspective. Backing and expressing the people's demands by religious institutions and leaders often draw a backlash from the state. Often states worldwide tend to portray such actions as attempts at religious destabilisation of peace. Consequently, this comes with stern warnings, harassment, banning religious groups and even violent crackdowns, to mention the least. Therefore, as much as religious institutions and leaders have subscribed to the state's perspective on religion's role in politics, in some instances, they have sided with society to support and advocate demands for socioeconomic and political rights.

## Interfaith Approach to Peacebuilding and Conflict Prevention

One way to understand the role of religion in peace is to look at its capacity for conflict management. Religious institutions and leaders use their influence to mediate and resolve conflicts (Alger, 2002). In line with Sustainable Development Goal (SGD) 16, pursuing a peaceful and inclusive society requires all people of different religious orientations to be on board. As religion and religious identities play a significant role in African societies, they can be tapped to promote peacebuilding, which ultimately realises SGD 16. It should be noted that most sub-Saharan African countries are multi-religious. Effective conflict management and peacebuilding are premised on an interfaith approach in multi-religious societies. This requires the religious institutions to maintain a harmonious relationship, not just amongst themselves, but also the state (Ahamed, 2014). Such a relationship must be built on trust and with a common interest for peace and peacebuilding. Also, an interfaith approach means that different religions come together to discuss issues affecting society and ultimately promote a common solution. Moreover, the approach implies embracing issues which bridge the gap among different faiths and enhance issues of common interests (Ahamed, 2014). Interfaith committees have emerged as the common types of religious conflict management and peacebuilding mechanisms. The effectiveness of interfaith committees is mainly a result of sustainability and institutionalisation, which implies sustaining the committees beyond the conflicts. To ensure this sustenance, the type of leaders, and their vision, legitimises the committees.

## METHODS AND OBJECTIVE

The objectives and activities of IPC feed to the SGD 16, which is about promoting just, peaceful and inclusive societies. The discussion of this chapter intends to understand the extent to which IPC in Tanzania is institutionalised. The objective draws from SGD 16, which emphasises strong institutions which are effective, accountable and inclusive. The data for this chapter was collected mainly from secondary sources and supplemented by interviews with members and leadership of IPC. Since the IPC lacks a permanent office and secretariat, it was difficult to capture its activities accurately. To mitigate this challenge, we relied heavily on past engagement with the topic and the work of the IPC. The analysis is guided by the premise that the effectiveness and success of conflict management and peacebuilding mechanisms are highly dependent on their institutionalisation. The institutionalisation presupposes sustainability and proactive mechanisms as opposed to ad hoc and reactive modes of operation. This chapter regards institutions as both actors and rules of the game. Thus, institutions entail both soft and hard institutions.

## INSTITUTIONALISATION OF INTERFAITH PEACE COMMITTEES

The institutionalisation of IPC is analysed by looking at six variables: constitution and regulations; governance structure; secretariat; permanent office; budget and funding; and relationship with other stakeholders.

### *Constitution and Regulations*

Formal institutions operate on rules. Rules are essential as they provide the "Modus Operandi" through which an institution should conduct its businesses (Thoenig, 2003). In Tanzania, the Interfaith Peace Committee was established in 2009. However, formal rules or regulations to guide the committees have never been created since its establishment. However, the lack of rules and regulations guiding the committee is primarily attributed to how it was born. The committee originated from the Interfaith Dialogue organised in 2009 to discuss how to end religious tension between Muslims and Christians (Interview 02, December 10, 2022). Present in the dialogue were the religious leaders from Christian and Islamic faiths, government officials and influential business people. Members of the dialogue resolved to create a committee of leaders with the mandate to follow up on what was discussed during the dialogue. The committee was also tasked to organise further peacebuilding and conflict resolution activities. The resolution contributes to achieving SGD 16, which among other things emphasises significantly reducing all forms of violence and related death rates everywhere through peaceful and inclusive ways. However, the formalisation of the committee into a formal structure or at least adopting rules and regulations of its engagement was off the discussion during the meetings. As a result, there was no motion to adopt regulations or rules to guide the activities of the created committee (Interview 09, January 11, 2023). This could be attributed to the fact that the delegates did not envision that these committees would last long and play a key role as they are today.

As a result, the operations, mandate, organisation and relationship between the committee with other structures need to be formally defined. The committee has been performing different activities, including resolving conflicts and conducting peacebuilding. However, such functions are done using what we can refer to as members' wisdom since the rules of engagement have never been developed and codified. Thus, the committee has no constitution. Lacking a constitution to guide the committee impacts its effectiveness. First, it affects how the activities are carried out, as no standard procedures guide the engagement defined by the institutional philosophy. For instance, what guides the committee's engagement in resolving conflicts arising or carrying out peacebuilding activities such as interfaith dialogues? Since there are no codified or uncodified rules, the leaders' engagement is guided by their perception of the context, and conflicts of the time. This affects the resolution of other future crises because if leaders or executives change, then those who follow will work without reference to what was done in the past. Since these committees are made up of religious leaders, when a religious leader who is a committee member has been transferred to another work station, suspended or retired, that leader leaves with the knowledge of how these committees work. Without a constitution or rules governing the committee it can only be leadership and action based on personal experiences.

Nevertheless, for these mechanisms to be effective, they should be institutionalised instead of personalised. For achievement of SGD 16, apart from advocating for a just, peaceful and inclusive society, there is need for institutionalisation of the mechanisms to achieve these goals. The analysis of the current state of the interfaith committee at regional and national levels indicates that, at the moment, they are mainly functioning on the personal profiles of their members—the religious leaders. This explains why there are no committees in some districts and regions, especially in rural areas, since there the leaders have no substantial public profile. Similarly, the role of personalities in the committees affects and influences the relationship with community members, who are also beneficiaries of the committee's peacebuilding and conflict resolution activities. For instance, when the community negatively perceives some of the IPC members, such misunderstandings may be generalised to the entire committee.

## *Governance Structure*

Interfaith Peace Committees are designed to operate at the national, regional and district levels. When the committee was established, it was supposed to function at all three levels nationwide. The committee at the national level is composed of national religious leaders and other influential people. At this high level the committee is tasked with nationwide peacebuilding and conflict resolution activities. The level is also mandated to facilitate discussions among the religious leaders, and between the religious leaders and the government (Interview 02, December 10, 2022). Moreover, the national level is required to oversee the committee's activities at regional and district levels.

The regional level is composed of regional religious leaders. The regional committees engage in peacebuilding and conflict resolution activities at a regional level and oversee the activities carried out by the committees at the district level. The activities performed by the regional committee are not different from those of the national level, except that they are limited to the respective region of the committee. For instance, the Dar es Salaam region IPC has actively participated in the fight against gender-based violence. Its leaders have given talks and presentations each year during the 16 days of activism against gender-based violence organised by the Coalition of Civil Societies in Tanzania (Tamwa, 2020). During this annual event, the IPC strategically use the religious profiles of its members to voice against gender-based violence among their followers and the general society. This feeds into SGD 16, which calls for reducing violence and exploitation.

At the district level, peace committees are mainly tasked with resolving conflicts in their respective district. In Tanzania, experience shows that most conflicts arise at the lower levels of society. Thus, the presence of the committee at the district is meant to resolve these conflicts. The primary modus operandi of peace committees is a dialogue between various stakeholders. Subsequently, the district level is well placed to bring together stakeholders from the lowest levels. Also, at the district level, the committee gets cooperation in carrying out its duties from the government authorities. Structurally, the District Commissioner (DC) is the chief in charge of peace and security of the respective district. Thus, DCs often work closely with various stakeholders to ensure security and peace. Interfaith Peace Committees are critical stakeholders whose primary goal is to ensure peace (Interview 09, January 11, 2023). The committees were conceived with the understanding that religious leaders are listened to and respected by their believers and society in general. As such, they could play a critical role in peacebuilding and conflict resolution in the respective areas.

Although the structure of these committees looks good in theory, implementation of their mandate has been a challenge, and this affects the execution of the committee's responsibilities at various levels. As noted at the outset, no constitutions or rules guide the committee's day-to-day activities. Thus, many committee affairs are conducted at the will of the leaders who are members of those committees. Further, since each higher level is in charge of the immediate lower level, without proper rules and regulations, this becomes a complicated process. Often, it is difficult for a leader from a higher level to interfere with the authority of another at a different level. It is even more complicated when the matter in question is not an official activity related to religious duties.

The peace committee has consistently existed at the national level since 2009. Although the committee claims to be present in several regions, a close analysis reveals that only some regions have functioning peace committees. Seemingly, it is only Dar es Salaam that has had a permanent committee. The committees in other regions are temporary, as they often meet during seminars or conferences organised by the government or civil societies. This is explained from the fact that Dar es Salam is the headquarters of many religious institutions, such as Muslim, Catholic, Lutheran, Anglican and other evangelical churches. Also, since it is a commercial city and the former administrative capital of the government, the possibility of getting resources to run the committee's activities is high, unlike other regions. Moreover, Da res Salaam hosts head offices of various national and international organisations. These have been the significant stakeholders and funders of conflict resolution and peacebuilding programmes and activities.

### *Secretariat*

An organisation's permanent bureaucracy helps the institution develop its culture and memory (Thoenig, 2003). Due to the nature of the meetings held by the peace committees, the need for permanent staff cannot be overlooked. However, the committee has been working without permanent staff since its inception. This means that religious leaders who are members of these committees also work as secretariats (Interview 04, December 16, 2022). Experience from other countries and organisations serving similar or related purpose shows that such committees constitute a body with permanent offices and staff. Usually, this entity has permanent registration and functions as a complete office. Once this body is constituted, it assumes the role of a secretariat of the peace committees through its professional and career staff. The secretariat helps implement daily activities, including monitoring and evaluating the peace committees at various levels as stipulated in its structure.

For IPC, this kind of secretariat does not exist. It has, therefore, been difficult for the peace committees to carry out their duties efficiently. For instance, information on the stock of activities carried out since its inception, the total amount of funds received and its use in committee activities and the planned activities to be carried out are not fully documented. It is also an arduous task to know the committee's plan of activities at various levels (Interview 09, January 11, 2023). Since the religious leaders who are committee members are the same ones who work as secretariats, who are unable to juggle the roles well. The committee leaders need help to perform their duties effectively. Lack of such an important office then challenges the efforts to institutionalise IPC.

## Permanent Office

The Interfaith Peace Committee was designed to function as a permanent conflict resolution office. It was therefore expected to develop into a permanent organisation that would discharge its activities countrywide. However, for that to be realised, the committee must have an office coordinating administrative activities. As it is, this is not the case. The committee members rely on their religious institutions' offices for committees' activities. Several challenges result from this arrangement. For instance, when the tenure of the leader, who is also an IPC member, ends for various reasons, the documents and facilities belonging to the committee cannot remain in the office. In January 2023, for instance, the Dar es Salaam region Chief Sheikh Alhad Salum, a famous regional and national IPC member, was removed from his religious leadership position. However, when he handed over the office to his predecessor, he had already moved the office facilities, including chairs, tables, computers and bookshelves, from the office (Interview 11, February 01, 2023). He explained that the facilities he removed belonged to the Interfaith Peace Committee. They had been obtained from various donors as part of the support to the committee's activities. The facilities were kept at the Dar es Salaam Chief Shekh's office because the committee had no office to store them.

Without a properly established office, IPC cannot be able to receive sustainable support. It is also not able to initiate and conduct activities of their planned programmes. Funding agencies prefer to work with institutions that have evidence of permanence and official structure. Once an institution is adequately constituted with a recognised structure and address, it is easy to engage with other organisations for funding or technical support. As a result, most of the support is for part-time activities such as conferences, seminars and visits. Such activities last a few days, with little monitoring or evaluation.

## Budget and Funding

Budgeting and mobilisation of funds are at the core of success of peacebuilding and conflict resolution processes. As noted, the peace committee carries out peacebuilding and conflict resolution activities at national, regional and district levels. To facilitate the committee's work, sustainable sources of funding are mandatory to enable the committee achieve their short- and long-term objectives. Constant source of funding also allows the committee to expand its operations in varied areas. Observably, since its establishment, the committee has conducted its activities without a specified budget. According to its members, committee activities primarily depend on volunteer work and minimal funds from well-wishers (Interview 04, December 16, 2022). It has been a practice for members of the committee to carter for some costs, such as transport, air time and meals, when carrying out the committee's activities.

The lack of reliable sources of funds hinders the activities of the committee. For instance, the committee is not autonomous in choosing the activities to implement. Since the government is the single biggest funder of the committee's activities, especially the annual national dialogue, IPC cannot initiate proper peacebuilding activities (Interview 06, January 24, 2023). Relying on government is encouraging partisanship, which had negative repercussions for organisations that aim at resolving communities' conflicts. In Tanzania, experience shows that the state is directly involved as a prime or secondary actor in many conflicts. Since the committee, which resolves such conflicts, depends heavily on government support, its neutrality is jeopardised. There have been complaints from various stakeholders that the committee at different levels tends to side with the government when delivering peace messages or engaging in peacebuilding activities (Interview 05, December 28, 2022). This is contrary to SGD 16 targets that, among other things, emphasise equal access to justice.

### *Relationship with Other Stakeholders*

The relationship between an organisation with other actors is critical to the success of the activities carried out by such an organisation. How the organisation interacts and is perceived by other entities or individuals impacts its institutionalisation. Specifically, to peacebuilding and conflict resolution mechanisms, their relationship with other stakeholders is critical in attaining its goals. Both government and non-state actors as partners in peacebuilding and conflict resolution should be able to engage IPC in more trustworthy ways, especially because of the crucial role that IPC plays in resolving various conflicts. For instance, in 2012, the national-level peace committee was the front mediator in resolving the conflict on the slaughtering of livestock between Christians and Muslims in Buseresere, Geita region. The intervention of the committee was positively received. All parties accepted the committee to resolve the conflict since it was regarded as neutral and credible. The committee was also involved in peacebuilding activities to prevent the conflict from reoccurring in the future. Accordingly, the intervention is arguably the most successful story of the committee since its establishment.

However, in recent years the committee has experienced a relatively negative view from some stakeholders, including society, opposition political parties and activists. They have raised concerns that the committee is biased towards the government while addressing issues of peace. There are also concerns that the committee tends to be silent when the government or its agencies commit injustices (Interview 02, December 10, 2022). In fact, there have been complaints that the annual peace dialogue organised by the committee is an arena to campaign for government rather than address issues threatening the country's peace, especially the injustices. The committee also faces accusations of offering peace messages biased in favour of the government and the ruling party. During the 2020 election, for example, the Dar es Salaam committee issued a statement condemning the participation of religious leaders in the 2020 general elections. The statement was spoken against the involvement of two prominent religious leaders, Sheikh Issa Ponda and Bishop Emaus Mwamakula, who had joined the opposition campaigns. It is then that the opposition and the public criticised the committee for its silence when other religious leaders participated in the ruling party's activities (Tanzania Election Watch, 2020). In 2022, the government relocated the Maasai, an indigenous community, from the Ngorongoro district. The activity faced opposition from the Maasai community members, activists and the public on the ground that it was not voluntary. The peace committee did not issue any statement on the issue. The government defended the relocation for adhering to national and international legal and humanitarian principles. It invited the delegation of the national-level peace committee to tour the area to see how the relocation had been carried out. At the end of the tour, the committee stated that it had been satisfied with the activity and the procedures employed (Michuzi, 2022). However, the public criticised the legitimisation of the relocation by the committee indicating that it was not a fact-finding but a political mission. They, for example, questioned the committee's silence on the complaints from the Maasai community towards the relocation. It was also noted that the government had funded the tour, thus making it a guided tour. The committee did not hold discussions with those opposing the relocation, as a conflict resolution process would require. Accordingly, the public accused the committee of becoming a conduit of violence against community members, which contradicts its purpose (Interview 10, January 12, 2023).

## Conclusion

Tanzania has been regarded as a peaceful country. This perceived state is as a result of a successful nation-building project. Nevertheless, the country experiences religious, political and economic conflicts that often threaten peace. The IPC has emerged as an essential mechanism of conflict resolution and peacebuilding. Its importance results from the religious nature of Tanzania society, which is anchored in the respect for religious institutions and leaders. The IPC committee's objectives and activities align with the SGD 16, which promotes just, peaceful and inclusive societies. Through an interfaith approach to conflict intervention and peacebuilding, the committee has aligned itself with SGD 16. This chapter sought to understand the extent to which the committee is institutionalised. The objective was premised on the supposition that the effectiveness of peace mechanisms, among other things, depends mainly on its institutionalisation.

The chapter discussed six aspects of institutionalisation: constitution and regulations; governance structure; secretariat; permanent office; budget and funding; and relationship with other stakeholders. Based on the analysis of these aspects the IPC has so far not been institutionalised, and this is necessary if sustainable conflict resolution mechanisms and peacebuilding processes are to be realised. We have argued that despite its potential in society and the promotion of SGD 16, the IPC operation needs to be better positioned to fulfil its mandate. The committee operates primarily on individual leaders rather than rules, lacks the permanent staff to execute activities, permanent office, budget and reliable funding sources and needs to maintain good relationships with non-state stakeholders. However, the committee remains vital as Tanzania's conflict resolution and peacebuilding mechanism. Based on this, first, the IPC should be supported by the government and other stakeholders to attain institutionalisation. Second, the activities of IPC should be streamlined to reflect the SGD 16's targets, thus ensuring inclusiveness and responsiveness. Lastly, IPC should not be reactionary but based on pre-determined programmes and projects rather than the current ad hoc modality.

## References

Ahamed, D. (2014). *Religion–State Relations: International IDEA Constitution-Building Primer 8.* International IDEA.

Alger, C. F. (2002). Religion as a peace tool. *The Global Review of Ethnopolitics, 1*(4), 94–109.

Appelby, S. R. (1999). *The Ambivalence of the Sacred: Religion, Violence, and Reconciliation.* Rowan and Littlefield.

Bakari, M. A. (2012). Religion, Secularism, and Political Discourse in Tanzania: Competing Perspectives by Religious Organizations. *Interdisciplinary Journal of Research on Religion, 8,* 1–34.

Bakari, M. A., & Ndumbaro, L. (2006). Religion and Governance in the Post-Liberalization Era. In R. S. Mukandala, S. Yahya-Othman, S. Mushi, & L. Ndumbaro (Eds.), *Justice, Rights, and Worship: Religion and Politics in Tanzania* (pp. 334–359). E & D.

Basedau, M., & de Juan, A. (2008). *The "Ambivalence of the Sacred" in Africa: The Impact of Religion on Peace and Conflict in Sub-Saharan Africa.* GIGA Working Papers, No. 70, German Institute of Global and Area Studies (GIGA).

Behrend, H. (1999). *Alice Lakwena and the Holy Spirits: War in Northern Uganda, 1985–97.* Currey.

Britain-Tanzania Society. (1993). Religion, Zanzibar Politics, Rev. Mtikila, and Indigenization Witch Craft in Modern Tanzania. Retrieved August 15, 2012, from http://www.tzaffairs.org/wp-content/uploads/pdf/tzaffairs_45.pdf

Daniel, K., & Napoo, N. G. (2013). The Relationship Between Church and State. *International Journal of Applied Sociology, 3*(2), 9–18.

Fox, J. (2004). Religion and State Failure: An Examination of the Extent and Magnitude of Religious Conflict from 1950 to 1996. *International Political Science Review, 25*(1), 55–76.

Frost, W. J. (2015, June 16–19). *Why Religions Facilitate War and How Religions Facilitate Peace.* A Lecturer delivered at Friends Association for Higher Education Conference at Haverford College.

Haynes, J. (1996). *Religion and Politics in Africa.* East African Educational Publishers Ltd..

Heilman, B. E., & Kaiser, P. J. (2002). Religion, Identity and Politics in Tanzania. *Third World Quarterly, 23*(4), 691–709.

Huntington, S. P. (1996). *The Clash of Civilisations and the Remaking of World Order.* Simon & Schuster.
Jeong, H. (Ed.). (1999). *The New Agenda for Peace Research.* Ashgate.
LHRC. (2012). *Tanzania Human Rights Report 2011.* LHRC.
LHRC. (2013). *Tanzania Human Rights Report 2012.* LHRC.
Makulilo, A. B. (2019). Who should slaughter animals and poultry? Rethinking the tensions between Muslims and Christians in Tanzania. In E. Chitando, & J. Tarusarira (Eds.), *Religion and Human Security in Africa.* Taylor & Francis Ltd.
Marx, K. (1959). *Das Kapital, A Critique of Political Economy.* H. Regnery.
Mesaki, S. (2011). Religion and the State in Tanzania. *Cross-Cultural Communication, 7*(2), 249–259.
Mhina, A. (Ed.). (2007). *Religions and Development in Tanzania: A Preliminary Literature Review.* Working Paper 11, Religions and Development Research Programme: International Development Department, University of Birmingham.
Michuzi Blog. (2022, June 30). Kamati ya Amani na Jumuiya ya Maridhiano Wapongeza Mchakato Wakazi Ngorongoro Kuhama Kwa Hiyari. https://issamichuzi.blogspot.com/2022/06/kamati-ya-amani-na-jumuiya-ya.html
Molner, T. (1988). *Twin Powers: Politics and the Sacred.* Eerdmans Publishing Company.
Muganda, A. (2004, May 25–27). *Tanzania's Economic Reforms—And Lessons Learned, Scaling Up Poverty Reduction.* A paper presented at A Global Learning Process and Conference Shanghai. Retrieved March 20, 2017, from http://www.tanzaniagateway.org/docs/Tanzania_Country_Study_Full_Case.pdf
Mukandala, R. S., Yahya-Othman, S., Mushi, S., & Ndumbaro, L. (Eds.). (2006). *Justice, Rights, and Worship: Religion and Politics in Tanzania.* E & D.
Njozi, H. M. (2003). *Muslims and the State in Tanzania.* Dar es Salaam Muslim Trustees.
Ramsbotham, O., Miall, H., & Woodhouse, T. (2011). *Contemporary Conflict Resolution.* Polity Press.
Ratzinger, J. (2001). *Church, Ecumenism and Politics.* St. Paul Publisher.
Reychler, L. (1997). Religion and Conflict. *International Journal of Peace Studies, 2*(1), 19–38.
Said, M. (1998). *The Life and Times of Abdulwahid Sykes (1924–1968): The Untold Story of the Muslim Struggle Against British Colonialism in Tanganyika.* Minerva Press.
Tambila, K. (2006). Intra-Muslim Conflicts in Tanzania. In R. S. Mukandala, S. Yahya-Othman, S. Mushi, & L. Ndumbaro (Eds.), *Justice, Rights, and Worship: Religion and Politics in Tanzania* (pp. 165–188). E & D.
Tanzania Elections Watch. (2020). *Final Observation Report on the General Election Held In Tanzania On 28 October 2020.* Retrieved March 9, 2021, from https://www.khrc.or.ke/publications/226-final-election-observation-report-on-the-general-elections-held-in-tanzania-on-october-28-2020/file.html
Terdiman, M. (2013). Slaughtering of Animals: A Bone of Contention Between Muslims and Christians in Tanzania. *RIMA Occasional Papers, 1*(8).
Thoenig, J. (2003). Institutional Theories and Public Institutions: Traditions and Appropriateness. In B. Guy Peters & J. Pierre (Eds.), *The Handbook of Public Administration* (pp. 127–148). Sage Publications Ltd.
Westerlund, D. (1980). *Ujamaa na Dini: A Study of Some Aspects of Society and Religion, 1961–1977.* Stockholm Studies in Comparative Religion.
Wijsen, F. J. S. (2004). *Seeds of conflict: Religious tensions in Tanzania.* Paulines Publications Africa.

CHAPTER 15

# Religion and Peacebuilding in the Democratic Republic of the Congo (DRC)

*Donatien M. Cicura*

## INTRODUCTION

In this chapter, I will address Christianity in the Democratic Republic of the Congo (DRC) and more broadly in sub-Saharan Africa as a missionary religion that exists and functions as a foreign worldview imposed by missionaries and colonial powers, and as a social institution that thrives on the violent crises born out of its adoption in African countries. The chapter will focus exclusively on Christianity in its multiple iterations as both a new worldview built on the belittling of traditional African religions and a social institution that serves the cause of peacebuilding in societies that now lack spiritual cohesion, cultural unity and public conception of justice, particularly the DRC plagued by endemic violence since the early days of its independence in June 1960. The broadest form of violence in the DRC started in 1996 and is still unresolved. Its main cause is a dispute about legal identity of Kinyarwanda-speaking groups in eastern Congo who claim they resort to using armed rebellion against Kinshasa as their last attempt to claim Congolese citizenship they believe has been unlawfully denied to them. In the case of the DRC, the Roman Catholic Church is uniquely qualified to provide a needed help at resolving this problem by using its rich archives of vital registry of its members who represent over 70% of the Congolese population. The originality of the chapter lies in the fact that it looks at Christianity as centrally responsible for the emergence of

D. M. Cicura (✉)
Department of Religious Studies, Georgia Gwinnett College, Lawrenceville, GA, USA
e-mail: dcicura@ggc.edu

© The Author(s), under exclusive license to Springer Nature Switzerland AG 2023
S. M. Kilonzo et al. (eds.), *The Palgrave Handbook of Religion, Peacebuilding, and Development in Africa*,
https://doi.org/10.1007/978-3-031-36829-5_15

violence in modern society by destroying, through its efforts of converting Africans, the traditional social, ethical and religious worldviews that nurtured the different societies that were integrated in the DRC, and by replacing these views by its own worldview presented as the unique truth. The disintegration of these traditional channels of spirituality and morality by the ridiculing discourse of missionaries led to building a modern society with abstract ethical principles that do not speak to individuals and communities. Thus, the lack of social, ethical cohesion in a society where people barely have political and economic power leads to endemic violence. To help resolve this problem of violence, Christianity, particularly the Roman Catholic Church, remains the only stable institution that builds educational and charitable institutions that contribute to the efforts of peacebuilding. These efforts of peace are based on the new paradigm of a modern state that builds its cohesion and internal peace through education, economic progress, and creation of a national identity based on common citizenship. Given that recent outbreaks of violence in the eastern province of the DRC are based on an acute crisis of citizenship, Roman Catholicism can help the government establish legal status (identity) to people, thus responding to one of the SDG 16 goals. The choice of the Roman Catholic Church is justified by the fact that it detains the largest record and database of birth registry of its members that covers over 70% of the population of the country, where the Congolese state lacks such records. If peace can be achieved by clarifying the citizenship status of armed group members in eastern Congo by using the database of vital registry created by the Catholic Church since the nineteenth century, thus contributing to the realization of one of the objectives of SDG 16, then the Catholic Church becomes an irreplaceable and strategic partner with the Congolese state in its efforts to bring peace in a region that has seen millions of deaths since 1996. As a matter of policy, building peace, resolving armed conflicts, ensuring inclusivity, and deciding on citizenship status of people are not the work of the Church, but that of the Congolese state. But in making such decisions, the Congolese state needs accurate historical records that only the Catholic Church can provide.

The first aspect of the chapter, the experiential essence of Christianity, will be addressed by analyzing the work of a few African critiques of Christianity in African societies in order to build an image of what religion represents for the people and for religious leaders. This first part of the chapter will be the longest. In the second part, I will briefly look at Christianity as a social institution in a deeply dysfunctional society, and gauge its contribution to efforts of peacebuilding, as envisioned by SDG 16.

In the first part, I will show that in its essence, Christianity as a missionary religion cannot and does not contribute to peace, because it is fundamentally about imposing a foreign worldview void of the spiritual richness of traditional African religions labeled as paganism, magic, or sorcery, and because it pretends to have the only infallible truth for what it portrays as salvation. Representing the negation of the traditional spirituality that bore the African humanity, Christianity is also the destruction of African anthropological identity in a way that is deeper and long lasting than the political and social violence of the colonization itself. Missionary religions like Christianity and Islam are fundamentally disruptive of traditional ethos and by that token, they create violence, hostilities, and divisions in any society they penetrate. Violence, hostilities, and divisions defeat any sustainable development goal. Thus, the claim to the one and only infallible truth excluding other worldviews and spiritualties is a source of physical, psychological, political, and religious violence. SDG 16 tries to remedy the effects of such violence.

## Congolese Identity and Christianity

In this section, the chapter will address the nature of Christianity as a foreign missionary religion that imposed its worldview on Congolese aggressively and violently destroying their traditional ethos, thus contributing to the development of modern endemic violence in DRC society. This view is based on the work of two philosophers and theologians who have become classic, at least in French-speaking African countries: the Cameroonian Fabien Eboussi Boulaga and the Congolese Vincent Yves Mudimbe. On the ashes of the traditional social and ethical beliefs, Christianity as a new social institution stands to help build new peace based on new grounds that are more administrative than spiritual.

The choice of Fabien Eboussi Boulaga and Vincent Yves Mudimbe as reflectors for this work is based on the fact that their work is descriptive of African reality; it is an engaged phenomenology of the African condition in time of transition: transition between the time of colonial yoke and the first years of postcolonial hopes and stumbles. Whether it be the novels, the essays, or formal books, their work, more than any other, describes the causes of the postcolonial violence as rooted in the psychological and physical suppression of traditional African voices of spirituality by the work of colonial Christian missionaries. They are competent and engaged theologians and philosophers who, both, have briefly flirted with clerical life, before rediscovering the traditional roots of their own personal and intellectual authenticity.

In *La Crise du Muntu*, the Cameroonian philosopher and theologian Fabien Eboussi Boulaga (1977) makes a poignant description of the "Muntu," that applies very well to the Congolese. He wrote his book after living for years in the DRC, teaching philosophy at the Institut de Philosophie Saint Pierre Canisius of Kimwenza, in the Southwestern suburbs of Kinshasa. *La Crise du Muntu* reveals a nothingness of identity, something floating without substance, and which can be bound in all directions according to circumstances. This lack of substance is arguably characteristic of sub-Sahara Africa in general beginning with the fifteenth century when the Portuguese navy first arrived in what is known today as Lagos (Nigeria) in August 1441. It is a pauperized identity, to use Engelbert Mveng's expression (Mveng, 1985). It is artificial because it is a byproduct of external forces integrating forcibly the African into a new system of production and self-reproduction in which he or she has no initiative; an identity bearing the marks of his or her defeat and the racialization of both the defeat and the victory. As it appears, Eboussi Boulaga conceives African identity at the cross-road of the West and the traditional African way of being, but this identity comes from the experience of domination. Historically, the African lost the decisive war of humanity and exists only under the terms of the Western master This relationship of dominated and dominating is also visible and experienced in religion and religious domain, whether this experience be dogmatic, social, or charitable.

## Religious Symbolism of Domination and Critique of Missionary Discourse

To understand contemporary violence in the DRC, violence and injustice targeted by the SDG 16, one must go to its symbolic and real roots in the missionary discourse during colonization. It is a discourse that, by suppressing the religious symbolism of traditional African societies, denies humanity to the black African.

The question of domination, subjugation, and negation of the humanity of black Africans dominates African philosophical, anthropological, and religious literature. This abundant literature asks for the introduction of new paradigms in the framework of the dogma received from Western Churches. As a major religion in Africa, Christianity, except in Ethiopia and north Africa, was introduced by missionaries who accompanied both slave traders and colonial powers. The experience of Christianity is fundamentally that of being a religion of domination, of the conqueror, and of his vision of the world, a religion, therefore, that predicates itself on a systematic and fundamental negation of traditional African spiritual experience. This experience is either considered as non-existent or ridiculed as fetishism, sorcery, magic, or idolatry.

Christianity takes roots in Africa on the demolition of the worldviews that defined sub-Sahara Africa for millennia. It is fundamentally a religion based on the violence against the African, who is coerced to abandon his traditions, the nurturing spirituality that fertilized its traditions for millennia. It is a religion in which genuine ancestors and their ideal of perfection, solidarity, their status of guardians of collective morality and justice are ridiculed as maleficent demons, zombies, and so on. One is accepted in this new religion only by severing his or her existential link to his or her kin, his or her traditions. It is a religion that, effectively, establishes an anthropological pauperization as the substratum of being of the African. A religion devoid of indigenous authentic spiritual imagination and which functions only either as a system of management of decrees poorly understood by the faithful or as a denatured syncretic practice in the new religious movements that abandon the missionary religion in order to build something that appeals to the existential needs of the followers more hypnotized by the spectacle of the supernatural, the miraculous (true or staged), than reciting dry formula received from Rome or London, formulas that mean really nothing understandable and of existential value to the new convert.

In *Savage Systems: Colonialism and Comparative Religion in Southern Africa*, David Chidester describes that same colonial religious violence exercised not only by missionaries but also by anthropologists. The classification of African traditions as "animist" or "polytheists" or primitive was aimed at establishing a system of superiority and inferiority that benefited the colonizer and legitimized colonial efforts at actively suppressing these religious, spiritual, and ethical systems (David Chidester 1996).

Understanding the symbolism of domination embedded into African Christianity becomes a task and a duty for every contemporary African who wants to participate in the movement of African liberation. In *Christianisme sans fétiches*, Eboussi Boulaga (1984) studies the reality and language of domination and their symbolism from a religious point of view. According to him, African identity in the contemporary world can be understood only in terms of the relationship of power and domination. Christianity, as a Western religion, participates in this *rapport de forces* and on an equal footing with colonialism. It deploys the same symbol of domination in a language of derision of African traditions and myths. One important and inspiring question he raises is this:

> Can tribal human beings, who have known the critique of their certitudes, have lived the death of both their myths and the irrefutable universe of those myths, seriously accept Christianity's pretension to be the foreordained truth and norm of all authentic existence and the solitary matrix of genuine human beings? Further: How is one to think and to live the necessity, supremacy, and universality of Christianity when the latter is imposed as the dominant religion, or the religion of the dominant? How are the truths, commandments, and rites to be inscribed in one's flesh, when they are received from below, in a state of social, political, economic, and cultural subordination and minority of age? (Eboussi Boulaga, 1984, p. 2)

Under these conditions, the deity proposed by Christianity cannot be internalized but only seen as "other people's god." This deity participates in the domination itself; it is the winning god that can ridicule the gods of others as mere idols. His acceptance or imposition, even when he enters in the realm of local folklore, is one of the biggest signs of domination. The exponential growth of Christianity on the African continent can be interpreted in terms of increased alienation and estrangement of Africans from their native and traditional substance.

If Christianity, which participates in the metamorphosis of African identity, astonishingly and effortlessly destroyed the gods of the Bantu, it is because it was coupled with colonial power, and using the language of derision, it put logic at the service of its "massive evidence." Christianity appears as having unquestionable evidence, claiming the allegiance of nations, races, and conditions. More importantly, it is the religion of the civilization that brought about the scientific and technological revolutions (Eboussi Boulaga, 1984, p. 3).

Christianity in Africa is the religion of power; it participates in the same civilizing mission of the nineteenth century and it remains its continuation. That is, it operates on the assumption that there are advanced, rational, and developed people, on the one hand, and primitive people who need to be brought from primitivity to the light of civilization, on the other hand. That is why its evidence appears as if it cannot be questioned. Opposing its evidence would be a sign, not of rebellion, but of the inability to knock at the door of true humanity and therefore condemning oneself to remain wretched not only on this earth but also in the eschatological world. That is why Christianity requires of Africans that they alienate themselves from their traditions, that they cut the roots by which they are tied to the African soil, that they become alien to themselves if they want to enter the kingdom of humanity. Any African cultural expression and anthropological sign must be "eradicated," according to the dominant theological stance of Christianity.

By not belonging to the Christian tradition, sub-Sahara Africans fall short of crossing the threshold of humanity, and the missionary discourse is constructed in order to make them accept this situation as self-evident. One becomes human only by converting to Christianity. Being born into a traditional Christian family makes one fully human. The convert is not yet fully trustworthy as he/she lacks the seal of the centuries-old Christian tradition. Therefore, the convert has to work hard to double his or her zeal in order to be counted among the new born to humanity, even if this humanity is still dubious. The new Christianity and humanity of the African convert do not enjoy the same privilege as the inherited ones, because they lack the absolute knowing and technology and the racial symbolism which goes with them. The language of missionaries is that of derision and mockery of African traditions, ancestors, and gods, a language refuting the coherence of the African worldview founded on traditional religions and ethical systems, and finally a language that demonstrates the superiority and self-evidence of Christianity as the only chance to have access to humanity.

Finally, that language proposes a corpus of doctrines presented as "orthodoxy," that is, a summary of what must be taken as the standard for any authentic Christian language and belief. An African appropriation of a non-doctrinal Christianity which leaves room for an African appropriation and creativity respecting the genius proper to the multiple African traditions is what Eboussi Boulaga had in mind. To realize his view, Eboussi Boulaga called for the end of missionary work in Africa in the early 1970s, and his call was taken as scandalous by African bishops, who hurried to call a special synod to condemn his view, expressing their solidarity with missionaries (Eboussi Boulaga, 1991, pp. 29–42). "La dé-mission" is famous for the sharp criticism of the missionary work and its solemn call for all missionaries to go back to their home countries that need more saving, more evangelizing than African societies.

This critique of Christianity as a religion of domination that creates and perpetuates violence and is, itself, built on an imaginary of violence in its eschatological proclamations is continued in the work of Vincent Yves Mudimbe, who places Christian dogmatism on par with the language of social sciences practiced in Africa by Westerners (Mudimbe, 1982, 1994, pp. 105–153).

## The Missionary Experience in the Work of V.Y. Mudimbe

Vincent Yves Mudimbe is a sharp critic of social sciences practiced by Westerners in Africa. His critique extends to Christianity as the religion of Western civilization imposed in the Congo by the work of missionaries. For Mudimbe, the missionary is a conqueror, materially and ideologically, an expansionist of his culture in the name of the gospel (Mudimbe, 1982, p. 62). He cannot speak of the original Jesus, but only the Jesus of the Western culture, with dogmatic pretense to truth and allegiance to the Roman papal and imperial power (Mudimbe, 1982, pp. 62–63). The missionary is an agent of the Church system with its practices, traditions, and pretense to perpetuate the truth comes from Israel. The mission is a political enterprise, and Christianity is an ideological structure (Mudimbe, 1982, p. 63). In this regard, mission does not consist in announcing Jesus Christ, but it is related to "the most clever techniques of psychological conditioning" and "the restructuration and (…) africanization of a Western *déjà-vécu*" (Mudimbe, 1982, p. 64).

The Africanization of the mission, the creation of schools of missiology or what Mudimbe calls "the science of mission," does not change substantively the damage done by the first wave of missionaries. Mudimbe's conclusion is clear: Congolese and Africans in general do not have anything to learn from missionaries nor from African priests or theologians (Mudimbe, 1982, p. 71). The challenge is to claim the right to difference, and, in the line of Foucault, *pouvoir assumer la folie* (Mudimbe, 1982, p. 81). The challenge is taken up by a new system of education which favors African creativity and takes its model not on the contemporary Western way of life which transforms the human being into an object of power, but on different models, like the Islamic model or the traditional African model of initiation, which promote, as Mudimbe believes, human freedom (Mudimbe, 1982, p. 81). However, the cooperation and dialogue between cultures will always be violent and dramatic, because the weaker culture will always lose its soul in the process. What is needed, in the end, is the act by which the Africans would speak for themselves about themselves and delineate the real meaning of their identity shaped by historical vicissitudes to the other in the encounter. This other who remains on the stage trying to continue to shape the dialogue according to his rules and his logic of domination.

Decades after Mudimbe's publication, there is an effort of bringing back elements of African traditions and incorporating them into Christian narratives. Inculturation is how this effort is known in the major theological schools in Africa (Luneau, 2002, pp. 78–84). Thus, Christian stories of apparitions become possessions by saints or heavenly beings (Luneau, 2002, pp. 107–110), and priestly ordination looks like a ritual of a traditional enthronement of the traditional king or tribal leader.

When it comes to thinking "inculturation," few theologians would rival Laurenti Magesa. His work, in his most important publications since 1994, is focused on the contributions that traditional African ethical values can have on this new religion implanted in Africa by Christian missionaries. He recognizes that every authentic Christian theology must take its roots in the cultural context of the theologian or the people being ministered to. He sees this to be true in early Christianity shaped by Hellenistic culture (Laurenti Magesa 2002, 2015) and argues that the cultural context of modern Africa has influenced and must continue to influence the development of an authentic African Christian theology. Thus, the work of Magesa tries to bring back the old and recalibrate it with the new context where Africans find themselves.

In this context he advocates the retrieval of African traditional practices, values, and beliefs that are compatible with Christianity; inculturation that finds a mutual locus of encounter between those traditional practices, values, and beliefs and the prevalent Christian theological positions; contextualization that adapts Christian theology to the specific cultural context of Africans; and finally liberation theology that calls for African theologians to use their teachings to address social, economic, and political injustices in African societies (Laurenti Magesa, 2004b).

Like Eboussi Boulaga and Mudimbe, Magesa's theology of inculturation recognizes the same ills of the missionary enterprise in Africa that suppressed African practice, moral and ethical values, and beliefs in the name of a totalitarian discourse presented as having no alternative. However, Magesa's position is less acerbically critical and more conciliatory toward Christianity. For Magesa, Christianity is in Africa with staying power and the African theologian's duty is to "inculturate" it, to adapt it to traditional values, and to adapt "compatible" values to the accepted theological discourse. This work of inculturation is necessary to heal the African from the violence of both the slave trade and colonialism that have generated poverty, ignorance, and disease (Magesa, 2007, p. 49). As a consequence of this colonial violence, Africans are faced with the challenge of being perceived by others as "nonpeople," "whose life and civilization are not of much significance, if indeed any at all, for humanity" (Magesa, 2007, p. 50). Inculturation that uses some of the traditional values of Africa such as the practice of the palaver, the value of the community properly understood in its African ethos, can be instrumental in equipping modern Africans with an invaluable tool to address violence and injustice (Laurenti Magesa 2004a, pp. 160–161). Put in perspective with the real spiritual needs of Africa, these forms of reappropriation of Christianity are cosmetic. If they "paraphrase" the language of traditional African religions and rituals, they still are serving a purely alien and heterogeneous canon of belief, which does not meet the real situation of Africans.

Thus, the effort of understanding Africa necessitates that one be aware of the system of correspondence between the old and the new and how the new is often reinterpreted and reappropriated in accordance with the old and traditional African canon. The necessity of reinterpretation is vital. It has the status of resistance against external forces which have historically demonized African traditions and religions as they introduced "alien deities" in the city.

It is clear that there is no way for Africans today to go back in the past and retrieve the purity of their old beliefs. Pre-colonial Africa is gone and cannot be resurrected. What Africans today have is the possibility to cover the new Christian system with old African vestments. The danger of the process, though, is to give Africans the impression of "having something authentic," while what survives is only the externality of folkloric practices. These practices, because they no longer spring from the very core of an authentic traditional African worldview, are crafted and presented in a way which mostly profits the leaders, religious or political, who brought them to light or who claim to legitimize themselves through recourse to tradition. One eloquent example can be taken from the politics of authenticity promoted and practiced by President Mobutu of the Democratic Republic of the Congo (former Zaire) from 1965 to 1997. A second example is what has been called the Zairian liturgical rite in the Roman Catholic Church.

Mudimbe's *The Invention of Africa* and *Tales of Faith* present the process of evangelization as obeying the categories of the nineteenth-century evolutionist anthropology. These categories oppose the civilized to the primitive and remain insensitive to the very African condition. There is a deep interpenetration between the enterprise of colonization and the work of anthropologists and missionaries (Mudimbe, 1988, p. 44). Missionary discourses have had such an undeniable positive and negative impact on Africa and the process of formation of African ideology that it is necessary to study their impact on the process of formation of contemporary African identities and to put them in perspective with the crisis of African societies at all levels. The crisis of African societies today can be interpreted as a crisis of transition: transition between the old that has been largely destroyed by Christianity and colonization and the new identity that is developing but does not yet have a clear contour.

Missionary discourse and the African response to it merge historically and ideologically in an anthropological locus and have *ad valorem* responsibility in the building of an African ideology of otherness (Mudimbe, 1988, p. 44). The problem is to grasp the process by which religion, particularly alien Christianity, contributes to the marginality of the African continent and generates violence in the process. It can clearly be noticed that the history of Christian missions in Africa has to be identified with cultural propaganda, patriotic motivations, and commercial interests, since the mission's program is indeed more complex than the simple transmission of the Christian faith. From the sixteenth century to the eighteenth century, missionaries were, through all the "new worlds," part of the political process of creating and extending the right of European sovereignty over "newly discovered" lands (Mudimbe, 1988, p. 45).[1]

The missionary work of propagation of Christianity in Africa is one important component of the colonial project of dehumanization of Africans reduced to being simple primitives. For missionaries, the propagation of Christianity as part of the political agenda of European monarchs was a divine mission. They knew very well and practiced the pope's principle of "*terra nullius*" (nobody's land) (Mudimbe, 1988, p. 45). After Vatican II Council, Pope Paul VI's *Populorum Progressio* which advocates the right for self-determination of people is meaningful, not only as a correction to his predecessors' ideas but also because the wind of history has blown in different directions and the sun of African independence has long since arisen. Even if the Reformation challenged the Pope's right to give, grant, and assign forever lands to European monarchs, Mudimbe notes that the new axiom, born after the European wars of religion consecutive to the Protestant reformation and the Treaty of Westphalia of 1648, "*cuius regio, eius religio*," enforced the complementarity between colonial activity and religious conversion (Mudimbe, 1988, p. 45).

On a "*terra nullius*," a mass celebrated somewhere with the royal symbols meant the possession of that territory on behalf of some European king, or planting a cross, or, for Anglo-Saxons, pronouncing a sacred formula or issuing a legal decree (Mudimbe, 1988, pp. 45–46). It becomes clear that "the missionary played an essential role in the general process of expropriation and, subsequently, exploitation of all the 'new found lands' upon the earth" (Mudimbe, 1988, p. 46). The concept of *terra nullius* originated within the Roman Catholic Church and legitimated the triumphant discourse of "discovery," and the subjugation and enslavement of non-Europeans, particularly Africans. It is noteworthy that the scramble for Africa in the nineteenth century took place in a context of a revival of Christian faith and the end of the Enlightenment's criticism of religion. The missionary participates with the explorer and the soldier of the trilogy associated with mastering, colonizing, and transforming Africa (Mudimbe, 1988, p. 46).

---

[1] Missionaries are agents of the political agenda of conquering new lands for European sovereigns. In doing so, as Oscar Bimwenyi showed in a brilliant dissertation, they were obeying the sacred instructions of Pope Alexander VI in his bull, *Inter Caetera* (1493), "to overthrow paganism and establish the Christian faith in all barbarous nations." *Dum Diversas* (1452) and *Romanus Pontifex* (1455) of Nicholas V "had indeed already given the kings of Portugal the right to dispossess and externally enslave Mahometans, pagans, and black people in general." "*Dum Diversas* clearly stipulates the right to invade, conquer, expel, and fight (*invadendi, conquirendi, expugnandi, debellandi*) Muslims, pagans, and other enemies of Christ (*Saracenos ac paganos, aliosque Christi inimicos*) wherever they may be. Christian kings, following the Pope's decisions, could occupy pagan kingdoms, principalities, lordships, possessions (*regna, principatus, Domina, possessions*) and dispossess them of their personal property, land, and whatever they might have (*et mobilia et immobilia bona quaecumque per eos detenta ac possessa*). The king and his successors have the power and right to put these peoples into perpetual slavery (*subjugandi illorumque personas in perpetuam servitutem*)" (Ibid.). See also Oscar Bimwenyi Kweshi, *Discours théologique négro-Africain: Problèmes de fondements* (Paris: Présence Africaine, 1981).

Better than the explorer and the soldier who expanded European jurisdiction to Africa, the missionary expanded "the absoluteness of Christianity," its virtues, and European culture (Mudimbe, 1988, pp. 46–47). He is considered the best symbol of the colonial enterprise, devoting himself "sincerely to the ideals of colonialism: the expansion of Civilization, the dissemination of Christianity, and the advance of Progress" (Mudimbe, 1988, p. 47). With their devotion aimed at converting the African mind and space, missionaries did the most to destroy African societies and their traditional spiritual worldviews. The missionaries' discourse is predetermined and preregulated; it is the discourse of colonization. It is fixed and absolute, with the pretention of bearing the ultimate truth about the world; it creates demons and instills fear of demons in order to present itself as offering salvation. This discourse establishes a vital connection between Christianity and Western culture as a whole. The missionary makes his discourse from above the primitive. He cannot dialogue with pagans and savages. He is convinced that he has to impose the law of God and that he incarnates that law.

That is why he believes that Christianity has to be imposed by all available means, including by violence. In this context, African conversion was not a free and deliberate acceptance of Christianity but "the sole position the African could take in order to survive as a human being" (Mudimbe, 1988, p. 48). Hence, African conversion to Christianity mirrors the imposition of Christianity to the Roman Empire by Theodosius in 380 CE.

## Transitional Violence

If there can be a correlation between Theodosius's imposition of Christianity to the Roman Empire and African conversion to Christianity through colonization and missionary work, then both contemporary violence and peacebuilding efforts spring from the same source: Christianity. Christianity imposes the notion that there is only one unique truth, its truth, that is imposable to all, not only as the means of salvation, but also as an organizational principle for society. Anything or anyone outside of that view is not only a pagan, but a representative of evil that can be object of legitimate violence (physical, social, psychological, etc.). The first lines of violence are thus drawn between converts and non-converts, between these new religious tribes and the old tribes. The second line of violence is drawn between the different denominational iterations of the unique truth.

After the old organizational systems have been destroyed by colonization and Christianity and the establishment of new social norms based on Christian principles, there is a period of chaos marked by violence (political, religious, social, economic). In the Roman Empire, this period of violence and transition lasted over four centuries between the collapse of Rome and the formation of the new Holy Roman Empire founded by Charlemagne. This is what I call transitional violence or violence of the transition between the old identities and the establishment of new identities. African and Congolese violence today fall in this category. It calls for new principles that determine the appropriation of the soil, the political identity of its inhabitants, and their social and political relations.

Achille Mbembe asserts that indigenous Africans resisted the notion of one dominant truth which was perceived as excluding the existence of any other religious truth beside it (Mbembe, 1988, 211). Africans can capitalize upon this resistance and invent a new form of African Christianity and identity. The existence of an African version of Christianity would not be a simple reactionary move of Africans unable to enter into the mindset of Western Christianity. It is rather in the essence of Christianity to exist in different versions which complement one another and enrich Christianity as a whole. It is in this sense that beside the Roman Catholic version of Christianity, we find different versions of the same religion in Western nations and cultures as well as different other forms of Christianity going under the generic denomination of "Orthodox" Christianity or Global Christianity to use Lamin Sanneh's expression.

Pluralism of theologies and modes of worship are unavoidable. There must exist an African heresy which breaks away from the mainstream Western version of Christianity: a heresy more respectful of African needs, cultures, and world visions. No longer will the question be that of contrasting mythical and superstitious forms of beliefs with the reputed rational and scientific Western Christianity, but that of attesting to oneself through the new, imposed but reappropriated religion. The experience of pluralism in African Christianity already comes with the competition between Catholic and Protestant missionaries during the missionary scramble for Africa (Mudimbe, 1997, pp. 40–41).

The same interest can be found in many African theologians (Meinrad Hebga, Engelbert Mveng, Kä Mana), even when they keep thinking under the guidelines of some dominant Western Christian denominations and dogmas. In this regard, conflicts between the will to authenticity and the duty to preconstructed orthodoxy appear and the African theologian is caught between these two lines of thought. This theological "rift" reminds us of the kind of misconception described in the case of social and human sciences, and if it does not lead to suicide as in the case of Nara, it is a factor of depersonalization and of corrosion of African substance. On one side, the theologian seems to be called to justify the position of the dominant Christianity, without always understanding the pre-conditions of that position; on the other side, he or she feels the call of his or her own traditional way of being that is a demand for articulating the new faith into a properly African ethos.

## PEACEBUILDING EFFORTS

A look at the old history of Christianity can help us draw similarities between what happened from the fourth to the ninth centuries of Christianity, even if it is in rather simplistic terms. After the Roman Empire imposed Christianity as the only official religion of the empire in 380 CE and began actively persecuting paganism, that is, the traditional religions of the empire, it took less than 100 years for the empire to collapse. In the aftermath of the fall of Rome in 476 CE, only the Church, its leadership, and ecclesiastical structures remained standing. Where political and social chaos developed, Christianity began to offer the antidote as people began to rely on Church services and charities in the absence of stable political structures. The Dark Ages, as that period is called, saw wars upon wars between the different temporary kingdoms and chiefdoms that formed on the ashes of the majestic empire.

In the Democratic Republic of the Congo, and in sub-Saharan Africa broadly, a similar dynamic can be observed. The demolition of traditional structures by colonial powers and Christian missionaries ushered in a period of endemic violence since the independence of the country. From the Katanga secession of 1960 to countless rebellions and wars (Pierre Mulele, Jean Schram, the Moba and Kolwezi wars, the South Kasai rebellion, the persecution of Kasaians in Katanga) to invasions disguised as endogenous rebellions in the 1990s to this day (AFDL, RCD/Goma, MLC, CNDP, M23, etc.), the Congo has been a theater of violence because of the breakdown of its traditional ethical fabric, and because its leaders have never been able to overcome the psychological and anthropologic trauma of colonial and missionary violence. They have never been able to reconnect with their land as a sacred trust inherited from their ancestors. Rather, recycling colonial exploitation and violence, they use the land as a rental good for short-term enrichment with no long-term plan for development: for building human and material infrastructure necessary for human, economic, and social development. When it comes to using the land and its riches with no plan other than quick enrichment for the political elite, the Church has proven to have no power to influence political elites to responsibly manage these natural riches.

Similar to what happened after the collapse of the Roman Empire, the vacuum left by political incompetence and corruption, endemic violence, is filled by the only functional institution left: religion. The Christian Church, in its different denominations, functions as an institution in the image of the different Western Churches it is the continuation of (Roman Catholicism, Anglicanism, different traditional Protestant denominations, evangelicals, etc.). It also continues to receive financial subsidies from these mother churches that allow her to build educational and charitable structures that serve the population mostly abandoned by the politicians.

The crisis and violence in the Congo and many other African countries can be interpreted as crises of transition toward a future marked by organizational principles of Christianity and modernity broadly understood. It takes time to build new moral, social, political, and economic infrastructures when the old ones have been dealt a fatal blow by colonization and religion. And as a sign of this effort of building new human, moral, social, political, and economic infrastructure, Christianity has been building schools, hospitals, and charitable institutions to implement its new paradigm of peace based on the abstract and universal moral principles of the gospels. Solidarity with any human being tries to supplant the old solidarity with the kin and the tribe's members.

Good schools inherited from the missionaries, or still in the hands of missionaries, or built by the different dioceses, religious congregations, or protestant missionaries contribute a great deal to the cause of peace by providing quality education to the youth and preparing them to better integrate civil society and the economy rather than joining the different militias and rebel groups. Schools are the best example of peacebuilding because their financing involves not only the religious leaders but also the state and the community (parents). In taking part in the financing of schools, parents and their community internalize that the work of development, progress, education, and peace necessitates the effective involvement of everyone. It is not something that comes down from above like the biblical manna through the magical powers of religious leaders or the government. To this extent, communities get involved in maintaining good, safe, and functioning schools, because they have directly invested in them and can see their own children get educated.

Functional hospitals and other charitable structures also advance the cause of peace and economic opportunity provided to local population. By maintaining these institutions in the backdrop of failing state institutions plagued by corruption and mismanagement, religion, here Christianity, advances the cause of peace and harmony in the community. Those who benefit from the services those hospitals provide come from all strata of the society: rich and poor, all tribal and ethnic groups with no discrimination. By providing these services where all the components of the society meet regardless of religious denomination, tribal identity, or economic status, hospitals maintained by the different religious denomination and mostly the Catholic Church serve as incubators of social cooperation, harmony, and peace. However, the rich who are able to pay for their healthcare enjoy better treatment than the poor in a society where no health insurance system exists.

Peace and Justice commissions function within diocesan structures as well. They are less effective than schools and hospitals, despite their name. Yes, they catalog violence committed, and make declarations, but they are less headed by political authorities, leaders of the civil society, and those who unleash violence. One of the most important weaknesses of these commissions is their financing. Instead of relying on local financing by the community or economic and political leaders who would, thus, invest in that work and be responsible for its success, they mostly rely on the financing by international donors, Western Churches, and other charities. Thus, they function like superstructures alien to the reality of the community, even when they try to address violence and injustice within the community. One other weakness of these commissions is that they are mostly centered on the denominations that operate them, instead of being inclusive of the diversity of the community in which they operate.

The success of these religious institutions demonstrates that if Congolese society can build a unifying religious and moral worldview, it may become easier to build and maintain peace, because religious solidarity based on a common worldview is one of the strongest social bonds that keep societies together and allow people to develop greater sentiments and acts of solidarity. This requires, however, good and trusted religious leadership that models the right behavior for their folks and that remains in permanent dialogue and consultations with leaders of different denominations, sects, and religions for the purpose of building bridges of solidarity, understanding, and common good.

## SDG 16 Targets

For some cryptic reasons, the United Nations Sustainable Development Summit has listed some goals that it thinks can help "significantly reduce all forms of violence and related death rates everywhere" by 2030. Among these goals at 16.9, we find this one: "By 2030, provide legal identity for all, including birth registration." If meeting this goal can reduce violence, then the Catholic Church can provide an invaluable help and expertise to the government of the DRC. If there is a domain where the expertise of a religious institution may prove to be invaluable and make a substantial and tangible difference, it would be in this domain.

The chapter previously spoke to the endemic violence in the Congo since its independence in 1960. There is a peculiarity to the violence that started in 1996 and which has been the deadliest and the most disruptive to Congolese society. When the AFDL (Alliance des Forces Démocratiques pour la Libération du Congo) made of Rwandese officers, Kinyarwanda-speaking Congolese who came to be known as Banyamulenge, and led by Laurent-Désiré Kabila surged on the national and international scene in 1996, they justified the use of armed violence in their rebellion against the government of Kinshasa by claiming that they have been denied their rightful Congolese citizenship, and thus wanted to forcibly bring the government to acknowledge not only their citizenship but also the part of territory they claimed to be theirs, the high plateau of Minembwe in the South Kivu province.

In subsequent peace agreements between the government of Kinshasa and the different rebel groups that developed in the Kivu (AFDL, RCD/Goma, M 23, etc.), rebel groups largely made of Tutsi and other Kinyarwanda-speaking people were mixed with the regular army (in operations locally known as "brassage") to only be pointed out as disloyal and as contributing to the creation of more instability and more rebel groups in the Kivu. One is only to think about the metamorphosis of the AFDL into RCD/Goma, and this one broke down into smaller militias under the leadership of officers like Jules Mutebusi, Laurent Nkunda, and Jean-Bosco Ntaganda, before the militias regrouped into the movement known as M23 that remains active to this day.

This claim to citizenship by Kinyarwanda-speaking groups in eastern Congo and its resistance by other Congolese groups and even the Congolese legislature make sense only because the Congolese government does not have a clear and practical way of determining who is Congolese and who is not, particularly for populations that live in border provinces and whose ethnic or tribal groups may spread to neighboring countries. Practically, anyone who is black can potentially claim Congolese citizenship, because the government does not have a registry of citizens and does not conduct regular censuses to determine how many citizens there are and who they are or how old they are. The last viable census in the Congo, then called Zaïre, was conducted in 1984. Because the government does not have a registry of birth, a record of naturalizations, nor a national identity system, it becomes impossible to know who is truly citizen and who is not, who can vote and who cannot, who qualifies to lead the country or its provinces and who cannot.

It is therefore imperative for the administration of the country to create a system that can provide legal identity to its citizens, instead of relying on a traditional system that was made obsolete and inoperable by colonization. The constitution defines a Congolese citizen as anyone who belongs to one of the ethnic groups of the Congo in 1885 when the country was created as Free State of Congo, and the late constitution promulgated in 2006 defines the citizen in similar terms: anyone who belongs to the tribes of the Congo at independence in 1960 (DRC Constitution, art. 10). Citizenship is now defined by tribality when tribes no longer function as nations the way they did prior to 1885.

To accomplish the task of providing legal identity to all, including birth registration, Christianity as a social institution can provide the help the country so desperately needs. The Roman Catholic Church, which is the majority religion in the country and which has the largest network of schools, universities, hospitals, charitable work, and peace and justice commissions, maintains also the largest vital registry of its faithful. The Catholic Church maintains baptism files for its current and former members that have the names, the date and place of birth, the date and place of baptism, confirmation, and marriage. These files can be used by the government to create or update its own registry and have accurate information that allows it to provide legal identity to more than 70% of its population. The government would, then, call for the service of other religious groups and have the information needed to provide that legal identity to the entire population.

If a serious collaboration is established between the government and the Catholic Church, this work can be done quickly and at a very reasonable price (less than a US $100 million), and be concluded in one year or less. Once this work is done, it can prove or disprove the claim to citizenship of many members of militias and rebel groups. The country could then create new laws and capacities that require every child born on its territory to be issued a legal birth certificate within days of their birth.

As stated above, Church archives can help contribute to the work of clarifying people's identity, and indirectly contribute to the work of peace and stability in the DRC. This would also help ease accusations of "being a foreigner" levied against groups and individuals, particularly those that come from border provinces, and more pointedly, those who come from eastern Congo. This work, if done with seriousness and competence, would contribute to national harmony and create a common public conception of justice and citizenship.

## Conclusion

In pluralistic and free societies, religion tends to transform itself into a consumer good of choice, catering to the feelings of individuals. As such, religion loses its capacity and power of building a unifying vision of the world that fosters peace and channels a common public conception of justice. Instead, it breaks down into rival sects at war of influence with one another, sects that battle to delegitimize one another at the dogmatic and moral levels. In African nations that were recently Christianized by missionaries accompanying the colonial enterprise, this battle is more visible. In older Christian nations open to foreign ideas, the crisis is somehow similar when facing new Muslim citizens, and believers of Asian religions such as Buddhism, Hinduism, Jainism, Sikhism, Shintoism, and so on.

In Western traditionally Christian nations and in Muslim countries, it is not religion that brought peace, justice, and progress, but the State asserting its power of organization over the different religious sects. This can be seen with Christianity adopted and organized by the Roman Empire, Ethiopia, and Armenia. Similar dynamics exist in Islam, not only when speaking about the divide between Suni and Shia Islam, but even when considering the different theological schools within each denomination of Islam. Whether it be the Umayyad, Abbasid dynasties imposing Suni Islam in their conquests, or the Safavid of Iran adopting Shia Islam for political reason, the peace that results from these impositions is not the fact of religion but that of the State. The wars of religion in the sixteenth and seventeenth centuries in Europe between the Catholics and the different iterations of Protestantism were concluded in the Peace of Augsburg and the Treaty of Westphalia by the States, not by the will of religious leaders who continued to demonize one another as heretical, illegitimate, and candidate for hell for the several centuries that followed. In weak and corrupt states like the DRC, religion itself, in its essence, is unable to bring about meaningful and lasting peace because of the competition between the different sects that build tribal religious solidarities. Despite its social, educational, and charitable work that incontrovertibly contribute to the cause of peace, religion cannot succeed on its own in building lasting peace. It is the work of the State, in pursuing its interests, that produces lasting peace and maintains it.

## Recommendations

Peace can only be achieved by concrete actions of political actors, specially by concrete choices made by national governments. Religion may help as a catalyst in societies where a unifying religious worldview exists as in societies dominated by one religion, or in pluralistic societies where religion has been transformed into a consumer good catering to people's individual feelings. In the case of the DRC, to achieve some of the SDG goals, the government should collaborate with established religions, particularly the Roman Catholic Church, in order to establish a registry of its citizen with accurate information that the Catholic Church can provide to the government. This would help provide legal status or legal identity to all individuals established in the Congo and help resolve a long simmering conflict of citizenship for groups of people in border provinces. This collaboration with the Catholic Church and other religious groups can also help provide a timely census of the population and provide accurate numbers of those who can participate in national and local elections, thus adding a layer of accuracy and legitimacy to elections and their outcome. This would be the most cost-effective way of realizing a task that has been elusive for four decades in the country: the census of the population.

The government should strengthen and broaden its partnership with religious institutions in order to develop and expand institutions of primary, secondary, and tertiary education that provide access to education to as many people as possible, thus reducing the temptation of militias and rebel groups for the youth. This would significantly contribute to ending abuse, exploitation, trafficking, and violence against children (SDG 16.2).

## References

Eboussi Boulaga, F. (1977). *La crise du muntu. Authenticité africaine et philosophie*. Présence Africaine.

Eboussi Boulaga, F. (1984). *Christianity without Fetishes: An African Critique and Recapture of Christianity*. Orbis Books.

Eboussi Boulaga, F. (1991). *A Contretemps: L'enjeu de Dieu en Afrique*. Karthala.

Chidester, D. (1996). *Savage Systems: Colonialism and Comparative Religion in Southern Africa*. University of Virginia Press.

Luneau, R. (2002). *Comprendre l'Afrique: Evangile, modernité, mangeur d'âmes*. Karthala.

Magesa, L. (2002). *Christian Ethics in Africa*. Acton Publishers.

Magesa, L. (2004a). *African Traditional Religion and Christian Faith*. Paulines Publications.

Magesa, L. (2004b). *Anatomy of Inculturation: Transforming the Church in Africa*. Orbis Books.

Magesa, L. (2007). Locating the Church among the Wretched of the Earth. In S. J. James F. Keenan (Ed.), *Catholic Theological Ethics in the World Church: The Plenary Papers from the First Cross-cultural Conference on Catholic Theological Ethics*. Continuum.

Magesa, L. (2015). *Theology and Identity: The Impact of Culture upon Christian Thought in the Second Century and Modern Africa*. Wipf and Stock.

Mbembe, A. (1988). *Afriques Indociles: Christianisme, Pouvoir et Etat en Société Postcoloniale*. Karthala.

Mudimbe, V. Y. (1982). *L'Odeur du Père: Essai sur des limites de la science et de la vie en Afrique noire*. Présence Africaine.

Mudimbe, V. Y. (1988). *The Invention of Africa: Gnosis, Philosophy and the Other of Knowledge*. University of Indiana Press.

Mudimbe, V. Y. (1994). *The Idea of Africa*. Indiana University Press.
Mudimbe, V. Y. (1997). *Tales of Faith: Religion as Political Performance in Central Africa*. The Athlone Press.
Mveng, E. (1985). *L'Afrique dans l'Eglise: Paroles d'un croyant*. L'Harmattan.

CHAPTER 16

# Religion, Peacebuilding, and Development in Uganda

*David Andrew Omona*

## INTRODUCTION

The discourse on religion, peacebuilding, and development brings to mind the interwoven nature of the triune. In Uganda, as elsewhere, while religion, the valuation of the ideal (Omona & Kiriaghe, 2020), has caused conflicts that have retarded peace and development. By and large, it has greatly contributed to peacebuilding and development. Given the dual role it plays, R. Scott Appleby (2000), in his book *Ambivalence of the Sacred: Religion, Violence and Reconciliation*, cites several examples right from the 1560s showing how religion has been a factor in both causing violence and reconciliation, and by extension development.

The participation of religion in peace and development has not just started with the advent of Abrahamic religions, but even before. Notwithstanding some excess involved, the local people have been using their religion in all matters of life including promotion of peaceful and inclusive societies for their development. Religious personalities and chiefs have been pivotal in providing justice for all and building effective, accountable, and inclusive community where everyone feel belonged. Both among the centralized and decentralized communities, the king, chief, or clan leader represented the unity of the people. On their part, the leaders worked toward ensuring their people were protected from external aggression, and they administer justice to all. In such enabling environment, the community members had the latitude to work for their

D. A. Omona (✉)
School of Social Sciences, Uganda Christian University, Kampala, Uganda

© The Author(s), under exclusive license to Springer Nature Switzerland AG 2023
S. M. Kilonzo et al. (eds.), *The Palgrave Handbook of Religion, Peacebuilding, and Development in Africa*,
https://doi.org/10.1007/978-3-031-36829-5_16

self-promotion and progress. To ensure peaceful coexistence, efforts were made to ensure issues that cause conflict among and between communities were sorted before they turn ugly.

Eventually, when foreign religions were introduced to Uganda, they have been used for addressing the tenets of Sustainable Development Goal (SDG) 16, even before its promulgation in 2015. In many areas, religious leaders have used the teaching and practice in the different religions to reduce violence and its related death rates (16.1); curtail abuse, exploitation, trafficking, and all forms of violence against and torture of children (16.2); promote the rule of law at the national and international levels and ensure equal access to justice for all (16.3); preach against illicit financial and arms flows, strengthen the recovery and return of stolen assets, and combat all forms of organized crime (16.1); campaign against corruption and bribery in all their forms (16.5); and agitate for developing effective, accountable, and transparent institutions at all levels (16.6). Furthermore, religion has also been used as a channel for ensuring responsive, inclusive, participatory, and representative decision-making at all levels (16.7); calling upon develop countries to broaden and strengthen the participation of developing countries in the institutions of global governance (16.8); agitating for the state to provide legal identity for all, including birth registration (16.9); and agitating for public access to information and protection of fundamental freedoms, in accordance with national legislation and international agreements (16.10). Religion has also worked toward strengthening relevant national institutions for building capacity at all levels so as to prevent violence and combat terrorism and crime (16.a) and promoting laws and policies for sustainable development (16.b).

While at times denominations within a religion or a religious group have worked toward addressing the tenets of SDG 16 single-handedly, in some instances they have joined hands at intra- or inter-religious level to work together for the good of the people so as to ensure the local population is using the dividends of peaceful coexistence for their personal development. Such initiative did not only help to build peace in the present, but also gave support for the formation of an interfaith council that helps to address the cancer of religious actors acting in isolation, hence breaking religious leaders and actors' operating in silos. Such initiatives predispose religious actors to work in tandem with or in support of other ethnic, civil society, or governmental actors to bring peace and development for the good of the people. Therefore, a symbiotic relationship that grows between religion, peacebuilding, and development usually helps people of diverse standing to come together for socio-economic development. The discussion that follows below highlights how that has played out in the case of Uganda.

## The Religious Characterization and Environment in Uganda

Uganda is a multi-religious country. Currently, the religions that are represented in the country range from the Baha'i Faith, Buddhism, Christianity, Hinduism, Islam, Judaism, Mormon, traditional religions, and other eastern religions in small numbers. Most of these religious groups have their origin from outside the country, except the traditional religions that each group practices. While the traditional religions have been there from time immemorial, the rest of the religions started showing up in Uganda from the mid-nineteenth century. During most of these years, the different religions have participated in enhancing or distorting the tenets of the United Nations Sustainable Development Goal 16. While the 2030 SDG "Agenda recognizes that sustainable development goes hand in hand with peace and security" (DCAF, 2021, p. 3), religion has worked both for and against peace and security—the tenets of SDG 16—during much of the colonial and postcolonial Uganda. This part of the chapter, therefore, focuses on highlighting how religions represented in Uganda have distorted the tenets of SDG 16.

Of all the foreign religions, Islam was introduced first, followed by Christianity, and the rest came thereafter. Introduced by Arab traders in northern and central Uganda in the 1850s, initially Islam did not gain a lot of attention among the local people like the two initial denominations of Christianity introduced in the 1875 and 1877. After the introduction of the foreign religions, trouble to peace and security started showing up at both inter- and intra-religious levels. At the inter-religious sphere, the first challenge to peace and security came between some Muslim converts and traditionalists that the King of Buganda represented. Influenced by the Egyptian Muslims to "strictly observe Islamic food laws" when the Muslim coverts refused "to eat meat slaughtered by the Kabaka's butchers" (Omona, 2019, p. 149), an ugly situation ensued that even saw the martyrdom of 100 Muslims, a contrary act to what SDG 16:1 aspires for, even before it was enacted.

The second inter-religious challenge to peace and security came when adherents of the new religions (Christianity and Islam) organized a standing army and ousted the traditionalists and their leader—the King of Buganda from leadership (Ward, 1991). While the common enemy was gone, who to install as a replacement of the ousted leader ushered in the third inter-religious crisis when the Muslims turned against the Christians, expelled them from the seat of the kingdom, and installed Kalema—who they referred to as Sheik—as a new king. On their part, the Christian forces fought back, and defeated the Muslim faction, and brought the ousted king back to the throne (Omona, 2019). The virulence that this chaotic episode ushered in was contrary to the aspirations of SDG 16.1, 3, 6, & 9. For example, given the Muslim traders did not introduce social services, during much of the colonial and immediate postcolonial administration, the majority of Muslims were excluded from enjoying such services, especially education, until the Anglican Church became somewhat lenient to them by opening space for them in church schools founded by the missionaries. The segregation the Muslims were subjected to was contrary to SDG 16 b that requires "promotion and enforcement of non-discriminatory laws and policies for sustainable development" (DCAF, 2021, p. 3). However, when Idi Amin Dada ascended to the presidency after the 1971 coup d'état, some Muslims tried to pay back the pain they went through, thus leading to the resurgence of the Muslim-Christian conflict (Odoi, 2009, p. 236).

The third inter-religious rivalry that worked against peace and security came during the expansion of the new religions to other parts of the country. Since this expansion, especially Christianity, went alongside the colonial administration, it came against the forces of traditional religion—represented by the chiefs in the different parts of the country. The conflict that ensued set people that used to be in harmony against each other. And depending on which brand of the new religion went to a particular place, the adherents of such religious brand got "special treatment" (Pirouet, 1998), as opposed to what SDG 16.7 & 16b promote.

At the intra-religious level, the challenge began right from the introduction of the two Christian denominations—Protestant and Roman Catholic—in 1877 and 1879, respectively. The conflictual relationship that existed between the two Christian denominations in Europe played out between their adherents in Uganda. To start with, after joining to expel the Muslims and the king they had installed, a fight ensued between the Protestants and the Roman Catholics in which the Protestant forces, aided by Captain Lugard's maxim guns (Ward, 1991), emerged victorious and chased the Roman Catholics away from the seat of power. During the expansion of the Christian religion outside Buganda, those who converted to the Protestant brand of Christianity enjoyed a privileged position as compared to the Roman Catholics. The division this brought was so deep in Ankole, as elsewhere in other parts of the country. For example, in Ankole most of the Bahima became Protestant and almost half of the Bairu became Roman Catholic. Since the Bahima were the ruling class, all privileged positions went to them (Karamura, 2019), as compared to the Bairu.

Then in the 1950s when Ugandans started to agitate for political independence from Britain, political parties that were formed, authors like Museveni (2007), Ngabirano (2010), Omona (2015), Mutiabwa (2010), and others say followed denominational affiliations. While there were people from other religious and denominational affiliations that belonged to these parties, the majority of the adherents of the earliest political parties belonged to the same denomination. Museveni (2007, p. 41), for example, observes that "at the time of independence … religion was used in secular matters such as winning political votes." He further argued that "[A]ll the independence political parties were involved in these practices-with the DP allied to the Roman Catholic, the UPC to Protestants and the KY to Protestants in Buganda" (Museveni, 2007, p. 41). To an extent, in Ankole, the modern religion and political inclination added to the existing precarious relations between the Bairu and Bahima ethnic groups. Accordingly, as Omona (2015, p. 54) observes, during much of the postcolonial time "to be a Muiru, a Roman Catholic and a Democratic Party (DP) member" was a double tragedy because of the exclusion that came with it. Whereas the abolition of kingdoms and their paraphernalia brought to rest aspects of the Bahima dominance over the Bairu, the rise of Museveni to power rejuvenated a sense of superiority in some of the Bahima Protestants over Bairu in general, and those who were Roman Catholics in particular (Omona, 2015; Omona, 2019). Given this intra-religious struggle, Ngabirano (2010), as quoted by Omona (2019), observes "the first years of independence up to 1967, the conflict factor was mainly between Protestants against Catholics ... from 1986 to date the Protestant and Catholic factor still remains" (Ngabirano, 2010, p. 61).

The intra-religious political rivalry in Acholi between the Roman Catholics and the Protestants made those in the DP (Roman Catholics) feel their exclusion was an intentional project by the British colonial administration. To express their dissatisfaction, some DP members composed a song in Luo that goes—"*Muni oyube me nyono wi wa*," literally translated as "it was a design by the Europeans to sit on us." On their part, the members of the Uganda Peoples' Congress—who were regarded Protestants—also composed a song that goes—"*kwon pa DP pe acama*," which literally means, "I cannot share food with the DP" (RLP, 2014, p. 66). While SDG 16 hopes to end such expressions that are tantamount to abuse, exploitation, and violence, the vestiges of such still continue in Uganda to date. While such acrimony plays against peace and development in Uganda at all levels, the religious feel in Ugandans is equally working to change the state, an act that is in line with what SDG 16 stands for.

## PARTICIPATION OF RELIGIOUS INSTITUTIONS IN PEACEBUILDING AND DEVELOPMENT IN UGANDA

Religious service provision pre-dates the rise of non-profit institutions. Invariably, as Welty (2014, p. 65) argues, "nearly all religious traditions contain peacebuilding and development practices such as the Christian traditions of diakonia and charity, tzedakah in Judaism and zakat, sadaqa and waqf in Islam." As increasingly powerful humanitarian actor, religion occupies a critical point in peacebuilding and development. Stemming from the early Christian conceptions of charity based on the premise of giving without expectation of reciprocity because charity was believed to add to the spiritual merits of the giver (Welty, 2014), religious leaders worked tirelessly to bring peace and development as acts of service to the society. The discourse that follows highlights instances of how religion has been deployed in peacebuilding and development in Uganda.

## Participation of Religious Institution in Peacebuilding in Uganda

In any conflict situation, religious power-brokers do play a great role, apart from formal institutions and chains of authority. At the core of its nature, religion is a critical consideration for peacebuilding because it often transcends geographic boundaries and the outcome of what is reached could spread to a wider network of followers. Accordingly, the USAID tool kit argues;

1. [R]eligion is often a core source of identity. A religious landscape taps into a narrative which, similar to ethnicity, is historical and personal. Both ethnicity and religion may exist interdependently. However, religion has the ability to transcend ethnic differences.
2. Actors in a conflict may employ religious authorities or religious language to mobilize followers and widen their base of support. This can occur at the political level, when leaders use religious discourse to garner popular support for specific policy aims or make space for their group that may feel discriminated and/or marginalized. Military or movement leaders may use religion in a tactical way, as a tool for recruitment or as a safeguard from defection. Religious actors engaged in peacebuilding can draw on a common worldview, theological language, and shared values by adherents to gain support for peace.
3. Religious teachings can provide justifications for extreme action or peace. This role is important to remember when in a conflict-zone with any or no religious overtone. As a powerful source of identity, the emergence of religion in a conflict dramatically raises the stakes of the conflict's outcome. (USAID, 2009, p. 9)

The above is a clear testimony that engaging religion and key religious actors in peacebuilding provides unique opportunities to intervene in ongoing conflicts or to reduce the risk that violence will erupt. For, religious teachings do provide important sources of: meaning, identity, and emotional support that can increase resilience in coping with adversity and facilitate mobilization to overcome it. They can also provide empathy and compassion that can sustain reconciliation and problem-solving across divisions. It further instills values, norms, and motivations that support nonviolent approaches to raising and confronting differences. Religious actors frequently have a special relationship with the affected populations that can dampen conflict drivers, strengthening conflict mitigation efforts, or both. Specifically:

> Religious leaders and institutions are often considered trustworthy and credible by the local population due to their established roles in their respective communities.
>
> Religious actors may have a shared and respected set of values with different sides of the conflict. Values, including forgiveness and reconciliation, in religious texts and teachings can inspire communities to change attitudes and actions at a

basic level and transform worldviews at a deeper level to understand "others" in the conflict positively.

Religious actors may have unique leverage as spiritual leaders that allows them to influence and sway communities in ways that secular players in the conflict may not. This unique leverage increases the likelihood of expanding support for peace.

Religious actors have a deep understanding of the local context giving them the ability to work successfully at a local level. Religious actors often have access to all levels of power—community, nation, and international—which gives them the ability to address conflicts on multiple levels. (USAID, 2009, p. 10)

In many settings religious organizations and their leaders, due to the trust and moral authority they hold from broad-based constituencies, are uniquely positioned to facilitate post-conflict reconstruction and reconciliation efforts.

Like in other parts of the world, in Uganda, religion has been effectively used in peacebuilding during many of the turbulences the country experienced. For example, the introduction of foreign religions in the country has broken the barriers that existed at local levels since the adherence of these religions comes from different ethnic groups who, instead of looking at each other as enemies, started to be at peace. And after the formation of the Uganda Joint Christian Council in 1963, religious leaders played a pivotal role during the political crisis that ensued soon after independence until date.

During and after the 1971 coup that saw Amin Dada coming to the political limelight (Omona, 2015), religious leaders worked to ensure peace at all levels. Although the fight for peace and security for the vulnerable led to the death of Archbishop Janani Luwum (NRC, 2004, p. 17), the determination of religious leaders to bring peace did not end. While the overthrow of Amin's regime in 1979 brought a sigh of relief, the arrogance that the Uganda National Liberation Army (UNLA) soldiers came with returned Uganda into chaos (Omona, 2015). The mass murder, looting, and rape of women that came to define the state, and the failure of the coalition government to work out proper administrative modalities leading to four presidents ruling Uganda within a span of two years, starting with Professor Yusuf Lule, Godfrey Binaisa, Paul Muwanga, and Milton Apollo Obote, made religious leader to swing to action so as to secure the state. Lamenting such rapid change of government, the religious leaders in Uganda wrote a letter to President Nyerere that reads in part:

> As soon as it (*the UNLF*) had seized power, among all other things we were promised peace, stability, and security; "never again Uganda shall be ruled by the power of the gun" … *but* … the development which have taken place within the UNLF government have not been very promising. For three times the UNLF has changed government within a period of less than two years—thus we realize instability still lives with us. Shooting and killing have continued as in the times of Amin at times even worse. We have seen families being exterminated; father, mother, and children all killed on the same day. (Nsubuga et al., 1980, p. 1)

The above is indicative that the hope of many people who celebrated the fall of Amin were not met because the liberators started to do exactly what they said they were liberating the masses from. Thus, prior to sending the above letter to President Nyerere, the religious leaders had drawn the attention of President Binaisa on the worsening situation in Uganda (Nsubuga et al., 1980, p. 1). This degenerating situation was also echoed by a statement issued by the Bishops and Clergy of the Church of Uganda (CoU) that met at Makerere University from June 16 to 19, 1980 (Wani, 1980, p. 1). Although in the letter to President Nyerere the religious leaders suggested that

> [t]he present government should use all possible means in its capacity to fight insecurity, not to wait until they were elected into power as one of the members of the military commission said (*published in the Uganda Times of Monday September 1, 1980*): "if the UPM is voted in power it will ensure total security for all Ugandans within its first two weeks in office." (Nsubuga et al., 1980, p. 1)

The campaign catchword from the Uganda Patriotic Movement (UPM) candidate in the quotation of the church leaders made the religious leaders skeptical. Citing the example of Lebanon, the religious leaders suggested peacekeeping forces from the UN, Organisation of African Unity (OAU), or the Commonwealth countries to be set up. Unfortunately, nothing like what they suggested was put in place to address the emergency. The action of religious leader to bring peace during such tough time resonates with the tenet of SDG 16.

At the intra-religious level, the establishment of Uganda Joint Christian Council (UJCC) in 1963 considerably changed the environment that was characterized by bitter conflicts between and among faith communities. The leaders of the Church of Uganda, the Roman Catholic Church, and the Uganda Orthodox Church at the time recognized a need for Christians to witness together and live in harmony (UJCC, 2017). Subsequently, the member churches became a vanguard of hope during the turbulent socio-political periods of Uganda's postcolonial era. To start with, the UJCC broke the segregation that used to manifest in provision of health, education, and other social services to persons. Hence, instead of only attending to the needs of the adherents of the particular faith group, the de-balkanization saw such services being opened to all the masses in a given location. In the area of education, the harmonization of Christian Religious Education syllabus helped to break the initial arrangement where Roman Catholics and Protestants schools did different papers.

Over the years, through its Good Governance arm, the UJCC has informed policy in the country through participating in giving guidance on bills tabled in parliament before such bills become laws (UJCC, 2017), conducting civic education, and election monitoring during elections at all levels so as to promote rule of law, equal access to justice for all, strengthen national institutions, prevent violence, and combat terrorism and crime (SDG 16.1 &

16 a). The action of the faith body has helped to "promote and enforce non-discriminatory laws and policies" (SDG 16. b) that works to pacify the different political groups, thus making them to know that politics is not an end itself but rather a means to an end-service to the people. Besides, the UJCC has also worked tirelessly, through its peacebuilding and humanitarian action, to carry out dialogue at different community levels in Uganda, an act in response to SDG 16.1. For example, it has played a key role in conducting dialogue over land in western, eastern, and northern Uganda; mediated between refugees and host communities in parts where refugees have been settled (UJCC, 2017); and also brokered peace between communities and state apparatus, especially in the Rwenzori sub-region and northern Uganda.

Furthermore, during the Juba Peace Talks between the Lord's Resistance Movement (LRM) and the Government of Uganda, religious leaders through para-religious organizations like the UJCC and Acholi religious Leaders Peace Initiative (ARLPI) participated in the peace process so as to bring peace to the people, deter wanton destruction of lives and properties, eliminate acts of terrorism, and end "abuse, exploitation, trafficking and all forms of violence against and torture of children" (SDG 16.2) in Lord's Resistant Army (LRA) custody and protected camps. The UJCC, under the chairmanship of Bishop David Zach Niringiye, did a commendable job by expressing the need for forgiveness and reconciliation among the local people, the Ugandan government, and the Lord's Resistant Army (LRA) rebels. The leaders opined that to attain peace in such a dilemma, the use of alternative justice system other than formal justice system could yield better results since there are some advantages that accrue when using alternative justice system. Thus:

- It offers flexible, accessible and cheap procedure for all.
- It insures community participation in resolving the conflict.
- It promotes mutual healing and restoration of broken relationship.
- It ensures satisfaction of both offenders and victims.
- It addresses the concern of the victims through payment of reparation.
- It ensures effective reintegration of combatants into the community.
- It facilitates documentation of crimes committed by the perpetrators.
- It insures against the culture of impunity because perpetrators of crimes that are unwilling to cooperate are subjected to the contemporary justice systems.
- It ensures creative collaboration with cultural and religious institutions. (UJCC, 2007, p. 17)

Since at the heart of the traditional justice system is the principle of acknowledgment of responsibility for wrongs committed by the offender (UJCC, 2007, pp. 22–23), using it could serve as a way of restoration of peaceful coexistence in Uganda. Indeed, such agitation became a basis for the realization of peace in parts of Uganda.

In a related development, with the backing of the ARLPI, the Anglican dioceses of Kitgum, northern Uganda, Lango, Soroti, and the Catholic Archdiocese of Gulu have been active participants in the peace process. For instance, Mark Baker Ochola II, the retired bishop of the Diocese of Kitgum who himself lost a wife during the insurgency, is an ardent supporter of seeking for a peaceful solution to the conflict (Omona, 2015). In several fora, he pleaded for the use of the traditional mechanisms for conflict resolution during settling conflict. Archbishop John Baptist Odama (Odama 2005) is in support of this plea on the need to use local mechanisms to resolve conflicts. Since the impact of conflicts is felt more among the local people, Odama (2005, p. 3) argues that "the traditional conflict resolution mechanisms work best in local conflicts because the local people consider crime as a communal aspect that involves the whole community," even if the crime would have been committed by one person. Hence, applying such a mechanism would easily make the communities forgive and reconcile with each other.

Knowing that peaceful coexistence starts at local level, over the years the UJCC has undertaken efforts aimed at achieving gender equality. To start with, its Human Resource policy clearly spells out that the recruitment of staff should be based on merit and not sex. With an active gender program, the UJCC was able to draft a gender policy. In addition to this program, it has developed family life materials aimed at emphasizing the role of parenting in child upbringing. To actualize this, it has mobilized women in the member churches to commemorate the World Women's Day of Prayer. Such an act has not only created harmony among women in the member churches but also provided space for women to discuss their own development and participation in church-related activities. The UJCC has also mobilized women to commemorate the sixteen days of Activism against Gender Based Violence, an activity which is being replicated by the women in the member churches in various dioceses across the country. Then in 2014, the UJCC through funding from the Church of Sweden implemented "the Gender Justice Project." Through the project's activities such as radio talk shows, dialogue with universities, and access to justice in terms of medical care and referrals (UJCC, 2016, p. 7), local communities are showing the value of working together in harmony.

Like the UJCC, the Interreligious Council of Ugadan (IRCU) is yet another religious organization that has greatly worked toward pacifying Uganda. The joint actions in health, policy dialogue, and promotion of peaceful coexistence among the religious and political groups have greatly contributed to the peacebuilding processes in Uganda. Besides, twice now, the IRCU has organized presidential debates for those vying to lead the country. Having the different candidates appear at a location at the same time is a testimony for cooperation, thus an encouragement for their supporters to tolerate "the other." The moderators have also used such moments to encourage the candidates to appeal to their supporters to maintain peace before, during, and after elections. While no one could say the outcome of such meetings brought in the much yearned for peace, at least, they have assisted in reducing the level of electoral violence around the country.

Apart from working jointly, the different religious groups and denominations have also weight in to bring peace to the country. For example, the Provincial Assembly of the Church of Uganda that sat in August 2008, among other things, reaffirmed its commitment to the then Juba Peace Process and maintained that the members it nominated in 2006 to continue monitoring the trend in the peace process (CoU, 2009, p. 30). The Roman Catholic Church, through its Justice and Peace docket in the different dioceses, is actively participating in community peacebuilding processes. Since, as Coeli Barry and Hippolyt Pul (2009) argue, religious leaders take on practical roles as connectors, mediators, and unifiers, among various actors, their inclusion of individuals and inter- or intra-religious groups has assisted greatly in pacifying Uganda. For, "[r]eligious leaders are the gatekeepers to their communities, as they leverage their authority, legitimacy, and knowledge of the structures and functioning of their communities to create and manage access for external actors who need to engage with or in the communities" (Barry & Pul, 2009, p. 7).

Through such, the leaders of the different faith groups have participated in peace-brokering efforts between different groups in Uganda. As Cissy Makumbi (2015/2021) asserts, in doing so "[t]he church's efforts towards the realization of peace and stability in ... Uganda cannot be overlooked."

In a way, the participation of religion in pacifying Uganda as seen above has set religion at the center of promoting peaceful and inclusive societies for sustainable development; providing access to justice for all; and building effective, accountable, and inclusive institutions at all levels (DCAF, 2021, p. 3).

## *The Participation of Religious Institution in Development in Uganda*

The participation of religion in fulfilling SDG 16 stretches right from antiquity to the present. Authors like Niringiye (2016), Mutiabwa (2010), Omona and Kiriaghe (2020), Odoi (2009), and others have succinctly attested to this. To an extent, even the current polity of Uganda is a result of the efforts of religious groups. Therefore, the role religion plays in the development—in line with SDG 16—of any society could not be oversimplified. As Omona and Kiriaghe (2020, p. 258), quoting James Wolfensohn (2011, p. 8), note:

> Religion is an omnipresent and seamless part of daily life, taking an infinite variety of forms that are part of the distinctive quality of each community. Religion could thus not be seen as something apart and personal. It is, rather, a dimension of life that suffuses whatever people do. Religion has an effect on many people's attitudes to everything, including such matters as savings, investment and a host of economic decisions. It influences areas we had come to see as vital for successful development, like schooling, gender quality, and approaches to health care. In short, religion could be an important driver of change, even as it could be a break to progress.

Wolfensohn, the first World Bank President to realize the import of religion in development, did understand the way religion opens the eyes of many people. Therefore, if well espoused, religion has the potential to be an engine to leapfrog a community to greater heights. Consequently, from the mid-1990s development donors have increasingly chosen to support the work of faith-based organizations (FBOs), even though religious organizations have been involved in various types of charitable, philanthropic, humanitarian, and development work for far longer and many have been funded by multi- and bilateral donors for years (Tomalin, 2012). To this end, since right from pre-colonial periods every community uses their religion to understand seasons and events in life (Omona & Kiriaghe, 2020, p. 258), they have been able to progress without being coarse. Hence, people in the present Uganda have used such knowledge to plan their lives in matters of hunting, planting, harvesting, and so forth. Invariably, therefore,

> cultivation of land and expansion of tribal wealth through agriculture and livestock farming involved performance of religious rituals. As individuals in a given community sought to improve their wealth through marrying many wives who will in turn produce many children to provide the required manpower to cultivate expansive chunks of land, they did not go against their religious ideals while engaging in agriculture, but rather observed the required practices methodically. (Mbogo 2015, pp. 172–173)

The introduction of the Christian and Islamic religions that ushered in the establishment of formal education system has greatly leapfrogged many communities into the development arena in Uganda. While initially it was the Christian missionaries that established formal education, after independence, the Muslims also joined in the venture. What formal education brought was to help people acquire new skills, change their outlook of things, and use the knowledge and skills acquired to their personal progress. The learning institutions became centers of technology and scientific advancement, which promote development. Besides, it also helped to develop people's administrative and management skills that help in overseeing resources as well as structures for maintaining social, political, and economic systems that sustain society (Omona & Kiriaghe, 2020, pp. 261–262). The education system introduced transformed the nation from the vestiges of some conservative traditional beliefs to modern knowledge, thus helping people to expand the horizons of their progress; work toward developing effective, accountable, and transparent institution at all levels (SDG 16.6); and enabled the masses to develop "responsive, inclusive, participatory and representative decision-making at all levels" (SDG 16.7).

The interest of religion in both the temporal and futuristic wellbeing of human beings need not be overemphasized. For example, when the Christian missionaries came to Uganda, they knew that for a person to be attentive to the world, his or her temporal life has to be taken care of. Hence, to help improve the temporal lives of the local people, the missionaries enhanced cash economy by encouraging the growth of tropical raw materials like coffee and cotton to satisfy the British industrialists urge. Bishop Burrup, for example, introduced cotton growing in Uganda (Omona & Kiriaghe, 2020, p. 263). This was somewhat an implementation of what David Livingstone had in mind when he advocated for the three "C" policy: Christianity, Civilization, and Commerce (Nkomazana, 1998, p. 45). Livingstone believed that "Christianity would provide principles for moral guidance, while legitimate commerce and education would encourage Africans to produce their own goods from their fertile soil to trade with Europeans" (Manala, 2013). The missionaries introduced cultivation of cash crops like coffee and cotton in large scales. The sales of the produce from these cash crops boosted the economy of the local people, thus helping them to avert poverty, pay their children's school fees, and afford to pay for their health bills (Omona & Kiriaghe, 2020, p. 263). This helped the local people to build their capacity (SDG 16a) so as to eliminate what sets them aback, broaden and strengthen their "participation ... in the institutions of global governance" (SDG 16.8).

While during the earlier period the acrimonious intra- and inter-religious relations brought pain to the citizenry in Uganda, the same religious groups helped in modernizing political organization in the country. The Christian missionaries of the Church Missionary Society (CMS) welcomed colonial administrators to set up a modern political system in Uganda, an act that helped the masses to occupy the political space to date—unlike in the previous years where politics was a matter of royalty. The new arrangement has enabled Ugandans from different parts of the country to look at themselves as belonging to a common polity and enjoy fundamental freedom as citizens (SDG 16.10). The sheer facilitation of free movement this has brought in is helping people who have seen what is happening in other parts to take such ideas to their areas of origin. Through such, a lot of both qualitative and quantitative changes are taking place across the country.

## Conclusion and Recommendations

The foregoing discourse does not assume that everything about religion, peacebuilding, and development in relation to the SDG 16 has been covered. However, notwithstanding some painful experiences, the issues highlighted have brought to bear that religion, peacebuilding, and development have worked in tandem for the good of the people in Uganda. For, apart from religion orchestrating conflicts that have seen a lot of drawbacks to development in the country over the years, by and large, it has been a force in peacebuilding and development. To enable the positives to be manifest and realize SDG 16, there is a need for a deliberate deployment of religion in peacebuilding and development. To this end, a deliberate move is required from all stakeholders to inculcate the right mindset among adherents of the different religions so that the achievements realized so far are sustained and enhanced.

## REFERENCES

Appleby, S. R. (2000). *Ambivalence of the Sacred: Religion, Violence and Reconciliation*. Rowman & Littlefield Publishers, Inc.

Barry, C., & Pul, H. (2009). *Understanding Religious Identity and Peacebuilding in the People-to-People Reconciliation Fund-Program End of Project Evaluation Report*. USAID.

CoU (Church of Uganda). (2009). The Provincial Assembly Resolutions. *The Courage News, 1*(8), 30.

DCAF. (2021). SSR Background: Sustainable Development Goal 16. DCAF, Retrieved January 26, 2023, from https://www.sdg16hub.org/topic/ssr-backgrounder-sdg-16

Karamura, G. P. B. (2019). *The Dynamics of Identity Politics: Interplay of Ethnicity, Religion, and Power in Ankole, Uganda-1953–1993*. New Vision Publishers.

Makumbi, C. (2015, November 25–updated January 04, 2021). Role of Catholic Church in bringing peace to Northern Uganda. *The Monitor*. Retrieved January 15, 2023, from https://www.monitor.co.ug/uganda/lifestyle/religion/role-of-catholic-church-in-bringing-peace-to-northern-uganda-1632040

Manala, M. J. (2013). *The impact of Christianity on Sub-Saharan Africa*. Available from http://hdl.handle.net/10500/13139. Accessed 29/3/2022.

Mbogo, R. W. (2015). Historical Factors for the Church's Involvement in Holistic Community Development in East Africa. *Developing Country Studies, 5*(21), 169–176.

Museveni. (2007). *Sowing the mustered seed: The struggle for freedom and democracy in Uganda*. London: Macmillan.

Mutiabwa, P. (2010). *Uganda Since Independence: A History of Unfulfilled Hopes*. Fountain Publishers.

Ngabirano, M. (2010). *Conflict and peace building: Theological and ethical foundation for a political reconstruction of the Great Lakes Region in Africa*. Kampala: Uganda Martyrs University book series.

Niringiye, D. Z. (2016). *The Church in the World: A Historical Ecclesiological Study of the Church of Uganda with Particular Reference to Post Independence Uganda-1962–1993*. Langham Publishers.

Nkomazana, F. (1998). Livingstone's Ideas of Christianity, Commerce and Civilization. *Pula: Botswana Journal of African Studies, 12*(1 & 2), 44–57.

NRC. (2004). *Uganda Index*. Retrieved December 2, 2022, from http://www.mongabay.com/history/uganda/uganda-the_national_resistance_council.html

Nsubuga, E., Mulumba, N., & Wani, S. (1980). A letter by four religious leaders of Uganda to His Excellency President Julius Nyerere of Tanzania on insecurity and the coming elections in Uganda, UCU Archive, box 120.2, Folder/Title: Ministry of Internal Affairs, Pm3/7(a).

Odama, J. B. (2005). Reconciliation Process *(Mato Oput)* among the Acholi Tribe in Northern Uganda, a Commemorative Address Made during the Ceremony for 21st NIWANO Peace Prize Award in Japan.

Odoi-Tanga, F. (2009). *Politics, Ethnicity and Conflict in Post Independence Acholiland, Uganda 1962–2006*. PhD Thesis, University of Pretoria.

Omona, A. D. (2015). *The Management of Postcolonial Intrastate Conflicts in Uganda: A Case of Northern Uganda*. PhD Thesis, Nairobi: Kenyatta University.

Omona, A. D. (2019). Religion and Human Security in Uganda. In E. Chitando & J. Tarusarira (Eds.), *Religion and Human Security in Africa*. Routledge.

Omona A. D., & Kiriaghe, U. M. (2020). Religion and Development in Uganda. In E. Chitando, M. R. Gunda, & L. Togarasei, eds., *Religion and Development in Africa* (BiAS 25/ERA 4, pp. 259–279). University of Bamberg Press.

Pirouet, M. L. (1998). *Black Evangelists: Spread of Christianity in Uganda, 1891–1914.* London: Africa Book Centre Ltd.

Refugee Law Project [RLP]. (2014). *Compendium of Conflicts in Uganda: Findings of the National Reconciliation and Transitional Justice Audit.* RLP.

Tomalin, E. (2012). Thinking about Faith-Based Organisations in Development: Where Have We Got to and What Next? *Development in Practice, 22*(5–6), 689–703. https://doi.org/10.1080/09614524.2012.686600

UJCC. (2007). *A Framework for Dialogue on Reconciliation and Peace in Northern Uganda.* Uganda Joint Christian Council.

UJCC. (2016). A Report on Dialogue Meetings Conducted in Boroli, Nyumanzi Baratuku and Ayilo 1, Establishing Structures at the Grass Root to Enable Collaborative Networks for Peaceful Co-existence between the Host Community and the Refugees.

UJCC. (2017). Strategic Plan (2018–2023): Positioning for Holistic and Sustainable Change. Retrieved January 15, 2023, from https://ujcc.co.ug/wp-content/uploads/2018/09/ABRIDGED-VERSION-SP-2018-2023-final-kmt.pdf

USAID. (2009). *Religion, Culture and Peacebuilding: An Introductory Programme Guide.* Available from http://www.partnerreligiondevelopment.org/fileadmin/Dateien/Resources/Knowledge_Center/Pnadr501.pdf. Accessed 20/5/2022.

Wani, S. (1980). A Statement from the Bishops and Clergy of the Church of Uganda Meeting at Makerere 16th–19th June 1980, UCU archive, Box 120.2, Folder/Title: Ministry of Internal Affairs, Pm3/7 (a).

Ward, K. (1991). A History of Christianity in Uganda. Retrieved January 26, 2023, from http://www.dacb.org/history/a%20history%20of%20christianity%20in%20uganda.html

Welty, E. (2014). Faith-Based Peacebuilding and Development. *Journal of Peacebuilding and Development, 9*(2), 65–70. Retrieved January 13, 2023. https://doi.org/10.1080/15423166.2014.938994

Wolfensohn, J. (2011). Foreword. In G. ter Haar (Ed.), *Religion and Development* (p. xvii). Colombia University Press.

CHAPTER 17

# Indigenous Spirituality, Peacebuilding, and Development in Eswatini

*Sonene Nyawo*

## INTRODUCTION

Religion remains key to human existence. Thus:

> The world's religious traditions, despite their profound differences, all coalesce around a multi-religious vision of "shared well-being." Such a vision puts the dignity of the human being at the center of the common good. Such a vision puts the golden rule, to treat others as they would be treated, as the guiding moral precept. Such a vision enjoins us to help the poor, the hungry, and the suffering, for they have the greatest needs, and possess the same human dignity as everybody else. And such a vision, finally, must recognize that moral virtues are not simply inherited, or present, or lacking—these virtues are cultivated by societies that hold the dignity of the individual as the highest purpose. (Annett et al., 2017, p. 2)

In Africa all human activities are performed, seen, and experienced from a religious perspective. It is difficult to distinguish one area of life from another because religion is perceived as being a component of all aspects of existence. The human element is perceived as playing a passive role in the pursuits of social and economic development, with everything left in the hands of spiritual beings. Thus, the relationship between religion and everyday life has a significant impact on the judgments, decisions, and practices of the people in

S. Nyawo (✉)
Department of Theology & Religious Studies, University of Eswatini, Kwaluseni, Eswatini
e-mail: snyawo@uniswa.sz

that particular location (Mzizi, 2003; Bediako, 2001). This is also true of traditional religions, alternatively known as primal religions, per the word "primal" being a positive term that is related to the word "primary." Primary carries with it connotations of prior, earlier in origin, basic, or fundamental substratum to all religious systems (Nyawo, 2004). Harold Turner is therefore right in his definition of primal religion when saying that the term conveys two ideas: "the primal religious systems are the most basic or fundamental religious forms in the overall religious history of mankind" and "they have preceded and contributed to the other great religious systems" (Turner, 1977, p. 27).

In light of this, we have doubts about attempts by certain scholars to create a hierarchy that places traditional religions at the bottom and other religions that are sequentially positioned above them as "world religions" (Bediako, 1992). When it comes to peace and development, Africans have always had their indigenous knowledge systems (IKSs) that engender order and tranquility in their lives. Regrettably, these indigenous epistemologies are repeatedly threatened by western hegemonic tendencies, which demonize the African legacy as diabolic, barbaric, and backward; thus some indigenous knowledge systems are gravitating toward extinction (Mawere, 2010). It is in this vein that Mawere further advocates for a correction to the vestiges of colonialism, neo-colonialism, and the western gaze that demonized African IKSs and posed fatal challenges to their (IKSs) potentials in improving African societies socially, economically, and morally (2010, p. 212). Many African scholars would agree with Mawere that Africa today is in the grips of high crime rates, conflicts, serious moral decadence, and other mishaps because of the marginalization, false, and pejorative label attached to the African IKSs (Ndlovu & Svodziwa, 2017; Mawere & Kadenge, 2010; Murithi, 2008).

Conflicts are a major mishap that occurs at all levels of society in Africa and the rest of the globe. The term conflict is ambiguous as it is used according to context. In this chapter it is understood as the product of differences in the interpretation of reality, data, issues, values, interests, relationships, and unsatisfied human needs (Szirmai, 2005). It is always the result of differences in a family, community, village, a tribe, and religion occasioned by incompatible desires and aims (Nader, 1986). By nature conflicts undermine interpersonal and social trust, and they consequently destroy social norms, values, and institutions that have regulated and coordinated peace, cooperation, and collective action for the wellbeing of the community (Francis, 2008).

The United Nations Organization has had concerns about intra-state conflicts; thus it has taken initiatives to attain Number 16 of the Sustainable Development Goals (SDGs) on peace, which is one of the cardinal pillars to development. Agreeing with the opening quote by Annett et al., which is in the spirit of SDG 16, human dignity is indeed core in all religions, whether traditional or modern; societies live by cultivated moral values drawn on these religions, which among other roles, aim at creating peace. Peace, in the words of Dauda (2017), is all about individuals demonstrating their commitment toward contributing to the flourishing of their community. However, in the context of indigenous spirituality peace and conflict are understood as encompassing a parameter that is beyond the physical to involve the spiritual and emotional dimensions (Kanu, 2017). Although Eswatini has not experienced intra-state conflicts, differences that result in hostilities internally do occur, but ritualized performances bring order and stability.

Religious figures and founders emphasize relational values like peaceful coexistence as essential in fostering harmonious relationships within communities; thus they are core to a society's belief system. To put it differently, the presence of religion in a community serves as a resource for managing conflict, which subsequently promotes development. In the case of indigenous spirituality, it can be conflicts, fear of impending disaster brought on by transgression, or a prayer for safety, success, and tranquility, all call for religious personages to execute rituals.

The obsession with the religio-cultural legacy is nearly incorruptible for an African mind in particular. It is strange, nevertheless, that a continent with such a rich history is wracked by wars, conflicts, and injustices. Thus, the chapter contributes to increasing awareness about indigenous knowledge and understandings that they are alternatives to the prevalent peacebuilding frameworks which often keep conflicts prolonged. It is further argued that African indigenous epistemologies are anchored on communitarian-based principles and values which shape their perspective of themselves, that as individuals, they are in a peaceful relationship with the community. It is from this angle that the chapter presents a peace-inclined ritualized performance, which reinforces the African communitarian ethic among Emaswati. To realize this mandate, religion, development, and peacebuilding as understood in this discussion are defined in the next section. It is worth mentioning that different from most African countries, the 1.2 million Eswatini population has not experienced intra-state conflicts ever since it attained independence in 1968. Nonetheless, internally and among themselves, there are hostilities, disagreements, and misunderstandings which result in clashes and opposition, hence the annual performance of *Incwala* ritual to restore national peace and stability.

## Religion, Development, and Peacebuilding in the Eswatini Context

Religion is a complex phenomenon whose nature makes it to be "notoriously" difficult to define (Thorpe, 1992). Over the centuries, influential theorists have offered their definitions, each emphasizing one characteristic or another of religion, to the exclusion of others. In the words of Sani, "[R]eligion, unlike other disciplines like Music, Geography, History, Mathematics, Chemistry and a host of others, has no universally acceptable and satisfactory definition; it is looked at from different perspectives based on the angle which one understands it." Virtually all of the definitions of religion have been found wanting by the majority of scholars; "all the definitions sound good, but all obviously need large amounts of 'unpacking' to give them sufficient scope and sufficient precision to be adequate as definitions," argues Tremmel (1983, p. 3). Thus, he suggests that scholars should come up with a working definition that will address two aspects of the religious phenomena—the functional and the sacred—if they expect to make any headway at all in religious scholarship. The distinction between the functional and sacred modes helps us understand that religion can refer to a person's natural aptitude and tendency to engage in operations and activities that are related to religious ideas, ritual practices, and the human condition (Tremmel 1983, p. 60). Agreeing with Tremmel, Menkiti (1984) advances that the functionalist approach does not only propose that religion should be identified according to what it does, but must be viewed as ritualistic acts of communal unification. Put differently, religious rituals unify a community and peace is ensured.

Until recently, the contribution of religion to social transformation has been relegated to the side lines mainly because it is considered irrational and stifling progress in the scientific innovations that came with the Enlightenment (Shah, 2013). While religion is steadily regaining its lost glory to science, Marshall (2001) still laments that it had been pushed to the peripherals in many of the global initiatives on development; yet it is the cornerstone of sustainable development. Given the influence religions have on societies, some scholars have come to the conclusion that religions have a double-edged sword in that they can either increase conflict or reduce it. They are such a potent force that they can be used to improve or damage societies, and depending on how they are applied, they can also be a tool for unification or division (Kanu & Ndubisi, 2020). The ambivalent nature of religion is well articulated by Chimuka (2020, p. 85) when he says:

> Although religion has been accused of fanning divisions and wars in the world, it has also brought unity and peace. In other cases, although it has been condemned and subverted by Enlightenment thinkers as whimsical and superstitious, it has re-surfaced in various modes in society. Although it has in some cases caused terror and extremism, in others it has been responsible for building bridges and reconstructing broken societies. Although it has caused wars in some areas, it has been responsible for receiving and caring for refugees and victims of natural disasters.

While religion has multiple definitions, the idea of "development" is also conceptualized differently by different people, and at different times; hence what may be termed as "development" is relative to time and space (Deneulin & Bano, 2009, p. 24). However, the general understanding of development centers on the improvement of a country's economic and social conditions so that it reaches an acceptable standard of living for all people (Nyawo, 2020).

In this chapter, development is defined as an inclusive and "people-centered" process that aims to improve the lives of people on a local, national, and global scale rather than being purely economic (Speckman, 2016, p. xxv). Development therefore has more to do with citizens' health, happiness, and sense of fulfillment than it does with statistics relating to economic growth, per capita income, and the size of the sovereign wealth fund (Szirmai, 2005, p. 8). Its main goal is to bring out the true person in each person, making the total human evident (Chitando, 2020, p. 403). Subsequent to the overemphasis on economic objectives of the United Nations Millennial Goals that aim at eradicating poverty and hunger in the world, countries understand development in narrow terms. Ultimately, using economic tactics is the only way to move toward achieving these goals. The Millennium Development Goals (MDGs) were the first to fall short of the 2015 deadline, and now the Sustainable Development Goals (SDGs) are taking up where the MDGs left off. By 2030, these development goals seek to improve local economies as well as those of the entire world, with a focus on the most vulnerable regions (Chitando, 2020). Until recently, religions (the so-called global religions) have been marginalized in favor of western scientific frameworks as societies ascended the development ladder; African religions have experienced even a double dose of repudiation. This chapter aims to show how ritualization in indigenous religious systems does indeed promote growth and peace.

Like development, peacebuilding is another amorphous concept defined differently, depending on context (Nyawo, 2021). While most definitions restrict the scope of peacebuilding to post-conflict interventions, common to all is the agreement that it seeks to improve human security by ensuring that people are safe from harm and they have access to law and justice (Nyawo, 2021). It also strives to protect people from political decisions that may affect them, and that they would have access to better economic opportunities and better livelihoods (Khodary, 2016). Although there are many varying peacebuilding strategies and tactics, they all ultimately aim to make sure that people are protected from harm, have access to justice and the law, are involved in political decisions that affect them, have access to better economic opportunities, and lead better lives (Moghadam, 2005). The term "peacebuilding" was first used in the context of post-conflict rebuilding efforts in war-torn countries, but this chapter employs it widely to refer to religious actors who, through ritualization, maintain a country's stability and integrity.

This understanding of peacebuilding is in line with Khodary's definition that peacebuilding is a "range of measures targeted to reduce the risk of lapsing or relapsing into conflict by strengthening national capacities at all levels for conflict management and to lay the foundation for sustainable peace and development" (2016, p. 499). Maseno (2020, p. 96) confirms by stating that peacebuilding as a concept encompasses not only internationally led forms of intervention, but bottom-up and locally led approaches. Also, it is not only restricted to post-war processes, but its methods are relevant to preventative diplomacy and peace processes. Lederach (1997) believes that religious actors are key in peacebuilding because they are both mediators and advocates for peace, as they tend to focus on building relationships and community. In the words of Maseno (2020) religious personages active in peacebuilding focus on encouraging empowerment and human rights among their people (2020, p. 97).

A discussion on how traditional religion and development interact is crucial because, despite the fact that religion penetrates Africans' daily lives, the development narrative that emerged seemed to see no value in religion in terms of development (Gunda, 2020). It is worthwhile to investigate religion's role in peacebuilding once more because it is believed that religion has contributed to the world's socio-political problems.

Kagema (2015) comments on intra-state conflicts in his article "The Role of the African Traditional Religion in the Promotion of Justice, Reconciliation and Peace in Africa in the Twenty-first Century: A Kenyan Experience." He poses a pertinent question which shares sentiments with this chapter: "Why should we wait for someone from Europe, America or China to help us resolve our conflicts while in fact by our very nature we believe in living together in harmony?" (2015, p. 7). With Africans, their indigenous epistemology is based on the understanding that "we are all related—each aspect relates with the whole: the dynamics of realty are based on the relationships and experiences of interrelationships and interconnections" (Kanu, 2017, p. 33). Their worldview has the "complexion" of peace and togetherness, and as Mbiti (1975) has noted, rituals, festivals, and ceremonies are carried out to keep this heritage alive. The discussion that follows presents the Emaswati indigenous perspective of a closely integrated world, which ensures that a functional relationship exists between the living and the dead. Through ritual performances by religious specialists the nation is collectively cleansed from sin, broken relationships are restored, and then peace will prevail.

Considering the indigenous epistemology that the cosmos is one, to deal with conflicts, at any level, there is a need for the incorporation of traditional peace processes that ensure unity. Such peace processes do not only declare a person right and the other wrong, but what heals the wounds or hurts that have emanated from the conflict in question (Kanu, 2017). This chapter therefore demonstrates how the monarch who serves as both king and chief priest converses with the nation's ancestors and engages in national rites that are thought to preserve the nation's stability and prosperity. *Incwala* in particular, where the king is the main celebrant, is one traditional peace process that ensures good health, wellbeing, order, and freshness among Emaswati. Also, broken relationships at all levels will be mended through sacrifices, as it shall be shown later. From this understanding of a united universe that upholds peace, poverty, insecurity, unemployment, waywardness, communal clashes, religious crisis, and other mysterious and human-made misfortunes are considered to be the opposite or negation of peace (Murithi, 2008).

## Methodology

Data for this chapter were generated through library research, which is a pivotal methodology that explores in-depth resources. Published books, journal articles, government documents, unpublished books, online sources, archival materials, and regional dailies were some of the library sources that were consulted. As a result, the research is restricted to the secondary sources. The search for information was primarily led by the phrases "religion," "development," "peacebuilding," and "*Incwala* ritual." In order to summarize the conclusion on the impact that a frequently marginalized religion can have on SDG 16, the chapter also pulls from and combines thoughts on the interaction that exists between religion, development, and peacebuilding.

## Theoretical Considerations: African Communitarian Ethic

Laying core in the traditional peace processes which are represented by *Incwala* in this discussion is relationality of all that is in the universe; that is one cannot function without the other. African communitarian thinkers (Tempels, 1959; Mbiti, 1969; Menkiti, 1984; Matolino, 2014) refer to this relationality as African communitarian ethic that regulates behavior (Murove, 2012). Murove further observes that colonial anthropology regretfully trivialized the African communalism that was inherent in this African ethic, and strongly condemned it for impeding modernization. He picks up on Ubuntu as a post-colonial effort to revive lost African identity, which holds that in order for human beings to achieve ultimate wellbeing, we must depend on one another. Echoing previous African communitarian philosophers, he asserts, "[I]t is in the reality of our dependence and interdependence with each other that we attain the fullest of our humanness" (Murove, 2012, p. 37). In their definition of Ubuntu, which is similar to that of Murove, Samkange and Samkange (1980, p. 3) list the values of Ubuntu as kindness, peace, courtesy, consideration, and friendliness in the relationship between people, a code of behavior, an attitude to other people and to life. Since the African communitarian ethic places a strong focus on coexistence and harmony, it conceptually better informs a discussion on a ritual performed to bring about peace among members of the society.

For an African, being a community rules over all other facets of African philosophy. Worship and dances are communal activities that bind Africans together. Prior to the colonial era, property was held communally, and current efforts aim to bring that tradition back. Individualism is always viewed as a deviation because of this ingrained leaning toward the community. Tradition therefore plays a big role in reinforcing the communal ethic. To illustrate this point, Mutiso gives an example of a father telling his son that the word "why" is not a common word in the African communal ethic:

> [T]radition never gives an answer because it never asks the question. To it there is only one law in life and that is obedience. Tradition is sacred. Custom is above all. To question tradition is to commit sacrilege. If men do not respect tradition how can society stand?

According to Niekerk, in a world where everything is undergoing a process of rapid development and change, the serenity and security that a person enjoys in the group to which he or she belongs, which contributes to development, is of enormous importance. The collective connection can aid in controlling a person's tendency toward selfishness and preventing unchecked individual advancement at the expense of the group. Thus, advancement or development of a group in all facets of life also becomes communal. The concept of power comes in here, as power is always related to the peace and harmony of a group. The increase of power, including economic development, that threatens the harmony of the group, is regarded as sin. According to Tempels, there is a connection between the idea of power and positive group dynamics. But where sin abounds, everything would be struck sterile, nothing would grow in the soil, and the women would not be able to produce children due to a disruption of the group's harmonious equilibrium (p. 71).

Premised on this conceptual framework, the chapter illustrates a situation in which ritualized performances that foster peace and growth uphold the communal ethic, which is based on the relational worldview. Also, the *Incwala* performances, led by the king as the facilitator of peace and unifier of the nation every year end, are meant to collectively cleanse the nation from sins, which would affect their advancement in the coming year. As a result, in African indigenous thought patterns, development is fully defined by the centrality of people rather than just economic output.

## Conflict and Religion in Africa

A wave of modernist, secular societal transformation that made religion obsolete dominated development, practice, and debate beginning in the second part of the twentieth century (Tomalin, 2012). However, a new trend in global development discourse and practice has emerged that suggests a shift toward acknowledging the important role of religion in maintaining peace and resolving conflicts. The notion of including indigenous systems in conflict handling was then advocated for as a fundamental pillar in resolving African conflicts and problems by the African Union (AU) and the African Centre for the Construction Resolution of Disputes (ACCORD) (Namakula, 2022). Establishing effective mechanisms that suit a given environment for preventing new flare-ups are now taken as a better solution to control resurfacing of intra-conflicts in Africa (Kanu, 2017).

Faith-based initiatives or organizations are now used to channel larger amounts of development aid, and religion is increasingly seen as a human resource rather than a barrier to development (Tomalin et al., 2019, p. 2). As such many faith actors had been involved in development policy, initially by adopting and heralding the Millennium Development Goals (MDGs), and more recently through a commitment to join the global collaboration around achieving the new SDGs. The 193 UN member nations agreed to the 17 goals and 169 targets of the SDGs in 2015. They have taken the role of the MDGs that were in effect from 2000 to 2015 and are a component of the larger Agenda 2030, which reflects the goal that they should be accomplished by the year 2030 (Dodds et al., 2017). The MDGs were established unilaterally within the UN, in contrast to the SDGs, with little to no input from civil society. The SDGs, in contrast, were developed after extensive negotiations inside the UN and the largest civil society participation (Tomalin et al., 2019, p. 2).

Intra-state and internal conflicts prevalent in African countries provide evidence that despite the initiatives of the United Nations to forge peace in the globe, and also through roping in religion, the problem persists. The question is, why would religion, which ordinarily has to permeate all facets of life, seem to be less effective in conflict resolution and sustainability of peace? The answer lies in the approaches adopted to engender peace, that they are largely informed by values, resources, and institutions that have been developed by Eurocentric western tradition, broadly defined as the Judeo-Christian heritage. This chapter therefore argues for the adoption of indigenous cultural approaches to conflict resolution, prevention, and sustainability of peace as the alternative. This position is well articulated by Francis (2008, p. 7) when he observes:

> [I]ncorporating the insights and best practices of indigenous processes into official peace, can improve the efficacy of peacemaking. The term indigenous refers to that which is inherent to a given society, but also that which is innate and instinctive … when we allude to indigenous approaches to peace and conflict resolution, we are simultaneously referring to processes that are inherent in a given society following years of tradition, but also to those that are generated and systematically reproduced by such a society.

The incorporation of the indigenous practices to peacemaking that Francis advocates is best illustrated in the Eswatini context, where the *Incwala* ritual is performed to keep the nation together. It is no surprise that the global state of peace shows Eswatini to have a high level of peace, but this does not imply that there are no conflicts there. Although not to the same extent as other political environments regionally and internationally, it does encounter its own difficulties related to the plurality of perspectives. According to some political observers, the Emaswati's resistance to dramatic change is a result of their loyalty to their culture, which is upheld by their king in his function as the keeper of tradition. Culture and tradition continue to play a significant part in Eswatini society despite the changes brought about by the money economy, a high level of literacy, and basic education, which constantly improve living standards and change lifestyles (DOKUMEN, 2012). This reflects the peace and unity of Emaswati as one nation under a traditional leader, whose authority according to Pobee is a "double pivot," meaning that he is both the political head of the tribe or a monarch and the center of the ritual expression. A cursory glance on monarchs as custodians of culture and thus a symbol of peace and unity is what follows in this discussion.

## *Incwala* Ritual as an Enhancer of Peace and Development in Eswatini

As established earlier, Emaswati perceive the cosmos as a united whole; their approach to peace and development always entails both a physical and a spiritual dimension. Through rituals that link the people with their past, the present, and their future, they create and restore damaged relationship with the ancestors, families, and neighbors. Thus, when it comes to promotion of peace and development, or settling disputes among people, indigenous African communities have well-defined religious methodologies, whose custodians are religious personages. This submission is best illustrated in the peace processes of the *Incwala* ritual of Emaswati, carried out by the monarch in his capacity as the chief priest of the nation.[1] The underlying philosophy to the *Incwala* is similar to that of the *Igwebuike* among the Igbo motivated by Kanu (2017). He advocates for its incorporation into peace processes because it understands peace and conflict as encompassing a parameter that is beyond the physical to involve the spiritual and emotional dimensions. For Kanu (2017, p. 37), this philosophy does not understand conflict merely as a fracas between two persons, or two groups; it rather understands conflict as a fracas touching on the harmony of reality.

Eswatini has its cultural norms and values embedded in its system of beliefs. Within their culture are rich ritualistic ceremonies like the *Incwala*. This is the main ritual of kingship in the Kingdom that the nation participates in during the summer solstice. It signals the end of the old and the beginning of a new year, when the first fruits of the new harvest may be eaten. *Incwala* is also important to Emaswati because it signals the continued health and prosperity of the king and his people. It is from traditions such as *Incwala* ceremony and the institutionalized monarchy that the monarch derives his legitimacy to rule. Most of the Swati population considers the king to be the benevolent father of the nation, and they refer to this ritual where the king is main actor as "prayer for the nation."

Before this ceremony can be performed, considerable organizational and preparatory activities must be undertaken during a three-week period each

---

[1] I also discuss the *Incwala* ritual in a chapter titled "Climate Crisis: Mitigation and Control Through Emaswati Indigenous Knowledge" (Nyawo, 2022). Here, *Incwala* is presented not as a facilitator and enhancer of peace and development but a climate ritual that enables traditional communities to respond to climate changes, hence the proposal on integration of indigenous knowledge and scientific interventions for the establishment of a creative multipronged climate change response.

year. For example, water and sacred plants are collected at distant points to strengthen and purify the king. Thereafter, the oldest warrior regiment opens the *Incwala*. Sacred songs that are concerned with the important events of kingship (a king's marriage to his main ritual wife, the return of ancestral cattle from the royal grave, and the burial of kings) as well as dances are performed. Themes of fertility and potency predominate. Celebrants are adorned in striking clothing, including feathers of special birds and skins of wild animals. Kuper (1947) maintains that the *Incwala* symbolizes the peace unity of the state and attempts to reinforce it.

One aspect of this rite, which unites the nation and entices the blessings of national ancestors, is the king savoring the first of the season's bounty. Additionally, it elevates the kingship. Only on this occasion are certain sacred melodies sung, which promote the nation's peace and prosperity. Ndlovu (2011, p. 85) adds that performance of rituals like *Incwala* revolves around the beliefs in the existence of a universal life force that is inherited in living, non-living, and spiritual entities in varying degrees. It is believed that this mysterious power can be controlled and manipulated by religious specialists for various purposes including enhancement of good health, long life, good fortune, and the common good, on the one hand, and the pursuit of malevolent and anti-social acts, on the other hand (Amenga-Etego, 2011, p. 626). The *Incwala* ceremony, as the apex and axis of Swazi Traditional Religion, is well articulated by Kasenene when he asserts:

> Besides sacrificing to the ancestors and tasting of the first fruits of the nation, the King strengthens the nation and blesses the people. During this ritual, the King dedicates the nation to national ancestors who in turn bless it. This yearly ceremony binds the nation and renews its collective strength. (Kasenene, 1993, p. 25)

Thus, the ritual does not only symbolize and promote the unity of the Swati people but also link them with their ancestors.

The King of Emaswati who doubles as the political leader and religious head of the nation is the main celebrant in the *Incwala* ritual, in his capacity as the king-priest (Nyawo, 2004). He is accompanied by other religious personages like water priests, diviners, and medicine men; hence he is described in super-human terms like "*umlimo longatsetsi emanga*" (the mouth that never lies). Vilakazi makes this observation about the deification of religious leaders:

> In historical times, anyone who was to be regarded and treated as higher than mere mortal, e.g. bishop, a pope, a king, a queen etc …, was treated/anointed with magical herbal mixtures which gave magical powers to that person, and also added powers of divine forces to the person. This is the process of deification, which magically transformed the person installed. (2013, p. 8)

According to the communitarian ethic, advancement or development of a group in all facets of life becomes a collective affair. What threatens peace of the group is sin, which encompasses immoral acts, ritual mistakes, and breach of covenant and violation of taboos. Rituals are therefore performed by the religious personage with magical powers to purge the entire group from sin. Failing which society will suffer social ills like constant misfortunes, incurable illnesses, disputes, and customary penury. Sins are forgiven through purification, confession, and reparation and sacrifice. The rituals are therefore performed to make the people acceptable to the deity, divinities, and spirits, and eventually escape the punishment attached to sin. Bringing this point to context, Emaswati share these sentiments; sin is perceived as a stain which can be washed off or cast off, respectively. The disappearance of sin brings new life just as the rejuvenated man takes on a clean white cloth and casts off the old one (Kuper, 1975). The king as the chief priest sends off water priests to the Red Sea in Mozambique and to where all the country's tributaries meet, so as to fetch water. The water fetched from the tributaries symbolize the filth of the whole nation that needs to be cleansed before it could venture into the New Year, while the medicated holy water from the sea will cleanse the nation from all the sins Emaswati have committed during the course of the year (Gamedze, 1980, p. 31). These ritualized performances stand for the renewal of the communitarian ethic, as social divisions are mended and broken relations are restored. The success of the ritual makes Emaswati believe that the New Year comes with freedoms from poverty, insecurity, unemployment, waywardness, communal clashes, religious crisis, and other mysterious and human-made misfortunes.

The king as the chief priest offers sacrifices to the national ancestors of sacred pitch-black bulls and oxen. Among the ritual black oxen is a sacred ox known as *incwambo* (a term applied to a muscle near the testicles) which is driven into the sanctuary by the "pure" youth. The *incwambo* is observed for a year and it holds a unique position in the royal herd. It must not be beaten, battered, or used for any mundane task, until it is sacrificed (1947). During the *Incwala* the king-priest, embodying the sins of the nation, sits on the king-priest washes with the sacred water earlier fetched by the water priests from the sea. It symbolizes the cleansing of the entire nation from all sins committed as the year progressed. The *incwambo* is then released into the wilderness and the original belief is that the sins of the past year are removed from the entire ration. Another ritual cow is offered during the final purification known as *kushisa lukhuni* (burning the wood). During this purification rite all the objects used throughout the *Incwala* ceremony are burnt in the fire meaning that all the "filth of the king priest and all his people now lies here on the fire" (Kuper, 1986). Also, as the king-priest bathes with the sacred water and the water drops down, rain that will quench the fire will fall; hence his title that he is the rainmaker (Kuper, 1963). The people who witness the event speak of the fire as purification and an offering to the ancestors, who must acknowledge it with rain (Kuper, 1947). The king then dresses in his normal, *Incwala* clothing and he joins his subjects as they sing and dance in jubilation that the nation will experience a peaceful and successful year.

In the Swazi religio-political context the ceremony of *Incwala* is a continuation of the ritual of deification of the monarchy, so that he remains separated and almost magical (Mzizi, 1995). The majority of Emaswati continue to practice these rituals because of their ability to keep society cohesive. It has long been believed that the king possesses magical abilities that keep the nation peaceful and stable. He must spend the entire month of December in solitude, where herbs and animal blood are collected, traditional national songs are sung, and priests of Zionist churches offer prayers to the Supreme Being in an effort to convince them to grant him magical abilities and strength (Ndlovu, 2011). What then follows after the annual celebration of the *Incwala* is good health, low infant mortality rate, long life, prosperity, freedom from disease and stress, security, harmonious relations among humans, including with the created order, and others (Mzizi 2004). This is what development is all about in indigenous thought.

## Conclusion

The MDGs are said to have accomplished less because they were perceived by many as a top-down Global North to Global South exercise, whereas the SDGs apply equally and contain goals and targets for countries of the Global North and South (Haustein & Tomalin, 2017). The SDGs have a changed approach in that it seeks to ensure a more grassroots and locally owned type of development based on the recognition that "local people" are better placed to both understand and respond to development challenges. Tomalin adds that since local societies mostly comprise faith communities, their engagement and the role they play become even more critical to the discussion on sustainable development. In the consultation process as well as the implementation phase, there has been a coordinated effort from within the UN to engage with civil society actors, including those who are faith based (2019, p. 4). The chapter therefore hypothesizes that Goal Number 16 on peace cannot succeed, especially in traditional societies, without the engagement of indigenous religious systems.

The nation is peaceful because of the Emaswati belief system, which is based on an African communitarian ethic that requires everyone to live in harmony. Development is all about living well, having peaceful relationships with other people, the dead, and the created order. Sustainable development is brought about by the harmony and peace that are maintained by yearly ritualized acts by the king, who serves as the father figure. One can fairly conclude that indigenous spirituality aids in development if one uses the notion of development, which according to African thought patterns is broader than the economic development filtered by western ideas. The discussion in this chapter confirms the insights of scholars who define development in much broad sense. Amartya Sen (1999), in particular, perceives development in terms of freedoms.

He describes development as an integrated process of expansion of substantive freedoms or the deliberate process of removing obstacles and unfreedoms. Cited by Gunda (2020), he asserts, "[A]mong the most important of these freedoms are freedom from famine and malnutrition, freedom from poverty, access to health care and freedom from premature mortality." This understanding of development places human beings at the center of development, and development is meaningless unless it improves the livelihoods of citizens in a particular community or society, as concluded by Gunda (2020). While the Enlightenment narrative popularizes that "nothing good can come out of Nazareth," indigenous religion does contribute to peacebuilding; thus peace, development, and religion become an intertwined web.

## References

Amenga-Etego, R. M. (2011). *Mending the Broken Pieces: Indigenous Religion and Sustainable Rural Development in Northern Ghana*. Africa World Press.

Annett, A., Sachs, J., Vendley, W., & Sorondo, S. (2017). A Multi-Religious Consensus on the Ethics of Sustainable Development: Reflections of the Ethics in Action Initiative, *G 20 Insights*. https://www.g20-insights.org/wp-content/uploads/2017/05/A--Multi-ReligiousConsensus-on-the-Ethics-of-Sustainable-Development-Reflections-of-the-Ethics-inAction-Initiative.pdf

Bediako, K. (1992). *Theology and Identity: The Impact of Culture upon Christian Thought in the Second Century and in Modern Africa*. Regnum.

Bediako, K. (2001). Scripture as the Hermeneutic of Culture and Tradition. *Journal of Christian Thought*, 4(1), 2–11.

Chimuka, T. A. (2020). Religion and Development in Sub-Saharan Africa Understanding the Challenges and Prospects. In E. Chitando, M. R. Gunda, & L. Togarasei (Eds.), *Religion and Development in Africa Volume 25 of Bible in Africa Studies* (pp. 75–88). University of Bamberg Press.

Chitando, E. (2020). The Bible as a Resource for Development in Africa: Ten Considerations for Liberating Readings. In E. Chitando, M. R. Gunda, & L. Togarasei (Eds.), *Religion and Development in Africa Volume 25 of Bible in Africa Studies* (pp. 401–417). University of Bamberg Press.

Dauda, B. (2017). African Humanism and Ethics: The Cases of Ubuntu and Omoluwabi. In A. Afolayan & T. Falola (Eds.), *The Palgrave handbook of African philosophy* (pp. 475–491). Palgrave Macmillan.

Deneulin, S., & Bano, M. (2009). Religion in Development: Rewriting the Secular Script. *11*(4). Retrieved November 12, 2022. https://doi.org/10.1177/146499341001100408

Dodds, F., David, D., & Jimena, L. Roesch. (2017). *Negotiating the Sustainable Development Goals*. Routledge. Retrieved December 16, 2022.

DOKUMEN. (2012). Integrating Africa: Decolonization's Legacies, Sovereignty and the Africa Union. Retrieved December 18, 2022, from DOKUMEN.PUB https://dokumen.pub

Francis, D. J. (Ed.). (2008). *Peace and Conflict in Africa*. Zed Books.

Gamedze, A. B. (1980, October 23). *Somhloloism—Its Place in Political Science*. BOLESWA Conference, University of Swaziland, Kwaluseni.

Gunda, M. R. (2020). Rethinking Development in Africa and the Role of Religion. In E. Chitando, M. R. Gunda, & L. Togarasei (Eds.), *Religion and Development, in Africa Volume 25 of Bible in Africa Studies* (pp. 37–57). University of Bamberg Press.

Haustein, J., & Tomalin, E. (2017). Religion and Development in Africa and Asia. In P. Amakasu Raposo, D. Arase, & S. Cornelissen (Eds.), *Routledge Handbook of Africa–Asia Relations*. Routledge.

Kagema, D. N. (2015). The Role of the African Traditional Religion in the Promotion of Justice, Reconciliation and Peace in Africa in the Twenty-first Century: A Kenyan Experience. *International Journal of African and Asian Studies, 15*, 1–9.

Kanu, I. (2017). Igwebuike as an Igbo-African Modality of Peace and Conflict Resolution. *Journal of African Traditional Religion and Philosophy (JATREP), 1*(1), 31–40.

Kanu, I. K., & Ndubisi, E. J. (2020, June 10th–11th). *Religion and Peace Building in Africa*. Proceedings of the International Conference of the Association for the Promotion of African Studies on African Ideologies, Human Security and Peace Building, Maryland, APAS.

Kasenene, P. (1993). *Religion in Swaziland*. Skotaville.

Khodary, Y. M. (2016). Women and Peace-Building in Iraq. *Peace Review, 28*(4), 499–507. https://doi.org/10.1080/10402659.2016.1237151

Kuper, H. (1947). *An African Aristocracy*. Oxford University Press.

Kuper, H. (1963). *The Swazi: A South African Kingdom*. Holt, Rinehart and Winston.

Kuper, H. (1975). The Supernatural. In A. B. T. Byaruhanga-Akiiki (Ed.), *Religion in Swaziland* (Vol. 1, pp. 53–72). BOLESWA, Department of Religious Studies.

Kuper, H. (1986). *The Swazi: A South African Kingdom*. Halt Rinehart and Winston.

Lederach, J. P. (1997). *Building Peace: Sustainable Reconciliation in Divided Societies*. United States Institute of Peace Press.

Marshall, K. (2001). Development and Religion: A Different Lens on Development Debates. *Peabody Journal of Education, 76*(3/4), 339–375.

Maseno, L. (2020). Gender in Religion and Development Research. In E. Chitando, M. R. Gunda, & L. Togarasei (Eds.), *Religion and Development in Africa, Volume 25 of Bible in Africa Studies* (pp. 89–102). University of Bamberg Press.

Matolino, B. (2014). *Personhood in African Philosophy*. Cluster Publications.

Mawere, M. (2010). Indigenous Knowledge Systems' (IKSs) Potential for Establishing a Moral, Virtuous Society: Lessons from Selected IKSs in Zimbabwe and Mozambique. *Journal of Sustainable Development in Africa, 12*(7), 209–221.

Mawere, M., & Kadenge, M. (2010). Zvierwa as African Indigenous Knowledge Systems: Epistemological and Ethical Implications of Selected Shona Taboos. *INDILINGA-African Journal of Indigenous Knowledge Systems, 9*(1), 244–257.

Mbiti, J. S. (1969). *African Religions and Philosophy*. Heinemann.

Mbiti, J. S. (1975). *Introduction to African Religion* (2nd ed.). East African Publishers.

Menkiti, I. A. (1984). Person and Community in African Traditional Thought. In R. A. Wright (Ed.), *African Philosophy: An Introduction* (pp. 171–181). University Press of America.

Moghadam, V. M. (2005). Peacebuilding and Reconstruction with Women: Reflections on Afghanistan. *Iraq and Palestine. Development, 48*(3), 63–72.

Murithi, T. (2008). African Indigenous and Endogenous Approaches to Peace and Conflict Resolution. In D. J. Francis (Ed.), *Peace and Conflict in Africa*. Zed Books.

Murove, M. F. (2012). Ubuntu. *Diogenes, 59*(3-4), 36–47. https://doi.org/10.1177/0392192113493737. http://www.sagepub.com/content/59/3-4/36

Mzizi, J. B. (1995). *Voices of the Voiceless: Towards a Theology of Liberation for Post-Colonial Swaziland*. [Unpublished doctoral thesis]. Vanderbilt University.

Mzizi, J. B. (2003). Church-state Tensions in the Kingdom of Swaziland: Honest Dishonesty or Dishonest Honesty? *BOLESWA Journal of Occasional Papers in Theology and Religion*, 1(10), 7–22.

Mzizi, J. B. (2004). The Dominance of the Swazi Monarchy and Moral Dynamic of Democratisation of the Swazi State. *Journal of Africa Elections*, 3, 94–119.

Nader, L. (1986). Conflict: Anthropological Aspects. In D. Sills (Ed.), *International Encyclopedia of Social Science* (pp. 34–45). The Free Press.

Namakula, E. B. (2022). Rethinking United Nations Peacekeeping Responses to Resource Wars and Armed Conflicts in Africa: Integrating African Indigenous Knowledge Systems. *Journal of Aggression, Conflict and Peace Research*, 14(4), 320–333. https://doi.org/10.1108/JACPR-01-2022-0671

Ndlovu, H. L. (2011). Swazi Religion and the Environment: The Case of the NCWALA. *BOLESWA. Journal of Theology, Religion and Philosophy*, 3(3), 83–99.

Ndlovu, L., & Svodziwa, M. (2017). The Role Of Indigenous Knowledge Systems in Peace Building: A Case of Umguza District, Zimbabwe. *International Journal of Politics and Good. Governance*, VIII(8.1), 1–16.

Nyawo, S. (2004). *The Early Encounter between Swaziland the Western Missionaries: The Establishment of the Evangelical Church in Swaziland, 1982–1950*. [Unpublished MA thesis], University of Natal.

Nyawo, S. (2017). Are Prayers a Panacea for Climate Uncertainties?: An African Traditional Perspective from Swaziland. *The Ecumenical Review*, 69(3), 362–374. https://doi.org/10.1111/erev.12299

Nyawo, S. (2020). Religion and Development in Swaziland1 Advances and Reversals in the Case of Religious Education. In E. Chitando, M. R. Gunda, & L. Togarasei (Eds.), *Religion and Development in Africa Volume 25 of Bible in Africa Studies* (pp. 305–318). University of Bamberg Press.

Nyawo, S. (2021). 'Swimming against the Current': Queen Labotsibeni, the Epitome of Effective Peacebuilding in Eswatini. In A. Chitando (Ed.), *Women and Peacebuilding in Africa* (pp. 199–212). Routledge.

Nyawo, S. (2022). The Climate Crisis: Mitigation and Control through Emaswati Indigenous Knowledge. In E. Chitando, E. M. Conradie, & S. M. Kilonzo (Eds.), *African Perspectives on Religion and Climate Change* (pp. 34–48). Routledge.

Samkenge, S., & Samkenye, T. (1980). *Hunhuism or Ubuntuism: A Zimbabwe Indigenous Political Philosophy*. Printopar.

Sen, A. (1999). *Development as Freedom*. Alfred A. Knopf.

Shah, S. T. (2013). In God's Name: Politics, Religion, and Economic Development. Presented at the Religious Freedom Center (pp. 1–26). Georgetown University. http://www.sivicouncil.org/history.htm

Speckman, M. (2016). Development, the Bible and the Role of the African Church. In I. A. Phiri et al. (Eds.), *Anthology of African Christianity* (pp. 1085–1091). Regnum Books International.

Szirmai, A. (2005). Developing Countries and the Concept of Development. In A. Szirmai (Ed.), *The Dynamics of Socio-Economic Development: An Introduction*. Cambridge University Press. https://doi.org/10.1017/CBO9780511817342

Tempels, P. (1959). *Bantu Philosophy*. Presence Africaine.

Thorpe, S. A. (1992). *Primal Religions Worldwide: An Introductory, Descriptive Review*. A Project of the Institute for Theological Research, Pretoria, University of South Africa.

Tomalin, E. (2012). Thinking about Faith-Based Organisations in Development: Where Have We Got to and What Next? *Development in Practice, 22*(5–6), 689–703.

Tomalin, E., et al. (2019). Religion and the Sustainable Development Goals. *Review of Faith & International Affairs, 17*(2), 102–118. https://doi.org/10.1080/15570274.2019.1608664

Tremmel, W. C. (1983). *Religion: What Is It?* (2nd ed.). Holt, Rinehart and Winston.

Turner, H. (1977). The Primal Religions of the World and their Study. In V. C. Hayes (Ed.), *Australian Essays in World Religions* (pp. 27–48). Bedford Park.

Vilakazi, H. (2013). *Religion and Historical Change*. Paper presented at the Peter Storey Lecture at Seth Mokitini Methodist Seminary, Pietermaritzburg.

PART III

# Diverse Religions in Africa, Peacebuilding and Development

CHAPTER 18

# The Role of Traditional Authorities in the Promotion of Electoral Justice and Peacebuilding in Ghana

*Christopher Appiah-Thompson and Jim Jose*

## Introduction

Disputed election outcomes and perceptions of electoral injustices can lead to political instability. This has consequences for the peaceful building of robust democratic institutions of good governance. In turn such consequences can negatively impair strategies for sustainable development because conflicts and violence often result in the "loss of lives, burning of houses, farmlands, farms, as well as property, including state assets. Monies meant for development, such as building of schools, roads, etc., are rather spent on peacekeeping" (Amoakohene, 2017, p. 29). Hence resolving disputed elections in a peaceful way is of some importance in a context where a country is aiming to realise just and accountable political institutions as per United Nations Sustainable Development Goal 16—Peace, Justice and Strong Institutions (hereafter UN SDG 16). While much has been written about the role of formal institutions in managing elections and disputed outcomes, very little attention has been paid to the role of traditional authorities such as chiefs and religious leaders.

C. Appiah-Thompson (✉)
Newcastle Business School, University of Newcastle, Newcastle, NSW, Australia
e-mail: christopher.appiahthompson@uon.edu.au

J. Jose
Newcastle Business School, University of Newcastle, Newcastle, NSW, Australia
e-mail: Jim.Jose@newcastle.edu.au

© The Author(s), under exclusive license to Springer Nature Switzerland AG 2023
S. M. Kilonzo et al. (eds.), *The Palgrave Handbook of Religion, Peacebuilding, and Development in Africa*,
https://doi.org/10.1007/978-3-031-36829-5_18

Traditional African religious institutions (including traditional authorities such as chiefs) constitute one major category of non-state actors whose diplomatic activities can effectively contribute to conflict prevention and peacebuilding in fragile African democracies. There is a strong link between conflict management (i.e., good governance) and (sustainable) development, on the one hand, and religion in Africa, on the other. Even though sustainable and effective socio-economic development is the result of constructive politics and responsive governance, this presupposes the mediating role of both traditional and modern religious institutions because religion is woven into every aspect of citizens' lives.

Our chapter examines the role of traditional authorities in mediating Ghana's disputed 1992 presidential election. This was a transitional election in the sense that it was the first democratic election following the democratisation of the then authoritarian-military regime. There was considerable "bitter" mistrust between the government and the opposition parties concerning the nature of the administration of the 1992 presidential election. There were allegations of manipulation of the electoral rules and rigging of the vote during elections that led to violent protests. The formal electoral institutions struggled to cope with the protests, in part because their efforts were also circumscribed to some extent by the legacy of a non-democratic past and authoritarian political actors still active in the new democratic setting (see, e.g., Agyeman-Dua, 2008; Gyimah-Boadi, 1994; Rothchild, 1995). It was in this context that the traditional authorities proved influential in helping to resolve a seemingly intractable electoral dispute.

Our principal focus is with how the traditional authorities contributed to the successful mediation of the dispute over the electoral outcomes; though we do consider how the dominant religious values and norms are woven into Ghanaian understandings because our argument recognises that the value of the traditional authorities as mediators is informed by and dependent upon their role in upholding traditional religious norms and values. For example, the concept of "peace" in African religious philosophy embodies not only the absence of violence but also the protection of the general welfare of a community. The evidence for our argument will be drawn from an analysis of the indigenous conflict resolution strategies of the traditional leaders and the reactions of the populace towards them. The focus here is on the shared cultural understandings and expressions of "peace" and "tolerance" through their religious symbols, proverbs and myths that are found among the Ghanaian populace. In this way we demonstrate the importance of religious values in realising just and accountable political institutions as per UN SDG 16.

Scholars have recognised that there is a need for comparative historical analyses to provide a nuanced examination of the variations in the scope and intensity of electoral violence both within and across specific African states (Laakso, 2019; Straus & Taylor, 2012). Our discussion of the role of traditional authorities in assisting with resolution of electoral disputes contributes to this recognition. It differs from studies like Pindiga et al. (2020) and Mboh (2021), for example, which concentrated primarily on the self-reporting of traditional leaders via survey questionnaires and interviews. Rather, our approach is to combine the insights of both formal institutional and politico-cultural explanations using qualitative-interpretive methods of process tracing and content analysis of the available historical documents such as newspapers, periodicals and international election observer reports. These constitute the primary empirical sources. Our analysis builds on the conventional wisdom of institutional theories by arguing for the importance of powerful traditional leaders to mediate crises like post-electoral disputes.

Our aim is to illuminate how the contribution of traditional authorities and cultural norms affected the mechanical conversion of electoral rules into non-violent, acceptable electoral outcomes. The underlying logic here is that understanding the diverse socio-cultural conditions for building democratic institutions and practices in Africa is very important for contributing to our understandings of democracy. Such understandings are crucial if African democracies are to bring to fruition efforts to realise justice and produce effective, accountable and inclusive institutions as per the UN SDG 16.

## Accounting for Electoral Conflicts and Violence in Africa

The extant literature on disputed elections, electoral violence and democratisation in Africa points to the diverse roles played by the major stakeholders such as political actors and citizens in disputing electoral outcomes. Examples of these studies include Norris et al.'s (2015) conceptualisation of the conditions responsible for opposition parties to challenge "the legitimacy of electoral actors, procedures, or outcomes" (2015, p. 2). Kuhn examined the social conditions that make it attractive for political actors to resort to pre-electoral violence during elections by exploring "the degree to which ethnicity determines vote choice associated with pre-electoral violence", concluding that "there is a positive relationship between ethnic voting and pre-electoral violence" (Kuhn, 2015, p. 93). Similarly, Bekoe and Burchard (2019) explored the strategic uses of electoral violence by African politicians in electoral and political competition to secure favourable electoral results in their electoral interests.

Laakso (2019) looked at the broader trends of electoral violence employing statistical datasets and argued that history, patrimonialism, political economy and institutions are the primary and secondary causes of electoral violence in Africa. Several examples were identified as scenarios whereby election results were disputed followed by small- or large-scale electoral violence and instability, which derailed the democratisation process. In measuring the intensity and scope of electoral violence, Burchard estimated that more than 50% of African elections held since the 1990s are characterised by some electoral dispute and violence (Burchard, 2015, pp. 2–3). Moreover, about 20% of the elections conducted between 1990 and 2008 resulted in "intense and destabilizing violence" (Laakso, 2019, p. 4; Straus & Taylor, 2012). Updated data for the years between 2004 and 2013 revealed a substantial increase in occurrences of intense electoral violence in Sub-Saharan African elections (Burchard, 2015, pp. 2–3). It is important to keep this in perspective because "most elections in Africa—80 percent, in fact—have not been as intensely violent as the ones in Nigeria (1992, 1993, 2003, 2007), Kenya (1992, 1997, 2007), Zimbabwe (1990, 2000, 2002, 2008) and Cote d' Ivoire (1990, 1995, 2000)" (Bekoe, 2012, p. 3; Straus & Taylor, 2012).

On the nature of electoral violence, Burchard distinguished pre-electoral violence from post-electoral violence, arguing that "strategic pre-election violence" constituted the efforts of electoral and political actors to manipulate an electoral outcome before Election Day through coercive acts calculated to influence "the behaviour of candidates and voters as part of the (electoral) process" (Burchard, 2015, p. 64). In contrast, "[s]trategic post-election violence" aimed "to change an electoral outcome after the fact through extra-judicial means, or those not previously agreed upon by political actors" (Burchard, 2015, p. 64). Moreover, post-electoral violence can also occur incidentally, often triggered by the perception of actual or imagined manipulation of the electoral institutions, process and outcomes (Burchard, 2015, pp. 12–13). As a result, in terms of "intensity" post-electoral violence can occur on a "smaller scale" in the form of "pockets of electoral violence, where violence is restricted to certain regions or areas" (Bekoe, 2012, p. 8) in a particular country. It may occur on a "larger scale" in the form of protests or violent riots over an electoral result where counter repression and violent suppression from the state security agencies are present. In all, post-electoral violence constitutes an enormous obstruction to a country's democratisation process and the legitimacy of its leaders (Bekoe, 2012, p. 4).

Despite the above research findings' attempts to describe the "scope, nature and patterns of electoral violence", none have been able to grasp fully "the (nuances, variations and) complexity of these (disputed) elections" (Laakso, 2019, p. 6). One important area for understanding and explaining the dynamics of electoral governance in Africa, particularly electoral justice that has been glossed over in the literature, is the role of the informal institutional strategies for resolving electoral disputes, often referred to as "alternative or traditional dispute resolution mechanisms" (Staino, 2011, p. 187). However, there are differential patterns of constitutional recognition and legitimisation of the mediation role of traditional authorities in the management of electoral disputes based on indigenous methods of conflict transformation in African states (Mboh, 2021; Momoh, 2021; Pindiga et al., 2020). This represents a major limitation of the neoliberal peace agenda of some international and national stakeholders in their selective disregard of "indigenous and endogenous" (Murithi, 2008, p. 16) strategies for peace-making such as reconciliation and restorative justice. These strategies are considered "central to peacebuilding and sustainable human development" (Mahamat, 2019, p. iv) in African states. Such strategies also align with the goals of the African Union (AU) Transitional

Justice Policy, which seeks to promote effective conflict resolution strategies based on shared African values and traditional justice principles and norms (AU, 2019, p. 4).

Much of the relevant scholarship has focused on the convergence or divergence of African politico-religious structures and customary norms with the imposed colonial and post-colonial conflict resolution institutions (such as the Judiciary and the electoral institutions) (Owusu, 2012). In this vein, the debates have been concerned with the colonial and post-colonial periods and the nature of the relationship that existed between the traditional authorities and the modern political institutions imposed during colonisation. The main lines of contention were on the relevance of these traditional authorities for the socio-economic and political development of the post-colonial African states. Particularly, it was assumed that traditional political institutions and the modern state structures operated under different logics of sovereignty, legitimacy and authority (Ray, 1994). There was little agreement on the ways the existing traditional authorities could complement the post-colonial political institutions in nation-building, socio-economic and political development (see also the AU, 2019). In turn this led to various degrees of scepticism about the role of traditional political institutions and cultural values in the transformation and developmental efforts of the modern African state. Traditional authorities were dismissed as essentially "undemocratic, divisive and costly"; thus, it was felt that there was a need to abolish them (see the ECA Report on African Traditional Institutions of Governance, 2007, p. 10 as cited in Peter, 2014, p. 140). Indeed, some African states such as Kenya and Tanzania went to great lengths to abolish their traditional political institutions, either through the efforts of missionaries or colonial powers or by the immediate post-colonial African leaders.

Another strand of literature contends that traditional political institutions and values are essential ingredients for the socio-economic and political transformation of the post-colonial African state since they constitute the major pillars in the political culture, history and governance systems of Africa (Peter, 2014, p. 140). Indeed, in most of the countries occupying the "vast areas of Western, Central, Eastern, and Southern Africa, traditional political (and religious) institutions still exist and participate in public affairs at the local, regional and state levels, either separately or as members of (civil) administrations" (Skalnik, 1994, p. 2). Traditional authorities such as the chief priests of the traditional religious belief systems take decisions regarding peace and the realisation of conflict resolution-based principles of reconciliation, consensus-building and tolerance aimed at establishing the basis for peaceful coexistence. These values and norms are expressed in religious myths, symbols and proverbial wisdom and constitute the primary tools of negotiation when mediating conflictual situations (Appiah-Thompson, 2020b; Appiah-Thompson et al., 2022). In this context, the myths, symbols, proverbs and their metaphysical assumptions manifest the deepest feelings in the minds of people which enable traditional authorities to serve as mediators to "empathize with the forces on both sides of the conflict and to dynamically interact with the spiritual language of frustration and anger that leads to violence" (Gopin, 2000, p. 14). The sacred basis of the authority of traditional leaders requires them to be impartial and fair in their conflict resolution decisions in reconciling aggrieved parties and restoring harmonious relations in the society (Opoku, 2011, p. 426. Also Momoh, 2021). The establishment of a peaceful political climate constitutes the precondition for sustainable socio-economic, political, cultural, spiritual, physical and human development of any progressive society as is recognised in the UN Sustainable Development Goals (especially SDG 16.3, 16.6 and 16.7).

## The Values, Norms and Precepts of Traditional Authorities

Ghana's 1992 Constitution empowers the traditional authorities through the "National and Regional Houses of Chiefs to have a corresponding responsibility to be more pro-active in dealing with potential tensions and disputes before they lead to breaches of the peace and damage to lives and property" (Annan, 1994, p. 20). As such, traditional authorities are formally recognised as the custodians of culture with a complementary role in democratic governance and development. To fully appreciate the "true range" of these (positive) religious and political values that influence the behaviour of Ghanaians towards conflictual situations there is a need to recognise the reality of some of the (positive) attitudes and values that the Ghanaian populace bring to the practice of democracy. These values have their roots in the pre-colonial period—their customary institutions such as Chieftaincy "are the survivors from that period, even if they are much changed" (Ray, 2003, p. 15). These values and attitudes are expressed in traditional oral-literary devices such as religious myths, symbols and proverbs. The mysteries of peace and violence as well as "life and death have been the themes for poetry, songs, proverbs, art and festivals" (Opoku, 1978, p. 13) in African societies. In what follows, we draw on material already published by Appiah-Thompson appearing respectively in a journal article (2020a), a working paper (2020b) and a doctoral dissertation (2021a).

Proverbs, wise sayings and cultural idioms provide powerful means for encouraging all the parties to a dispute (including their supporters) to share and understand the wisdom contained therein. For example, a proverb of the Akan people of Ghana advises that "conflicts are resolved best with the tongue and not with an axe" (Opoku, 2005, p. 14). This maxim emphasises "peaceful rather than forceful or violent means for promoting social harmony and peace" (Opoku, 2011, p. 426). Given this precept, it can be predicted that the rational behaviour of a well-cultured Ghanaian is to "veer away, as far as possible, from such activist political manifestations such as demonstrations and civil disorder" (Ansah-Koi, 1993, p. 67). Embedded within this understanding is the principle that every human dispute and violent action originate from the mind, as in the maxim *onipa nneyea nyinaa, akese o, nketewa o, efi ne yam. (n'adwenem)* ("whatever a man does is first conceived in the mind" or "all human actions come from the mind") (Akrofi, 1958, p. 7). Fundamental to this maxim are the values favouring stability and harmony (Atiemo, 2013, p. 120) as the basis for a well-ordered and peaceful polity (Gyekye, 2013, p. 141). Often these religious sayings and proverbs "succeed in achieving their effects quite often with little or no reason", yet quite frequently they "enable and persuade people" to refrain from violence and to peacefully "participate, to collaborate, and to see reason with each other and act together" (Eze, 1997, p. 317). More importantly, the ability of the chiefs and elders to invoke the supreme judgement and punishment of God (*onyame*) and the spirits of the ancestors (*nananom mu sunsum*) during situations of tension makes it imperative for the conflicting parties to accept the solutions proposed by the elders (Gebrewold, 2011, p. 434).

In the African worldview, political activity, religion and culture are part of a "seamless whole and no part of it could stand on its own", which means that "African traditional religion is inextricably linked to the culture of the African people", an integral part of daily living (Opoku, 2006, p. 537; Busia, 1968). The "Supreme Being, regarded as the source and giver of peace and the origin of the harmonious order and equilibrium of the universe, [.] is each person's responsibility to maintain by his or her life in the community" (Opoku, 2011, p. 418). In this context, religion needs to be understood as the source of the ideology in myths, sayings and proverbs that are applied to peace, violence and political development in the African society. The belief is that peace will prevail only "if there is justice, and justice is what ('*Nyame*' the Akan word for God) decide it to be" (Sarpong, 1989, p. 354). For example, we can see this expressed in the Akan proverb, "if you trample on another person's property in looking for your own, you will never find your own" (Opoku, 1975, p. 26).

This resonates with the concept of the "sustainable development" that can readily be found in the traditional religious belief systems of the Akan people of Ghana in which futuristic values serve to preserve the natural environment as well as all other visible and invisible cultural heritage for the sake of future generations. For instance, the *adinkra* symbols such as *asaase ye duru* ("the earth is heavily resourced") and *Sankofa* ("go back and take it") show the "need to revere the earth as we benefit from its abundant resources, and the need to constantly look back at the effects of our actions as we move forward, respectively" (Lettau et al., 2023, p. 4). Other scholars point out that in some West-African societies (including Ghana), some primary economic activities such as fishing and farming are regulated by religious precepts to "ensure that the land and water bodies are not just protected but are regimented to improve their productivity", and there are also cultural norms that prevent the killing or eating of certain animals (Lettau et al., 2023, p. 4). These are all geared towards protecting the environment through religiously guided practices of sustainable development.

These positive elements in the traditional religious and cultural heritage of Africa can be effectively harnessed to complement the efforts of development practitioners in the implementation of the goals of the UN SDG 16 pertaining to the building of strong (electoral) institutions (e.g., SDG 16.6, 16.7, 16.8 and 16.A) and sustaining peace and justice in African states. For instance, in the Akan community in Ghana, the unscripted and acceptable moral rules of conduct (*Amammere*) like the formal Constitution of Ghana are "imbibed through the socialisation process" of the family and society. The *Amammere* serves as the cultural markers or the shared socio-cultural and religious norms and values of tolerance, peace, unity, consensus-building, social justice or the manner of "emotional reactions to phenomena" in conflictual situations (See also Lettau et al., 2023, p. 4).

Of equal importance is the fact that the African concept of peace includes, as we have already noted above, not just the absence of violence but also non-material aspects such as the morality and ethics that contribute to the welfare, harmony and the prosperity of the people (Opoku, 2011, p. 417). That is, African people "have always had recourse to beings and potencies believed to possess knowledge and abilities far superior to them" (Sarpong, 1989, p. 351). For instance, the Akan saying of *fa ma nyame* ("leave it to God") implies absolute faith in the "Supreme Being" to bring about divine judgement and justice at critical moments. This proverb and similar wise sayings and symbols hold the key for understanding the mechanisms that traditional authorities (or peacemakers) employ to mitigate or avoid the escalation of violent behaviour associated with post-electoral disputes. Indeed, as we demonstrate below, through these cultural values and norms we can understand how electoral disputes and ensuing, potentially violent, protests are peacefully resolved in the Ghanaian context.

## THE CONTENTIOUS TRANSITION TO DEMOCRATIC RULE IN GHANA

Democratic prospects after the 1992 transitional election remained "uncertain" at that time (Gyimah-Boadi, 1994). The nature and politics of the electoral process for Ghana's transitional election involved claims and counterclaims concerning "the establishment and control of the electoral body, abuse of the electioneering process, voters' registration and the conduct of elections" (Adejumobi, 2000, p. 67). During the pre-election phase, there was a lack of civic education, civil society institutions and an independent media environment which meant that "critical election support activities such as advocacy for transparency and fairness, independent monitoring and observation of the balloting process" (Agyeman-Dua, 2008, p. 164). There was a mood of scepticism among the political actors and ordinary citizens alike. The governing military-civilian regime of the Provisional National Defence Council (PNDC) led by Flt Lt. Rawlings metamorphosed into a political party, the National Democratic Congress (NDC), and hence had the benefit of incumbency during the transition process. This gave Rawlings an "advantage over the other presidential candidates" (Rothchild, 1995, p. 61) since he had at his disposal state resources such a "money, government vehicles, helicopters, the press, everything", while the other parties struggled for funds and resources which placed them at a distinct disadvantage (Abdulai, 1992, quoted in Rothchild, 1995, p. 61; Afari-Gyan, 1994). The political context in 1992 did not favour competitive, free and fair elections. In spite of all these unfavourable conditions, the leader of the dominant opposition party (the New Patriotic Party, NPP), Prof. Adu Boahen, believed that "if the (Interim Electoral Commission) INEC were to discharge its functions fairly, honestly and transparently … we were going to win hands down" (Boahen, 1995, pp. 277–278).

As it turned out, Rawlings officially won the presidential election with 58.3% of the vote to Prof. Boahen's NPP with 30.4% (Jeffries & Thomas, 1993, p. 331), with a turnout of 48.3% (*West Africa*, 16–29 November 1992a, p. 1963). Not surprisingly, in the subsequent days that followed the declaration of the polls, the main opposition leaders questioned the results. Prof. Boahen issued a joint statement on behalf of the NPP and the other contesting opposition parties (including the PNC, PHP and NIP) expressing "shock and dismay" over what they perceived as "fraudulent manipulation of the presidential election just concluded", further stating that it was evident that "a combination of intimidation and manipulation of ballot boxes and the voting process" that the poll was in effect rigged (*West Africa*, 23–29 November 1992e, p. 2004). A complete account of their evidence was catalogued in *The Stolen Verdict: Ghana November 1992 Presidential Election* (Boahen, 1995, p. 280). On the other hand, international observers like the Commonwealth Observer Group (COG), though acknowledging that there were some shortcomings and irregularities, reported that "the conduct of the election has been free and fair, and free from fear" (Commonwealth Secretariat, 1992, p. 79). Similarly, the Carter Center (CC) reported that "despite the occurrence of serious irregularities in the election process, what we have observed does not lead us to question the validity of the results"; although this view was qualified by the caveat that the irregularities that were observed "raise troubling questions about the electoral process" (Carter Center, 1992, p. 1).

In an interview with a reporter from the *West-Africa* magazine, Prof. Boahen condemned the "favourable comments" of the Commonwealth Observer Group (COG) because they had been "issued before the conclusion of the actual voting" and hence were "premature, and therefore absolutely unreliable" (*West Africa*, 16–22 November 1992c, p. 1964). He preferred the verdict of the Carter Center (CC) observers as presenting a truer "reflection of what transpired on the election day", asserting further that "reading between the lines, they're saying that the results should be rejected" (*West Africa*, 16–22 November 1992c, p. 1964). One reporter commented about the opposition's opinion of the Carter report that perhaps "the opposition obviously believes in the Akan proverb that says the stranger may have big eyes, but he/she doesn't necessarily see everything, hence their dismissal of the 'fair and free' reports" (*West Africa*, 16–22 November 1992c, p. 1964). According to Prof. Boahen, the major reason why the losing parties disputed the results of the presidential election was because he and the other opposition leaders adopted the view "that the Ghanaian public overwhelmingly and unequivocally rejected the outcome of the presidential election!" (Boahen, 1995, p. 278). Some scholars also thought it reasonable for the opposition leaders to heed the reactions of the public as that might "compel the parties to the conflict to settle the matter by negotiation either directly or by means of a go-between" (Radcliffe-Brown, 1969, p. xviii).

In the aftermath of the polls on 3 November, some demonstrations occurred in Kumasi, the second largest city and the stronghold of the dominant opposition party (NPP) (*West Africa*, 23–29 November 1992e, p. 2004). Indeed, the intensity of the riots in Kumasi led to the "imposition of a 6pm to 6am curfew for a few days, fortunately lifted on November 9" (*West Africa*, 16–22 November 1992b, p. 1963). Some riots over the election results also "erupted in some parts of the country like Tamale, Sunyani" (*West Africa*, 16–22 November 1992b, p. 1963). In Accra, the state-owned *Daily Graphic* reported that "violence broke out when some jubilant NDC supporters stopped in front of an NPP office" (*West Africa*, 23–29 November 1992e, p. 2004). There were also reports of the detonation of explosives and violence in various regions of the country, for example, in Accra and Tema (*West Africa*, 16–22 November 1992b, p. 1963) and there were reports of an explosion "on the campus of the University of Ghana on November 10" (*West Africa*, 23–29 November 1992e, p. 2004). Given the nature of these incidents, and despite the climate of fear it engendered, "many people doubted that these frightening acts of violence could be the work of opposition", but rather interpreted them as "attempts to give the opposition a bad name" (*West Africa*, 16–22 November 1992b, p. 1963). Such incidents were condemned by the opposition, especially Prof Boahen who stressed his party's commitment to non-violent political change, although he did interpret these incidents as "indicative of the fact that the Ghanaian public does not approve of the results" (*West Africa*, 16–22 November 1992c, p. 1964). The opposition parties saw the eruption of violent protests and demonstrations in their stronghold as the only legitimate means for their supporters to express their dissatisfaction to the conduct of the elections, but the existing traditional authorities had a different perspective and strategy for the peaceful resolution of the post-electoral dispute and the de-escalation of the violent protests and demonstrations in their communities.

## Traditional Authorities and Conflict Prevention in the Post-Election Period

The apparent breakdown of order and law indicated to the international community (e.g., the Commonwealth Observer Group [COG], Organisation of African Unity [OAU] [later to become the African Union, AU, in 2002], Observer Group and the European Commission [EC] Observers) that the formal conflict resolution mechanisms were not able to mitigate the escalating violence and protests. The international observers took the initiative to mediate and negotiate for peaceful solutions to the post-electoral dispute with the leaders of the two dominant political parties. However, their efforts were not successful. The COG reported that their initial attempts to meet with the NPP leadership were rebuffed, whereupon they tried to work with the OAU to meet with the respective leaders, but again their overtures were declined, both jointly and separately (COG, 1992, p. 60).

The failure of these international organisations to mediate the post-electoral dispute, coupled with the ineffectiveness of the Interim Electoral Commission and Judiciary, prompted calls for the traditional authorities to intervene. As we have established above, traditional political authorities are "identified with a social purpose and permanence", with spiritual powers to enforce "rules governing cooperative human behaviour" (Ololajulo & Awodola, 2010, p. 361). It was also reported that a former Justice of the Supreme Court and member of the incumbent government, Justice D. F. Annan, pointed out that as the "custodians of culture and partners in modern governance and development" the traditional political actors (chiefs) needed "to deal with potential tensions and disputes before they reach damaging parameters" (*Daily Graphic* newspaper report in van Rouveroy van Nieuwaal, 1994, p. 535). Hence on 6 November 1992, and consistent with their authoritative role in the peaceful mediation and resolution of individual and inter-group conflicts in their communities, the traditional leaders intervened. The socio-cultural logic here is that these violent protests and demonstrations were a consequence of the divisive and acrimonious tendencies of multiparty competitive elections with the potential to unravel the harmonious social fabric of the communities under the jurisdictions of these "sacred" traditional authorities. The traditional authorities recognised the need to mediate and enforce the well-established religious values and norms of tolerance, consensus-building, reconciliation and restorative justice in line with the AU Transitional Justice Policy (2019).

As the discussion below shows, these norms and principles constituted the core underpinnings for the informal resolution of the post-electoral disputes, particularly the peaceful traditional diplomatic activities with the political elites and their supporters. On that basis, the traditional authorities adopted the strategies of mediation and negotiation as their main approaches. These strategies are among those commonly used by traditional authorities to resolve conflicts (Momoh, 2021). The two strategies aimed to resolve the electoral dispute and identify (if possible) the root causes of the electoral conflict, and in so doing mitigate or at least de-escalate the conflict and address the attendant humanitarian crises (Wamai, 2018, p. 127). These outcomes constitute the parameters for examining the effectiveness of the conflict prevention strategies of the traditional authorities, and hence their prospects and limitations in the promotion of electoral justice and peacebuilding in the democratisation processes in Africa and beyond (Murithi, 2012; Staino, 2011).

In the public domain the chiefs were reported as delivering peace messages to the dissatisfied and aggrieved supporters of the opposition parties and the general citizenry, exhorting their subjects to halt all political actions and symbols associated with the conduct of political party activities. Such activities were seen as the source of the divisiveness, violence and acrimonious emotions expressed by the supporters of the various political parties. For example, the *Asantehene* (the Paramount Chief of the Ashanti people) announced a ban on further political activities and the enforcement of the societal norms of peace and tolerance under his jurisdiction. He also requested that the parties "ban their members from wearing any political party T-shirts and other insignia, such as badges and stickers on cars" as a way of easing tensions and removing potential causes for provocation or molestation (*West Africa*, 22–25 November 1992d, p. 2005).

Beyond the public domain, the traditional authorities also engaged in discussions with the leaders of the two dominant political parties in closed-door negotiations in order to find amicable solutions to the political impasse and crises. In a special meeting of the representatives of "political parties in Ashanti, the Regional Security Council, the Police Service and the Kumasi Metropolitan Assembly", the *Asantehene* advised the "various political parties to restrain their supporters to desist from such unwarranted behaviour so as to help preserve the relative peace prevailing in the country" (*Ghanaian Times*, 6 November 1992b, p. 1). Further, he also appealed to the "Regional Security Council to lift the curfew in order not to create any unnecessary tension or fear among the people". The party representatives responded to the entreaties of the *Asantehene* by agreeing unanimously to comply with his suggestions. Finally, the *Asantehene* instructed the "Regional Police Commander not to embark on arbitrary arrest as that would not augur well for peace in the metropolis" (*Ghanaian Times*, 6 November 1992b, p. 1). Similarly, in the Brong Ahafo region, the President of the Brong Ahafo Regional House of Chiefs, Nana Adu Gyamfi Ampem, Omanhene of *Acherensua*, advised the PNDC Chairman to rise above the negative statements being made about him and be like "the hen which only steps on her chicks but does not trample upon them" and to "gather his brood and promote unity" (*West Africa*, 22–25 November 1992d, p. 2005).

These diplomatic actions by the traditional authorities had a ripple effect of calming the high political tensions and paved the way for the peaceful informal resolution of the post-electoral dispute by the political parties. They had the effect of de-escalating the post-electoral violent protests and riots. They also served as the medium for the transformation of the causes of the electoral dispute in the peacebuilding processes, thereafter. In these ways the chiefs and traditional authorities assisted in restoring confidence in the electoral process and thus shored up a key institution of governance (as per SDG 16.6). They broadened the scope of the means of resolving the dispute by including as many of the stakeholders as possible in the process, while at the same time reminding them of their common cultural and religious precepts as guides for their behaviour. This contributed to developing an outcome based on a participatory and representative process (SDG 16.7) that reflected and reinforced the rule of law (SDG 16.3).

The efforts of the traditional authorities were widely reported in the local print media. For instance, in an article featured in one of the local daily newspapers, *Ghanaian Times*, the *Asantehene*, Otumfuo Opoku Ware II, was reported as urging all "Ghanaians to avoid violence and endeavour to exhibit political maturity during the crucial stage of the country's transition to constitutional rule", while at the same time exhorting the political elites to cultivate the democratic values of "tolerance and respect for opposing views" as these constituted the "main ingredients for political maturity and were highly essential for a smooth transition to constitutional rule" (*Ghanaian Times*, 31 October 1992a, p. 1). The *Asantehene* was also reported as "expressing regret" over the outbreaks of violence in his community, describing it as "greatly embarrassing to him personally, and to Ashanti Region in general", especially as "no area in the country had recorded such a nasty incident over the election results" (*Ghanaian Times*, 6 November 1992b, p. 1). In general, due to the peaceful mediation and negotiations by the traditional authorities, it was reported that the parties and their supporters, as well as the public in general, heeded the wisdom and the effective judgement of their traditional political leaders.

The disputing parties agreed to disagree and, in effect and in order for the country to move forward in its democratising processes, accepted the electoral outcome as announced, as indeed did the general citizenry. As one journalist reported on the mood of Ghanaians, they became "nothing if not philosophical. In offices and homes all over the country … one can hear more and more the unwritten motto of Ghanaians: '*Let's leave it to God*'" (*West Africa*, 16–22 November 1992c, p. 1964). As one of Ghana's leading political scientists, Ransford Gyampo, noted, Ghana's culture of tolerance mostly eschews violence and when there is violence Ghanaians take a "give it to God" approach in the sense that "It's not your time; your time will come, wait for your time and all the rest" (cited in Issacharoff & Scher, 2010). This is a deeply ingrained socio-cultural norm and is often invoked "whenever the people feel overwhelmed by what is perceived to be a circumstance beyond their control" (Ansah-Koi, 1993, p. 66).

In sum, the peaceful mediation, persuasion and negotiation activities of the traditional authorities paved the way for mediation of the Electoral Commission in its attempts to foster consensus-building surrounding the contentious issues of the electoral processes and their resolution. Nevertheless, the last two steps in the peacebuilding efforts, namely finding solutions for the resolution of the technical issues of the electoral dispute and addressing root causes of the electoral conflict, were major limitations of the mediation efforts of traditional authorities. Disputes over election results are very difficult and politically sensitive issues, which require highly skilled expertise and politico-legal solutions which were beyond the scope of the powers of the traditional authorities.

Indeed, the conflict prevention decisions made by traditional authorities are guided by religious, moral and cultural customs rather than by the principles underpinning the electoral rules and laws and as such "may not protect the electoral rights as well as the formal mechanism established within the legal framework" for ensuring electoral justice (Staino, 2011, p. 188). For example, as the traditional authorities' efforts geared towards the de-escalation of the violent protests and demonstrations show, issues of accountability (in terms of investigations and sanctions concerning the incidents of electoral fraud and physical assaults) became less important when their short-term "negative" peace was sought.

Finally, the mediation and negotiation efforts of the traditional authorities were also less influential in terms of tackling the root causes of the electoral dispute through sensitive political and electoral reforms for "long-term" political transformation of the country. These endemic deficits still continue to plague the effectiveness of national elections and the consolidation of democratic governance, after "a quarter-century of constitutional rule in Ghana" (Mensa-Bonsu, 2021, p. 185). For instance, crucial electoral reforms are still needed to curb the excessive powers enjoyed by the executive to appoint individuals to sensitive official positions in the Judiciary and the Electoral Commission (Appiah-Thompson, 2021b; Appiah-Thompson & Jose, 2021). Reforms are needed to moderate the "first-past-the-post" electoral system, as well as the measures to curb electoral corruption and promote good governance and sustainable socio-economic development in the country (Mensa-Bonsu, 2021).

## Concluding Remarks

Our discussion has outlined the diplomatic role of traditional authorities in Ghana's disputed 1992 election. We have shown how their intervention in the post-electoral dispute and the promotion of peace and tolerance were based on the traditional strategies and logic of conflict resolution norms and principles. These actions were undertaken with the twin aims of de-escalating outbreaks of violence and of finding an amicable solution to the seemingly intractable electoral conflict. In so doing, their actions resonated with various UN SDG goals—16.3, 16.6, 16.7 and 16.A. As importantly, the response and attitudes of Ghanaians towards these traditional mediation efforts also reveal the rich heritage and pride the citizens have for their politico-cultural norms, values and authority. The pockets of violent incidents in some parts of the country were curbed and the electoral dispute was brought to a satisfactory outcome. What insights can we distil from these post-electoral conflicts as illustrated in the Ghanaian 1992 disputed presidential election in Ghana?

In the first place there is a need for the informal alternative traditional dispute resolution mechanisms to complement the formal mechanisms overseen by the Electoral Commission and the courts. Hence beyond their recognition in the Ghanaian Constitution, the traditional political authorities and institutions should also be empowered to apply their traditional tools of conflict transformation in critical situations of electoral disputes. Innovative and creative strategies need to be designed for building the capacities of these traditional authorities to perform such complementary roles in order to contribute to the consolidation and sustainability of democratic governance in Ghana and beyond. These recommendations are directly in line with international and national efforts aimed at achieving the UN SDG 16 which specifically concerns the strategies for building effective (electoral) institutions and the achievement of sustainable electoral justice, peace and stability.

Our discussion has provided some important insights concerning the relevance and importance of traditional authorities for the democratic governance of Ghana. In doing so we have highlighted the importance of a comprehensive approach for electoral justice and peacebuilding. In so doing our discussion should be of benefit for policymakers and international democracy promoters in their efforts to build sustainable and effective political institutions and cultures in emerging African democracies.

## References

Adejumobi, S. (2000). Elections in Africa: A Fading Shadow of Democracy? *International Political Science Review, 21*(1), 59–73.

African Union (AU). (2019). *Transitional Justice Policy*. Addis Ababa: AU.

Afari-Gyan, K. (1994). Elections and Related Issues during Transition from the Military Rule to Civilian, Multiparty System: The Case of Ghana. In Omoruyi, O., Schlosser, D. B., Sambo, A. and Okwuosa, A. (Eds.), *Democratization in Africa: African Perspectives* (Vol. 2. pp. 39–46). Abuja: Centre for Democratic Studies.

Agyeman-Dua, B. (2008). Elections Management and Electoral Politics. In B. Agyeman-Dua (Ed.), *Ghana: Governance in the Fourth Republic* (pp. 155–194). Ghana Centre for Democratic Development (CDD).

Akrofi, C. A. (1958). *Twi mmebusem (Twi Proverbs): With English Translations and Comments*. Macmillan.

Amoakohene, M. (2017). The Role of Media in Conflict and Peacebuilding. In A. S. Gadzekpo (Ed.), *Conflict-Sensitive Coverage: A Manual for Journalists Reporting Conflict in West-Africa* (pp. 24–29). School of Information and Communication Studies, University of Ghana, Legon/African Peacebuilding Network (APN).

Annan, D. F. (1994). Speech Delivered on the Opening Ceremony of the International Conference on Traditional Authority and Development in Africa. In *Proceedings of the Conference on the Contribution of Traditional Authority to Development, Human Rights and Environmental Protection: Strategies for Africa*, 2–4 September, African Studies Centre, Leiden.

Ansah-Koi, K. (1993). The Socio-cultural Matrix and Multi-party Politics in Ghana: Observations and Prospects. In K. A. Ninsin & F. K. Drah (Eds.), *Political Parties and Democracy in Ghana's Fourth Republic* (pp. 63–71). Woeli Publishing Services.

Appiah-Thompson, C. (2020a). The Concept of Peace, Conflict and Conflict Transformation in African Religious Philosophy. *Journal of Peace Education, 17*(2), 161–185.

Appiah-Thompson, C. (2020b). The Usage of African Religious Symbolism, Proverbial Wisdom and Myths in Conflict Transformation and Peacebuilding. Retrieved January 8, 2023, from https://ssrn.com/abstract=3639682 or https://doi.org/10.2139/ssrn.3639682

Appiah-Thompson, C. (2021a). Ghana's Disputed Elections of 1992 and 2012: The Significance of Political Culture. Unpublished doctoral dissertation. The University of Newcastle, Australia.

Appiah-Thompson, C. (2021b). The Politics of Judicial Review of Elections in Ghana: Implications for Judicial Reforms and Emerging Electoral Jurisprudence. *African Review, 13*(2), 251–269.

Appiah-Thompson, C., & Jose, J. (2021). Adjudicating Electoral Disputes or Judicializing Politics? The Supreme Court of Ghana and the Disputed 2012 Presidential Election. *The Round Table: The Commonwealth Journal of International Affairs, 110*(6), 694–708.

Appiah-Thompson, C., Jose, J., & Moore, T. (2022). Examining the Mediating Role of Customary Institutions in the Resolution of Electoral Conflict in Ghana. *African Identities.* https://doi.org/10.1080/14725843.2022.2146050

Atiemo, A. O. (2013). *Religion and the Inculturation of Human Rights in Ghana.* Bloomsbury.

Bekoe, D. A. (2012). Introduction: The Scope, Nature, and Pattern of Electoral Violence in Sub-Saharan Africa. In D. A. Bekoe (Ed.), *Voting in Fear: Electoral Violence in Sub-Saharan Africa* (pp. 1–14). United States Institute of Peace Press.

Bekoe, D. A., & Burchard, S. M. (2019). The Use of Electoral Violence. In Lynch, G. & VonDoepp, P. (Eds.), *Routledge Handbook of Democratization in Africa* (pp. 258–273). Routledge.

Boahen, A. (1995). A Note on the Ghanaian Elections. *African Affairs, 94*(375), 277–280.

Burchard, S. M. (2015). *Electoral Violence in Sub-Saharan Africa: Causes and Consequences.* Lynne Rienner Publishers.

Busia, K. A. (1968). *The Position of the Chief in the Modern Political System of Ashanti: A Study of the Influence of Contemporary Social Changes on Ashanti Political Institutions.* Frank Cass.

Carter Center. (1992). *Final Report: Observing the 1992 Ghana Election.* The Carter Center of Emory University.

Commonwealth Observer Group (COG). (1992). *The Presidential Election in Ghana, 3 November, 1992: The Report of the Commonwealth Observer Group.* London: Commonwealth Secretariat.

Eze, E. C. (1997). Democracy or Consensus? A Response to Wiredu. In E. C. Eze (Ed.), *Postcolonial African Philosophy: A Critical Reader* (pp. 313–323). Blackwell Publishers.

Gebrewold, B. (2011). T'ummu: An East African Perspective. In W. Dietrich (Ed.), *The Palgrave International Handbook of Peace Studies: A Cultural Perspective* (pp. 428–441). London: Palgrave Macmillan.

*Ghanaian Times.* (1992a, October 31). Ghanaians Must Avoid Violence during Elections.

*Ghanaian Times.* (1992b, November 6). Asantehene Urges End to Violence. p. 1.

Gopin, M. (2000). *Between Eden and Armageddon: The Future of World Religions, Violence, and Peacemaking.* Oxford University Press.

Gyekye, K. (2013). *Philosophy, Culture and Vision: African Perspectives*. Sub-Saharan Publishers.

Gyimah-Boadi, E. (1994). Ghana's Uncertain Political Opening. *Journal of Democracy*, 5(2), 75–86.

Issacharoff, L., & Scher, D. (2010). Interview with Ransford Gyampo. Innovations for Successful Societies. Princeton: University of Princeton. Retrieved December 3, 2022, from https://successfulsocieties.princeton.edu/interviews/ransford-gyampo

Jeffries, R., & Thomas, C. (1993). The Ghanaian Elections of 1992. *African Affairs*, 92(368), 331–366.

Kuhn, P. M. (2015). Do Contentious Elections Trigger Violence? In P. Norris, R. W. Frank, & F. M. I. Coma (Eds.), *Contentious Elections: From Ballots to Barricades* (pp. 89–110). Routledge.

Laakso, L. (2019). Electoral Violence and Political Competition in Africa. In *Oxford Research Encyclopaedia of Politics* (pp. 1–16). Oxford University Press.

Lettau, M., Mtaku, C. Y., Otchere, E. D., & Kagan, S. (2023). Cultural Practices and Policies for Sustainable Development: Theoretical and Methodological Approaches to Researching Culture in Conflict Situations in West-Africa. In M. Lettau, C. Y. Mtaku, & E. D. Otchere (Eds.), *Performing Sustainability in West Africa: Cultural Practices and Policies for Sustainable Development* (pp. 1–24). Routledge.

Mahamat, M. F. (2019). Forward. In *African Union (AU) Transitional Justice Policy* (pp. iv–v). AU.

Mboh, L. (2021). An Investigation into the Role of Traditional Leaders in Conflict Resolution: The Case of Communities in the Mahikeng Local Municipality, North West Province, South Africa. *African Journal of Conflict Resolution*, 21(2), 25pp. Online journal at: https://www.ajol.info/index.php/ajcr/article/view/232007

Mensa-Bonsu, M. A. S. (2021). Why Electoral Reforms are Urgently Needed in Ghana. *African Journal of International and Comparative Law*, 29(2), 185–203.

Momoh, H. B. (2021). The Role of Traditional Leaders in Peacemaking and Conflict Management among the Mende of Sierra Leone. *International Journal of Sciences: Basic and Applied Research*, 35(2), 156–171.

Murithi, T. (2008). African Indigenous and Endogenous Approaches to Peace and Conflict Resolution. In D. J. Francis (Ed.), *Peace and Conflict in Africa* (pp. 16–30). Zed Books.

Murithi, T. (2012). Peacemaking and African Traditions of Justice and Reconciliation. In S. A. Nan, Z. C. Mampilly, & A. Bartoli (Eds.), *Peacemaking: From Practice to Theory* (Vol. I, pp. 275–294). Praeger Security International.

Norris, P., Frank, R. W., & Coma, F. M. (2015). Contentious Elections: From Votes to Violence. In P. Norris, R. W. Frank, & F. M. Coma (Eds.), *Contentious Elections: From Ballots to Barricades* (pp. 1–20). Routledge.

Ololajulo, B. O., & Awodola, B. F. (2010). Nigerian State and Institutional Capacity: Rethinking the Role of Traditional Rulers in Post-election Conflict Management. In I. O. Albert & O. I. Oloyede (Eds.), *Dynamics of Peace Processes* (pp. 361–370). Centre for Peace and Strategic Studies, University of Ilorin.

Opoku, K. A. (1975). *Speak to the Winds: Proverbs from Africa*. Lothrop, Lee & Shepard Company.

Opoku, K. A. (1978). *West African Traditional Religion*. FEP International Private Limited.

Opoku, K. A. (2005). Introduction. In J. Halperin & H. Ucko (Eds.), *Worlds of Memory and Wisdom: Encounters of Jews and African Christians* (pp. 9–14). World Council of Churches Publications.

Opoku, K. A. (2006). Traditional African Religious Society. In M. Juergensmeyer (Ed.), *The Oxford Handbook of Global Religions* (pp. 537–544). Oxford University Press.

Opoku, K. A. (2011). Asomdwoe: A West African Perspective. In W. Dietrich (Ed.), *The Palgrave International Handbook of Peace Studies: A Cultural Perspective* (pp. 417–427). Palgrave Macmillan.

Owusu, M. (2012). Africa. In B. Isakhan & S. Stockwell (Eds.), *The Edinburgh Companion to the History of Democracy* (pp. 223–232). Edinburgh University Press.

Peter, I. (2014). Reconsidering Place of Traditional Institutions under the Nigerian Constitution: A Comparative Analysis. *Journal of Law, Policy and Globalisation, 31*, 135–148.

Pindiga, H. A., Wakili, S. G., & Mohammed, M. I. (2020). Traditional Rulers and Peace Building in Gombe Emirate, Gombe State. *FUDMA: Journal of Politics and International Affairs, 3*(1), 11pp. Online journal available at: http://journal.fudutsinma.edu.ng/index.php/FUJOPIA/article/view/1587

Radcliffe-Brown, A. R. (1969). Preface. In M. Fortes & E. E. Evans-Pritchard (Eds.), *African Political Systems* (pp. xi–xxiii). Oxford University Press.

Ray, D. I. (1994). Indicators of Divided Sovereignty: Traditional Authority and State in Ghana. In *Proceedings of the Conference on the Contribution of Traditional Authority to Development, Human Rights and Environmental Protection: Strategies for Africa* (pp. 97–123). African Studies Centre, Leiden, 2–4 September.

Ray, D. I. (2003). Rural Local Governance and Traditional Leadership in Africa and the Afro-Caribbean: Policy and Research Implications from Africa to the Americas and Australasia. In D. I. Ray & P. S. Reddy (Eds.), *Grassroots Chiefs in Africa and the Afro-Caribbean Governance?* (pp. 1–30). University of Calgary Press.

Rothchild, D. (1995). Rawlings and the Engineering of Legitimacy in Ghana. In I. W. Zartman (Ed.), *Collapsed States: The Disintegration and Restoration of Legitimate Authority* (pp. 49–68). Lynne Rienner Publishers.

Sarpong, P. A. (1989). African Traditional Religion and Peace (with Special Reference to Ashanti). *Studia Missionalia, 38*, 351–370.

Skalnik, P. (1994). Authority Versus Power: Democracy in Africa Must Include Original African Institutions. In *Proceedings of the Conference on the Contribution of Traditional Authority to Development, Human Rights and Environmental Protection: Strategies for Africa* (pp. 125–145). African Studies Centre, Leiden. 2–4 September.

Staino, S. (2011). Preventing and Mitigating Election-Related Conflict and Violence: The Role of Electoral Justice. In D. Gillies (Ed.), *Elections in Dangerous Places: Democracy and Paradoxes of Peacebuilding* (pp. 171–189). McGill-Queen's University Press.

Straus, S., & Taylor, C. (2012). Democratization and Electoral Violence in Sub-Saharan Africa, 1990–2008. In D. A. Bekoe (Ed.), *Voting in Fear: Electoral Violence in Sub-Saharan Africa* (pp. 15–38). United States Institute of Peace Press.

Van Rouveroy van Nieuwaal, E. A. B. (1994). Synthesis of the Conference. In *Proceedings of the Conference on the Contribution of Traditional Authority to Development, Human Rights and Environmental Protection: Strategies for Africa* (p. 535). African Studies Centre, Leiden, 2–4 September.

Wamai, N. (2018). The 2008 Kenyan Mediation Process: Lessons and Dilemmas for Conflict Prevention in Africa. In T. Karbo & K. Virk (Eds.), *The Palgrave Handbook of Peacebuilding in Africa* (pp. 119–136). Palgrave Macmillan.

*West Africa*. (1992a, November 16–29). Presidential Election Results: Results at Region Level. p. 1963.

*West Africa*. (1992b, November 16–22). Post-election Thoughts. p. 1963.

*West Africa*. (1992c, November 16–22). I was … Shocked. p. 1964.

*West Africa*. (1992d, November 22–25). Violence Creates Tension. p. 2005.

*West Africa*. (1992e, November 23–29). Opposition Parties Cry Foul. p. 2004.

CHAPTER 19

# Rastafari Insights into Peace-building and Sustainable Development

*Fortune Sibanda*

## Introduction

The world over, the call for promoting peace, love and harmony is a common phenomenon among, for instance, the developed and the emerging nations, individuals and groups, the rich and the poor. Apparently, the calls for political and economic independence, democracy and human rights have seen the world continuously being torn apart for these ideals. The two World Wars culminated in the formation of the United Nations whose mandate is to, inter alia, be a mediator and watchdog for peace even in the post-Cold War era. Currently, Goal number 16 of the United Nations Sustainable Development Goals is anchored on the aspiration to "[p]romote peaceful and inclusive societies for sustainable development, provide access to justice for all and build effective, accountable and inclusive institutions at all levels" (https://sdgs.un.org/goals). The quest for peace in Africa (Nhema, 2004) has also seen the participation of private mediators such as the World Council of Churches (WCC) and the All Africa Conference of Churches (AACC) as peace-makers in African conflicts (Okoth, 2004). In fact, in recent years, peace studies have taken the centre stage in the social sciences, economics, law, politics and Diaspora studies. A variety of research work, articles, journals, books, courses, centres, institutes and organisations devoted to the study of the problems of peace are emerging (Kaur, 2006, p. 41). For instance, UPEACE is a United

F. Sibanda (✉)
Department of Theology and Religious Studies, University of Eswatini, Kwaluseni, Eswatini

© The Author(s), under exclusive license to Springer Nature Switzerland AG 2023
S. M. Kilonzo et al. (eds.), *The Palgrave Handbook of Religion, Peacebuilding, and Development in Africa*,
https://doi.org/10.1007/978-3-031-36829-5_19

Nations-mandated University for Peace that was established with a mission to stimulate and strengthen capacities in Africa to teach, research and provide services to communities on matters of peace, conflict and development in Africa. Therefore, 'weaving peace' (Ewusi, 2012) has taken the centre stage in different forums and different stakeholders.

This chapter adopts a religious perspective to the issue of peace-building and sustainable development. The study examines Rastafari insights on peace-building, love and harmony towards promoting sustainable development and nation-building in Zimbabwe. Although Rastafari has been grossly criminalised, misunderstood, exploited, underutilised, excluded, misused and abused (Afari, 2007; Sibanda, 2017), the chapter argues that Rastafari insights on peace-building and sustainable development can be viewed in ambivalence on the basis of their worldview, spirituality, symbols and practice. On the one hand, Rastafari have the potential to enforce sustainable development through the promotion of national healing, reconciliation, peace, love and harmony with mother earth and humanity. Thus, the watch phrases like 'peace, love and harmony' and 'One love' are more than mere clichés that Rastafari reggae artists and adherents are known for, but represent the essence of Rastafari philosophy and religion alongside the universal ideal of the concept of 'One God, One Aim, One Destiny, One Heart and One Earth'. On the other hand, the major critique on Rastafari lies under their homophobic attack towards same-sex relations through music and other communication avenues, which tend to atrophy the positive insights towards peace-building efforts and sustainable development. Therefore, the chapter seeks to demonstrate that whereas Rastafari music and related symbolic material culture have the potential to significantly contribute to the establishment of peace and religious tolerance in a politically volatile and religiously pluralistic society, they can also be manipulated to create aggression and social disharmony. This echoes Strijdom & Tarusarira's (2017, p. 1) assertion that religions (Rastafari included) are "not inherently violent or non-violent, but can be instrumentalised in either way by individuals or groups". The human agency is key for better or for worse in peace-building and sustainable development in Africa.

## Theoretical Framework and Research Methodology

This qualitative study was informed by the Afrocentric theory, which is also known as Afrocentricity, Afrology or Africology (Asante, 1998, p. 19). The theory was popularised by scholars such as Molefi Kete Asante. Afrocentricity emerged as a reaction to the mythology of white racial superiority enmeshed in Eurocentric ideology and its essentialist philosophy of the centre and the periphery dichotomy. In that way, Afrocentricity is the study and examination of phenomena from the standpoint of Africans as subjects rather than objects (Asante, 2007). The history, culture and philosophy of African people are used as reference point for determining one's approach to reality and understanding of the world. Being an Afrocentric movement, Rastafari culture is rooted in the

African worldview from which it emerged. Afrocentricity is helpful to the study as it "stands as both a corrective and a critique" (Asante, 2007, p. 27; Sibanda, 2016a, p. 347). It is a corrective to the European Christian universal claims to reality and peace-building that denied the agency and action of African people. However, the Afrocentric theory can also be utilised as a critique to the Rastafarian position of homophobia that implicates the movement in matters of violence and non-tolerance.

In terms of research methodology, the study used a phenomenological research paradigm to explore Rastafari insights into peace-building and sustainable development in Zimbabwe. The research combined in-depth interviews, documentary analysis and observation to collect data among Nyahbinghi Rastafari communities in Zimbabwe. On in-depth interviews, both Rastas and non-Rastas were engaged to collect data. Documentary analysis was vital towards understanding material from the print and electronic media covering events such as Rastafari festivals and peace concerts. In addition, the research used the sociological approach and the phenomenological approach to analyse the phenomena under study. The phenomenological approach provided an insider perspective of Rastafari activities inclined towards peace. The approach comprises a number of elements such as *epoche* in which the researcher's prior judgements were kept in abeyance, respecting the believer's point of view, empathy, descriptive accuracy, intentionality and establishing the essence or meaning of the phenomena under study through *eidetic* intuition (Chitando, 1998; Cox, 1996). Some of these elements of phenomenology are dimensions that constitute the self as a source of agency in day-to-day life activities. In this manner, despite the shortcomings of the phenomenological approach, the study regarded it as an ideal hermeneutical tool that would be a basis for evaluating the extent to which Rastafari peace-building efforts towards sustainable development were recognised and adopted in the often politically volatile milieu of postcolonial Zimbabwe. In order to cover up for the weaknesses of the phenomenological approach, the sociology of religion came in handy as a complimentary method. The sociological method looks at how religion affects society, and how it is in turn affected by other institutions and events in society (Bourdillon, 1990, p. 2). Sociological elements useful in the study included conflict and consensus, which bring issues of peace-building and sustainable development to the fore. Therefore, the two methods were used in a complimentary way.

## Religious and Political Landscapes in Zimbabwe

The Zimbabwean religious landscape shows that a plethora of religious traditions have registered themselves from antiquity to contemporary times. Evidently, the nation is marked by radical pluralism as it is a home to religions such as African Indigenous Religion, Judaism, Christianity, Islam, Buddhism, Hinduism, Bahai Faith and Rastafari (Chitando, 2010, p. 107; Sibanda, 2010). This suggests that the religious picture cannot be explicated in monolithic terms. In this whole maze, Christianity has had a long-standing campaign to declare Zimbabwe a Christian state. This is an ideologically charged move that emanates from the western missionary colonial historiography. Because Christianity claims to have a large following of up to approximately 80% of the population (Shoko, 2010, p. 102), the Zimbabwean community has taken little or no notice of the potential of other religious traditions such as Rastafari in issues of peace-building and tolerance towards humanity and the environment, which have implications on sustainable development. In fact, the imbalance on the religious landscape where Christianity dominates stultifies a multi-faith approach, which excludes voices and perspectives of Rastas in various circles of life including the campaign for establishing peace, love, democracy, human rights and environmental consciousness.

The political landscape of Zimbabwe has a long history. Following a century-old of colonial rule, the nation has had a fair share of some successes and challenges in the postcolonial period. For instance, the first decade had a political turmoil that resulted in Gukurahundi massacres in Matabeleland and Midlands provinces which culminated in the 1987 Unity Accord between Zimbabwe African National Union -Patriotic Front (ZANU-PF) and Patriotic Front-Zimbabwe African Peoples Union (PF-ZAPU) (CCJP & LRF, 1997). The 'Zimbabwe crisis' which began in 2000 on account of the contentious land reform programme has been another significant landmark to the economic and political challenges. As a result of this crisis, Zimbabwe suffered a number of social, legal, economic and political woes to the detriment of both Zimbabwe and the international community. Currently, under the New Dispensation led by President Emmerson D. Mnangagwa since 2018, people have been polarised between ZANU-PF Party and the opposition political formations such as the Citizens Coalition for Change (CCC) led by Nelson Chamisa. As these political parties continue to contest for political dominance in Zimbabwe, some callous Machiavellian strategies are being employed over the ordinary people as brother has been made to fight against brother in politically motivated violence (Masunungure, 2009; Muchacha, 2016). Machacha (2016) further asserts that politically motivated violence is a political tool for consolidating power and suppressing social movements, dissenting voices and political parties. One opposition leader once lamented that violence was the biggest crisis bedevilling Zimbabwe, given that the country had never enjoyed a mere decade of peace since independence in 1980 due to political violence (News Day 30 October 2012). The general suspicious attitude of Rastafari towards politics often referred to as *poly-tricks* is informative to a study of this magnitude and thrust. Rastas tend to be apolitical and typical lovers of peace as well as ardent peace-makers. This scenario makes it timely to explore Rastafari insights into peace-building and sustainable development in a religiously pluralistic context punctuated by sporadic politically unpredictable situations.

## HISTORICAL OVERVIEW OF RASTAFARI

Rastafari is an Afrocentric religio-political New Religious Movement that originated from Jamaica. It began as an Afro-Caribbean movement stimulated by the ideas and influence of an early twentieth-century Jamaican evangelical preacher and Black Nationalist, Marcus Garvey, whose ideas were appealing to the majority of black ex-slaves exposed to untold suffering due to bondage, unemployment, racial discrimination and harassment. This made Rastafari a beacon of hope for the affirmation of Black traditions, identity and history (Parsons, 1993, p. 266; Sibanda, 2012, p. 66; 2017). The coronation of Ras Tafari as Negus of Ethiopia on 2 November 1930 to become Emperor Haile Selassie I brought a paradigm shift to the movement of Rastas, which was named after his pre-coronation name Ras Tafari Makonnen. In Rasta theology, the crowning of Haile Selassie was a fulfilment of the spiritual revelation by God from Marcus Garvey to look to Africa for a Black king who would be crowned to redeem the oppressed Black people (Afolabi, 2004, p. 37).

Rastas identify themselves with Ethiopia and Africa. Ethiopia symbolises freedom because it was never colonised and as such Rastafarians have adopted the red, green and yellow colours of Ethiopia into their movement. Gerald Parsons (1993, p. 267) cited in Sibanda (2012, p. 66) concisely writes in reference to Rastas thus: "Having suffered enslavement at the hands of the white Babylon, they look forward to redemption from slavery and return to the promised land in Africa, symbolised above all by Ethiopia, the seat of ancient African civilization and symbol of a free and uncolonized African identity". In this way, the ancient Nyahbinghi philosophy that refers to all 'downpressors' and repressive structures, whether from Blacks or whites as 'Babylon', has been inspirational to Rastafari.

In addition, Rastafari as an existential reality in Jamaica grew and spread far and wide. In this way, whereas some Rastas have come to settle in Africa as part of repatriation emerging from the global Pan-Africanism, yet others have remained in the Diaspora where they transformed their focus from the idea of a physical repatriation to Africa to a spiritual conception based on self-worth (Sibanda, 2012). The message of liberation has been made popular through Rastafari culture including reggae music the world over. Apparently, it was through reggae music that Bob Marley drummed a variety of messages which sought to promote, *inter alia*, Pan-Africanism, African unity, peace, love, harmony and liberation. Marley used the power of music and Rastafari to influence and change Jamaica and eventually the rest of the world. In this regard, Yasus Afari (2007) is correct to describe Rastafari phenomenon as "Jamaica's gift to the world". The importance of reggae in Jamaica is noted when the political rivalry between Michel Manley and the opposition party became violent in the 1970s. In 1978 the Rastafarian reggae music helped to restore law and order in Jamaica. As such, Bob Marley staged his 'peace concert' that helped to patch up the political struggle between Manley and his arch-rival, Edward Seaga. The fact that both the 1976 'Smile Jamaica Concert' and the 1978 'Peace Concert' placed Bob Marley at the centre confirmed Rastas as peace-makers (Edmonds, 2012). Evidently, the Rastas played a small but significant role as agents of change, accorded a measure of respectability. Marley through music encouraged Black people the world over "to stand up for their rights and to project themselves as peaceful, loving people who wanted to change society in a way that would benefit everybody" (Catchpole, 1983, p. 108).

The emergence of Rastafari communities in Zimbabwe is largely linked to the historic performance of Bob Marley at the eve of Zimbabwe's independence in April 1980. The development of Rastafari in postcolonial Zimbabwe has found a fertile ground mainly among youths who particularly listened to reggae music. It is a paradox that despite the popularity of reggae music, Rastafari experienced remarkable prejudice that was initially fuelled by western scholarship and colonial administrators but has been maintained in some African States including Zimbabwe (Campbell, 1988, p. 81). This irony has resulted in a continual criminalisation of Rastafarians as 'rogues', social outcasts and dagga-smokers. Yet, notwithstanding the negative images a section of the Zimbabwean society has held, today, the country is a home to several Nyahbinghi Rastafari Houses or mansions. These include Chaminuka Rastafari House in Chitungwiza; Dzimbadzemabwe Rastafari House of Glen Norah; Marcus Garvey Rastafari House in Epworth; Murahwa Rastafari House in Mutare; Chirorodziva Rastafari House in Chinhoyi; Khami Army Rastafari House in Bulawayo; the Mwenemutapa Rastafari House in Kwekwe; and the Cherutombo Rastafari House in Marondera (Sibanda, 2012, p. 67). This study focuses on the activities of some of these Rastafari mansions to interrogate the extent to which Rastafari cultural identities such as reggae music are employed to present the Rastafari message of literacy for peace and sustainable development in Zimbabwe.

## Rastafari Insights on Peace-building and Sustainable Development in Zimbabwe

The Rastafari understanding of peace, love and harmony is part and parcel of their living philosophy. The study established that the Rastafari aim for peace, love, harmony and religious tolerance is pervasive and evident in some of their teachings, beliefs and practices in relation to humanity and the environment. This section will present findings from interviews, observation and documentary analysis. Themes that emerged from the study have been used to organise this section.

### *Becoming Members of a New Race*

Rastas have a global slogan and clarion call for peace and love to ensure that people enjoy full respect of their human rights to live with dignity. Unity is regarded as a key concept in the process of attaining peace-building and sustainable development. Zimbabwean Rastas claim that they have two main sources of inspiration to cascade unity, peace and love. The first one is His Imperial Majesty (H.I.M.), Emperor Haile Selassie I, whom Rastas deify and consider as JAH Rastafari, and the second one is the Jamaican reggae king, Bob Marley. Using documentary analysis, it was learnt that His Imperial Majesty spoke on various subjects including unity, peace and love. Two excerpts can suffice to illustrate this point. On one occasion H.I.M. Emperor Haile Selassie I said: "We must be ever mindful that our greatest weapon is the oneness which we share as Africans. But it is not enough to be Africans. That which pulls us apart and divides us must be resisted with all our strength. That which unites us must be pursued relentlessly and inexorably *to promote peace and love*" (emphasis in italics added). In a historic "War" Speech to the United Nations General Assembly in New York City on 4 October 1963, Emperor Haile Selassie I remarked: "And we must look into ourselves, into the depth of our souls. We must become something we have never been and for which our education and experience and environment have ill-prepared us. We must be bigger than we have been: more courageous, greater in spirit, larger in outlook. We must become members of a new race, overcoming petty prejudice, owing our allegiance not to nations but to our fellow men within the human community" (Selassie, 1963). The "War" speech reveals Selassie's hope for an inclusive world with peace, tolerance and upholding of human rights for sustainable development in the context of existential challenges anchored on race, gender, class and religion (Sibanda, 2021, p. 127). Through such wise counsel from Emperor Haile Selassie I, Rastas claim that they choose good over evil. They seek to attain 'One Nation, One Love, One Aim, One Destiny, One Creation'. On this basis, it becomes a shared responsibility for people to promote unity, peace and love.

Along the same lines, according to Rastas, the reggae artist, Bob Marley, has left a legacy of promoting peace, love and harmony through song. Two songs from Bob Marley will suffice to illustrate the point. What is important to note is that the lyrics of Bob Marley's song entitled "War" (1976) are mainly derived from the "War" Speech of H.I.M. at the UN General Assembly. The lyrics captured in part here, declare thus: "Until the philosophy which hold one race// superior and another inferior// is finally and permanently discredited and abandoned// Everywhere is War. … That until that day// the dream of lasting peace world citizenship// rule of international morality// will remain in but a fleeting illusion// to be pursued, but never attained// Now everywhere is war, war." For Rastas, the "War" song implies that for peace to be established it is necessary to fight and declare war every place where there are oppressive 'Babylon' systems. They have confidence that good will triumph over evil. The album, *One Love*, made Bob Marley to be declared by *The Beat* Magazine in 2000 an artist of the century. BBC declared *One Love* the "Song of the Millennium" at the end of 2000. Through documentary analysis, Seth Nelson and Daniel Nelson (Nelson & Nelson, 2000, p. 54) described Marley as "[a]n eternal teacher, a unifier of all, a healer, a man crossing all boundaries between races of people, locations, classes, genders and ideologies". Thus, Marley became a conduit of humanity's hopes, dreams and foundations for freedom, human rights, justice, peace, love and harmony. This dovetails with SDG 16 that is dedicated to the promotion of peaceful and inclusive societies for sustainable development. The element of 'One Creation' has made Rastas to consider nature as an indispensable ally by making peace with nature.

## *Making Peace with Nature*

In all Nyahbinghi Rastafari Houses in Zimbabwe, the adherents gather every Sabbatical (Sabbath) to worship at *binghis* (shrines) pronouncing and chanting praises to Jah Rastafari for peace and love to prevail. With most *binghis* being located in natural environments, far away from the 'madding crowd', Rastas operate in serene places in harmony with nature. Rastas are environmentalists who emphasise the importance of preventing the destruction of nature through "Rastafari green philosophy" (Sibanda, 2015, 2017), since humanity and nature are inseparable. In this way, a rediscovery of a spirituality firmly based upon the sacredness of all life can be realised through Rastafari. Besides fulfilling SDG 16 where peaceful and inclusive societies are promoted among humankind, Rastafarian environmentalism is a collective consciousness that promotes a peaceful co-existence with nature, which fulfils SDG number 13 on urgent action to combat climate change and its impact. Therefore, instead of *trodding* the reckless and suicidal path of waging war on nature, which has left mother earth broken, Rastafarians are "making peace with nature" (UN Environmental Programme, 2021). Put differently, the Rastafari environmental ethic basically shows that Rastas do not only focus on being at peace with fellow brethrens and sistrens but with nature as well. In a previous study on their attitude to the environment, it was established that the 'Rastafarian green philosophy and *livity*' (Sibanda, 2012, p. 73, 2015) are in tandem with the ideals of peace, love and harmony. These ideals support all forms of life sustained by mother earth.

## *Prayer for Peace*

Rastafarians have occasions when they pray for peace to the extent of holding national prayer meetings. On one such occasion of a national prayer, hundreds of people, especially of Rastafari orientation, came from across the country and converged at Cherutombo Nyahbinghi Rastafari House in Marondera to pray for peace in the country and for its leadership. The high priest of Cherutombo Rastafari House, Ras Alexander Munyukwi, led the procession and made some remarks that ended in the reading of the Nyahbinghi prayer. Among the key points raised were the need to promote peace and to shun violence. What emerges from this particular event is that the Rastafarians consciously set aside time, 'sacred time' at a 'sacred space', to pray for peace. A 'peace pipe'/chalice pot was specially prepared and dedicated to the cause of promoting peace and sustainable development. The Rastas proved to be religiously tolerant by inviting 'all church denominations' to their prayer meeting on this occasion. The march and meeting was punctuated by drumming and chanting of Rastafari songs that engendered the call for peace, love and harmony.

In line with the above, following the marching in the streets of Marondera and clad in Rastafari attire of red, gold and green, the procession at that national prayer meeting later gathered and preached at Cherutombo Shopping Centre, situated near the *binghi* (place of worship) of the Cherutombo Nyahbinghi Rastafari House. Different Rastas Elders took turns to explain the essence of Rastafari and its ideals that seek to promote a platform for exercising One Love, peace and unity. The explanations and 'reasonings' were interspaced with singing and drumming Nyahbinghi chants. The reggae beat was evidently inspiring to all and sundry. The power of reggae music cannot be underestimated as it cascades education and entertainment through its lyrics reminiscent of the reggae king, Bob Marley.

### *Symbolism of Heart and Spear*

A symbolic gesture for Rastafari peace and harmony noted at the prayer meeting just as in other settings is the use of fingers, whereby the adherents hold the tips of their thumbs and index fingers together in a shape of a triangle. This can be done both individually and/or in pairs. Rastas believe that the shape of their hands represent a heart and a spear. The sign of a heart and spear represents the key Rastafari principle of peace and the desire to combat oppression. Yasus Afari (2007, p. 102) says that this symbol is "the Rastafarian Seal of the Trinity that balances between the spiritual, mental and physical. It stimulates and inspires meditation, harmony, balance, tranquillity and relaxation; in goody/body, mind and spirit." This shows that, on the one hand, Rastas can preach, teach and live a levity that promotes peace and harmony as symbolised by the heart. In a bid to fight evil in order to attain good, Rastas readily declare death to Satan and forces of darkness, on the other hand. Symbolised by the spear, Rastas pronounce "fire", "war", death and destruction to darkness and oppressive "Babylon" systems. As one Elder explained, "Rastas do not shy away from physical confrontation. It is the law of nature that darkness must be annihilated." This is done as a way of fighting in defence of good over evil. In Rastafari circles, it brings to the fore the question of justified and unjustified war as will be illustrated by the issues of homophobia.

### *Homophobia and Same-Sex Relations*

Although Rastafarians are known for propagating the ideals of peace, love and harmony at all costs, they are found wanting from a western perspective of human rights because of declaring "war" on homosexuality. Guided by the Afrocentricity where the pro-life African philosophy is central, Rastafarians regard same-sex relations as "unnatural", "un-African", "alien", "abnormal", "unbiblical" and "non-productive". Rastas seek to fulfil the biblical command in Gen. 1:28 to be "fruitful and multiply, and fill the earth". This implies that the Creator designed male and female for procreation and homosexuality is regarded among Rastas as a dissident and non-acceptable practice (Sibanda, 2016b, p. 189; Sibanda 2021, p. 137, 138). Therefore, Rastas equate homosexuality to 'witchcraft', which is anti-life and is opposed in all progressive societies. In defence of Afrocentric pro-life agenda perpetrated by Rastas, one Elder said "Rastas are not homophobic but death-phobic". The fact that homosexuality does not promote reproduction, it becomes anti-life and this affects population growth, just as the use of contraceptives. The practice was attacked through songs by some reggae artists such as the Jamaican Buju Banton (Sibanda, 2016b). Thus, Rastafari insights on peace attract criticism from human rights players for homophobia.

## Chanting Peace, Love and Harmony for Sustainable Development: Critical Reflections

The Rastafari call for peace, love and harmony as expressed through various avenues including music is evident among Rastafari communities in Zimbabwe. The use of music to drum important messages can be traced back to Rasta personalities such as Bob Marley. Marley was a great ambassador for peace, love and harmony through the lyrics of reggae music. Roger Steffens (2000, p. 60) refers to the lyrics of Bob Marley when he writes, thus: "His lyrics are a one-world sermon, championing Rastafarianism [sic], marijuana, pacificism, equal rights and all degrees of love, physical and spiritual. With prophetic fervor, Marley's melting tenor broadcast hope and redemption from the third world to the first." In other words, Marley was a real champion worth emulating in an era bedevilled by spates of political violence, gender-based violence and unbridled "environmental terrorism" (Sibanda, 2010), which come to the fore with challenges associated with election period.

In line with the above, Fresh (2003, L5) stressed Marley's contribution when he says "the man preached peace and love all over the world, one of his songs was voted the best ever by listeners around the world, he united warring factions in his country and is also the first musician to be conferred that honour". In 1978, the UN awarded Marley the 'Medal of Peace'. This shows that Rastafari insights on peace and religious tolerance are not a new concept but an ongoing phenomenon that requires practising at a more grand magnitude. Practising violence in all its various forms is equivalent to being illiterate. In fact, a new understanding of *illiteracy* proffered by Alvin Toffler is informative towards upholding Rastafari insights on peace-building for sustainable development in Zimbabwe. He writes in this regard, thus: "[T]he illiterate of the 21st century will not be those who cannot read or write but those who cannot learn, unlearn and relearn". This shows that people must not just adopt but also adapt and critically examine messages cascaded through music that they listen to. Peace is not just the presence of comfort but the presence of justice. In contemporary times, performing Dance Hall artists such as Winky D have also cascaded messages of peace in the period towards national elections. This shows the continued relevance of music to encourage peace-building and sustainable development.

## Conclusion

The chapter has demonstrated that Rastafari communities can immensely contribute to matters of peace, love, harmony and religious tolerance through, *inter alia*, reggae music in Zimbabwe. Perhaps the words of Yasus Afari (2007, p. 128), are apt in this regard: "Like its parent, Niah Binged music, reggae is used as a conduit for the message and Livity of the RASTAFARIANS as well as a tool of liberation; communicating the values and concepts of the faith and movement of RASTAFARI. Promoting and spreading a universal message of one love, African redemption, hope, inspiration, justice, equality, peace and goodwill to all mankind/humanity." Thus, the essence of reggae music is noted in its message that appeals to the local and global community. On the one hand, Rastafari have the potential to enforce sustainable development through the promotion of peace, love and harmony. On the other hand, the major critique on Rastafari lies under their homophobic attack towards same-sex relations through music and other communication avenues, which tend to atrophy the positive insights towards peace-building efforts and sustainable development. Rastafarians have declared a "war" against evil, including same-sex relations. The advice of H.I.M. Emperor Haile Selassie I to shun petty prejudices and become members of a new race is not compatible with Rastafari stance on homosexuality. The chapter concludes that despite the shortcomings of Rastafari, the quest for sustainable development can be fulfilled through integrating the Rastafari insights into peace, love and harmony with a full conviction that when the power of love overcomes the love of power, the world at large and Zimbabwe, in particular, would know genuine peace among people and nature. Rastas have insights that can be used to conscientise people to promote peace-building.

## References

Afari, Y. (2007). *Overstanding Rastafari: Jamaica's Gift to the World*. Senya-Cum.
Afolabi, J. A. (2004). By the Rivers of Babylon: The Bondage Motif in Performing Arts, Life and Aesthetics of Rastafarians. *Tinabantu: Journal of African National Affairs*, 2(1), 37–49.
Asante, M. K. (1998). *The Afrocentric Idea*. Philadelphia: Temple University Press.
Asante, M. K. (2007). *An Afrocentric Manifesto: Toward an African Renaissance*. Maldem: Polity Press.
Bourdillon, M. F. C. (1990). *Religion and Society: A Text for Africa*. Mambo Press.

Campbell, H. (1988). Rastafari as Pan Africanism in the Caribbean and Africa. *African Journal of Political Economy*, 2(1), 75–88.

Catchpole, B. (1983). *A Map History of Our Own Times: From the 1950s to the Present*. Heinemann Educational Books Ltd.

CCJP & LRF. (1997). *Breaking the Silence, Building True Peace: Report on the Disturbances in Matabeleland and Midlands, 1980–1989.* Harare: CCJP and LRF.

Chitando, E. (1998). The Phenomenological Method in a Zimbabwean Context: To Liberate Or to Oppress? *Zambezia*, XXV(i), 99–114.

Chitando, E. (2010). African Jews: Expressing Identities in Tight Spaces. In L. Togarasei & E. Chitando (Eds.), *Faith in the City: The Role and Place of Religion in Harare* (pp. 107–136). Swedish Science Press.

Cox, J. L. (1996). *Expressing the Sacred: An Introduction to the Phenomenology of Religion*. University of Zimbabwe Publications.

Edmonds, E. B. (2012). *Rastafari: A Very Short Introduction*. Oxford University Press.

Ewusi, S. K. (Ed.). (2012). *Weaving Peace: Essays on Peace, Governance and Conflict Transformation in the Great Lakes Region of Africa*. Trafford Publishing.

Fresh. (2003). When the Youthful Crowd Went Wild. *The Sunday Mail*, April 6. https://sdg-tracker.org/peace-justice

Kaur, B. (2006). *Teaching of Peace and Conflict Resolution: New Trends and Innovations*. Deep and Deep Publications Pvt Ltd.

Masunungure, E. V. (2009). A Militarized Election: The 27 June Presidential Run-Off. In E. V. Masunungure (Ed.), *Defying the Winds of Change: Zimbabwe's 2008 Elections*. Weaver Press.

Muchacha, M. (2016). Politically Motivated Violence (PMV) in Zimbabwe and the Role of Social Work, J. *Human Rights Social Work 1*, pp. 156–164.

Nelson, S., & Nelson, D. (2000). Bob Marley as Artist of the Century. *The Beat*, 19(3), 54.

News Day. (2012). Violence Biggest Crisis in Zimbabwe. *News Day*, October 30.

Nhema, A. G. (Ed.). (2004). *The Quest for Peace in Africa: Transformations, Democracy and Public Policy*. OSSREA.

Okoth, P. G. (2004). Conflict Management in Post-Cold War Africa: The Role of International Actors. In A. G. Nhema (Ed.), *The Quest for Peace in Africa: Transformations, Democracy and Public Policy* (pp. 73–92). OSSREA.

Parsons, G. (1993). Filling a Void?: Afro-Caribbean Identity and Religion. In: G. Parsons (Ed.) The Growth of Religious Diversity in Britain from 1945, Vol. 1, (pp. 243–273). London: Routledge.

Selassie, H. (1963). Address to the United Nations, 1963. https://bit.ly/3qhDhSd

Shoko, T. (2010). Traditional Healing: Continuity and Change. In L. Togarasei & E. Chitando (Eds.), *Faith in the City: The Role and Place of Religion in Harare* (pp. 85–106). Swedish Science Press.

Sibanda, F. (2010). Turning the Wheel of Dharma:The Implantation, Development and Impact of Tibetan Buddhism. In L. Togarasei and E. Chitando (Eds.) Faith in the City: The Role and Place of Religion in Harare. Uppsala: Science Swedish Press (pp. 153–180).

Sibanda, F. (2012). The Impact of Rastafari Ecological Ethic: A Contemporary Discourse. *Journal of Pan African Studies*, 5(3), 59–76.

Sibanda, F. (2015). Rastafari Green Philosophy for Sustainable Development in Postcolonial Zimbabwe: Harnessing Eco-theology and Eco-justice. In F. H. Chimhanda, V. M. S. Molobi, & I. D. Mothoagae (Eds.), *African Theological*

*Reflections: Critical Voices on Liberation, Leadership, Gender and Eco-justice* (pp. 187–206). UNISA: Research Institute for Theology and Religion.

Sibanda, F. (2016a). Avenging Spirits and the Vitality of African Traditional Law, Customs and Religion in Contemporary Zimbabwe. In P. Coertzen, M. C. Green, & L. Hansen (Eds.), *Religious Freedom and Religious Pluralism in Africa: Prospects and Limitations* (pp. 345–359). Sun Media.

Sibanda, F. (2016b). One Love, Or Chanting Down Same-sex Relations?: Queering Zimbabwean Rastafari Perspectives on Homosexuality. In A. Van Klinken & E. Chitando (Eds.), *Public Religion and the Politics of Homosexuality in Africa* (pp. 180–196). Routledge.

Sibanda, F. (2017). Praying for Rain? A Rastafari Perspective from Zimbabwe. *The Ecumenical Review*, 69(3), 411–424.

Sibanda, F. (2021). Law and the Competing Interests of Parents and the State in Child-Rearing in Africa: Zimbabwe Rastafari Perspectives. In M.C. Green and F. Kabata (Eds.) *Law, Religion and the Family in Africa*. Stellenbosch: African Sun Media, (pp. 127–139).

Steffens, R. (2000). Wailers' Scrapbook. *The Beat*, 19(3), 60–62.

Strijdom, J., & Tarusarira, J. (2017). Editorial: The Role of Religion in Violence and Peacebuilding. *Journal for the Study of Religion*, 30(1), 1–4.

UN Environmental Programme. (2021). *Making Peace with Nature: A Scientific Blueprint to tackle the Climate Biodiversity and Pollution Emergencies.* Nairobi: UN Environmental Programme.

CHAPTER 20

# Islamophobic Agenda: An Analysis of Media Representation of Radicalization and Terrorism in Kenya Since 2000

*Suleiman A. Chembea*

## Introduction

Radicalization into violent extremism and climate change are arguably the most serious concerns facing humanity in the twenty-first century. Unlike climate change in which stakeholders seem to agree on the root causes and how to arrest the challenge, there is little consensus on 'radicalization', 'terrorism' and 'violent extremism' with regard to what they structurally constitute and subsequently what may be included as effective ways of dealing with the threat. Moreover, the lack of common perception and definition of the key concepts not only confuses efforts to rational prognosis but also provides room for the media[1] to frame and propagate a public narrative of hate and fear against Islam and Muslims as not only inherently violent but also condone terrorism.

---

[1] I use media to imply means of mass communication such as the press, television, radio, newspapers, magazines and the internet. See Ahere, J. R.. (2019). Can the Media Be Conflict Sensitive? An Analysis of Kenya and South Africa. *Open Access Library Journal*, 6: e5569, 1-22. DOI: 10.4236/oalib.1105569.

According to the Advanced English Dictionary (AED), 'radical' is a synonym of 'extremist' in relation to "opinions and actions far beyond the norm" and with the propensity to introduce "markedly new or radical change". Again, the Dictionary defines a terrorist as "a radical who employs terror as political weapon [and] usually organizes [his/her activities] with other terrorists in small cells [that] often use religion as a cover for terrorist activities". The AED further views radicalism as "the political orientation of those who favor revolutionary change in government and society". Thus, AED clearly points out the main goal of terrorism as attainment of political ends with religion merely appropriated as a means rather than an end in itself. Besides, understood from the view point of the AED, one could argue that advocating for 'opinions and actions far beyond the norm' such as lesbianism and gayism as propounded by the Lesbians, Gays, Bi-sexual, Transgender, Intersex and Queer (LGBTIQ) movement rightfully qualifies to be 'radicalization' and 'extremism' in conservative African communities, though not necessarily in European societies. This is because opinions and actions of LGBTIQ enthusiasts remain appealing only to a few across African communities with the vast majority perceiving such acts as 'markedly new', 'un-African' and 'un-natural' (Ndzovu, 2016). In a nutshell, the biggest challenge lays on the authority that reserves the right to determine what is 'extreme' or 'radical' in a given society and context, and whether or not such right extends beyond the geographical boundaries and political jurisdictions of the concerned authority.

Invoking the AED was meant to emphasize the view that words attain meaning depending on how they are framed thereby shaping peoples' choices on how and where to place them (Aziz, 2007). According to Aziz, framing of media news items is a deliberate and systematic process involving selection and salience where the presenter, under the influence of various factors including political, religious, moral, ideological and cultural inclinations, places prominence on certain aspects of the story with a view to promoting a select stand point (Aziz, 2007, pp. 10–11). The significance of framing, therefore, is that it helps shape peoples' reasoning thereby affecting opinion. In the words of Aziz, "media has the capability of informing the public about what issues to think about and also how to think about them" (2007, p. 12). In the context of terrorism and radicalization into violent extremism, therefore, media framing and representation of these components of security threat as caused exclusively by Islam and Muslims fanned the fear for and hatred against Islam and Muslims, hence Islamophobia.

Moreover, framing and presentation of 'radicalization', 'terrorism' and 'violent extremism' by the media remarkably influenced policy making with regard to security subsequently affecting coexistence and peace building in contemporary times. Essentialist representation, for instance, accorded the media the near monopoly to define and shape the security discourse rendering the borders of 'radicalization', 'violent extremism' and 'terrorism' so fluid to include "people embracing opinions, views and ideas which could lead to acts of terrorism" (European Commission, 2008, as cited in Nandwa, n.d., p. 5).

Consequently, the fluidity not only became part of concerted effort to secure the global society but also gave state institutions the cleavage to infringe on fundamental rights and freedoms including those of thought, religion, belief and conscience of those harboring contrary view points (Article 32, Constitution of Kenya, 2010).

To sample how framing shapes reasoning thereby affecting opinion, we draw from Hassan Nandwa's article, "The Impact of criminalizing 'Radicalization' on the Freedom of Thought, Conscience and Religion or Believe in Kenya" (n.d.). In this article, Nandwa presents 'radicalization' as the process of attaining "new or different idea or entity whose implementation entails a great effect". 'Radicals', opines Nandwa, is a group of people that are "distinct from the rest in attributes, characteristics and behaviour" (n.d., p. 2). Looked at from this perspective, Nandwa does not depart sharply from the AED in framing radicalization as not entirely a negative process despite the proclivity to be perceived as such especially where the radicals manifest the capacity to challenge the status quo.

On their part, Boga et al. (2021) define radicalization as "a gradual or phased process that employs the ideological conditioning of individuals and groups to socialize them into violent extremism, and recruitment into terrorist groups or campaigns" (2021, p. xv) 'Radicalization', argue Boga et al., is "dependent on a fanatical ideology [and] the willingness to use mass violence to advance political aims" that are defined in racial, ethnic, sectarian and religious terms (2021, pp. xv–xvi). Further, Boga et al. opine that 'violent extremism' is "an ideology that drives radicalized individual(s) to engage in, or actively support acts of violence in furtherance of religious, socioeconomic or political ideologies or objectives" (2021, p. xvii).

Botha (2013) and Boga et al. (2021) show 'radicalization' "as a slow process that works over a period of time" during which religious indoctrination is undertaken in mosques and *madrassas* (Qur'an schools) with messages of hatred and intolerance preached and spread through literature, mass media and organizing of youth meetings (2013, p. 18). While both Boga et al. (2021) and Botha (2013) are cognizant of 'violent extremism' and 'terrorism' appropriated as a vehicle toward unresolved socio-economic and political grievances, their further discourse point to concerted efforts to link a certain religious ideology with the vice falling short of explicitly pronouncing that indeed some faiths and religious communities teach and abet violence.

The position held by Boga et al. (2021) and Botha (2013) above is also shared by the International Center for the Study of Violent Extremism (ICSVE). ICSVE perceives radicalization and the making of a terrorist as a multi-faceted process with three variables in force—group, ideology and social support. It alleges that

> to make a terrorist, there must be a *group* purporting to represent some segment of a society (i.e. disenfranchised and, therefore vulnerable or 'at risk') and presenting violence as an answer to contentious socio-political issues facing that

particular segment of the society. The *group* also provides an *ideology* to justify terrorist violence and garner social support for both the *group* and its *ideology*. (Speckhard et al., 2018, p. 34, emphasis added)

In the majority of the perceptions on 'radicalization', 'terrorism' and 'violent extremism' as exemplified in the ICSVE, Boga et al. (2021) and Botha (2013), talks of a *group* would often refer primarily to organized 'Muslim extremists' like the *al-Shabaab*, *al-Qaeda* and Boko Haram on one hand, with (Islamic) religious teachings, allegedly based on ultraconservative scriptural interpretations calling for return to puritan Islam (Salafism), as the ideology on the other. Placing prominence on the 'extremists' as identified by the ICSVE, security agencies and the media, therefore, it becomes clear of an existing campaign to propagate a viewpoint that, first, associates Islam with 'terrorism' and 'violent extremism' and, second, divides Muslims into two camps—'the peaceful and accommodative Sufi [i.e. African] oriented' and the 'exclusive and puritanical Salafi [also Wahabi, Arab]' with the latter allegedly inclined toward promoting division, intolerance and conflict (Boga et al., 2021, p. 20; Mamdani, 2002; Seesemann, 2006, 2007).

While analyzing the security threat in the East African region, however, Shinn (2003) identified three types of terrorism. First was 'international terrorism' where terrorist organizations from outside the region carried out acts of 'terrorism' mainly against foreign interests including those of USA and Israel (2003, p. 1). The twin bombing of the American embassies in Nairobi and Dar es Salaam by *al-Qaeda* in 1998 as well as the simultaneous attacks at Mombasa in 2002 against an Israeli airliner and the Paradise Hotel at Kikambala popular with Israeli tourists by the same group suffice as examples of 'international terrorism' (Boga et al., 2021; Seesemann, 2006; Seesemann & Soares, 2009). Second were acts of terrorism by organizations within the region but aimed at neighboring countries (Shinn, 2003, p. 1). This type could be manifested in various acts often associated with the Somali-based *al-Shabaab* and its international allies, the *al-Qaeda* against Kenya. The two organizations have continued to claim responsibility for acts of 'terrorism' in the country including the Dusit D2 (2019)[2] and West Gate shopping Mall (2013)[3] both in Nairobi; the Garissa University College (2015)[4]; Mandera quarry massacre

---

[2] Kenya Attack: 21 Confirmed Dead in DusitD2 Hotel Siege. (2019, January 16). *BBC News*. http://www.bbcnews.com.; Nyanchama, V. (2019, January 16). Dusit Attack at 14 Riverside Nairobi: Latest News, Photos and Videos. *TUKO*. 14 Riverside attack in Nairobi: latest news, photos and videos (tuko.co.ke).

[3] Omabti, C. (2022, September 19). What We Know about Westgate Mall Attack Nine Year Later. *The Star*. What we know about Westgate mall attack nine year later. (the-star.co.ke); Dhanji, K.. (2013, October 4). Terror in Nairobi: The Full Story Behind al-Shabaab's Mall Attack". *The Guardian*. Terror in Nairobi: the full story behind al-Shabaab's mall attack | Westgate mall attacks | The Guardian.

[4] Garissa University College Attack in Kenya: What Happened? *BBC News*. http://www.bbc-news.com.

(2015)[5] as well as the Mandera Bus incident (2014).[6] The third type of terrorism, according to Shinn (2003), are acts instigated by internal insurgent groups against the state as grievances against socio-economic and political exclusions (2003, p. 2; Mickolus, 2016). Terrorist acts by the Lord Resistance Army (LRA) and Alice Lakwena's Holy Ghost Movement in Uganda; the Mombasa Republican Council (MRC) as well as the Sabaot Land Defense Forces (SLDF) in Kenya aptly fit this category. Unlike the positions held by the ICSVE, Boga et al. (2021) and Botha (2013), therefore, framing and presentation of 'terrorism' by Shinn (2003) take cognizant of the various types and associated dynamics that foment and sustain the threat beyond religious ideologies and faith communities.

This is to say that the near lacuna in the common perception of the key terminologies driving (in)security in the twenty-first century has made it increasingly challenging to establish the boundaries between prohibited radicalization and freedom of thought and expression on one hand, and objective analysis of the root concerns that provoke and uphold the choice of terrorism as a means to expressing unresolved grievances on the other (Nandwa, n.d., p. 1). Despite the apparent void on the consensus, nonetheless, it is undeniable that media framing and representation of the phenomenon have continued to impact policies on security and peace building in the present age. Defeating the security threat to promote a just, inclusive, secure and participatory society (UN SDG 16),[7] however, demands a rational and objective analysis and representation of the root causes sustaining it. It is argued that narrow framing and representation of radicalization, terrorism and violent extremism on the lenses of a religious ideology and faith community is, therefore, defeatist and undesirable. The essentialist representation of the threat fuels stereotyping, profiling, hatred and irrational fear against Islam and Muslims thereby confusing rational efforts to mitigate the menace.

## Methodology and Structure

Kenya boasts of a robust media sector composed of national and international outlets. Data was, therefore, largely drawn from daily newspapers and weekly magazines including the *Daily Nation, The Standard, BBC News, Aljazeera, The Star, The Independent*, and the *Friday Bulletin*. Others were local and translocal TV channels, national and regional legal statutes on terrorism and money laundering, deradicalization and counter-terrorism programs as well as

---

[5] Kenya: Al-Shabab Kills Quarry Workers in Mandra Gun Attack. (2015, July 7). BBC News. http://bbcnews.com.

[6] Ombati, C. (2021, June 8). Death Toll from Mandera Bus Attack Rises to Three as Two More Cops Succumb. *The Star*. Death toll from Mandera bus attack rises to three as two more cops succumb (the-star.co.ke).

[7] SDG 16: Promote peaceful and inclusive societies for sustainable development, provide access to justice for all and build effective, accountable and inclusive institutions at all levels – SDG Compass.

social media. The choice of these media was strategic owing to their wider readership and coverage of the subject subsequently shaping public opinion throughout the two decades during which the concern has been in the limelight. A casual search of the main terms in all these outlets unearthed hundreds of entries since 2000 whose textual analysis enriched the chapter.

To understand how the media actively shapes and drives the Islamophobic narrative, this chapter proceeds in four sections. The preceding introductory section set the pace in highlighting the challenges of perception and defining 'radicalization', 'terrorism' and 'violent extremism', thus contributing to the disconnect in mitigating measures. Section two on Islam and Muslims disabuses the essentialist representation of the faith and religious community with regard to radicalization into violent extremism. By essentializing Islam and Muslims as a monolithic society and religion, the media has progressively succeeded in building a picture of a belief and faith community opposed to peace, development and coexistence. Section three moves away from essentialist Islam and Muslims to balkanizing the faith and religious community. In the attempt to attribute terrorism to a specific ethno-religious group, the media (and a cross-section of the academia) have relentlessly depicted Islam and Muslims in racial and theological underpinning in relation to being moderate, accommodative and peace loving (African/Sufi) on one hand, and ultraconservative and prone to violence (Arabic/Salafi) on the other. The final section demonstrates how media framing and representation of acts of terrorism by Muslims differ from those by non-Muslims. This section not only overlooks the plight of victims of insecurity by the latter group but also impedes rational prognosis of the problem whose elimination significantly contributes to peaceful and inclusive societies as well as access to justice in the society.

## 'ISLAM' AND 'MUSLIMS': ALIGNING VIOLENT EXTREMISM AND TERRORISM WITH ETHNO-RELIGIOUS COMMUNITIES

While framing and representations of violent extremism and terrorism, we could discern two paths: The first, drawn from the UN SDGs and Shinn (2003), seemingly objective and inclusive. Here, 'violent extremism' and 'terrorism' tend to be rationally explored, the root causes interrogated, analyzed and plausible mitigating measures arrived at and tested from a participatory perspective. The second, expounded by the ICSVE, Boga et al. (2021) and Botha (2013) where 'radicalization', 'terrorism' and 'violent extremism' are presented mainly on the basis of a religious ideology and group identity. All other socio-economic and political grievances aside, the latter group tends to accord premium to a religious ideology as the driving force in the choice of the path of violence in attaining set objectives. In its view, therefore, 'radicalization', 'violent extremism' and 'terrorism' are essentially and exclusively Islamic problems (Costanza, 2015; Kundnani, 2015; Speckhard et al., 2018). But who are the 'Muslims', or which 'Islam' if one may ask?

Muslims in Kenya are the largest minority group accounting for 11% of the total population (KBS, 2019)[8] and spread across ethnic, racial, geographical as well as theological affiliations none of which are homogeneous. While it could be true that the majority of Muslims in the country identify themselves with the Sunni-Shafi'i *madhaheb* (school of law) (Botha, 2013; Mraja, 2007), there are also pockets of Hanafi, Hanbali and Malik as well as Ahmadiyya and Bahais. Others are the minority Shia that also offer allegiance to various *madhaheb* including the *Ithna' Ashari* (Twelvers), Ismailiyyah (the Seveners) and Bohras (Oded, 2000, pp. 15–19). Racially and geographically, there are African and Asian Muslims from the Somali, Arab, Swahili and Mijikenda on one hand, and coastal, North-eastern and upcountry on the other. It becomes simplistic within this context, therefore, to construct and qualify 'Muslims' along abstract binaries of 'Suni-Shia', 'Sufi-Salafi' and 'accommodative-puritanical' lenses.

Islam and Muslims could best be understood as categories of census and labeling in relation to the principle of 'Categories of Practice and Categories of Analysis' (Brubaker, 2012). In the Categories of Analysis, 'Muslims' are a category in the taxonomical religious or faith affiliation with regard to "identifying oneself and to identify others", that is, the self (internal) and other (external) identification (Brubaker, 2012, p. 2). In this categorization, religion becomes the denominator where 'Muslims' are constructed and represented in the perspective of 'collective and organizational structures' in contrast to other religious communities like Christians, Buddhists, Jews, and Hindus for the purposes of data or census (Hausner & Gellner, 2012, p. 974). Further, 'Muslims' could be used for categorization in the internal identification within the Muslim community of believers (*umma*), that is, the collective 'we' (us) that transcends racial, geographical and national boundaries, and bonded by faith. The later categorization is how 'Muslims' are constructed and represented in sections of the policy and security studies as well as the majority of the media news items in the unrelenting 'war on terror'.

The *umma* is, nonetheless, heterogeneous, and the 'prevailing other' identification of 'Muslim populations' could as well apply in reference to the various ethnic, racial and regional origins like the Asians, Africans, Somali, Swahili, coastal and upcountry. The 'prevailing other' identification draws prominence from Qur'an 49:13 where God reminds us of having created mankind in nationalities and confederacies as part of the divine plan. This component is often overlooked by the media and academic pieces in policy and security studies representing 'Muslims' as a homogeneous entity. Consequently, this form of representation confronts us "with an essentialist and totalizing discourse that negates the existence of multiple cultures and identities within a single society" (Borg & Mayo, 2006, p. 153).

In the Categories of Practice, 'Muslims' could further be understood as an object of Practice-Analysis in relation to spiritual performances. Hausner and

---

[8] Kenya Population and Housing Census (2019) Vol. IV: Distribution of Population by Socio-economic Characteristics. Kenya National Bureau of Statistics (knbs.or.ke).

Gellner (2012) refer to 'practice' as the "activities engaged in by individual people, agents capable of modifying and adjusting exigencies of their daily lives" (2012, p. 974). Included in this is a wide range of ritual practices that generally fall under the class of *ibada* (worship) in Islam. They include *fardh* (obligatory) like prayer, fasting and alms; *sunna* (optional), such as night vigil, some fasts and prayers too; and *halal* (permitted), like eating good food. While it is easy to regard these acts generally as 'Muslim practices', they are also subject to diverse interpretative and jurisprudential discourses of the *madhaheb* in relation to 'accommodative and peaceful' or 'modernity and reforms' in the faith.

In the Practice-Analysis, therefore, 'Muslims' are categorized as either Sunni or Shi'a and often juxtaposed with 'conservative-modernity' discourse in relation to how the spiritual practices above are observed. In essence, however, all theological dispositions, taking cognizance of the various sub-sects under them, are reformist in their own perspectives. These include the different strands under the two main Sunni and Shia *madhaheb* identified elsewhere in the chapter. As is the norm, however, the Shi'a are often depicted in essentialist terms as 'modernists' and inclined toward 'logical' interpretations of the spiritual practices confining religion to the private life. A small group within the majority Sunni Islam, specifically the Salafis are, nonetheless, alleged to champion a return to the first century 'true and puritan Islam' through rigid and literal interpretation of some religious practices including jihad (literally, to strive) (Boga et al., 2021; Botha, 2013; Speckhard et al., 2018). This is the essentialist perception of Islam that accords Salafis a disproportionate attention as 'ultraconservatives', 'fundamentalists', 'radicals', 'extremists' and 'terrorists' and by extension, the face of 'Islam' and 'Muslims' in both local and international media coverage. It is submitted in here that this view of 'Islam' and 'Muslims' is not only simplistic but also misguided in the effort toward promotion of a just, inclusive and participatory society as argued in the subsequent section.

## Islamic Extremism and Radicalism: Positioning Terror in the Global Challenges of (in)Security and Inclusivity

This chapter disabuses essentialist definitions of Islam and Muslims for being narrow and creating a non-existent homogenic community of believers. Moreover, essentialist perceptions of Islam and Muslims have serious misgivings that obscure global efforts toward peacebuilding and coexistence. First, the essentialist ideas suggest 'non-radical', 'peaceful and accommodative' African Islam that ought to be promoted at the expense of 'exclusivist puritanical Arab Islam'. That 'reformism', 'radicalism' and 'puritanism' in Islam are inherently Arabic and were only imported to Africa from South Asia and the Middle-East (Kimunguyi, n.d.; Seesemann, 2006, 2007). Such sentiments are prominent in Boga et al. (2021) and Botha (2013) who claim that though East Africa was traditionally seen as 'accommodative Shafi'i [Sufi] oriented', this gradually changed from the 1980s following settlement of immigrants from South Asia as well as

> return of the Saudi trained scholars ... who started fanning, across the coastal region, teachings of what they be termed as 'correct type of Islam' with a strong Wahhabi orientation in *madrassas*, mosques, Friday sermons (*khutbahs*) and regular *darsas*. (Boga et al., 2021, p. 25)

While it could be correct to observe that the reformist agenda increasingly succeeded in rendering the Shafi'i theology impotent and irrelevant (Botha, 2013) following return of the foreign trained local scholars as well as immigrants from Saudi Arabia and South Asia, it would be insincere to exclusively associate Salafism with 'extremism' and 'terrorism'. Calls to purge Islam of religious innovations (*bida'a*) and return to 'true and puritan Islam' were evident in the local Muslim community long before immigration of Muslims from South Asia and return of the foreign trained *ulamas* as manifested in the efforts by Sheikh al-Amin Mazrui and his students (Mraja, 2007; Seesemann, 2006). Despite these early efforts, nonetheless, incidents of terrorism and violent extremism attributed to Islam were hard to come by owing to the fact that the vast majority of Muslims have no interest in Islamic fundamentalism or even political Islam (Shinn, 2003). Moreover, many Muslims, Kenyans being no exception, tend to oscillate between theological schools, teachings and practices making it practically impossible, if not unnecessary, to confine a believer to a particular line of thought. In other words, as far as religious practices are concerned, the so-called Salafi is at times 'Sufi', making them one and the same in different contexts.

Secondly, essentialist perceptions of Islam and Muslims are more of selective amnesia for being alive to terrorism purportedly carried out in the name and on behalf of Islam and Muslims but remain blind to unresolved historical, socio-cultural and political grievances by the community that significantly contribute to the security challenge in the society. Seminal works on security and radicalism acknowledge an array of 'push and pull' factors including personal, sociological and political motives to radicalization and extremism (Botha, 2013; Turner, 2011). As correctly documented by others, predominant Muslim regions in Kenya "have been kept on the fringes of the national agenda" consequently lagging behind in economic development and political inclusion compared to the mainly Christian upcountry (Botha, 2013, p. 15; Ndzovu, 2014). This suggests that Muslims across the country suffer socio-economic disadvantages and "general feelings of exclusion and injustice" that successive political administrations have failed to address (Götsch, 2016, p. 42; Belquis, 2015; Job, 2019). Coupled with endemic corruption, high unemployment rate despite good levels of quality education, systemic injustices and police brutality as well as collapsed social systems, Muslim youths often find themselves vulnerable to extremist ideologies owing to failure by the government to help them redirect their energies positively (Costanza, 2015; Maiangwa et al., 2021; Rabasa, undated). Thus, to the marginalized and disenfranchised youths, extremist groups only tend to fill an existing void created by systemic state failure in its core mandate by offering social warmth, recognition, belonging and identity that youths continuously yearn for (Botha, 2013; Götsch, 2016).[9]

In her study "*Afghan Youth and Extremists: Why Are Extremists' Narratives so Appealing?*", Belquis (2015) further observed that pop and youth culture provided invaluable vehicles through which radicalization campaigns were disseminated as videos, sound messages and heroic pictures of fighters. In her view, the messages were often packaged as chants and folk poetry appealing to youths to take action against ineffective governments (2015, p. 3). To some extent, therefore, youth culture helped expose large section of the Muslim community in the country that accounts for close to 65% of the Muslim population to extremist ideas and practices (Botha, 2013, p. 2). The belief adopted by extremists as key to recruitment and motivation to act being that their interpretation of the Sharia and establishment of an Islamic state would be the panacea to the socio-cultural decay occasioned by non-Muslim economic and political systems. Retrospectively, this calls for responsive, participatory and representative decision-making measures (SDG Target 16.7) in addressing the demands and expectations of youths as well as sections of the society that feel economically and politically marginalized hence vulnerable to radicalization and recruitment to extremism. Governments have a moral responsibility to ensure equitable distribution of resources and improve socio-economic and political inclusivity to stem dissent and radicalization occasioned by feelings of exclusion. The narrow perception of radicalization into violent extremism is, therefore, a subtle attempt to exonerate the government from failure of its core mandate to reduce forms of violence and related deaths by providing for the youth and the marginalized in the society as envisioned in SDG Target 16.1.

Moreover, Kenya shares porous borders with the fragile state of Somalia that has experienced civil war since the 1990s. This has allowed free flow of refugees, members of insurgent groups as well as small arms thereby making security management challenging (Botha, 2013; Shinn, 2003). This contributed significantly to terrorist activities by non-Muslim militias as well that equally employed terror and armed violence to express socio-economic and political grievances. To perceive religious ideology as the exclusive basis of radicalization into violent extremism was, therefore, to conflate Islam with terrorism while remaining blind to the various forms of terrorism and root causes fomenting and sustaining them.

---

[9] To emphasize the view that extremists capitalize on socio-economic and political grievances, it was observed that they are shifting their recruitment campaigns to non-Muslim regions where recruits would either be new converts or even non-Muslims enticed by the allure for jobs and quick money. See Wambui, M. (2021, November 24). Kenya's new terror hot spots raise alarm. *Daily Nation*. Kenya's new terror hotspots raise alarm | Nation.

The largest beneficiaries of the narrow framing of radicalization into violent extremism and terrorism in the East Africa region are a host of non-Muslim insurgent groups operating locally as elaborated elsewhere in the chapter. Kenya has experienced forms of violent extremism and terror-related incidents since 1990s with the earliest being the USA Embassy bombing, the Norfolk Hotel attacks in Nairobi, as well as the Paradise Hotel bombing in Mombasa. These were acts of 'international terrorism' imported into the country and inclined toward religio-political ideologies targeting Western and Israel interests. Kenya became a collateral damage owing to its perceived position as an alley of the USA and Israel (Boga et al., 2021; Shinn, 2003). The majority of terrorist incidents, however, had very little or nothing to do with specific religious ideologies and were carried out by local militant groups like the MRC, Chinkororo, Mungiki, and the SLDF. It could rightfully be claimed that these local militant groups were (still do) influenced by a political and/or socio-economic ideology aligned to violence and terror in achieving set objectives that included quick and illegal acquisition of wealth and property as well as political ambitions (Nandwa, n.d.; Shinn, 2003). In all types of terror incidents, both 'local' and 'imported' nonetheless, it was evident that extremists merely tapped into the pool of existing grievances and local vulnerabilities. However, what seemed to qualify an attack as 'terrorism' or 'violent extremism' in the view of the media was the religious identification of alleged radicalized and extremist masterminds with Islam, either by name, ethnicity or even race (Boga et al., 2021; Speckhard et al., 2018).[10] Any other form of violence and extremism simply fell under the radar of terrorism and radicalization for its failure to be associated with Islam and Muslims.

Further, representing radicalization and extremism as a group and a religious ideologically influenced process is to refuse to acknowledge various acts of terrorism carried out by the so-called lone rangers. There are various acts of violent extremism perpetrated by lone non-Muslim gun-men and women that the media often explained in terms of psycho-social traumas despite bearing all features of terrorism.[11] Thus the idea, as adopted in a cross-section of the academia, policy and security studies, was to depict 'Muslims' as adherents of a dangerous ideology incompatible with Western democracy and culture (Kundnani, 2015) while negating what were clearly terrorist acts by non-Muslim extremists and radicals.

The attempt to narrowly present terrorism and radicalization as a unitary phenomenon that is exclusively Islamic (Mickolus, 2016) is what I call the

---

[10] Wanjohi, J. (2021, August 11). Missing lawyer Prof. Hassan Nandwa found Alive in Kitui. *Mwakilishi.com*. Missing Lawyer Prof. Hassan Nandwa Found Alive in Kitui | Mwakilishi.com.; Cece, S. (2001, August 23). Police arrest two suspected terrorists at Likoni ferry Crossing. *Daily Nation*. Police arrest two suspected terrorists at Likoni ferry crossing | Nation.

[11] Mutambo, A. (2021, August 26). Tanzania gunman was a good boy 'turned bad – Neighbours. *Daily Nation*.. Tanzania gunman was a good boy 'turned bad'—Neighbours | Nation.; Echenje, M, (2022, January 20). The war at Home: We need to Open up to Stem the violence. *Daily Nation*, The war at home: We need to open up to stem the violence | Nation.

'dominant ideology of Islamophobia'. By dominant ideology I refer "to the organizing principles that generate, shape, and sustain" a discourse on intense dislike and the belief of Islam and Muslims as inherently terroristic (Macedo & Gounari, 2006, p. 3; Allen, 2010). Founded on the view of Islam as a homogeneous cultural entity, the dominant ideology perceives Muslims as "either unable or unwilling to co-exist with the civilization" and modernity often associated with the West (Hendrick, 2013, p. 12). While obfuscating the underlying causes that fuel and sustain violence perpetrated by both Muslim and non-Muslim extremists and individuals, the dominant ideology blocks the objective interrogation and understanding of terrorism and radicalization thereby confusing efforts to mitigate the menace. Consequently, this cripples rational thinking toward an inclusive, just and participatory measures to combat the threat.

To arrest the dominant ideology of Islamophobia as advocated by the media, state agencies and sections of academia, the cure lays in securitization of institutions and systems to check on alleged financial and logistical support to Muslim terrorists.[12] Establishment of the Prevention of Terrorism Act (2012); The Prevention of Terrorism (Amendment) Act (2018); Security Amendment Act (2014) and The Proceeds of Crime and Anti-Money Laundering Act (2009) bear witness to this assertion. As a member of the Intergovernmental Authority on Development (IGAD), Kenya also adopted the IGAD Building Program against Terrorism (ICPAT) funded by the European Union (EU) and other foreign donors (Kimunguyi, n.d., p. 14). The enactment and implementation of these statutes faced spirited resistance by Muslims owing to the apparent targeting of the community and some of its religious practices as well as imposition and sponsorship by the West. The visible and active presence of the EU and the USA in the 'war on terror' at the local level thus continued to cement suspicions by Muslims that local statutes and efforts in the 'war on terror' were wrongly crafted and without regard to local contexts.[13]

As part of the securitization measures, deradicalization and counter-terrorism programs were established. Other than being significantly crafted along Western anti-terrorism frameworks, the programs were also funded by foreign governments and involved particularly alleged radicalized Muslims being consciously directed "to cause them to change their views to reject violent extremist ideologies and act within acceptable, religious, legal and constitutional bounds" (Boga et al., 2021, p. xv). Disdain to public display of religiosity by Muslims became common, not to mention military incursions

---

[12] Mukinda, F. (2014, September 2). Police to join hands in war on crime. *Daily Nation*,. Police to join hands in war on crime | Nation.

[13] Nandwa, H. (n.d). "The Impact of criminalizing 'Radicalization' on the Freedom of Thought, Conscience and Religion or Believe in Kenya". (DOC) Radicalization | Hassan Nandwa - Academia.edu. See also Kahongeh, J. (2021, September 12). How the global war on terror changed Kenya'. *Daily Nation*. How the global war on terror changed Kenya | Nation.; Gordon, O. (2021, November 8). Sudan-educated Nandwa believes radicalization poorly framed. *The Star*. Sudan-educated Nandwa believes radicalization fight poorly framed (the-star.co.ke).

against perceived Islamists.[14] Others were collective condemnation of the community while calling upon them to account for terrorism carried out in the name of the faith.[15] For some time, Muslim religious institutions like the *madrassas* and *masjids* (mosques) were also misconstrued to be breeding grounds for terrorists (Belquis, 2015; Speckhard et al., 2018).[16]

But why were *madrassas* and *masjids* targeted in the 'war on terror'? Despite there being no scientific relation between *madrassa* education and terrorism, the fear that the religious centers incubated terrorists stemmed from the historical relation of the term *taliban* (seekers), literally, *madrassa* students' movement, with *mujahidin* (freedom fighters). During the anti-Soviet war in Afghanistan, the Taliban, instead of being trained on religious sciences in the *madrassas*, were exposed to radical interpretation of Islam, *jihad* and terror tactics with the support of allied forces (Pakistan, Saudi Arabia and the UAE). Consequently, the group morphed into a splinter military and dominant player controlling large sections of the country different from the mainstream *mujahidin* before felling out of favor to be branded as terrorists (Campo & Elfenbein, 2004; Mamdani, 2002).

Research, nonetheless, suggests that majority of alleged terrorists have only basic knowledge of Islam with the bulk of information on the faith sourced from their sheikhs, the internet, media and heroes, but not necessarily due to critical studies of religious sciences in *madrasas*.[17] For instance, the suspects in the twin bombing of the US embassies in Nairobi and Dar es Salaam in 1998 had no record of *madrassa* training (Oded, 2000, p. 82; Shinn, 2003). A large number of the supposed Islamists elsewhere were also known to have had prior records of crime and got converted to Islam while serving jail sentences (Mickolus, 2016, pp. 57, 66). To such zealots, therefore, religion only provided a cover to enhance and justify long-held traditions of violence and lawlessness. To the majority of Muslims, nonetheless, *madrassas* have historically supplemented formal education and in certain circumstances served as the only source of education, among minority marginalized Muslim communities deprived of formal education as was evident in pre-independence Kenya (Chembea, 2017). The narrow framing and representation of radicalization as exclusively Islamic and the fear for *madrassas* as incubators of terrorists, in particular, partly explains the incorporating of *imams* and religious leaders "to

[14] Kenya invaded Somalia in 2011 to fight the *Al-Shabaab* extremist group in a military expedition known as *Operation Linda Nchi*. This was in response to a string of terrorist activities in the country. Kenyan forces were later joined in a larger operation—the African Mission in Somalia (AMISOM) to rid Northern Somalia of the terrorist group.

[15] Mahdawi, A. (2017, March 29). Dossier: Muslim Condemn Terrorism. *IslamiCity*.. Dossier: Muslims Condemn Terrorism - IslamiCity; Heard, L. (2005, July 26). Muslims are Condemning Terror, But Who's Listening? *Arab News*. Muslims Are Condemning Terror, But Who's Listening? | Arab News

[16] Mayoyo, P. (2014, March 2). Mosques turned to avenues for recruiting youth into terrorism'. *Daily Nation*. Mosques turned to avenues for recruiting youth into terrorism | Nation.

[17] Roy, O. (April 13). Who are the New *Jihadis*? *The Guardian*. https://www.theguardian.com/news/2017/apr/13/who-are-the-new-jihadis.

work with youth and encourage their development in the areas of education, careers, and personal development" in the so-called deradicalization programs (Speckhard et al., 2018, p. 37).[18] On the flip side, this is a pointer that *madrassas*, once well taped, could play a significant role in the 'war on terror' by imparting positive religious knowledge and values than are presently demonized.

Global profiling and collective condemnation of Islam and the Muslim community as inherently violent is, in the words of Botha (2013, p. 19), "not only ineffective but also counterproductive". Moreover, it is an exclusivist approach contrary to the United Nations (UN) Sustainable Development Goal (SDG) on the promotion of just, peaceful and inclusive societies.[19] When a particular community is viewed to be the problem rather than part of the solution, it becomes isolated and targeted in the search for solutions. Whereas Muslims are equal victims of terrorism despite being collectively viewed as "terrorists or potential terrorists" themselves (Botha, 2013, p. 19), attempts to craft solutions against radicalization from a narrow perspective risk overlooking invaluable contributions by Muslims, thereby emboldening the problem. Embracing a wider understanding of and approach to the phenomenon by unraveling and addressing socio-economic and political conditions fomenting and sustaining the threat cannot, therefore, be gainsaid. This would be an invaluable effort to attain a just, peaceful and inclusive society contrary to how the menace is being framed and represented across the media as elaborated in the following section.

### *Terrorism, Far-Right Extremism and Socio-emotional Instability: The Shifting Constructions and Representations of a Global Challenge*

The dominant ideology of Islamophobia has unwavering support of the media in representing radicalization as exclusively Islamic, not only specific to Africa and Kenya in particular, but also across the globe. Whenever terrorist attacks happen anywhere in the world, media coverage helps shape the discourse on perception and resentment against Islam and Muslims that are made to explain events undertaken in the name of their faith or even apologize for the same. Consequently, this not only creates fear and suspicion against a single faith and religious community but also blinds our vision toward an objective analysis of the threat, thereby impeding the formulation and application of appropriate measures to arrest the challenge.

Radicalization and terrorism remain global challenges to 'promoting a just and inclusive society' (SDG 16) and are difficult to associate with any particular socio-religious group, political faction, or state. Above all, religious motive could not be the primary factor in perpetrating terrorism as the dominant ideology would make us believe. With the religious motive out of the matrix,

---

[18] See also Atieno, W. (2021, October 23). Muslim Religious Leaders in Push to stop Radicalization. *Daily Nation*. Muslim religious leaders in fresh push to stop radicalization | Nation.

[19] SDG 16: Targets and Indicators – Sustaining Development.

therefore, understanding why people are susceptible to extremism becomes complex than is narrowly presented (Botha, 2017; Turner, 2011).[20]

A casual review of the media undertaken for this chapter revealed a seemingly deliberate campaign to disproportionately frame and represent the Islamization of terror and radicalization. The article, "From Top Student to ISIS Butcher, Salim Rashid Shocks Friends and Family" bears testimony to such subversion.[21] Apart from arresting a *Swahili Muslim* suspect, the article claimed that security officers had identified the suspect in a video beheading an alleged ISIS defector during which he is alleged to have uttered the phrase *Bismillah rahmani raheem* (in the name of Allah the beneficent the merciful). Other phrases that are often misconceived as *jihadists*' war cry calls include *Allah Akbar* (God is greatest), *laailaha illa Allah* (there is no deity but Allah), *Subhanna Allah* (all praise be to the Lord), *Alhamdulillah* (thanks be to the Lord) and *takbir* (praise be the Lord). Others include graphics of women in *niqab* (face veil) and *burqa* (full body covering) (mis-)representing 'oppression' and 'backwardness' of Muslim women while men in turbans and beards are adopted as markers of Islamism. Polemical images of the *mashaf* (hard copies of Qur'an) were (still do) also common subtly suggesting that indeed the Muslim holy book condones violent extremism. Distorting Islamic concepts only serve to criminalize sections of religious rituals that in essence form the everyday pronouncements of vast majority of Muslims who have nothing to do with Islamism. Moreover, this type of framing borders on deliberate misinformation in what Borg and Mayo (2006) refer to as the 'culture of *alterity*' that disregards the religious values and sensibilities of others (2006, p. 151). As correctly summarized by Allen (2010), it is what "newspaper editors sell newspapers with: Muslims as threat, Muslims as against 'our' way of life" (2010, p. 92).

While reporting similar acts of terrorism by non-Muslims, however, the media would meticulously gloss the violence. The articles, "The War at Home: We Need to Open up to Stem the Violence"[22] and "Tanzania Gunman Was a Good Boy 'Turned Bad'—Neighbours"[23] are a case in point. Unlike in the Kenyan student case above, the ethnic and religious identities of the suspects in the present incidents were not emphasized, neither was the violence associated with some religious motive despite appearing to be deliberate and well planned. This trend was also common with violent extremism perpetrated by non-Muslims who owed no allegiance to any particular group with a view to attracting attention in relation to domestic, social and emotional matters, and even

---

[20] See also Mehdi, H. (2017, March 29). You Shouldn't Blame Islam for Terrorism: Religion Isn't a Crucial Factor in Attacks. *The Intercept*. http://www.theintercept.com.

[21] Ocharo, B. (2021, September 8). From top student to ISIS butcher, Salim Rashid shocks friends and family. *Daily Nation*. From top student to Isis butcher, Salim Rashid shocks friends and family | Nation.

[22] Echenje, M. (2021, January 20). The war at Home: We need to Open up to Stem the violence. *Daily Nation*. The war at home: We need to open up to stem the violence | Nation.

[23] Mutambo, A. (2021, August 26). Tanzania gunman was a good boy 'turned bad' – Neighbours. *Daily Nation*. Tanzania gunman was a good boy 'turned bad'—Neighbours | Nation.

economic gains as was the case with armed robbery. In such incidents, suspects were exonerated from their heinous acts through speculations into financial stress, depression, family breakdown and socio-emotional instability.[24] The media would not, therefore, hesitate to brand violence by Muslim suspects as 'terrorism' or an 'Islamist attack', but would belabor to downplay similar violence by non-Muslims as 'far-right extremism', 'hooliganism', or merely 'acts of lawlessness'. Even where further investigations exonerated Muslim suspects from alleged terrorism rarely were apologies issued despite the religious insensitivity inflicted.

As emphasized elsewhere in this chapter, there are non-Muslim extremists that benefited from the shifting construction and misrepresentation of radicalization in the region and beyond. Since violence by non-Muslims was (still do) perceived in the prism of 'non-state resistance' undermining state policies, or more broadly, struggles for 'freedom and liberation' (Mickolus, 2016), seldom were such acts regarded as terrorism.[25] Like in Islamism, therefore, subversively representing terrorism on the viewpoint of an explicit Islamic ideology resulted in overlooking not only the local socio-economic and political dynamics of actors that fueled and sustained the violence across the globe but also efforts to address such grievances for lasting peace in the society. Consequently, this has hindered inclusivity and representation in crafting responsive measures against a global phenomenon as envisioned in the SDGs.

What makes Islamists particularly victims of the shifting construction is their perceived belief in the existence of *dar al-Islam* (land of Islam) and *dar al-harb* (land of war), thereby making their violence to attract global attention as *jihad* aimed at creating "a return to the era of Muhammad" (Mickolus, 2016, p. 7). It is, however, significant to note that people in the alleged *dar al-harb* have not been the exclusive target of 'Islamist attacks' to warrant the disproportionate media coverage as *jihad*. It is, rather, the continued selective framing and representation of violence and extremism as exclusively Islamic that accords groups like the *al-Shabaab*, al-Qaeda and Boko Haram the courage to claim responsibility on terrorist acts even where they never deserved. Moreover, misrepresentation has also made suspects to be perceived as accomplices of Islamists with 'incriminating evidence' pieced together to corroborate the claims. This partly explains the tens, if not hundreds, of 'Islamist groups' and 'major terrorist leaders' in the watch list of international security agencies that entirely include Muslims who end up facing extrajudicial extermination,

---

[24] See also Andrews, F. (2022, September 23). 'Riverdale' actor Ryan Grantham sentenced to life for killing his mother. *The National News*. 'Riverdale' actor Ryan Grantham sentenced to life for killing his mother (thenationalnews.com).

[25] Mito, W. (2022, February 18). 15 High School Students Injured, Driver Killed after Bus Sprayed with Bullets. *Kenyans.co.ke*. 15 High School Students Injured, Driver Killed After Bus Sprayed With Bullets – Kenyans.co.ke; Abdikadir, H. (2017, June 9). Pokoto Bandits Kill KDF Soldier in Brutal Morning Attack. *TUKO*. Pokot bandits kill KDF soldier in brutal morning attack – Tuko.co.ke.

enforced disappearance as well as arbitrary detention and torture (Mickolus, 2016, pp. 9–11, 13–15; SDG Target 16.10.1).[26]

The shifting construction and representation of radicalization propagates a non-existent dialectic relationship between Islam and terrorism. Consequently, this breeds religious intolerance manifested in a wide range of incidents curtailing fundamental rights and freedoms of Muslims in the country. Despite public display of religiosity not being uncommon in the Kenyan society, for instance, Muslim girls have increasingly experienced hostility in schools for wearing the *hijab* compared to the Akorino, Catholic nuns and a section of Hindus that also put on head scarves.[27] Again, Muslims have reported cases of being segregated on the basis of religious affiliation where they have been profiled by dress, like the flowing robes (*kanzu*) and *buibui;* race and ethnicity such as the Somali and Afro-Arabs (Swahili) as well as regions of origin, like the coast and North-Eastern with the later particularly stereotyped as *waria* or *shifta* (bandits) (Botha, 2013). As a matter of fact, the question of public display of religiosity remains controversial even across Europe where unlike adherents of other faiths, Muslims have been banned from adorning the *niqab* and *burqa* in certain countries (Durham et al., 2012).

Further to Islamophobia, ethnic Kenyan-Somali Muslims have often lamented the difficulty in acquiring travel documents like passports and identity cards thereby hampering free movement for socio-economic development (Ndzovu, 2014). At some point in the height of the 'war on terror', Kenyan-Somali Muslims were attacked by their non-Somali Christian compatriots following detonation of an explosive device on November 18, 2012, in the predominantly Muslim neighborhood of Eastleigh in Nairobi (Botha, 2013, p. 19). Owing to ethno-religious and racial profiling, there were also calls to deport Somali Muslims to refugee camps in Kakuma and Dadaab or close the camps altogether for allegedly abetting terrorism.[28] Narrow representation of radicalization, therefore, has not only caused stereotyping and profiling of Muslims and Islam but also denial of fundamental rights and freedoms including those of religion, conscience, belief and movement (Article 32 Constitution of Kenya, 2010; SDG Target 16.B; 16.10). What has conspicuously been lacking, however, in the shifting construction and misrepresentation of terrorism is the objective interrogation of the root causes and the forces sustaining the vice. The skewed gaze propagated by the media instead pays attention to the

---

[26] The most prominent of such cases include that of Saifullah Paracha, a Pakistan Muslim and businessman who was arrested in Thailand and held at Guantanamo Bay for close to 20 years without charges for allegedly supporting terrorism. Saiffulah was released in 2022 following a Presidential (Bidden) pardon. See (10) Facebook.

[27] Andrww, W. & Magdalene, M. (2018, April 28). Muslims at Kenya college barred for wearing hijab. Muslims at Kenya college barred for wearing hijab (aa.com.tr); http://www.aljazeera.com/news.

[28] Langat, A. (2016, July 11). Somali Refugees in Kenya Fear Being Repatriated. *Aljazeera*. Somali refugees in Kenya fear being repatriated | Refugees | Al Jazeera.

devastating results with a view to justifying punitive policies against an entire religious community as well as military engagement against alleged Islamists.

In summary, the impact of media obsession with religious extremism and terrorism as exclusively Islamic is three-fold. Firstly, it blinds us from objective analysis of similar acts of terrorism by non-Muslims across the world that receive little attention leaving victims without recourse. These include religiously inspired acts of terrorism by the anti-abortion group 'Operation Rescue' in the USA[29]; the 'Cow Protection Vigilante' groups in India[30] as well as a host of local militias in Kenya and Uganda mentioned elsewhere in the chapter. Without doubt, non-Muslim perpetrators of violence equally anticipate spiritual rewards and glory. As correctly observed by Mamdani (2002, pp. 1–2), "if there are good Muslims and bad Muslims, there must also be good" and bad Christians, Hindus, Buddhists, Confucians and Jews. These groups should not, therefore, be allowed to evade the scrutiny of terrorism as well.

Secondly, the perception that terrorism is exclusively Islamic has inhibited the global urge to go beyond the surface to interrogate what lays beneath the violence by both Muslim and non-Muslims, with some of them turning to be black market cartels of drugs, prostitution, human organs, and slavery.[31] More so, shifting constructions and bias analysis of radicalization obscures the castigation of terrorism by a section of peace-loving Muslims, some of whom have paid the ultimate price protesting against Islamic fundamentalism.[32] This is a misdemeanor that peace-loving Muslims have continued to endure and belabor to correct as Abou el-Fadl (2005) lamented:

> The vast majority of Muslims are not terrorists, and do not condone terrorism. Yet hardly a time passes without a group of extremist Muslims featured in the news, typically because of an act of violence that shocks the world. For those who know Islam only through the media, the legacy of modern Muslims seems to be a long sequence of morally repugnant acts ... Islam has intimately become associated with ... ugliness—intolerance, persecution, oppression, and violence. (2005, pp. 3–4)

---

[29] See http:www.pro-lies.org/operation-rescue/Operation Rescue - Pro-Lies.org | Extreme. Toxic. Out of Touch.

[30] India: Vigilante 'Cow Protection' Groups Attack Minorities. (2019, February 18). Human Rights Watch. (http://hrw.org); See also Rana, A. (2018, July 20). Mobs are killing Muslims in India. Why is no one stopping them. *The Guardian*. Mobs are killing Muslims in India. Why is no one stopping them? | Rana Ayyub | The Guardian.

[31] Sylvia, L. (2019, July 12). How do terrorists fund their activities? Some do it legally. *The Conversation*. How do terrorists fund their activities? Some do it legally (theconversation.com).

[32] Arwa, M. (2017, March 26). The 712-page Google doc that proves Muslims do condemn terrorism. *The Guardian*. The 712-page Google doc that proves Muslims do condemn terrorism | Race | The Guardian; Willa Frej. (2015, December 11). How 70,000 Muslim Clerics Are Standing Up To Terrorism. Huffpost. How 70,000 Muslim Clerics Are Standing Up To Terrorism | HuffPost The WorldPost.

Statistics on terrorist attacks by Islamists and the unrelenting 'war on terror' suggest that Muslims are, arguably, the greatest victims (Mickolus, 2016). However, owing to shifting constructions and subversive representations, Muslims continue to be blamed for not doing enough to condemn terror. This attitude has forced majority of Muslims to be apologetic denouncing terrorism as acts by certain people who were merely 'incidental Muslims' or explaining them as manifestations of 'economic, political, and socio-cultural' grievances that were not exclusively Islamic (Abou el-Fadl, 2005, p. 12). This line of argument is particularly invoked with regard to Islamists like the *al-Qaeda* and the Taliban who, during the anti-Soviet war in Afghanistan (1979–1988), were used as *mujahidin* before falling out of favor to be condemned as terrorists in the contemporary times (Tayob, 2015, p. 165; Campo & Elfenbein, 2004).

Media framing and misrepresentation of radicalization, therefore, other than forcing respective religious communities to be excusatory, fails in establishing the root causes of the vice as well as inclusive and participatory policies to mitigate it. By blindly taking what we are being fed by the media, we not only obfuscate the underlying socio-economic and political dynamics fomenting and sustaining terrorism but also overlook violence perpetrated by non-Muslims that are equally inspired by some ideologies, whether religious, economic or political, hence closing our eyes to the victims of such terror.

## Conclusion

Radicalization into violent extremism and terrorism are multi-faceted phenomena with no single cause, community, or panacea attributable to it. Though forms and styles of insurgent groups and ways of expressing grievances may differ, the message always remain constant—unresolved socio-economic and political circumstances fuel and sustain the menace. Religion in most of the scenarios is only appropriated to legitimize violence and terrorism to remove the guilt, if any, that comes with the commission of heinous acts. By perceiving terrorism as exclusively and inherently Islamic, therefore, the dominant ideology of Islamophobia seeks to hoodwink us into believing that extremism is 'genetic' and an inborn vice. However, we are rightfully aware that violent extremism and terrorism are socially acquired and politically specific behaviors with no region, race or religion predisposed to the vice. In the majority of cases where violence and terrorism occur, perpetrators, often weak and subordinate, vent out their frustrations arising out of suppressed and unaddressed grievances.

The urgency to objectively interrogate and understand terrorism and violent extremism by addressing the grievances cannot, therefore, be overemphasized to save humanity from the never-ending mutating threat to security. Like a wrongly prescribed medical condition, two decades of mis-framing and misrepresentation is a long period that has made terrorism and radicalization resistant to every possible fronted solution so far. Without doubt, securitization touted as the panacea to terrorism and radicalization has proved inefficient. Excessive force by law enforcement agents, enforced disappearance and extrajudicial extermination of alleged 'fathers of jihadist ideology' only serve to breed sympathy among locals which have in turn become conducive push factors to radicalization, recruitment to extremism as well as according financial and logistical support to terrorist organizations. What the global society requires, therefore, is a rational approach manifested in the SDG 16 to interrogate and understand the diverse social, political and economic conditions fomenting the threat and encourage participatory and inclusive efforts in addressing the vice rather than seeking to solve it based on narrow assumptions as is presently the norm.

## REFERENCES

Abou el-Fadl, K. (2005). *The Great Theft: Wrestling Islam from the Extremists*. Perfect Bound.

Ahere, R. (2019). Can the Media be Conflict Sensitive? An Analysis of Kenya and South Africa. *Open Access Library Journal*, 6(e5569), 1–22. https://doi.org/10.4236/oalib.1105569

Allen, C. (2010). *Islamophobia*. Ashgate Publishers.

Aziz, M. (2007). *An Analysis of Print Media Coverage of the Palestinian-Israel Conflict During the Second Israel Invasion of Lebanon in 2006* (pp. 1–79). Clemson University.

Belquis, A. (2015). Afghan Youth and Extremists: Why Are Extremists Narratives So Appealing? *US Institute of Peace Brief*, 188, 1–5.

Boga, H., Shauri, H., Mwakimako, H., & Mraja, M. (2021). *Radicalization into Violent Extremism in Coastal Kenya: Genesis, Impact and Responses*. HORN International Institute for Strategic Studies.

Borg, C., & Mayo, P. (2006). Toward an Antiracism Agenda in Education: The Case of Malta. In D. Macedo & P. Gounari (Eds.), *The Globalization of Racism* (pp. 148–164). Paradigm Publishers.

Botha, A. (2013). Assessing the Vulnerability of Kenyan Youths to Radicalization and Extremism. *Institute for Security Studies (ISS)*, 245, 1–28.

Botha, A. (2017). *Practical Implications in the Attempt to Prevent and Counter Radicalization in Africa*. Research on Islam and Muslims in Africa (RIMA) Policy Papers, 5(1). https://muslimsinafrica.wordpress.com/2017/04/07/practical-implications-in-the-attempt-to-prevent-and-counter-radicalisation-in-africa-dr-anneli-botha/

Brubaker, R. (2012). Categories of Analysis and Categories of Practice: A Note on the study of Muslims in European Countries of Immigration. *Ethnic and Racial Studies*, 1-8. https://doi.org/10.1080/01419870.2012.729674

Campo, J., & Elfenbein, C. (2004). Terrorism. In C. Martin (Ed.), *Encyclopedia of Islam and Muslim World* (pp. 691–993). Macmillan.

Chembea, S. (2017). *Competing and Conflicting Power Dynamics in Waqfs in Kenya, 1900–2010*. Bayreuth International Graduate School of African Studies (BIGSAS), University of Bayreuth. http://www.uni-bayreuth.de

Chitando, E. (Ed.). *Public Religion and the Politics of Homosexuality in Africa* (pp. 80–93). Routledge.

Costanza, W. (2015). Adjusting Our Gaze: An Alternative Approach to Understanding Youth Radicalization. *Journal of Strategic Security, 8*(1), 1–15. https://doi.org/10.5038/1944-0472.8.1.1428

Durham, W., Torfs, R., Kirkham, M., & Scott, C. (Eds.). (2012). *Islam, Europe and Emerging Legal Issues*. Ashgate.

Götsch, K. (2016). Alleged Terrorists, Refugees and Radicalized Muslims in Europe: A Wicked Discursive Conjunction. *Security and Peace, 34*(1), 38–45.

Hausner, L., & Gellner, N. (2012). Category and Practice as Two Aspects of Religion: The Case of Nepalis in Britain. *Journal of the American Academy of Religion, 80*(4), 971–997.

Hendrick, J. (2013). *Gülen: The Ambiguous Politics of Market Islam in Turkey and the World*. New York University Press.

Job. (2019). TOR Radicalization and Recruitment into Violent Extremism in Kenya: Trends, Status, Progress and Challenges in Preventing & CVE (ACT-RRVE-07-2019) Act Change Transform.

Kenya Population and Housing Census. (2019). *Vol. IV: Distribution of Population by Socio-Economic Characteristics*. Government Press.

Kimunguyi, P. (n.d.). *Terrorism and Counter Terrorism in East Africa*. Global Terrorism Research Center and Monash European and EU Center Monash University.

Kundnani, A. (2015). *The Muslims are Coming: Islamophobia, Extremism, and the Domestic War on Terror*. Verso.

Macedo, D., & Gounari, P. (Eds.). (2006). *The Globalization of Racism*. Paradigm Publishers.

Maiangwa, B., Ufo, O., Uzodike, A. W., & Hakeem, O. (2021). Baptism by Fire: Boko Haram and the Reign of Terror in Nigeria. *Africa Today, 59*(2), 41–57.

Mamdani, M. (2002). Good Muslim, Bad Muslim: A Political Perspective on Culture and Terrorism. *American Anthropological Association, 104*(3), 766–775.

Mickolus, E. (2016). *Terrorism, 2013–2015. A Worldwide Chronology*. McFarland Publishers.

Mraja, M. (2007). *Islamic Impacts on Marriage and Divorce among the Digo of Southern Kenya*. Ergon Verlag.

Nandwa, H. (n.d.). *The Impact of criminalizing 'Radicalization' on the Freedom of Thought, Conscience and Religion or Believe in Kenya*. (DOC) Radicalization | Hassan Nandwa—Academia.edu.

Ndzovu, H. (2014). *Muslims in Kenyan Politics: Political Involvement, Marginalization, and Minority Status*. Northwestern University Press.

Ndzovu, H. (2016). *'Un-natural', 'Un-African' and 'Un-Islamic': The Three-Pronged Onslaught Undermining Homosexual Freedom in Kenya*. In A. van Klinken.

Oded, A. (2000). *Islam and Politics in Kenya*. Lynne Rienner Publishers.

Prevention of Terrorism Act. (2012). Government Press.

Rabasa, A. (undated). Al-Qaeda in East Africa. In A. Rabasa (Ed.), *Radical Islam in East Africa*. RAND.

Security Amendment Act. (2014). Kenyan Government Press.

Seesemann, R. (2006). African Islam or Islam in Africa? Evidence from Kenya. In R. Loimeier & R. Seesemann (Eds.), *The Global Worlds of the Swahili: Interfaces of Islam, Identity and Space in 19$^{th}$ and 20$^{th}$ Century* (pp. 229–250). Lit.

Seesemann, R. (2007). Kenyan Muslims, the Aftermath of 9/11, and the 'War on Terror'. In B. Soares & R. Otayek (Eds.), *Islam and Muslim Politics in Africa* (pp. 157–176). Palgrave Macmillan.

Seesemann, R., & Soares, B. (2009). 'Being as Good Muslims as Frenchmen': On Islam and Colonial Modernity in West Africa. *Journal of Religion in Africa, 39*(1), 91–120.

Shinn, H. (2003). Terrorism in East Africa and the HORN: An Overview. *Journal of Conflict Studies, 23*(2), 1–13.

Speckhard, A., Shajkovci, A., & Ahmed, M. (2018). Intervening in and Preventing Somali-American Radicalization with Counter Narratives: Testing the Breaking the ISIS Brand Counter Narrative Videos in American Somali Focus Group Settings. *Journal of Strategic Security, 11*(4), 32–71. https://doi.org/10.5038/1944-0472.11.4.1695

Sustainable Development Goal (SDG) Target 16.7. https://indicators.report/targets/16-7/

Tayob, A. (2015). Religion and Life Trajectories: Islamists against Self and Other. In C. Bochinger & R. Jörg (Eds.), *Dynamics of Religion: Past and Present* (pp. 155–169). CPI Books GmbH.

The Prevention of Terrorism (Amendment) Act. (2018). Government Press.

The Proceeds of Crime and Anti-Money Laundering Act. (2009). Government Press.

Turner, S. (2011). *Religion and Modern Society: Citizenship, Secularization and the State*. Cambridge University Press.

CHAPTER 21

# Islam, Conflict, Peace and Security in Africa

*Mohamed Suleiman Mraja*

## INTRODUCTION

The quest for peaceful and inclusive societies, free of conflict and insecurities, have been an ideal that all human societies have come to cherish and aspire. This has been succinctly expressed in the formulations of one of the Sustainable Development Goals thus: "Promote peaceful and inclusive societies for sustainable development, provide access to justice for all, and build effective, accountable and inclusive institutions at all levels" (SDG, Goal 16). It is worth noting that peace, broadly understood as "not merely the absence of war", is a key ingredient to the sustainable development of any nation or society. A cursory survey of the *Africa SDG Index and Dashboards Report 2020* shows that many countries in Africa depict a continent that is far from the above ideal. The report, for instance, listed the goals facing the greatest challenges as being SDG 3 (good health and wellbeing), SDG 9 (industry, innovation and infrastructure), and SDG 16 (peace, justice and strong institutions). Conflicts and insecurity within and among nations abound. While there may be many causative factors contributing towards fragile and unstable nations in Africa, the low pace of economic and social development is generally inexcusable, given the abundance of both natural and human resources in the continent.

One of the major institutions that is pervasive within the continent is religion. Though the term has defied precise definition, what is generally acceptable is that "Africans are notoriously religious" (Mbiti, 1969, p. 1) and the

M. S. Mraja (✉)
Department of Religion, Culture and Gender Studies, Bomet University College, Bomet, Kenya
e-mail: mraja@buc.ac.ke

© The Author(s), under exclusive license to Springer Nature Switzerland AG 2023
S. M. Kilonzo et al. (eds.), *The Palgrave Handbook of Religion, Peacebuilding, and Development in Africa*,
https://doi.org/10.1007/978-3-031-36829-5_21

African continent is home to the African Traditional Religions, Christianity, Islam and other religions (Grillo et al., 2019). This chapter utilizes Islam to situate the normative precepts that the quest for enduring peace in the continent may be found. For one, Islam is understood, from its etymology, as a "religion of peace", with one being at peace with Allah, with fellow human beings, self and other elements in the universe (Malik et al., 2012, p. 444b; Maududi, 1992). Islam is also Africa's second largest religion (Moller, 2006, p. 19). As a civilization and a way of life to over 40.5% of Africa's religious population (Moller, 2006, p. 10), one cannot underestimate the impact of the norms and values that Islam holds in any peace and security initiatives in the region. What follows is a brief survey of some of the causes of conflict and insecurity in Africa.

## Causative Factors for Conflict and Insecurity in Africa

Knowledge of what triggers conflict may be one of the key ingredients in finding lasting solutions to civil wars, intertribal and interfaith feuds, intercommunity animosities, xenophobic outbursts, extremism, ethnic tensions and fights over resources. The proposed outlines are only meant for coherence in the discursive tradition and not in any way suggestive that there is only a single reason that caused a given conflict. Social dynamics are complex and a myriad of factors may be at play in any given conflict. Among the factors that have exacerbated conflict in Africa over time include the following.

### *Poor Political and Governance Structures*

Yabi (2016) identified Africa and the Middle East as the two regions of the world with the highest conflict burden with weak governance structures and global governance failures as among the contributors of conflict. He noted that violence in many parts of the continent is primarily centred on rivalries between strong political personalities backed by their political supporters who are also often partly defined by ethnic, regional and religious identities. The alignment of political parties with ethnic identity affiliation exacerbates conflicts and has been a constant threat to peace and security. Furthermore, throughout the continent, political systems have not yet been stabilized and African societies, which are characterized by their immense cultural diversity, are finding it difficult to adopt a shared vision of governing principles and values for their countries. Political crises are associated with various forms of violence, including tribal clashes, rape, theft and vandalism of properties and death. The post-election violence that occurred in Kenya in 2007 where more than 1200 people were killed, 1000 more injured, over 300,000 people displaced with many homes and businesses looted or destroyed and with 94 deaths, 201 cases of sexual violence and more than 300 injuries reported in 2017 (Africanews with AFP, 2022; Human Rights Watch, 2017; Office of the United Nations High Commissioner for Human Rights [OHCHR], 2008), as well as the civil war that broke out in Côte d'Ivoire in 2011 that claimed 3000 victims are cases in mind. In the Democratic Republic of Congo (DRC), recent efforts in political stabilization have not put an end to the killings of civilians by various rebel groups in the east. The return of political violence in Burundi has raised deep concerns about the Great Lakes region's possible relapse into widespread violence, igniting tensions between ethnic groups.

Many of the African states and the instability they exhibit may be a product of poor leadership. Most of the leaders seem to ascend to power not on the basis of merit but rather on political patronage and exploitation of "tyranny of numbers" drawn from corruption and negative ethnicity. Their legitimacy is often imposed upon the masses through repressive leadership, lack of respect for the rule of law, police brutality and extra-judicial killing of their perceived opponents. Where national resources (including employment opportunities and infrastructural developments) are distributed unevenly based on patronage and political allegiance, such may fuel dissidence and disunity in a country. The history of Africa is full of despotic and dictatorial leaders. It may thus not be surprising that peace and security has been a mirage (Mbandlwa, 2020).

## *Weak Electoral System*

Many countries in Africa hold periodic elections to elect leaders to various national, regional and local administrative positions. While most of these countries have national election bodies that are supposed to be "independent", the contestations that have marred many election results, except for a few countries such as Ghana and South Africa, are a far outcry from the ideals of "free and fair" elections. Africa is replete with cases of elections that have turned violent. Claims of bribery, corruption and manipulation of results in favour of a given candidate often result in election disputes and conflict. Where the courts have been seen as the last arbiter of political contestations of elections results, losers often cry foul, accusing the judiciary of "state capture" or corruption (Gadjanova, 2017; Omotola, 2010).

## *Civil Wars and Coups d'etat*

Africa has had its share of civil wars. A report by the Norwich University Online (2017) noted that armed conflicts in Africa during the twentieth century caused an enormous loss of human life, the collapse of socio-economic systems and the degradation of health and education services across the continent. For instance, the Nigerian Civil War in 1967, caused by ethnic tensions and the military coup of the first civilian government, resulted in different ethnic factions fighting one another, creating chaos and leading to a massive crisis, including the deaths of countless civilians (Baxter, 2014, p. 63; Thomas, 2022). The late 1980s saw the Lord's Resistance Army (LRA), led by Joseph Kony, being responsible for the longest-running rebel upheaval in Uganda and its neighbouring countries, resulting in the displacement of nearly two million people and the deaths of thousands. The LRA originated in 1987 with the rebellion against Yoweri Museveni's leadership in Uganda, when Kony (having succeeded Alice Lakwena) dubbed himself a spiritual leader and the liberator of the Acholi people of northern Uganda. Since then, Kony and his movement have become notorious for abducting and forcibly recruiting children, and the LRA has kidnapped more than 60,000 civilians and forced them to serve as soldiers and sex slaves. By September 2002, it was estimated that 552,000 Ugandans were displaced or at risk of having no harvest, with tens of civilians reported to have been killed in this conflict since March 2002 in both northern Uganda and southern Sudan (Human Rights Watch, 2002).

The Horn of Africa region has also witnessed its share of civil instability and conflict (see e.g., Bach et al., 2022). Since 1991 Somali has gone through Civil War originally as a result of ouster of President Mohammed Siad Barre through a coup. The 20-plus-year civil war has killed as many as one million Somalis via violence, famine or disease, in a country that is essentially religiously and ethnically monolithic. Many of its citizens had to flee the country as refugees, with Kenya hosting the largest portion of the displaced Somalis. There was also the two-year (1998-2000) war between the neighbouring countries of Eritrea and Ethiopia which was triggered by a border dispute and claimed approximately 80,000 lives. And from 2020 to 2022, the Ethiopian government has been fighting an internal war against the separatist movement among the Tigray People Liberation Front (TPLF). There is also simmering tension between Ethiopia and its Sudanese and Egyptian neighbours over the use of the waters of the Nile River following the recent construction of a dam by the Ethiopian government. It has been noted that while water rights along the Nile have been in dispute since 1959 among these countries in the region, today, the conflict, if not resolved, threatens to escalate into a war (Polakovic, 2021). Thus, one may opine that competition over resources may trigger armed conflict between nation states and communities. The recently witnessed border and land disputes between Kenya and Uganda over the Migingo Islands as well as Kenya and Somali over maritime border mostly have the underlying factor of disputation over resources.

Perhaps the worst civil war that was propelled by ethnic animosity between the Tutsis and Hutus was the 1994 Rwandan genocide. The murder of Rwandan President Juvenal Habyarimana is viewed as having jumpstarted the systematic and brutal genocide of approximately 800,000 Tutsis, the ethnic minority of Rwanda's population. The hundred-day genocide was relentless, pitting neighbour against neighbour and in some instances, even forcing Hutu husbands to kill their Tutsi wives. The Rwandan genocide was caused by state-sanctioned hatred and dehumanization of the ethnic minority Tutsis (Hintjens, 1999; Norwich University Online, 2017; Prunier, 2009).

Prior to the Rwandan genocide, the South African apartheid system or policy that governed relations between South Africa's white minority and non-white black majority for much of the latter half of the twentieth century sanctioned through a series of legislations the racial segregation and political and economic discrimination against non-whites. Although the legislation that formed the foundation of apartheid had been repealed by the early 1990s, the social and economic repercussions of the discriminatory policy persisted into the twenty-first century. As a way of remonstration against the oppression and injustice caused by the system, black African groups, with the support of some whites, held demonstrations and strikes, with many instances of violent protest and of sabotage being staged (Britannica, 2022).

South Sudan, however, presents a different case of violent competition over control of power. South Sudan, the world's newest country, was born out of a decade-long civil war, and soon after its independence, in 2011, it itself descended into war. This renewed war took on an ethnic dimension and was started due to an inability to successfully share power between two ex-rebel leaders. A new peace accord has been signed and it brought the power-sharing agreement back to a pre-civil war status quo. The last two years in South Sudan have been characterized by violence against civilians (Yabi, 2016).

### *Extremism and Religious-Based Violence*

According to Basedau (2017), religious-based conflicts and the attendant violence have apparently become a widespread phenomenon in sub-Saharan Africa, while terrorist attacks have killed many civilians in Burkina Faso, Chad, Côte d'Ivoire, Kenya (Al-Shabab), Mali (Ansar Dine), Nigeria (Boko Haram) and Somalia (Al-Shabaab). In Mali, Nigeria and Somalia, jihadist organizations have staged rebellions and managed to at least temporarily control large parts of the territory of these states. Østebø (2022, p. 182) further commenting on Al-Shabab and Boko Haram as the main militant Salafi groups in Africa argues that although their activities may have caused great human suffering, they are far from representative of African Salafism, or indeed the main body polity of Islam in general. The emergence of a militant Salafi movement in Somalia obviously needs to be related to the particular violent context where the precarious security situation inhibited the possibility of peaceful *dawa* (propagation) and laid the groundwork for a programme of religious reform to be carried out with guns. Boko Haram, on the other hand, was founded in Nigeria in 2002 by Muhammad Yusuf. In the formative stages, the question of an Islamic state was not much emphasized, and neither did the founder espouse or engage in any form of organized violent political activism. Boko Haram focused on the denunciation of any form of secular education which was viewed as overly influenced by Western ideology and thus contradictory to Islam. Boko Haram initially embarked on a somewhat defensive path by carving out symbolic and territorial space for the purpose of implementing and securing religious purity. Tensions with the state escalated after Muhammad Yusuf was killed by Nigerian police in 2009. Lately, the group has gained widespread attention through a number of violent attacks against state establishments, abduction of women and children and burning homes and schools as well as killing of people, both Muslims and non-Muslims in the country. In the Central African Republic

(CAR), a Muslim rebellion ousted a Christian-dominated government; the ensuing turmoil escalated into bloody confrontations between Muslim and Christian militias and left thousands of civilians dead. While the causes of these conflicts are not yet fully understood, Basedau suggests that they appear to demonstrate a mixture of religious and secular roots. Parallel ethnic- and religious-identity boundaries increase the risks of interreligious confrontation. Weak states both enable the activities of religious extremists and make their ideology a tempting alternative for the population. In addition, external support for religious extremism from countries in North Africa and the Middle East poses a special problem. Other studies have also reported growing cases of Islamic radicalism in East Africa in recent times, with a more radical understanding of Islam of the "fundamentalist"/Islamist variety being espoused and with sporadic cases of violent extremism having been reported (Boga et al., 2021; Chande, 2000).

Suggesting the potential of manipulating religion for non-religious ends, Moller (2006) posits that in a few cases, parties to an armed conflict have gone so far as to proclaim "holy war" (*jihad*) against their respective opponents, be they foreigners or indigenous adversaries—as has been the case on several occasions in Sudan. More often, however, Islam has been merely one element in armed conflicts, which are mainly about something else, for example, by couching political grievances or demands in religious terms or by fusing ethnicity with religion. As Issaka-Toure (2020, p. 86) observes that in the post September 11 era Africa, the militant rhetoric surrounding the attacks gave new impetus or legitimacy to a modern concept of jihad. This phase of *jihad* on the continent has taken a different turn as the jihadist leaders attempt to capture power in order to reform the system that they perceive as having been corrupted by non-Islamic values. This has created a situation of conflict and power struggle between armed jihadist and local government security forces. However, in most cases Islam is used to rally support, despite the fact that there may be other ethnic, political and economic motivations. Be that as it may, religious ideas in themselves do not necessarily cause radicalisation and violent extremism. For the most part, the religious values and norms within Islam, Christianity and other faiths are actually in favour of peace (Basedau, 2017).

From the forgoing discussion, it is apparent that Africa is bleeding internally for want of enduring peace. The contributing factors leading to conflict and instability are varied, as outlined above. And although some of the glaring conflicts were resolved through internal (and in some instances, external) mechanisms, most of these interventions failed to ingrain value-systems that assure sustainable peace and security in the continent. It is clear that these conflicts subjected civilians to intense physical and psychological trauma that negatively impacted development throughout many African nations. It is to the values and norms of Islam that the remaining sections will proceed to analyse as a way of bolstering the existing peace-building frameworks, which have largely failed to deliver meaningful and lasting peace—devoid of wars and creating cohesive nations guided by the principles of justice (*adalah*), and promotion of social good or welfare (*maslaha*) of all the citizenry regardless of colour, creed, sex or social or political considerations. In rooting for Islam as a peaceful civilization, Funk and Said (2009, p. 50) observed that not only do Islamic precepts provide a coherent and affirmative position on the desirability of peace for human flourishing, but also its culture provides not one but multiple paradigms through which efforts to translate these precepts into reality may be pursued.

## Islamic Framework for Peace

There are several studies that have treated the subject of Islam and peace (and its antithesis, war). Wahyuddin and Hanafi. (2016) use the Qur'ān, Hadith and the Medina Charter as the basis of analysis on the message of peace inherent in Islam. Their library-based work argues that Islam leads to the path of peace and patience—all on the basis of truth and justice. The work is significant in outlining general principals of Islam on justice, equality, freedom, mutual cooperation and social solidarity, as well as tolerance as a way of preventing conflict. The work by Malik et al. (2012) also delves into the role of Islam towards peace and progress. In general, the study explores the relationship between Islam and peace-building and attempts to understand how Islamic traditions can be employed for peace-building and progress of a nation. Islamic religion, the study argues, can be a positive force to establish justice and peace through nonviolent activism.

The work of Baderin (2020) is country-specific and focuses on how relevant Islamic normative precepts on peaceful coexistence, security and socio-economic development may have a positive persuasive impact in Nigeria. Building on these studies, this chapter underscores the primacy of the Qur'ān and Sunnah (Prophetic Traditions) as the authoritative sources of norms on peace and harmonious coexistence in society within the Islamic religious motif. It will seek to apply these normative values and principles beyond the Nigerian confines and relate them to the quest for peace and security in Africa as a whole. In so doing, historical anecdotes (*sirah*) drawn from the practical examples from the life of Prophet Muhammad will be cited to illustrate the potential of realization of enduring peace in human societies. Below is a discursive elucidation on specific precepts of the Qur'ān, the Hadith and *sirah* of the Prophet as the peace and security building blocks for the African continent.

### *Condemnation and Prohibition of Racial Discrimination and Tribal Acrimony*

It is common knowledge that communities and nation states are made up of people who may belong to diverse configurations or profiles in terms of colour complexions, race, language, physique and economic endowments. Our earlier historical survey has shown that several countries in Africa, including South Africa, Nigeria, Rwanda, have experienced civil wars and social ruptures whose prime genesis could be traced to the question of discrimination on the basis of racial/ethnic bigotry. Recent spates of xenophobic attacks against immigrants from other African countries in South Africa all bear a slur of ethnic profiling. In other African countries, cases of economic marginalization have been attributed to exclusion from national resource distribution by those in power on account of minority and/or ethnic status.

From an Islamic perspective, ethnicity/tribe is a natural phenomenon that represents the creative powers of God. Thus, Islam advocates that it should be positively appreciated and accommodated, not negatively exploited to threaten peace and security or marginalize others in human society. This principle is well enshrined in Qur'ān 49:13:

> O People! We created you from a male and a female, and made you into nations and tribes, that you might come to know one another. The noblest of you in the sight of God are those who are most deeply conscious of Him.

In another place, the Qur'ān 30:22 states: "and part of His [God's] signs is the creation of the heavens and earth and the diversity of your tongues [languages] and colours; surely there are signs in this for those who are knowledgeable".

The Qur'ān condemns use of hate-speech (as political leaders often do) to spur negative ethnicity, tribal animosity and division in society for social and political expedience; thus, "Believers, let no man mock another, who may perhaps be better than himself. And let no woman mock another, who may perhaps be better than herself..." (Qur'ān 49:11).

Turning to the Sunnah, Prophet Muhammad underscored the equality of mankind based on a common ancestry. He is reported to have said: "Verily, Allah has removed from the pride of the time of ignorance with its boasting of ancestors. Verily, one is only a righteous believer or a miserable sinner. All of the people are the children of Adam, and Adam was created from dust" (Tirmidhi: 3955).

Ghazali (2000, p. 579), while commenting on these verses, posits that they point to vile behaviour that humans must avoid. It is vulgar and foolish to mock or ridicule other people or be condescending towards them. Furthermore, Islam condemns slandering others or scoffing at them. It denounces snooping, maligned suspicion, backbiting and defamation. Regrettably, these are widespread in human intercourse, and if people were to avoid these negative traits in their dealings with one another, they would spend half their lives in silence! This, one may opine, will invariably lead to peace. According to Bederin (2020, pp. 8-9), these Islamic precepts establish the powerful social norm that, despite ethnic or tribal differences, all human beings belong to a single human family as they are all created by one God and descended from the same ancestral root. In addition, while ethnic/tribal solidarity and cooperation is natural, Islam enjoins that this should be harnessed for positive human development and not for enmity or negative discrimination leading to threat to peace and security or corruption in human society.

It is instructive that some African countries have taken the right steps to enact laws that proscribe discrimination. For instance, the *Constitution of Kenya, 2010*, undertakes to accord its citizens' equality and freedom from discrimination. In one of its articles, it states: "The State shall not discriminate directly or indirectly against any person on any ground, including race, sex, pregnancy, marital status, health status, ethnic or social origin, colour, age, disability, religion, conscience, belief, culture, dress, language or birth" (*Constitution of Kenya, 2010*, 27, (4)). If fully implemented, such provisions will undoubtedly enhance the dignity and welfare of the people and quash societal conflicts.

### *Promotion of Justice and Warding off of Oppressive Practices*

Malik et al. (2012) have argued that justice (*adl*) has been an integral aspect of the Islamic discourse of peace, since the Qur'ān clearly states that the aim of religion is to bring justice. This is evident in Quranic verses such as: "We sent Our messengers with veritable proof, and with them We sent the Book and the criterion, so that men might establish justice" (Qur'ān 57: 25). Without justice, there can be no peace and sustainable development. Therefore, justice is the essential component of peace, according to the Quranic message.

Furthermore, it is stated in the Qur'ān that "O ye who believe! Stand firmly for justice as witnesses to Allah to even as against yourselves, your parents, your kin, and whether it be (against) the rich and poor…" (Qur'ān 4: 135). While in most countries in Africa one would find political opponents or regions being perceived by national leaders as opposition facing all manner of injustices and repression, the Quranic principles warn against such. Thus, Allah directs, "O believers! Stand firm for Allah and bear true testimony. Do not let the hatred of a people lead you to injustice. Be just! That is closer to righteousness" (Qur'ān 5: 8). Thus, according to Azzām (1979: 105), Islam has placed justice above everything, weighing in an equitable balance between the infidel and the Muslim, the enemy, associate (*mawalā*) and the ally; for in Islam's sight they are all the same and equal before justice. In support, Malik et al. (2012) have opined that the Islamic understanding of peace suggests that justice is the overriding principle and it must transcend any consideration of kinship, social status, religion, race or even animosity. Consequently, tyranny, which is a system that perpetuates injustice, is viewed as one of the greatest evils that must be removed.

The state, through its leadership and the judiciary, must uphold justice. The Prophet was emphatic on this principle. The Prophet warned people against mistrial of the justice system, saying, "If a reputable man amongst the children of Bani Israel committed a theft, they used to forgive him, but if a poor man committed a theft, they would cut his hand. But I would cut even the hand of Fatima (i.e. the daughter of the Prophet) if she committed a theft" (Bukhari: 3733). One may opine that making the justice system impartial and accessible to all citizenry in the African continent, regardless of one's social status, age or gender will be an essential building block towards sustainable peaceful societies, as envisioned under SDG 16.

Warding off oppression and injustice against a people is also the role of a leader in Islam, as was exemplified by the Prophet, even when such people are not Muslims. In the late period of the Prophet Muhammad's (PBUH) life, the tribe of Banu Khuza'ah became his ally through a treaty of joint defence. They were living near Makkah which was under the rule of the pagan Quraysh, Prophet Muhammad's (PBUH) own tribe. The tribe of Banu Bakr, an ally of Quraysh, with the help of some elements of Quraysh, attacked the Banu Khuza'ah and inflicted heavy damage. The Banu Khuza'ah invoked the treaty and demanded the Prophet Muhammad (PBUH) to come to their help and punish the Quraysh. The Prophet Muhammad (PBUH) demanded an immediate redress for not only violating the treaty but also slaying people allied to him. As a measure of justice, the Prophet gave the aggressors three demands, the acceptance of any one of them being imperative: either to pay blood money for the victims of Khuza'ah, or to terminate their alliance with Banu Bakr, or to consider the truce to have been nullified. The Quraysh rejected all these options, thus forcing the Prophet to organize a campaign against them, ending finally in the peaceful conquest of Makkah, without any battle (Mubarakpur, 1995, pp. 388-398).

According to Ghazālī (2000, pp. 80-81), society as a whole can grow and survive only on the foundation of equity and justice among its members. Conversely, oppression and the absence of justice affect a society and threaten its cohesion and the safety and quality of life within it. Where the Islamic principles of justice are enshrined in a society, in the words of Azzām (1979, p. 104), it will eradicate communal prejudices and bigotry and places equality above all consideration.

## Establishing Cohesive and Harmonious Societies

There is no doubt that Africa represents one of the most diverse and plural societies in the world in linguistic, religious and cultural respects. On the religious sphere, Ibrahim (2022, p. 153) noted that perhaps nowhere in the world do so many Muslims and Christians live in such close proximity, often in the same family, as in Africa. This has been a characteristic feature of religious pluralism in the past, but under the contemporary global conditions of politicized religion, the peaceful coexistence of different religious traditions is now generating conflicts. How then can the Islamic norms and traditions, beyond the narrow politicization of religion, still help resolve the emerging conflicts?

The plural nature of human societies in their linguistic and social configurations has been acknowledged in the Qur'ān. In Qur'ān 11: 118, God says, "Had your Lord wished, he would have made the whole of the mankind as one nation". Most of the atrocities committed by extremists groups in the name of religion in Africa, by, among others, Boko Haram in Nigeria and the Al-Qaeda in Somalia, are a far outcry of the vision of Islam as espoused in its primary texts. A hermeneutical reading of the Qur'ān reveals that a harmonious society that is cohesive in its diversity is realizable, based on the principles of freedom of worship, tolerance and mutual cooperation. Azzām (1979, pp. 105-107) notes that "Freedom in Islam is one of the most sacred rights; political freedom, freedom of thought, religious freedom, and civil freedom are all guaranteed by Islam….

The hearts of the Muslims were filled to overflowing with the meaning of freedom. They oppressed no man who delved into the mysteries of the universe and adopted for himself a theory or claimed a certain opinion. Freedom of learning was guaranteed to the Sabaeans and the Magians, and the Christians and the Jews, who were permitted to express their beliefs unmolested. Muslims likewise enjoyed considerable freedom in this respect and were not restrained by their Sharī'ah—the restrictions placed on the freedom of opinion, belief, and expression in Islamic states were those aimed at eliminating disturbances, riots and unrest endangering the safety of the state."

On freedom of worship, the Qur'ān states, "There shall be no compulsion in [acceptance of] the religion" (Qur'ān 2: 256). In another verse, God says, "Say, 'O Disbelievers! I do not worship what you worship, nor you worship what I worship. I shall never worship what you worship, nor will you worship what I worship. You have your own religion, and I have mine" (Qur'ān 109: 1-6).

On tolerance and mutual cooperation, the Qur'ān (60:8-9) states thus: "God does not forbid you from showing kindness and dealing justly with those who do not make war against you and have not driven you out of your homes; surely, God loves those who do justice. God only forbids you in respect of those who make war against you because of your religion, and drive you out of your homes and back others in your expulsion; that you make friends with them, and those who make friends with them are unjust". In another verse, Allah says: "And had your Lord willed, those on earth would have believed - all of them entirely. Then, [O Muhammad], would you compel the people in order that they become believers?" (Qur'ān 10: 99).

It is possible for Muslims and non-Muslims to cooperate on matters that promote the common good or welfare. There is no mutual cooperation in the perpetuation of evil, corruption and hostility against fellow members of the society, whether Muslims or non-Muslims. This is expressed in Qur'ān 5:2: "And cooperate in goodness and righteousness but do not cooperate in evil and enmity and be God-conscious".

It has been noted that these verses lay down one of the most fundamental principles in international relations: the recognition of all religious faiths, and the promotion of good neighbourliness and constructive dialogue. Moreover, the verses confirm that it is impossible for one religious faith to be universally accepted. Islam acknowledges the existence of different ideologies and beliefs and endeavours to coexist with them. And that the overwhelming majority of Muslim scholars and jurists are of the view that Muslims should only take up arms in order to confront insurgency, sedition, or hostility. No use of force can ever be justified to compel or coarse people to accept a particular religion or creed (Ghazālī, 2000, pp. 760-761).

### Signing of Peace Accords and Reconciliation among Parties to a Conflict

There are many instances in the Qur'ān and in the life of the Prophet that call for parties to a conflict to resolve their differences through accords and reconciliation, both among the Muslims themselves or between the Muslims and non-Muslims.

In the case of aggression by one Muslim group on another, all Muslims must oppose the wrongdoers until the latter yields to peace and accept arbitration. This principle of peace-building through reconciliation is founded on the following verse:

> If two parties of believers take up arms against each other, then make peace between them. If either of them commits aggression against the other, then fight the aggressors until they submit to the will of God. Once the aggressors desist, reconcile the two parties with equity and justice, for God loves those who exercise justice. (Qur'ān: 49:90)

The above verse underscores two principal conditions of reconciliation through arbitration, namely equity and justice (Azzīm, 1979, p. 134). One may opine that while the above verse may address specifically the Muslims, African countries and the international world may equally institute reconciliation between warring parties or nations. The recent (2022) African Union initiative to bring about cessation of hostility between Ethiopian government forces and those of the Tigray People Liberation Front is commendable.

With regard to entering into peace alliances and treaties with non-Muslims, the Quranic ideals were exemplified by the Prophet Muhammad himself as shown in the signing of the Medina Charter with the Jews and other tribes in Madinah, and the Treaty of Hudaybiyah with the Quraysh of Makkah (Mubarakpur, 1995, pp. 189-198, 339-348; Haykal, 2007, pp. 179-183, 340-356). One may posit that Africa and the world at large may require more of the peace and unity conventions as articulated by such prophetic models. It is a cardinal principle of Islam that all agreements are sacred once entered into in that they are conducted within the sight of God, in Whose name they are guaranteed. They enjoy a religious sanctity which does not permit deception or hypocrisy (Qur'ān 4:1). Thus, a pledge may never be betrayed. Islam forbids the betrayal of a pledge, secretly or openly, as it forbids the betrayal of a trust, materially or spiritually.

According to Azzām, (1979, p. 141), the Sharī'ah has also forbidden a Muslim to aid another Muslim against a non-Muslim who enjoys the protection of a security pledge or alliance even for a religious cause. The Qur'ān states, "But if they seek help from you in the matter of religion then it is your duty to help (them) except against a folk between whom and you there is a treaty" (Qur'ān 8:72).

Furthermore, fulfilment of a pledge may be withheld only when the common welfare of the Muslims is betrayed by the other party whose deception and ill will are apparent. Only in these exceptional circumstances is it permissible to cast off an accord. This principle is echoed in the Qur'ān thus: "And if you fear treachery from any folk, then throw back to them (their treaty) fairly. Lo! Allah loves not the treacherous" (Qur'ān 8:58). It has been argued that even in such circumstances, Muslims should not employ artifice, nor are they to surprise the other party with its denunciation, without prior warning and a period of delay or consideration (Azzīm, 1979, pp. 142-143).

The Qur'ān also gives room for parties to restore fractured relations through forgiveness and restitution. God says, "And not equal are the good deeds and the bad. Repel (evil) by that (deed) which is better; and thereupon the one whom between you and him is enmity (will become) as though he was a devoted friend" (Qur'ān 41:34). In his comments on this verse, Ibn Kathir observed that if a person (or party) treats well those who treated them badly, this good deed will lead to reconciliation, love and empathy. The spirit of forgiveness was exemplified by Prophet Muhammad to the people of Quraysh following the conquest of Makkah (Mubarakpur, 1995, pp. 395-396). Thus the Truth and Reconciliation efforts in post-Apartheid South Africa and the Justice and Reconciliation initiatives in post-genocide Rwanda, including those under the traditional Gacaca system, whose aim is "to bring about justice and reconciliation at the grassroots level" (United Nations, 2012) are in line with the tenets of peace-building in Islam and the SDG 16 ideal of providing access to justice to all. Concerning restitution in the event of loss of life or injury, the Qur'ān (2:178) directs, "O you who believe! The law of retaliation is prescribed for you in case of murder. The free for a free, the slave for a slave, the woman for the woman. But if any remission is made by the brother of the slain, then grant any reasonable demand and compensate him with handsome gratitude. This is a concession and mercy from your Lord. After this whoever exceeds the limits shall be in grave penalty. In another verse, it states, "And We ordained therein for them a life for a life, an eye for an eye, a nose for a nose, an ear for an ear, a tooth for a tooth and for wounds retaliation. But if anyone remits the retaliation by way of charity, it is an act of atonement for himself" (Qur'ān 5:45). Compensation for loss of life or injury may thus take the form of *diyat* (blood money) or anything of value given to the heirs of the victim (Anwarullah, 2006, p. 95-96).

### *Entrenching the Ethic of Responsible Leadership*

Islam has placed the enormous responsibility of good stewardship to leaders as the primary agents in promotion of a just, inclusive and prosperous society. Most of the conflicts in Africa and elsewhere in the world may be attributed to self-seeking leaders who use their offices to amass wealth at the expense of the welfare of their citizenry. Quite often, coups d'etat and social disorder (corruption, demonstrations, strikes and revolts) become the avenues of people expressing discontent with such leadership. One of the key tenets of Islam that can engrain good governance is shared or collective responsibility in decision making. Leaders should govern through mutual consultation (*shura*). On this leadership norm, the Qur'ān (42:38) states, "Their (the Muslims') affairs are (decided) by mutual consultation among themselves". It is imperative to note that the Constitution of Kenya, 2010, has made public participation a key component of the country's parliamentary and country assemblies' legislative functions. It also encourages public participation in the management, protection and conservation of the environment. Such initiatives can broadly be seen as part of the efforts towards the realization of the ideals of SDG 16, especially that of building inclusive and participatory societies and institutions.

The leader should also not be tyrannical, despotic or corrupt when discharging the affairs of the state or institution. The Qur'ān thus directs, "God commands you to treat (everyone) justly, generously and with kindness" (Qur'ān 16:90). In another verse, the Prophet Muhammad, as a leader of the Muslims, is reminded thus: "And by the Mercy of Allah, you dealt with them gently. And had you been severe and harsh-hearted, they would have broken away from about you; so pass over (their faults), and ask (Allah's) Forgiveness for them; and consult them in the affairs. Then when you have taken a decision, put your trust in Allah" (Qur'ān 3: 159).

It is a cardinal principle of Islam that leaders should also be accountable for their decisions and actions while discharging their duties. In one hadith, Prophet Muhammad (PBUH) said, "Every one of you is a shepherd and is responsible for his flock. The leader of a people is a guardian and is responsible for his subjects. A man is the guardian of his family and he is responsible for them. A woman is the guardian of her husband's home and his children and she is responsible for them. The servant of a man is a guardian of the property of his master and he is responsible for it. No doubt, every one of you is a shepherd and is responsible for his flock" (Bukhari, 7138; Muslim, 1829).

Given that Islam looks at leadership as a trust from God, a leader should exercise such a trust in a manner that is in accord with the laws of Allah, whose objective is to promote the wellbeing of all mankind, which is, safeguarding their faith (*deen*), their self (*nafs*), their intellect (*aql*), their posterity (*nasab*) and their wealth (*mal*), (Zaghloul et al., 2022, p. 633) and for which people will be held accountable in the Day of Judgement (Qur'ān 102: 8).

When these principles are enacted in society, they would meet the spiritual needs and physical needs of the people, thereby affording civilization and human life the requisite ingredients for peace, stability and prosperity (Azzīm, 1979, p. 123). Thus, it cannot be gainsaid that the development of Africa and any other society cannot thrive except in an environment of peace and security—free from fear, oppression and injustice.

## Conclusion

In this chapter, effort has been made to delineate specific values and principles that are enshrined in the religious traditions of Islam which may be integrated in country-specific and regional initiatives towards peace and security building in Africa. The quest for lasting peace amidst myriad of historical and ongoing conflicts in different parts of Africa is undoubtedly a work in progress. By integrating Quranic, Sunnah and *Sirah* based peace normative precepts of non-discrimination, the upholding of justice (*adl*) to all, and the ethos of harmonious coexistence in increasingly pluralistic societies under the auspices of responsible leadership, sustainable peace devoid of civil wars and ethnic rivalries and animosities may be realizable. While most of the targeted consumers and implementer of these precepts are, by nature, the Muslim faithful, the chapter has shown that already a number of countries have begun implementing some of the Islamic norms that have "universal" appeal. The cases of conflict resolution through the signing of peace accords, reconciliation, and restitution, as well as public policy formulation through the involvement of the citizenry are quite visible. Given the magnitude of human loss and stunted pace of development in much of Africa borne out of insecurity, every plausible initiative and contribution from the diverse religious traditions in Africa will certainly be a boon in the realization of the SDGs by 2030. This essay has made a case for Islam, at least, in the context of ethos of enduring peace, justice, cohesion and accountability among Africa's leadership.

## References

Africanews with AFP. (2022, October 28). Kenya charges police officers over 2017 post election violence. https://www.africanews.com/2022/10/28/kenya-charges-police-officers-over-2017-post-election-violence//

Anwarullah. (2006). *The Criminal Law of Islam*. Kitab Brahvan.

Azzīm, A. (1979). *The Eternal Message of Muhammad*. Quartet Book.

Baderin, M. (2020). Advocating for Islamic Precepts for Peace, Security and Social Development in Nigeria. *ResearchGate, 1*, 1–17. https://www.researchgate.net/publication/348649769

Bach, J.-N., et al. (Eds.). (2022). *Routledge Handbook of the Horn of Africa*. Routledge.

Baxter, P. (2014). *Biafra: The Nigerian Civil War, 1967-1970*. Helion & Company Ltd and 30° South Publishers.

Boga, H. I., Shauri, H. S., Mraja, M., Mwakimako, H., & Akoth, O. (2021). *Radicalization into Violent Extremism in Coastal Kenya: Genesis, Impact and Responses*.

*Britannica*. https://www.britannica.com/topic/apartheid

Bukhari, M. Companions of the Prophet. *Sahih al-Bukhari*. 5(57), Hadith 79. https://sunnah.com/bukhari:3733

Bukhari, M. Obey Allah and obey the Messenger. *Sahih al-Bukhari*. 9(89), Hadith 252. https://sunnah.com/bukhari:7138

Chande, A. (2000). Radicalism and Reform in East Africa. In N. Levtzion & R. L. Pouwels (Eds.), *Islam in Africa* (pp. 349–369). Ohio University Press.

Funk, N. C., & Said, A. A. (2009). *Islam and Peace-making in the Middle East*. Lynne Rienner Publishers.

Gadjanova, E. (2017, August 16). Kenya's 2017 election and its aftermath. *Max-Planck-Gesellschaft*.. https://www.mpg.de/11436923/elections-kenya

Ghazālī, M. (2000). *A Thematic Commentary on the Qur'an*. The International Institute of Islamic Thought.

Grillo, L., van Klinken, A., & Ndzovu, H. J. (Eds.). (2019). *Religion in Contemporary Africa: An Introduction*. Routledge.

Haykal, M. H. (2007). *The Life of Muhammad*. The World Forum for proximity of Islamic Schools of Thought.

Hintjens, H. M. (1999). Explaining the 1994 genocide in Rwanda. *The Journal of Modern African Studies., 37*(2), 241–268.

Human Rights Watch. (2017, August 27). Kenya: Post-Election Killings, Abuse.. https://www.hrw.org/news/2017/08/27/kenya-post-election-killings-abuse

Human Rights Watch. (2002, October 29). LRA Conflict in Northern Uganda and Southern Sudan, 2002. https://reliefweb.int/report/uganda/lra-conflict-northern-uganda-and-southern-sudan-2002

Ibrahim, A. (2022). Islam and Politics in Africa: Politics within and without the State. In T. Østebø (Ed.), *Routledge Handbook of Islam in Africa* (pp. 145–157). Routledge.

Issaka-Toure, F. (2020). Interpretations of Jihād in Africa: A Historical Overview. In F. Ngom, K. F. Mustafa, & T. Falola (Eds.), *The Palgrave Handbook of Islam in Africa* (pp. 77–92). Palgrave Macmillan.

Malik, A. A., Sheikh, M., & Rafaqi, M. Z. (2012). Role of Islam towards Peace and Progress. *Research Journal Humanities and Social Sciences, 3*(4), 443–449.

Maududi, S. A. (1992). *Towards Understanding Islam*. International Islamic Publishing House.

Mbandlwa, Z. (2020). Challenges of African Leadership after the Independency. *Solid State Technology, 63*(6), 6796–6782.

Mbiti, J. S. (1969). *African Religions and Philosophy*. Heinemann Kenya.

Mubarakpur, S. (1995). *Ar-Raheeq Al-Makhtum (The Sacred Nectar): Biography of the Noble Prophet*. Maktaba Dar-us-Salam.

Norwich University Online. (2017, September 4). Five Major African Wars and Conflicts of the Twentieth Century.. https://online.norwich.edu/academic-programs/resources/five-major-african-wars-and-conflicts-of-the-twentieth-century

Omotola, S. (2010). Explaining Electoral Violence in Africa's 'new' Democracies. *African Journal on Conflict Resolution, 10*(3), 51–74.

Østebø, T. (2022). African Salafism. In T. Østebø (Ed.), *Routledge Handbook of Islam in Africa* (pp. 173–188). Routledge.

Polakovic, G. (2021, July 13). Water dispute on the Nile River could destabilize the region. https://news.usc.edu/188414/nile-river-water-dispute-filling-dam-egypt-ethiopia-usc-study/

Prunier, G. (2009). *Africa's World War: Congo, the Rwandan Genocide and the Making of Continental Catastrophy*. Oxford University Press.

Tirmidhi, I. About the Virtue of Ash-Sham and Yemen. *Jami at-Tirmidhi*. 1(46), Hadith 3955. https://sunnah.com/tirmidhi:3955

The Republic of Kenya. The Constitution of Kenya, 2010. National Council for Law Reporting with the Authority of the Attorney-General.

The Sustainable Development Goals Center for Africa and Sustainable Development Solutions Network. (2020). *Africa SDG Index and Dashboards Report 2020.* SDG Center for Africa and Sustainable Development Solutions Network.

Thomas, D. (2022). The Nigerian Civil War (1967-1970): New Theories, Old Problem, Fresh Crisis. *International Relations and Diplomacy, 10*(3), 131–139.

Office of the United Nations High Commissioner for Human Rights [OHCHR] (2008, March 18). UN Human Rights Team Issues Report on Post-Election Violence in Kenya. https://www.ohchr.org/en/press-releases/2009/10/un-human-rights-team-issues-report-post-election-violence-kenya

United Nations. (2012, March). Outreach Programme on the Rwanda Genocide and the United Nations.. https://www.un.org/en/preventgenocide/rwanda/pdf/bgjustice.pdf

Wahyuddin, W., & Hanafi. (2016). Message of Peace in the Teaching of Islam. *Alqalam, 33*(2), 70–85.

Zaghloul, S. G., Ahmed, A. R., & Abu Bakar, M. (2022). The Purposes of Sharia (Maqasid Al-Shariah) from Contemporary Scientific Research. *International Journal of Academic Research in Business & Social Sciences, 12*(1), 629–639.

CHAPTER 22

# Apostolic Churches and Youth Response to Social Challenges Post-Violence in Zimbabwe

*Obadiah Dodo*

## INTRODUCTION

The discussion looks at the role of an African Independent Apostolic church to the youth's response to social challenges post-violence in Zimbabwe. Particularly, it focusses on Johane Masowe Apostolic Church. This is in relation to the dictates of the Sustainable Development Goal (SDG) 16, which seeks to stimulate peaceful and all-encompassing societies for viable development, afford access to justice for all and create effective, responsible and inclusive institutions at all levels (Kasirye et al., 2020). Particularly, the discussion focuses on ensuring a responsive, inclusive, participatory and representative decision-making and justice at all levels. The discussion looks at the youth in urban areas who would have participated in violence and now encountering social challenges that require attention and possible redress. It suffices to highlight the fact that often, it is the youth who are put on the frontline in times of violence and consequently, it is also the youth who face various challenges post-violence.

The review looks at apostolic churches since they are the most common religious groups that are found in most urban settlements in Zimbabwe, often offering free services. Because they operate in public spaces on almost every street corner, they are easily available and easy to visit particularly by the troubled youth. The discussion is based on extensive analysis of literature drawn from a broad spectrum of disciplines over time. Deliberately, most of the

---

O. Dodo (✉)
Department of Peace and Governance, Bindura University of Science Education, Bindura, Zimbabwe

© The Author(s), under exclusive license to Springer Nature Switzerland AG 2023
S. M. Kilonzo et al. (eds.), *The Palgrave Handbook of Religion, Peacebuilding, and Development in Africa*,
https://doi.org/10.1007/978-3-031-36829-5_22

consulted literature directly relates with the youth situation in Zimbabwe thus giving it a real, credible and impactful outlook.

Zimbabwe is traditionally characterised by periodic political elections that are held usually after every five years. In between, there are by-elections and other isolated local government elections, wherever there is need. Since the 1960s to the 1970s liberation war, the political environment has been defined by violence instigated by political elites and unfortunately waged by innocent and defenceless youth. This situation has escalated with the attainment of the independence in 1980.

From 1980, Zimbabwe has held 15 national elections and plebiscites. With each activity, allegedly, the ruling party has always employed the services of the youth to campaign and unleash violence on the opposition and other moderate citizens (RAU, 2018a; Dodo, 2021). The opposition only joined in the practice of mobilising its youth for violence from the 2000 Parliamentary elections but only as a response to the ruling party provocation (RAU, 2018a).

Violence involving youth in Zimbabwe has manifested through various activities outside of politics; service delivery protests and demonstrations, electoral disputes, and poor governance protests as given in the figure below. These activities are preceded by an election related activity as in the Table 22.1.

Given the frequency of youth involvement in violence, there are more problems that equally bedevil them. In each national election process, there are over 1000 arrests, over 500 prosecutions of the youth with an average of 10 losing their lives and over 200 getting maimed through violence and over 500 internal displacements. In each of the protests in the urban areas, there are over 1000 arrests, about 500 criminal convictions, over 5000 injuries and at least 100 internal displacements (Dodo, 2021; RAU, 2018a). It is therefore against this background of increased incidents and exposure to violence that most youth find themselves seeking assistance from the apostolic churches largely on

Table 22.1 Zimbabwe National Elections

| YEAR | Electoral Activities | Matching Violence Instigating Events |
| --- | --- | --- |
| 1980 | General election | |
| 1985 | General election | Post-election celebrations dubbed Operation Perm organised by ZANU PF in 1985 |
| 1990 | General election | Economic melt-down protests against ESAP organised by ZCTU in 1995 |
| 1995 | Parliamentary elections | Service delivery national protests organised by ZCTU in 1995 |
| 1996 | Presidential election | Food riots organised by ZCTU in 1998 |
| 2000 | Constitutional referendum | Land invasion in 2000 |
| 2005 | Senatorial & Parliamentary elections | Final push organised by MDC in 2008 |
| 2008 | Harmonised elections | |
| 2018 | Harmonised elections | Electoral dispute in 2018 and 2019 |

account of their free services, proximity to their residences, desperation for relief and growing promises of instant deliverance.

This discussion primarily focuses on the youth in the urban areas where apostolic churches are more prevalent. It should be noted that most of these apostolic churches operate on public open spaces where they pay no statutory taxes, with no requisite water and sanitary facilities. Regularly, these churches receive threats of eviction while others, without notice find their spaces legally sold and developed for some purposes. Such matters often make them susceptible to abuse by some political elites (RAU, 2018b). By definition, youth is a wide cohort defined by age and responsibilities. Different institutions have defined it differently taking into account either age or their responsibilities in society.

## Theoretical Framework

The discussion leans heavily on the employment of the Strengths Based Perspective theory which argues that people have capabilities and internal properties that help them to cope successfully with the problems of living (Rothman, 1994). The theory further argues that even persons ordinarily perceived as desperate, hopeless and impervious to help are presumed capable of making noteworthy steps in facing tough challenges when supported to revive their capabilities.

According to the discussion, this is the perception held by the Johane Masowe apostolic church about the youth post-violence especially when they are in various forms of trouble. Most apostolic churches adopt a case-management approach when helping their clients as they deliberately pay individual attention and seek to understand their weaknesses and challenges, before retracing how they failed and prescribing some rituals till finality of the case.

It is guided by a case of what the discussion calls a 'galloped and benefit' situation among the youth, apostolic churches and the government with each entity prepared to be galloped in order to benefit at some point in the future. Apostolic churches appear to help youth's response to social challenges in an effort to appease government whose governing political party also targets to fish from the church for political abuse. In return, the government allows apostolic churches to exist without adherence to any health and urban planning requirements. Basically, it is a 'scratch my back and I scratch your back' situation.

Today's youth in Zimbabwe lack social protection, jobs and are exposed to chronic poverty, malnutrition and poor health systems among others (Hallsworth, 2013; Maguranyanga, 2011; RAU, 2018). Yet to the church, they are a pool of potential membership while to the government, they are a pool of potential vanguards of political parties to be abused at some point in the future. While this arrangement seems to benefit all the three parties, particularly the churches, it has salient implications particularly to the youth whose future will be gradually getting ruined while they also get wasted in terms of ages and health except for those who are able to recognise a window for transformative empowerment.

## Apostolic Churches in Zimbabwe

Zimbabwe is a secular state with the 2013 Constitution clearly providing for equal statuses to all religions. This is clearly stated in the constitution which pronounces as such: Zimbabwe is a republic and supposedly a constitutional democracy [Section 3(a)]. The State is based on: (i) fundamental human rights and freedoms [Section 3(c) and 49]; and (ii) the recognition of the equality of all human beings [Sections 3(f) and 56] (GoZ, 2013). This position was inherited from the previous colonial Constitutions. This set-up has seen hundreds of African Initiated Churches (AIC) mushrooming all over the country. Among these AICs is Johane Masowe apostolic church (JMAC), which has over time gained confidence and trust among some citizens largely owing to its promises and preparedness to address political, social and economic challenges bedevilling most households.

Scholarly studies complimented by Zimstats (2017) have established that, Christianity commands the majority population with about 84%. However, over 60% of the 84% consult traditionalists for advice and wisdom through their strict adherence to traditional rites and processes. It is also on record that the demographic statistics for various other religious followings is that Hinduism has 0.1%, Islam, 3%, African Traditional Religion (ATR) 18%, Judaism with 0.1% and other 0.1%. It is also given out that of the 84% Christians, 34% over 15 years are apostolic (Chitando, 2013, Dodo, 2014 and Dodo et al., 2018).

Demographics for the membership of the apostolic churches fluctuate depending on the time of the year, prevailing prominent national activities, levels of poverty and the emergency of some prominent 'prophet'. What has usually defined the existence and growth of the apostolic churches, especially in the urban areas in Zimbabwe, is the ability of a church group to instil confidence and hope in a vulnerable society (Chitando, 2013; Maguranyanga, 2011). RAU (2018b) further posits that because these apostolic churches appreciate their weaknesses and deficiencies with regard to legal documentation and requirements, they are forced to toe the line of the ruling political party for protection.

## Sustainable Development Goals (SDG) and the Youth

By virtue of the economic, political and social structure of the Zimbabwean system, the country faces wide-ranging challenges in implementing the SDG 16 Agenda particularly ensuring a responsive, inclusive, participatory and representative decision-making and justice at all levels. Exhibitions of these challenges are usually anecdotal, grounded on the government's failure to take care of all its citizens, especially the vulnerable youth constituency and the lack of tangible and credible data on the youth needs vis-a-vis their susceptibility to both violence and exposure to challenges of post-violence situations. The SDGs were crafted to avert restricted access to information, which is a serious impediment in the way of youth and their right to development. Most youth were seen to be suffering compounded forms and layers of inequality and subjugation (Mercy Corps Zimbabwe, 2019), which naturally limited their choices and prospects for improvement.

Goal 16 demands governments to make sure that all people are given security by the state and to cultivate principles that do not depend on violence as a way of solving conflict (Jayawardena, 2018). The Goal is a multi-dimensional and multifaceted development agenda whose objects are deeply interrelated as an indissoluble whole. The Goal represents a rights-based approach to a cohesive, transformative and broad development model. Violence has traditionally been adopted in most developing countries, Zimbabwe included, applying as a means of resolving conflicts and disputes. In most of the cases of violence, it is the youth who are tasked with the responsibility without paying attention to all the long-lasting repercussions. Though the scope of the Goal has not been fully satisfied, it seeks to safeguard the youth from such abuse especially by politicians. While the Goal also encourages non-discriminatory policies and laws for sustainable development (Gunasekara, 2017), in Zimbabwe, there are a raft of discriminatory laws that have shut most youth out of lucrative opportunities. In an effort to help the youth respond to some of the social challenges, some of the apostolic churches try to embrace the scope and agenda of the Goal, though they could be doing it unknowingly. The aspect of ignorance on the part of the church emanates from the fact that nothing is documented in the church and no-one adheres to any documented system or policy (Dodo et al., 2014).

## YOUTH IN ZIMBABWE

Youth in Zimbabwe constitute the majority of the population with over 67% and yet make up the least numeric consideration in terms of conventionally active political participation and economic and governance involvement. According to the Ministry of Youth, Indigenization and Empowerment records, there are an average of between 15000 and 17000 youth in each district in Harare and about 9000 in each district in other cities like Bulawayo, Gweru and Mutare. Of these, over 80% are formally unemployed and are known to be loitering in the streets idly (Mercy Corps Zimbabwe, 2019). Youth are a critical pointer of the condition of a nation, its politics, economy, religious and social and cultural life (Honwana, 2012). The bulk of African youth are currently struggling with a non-existence of jobs and poor education. After leaving school with limited expertise, they cannot find jobs and become autonomous. Resultantly, they are exposed to potential abuse by both political and economic elites for a pittance unless they adopt a 'galloped and benefit' mentality.

Traditionally, the changeover from childhood to adulthood has been known to be linear in practice whereby individuals move from one phase to another, each with its distinct social and cultural roles: schooling, work, independence, marriage and parenthood. The manner by which youth got liberated and independent could be evidently trailed as they progressively abandoned their more youthful duties and took on new ones (Hallsworth, 2013). The circumstances to which youth are subject and the prospects that are available to them have, however, tended to create a more varied set of conduits for the changeover to independence.

The immediate surroundings for youth in different socioeconomic echelons set them on ever more unpredictable life situations as they move back and forward between education, joblessness, work, family and indolence (Moon et al., 2010). A picture thus appears of intermittent changeover patterns in which the youth swing from one situation to another, thus exposing them to abuse by some political elites and institutions. While the majority of the people in Zimbabwe live in the rural areas, the majority of the politically and economically active ones are in urban areas.

## YOUTH VIOLENCE

Youth violence is a regular problem to both families and local communities. It is a problem that different participants have tried various methods to address but with minimum success. Youth studies show that while the problem is all over, it is more widespread and life threatening in the urban areas. According to RAU (2012) and Dodo et al. (2018), youth in urban areas are at higher risk to exposure to violence than those in the rural areas. The same studies estimate that between 20 and 35% of rural youth and about 60 to 90% of the urban youth have either seen or experienced some type of violence in their communities in that order.

In the context of this discussion, violence has at all times occurred in different environments since time immemorial. It has only become a problem when it is perpetrated on the blameless and young people. Exposure to violence through direct victimisation and secondary exposure during youth-hood sets the youth at risk for different debauched behavioural and health eventualities (Seal et al, 2014). Some of these unpleasant effects include hopelessness, apprehension, violent behaviour, and regression in academic performance (Lambert et al., 2012:1-9). Dahlberg, stemming from Bronfenbrenner's Ecological Systems theory (Bronfenbrenner, 1979) mentions four phases of stimulus elucidating the risk factors that aggravate the probability of exposure to violence as individual, peer, family and environmental.

Studies show that the earlier a youth joins a life of violence, the longer the youth is likely to engage in criminality and grow into a habitual criminal extending into adult life (Kethini et al., 2004:697–720). According to Kethini et al. (2004:697–720), the youth who grow up under violent situations imitate the practice either from their family members or role models as a decent conduct before embracing it into their personalities. Further issues that contribute to youth violence and prolonged offending include lack of interest in education and poor academic performance. According to Moon et al. (2010:839–856), factors like family, peer closeness, school, and drug abuse also have significance on youth violence. Coincidentally, the latter is rife in most high density areas. It has also been proven that the youth who drop out of school are more probable taking part in some form of misdemeanour than those who do well (Davalos et al., 2005:57–68). Youth violence can also be a consequence of social segregation which is a practice whereby other community parties are methodically deprived and segregated because of particular explanations like ethnicity, religion or political alignment.

Generally the youth in the global south where Zimbabwe also falls, have encountered and gone through most of the trying experiences so much so that they are now hardened. The youth have not submitted themselves to the adversities of their circumstances, but are employing their agency and ingenuity to fashion new means of running away from their challenges with alternative forms of livelihood and social relationships in the boundaries of conventional society (Sukarieh & Tannock, 2015). Such new initiatives like the 'galloped and benefit' mentality have unfortunately landed them in some immoral and illegal activities. They have over the period ventured into drugs and prostitution before trying violence (Hallsworth, 2013). While all the attempts have accessed them to some financial incentives, they have equally exposed them to crime and encounters with the law enforcement agencies. The youth are facing more globally, the problems confronting them by drawing upon and remodelling prevailing practices and by creating new ones. They draw encouragement from actions, experiences, [sometimes an 'Oxford' comma is used, whereas elsewhere it is not. This suggests an inconsistency] and interactions that transpire both within and far from their immediate environs, both in virtual and in the physical world, generating an interconnecting network that connects local, national, and global realities (Hassan, 2015).

There are instances when Zimbabwe has recorded cases of violent extremism by the youth owing to a variety of factors. During political campaign periods, there are groups of youth who, ostensibly on orders of some 'senior' politicians, go on terrorism sprees injuring, killing, intimidating, robbing and raping and causing untold suffering to other members of the society. This was evident in Chipangano group in Harare (RAU, 2012; RAU, 2018a). There are also some youth who have assembled themselves to specifically kill, maim and rob other miners of their minerals. This has become common in gold and lithium mining areas. These developments have a risk leading some of the youth to embark on some form of dissent before resorting to unconventional systems of organisation in the absence of apposite socialisation structures for citizens. Some of these forms of delinquency are a clear sign of outright absence of the basic pillars for the protection of the rights and interests of the youth as advocated in the SDGs.

## Youth's Social Challenges

What the youth go through, throughout the age period and as they undertake the various responsibilities, are unbelievable and often horrific. It is therefore the un-believability and horrifying aspects that then generate the youths' social challenges.

Zimbabwe, just like most developing countries, has experienced various diseases, most of which have impacted on the poor and marginalised communities. Historically, it has been the poor and marginalised communities that are abused by politicians to unleash violence either during political campaigns or during some protests. Because they are poor, they normally do not afford meaningful medical services should they require some attention, thus exposing them to avoidable and preventable diseases.

Closely akin to youth health is the challenge of youth pregnancy. This is not only a demographic occurrence, but an intricate social one as well, with an undesirable effect on development and the country through truncation of scholastic goals, alteration of life plans and restricting the enjoyment of youth mothers' rights. Studies have shown that there is a sizeable figure of female youth who are impregnated in political bases where they live during some of the violence episodes like political campaigns (Dodo & Dodo, 2018). Besides pregnancies, they risk contracting sexually transmitted infections. Therefore, JMAC comes in to offer counselling services through women members of the advisory panel called '*Vasadare*', re-instil confidence to continue with the life journey again and re-establish spiritual hope. This form of assistance to the youth is an important pillar in the protection of the youth as espoused in the SDG 16.

Some youth, realising that they have committed serious crimes during violence episodes, begin to regret and possibly find ways of containing the ill-feeling. This could be through drug and substance abuse. Studies show that factors that prompt the start of substance use are found at the individual level and in interpersonal relationships with colleagues (Alleyne & Wood, 2013). Though several elements including peer pressure and individual qualities can also lead youth to substance abuse behaviours, in most of these areas where cases of violence are recorded the most, it is an escape route from the regrets of partaking in violence. In some areas, substance abuse is an effect of the level of trauma that one might have gone through during violence episodes.

Studies show that drug abuse among youth has substantial direct and indirect costs for the individual families of the youth and society. These can be summed up in expenses associated with the health care and criminal justice system and years of productive life lost among youth with dependence (UN, 2014). Therefore, because most of the affected youth are from the poor and marginalised communities, the impact on their families is unbearable.

There is lack of a sense of belonging also understood as non-adherence to shared values, reluctance to recognise others in relation to views of discrimination and non-existence of trust in social structures and of confidence in the future which is a serious effect of post-violence trauma. This is common in youth who would have wronged their communities. Out of guilty conscience, they choose to isolate themselves on assumption that they are being discriminated and also lose confidence in their actions and behaviours. There are also some youth, such as those from urban areas usually associated with violence, who are stigmatised. In the collective imaginary, youth from poor urban areas are usually stigmatised as a possible risk and sign of violence (UNICEF, 2014). This is a serious social challenge that affects most youth post-violence regardless of whether they have participated or not.

The majority of the youth who usually participate in some of these political and service delivery protests are mobilised from the high density suburbs where poverty and desperation are on the higher side. Convenors of such violence actually bait these youth on promises of a better life through the distribution of free alcoholic substances, free basic foods, free drugs and some aspect of impunity should they break the law (Dodo & Dodo, 2018). Naturally, such promises could not be made to the youth from privileged families in low density areas. These promises for a better life have not changed anything as the level of poverty continues to rise. While the element of poverty is glaring as a push factor, there is also an aspect of hopelessness on the part of the youth. In the tunnel, they see no light in any foreseeable future before they realise that they were duped.

Poverty and hopelessness cannot be separated from joblessness. OAS (2014), Paynevandy (2016) and Dodo (2021) give out that unemployment is a serious challenge in the developing world that the selection of potential workers assumes an exaggerated diligence, thus spiralling academic inflation. While Zimstats (2022) reports that employment levels have improved drastically, the situation on the ground does not seem to save the youth crisis. However, studies show that most of the youth who have a history of partaking in violence stand little chances of securing jobs in their local communities. Those who would have had their violence activities recorded by law enforcement authorities equally risk missing on other nationally advertised jobs. Therefore, joblessness attracts poverty and hopelessness. Studies show that youth unemployment can result in mental illness, malnourishment and loss of self-confidence causing depression (Thomas et al., 2010). It is also linked to anxiety leading to possible suicide and poor physical health. Most of such cases are recorded post-political campaign periods (Dodo, 2021; Honwana, 2012; Kethini et al., 2004) and businesspeople will be uncomfortable associating with youth who would have persecuted fellow members of the community.

Youth social challenges have played a part in the rise in illegal migration as troubled youth go in pursuit of a renewed and better life. It has been noted that soon after each national election that is characterised by violence, Zimbabwe records the worst brain drain to the neighbouring countries. It is the same period when some of the youth who would have committed crimes skip the borders for sanctuary in the neighbouring states. To some extent, this explains an increase in the number of Zimbabweans committing crimes, especially in South Africa.

## Role of the Church

Through the Zimbabwe Constitution of 2013, religious institutions like churches, synagogues, mosques and temples among others are allowed to operate freely and anywhere in Zimbabwe (GoZ, 2013). Besides the religious object of worshipping, these institutions are known to drive other noble societal responsibilities. In the context of this discussion, the roles of JMAC are narrowed to focus on their assistance and contribution towards the development of the youth and particularly rescuing them post-violence. This approach strongly derives from the Strengths Based Perspective theory which argues that youth have skills and internal systems that enable them to cope effectively with problems in their respective communities. From a society and youth lenses, JMAC only seeks to address peoples' concerns spiritually and socially. According to Ekeke (2011) and Matiure (2011), various religious groups in different societies play distinctive roles depending on their capability and the extent of reverence that they enjoy among the people. Depending on the nature of problems prevalent in individual communities, religious groups move in with different problem-specific solutions. In the case of Zimbabwe, apostolic churches have always presented Christian based traditional prescriptions that they believe are acquiescent to the belief systems and cultures of local people.

The discussion points out that it were the mainstream churches that have played a critical role in both social upbringing of the people, active mobilisation of resources during the liberation war and infrastructural development across the country (Bhebe, 1979; Mudenge, 1986). However, apostolic churches have also helped morally and spiritually during the liberation struggle of Zimbabwe from the 1950s till the attainment of the independence in 1980. There have also been some church leaders who have spoken out against social injustice, poverty, violence and abuses of human rights among others. Particularly after independence in 1980, some apostolic churches have assumed development work and peacebuilding in different parts of the country (Dodo et al., 2014). The most notable development and peacebuilding initiatives include the Noah Taguta High School in Marange run by Johane Marange AC and Centre Zimbabwe Africa High School and health centre in Madziva run by Johane Masowe Vadzidzi AC. In recent times, it has been established that some of the roles played by Apostolic Churches in local communities have evolved embracing modernity and civilisation. Literally, these modern apostolic churches have created social institutions that have the capacity to remodel compact family systems through their regular prophetic sessions and rituals. These institutions have managed to build imaginary threats to households and individuals that have managed to restrain them from either engaging in illegal activities or perpetuating immorality.

Economic partnerships and empowerment are critical aspects in the survival of humanity. Paynevandy (2016) describes empowerment as a process of providing influence, information, expertise and inspiration to an individual to improve on performance and gain control over one's life. To the apostolic church, since the church's resource pool is shallow, they then primarily focus on the inspiration aspect which, according to them instils confidence and hope for continuity and development. This shows that empowerment is about increasing knowledge, skills and inspiration required to gain the needed practice to thrive in the youth's endeavours. This 'transformative empowerment' is also expected to stir development of youth potential in order to get them ready for nation-building and contribute to the upgrading of their standard of living. This also comes against the backdrop of a belief that the youth have skills that help them to cope well with the problems as explained in the Strengths Based Perspective theory.

Empowerment can transpire in varied ways in different community settings (Jayawardena, 2018). Therefore, apostolic churches seek to impress on activities that include social processes that transpire at various stages of societal life like community and family. They also generate a facilitating atmosphere where the youth can take charge of their actions, rather than blame the other part in violence. Their efforts simply seek to build the capacity of the youth to produce broad-minded, impartial and peaceful societies. It should also be realised that most of the inspiration is socially generated without any reference to Christian scriptures, as apostolic churches do not refer to the bible.

JMAC strongly believes in strong leadership in communities. This church's leadership structures are headed by one who is referred to as a prophet. Under the prophet is a panel of men and women who give guidance and advice. They are called '*Vadare*' for men and '*Vasadare*' for women. They believe in accountability. Therefore, they seek to build a robust and responsible leadership founded on effective participation.

According to Weyers (2011), community development pays attention to the supremacy of oppressed people in the course of crushing externally forced social challenges. Contextually, the youth who would have undergone serious violence either in politics or in some social service delivery protest are what Weyers regard as the oppressed. Others view the employment of community structures to address social needs and empower the youth as another form of community development.

The sessions and rituals that are conducted by JMAC in its endeavour to heal have the capacity to shape the recipients' mind-set and faith into believing that indeed, the rituals do work perfectly well. Chitando (2013) talks about prayers and players in his depiction of how apostolic churches operate, convincing the outside world. This psychology has over the years managed to help erase all the scars and stigma attached to known participants in violence episodes from the community, friends and schools.

The church is helping to rebuild trust that might have been lost following the youth's participation in violence. According to the church, building trust is a way of controlling ones behaviour, as it is believed that engaging in violence is a sign of hopelessness and failure to manage one's temper and emotions. Closely related to emotions are the aspects of submission and respect (Akanbi & Beyers, 2017; Dodo et al., 2014). The church encourages its members to be submissive and respect each other as a way of managing disputes, conflicts and co-existence in various communities.

The church helps in fostering governance within the community. The various leadership structures in the church have traditionally helped in ensuring that the surrounding communities imitate their functional efficiencies (Akanbi & Beyers, 2017). The church also helps in creating order and instilling a sense of belonging and accountability into the people, particularly the youth who would have participated in violence in some instances vandalising property and injuring other community members.

## Youth Responses to Social Challenges

The modern day youth have a great potential for transformation. Youth today recognise that the fight to overcome their quandary needs drastic social transformation (Dodo, 2018; Honwana, 2012; RAU, 2018b). No longer characterised by political parties' philosophy or any religious orientation yet declining being cast as lethargic, they are resorting to civil groups and employing popular culture as well as communication, new technologies of information and social networking to challenge the status quo. It is against this background that some of the youth in urban areas particularly Harare resort to the commercialisation of their energy and competences for some sustenance.

There has been an observation in the youth constituency in urban areas that the youth, in-between political campaigns, flock to gatherings where they anticipate to access opportunities to enrich or improve themselves rather than get abused for a pittance. In some areas, the youth have created groups that are available for hiring to execute various assignments like close security service, night guard services and household cleaning services among others. These are just measures meant to cushion some of the troubled youth pending availability of sustainable solutions to their quandary. From a social point of view, economic challenges have forced some youth to take risky methods of survival. As a means of revenue creation, some young women especially in Harare: Chitungwiza, Mbare, Highfields, Mabvuku, Kuwadzana, Mutare: Sakubva and Dangamvura have taken up transactional and commercial sex to satisfy their basic economic requirements (Mercy Corps Zimbabwe, 2019). Some of these women have gone to an extent of organising themselves in groups for ease of coordination and protection from criminals and sexual predators.

As a response to the social challenges, the youth are teaming up in respective communities and building confidence in each other. This strategy is helping restore buoyancy that would have been eroded as a result of the stigma and discrimination in their communities. The youth are seeking to equip themselves with trainings in leadership, business entrepreneurship, life skills and peacebuilding, which they hope will positively transform their lives and their communities.

With the assistance of *Mapostori4Ed*, some youth have introduced sporting activities as a means of creating and bolstering relationships as they are now connecting and socialising with youth from previously rival groups through sport. Some of the activities drawing participants from across the youth in Harare are centred at the City Sports Centre and Belvedere Teachers' College in Harare. The sporting activities availed a chance to mingle and taught the youth on how to collaborate and contest fairly. They are primarily meant to ensure that any future political contestation is free of violence. Life skills training through sports have also inspired the youth to develop community based groups where personal and social matters can be shared and talked over. The youth also deliberate different cross cutting subjects through the peer-to-peer linkages that they have formed in various residential areas. It has been established that various peer-to-peer networks have drastically helped to disseminate information and transform the conduct of several youth previously known to be substance abusers and rowdy in nature.

Peer-to-peer networks are serving as mechanisms for safety in the communities and as Ward-based group meetings and structures to help each other on matters distressing the youth. It has become easy, convenient and cheap for the youth to seek counselling services to help them clear past distressing experiences. In instances where they cannot afford to secure the services of professional counsellors, they simply approach apostolic churches who, unknowingly guided by the Strengths Based Perspective theory, offer free counselling.

## CHALLENGES TO EFFECTIVE TRANSFORMATION

The efforts by the AC in helping to rebuild the youth constituency post-violence are applauded as they are leaving a noticeable trail on the ground. However, it has been evident on the ground that like most developing countries, Zimbabwe has its fair share of challenges that are impeding planned progress. Most noticeable is the presence of a weak civil society base, limited civic spaces and underdeveloped private sector. As argued by Kasirye et al. (2020), these are prominent challenges for creating partnerships that are necessary for an effective re-establishment of the youth post-violence. In most urban settlements in Zimbabwe, it has been noted that whenever there are instances of violence or any other disturbance, there are hordes of youth who are left facing various criminal, political, economic and social challenges without anyone assisting them.

As it has been noted above, Zimbabwe lacks a clear and credible database on the youth needs, especially around economic empowerment and social and political development. There is also a dearth of information on the demographic distribution of the youth, especially those in need, post-violence episodes and the distribution of AC and their capacities in respective areas across the country. These deficiencies naturally impact effective programming around youth in cases where they have been affected by violence and other disturbances. Similarly, the assumption by the Strengths Based Perspective theory that youth have some internal mechanism that helps them reignite to full functionality might not help owing to these several challenges.

The adoption and domestication of some of these SDGs by some countries has not been to the satisfaction of its dictates. Particularly, Zimbabwe has selectively adopted the Goals, in some cases choosing to separate complementing aspects. Specifically, regarding SDG 16, which seeks to stimulate peaceful and all-encompassing societies for viable development, afford access to justice for all and create effective, responsible and inclusive institutions at all levels (Bhattacharya et al., 2016), the government has been evasive on the establishment of peace, justice and strong institutions. It is evident that impartiality in most governance institutions in Zimbabwe has led to the suffering of the youth post-violence. The security sector, penal systems and the judiciary are either captured or heavily biased, so much so that the vulnerable and often defenceless youth are left suffering, while the fourth estate, mandated to play an oversight role is equally polarised that it has lost its credibility. It has also been established that the justice system has remained a preserve of the few elite constituency exposing the youth to its dangerous side. While JMAC has tried to empower some of the youth against political, social and economic injustices, the reality on the ground points otherwise, exposing a 'galloped and benefit' mentality, especially in view of the dictates of the SDGs' targets.

There has been a challenge to do with the mapping of conflicts on the ground especially around the areas of the youth post-violence. First and foremost, most efforts to identify youth challenges have been marred by serious fabrication, disinformation and ignorance on the part of the implementers. What has been programmed as conflict is often mere disputes, determinants or problems. Therefore, failure to appreciate these three terms and mistaking them for conflicts has hampered all well-meant initiatives directed at addressing youth challenges.

Most apostolic churches involvement in youth responses to social challenges require substantial funding. By their nature, most JMAC do not have abundant sources of finances on account of the fact that the membership is drawn from the marginalised and poor communities who immediately shift to other non-apostolic groups once their social and economic challenges are resolved. Therefore, JMAC has serious limitations when it comes to availing financial and other material assistance to the needy youth post-violence. These churches usually find themselves only helping from a social and spiritual perspective. It is only during political campaign periods that some apostolic churches are exposed to some material freebies courtesy of the contesting political parties that might be 'buying' votes.

Coordination is crucial in the delivery of strong institutions (Kasirye et al., 2020) as defined in SDG 16. However, this critical aspect lacks, as there is no proper coordination between JMAC, the youth and the government so that any efforts towards helping the youth are in alignment with the SDG and the appropriate needs of the youth. The initiatives on the ground by the churches are haphazard and appear to be results of chance and unintended goals. Ultimately, this lack of coordination has in some instances created more challenges for the youth as the church ends up on a collision course with government agencies thereby exposing the youth to either potential crimes or poverty.

Policy configuration can support governments and other bodies to have their engagements and approaches synchronised, unswerving and unified to accomplish common objectives. Policy alignment enables countries appreciate the impacts of their policy engagements (Bhattacharya et al., 2016). It is unfortunate that in the case of JMAC, it exists and operates informally without any legal paperwork. This then makes it very difficult to have specific policies, subsequent enforcement and then align them to any initiative on the ground. This lack of formalisation of most of the apostolic churches is capitalised by government, especially during political campaign periods as the former are expected to toe 'some defined' line in exchange for 'protection', which the discussion calls 'galloped and benefit' approach. On the other hand, these informal churches ride on their association with government to operate 'illegally' and on public spaces without attempting to meet any of the public health and urban planning requirements.

Some youth have attempted to do away with violence and improve their welfare by becoming entrepreneurs, but encounter challenges with the competition from long-established companies. They also find it difficult to compete with foreign-run business entities especially when these foreigners, most of whom might be illegal migrants are given priority over the locals (RAU, 2018). The attempts by youth to embark on some entrepreneurial activities is a confirmation of the Strengths Based Perspective theory, which argues that individuals usually seen as hopeless and resistant to assistance are presumed capable of initiating noble projects when supported to resuscitate their competences.

## Recommendations

Relevant authorities are recommended to review laws around the existence and operations of local apostolic churches in relation to the people around and the government system. This is meant to create a sustainable and formal relationship where there is accountability and sincere interaction devoid of the 'galloped and benefit' attachment. This also ensures creation of responsive, participatory, inclusive decision-making and justice for the youth.

There is need to establish and strengthen both entrepreneurship and peace education in schools and tertiary institutions to nurture the growth of an entrepreneurial culture among the youth to expedite self-employment and keep them off the streets. This form of education and training is also expected to inspire the youth from staying away from violence hot-spots. There is also need to evaluate the extent to which entrepreneurial development institutions and systems have promoted and supported viable entrepreneurship which generates employment for the active youth. This clearly supports the spirit espoused in the Strengths Based Perspective theory of seeking to support the suppressed capacities in the youth with a view to helping them exude their full potential.

## Conclusion

The discussion which looked at the nexus between youth post-violence and apostolic churches revealed the clandestine role that is played by some government agencies to their advantage through what the author called 'galloped and benefit' approach. However, it is undeniably clear that most JMACs in urban areas are critical in helping restore value, dignity, morality, discipline and growth in both youth and the society in general, albeit with some conditionalities.

The analysis has also established that exposure to violence has indubitably been proven to lead to high levels of anxiety among youth which has been associated with the development of a host of psychological problems. The discussion observed that while most studies on youth violence regard youth as reprobates, JMAC views the same youth as either victims of adults' sins or roaming family evil spirits violently demanding redress. Therefore, JMAC ensures that it takes the youth who would have participated in violence through individualised cleansing processes, which are believed in most communities to help invaluably. Some of the ritual processes are believed to cleanse off avenging spirits, traumatic episodes of hallucinations, anxiety and depression among others. In most urban residential areas, this approach has worked well and it is embraced by local people as a sustainable solution.

The discussion notes that while JMAC has been making efforts to help urban youth positively respond to social challenges post-violence, it is hamstrung by lack of resources. It has been established that the most essential component of support including empowerment requires financial backing, which unfortunately lacks within this constituency. While spiritual guidance and other forms of support may be rendered, the fact that these youth are in urban settlements where lives revolve around finances, the support remains inadequate. The support's lack of other crucial aspects like health, education, and sexual health and reproduction also negatively impacts the gains.

As it is defined by the SDGs that "sustainable development" is change that satisfies the requirements of the present without affecting those of the future and that it starts with the respect for the coming generation as a significant stakeholder, any efforts by both JMACs and the government should consider the future well-being of the youth. This comes against the background of abuse by both the church and government as aptly explained in the case of 'galloped and benefit' situation. Ultimately, this 'galloped and benefit' mentality erodes the spirit of building lasting pillars for the protection and growth of the youth in their communities as argued in the Strengths Based Perspective theory. On the part of the church, it has to be development moulded in line with the constitution and other progressive policies.

## References

Akanbi, S. O., & Beyers, J. (2017). The Church as a Catalyst for Transformation in the Society. *HTS Theological Studies, 73*(4), 1–8.

Alleyne, E., & Wood, J. L. (2013). Gang-related Crime: The Social, Psychological and Behavioural Correlates. *Psychology, Crime and Law, 19*, 611–627.

Bhattacharya, D., Khan, T. I., Rezbana, U. S., & Mostaque, L. (2016). *Moving Forward with the SDGs: Implementation Challenges in Developing Countries.* Friedrich-Ebert-Stiftung (FES).

Bhebe, N. (1979). *Christianity and Traditional Religions in Western Zimbabwe, 1859-1923.* Longman Publishing Group.

Bronfenbrenner, U. (1979). *The Ecology of Human Development: Experiments by Nature and Design.* Harvard University Press.

Chitando, E. (2013). *Prayers & Players: Religion and Politics in Zimbabwe.* Sapes Books.

Davalos, D. B., Chavez, E. L., & Guardiola, R. J. (2005). Effects of Perceived Parental School Support and Family Communication on Delinquent Behaviours in Latinos and White Non-Latinos. *Cultural Diversity & Ethnic Minority Psychology, 11*(1), 57–68.

Dodo, O. (2018). Clash of Two Religions: Erosion of Indigenous Systems by Pentecostalism in the Shona People. *Zimbabwe, Journal for the Study of Religions and Ideologies, 17*(49), 90–104.

Dodo, O. (2021). Revolutions and the Power of the Youth in Regime Configurations. *World Applied Sciences Journal, 39*(1), 56–64.

Dodo, O., & Dodo, G. (2018). Youth, Parental Absenteeism and Political Bases in Mazowe District. *Child & Youth Services, 39*(1), 4–16.

Dodo, O., Banda, G., & Dodo, G. (2014). African Initiated Churches in Peace-building: Case of the Johane Mosowe Church. *Journal of Religion and Society, 16*, 1–12.

Dodo, O., Makoni, M., & Mutandi, T. (2018). Inter-Religious Conflicts: A Review of Zimbabwe's Religious Landscape, Post-Independence. *Dialogue & Alliance, 31*(2), 29–44.

Ekeke, E. C. (2011). African Traditional Religion: A Conceptual and Philosophical Analysis. *Lumina, 22*(2), 1–18.

Government of Zimbabwe (GoZ). (2013). *Constitution of Zimbabwe.* Government Printers.

Gunasekara, V. (2017). *Coming of Age in the Classroom: Religious and Cultural Barriers to Comprehensive Sexuality Education.* Asian-Pacific Resource & Research Centre for Women (ARROW).

Hallsworth, S. (2013). *The Gang and Beyond: Interpreting Violent Street Worlds.* Palgrave Macmillan.

Hassan, A. F. (2015). *Media, Revolution and Politics in Egypt. The Story of an Uprising.* I.B.Tauris & Co..

Honwana, A. (2012). *The Time of Youth: Work, social change and politics in Africa.* Kumarian Press.

Jayawardena, S. (2018). 'Sustainable Development Agenda and Young People: Recognising Voices and Claiming Rights', the Asian-Pacific Resource and Research Centre for Women, Kuala Lumpur.

Kasirye, I., Ntale, A., & Venugopal, G. (2020). Implementation Progress of the SDGs: Sub-Saharan Africa Regional Survey, Occasional Paper Series No. 66, Southern Voice.

Kethini, S., Blimling, L., Madden-Bozarth, J., & Gaines, C. (2004). Youth Violence: An Exploratory Study of a Treatment Program in Central Illinois County. *International Journal of Offender Therapy and Comparative Criminology*, 48(6), 697–720.

Lambert, S. F., Boyd, R. C., Cammack, N. L., & Lalongo, N. S. (2012). Relationship Proximity to Victims of Witnessed Community Violence: Associations with Adolescent Internalizing and Externalizing Behaviours. *American Journal of Orthopsychiatry*, 82(1), 1–9.

Maguranyanga, B. (2011). *Apostolic Religion, Health and Utilization of Maternal and Child Health Services in Zimbabwe. A Study conducted for Collaborating Centre for Operational Research and Evaluation.* UNICEF.

Mercy Corps Zimbabwe. (2019). Trusting in Youth in Zimbabwe Project, Final Report.

Moon, S. S., Patton, J., & Rao, U. (2010). An Ecological Approach to Understanding Youth Violence: The Mediating Role of Substance Use. *Journal of Human Behaviour & Social Environment*, 20(7), 839–856.

Mudenge, S. I. G. (1986). *Christian Education at the Mutapa Court.* Zimbabwe Publishing House.

Organization of American States (OAS). (2014). 'The OAS Drug Report: 16 Months of Debates and Consensus', Washington, D.C.

Paynevandy, S. G. (2016). The Role of Empowerment in Organization Development. *Human Resource Management*, 3(5), 9–16.

RAU. (2012). *'Political Violence and Intimidation of Teachers in Zimbabwe'. Report Prepared for the Progressive Teachers Union of Zimbabwe* (pp. 1–23). Research and Advocacy Unit.

RAU. (2018). *Social Capital and Active Citizenship in Zimbabwean Youth: a Statistical Study.* Research & Advocacy Unit.

Research and Advocacy Unit (RAU). (2018a). 'Political Violence'. Harare.

Research and Advocacy Unit (RAU). (2018b). *Religion and Politics in Zimbabwe.* Research & Advocacy Unit.

Rothman, J. (1994). *Practice with Highly Vulnerable Clients: Case Management and Community-based Service.* Prentice Hall.

Sukarieh, M., & Tannock, S. (2015). *Youth Rising? The Politics of Youth in the Global Economy.* Routledge.

Thomas, J. L., Wilk, J. E., Riviere, L. A., McGurk, D., & Castro, C. A. (2010). Prevalence of Mental Health Problems and Functional Impairment among Active Component and National Guard soldiers 3 and 12 months following combat in Iraq. *Archives of General Psychiatry*, 67, 614–623.

United Nations. (2014). 'Mental Health Matters: Social Inclusion of Youth with Mental Health Conditions'.

United Nations Children's Fund, (UNICEF). (2014). 'Hidden in Plain Sight: a Statistical Analysis of Violence against Children', New York.

Weyers, M. L. (2011). *The Theory and Practice of Community Work: A Southern African Perspective* (2nd ed.). Keurkopie.

Zimbabwe Statistical Agency (Zimstats). (2017). *Inter-Censal Demographic Survey (ICDS) of 2017.* Zimbabwe Statistical Agency.

PART IV

# Actors in Religion, Peacebuilding and Development

CHAPTER 23

# African Traditions in the Study of Religion, Peacebuilding and Development in Africa: Engaging with Emmanuel Katongole

*Ezra Chitando*

## INTRODUCTION

The United Nations (UN) Sustainable Development Goal (SDG) 16 envisages the promotion of peace, justice and strong institutions in all parts of the world. While there have been critical voices regarding the SDGs, particularly regarding perceived inconsistencies among the SDGs (see e.g. Swain 2018), preoccupation with indicators, targets and numbers (see e.g. Choudhary 2022), relying on the capitalist model of development and the need for a new ideological orientation (see e.g. Bendell 2022), inadequate focus on women's issues (see e.g. Struckmann 2018), lack of enforcement mechanisms (Sengupta 2018) and Africa's struggle to maintain peace (see e.g. Jaiyesimi 2016), only the most pessimist of analysts would quarrel with the need and quest for peace, justice

---

I am grateful to Nyambura Njoroge for introducing me to, and continuing to encourage me to retain interest in, the works of Emmanuel Katongole. I am also grateful to the Nagel Institute, through the Africa Theological Advance, for a Research Grant for the project, "An Exploration of Christian Perspectives on Forgiveness in Light of the Gukurahundi Atrocities of the early 1980s in Zimbabwe," 2018-2020, which was headed by Nisbert T. Taringa.

---

E. Chitando (✉)
Department of Philosophy, Religion and Ethics, University of Zimbabwe, Harare, Zimbabwe

and strong institutions. Indeed, without peace there is no development. This remains true, irrespective of whichever definition of the two concepts is used. For Africa, peace, justice and strong institutions are imperative, given the deleterious and ongoing impact of the slave trade, colonialism, neo-colonialism and globalisation. Thus, while acknowledging the challenges associated with the SDGs, this chapter appreciates the imperative of peace, justice and strong institutions in Africa and their contribution to development (for an earlier commentary, see e.g. Phiri, Ross and Cox 1996). It underscores the strategic role of African academics researching and publishing on religion and peace to propel this agenda forward. More critically, the chapter concurs with the notion of interconnectedness between SDG 16 and other SDGs. This is so because, "peace cannot be achieved in abstraction from education, gender equality, and climate change, to name just three related challenges" (Schliesser, Kadayifci-Orellana and Kollontai 2021: 135). Nonetheless, it remains important to bear in mind the warning that, "[T]here is an unstated risk in linking peace to 'development' given the broad definition of the term and the competing understandings of what development ought to look like" (Sharra 2009: 93).

The key argument of this chapter is that in order for religious institutions and individuals in Africa to make sustainable contributions to development, it is critical for African scholars, that is, those who are pursuing academic careers (including activism), working in the field of religion, peacebuilding and development to be more visible and consistent in generating and applying relevant knowledge. If religion is to make an effective contribution to peacebuilding and development in Africa, it is absolutely critical that African scholars who are mandated to study religion be at the forefront in the production of the relevant knowledge, its dissemination and uptake. African scholars of religion cannot abdicate responsibility for theory formation and methodological approaches in religion, peacebuilding and development to academics and practitioners in the global North. Where critics might charge that the claim of identity is a fallacy (as it does not automatically translate to knowledge), I would insist that, as feminists and womanists have ably and consistently demonstrated, personal experience constitutes a sound foundation for knowledge. After all, it is their (our) continent's very survival and flourishing that is at stake! As the COVID-19 emergency confirmed through vaccine nationalism and hoarding by many countries in the global North (see e.g. McCann and Matenga 2021), Africa must take responsibility for the continent's own vibrancy. Earlier, Emmanuel Katongole (2017b: 86), whose work constitutes the focus of this chapter, had expressed how he wrestled with the evacuation of Western nationals and abandonment of Rwandans as the genocide got underway in Rwanda. The chapter maintains that Katongole provides valuable insights into the potential and desired outlook of African traditions in the study of religion, peacebuilding and development in Africa. While the chapter provides additional details on Katongole below, it is helpful to appreciate that he positions himself as an African philosopher-theologian who has invested in painting how a re-imagined future in Africa might look like (Katongole 2008: 92). Katongole challenges the Church in Africa (conceptualised ecumenically) to be the locus of hope for a brutalised, ignored and battered continent. He regards his task as one of understanding (theologically and philosophically) Africa's past in order to be able to re-imagine Africa's future. In his own words, he says:

> It is because I have been set on a journey towards that 'New Creation' and have come to realize that being set on that journey involves living and working at different locations, using whatever gifts are at hand; constantly on a journey, grounded in the present, but ever straining to see and live in a new future, a different world right here. (Katongole 2008: 93)

Cognisant of the conviction outlined above, this chapter interrogates the presence of African traditions (Adogame, Chitando and Bateye 2012) in the study of religion, peacebuilding and development in Africa. The first section of the chapter outlines the ideological context of Africanisation. It discusses the calls for Africanisation in the study of Africa in general and makes some references to the study of religion in particular. The second section of the chapter summarises the contribution of Emmanuel Katongole to the field of religion, peacebuilding and development in Africa. This is followed by a third section that engages in a consolidated analysis of the Katongole's works in the context of Africanisation for Africa's development, as envisaged by SDG 16. In conclusion, the chapter argues that African institutions of higher learning need to be more deliberate in investing in research, publication and activism in religion, peacebuilding and development in Africa. Whereas some earlier works have explored some key aspects of Katongole's work (see e.g. Matthews 2014, Ngong 2020 and Maluleke 2020), in this chapter I provide an appreciative enquiry reading of Katongole in the context of Africanisation of research, teaching and publication on religion, peacebuilding and development in Africa.

## AFRICANISATION AND THE QUEST FOR AFRICAN TRADITIONS IN THE STUDY OF RELIGION, PEACEBUILDING AND DEVELOPMENT IN AFRICA

In order to place the review of the contributions by Katongole to the study of religion, peacebuilding and development in Africa in its proper ideological context, there is a need to appreciate the call for Africanisation in African Studies. However, space considerations imply that I can only highlight the key issues relating to Africanisation of the disciplines in Africa (and beyond). Central to this move is the observation that the dominant personalities, paradigms and positionalities in the field are those from the global North. For example, European traditions remain highly influential in the study of religion in Africa (see e.g., Ludwig and Adogame 2004). Across the disciplines in Africa, the formulations, whims and serious convictions of theorists from the global North continue to hold sway. This has resulted in the hegemony of Euro-American scholarship in African Studies, including in Africa (see e.g.

Daley and Marrey 2022 for the field of African geographies). This is a result of colonialism, where knowledge construction was essentially about knowing the native in order to be able to control him/her more effectively. Thus,

> "[C]olonialism and coloniality can be defined teleologically: the subjugation and subjection of people, societies, and experiences for the purposes of accumulating knowledge, wealth and power that serve, directly or indirectly, white Western hegemony" (Kessi, Marks and Ramugondo 2020: 271-272).

As the history of struggles globally confirms, no oppression has gone without meeting resistance, however such might be expressed. This resistance might take the force of arms, as in the liberation struggles, or the oppressed might opt for "weapons of the weak" (Scott 1985) such as creative works that critique the oppressor, sabotage, refusal to subscribe to the tenets set by the oppressor, foot-dragging, false compliance, feigned ignorance and others. In the case of epistemic violence, Africans have resorted to epistemic liberation. This refers to the conviction by African scholars that they can produce knowledge that is legitimate and sustainable (see e.g. Masaka 2021). Generations of African scholars have engaged in intellectual resistance to unsettle and displace the hegemony of Euro-American scholarly formulations. This has happened across the various fields, particularly during and after the 1960s decade of decolonisation for much of the continent. In African history, literature, languages, classical studies, philosophy and others, there is a revolution that decolonial scholars have dubbed epistemic disobedience and epistemic freedom (see e.g. Ndlovu-Gathsheni 2018; Tamale 2020). There is an ongoing protest against epistemicide (Tshaka 2019), which is the denial of African ways of knowing, in African academia. In African theological (see e.g. Mashabela 2017), biblical (Abogunrin 2005) and religious studies (Wiredu 1998; P'Bitek 2011), there is a questioning of the assumptions, approaches and fixations of the global North contributors to the disciplines. To be sure, African scholars who are regarded as following these assumptions uncritically also come under critique (or attack, in the case of P'Bitek!)

One of the abiding questions in this discourse, the focus of this chapter, relates to the place of African scholars in the production, dissemination and uptake of knowledge. In most instances, knowledge produced by African scholars is regarded as having less weight and relevance than that produced by their counterparts from Europe and North America. Indeed, there is the tendency of regarding African scholars as perpetual research assistants under the tutelage of Euro-American "experts" in the field (Ndlovu-Gatsheni, Seesemann and Vogt-William 2022). However, African scholars have made, and are making, significant contributions to their areas of expertise. They are overcoming formidable odds that include operating in environments that are extremely challenging (sometimes disabling administrative systems, struggles to access relevant publications, unprogressive compensation systems, etc. See e.g. Mulisa 2021).

In the specific case of religion and peacebuilding in Africa, one can acknowledge that African scholars are producing valuable knowledge, although the field is yet to take a more or less defined shape (see e.g. Carney 2010). That such a strategic publication as *Peace Research for Africa: Critical Essays on Methodology* (McCandless et al. 2007) could not make any reference to religion calls for African scholars of religion and theologians to redouble their efforts in order to become more visible and relevant to policy makers. However, it might also suggest that many social scientists in Africa need to acquaint themselves more with the work that is being produced within African religious studies and theology more generally. However, a more recent publication, namely, *The State of Peacebuilding in Africa* (McNamee and Muyangwa 2021) does carry an essay on religion and peacebuilding in Africa (Ludovic 2021). More reflections in this field are necessary as the strategic role of religion in peacebuilding and development in Africa requires attention (see e.g. Hayward and Wilson 2022 for an overview of the discourse in its global context).

One of the key tasks is that of outlining what constitutes specifically *African* contributions to the field. Here, I provide some operating principles that can serve as a guide. Writing with special reference to African psychology, Ratele et al. say that it is the same as "psychology *in*, *by*, *from*, or *of* Africa or Africans" (2018: 332). Thus, in reflecting on African contributions to the field of religion, peacebuilding and development in Africa, the emphasis should be on whether the material meets the criteria so outlined. In this regard, "the Africanization of religious studies implies that the discipline reflects seriously on its African context, takes on board African issues, and has an African flavour or outlook" (Chitando, Adogame and Bateye 2013: 2). Some of the relevant questions include: Is the publication by an African scholar (black or white, born or raised in Africa or its diaspora)? Are they addressing African issues? Do they engage with African scholars? Do they utilise African resources (e.g. indigenous knowledge systems, reflections by fellow Africans) in their reflections? Are they committed to Africa's transformation/progress/development/flourishing? Africanisation, therefore, implies the presence of African scholars, who are acutely aware of their identity as such, willingness to respect and engage with fellow African scholars, recognition and deployment of African resources and unwavering commitment to the African agenda (see also, Chitando 2016, and Chitando and Mateveke 2017). Africanisation does not mean cataloguing the ills of Africa, but implies a commitment towards searching for and contributing towards the resolution of the same. Africanisation is not neutral: it is taking a stand for Africa in the face of multiple forces that seek the continent's demise (or its ongoing exploitation).

As the growing literature on Africanisation (and decolonisation and decoloniality) in African Studies confirms, African scholars are agitating to have African contributions to knowledge production, dissemination and uptake acknowledged and confirmed. In the study of religion, the dominance of European traditions (Ludwig et al. 2004) is being challenged by the notable increase in the number of publications by African scholars. African scholars are grappling with the question of how religion can contribute to human flourishing in Africa. They are seeking to understand how religion can become a major factor in the quest for abundant life in Africa. Below, I provide the example of one African scholar who has made, and continues to make, a significant contribution to field.

## Katongole: Setting the Agenda for African Traditions in Religion, Peacebuilding and Development

In the foregoing sections, this chapter outlined the quest for Africanisation in African Studies in general and broached the theme of how to place material in religion, peacebuilding and development in Africa. In this section, the focus is on the work of one of the continent's most consistent contributors to this field, namely, Emmanuel Katongole. Katongole has emerged as one of the most productive, creative and dedicated African scholars writing on theme. Since I will not be able to do justice to his oeuvre in the context of this chapter, I proceed by way of summarising his academic and professional background. I then move on to drawing attention to some of the major themes emerging from his works. From the onset, I must declare that I stand with Adogame (2018: 31) when he opines that, "Katongole brings fresh critical insights into theoretical and methodological discourses in public theology, social ethics and peace studies in Africa." Katongole's determination to listen and observe closely in order to identify grassroots initiatives that represent hope for the future in Africa (Katongole 2022) is highly commendable.

A Catholic priest born on 27 November 1960 in Malube, Uganda, to parents who were originally from the neighbouring Rwanda, Katongole studied philosophy and theology at seminaries in Uganda and was ordained in June 1987 (https://emmanuelkatongole.org/biography/). A high flying student, he graduated with high pass rates for his degrees, including his doctorate in philosophy at the Catholic University of Louvain in 1996. He has held teaching positions at the Universities of Notre Dame and Duke in the United States. From 2005-2011 he was the founding Co-Director, Centre for Reconciliation at Duke University Divinity School. Katongole is a scholar-activist (see e.g. Desai 2013 for the possible tension) who recognises the diversity, complexities and holistic character of strategies for peacebuilding and development in Africa:

> the various forms—prayers, songs, counseling, medical healing, education, and leadership formation—reflect a re-enlivened theology, discovered in the midst of the devastation through which the leaders engage scripture and other resources from the Christian tradition to innovate, shape and lead programs that seek to heal, restore and rebuild the shattered lives of individuals and communities and to re-imagine a new future in the midst of ruins. (Katongole 2018: 111)

Katongole's theology of reconciliation in Africa is closely tied to his political theology. An original thinker, he is constantly wrestling with the pain and suffering that many Africans encounter and the dynamism and hope that millions of Africans exude. Sharply critical of the images of doom, destruction and death that are often deployed by the western media about Africa, he senses that "[Africans] do not live … kind of waiting for western media and other perceptions to tell them whether they are hopeless or hopeful. There is a lot of energy and innovativeness … resourcefulness that is going on … an incredible resilience that needs to be discovered … African Christians [are able to] stand at the intersection of pain and hope."[1]

Katongole writes elegantly and deploys poems, stories and biblical narratives in a very effective way. He is not one to stand aside and critique dispassionately, declaring, "the theologian cannot remain a detached, armchair theologian, but an engaged participant" (Katongole 2012b: 25). He is deeply immersed, bringing his entire self to the peacebuilding ministry in Africa. When Africa laments, he laments. When he senses the small signposts of healing and reconciliation, he rejoices. When God asks, "Who are My People?" (Katongole 2022), Katongole also asks himself, "Who am I?" on the basis of his multiple identities (born in Uganda to parents who were Hutu and Tutsi, originally from Rwanda, moving constantly between the US and Uganda, etc. see e.g. Katongole 2022). Katongole is brutally honest about the shortfalls of his continent, daring to say some beliefs and practices must actually die before Africa resurrects and flourishes (Katongole 2012b). He plumbs the depth of his soul in an effort to fathom Africa's "sickness unto death." He seeks to understand how the gospel can remain good news to a people who experience violence regularly. How do African Christians negotiate violence and create places to feel at home?

This commitment towards understanding the setting in life of regular Africans (see e.g. Katongole 2002: 207) forms the foundation of Africanisation, as I have outlined it above. Katongole's approach to peacebuilding, political theology (see e.g. Katongole 2019 for his review of political theology in Africa) and activism for development do not begin with abstract reflection, but with an acute awareness of the local struggle. For him, "our discussion must begin with the sociological reality of the African church. Such a starting point, by drawing attention to the African context within which the church is located, will highlight the social and existential challenges that confront millions of Africans on a daily basis"(Katongole 2016: 164). This would imply that research, community engagement and teaching by African scholars must always be informed by the concrete and lived African realities. According to him:

> In all my teaching I find myself in search of something better than the tribalization that divides so much of Africa, or categories such as North and South, black

---

[1] Emmanuel Katongole, Eerdmans Author Interview Series. YouTube. See also, EEDWORD: The EEDMANS Blog. "Five Questions with Emmanuel Katongole," Eedmans, May 16, 2017. Available at https://eerdword.com/five-questions-with-emmanuel-katongole/, accessed 30 December 2022.

and white. Here I am, pressing the question as I teach, "But what does this theology mean for my mother?" What does this mean back in Malube, where trees are being cut down by powerful businesses, where roads are in disrepair, where the priest lives in a faraway town? What does it mean for our conversations about God and peace never to be disconnected from the challenges or real, local places from digging wells, organizing education and planting trees (Katongole and Rice 2008: xi).

Katongole is as much an African theologian and historian of Christianity in Africa as he is a creative writer, a portraitist (see, e.g. Katongole 2017a: 37) and therapist. His creativity comes through in the approach that he adopts, his identity as a portraitist can be discerned in the thick descriptions that he provides, while his work as a therapist is confirmed by his proposals for Africa's healing and reconciliation. If in an earlier period Gifford (2008: 31) felt that Katongole's formulations had not yet taken a more definite shape, the situation has since changed in a significant way. Katongole has been quite prolific and articulate in detailing healing and reconciliation in Africa. Katongole's publications, including *The Sacrifice of Africa: A Political Theology for Africa* (Katongole 2011), *Stories from Bethany: On the Faces of the Church in Africa* (Katongole 2012a), *Born from Lament: On the Theology and Politics of Hope in Africa* (Katongole 2017a), *The Journey of Reconciliation: Groaning for New Creation in Africa* (Katongole 2017b) and *Who Are My People? The Invention of Love in Sub Saharan Africa* (Katongole 2022), as well as co-authored books, book chapters and journal articles, are strategic resources for the emergence of African traditions in the study of religion, peacebuilding and development in Africa. Critically, his interpretation of the role of the African scholar in the process of social transformation (see e.g. Katongole 2018: 23; Katongole 2022) is consistent with my reflections on African traditions in the study of religion in the foregoing section. It does not come as a surprise, therefore, that in *Stories from Bethany* he utilises quotations from the African Bible, whose contributors are mostly African biblical scholars. He does this because, "The African Bible contains notes and commentaries based on the African context, helping the readers see the relevance of the word of God in Africa today" (Katongole 2013: 10). When reflecting on the task of African academic, he writes:

> On a scholarly level, the Rwanda genocide had a number of immediate and long-time impacts. In the wake of the genocide, there was a sense of the utter irrelevance and even uselessness of my scholarly pursuits. Here I was doing a doctorate in philosophy (and studying interesting figures like Hegel, Habermas, and Heidegger), and there were my brothers and sisters killing each other in the name of ethnicity. The long-term effect of this desolation was a nagging question about not simply my own studies but about scholarship in general, especially as it relates to Africa. For I was beginning to get a feeling that unless my academic pursuit was able to shed light on events like this, which threatened the very foundations of social existence in Africa, it was totally useless and in fact a distraction (Katongole 2017b: 86).

Katongole is critical of triumphalist narratives relating to the shift in the center of gravity from the west to Africa (as presented by the "Translatability School" of Lamin Sanneh and Kwame Bediako. See particularly Katongole 2002 for his critique of Bediako and Mugambi). For him, numerical superiority is of little or no consequence as long as Christianity remains reticent. Thus, "Even though Christianity, statistically has a powerful presence in Africa, when it comes to facing the critical challenge of social imagination, it tends to remain shy and self-effacing" (Katongole 2011: 52). Katongole's own approach is to challenge the same Christianity to make a qualitative difference in the lives of women and men in the villages and cities of Africa. It must, Katongole insists throughout his works, lead the way by way of generating a new social imagination/imaginary (see, particularly, Katongole 2005). Where the colonial and the independent African states remained trapped in logics of violence, the Church must do better in authoring new forms of identity and visions of the future. Unfortunately, the Church is equally a victim of failure of imagination. Katongole's analysis of the genocide in Rwanda is instructive (see also Katongole and Hartgrove 2009). His basic argument is that the church in Rwanda failed to critique (and therefore uncritically upheld) the invented identities of "Hutu" and "Tutsi" and suggests that church in Africa needs to imagine afresh. Thus:

> However, perhaps by far the most disturbing questions were related to the realization that Rwanda was an overwhelmingly Christian count[r]y, one in which Catholics made up more than 80 percent of the population. That the Christian churches where the majority of Rwandans worshipped became killing fields during the genocide raised fundamental questions about mission. How could Christians kill one another, often within the same churches they worshipped in? Is the blood of tribalism deeper than the waters of baptism? The fact that the genocide unfolded during Holy Week made the question even more poignant (Katongole 2017b: 86).

Given the ongoing climate emergency, it is important to highlight that Katongole (2022) includes ecological violence and reinvention of the land into consideration in his approach to peacebuilding and development (see e.g. Machingura and Gusha 2020). He shows how ecological violence has a devastating impact on the poor, including food insecurity, diminishing livelihoods, loss of water and spiritual wounds. Reflecting on the papal encyclical *Laudato Si': On Care for Our Common Home* (2015), Katongole (2022) evokes the idea of the connection between African spirituality and the land. He critiques the contemporary development economics for encouraging an exploitative and extractive relationship to nature and the land. Thus, although he does not write on "sustainable development" in an engaged way, Katongole's body of works has clear implications for sustainable development. In fact, as this chapter confirms, his reflections seek to promote holistic healing, peace, integration and wholesome lives for millions of Africans and creation.

## Major Themes in Katongole's Reflections and Activism in the Field of Religion and Peacebuilding in Africa

Having outlined Katongole's understanding of and approaches towards peacebuilding and healing in Africa in the preceding section, in this section I seek to summarise the key issues that emerge from his work in the context of SDG 16.

### Reconciliation, Peacebuilding and Development as Deeply Theological Acts done by Regular Lay African Christians

The temptation is high to regard grand institutions such as the World Bank and the global church as the enablers and undertakers of peacebuilding and development. At face value, SDG 16 is to be realised through the activities of "big institutions doing massive works." Yet, Katongole reminds his readers that it is regular lay African Christians who are movers of healing, reconciliation and development in their small and modest, but exceedingly significant, ways. Throughout his works, Katongole concentrates on local action for local transformation, but with global implications. It is 'ordinary' women and men doing extraordinary works who constitute the locus of peacebuilding and development in Africa. It is local individuals who must transform "the same story of the politics of greed, dispossession and state brutality" (Katongole 2011: 15) into new stories of healing, hope and restoration.

Here, I would categorise Katongole among those African intellectuals and activists who insist on peacebuilding and development "from below." He categorically stands for and with those who are at the coalface of the struggle. He is suspicious of grand programmes for healing, reconciliation and development "from above." While global religious centers such as the Vatican (for the Roman Catholic Church), Geneva (for the World Council of Churches) are helpful in formulating approaches for peacebuilding and development, Katongole's work shifts and retains focus on local people acting in the local context.

### Appreciating the Stories of Regular People doing Extraordinary Peacebuilding and Development Work

Related to the foregoing is Katongole's highly impressive and effective deployment of stories. Where many African theologians and scholars of religion devote a lot of space to debating lofty ideas and concepts, Katongole shares the powerful narratives of regular people undertaking outstanding work in the field of peacebuilding and development. He is able to synthesise how they are driven by their faith and biblical interpretation. In his works, African women and men who would never be known in academia come alive. They sacrifice and they are sacrificed for the lives of others: Sister Félicitée chose death and prayed for her executioner during the genocide in Rwanda (Katongole 2012a: 31-32). Angeline Atyam, sacrificed her daughter Charlotte in Northern Uganda

(Katongole 2011: 155-165). Jo and Lyn Lusi opened a holistic healing hospital and center in Eastern Democratic Republic of Congo (Katongole 2017b: 167-181). Maggy Barankitse, a Tutsi, adopted seven children, three Tutsi and four Hutu, in Burundi (Katongole 2022). Further examples could be shared, but the underlying theme is the same: narrating gripping stories of regular people moved by faith to do exceptional peacebuilding and development work in Africa.

Through storytelling, Katongole recovers a distinctive, powerful and popular genre in Africa. For example, the Circle of Concerned African Theologians has made storytelling central to the methodology of its members and practitioners (see e.g. Mombo 2003). For her part, Nadar (2014) proclaims that, "stories are data with Soul." Katongole (2022) insists, rightly, that stories matter. His deployment of stories is consistent with the call for Africanisation that I raised in an earlier section in this chapter. Stories have an important role to play in the lives of most Africans. Katongole utilises stories to capture and express the creative peacebuilding and development work that Africans are undertaking in diverse contexts.

### *The Emergence of African Faith Communities Capable of Undertaking High-Level Social Analysis*

Katongole's work confirms the urgency of African faith communities engaging in high-level social analysis. If the World Council of Churches popularised the call for "HIV Competent Churches" (see e.g. Parry 2008), Katongole's reflections highlight the need for faith communities in Africa to deepen their social analysis. This will enable them to overcome divisive ethnicity and manipulation by politicians, challenge the cheapening of African lives ("sacrifice" in Katongole's parlance), defend African resources against domestic thieves acting in cahoots with foreign looters, as well as build and solidify resilient and flourishing communities. Reading the raising of Lazarus, Katongole makes the following submission:

> Jesus['s] invitation to those around him to "take away the stone" can be seen as pointing to the need to remove the structural, institutional obstacles; political and economic policies, systems and cultural traditions that entomb millions in Africa or hold them back from realising their full potential. One critical role of a theologian is not only to point to these structural and institutional systems but to call for their lifting. For without a re-inscription of African villages within a new and more promising economic and political systems, millions of Africans will remain entombed in a life of misery, poverty and unrealised potential (Katongole 2012b: 31).

Although he does not position or describe himself an African liberation theologian (and neither do his extant reviewers), I contend that there are adequate grounds for locating Katongole within the tradition of radical African

(Cameroonian) Catholic liberation theologians such as Jean-Marc Ela and Engelbert Mveng (see e.g. Ogbonnaya 2015, Iheanacho 2021 and Ndongala 2021). Katongole is keen to see Africans liberated from the tyranny of oppressive African regimes and global financial systems. For example (Katongole 2022), he exposes the collusion of powerful external and local interests who have "owned" Central Africa and who have abused and neglected the majority of the citizens. While he adopts a different mode and style of expressing his liberation theology, he is unwavering in his call for sustainable peace and development in Africa.

### The Bible as a Resource for Peacebuilding and Development in Africa

Katongole (see e.g. Katongole n.d.) engages in Contextual Bible Studies to invite individuals and communities to peacebuilding and development work. Whereas the Bible might be experienced as a violent text (see e.g. Melanchthon and Whitaker 2021), Katongole mines it to convert people to peacebuilding and development. His reflections on lament, new creation, hope and resurrection emerge from his interpretation of biblical passages. His readings of the text are highly creative and mobilise individuals and communities to eschew violence and commit to peacebuilding and development. His conviction that Africa is a continent that is loved by God, but which must allow certain ideas and practices to die in order for it to resurrect and prosper, is derived from the Bible. Perhaps this is one of the direct outcomes of Katongole's immersion in Protestant settings (Katongole 2022). Katongole's appropriation of the Bible as a resource for peacebuilding and development in Africa is also consistent with the extent to which the Bible is widely engaged with Africa (for an expansive reflection on the "Word of God" and reconciliation in Africa, see e.g. Béré 2011).

Reflecting on Katongole's deployment of the Bible as a resource (see e.g. Chitando 2020b) is a necessary undertaking, as it constitutes a valuable source of his political theology. Further, there is a real danger that reviews of peacebuilding and development initiatives by individuals and organisations inspired by faith can miss out the distinctively religious factors that drive their engagement. Katongole himself reflects on the story of Martha and Mary in the Bible by drawing attention to Mary's ability to see in the midst of a flurry of activities. According to him, "Without a clear sense of priority and discipline the African Church will continue to be pulled in so many directions and may simply come to resemble just another NGO, constantly busy, constantly seeking to be relevant and useful in tending to the plethora of Africa's needs" (Katongole 2012a: 61).

## The Special Place of African Women in Religion, Peacebuilding and Development

Several narratives are required to do justice to the role of African women to peacebuilding in general (see e.g. Chitando 2020a), as well as in religion in particular. Katongole is painfully aware of the extent to which patriarchal attitudes in church and society lead to the exclusion of women in peacebuilding, leadership and development initiatives in Africa. He anticipates a Vatican III where the gifts and leadership abilities of women will be embraced (Katongole 2016: 172). His heroines are consistently everyday African women of faith who are involved in exceptional tasks of forgiveness, reconciliation, leadership and development. If there is the prior question, "Who cooked the last supper?" (Miles 2001), Katongole poses his own, equally relevant question, "Where are the African women in religious peacebuilding?" and proceeds to provide numerous, empowering examples.

In the opening paragraph, I referred to the intractable character of the SDGs. Whereas SDG 16 focuses on peacebuilding, SDG 5 prioritises "gender equality and women's empowerment." Katongole's work bears testimony to the extent to which the SDGs are closely interwoven. He demonstrates how women are at the forefront of religious peacebuilding in Africa, justifying his call for a profound ecclesiological shift. This ecclesiological shift will see African women taking up leadership in church and having access to quality theological education that exposes misleading theologies (see e.g. Bosela and Njoroge 2020) and problematic approaches to development.

Overall, one might critique Katongole for not being more forthcoming in terms of outlining the concrete steps that the Church in Africa can/should/could take for it to contribute towards peacebuilding in Africa. Is this by way of transforming theological education to mainstream peacebuilding, for example? How can African Christians join hands with people of other faiths to challenge cultures of violence and nurture cultures of peace? What would the place of young people in the struggle for peacebuilding? While stories are powerful, can they move those who are committed to not moving? These are some of the challenges that Katongole might need to address as he continues to provide reflections on the role of the Church in peacebuilding in Africa.

## Conclusion

Katongole provides valuable insights into the Africanisation of the scholarly field of religion, peacebuilding and development in Africa. Embracing an ecumenical vision (Katongole 2022), remaining passionately committed to Africa while working in the US and striving to locate signs of hope in an Africa facing multiple challenges, Katongole's approach is impressive. Eschewing abstract theological reflections, he grapples with his multiple identities and demonstrates the complex relationship between identity, peacebuilding and sustainable development in contemporary Africa. His work serves as a valuable pointer to African institutions seeking to promote research, publication, teaching and activism in the field of religion, peacebuilding and development. It paints a helpful picture of the importance of personal engagement, fieldwork, patient analysis, clarity of thought and creativity in establishing African traditions in this field of study. As the continent strives to achieve the targets set in SDG 16 and sustain African traditions in the study of religion, peacebuilding and development in Africa, Katongole's lament, sacrifice and storytelling can serve as reservoirs of strength and imagination.

## References

Abogunrin, S. O. (Ed.). (2005). *Decolonization of Biblical Interpretation in Africa*. Ibadan: Nigerian Association of Biblical Studies.

Adogame, A. (2018). Remembering to Forget: Forgetting to Remember: Memory, Trauma, and Religious Imagination in Africa. In M. Girma (Ed.), *The Healing of Memories: African Christian Responses to Politically Induced Trauma* (pp. 17–35). Lexington Books.

Adogame, A., Chitando, E., & Bateye, B. (Eds.). (2012). *African Traditions in the Study of Religion in Africa: Emerging Trends, Indigenous Spirituality and Interface with Other World Religions*. Ashgate.

Bendell, J. (2022). Replacing Sustainable Development: Potential Frameworks for International Cooperation in an Era of Increasing Crises and Disasters. *Sustainability, 14*, 8185. https://doi.org/10.3390/su14138185

Béré, P. (2011). The Word of God as Transformative Power in Reconciling African Christians. In A. E. Orobator (Ed.), *Reconciliation, Justice, and Peace: The Second African Synod* (pp. 48–58). Orbis Books.

Bosela, E. E., & Njoroge, N. J. (Eds.). (2020). *Addressing Contextual Misleading Theologies in Africa Today*. Regnum.

Carney, J. J. (2010). Roads to Reconciliation: An Emerging Paradigm. *Modern Theology, 26*(4), 549–569.

Chitando, E. (2016). The Africanization of Biblical Studies in Zimbabwe: Promises and Challenges. *Journal of Theology for Southern Africa, 156*, 54–70.

Chitando, A. (Ed.). (2020a). *Women and Peacebuilding in Africa*. Routledge.

Chitando, E. (2020b). The Bible as a Resource for Development in Africa: Ten Considerations for Liberating Readings. In E. Chitando, M. R. Gunda, & L. Togarasei (Eds.), *Religion and Development in Africa* (pp. 401–417). University of Bamberg Press.

Chitando, E., & Mateveke, P. (2017). Africanizing the Discourse on Homosexuality: Challenges and Prospects. *Critical African Studies, 9*(1), 124–140. https://doi.org/10.1080/21681392.2017.1285243

Chitando, E., Adogame, A., & Bateye, B. (2013). Introduction: African Traditions in the Study of Religion in Africa: Contending with Gender, the Vitality of Indigenous Religions, and Diaspora. In A. Adogame, E. Chitando, & B. Bateye (Eds.), *African Traditions in the Study of Religion, Diaspora and Gendered Societies Essays in Honour of Jacob Kehinde Olupona* (pp. 1–9). Ashgate.

Choudhary, N. (2022). Critiquing the SDG Framework through the Lens of Goal Two: Empirical Reflections from Two Case Studies in India. *Forum for Development Studies*. https://doi.org/10.1080/08039410.2022.2099459

Daley, P. O., & Murrey, A. (2022). Defiant Scholarship: Dismantling Coloniality in Contemporary African Geographies. *Singapore Journal of Tropical Geography, 43*(2), 159–176.

Desai, M. (2013). The Possibilities and Perils for Scholar-Activists and Activist-Scholars Reflections on the Feminist Dialogues. In J. S. Juris & A. Khasnabish (Eds.), *Insurgent Encounters: Transnational Activism, Ethnography, and the Political* (pp. 89–107). Duke University Press.

Gifford, P. (2008). Africa's Inculturation Theology. *Hekima Review, 38*, 18–34.

Hayward, Susan, & Erin Wilson. (2022). Religions, Peace, and Conflict. In *The State of the Evidence in Religions and Development*, edited by Joint Learning Initiative on Faith and Local Communities (JLI), 59-64. Washington, DC: JLI, 2022, 55-60.

Iheanacho, V. U. (2021). Engelbert Mveng and Jean Marc Éla: Bridging the Gulf between Liberation and Inculturation. *Stellenbosch Theological Journal, 7*(1), 1–22.

Jaiyesimi, R. (2016). The Challenge of Implementing the Sustainable Development Goals in Africa: The Way Forward. *African Journal of Reproductive Health, 20*(3), 13–18.

Katongole, E. M. (2002). "A Different World Right Here, A World Being Gestated in the Everyday." The Church within African Theological Imagination. *Missionalia, 30*(2), 206–234.

Katongole, E. (2005). *A Future for Africa: Critical Essays in Christian Social Imagination*. University of Scranton Press.

Katongole, E. (2008). A Tale of Many Stories. In D. C. Marks (Ed.), *Shaping a Global Theological Mind* (pp. 89–93). Ashgate.

Katongole, E. (2011). *The Sacrifice of Africa: A Political Theology of Africa*. W. B. Eerdmans.

Katongole, E. (2012a). The Raising of Lazarus and the Sites for African Theological Exploration and Engagement. In A. J. Bwangatto (Ed.), *Africa Is Not Destined to Die: Signs of Hope and Renewal* (pp. 21–32). Paulines Publications Africa.

Katongole, E. (2012b). *Stories from Bethany: On the Faces of the Church in Africa*. Paulines Publications Africa.

Katongole, E. (2016). The Church of the Future: Pressing Moral Issues from Ecclessia in Africa. In A. E. Orobator (Ed.), *The Church We Want: African Catholics Look to Vatican III* (pp. 161–173). Acton.

Katongole, E. (2017a). *Born from Lament: The Theology and Politics of Hope in Africa*. William B. Eerdmans.

Katongole, E. (2017b). *The Journey of Reconciliation: Groaning for a New Creation in Africa*. Orbis.

Katongole, E. (2018). "When the Foundations are Destroyed" (Psalm 11: 3): Lament, Healing, Social Repair, and Political Reinvention in Eastern Congo. In M. Girma (Ed.), *The Healing of Memories: African Christian Responses to Politically Induced Trauma* (pp. 95–112). Lexington Books.

Katongole, E. (2019). Political Theologies of Africa. In W. T. Cavanaugh & P. M. Scott (Eds.), *Wiley Blackwell Companion to Political Theology* (pp. 346–359). John Wiley and Sons.

Katongole, E. (2022). *Who Are My People? Love, Violence, and Christianity in Sub-Saharan Africa*. University of Notre Dame Press.

Katongole, Emmanuel M. (n.d.). The Great Lakes Initiatives: Duke Center for Reconciliation: Identity, Community and the Gospel of Reconciliation Christian Resources in the Face of Tribalism. Retrieved January 3, 2023, from https://divin-

ity.duke.edu/sites/divinity.duke.edu/files/documents/cfr/identity-and-reconciliation.pdf.
Katongole, E., & Hartgrove, J. W. (2009). *Mirror to the Church: Resurrecting Faith After Genocide in Rwanda*. Zondervan.
Katongole, E., & Rice, C. (2008). *Reconciling All Things: A Christian Vision for Justice, Peace and Healing*. InterVarsity Press.
Kessi, S., Marks, Z., & Ramugondo, E. (2020). Decolonizing African Studies. *Critical African Studies, 12*(3), 271–282.
Ludovic, L. T. (2021). Religion and Peacebuilding in Sub-Saharan Africa. In T. McNamee & M. Muyangwa (Eds.), *The State of Peacebuilding in Africa: Lessons Learned for Policy Makers and Practitioners* (pp. 47–64). Palgrave Macmillan.
Ludwig, F., et al. (Eds.). (2004). *European Traditions in the Study of Religion in Africa*. Harrassowitz Verlag.
Machingura, F., & Gusha, I. (2020). Biblical Texts, Ecology, and Sustainable Development: An African Eco-theological Discourse. In E. Chitando, M. R. Gunda, & L. Togarasei (Eds.), *Religion and Development in Africa* (pp. 455–471). University of Bamberg Press.
Maluleke, T. S. (2020). Forgiveness and Reconciliation in the Life of Desmond Tutu. *International Review of Mission, 109*(2), 210–221.
Masaka, D. (2021). Knowledge, Power, and the Search for Epistemic Liberation in Africa. *Social Epistemology: A Journal of Knowledge, Culture and Policy, 35*(3), 258–269.
Mashabela, J. K. (2017). Africanisation as an Agent of Theological Education in Africa. *HTS Teologiese Studies/Theological Studies, 73*(3), a4581. https://doi.org/10.4102/hts.v73i3.4581
Matthews, M. (2014). African Theology and the Paradox of Missions: Three Intellectual Responses to the Modern Missions Crisis of the African Church. *Transformation, 31*(2), 79–98.
McCann, G., & Matenga, C. (2021). COVID-19 and Global Inequality. In P. Carmody et al. (Eds.), *COVID-19 in the Global South Impacts and Responses* (pp. 161–171). Bristol University Press.
Melanchthon, M. J., & Whitaker, R. J. (Eds.). (2021). *Terror in the Bible: Rhetoric, Gender, and Violence*. SBL Press.
Miles, R. (2001). *Who Cooked the Last Supper? The Women's History of the World*. Three Rivers Press.
Mombo, E. (2003). Doing Theology from the Perspective of the Circle of Concerned African Women Theologians. *Journal of Anglican Studies, 1*(1), 91–103.
Mulisa, F. (2021). Challenges for African Scholars in the Globalization Era: Contexts Speak. *Journal of the Knowledge Economy, 12*, 923–942.
Nadar, S. (2014). "Stories are Data with Soul" – Lessons from Black Feminist Epistemology. *Agenda, 28*(1), 18–28.
Ndlovu-Gatsheni, S. J. (2018). *Epistemic Freedom in Africa: Deprovincialization and Decolonization*. Routledge.
Ndlovu-Gatsheni, S. J., Seesemann, R., & Vogt-William, C. (2022). African Studies in Distress: German Scholarship on Africa and the Neglected Challenge of Decoloniality. *Africa Spectrum, 57*(1), 83–100.
Ndongala, I. (2021). Decolonial Approaches and Practices in African Theology: Genealogies of Research. *Interreligious Studies and Intercultural Theology, 5*(1-2), 103–120.

Ngong, D. T. (2020). Recent Developments in African Political Theology. *Religion Campus, 14*(10), 1–11.

Ogbonnaya, J. (2015). African Liberative Theologies. In M. A. De La Torre (Ed.), *Introducing Liberative Theologies* (pp. 26–46). Orbis Books.

P'Bitek, O. (2011). *Decolonizing African Religion: A Short History of African Religions in Western Scholarship*. Diasporic African Press.

Parry, S. (2008). *Beacons of Hope: HIV Competent Churches: Framework for Action*. World Council of Churches Publications.

Phiri, I., Ross, K., & Cox, J. (Eds.). (1996). *The Role of Christianity in Development, Peace and Reconstruction*. All Africa Conference of Churches.

Ratele, K., et al. (2018). Some Basic Questions about (a) Decolonizing Africa(n)-centred Psychology Considered. *South African Journal of Psychology, 48*(3), 331–342.

Schliesser, C., Kadayifci-Orellana, S. A., & Kollontai, P. (2021). Now What? Implications for Academics, Policy Makers, and Practitioners. In S. Christine Schliesser, A. K. Orellana, & P. Kollontai (Eds.), *On the Significance of Religion in Conflict and Conflict Resolution* (pp. 133–140). Routledge.

Scott, J. C. (1985). *Weapons of the Weak: Everyday Forms of Peasant Resistance*. Yale University Press.

Sengupta, M. (2018). Transformational Change or Tenuous Wish List? A Critique of SDG 1 ('End Poverty in All Its Forms Everywhere'). *Social Alternatives, 37*(1), 12–17.

Sharra, S. (2009). African Paradigms for African Peace. *Journal of Peacebuilding & Development, 4*(3), 92–96.

Struckmann, C. (2018). A Postcolonial Feminist Critique of the 2030 Agenda for Sustainable Development: A South African Application. *Agenda, 32*(1), 12–24. https://doi.org/10.1080/10130950.2018.1433362

Swain, R. B. (2018). A Critical Analysis of the Sustainable Development Goals. In W. L. Filho (Ed.), *Handbook of Sustainability Science and Research* (pp. 341–355). Springer International.

Tamale, S. (2020). *Decolonization and Afro-Feminism*. Daraja Press.

Tshaka, R. S. (2019). The Advocacy for Africanity as Justice against Epistemicide. *Black Theology, 17*(2), 132–149.

Wiredu, K. (1998). Toward Decolonizing African Philosophy and Religion. *African Studies Quarterly, 1*(4), 17–46.

CHAPTER 24

# Traditional Leaders and the Quest for Sustainable Peace in Kenya

*Shamsia Ramadhan*

## Introduction

African cultures have a comprehensive social, economic, political, and environmental governance system that regulates relations within an ethnic group and other groups. It is also a system that ensures balance in society by regulating the use and access of resources using traditional rules and regulation that ensures checks and balances. A fundamental structure within the African system is the traditional elders. In Kenya, traditional leaders have traditional law that governs the community though they may have different practices and rituals for governance, community resource mobilization, dispute resolution, and mediation, among others (Kariuki, 2022).

Traditional leaders, including Kaya elders at the Coast, the Njuri Nceke from Meru, the Wanga in Mumias, the *Kokwo* in Pokots and Marakwets, and the Ker of the Luo, have guided their communities in traditional matters to resolve disputes across the various historical periods. For example, they have used the traditional justice system to resolve marital problems and address land disputes between families and community members (ICJ Kenya, 2011). The traditional elders, also known as the Council of Elders, that exist in almost all communities in Kenya are organized in two ways: the Council of Elders is a collection of more than one elder responsible for solving problems within the community and individuals recognized by the community as an elder based on

S. Ramadhan (✉)
Institute of Social Transformation, Tangaza University College, Nairobi, Kenya

© The Author(s), under exclusive license to Springer Nature Switzerland AG 2023
S. M. Kilonzo et al. (eds.), *The Palgrave Handbook of Religion, Peacebuilding, and Development in Africa*,
https://doi.org/10.1007/978-3-031-36829-5_24

leadership roles assigned to the individual (Muigua, 2018). In many communities, they are tasked with guiding the community to make collective decisions.

Among the Luo community, for one to be considered an elder, they have to be respected, wealthy, and able to feed visitors and their families and be spiritually connected to the mystical powers known as *Jwogi* (Achar et al., 2017). For the Maasai, to be recognized as an elder one has to go through the Maa rite of passage. It involves transitioning from Moran to adult, and one belongs to a specific age group that instills a sense of community and collective responsibility in those in the group. The ability to resolve disputes among age groups is a point of reference when elders are being identified. Other characteristics include effective communication and impartiality, demonstrated by the capacity to transcend divisions between groups or individuals in conflict (Achar et al., 2017). Thus, traditional elders in many communities comprise a group of old male members of society who have gone through the rites of passage and conducted themselves righteously to earn respect from members of society. In many cases, they are married and head of the family, providing leadership at the micro level, a mark of stewardship and recognition in the community. So, the responsibility of being an elder in the community is a socialization process nurtured at the lowest unit in society, the family.

However, colonization disrupted the long-standing ingrown traditional system that criticized the traditional governance system for being incompatible with the modern state. Instead, communities were introduced to a leadership and governance system based on a Western philosophy that destroyed the traditional functions that emphasized social cohesion and responsibility for natural resources in the community and the African philosophy of Ubuntu that put a responsibility on individuals and communities for the well-being of others. Nevertheless, with the increase of community-level protracted conflicts driven by competition for control and access to resources, including land, competition for political positions, and the need for reconciliation and healing, traditional leaders are increasingly involved in conflict prevention and peacebuilding activities, especially in the community level, where they have a massive influence.

This chapter explores traditional leaders' role in the broader Sustainable Development Goals (SDGs) process, with special reference to SDG 16, namely, "Promote peace and inclusive societies for sustainable development…", focusing on conflict prevention and peacebuilding in Kenya. It argues that sustainable peace, justice, and inclusion in Kenya can be realized if approaches go beyond the inclusion of groups such as traditional elders in peacebuilding, and instead considers the social and cultural resources that can add value to building sustainable peace. In reality, it will require, among other actions, aligning and harmonizing local resources, including traditional governance systems and institutions, to the peacebuilding and development processes. The chapter begins by laying out the conceptual framework for a sustainable peace encompassing justice and inclusion from a social transformation perspective, situating the traditional leaders as crucial actors in advancing the SGDs.

In this chapter, the term "traditional leaders" is used to encompass recognized traditional authorities within an ethnic community located at the community level who play an advisory role at the community level and are recognized as leaders, either as a group or as individuals (Miller & Skinner, 1968). These include, but are not limited to, chiefs, sub-chiefs, community sages, the community of elders, etc.

## Kenya: Integration of Traditional Leaders in the National Peacebuilding Infrastructure

As noted earlier, this study focuses on SGD 16, which focuses on peaceful and inclusive societies, access to Justice, and building strong institutions. Traditional elders play a key role in the African governance system: peacemaking and resolving disputes using traditional customs and mechanisms (Momoh, 2021). "The system relied on cultural sources to uphold the values of peace, tolerance, solidarity, and respect for and of one another" (ACCORD, 2019). Although adulterated by the process of colonization, traditional elders remain a critical aspect of community-based dispute resolution because of its people-centered approach centering on social relations and right relationships (Kariuki, 2022). This is rooted in the African philosophy of collective action and responsibility and is a critical aspect that dovetails well with the Sustainable Development Goal (SGD) 16. It taps into the potential of local participation and utilization of resources in addressing social disputes. Its proximity to the community and its use of local resources enable effectiveness and legitimacy, especially in community conflict prevention and peacebuilding.

With the wars in the post-Cold War era being increasingly within states and between communities, the approaches used to address conflicts between states that were common in the Cold War era were not applicable. Still, external actors were key mediators and provided financial resources for peacebuilding in the post-Cold War era based on their geopolitical interests. In the 1990s, the conflicts in Somalia (1992–1993) and Bosnia (1992–1995), and the genocide in Rwanda challenge the predominantly Western approach to dealing with conflict (Ramsbotham et al., 2005). In addition to the focus on human rights, reforming institutions, and building democracy, among other liberal peacebuilding approaches, the influence of globalization on conflict resulted in increased vulnerabilities of communities affected by conflict. The conflicts had more casualties because of modern weaponry and increased illicit weapons used in community conflicts. Additionally, the intra-state and inter-community conflicts were more driven by greed and grievance. The approach focused on mediation and building consensus did not address the conflict's underlying causes and drivers, leading to a perpetual relapse to violence (Ramsbotham et al., 2005). It is complicated further by the entry of armed groups in a conflict context, especially in areas with weak states. The approaches to address these engaged more with formal institutions, including the government and non-state actors. The interventions led to the end of violence leading to negative peace and temporary resolution of the dispute between adversaries.

The structural issues causing and driving the conflicts that are systemic and require long-term engagement were not adequately addressed, leading to recurrent conflicts. For instance, in Kenya, community conflicts over inequality and competition for resource are amplified every election cycle, leading to election-related violence. The conflict prevention strategies before the election that include community dialogues and preventative mediation are strategies for de-escalation and do not address the underlying systemic factors of conflict. To effectively address these conflicts required a change of tact, focus on addressing underlying causes of conflict, and the inclusion of other actors (formal and informal) within the context.

Kenya experiences different types of violent conflicts. Every election cycle, the population is apprehensive of the electoral process stemming from the ethnic clashes in 1991 in the advent of multiparty elections and post-election violence in 2007/2008 that led to 1000 deaths and over 500,000 displacements. Long-standing historical injustices are at the backdrop of election-related violence, as was mentioned in the WAKI report (see http://www.knchr.org/Portals/0/Reports/Waki_Report.pdf). These political conflicts are also connected to community conflicts and tensions over grazing land, control of resources at the county level, climate change-induced conflicts, and unequal sharing of resources, among other factors that drive communal conflicts.

In addition to the above, reports show that gender inequality is increasing, especially in rural communities in Kenya. Further, issues such as climate change have resulted in climate change-induced conflicts due to changing weather patterns that have increased competition for already scarce resources. As a result, there are changes in livelihood patterns, especially in pastoral communities. Research shows that due to climate change, there is an increase in female-headed homes accompanied by an increase in gender-based violence. Also, the patriarchal nature of many African communities has perpetuated gender inequalities that greatly contribute to injustices against women and girls. This is one issue that traditional leaders can be empowered to help change cultures that view women as incapable of managing communal affairs.

## Traditional Dispute Resolution in Kenya

In Kenya, traditional dispute resolution is recognized in the constitution under Article 159 (2) (c) which recognizes customary jurisprudence, acknowledging that it is linked to community traditions and was used to resolve conflicts in the community (Muigua, 2018). Traditionally dispute resolution used by elders focuses on common well-being, unlike the alternative dispute resolution (ADR) mechanism that focuses on the needs of parties reflecting the Western common law and statutory regulations. According to Zamisa and Mutereko (2019), communities benefit from traditional leaders' nurturing and advisory role that enforces their rights and responsibilities in the community. They also engage to ensure that individual and collective roles for the well-being of the communities are well played. As a result, communities rely on the wisdom and experience of traditional leaders to facilitate conflict resolution processes that build relations through fair and just processes.

Traditional elders engaging in community dispute resolution rely on communication between the conflict groups based on mutual interest that relies on the negotiation skills of those involved in the disputes. It is recognized that traditional leaders' proximity to the community and their process is bidding for the community members as it invokes rituals and practices (Kariuki, 2022). Additionally, communities respected the decision reached in the traditional conflict resolution process because the elders were respected and trusted. Their decisions were binding because the process was guided by the African philosophy of "I am because we are". In essence, an individual lives in a community and thrives because of connections to families that result from inter-marriages, these relationships are critical for the community's welfare (ACCORD, 2019). In light of Article 159 (2) and relevant community conflicts, the traditional leaders are key actors in helping resolve community disputes, such as those around building social cohesion and accessing common and natural resources (Muigua, 2018). In regions where they have effectively helped address conflicts, their resolutions are recognized by the government.

The African principle of community well-being, which depends on interdependency, is a critical aspect that makes traditional leaders relevant and effective in helping with early warning and response. For instance, the Kaya elders among the *Miji Kenya* (Nine Villages) people are used as dialogue facilitators in land disputes, including trespassing cases. The two persons involved in the disputes do not speak directly to each other on the issue. Instead, the person whose land was encroached on sends the Kaya elders to the trespasser and they provide details of their origin and native home. The discussion is relational and does not begin with the dispute that needs to be addressed. This restorative approach creates an enabling environment for discussion that builds on empathy and interest in the well-being of all parties.

An example of a traditional resolution mechanism that helped resolve conflict is the Modogashe Declaration, first drafted in 2001, then updated in 2005, and further revised in 2011 that involved the Council of Elders from Marsabit, Isiolo, Mandera, Garissa, Tana River, and Samburu. On the tenth anniversary of the first agreement, the elders deliberated further issues that need to be addressed in their locations, including unauthorized grazing, livestock raiding, control of livestock diseases, acquisition of identity cards by non-Kenyans, social and economic empowerment, the role of peace structures, among other. This shows that engaging traditional leaders with various peacebuilding skills enables them to address social, economic, and political issues in their context. Traditional elders also address exclusion issues common in rural areas and among pastoralist communities (Pkalya et al., 2004).

However, due to their patriarchal orientation, traditional institutions face some limitations, such as gender inequality, that may be challenging to achieve

SDG 16. The Council of Elders are predominantly male, and women are often not involved publicly in critical community discussions or implementation; hence, gender issues are not adequately addressed. But, some traditional leaders are discussing including women to conform to the two-thirds gender requirement (Wanyoro, 2023). In Meru, the Ameru Council of Elders (*Njuri Ncheke*) have commenced discussions on the possibility of including women in alternative dispute resolution that includes their customary court system. However, they are concerned about including women in a role that excluded them to protect community secrets. The elders have agreed that out of the nine judges in the traditional court, three will be women. The elders hope that women judges seeking justice through the courts will share their issues with the women judges, something they were hesitant to do before the male elders (Wanyoro, 2023). According to the UNSCR 1325, including women in peace and security matters from analysis to implementation is critical in realizing sustainable peace. The presence of women in peacebuilding and conflict resolution platforms brings in the unique perspectives of women in violence and conflict. Acceptance of women by the *Njuri Ncheki* is good progress toward achieving SGD 16. It shows that the Council of Elders operate within a dynamic institution and are amenable to change from within. As a strategy of including traditional leaders in achieving SGD 16, there is a need for their recognition as critical actors and support for indigenous peacebuilding processes while slowly integrating human rights to enable the traditional system to conform with international human rights standards.

## Traditional Leaders as Protagonists of Peace Within the Local Peace Committees

The complexity of conflicts forced peacebuilding actors to explore approaches that will contribute to conflict de-escalation and interventions that would lead to sustainable peace. This thinking led to evaluating peacebuilding models and critically looking at effectiveness, inclusivity, and ownership. For example, a critique of liberal peace, a leading approach in developing peacebuilding models in the post-Cold War era, revealed the weaknesses of the top-down model that left out a large segment of the population critical in building sustainable peace. To address the model's weaknesses, a "liberal-local" hybrid form of peace was developed that focused on intellectual engagement with the lives of ordinary people in their contexts (Kariuki, 2022). Further, following a critique of externally driven peace initiatives, the local turn was introduced as a model that includes the local in the peacebuilding process from analysis to implementation. Local Peace Committees (LPCs) in Kenya were created to involve communities in peacebuilding activities, embracing a bottom-up approach to addressing conflicts.

The origin of LPCs is connected to Wajir Peace and Development Committee (WPDC), a community peacebuilding process in Wajir that was created in

1993 to address perennial inter-clan and inter-community conflict initiated among the pastoralist communities (Ndegwa, 2001). The WPDC was formed by six women without any support from external actors to deal with the conflict in their region that affected their families (Berkley Center for Religion, 2010). Contrary to the idea that women are excluded in traditional conflict resolution mechanisms, the women mobilized elders from the warring communities to discuss ending their community's suffering. Through the mobilization of community elders creating a path for dispute resolution in an active conflict, the women's leadership demonstrates that though there may be resistance, traditional structures are open to change. The WPDC's success led to its recognition by other peace actors, including government and non-state actors, as a platform to resolve communal disputes. Because of the influence in the community, it was included in formal peace and security processes in the community process that used innovative ways that incorporated state law with Somali traditional conflict management in addressing peace and security matters (Ndegwa, 2001). Its success led to the creation of peace committees in other pastoralist locations that were also experiencing conflict.

In the 1990s, peace committees grew in tandem with the discourse on the "local turn" in peacebuilding that called for more homegrown solutions and the involvement of local actors in peacebuilding (Nganje, 2021). The LPCs were created in the early 1990s to help address the perennial conflict in Northeastern Kenya after several failed attempts by the government, a multi-stakeholder platform that steers peace efforts at the county and community levels. The LPCs have shaped Kenya's peace architecture and have played a critical role in addressing inter-communal conflict and preventing violent conflict during elections. They are recognized for their influence in society and have been included in formal processes because of their approach to using customs and traditional values in dealing with community matters.

Traditional elders are recognized as key players in early warning, response, and peace initiatives, including community dialogue, mediation, and negotiation (Peacebuilding and Conflict Management Directorate, 2023). Traditional leaders are part of the LPCs.

Practically, it means including formal, informal, and key influential individuals in the communities that comprise the diverse ethnic communities in the conflict context in peace processes. Scholars and practitioners advancing the "local turn" argued that those in the conflict context affected by violent conflict have higher motivation to establish and keep the peace than outsiders (Mac Ginty & Richmond, 2013).

Involving the communities would mean being alive to everyday experiences of violent conflict and how communities deal with the conflict. Such an approach would lead to sustainable peace supported by local ownership and legitimacy (Van Leeuwen et al., 2019). The "local turn" debate emphasized the need to understand the local context from the perspective of those affected by the conflict, including local initiatives, whether formal or informal, in preparing and implementing interventions and empower on local agencies in conflict prevention and sustainable peace. Others pushed for local inclusion to overcome implementation challenges in communities and explored the possibility of engaging local powers to influence agency at the community level (Randazzo, 2021). Paffenholz (2015) opines that "local turn" attempts to develop appropriate, context-specific peace strategies. Proponents also emphasized local actors and local knowledge in developing interventions (Powers & Connoly, 2020). Edomwonyi (2003, p. 43) contends that because peacebuilding intends to bring about fundamental social change, the process ought to be internally generated and led if it is to lead to sustainable peace and actual social changes. A study by Ahmad et al. in Pakistan (2013, p. 105) showed that local people's involvement is essential. They argue that local citizens have a much better understanding and a higher level of expertise in understanding conflict because of familiarity with the context. Conflict-specific strategies involve recognizing existing formal and informal resources that can add value to strategies to build sustainable peace. It begins with recognizing that even in conflict situations, there are structures and social resources, including local culture and informal structures, that the communities identify with (Nganje, 2021). These can be a more sustainable channel for initiating reconciliation and building social cohesion.

Traditional leaders are part of the national peace architecture in Kenya. They are included in the peace committee because of their proximity to communities and critical role in their social, political, economic, and environmental life (Peacebuilding and Conflict Management Directorate, 2023). Their role in the conflict context is to initiate and facilitate peace activities in their locations alongside other stakeholders. They were included because traditional dispute resolution mechanisms effectively resolved community disputes, restoring relations between individuals and communities. They exemplify preserving the community's culture, traditions, customs, and values (ACCORD, 2019). At the same time, they represent forms of societal organization and governance that are participatory and innovative that can lead to achieving SGD 16, which emphasizes peaceful and inclusive societies as a precondition for sustainable peace and development. Most importantly, the traditional mechanism resonated with the parties in dispute. It led to an amicable resolution of the conflict because the approach mirrored the social and political orientation of the community embracing the communal way of living. Additionally, unlike conflict management being led by outsiders that often happens away from the conflict context, the traditional dispute resolution process took place in the community for transparency and accountability.

Communities in Kenya have used traditional leaders to resolve conflicts through mediation, though they may not have called it that. In every ethnic community, there is a tradition of converging at a familiar place, often a central place that is accessible to all community members. In this space, elders and community members sat to deliberate and agree on common community issues, such as the allocation of resources. Without a formal justice system, traditional elders addressed all disputes and provided guidance on key decision-making for individuals and communities. For example, among the Kikuyu ethnic community, the *Kiama* or Council of Elders acted as an arbitral forum and mediator. Even when the colonizers introduced a legal system based on Western (British) Common Law and established courts, community members continued to utilize their traditional customs, especially to resolve disputes, inter-personal and inter-communal disputes. Later, the traditional justice system would be faulted for violating human rights and, in some cases, being unjust.

Communities have used mediation to resolve their conflicts for centuries, but it was not known as mediation as it is today. It was customary and an everyday affair to see people sitting down informally and agreeing on specific issues, such as allocating resources. They did not have formal courts of law to deal with their conflicts. For instance, the Kiama or Council of Elders among the Kikuyu community acted as an arbitral forum and a mediator. These elders and institutions were accessible to the populace, and their decisions were respected. They deliberated within the Council of Elders to reach decisions, and their decisions reached by consensus were effective immediately after the pronouncement (Pkalya et al., 2004). Below, the chapter summarizes another community-based peacebuilding initiative in Kenya.

## Amani Mashinani: An Example of a Traditional Approach That Contributed to Sustainable Peace

Amani Mashinani (Peace at the grassroots) is a community peacebuilding initiative implemented in the North Rift Region of Kenya. The intervention was formulated by Bishop Korir, a Catholic Priest who worked in a conflict-affected region. The conflict was between nomadic communities—Marakwet and Pokot and during elections between Kalenjins and Kikuyus (Omondi, 2020). These overlapping conflicts not only affected relationships between communities but also led to underdevelopment because of the destruction resulting from the cycle of violence created by the violence. For instance, every election year, members of non-Kalenjin communities became self-displaced people leaving their property and closing their businesses during the election for fear of attacks. Many externally led interventions were implemented without success. Interventions included meetings involving only a few members of the warring groups, leaving others with no access to such spaces, such as women and youth, excluded from such interventions.

Bishop Korir resolved to have community meetings and changed the venues from hotels to community spaces under trees and other common spaces. Being a Catholic Bishop, he was guided by the Catholic Social Teachings (CST principles) that call for protecting the sanctity of life and upholding human dignity (Omondi, 2020). These principles are universal and are accepted across ethnic and religious divides. Utilizing shared values is one way of building confidence and trust through inclusion, not only physically by ideologically as a strategy for forging solidarity among warring groups. The Bishop understood that inclusion is critical to allow interaction that would enable an exchange of information and ideas that would result from changing of attitude, perception, and behavior between the warring groups. For Amani Mashinani, this meant having all categories of groups in the community, including women, youth, and men from all ethnic groups, including in the community discussions and processes to find a collective solution. Building peace is a never-ending process. Hence, including community members builds ownership and empowers the community to adopt attitudes and behavior that will nurture peace. Strategic peacebuilding, therefore, is a worthwhile investment (Lederach & Appleby, 2010).

The process that a Catholic Bishop led adopted an African dispute resolution system. First, the meetings happened in the community spaces under trees. This exemplifies the ownership and legitimacy of the critical process for sustainable peace and social cohesion. Having peacebuilding processes at community levels ensures inclusion as the participation of people is increased, and all views on how to address structures and drivers of violence are discussed by community members (Omondi, 2020). Second, the process adopted traditional reconciliation principles and values. During the meetings, the participants from warring groups shared a meal. In the traditional culture, eating together signifies friendship, unity, and trust. Unlike an externally driven process, the Amani Mashinani is an ingrown approach facilitated by insiders using their traditional resources that make it legitimate and successful.

## Engaging Traditional Leaders as Gate Keepers Toward Achieving SDG 16

As indicated earlier, the discourse on the "local turn in peacebuilding" emphasized in the inclusion of local actors in peacebuilding processes. Proponents argued that local actors have resources that can add value to peacebuilding. For the traditional leaders, the following principles make them useful in advancing the SGDs agenda to foster peace among communities.

### Local Ownership and Legitimacy

Historically, traditional leaders have been their communities' mediators and problem solvers. To the community, they are the custodians of traditional law that help keep order and build social cohesion even in times of turbulence. The traditional values and practices enable them to deal with domestic or community disputes, including anti-social behavior. Through this role, they are accepted by society and have cumulative knowledge to prevent and address violence. Since they engage at the community level and have a history of acting for the community's well-being, implementing SGD 16 through the traditional leaders is likely to be well received by the community instead of being championed by outsiders.

## COMMON HUMANITY

Peacebuilding involves nurturing constructive human relationships, and building sustainable peace requires building strategic relationships across existing divides (Lederach & Appleby, 2010). Traditional African communities are organized around building relationships that enable sharing of resources and the general responsibility of community members. Community structures and laws are strategically positioned to facilitate interaction and enable communal living where everyone is responsible for individual and communal well-being. Those from one ethnic group considered themselves as "one people". Peaceful co-existence emphasizes that despite differences, human beings are the same. The communal setting was a sign of acceptance that each person and each group are entitled to access resources and utilize them for the betterment of society. This principle enabled the LPCs to address environmental conflict among the Maasai community. The post-independence land tenure system intensified land-related conflict over pasture and access to water for nomadic pastoralist communities. Land that was historically shared communally became individual land reducing the grazing lands. Changing land use patterns resulted in deforestation, leading to climate change and unreliable rain. The scarcity of resources led to intense violence between pastoralist communities resulting in more deaths and increased cases of sexual and gender-based violence (SGBV). To help address the increasing conflicts, traditional elders from warring communities have used tradition to resolve disputes over grazing land and water catchment areas (Muigua, 2018). Traditional dispute resolution thrives because they operate within a social and cultural context that is an entry point for formal conflict resolution mechanisms that is locally owned and locally lead the increase the chances of acceptance by the community.

## RECIPROCITY

Among the focus of SGD is building institutions that promote peaceful and inclusive societies for sustainable development (SGD Tracker, 2018). Building sustainable peace requires addressing conflict's structural, cultural, relational, and personal dimensions. The four aspects are connected, and the likelihood of perpetual conflict increases if one is addressed. In traditional African societies, sharing goods and services ensured a balance in all aspects, including addressing structural issues through equitable resource-sharing. According to Francis Muigua (2018), sharing goods and services was common in African communities. Communities exchanged "privileges, goods, favors, obligations, among others, thus fostering peaceful coexistence and eliminating the likelihood of wars and conflicts". The communal way of life ensured that people cared for the resources and environment to ensure enough for everyone. Management of resources was for posterity and future generations. However, communities, especially in urban centers, have changed from communal to individualistic ways of life that have contributed to economic, social, and political inequalities intensifying competition for resources and affecting social cohesion.

Underdevelopment and inequalities are the underlying cause of conflict between communities as they compete for scarce resources. The violent conflicts between communities further contribute to increased underdevelopment and inequality. However, peacebuilding can create an enabling environment for development that will deal with the structural issues that engender conflict. The African philosophy of interdependency is a key value in peacebuilding. Traditional leaders have used this principle to build social cohesion based on mutual interest to resolve disputes through mediation and negotiations. In rural areas with no formal justice system, traditional leaders, although faulted for violating some international human rights standards, have been able to resolve disputes.

## Possible Entry Points for Traditional Leaders' Engagement in Advancing SGD 16

The success of building sustainable peace relies on the inclusion and participation of all stakeholders in interventions, as this chapter continues to assert. Stakeholder involvement in all steps of planning peace and development activities will increase the success rate, and the projects will be well managed. In community contexts, among key stakeholders are traditional leaders who are the custodians of culture and stewards of community governance. They can influence the attitude, perceptions, and behavior of the community. In advancing SGD 16, community leaders can use the community platform to mobilize the community toward addressing structural challenges through collective action. As shown in the cases shared above, traditional leaders leverage cultural values and principles to catalyze change in the community. To advance SGD 16, the traditional leaders can be involved in the following ways.

1. Engage traditional elders in their community/indigenous spaces.

    Community spaces are considered sacred. In African tradition, sacred places exist to inspire, inform, and guide social and communal living for the community's well-being. Historically, these spaces have been used to unify communities and are safe spaces to discuss social matters. Engaging traditional elders in their spaces exemplifies the bottom-up approach, a strategy for building ownership and sustainability critical for SGD 16.
2. Traditional leaders use traditional values and customs to enforce decisions reached by communities. Many of these spaces are male-dominated and undermine the principle of inclusion which is key to achieving SGD 16. Including women in peace and development processes involving traditional leaders will require a change of perception and attitude. Engaging in gender sensitivity using simple language and evidence showing the value of including women in traditional spaces will contribute

to changes allowing women to enter some traditional spaces. Further, providing gender-inclusive language that equips traditional leaders with additional analytical leverage to develop their understanding of the role of women in building sustainable peace is very strategic.
3. It is helpful to engage traditional leaders in developing interventions focusing on local specificities that enable or prevent transformative change. A good example is the Modogashe Declaration or the Amani Mashinani model. Both were local processes led that engaged local tradition that merged religion and traditional value systems to find a workable solution for the community.

## Conclusions and Recommendations

Traditional leaders are strategic stakeholders in advancing SGD 16 at the community level. Their role as governance and custodian of traditional values and practices makes them influential in communities. Tapping into their potential by peace actors has helped improve the community's effectiveness and legitimacy of peacebuilding initiatives. Traditional processes, such as conflict resolution practices within community spaces, are a strong feature that can build sustainable peace and create an enabling environment for development.

Sustainable peacebuilding, justice, and inclusion are values that society requires to ensure the well-being of everyone. In traditional society, these values were transferred through socialization at the micro level. At the macro level in the community, traditional leaders are the stewards and custodians of the traditional culture. In these roles, they have the power to mobilize and influence communities toward a transformation that includes addressing violence and underdevelopment through inclusion. That places traditional leaders in addressing sensitive cultural matters that hinder the achievement of SGD 16. Given their proximity to society and traditional leaders' goodwill in the community, they can play a catalytic role in meeting the central goal of SDG 16, namely, promoting peace, justice, and inclusion and countering the factors that drive conflicts through interrogation of culture and traditions vis-à-vis current social, economic, and political realities.

## References

ACCORD. (2019, March 12). *Traditional Methods of Conflict Resolution*. ACCORD. Retrieved April 10, 2023, from https://www.accord.org.za/conflict-trends/traditional-methods-of-conflict-resolution/

Achar, G. O., Wepukhulu, R. N., & Angeline, S. (2017). The Traditional Integrated Ways of Conflict Resolution between the Luo-Maasai Communities, Kenya. *The International Journal of Humanities & Social Studies, 5*(9), 340–344.

Ahmad, N., Shah, S., Ullah, F., & Aad, A. Z. (2013). Local Peace Committees: Potentials Contributing Factors in the Peace-Building Process in Conflict-Affected Areas of Pakistan {A Case Study of Maidan, (Lower Dir) in the Province Khyber Pakhtunkhwa}. *Pakistand Journal of Criminoloty, 5*(2), 103–115.

Berkley Center for Religion, B. C. Fo R. P. and W. A. (2010, May 29). *A Discussion with Dekha Ibrahim, Founder, Wajir Peace and Development Committee, Kenya*. Berkley Center for Religion, Peace and World Affairs. Retrieved April 6, 2023, from https://berkleycenter.georgetown.edu/interviews/a-discussion-with-dekha-ibrahim-founder-wajir-peace-and-development-committee-kenya

Edomwonyi, O. (2003). (rep.). Rwanda: The Importance of Local Ownership of the Post-Conflict (Vol. 4, pp. 43–47). Durban, Durban: ACCORD - Conflict Trends.

ICJ Kenya, (2011). (rep.). *Interface between Formal and Informal Justice Systems in Kenya*. ICJ Kenya.

Kariuki, F. (2022). Harnessing Traditional Knowledge Holders' Institutions in Realising Sustainable Development Goals in Kenya. *Journal of CMSD*, 6(1), 1–54. https://doi.org/10.5772/intechopen.98802

Lederach, J. P., & Appleby, R. S. (2010). Strategic Peacebuilding. In D. Philpott & G. F. Powers (Eds.), *Strategies of Peace Transforming Conflict in a Violent World* (pp. 19–44). Oxford University Press.

Mac Ginty, R., & Richmond, O. P. (2013). The Local Turn in Peace Building: A Critical Agenda for Peace. *Third World Quarterly*, 34(5), 763–783. https://doi.org/10.1080/01436597.2013.800750

Miller, N. N., & Skinner, E. P. (1968). The Political Survival of Traditional Leadership: The 'Paradox' of Rural Leadership: A Comment. *The Journal of Modern African Studies*, 6(2), 183–202. https://doi.org/10.2307/159466

Momoh, H. B. (2021). The Role of Traditional Leaders in Peacemaking and Conflict Management among the Mende of Sierra Leone. *International Journal of Sciences: Basic and Applied Research (IJSBAR)*, 55(2), 156–171.

Muigua, K. (2018, August). Traditional Dispute Resolution Mechanisms Under Article 159 of the Constitution of Kenya of 2010. Retrieved April 9, 2023, from http://kmco.co.ke/wp-content/uploads/2018/08/Paper-on-Article-159-Traditional-Dispute-Resolution-Mechanisms-FINAL.pdf

Ndegwa, S. (2001). (rep.). *Peace Building Among North Eastern Pastoralist in Kenya: Wajir Peace and Development Committee* (pp. 1–33). USAID—Greater Horn of Africa Peacebuilding Project.

Nganje, F. N. (2021). Local Peace Committees and Grassroots Peacebuilding in Africa. In T. McNamee & M. Muyangwa (Eds.), *The State of Peacebuilding in Africa: Lessons Learned for Policymakers and Practitioners* (pp. 164–166). Palgrave Macmillan.

Omondi, E. O. (2020). Amani Mashinani Conflict Transformation Model: Bishop Korir's Amani Mashinani Conflict Transformation Model: Bishop Korir's Legacy on Peace and Reconciliation Legacy on Peace and Reconciliation. *The Journal of Social Encounters*, 4(1), 9–21.

Paffenholz, T. (2015). Inclusive Politics: Lessons From and For the New Deal. *Journal of Peacebuilding & Development*, 10(1), 84–89. https://doi.org/10.1080/15423166.2015.1013845

Peacebuilding and Conflict Management Directorate, N. (2023). National Peace Coordination. NSC Peace. https://www.nscpeace.go.ke/work/national-peace-coordination

Pkalya, R., Adan, M., Masinde, I., Rabar, B., & Karimi, M. (2004). *Indigenous Democracy: Traditional Conflict Resolution Mechanisms: Pokot, Turkana, Samburu, and Marakwet*. Intermediate Technology Development Group--Eastern Africa.

Powers, L., & Connoly, L. (2020, May 12). *Local Networks for Peace: Lessons from Community-led Peacebuilding*. International Peace Institute. Retrieved April 25, 2023, from https://www.ipinst.org/2018/09/local-networks-for-peace-lessons-from-community-led-peacebuilding

Ramsbotham, O., Miall, H., & Woodhouse, T. (2005). Introduction to Conflict Resolution: Concepts and Definitions. In *Contemporary Conflict Resolution* (pp. 3–31). Blackwell.

Randazzo, E. (2021). The Local, the 'Indigenous' and the Limits of Rethinking Peacebuilding. *Journal of Intervention and Statebuilding, 15*(2), 141–160. https://doi.org/10.1080/17502977.2021.1882755

SGD Tracker, S. G. D. T. (2018). *Goal 16: Peace, Justice and Strong Institutions—SDG Tracker*. Our World in Data. Retrieved April 13, 2023, from https://sdg-tracker.org/peace-justice

Van Leeuwen, M., Nindorera, J., Kambale Nzweve, J.-L., & Corbijn, C. (2019). The 'Local Turn' and Notions of Conflict and Peacebuilding—Reflections on Local Peace Committees in Burundi and Eastern DR Congo. *Peacebuilding, 8*(3), 279–299. https://doi.org/10.1080/21647259.2019.1633760

Wanyoro, C. (2023, March 3). *Meru Elders Heed Calls to Include Women in Traditional Courts*. Nation. Retrieved April 25, 2023, from https://nation.africa/kenya/news/gender/meru-elders-heed-calls-to-include-women-in-traditional-courts-4144820

Zamisa, N. A., & Mutereko, S. (2019). The Role of Traditional Leadership in Disaster Management and Disaster Risk Governance: A Case of Ugu District Municipality By-Laws. *Jàmbá: Journal of Disaster Risk Studies, 11*(1), 1–9. https://doi.org/10.4102/jamba.v11i1.802

CHAPTER 25

# Decolonising Peacebuilding for Development in South Africa: African Traditional Spiritual Leaders as Critical Assets

*Beatrice Dube and Sinenhlanhla S. Chisale*

## INTRODUCTION

While peacebuilding is prioritised in countries that have recently been at war or are still at war, the need to re-build peaceful and inclusive societies elsewhere in non-warring Africa is also growing due to identity politics that separate people by nationality, gender, race, ethnicity, etc. The colonial logic that created social relations based on categories of ethnicity, gender, race and/or nationality destroys African values of relationality which have since time immemorial held together communities, making peacebuilding a proactive rather than reactive approach.

Credit for the peacebuilding concept is given to Johan Galtung, a peace studies scholar who coined the term in his publication: *Three Approaches to Peace: Peacekeeping, Peacemaking, and Peacebuilding* (1976). According to Galtung, peace has a structure; therefore, peacebuilding structures should promote sustainable peace. He argued that,

---

B. Dube (✉)
Department of Development Studies, University of South Africa, Pretoria, South Africa
e-mail: maphob@unisa.ac.za

S. S. Chisale
Department of Practical Theology and Mission Studies, University of Pretoria, Pretoria, South Africa

© The Author(s), under exclusive license to Springer Nature Switzerland AG 2023
S. M. Kilonzo et al. (eds.), *The Palgrave Handbook of Religion, Peacebuilding, and Development in Africa*,
https://doi.org/10.1007/978-3-031-36829-5_25

> The mechanisms that peace is based on should be built into the structure and be present there as a reservoir for the system itself to draw upon…More particularly, *structures must be found that remove causes of wars and offer alternatives to war in situations where wars might occur.* (1976, p. 298) (emphasis in original)

What Galtung, however, is referring to is not a structure with a superpower on top that supersedes others, but one where there is interconnection and interaction between different groups.

The sixth Secretary-General of the United Nations, Boutros Boutros-Ghali (1992), introduced peacebuilding to the UN Assembly where he quantified the term peacebuilding by introducing post-conflict. Boutros-Ghali defined the concept of post-conflict peacebuilding, as "action to identify and support structures which will tend to strengthen and solidify peace in order to avoid relapse into conflict" (Boutros-Ghali 1992, Par 21). In this definition, peacebuilding takes place after a war or conflict has occurred. Since then, UN rolls out efforts on peacebuilding after conflict has taken place. The United Nations is an institution with capacity to operate on a global scale but not necessarily rooted in any local context. Its focus on peacebuilding, however, tends to focus on the so-called developing world, ignoring the so-called developed nations, which in most cases are the instigators of conflict in the so-called developing nations. While the efforts of the United Nations are sometimes commendable, homegrown efforts to curb conflicts and sustain peaceful societies should be encouraged and evidence shows that religious institutions do play a big role in peacebuilding for development in African contexts. When considering African traditional spirituality, religion is not a new baby in the field of development and peacebuilding in Africa (see e.g. Kagema, 2015).

The interplay of religion, human dignity and freedom has challenged religious leaders to take centre stage in public policy initiatives (see African Union Transitional Justice Policy, AU, 2019, p. 15). According to Hayward (2012, p. 2), religious peacebuilding work evolves from decades-old discussions on the role of religion in causing and preventing conflict. Hayward (2012) asserts that the visible interest by the international community including academics started after the Iranian Revolution in 1979, the Cold War and the September 11 attacks. These conflicts challenged the US government to take into consideration engagements with religion, religious actors and institutions in promoting peace, security and development (Hayward, 2012, p. 2). In this context, religion is seen as the driver of conflict and is often used to foster and tolerate conflict on the one hand and significantly important in preventing and resolving conflict and fostering peace on the other (Silvestri & Mayall, 2015, p. 15, 28). The Sustainable Development Goals (SDGs) highlight that peace, justice and inclusivity are key pillars to development. To be specific, SDG 16 seeks to "promote peaceful and inclusive societies for sustainable development, provide access to justice for all and build effective, accountable and inclusive institutions at all levels" (United Nations (UN), 2020, p. 71).

Religion and engagement with religious stakeholders in bringing about peace is significant for sustainable development to take place. This is because Africa is a religious continent, hence John Mbiti's statement "the African is notoriously religious" (1969, p. 1). This statement is still relevant to the contemporary African who in some ways is very spiritual and religious in a way that any life occurrence has a spiritual or religious explanation and significance. Before the onslaught of colonialism, Africans had belief systems and practices, sacred and specific to their way of being and knowing (Gomez, 2013, p. 78), otherwise known as African Traditional Religion (Kagema, 2015) or organised spirituality (Gomez, 2013). Thus, this chapter focuses on peacebuilding efforts of spiritual leaders in South Africa; this is because South Africa is slowly returning to ATR and gives ATR the respect it deserves. For instance, there is a noticeable paradigm shift in South African spirituality with some public figures openly sharing that they have accepted ancestral calling to be *sangoma*s (healers) and are freely sharing their spiritual journey of *ukuthwasa* (initiation/ training) with the public. This paradigm shift has potential to influence perspectives, where African ways of knowing and being get to be appreciated again. ATR has strong personalities in South Africa who could be assets in facilitating peacebuilding for sustainable development, considering that ATR is viewed as a peaceful religion (Nkonge 1024 in Kagema, 2015, p. 6). Some of these leaders include Baba Credo Mutwa, Gogo Dineo Ndlanzi and Gogo Aubrey Matshiqi, who will be the focus of this chapter.

Written from a case study approach and decolonial epistemic perspective, this chapter thus seeks to explore how traditional spiritual leaders are assets in peacebuilding in the South African context. Hence the chapter taps into the voices of these spiritual leaders to explore how their messages influence and lead towards peacebuilding initiatives that facilitates the achievement of Sustainable Development Goal 16 in South Africa. This chapter is divided into four sections. Firstly, it reviews relevant literature on religion and peacebuilding and locates this debate into the SDG 16. Secondly, it describes the underlying methodology and framework used by the chapter. In this section, the decolonial epistemic framework is discussed in connection to religion and SDG 16. Thirdly, the chapter presents three cases of African traditional spiritual healers and custodians of indigenous knowledge, particularly how their voices are critical in achieving SDG 16 and addressing xenophobia in the country. Lastly is the conclusion, where the chapter draws the argument together by presenting an analysis of the presented cases in connection with addressing xenophobia and promoting peace and inclusion that fairly delivers access to justice for all.

## METHODOLOGICAL CONSIDERATIONS

The chapter employs three case studies of South African spiritual leaders to highlight how their messages influence and lead towards peacebuilding initiatives that facilitates the achievement of Sustainable Development Goal 16 in South Africa. In particular, the chapter focuses on Baba Credo Mutwa,

Gogo Dineo Ndlanzi and Gogo Aubrey Matshinqi's messages. The three were chosen using purposive sampling simply because "who a person is and where that person is located within a group is important" (Palys, 2008, p. 697). Criterion sampling, a purposeful sampling method which allows researchers to pick a case (cases) that meet "prespecified criterion" (Harley et al., 2013, p. 350) was used. The criteria in this case were South African, vocal and visible spiritual healer with content that could be accessed for study purposes. The authors recognise the existence of many other spiritual leaders whose voices could be drawn from, and also the existence of other discourses on liberal peacebuilding and local peacebuilding. The chapter will however be limited to the three South African traditional spiritual leaders but will not claim to be exhaustive as the focus will only be on snapshots on messages that influences peacebuilding.

Having selected the three spiritual leaders, purposive selection of texts from different source formats: written, audio (podcasts) and video was employed. Social media platforms such as Twitter and YouTube provide a media presence for the three cases, becoming a source of at times verbatim information for researchers and other general readers and listeners alike. Supporting the use of social media data, Stieglitz, Mirbabaie, Ross and Neuberger (2017, p. 156) suggests that "social media data can be analysed to gain insights into issues, trends, influential actors and other kind of information". For Baba Credo Mutwa who was also a published author, some texts are also sourced from his published works. Data for the chapter were thus purposively selected and limited to texts on peace or those that were of relevance to peacebuilding and social cohesion. The main limitation of this selection process is that some of the videos are long and one may miss some points as all three cases have video recordings with potential relevance to the peacebuilding subject. With download options for watching later, it was, however, easy to circumvent this problem as one could always listen again or rewind the videos or podcasts.

## The Question of Peacebuilding in South Africa

Goal 16 of the Sustainable Development Goals directs the UN and member states to maintain peace and justice in societies (UN, 2020). Thus, South Africa is known for its peacebuilding missions in African countries such as Darfur, Burundi and the Democratic Republic of the Congo (DRC) (cf. Kok, 2014; Nyuykonge & Zondi, 2017). The external efforts on peacebuilding by the South African government may seem to suggest that the country itself is at peace. It, however, often experiences civil unrests as a result of disgruntlements levelled at the government, and also at foreigners, particularly of African descent (Behr, 2021). There has not been any armed conflict in the country following the move to democratic rule in 1994; there have, however, been skirmishes between political parties, different cultural groups, genders and races. What stands out the most in South Africa in the current epoch is the friction between the different cultural groups and nationalities, mostly informed by the colonial logic that divided Africa into different nations, and the apartheid tactics of divide and rule. Makhado and Tshisikhawe (2021) posit that apartheid turned South Africa "into a hotbed of tribalism and xenophobia" with the use of segregationist legislations and an emphasis on the differences between races and ethnicities. This conviction is shared by Mpofu (2020, p. 39) who points out that "xenophobia is in practice and effect part of the classification of human beings according to colour, ethnic, cultural, religious, and even gender difference, a classification that began in 1492 with the conquest of the Americas and the spread of slavery and colonialism into the Global South".

## Xenophobia, Religion and Peaceful Coexistence in Africa—A Decolonial Approach

The narrative of peacebuilding for development is distorted by approaches that fail to recognise coloniality as a strong force that impedes long lasting peace as the brutality of colonialism on the African psyche remains unhealed. Although peaceful coexistence is crucial in contexts of conflicts such as xenophobia, it should not be dictated by the Euro-Western countries or countries from the Global North. Rather peaceful coexistence should be defined and applied in African terms that do not undermine the African heritage. This is because African countries, particularly those in Southern Africa, have ethnicities that share ancestral heritage; as a result, some conflicts that divide and discriminate against some people on grounds of ethnicity and nationality such as xenophobia undermines that heritage. Notably, some forms of conflict have a potential of leading progressive social change; however, when conflict is violent and destructive to other humans or creations, it should be denounced.

Current approaches to peacebuilding in Africa are framed within a liberal approach in which driving forces for peace are informed by the "promotion of democracy, market-based economic reforms and other institutions associated with 'modern' states" (Newman, 2009, p. 3). These have been criticised by Ottoh (2022, p. 30) who views them as "top-down … state-centric strategies that do not address everything needed for peace". This chapter deploys the decolonial approach as it implores us the need to face the experience of colonialism as well as recognising the precolonial (Bernasconi in Mignolo, 2002, p. 72) in the understanding of peace processes, thereby placing indigenous approaches at the centre of "intellectual inquiry" (Ottoh, 2022, p. 26). Decolonising peacebuilding is therefore about remembering the local, including indigenous knowledge, as capable of building peace, while also recognising that what is at the centre of conflict manifesting as xenophobia, that is, nationality and ethnicity are categories that served the coloniser. It is Wiredu's (1998, p. 20) argument that "minds that think about and expound their own culture in terms of categories of a colonial origin without any qualms as to any possible conceptual incongruities" are "what may justly be called colonized".

The coloniser indoctrinated the African's mind, as explained by Taylor (1992), to self-hate and to feel inferior. With specific reference to black people, Taylor suggests that,

> white society has for generations projected a demeaning image of them, which some of them have been unable to resist adopting. Their own self-depreciation, on this view, becomes one of the most potent instruments of their own oppression. Their first task ought to be to purge themselves of this imposed and destructive identity. (Taylor, 1992, p. 26)

As such, personhood in postcolonial Africa has a different meaning to that in precolonial Africa, as also observed by Ndlovu-Gatsheni when he avers that,

> the coalescence of various historical processes that combined to produce Africa as an idea and cartographic reality and African identity as a contingent phenomenon are useful in explaining the postcolonial problems of territorialised autochthony, nativism and xenophobia. (Ndlovu-Gatsheni, 2010, p. 282)

Global approaches to peacebuilding in many cases are far removed from the local issues to offer necessary changes, hence a decolonial approach that privileges local voices and indigenous knowledge. Zvaita & Mbara (2019, p. 156) have also opined that global approaches to peacebuilding reduce effectiveness of the locals, criticising them as "mechanised … calculated outcomes … within the reach or influence of those who plan" (see Lederach, 2019).

Africans are spiritual, and spirituality has long been the social glue of the African society. In African ways of knowing and being, xenophobia does not exist. Thus, Kwame Nkrumah points out that

> pre-Islamic and pre-Christian Africa had a specific "face" which includes an attitude towards man which can only be described, in its social manifestation, as being socialist. This arises from the fact that man is regarded in Africa as primarily a spiritual being, a being endowed with a certain inward dignity, integrity and value. (Wiredu, 1998, p. 252)

This thus makes xenophobia a modernity or postcolonial problem as predicted by Franz Fanon that "Africa would sink into acts of xenophobia at some stage post-liberation" (Mafukata, 2021, p. 71). Mafukata (2021, p. 72) also observed that "[T]he post-colonial and post-apartheid state in Africa is being anchored on a xenophobic political rhetoric which creates biases against immigrant nationals". This shows how Africans have been, and continue to be brainwashed when it comes to humanness, respecting differences and resolving conflicts nonviolently, what Khaminwa (2003) calls "coexistence". Coexistence is crucial in contexts of diversity, difference, insider and outsider politics. Peaceful coexistence is similar to *Ubuntu* where mutual respect is crucial for meaningful lives and sustainable societies.

The need to prioritise conflict prevention, management, resolution and transformation (CPMRT) in communities has led peacebuilding scholars such

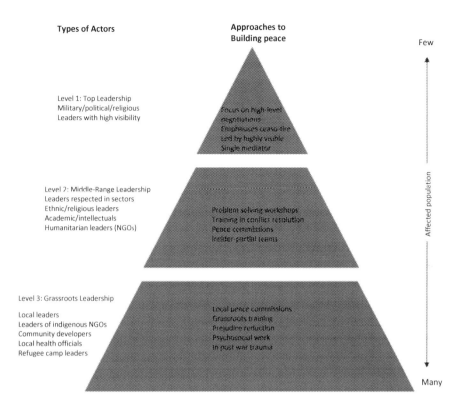

**Fig. 25.1** Lederach's peacebuilding pyramid (Lederach, 1997, p. 39)

as John Paul Lederach (1997) to develop a peacebuilding pyramid. The pyramid (Fig. 25.1) presents a case for a multi-level peacebuilding process with different players at different levels. The peacebuilding pyramid's strength lies in its ability to recognise how local level issues, presented as Level 3, should be dealt with using localised solutions. Xenophobia, racism, gender-based violence, tribalism, sexism, etc. are forms of cold-wars that are perpetuated by fear or lack of tolerance for diversity, leading to the struggle for peaceful coexistence. Lederach's peacebuilding pyramid targets issues such as prejudice at the local/grassroots level where he also sees large numbers of affected population being high.

## Grassroots Peacebuilding: Case Analyses of African Traditional Spiritual Leaders

Traditional approaches to dealing with conflict and pursuing social and cultural justice have been encouraged by scholars such as Te Maihāroa et al. (2022, p. 2) as they see a need for peace studies to affirm "indigenous ways of knowing and being". The decolonial epistemic approach advocates for local ways of knowing and being, seeing as the formerly colonized were ontologically exiled from their "languages, cultures, names, and even from themselves" (Ndlovu-Gatsheni, 2018, p. 16). The idea of peacebuilding as interventions from outside have, according to Docherty and Lantz-Simmons (2016), been encouraged by the UN definition of peacebuilding where the role is played by external parties. Docherty and Lantz-Simmons argue that there are also other approaches to peacebuilding that look at internal/local role players (see also Van Leeuwen et al., 2019) which they illustrate using John Paul Lederach and Katie Mansfield's 2010 peacebuilding wheel.

The three local traditional spiritual leaders focused on in this chapter, Credo Mutwa, Dineo Ndlanzi and Aubrey Matshiqi, often remind the African about their roots, philosophy and ancestry which is critical for initiating peacebuilding for development. They will be written on and about, using honorifics suiting their standing, and also in line with the African culture of respect of the elders within which this chapter is written. While all cultures have respect for their elders, in African culture, elders are not called by their first names or their surnames without honorifics that show the speaker's relationship with the other, or in this case, the spiritual standing of the spiritual leaders discussed in the chapter. Thus, we have Baba (father) for Credo Mutwa, and Gogo (loosely translated as grandmother) for Aubrey Matshiqi and Dineo Ndlanzi. The title Gogo is bestowed upon Aubrey Matshiqi who is male because the spirit that possesses him is female (Mpofu-Walsh, 2020). Unlike mainstream religions, spiritual healers are seldom heard from by the general public. However, the three spiritual leaders of focus in this chapter are visible on digital and social media, such as television, YouTube, Instagram and Twitter, platforms that make their messages easily accessible to the public. While there is a gap in literature with regard to social media presence of traditional spiritual leaders/healers, Cheong (2011) observes the proliferation of religious tweets with Scriptures being adapted "for wider dissemination". Cheong (2011, p. 454) suggests that "In an era of global communications, it is also productive to consider the diffusion of ... religious discourse to effect social change across local and transnational communities in need". Similarly, the social media presence of the three leaders in this chapter can similarly effect peacebuilding.

### *Case Analysis 1: Credo Mutwa—Institution of Healing*

Baba Credo Mutwa was a well-known healer, author, artist and philosopher who passed away in 2020 (South African History Online (SAHO), 2020) in his 99th year. Among his many predictions as a prophesier, Baba Credo is said to have predicted the 1976 youth uprising, a prediction which became misinterpreted by the youth as support for the then apartheid government resulting in the burning down of his Soweto home by the youth (South Africa Broadcasting Corporation (SABC), 2020). In a talk with his daughter on the SABC programme *Leihlo La Sechaba* (510,000 views), Baba Credo told his daughter to not be "*angry over shadows. Let the pains of the past go by, because if you do, your soul becomes corrupted, your soul becomes warped ... I don't want the Mutwa name to become a name of anger*" (sic) (SABC, 2020). This message inculcates the ethic of forgiveness, which, according to Vorster (2009, p. 366), has capacity to "break the cycles of violence and suspicion". Taken to the national level, the idea that not letting go of past angers corrupts and warps the soul has meaning for post-1994 South Africa, still healing from apartheid and other atrocities of colonial-apartheid. While Vorster (2009) speaks from a Christian-centred perspective of forgiveness, the concept as it is addressed by Baba Credo should be understood similarly. Baba Credo, however, cautions that "*peace should not be prayed for*" (African Wisdom, 2022). He instead calls for inward looking and says, "*we human beings ... got to rethink ourselves, who we are*", which is a proactive stance on building peace. Events around Baba Credo Mutwa seem to have largely defined his outlook on life; while pained, he was able to create lasting statements, sculptures, a cultural village and books out of the experiences.

The idea that African traditional spirituality does not separate humanity based on nationality, ethnicity, gender, etc. emerges from Baba Credo's book: *Africa's Hidden History – The Reptilian Agenda*. He explains in the book that when Europeans "write about the people of Africa they deliberately separate them" as they do with the Khoi san (n.d., p. 12). He argues that the "writers deliberately view the Khoi san as if they were an entity completely isolated from the rest of the African people, and yet ... the cultures of many black nations in Southern Africa were intimately interconnected with the Khoi San cultures" (n.d., p. 12). Hamilton (1982, p. 6) had a similar observation that,

> divisions are repeated and emphasised in ... text-books, in which the histories of the different language groups of southern Africa are treated separately, and cultural differences are stressed. Obviously, the continued presence and manipulation of ethnic divisions presents an immense tactical problem for anybody working for change in South Africa.

The identity politics that separate one African from another is clearly a colonial agenda. Lamenting this, Mutwa says that "the deliberate separation of Africa, the creation of some separate races and tribes has resulted in great disaster for the people of Africa as a whole" (n.d., p. 12). What Baba Mutwa's message essentially does is seed a message of oneness among Africans, in line with SDG 16's broader goal of promoting peaceful and inclusive societies.

Baba Credo's wealth of indigenous knowledge has been described by Naidoo (2018) as a national treasure, whose knowledge, if taught in schools and universities, would create "*doctors of Life. People who know what it means to be human. And be kind*". What poet and writer Wally Serote said about Baba Credo that "if we claim his knowledge, the first port of all that claim would be the institution of healing" (SABC News, 2020), thus makes it clear what role the healer played and continue to play in national peacebuilding. The works of Baba Credo Mutwa have in a way been curated by the University of South

Africa (UNISA) as evidenced by the several seminars held in honour of the late healer. At the commemoration of what would have been his 100th birthday, the UNISA College of Graduate Studies convened a community engagement indaba to engage on his wealth of indigenous knowledge which is regarded as important for the transformation journey the country in general and the academy in particular is journeying on through the "decolonisation, Africanization and indigenization" focus. The indigenous knowledge for which Baba Credo is considered an institution provides for African centred ways of knowing and departs from the colonial border politics of nationality, race, ethnicity or gender. He thus calls for humanity to "*awaken the mother mind within us, we must feel what is going on in the world, we mustn't just listen to newspapers...*"

### Case Analysis 2: Gogo Aubrey Matshiqi: Call for Justice

In its focus on sustainable peace, one of the proposed targets for Goal 16 of the SDGs is the focus on reducing corruption and bribery. There is quite substantive literature on the topic of corruption in the country and one by Tom Lodge (1998) is particularly interesting as it locates the origins of corruption as "a legacy from the homeland civil services". In his calling as a healer and political analyst, Gogo Aubrey Matshiqi provides insights on South African politics and as an independent analyst; he does not seem to have alliance with any one particular political party. In an interview which touched on many issues including the issue of corruption in South Africa (Insight Factor, 2021 (14412 views)), Gogo Aubrey describes the main problem in the country as that of inequality, adding that the focus on corruption is wrong. In his words, he states that,

> We buy into this narrative, ... of focusing narrowly on corruption because, when you do so, the finger is pointing away from those who are responsible for the neo-apartheid our people still have to live through today. So, if we focus on inequality, the finger will be pointing in the direction of those who benefitted from colonial-apartheid. If you talk corruption, you achieve two things; you give corruption a black face but more importantly, you erase the sin of apartheid. (Insight Factor, 2021, 29:38–30:26)

The same can be extrapolated to issues of xenophobia. By pointing fingers in the direction of black and brown foreigners as reasons for excessive unemployment, the colonial logic of divide and rule wins and colonial beneficiaries remain blameless. The prerequisite for solving South Africa's problems according to Gogo Aubrey hence lies in addressing historical inequalities. This line of argument is supported by Zondi (2017) who avers that the failure to change the conditions arising out of Africa's historical experience challenges peacebuilding efforts as whatever peace that is achieved is not long lasting. The approach of 'pointing fingers' on colonial-apartheid beneficiaries may, however, be viewed as countering reconciliation and peacebuilding efforts. Yet still, tribalism, xenophobia and racism are all symptoms of a deeper problem, what Furnivall (in Sörensen, 2014, p. 242) describes as the 'plural society', a result of liberal colonial policy in which migration and ethnic division of labour were encouraged, "resulting in both social disintegration and inter-ethnic animosity". Gogo Aubrey claims that South Africans are an angry society and xenophobia, according to him, should not be seen as a simple matter as it is complex (Democracy Development Programme (DDP), 2015). He adds that the attacks resulting in the killings of fellow Africans are a sign that South Africans are still human as colonialism and apartheid did not take their human capacity for evil away, but questions if Ubuntu still exists. An answer to his question is proffered by Sesanti (2022) who avers that Ubuntu is not a 'soft' philosophy as falsifiers wish to make of it. Sesanti (2022) argues that while Ubuntu champions kindness and forgiveness, it should also be understood as a philosophy that also seeks for justice.

Through some of his social media messages, Gogo Aubrey has also shared his stance on peace while also reaffirming African traditional spirituality. While Baba Credo says, "peace is not something to be prayed for", Gogo Aubrey called people to pray saying, "*At 3AM we will be praying for peace - for God to help us be truthful when we talk about the causes of the violence… State-sponsored vigilantism is not the answer*". By using the broadly familiar, "God", "pray" instead of the indigenous terms, *ukuphahla* (communicating with one's ancestors) for example, Gogo's message becomes far reaching while also preserving African traditional spirituality as communicated through the call for prayer at 3 AM, the time for connecting with the spiritual realm. Thus, as a spiritual healer, Gogo Aubrey's role can be interpreted as that of re-centring African consciousness. This is so necessary as imperialism continuously unleashes its cultural bomb "to annihilate a people's belief in their … heritage of struggle, in their unity, in their capacities and ultimately themselves" (Ngugi wa Thiong'o, 1994, p. 3). Teachings on African traditional spirituality are therefore essential as they point to a shared African way of being which is at the centre of Gogo Dineo's teachings.

### *Case Analysis 3: Gogo Dineo Ndlanzi: Spirituality, Identity and Healing*

Gogo Dineo Ndlanzi calls herself a *sangoma*, which means child of the spirit song, *ingoma*. She is also a spiritual healer, teacher, life and systems coach and performing artist (Gogo Dineo, 2020). Central to her teachings is African traditional spirituality whose essence she puts forth in the greeting *Thokozani* which she explained as meaning "the divine in me honours the divine in you and an entourage of ancestors that you walk with". She intentionally teaches in order to ground the Africans in their identity; hence, she says, "where we are born is our geographical location but we are Africans" (2020, 51:44) and also asks a critical question *who were we before we were taught who we are*. Coloniality of power has meant that for many Christianised Africans, knowledge of self has been replaced by the distorted knowledge of self. While the words Gogo Dineo pronounces do not include terms such as xenophobia, racism, etc., they plant a seed necessary for building peace by re-positioning the African as one with another African. Clashes between Africans may then be interpreted as failing to recognise the divine in the other. The imposition of Christianity and its accompanying European experience (Mazama, 2002) and the colonial and apartheid experiences were in themselves cultural bombs that dismembered the African. Gogo Dineo thus suggests that the nation needs healing through cleansing, *nhlambuluko (inhlambuluko or ihlambo)*, as "*the bloodshed that was never cleansed is haunting us. We are also divided not only by race but the black race is divided by class, by ethnicity and by religion. The psychological impacts of divide & conquer also needs healing*!" (Gogo Dineo Ndlanzi on Twitter, 13 July 2021, Fig. 25.2 with responses). Ordinarily, the cleansing or *inhlambuluko* ritual is supposed to take place 30 days after the passing of a family member (Edwards et al., 2009). The call for the whole nation therefore symbolises the need for healing that transcends the involvement of the living, but incorporation of the ancestors into the healing process.

Citing the work of Jobling et al. (2004) and Myers (1993), Edwards et al., (2009) posit that "contemporary humanity has survived primarily because of a remarkable facility to form and maintain social relationships". Through the shared philosophy of Ubuntu, African communities have been viewed as human centred where one's being is complemented and/or accentuated by that of another. Ndlovu-Gatsheni (2012, p. 411), however, avers that it was the colonial encounters which acted as identity markers for South Africa, differentiating between one and the 'other'. This thus begs the question: where does Gogo Dineo's idea of "we are Africans" fit in the fight for belonging in a

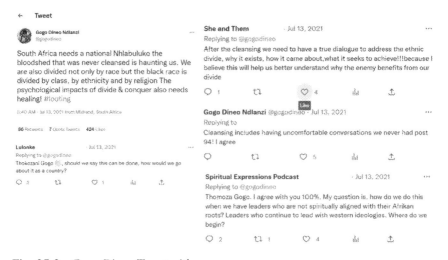

**Fig. 25.2** Gogo Dineo Tweet with responses

South Africa where "ethnic identities were emphasized"? (Makhado & Tshisikhawe, 2021). Perhaps as a healer, Gogo Dineo through her Ubuntu eyes sees Africa as explained by Ndlovu-Gatsheni as:

> a continent that is ceaselessly seeking to regain and negotiate itself above the Eurocentric egoisms of singularities that continue to inform conventional and often insensitive notions of identity imposed on it and its people by external agents. (2010, p. 283)

The greeting *Thokozani*, according to Gogo Dineo, is thus a way of getting rid of the egos as one gets to be seen as something greater than previously assumed, that is, one with an entourage of ancestors walking with them (702 FM, 2018). The decolonial project in which Gogo Dineo also participates in re-centres "Afrikan consciousness" (UNISA, 2018), a necessary building step towards peace not only in the country but on the continent.

## SITUATING THE ROLE OF AFRICAN SPIRITUAL LEADERS— CENTRING UBUNTU IN PEACEBUILDING

An essential component of grassroots peacebuilding as highlighted in the discussion of Gogo Aubrey has been the philosophy of Ubuntu, whose continued existence is doubted when one considers the xenophobic attacks from 2008 to date. Ubuntu principles are championed by Ottoh (2022, p. 30) as promoting social order as they highlight the "importance of peacemaking through the principles of reciprocity, inclusivity, and a sense of shared destiny between peoples". This principle is in line with the Sustainable Development Goal 16 of peaceful and inclusive societies, and as an indigenous way of knowing, it appeals to most Africans (including non-black Africans) as an expression of good will.

With justice and healing having been identified as key in advancing peace and inclusivity in South Africa, this chapter recommends a wheel of peacebuilding that puts Ubuntu at the centre of peacebuilding processes (Fig. 25.3). Ubuntu according to Letseka (2015 in Dube, 2021, p. 4) "upholds humaneness and 'has the capacity to constitute order, to restore peace, and to maintain the balance between conflict and harmony'". Human dignity is a human right and spiritual component. It is an inherent right for all people linked to the spiritual realm and through SDG 16, the UN reaffirms the need for peace and therefore rejects all forms of oppression or inequality that leads to the dehumanisation of the other humans. Oppression and inequality create wounded souls as it emerges from the case analysis. Wounded souls disrupt peace, and if left untreated, the infesting wounds spread from generation to generation infecting the whole society which grows into anger and hatred.

The three leaders emphasise the significance of healing from the hurts and pains of the past, in order to sustain peace. Peace was never negotiated or reminded; in the precolonial Africa, peace came naturally according to the

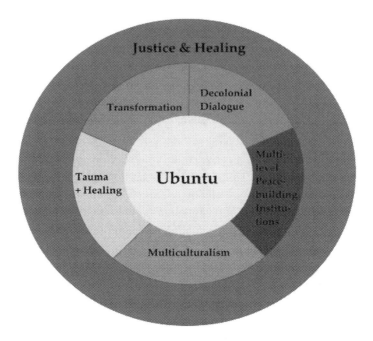

**Fig. 25.3** Centring Ubuntu for justice and healing in peacebuilding. (Source: Adapted from Lederach and Mansfield (2010))

spiritual leaders. This is supported by Mugambi (1995 in Kagema, 2015, p. 3) who opines that Christian missionaries taught Africans about tribalism based on their European experiences. As custodians of ATR, the spiritual leaders highlight how natural peace that existed could heal communities and bring harmony. The three leaders emphasise the significance of healing from the hurts and pains of the past, in order to sustain peace.

Emanating from the case analyses of the spiritual leaders are pointers to processes that may be required to achieve justice and healing for the sake of peace. In the middle circle of the proposed peacebuilding wheel is Ubuntu, as it has catalyst characteristics that can assist in the spinning of the wheel of peace. The five processes suggested which are hoped to assist in the regaining of peaceful, inclusive and sustainable communities include transformation and redress, trauma healing, decolonial dialogue, multi-culturalism and creation of multi-level peacebuilding institutions.

## JUSTICE AND HEALING

Central theme from the messages of the three spiritual healers discussed above is the idea of healing and justice. Peacebuilding as healing is often discussed in connection with reconciliation, where healing and reconciliation are intertwined. Healing is used in a clinician-patient context, highlighting that it involves a process of health and curing. According to the spiritual leaders, the nation is wounded and not healed from the many years of being seen as non-beings, hence also the call for justice. The hatred of other black Africans resulting from the severing of the African common heritage is but a symptom of the wounded state. Thus, for South Africa to heal from past traumas, there is a need to heal from those pains in order to desist claiming their humanity by any means necessary.

Justice on the other hand demands that the wrongs of the past be righted as the struggle for livelihoods remains the battle of the average South African. It is Bhattacharjee's (2020, p. 1) conviction that "even on grounds of altruism", the minorities have historically not been accepted in other states, no matter their circumstances. Bhattacharjee observes that for most migrants "[A]part from economic and cultural subordination, there is a subalternity about their displacement and existence". Justice, therefore, ceases to be a requirement for nationals only, hence Gogo Dineo's emphasis on being African first before identifying oneself by the somewhat divisive tribal groupings. Baba Mutwa says, "the deliberate separation of Africa, the creation of some separate races and tribes has resulted in great disaster for the people of Africa as a whole" (nd, p. 12). Peace was never begged or reminded, but in the precolonial Africa, peace came naturally according to the spiritual leader.

Justice, as gleaned from Gogo Aubrey, goes beyond bringing the corrupt to court, but addressing the "sin of apartheid". Processes of justice and healing that have taken place already include the Truth and Reconciliation Commission, but more processes need to be investigated. Gogo Dineo suggests an *inhlambuluko* ritual. In her discussion of Motsei's *Reweaving the Soul of the Nation*, Segalo (2019) expresses that it is important for people to understand who they are. Edwards, Makunga, Thwala and Mbele (2009, p. 5) also add that "ancestors are regarded as custodians of our lives ... healing by ancestors is achieved in a sense that they provide us with a sense of rootedness; they anchor us, and they confirm our identity".

## Conclusion

The aim of this chapter was to explore how traditional spiritual leaders are assets in peacebuilding in the South African context. The chapter analysed three spiritual leaders' messages in efforts to highlight how they promote peaceful communities and facilitate the achievement of Sustainable Development Goal 16 in South Africa. A peacebuilding wheel that is grounded on the South African reality was suggested. At the centre of the wheel is Ubuntu, around which the five peacebuilding blocks will orbit around and get energy to reach their objectives.

The chapter recognises that xenophobia is not inherently African but something that is taught through the violent encounter with colonialism and apartheid. Xenophobia in South Africa is rather colonial than ontological. This colonial mindset is contested by African traditional spiritual leaders who call for

Ubuntu that promotes peaceful coexistence. It is therefore concluded that achieving justice and healing by centring Ubuntu becomes the ultimate goal of the peacebuilding processes. Promotion of Ubuntu principles aids in the reduction of conflict-related deaths and population subjected to physical or psychological violence. It also fortifies the significance of custodians of the principles, the traditional spiritual leaders, as relevant institutions for guiding societal behaviours and morals towards peaceful coexistence.

Lastly, peacebuilding in non-warring but post-conflict countries in the sense of being new democracies requires that local cultures be part of the structures where peace is built on. The chapter concludes that the messages from the three spiritual leaders has potential to generate social cohesion and thus spiritual leaders can indeed be assets in building peace. A lot can be learnt about Africa and humaneness from them.

## References

1 FM. (2018). Traditional Healing with Gogo Dineo Ndlanzi. Interview with Eusebius McKaiser, December 6. Retrieved June 26, 2022, from http://www.702.co.za/articles/329843/watch-traditional-healer-gogo-dineo-ndlanzi-in-conversation-with-eusebius

African Wisdom. (2022). We Don't Worship Spirits: Credo Mutwa. Retrieved June 26, 2022, from https://www.youtube.com/watch?v=XR3PHkwrBYM

AU. (2019). Transitional Justice Policy. African Union. Retrieved January 3, 2023, from https://au.int/sites/default/files/documents/36541-doc-au_tj_policy_eng_web.pdf

Behr, A. W. (2021). Xeno-Afrophobia and Pan-Africanism: What Lies Beneath the Mask of an Identity? In S. Ogbobode-Abidde & E. K. Masando (Eds.), *Xenophobia, Nativism and Pan-Africanism in 21st Century Africa: History, Concepts, Practice and Case Study* (pp. 43–60). Springer.

Bhattacharjee, S. (2020). The Subaltern Migrant in the Era of Neoliberal Empires. Retrieved August 22, 2022, from http://www.mcrg.ac.in/RLS_Migration_2020/Researchers_Abstracts_Fullpapers/Abstracts_Worshop_2020/Module%20D/Full%20Paper%20Srinita%20Bhattacharjee.pdf

Cheong, P. H. (2011). Religious Leaders, Mediated Authority, and Social Change. *Journal of Applied Communication Research, 39*(4), 452–454.

DDP Democracy. (2015). Xenophobia Guest Speaker: Audrey Matshiqi. Retrieved June 22, 2022, from https://www.youtube.com/watch?v=ErC08lNqRnw

Docherty, J. S., & Lantz-Simmons, M. (2016). A Genealogy of Ideas: What Is Old Is New Again. The Centre for Justice and Peacebuilding. Retrieved June 26, 2022, from https://issuu.com/easternmennoniteuniversity/docs/a-genealogy-of-ideas-journal-1-2016

Dube, B. (2021). Deficit Thinking in South Africa's Water Allocation Reform Discourses: A Cultural Discourse Perspective. *Journal of Multicultural Discourses, 16*(4), 293–312.

Edwards, S. D., Makunga, N. V., Thwala, J. D., & Mbele, P. B. (2009). The Role of the Ancestors in Healing. *Indilinga. African Journal of Indigenous Knowledge Systems, 8*(1), 1–11.

Galtung, J. V. (1976). Three Approaches to Peace: Peacekeeping, Peacemaking, and Peacebuilding. In J. Galtung (Ed.), *Peace, War and Defense: Essays in Peace Research, Vol. II* (pp. 297–298). Christian Ejlers).

Gogo Dineo Ndlanzi. (2020, July 6). Joshua Maponga Interviews Me on African Spirituality and Religion. Retrieved September 10, 2022, from https://www.youtube.com/watch?v=9OzykJfmisQ

Gomez, M. A. (2013). Africans, Religion, and African Religion Through the Nineteenth Century. *Journal of African Religions, 1*(1), 78–90.

Hamilton, C. A. (1982). The Study of Southern African Precolonial History: "Bantustan propaganda"? Reality, May, pp. 6–9. Retrieved September 10, 2022, from https://disa.ukzn.ac.za/sites/default/files/pdf_files/remay82.6.pdf

Harley, A. E., Buckworth, J., Katz, M. L., Willis, S. K., Odoms-Young, A., & Heaney, C. A. (2013). A Grounded Theory Study – "Developing Long-Term Physical Activity Participation: A Grounded Theory Study with African American Women". In J. W. Creswell (Ed.), *Qualitative Inquiry and Research Design: Choosing Among Five Approaches* (3rd ed.). Sage Publications.

Hayward, S. (2012). *Religion and Peacebuilding: Reflections on Current Challenges and Future Prospects.* Special Report 313. Unites States Institute of Peace, Washington, DC.

Insight Factor. (2021). Aubrey Matshiqi. Retrieved February 10, 2022, from https://www.youtube.com/watch?v=zrv59O91A4U

Kagema, D. N. (2015). The Role of the African Traditional Religion in the Promotion of Justice, Reconciliation and Peace in Africa in the Twenty-First Century: A Kenyan Experience. *International Journal of African and Asian Studies, 15*, 1–9.

Khaminwa, A. N. (2003). Coexistence. Retrieved September 10, 2022, from https://www.beyondintractability.org/essay/coexistence

Kok, N. (2014). South Africa's Peacebuilding and PCRD Activities. The Role of IBSA and BRICS. Institute for Security Studies. ISS Paper 267.

Lederach, J. P. (1997). *Building Peace: Sustainable Reconciliation in Divided Societies.* United States Institute of Peace Press.

Lederach, J. P. (2019). Sustaining Peace: Concluding thoughts. Keynote Address: Building Sustainable Peace Conference, November 2019. Available on https://www.youtube.com/watch?v=GE_XNFVfO7o. Accessed 6 June 2022.

Lederach, J. P., & Mansfield, K. (2010). Strategic Peacebuilding Wheel. Kroc Institute for International Peace Studies. Retrieved February 10, 2022, from https://www.uml.edu/docs/pcs%20career%20pathways%20print2_tcm18-90734.pdf

Lodge, T. (1998). Political Corruption in South Africa. *African Affairs, 97*(387), 157–187.

Mafukata, M. A. (2021). The Influence of Political Rhetoric on the Evolution of Xenophobia in Africa. In M. A. Mafukata (Ed.), *Impact of Immigration and Xenophobia on Development in Africa* (pp. 72–89). IGI Global.

Makhado, M. P., & Tshisikhawe, T. R. (2021). How Apartheid Education Encouraged and Reinforced Tribalism and Xenophobia in South Africa. In M. A. Mafukata (Ed.), *Impact PF Immigration and Xenophobia on Development in Africa* (pp. 131–151). IGI Global.

Mazama, M. A. (2002). Afrocentricity and African Spirituality. *Journal of Black Studies, 33*(2), 218–234.

Mbiti, J. S. (1969). *African Religious and Philosophy.* Heinemann.

Mignolo, W. (2002). The Geopolitics of Knowledge and the Colonial Difference. *South Atlantic Quarterly, 101*(1), 57–96.

Mpofu, W. (2020). Xenophobia as racism: The colonial underside of nationalism in South Africa. *International Journal of Critical Diversity Studies, 3*(2), 33–52.

Mpofu-Walsh, S. (2020). Aubrey Matshiqi: 'South Africa needs a new revolution'. Retrieved February 10, 2022, from https://www.youtube.com/watch?v=ApsL29r7JR4

Mutwa, C. (n.d.). Africa's hidden history: The reptilian agenda (pp. 1–110). Available on https://www.scribd.com/document/499050730/Mutwa-Credo-Africa-s-Hidden-History-the-Reptilian-Agenda-PDF. Accessed on 6 June 2022.

Naidoo, J. (2018). Credo Mutwa: Tapping into the Wisdom of the Ancients. *Daily Maverick*, August 10. Retrieved August 22, 2022, from https://www.dailymaverick.co.za/opinionista/2018-08-10-credo-mutwa-tapping-into-the-wisdom-of-the-ancients/

Ndlovu-Gatsheni, S. J. (2010). Do 'Africans' Exist? Genealogies and Paradoxes of African Identities and the Discourses of Nativism and Xenophobia. *African Identities, 8*(3), 281–295.

Ndlovu-Gatsheni, S. J. (2012). Racialised Ethnicities and Ethnicised Races: Reflections on the Making of South Africanism. *African Identities, 10*(4), 407–422.

Ndlovu-Gatsheni, S. J. (2018). The Dynamics of Epistemological Decolonisation in the 21st Century: Towards Epistemic Freedom. *Strategic Review for Southern Africa, 40*(1), 16–45.

Newman, E. (2009). "Liberal" Peacebuilding Debates. In E. Newman, R. Paris, & O. P. Richmond (Eds.), *New Perspectives on Liberal Peacebuilding* (pp. 26–53). United Nations University Press.

Ngugi wa Thiong'o. (1994). *Decolonising the Mind: The Politics of Language in African Literature*. Zimbabwe Publishing House.

Nyuykonge, C., & Zondi, S. (2017). South African Peacebuilding Approaches: Evolution and Lessons. In C. T. Call & C. de Coning (Eds.), *Rising Powers and Peacebuilding: Breaking the Mold?* (pp. 107–126). Palgrave Macmillan.

Ottoh, F. O. (2022). Decolonizing Peacebuilding Research in Africa Through Indigenous Knowledge Systems: Experience of Igbo-Speaking Group of Niger-Delta Region, Nigeria. In K. Te Maihāroa, M. Ligaliga, & H. Devere (Eds.), *Decolonising Peace and Conflict Studies Through Indigenous Research* (pp. 23–40). Springer.

Palys, T. (2008). Purposive Sampling. In L. M. Given (Ed.), *The Sage Encyclopedia of Qualitative Research Methods* (Vol. 2, pp. 697–698). Sage.

SABC News. (2020). Leihlo La Sechaba: Credo Mutwa. February 3. Retrieved March 28, 2022, from https://www.youtube.com/watch?v=Xx3CGvwUqi0

SAHO. (2020). Vusamazulu Credo Mutwa. South Africa History Online. Retrieved February 10, 2022, from https://www.sahistory.org.za/people/vusamazulu-credo-mutwa

Segalo, P. (2019). Poison in the Bone Marrow: Complexities of Liberating and Healing the Nation. *HTS Theological Studies, 76*(3), a6047. https://doi.org/10.4102/hts.v76i3.6047

Sesanti, S. (2022). Rescuing and Reclaiming Ubuntu for Justice (Gender and Environment Included) from Its Falsifiers. UNISA Africa Speaks, April 13.

Silvestri, S., & Mayall, J. (2015). *The Role of Religion in Conflict and Peacebuilding*. British Academy.

Sörensen, J. S. (2014). The Return of Plural Society: State Building and Social Splintering. *Peacebuilding, 2*(3), 270–285.

Stieglitz, S., Mirbabaie, M., Ross, B., & Neuberger, C. (2017). Social Media Analytics – Challenges in Topic Discovery, Data Collection, and Data Preparation. *International Journal of Information Management, 39*, 156–168.

Taylor, C. (1992). The Politics of Recognition. In A. Gutmann (Ed.), *Multiculturalism and the Politics of Recognition* (pp. 25–74). Princeton.

Te Maihāroa, K., Ligaliga, K. M., & Devere, H. (Eds.). (2022). Introduction. In K. Te Maihāroa, M. Ligaliga, & H. Devere (eds.), *Decolonising Peace and Conflict Studies Through Indigenous Research*. Springer.

UN. (2020). Peace, Justice, and Strong Institutions: Why They Matter. United Nations. Retrieved September 10, 2022, from https://www.un.org/sustainabledevelopment/wp-content/uploads/2019/07/16_Why-It-Matters-2020.pdf

UNISA. (2018). College of Human Sciences Leads Decoloniality Conversations. https://www.unisa.ac.za/sites/corporate/default/Colleges/Human-Sciences/News-&-events/Articles/College-of-Human-Sciences-leads-decoloniality-conversations

Van Leeuwen, M., Nindorera, J., Nzweve, J.-L. K., & Corbijn, C. (2019). The 'local turn' and notipns of conflict and peacebuilding – Reflections on local peace committees in Burundi and eastern DR Congo. *Peacebuilding, Taylor & Francis Group*, pp. 1–22.

Vorster, J. M. (2009). An Ethics of Forgiveness. *Verbum Et Ecclesia JRG, 30*(1), 365–383.

Wiredu, K. (1998). Toward Decolonizing African Philosophy and Religion. *African Studies Quarterly, 1*(4), 17–46.

Zondi, S. (2017). African Union approaches to peacebuilding: Efforts at shifting the continent towards decolonial peace. *African Journal on Conflict Resolution, 17*(1), 105–131.

Zvaita, G. T., & Mbara, G. C. (2019). Engaging the Values of Local Participation in African Peacebuilding Processes. *Journal of African Union Studies (JoAUS), 8*(2), 155–178.

CHAPTER 26

# Religious Peacebuilding's Response to Violent Extremism in Informal Settlements in Egypt

*Patrick Karanja Mbugua and Nahed Talaat Ayoub*

## INTRODUCTION

One of the lines of argument in religious peacebuilding holds that implementing inter-religious activities involving youth from different religions and cultures reduces religious radicalisation and extremism, enhances pluralism and reconciliation, and promotes peaceful relations. Accordingly, increased interaction between followers of different religions and cultures demystifies the pre-existing stereotypes, prejudices, and misconceptions and shapes attitudes and behaviour. Further, such interactions increase knowledge and understanding of the commonalities and differences between the various religious formations, enhance cross-religious and cross-cultural communication, and instil the values of acceptance, tolerance, and respect (Dubois, 2008). This chapter assesses these arguments using empirical evidence from the interventions by the Anglican Diocese of Egypt with North Africa and the Horn of Africa (ADE) in three slums in Cairo, namely Ezbet El-Nakheel, Miser El-Kadima, and Madient

The CRID consortium published a simplified general readers version of this study using some of the evidence cited in this chapter as Case Study Series No. 2 in April 2022, which is available here: https://www.faithtoactionnetwork.org

P. K. Mbugua (✉)
Peace & Conflict Studies Academic and Consultant, Peacebuilding, Conflict Transformation, and Preventive Diplomacy, Nairobi, Kenya

N. T. Ayoub
Independent Consultant, Cairo, Egypt

© The Author(s), under exclusive license to Springer Nature Switzerland AG 2023
S. M. Kilonzo et al. (eds.), *The Palgrave Handbook of Religion, Peacebuilding, and Development in Africa*,
https://doi.org/10.1007/978-3-031-36829-5_26

El-Salam. The Diocese implemented the project from November 2018 to December 2020 and targeted youth aged between 18 and 29 years from the Muslim and Coptic Christian communities.[1] The chapter views religion and culture as conceptually and socially distinct, although religion is a subset of culture (Roy, 2013; Dawson, 2013; Beyer, 2017).

The Diocese aimed to respond to issues it had observed since the 1990s, including increased violent extremism, religious radicalisation, and tensions in the informal settlements that encircle Cairo, which, as Bayat (2007) observes, are the embodiment of urban dispossession, marginalisation, and poverty in Egypt. According to some scholarly studies, the rise of Islamist movements, which rejected the secular state and privileged Islam, greatly affected the relations between different religious formations in the country (Weaver, 1999; Zeidan, 1999; Abdo, 2000; Kepel, 1993; Iskander, 2012; Farid, 2012). Moreover, the ADE staff explained that their interventions showed that these problems were rampant in the informal settlements. The Diocese was particularly concerned by religious radicalisation, intolerance, and violence, which intended to incite hatred and animosity between Muslims and Christians. Further, the ADE experience showed that youth in these communities contributed to tensions and violence because they had internalised intolerance and extremism due to ignorance of other religious beliefs, dogmas, and rituals.

Therefore, the Diocese aimed to build and promote understanding, tolerance, pluralism, and peaceful relations between followers of different religions through activities which appeal to the youth, such as visual and performing arts, as well as joint community work that encourages and promotes solidarity and common civic identity. Activities under performing arts included drum circle practices, story-telling sessions, pantomime workshops, and film screening forums, while activities under visual arts included painting, photography, Arabic calligraphy, and sculpture. Meanwhile, community work involved cleaning and lighting the streets and solidarity visits to schools and marginalised communities. The ADE's interventions directly reached 2467 male and female youth from the Muslim and Christian religions from November 2018 to December 2020. Also, ADE assembled a group of 30 young imams and 30 young priests, who conducted diverse activities such as seminars, outreach missions, and training sessions on youth involvement in community development. From a global perspective, this study suggests that ADE interventions demonstrated its recognition that building sustainable peace needs all levels of society and also were in line with UN's Sustainable Development Goal (SDG) 16, specifically target 16.1, which calls for the reduction of all forms of violence and related deaths everywhere, and indicators 16.1.2 and 16.1.3, which encourage the reduction of conflict-related deaths and physical violence.

---

[1] Documents from the Government of Egypt show that 18 to 29 years old is the official definition of youth in the country. See Capmas https://www.capmas.gov.eg. Also, UN Security Council Resolution (UNSC) 2250 (August 2017) on Youth, Peace and Security defines "youth" as people aged from 18 to 29 years.

Research for the study collected empirical data using different methods. The first method was desk review which analysed 17 secondary sources, that is, 13 project reports, one baseline survey, one endline survey, and two ADE's video documentaries. The second method was Outcome Mapping (OM), which tracked the relationship between project objectives and the intended behaviour change. The third method was semi-structured interviews with 7 ADE staff members and 58 project participants and beneficiaries in the 3 informal settlements, that is, 8 Muslim and Christian religious leaders and 50 young men and women. The following sections will provide an overview of the context of religious extremism and radicalisation in which ADE interventions occurred, the analytical approach employed, and the path of change chosen by ADE. Then the subsequent section will present empirical evidence of behaviour change, discuss the transformation of individuals and their relationships, and conclude the study.

## Religious Extremism and Radicalisation in Informal Settlements in Cairo

ADE implemented its peacebuilding interventions at the Gusour Centre in its premises in Cairo and three sprawling *ashwa'iyyat*.[2] The first *ashwa'iyyat*, Ezbet El-Nakheel, lies between Cairo and Qalubia governorates and has a population of 824,000, while the second one, Miser El-Kadima, is smaller and has around 258,000 inhabitants. According to ADE staff, a distinctive feature of the Miser El-Kadima slum is the presence of Muslim and Christian deaf communities, who rarely interact because each community lives in its own neighbourhood. The third informal settlement, Madient El-Salaam, is in eastern Cairo and has a population of 500,000. Documents from the UN-Habitat claim that there are 1171 informal settlements in Egypt, and 60% are in the Greater Cairo region. Aspects of structural violence in these slums include poverty, overpopulation, limited opportunities, high unemployment, low literacy levels, and a lack of social services and basic infrastructures such as electricity, running water, and sewage systems (Bayat, 2007). Explaining their choice of the three informal settlements for peacebuilding interventions, the ADE team argued that these settlements are prone to recurrent violent religious clashes, as Islamists and many followers of the Muslim Brotherhood[3] and other *Salafist* ideologies inhabit and provide welfare programmes in these slums.

The attraction and prominence of Islamist humanitarian projects in these informal settlements are in line with the observations in the scholarly studies

---

[2] *Ashwa'iyyat* is the Arabic word used for informal settlements or slums in Egypt and means "random or haphazard". The UN-Habitat calls them slums while the Egyptian government authorities refer to them as *ashwa'iyyat*, slums and informal settlements/areas, and categorise them as unsafe. See https://pubs.iied.org/sites/default/files/pdfs/migrate/10572IIED.pdf. For a sample study on slums and urban poverty in Egypt, see Sabry, S. (2009).

[3] For selected studies on Muslim Brotherhood, see Wickham, C.R. (2015); Al-Awadi, H. (2013); Zollner, B. (2008); Roy, O. (1999); Kepel, G. (1993).

that depravity and the dominance of the secular state by the military make the Islamist vision of an alternative world attractive to the slum inhabitants. This attraction is not a uniquely Egyptian phenomenon but a common observation in North-East Africa and the Middle-East, where Islamist movements are known to adroitly interweave their extremist ideologies, which are centred on monist and totalising conceptions of society, with humanitarian welfare programmes and everyday struggles against poverty and economic and political marginalisation (Sullivan & Sana, 1999; Ayoob, 2005, 2004; De Waal, 2004; Volpi & Stein, 2015; Korotayev, 2019; Sigillò, 2020). As De Waal (2004, p. 2) notes, "Islamism has been adept at the 'little projects' of delivering public services and mobilising the piety of young Muslims for social change in Muslim communities. Islamists are likely to improvise new forms of political mobilisation." Islamists opt for the approach because they consider it to be effective in providing practical solutions to the immediate problems facing the slum inhabitants as well as advancing their aims of Islamising society from below (De Waal, 2004).

Therefore, the ADE targeted the youth in these slums who are exposed to extremist ideas that affect their perceptions towards members of other religions, the use of violence, and the need for peaceful coexistence. The Diocese identified the Islamist demands for the installation of Islamic rule and the legal provision in the constitution that identifies Islam as the state religion as some of the factors that were plausibly predisposing the slum dwellers to direct violence against religious minorities such as Christian Copts. More fundamentally, as the Islamists implemented community welfare programmes which addressed the depravity of the slums, they also used these programmes as sites of radicalisation and recruitment into religious extremism. According to ADE, the youth bulge in the country probably contributed to predisposing the youth in slums to the risk of recruitment into religious radicalisation and violent extremism.

Consequently, the Diocese opted to engage the youth in activities that promoted dialogues across religious boundaries, mutual understanding, cultural diversity, and peaceful coexistence between Muslims and Christians. Since the ADE collaborated with the office of the Grand Mufti, the Government of Egypt endorsed their model, encouraged dialogues between religious leaders and theologians from different religious backgrounds, and supported the use of visual and performing arts to reach the youth at the risk of radicalisation in the three informal settlements. In the subsequent sections, this chapter will interpret the ADE's de-radicalisation and counter-extremism interventions using the broader peacebuilding framework. The study views the ADE's inter-religious and intercultural dialogues and peaceful coexistence activities in the slums as integral components of grassroots peacebuilding because such interventions are core constituents of peacebuilding theory and practice.

## Analytical Approach and ADE's Pathway to Change

The chapter examines how and why young men and women changed their behaviour after participating in ADEs activities. To understand behaviour change, the study draws on insights from behavioural theories and peacebuilding theory and practice. For behavioural theories, the chapter turns to the Theory of Planned Behaviour (TPB), which employs a cognitive approach to explain behaviour that centres on individual attitudes and beliefs (Rhodes & Courtney, 2003; Ajzen, 2011; Armitage & Conner, 2001). According to TPB, behaviour is a function of individuals' pre-existing attitudes and behavioural intentions, and, therefore, an individual's decision to engage in a particular behaviour is based on the expected outcomes (Doswell et al., 2011). Colman (2015) argues that stronger intentions lead to increased effort to perform the behaviour. The TPB postulates that attitudes and behavioural intentions occur within the framework of social norms and are self-regulated by perceived behavioural control (O'Brien et al., 2017). In this conceptualisation, behaviour as human practices (ways of doing, routinised behaviour, and habits) constitute arrangements of various interconnected elements, such as physical and mental activities, norms, meanings, technology use, and knowledge, which form people's actions or 'behaviour' as part of their everyday lives (Reckwitz, 2002).

This chapter uses the above theoretical insights to analyse the change experienced by the youth in Ezbet El-Nakheel, Miser El-Kadima, and Madient El-Salaam informal settlements. Arguing that the behaviour of young men and women in the three slums does not occur in a vacuum, the chapter postulates that their behaviour is affected and shaped by their environment. Therefore, the ADE strategically involved these young men and women because they belong to groups that are disproportionately affected by poverty, illiteracy, and unemployment and thus are predisposed to violence in the slums. Included in the activities were young men and women from the Christian and Muslim communities and the disabled minority, specifically the deaf people. Such planned interactions allowed the involved youth to be together and provided supportive spaces that were physically, socially, and emotionally safe for them to share their experiences and express their feelings, threats, worries, and fears. As the TPB postulates, the ADE team hoped these spaces and open engagements would help the involved youth change their behaviour. The Diocese reasoned that providing them with knowledge about the religious and cultural 'other' through shared experiences and awareness sessions would change their perceptions and lead to positive attitudes towards 'others'. Therefore, the ADE interventions created spaces that allowed behavioural intentions, which, in turn, changed the perceptions and practices of the youth in the slums, that is, de-radicalise them and reduce their attraction to extremist ideologies.

For a deeper understanding of the ADE's response to religious radicalisation and extremism, as well as the youth's behaviour change, this study draws additional insights from peacebuilding theory and practice. In particular, the study utilises the notion of everyday peace at the micro-level (Mac Ginty, 2014, 2015, 2021; Mac Ginty & Firchow, 2016; Richmond, 2009a, 2009b; Richmond & Mac Ginty, 2019; Dery et al., 2022). Peacebuilding literature conceptualises everyday peace as social practices that ordinary people perform as they seek to conduct their daily lives in conflict contexts to minimise the effects of direct and structural violence (Mac Ginty, 2014, 2015, 2021; Mac Ginty & Firchow, 2016). The literature adds that there are no universal indicators of everyday peace due to its contingent, contextual, and temporal nature. In other words, individuals and groups in a particular context and at specific time determine their indicators of everyday peace. Additionally, Berents and McEvoy-Levy (2015) have theorised the role of youth in everyday peace, arguing that young people engage in their everyday worlds in complex and diverse ways and their involvement in peacebuilding practices are multi-faceted. Since young people are involved in the daily processes that create everyday peace in contexts of direct and structural violence, their engagements influence the ways in which other young people, adults, and the structures within which they exist understand them.

Thus, from its understanding of the three slums, the Diocese believed that the majority of the population, including the youth, rejected the violence propagated by the religious radicals and violent extremists, even though many in the population probably shared the stereotypes, fears, prejudices, and misconceptions of the religious and cultural 'other' inherent in the extremists' narratives. Therefore, the ADE team chose tolerance, conciliation, understanding, and peaceful relations between Muslims and Christians as indicators of everyday peace in the three informal settlements. This approach was necessary because changing the behaviour of youth who are exposed to extremist discourses was a prerequisite to the cessation of violence and prevention of conflicts in the three slums.

According to Maria Sellevold (2012), there are three approaches to addressing youth in peacebuilding contexts. The human rights-based approach de-emphasises youth agency and views them as victims, the economic approach stresses the role of youth as threats, and the peacebuilding approach recognises youth agency in violence de-escalation and attainment of peaceful coexistence. Because the peacebuilding approach prioritises youth involvement in promoting peace and improving relations, it considers their voices, perceptions, ideas, and roles in violence de-escalation and improvement of relations at the micro-levels. Therefore, providing opportunities for the youth to participate in peacebuilding interventions could probably lead to sustainable peace. Braunsteiner and Mariano-Lapidus (2014) similarly argue for the inclusion of young people's experiences and understanding of the proximate reasons that drive them to radicalisation and extremism. This study posits that the ADE interventions intended to transform the involved youth in the three informal settlements into agents of tolerance, conciliation, religious diversity, and peaceful relations between Muslims and Christians. The Diocese acknowledged them as valuable agents of change, supported their contributions, and emphasised empathy, pro-social behaviours, and civic engagement, which, as McKeown and Taylor (2017) state, are antecedents for peacebuilding and development activities.

Applying the above theoretical and praxiological insights, the chapter contends that ADE interventions aimed not just to develop mutual understanding between Muslim and Coptic youth in the three informal settlements but also to transform their behaviour and inspire them to build sustainable peace in their neighbourhoods. The ADE team hoped that the transformed individuals would promote tolerance and peaceful relations by influencing and motivating their peers and families and contribute to reducing religious extremism and radicalisation. In other words, the ADE pathway to change focused on two levels of transformation: *individual transformation* and *relational improvement*. While individual transformation aimed to change perceptions, attitudes, and behaviour towards the religious and cultural 'other', relational improvement aimed to change relations between members of different religions and cultures as groups and collective identities. In particular, the focus on the slum inhabitants considered that extremist groups had interwoven their ideologies with welfare programmes that sought to address structural violence. Since the approach enabled the Diocese to move from the level of religious leaders to the grassroots, the ADE team referred to it as "the practical daily life dialogue" between ordinary citizens. A global perspective would suggest that this approach addresses the UN Sustainable Development Goal (SDG) 16, specifically target 16.1 that calls for reducing all forms of violence and deaths associated with them, as well as indicators 16.1.2 and 16.1.3 that call for reducing conflict-related violence.

As part of the approach, *edutainment* provided a platform through which individuals and groups could appreciate, understand, and learn about the religious and cultural 'other' through entertaining visual and performing arts. For example, ADE utilised music, drums, painting, mimes, and photography to introduce, in a simple but effective manner, subjects, issues, taboos, and religious viewpoints which could not be discussed publicly, while the story-telling sessions created a safe and friendly space for individuals to share personal stories, including engagements with extremist ideas, with their peers. A notable innovation was the use of pantomimes which allowed members of the Muslim and Christian deaf communities to participate in the discussions and break their separation from each other. Since these activities challenged preconceived prejudices and demystified certain religious and cultural viewpoints, they busted each group's fear of the other's holy shrines, enhanced knowledge and understanding of each other's religious dogmas and rituals, built individuals' self-confidence, and promoted neighbourhood solidarity and development. Joint community development work included street cleaning and lighting, solid waste management, and slum beautification activities, which served as an alternative to violence. In summary, the ADE interventions became a bridge for cross-cultural and cross-religious understanding as followers of different religions realised they shared a common Egyptian civic identity and the same humanity.

## Individual and Relational Transformation

The following outcome mapping table summarises the achievements and impacts of the ADE interventions. It shows the various interventions and their outcomes, which helped the youth in the three informal settlements change their perceptions, attitudes, and behaviour.

**Problem statement:**
In the last few decades, religious extremists have exposed youth in three informal settlements in Cairo, Ezbet El-Nakheel, Miser El-Kadima, and Madient El-Salaam, to an exclusivist ideology, which affects their views and perceptions towards religious and cultural 'others', religious tolerance, peaceful coexistence, and the use of direct violence. This exposure has contributed to increased tensions and violent clashes between the majority Muslim and the minority Christian population.

| | Who participated? | Helping factors | Hindering factors |
|---|---|---|---|
| | A total of 2467 individuals had the opportunity to participate in ADE peacebuilding activities, including those who were at risk of being recruited into or affected by religious radicalisation or violent extremism. There were also some young religious leaders who participated actively in the project. | • The political will that encouraged inter-religious dialogues.<br>• Supportive policy environment for youth participation in general.<br>• Strong support from senior religious leaders.<br>• Successful previous experience of ADE in this domain.<br>• Availability of required funds. | • Some youth feared to participate in the project activities.<br>• The topic of religious radicalisation and extremism is sensitive in Egypt.<br>• At the start of the activities, the targeted youth were very suspicious.<br>• Limited democratic space.<br>• Discrimination based on gender and religion.<br>• COVID-19 situation delayed some activities. |
| **Interventions** | **Discourse through art**<br>• Music, drums, art, and photography sessions<br>• Story-telling sessions, and pantomime plays. | **Integration and dialogue**<br>• Training workshops<br>• Physical education and sports sessions. | **Community development activities**<br>• Cleaning, painting, and beautification<br>• Solid waste management activities |

*(continued)*

(continued)

| | | | |
|---|---|---|---|
| Process | • Cultural sessions on the importance of acceptance and peaceful coexistence were presented. For example, music, art, photography sessions introduced new lessons and shared different religious views, that otherwise could not be accepted.<br>• Introducing effective ways to deal with conflict through various art sessions.<br>• Story-telling sessions also allowed everyone to share their personal stories with their peers from different culture and religion. Participants had the chance to learn about each other's culture on an equal footing. So, the activity nurtured mutual understanding that built bridges.<br>• Participants realised they shared a common Egyptian civic identity and a common humanity.<br>• Pantomimes served as a means to engage Muslim and Christian deaf communities and break down barriers between them. | • Training workshops and sports sessions at the ADE training Centre developed the participants' skills and enhanced their knowledge as they explored, learned, and understood each other's culture and religious worldviews.<br>• The Centre provided a safe space for the participants to interact and learn through edutainment and sports activities.<br>• Diverse activities at the Centre and in the slums improved religious and cultural interactions. | • ADE interventions promoted harmony and non-violent resolution of disputes in the slums.<br>• Participation in beautifying and lighting streets and common spaces improved interactions across religious and cultural lines and reduced religious inspired violence in the slums.<br>• Painting, neighbourhood beautification programme, and solid waste management engaged the youth and provided alternative income generating activities. |
| Personal outcomes | Increased knowledge, self-confidence, and resilience<br>• Changes in attitudes and behaviour.<br>• Raising voices and reducing the sense of marginalisation.<br>• Enhancing life skills as well as communication skills. | | |

(*continued*)

| (continued) | | | |
|---|---|---|---|
| Intermediate development outcomes | • Enhanced the understanding, tolerance, and respect for cultural and religious diversity among 2467 youth.<br>• Pluralist discourses, practices, and tools promoted amongst 60 religious' leaders, and 426 youth leaders.<br>• Improved leadership capacity of 60 religious' leaders and 426 youth leaders. | • Increased knowledge on the commonalities and differences between religious and cultural groups.<br>• Negative stereotypes about the religious and cultural 'other' demystified. | • 655 Muslim and Christian youth participated in the ADE activities. |
| Ultimate development outcomes | • Reduced attraction to violent religious extremism and de-radicalisation of those already exposed to extremism in three informal settlements, Misr Kadima, Ezbet El-Nakheel, and Madinet El-salaam.<br>• Improved relations between Muslims and Christians in the three settlements.<br>• Enhanced tolerance and respect for religious and cultural diversity among 2467 Muslim and Christian youth. | | |
| Expected impact | To influence youth behaviour by cultivating everyday peace at the micro-level, promoting religious and cultural diversity, and respecting the equal dignity of all Egyptians. | | |

One can discern from the mapping outcomes table that the young men and women from the three informal settlements who participated in the ADE activities increased their knowledge and understanding of the religious and cultural 'other' and, consequently, discarded their pre-existing stereotypes and hostilities. A young Christian male admitted that he had very little knowledge about Muslims at the beginning of the project. "We have very little knowledge about Muslims," he stated. "We view them as fanatics and blame them for deciding matters without paying attention to us because we belong to a different religion."[4] A Muslim male shared similar sentiments about Christians. As he claimed, "I do not understand Christians; I do not understand their way of thinking." This lack of understanding was widespread in the three informal settlements before ADE interventions.

However, the ADE edutainment interventions and community work in the three informal settlements transformed perspectives by demystifying each

---

[4] The interview data used in this chapter was collected during three phases of research. While the first phase took place from August 2019 to October 2019 during the life of the ADE project, the second phase occurred from August to October 2020 after the end of the ADE project. Additional follow-up interviews were conducted in January and February 2022 to explore parts of the previous empirical evidence in detail.

religion and promoting learning and understanding of the religious and cultural 'other'. A Muslim male from Ezbet El-Nakheel revealed that he had "misconceptions about Christians and their practices in the church." Accordingly, he thought they were doing improper actions that they named prayers. However, after he interacted with them at the ADE Centre and he participated in group activities, they explained to him their religious beliefs and rituals. As he admits, that is when "I realised I was wrong about their religion; I was ignorant and lacked knowledge about Christianity. I have accepted them as my neighbours." Others shared such moments of transformation, as a female Christian revealed: "I feared the Muslim youth because I thought Islam ordered them to attack Christians, steal our money, and violate our women and girls." After interacting with the Muslim youth in group activities and knowing about their religious values, she understood that Islam, as a religion, is not violent. "It was individuals who misinterpreted some verses of the Qur'an to advocate violence against Christians," she concluded.

Both the endline survey and research for this study showed that the youth who participated in the ADE interventions increased their knowledge and understanding of the religious and cultural 'other'. According to the endline survey, 86.0% of the youth who participated in the activities indicated they had acquired more knowledge about the 'other', whereas 76% demonstrated awareness of the similarities and differences between Christians and Muslims. In addition to increasing knowledge and understanding of the religious and cultural 'other', participants reported an increase in self-knowledge, self-confidence, and resilience, indicating that their participation in most interventions was a great learning experience. Subsequently, increasing understanding of each other led to knowledge exchange among the youth and an increase in social capital.

During research for this study, young men and women explained how ADE empowered them, strengthened their bond, and opened new opportunities for friendships across religious and cultural lines. According to a male drum circle participant, the drumming activity made him feel he was raising his voice and the 'others' were listening to him. "I felt like I was releasing energy and sounds within others who were drumming with me in the circle," he explained. A female participant espoused a similar viewpoint. "While drumming, I feel we are singing one common song in a fabulous harmony without pronouncing any words, and our minds are together as singers. I feel empowered and inspired," she affirmed. Narrating the same experience, a male participant claimed that the drum rhythm developed a strong bond among followers of different religions and cultures in a magical way. He added: "all participants forgot about their religious and cultural differences and remembered only one thing: we should follow the drum's rhythm and express ourselves." To him, the drum rhythm symbolised the shared humanity that bound them together as Egyptians. Therefore, they were bound by the same values, energies, and life principles regardless of their methods or shrines of worship or types and postures of prayers.

Similarly, those who participated in story-telling and pantomime workshops mentioned that they became familiar with each other during rehearsals and developed friendships. Subsequently, they often organised group outings and frequently held get-togethers. While acting or telling the stories, they felt they were expressing their true feelings and freely sharing their happiness and sorrows in front of others. Thus, open sharing of individual experiences in a safe space became therapeutic because it allowed them to espouse hitherto suppressed viewpoints and perceptions towards the religious and cultural 'other'. For example, during the research for this study, 80% of young men and women confirmed that they regularly engaged in conversations with their neighbours and others who follow different religions, cultures, or spiritual traditions. Another 84% affirmed that they understood the religious and cultural viewpoints of their friends and neighbours. This was a significant improvement from the baseline survey which found that only 40% engaged in conversations with their neighbours from another religion and culture, and only 34% understood their neighbour's religious and cultural viewpoint. Practically, while only 30 Muslim and 30 Christian youth in Ezbet El-Nakheel planned and participated in beautification activities to transform their slum, they organised public exhibitions in the informal settlement which attracted thousands of people and, thus, created a space for the slum women to sell their homemade products. Such cross-cultural understanding, cross-religious interaction, and joint public events were new to the slum inhabitants. These achievements were in line with SDG 16 because they promoted peaceful and inclusive society and reduced conflicts and direct violence at the micro-levels.

An invaluable achievement for ADE was bringing together hitherto separated Christian and Muslim deaf communities in Misr El-Kadima informal settlement. After participating in the same pantomime performances, 35 deaf Muslims and 35 deaf Christians teamed up and organised joint reflection forums and cleaning, painting, and tree-planting campaigns in the slum, starting with Game'a Amor Street, which is the oldest street in Misr El-Kadima. As a Christian male who participated in the campaign explained: "I was so proud because all the deaf, Muslims and Christians, worked together to change our slum. We contributed to developing our neighbourhood as part of our national duty to Egypt." This inclusion of deaf people was a salient innovation on the part of ADE for several reasons. First, inclusion in the pantomime performances promoted their active participation in activities that demystified their individual and group stereotypes and prejudices towards the religious 'other'. Second, their involvement in pantomime performances, slum beautification activities, and the tree-planting campaign recognised their humanity and Egyptian civic identity, built individual and group confidence, and fostered an inclusive society. The inclusion, therefore, contributed to the achievement of SGD 16. Third, their inclusion reduced psychological violence engendered by a combination of structural violence inherent in the slum environment and separation from each other. This achievement aligns with target 16.1.3, which calls for the reduction of all forms of violence, including psychological violence. Lastly, the involvement of hearing-impaired communities in various activities empowered them and promoted their safety in line with SDG 16, target 16.1.4.

Such positive changes in attitude were widely shared by the youth who participated in all ADE activities and addressed the core concerns of SDG 16, specifically the building of an inclusive society. Research for this study found that 96% of the interviewees changed their general attitude towards the religious and cultural 'other', whereas 88% had started interacting and dealing with their neighbours and religious 'other' on an equal footing. This was a significant improvement from 64% who said the same during the baseline survey. Further, the research found that more than 60% of the participants could now trust the religious and cultural 'other' compared to 26% during the baseline survey.

While such changes were essentially at the micro-level, specifically among the participants of the ADE activities, they are good indicators of change in perceptions towards the overall religious and cultural value systems and acceptance of everyday peace. All participants mentioned that they promoted love, honour, solidarity, and acceptance of others as the most important values they gained from the ADE interventions. According to a female Muslim who participated in all the activities at the ADE's Gusour Centre:

> Our painting and creativity in sculptures and beautiful drawings gave us knowledge and courage to face those with extremist views. We encountered them and explained our shared Egyptian civic identity. I do not see the difference between Muslims and Christians; we are Egyptians with a shared national identity.

Such evidence proves that the ADE interventions engendered positive behavioural change among the youth by creating opportunities and spaces for them to demystify their preconceived biases against the religious and cultural 'other', acquire knowledge and understanding of the 'other', and, subsequently, pursue common goal and interests as subalterns. In other words, the ADE interventions gave them space and opportunity to espouse an alternative identity, the subaltern, which unified inhabitants of the three slums. For example, a Muslim youth, who was among the 20 Christians and Muslims that organised a cleaning campaign in Madinat El-Salaam, insisted that Muslim and Coptic youth were not just partners in a group. "We became one family; we all stood up and rose together." In essence, the young male is confirming that the ADE interventions helped them see each other as subalterns who joined to improve their slum environment, rather than followers of different religions and cultures.

This study posits that the ADE engendered change by providing the opportunity and space for the Muslim and Christian youth to participate in activities that changed their perceptions towards the religious and cultural 'other'. Indeed, research for this study found that 94% of the participants viewed extremists and radicalised persons as individuals rather than as representatives of religious communities. After ADE interventions, they felt they could engage with their neighbours without emphasising their religious affiliations and interact cooperatively and not competitively. Such changes affirmed the position of the ADE Bishop, who argued that the "Muslim and Copts youth came together and developed a mutual understanding. ... Let us cooperate and encourage them to build our Egypt". Sharing the same observation, the Grand Imam of Egypt insisted that this "is not a philosophy far from reality; these are real thoughts being implemented through practical initiatives in different locations. The spread of good is stronger and faster than the spread of evil." In summary, the ADE's inter-religious activities enhanced the understanding, tolerance, and respect for cultural and religious diversity among 2467 youth and promoted pluralist discourses and practices among 60 religious leaders and 426 youth leaders. Among external factors that contributed to these changes was an improved and supportive political and policy context. Nonetheless, the changes were at the micro-level and mostly centred on the transformation of individual worldview, improvement in relations between Muslims and Christians, and attainment of everyday peace in the three informal settlements.

Therefore, this study suggests that the ADE's micro-level transformations can be understood and universalised, using the postulates of the Theory of Planned Behaviour (TPB) and the peacebuilding theory and praxis, especially the notion of everyday peace. As noted earlier, social scientists use the TPB to predict the behaviour of individuals based on their pre-existing attitudes and behavioural intentions. The theory postulates that individual attitudes, societal norms, and perceived behavioural control shape an individual's intentions and behaviours. It also posits that the desire to perform any behaviour precedes the actual action, and the underlying intention is the belief that performing the behaviour will lead to a specific outcome. Conceivably, this study asserts that the ADE interventions synthesised behavioural approaches and peacebuilding perspectives. Since the ADE team designed their interventions to create positive attitudes and behavioural intentions, it explicitly intended to achieve everyday peace between Christians and Muslims. Specifically, the ADE interventions aimed to promote the values of tolerance and acceptance of the religious and cultural other and thus, deliberately targeted changing attitudes and pre-existing prejudices. Such interventions were in line with the TPB's postulates and peacebuilding praxis that intentions to do actions, as shaped by pre-existing attitudes, are central to behaviour change, which is a key indicator of everyday peace.

Therefore, the ADE instituted activities that transformed attitudes and mindsets, including knowledge sharing and active participation in visual and performing arts and community work. Armed with the belief that performing the behaviours would lead to specific outcomes, the ADE team involved the youth in interventions that inspired them and encouraged them to be peace agents and community builders by countering their radicalised peers who had been attracted by extremist ideologies. Activities such as discourse through art aimed to change the pre-existing prejudices and religious extremism, while drum rhythms and non-verbal pantomimes symbolised a common civic identity and shared humanity. Therefore, understanding and acceptance of a shared humanity were central to acceptance of the religious and cultural 'other' and everyday peace between Muslims and Christians. Additionally, in line with TPB's postulates, the ADE interventions, through transforming adversarial relations between Muslims and Christians, empowered the participating youth with knowledge, confidence, improved self-identity, and positive attitudes towards the vulnerable subalterns inhabiting the three slums. Overall, improved communication, regular interactions, sharing of individual experiences, and increased awareness of their shared civic identity became a bridge for conciliating contested viewpoints and religious beliefs. The TPB speaks to the evidence of free engagement spaces as the intention to perform certain behaviour precedes the actual action. Therefore, ADE's free space allowed interactions that promoted an understanding of different viewpoints, confidence building, sharing common interests and issues, and new skills acquisition. In other words, as the ADE's interventions fostered changes at the individual and relational levels, they advanced the quest for everyday peace.

Moreover, the TPB postulates that an individual's decision to engage in a particular behaviour is based on the expected outcomes. Therefore, stronger intentions lead to increased effort to perform behaviour or to change it. This insight applies to ADE interventions because most of the youth whom the research interviewed responded that they had changed their behaviour after participating in the Diocese's activities. All argued that they had advanced their ability to control self-perceptions, to listen to the concerns of others, and to avoid making judgements about others. For example, while performing and visual arts fired their imaginations and allowed them to express their viewpoints, concerns, and pre-existing prejudices, community activities, such as cleaning and beautification campaigns, built confidence and improved group solidarity. Such community activities fostered a feeling of belonging and improved understanding of the collective identity. In turn, improved group solidarity and collective identity enhanced their shared humanity and gave them a chance to contribute to developing their communities. In summary, therefore, the ADE activities transformed the behaviour of the involved youth, improved the relationships and practices as intended, and built everyday peace between Christians and Muslims.

Lastly, the theory avers that human practices and routinised behaviour create habits that become the basis for various activities and social norms. In line with this argument, the ADE designed and implemented different activities which led to routinised behaviour such as responses to the drum rhythms or the non-verbal pantomime actors. In turn, story-telling and film discussions fired their imaginations and reinforced the messages of a shared humanity and future. Continuously repeating these activities led to a 'routinised practice' and contributed to positive change at the personal and relational levels. Indeed, 90% of interviewees during the research for this study responded that they had experienced positive personal transformation in their attitudes and behaviours.

For example, while some reported that they had gained many new friendships and felt accepted by others, others praised the various activities for promoting group solidarity and helping them improve and beautify their local communities. Overall, the ADE interventions turned into a bridge for reconciling contested viewpoints and religious beliefs, fostering behavioural changes at the individual and group relational level, empowering the transformed individuals to counter their radicalised peers and neighbours, and consolidating everyday peace in the three informal settlements. Further, they clearly addressed the core lines of SDG 16, target 16.1, and indicators 16.1.2 and 16.1.3 because they promoted peaceful and inclusive society by reducing violence and conflict-related deaths in the three informal settlements.

## Conclusion

This study has analysed empirical evidence from the interventions implemented by the Anglican Diocese of Egypt in three informal settlements, namely Ezbet El-Nakheel, Miser El-Kadima, and Madient El-Salaam, in Cairo. From the evidence, the chapter has argued that the ADE implemented diverse activities, among them performing and visual arts and slum cleaning and beautification, which transformed the perceptions and the behaviour of the youth, who were at risk of religious radicalisation and recruitment into violent extremism. The ADE activities promoted interaction, communication, knowledge, and understanding of the religious and cultural 'other', and demystified and deconstructed pre-existing stereotypes, prejudices, beliefs, misconceptions, and hostilities. After demolishing pre-existing religious boundaries, which ideologues of extremist organisations had adroitly exploited by interweaving their welfare and charity programs with everyday struggles against structural violence, ADE provided the inhabitants of the three slums with alternative identities, specifically slum subalterns and the Egyptian civic identity.

The study has argued that the ADE model sought to engender change at the individual and relational levels and promote tolerance, conciliation, understanding, religious and cultural diversity and, consequently, everyday peace between Muslims and Christians in the three informal settlements. While at the individual level the Diocese instilled new skills, built confidence, enhanced self-identity, and improved perceptions towards the religious and cultural 'other', change at the group relational level involved cultivating the values of tolerance, respect for religious and cultural diversity, acceptance of common Egyptian civic identity, and embracing shared humanity. One of ADE's main achievements was uniting separated Christian and Muslim deaf communities in Misr El-Kadima informal settlement through non-verbal pantomime performances and cleaning, painting, and tree-planting campaign. Overall, this chapter concludes that the ADE model can be universalised for two main reasons. First, the interventions turned into a space and a bridge for engaging conflicting cultural viewpoints and conciliating divergent religious beliefs. Second, the interventions fostered behavioural changes at the individual and group relational levels and empowered the transformed individuals to articulate alternative narratives to their radicalised peers and neighbours. Overall, in addition to promoting everyday peace by championing religious and cultural diversity and offering an attractive alternative to religious radicalisation and violent extremism in the three informal settlements, it addressed the UN SDG 16, specifically target 16.1, indicators 16.1.2 and 16.1.3.

## References

Abdo, G. (2000). *No God but God: Egypt and the Triumph of Islam.* Oxford University Press.
Ajzen, I. (2011). The Theory of Planned Behaviour: Reactions and Reflections. *Psychology & Health, 26*(9), 1113–1127.
Al-Awadi, H. (2013). Islamists in Power: The Case of the Muslim Brotherhood in Egypt. *Contemporary Arab Affairs, 6*(4), 539–551.
Armitage, C. J., & Conner, M. (2001). Efficacy of the Theory of Planned Behaviour: A Meta-analytic Review. *British Journal of Social Psychology, 40*(4), 471–499.
Ayoob, M. (2004). Political Islam: Image and Reality. *World Policy Journal, 21*(3), 1–14.
Ayoob, M. (2005). The Future of Political Islam: The Importance of External Variables. *International Affairs, 81*(5), 951–996.
Bayat, A. (2007). Radical Religion and the Habitus of the Dispossessed: Does Islamic Militancy Have an Urban Ecology? *International Journal of Urban and Regional Research, 31*(3), 579–590.
Berents, H., & McEvoy-Levy, S. (2015). Theorising Youth and Everyday Peace(Building). *Peacebuilding, 3*(2), 115–125. https://doi.org/10.1080/21647259.2015.1052627
Beyer, J. (2017). Religion and Culture: Revisiting a Close Relative. *HTS Theological Studies, 73*(1), 1–9.
Braunsteiner, M. L., & Mariano-Lapidus, S. (2014). A Perspective on Inclusion: Challenges for the Future. *Global Education Review, 1*(1), 32–43.
Colman, A. (2015). Availability Heuristic. In *A Dictionary of Psychology.* Oxford University Press.
Dawson, C. (2013). *Religion and Culture.* The Catholic University of America Press.
De Waal, A. (2004). *Islamism and Its Enemies in the Horn of Africa.* Indiana University Press.
Dery, I., Baataar, C., & Khan, A. R. (2022). Everyday Peacebuilding among Ghanaian Men: Ambiguities, Resistances and Possibilities. *Journal of the British Academy, 10*(s1), 35–53. https://doi.org/10.5871/jba/010s1.035
Doswell, W., Braxter, B., Cha, E., & Kim, K. (2011). Testing the Theory of Reasoned Action in Explaining Sexual Behaviour among African American Young Teen Girls. *Journal of Paediatric Nursing., 26*(6), e45–e54. https://doi.org/10.1016/j.pedn.2011.03.007
Dubois, H. (2008). Religion and Peacebuilding: An Ambivalent Yet Vital Relationship. *Journal of Religion, Conflict and Peace, 1*(2), 1–21.
Farid, S. A. (2012). Toleration or Recognition: Towards a New Account of Religious Diversity in Contemporary Egypt. *European Scientific Journal, 8*(1), 207–238.

Iskander, E. (2012). The 'Mediation' of Muslim–Christian Relations in Egypt: The Strategies and Discourses of the Official Egyptian Press during Mubarak's Presidency. *Islam and Christian–Muslim Relations, 23*(1), 31–44.

Kepel, G. (1993). *Muslim Extremism in Egypt: The Prophet and the Pharaoh* (2nd ed.). University of California Press.

Korotayev, A. (2019). Islamism and Its Role in Modern Islamic Societies. *Islamic Quarterly, 63*(3), 27–452.

Mac Ginty, R. (2014). Everyday Peace: Bottom-up and Local Agency in Conflict-Affected Societies. *Security Dialogue, 45*(6), 548–564.

Mac Ginty, R. (2015). Where Is the Local? Critical Localism and Peacebuilding. *Third World Quarterly, 36*(5), 840–856.

Mac Ginty, R. (2021). *Everyday Peace: How So-called Ordinary People Can Disrupt Violent Conflict*. Oxford University Press.

Mac Ginty, R., & Firchow, F. (2016). Top-Down and Bottom-up Narratives of Peace and Conflict. *Politics, 36*(3), 308–323.

McKeown, S., & Taylor, L. K. (2017). Intergroup Contact and Peacebuilding: Promoting Youth Civic Engagement in Northern Ireland. *Journal of Social and Political Psychology, 5*(2), 415–434.

O'Brien, L., Morris, J., Marzano, M., & Dandy, N. (2017). Promoting Sustainability Behaviours Through Forestry. *An International Journal of Forest Research, 90*(1), 88–98.

Reckwitz, A. (2002). Toward a Theory of Social Practices: A Development in Culturalist Theorising. *European Journal of Social Theory, 5*(2), 243–263.

Rhodes, R. E., & Courtney, K. S. (2003). Modelling the Theory of Planned Behaviour and Past Behaviour. *Psychology, Health & Medicine, 8*(1), 2003.

Richmond, O. (2009a). A Post-Liberal Peace: Eirenism and the Everyday. *Review of International Studies, 35*(3), 557–580.

Richmond, O. (2009b). Becoming Liberal, Unbecoming Liberalism: Liberal-Local Hybridity via the Everyday as a Response to the Paradoxes of Liberal Peacebuilding. *Journal of Intervention and Statebuilding, 3*(3), 324–344.

Richmond, O., & Mac Ginty, R. (2019). Mobilities and Peace. *Globalizations, 16*)5), 606–624.

Roy, O. (1999). *The Failure of Political Islam*. I.B. Tarus.

Roy, O. (2013). *Holy Ignorance: When Religion and Culture Part Ways*. Oxford University Press.

Sabry, S. (2009). *Poverty Lines in Greater Cairo: Underestimating and Misrepresenting Poverty*. Working Paper Series 21. International Institute for Environment and Development.

Sellevold, M. (2012). *Youth as Peace Builders: A Comparative Study of Educational Response in Post-Conflict Burundi*. Unpublished MA dissertation. University of Oslo.

Sigillò, E. (2020). Islamism and the Rise of Islamic Charities in Post-revolutionary Tunisia: Claiming Political Islam through Other Means? *British Journal of Middle Eastern Studies*. https://doi.org/10.1080/13530194.2020.1861926

Sullivan, D. J., & Sana, A. K. (1999). *Islam in Contemporary Egypt: Civil Society vs the State*. Lynne Reinner.

Volpi, F., & Stein, E. (2015). Islamism and the State after the Arab Uprisings: Between People Power and State Power. *Democratization, 22*(2), 276–293.

Weaver, M. A. (1999). *A Portrait of Egypt: A Journey through the World of Militant Islam*. Farrar, Straus, and Giroux.

Wickham, C. R. (2015). *The Muslim Brotherhood: Evolution of an Islamist Movement*. Princeton University Press.

Zeidan, D. (1999). The Copts—Equal, Protected or Persecuted? The Impact of Islamization on Muslim Christian Relations in Modern Egypt. *Islam and Christian–Muslim Relations, 10*(1), 53–67.

Zollner, B. (2008). *The Muslim Brotherhood: Hasan al-Hudaybi and Ideology*. Routledge.

CHAPTER 27

# Peace, Justice, and Strong Institutions: The Role of Church Leaders During Political Electioneering Periods in Kenya

*Simon Omare and Eunice Kamaara*

## INTRODUCTION

African nations through time have been affected consistently by internal and external conflicts before and during elections. Historically, Ethiopia, the Democratic Republic of Congo, Somalia, Libya, Chad, Morocco, Eritrea, Zimbabwe, Northern Mozambique, South Sudan, Nigeria, and Cameroon have been having politically motivated ferocious conflicts (Kamaara & Omare, 2013). Similarly, Kenya, Uganda, and Ghana have been experiencing latent conflicts which are likely to escalate in future (PSC report, 2021). Despite regular peace conventions, there is a minimum impact yet the majority of Africans claim to be staunch Christians. In nearly all situations, conflict revolves around competition for power and the absence of strong electoral institutions that promote peace and justice. In Kenya, the focus of this chapter, national elections almost always end up acrimoniously with losers claiming injustice. The option of going to court is rarely taken; it is perceived to be a waste of time because of alleged corruption.

Religion with its strong ethical dimension is expected to be a strong force with the potential to promote peace and justice for sustainable development in Africa. By religion we mean a set of beliefs and practices generally agreed upon by a number of persons or sects. The Church is one of the key development

S. Omare (✉) • E. Kamaara
Department of Philosophy and Religion, Moi University, Eldoret, Kenya

© The Author(s), under exclusive license to Springer Nature Switzerland AG 2023
S. M. Kilonzo et al. (eds.), *The Palgrave Handbook of Religion, Peacebuilding, and Development in Africa*,
https://doi.org/10.1007/978-3-031-36829-5_27

agents in all spheres of life that is next only to national governments in provision of public goods and services such as education, health, and employment. In many places, it is the 'government' that people know. According to the 2019 Kenya Population and Housing Census, Christianity is the most widely practiced religion in Kenya, comprising over 85% of the national population (KNBS, 2019). The religion provides 40% of all health services either directly or through Church-based institutions. Yet, sustainable development remains elusive due to injustice and poor governance manifested in elections-related violence and other malpractices. In a context where a great majority of the political leadership claims to be Christian, one would be interested in understanding the role of Church leaders in promoting strong electoral institutions for justice and peace.

Basing on the foregoing, this chapter postulates that unfair, unjust, and undemocratic elections are barriers to peace and justice and that the outcome of elections always depends on strong electoral institutions. To keep electoral institutions strong, the Church as the conscience of society has a critical role of keeping institutions in check (Benestad, 2011; Bretzke, 2013). In order to meet its objective, this chapter analyses activities of Church leaders during national political electioneering periods to establish if the identified activities promote justice, peace, and strong political electoral institutions.

The first section of this chapter after this introduction explains the democratic peace theory which guides the discussion that follows. The second section presents what makes a strong electoral institution. Thereafter, the chapter interrogates activities of Church leaders during Kenya's national political electioneering periods since Kenya's independence up to 2022 to grasp how they promote justice, peace, and strong political institutions. Lastly, it makes some conclusions and offers lessons for Church leaders in Kenya.

## THE DEMOCRATIC PEACE THEORY

The democratic peace theory suggests that democracies are less prospective to go to war with each other than nondemocratic countries (Doyle, 2011). Further, it suggests that democracies have political systems which are relatively open, transparent, and accountable and therefore allow for peaceful resolution of conflicts through dialogue and compromise (Tomz, 2013). Generally, the theory is in line with Sustainable Development Goal (SDG) 16, with the postulation that strong electoral institutions allow for justice and peace.

The basic philosophy of democratic peace theory was laid out by Immanuel Kant and Thomas Paine in the 1700s. In his essay, Kant (1775) claimed that the public would never vote to go to war unless in self-defence, which means that injustice (and lack of strong democratic electoral systems to prevent and resolve disagreements) is what leads to electoral violence. Consequently, Paine (1986), in his work, *Common Sense*, contends that monarchies easily go to war because of pride; pride is negatively related to justice.

The structural explanation of this theory is that weak electoral institutions make war a poor choice for both the government and its citizens (Rosato, 2003). Since war and its aftermath affect people negatively, elected officials who are accountable to the government and the citizens look for viable options as the electorate would otherwise vote them out of power. This means that democratic structures give citizens the power to change governments through elections. Consequently, the democratic political culture endeavours towards non-violent and peaceful means of conflict resolution (Tomz, 2013). In spite of various criticisms against the democratic peace theory (e.g., Jakobsen et al., 2016; Pazienza, 2014), the philosophy remains one of the most plausible explanations of what causes war before, during, and after national elections.

Without getting into the chicken-and-egg debate on whether peace and justice lead to strong institutions or strong institutions lead to peace and justice, we acknowledge the need for strong institutions in national political electioneering processes to promote justice in order to resolve differences related to competition for power without war. With their presence, dominance, and social mandate, Church leaders in Africa are expected to play a major role in promoting strong institutions for peace and justice (Benestad, 2011; Carlson, 2008). Through an analysis of the case of Kenya's past political electioneering periods, we interrogate this role and provide lessons for the future.

## What Makes Strong Electoral Institutions?

Elections matter. According to the International Institute for Democracy and Electoral Assistance (2017), elections are part of the governance process that determine key issues associated with democratic principles, including (1) leadership, (2) length of terms of leadership including continuation or change of leadership, and (3) institutionalization of electoral integrity. In so doing, elections serve to legitimize leaders, offer accountability to voters, offer opportunity for citizens to choose their leaders, exercise agency and voice, as well as aggregate preferences (IIDEA, 2017). Therefore, regular, transparent, peaceful, and free and fair elections remain one of the key indicators of democracies. Towards regular, transparent, peaceful free and fair elections, governments create electoral institutions. In Kenya, the focus of this chapter, electoral institutions fall under the executive, legislature, judiciary, Kenya police, the anticorruption authority unit, and Independent Electoral and Boundaries Commission (IEBC), among others.

Beyond working towards regular, transparent, free, and fair elections, a country's electoral institutions, also known as electoral system, contribute to economic development by determining voter's attitudes, motivations, and circumstances (Moya, 2020). It is not enough to have electoral institutions; these institutions have to be strong if they are to (or at least to be seen to) deliver credible elections. We maintain that strong electoral institutions are not just the bedrock of democracies but also the cornerstone of sustainable development. But what exactly makes electoral institutions strong?

First and foremost, electoral institutions have to operate independently from their appointing bodies if they are to conduct their business in an impartial manner (Joseph, 2021). For example, the judiciary should be independent of the legislature and vice versa. It is only with independence that the institutions can fight for and maintain the rights of all regardless of whether they are current leadership or not. They should strengthen accountability, empower voters, and fight any form of corruption such as bribery and tribalism (UN, 2013) without protecting anyone who violates human rights. It suffices to note that perceptions matter; even if there was no foul play, any perception that an electoral institution is operating under any amount of coercion or inducement would make voters lose confidence in the process and the outcome of elections leading to election violence. Subsequently, strong electoral institutions provide an enabling environment that does not deter justice for all (López, 2000). This means that access to justice and the rule of law enable people to resolve election-related conflicts, claim their rights, and obtain remedies. It helps to level the playing field between the vulnerable and the powerful by addressing issues of impunity, corruption, and discrimination in elections.

As a way of ensuring peace and sustainable development, strong electoral institutions strengthen the rule of law (UNDP, 2010). Strengthening the rule of law and promoting human rights are always key to sustainable peace before, during, and after elections. The rule of law encourages participatory decision-making and all-inclusive public electoral policies without which there can be no sustainable development. The law shapes the institutional norms as well as attitudes and behaviour of election officials. Further, the rule of law provides a viable framework for peaceful management of electoral conflicts due to its defining features: establishing the election rules of a society and therefore providing reliable, just, and stable elections; norms defining apt societal behaviour elections; electoral institutions that can resolve conflicts, enforce laws, and regulate the political and judicial system.

Strong electoral institutions are relatively permanent in their structure (Hix, 2004). They are not swayed in terms of decision-making since they are defined by what they stand for. This means that they stick to their core objectives in elections structure and function. Since strong electoral institutions are necessarily value laden, they are guided strictly by their code of conduct. These institutions promote justice and peace in an inclusive manner leading to sustainable development. Yet, no matter how strong or independent an institution is, every institution requires an external force to hold it accountable. In the context of this chapter, we aver that the Church in Kenya, being next only to national governments in terms of development, has a key role to play. Therefore, Church leaders have an obligation to keep electoral institutions on their toes before, during, and after elections to promote justice and peace. How has the Church in Kenya played this role during political electioneering periods? This is the focus of the next section.

## Activities of Church Leaders in Kenya During National Political Electioneering Periods

Many African countries, Kenya included, have made significant progress in democratizing their election processes by institutionalizing them (AU, 2021). Religions are expected to be watchdogs of these institutions so that they can offer just and peaceful elections for sustainable development (Gumo et al., 2012). Kenya is a multireligious country, with an estimate of 83% of the national population being Christians; followed by Muslims at 11%, Hinduism, Sikhism, Baha'i, Buddhism, and African traditional religions accounting for 4% of the Kenyan population, while 2% of Kenyans do not believe in any religion (KNBS, 2019). It is crucial to state that the Kenya Constitution (2010) maintains that there shall be no state religion and guarantees religious freedom and equal protection to all religions. In spite of majority of Kenyans being Christians, the country has and continues to experience many forms of conflicts and insecurity intermittently during and after presidential elections (Cox & Ndung'u, 2014). Most conflicts recur due to ethnic and political tensions linked to the leading political contesters. One would wonder how Church leaders have been involved.

As mentioned in the introductory section of this chapter, the Church is a major development agent. It is only next to government in provision of public services especially in the areas of education and health. This implies that Church leaders unify ethnic groups at the local level through shared religious practices, experiences, and service provision. Yet, a report produced by the Truth, Justice, and Reconciliation Commission (TJRC) in Kenya found out that some Church leaders incited ethnic-based violence, particularly during the 1992 and 2007 general elections (Cox & Ndung'u, 2014). The foregoing indicates that Church leaders in Kenya may be likened to a double-edged sword; they unite Kenyans during electioneering periods and at the same time generate social fragmentation and inter-group mistrust at the national political level.

In this section, we analyse the role of Church leaders in three distinct political eras: (1) between 1963 and 2002 (when Kenya gained self-rule—this was under a multiparty state but sooner than after the nation became single party), (2) elections of 2002, 2007, 2012, and 2017 when Kenya had effectively reverted back to multipartyism, and (3) the immediate past 2022 elections in order to bring out the role of Church leaders in Kenya's electioneering politics. In this, we limit ourselves to SDG 16 and specifically to five of its targets namely: 16.1, significantly reduce all forms of violence and related death rates everywhere; 16. 3, promote the rule of law at the national and international levels and ensure equal access to justice for all; 16.5, substantially reduce corruption and bribery in all their forms; 16.6, develop effective, accountable, and transparent institutions at all levels; and 16.7, ensure responsive, inclusive, participatory, and representative decision-making at all levels. This enables us to draw lessons for the Church, now and in future.

## Activities of Church Leaders in Kenya's Electioneering Periods Between 1963 and 2002

Kenya is a religious pluralistic state; equal treatment of religious diversity in a country is very crucial to its peace and stability. The Kenyan constitution demands, equal treatment of all persons and respect for religions and protection of religious diversity as the cornerstone of national peace. In Kenya, the management of religious diversity is governed by the constitution and the laws of the country with major opportunities but not without major challenges (IPI, 2011; Moywaywa, 2018). It advocates for separation of the state and religion. Still, given the numerical strength of the Church in the country, the role of Church leaders in electioneering has been and continues to be significant. Since independence, various Church leaders and religious groups have been active in promoting political candidates, parties, and issues that align with their beliefs and values.

When the first president of Kenya (Jomo Kenyatta) took over from the colonial masters, the Church was actively involved in matters of development such as preparation of national education syllabus and starting missionary schools and hospitals. After the death of Kenyatta, Daniel Arap Moi succeeded him with an aim of continuing with Kenyatta's ideologies. However, following an attempted coup in 1982, Moi's government came up with a coercive centralization process which curtailed freedom of expression (including that in parliament) and autonomy of the judiciary (Galia, 1997). Moi introduced *a de jure* one-party state which criminalized and persecuted those who opposed him, and limited the activities of professional, ethnic, and cultural organizations. Consequently, Church leaders became a channel for expression of discontent and desire for political transformation in Kenya as per their Christian obligation to social justice and compassion. During this period, churches, and particularly the Church of the Province of Kenya (CPK), the Roman Catholic Church, and the Presbyterian Church of East Africa (PCEA), had both external donor funding and global organizational networks which gave them greater immunity from governmental control.

During Moi's era, five Church leaders were leading critics of the ruling party, namely CPK bishops Henry Okullu, Alexander Kipsang Muge, and David Gitari; the Rt. Rev. Timothy Njoya then based at St. Andrew's Church, Nairobi, the most prominent Presbyterian Congregation in Kenya; and the Rt. Rev. Ndingi Mwana wa Nzeki, the then Roman Catholic Bishop of Nakuru and former secretary of the Kenya Catholic Bishop's Conference (Kioko et al., 2016). These leaders educated their followers on the normative basis of good rulership and the legitimate political role of the Church. Implicitly, the Church and the state were seen as two antagonistic power constellations. Church leaders were the voice of the voiceless as they stood up against the pressures of totalitarianism in the name of one-party system. For instance, in 1986, President Moi changed the provincial electoral procedures by removing the secret balloting system and substituting it with queue-voting where voters queued physically behind their favourite candidate (Sabar-Friedman, 1997). Immediately, 1200 pastors protested against the new regulations and threatened to boycott elections if the queue-voting system remained with a claim that the new system would diminish confidence in the integrity of the electoral system and expose voters to violence from the powerful elements within the political system.

By protesting against queue-voting in favour of secret ballot, the Church leaders were promoting achievement of target 16.7 towards 'responsive, inclusive, participatory and representative decision-making' about the people who would lead them for the next so many years. Through secret ballot, people would vote without intimidation and violence would be reduced since it would be difficult to know who voted for who and therefore people would believe that they were included in this aspect of decision-making.

In June 1987, Bishop Gitari publicly attacked and declared 'unconstitutional' the newly Moi instituted conditions for registration in general elections. Gitari reminded the authorities that membership of the KANU (the sole party at the time) was not a prerequisite for registration as a voter (Maupeu, 2005). In addition, Maupeu further notes that Gitari maintained that in case membership of KANU was to be made a condition, then there would be many poor people who would not afford the party membership fee, hence denying them their democratic right to vote. Further, the Bishop postulated that there would be a danger that some rich politicians would pay fee for party membership on behalf of poor people on condition that they vote for them. He recommended that in order to avoid this, the constitution be upheld to allow every Kenyan over 18 years old to register and vote without membership to KANU. This single act of ensuring that adult Kenyans would vote regardless of whether they were registered KANU members or not would promote inclusiveness regardless of social class and would reduce electioneering violence and related deaths. Thus, the Christian leaders contributed to the ideals of SDG 16, although these had not yet been formulated.

The year 1990 was a turning point in Kenya's political history due to international and internal pressure from the Church and other bodies (Maupeu, 2005), leading to the first multiparty elections in 1992. Specifically, the most important achievements of 1990 were changes in the right to vote and the cancellation of the queuing system in elections. Further, Rev. Timothy Njoya and Bishop Okullu echoed the call by the former MP for Butere, Martin Shikuku, for the constitutional repeal of section 2A and called for a two-term limitation of presidential tenure under the multiparty system. Sadly, the period prior to the 1992 elections saw ethnic clashes erupt in various parts of the Rift Valley region of Kenya as then President Moi resisted multipartyism.

Subsequently, on 11 May 1992 the National Council of Churches of Kenya (NCCK) organized a two-day inter-party symposium to discuss national issues, including the then ongoing ethnic clashes (Sabar-Friedman, 1997). Sabar-Friedman explains that, in the absence of the ruling party that had turned down their invitation, the gathering turned into a forum to unite the opposition.

Consequently, the symposium agreed to present the government with a number of demands, including the abolition of the Electoral Commission of Kenya then chaired by Mr Justice Z. Chesoni and that it be replaced by a team selected by opposition parties. In addition, they demanded immediate cessation of the ethnic clashes and commanded the government to provide assistance to the victims of the clashes and the liberation of all political prisoners. Further, the forum commanded that all steps leading to the general elections, including the intended review of electoral boundaries and voter registration procedures, be stopped until all their demands were met.

Beyond this, Church leaders were continually engaged in 'Civic Education' alongside their eclectic range of educational programmes (Chacha et al., 2018). This was designed to focus on issues related to political revolution such as voter education, election monitoring, and the rights and duties of both the rulers and the ruled within democratic systems. Chacha further explains that, in 1992, the National Ecumenical Civic Education Programme (NECEP) was established by the NCCK, the CPK, and the Kenya Episcopal Conference. The formal long-term objectives of the NECEP were the promotion of public political awareness, protection of fundamental human and civil rights, and on democratic politics through peaceful free and fair elections. To meet these objectives, the NECEP produced instrumental guidelines in pamphlets form, such as *Why You Should Vote* and *A Guide to Election Monitoring*. These publications were circulated through numerous church organizations, services, and programmes all over the country. In addition, the *Daily Nation* published a number of NECEP articles explaining the rights and duties of all Kenyans in the first multiparty elections since 1963.

All these activities of the Church were geared towards promotion of the rule of law, reduction of corruption and bribery to all levels, development of effective accountable and transparent electoral institutions, and responsive, inclusive, and participatory representative decision-making in national elections. The 1990s were characterized by ethnic clashes where a sizeable number of Kenyans suffered mortalities and morbidities. But it was not in vain. The repeal of Section 2A of the Kenya Constitution to introduce multipartyism is arguably one of the major political developments that Kenya has had and sustained. The activities of Church leaders would go a long way towards this success.

Nevertheless, it is worth mentioning that Church leaders were not entirely innocent. The foregoing is against a backdrop where the map of Christian denominations in Kenya is synonymous with the map of ethnicity, which is also in line with key political camps on certain occasions. Generally, Church leaders and their various denominations are often associated with specific ethnic groups (Kamaara & Omare, 2013). For example, the Presbyterian Church of East Africa (PCEA) is associated with the Kikuyu and thus Central Province; the Seventh Day Adventist as largely Abagusii and Luo and thus associated with Nyanza province; the African Inland Church is largely Kalenjin and thus associated with Rift valley province; and the Quakers (Friends) as largely Luhyia and therefore associated with Western Province. Consequently, many Church leaders played the party-political game based on ethnic grounds, even as they supported the opposition (Sabar-Friedman, 1997). For example, while Archbishop Manasses Kuria and Rev. Timothy Njoya supported a Kikuyu presidential candidate, Kenneth Matiba, Bishop Henry Okullu of the Anglican Church supported Odinga, a Luo presidential candidate.

The foregoing observations raise questions on whether the Church is a strong instrument against ethnic polarization in Kenya. Generally, other Church denominations operated more or less the same. The only exception was the Roman Catholic Church which remained neutral and consistently issued pastoral letters signed by the whole Kenyan hierarchy or made joint statements through the chairman of the Kenya Episcopal Conference.

One would expect that Church leaders would rise above their ethnic belonging to promote democratic practice. But reality indicates otherwise. There is a tendency of Church leaders to campaign for political leaders along ethnic lines. This goes against the targets of SDG 16, and especially target 16.5 which seeks to reduce corruption and bribery in all its forms. In aligning themselves to their ethnic groups, Church leaders promoted tribalism which is heavily associated with electioneering violence and related deaths. This explains why President Moi went on to win the 1992 and 1997 elections in spite of massive opposition. The opposition was heavily divided along ethnic lines and Church leaders supported them along the same lines.

In all, the 1990s may be described as the golden age of the Church in Kenya as far as Church leaders were key players in the movement for political and economic reformation during electioneering periods. Church leaders rose above their doctrinal and historical differences to express their opposition to the government's corruption and human rights abuses and to push for justice, peace, and strong electoral institutions. They used their pulpits and networks to mobilize citizens to demand change and to support opposition candidates and parties, a key step towards peaceful and just elections.

## Activities of Church Leaders in the 2002, 2007, 2012, and 2017 Kenya's Electioneering Periods

Church leaders in Kenya were actively involved in peace building and reconciliation activities in the electioneering periods preceding the 2022 elections. Some Church leaders conducted civic education on how to vote, why vote, and how to choose the right leader. An example of a past initiative is a civic education programme in Kibera, a large and densely populated informal settlement in Nairobi, Kenya (Bodewes, 2010). This programme was implemented by the human rights ministry of a Catholic parish with significant positive impact on participants' democratic values and behaviour. The impact was evident in the 2004 small Christian communities' leadership elections where about 75% of the leaders were voted out of office. Bodewes notes that the programme also enhanced parishioners' willingness to speak openly about a range of subjects, to tolerate and respect other views, and to counter prejudices.

The constitution is a crucial item in the regulation of institutions in a country. Strong institutions coupled with promotion of rule of law significantly reduce elections conflicts and the associated morbidities and mortalities. During the 2010 constitutional review process, Church leaders were strongly united not just among themselves but also with other religious leaders in the country through the *Ufungamano* initiative which forced the government to listen to the will of majority Kenyans through a referendum (Mati, 2012). Besides, Church leaders mobilized their faithful to take seriously the constitutional review process and participation in the transformation of the society. Notably, Pentecostal leaders rallied their members alongside the Orange Democratic Movement (ODM) to reject the Bomas Constitution draft during a referendum that took place in November 2005.

However, after the constitutional review, religious actors became divided along ethnic and political lines (Willis, 2007). Willis gives an example of the National Council of Churches of Kenya (NCCK) which transformed from 'principled' opposition under Kibaki to become part of the leadership to satisfy the then NCCK secretary general Rev. Mutava Musyimi's political ambitions. Musyimi was appointed by Kibaki to head the steering Committee on Anticorruption, thereby compromising his ability to point out massive corruption in government independently. In 2007, he resigned from NCCK to seek a parliamentary seat under the ruling party, which he won.

Later, the process of review of the Constitution of Kenya emerged as a duel between Church leaders and the state, thereby dividing Christians (Mujuzi, 2011). Notably, many Church leaders opposed the proposed constitution; Church leaders such as Cardinal John Njue (Catholic Church), Reverend Peter Karanja (National Council of Churches of Kenya, NCCK), Bishop Stephen Kewasis (Anglican Church of Kenya, ACK), Reverend Patrice Chumba (African Inland Church, AIC, North Rift), and Reverend Geoffrey Songok (Reformed Church of East Africa) opposed the proposed constitution (Kapinde, 2018). They opposed the constitution with allegations that it authorized LGBTQ (Lesbian, Gay, Bisexual, Transgender, Queer, or questioning persons) and that it would give advantage to Muslims over Christians through *Kadhi* courts.

From 2002 to 2017, Church leaders played a big role in shaping voting patterns in Kenya's elections. Surprisingly, some of the Church leaders such as Pastor Pius Muiru, Bishop Margaret Wanjiru, Kamlesh Pattni (also known as Paul), and Mutava Musyimi who expressed their interest in joining politics did not succeed. It seems their large congregations during their ministries could not be translated into voters. For instance, Bishop Pius Muiru, the head of the Maximum Miracle Ministries, vied for presidency in 2007; however, despite his large following, he did not win.

During these electioneering periods (2002–2017), Church leaders were in the forefront in spreading the message of peace. Notably, the role of Church leaders as peace-makers came out strongly, especially after the 2007 post-election violence, in which upward of a 1000 people were killed and thousands displaced from their homes (Throup, 2015). Throup further explains that at least 1200 people had been killed and over 600,000 forced into camps during the violence that occurred between 27 December 2007 and 28 February 2008. The violence was ignited after Mwai Kibaki, the incumbent president, was declared the winner and the main opposition leader Raila Odinga rejected the result as rigged.

Most Church leaders were involved in campaigns against the 2007 post-election violence. For instance, during the violence, Catholic bishops such as Bishop Cornelius arap Korir of Eldoret Diocese worked hard to bring the warring ethnic groups together through interethnic dialogue through *Amani Mashinani*—a Christian organization involving locals in peace building (Kilonzo, 2009). Later, inter-religious forums such as the NCCK took the initiative of mobilizing Kenyans to support the prosecution of leaders who had instigated the post-election violence. However, it is important to note that not all Church leaders were for the idea of prosecution as others were advocating for 'forgiveness' and praying for those accused to be vindicated. Meanwhile, some Church leaders in the NCCK educated warring communities on peaceful political processes and the dangers of conflicts through educational trips to countries that had earlier experienced conflicts such as Rwanda (Cox & Ndung'u, 2014). Other Church leaders were involved in peace rallies and caravans. For instance, in 2012, Prophet Dr David Owuor held a national prayer and repentance event attended by nearly all the presidential candidates who swore in front of his congregation that they shall not promote violence whatever the outcome of the elections (Deacon, 2015).

In all, it seems during this period most of the activities of the Church leaders dwelt on the making of the new constitution and peace building unlike the previous period where they spent time correcting governance institutions dealing with electioneering for peace and justice. For peace building, Church leaders made efforts to shape institutions in charge of elections and justice such as IEBC and the judiciary. During this period, most Church leaders appeared to be friendly with the two leaders of state; Mwai Kibaki and Uhuru Kenyatta, as the vocal Church leaders, went mute irrespective of the social evils witnessed during this period. We expect Church leaders to emulate Old Testament Prophets such as Samuel, Elijah, Jeremiah, Isaiah, and Nathan who played a key role as God's messengers challenging the political leaders of Israel; a role that is absent in the contemporary Kenyan Church. Consequently, it seems Church leaders are blindfolded; they are not openly correcting the current political leaders but uncritical towards their evil actions. Most people often accuse the current Church leaders for supporting politicians from their ethnic cocoons. This discussion leads into an inquiry on the activities of the Church in the most recent 2022 electioneering period in Kenya.

## ACTIVITIES OF CHURCH LEADERS IN KENYA'S 2022 ELECTIONS

Just like the earlier period, Church leaders were in the forefront disseminating messages encouraging politicians and Kenyans to unite towards just and peaceful elections during the 2022 electioneering period. As an attempt to regulate political divisions in Church, the Kenya Conference of Catholic Bishops banned political campaigns in Churches ahead of the 2022 general election (Ndunda, 2019). In the same vein, the Chairman, Archbishop Martin Kivuva, directed Catholic officials not to allow politicians to take advantage of their congregation to make political statement in churches. Moreover, Church leaders directly called and prayed for peaceful elections. For instance, Archbishop Jackson Ole Sapit of the Anglican Church of Kenya (ACK) urged political leaders to accept the outcome of 9 August General Election and avoid inciting their supporters to cause violence (Rop, 2022). The archbishop appealed to Kenyans to use the power of their vote to make right choices when electing leaders in elections (Khaduli, 2022). Apart from Sapit, other leaders held worship services to pray and fast for 9 August 2022 peaceful elections (ACI Africa Staff, 2022). Archbishop Anthony Muheria of the Roman Catholic Diocese of Nyeri joined in the call for peace and calm amid tension following the declaration of the final results of the presidential elections which declared Dr Samuel Ruto the president-elect. Here we see many Church leaders directly working towards the achievement of SDG 16.

However, some Church leaders provided platforms in their worship places to politicians who made statements that would divide Kenyans without correcting them. For example, speaking to supporters in Machakos, the Azimio la Umoja presidential candidate Raila Odinga claimed that he was an ardent advocate of the rights of other religious groups in the country and promised to assist a group of Muslims in case he won elections to make Christianity and Islam equal. He alleged that the colonial masters came up with an ideology that elevated Christianity above all other religions (Otieno & Mathew, 2022). The foregoing remark did not go well with some sections of Christians who condemned interpreted that he intended to make Islam more popular than Christianity in Kenya (Muia, 2022). Such remarks made by the Church leaders seem to undermine the 2010 Kenyan constitution which acknowledges that Kenya is a secular state and advocates for freedom of worship. Some politicians took advantage to compete, brag, and struggle to outweigh each other on the pulpit on who was more Christian than the other. While in one of the churches, Ruto of the Kenya Kwanza Alliance criticized the Azimio coalition as one led by people who did not value religion (Nyamasege, 2022). In response to Ruto's claims, Odinga declared himself an Anglican—an allegation disputed by Archbishop Jackson Ole Sapit, the head of the Anglican Church of Kenya. Sapit claimed that the Church did not have any records showing that Odinga was a member of the Maseno Diocese and urged him to forward his baptismal card as evidence (Gichuhi, 2022). On another incident while scoffing at Ruto, Martha Karua, the deputy presidential candidate of Azimio, responded: 'Jesus

Christ has no deputy … stop pretending to be his deputy on earth, he belongs to all of us' (Mary, 2022). Such kind of utterances in church places create disharmony which is positively associated with electioneering violence and deaths.

Some Church leaders such as David Mwaure Waihiga took the bold decision of joining in the 2022 politics. Waihiga, who is a lawyer and cleric, registered to vie for presidency under the Agano Party. Waihiga pronounced himself as new, clean, never been a part of past failures, and never been recycled (Kalekye, 2022). He likened himself to one of the most popular biblical characters—David. David was a shepherd boy, lacking the experience to win a battle, but who was able to slay the giant-sized and seasoned warrior, Goliath, with a sling. Since elections are competitive, David did not shun from the politics of downplaying other political leaders. He participated in the dissemination of messages that seemed to be of hatred. However, after elections, Waihiga trailed fourth in the presidential contest. One wonders, if Kenyans wanted a Christian leader as a president, why did they not vote for Waihiga?

Some Church leaders spread confusing messages which could lead to violence and injustice. Leaders of the charismatic churches prophesied on who was to win elections which were biased. The Azimio supporters relied on the prophecy of *Dini ya Msambwa*. Elijah Masinde the leader of Dini ya Msambwa had predicted that the leadership of the Mulembe Nation would come from the Lake Victoria region (Amalemba & Thiongó, 2022). Of course, this did not materialize. In another incident, Pastor Mwai of the Jesus Winner Ministry, Roysambu, made his prophecy that Ruto would win the 2022 elections (Wandede, 2022). These prophecies may have injured supporters in the congregation who supported the opposite political wings of whatever they prophesied. This kind of behaviours and utterances often lead to electoral violence and, worse, erode the trust and confidence that populations have in religious leaders.

The foregoing incidents indicate that Church leaders were actively involved in the 2012 Kenya's electioneering period. Some participated in advancing their interests for certain political leaders and parties, rather than truly promoting democracy and good governance. The Church leader's use of their religious authority to influence the political views of their congregations contributed to political divisions of Church members. We hold that as much as Church leaders are voters in their personal capacity, as public leaders they must take their appropriate role as universal chaplains who promote peace, justice, and strong electoral institutions. They should have their personal convictions and still carry a transcendent vision. In the context of this chapter, Church leaders would need to rise above tribal and personal interests if they are to promote justice, peace, and strong institutions in electioneering periods in Kenya.

## Conclusions and Lessons for the Future

Everyone, Church leaders included, agrees that Church leaders have a duty of promoting justice, peace, and strong political institutions. In the context of electoral processes in a country whose population is overwhelmingly Christian, this role is indisputably necessary. However, what specific activities comprise this role is the controversial question. This chapter has discussed the role of Christian leaders in Kenya's electioneering history since 1963 with reference to SDG 16. The overall assumption of this chapter is on the basis that activities of Church leaders should be in line with SDG 16 (Sustainable Development Goal 16) in terms of aiming to promote peaceful and inclusive societies. Church leaders are expected to concentrate on activities which promote electoral systems that provide access to justice for all and build effective, accountable, and inclusive institutions at all levels during elections. The targets for SDG 16 which Church leaders should promote through strengthening electoral systems are as follows: significantly reduce all forms of violence and related death rates during elections; promote the rule of law during elections levels and ensure equal access to justice for all during and after elections; substantially reduce corruption and bribery in all their forms during elections; develop effective, accountable, and transparent electoral institutions; ensure responsive, inclusive, participatory, and representative decision-making during elections; ensure public access to electoral information; and protect fundamental freedoms and in accordance with national legislation and international agreements during elections. These targets are all interconnected and reflect the overarching goal of promoting peaceful and inclusive societies that are built on effective and accountable electoral institutions in our case.

One thing is clear: Church leaders have significantly played a major role in Kenya's electioneering periods. But this role has been dualistic, even within individual leaders and among individual leaders within the same denomination. On some occasions, Christian leaders have positively contributed to SDG 16, while in others they have contributed negatively. We note that whenever Christian leaders have risen above their personal, ethnic, religious identities, they have become united to take common action with great success.

Among the positive contributions that Christian leaders have made, we include praying for peace; offering civic education on the need for peace, justice, and strong institutions; calling for unity across the country; calling for respect for the rule of law and acceptance of election results; supporting the opposition against oppressive electioneering practices of the government of the day; and also opposing government actions against violence and human rights. These activities have often yielded great fruits, as witnessed during the 1990s when mainstream Church leaders took a pro-democratic stand by speaking against authoritarianism, holding conferences that created new constitutions, as well mobilizing their Church members to join in the call for specific democratic reforms such as constitutional review.

On the other hand, Church leaders have fallen short of promoting SDG 16 by making divisive statements and openly supporting specific political candidates, not on the basis of issues, but on the basis of ethnic and religious association. In such situations, some Church leaders have failed to rise above their personal, ethnic, and denominational identities for justice and peace. This has greatly eroded trust and confidence which the Kenyan population has bestowed on them.

Three key lessons may be derived from the preceding conclusions. First, Church leaders, as with all other leaders, need to unite if they hope to build strong institutions and thereby win any war against injustice and violence. For them to be united, Church leaders have to focus on issues rather than focus on candidates. Given the divisive history of the Church in Kenya and its continued alignment with ethnic identities, focus on candidates who necessarily belong to specific identities is bound to create division among the leaders.

Second, given that conflict is part of human life and electioneering is a competitive process, there is bound to be tensions and moments of conflict. The basic fact that every election has winners and losers is worth emphasizing. Therefore, before, during, and after elections, Christian leaders should find ways of preparing political contenders and their supporters for either outcome. For example, before elections, Christian leaders should work to promote structures, systems, institutions, and elements of culture work that provide constructive, non-violent pathways for decision-making, resolving conflicts, and addressing societal injustices. During elections, Christian leaders may be involved in monitoring the electoral process to ensure that it is free, fair, and transparent, while after elections, Christian leaders may engage the contending actors through outreach, negotiations, mediation, and acknowledgement of grievances and avoid chest thumping by the victorious since this naturally makes the losers feel aggrieved. Through the practices of human rights advocacy, restorative justice, reconciliation, and community healing, Church leaders are effectively well-placed promoting peace, justice, and strong institutions for sustainable development.

From the discussion of the Kenya's electioneering periods presented in this chapter, it would appear that Christian leaders risk losing their trust and confidence to levels that would make it difficult for them to play their public role in future. This would be a dangerous point for Kenya to be in, because as the democratic peace theory holds, democratic structures give citizens power to influence governments through elections. Church leaders are among the major groups with the potential to change the future of country threatened with conflict before, during, and after national elections by promoting democratic structures and practices. We hold to the Sankofa saying from the Akan ethnic group in Ghana that *'it is not taboo to fetch what is at risk of being left behind'*.

# References

ACI Africa Staff. (2022, August 15). Kenya's Faith Leaders Call for Peace amid Tension after Declaration of Presidential Result. Retrieved January 25, 2023, from https://www.aciafrica.org/news/6478/kenyas-faith-leaders-call-for-peace-amid-tension-after-declaration-of-president

Amalemba, R., & Thiongó, J. (June 18, 2022). Is George Wajackoyah the promised Mulembe Prince? Retrieved October 20, 2022, from https://www.standardmedia.co.ke/health/national/article/2001448186/is-george-wajackoyah-the-promised-mulembe-prince

AU. (2021, November). AU Institutionalizing Electoral Democracy in Africa. *AU Monthly Bulletin*. Retrieved January 25, 2023, from https://au.int/en/treaties/african-charter-democracy-elections-and-governance

Benestad, J. B. (2011). *Church, State, and Society: An Introduction to the Catholic Social Doctrine*. CUEA Press.

Bodewes, C. (2010). Civil Society and the Consolidation of Democracy in Kenya: An Analysis of a Catholic Parish's Efforts in Kibera Slum. *The Journal of Modern African Studies, 48*(04), 547–571. Retrieved January 23, 2023, from https://doi.org/10.1017/S0022278X10000467

Bretzke, J. T. S. J. (2013). *Handbook of Roman Catholic Moral Terms*. Georgetown University Press.

Carlson, J. D. (2008). Is There a Christian Realist Theory of War and Peace? Reinhold Niebuhr and Just War Thought. *Journal of the Society of Christian Ethics, 28*(1), 133–161. Retrieved February 22, 2022, from http://www.jstor.org/stable/23562839

Chacha, B., et al. (2018). The Role of Church in State and Public Affairs during the Moi Era, 1978–2002. *Journal of Philosophy, Culture and Religion, 1*(1), 54–76.

Cox, F. D., & Ndung'u, J. (2014). *Social fault lines: Identity and insecurity in modernising Kenya: DRAFT*. University of Denver.

Deacon, G. (2015). Kenya: A Nation Born Again. *PentecoStudies, 14*(2), 219–240. Retrieved February 10, 2022, from https://ssrn.com/abstract=2646766

Doyle, M. W. (2011). *Liberal Peace: Selected Essays*. Routledge.

Galia, S. (1997). Church and State in Kenya, 1986–1992: The Churches' Involvement in the 'Game of Change'. *African Affairs, 96*(382), 25–52.

Gichuhi, G. (2022, August 8). No, Kenya's Anglican Archbishop Didn't Say Church Had No Record of Presidential Candidate Odinga Being a Member. Retrieved January 25, 2023, from hhttps://africacheck.org/fact-checks/meta-programme-fact-checks/no-kenyas-anglican-archbishop-didn't-say-c

Gumo, S., et al. (2012). Religion and Politics in the Contemporary Kenya. *European Scientific Journal, 8*(18), 29–41.

Hix, S. (2004). Electoral Institutions and Legislative Behavior: Explaining Voting Defection in the European Parliament. Retrieved March 3, 2023, from https://www.jstor.org/stable/25054255

International Institute for Democracy and Electoral Assistance. (2017). *Elections, Electoral Systems and Party Systems, A Resource Guide. Stockholm: International Idea*. Elections, Electoral Systems and Party Systems: A Resource Guide (idea.int). Retrieved March 3, 2023, from https://www.idea.int/

International Peace Institute (IPI). (2011). Elections in Africa: Challenges and Opportunities. Retrieved January 25, 2023, from www.ipinst.org

Jakobsen, J., Jakobsen,T. G., & Ekevold, E. R. (2016). Democratic Peace and the Norms of the Public: A Multilevel Analysis of the Relationship between Regime Type and Citizens' Bellicosity, 1981–2008. *Review of International Studies, 42*(5), 968–91. Retrieved January 25, 2023, from https://www.jstor.org/stable/26618698

Joseph, O. (2021, November 29). Independence in Electoral Management. Retrieved March 3, 2023, from https://doi.org/10.31752/idea.2021.103

Kalekye, M. (2022, July 24). Uhuru Succession: David Mwaure Waihiga, a Man of Many Hats. Retrieved September 24, 2022, from https://www.kbc.co.ke/uhuru-succession-david-mwaure-waihiga-a-man-of-many-hats/

Kamaara, E., & Omare, S. (2013). *Ethnicity and Political Violence in Kenya and the Role of the Church in Kalengyo E.* Our Burning Issues. A Pan African Conference. All African Conference of Churches.

Kant, I. (1775). Perpetual Peace: A Philosophical Sketch. Retrieved January 14, 2022, from http://fs2.american.edu/dfagel/www/Class%20Readings/Kant/Immanuel%20Kant,%20_Perpetual%20Peace_.pdf

Kapinde, S. A. (2018). The Church and Constitutional Reforms in Kenya, 1992–2002: A Retrospective-Historical Analysis. *European Scientific Journal, 14*(5). https://doi.org/10.19044/esj.2018.v14n5p216

Kenya National Bureau of Statistics (KNBS). (2019). *National Population Census Report.* Retrieved February 12, 2022, from https://www.knbs.or.ke/2019-kenya-population-and-housing-census-reports/

Khaduli, B. (2022, July 12). Elect Leaders of Integrity—Ole Sapit. Retrieved January 25, 2023, from https://www.kenyanews.go.ke/elect-leaders-of-integrity-ole-sapit/

Kilonzo, S. (2009). Ethnic Minorities Wedged Up in Post-Election Violence in Kenya: A Lesson for African Governments. *Critical Arts, 23*(2), 245–251. Retrieved March 4, 2022, from https://doi.org/10.1080/02560040903047342

Kioko, D., et al. (2016). The Church State Relationship in Kenya after the Second Liberation Struggle. *Journal of Educational Policy and Entrepreneurial Research, 3*(1), 44–59.

López, R. (2000). *Electoral Management Bodies as Institutions of Governance.* UNDP: Bureau for Development Policy.

Mary, A. (2022, July 29). Raila Clarifies His Controversial Christianity Remarks, Says He Is a Practicing Anglican. Retrieved January 25, 2023, from https://www.k24tv.co.ke/news/raila-clarifies-his-controversial-christianity-remarks-says-he-is-a-practicing-anglican-73243/

Mati, J. M. (2012). Social Movements and Socio-Political Change in Africa: The Ufungamano Initiative and Kenyan Constitutional Reform Struggles (1999–2005). *Voluntas: International Journal of Voluntary and Non-profit Organizations, 23*(1), Civil Society in Africa, pp. 63–84. Retrieved January 20, 2023, from https://www.jstor.org/stable/41427513

Maupeu, H. (2005). Religion and the Elections. In H. Maupeu, K. Musambayi, & W. Mitullah (Eds.), *The Moi Succession Elections 2002.* Trans Africa Press.

Moya, C. (2020, March). The Importance of Electoral Design in Economic Development Retrieved January 18, 2022, from https://www.globaldevblog/

Moywaywa, C. K. (2018). Management of Religious Conflicts in Kenya: Challenges and Opportunities. *International Journal of Education and Research, 6*(1), 129–142.

Muia, J. (2022, July). Raila Clarifies on 'Christianity Discriminatory' Remarks, Says He Was Misunderstood. Retrieved March 4, 2023, from https://www.citizen.

digital/news/raila-clarifies-on-christianity-discriminatoryremarks-says-he-was-misunderstood-n303129

Mujuzi, J. D. (2011). Separating the Church from State: The Kenyan High Court's Decision in "Jesse Kamau and 25 Others v Attorney General" (Judgment of 24 May 2010). *Journal of African Law*, 55(2), 314–319. http://www.jstor.org/stable/41709866

Ndunda, E. (2019, July). No Campaigns in Churches, Bishops Now Tell Aspirants. Retrieved January 25, 2023, from https://www.standardmedia.co.ke/coast/article/2001421511/no-campaigns-in-churches-bishops-now-tell-aspirant

Nyamasege, W. (2022, June 20). Karua: Quoting Bible verses Doesn't Make You a Christian. Retrieved January 25, 2023, from https://www.pd.co.ke/news/karua-bible-verses-christian-133458/

Otieno, R., & Mathew, N. (2022, July). Raila Pledges to Protect Religious Rights if Elected. Retrieved March 4, 2023, from https://www.pd.co.ke/august-9/raila-pledges-to-protect-religious-rights-if-elected-140449/

Paine, T. (1986). *Common Sense* (I. Kramnick, Ed.). Penguin Classics.

Pazienza, T. A. (2014). *Challenging the Democratic Peace Theory—The Role of US-China Relationship*. Graduate Theses and Dissertations. Retrieved January 25, 2023, from https://scholarcommons.usf.edu/etd/5098

PSC. (2021). Religion and Peace. Retrieved December 11, 2022, from https://issafrica.org/pscreport

Rop, J. (2022, July 29). Accept Election Results, Ole Sapit Urges Politicians. Retrieved January 25, 2023, from https://www.kenyanews.go.ke/accept-election-results-ole-sapit-urges-politicians/

Rosato, S. (2003). The Flawed Logic of Democratic Peace Theory. *American Political Science Review*, 97(4), 585–602. https://doi.org/10.1017/S0003055403000893

Sabar-Friedman, G. (1997). Church and State in Kenya, 1986–1992: The Churches' Involvement in the 'Game of Change'. *African Affairs*, 96(382), 25–52 (28 pages). Retrieved February 28, 2023, from https://www.jstor.org/stable/723749

Throup, D. (2015). Politics, religious engagement, and extremism in Kenya. In Cooke, J. G. & R. Downie (Eds.), *Religious Authority and the State in Africa* (pp. 29–48). Washington, DC: Centre for Strategic Studies. Retrieved from: https://csis-prod.s3.amazonaws.com/s3fs-public/legacy_files/files/publication/151028_Cooke_ReligiousAuthorityStateAfric_Web.pdf

Tomz, M. R., & Weeks, J. L. P. (2013). Public Opinion and the Democratic Peace. *The American Political Science Review*, 107(4), 849–865. http://www.jstor.org/stable/43654037

UN. (2013). Eliminating Corruption is Crucial to Sustainable Development. Retrieved March 3, 2023, from https://www.unodc.org/unodc/en/press/releases/2015/November/eliminating-corruption-is-crucial-to-sustainable-development.html

UNDP. (2010). *Participation UNDP Contribution to Strengthening Local Governance*. A.K. Office Supplies, Ltd..

Wandede, N. (2022, June). Jesus Winner Ministry Bishop Predicts Kenya Kwanza Will Win August Polls: 'Siwadangayi'. Retrieved March 6, 2023, from https://www.tuko.co.ke/politics/458963-jesus-winner-ministry-bishop-predicts-kenya-kwanza-will-win-august-polls-siwadangayi/

Willis, J. (2007). What Has Kibaki Got Up His Sleeve? Advertising the Kenyan Presidential Candidates in 2007. *Journal of Eastern African Studies*, 2(2), 264–271.

CHAPTER 28

# Religion, Conflict Transformation, Peacebuilding, and Development in Ghana: The Role of the National Peace Council

*Edmond Akwasi Agyeman*

INTRODUCTION

Ghana has a long tradition of religious tolerance, inter-religious dialogue, and harmonious multi-faith coexistence in spite of the wide diversity of its religious and ethnic composition (Owusu-Ansah & Akyeampong, 2019; Iheduru, 2020). The major religions in Ghana include myriad Christian religious denominations, competing traditions of Islamic groups, traditional African religion, various groupings of Asian religions, and several elements of syncretic religious groups (Ghana Statistical Service, 2021).

Alongside the religious diversity are the various ethnicities and ethnic identities that constitute Ghana. In most cases, religious divisions are drawn along ethnic lines. Southern Ghana, which is largely Christian, is dominated by people of the Akan ethnic group, the Guans, the Ewe, and the Ga-Adamgbe, as well as several other minority ethnic groups such as the ancient Koulango/Nkoran and the Nafana. In this part of the country, Muslims are largely considered settlers. In the urban areas, Muslims live in enclaves commonly known as the *zongo* where development generally lags and social problems are more rampant (Prempeh, 2022). Islam is dominant in the northern half of the country. The major ethnic groups such as Mole-Dagbani and Gonja are largely

E. A. Agyeman (✉)
Department of Interdisciplinary Studies, Akenten Appiah-Menka University of Skills Training and Entrepreneurial Development (AAMUSTED), Kumasi, Ghana

Muslim and have integrated Islamic traditions into their culture, education systems, and traditional political institutions (Wilks, 1963). However, the Dagaare, which is one of the major ethnic groups in North Western Ghana, is largely Christian. These various ethnicities and their various religious identities make competing claims for recognition, political representation, and an equal share of national development projects. Moreover, political divisions and the increasing polarisation of the Ghanaian politics are taking place largely along ethnic lines (Alidu, 2022; Osei-Tutu, 2021).

In the case of Ghana, the ability to manage such diversities has played a key role in the political stability, peace, and steady economic development that the nation has experienced in the past decades. However, stability and equilibrium have not been achieved without effort. It is this effort that I intend to unpack in this chapter. First, following Amartya Sen, I conceptualise development in post-colonial Africa as freedom in the first section of this chapter. I then look at the geography of conflict within the Ghanaian society, followed by the role of religion in the development of Ghana's peace architecture, with a focus on the National Peace Council (NPC). The NPC's operating procedures are detailed, outlining with examples how the NPC was able to mediate critical conflict situations in order to prevent escalation and maintain the nation-state's equilibrium during key moments in the country's recent history. I focus on cases that were widely reported in the dailies and electronic media. This is then followed by analysis and a conclusion. The chapter draws primarily on secondary data, the NPC reports, and newspaper reports.

## Development as Freedom

The development economist and Nobel Prize winner Amartya Sen has advanced the thesis that development is "a process of advancing the real freedoms that people enjoy". He argues that "[d]evelopment requires the removal of major sources of unfreedom: poverty as well as tyranny, poor economic opportunities as well as systematic deprivation, neglect of public facilities, as well as intolerance or overactivity of repressive states" (Sen, 1999, p. 3). For Sen, unleashing the free agency of people through capacitation is very essential in the development discourse. His vision of development is connected with capability building, and for him, development should concern itself with building "our capability to lead the kind of lives we have reason to value" (Sen, 1999, p. 285). Sen's way of viewing development whereby human freedom is taken as the precondition aligns best with UN Sustainable Development Goal (SDG) 16 which aims to promote an inclusive society and access to justice for all. It is against this background that peacebuilding is essential for promoting development in Africa.

Post-colonial societies in Africa have experienced violence of various kinds and degrees, which has created insecurities, harmed the environment, displaced people, caused involuntary migrations, and robbed people of their livelihoods (Setrana et al., 2017; Mbembe, 1992). This violence, which is often the perpetuation of colonial violence, has robbed African peoples and citizens of their humanity, freedom, and long-expected development (Mbembe, 1992). In fact, in parts of Africa where armed conflict is widespread, economic development and social progress have eluded the population.[1]

Within West Africa, violent conflicts have stagnated socio-economic development in many parts of the sub-region. In parts of Nigeria, Niger, Burkina Faso, and Mali, these conflicts have forced people to abandon their homes to seek refuge elsewhere. The high degree of refugee movement in West Africa is attributed to the rampant conflicts and insecurity that the sub-region has experienced in recent decades. This has stagnated development projects in many places.

In light of this, peaceful means of conflict resolution and peacebuilding initiatives are crucial for unleashing the full development potential of African populations. The absence of internal peacebuilding mechanisms has exposed the vulnerability of many African nations, who in times of conflict have to depend on external, often military, sources for arbitration. This situation has contributed to undermining the independence of many African states and denigrated these states into the abyss of poverty, thereby worsening their conditions rather than ameliorating the lives of people. For example, in the ongoing political crisis in Mali and Burkina Faso, the military governments that have taken the helm of affairs in both countries have accused France, which has stationed peacekeepers in their territory, of being the cause of the protracted armed conflict and insecurity that the countries are experiencing. Therefore, while countries are bound to experience some forms of conflict at some points of their history, their capacity to build internal structures for the maintenance of peace is essential for their socio-economic progress.

## Conflicts in Ghana

Since the 1980s, development initiatives within West Africa have been greatly marred by conflicts of all kinds. Many West African countries, including Sierra Leone, Liberia, Mali, Nigeria, Ivory Coast, and Guinea, have experienced conflicts of various degrees in recent years. At the time of writing, the security situation in the West African sub-region was threatened by the activities of Islamic insurgencies that had taken hold of Burkina Faso, Mali, Niger, and Northern Nigeria. These groups had also committed terrorist acts in Cote D'Ivoire and Togo. As a result, the entire sub-region was on high security alert.

Even though Ghana is generally considered an "oasis of peace" within West Africa, it shares the "same mix of structural variables that have plunged other African countries into violent and often protracted conflicts" (Iheduru, 2020, p. 66). This vulnerability is exemplified in the various degrees of violent

---

[1] For example, the Horn of Africa region, as well as the Sahel where there is a high degree of conflict and insecurity has experienced high poverty levels as compared to other places in Africa that have enjoyed an extended period of peace.

communal conflicts that the country has experienced in the post-independence period, some of which have attracted national and international attention (Kendie et al., 2014; Anumiel, 2017). The key difference between Ghana and the other West African states, however, is its capacity to deploy inbuilt local mechanisms to manage and resolve the conflicts internally without resorting to external help and thus preventing the conflicts from escalating (Iheduru, 2020). Yet, though the conflicts have not blown into full-scale civil strife, the threat of war is a reality due to the obstinate and recurrent nature of some of the conflicts, with national politics becoming increasingly implicated (Tonah, 2012). Thus, communal violence, though isolated in nature, poses a serious threat to Ghana's young democracy and national cohesion.

## *Causes of Conflicts in Ghana*

Most of the conflicts are ethno-political in nature and are caused by electoral disputes, chieftaincy and succession disputes, disputes over lands and natural resources, ethnic disputes, religious disputes, and several other forms of socio-cultural disputes (Issifu, 2015; Kendie et al., 2014; Draman et al., 2009). Some of the conflicts are also caused by disputes over the names of places and mineral resources, as well as historical factors (Lund, 2013; Shale, 2017). In more recent times, political vigilantism and disputes between farmers and Fulani herdsmen have been the frequent sources of conflicts in some parts of the country (Setrana & Owusu-Kyei, 2020; Owusu-Kyei & Berckmoes, 2021).

Since the beginning of the post-independence era, politics has contributed to the polarisation of the Ghanaian society. This situation is a contributory factor to all sorts of conflicts in the country. Ghana has essentially run a two-party system since returning to democratic rule in 1992, with the National Democratic Congress (NDC) and the New Patriotic Party (NPP) alternating power. The rivalry between these two political parties has raised the stakes in the country's politics and become the source of several other conflicts, including chieftaincy, religious, and ethnic conflicts in the country (Draman et al., 2009).

More often than not, these communal conflicts expose the inefficiencies of the state apparatus in conflict resolution, while the politicisation of the conflicts has led them to acquire the "character of pattern entrenching conflict" (Lund, 2013, p. 589). Whereas all parts of the country have experienced conflicts of some sort, most of the violent conflicts in Ghana are disproportionally concentrated in the northern half of the country.

## TYPES OF CONFLICTS

Communal conflicts in Ghana are classified as inter-ethnic, intra-ethnic, inter-religious, intra-religious, and political (Kendie et al., 2014; Mahama & Longi, 2013). In recent years, there has been an increasing spate of farmer-herder conflicts, especially due to the activities of transhumance Fulani herdsmen in farming communities in central and southern Ghana (Kuusaana and Bukari, 2015; Tonah, 2006).

## *Inter-ethnic Conflicts*

Inter-ethnic conflicts are usually between two ethnic groups disputing over land, boundaries, mineral resources, and political authority (Nonterah, 2016; Dennis & David, 2019). The most notorious and recurrent ones are concentrated in northern Ghana. They include the Bawku conflict between Kusasi and Mamprusi people in the Upper West region; the Bimbila conflict between the Konkomba and Dagomba in the Northern Region; and the century-old violent land dispute between the Alavanyo and Nkonya people in the Oti region (Kendie et al., 2014; Penu & Essaw, 2019).

The Bawku conflict, which has raged to date between the Kusasi people and the Mamprusi people since the 1930s, has become a serious threat to national peace and stability due to Bawku's geographical proximity to Burkina Faso, where Islamic insurgents have rendered the country ungovernable in recent years. In 2022, the clashes in the Bawku area resulted in the assassination of several individuals. The longstanding conflict is the result of disputes over lands and chieftaincy rights between the previously acephalous Kusasi and the more politically institutionalised Mamprusi, who had ruled the place in pre-colonial times. Another example of recurring intra-ethnic conflict in the northern half of the country is the conflict between acephalous Konkomba and ruling Dagomba people in the Bimbila area of the Northern Region. In both cases, the remote cause is the British colonial strategy of indirect rule, which required "giving power to chiefly groups to control the non-chiefly ones without recourse to the traditional jurisprudence" (Mahama & Longi, 2013, p. 122). During the period of colonial rule, the British colonial administration vested power in groups that had developed centralised political institutions over autochthonous populations that did not have such institutions. However, these acephalous groups, such as the Konkomba and Kusasi, vested authority in the earth priest, known locally as *tindana*, who wielded unrivalled power and control over the lands, despite the lack of centralised political systems. During the time of Nkrumah's rule, his resentment for chiefly authority led him to enact a series of policies to undermine chiefs. The protracted chieftaincy and inter-ethnic conflicts have been blamed on this and subsequent governments' attempts to transfer chiefly powers from previously recognised groups to autochthonous acephalous populations without recourse to previously laid down political structures and customs.

Furthermore, attempts by settler groups to seize control of lands that autochthonous populations had exclusive rights to and invest such powers in their *tindana* have resulted in clashes between groups that had previously lived and interacted peacefully. Therefore, in most situations, these conflicts are traceable to colonial administration and post-colonial governments' interference in local politics and customs (Lund, 2013).

## Intra-ethnic Conflicts

Intra-ethnic chieftaincy conflicts are pervasive in Ghana. Succession disputes are prevalent and recurrent in the Ga traditional areas in Accra, Winneba, and several other places in the south. The 2002 Dagbon succession crisis is considered one major intra-ethnic conflict which threatened the peace and stability of the nation. This is due to the fact that the Dagbon constitutes the second-largest ethnic group in Ghana after the Akan. In this case too, political interference in a succession dispute between the families of the two sons of *Yaa Naa*, the king of Dagbon, from the Abudu and Andani gates led to the crisis (Tonah, 2012). During the rule of Ya Naa Yakubu I (1829–1849), a succession arrangement based on a gate system (rotational system) was introduced, which specified that upon the death of the King his three sons would rule in turn. This practice later metamorphosed into two rotational gates: the Abudu gate and the Andani gate. The crisis began in 1974, when upon the death of king, Yaa Naa Mohammudu Abudu IV from the Abudu gate was enskinned. Those at the Andani gate protested, claiming it was not the turn of the Abudus. The government of the ruling National Redemption Council (NRC), led by Col. I. K. Acheampong, set up a Commission of Inquiry to look into the matter. Upon the commission's recommendation, the king was removed and Yaa Naa Yakubu Andani IV from the Andani gate was enskinned in replacement; and later, in 1988, Yaa Naa Mohammudu Abudu IV died and was buried without receiving the fitting burial he deserved as a Dagbon king. This did not go down well with the Abudus who waited till 2002, when they believed they had the political leverage with the coming to power of the New Patriotic Party (NPP). Therefore, on 27 March 2002, a faction of the Abudu gate broke into the Gbewaa Palace in Yendi, the seat of Yaa Naa Yakubu Andani IV, set the place ablaze, and killed everyone on sight, including the king, his elders, and his family. In addition, several houses were set ablaze and property was destroyed (Mahama & Longi, 2013). Later, there were reprisal clashes in distant communities where there were factions of Abudus and Andanis. This crisis threatened the stability of Ghana's democracy, as there were accusations of political complacency by the ruling government. It was not until 2018 that the problem was solved, a new Yaa Naa was enskinned, and peace finally returned to Dagbon.

## Inter-religious Conflicts

Incidences of inter-religious conflicts are very rare in Ghana due to a strong culture of tolerance and inter-religious dialogue between the mainstream Christian churches, traditional African religion, and Islam (Owusu-Ansah & Akyeampong, 2019; Nonterah, 2016). Most of the violent religious conflicts that Ghana has experienced in recent times have been intra-religious, especially among different confessions of Muslims (Iheduru, 2020; Nonterah, 2016; Mahama & Longi, 2013). Contestations over doctrinal difference, foreign influence, and competition for recognition and dominance have led to bloody conflicts among Muslim groups in Ghana (Iheduru, 2020).

Despite this reality, clashes have occurred between traditionally established authorities and some Charismatic and Pentecostal churches that have attempted to defy traditional customs considered pagan and fetishistic by theses churches, particularly during festivals. In the Greater Accra region, these incidents are very frequent. Often, the clashes happen between traditional authorities enforcing their ancestral traditions, customs, and religio-cultural values and Christian groups defying such customs, which they consider fetishes. One common cause of such conflicts is the ban on drumming and noise-making which precede the celebration of traditional festivals in several chiefdoms in Ghana. Since the 1990s, there have been violent clashes between community task forces enforcing bans on drumming and Christian groups, particularly Pentecostal and Charismatic churches that attempt to defy such orders (Atiemo, 2014). In the Ga traditional area of Accra, these clashes have become an annual ritual. Ga youth led by their chief priest with the backing of the Ga Traditional Council have year in and year out patrolled the Ghana traditional area to enforce the ban during the celebration of the Homowo Festival, and non-compliant churches have been attacked, their musical instruments have been seized, leading to violent clashes between church members and the task force, the burning of churches, and gun shots, with church members sustaining injuries in several cases.[2]

What is worrying about these incidents is that they keep repeating themselves each year. Also, both the traditional authorities and the churches have accused the state of complacency and failing to address their rights. Whereas the Christian groups argue that the Constitution of Ghana grants them freedom to worship, the traditional authorities also appeal to the constitution, arguing that it recognises the full force of customary law. In fact, Article 21 (1) of Ghana's 1992 Constitution states that "[a]ll persons shall have the right to freedom to practice any religion and to manifest such practice", while Article 26 (1) specifies that "[e]very person is entitled to enjoy, practice, profess, maintain and promote any culture, language, tradition or religion subject to the provisions of this constitution" (Republic of Ghana, 1992). Based on this, the Christian groups maintain that they are not bound to respect customary laws being enforced by traditional authorities as they are grounded in traditional African religious values which they consider heathen.

Interestingly, the 1992 Constitution also recognises the full force of customary law as one of the laws of the state. Article 11 (1) states: "The laws of Ghana shall comprise: (a) this Constitution; (b) enactments made by or under

---

[2] In May 2001, Rev. Annor Yeboah, the general secretary of the Christ Apostolic Church, reported to have pulled a gun when his church was attacked by Ga youth enforcing the ban on drumming for non-compliance. Before the incident, Rev. Annor Yeboah was reported to have organised a press conference inviting all Christian churches to take up arms to defend rights (Cf. Atiemo, 2014).

the authority of the Parliament established by this Constitution; (c) any orders, rules and regulations made by any person or authority under a power conferred by this Constitution; (d) the existing law; and (e) the common law". Article 11 (2) lists customary law as part of the common law and paragraph (3) of the same article specifies: "For the purposes of this article", customary law "means the rules of law, which by custom are applicable to particular communities in Ghana" (Republic of Ghana, 1992). Based on this provision, the traditional authorities have also claimed the right to enforce their customs on anybody, institution, or organisation that is found within their territory. In addition, they claim they are the owners and custodians of the land, and they have the right to banish from their community anyone who defies their customs. These arguments further expose the fragility of post-colonial African states that have been superimposed on pre-existing ethnic states, which Davidson (1992) has described as the curse of the nation-state in Africa.

## Conflict Resolution in Ghana

The state has struggled to resolve the conflicts despite its power and the existence of bodies of arbitration such as the courts. In some cases, the state has strategically avoided enforcing the full force of the law and its powers in resolving some of the conflicts in order to avoid escalation. Instead, the state has tacitly relied on non-state institutions to mediate and resolve the conflicts through dialogue. These are the areas where religious institutions have played a key role in Ghana, being both the cause and the arbiter of conflicts. Nordås (2014) has observed that despite Ghana and Cote d'Ivoire sharing a similar religious and ethnic demography, the former has not experienced civil war as compared to the latter because of its policy of inclusion and non-repression of any group, be it religious or ethnic. Thus, the neutrality of the state has played a key role in conflict resolution and peacebuilding.

The state uses three main strategies to resolve communal conflicts. These include military intervention, which involves the imposition of curfews in affected areas; the use of the courts, especially to bring perpetrators to book; and reliance on the soft power of religious leaders and eminent chiefs, which has resulted in the establishment of the National Peace Council (Atiemo, 2014; Kendie et al., 2014).

## The National Peace Council

The National Peace Council (NPC) is a statutory body mandated to work with other state and non-state agencies to spearhead the country's peacebuilding effort through conflict resolution and prevention. The NPC is described as the lynchpin of Ghana's infrastructure for peace (Draman et al., 2009). According to Kotia and Aubyn (2013, p. 4) the concept of peace infrastructure was first introduced by Lederach[3] and it signifies "a functional network that spans across the divisions and levels of society, which ensures optimum collaboration between the main stakeholders in the resolution of conflicts with minimal external contribution".

The establishment of the NPC in Ghana can be considered an important strategy by the state to foster national development in accordance with UN Sustainable Development Goal 16. This is premised on the recognition that Ghana's economic development is dependent on its ability to ensure that there is peace and stability as well as social inclusion and freedom.

Ghana is not unique as far as establishment of national peace infrastructures is concerned. However, with regard to the development, nature, structure, and functions of Ghana's peace council, the country's experience is unique. This is because religious organisations have played a central role in the establishment and sustenance of peacebuilding infrastructure in Ghana (Kotia & Aubyn, 2013).

## THE CATHOLIC CHURCH AND THE ORIGINS OF THE NPC

The origins of the NPC are traced to the activities of Archbishop Philip Naameh, the Metropolitan Archbishop of the Catholic Diocese of Tamale and former bishop of the Diocese of Damango. In a bid to prevent the various land, chieftaincy, and communal conflicts in Northern Ghana from escalating, the Bishop, upon his appointment as Bishop of the newly created Damango Diocese in 1995, decided to dedicate his initial apostolate to erecting the necessary structures and processes for peacebuilding in the Northern Region (Awinador-Kanyirige, 2014; Issifu, 2014). With the backing of the Ghana Catholic Bishops Conference, he started the Northern Ghana Peace Project in 1995, which later developed into the Center for Conflict Transformation and Peace Studies (CECOTAPS). With the support of the Catholic Relief Service, Civil Society Organisations (CSO), and other development agencies, the CECOTAPS was able to prevent violent conflicts and broker peace in the region through mediation.

According to Issifu (2014), the role of the Catholic Church and other non-state agencies in conflict prevention and resolution became crucial in Northern Ghana because the state law enforcement agencies, such as the National Security Council (NSC), "were not only financially challenged but also lacked the requisite mediation capacity, particularly the skills in dealing with chieftaincy-related conflicts and land disputes, a characteristic of the northern region's violent conflicts" (Issifu, 2014, p. 3). In addition, traditional authority had in many instances lost the trust of the people to be able to resolve conflicts through traditional and customary processes because, in many cases, it was accused of being compromised (Issifu, 2014; Lund, 2013). In the mid-1990s, there was a successful collaborative action between CECOTAPS, the Catholic

---

[3] See John Paul Lederach, *Building peace: sustainable reconciliation in divided societies*, (United States Institute of Peace, Washington, 1997), pp. 112–127.

Relief Service, and other CSOs such as Action Aid, World Vision, the Christian Council, and Oxfam International to resolve the conflict between the Konkomba and Nanumba people in Northern Ghana. This initiative prevented this conflict from becoming protracted and therefore attracted the attention and admiration of the state.

In the course of the period, the non-state peacebuilding agencies kept multiplying, and the coordinating effort was lacking due to the absence of institutions similar to CECOTAPS in the other regions, whose peacebuilding coordinating initiative has been crucial in resolving conflicts. Therefore, in order to ensure that the actions of the various stakeholders and agencies involved in peacebuilding are coordinated, the state established its first regional security council in Northern Ghana and later replicated the same in other regions of the country. Following that, a proposal was floated through the Ministry of the Interior in 2005 for the establishment of a national infrastructure for peace to coordinate the activities of the various agencies involved in the country's peace building. This request received cabinet approval, and in 2006, the government of President John Agyekum Kufuor established the National Peace Council. However, the National Peace Council Act (Act 818) giving parliamentary approval to the statutory body was passed in 2011.

## Religious Organisations and NPC Membership Board

The NPC board consists of 13 eminent persons nominated by religious organisations, traditional authorities, and the president of the Republic of Ghana for a 4-year term and eligible for reappointment. According to Draman et al. (2009, p. 16), the National Architecture for Peace document specifies that the eminent persons constituting the NPC board "shall be distinguished Ghanaians, without blemish and well trained in facilitating dialogues, negotiation, mediation, conciliation and reconciliation, tolerance, trust and confidence building, etc." In lieu of this, most of the members of the NPC board are drawn from the leadership of religious organisations.

The breakdown of the membership is as follows: Christian bodies (one member each from the Catholic Bishops Conference, Christian Council, Ghana Pentecostal Council, and National Council for Christians and Charismatic Churches); Muslim bodies (one member each from the Ahmadiyya Muslim Mission, Al-Sunnah Muslims, and Tijaaniya Muslim group); and Traditional bodies (one member each from practitioners of African Traditional Religions and the National House of Chiefs). In addition, the president of the Republic of Ghana has two nominees, one of whom should be a woman. There are also two other people who are nominated by identifiable groups. Therefore, 9 out of the 13 members are from religious bodies and traditional authorities.

Some scholars have questioned the dominance of religious leaders in Ghana's Peace Council. They claim that this has disadvantaged other groups such as trade unions, youth, women, people with disabilities, academia, as well as business and industry partners. It is further argued that the dominance of religious groups has created a situation where male presence on the board is dominant as compared to female presence. This is because leadership in Christian and Islamic religious groups is predominantly in the hands of men, and for that matter, these groups have a greater tendency to send male nominees at all times (Kotia & Aubyn, 2013).

Regardless of the criticisms, the board's composition demonstrates the state's trust in the ability of religious organisations to mediate peace in the country due to the privileged position they occupy in such matters. This privilege is largely drawn from the soft power and influence these religious leaders have, their supposed neutrality, and the experience they have acquired over the years in mediating and resolving all forms of conflicts in the country.

Members of the board elect a chairperson from their own ranks. However, since its establishment, three distinguished religious leaders have chaired the board. The first chair was His Eminence Peter Kwadwo Appiah Turkson, a cardinal of the Roman Catholic Church and member of the Roman Curia. He was succeeded by Rev. Prof. Emmanuel Asante, an academic and Bishop of the Methodist Church. The chair at the time of writing was Rev. Dr Ernest Adu-Gyamfi, who was a member of the previous board. Rev. Adu-Gyamfi was a minister of the Baptist Church and former Chairman of the Christian Council of Ghana. He also served as the Executive President of the Ghana Baptist Convention and as the Chancellor of Ghana Baptist University College. This calibre of leaders appears to satisfy the NTC's requirements for eminent personalities meant to lead conflict resolution and peace mediation in Ghana.

## The NPC and Peacebuilding in Ghana

Over the years, the Council has executed its duties creditably. Since 2012, they have played an indispensable role in electoral dispute resolution and helped to prevent possible post-electoral conflicts that have conflated and pushed some West African nations into civil wars. They have also played a key role in preventing possible inter-religious and inter-ethnic conflicts and have played an active role in resolving chieftaincy, religious, and ethnic disputes between groups in Ghana (Shale, 2017).

The NPC does not work in isolation but within a network of security and peacebuilding organisations such as national security agencies, religious bodies, civil society organisations, traditional authorities, and international bodies like the UNDP. The UNDP and the government of Ghana are the main sources of financial support for its activities. In addition, the UNDP has provided a lot of technical assistance to the peacebuilding body over the period of its existence. The NPC reports to the Parliament of the Republic of Ghana through the Ministry of Interior. The NPC also has sub-national structures, which include district and regional peace councils. In the subsequent sections I focus on the peacebuilding strategy of the NPC, with religious leaders at the helm.

## MODUS OPERANDI OF THE NPC

The operational strategy of the NPC has two goals, namely, conflict prevention and conflict resolution through non-violent means. To prevent conflicts, the NPC undertakes early warning initiatives and embarks on public education and training through workshops at national and grassroots levels. In times of conflict, it engages the relevant leaders and undertakes broader stakeholder consultations. The media is strongly involved, and in some cases, it undertakes regular press briefings to inform the public about progress in resolving the issue while warning the affected individuals to stay calm. During mediation processes, relevant state and non-state institutions, agencies, and stakeholders are involved, yet the NPC ensures that its position as a neutral and trusted arbiter is not undermined. To elucidate this, let us look at two cases of recent interest: the Wesley Girls' Senior High School incident and NPC intervention in the period after the 2016 and 2020 general elections.

### Case 1: Wesley Girls' School Banning of Fasting for Muslims Students in Ramadan

During the month of Ramadan in 2021, it was reported in the media that Wesley Girls' Senior High School, one of Ghana's foremost boarding secondary schools for girls, had barred all Muslim students from fasting. The school argued that it did so on health grounds. Yet, the decision infuriated Islamic parents and several Muslim groups in the country, who interpreted it as an attack on their religion. Some past students of the school also waded into the matter. While some, such as one former Muslim student, accused the school of not allowing Muslim students to observe *salat* (the Muslim's five daily prayers), others argued that the fasting ban is based on health, academics, and school routine, and that the rule applies to all religious confessions in the school, not just Muslims.

A directive from the Ghana Education Service (GES) instructing the school to allow the students to fast was rejected by the school authority, which had the backing of the Methodist Church, the Association of Former Students, and several others. At the 2021 Eid festival, the president of the Republic of Ghana urged all stakeholders not to reduce the schools to religious and ideological battlegrounds. He urged tolerance and promised the Muslim population that in the matter of the Wesley Girls' School, Christian and Muslim leaders would be engaged to find "a satisfactory solution".[4]

The Office of the Chief Imam also waded into the conflict, with the spokesperson Sheikh Aremeyaw Shaibu encouraging school authorities to show sympathy and tolerance in order to "make the children in all our schools all-time

---

[4] https://www.myjoyonline.com/dont-reduce-our-schools-to-ideological-and-religious-fighting-grounds-akufo-addo-tells-religious-leaders/

defenders and promoters of interface, harmony, and dialogue".[5] As the matter dragged on, the Islamic Caucus of Parliament also visited the school. They urged Muslim youth to remain calm, warning that what dialogue cannot resolve, neither can war resolve it.

In a similar incident, that year, Achimota College had denied admission to a Rastafarian student who had refused to cut his dreadlocked hairstyle. After a long tussle between the student's parents and the school authority, and a lot of negative reportage and debate in the print media and on the airwaves about the school's position, the school's authority refused to take the student in until the matter was settled in court. Therefore, the Wesley Girls' incident which happened in sequence only added to already high tempers from the affected religious groups. But this time, it pitted Methodist educational values against Islamic religious values, and the incident posed a serious threat to national peace, coexistence, and the religious tolerance that the nation is known for.

During the impasse, the NPC played a key role in ensuring that the affected persons used dialogue to resolve the conflict. The NPC provided the platform for the leadership of all affected parties including the school authorities, leadership of the Methodist Church, and leadership of various Islamic organisations, the Office of the National Chief Imam and Ghana Education service, to dialogue. In addition, the Council briefed the National Chief Imam about progress of events and requested him to add his voice to efforts aimed at calming down the Muslim population. The Council also organised regular press briefings to keep the population abreast with the proceedings and encouraged everybody to remain calm as they resolved the issue. By this strategy, the NPC was able to show the way and enforced the use of dialogue as the best preference for resolving the impasse. In fact, the Muslim Caucus of Parliament that visited the school declared after the visit that "what cannot be addressed through dialogue cannot be addressed through war either". Eventually, the conflict was not resolved in the Muslim's favour but peace prevailed over violence in resolving the conflict.

### Case 2: The Presidential and Parliament Elections of 2012, 2016, and 2020

In Ghana's fourth republic which started in 1992, there has been a peaceful transfer of power between the two major political parties in 2000, 2008, and 2016. However, the 2016 general elections marked the only period in Ghana's political history where there was a transfer of power from an incumbent president to an opposition leader. Usually, incumbent presidents are able to secure a second term whenever they win power.

Going into the three elections, the stakes were high between the two major political parties: the NDC and NPP. The political scenes were characterised by

[5] Cf. https://www.myjoyonline.com/schools-must-change-their-modus-operandi-in-dealing-with-muslim-students-sheikh-aremeyaw/

acts of violence including hate speech, physical and verbal assaults, ethnic profiling, and many others which threatened the peace of the country (Kotia & Aubyn, 2013; Shale, 2017). Therefore, in order to sustain the peace and stability of the nation, the NPC embarked on a number of interventions before, during, and after the elections. Prior to the elections, the NPC organised several stakeholder engagements with political parties, media houses, and key stakeholders across the country. During these forums participants received education and training on the dangers of political vigilantism and electoral violence and strategies to manage such occurrences. In addition, electoral-related conflict hotspots at the grassroots were identified where stakeholder consultations and training programmes were intensified.

The three elections under consideration have all ended in an impasse. The 2012 election, for example, ended in a dramatic fashion which took the intervention of the NPC in averting a possible national strife. As things turned out, there was a delay by the Electoral Commission in announcing the results of the polls which ended in the evening of 7 December. This prompted the General Secretary of the NPP to organise a press conference to declare the leader of the opposition party as the winner on 8 December. The atmosphere was charged until the intervention by the NPC Chairperson Most Rev. Prof. Emmanuel Asante. As the most trusted person in that crucial moment, he issued a press statement at mid-night of 9 December to call for calm. He described the NPP General Secretary's declaration as "premature" and unconstitutional and admonished the media houses not to provide their platforms for such acts that can jeopardise the peace of the nation (Kotia & Aubyn, 2013). This was then followed by a long electoral petition at the Supreme Court where the opposition finally conceded defeat.

In the 2016 election, President John Dramani Mahama's hope of winning a second term suffered a setback. However, as has become characteristic of Ghana's election, there were complaints of violence and a late drama when the incumbent refused to concede defeat. Here too, it took the intervention of the NPC Chairman to ensure there was peace through back door consultations to encourage the president to concede, which he did. The 2020 elections also ended in the Supreme Court with the opposition party claiming it had won the elections. Therefore, as Shale (2017) has observed, the role of the NPC has become crucial in Ghana's electoral politics and for sustaining peace in Ghana. Therefore, the NPC has become a key player in ensuring that the tenets of SDG 16 are fully realised in Ghanaian politics in order to achieve peaceful change and development.

## The Role of Religion and African Traditions

Essentially, the NPC is reliant on two philosophical/cultural traditions: the African/Ghanaian notion of the elder or family head who is supposed to settle all family feuds and conflicts without resorting to the court system, and the Catholic tradition of inter-religious dialogue. In both instances, mediation is the principal means of conflict resolution. Over the centuries, the Catholics have acquired a lot of experience in preventing and resolving conflicts between different religious faiths and building a conducive environment for multi-faith coexistence. This experience has been utilised by the Church in Africa where greater religious competition, diversity, and inter-religious conflicts are rampant (Basedau & Schaefer-Kehnert, 2019; Nonterah, 2016).

During the NPC's mediation process, a platform is created for each of the feuding parties to express their grievances. Parties are expected to use dialogue as a means of reconciliation and be ready to make compromises in the interest of peace. They are expected to listen to their opponents and understand their situation too. The feuding parties are expected to give maximum respect and trust to the elder mediating the conflict who is to be seen as repository of continuity between present, past, and future generations. He or she mediates on behalf of the ancestors to ensure fairness, justice, peace, and progress of the family.

Thus, the goal of the NPC mediation is not to find winners or losers, as is the case with the law courts. Both parties are expected to soften their positions and in some instances let things go in the interest of unity and peace. The interests of the whole society are set above those of individuals or specific interest groups. This is contrary to human rights principles, which focus on the rights of the individual. It goes in line with African ideals of rights, which not only focus on the individual but also on the group as captured in the African Charter for Human and Peoples Rights. Therefore, in their peacebuilding process, the NPC's style is to invite all aggrieved parties to the negotiating table. Leaders of feuding parties are discouraged from making pronouncements that will escalate the conflict. The elders mediating the conflict are not to judge in the Western sense. They are to listen and encourage the parties to make compromises where necessary in the interest of conviviality and peace.

Therefore, as we saw in both the Wesley Girls and electoral dispute cases, leaders of feuding parties were reminded to also control their utterances and bear in mind their role as elders and their responsibility to ensure peace. Here, the NPC's strategy of appealing to the Ghanaian ideal of the elder (*abusuapanyin*), who is supposed to be the source of peace and unity, is evident. In Ghanaian traditions, the elder is supposed to hold the group together and not to disintegrate it. Therefore, the responsibility for holding a position as elder is great. Unlike other African countries, Ghanaians have been able to resolve conflicts and maintain peace not only by enforcing social inclusions as Nordås (2014) has argued but also by remaining closer to African traditions, cultures, and means of conflict resolution. This is in line with the argument by Owusu-Ansah and Akyeampong (2019) that the Ghanaian culture is tolerant. It appears, therefore, that the more Africans remain faithful to their culture, the more they are likely to be in a position to resolve their conflicts through peaceful means.

However, one thing that is central in Ghana's peacebuilding process is the role of the state. What is clear from Ghana's case is the state's ability to utilise the virtues of Ghanaian culture and religion, the two possible causes of conflicts, for the purpose of peacebuilding. Indeed, the state has played a significant role in giving support to religious leaders to forge peace on its behalf in critical situations. This has helped the state to often avoid the situation where feuding parties will accuse it of bias and thus leading to escalation. This action is also a sign of recognition by the state of the power that religious groups and traditional authority have, which the state authority needs in order to run the affairs of the state satisfactorily.

## The Soft Power of Religious Leaders and Eminent Chiefs

Religious leaders in Ghana, like many other African nations, wield a lot of power due to the large followings they command. In fact, Ghanaians are deeply religious, and for that reason, religion has a lot of control over their social and economic lives (Agyeman & Carsamer, 2018; Atiemo, 2014; Meyers, 1998; Tweneboah & Agyeman, 2021). The 2021 Population and Housing Census of Ghana shows that out of a total population of approximately 31 million people, about 22 million, representing 71.3%, are Christians, of which 10% are Catholics, 17.4% are Protestants, 31.6% belong to the Pentecostal/Charismatic Churches, and 12.3% belong to other Christian denominations. Muslims make up 19.9% of the population, Traditionalists constitute 3.2%, and 4.5% belong to other religions, while the remaining 1.1% claim no religious affiliation. Moreover, of the over 6 million Muslims in Ghana, more than half (51.5%) live in the five regions of Northern Ghana, with the highest concentration in the Northern Region where over 80% of the population are Muslims (Ghana Statistical Service, 2021). In the light of the above, religious bodies and organisations such as the Catholic Bishops Conference of Ghana, the Christian Council of Ghana, Ghana Pentecostal and Charismatic Council, and the Islamic Council of Ghana and the Office of the Chief Imam constitute an important force in the country.

Further, it is argued that the traditional political institutions encapsulated in the chieftaincy institution, which were suppressed during colonial times, have remained resilient and relevant in modern politics. Boafo-Arthur (2003, p. 134) has argued that "the chief is a political and social power center (if even in a circumscribed sense) in the area he rules and ipso facto a microcosm of authority who at times rivals the central government in legitimacy, recognition and loyalty by subjects". Consequently, the chiefs also wield soft power, which, in some situations, the central government and organisations cannot do without in the area of conflict resolution (Agyeman et al., 2020; Iheduru, 2020). An important case is the Dagbon Chieftaincy Crisis, where the government of John Agyekum set up a committee of four eminent chiefs led by the King of the Asante Kingdom, Otumfuo Osei Tutu II (Issifu, 2015). Even after the first committee of eminent chiefs failed to resolve the conflict in 2003, it was still another committee of three eminent chiefs set up by the president of Ghana, Nana Addo Dankwa Akufo-Addo, in 2018 that eventually resolved the crisis the same year. The three eminent chiefs were Otumfuo Osei Tutu II, King of Asante; Nayiri Na Bohagu Mahami Sheriga, Paramount Chief of Mamprugu; and Yagbonwura Tumtumba Boresa, King of the Gonja kingdom.

In view of their influence and the important role that traditional authorities and religious leaders play in the affairs of the country, the chieftaincy and religious institutions are represented in government by the Ministry of Chieftaincy and Religious Affairs. The National House of Chiefs and the religious organisations already mentioned are often called upon when the situation demands brokering peace in the nation. In view of this, the chieftaincy and religious institutions play a dominant role in Ghana's National Peace Council, which developed out of the peacebuilding initiative of the Catholic Church in Northern Ghana. Therefore, we see clearly here that the strategy of inclusion and responsibility sharing which the state has adopted has played an essential rule in building Ghana's peace infrastructure.

## Conclusion

In this chapter, I have analysed the genesis and activities of the National Peace Council (NPC), whose architect is the Roman Catholic Church. The NPC is a national infrastructure for peace and conflict resolution in Ghana. It brings together actors from Christian organisations, Muslim groups, African Traditional Religion, the Chieftaincy institution, NGOs, and state institutions. Actions by religious groups and organisations to build and maintain peace in Ghana are embodied in the activities of the NPC. The chapter assessed the NPC's strategy of leveraging the resources of religious institutions and other bodies for conflict prevention and mediation during crisis periods in order to promote freedom, peace, stability, and development in Ghana. The role of the NPC in conflict prevention and resolution was analysed by focusing on two case studies: electoral politics and an incidence of inter-religious conflict in one of Ghana's foremost senior high schools.

Following Sen, development was conceptualised and analysed as freedom. It was argued that the peace that Ghana has enjoyed over the years has played a key role in its recent economic progress. Without peace, there could be no freedom, and without freedom it is impossible for people to pursue their development aspirations. The chapter has shown that the platform created through the NPC to enable key actors from various religious faiths, ethnic groups, and NGOs to work together, with the backing of the state, is an important recognition by the state of the soft power which the religious bodies wield, which should be further exploited to foster national development. However, given the important role that the NPC play in promoting Ghana's peace and development, effort should be made to achieve gender balance in the composition of the NPC board.

## References

Agyeman, E. A., & Carsamer, E. (2018). Pentecostalism and the Spirit of Innovation and Entrepreneurship in Ghana: the Case of the Maame Sarah Prayer Camp at Goka in the Jaman North District of Ghana. *Journal of Contemporary African Studies*, 36(3), 303–218.

Agyeman, E. A., Tamanja, M. J. T., & Bingab, B. B. B. (2020). University-Community Relations in Ghana: Traditional Authority as a Stakeholder. *Africa Development*, 45(4), 1–22.

Alidu, S. (2022). Balancing the Ticket: Ethnicity and Regional Politics in Ghana's Fourth Republic (1992–2016). In E. Chitando & E. Kamara (Eds.), *Religion, Identity & Values: Rethinking Africa's Development*. Palgrave.

Anumiel, B. (2017). *Assessing the Effectiveness of Conflict Resolution Mechanisms Used by National Peace Council in Resolving the Alavanyo/Nkonya and Hohoe Conflicts in Ghana*. MA Thesis submitted to the Institute for Development Studies of the Faculty of Social Sciences, College of Humanities and Legal Studies, University of Cape Coast.

Atiemo, A. (2014). Fighting for the Rights of the Gods: Tradition, Religious Human Rights, and the Modern Nation-State in Africa – A Ghanaian Case Study. In C. N. Omenyo & E. B. Anum (Eds.), *Trajectories of Religion in Africa* (pp. 233–247).

Awinador-Kanyirige, W. A. (2014). *Ghana's National Peace Council*. Policy Brief: Global Centre for the Responsibility to Project. Ralph Bunch Institute for International Studies. http://www.globalr2p.org

Basedau, M., & Schaefer-Kehnert, J. (2019). Religious Discrimination and Religious Armed Conflict in Sub-Saharan Africa: An Obvious Relationship? *Religion, State & Society*, 47(1), 30–47.

Boafo-Arthur, K. (2003). Chieftaincy in Ghana: Challenges and prospects in the 21st Century. *African-Asian Studies*, 2, 125–153.

Davidson, B. (1992). *The Blackman's Burden: Africa and the Curse of the Nation-State*. James Currey.

Dennis, A. K. P., & David, W. E. (2019). Geographies of Peace and Violence During Conflict: The Case of The Alavanyo-Nkonya Boundary Dispute in Ghana. *Political Geography*, 71, 91–102. https://doi.org/10.1017/S0022278X03004373

Draman, R., Adama, J. M., & Peter W. (2009). *The Conflict Prevention and Resolution Portfolio of UNDP Ghana: Evaluation Report. Collaborative Learning and Resolution Projects*, Cambridge, MA.

Ghana Statistical Service. (2021). *Ghana 2021 Population and Housing Census. Volume 3C. Background Characteristics*. Ghana Statistical Service.

Iheduru, O. C. (2020). The National Chief Imam of Ghana: Religious Leadership and Peacebuilding in an Emerging Democracy. *Journal of Transdisciplinary Peace Praxis*, 2(2), 66–98.

Issifu, A. K. (2014). *The Evolution of Ghana's National Peace Council: Successes and Failures*. University of Cape Coast.

Issifu, A. K. (2015). An Analysis of Conflicts in Ghana: The Case of Dagbon Chieftaincy. *The Journal of Pan African Studies*, 8(6), 28–44.

Kendie, B. S., Boakye, K. A., Mensah, E., Osei-Kuffour, P., & Addo, K. T. (2014). *Mapping Conflict Zones in Ghana: An Exploratory Study of Northern Ghana (Background Study for the National Peace Council of Ghana)*. National Peace Council.

Kotia, E.W. & Aubyn, F.K., (2013). *Building National Infrastructures for Peace in Africa: Understanding the Role of the National Peace Council in Ghana*. Kennesaw State University. 1-20. htps://works.bepress.com/emmanuel_kotia/10/.

Kuusaana, E. D., & Bukari, K. N. (2015). Land conflicts between smallholders and Fulani pastoralists in Ghana: Evidence from the Asante Akim North District (AAND). *Journal of Rural Studies, 42*, 52–62.

Lund, C. (2013). 'Bawku is Still Volatile': Ethno-Political Conflict and State Recognition in Northern Ghana. *Journal of Modern African Studies, 41*(4), 587–610.

Mahama, E. S., & Longi, F. T. (2013). Conflicts in Northern Ghana: Search for Solutions, Stakeholders and Way Forward. *Ghana Journal of Development Studies, 10*(1&2), 112–129. https://doi.org/10.4314/gjds.v10i1&2.7

Mbembe, A. (1992). Provisional Notes on the Postcolony. *Africa, 62*(1), 3–37.

Meyers, B. (1998). 'Make A Complete Break with The Past.' Memory and Post-Colonial Modernity in Ghanaian Pentecostalist Discourse. *Journal of Religion in Africa, 28*, 316–349. https://www.jstor.org/stable/1581573

Nonterah, N. K. (2016). The Challenges of Interfaith Relations in Ghana, A Case Study of Its Implications for Peace-Building in Northern Ghana. In V. Latinovic, G. Mannion, & P. C. Phan (Eds.), *Pathways for Interreligious Dialogue in the Twenty-First Century* (pp. 197–198). Palgrave Macmillan. https://doi.org/10.1057/9781137507303-15

Nordås, R. (2014). Religious Demography and Conflict: Lessons from Côte D'Ivoire and Ghana. *International Area Studies Review, 17*(2), 146–166. https://doi.org/10.1177/2233865914529118

Osei-Tutu, A. R. (2021). *A Study of Manifestations of Political Polarization as Structural Violence, A Case Study of Ghana's 2020 Election*. Master's Thesis in Peace and Conflict Transformation SVF-3901, Faculty of Humanities, Social Sciences, And Education Centre for Peace Studies. The Arctic University of Norway.

Owusu-Ansah, D., & Akyeampong, E. (2019). Religious Pluralism and Interfaith Coexistence: Ecumenicalism in the Context of Traditional Modes of Tolerance. *Legon Journal of the Humanities, 30*(2), 1–18. https://doi.org/10.4314/ljh.v30i2.1

Owusu-Kyei, J. R. K., & Berckmoes, L. H. (2021). Political Vigilante Groups in Ghana: Violence Or Democracy? *Africa Spectrum., 55*(3), 321–338. https://doi.org/10.1177/0002039720970957

Penu, D. A. K., & Essaw, D. W. (2019). Geographies of Peace and Violence During Conflict: The Case of the Alavanyo-Nkonya Boundary Dispute in Ghana. *Political Geography, 71*, 91–102. https://doi.org/10.1016/j.polgeo.2019.03.003

Prempeh, C. (2022). *Nima-Maamobi in Ghana's Postcolonial Development: Migration, Islam and Social Transformation*. Langaa Publishers.

Republic of Ghana. (1992). *The 1992 Republican Constitution of Ghana*. Ghana.

Sen, A. (1999). *Development as Freedom* (1st ed.). Knopf.

Setrana, B. M., Agyeman, E. A., & Kyei, M. R. K. O. (2017). Internal Displacement and Cross Boarder Movement of Nigerian Nationals. In *IOM, Compilation of Research Papers Presented at the Conference on National Migration Policy Thematic Areas* (pp. 39–55). IOM.

Setrana, M. B., & Owusu-Kyei, J. R. K. (2020). Migration, Farmer-Herder Conflict and The Challenges of Peacebuilding in the Agogo Traditional Area. Ghana. *Ghana Journal of Geography, 13*(2), 340–357. https://doi.org/10.4314/gjg.v13i2.13

Shale, V. (2017). *Evaluation of the Ghana National Peace Council's Performance During the 2016 Election Cycle*. Commonwealth Secretariat.

Tonah, S. (2006). Migration and Farmer-Herder Conflicts in Ghana's Volta Basin. *Canadian Journal of African Studies, 40*(1), 152–178.

Tonah, S. (2012). The Politicisation of a Chieftaincy Conflict: The Case of Dagbon, Northern Ghana. *Nordic Journal of African Studies, 21*(1), 1–20. https://doi.org/10.53228/njas.v21i1.177

Tweneboah, S., & Agyeman, E. A. (2021). Traditional African Religion and Trans-Saharan Migration from Ghana: Analysis of the Role of Nkoranza Deities in the Youth Migration to Libya. *African Diaspora, 13*(1-2), 204–229. https://doi.org/10.1163/18725465-bja10016

Wilks, I. (1963). The Growth of Islamic Learning in Ghana. *Journal of the Historical Society of Nigeria, 2*(4), 409–417.

CHAPTER 29

# The All Africa Conference of Churches (AACC): Youth, Peacebuilding, and Development in Africa

*Brian Muyunga*

## INTRODUCTION

The All Africa Conference of Churches (AACC) is a significant faith-based organization fostering peacebuilding and development in Africa. Representing more than 140 million Christians in 42 African countries, AACC is the largest ecumenical organization on the continent. This chapter discusses the role of youths in AACC's peacebuilding and development work in Africa. The chapter is organized into six sections and the second section discusses the relationship between peacebuilding and development. The third section highlights the relationship between religion, peacebuilding, and development. These two sections provide the foundation upon which the fourth section which discusses the AACC's involvement in peacebuilding and development in Africa is built. The discussion in the fourth section demonstrates how the AACC's past General Assemblies sustained the organization's commitment to peacebuilding and development. The General Assemblies define the agenda of the AACC and this provides the framework under which the youth in the AACC member churches contribute to the organization's peacebuilding and development work. The fifth section of the chapter discusses the role of youth in the AACC's peacebuilding and development work, focusing on the period between 2013, the year when the AACC marked its 50th anniversary, and 2023, the year when

B. Muyunga (✉)
All Africa Conference of Churches (AACC), Nairobi, Kenya

© The Author(s), under exclusive license to Springer Nature Switzerland AG 2023
S. M. Kilonzo et al. (eds.), *The Palgrave Handbook of Religion, Peacebuilding, and Development in Africa*,
https://doi.org/10.1007/978-3-031-36829-5_29

the organization marks its 60th anniversary. The chapter's interest in this specific period of time is influenced by the fact that it was also during this period that the first ten-year plan of the AU Agenda 2063 "The Africa We Want" was being implemented. Sustainable Development Goal (SDG) 16 is strongly reflected in the seven aspirations of Agenda 2063, now considered the blueprint of Africa's development since 2013.

### *Methodological Note*

To develop this chapter, a desk review of published literature was done, on AACC's past General Assemblies, published AACC General Assembly reports, and unpublished reports about AACC's peacebuilding and development projects and activities carried out between 2013 and 2023.

## PEACEBUILDING AND DEVELOPMENT

Peacebuilding is a complex and multifaceted endeavor. According to Boutros-Boutros Ghali's *Agenda for Peace*, peacebuilding was conceptualized as the penultimate phase in a series of intervention moments including conflict prevention, peacemaking, and peacekeeping (Khadiagala, 2021). In this chapter, peacebuilding refers to the process of addressing the root causes of conflicts and building social cohesion through the development of institutions, attitudes, and practices that promote cooperation, understanding, and reconciliation among different individuals and groups (Uzondu, 2020). Peacebuilding is part and parcel of the sustainable development Agenda 2030, particularly the Sustainable Development Goal (SDG) 16 which calls for states to promote peaceful and inclusive societies for sustainable development, provide access to justice for all and build effective, accountable and accountable and inclusive institutions at all levels.

Development could be defined as a process of economic and social transformation that is based on complex cultural and environmental interactions. According to Seers (1979), the purpose of development in society is to reduce poverty, inequality, and unemployment. For Sen (2000), development involves reducing deprivation or broadening choice. Deprivation represents a multidimensional view of poverty that includes hunger, illiteracy, illness, and poor health, powerlessness, voicelessness, insecurity, humiliation, and a lack of access to basic infrastructure (Okechukwu, 2012). The relationship between peacebuilding and development is complex and multifaceted, but it is very clear that without peace, development cannot take place, yet there can never be peace without the conditions of development (Dehman, 1991).

Conflicts pose a direct threat to development. Subsequently, peacebuilding becomes a goal of all individuals and communities pursuing any aspect of development (OHCHR, 2016). Peacebuilding and development in Africa are, therefore, interdependent and closely linked processes aimed at addressing the root causes of conflict and building sustainable peace. The challenges of peacebuilding and develop ment in Africa are significant, given the continent's history of conflict, poverty, and underdevelopment. Africa is a continent that has seen its fair share of conflict, violence, and poverty over the years. In recent decades, however, there has been much progress in terms of peacebuilding and development. Peacebuilding efforts in Africa involve a wide range of actors, including governments, civil society organizations, international institutions, and faith-based organizations.

## Religion, Peacebuilding, and Development in Africa

It is difficult to have a definite definition of religion because it has many facets, many of which do not appear to be religious by themselves. For example, religion involves gathering in groups. It involves communal eating. It involves theoretical discourse about the nature of the universe and so forth (Okechukwu, 2012). In Kirkpatrick's view, religion is a psychological attachment, a powerful emotional relationship to things. It is a system of social coherence commonly understood as a group of beliefs or attitudes concerning an object, person, unseen or imaginary being, or system of thought considered to be supernatural, sacred, divine, or highest truth, and the moral codes, practices, values, institutions, and rituals associated with such belief or system of thought. It is a framework within which specific theological doctrines and practices are advocated and pursued, usually among a community of like-minded believers (Kirkpatrick, 2005). In this chapter, religion is defined as the belief in the existence of a supernatural being and how this influences the worldview and practices of an individual or a group of people (Uzondu, 2020).

The relationship between religion, peacebuilding, and sustainable development is complex and interdependent. Religion can both be a source of conflict and be a force for peacebuilding, depending on how it is practiced and interpreted (Haynes, 2007). At the same time, sustainable development cannot be achieved without addressing the root causes of conflict and promoting peace. Religion can contribute to conflict in various ways. For example, religious differences can fuel sectarian violence, as seen in many parts of the world, and religious beliefs can be manipulated by politicians and extremist groups to justify violence and oppression (Haynes, 2005). However, religion can also play a critical role in promoting peacebuilding. Many faith traditions emphasize the values of compassion, forgiveness, and non-violence. Religious leaders can leverage their moral authority to encourage dialogue and reconciliation between conflicting parties (Lado, 2021). Moreover, religious organizations can provide essential services and promote community development, which can help reduce poverty and inequality both of which are major drivers of conflict. Additionally, many faith traditions emphasize the importance of social and environmental responsibility, which can be harnessed to promote sustainable development practices.

Religious organizations can also play a crucial role in delivering education, healthcare, and other basic services to marginalized communities, thereby promoting the human development necessary for sustainable development. In many African contexts, religion remains a significant factor in social life and greatly shapes people's attitudes, worldviews, and behaviors (Rakodi, 2012). Perceived to pervade all aspects of life, religion is thus interpreted as being integral to the African understanding of the world and the place of humanity in it (Ver Beek, 2000). In this vein, religion in Africa is often construed as part of the African holistic worldview. Many argue that in most African contexts, religion is widely recognized as a fundamental social, political, and development force (Bompani, 2015, p. 100) and thus considered to be an integral aspect of public culture (Englund, 2011, p. 8; Sakupapa, 2019, p. 109). Religion remains a significant component of social life on the African continent and recent projections suggest that this importance will continue for the next four decades. The role of religion in peacebuilding in Africa has to be located within the wider framework of the role of religion in the public space in Africa more generally. Religion has always been perceived, by a majority of Africans, "as having the power to radically change social life and history." It is, therefore, no surprise that people in Africa turn to religion for resources to prevent conflicts or to restore peace. (Lado, 2021).

Given that this chapter focuses on the AACC, this discussion will narrow down from religion in its entirety to Christianity. Christianity, simply put, is the Abrahamic faith tradition that focuses on the figure of Jesus Christ. As a religious tradition, Christianity grounds itself in the biblical scriptures and Christians often read and refer to the Scripture for guidance.

Peacebuilding is a concept that can be traced to the Bible, which contains numerous passages emphasizing the importance of building and maintaining peaceful relationships. One of the most famous biblical references to peacebuilding comes from Jesus' Sermon on the Mount in Matthew 5:9, where he states, "Blessed are the peacemakers, for they shall be called sons of God." This passage suggests that those who actively work toward peace will inherit a divine blessing. In other parts of the Bible, there are various calls for reconciliation and forgiveness. For example, Paul's letter to the Ephesians (2:14-16) speaks of Christ reconciling Jews and Gentiles into one body by breaking down the walls between them in order to build unity. Colossians 3:12-15 advises believers to clothe themselves with compassion, kindness, humility, gentleness, and patience and to forgive each other as Christ forgave them, stating that love and peace should govern their relationships. Additionally, in the Old Testament, several prophecies speak of a time when humanity would be united in peace under the Messiah's rule. For example, Isaiah 2:4 reads, "He shall judge between the nations, and shall decide disputes for many peoples; and they shall beat their swords into plowshares, and their spears into pruning hooks; nation shall not lift up sword against nation, neither shall they learn war anymore."

These among other scriptures form the biblical basis from which African Christians derive their mandate to engage in peacebuilding. Furthermore, Christians believe that the Church is called to participate in God's holistic mission to the world. The Bible is rich with stories of God reaching out to mankind and freeing them from circumstances that limited their socioeconomic development. Among these include stories of Jesus feeding the hungry, healing the sick and lame, and recovering sight to the blind in the New Testament and the liberation of the Israelites from forced labor in Egypt in the Old Testament.

In the document "Called to Transformative Action, Ecumenical Diakonia," jointly produced by the World Council of Churches (WCC), the Lutheran World Federation, and ACT Alliance (2022), it is argued that the Church is called to serve in the world by participating in God's mission of healing and reconciliation and of lifting up signs of hope, announcing by word and deed God's reign, its justice, and peace. In responding to the call to serve the world, it is inevitable for the Church to respond to contextual challenges that limit people's well-being and hinder individual and communal development. The handbook emphasizes that the United Nations (UN) SDGs provide a public platform for the church's engagement in developmental matters and invite faith-based actors to contribute to their realization.

Since its founding in 1963, the AACC has been involved in Africa's development matters through its holistic approach to mission that seeks to foster the social transformation of the continent. Peacebuilding occupies a pivotal place in the developmental work of the AACC. Throughout the organization's 60 years of existence (up to the time of writing), peacebuilding has always been featured in the strategy as part of the work that the organization and its members must do as they participate in God's mission to the world.

## The AACC's Involvement in Peacebuilding and Development in Africa

The AACC is a Pan-African ecumenical movement deeply committed to peacebuilding as a way of advancing Africa's development. Its enduring commitment is reflected not only in the organization's vision statement, "Churches in Africa together for life, Justice and peace," but also in all its programmatic and governance work. The AACC's involvement in peacebuilding can be traced throughout the history of its missional work right from the time of its inauguration in 1963 (AACC, 1963). AACC's General Assemblies, the highest decision-making governing bodies of the conference, are major historical stages in the life and work of the AACC given their central role in determining the agenda and direction of the organization's work. Since the first General Assembly in 1963, peacebuilding and development have emerged as two closely related themes that have been featured in every assembly's business. This has sustained the AACC's commitment to peacebuilding and fostering development in Africa (Utuk, 2007). This section will discuss the AACC's involvement in peacebuilding and development by demonstrating how these two themes featured in the previous 11 General Assemblies and the steps taken in between to foster peace and sustainable development in Africa.

The first assembly of the AACC took place in 1963 in Kampala, Uganda. It happened at a time when nationalist movements were very active on the continent, working for the total liberation of African states from colonial dominance (Sakupapa, 2018). A number of countries had obtained their independence while others were still agitating for theirs. In South Africa, anti-apartheid movements were also calling for its abolition, and given all these realities, there was an obvious need for peacebuilders across the continent. During that inaugural assembly, it was stated through a public outcome statement on Church and nationalism that the task of the Church was: (1) to be a watchman in the midst of a nation, prophetically witnessing to the Divine demands for truth, justice, and peace, and against all forms of oppression, discrimination, injustice, and corruption; (2) to witness the reconciliation which is in Jesus Christ in the midst of those situations where political leaders, parties, nations, and power blocs are in conflict; and (3) to witness by her own life and example the love and peace which she commends to the nation. This threefold definition of the task was basically a call for the Church to exist as not only an agent of peace but also a key player in addressing all forces that limited the holistic development of individuals and communities in Africa (AACC, 1963).

The assembly condemned the indiscriminate use of violence for the achievement of any purpose, affirmed Christian participation in partisan politics, and encouraged Christians to engage in labor-intensive programs to generate economic activities. The assembly urged the Church to cater for the needs of the people in growing African cities but also ensure that rural areas grow and compete with urban centers through its action. These, together with the threefold task of the Church described above, became a cornerstone upon which the programmatic work of the conference would be built until the next assembly and beyond. In all this, the AACC saw its role as one of promoting unity and joint action among its members in a way that enables them to fulfill the three elements of their task described above. In between the first and second assemblies of the AACC, the organization made remarkable contributions to peacebuilding and development. These included capacity-building seminars for church leaders on developmental matters, responding to the plight of refugees in Africa and supporting the resettlement of some refugees, and intervening in the Sudanese Civil disputes (AACC, 1963).

Held in 1969 in Abidjan, Cote d'Ivoire, the second assembly of the AACC emphasized the need for the AACC to champion the development of African Christian theologies, which was a very important contribution to the peace and development work of the churches in Africa. The assembly also acknowledged the tensions between Christians and non-Christian religious groups on the continent and examined how Christians would relate with Muslims in a way that fosters peaceful coexistence between the two religious groups. The assembly recognized education as a developmental tool and emphasized the need for high-quality training programs for teachers to enable them to offer quality education services. The assembly called upon indigenous communities to fight ignorance—one of the factors that impede development and also appraised the use of mass media to ease and fasten communication (AACC, 1970).

The assembly was held at a time when a number of coup d'états had disrupted the political peace of a number of African states. Subsequently, there was a high level of instability across many independent African states. Amidst this reality, the assembly called upon churches to enhance their involvement in promoting stability and constitutional governments. Member churches were called upon to show concern for the oppressed and compel political parties to act to exist as vessels for freedom, justice, democracy, and peace. The assembly argued churches to act against divisions and conflicts that sprout from racism, tribalism, and other forces of division and have a fundamental concern for the well-being of all human beings (Utuk, 2007). In the years that followed the Abidjan assembly, the AACC worked in collaboration with several continental and international organizations to address the root causes and effects of conflicts in various African communities. Some of these organizations include the WCC, the Organization of African Union (OAU), the Christian Peace Conference (CPC), and the World Peace Council (WPC).

The third assembly was held in Lusaka, Zambia, 1974 and it engaged participants in deliberations on the causes of ethnical rivalry and conflicts that are widespread in Africa. The assembly also emphasized the need for the churches in Africa to prevent civil strife and also act against perennial poverty (AACC, 1975). During the fourth General assembly in Nairobi Kenya, on the theme "Following the Light of Jesus Christ, John 8:12", the Church was mandated to further its developmental work when it was urged to work for an ideal society where all people are actively involved in building their communities (AACC, 1982). The assembly challenged churches to give men and women equal opportunities to develop skills and effectively participate in the development of society. The assembly took a strong stand against prevailing gender disparities and the marginalization of people. Condemning the use of militarism by oppressive states to tighten their grasp on power and the excessive military budgets at the expense of food and medical care. The assembly also called for the demilitarization of governance across Africa. The same assembly, however, supported the use of counter-violent methods of seeking liberation that was influenced by a real desire for peace and human fulfillment such as those that were used by the nationalists fighting against apartheid in South Africa at that moment. The assembly mandated the conference to broaden its peacebuilding work and support theological institutions to develop peace studies. Theologically, the assembly emphasized the role of the Church in the development of the language of the prophetic and serving Church. This entailed an understanding of the mission of the Church as prophetic service in terms of the institution being involved and sensitive to the well-being of the society (Sakupapa, 2018).

Acknowledging that unequal distribution of resources was a major cause of conflicts in many African states, the fifth assembly held in Lome, Togo, in 1987, criticized national governments whose leaders exploited natural resources for their selfish interests and condemned their self-centeredness and arrogance. The assembly urged all churches to embark on sustainable socioeconomic development, promote equal sharing of resources, and work for the eradication of poverty. It also decried the unnecessary brutality and terrorism against southern Africans that characterized the apartheid system (AACC, 1988).

In the sixth assembly held in Harare, Zimbabwe, in 1992, the churches' pursuit for peaceful coexistence between Muslims and Christians was expanded and churches were encouraged to work for the replacement of religious acrimony with comity, hate with love, and intolerance with tolerance. This assembly also called for the protection of the integrity of creation and the total transformation of social relationships. The sixth General Assembly acknowledged that the consequences of climate change arising from the exploitation of natural resources, loss of vegetation cover, and biodiversity, among others, would escalate conflicts but also impede Africa's development. The assembly called upon member churches to care for the welfare of the earth and serve as good stewards to God's creation (Utuk, 2007).

At the AACC seventh General Assembly in Addis Ababa in 1997, the Church was portrayed as the "facilitator of social transformation" and several issues related to the political and socioeconomic state of Africa were discussed. Issues pertaining to Africa's debt burden received special attention in this assembly and AACC member churches and National Christian Councils (NCCs) were urged to commit themselves to "advocate for debt cancellation in accordance with the biblical jubilee principle" (AACC, 1997).

The eighth General Assembly held in Cameroon in 2003 declared that peace and justice formed the heart of development and appealed to member churches to foster good governance and democratic practices in Africa. The churches were implored to recommit themselves to the struggle for peace and justice as they worked to rebuild their communities. The assembly acknowledged the New Partnership for Africa's Development (NEPAD) as an appropriate framework for Africa's economic and sustainable development. The assembly called upon member churches to embrace and popularize NEPAD, get involved in its implementation, and enrich its spiritual and cultural vision. Following this assembly, the General Secretariat established a working relationship with the NEPAD secretariat to enhance the implementation of NEPAD in ways that promoted faith, order, dignity, peace, and justice. Additionally, the assembly called upon churches in Africa to establish and strengthen healing ministry programs so as to promote medication and trauma healing as a way of facilitating peacebuilding, reconciliation, and development. Churches were also challenged to empower young people such that they can actively participate in developing the continent (Sakupapa, 2020).

Before the ninth General Assembly, AACC extensively advocated for the overhaul and review of the EU's neoliberal external trade policy with respect to the European Union's Economic Partnership Agreements. Additionally, the AACC-NEPAD program published three books in 2006 on the African Peer Review Mechanism (APRM), one of which was on "Peace, Diakonia, and

Development." In 2007, the AACC set up a liaison office at the African Union (AU) in Addis Ababa, Ethiopia, in an attempt to strengthen its collaboration with the AU in peacebuilding and development. (AACC, 2007a, 2007b).

The ninth assembly held in Maputo in 2008 appraised women as agents of peace. It was recognized that where sexual and gender-based violence (SGBV) has been used as a weapon, women undergo intolerable levels of suffering and suffer immeasurable trauma. Nevertheless, they never lost their agency to break the walls of enmity created by wars and conflicts. The assembly stressed that women must be an integral part of all peace processes. To effect this, the churches were called upon to affirm the nurturing role played by women as a means of instilling and establishing a culture of peace, enhancing the capacity for women to be agents of reconciliation, and peace, and advocating for the implementation of international instruments that promote the role of women in peacebuilding and development. At this assembly, the AACC reflected on the churches' advocacy for economic justice and fair trade, and in its final message to member churches (known as the Maputo Covenant), the AACC noted that with the prevailing forces of globalization, Africa experienced a new form of oppression with crippling economic burden through unjust international relations, trade, and hopeless foreign debts. Churches were, therefore, encouraged to focus their peacebuilding initiatives on advocating for economic justice (AACC, 2012).

At its tenth General Assembly held in Kampala Uganda in 2013, the AACC continued on this trajectory of advocacy for economic justice as an essential aspect of peacebuilding and sustainable development but also extended this to include climate justice (AACC, 2015). The assembly encouraged the conference to adopt the AU development plan, namely, "Agenda 2063: The Africa We Want," and provide the African continent with the spiritual pulse needed to achieve the seven aspirations of this Agenda which would lead to AU's vision for an integrated, prosperous, and peaceful Africa (AACC, 2015).

The AACC's 11th General Assembly held in Kigali Rwanda, in 2018, challenged the conference to continue engaging with both global and continental development agendas in its approach to peacebuilding in Africa (AACC, 2018a). Following this assembly, the AACC developed a new strategy with four main programmatic pillars: theology, interfaith relations, and ecclesial leadership; gender, women, and youth; advocacy at the African Union; and peace, diakonia, and development. The latter of these programmatic pillars has sustained AACC's peacebuilding and developmental work since 2019 to date (AACC, 2019).

As shown above, all 11 former General Assemblies of the AACC had a special interest in peacebuilding as a central developmental process for Africa. Each assembly left the conference with a specific mandate to fulfill as far as peacebuilding and development are concerned. This ensured that the programmatic work of the conference is structured in such a way that these two closely related themes are given key priority even in the allocation of the organization's resources.

## The Role of Youth in the AACC's Peacebuilding and Development Work

According to the AU Youth Charter, a youth is a person aged between 15 and 35 years (AU, 2006). Africa has the youngest population in the world over 70% of the continent's population is under the age of 30 years. This high number of young people is not only very vital in sustaining the work and life of churches in Africa but also in Africa's sustainable development agendas (UN, 2022). Since 1963, Youth has always been at the heart of AACC and a major stakeholder in the conference's work on peacebuilding and development (Utuk, 2007). In this discussion, the chapter demonstrates how the youth have contributed to AACC's work on peacebuilding and development in Africa during the 2013–2023. The 2013–2023 decade is also the first of implementing the African Union's 50-year development plan, the AU Agenda 2063 for the Africa we want, a developmental strategy that greatly informed AACC's programmatic work since 2013. This vision and seven aspirations of this Agenda strongly reflect the AU's commitment to the realization of SDG 16 and its desire for all developmental organizations on the continent to work toward achieving this goal. During this decade (2013–2023) there were two AACC General Assemblies and each of these demonstrated commendable interests in the role of young people in Africa's development. These were the 10th General Assembly held in Uganda in 2013 and the 11th General Assembly held in Rwanda in 2018.

Prior to the 10th Assembly of the AACC held in Uganda in 2013, the youth delegates from the member churches held a youth pre-assembly where they developed and issued a statement to the General Assembly for consideration in the formulation of the assembly resolutions. In this statement, the young people noted that they found inspiration in their Christian faith and God-given mandate to be good stewards of God's work. Out of this inspiration, the youth committed to being actively involved in all activities that would generate a better livelihood, uphold the values of the church and society, and free themselves from the dependency syndrome. To enable them to fulfill their commitment, the young people recommended that churches should work toward putting an end to the marginalization, manipulation, and exploitation of young people in Africa. To this end, the delegates called upon the churches to empower and create for them opportunities to actively participate in dialogues with governments, regional developmental bodies, and the AU, and to ensure that their voices are heard and interests prioritized. They expressed concern over the exploitation of natural resources and environmental degradation, observing that their future was threatened by the replenishing resources that God created for their survival. The young people also stressed the need for the member churches to foster transformative education across the continent, emphasizing that education is the most powerful tool that could be used to change the world (AACC, 2015). From this assembly, youth delegates were elected to serve on the AACC general committee. These youth members of the general committee represented the interests of the young people in the decision-making processes of the conference. The AACC established a scholarship program that enabled youth leaders nominated by member churches to pursue studies at various institutions of higher learning across the continent. The conference also encouraged member churches to manage their schools efficiently and effectively such that they become centers of transformation on the continent. Additionally, the annual theological institute that had begun during AACC's ninth General Assembly continued to build the capacity of lay and ordained young theologians to lead theological discussions on the contextual challenges and theological matters in their communities' countries. The majority of the beneficiaries of the theological institutes took up key leadership positions in their churches and influenced the development and implementation of their Church's mission agenda with an obvious commitment to peacebuilding and development (AACC, 2018a).

Toward the 11th General Assembly that would take place in Kigali in 2018, the young people took up advocacy against violent extremism. To accelerate their efforts, AACC began engaging youth leaders from member churches on the content of the UN Security Council Resolution 2250 on Youth, Peace, and Security and encouraged them to advocate for its implementation in their respective countries. In addition to combating violent extremism, the young people also arose against religious radicalization and engaged in various interfaith dialogues organized in collaboration with the Program for Christian and Muslim Relations in Africa. The young people in AACC member churches also initiated and engaged in various campaigns against the spread of HIV and AIDS, and HIV stigma and discrimination, and in the promotion of uptake of HIV testing and treatment services. Understanding that the HIV pandemic and its consequences persisted as a major threat to the development of many African communities, the AACC deepened its working relationship with the WCC Ecumenical HIV and AIDS initiatives and advocacy to strengthen the capacity of young people in confronting the HIV pandemic. A number of young people who benefited from this work have continued to promote holistic health and healing as central aspects of development and peacebuilding. Some of them have grown into leaders of national networks of people living with HIV and interfaith platforms supporting the contributions of people living with HIV to national development and in the elimination of the pandemic. The other area where the youth began making significant contributions to AACC's work on peacebuilding and development was in the promotion of gender justice. Through the directorate for Gender, Women, and Youth (as it was called then), youth occupied the AACC's spaces of advocacy for gender justice. In these spaces, they engaged in dialogues aimed at identifying and addressing the root causes of sexual and gender-based violence. Young people in some AACC member churches embraced the faith-based advocacy campaigns for gender justice supported by the AACC and popularized them in their local communities. Among these included the WCC Thursday's in Black campaign against rape and defilement. In such initiatives, the youth were also partly responding to the calls of the previous assemblies that recognized sexual and gender-based violence as a major threat to Africa's peace and development (AACC, 2018a).

Ahead of the 11th AACC General Assembly, the youth delegates still held a pre-assembly to agree on what to pursue while they participated in the assembly. In the communique that resulted from this pre-assembly, the youth urged church leaders to take seriously the need to promote the inclusion of young people in all decision-making processes and the need to mainstream youth concerns in efforts seeking for solutions to the persistent challenges confronting the African continent—of which poverty, conflicts, and insecurity were key. They expressed their commitment to working for an integrated, peaceful, and prosperous Africa and sought their leaders' support in lobbying for policies that protect the rights of the African child and safeguard young people from irregular migration and human trafficking. The young people called upon every member of their churches and the African governments to support and join in their campaign for peace in Africa. They stressed that the churches should never relax in advocating and working for peace and security but also emphasized the need to include young people in missions to states and regions experiencing instability, insecurity, and conflict as major agents of peace in Africa. Noting that the level of unemployment among young people was alarming and yet still escalating, the youth delegates urged the Church and African governments to encourage and provide resources for the youth to explore employment opportunities offered by the growth and expansion of technology and digitalization. They committed to intensifying their advocacy campaigns against gender-based violence, stigma, and discrimination against youth and children living with HIV, and disabilities, and to promote the rights of freedoms of children and all young people in Africa. In their commitments, the youths further noted that they would serve as examples of good stewardship over resources and the natural environment and to remain committed to championing the realization of the SDGs by 2030 as a step toward the achievement of the AU Agenda 2063 (AACC, 2018b).

The 11th General Assembly recognized the high rate at which the tendency of young people desiring to leave the African continent for other parts of the world in search of opportunities to study and work in addition to other reasons was growing. The assembly decried the persistence of armed conflicts and wars and corruption on the African continent whose consequences have made many African young people flee from their home communities, some through very dangerous routes such as the Mediterranean Sea and the Sahara Desert, to destinations where they think they would find opportunities to grow and develop but also live in peace. The assembly, thus, tasked churches to support and accompany the young people committed to transforming the continent into a peaceful and prosperous home that they would love to live in, such that their efforts can bear the desired fruit (AACC, 2018c).

Following this 11th assembly, the youth leaders in AACC member churches formed the All Africa Youth Network (AAYN) as an ecumenical youth leadership forum responsible for mobilizing and coordinating youth advocacy for peace and development in Africa, among other youth interests. Through the AANY, youth in AACC member churches began an advocacy campaign in favor of the "silencing the guns" project of the AU. This flagship project of the AU in Agenda 2063 has many positive implications for the realization of SDG 16. The young people engaged in the campaign by producing documentaries and through social media activism calling upon the AU heads of state and Intergovernmental Authority on Development (IGAD) to committee to the promise for all the guns to be silent in Africa by 2020. Despite their lobbying, however, 2020 came to an end before AU meeting this target, a new deadline 2030 was set as the deadline for the end of all armed conflicts on the African continent. Working with AACC's Eminent Person's Ecumenical Program for Peace in Africa (EPEPPA) and in close relationship with AU Liaison Office at the AU, the youth continue calling upon the AU heads of state to demilitarize political processes on the African continent and stop war and conflicts in Africa by 2030. The youth also always joined the EPEPPA members in observing elections in the different African states where AACC is invited as an election observer. Through the AAYN, the youth advocacy was not limited to only the silencing the guns initiatives but also other peace and developmental issues such as the debt crisis, tax injustices, oppressive financial systems, and gender justice (AACC, 2021). With the rampant rise in the rate of teenage pregnancies, increase in occurrence of SGBV, and persistent spread of HIV and AIDS among young people, the need to intensify the promotion of sexual and reproductive health and rights of the young people among AACC member churches was realized. Through the youth desk at AACC, young people began engaging in intergenerational dialogues equipping the youth with skills and knowledge to promote and protect sexual and reproductive heal and rights, as an element of holistic development in Africa.

As mandated by the 11th General Assembly, the AACC, in 2020, initiated a campaign on youth and pan-Africanism to inspire young African people and young people of African descent in the diaspora to love Africa and their continent and work for its holistic and sustainable development. This campaign runs on the theme: Africa; My Home, My Future, which is an acknowledgment that Africa is the only place that people of African descent can fully identify with as their home and it is in Africa they can build a stable future for their descendants. Under this campaign, youth mobilized one another to get actively involved in the democratic processes of their countries and in fostering creativity, innovation, and entrepreneurship to foster job creation on the continent. Furthermore, the young people began creating awareness about the dangers of irregular migration and human trafficking in their communities as they called upon churches and communities to ease access to legal paths through which people can migrate from one part of the African continent to another, but also in and out of Africa for trade and other developmental reasons. This youth work led to the All Africa Youth Congress that was held in 2022 in Accra, Ghana, as the official launch of AACC's campaign for youth and pan-Africanism on the theme—Africa; My Home, My Future. A thousand young people from 43 African countries and some from the diaspora physically participated in this event and committed to championing peacebuilding and development work in Africa through individual and communal initiatives. They asked the Africa Union to fasten the process of opening up the continent as a free trade area and also institute the African Passport that would allow Africans to travel across the continent without major limitations (AACC, 2022).

Since 2021, youth in the AACC member churches have intensified their campaign for ecological justice and creation care, responding to the climate change crisis. Through the Climate Young Ecumenical Summit (Climate-YES) Campaign, hosted at the AACC, the young people participate in the negotiation processes at the COP meetings, alongside the Africa Faith Actors Network for Climate Justice (AFAN-CJ). Besides their participation in the COP, the young people run local and national campaigns creating awareness about the climate change crisis and its potential to escalate conflicts over natural resources, land, water, and basic needs. They thus call for mitigation processes but also promote adaptation to the climate change challenges for peace to prevail.

## Conclusion

In summary, young people's contribution to the AACC's peacebuilding and development work described in this chapter can be categorized into two major roles: (1) informing and participating in decision-making processes of the conference, and (2) providing the needed human force for advocacy and activism on peacebuilding and developmental matters. The 12th General Assembly of the AACC scheduled for November 2023 will mark the end of the AACC's work on peacebuilding and development as mandated by the 11th assembly and also begin a new phase in the AACC programmatic work. Given that Africa is still a developing continent where peacebuilding is an ongoing process, it is very likely that the AACC's strategy for the period of time after the 12th General Assembly until the 13th General Assembly will still have a special focus on peacebuilding and development, but prioritizing the contributions of the African young people who now constitute over 70% of the African population.

## References

AACC. (1963). *Drumbeats from Kampala : report of the first assembly of the All Africa Conference of Churches, held at Kampala, April 20 to April 30, 1963*. London: Lutterworth Press.

AACC. (1970). *Engagement: The Second AACC Assembly, Abidjan 1969*. AACC.

AACC. (1975). *The Struggle Continues: Official Report, Third Assembly of the All Africa Conference of Churches, Lusaka, Zambia 12–24 May 1974*. AACC.

AACC. (1982). *Follow Me ... Feed My Lambs! Nairobi 1981: Official Report, Fourth Assembly All Africa Conference of Churches Nairobi, Kenya, 2–12 August 1981*. Alliance Printing.

AACC. (1988). *Lomé 87, You Shall Be My Witnesses: Official Report of the Fifth AACC General Assembly.* AACC.
AACC. (1997). *Seventh AACC Assembly Report: October 1997 Addis Ababa, Ethiopia.* AACC.
AACC. (2007a). *Report of the Study on African Ecumenical Engagement with the Consultation Process Towards a Joint EU-Africa Strategy.* AACC.
AACC. (2007b). *Economic Partnership Agreements (EPAs): Hopes, Fears and Challenges.* AACC.
AACC. (2012). *Africa Step Forth in Faith: The 9th AACC General Assembly Report.* AACC.
AACC. (2015). *God of Life, Lead Africa to Peace, Justice and Dignity: 10th General Assembly and Golden Jubilee Celebrations Report.* AACC.
AACC. (2018a). From Kampala to Kigali: Condensed Report, 2013–June 2018. http://assembly.aacc-ceta.org/index.php/downloads?download=26:all-africaconference-of-churches-general-secretariat-condensed-report-2013-june-2018
AACC. (2018b). Report of The Youth Pre-Assembly Held on 2nd July 2018. Unpublished Document.
AACC. (2018c). Respecting The Dignity And God's Image In Every Human Being (Genesis1:26–27), Report of the 11th General Assembly, Kigali, Rwanda, 01–07 July 2018. Nairobi: AACC.
AACC. (2021). *Annual Report, 2020.* AACC.
AACC. (2022). *Report About the All Africa Youth Congress Held in Ghana from October 31 to November 5, 2022.* AACC.
African Union. (2006). African Youth Charter. African Union: Addis Ababa. https://au.int/en/treaties/african-youth-charter
Bompani, B. (2015). Religion and Development in Sub-Saharan Africa: An Overview. In E. Tomalin (Ed.), *The Routledge Handbook of Religions and Global Development* (pp. 115–127). Routledge.
Dehman, M. E. (1991). Peace, Development, and Human Rights: Complementary Perspectives – Complementary Content. *The Canadian Journal of Peace and Conflict Studies, 23*(4), 49–56.
Englund, H. (2011). Introduction: Rethinking African Christianities: Beyond the Religion-politics Conundrum. In H. Englund (Ed.), *Christianity and Public Culture in Africa.* Ohio University Press.
Haynes, J. (2005). Religion in African Civil Wars. In M. Hildebrandt & M. Brocker (Eds.), *Unfriedliche Religionen?. Politik und Religion.* VS Verlag für Sozialwissenschaften. https://doi.org/10.1007/978-3-322-80796-0_14
Haynes, J. (2007). Religion and Development: *The Ambivalence of the Sacred.* In *Religion and Development.* Palgrave Macmillan. https://doi.org/10.1057/9780230589568_3
Khadiagala, G. M. (2021). The African Union in Peacebuilding in Africa. In T. McNamee & M. Muyangwa (Eds.), *The state of Peacebuilding in Africa: Lessons Learned for Policymakers and Practitioners* (pp. 197–214). Palgrave Macmillan.
Kirkpatrick, L. A. (2005). *Attachment, evolution, and the psychology of religion.* The Guilford Press.
Lado, L. T. (2021). Religion and Peacebuilding in Sub-Saharan Africa. In T. McNamee & M. Muyangwa (Eds.), *The State of Peacebuilding in Africa: Lessons Learned for Policymakers and Practitioners* (pp. 197–214). London.

Office of the United Nations High Commissioner for Human Rights. (2016). *2016 information Note: The Right to Development and Peace.* OHCHR.
Okechukwu, O. A. (2012). Religion and National Development in Nigeria. *American Academic & Scholarly Research Journal, 4*(4), 1–6. Washington, DC.
Rakodi, C. (2012). A Framework for Analyzing the Links Between Religion and Development. *Development in Practice, 22*(5-6), 634–650. https://doi.org/10.1080/09614524.2012.685873
Sakupapa, T. C. (2018). The Ecumenical Movement and Development: The Case of the All Africa Conference of Churches (AACC), 1963–2000 (Part 1). *Studia Historiae Ecclesiasticae*: Pretoria. http://orcid.org/0000-0002-6837-0310
Sakupapa, T. C. (2019). Ethno-Regionalism, Politics and the Role of Religion in Zambia: Changing Ecumenical Landscapes in a Christian Nation, 2015–2018. *Exchange, 48*(2), 105–126. Brill, Cambridge.
Sakupapa T. C. (2020). Reframing African Ecumenical Development Discourse: Case of the All Africa Conference of Churches (AACC) 2000–2018 (Part 2). *Studia Historiae Ecclesiasticae*. Pretoria. https://doi.org/10.25159/2412-4265/6822
Seers, D. (1979). *The Meaning of Development. Development Theory: Four Critical Studies.* Routledge.
Sen, A. (2000). *Development as Freedom.* Anchor Books.
United Nations. (2022). Young People's Potential, the Key to Africa's Sustainable Development. https://www.un.org/ohrlls/news/young-people%E2%80%99s-potential-key-africa%E2%80%99s-sustainable-development
Utuk, E. (2007). *Visions Of Authenticity: The Assemblies Of The All Africa Conference Of Churches, 1963–1992.* Nairobi: AACC.
Uzondu, I. C. (2020). Education and Religion: The Harbingers of Peace Building in Africa Ignatius. In A. Ikechukwu & K. Ejikemeuwa (Eds.), *Religion and Peace Building in Africa: Proceedings of the International Conference of the Association for the Promotion of African Studies on African Ideologies, Human Security and Peace Building, 10th–11th June 2020* (Vol. 1, pp. 1–22). APAS.
Ver Beek, K. A. (2000). *Spirituality: A Development Taboo. Development in Practice.* Routledge. https://doi.org/10.1080/09614520052484

PART V

# Interfaith Networks, Peacebuilding and Development in Africa

CHAPTER 30

# Interfaith Networks, Peacebuilding and Development in Africa: Analysis of the Contribution of the Fellowship of Christian Councils and Churches to Peacebuilding

*Elias Opongo*

## INTRODUCTION

Religious institutions have for centuries contributed to the social well-being of society, whether in education, health, development, peace and social cohesion. As such, religion has played a significant role in shaping society, influencing government policies, promoting peace and driving the agenda of safeguarding human dignity and common good (Welty, 2014). At the same time, religious groups have been at the centre of conflicts as active agents promoting violence and division. With the number of people professing a religion globally set to increase in the next 40 years (Pew Research Centre, 2015), it is important to analyse the role that interfaith networks have played or can play in conflict resolution. One such interfaith network has been the Fellowship of Christian Councils and Churches (FECCLAHA) which has done peacebuilding work at the grassroots and decision-makers level, networking with different faiths, civil society organizations, cultural leaders and government officials.

E. Opongo (✉)
Centre for Research, Training and Publications, Hekima University College, Nairobi, Kenya

The work of FECCLAHA is in line with the United Nations Sustainable Development Goal number 16 (SDG 16), which aims to reduce all forms of violence; end abuse, trafficking and all forms of violence against children; promote the rule of law and access to justice; significantly reduce illicit financial and arms flow; reduce corruption and instil accountability in governance while advocating for peaceful and inclusive societies, with the end goal of sustainable development (United Nations Statistics Division, n.d.). SDG 16 recognizes a multidimensional approach to peacebuilding and the intrinsic link between the promotion of peace and development. The Goal emphasizes the role played by grassroots religious organizations like FECCLAHA, non-government organizations (NGOs) and civil society organizations in promoting peace and development. Hence, FECCLAHA's commitment to finding peace in Eastern, Horn and Central African regions through interfaith networks is a significant contribution to peace, despite the complexity and the protracted nature of conflicts in this region.

Africa continues to face instabilities of different forms ranging from protracted conflicts, socio-economic conflicts, marginalization of the majority of the population, poor governance, gender-based violence (GBV), poor economic structures and unstable democracies, among others. In 2021, there were high-intensity armed conflicts in 12 states, namely: "Burkina Faso, Cameroon, the Central African Republic (CAR), the Democratic Republic of the Congo (DRC), Ethiopia, Mali, Mozambique, Niger, Nigeria, Somalia, South Sudan and Sudan. Low-intensity, subnational armed conflicts occurred in 6 states: Benin, Burundi, Chad, Kenya, Madagascar and Uganda" (Davis, 2022). Of the 18 states, 11 recorded a higher number of conflict-related fatalities in 2021 compared to 2020, a 19% increase in conflicts (Davis, 2022). The Horn of Africa and Great Lakes regions continue to face diverse threats to peace such as terrorism, armed conflicts, extreme weather conditions, the proliferation of small arms and light weapons (SALWs) and subsequent forced migration. The situation has further been worsened by the negative social-economic impact of the COVID-19 pandemic.

What can we learn from interfaith networks committed to peace and conflict resolution? What strategies do such institutions apply to achieve peace sustainability? The Fellowship of Christian Councils and Churches (FECCLAHA) is one such religious institution that has since 1999 worked in the Horn of Africa, Great Lakes and Eastern Africa regions (FECCLAHA, n.d.). Its primary mission is to "foster ecumenical fellowship that promotes justice, sustainable peace and development in the Great Lakes Region and the Horn of Africa through advocacy, capacity building, networking and partnership, and documentation" (FECCLHA, n.d.). Hence, this chapter focuses on understanding the peacebuilding strategies applied by FECCLAHA, in the light of the Sustainable Development Goal (SDG) 16, and the extent to which these interventions have brought positive changes to the region of operation. FECCLAHA has since its inception in 1999 committed itself to the promotion of peace, reconciliation and conflict transformation in the Great

Lakes, Eastern Africa and the Horn of Africa. Its core values include human dignity, compassion, peace, justice, integrity, and ecumenism, while its vision is articulated as "Together for justice, sustainable peace and development" (FECCLAHA, n.d.).

## Contextual Analysis

The region in which FECCLAHA operates has been volatile for the last five decades, with Somalia, South Sudan, Burundi, Ethiopia, the Democratic Republic of the Congo (DRC) and Eritrea facing protracted conflicts. Ethiopia's conflict is the most recent, breaking out in November 2020 in the northern Tigrayan region. The conflict escalated into military combat between the Tigrayan and government forces, leading to thousands of deaths and displacements of more than 5.4 million people (UN, 2022a). For the last four decades, Ethiopia has faced inter-ethnic conflicts, rendering the country fragile and unstable. A peace agreement was signed in Addis Ababa in November 2022 between the Ethiopian government and Tigrayan leadership, bringing an end to the two years of war. Religious institutions have made attempts to broker peace between the different ethnic communities, as well as with the government, but often the political and military intensity has made it difficult for the religious leaders to succeed in their efforts (International Crisis Group, 2022). The Orthodox Church is the dominant Christian denomination covering 43% of the population, while 19% are Christians and 35% are Muslims (Diamant, 2017). In fact, Ethiopia holds the largest Orthodox Christian population outside Europe (ibid.). The Interfaith Peace-building Initiative (IPI), which was founded in 2003, works with different faiths to promote peace and national dialogue. The faith network advocates for a culture of peace, tolerance, constructive dialogue and mutual understanding (United Religions Initiative, n.d.-b).

South Sudan, which gained independence in 2011 and became the youngest country in Africa, has experienced intermittent conflicts marked by uncontrolled proliferation of arms, ethnicized politics, ethnic violence, mass displacements, poor governance, food insecurity and poverty (Modi et al., 2019). The current government has severally failed to hold elections, contain sporadic and regional conflicts, and foster national cohesion (Nyadera et al. 2023). Hence, South Sudan is a fragmented country that struggles to stand together.

According to Human Rights Watch, in 2022, violence between different armed groups in the Upper Nile, southern Central Equatoria and southern Unity states has led to population displacements and human rights abuses, some of which may be categorized as crimes against humanity (Hassan, 2023). South Sudan is one of the largest sources of refugees in the world, with 2.4 million of its population displaced out of the country and an additional 2 million displaced internally (UNHCR, 2022b). Religious institutions have played a major role in efforts towards peace, both with the government and with community leaders. The South Sudan Council of Churches (SSCC) has been at the forefront of campaigning for peace and contributing to humanitarian support for millions of displaced populations. FECCLAHA has collaborated closely with the SSCC in contributing to peace in South Sudan through the training of religious leaders, and advocacy for peace with political leaders and government officials.

The Democratic Republic of the Congo (DRC) is yet another country that has experienced protracted conflicts since its independence. The eastern part of the country, which is rich in natural resources, has been a theatre of violent conflicts, and according to International Rescue Committee, between 1998 and 2007 more than 5.4 million died (International Rescue Committee, 2007), and more continue to die from secondary effects of conflict such as hunger, diseases and injuries. According to the United Nations High Commission for Refugees (UNHCR), there are more than 5.6 million people displaced in the DRC (UNHCR, 2022b). The conflict in South and North Kivu has been worsened by the return of the M23 rebel group that has been fighting the government forces. The UN and other Western nations have accused Rwanda of backing the M23, claims that Rwanda has denied (Al Katanty, 2023). The conflict has exacerbated the already fragile region, which is known to have about 120 armed groups (Global Centre for Responsibility to Protect, 2022). The country is struggling to hold together, and elections have become very divisive, while corruption, insecurity, poor infrastructure, unemployment and poverty stand out as major issues of concern.

Close to 90% of the DRC population is Christian, of which 55% are Catholic (US Department of State, 2022). The Catholic Church has strongly advocated for justice and peace in the country, constantly calling on the government to end the violence and restore peace (ACSS, 2018). Pope Francis' visit to the country in January 2023 marked a special moment for the country, with the Pope calling on foreign governments to leave the Congo minerals to the Congolese and stop financing violence. At the same time, the Pope called for an end to corruption and poor governance (Puella & Lorgerie, 2022).

Religious institutions have been involved in peace interventions and humanitarian support (Alfani, 2019). For example, the All Congo Inter-Faiths Platform (ACIP) brings together eight officially recognized religious communities in the DRC, while being open to working with other traditional religious groups. ACIP was founded in 1992 during the Sovereign National Conference called by then-President Mobutu Sese Seko to drive national dialogue and reconciliation in the country (United Religions Initiative, n.d.-a). The Inter-Religious Council of DRC has equally contributed to bringing together interfaith platforms for peace.

FECCLAHA facilitated in July 2021 the National Chapter of the Women Mediators in Eastern DRC to participate in the high-level national multi-stakeholder Intercommunity Dialogue held in Kinshasa, DRC. The dialogue forum addressed the protracted intercommunity conflicts in Fizi, Uvira, and Mwenga Provinces in the South Kivu region. It provided an opportunity to follow up on the interfaith dialogue held in 2022 in Bukavu, DRC (FECCLHA,

2021, pp. 11–12). It aimed to facilitate social cohesion and restore peace among the Babuyu, Bafuliru, Banyindu, Barundi, and Bavira communities. The women, including a young woman mediator, were incorporated into a church leaders' delegation and were deployed to accompany the intercommunity dialogue as peace mediators, given they are viewed as neutral. The role of the church leaders and women mediators included moderating breakout groups, contributing towards reducing tensions and mediating in case tensions arose during the dialogue sessions. The delegation of church leaders and REFWOMEN (Regional Faith Women Mediators Network) members held side meetings with the head of the Civil House of the president of DRC, who was the moderator of the dialogue where they presented their position paper that outlined various concerns, including the plight of women and the recommendations on how to the address the ongoing intercommunity conflicts in the region (FECCLAHA, 2021, p. 11).

Eritrea, Burundi, Djibouti, Rwanda, Kenya, Uganda and Tanzania have been relatively peaceful in recent years, except for election periods that often create tension and sometimes ethnic tensions or civilian violence. Burundi, Kenya and Uganda have experienced state violence during electioneering periods, with Kenya's worst period being the 2008 post-election violence that led to the deaths of more than 1500 people (Burchard, S. M., & Djak, I. 2013, p. 5). Kenya continues to struggle to achieve social cohesion due to its ethnicized politics, historical injustices, regional economic imbalances and corruption. Uganda has for years weaponized governance through the militarization of electoral processes and victimization of opposition politicians and their members. According to the 2022b Human Rights Watch (HRW) Report on Uganda, during the 2021 elections "security forces arbitrarily arrested and beat opposition supporters and journalists, killed protestors, and disrupted opposition rallies. There has yet to be any commitment to end the violation of freedom of association, assembly, and association which persist in Uganda" (HRW, 2022b). Rwanda has made milestone progress in the post-genocide period. The country experienced one of the worst human catastrophes in the twentieth century, a genocide that left more than 8000,000 people dead, mainly targeting the Tutsis and moderate Hutus. The current government, under the leadership of President Paul Kagame, has prioritized development and national cohesion, keeping the country peaceful for 27 years. However, according to Human Rights Watch (2022), opposition leaders have often decried the heavy-handedness of the government in dealing with dissent and any form of opposition, leading victimization of groups and individuals.

Religious institutions have been active in advocating for peace and reconciliation in Eritrea, Burundi, Kenya, Rwanda, Uganda and Tanzania. In Tanzania, the Inter-Religious Council for Peace in Tanzania (IRCPT) has been working with different religious faiths in promoting peace and reconciliation in the country. The IRCPT focus on providing "religious leaders and their communities with a platform for constructive dialogue, peace building, capacity building and advocacy for peaceful development" (United Religions Initiative, n.d.-c). The IRCPT operates at different levels to achieve peace through Inter-Faith Committees (IFCs) and Inter-Religious Village Community Banks (VICOBA). Uganda Joint Christian Council (UJCC), which was founded in 1963, has as its main mission: "To promote consensus among men, women, youth and children in member churches to uphold Christian values and address issues of economic and social justice through representatives at various levels, and Inter-Religious Council of Uganda (IRCU) have been active inter-faith networks" (UJCC, n.d.). The IRCU was founded in 2001 to address common issues of national concern. The interfaith network brings together "the Roman Catholic Church (RCC), the Church of the Province of Uganda (Church Of Uganda-COU), the Uganda Orthodox Church (UOC), the Uganda Muslim Supreme Council (UMSC), the Seventh-day Adventist Uganda Union (SDAUU), the Born Again Faith in Uganda (BAF) and the National Alliance of Pentecostal and Evangelical Churches in Uganda (NAPECU)… the Spiritual Assembly of the Baha'i, the Methodist and Lutheran Churches" (IRCU, n.d.). In Burundi, the Inter-Religious Council of Burundi (IRCB), established in 2008 by religious leaders from the Christian, Protestant and Islamic faiths, has focused on the promotion of inter-religious cooperation aimed at achieving peace "through reconciliation, social justice and sustainable development" (URI, n.d.-d). In light of SDG 16's target of achieving an inclusive society, the IRCB is "combatting political and religious violence, radicalization and extremism through multi-religious collaboration in Burundi" (Faith Action Network, n.d.).

FECCLAHA has closely worked with all the above interfaith networks in promoting peace, civic education, human rights advocacy and conflict resolution. Coupled with this have been the local networks for peace driven by civil society organizations (CSOs). The CSOs in Kenya have been active agents of peace and conflict resolution, often working with marginalized communities at the grassroots and keeping the government in check over cases of human rights abuse (Kirimi, 2018).

## FECCLAHA's Engagement in Peacebuilding and Conflict Transformation

From the contextual analysis above, it is evident that FECCLAHA operates in a region that is most volatile and susceptible to intermittent and protracted conflicts. While FECCLAHA cannot pretend to solve all the socio-political problems of the region, the organization nevertheless uses its regional influence under the auspices of a network of churches, other religions and civil society organizations, to impact social change. In line with the SDG 16 target of promoting just, peaceful and inclusive societies, FECCLAHA focuses on grassroots mobilization for peace and development while also working closely with civil society organizations and government officials. Hence, its strategy has largely been through interactive peacebuilding founded on direct engagement with different stakeholders at multiple levels of society. FECCLAHA has mainly focused on five main strategic responses to peacebuilding and conflict transformation for inclusive societies. The first is the social cohesion approach which fosters unity between communities in conflict and draws attention to potential conflicts that could emerge if they are not addressed. The second is the gender rights and peacebuilding initiatives. The third is youth engagement in conflict resolution. The fourth entails advocacy against the proliferation of small arms and light weapons, and the fifth is advocacy for good governance and accountability. These activities are closely linked and represent a much broader perspective on peacebuilding.

## *Social Cohesion Approach*

The term 'social cohesion' is very fluid without any standard definition. However, it refers to the state of a society in which there is a positive level of harmony in the relationship between different communities and social sectors, as well as between governance and citizen, to the extent that such a harmonious relationship sustains peace and stability. Langer et al. (2017, p. 322) define social cohesion as "the notion that relationships among members and groups in society are sufficiently good that all feel a sense of belonging, that they perceive the whole society as greater than the parts, and when difference develop, they can be dealt with peacefully." Efforts towards social cohesion may include peacebuilding activities such as justice for survivors of violence, forgiveness and reconciliation, economic justice and strategies for improving inter-ethnic/racial/religious/political relations. Social Cohesion Hub measures social cohesion under three variables: inequality, social trust and identity (Leininger et al., 2021). Inequality refers to unfair disparities between different groups in social, political and economic spheres. Perceived inequalities between groups can lead to violent conflicts. Social trust refers to the levels of trust towards the state and other groups in society. Where there is a low level of trust there is likely to be agitations, violence and disintegration of the society. Identity is the level of adherence to the national identity and values in comparison to one's immediate ethnic or racial identity (ibid.). Hence, in situations where people identify strongly with their national identity, and less with ethnic or racial identity, there are likely to be high levels of social cohesion. The above indicators of social cohesion should however be contextually tested to confirm the advanced hypotheses.

SDG 16 calls for the reduction of violence and related death rates. To contribute to this sub-theme of SDG 16, and in light of the social cohesion, FECCLAHA has worked with churches, NGOs and CSOs, mostly in Sudan and the DRC, two countries that have experienced political turmoil and conflict. The organization has conducted leadership training for religious leaders, women, youth and community leaders. In the DRC, in November 2020, FECCLAHA facilitated an Inter-Religious Dialogue Forum on Peace and Security in Bukavu, DRC, which was meant to address the conflicts in the territories of Uvira, Fizi and Mwenga (Itombwe Sector). This dialogue forum gave a platform for discussions on building partnerships between religious leaders and politicians (FECCLAHA, 2021). Participants included different church leaders and CSOs working on peace and youth groups from churches and general society.

Further, FECCLAHA, in collaboration with the National Council of Churches of Kenya (NCCK), formed, in 2018, the Kenya Women Mediators Network, drawing its membership from women leaders who have been involved in peacebuilding and mediation processes at different levels of the country, from the grassroots to county and national levels. In resonance with SDG 16, sub-goal 6 of ensuring responsive, inclusive, participatory and representative decision-making at all levels, FECCLAHA and NCCK equipped the women mediators with "peace building and mediation from the local to national level; and to advocate for women participation in decision making as well as elective positions both in church and political arena" (FECCLAHA, 2021, p. 11). Equally, FECCLAHA, in collaboration with the Ethiopian Evangelical Church Mekane Yesus (EECMY), Department of Women Ministry, carried out dialogue forums on peacebuilding, social healing and reconciliation (ibid., pp. 11–12). This was motivated by the fact that Ethiopia was experiencing violent conflict in the northern part of the country and the church was in a better position to mediate for peace.

FECCLAHA has also worked on the Sudan Social Cohesion Project under the Regional Peace Program (RPP) in collaboration with the Sudan Council of Churches (SCC) and Sudan Inter-Religious Council (SIRC) (2019). This strategy of multi-level engagement for peace is in line with one of the SDG 16 targets of promoting the rule of law and ensuring equal access to justice. The initiative, which focused on Freedom of Religion and Belief (FORB), was meant to strengthen social cohesion between different faith groups with a view to protecting and promoting the fundamental rights of faith minorities in Sudan. Projects carried out under the Sudan Social Cohesion Project included the Caravan of Faith in September 2020, which gave religious leaders a forum to push for increasing women's participation in the country's decision-making and policy-making processes; the signing of the Sudan Peace Deal in October 2020, which was a high-level strategic event drawing representatives from the United Nations, the African Union (AU), the European Union (EU), heads of state and governments and civil society organizations, among others; Church Leaders' training of trainers Advocacy on Freedom of Religion and Belief (FORB), which was held in December 2020 in Khartoum, Sudan (FECCLAHA, 2021).

FECCLAHA equally organized interfaith forums in Khartoum in December 2020, bringing together women, youth and church leaders for training meant to improve their knowledge of FORB and human rights in order to strengthen social cohesion in the country. Another activity was the Sudan High-Level National Interfaith Consultative Dialogue Forum for Faith Leaders in December 2021 in Khartoum, Sudan. This was conducted in collaboration with the Sudan Council of Churches (SCC) and the World Council of Churches (WCC). The discourse aimed to promote unity, national cohesion and trust among Sudan's religious communities which mainly include Muslims and Christians (FECCLAHA, 2021). To strengthen the church agency in conflict resolution, FECCLAHA conducted, in December 2020, training for church leaders on conversation management, conflict transformation tools, the culture of dialogue and effective communication, among other things (FECCLAHA, 2021).

## Gender Rights and Peacebuilding

FECCLAHA focuses on raising awareness on the marginalization of women as well as the latter's experience of violence and sexual abuse. While the organization advocates for the rights of the affected women, it also seeks women's agency in finding solutions to the drivers and causes of gender-based violence. To achieve this, FECCLAHA has collaborated with different organizations to conduct training workshops aimed at raising awareness on levels of gender violence, strategies of response through policy reviews, enforcement of legislation clauses meant to protect women's rights and provision of protection mechanisms for vulnerable women. Such initiatives have been undertaken in Ethiopia, Burundi, the Democratic Republic of the Congo (DRC), Kenya, Rwanda, South Sudan and Uganda (FECCLAHA, 2022).

FECCLAHA's support for women has been bolstered by the United Nations Security Council Resolution (UNSCR) 1325, which highlights the importance of women's equal participation and full involvement in all efforts to maintain and promote peace and security, conflict prevention and resolution, peace negotiations, peacekeeping, humanitarian response and post-conflict reconstruction (UNSCR, 2000). Women have participated in various peacebuilding efforts aimed at contributing to conflict transformation and human rights advocacy (Opongo et al., 2021; Yayboke & Abdullah, 2020). To a great extent, women are active mediators and are often considered to be creators of conducive environments for peace negotiations—in other words, "ripening the ground" for peace (Opongo et al., 2021). In the same line, the African Union's Assembly of Heads of State voted to establish the FemWise-Africa (Network of African Women in Conflict Prevention and Mediation) in July 2017. This Network was meant to increase the role of women in conflict prevention and mediation activities (AU, 2018). Women have participated in various peacebuilding efforts aimed at achieving conflict transformation and human rights advocacy (Opongo et al., 2021). Diop (2002, p. 144) notes that to address concerns about conditions restricting women's involvement in peace processes, African women came together to build national NGOs, such as the Liberian Women Initiative and Save Somali Women and Children, and eventually to create a continent-wide women's platform for peace, of which the African Women's Committee for Peace and Development (AWCPD), the Federation of African Women's Peace Networks (FERFAP) and Femmes Africa

Solidarité (FAS) are a part. The women sought to develop more comprehensive, gender-sensitive policies and practices for conflict prevention and resolution through this platform.

African women came together to build national NGOs, such as the Liberian Women Initiative and Save Somali Women and Children, and eventually to create a continent-wide women's platform for peace, of which the African Women's Committee for Peace and Development (AWCPD), the Federation of African Women's Peace Networks (FERFAP) and Femmes Africa Solidarité (FAS) are a part. Through this platform, the women sought to develop more comprehensive, gender-sensitive policies and practices for conflict prevention and resolution.

FECCLAHA has collaborated with different organizations to train women in peacebuilding and conflict resolution processes. For example, FECCLAHA collaborated with the African Centre for Constructive Resolution of Disputes (ACCORD) and the Norwegian Church Aid (NCA), to train Regional Faith Women Peace Mediators in the Great Lakes and the Horn of Africa in mediation (ACCORD, 2017). The trained women have been committed to conflict intervention and advocacy against gender violence. Further, according to FECCLAHA's 2018 report, three members of the Regional Faith Women Mediation Network were accredited to FemWise-Africa, hence broadening their platform for women's rights and peace advocacy (FECCLAHA, 2019).

FECCLAHA has worked with churches to enhance peacebuilding and conflict transformation. The organization has collaborated closely with various church institutions like the Church of Christ in Congo (ECC), Ethiopian Evangelical Church Mekane Yesus (EECMY), Uganda Joint Christian Council (UJCC), the National Council of Churches of Kenya (NCCK), South Sudan Council of Churches (SSCC), All Africa Conference of Churches (AACC), Africa Council of Religious Leaders (ACRL-Rfp), Arigatou International, Norwegian Church Aid (NCA), and Hekima Institute of Peace Studies and International Relations (HIPSIR), among others (FECCLAHA, 2021).

FECCLAHA has also put in efforts to promote gender justice. The organization has carried out this in two important areas: protection against gender-based violence (the Tamar Campaign) and women's participation in the life of the Church. For example, in 2005, FECCLAHA launched the Tamar Campaign, a programme aimed at advocating against gender-based violence (GBV) and educating women, men and youth on gender-based violence by providing resources for structured sensitization. FECCLAHA (2019) has developed manuals on gender-based violence and contextual Bible Study, which have served as important resources and guidance materials for Church ministers and workers dealing with GBV. For example, in the DRC alone in "2018, more than 35,000 cases of sexual violence were still recorded, the majority of them in the East. During the COVID-19 epidemic, violence increased by 99% in North Kivu Province" (UN Women, 2020). In collaboration with the International Conference on the Great Lakes Region's Regional Training Facility on Prevention and Suppression of SGBV in the Great Lakes

Region (ICGLR-RTF), FECCLAHA conducted a baseline survey on the state of GBV and the role of religious institutions on GBV prevention and protection of women in the Great Lakes and Horn of Africa regions in 2019 (FECCLAHA, 2019). The survey revealed the serious situation of violence against women and the extent to which the governments had not done enough to create safety nets for women experiencing violence (ibid.). The survey equally revealed that efforts towards SGBV awareness had helped reduce incidences of women abuse.

According to the World Health Organization (WHO), "domestic violence is a global problem affecting millions of women" (WHO, 2021). The WHO points out that some factors leading to GBV include illiteracy, witnessing family violence, drug abuse (including alcohol abuse), gender inequality, historical exposure to the perpetrators' maltreatment, community norms and harmful masculine behaviours, among others (WHO, 2021). The COVID-19 pandemic contributed to women's vulnerability to domestic violence, especially during the lockdown periods when families were confined to their homes.

The UN Women reported that the increased cases of domestic violence during the COVID-19 pandemic drew attention to women's vulnerability in their homes and noted that there were high demands for safe shelters across the world compared to the period before the pandemic (Mlambo-Ngcuka, 2020). The United Nations Development Programme observed that as COVID-19 spread over the world, various quarantine and lockdown protocols (including stay-at-home orders) were implemented to protect people from the virus. However, the measures exposed women to maltreatment and domestic and gender-based violence (UNDP, 2020).

During the peak of the pandemic period, FECCLAHA conducted a number of awareness campaigns. For instance, in June 2020 they assisted the Protestant Council of Rwanda (CPR) through the Rwanda Faith Women Peace Mediators (RFWPM) to launch a public awareness campaign through a local radio station, Radio Inkoramutima. In June and July 2020, FECCLAHA assisted the Federation of Women in Protestant Churches (FFP/ECC) in South Kivu in raising awareness among religious leaders about the elevated threat of GBV during the COVID-19 epidemic (FECCLAHA, 2021). Through different initiatives, FECCLAHA sensitized church leaders, women and youth leaders to adequately address the issue of GBV. These initiatives were held in partnership with the Church of Christ in Congo (ECC/South Kivu), the Protestant Council of Rwanda (CPR), the South Sudan Council of Churches (SSCC), the Christian Council of Tanzania (CCT) and the National Council of Churches of Kenya (NCCK) (FECCLAHA, 2021).

As a sign of commitment, women trained by FECCLAHA have established country interfaith and intra-faith structures seeking to consolidate the voice of women in the faith communities. Six country chapters have been established in Kenya, DRC, Rwanda, Ethiopia, South Sudan and Sudan. Through these platforms, the women have undertaken sensitization forums on gender-based violence as well as advocacy peace forums and dialogues. The women have also observed elections in Burundi and Kenya (FECCLAHA, 2020, p. 18 & 19).

Further, the women have participated in national and regional dialogues. For example, in November 2022, through FECCLAHA partners in Bukavu, South Kivu (ECC/RIO), the women mediators were invited by the Office of Coordination of the Civil Society of South and North Kivu to participate in the East Africa Community (EAC)-led Peace Process in Nairobi on the restoration of peace and security in Eastern DRC. The selection of ECC/RIO as participants in this process was based on its leadership in research for peace, its positioning among government officials and local authorities, and its sustained peace engagements with the local communities. The women's technical skills in facilitating dialogue processes and mediation were also considered. Finally, four women mediators from the RFMCP participated in the mediation process (FECCLAHA, 2022).

Under the REFWOMEN platform established by FECCLAHA in collaboration with the African Centre for the Constructive Resolution of Disputes (ACCORD) and Norwegian Church Aid (NCA), an advocacy mission in Ethiopia, Kenya, Sudan and South Sudan was undertaken in December 2018 in which a total number of 14 faith women undertook the successful advocacy mission in Ethiopia, Kenya, Sudan and South Sudan. This was in an effort to accompany the Women Link for Peace in South Sudan in their efforts towards advocacy for peace. This initiative aimed at lobbying and advocating for the full participation of women and youth in South Sudan in the implementation of the Revitalized Agreement on the Resolution of Conflict in the Republic of South Sudan (R-ARCSS) and their inclusion in different structures and mechanisms (FECCLAHA, 2018, p. 6).

FECCLAHA has also used social media platforms to raise awareness on GBV during COVID-19 by disseminating campaign messages against women's violence through social media platforms like WhatsApp, Twitter and Facebook (FECCLAHA, 2021). During the commemoration of the "16 Days of Activism Against Violence on Women" in November 2020, FECCLAHA used the opportunity to raise awareness on GBV in Uganda. This was done in collaboration with the Uganda Joint Christian Council (UJCC) (FECCLAHA, 2021). To complement its efforts against SGBV and to bolster its commitment to the SDG 16 target of inclusivity in peacebuilding, FECCLAHA equally works with the youth as key agents of peace and conflict.

## Youth Engagement in Conflict Resolution

According to World Social Forum (El Habti, 2022), more than 60% of Africa's population is below the age of 25, with the majority of these unemployed and subsequently vulnerable to recruitment by armed groups. In fact, many youths have been used by political leaders as militia to advance political agenda, whereas others have been given arms to fight in a particular conflict that often has nothing to do with their well-being (Raleigh, 2016). FECCLAHA has had numerous initiatives for the youth under the Regional Youth Peace Building Programme, aimed at empowering the latter to be active agents for peacebuilding and conflict transformation. The United Nations Security Council Resolution 2250 on Youth, Peace and Security, passed in December 2015, urges member states to give youth a greater voice in decision-making procedures at the local, national, regional and international levels while setting up mechanisms that enable young people to participate meaningfully in peace and conflict resolution processes (UNSCR, 2015).

FECCLAHA has provided safe spaces for young people to engage, share their experiences and learn from each other. For example, the organization has established 228 Youth Peace Clubs (YPCs) since 2013, bringing together over 10,000 members of the peace clubs across the region. These Youth Peace Clubs have provided a good opportunity to train the youth into becoming ambassadors of peace in their respective countries (FECCLAHA, 2019). The clubs have created a platform for the youth to identify issues of concern and design strategies for conflict interventions and support mechanisms for peacebuilders (ibid.).

There have been a series of capacity-building and advocacy initiatives through the peace clubs. FECCLAHA has reached youths from different countries, including Ethiopia, Tanzania, Uganda, Mukuru slums in Kenya and North Kivu in DRC. FECCLAHA has also engaged the youth in sports mentorship for peace and worked with the Resilient Men Peace Programme, which aimed at educating and raising awareness among the youth in Mukuru informal settlements in Nairobi. The programme encouraged the youth to desist from joining violent extremist groups and engaging in substance abuse (FECCLAHA, 2019), hence resonating with SDG 16's target of promoting the rule of law.

To foster SDG 16's target of developing effective, transparent and accountable institutions at all levels, FECCLAHA in 2020 collaborated with the Christian Council of Tanzania (CCT), South Sudan Council of Churches (SSCC) and Uganda Joint Christian Council (UJCC) in holding a series of capacity-building engagements on human rights awareness, violent communication, and the effects of COVID-19 on youth and implications on peace and security. In South Sudan, peace training focused on youth participation in peacebuilding initiatives by providing alternative narratives to armed violence while emphasizing non-violence as a strategy for peace. In Uganda, the focus has been on the enhancement of peaceful coexistence and the development of counter-narratives to youth radicalization. In Mtwara, Tanzania, FECCLAHA conducted training with the youth, religious leaders and civil society organizations on advocacy for extractive justice and accountable governance (FECCLAHA, 2021). Hence, efforts by FECCLAHA and other organizations to involve the youth in peacebuilding initiatives have to a great extent been successful, although the fluidity of conflict dynamics has been such that for peace initiatives to bear fruit, they have to be supported by local initiatives for peace. Besides, addressing the proliferation of illegal small arms is fundamental for sustainable peace.

## Advocacy Against Proliferation of Small Arms and Light Weapons

The Eastern Horn and Central Africa regions are awash with illegal small arms and light weapons (Tar & Onwurah, 2021). The conflicts in the DRC, Ethiopia, South Sudan and Somalia have been sustained by illegal arms at the hands of the militia. The easy access to these arms has led to increased armed conflicts and subsequent protraction of the conflicts. In light of SDG 16's target of significantly reducing illicit arms flow by 2030, FECCLAHA has lobbied different organizations, religious leaders and CSOs to raise awareness on small arms proliferation and its implications on peace and security in the region. The African Union (AU) has been committed to ending the proliferation of illegal small arms in Africa as well as related conflicts that have made the continent unstable. Through its initiative of *Silencing the Guns* by 2020, the AU called on member states and the regional economic communities (RECs) to commit themselves to end violent conflicts by involving the "youth and women in addressing the problems of proliferation, and the use and movement of illegal weapons and illicit goods" (AU, 2020).

The AU did not meet its 2020 target and pushed the deadline to 2030. However, the task of ending armed conflicts has been slowed down by the increase of violent extremist groups, the resurgence of coup d'états, especially in West Africa, resource-based conflicts in the DRC and intra-state conflicts in Nigeria, Ethiopia, South Sudan, Sudan, Cameroon and Libya, among others. The *Silencing the Guns* initiative was part of Agenda 2063 of the AU that aimed at achieving inclusive and sustainable development by the year 2050. Agenda 2063 calls for accountable governance, promotion of democracy, social inclusion, sustainable development and respect for human rights, justice and the rule of law as vital pre-conditions for a peaceful and conflict-free continent (AU, 2015).

FECCLAHA collaborated with the African Council of Religious Leaders through Religions for Peace, to advocate against the proliferation of small arms and light weapons (SALWs). Through this initiative, the National Council of Burundian Churches (NCBC) developed materials to educate local communities about the risks of SALW possession and its implications for peace and security. More than 40,000 individuals attended the SALW awareness sessions within six months, and the churches have committed themselves to continue the initiative to curb violent conflicts in the country (African Council of Religious Leaders, 2020). FECCLAHA has also worked with the SSCC to influence policy and legislation related to SALWs' control and management in the country. Through networking with the South Sudan Action Network on illicit SALWs, SSCC advocated and lobbied for the drafting and enacting of "The Fire Arms Act 2016." FECCLAHA not only undertook capacity-building and sensitization forums with religious actors but also supported SSCC participation in the advocacy and lobbying of this law (FECCLAHA, 2019, p 13).

FECCLAHA, on the other hand, has engaged in a number of initiatives against the proliferation of illicit arms. The organization had a programme in 2016–2018 on small arms and light weapons, and in 2019, it completed the evaluation of SALWs to assess the degree of achievements of the objectives and results of the programme (FECCLAHA, 2019). The organization was also part of a regional workshop on the ratification process of the Arms Trade Treaty (ATT) hosted by the Regional Centre on Small Arms (RECSA) in Nairobi, Kenya. In 2018, FECCLAHA collaborated with the Regional Centre for Small Arms (RESCA) in holding a regional stakeholders forum to analyse the state of SALW in the region and strategies that can be used to curb the proliferation. In 2019, FECCLAHA collaborated with Uganda Joint Christian Council (UJCC) to organize a national stakeholder meeting on SALW, in order to design short- and long-term strategies of response.

Given that SALW proliferation is a very complex and difficult issue to curb, it would be important for FECCLAHA to collaborate with the AU and other international networks that advocate against SALW, in order to do a more comprehensive analysis of the phenomenon, and how best to address to it. This requires a sustained strategy of response that brings together local stakeholders who have the capacity to network with regional and international bodies committed to advocacy against SALW. Finding partners in regions and countries that supply arms to Africa, such as Europe, Asia and the United States, is critical for the success of the campaign against SALW.

## Governance and Accountability

FECCLAHA has constantly advocated for good governance and accountability in the region. This is in line with SDG 16's target of developing effective, accountable and transparent systems of governance. FECCLAHA thus advocates for electoral justice, political engagement, extractives advocacy and engagement with regional intergovernmental bodies. The ultimate goal of this strategy is to attain transparent and accountable governance (FECCLAHA, 2019). Elections in Africa have been faced with diverse challenges, often leading to inter-ethnic conflicts, coup d'états and persistent political tensions that can easily destabilize a country (Opongo & Murithi, 2022). Electoral justice is a key instrument of the rule of law and the ultimate guarantee of compliance with the democratic principle of holding free, fair and transparent elections. Electoral justice "goes beyond simply enforcing the legal framework; it is also a factor in the overall design and conduct of all electoral processes and influences the actions of the stakeholders within them" (Institute for Democracy and Electoral Assistance, 2010, p. 5).

FECCLAHA has been involved in pre-election engagements in some countries like Burundi, Tanzania, Kenya and Uganda, as well as election monitoring in Kenya and DRC. For example, following consultative forums in South and North Kivu provinces held in June 2018, FECCLAHA accompanied the Church of Christ in Congo (CCC) to undertake domestic election observation missions (FECCLAHA, 2019). The CCC, in partnership with other churches, were able to carry out election observation in the region as a way of enforcing transparency in electoral processes. FECCLAHA also trained 30 religious leaders and legal representatives from the National Council of Churches of Burundi (CNEB) in election observation and electoral justice. The training explored different outcomes and scenarios before, during and after the 2020 elections (FECCLAHA, 2019). It also provided, in May 2020, an avenue for Burundi religious leaders to consolidate and enhance their unity ahead of the country's national elections (FECCLAHA, 2019).

To increase the agency of the church in responding to political challenges, and in the light of SDG 16 target against bad governance, corruption and poor development policies, FECCLAHA made efforts in training the church leadership on advocacy strategies for political accountability and good governance. For example, in 2019, it held a Regional Ecumenical Forum (REF) in Addis Ababa, Ethiopia, to strategize on how Churches within the region can proactively engage in political governance (FECCLAHA, 2019). The Regional Ecumenical Forum (REF) framework allowed for in-depth theological and biblical reflection on the Church's role in promoting accountable political governance (FECCLAHA, 2019). FECCLAHA seeks to continue engaging churches and other actors in examining the regional political frameworks charged with the responsibility of accountable political governance.

Given that the region in which FECCLAHA operates has vast amounts of minerals, especially the DRC, the organization has engaged religious leaders, civil society and government agencies to advocate for extractive justice. The conflict in Congo has largely been driven by the competition for extractive industries, leading to the multiplication of armed groups (Titeca, 2011). To increase the capacity of religious leaders in extractive industry advocacy, FECCLAHA developed 2018 a *Handbook for Churches on Advocacy on Extractives Justice*. The handbook provides religious leaders with biblical resources that can guide and motivate the leaders in advocating for civilian justice and accountable governance in the extractive industry (FECCLAHA, 2019). Further, in 2019 FECCLAHA developed yet another guide for religious leaders titled *Handbook for Religious Leaders on Advocacy in the Extractive Sector: A Faith Perspective*, which was produced in collaboration with the Hekima Institute of Peace Studies and International Relations (HIPSIR) (FECCLAHA, 2019). FECCLAHA has also promoted community dialogue on awareness and advocacy on extractives in Kenya and Uganda. In collaboration with Norwegian Church Aid (NCA), FECCLAHA organized a hybrid Regional Forum on Extractives in the Great Lakes and the Horn of Africa in August 2021 in Nairobi, Kenya, with the theme "Governance of Extractives for Sustainable Development and Peace: The Role of Religious Leaders" (Omondi, 2021). These strategies of advocacy for governance and accountability by FECCLAHA have contributed to citizen awareness about holding their governments accountable.

## Conclusion

The above discussion on the role that FECCLAHA has played in social transformation demonstrates that religious institutions have an important role to play in addressing human rights abuses and advocating for accountability in socio-political governance. FECCLAHA enjoys a wide regional network of churches and civil society organizations as partners on the ground. The organization is a catalyst for social change through its strategy of engaging with key players on the ground within the church networks. This strategy has led to the formation of peace leaders such as women and youth mediations, advocacy groups against gender-based violence and political activists calling for political accountability.

While SDG 16 recognizes a multi-stakeholder approach to peace and development, at the grassroots and decision-making level, interfaith networks tend to be marginalized in the policy and decision-making processes. However, their contribution has nevertheless been immense in realizing social change. One of the main challenges for religious institutions engaged in peacebuilding work has been the sustainability of the initiatives undertaken for social change. This is mainly due to a number of limitations, such as competing needs of the society, particularly given that livelihood needs tend to take a higher priority; multiple players on the ground, often with different agendas for social change, which may lead to misconceptions and sabotage of one's initiative for social change; volatility to armed conflicts which may derail initiatives for peace; and limited funding to sustain the peace initiatives for a longer period, among others.

One of FECCLAHA's main challenges has been working in regions that have experienced protracted conflicts such as the DRC, Somalia and Burundi. Besides, situations of active conflict have led to the suspension of some of the peace activities as well as the displacement or death of actors who had hitherto been active peacebuilders. At the same time, the reality of peacebuilding in volatile situations means that one has to be open to the contingent nature of peacebuilding, with the realization that such peace initiatives have both short- and long-term impacts despite the challenging limitations on the ground. Hence, it is important to have resilience in carrying out peace activities.

## References

ACCORD. (2017). ACCORD Trains Regional Faith Women in the Great Lakes and Horn of Africa Region on Mediation. *Reliefweb*. https://reliefweb.int/report/burundi/accord-trains-regional-faith-women-great-lakes-and-horn-africa-region-mediation.

Africa Centre for Strategic Studies. (2018). Catholic Church Increasingly Targeted by Government Violence in the DRC. https://africacenter.org/spotlight/catholic-church-increasingly-targeted-by-government-violence-in-the-drc/.

African Council of Religious Leaders. (2020). Small Arms and Light Weapons: Africa. *Religions for Peace*. https://www.rfp.org/wp-content/uploads/2020/10/Small-Arms-and-Light-Weapons-Africa-English.pdf.

Al Katanty, J. (2023). U.N. Condemns M23 Rebel Offensive on Congo Town, Hundreds Flee. *REUTERS*. https://www.reuters.com/world/africa/un-condemns-m23-rebel-offensive-congo-town-hundreds-flee-2023-01-26/.

Alfani, R. B. (2019). *Religious Peacebuilding in the Democratic Republic of Congo*. Peter Lang Publishing Incorporated.

Burchard, S. M., & Djak, I. (2013). History of Elections, Ethnicity and Electoral Violence in Kenya. In *Elections and Electoral Violence in Kenya: Insights from the 2007 Elections—Implications for the 2013 Elections* (pp. 2–7). Institute for Defense Analyses.

Davis, I. (2022). Armed Conflict and Peace Processes In sub-Saharan Africa. SIPRI. https://www.sipri.org/yearbook/2022/07.

Diamant, J. (2017). Ethiopia is an Outlier in the Orthodox Christian world. Pew Research Centre. https://www.pewresearch.org/fact-tank/2017/11/28/ethiopia-is-an-outlier-in-the-orthodox-christian-world/.

Diop, B. (2002). Engendering the Peace Process in Africa: Women at the Negotiating Table. *Refugee Survey Quarterly, 21*, 142–154.

El Habti, H. (2022). Why Africa Youth Hold the Key to Its Development Potential. *World Social Forum*. https://www.weforum.org/agenda/2022/09/why-africa-youth-key-development-potential/#:~:text=Today%2C%20more%20than%2060%25%20of,under%20the%20age%20of%2025.

Faith to Action Network. (n.d.). Combatting Political and Religious Radicalisation through Multi Religious Collaboration in Burundi. https://www.faithtoactionnetwork.org/what-we-do/peaceful-justice-and-inclusive-communities/pluralism-burundi/

FECCLAHA. (2018). Annual Report 2018. http://fecclaha.org/annual-reports/

FECCLAHA. (2019). Annual Report 2019. http://fecclaha.org/annual-reports/

FECCLAHA. (2020). Annual Report 2019. https://fecclaha.org/annual-reports/file:///Users/elly/Downloads/fecclahaann-report-2019-english-final.pdf.

FECCLAHA. (2021). Annual Report 2020. https://fecclaha.org/annual-reports/

FECCLAHA. (2022). Annual Report. http://fecclaha.org/annual-reports/

FECCLAHA. (n.d.). About Us. https://fecclaha.org/who-we-are/.

Global Centre for the Responsibility to Protect. (2022). Democratic Republic of Congo. https://www.globalr2p.org/countries/democratic-republic-of-the-congo/#:~:text=Attacks%20by%20armed%20groups%20and,and%20armed%20groups%20actively%20operate.

Hassan, T. (2023). South Sudan: Events 2022. *Human Rights Watch*. https://www.hrw.org/world-report/2023/country-chapters/south-sudan#:~:text=In%20September%2C%20the%20United%20Nations,12%20people%20sustained%20serious%20injuries.

Human Rights Watch. (2022a). Rwanda: Events 2021.World Report. https://www.hrw.org/world-report/2022/country-chapters/rwanda.

Human Rights Watch. (2022b). Uganda. https://www.hrw.org/africa/uganda.

International Crisis Group. (2022). Turning the Pretoria Deal into Lasting Peace in Ethiopia. https://www.crisisgroup.org/africa/horn-africa/ethiopia/turning-pretoria-deal-lasting-peace-ethiopia.

International Institute for Democracy and Electoral Assistance. (2010). *Electoral Justice: An Overview of the International IDEA Handbook.* https://www.idea.int/sites/default/files/publications/chapters/electoral-justice-handbook/electoral-justice-handbook-overview.pdf.

International Rescue Committee. (2007). Mortality in the Democratic Republic of Congo: An Ongoing Crisis. https://www.rescue.org/report/mortality-democratic-republic-congo-ongoing-crisis.

Inter-Religious Council of Uganda (IRCU). (n.d.). Our History. https://www.ircu.or.ug/

Kirimi, S. (2018). The Role of Local Networks for Peace in Kenya. *Local Network for Peace: Lessons from Community-Led Peacebuilding.* JSTOR. http://www.jstor.org/stable/resrep19651.8

Langer, A., Stewart, F., Smedts, K., & Demarest, L. (2017). Conceptualising and Measuring Social Cohesion in Africa: Towards a Perceptions-based Index. *Social Indicators Research, 131,* 321–343.

Leininger, J., Burchi, F., Fiedler, C., Mross, K., Nowack, D., von Schiller, A. & Ziaja, S. (2021). *Social Cohesion: A New Definition and a Proposal for its Measurement in Africa* (No. 31/2021). Discussion Paper.

Mlambo-Ngcuka, P. (2020). *Violence Against Women and Girls: The Shadow Pandemic.* UN Women. https://www.unwomen.org/en/news/stories/2020/4/statement-ed-phumzile-violence-against-women-during-pandemic.

Modi, L. P., Opongo, E., & Drew Smith, R. (2019). South Sudan's Costly Conflict and the Urgent Role of Religious Leaders. *The Review of Faith & International Affairs, 17*(2), 37–46. https://doi.org/10.1080/15570274.2019.1608660

Nyadera I. N., Islam M. N. & Shihundu, F. (2023). Rebel Fragmentation and Protracted Conflicts: Lessons from SPLM/A in South Sudan. *Journal of Asian and African Studies (20230214).* https://doi.org/10.1177/00219096231154815.

Omondi, D. (2021). *Regional Forum on Extractives in the Great Lakes and Horn of Africa.* FCCLAHA. http://fecclaha.org/regional-forum-on-extractives-in-the-great-lakes-and-horn-of-africa/.

Opongo, E. O., & Murithi, T. (Eds.). (2022). *Elections, Violence and Transitional Justice in Africa.* Routledge.

Opongo, E. O., Muthui, C. W., & Ondeng, F. (2021). Levels of Change in Women Participation in the Peacebuilding Process in Africa. *HIPSIR Research Series, 4*(01), 72.

Pew Research Centre. (2015). Future of World Religions: Population Growth Projections 2010–2050. https://www.pewresearch.org/religion/2015/04/02/religious-projections-2010-2050/.

Puella, P., & Lorgerie, P., (2022). Shun Ethnic Rivalry and Corruption, Pope Tells African Youth. https://www.reuters.com/world/africa/young-people-gather-big-meeting-with-pope-dr-congo-2023-02-02/.

Raleigh, C. (2016). Pragmatic and Promiscuous: Explaining the Rise of Competitive Political Militias Across Africa. *Journal of Conflict Resolution, 60*(2), 283–310.

Tar, U. A., & Onwurah, C. P. (Eds.). (2021). *The Palgrave Handbook of Small Arms and Conflicts in Africa.* Palgrave Macmillan.

Titeca, K. (2011). Access to Resources and Predictability in Armed Rebellion: The FAPC's Short-lived "Monaco" in Eastern Congo. *Africa Spectrum, 46*(2), 43–70.

Uganda Joint Christian Council. (n.d.). Mission. https://ujcc.co.ug/.
UN Security Council Resolution. (2000). *UN Security Council resolution 1325 on women and peace and security (2000)*. United Nations Women. https://www.unwomen.org/en/docs/2000/10/un-security-council-resolution-1325.
Union, A. (2015). *Agenda 2063 Report of the Commission on the African Union Agenda 2063: The Africa we want in 2063*. https://www.un.org/en/africa/osaa/pdf/au/agenda2063.pdf.
Union, A. (2018). Strengthening African Women's Participation in Conflict Prevention, Mediation Processes and Peace Stabilisation Efforts: Operationalisation of FemWise-Africa. https://www.peaceau.org/uploads/final-concept-note-femwise-sept-15-short-version-clean-4-flyer.pdf.
Union, A. (2020). Orientation Concept Note on the AU Theme of the Year 2020: Silencing the Guns-Creating Conducive Conditions for Africa's Development.
United Nations. (2022a). *Ethiopia: Peace Agreement between Government and Tigray 'a Critical First Step': Guterres*. UN News. https://news.un.org/en/story/2022/11/1130137.
United Nations (2022b). Somalia: UN Welcomes End of Fairly Contested Presidential Election, Calls for Unity. https://news.un.org/en/story/2022/05/1118292.
United Nations Development Programme. (2020). *No Safer Place Than Home?: The Increase in Domestic and Gender-based Violence During COVID-19 lockdowns in LAC*. https://www.latinamerica.undp.org/content/rblac/en/home/presscenter/director-s-graph-for-thought/no-safer-place-than-home%2D%2D-the-increase-in-domestic-and-gender lid.
United Nations High Commission for Refugees. (2022a). *Figures at a Glance*. https://www.unhcr.org/figures-at-a-glance.html.
United Nations High Commission for Refugees. (2022b). *UNHCR Gravely Concerned by Death Toll of Displaced in DR Congo's East*. https://www.unhcr.org/news/briefing/2022/7/62da4d724/unhcr-gravely-concerned-death-toll-displaced-dr-congos-east.html.
United Nations Security Council Resolution 2250. (2015). *UNSCR 2250 | Introduction*. Youth For Peace. https://www.youth4peace.info/UNSCR2250/Introduction.
United Nations Statistics Division. (n.d.). SDG Indicators: Metadata Depository. https://unstats.un.org/sdgs/metadata/?Text=&Goal=16&Target=.
United Nations Women. (2020). DRC Takes a Step Towards Zero Tolerance Against Gender-Based Violence. https://africa.unwomen.org/en/news-and-events/stories/2020/09/.
United Religions Initiative. (n.d.-a). All Congo Inter-Faith Platform. https://www.uri.org/who-we-are/cooperation-circle/all-congo-interfaith-platform.
United Religions Initiative. (n.d.-b). The Inter-Faith Peacebuilding Initiative. https://www.uri.org/who-we-are/cooperation-circle/interfaith-peace-building-initiative.
United Religions Initiative. (n.d.-c). Inter-Religious Council for Peace. https://www.uri.org/who-we-are/cooperation-circle/inter-religious-council-peace-tanzania.
United Religions Initiative. (n.d.-d). Inter-Religious Council of Burundi. https://www.uri.org/who-we-are/cooperation-circle/inter-religious-council-burundi
US Department of State. (2022). *2021 Report on International Religious Freedom: Republic of the Congo*. https://www.state.gov/reports/2021-report-on-international-religious-freedom/republic-of-the-congo/.

Welty, e. (2014). Faith-based Peacebuilding and Development: An Analysis of the Mennonite Central Committee in Uganda and Kenya. *Journal of Peacebuilding & Development, 9*(2), 65–70.

World Health Organization. (2021). *Violence Against Women.* https://www.who.int/news-room/fact-sheets/detail/violence-against-women.

Yayboke, E., & Abdullah, H. F. (2020). *Elevating Women Peacebuilders Amidst Covid-19.* Center for Strategic and International Studies (CSIS). http://www.jstor.org/stable/resrep25662.

CHAPTER 31

# Interfaith Dialogue, Peacebuilding, and Sustainable Development in Nigeria: A Case of the Nigeria Inter-Religious Council (NIREC)

*Dodeye Uduak Williams*

## INTRODUCTION

Contemporary global challenges have necessitated critical assessments of religion and religious entities as it has become almost impossible to discuss these challenges without referring to religion in one way or another. Whether one is looking at conflicts within and across national boundaries, environmental issues like climate change, migration issues, or terrorism and violent extremism, religion and the role of religion can no longer be ignored. Religion is "a key identity marker, an integral aspect of social and cultural life, and also an important source of division" (Kadayifci-Orellana, 2013: 150). But while it is often the case to emphasize religion only as the source of conflicts, at various levels religion has also been acknowledged as an important tool for peace. In light of this, many organizations agree that the United Nations (UN) Sustainable Development Goals (SDGs) can only be achieved through the involvement of religious leaders and their various communities as they utilize the resources available within religions to effect change (KAICIID, 2019), largely through grassroots dialogue. The SDGs represent the most elaborate global development agenda aimed at achieving certain targets for sustainable development, including peace, by 2030. While none of the 17 SDGs speaks directly to eliminating or mitigating violence in the name of religion, the goal of peace appears

---

D. U. Williams (✉)
University of Calabar, Calabar, Nigeria

© The Author(s), under exclusive license to Springer Nature Switzerland AG 2023
S. M. Kilonzo et al. (eds.), *The Palgrave Handbook of Religion, Peacebuilding, and Development in Africa*,
https://doi.org/10.1007/978-3-031-36829-5_31

to be a significant variable for achieving sustainable development as indicated by SDG 16—Peace, Justice, and Strong Institutions. SDG 16 emphasizes the promotion of peaceful and inclusive societies for sustainable development, provision of access to justice for all, building effective accountable, and inclusive institutions at all levels, and promoting peaceful societies at national levels as well as international cooperation (UN, 2022).

While religion is not originally incorporated into the SDGs, the UN recognizes its salience, as one of its reports in 2020 clearly states:

> Recognizing that the underpinning of peaceful and inclusive societies is respect or the equality of persons regardless of race, sex, ethnicity, nationality, culture, religion or belief, birth or other status, SDG 16 seeks inter alia to significantly reduce violence, abuse, and exploitation; to promote and enforce non-discriminatory laws and policies for sustainable development; to promote rule of law and equal access to justice, strengthen transparency and accountability of institutions; and to broaden and strengthen participation without discrimination on any grounds. These targets will only be achieved through effective integration of minority and marginalized voices, including members of religious communities. (OHCHR, 2020)

One of the ways that religion contributes to peace is through interfaith dialogues. The UN's decision to engage with civil society actors, including those that are faith-based is a clear recognition of the role of faith communities in sustainable development (Karam, 2014, 2016). Interfaith dialogue is a critical component of global efforts to build peace "as religious and traditional leaders provide a very unique lens" through which nations can view and solve global challenges (KAICIID, 2019). However, the nexus between interfaith dialogue and peace is sometimes contested, as some like Scheffler (2007: 173) argue, interfaith dialogues are "politically irrelevant and have in the past ushered in bloody wars". On the other hand, others like Kung (1999: 92) state categorically that "there will be no peace between the civilizations without a peace between religions, and there will be no peace between the religions without a dialogue between the religions". The UN has continued to provide support to its member states in this direction. In Nigeria, one of the ways of support has been in establishing a functional national infrastructure for peace, as well as supporting other dialogue initiatives.

Interfaith dialogue in Nigeria gained prominence against the background of cultural and religious plurality that has led to violence, loss of lives, vandalism, and disruption of peaceful coexistence (Olorunnisola, 2019: 28). Ethnic identity and economic and social conditions are some of the factors that contribute towards violent communal clashes, political clashes, and ethno-religious violence (Salawu, 2010). The purpose of interfaith dialogue, according to Akinwumi (2021: 5–6), "is largely three-fold: to eliminate ignorance and misconceptions of other faiths and practices and promote informed understanding, critical appreciation and balanced judgment on matters of faith;

to work together for a common purpose in society, particularly where human rights, social and economic justice and peace are concerned; and to bring to bear the deeper resources of different faiths on the basic problems of human existence that arise because of human finiteness". Hence understanding religious dynamics and the role of faith communities and actors is crucial for sustainable development (Tomalin et al., 2019: 102). However, it is difficult to say that interfaith dialogues have contributed significantly to building peace and preventing conflicts in Nigeria. Rather, the worsening situation of religious conflicts in Nigeria tends to be an indictment of the interfaith dialogue project in the country (Igwe, 2022). The immediate reason as some suggest could be that interfaith dialogues may contribute to peace only under certain conditions, but scholars like Olorunnisola (2019: 30) argue that these conditions are almost non-existent in the context of interfaith dialogues in Nigeria. Is this the case? What are these conditions? Are they being fulfilled in Nigeria? What are the dynamics of interfaith dialogue in Nigeria? To what extent can interfaith dialogues contribute to peacebuilding for sustainable development in Nigeria? These are some of the questions we attempt to answer in this chapter using Cornille's (2013) conditions for interfaith dialogue: epistemic humility, mutual commitment, interconnection, empathy, and hospitality.

## Interfaith Dialogue and Peacebuilding: The Nexus

Interfaith dialogue, also known as inter-religious dialogue, aims at "the resolution of important problems between two or more religious entities (persons or groups) in order to enhance peaceful co-existence and mutual benefit" (Marbaniang, 2018: 103). It refers to the "cooperative, constructive and positive interaction between people of different religious traditions at individual and institutional levels with each party remaining true to its own beliefs while respecting the rights of other parties to practice their faith freely" (Forde, 2013: 7). For Cornille (2013: 20) it is "a constructive engagement between religious texts, teachings and practices oriented towards the possibility of change and growth". Interfaith dialogues have a long history and are borne out of the realization that unity and diversity of faith traditions must be harnessed for peaceful coexistence (Patrick, 2022: 22). Busquet (2012: 97) rightly asserts that "interreligious dialogue is ultimately not about exchanging information and knowledge, but about communion of hearts in the deepest layer of human existence". Increased awareness of religious plurality, the potential role of religion in conflict, and the growing place of religion in public life present urgent challenges that require greater understanding and cooperation among people of diverse faiths to increase acceptance of others and to better understand their identity (Greenebaum, 2014: 4, 17). Interfaith dialogue can take a wide variety of forms, ranging from joint appeals by high-level religious leaders, to attempts to develop mutual understanding and the recognition of shared values and interests, to grassroots efforts to encourage repentance and promote reconciliation (Smock, 2002: 16) among conflicting parties, for sustainable peace and development.

Interfaith dialogue is premised on a pluralist relationship—theologically and in a humanistic sense (Marbaniang, 2018: 107). Theologically, pluralism regards all religions as equally valid and fundamentally truthful, but it suffers from the problem of exclusivism by taking up a position of itself making a claim to truth, thus invalidating its own claim of many truths. Humanistic pluralism, on the other hand, focuses on mutual respect, peaceful coexistence, dialogue towards peace, and humanitarianism. It is within the humanistic approach that one is able to find common goals for active collaboration while not compromising one's core beliefs. It fulfils the idea of "living radically according to one's own religion but being attentive and interested in the others" (Marbaniang, 2018: 107). The humanistic pluralism relationship is the foundation of dialogue and is fundamental to the success of interfaith dialogue, dialogue that works through partnerships—dialogue for peace and social cohesion. This is in line with the purpose of peacebuilding which is to rebuild specific political institutions with sustainable relationships to create lasting peace between the former conflicting parties (Jeong, 2005: 21). Peacebuilding involves several dimensions including security and military; social, economic, developmental humanitarian; political and diplomatic; and justice and reconciliation (Barnett et al., 2007: 45). The activities within the justice and reconciliation category include "leader dialogue to provide dialogue opportunities between leaders, community dialogue to provide dialogue opportunities between members of antagonistic groups in community, bridge building to strengthen and reinforce interethnic confidence, tolerance and trust in the state institutions; and truth and reconciliation through commissions or other means of inquiry into recent and violent pasts using knowledge as a basis for reconciliation" (Barnett et al., 2007: 57). It is within this dimension that interfaith dialogue can be beneficial for peacebuilding. Peacebuilding like interfaith dialogue requires constant negotiation, mutual concessions, and respect for each side (Gaitanos, 2020: 55). Coward and Smith (2004: 6) use the term religious peacebuilding to describe "the range of activities performed by religious actors and institutions for the purpose of resolving, or transforming deadly conflict, with the goal of building social relations and political institutions characterized by a mission of tolerance and non-violence". Religious peacebuilding includes individual and grassroots efforts for promoting human rights and cross-cultural interfaith dialogue (Uysal, 2016: 265). It includes the beliefs, norms, and rituals that pertain to peacebuilding, as well as a range of actors, from religious institutions, faith-based private voluntary organizations that are not formally part of a religious institution, and individuals and groups for whom religion is a significant motivation for their peacebuilding (Philpott & Powers, 2010: 322).

Religious peacebuilding intervenes in various stages of conflict through a broad array of roles and activities at the local, national, and international levels. The activities can be categorized into four types: observation and witness (e.g., fact-finding, monitoring of ceasefires, accompaniment of victims), education and formations (e.g., conflict resolution training, education on peace and justice issues), advocacy and empowerment (e.g., mass protests, efforts to change specific policies), and conciliation and mediation (participation in truth and reconciliation commissions, facilitating peace processes, interfaith dialogue) (Philpott & Powers, 2010). Peacebuilding also involves multiple time horizons: before ceasefires and regime changes, during the conflict itself, in the immediate aftermath, and during the often decades-long process of reconstruction and reconciliation after the violence ends (Philpott & Powers, 2010: 323). The concept of religious peacebuilding, according to Wang (2011), infuses the religious sphere with the political sphere. One part of the process is cultural peacebuilding, that is, building good relations between the groups on social levels. And the other part is structural peacebuilding, meaning changing those structures of society that legitimate the conflict. Such structures can be unequal power relations, lack of freedom of movement, or other discriminating practices. The third approach to peacebuilding is elite peacebuilding, which is connected to the decision-makers or negotiation partners among the political authorities. In these ways, Wang explains, religious peacebuilding can promote peace (Wang, 2011: 53).

In summary, the relevance of interfaith dialogue to peacebuilding for sustainable development lies in the fact that religious leaders at the local, national, and international levels often have moral credibility that political, governmental, media, and corporate leaders lack; this moral credibility allows them to be effective advocates for peaceful social change, mediate between conflicting parties, and provide new visions for the future in societies torn by conflict (Philpott & Powers, 2010: 327–328). It helps to avoid frictions and frustrations between religions and religious communities. It creates space for people of different religions to coexist and learn from each other and engages the resources within religion from a broader political, sociological, economic, and community context (Paneer et al., 2022: 8). It also creates opportunity for different religions to clarify their misconceptions and misunderstandings about other faiths for the purpose of cooperative, constructive, and positive interaction (Alatas et al., 2003). It aims at promoting a culture of interfaith understanding in the context of contemporary global challenges (Halsall & Roebben, 2006). Interfaith dialogue allows religion to promote peace, justice, and strong institutions. However, regardless of these potentials, interfaith dialogue cannot replace political negotiations and does not seek to do so (Bakkevig, 2016). It is clear therefore that there are certain conditions under which religious dialogue initiatives can contribute to peacebuilding and sustainable development. Kung (1999) emphasizes rightly the need for respect and recognition of other religions and their values and norms. Flecha (2000) highlights the importance of equality of differences; Habermas (2010) emphasizes communication as an important condition, and Cornille (2013) rightly identifies epistemic humility, mutual commitment, interconnection, empathy, and hospitality as necessary conditions. In the next section we use Cornille's conditions, as broad categories to examine the dynamics of interfaith dialogue in Nigeria, using the Nigeria Inter-Religious Committee (NIREC), in relation to peacebuilding in support of fulfilling SDG 16.

## Dynamics of Interfaith Dialogue in Nigeria: Interrogating the Nigeria Inter-Religious Committee (NIREC)

Interfaith dialogue is significant for peace in Nigeria mainly because of its multi-religious and pluralistic nature. Interfaith conflicts have become more frequent as relations between Christians and Muslims, in particular, have been on the decline since the early 1980s. From 1980 to date, Nigeria has battled with relentless religious conflicts which have promoted violence and impeded national development (Paul, 2019). The three major religious identities in Nigeria include Islam, Christianity, and African traditional religions (ATRs). Nigeria is polarized roughly along a North and South divide with a majority of the north dominated by Islam and a majority of the South dominated by Christianity, while the ATRs are minorities in both parts of the country but very significant. While some still deny the direct influence of this polarization on the political, social, and economic landscape of the country, history is clear that religion is central to the character of the Nigerian state and is entrenched in the social fabric and political culture of the state with implications for peace, unity, security, and its continued existence. Christianity and Islam in Nigeria, as Lewis and Bratton (2000: 5) rightly describe, continue to be "the backbone of religious disparity and conflict". This is not to suggest that these are homogenous as there are several sub-groups and factions within each of these religious traditions (Osaghae & Suberu, 2005: 11). The issues that breed conflicts in Nigeria cut across various facets and include the forceful amalgamation of various ethnic and cultural groups, ethnicity, resource control, state creation, religious intolerance, youth unemployment, poverty, insecurity, land ownership issues, boundary disputes, and party politics to mention a few (Adegbami, 2020: 59).

Interfaith dialogues in Nigeria can be classified broadly as formal and informal dialogues (Onaiyekan, 2011: 11). They can also be said to take place within three interrelated frames, namely, local (traditional) communities, academia, and government. As Olorunnisola (2019: 32–33) suggests, these frames are intertwining: first, at the local communities, various religious leaders, practitioners, and traditional community leaders assemble occasionally or when the need arises to deliberate on how to promote communal peace and harmony; second, in academic circles, scholars gather periodically to challenge one another on the ideal ways of relating in a religiously plural country while focusing on educating the religious other about basic theological concepts underpinning beliefs and practices in a religion; and third, the institutional or structured inter-religious dialogue. While all three categories exist in Nigeria, institutional or structured dialogue is the most visible and dominant form. Some of the associations and agencies saddled with the responsibility of interfaith dialogue in Nigeria include the Universal Peace Federation (UPF), Nigerian Interfaith Action Association (NIFAA), the Interfaith Mediation Centre (IMC), Advisory Council for Religious Affairs in Nigeria (1987), the Centre of Interfaith Relation and Outreach in Ogbomosho (2004), the National Conference on Religions, Ibadan (2006), and various initiatives of inter-religious understandings recorded between the Nigerian Supreme Council for Islamic Affairs (NSCIA), the Christian Association of Nigeria (CAN) August–September 2004, and the Nigerian Inter-Religious Council (NIREC) (1999). What makes the NIREC unique is that "it is the sole government-established interfaith organization saddled with the primary responsibility of mediating the two dominant religions in Nigeria" (Fadeke, 2015: 201).

NIREC was created by representatives of Christianity and Islam to foster interfaith peace and dialogue. The association currently comprises 60 members based on an equal ratio of Muslim to Christian (Article 2, NIREC Amended Constitution, 2020). The association is co-chaired by the President-General of the Nigerian Supreme Council for Islamic Affairs (NSCIA) and the President of the Christian Association of Nigeria (CAN) (NIREC Website, 2020). NIREC was created in 1999 as a response to the incessant ethno-religious crisis that threatened the political stability and socio-economic development of Nigeria. According to the information on its website, NIREC is "a permanent and independent body established to provide religious leaders and traditional rulers with a viable forum for greater interaction and understanding among the leaders and followers as well as lay foundations for sustainable peace and religious harmony in Nigeria" (NIREC Website, 2020). According to its mandate, NIREC is expected to hold quarterly meetings and its activities are to include not only theoretical dialogue but a dialogue of action which promotes joint actions on multi-religious platforms to address the major problems of the society such as insecurity, poverty, corruption, unemployment, and diseases. Its sub-committees include research and planning, international relations, public issues, education, dialogue and peacebuilding, and finance. Political leaders, religious leaders, traditional leaders, and opinion leaders in various zones attend meetings at the invitation of the Governor of the State hosting the meeting. NIREC is funded by the Office of the Secretary to the Government of the Federation (OSGF), host states, collaborating agencies, members of NIREC, and free-will donations from Nigerians. NIREC is affiliated with the West African Inter-Religious Council (WAIRC), the African Council for Religious Leaders (ACRL), and Religions for Peace (RFP). The Dialogue and Peace Building Committee is to "be responsible for initiating moves to nip in the bud any anticipated conflicts. It shall liaise with the Research and Planning Committee with a view to making effective and optimum use of the Committee's findings for peacebuilding and conflict resolution. The Committee shall also be responsible for networking with other national organizations with similar objectives" (Article 7(e) NIREC Constitution, 2020).

The mandate of NIREC is to enhance interfaith dialogue for the purpose of building sustainable peace in Nigeria. But there are certain conditions that must be present to enable it to fulfil this core objective. Using Cornille's (2013) conditions for meaningful interfaith dialogue, we discuss some of these conditions below.

## *Epistemic Humility*

Epistemic humility refers to the idea that no one knows it all, and no religion contains the ultimate truth. It is "an intellectual virtue grounded in the realization that one's knowledge is always provisional and incomplete" (Angner, 2020). One of the objectives of NIREC is to create a permanent and sustainable channel of communication and interaction in order to promote dialogue between Christians and Muslims (Oloyede, 2015). Interfaith dialogue in Nigeria mainly involves representatives from two major Abrahamic faith traditions—Islam and Christianity. As Borchert (2013) rightly observes, embracing epistemic humility is the antidote to having a worldview of one's religion as the ultimate repository of spiritual truth. In real day-to-day interactions, Muslims try to convert Christians and Christians try to convert Muslims, and as Ahmed-Hameed (2015) posits, the idea that faith must be propagated, evangelism for Christians and *dawah* for Muslims, is one of the major factors that has orchestrated religious extremism and volatility in Nigeria. NIREC excludes representatives of other faith and non-faith traditions in its activities. It has a restricted and exclusive membership of Muslims and Christians and is often criticized as being "an inter-Abrahamic faith dialogue, Muslim-Christian Dialogue, or a dialogue of the people of the book" (Igwe, 2022). The representatives do not engage in learning about each other but rather come to meetings to defend their respective religious positions on issues (see Fadeke, 2015). In addition to this, NIREC's inter-religious committee is non-representative and does not adequately include women. As Fadeke (2015: 211) rightly observes, "the place of women in NIRECs peace efforts has been slightly obscure". Outside the framework of NIREC, however, some local initiatives have emerged to mitigate the challenge of female unrepresentativeness. One of these initiatives is the Women's Interfaith Council (WIC) formed in 2010 to build peace and stability in Kaduna, a state in Northern Nigeria, by addressing conflict issues and issues of concern to women with a primary focus on conflict, poverty, insecurity, and vulnerability (McGarvey, 2022). The WIC is a consortium of leaders and members of women's faith groups including the women's wings of CAN, Pentecostal Fellowship of Nigeria (PFN), and several Muslim groups. WIC provides activities, training, and experiences of interfaith peacebuilding and spirituality to women's faith group leaders, as well as youth groups (McGarvey, 2022: 100).

## Mutual Commitment

Commitment here represents the idea of a particular tradition being accountable to that tradition and speaking for it for the purpose of spiritual enrichment, as separate from mere exploration of head knowledge. As Cornille (2013: 24) explains, "speaking from and for a particular religion plays an important role in dialogue for the partners and the religion itself". It is expected, therefore, that representatives of religions in dialogue must be seen to represent and speak for their religions without compromising, to further the goals of spiritual enrichment rather than self-aggrandizement. In practice, spiritual enrichment appears to be far from the goals of NIREC as it appears that the revenue generation from being members of the council is more attractive (Igwe & Ugorie, 2013: 20). NIREC is government funded and its ability to pull itself from the apron-strings of government is limited as "he who pays the piper dictates the tune". Apart from the general funding of operations, the sitting allowance of NIREC is also paid by the government (Igwe & Ugorie, 2013: 20). Beyond the communiqués and press releases to publicly condemn acts of religious violence and conducting public awareness programmes, NIREC does not clearly harness the resources within religions to solve religious tensions. The politicization of religion in Nigeria prevents religious leaders from speaking truth to and being accountable to their religions. Igwe (2022), in a critique, notes that there is very little contribution to real dialogue in NIREC, as representatives are more concerned with "taking pictures with the President or governors and issuing press releases". In explaining this dynamic, Adogame (2005: 128) rightly posits that "the inner dynamics of religion and politics equally aggravate an unhealthy interaction and dialogue in a religious space in the form of religionalization of politics and politicization of religion". Political influence within the group is possible because many of the meetings tend to be with government officials and politicians at federal and state levels, with limited engagement with stakeholders even at the grassroots. Grassroots engagement is key in sharing knowledge and influencing behaviour at community levels. However, despite the rotational meetings NIREC holds in all the geopolitical zones and states, as well as the interactions with religious and community leaders, grassroots engagement has been ineffective as these interactive sessions hardly clear doubts and misconceptions, let alone of resolving the irreconcilable differences among the religions (Fadeke, 2015). To spread its message at the grassroots level, NIREC has clubs in secondary schools to promote inter-religious interaction, mutual respect, and understanding among the youth, but these clubs cannot influence policy and are merely to educate the young students. It is important to add that while these clubs may not provide immediate results in terms of transformations of existing religious conflicts, they provide, as Babagario (2022: 260) rightly argues, opportunities for long-term conflict transformation in these communities through education "to break stereotypes, mitigate violence, create understanding and enable cooperation and peaceful coexistence despite religious differences".

## Interconnection

The possibility of constructive inter-religious dialogue requires that every religious tradition involved develops a religious self-understanding in which at least some of the teachings of other religions are related to or relevant to one's own religious conception of truth. The idea of interconnection implies that other religions have a part to play in what resources exist within religions to connect them with others and this requires trust on some level. It does not appear that there is any degree of trust to cultivate this level of interconnection in NIREC. NIREC's objectives include articulating cordial relationships among and between the various religious groups and the government and assisting the federal, state, and local governments accentuate the positive roles that religion can play in nation-building and development (Oloyede, 2015). But there have been increasing levels of mutual mistrust within NIREC and this kind of interconnection is absent as the level of cooperation within the organization has deteriorated relative to how it was at its inception (Ugorie, 2017). NIREC was established in 1999 and at the time the idea of introducing Islamic Sharia Law across the Northern states where the Muslim population was dominant but with significant Christian communities was heating up the religious and political landscape. The debate sharply divided both religious communities, but regardless of how the Christian community felt and the arguments they raised to prevent the introduction of Sharia Law, the very next year, in 2000, Islamic Sharia Law was allowed to be established in several States in the North with a significant Christian population, creating doubts as to the sincerity of government to foster peace and mutual coexistence. In 2015, during an internal crisis of leadership, the divisions within the Christian Association of Nigeria (CAN) were attributed to selfish and political interests, which, according to the National Secretary of NIREC, Ishaq Oloyede, "sabotaged NIRECs operations" (Fadeke, 2015: 216). In reaction to this and the increased levels of mistrust in the body, the CAN opined that "NIREC cannot function because it is a conglomeration of religious leaders from one group (CAN) and mix-grill of politicians and traditionalists on the other hand. That is the reason for all the confusion in NIREC" (Nnamdi, 2015). Among the Muslims, the composition of representatives was equally criticized for excluding certain Sheikhs and astute preachers (Nnamdi, 2015). These schisms impacted very negatively on the public perception of NIREC.

## Empathy

- Empathy is the "ability to take the perspective of others and experience their emotions, combined with the motivation to care about their welfare" (Sirin et al., 2021: 20). Dialogue across religions requires the possibility of understanding one another across religious traditions. Empathy suggests that it is not just knowledge that is important but affective and intellectual understanding. The lack of a holistic and comprehensive framework limits the capacity of NIREC to have forums where empathy can be cultivated, given that the meetings are almost too political. One of the important objectives of NIREC is to foster mutual cooperation and promote the welfare of Nigerians, as well as create channels for peaceful resolution of misunderstandings (Oloyede, 2015). But as Igwe and Ugorie (2013: 20) rightly observe, "NIRECs national and international social connections generate enormous personal benefits and financial remunerations, which some of the members are primarily interested in". The lack of group empathy limits the capacity of any group to improve intergroup relations, let alone contribute to peace and social justice (Sirin et al., 2021: 231). Although Nigeria is a secular state, the centrality of religion in public and private lives across various ethnic nationalities cannot be ignored (Fadeke, 2015: 200). The mandate of NIREC includes serving as a forum for achieving national goals like economic and political growth, making recommendations to government on matters that might foster the spiritual development of Nigerians (Oloyede, 2015). But in a recent development, the ruling political party in its choice of the presidential and vice-presidential candidate, decided to field a Muslim-Muslim ticket for the 2023 elections. This coming at a time when the country is neck deep in ethno-religious tensions is an indictment on NIREC.

### *Generosity or Hospitality Towards the Truth*

This involves recognition of actual truth in another religion and hospitality towards integrating that truth in one's own tradition, given that there is a possibility of truth in other religions that must be accepted. None of these religious traditions within NIREC wants to be questioned. The missionary orientation of Christianity and Islam tends to defeat the purpose of dialogue just as the unfortunate assumption that either religion has a monopoly of knowledge. While the main aim of interfaith dialogue is not unity, but harmony, it is important to emphasize the similarities inherent in the separate religious doctrines (Fadeke, 2015: 200). Representatives need to accept that there can be truth in other religions even if they are different from the one's own religion. In Nigeria, religious intolerance is rooted in teachings, indoctrinations, and traditions of exclusivity (Igwe, 2021). One of the major objectives of NIREC is "to honestly and sincerely endeavour, by themselves, to understand the true teachings of the two religions—Christianity and Islam—including their peculiarities and personal mannerisms through dialogue, discussions, workshops, seminars, conferences, pamphleteering" (Oloyede, 2015). But the representatives of the two religions appear to be more of political leaders than religious leaders. Also, the nature of dialogue within NIREC so far has been an "unyielding one-way-religious communication" as Igwe (2021) rightly observes. Even the basic common resources contained in teachings, truths, and doctrines of Christianity and Islam such as those that emphasize love, tolerance, and compassion have not been harnessed enough. Top religious clerics are often found inciting their followers to violence and extremism on both sides. In addition, the absence of representatives of traditional religions in NIREC is an indication of the faulty assumption that whole community is irrelevant in the peacebuilding process and there is nothing to learn from them.

## IMPLICATIONS FOR SDG 16

SDG 16 aims to promote peaceful and inclusive societies for sustainable development, provide access to justice for all, build effective accountable and inclusive institutions at all levels, and promote peaceful societies at national levels as well as international cooperation (UN, 2022). The limitations and challenges of NIREC, whether internal or external to it, have implications for its ability to contribute to and strengthen the SDGs, particularly SDG 16 in Nigeria. Some of these implications can be listed as follows:

1. Inability to build the increasing levels of trust among religious communities needed to bring about societal change now and in the future. The nature of NIREC tends to reinforce interfaith divisions, exclusion, and alienation. It even appears that within its structures, interfaith dialogue exacerbates tensions and aggravates the problems it was meant to solve.
2. The exclusion of certain parts of society like women, traditional religious communities, and non-believers in dialogue defeats the purpose of interfaith dialogue which is expected to promote inclusivity for mutual understanding and peace.
3. Inability of religious communities to overcome barriers as a result of not seeing truth in other religions limits the prospects for peace.
4. Inability to harness the resources within religion to positively impact the social, cultural, spiritual, and ethical landscape in the country limits the prospects of peace.
5. Politicization of interfaith dialogue hinders the ability of parties to experience spiritual fulfilment borne out of new insights and so prevents the parties from fostering the kind of understanding needed for tolerance. Government influence and partisan politics limit NIREC's ability to be objective and leave religious extremism to thrive.
6. The constant infighting within NIREC reinforces the image of religion as a tool of conflict, not cooperation or peace, and hinders the prospects of seeing the positive resources within religion in Nigeria.

Consequently, there is a need for major adjustments within NIREC for interfaith dialogue in Nigeria to deliver the needed impact and support SDG 16. At the level of leadership, there has to be dialogue among the religious leaders first and then with the political leadership to set boundaries and give room for real interfaith dialogue that emphasizes the resources within religion to support peace initiatives. Also, at the level of the community, members need to be given opportunities to dialogue, especially members of antagonistic groups, women, and youths as well as traditional religious groups and the non-religious community. This will help to build bridges, as Barnett et al. (2007) rightly posit, "to strengthen and reinforce interethnic confidence, tolerance and trust within the community and in the state institutions" in line with SDG 16. In order to harness the numerous benefits of interfaith dialogue NIREC needs to address its internal and external challenges. The entire framework and structure need to be disconnected from some government control and given a high degree of independence to operate. Recommendations made by the group to deal with religious tensions, violence, and extremism must be taken seriously to be reflected in policy decisions of government. As a religious group, NIREC leaders must be seen to emphasize spirituality rather than material gain. The leaders must also be seen to be representing their various religious constituencies and not themselves. Programmes need to be designed that actually give opportunities for learning about each other's religion to foster understanding. In order to contribute to promoting peace, justice, and strong institutions in Nigeria, interfaith dialogue needs to be inclusive of other religions outside Christianity and Islam.

## Conclusion

There is sufficient evidence to show that interfaith dialogue contributes to building peace and can be a great resource, to support peace, justice, and strong institutions, if harnessed properly for this purpose. While this is not yet the reality in Nigeria, given the dynamics within NIREC, there is still a lot that can be done to reposition the organization for better results. The necessary conditions need to be fulfilled to give interfaith dialogue a chance to support SDG 16 in Nigeria.

## References

Adegbami, A. (2020). Peacebuilding in a Disparate Federation: Nigeria's Experience. *Acta Universitatis Danubius Relationes Internationales (AUDRI)*, *13*(1), 59–77.

Adogame, A. A. (2005). Politicization of Religion and Religionization of Politics in Nigeria. In C. J. Korieh & G. U. Nwokeji (Eds.), *Religion, History and Politics in Nigeria Essays in Honor of Ogbu U. Kalu* (pp. 128–139). University Press of America.

Ahmed-Hameed, A. (2015). Interfaith Dialogue: Preventing Extremism and Interreligious Conflict in Northern Nigeria. *International Journal of Humanities and Social Science Invention*, *4*(11), 82–89.

Akinwumi, O. S. (2021). Interfaith Dialogue and Peaceful Co-Existence in Nigeria. *International Journal of Advanced Research in Management and Social Sciences*, *10*(3), 1–12.

Alatas, S. F., Ghee, L. T., & Kuroda, K. (2003). *Asian Interfaith Dialogue: Perspectives on Religion, Education and Social Cohesion*. World Bank.

Angner, E. 2020. Epistemic Humility—Knowing Your Limits in the Pandemic. https://behavioralscientist.org/epistemic-humility-coronavirus-knowing-your-limits-in-a-pandemic/

Babagario, E. A. (2022). Education and Interfaith Development in Northern Nigeria. In E. Chitando & I. S. Gusha (Eds.), *Interfaith Networks and Development* (Sustainable Development Goals Series) (pp. 255–272). Palgrave Macmillan.

Bakkevig, T. (2016). *Interfaith Dialogue Can Help Build Peace.* PRIO Blogs, June 29. Retrieved January 18, 2023, from https://blogs.prio.org/2016/06/interfaith-dialogue-can-help-build-peace/#:~:text=They%20must%20respect%20and%20acknowledge,for%20further%20conversation%20and%20negotiation

Barnett, M., Kim, H., O'Donnell, M., & Sitea, L. (2007). Peacebuilding: What Is in a Name? *Global Governance, 13*(1), 35–58.

Borchert, D. M. (2013). *Embracing Epistemic Humility: Confronting Triumphalism in Three Abrahamic Religions.* Rowman and Littlefield.

Busquet, C. (2012). A Budhist-Catholic Dialogueof Life in Japan: Finding Shared Values for Global Collaboration for the Common Good. *Claritas: Journal of Dialogue and Culture, 1*(1), 85–97.

Cornille, C. (2013). Conditions for Interreligious Dialogue. In C. Cornille (Ed.), *The Wiley and Blackwell Companion to Interreligious Dialogue* (pp. 20–33). Wiley and Blackwell.

Coward, H., & Smith, G. (2004). *Religion and Peacebuilding.* SUNY Press.

Fadeke, B. O. (2015). Forging an Interfaith Cooperation in A Multi-Religious Society: The Case of Nigeria Inter-Religious Council (NIREC) 1999–2015. In E. O. Akubor & B. S. Shabayang (Eds.), *Religion, Religious Education and Nation Building: Nigeria and the World in the 21st Century Festschrift in Honour of Very Rev. Fr. Prof. Joseph Haruna Mamman* (pp. 199–222). Darosat Global Limited.

Flecha, R. (2000). *Sharing Words: Theory and Practice of Dialogic Learning.* Lanham.

Forde, G. (2013). *A Journey Together, Muslims and Christians in Ireland: Building Mutual Respects, Understanding and Cooperation, a Resource for Christian Muslim Dialogue.* Cois Tine.

Gaitanos, G. (2020). Interfaith Dialogue as a Medium of Peacebuilding: Official and Unofficial Mediation Platforms. *Theology & Culture, 1*(2), 55–63.

Greenebaum, S. (2014). *Practical Interfaith—How to Find Our Common Humanity as We Celebrate Diversity.* Skylight Paths Publishing.

Habermas, J. (2010). *An Awareness of What is Missing?: Faith and Reason in a Post Secular Age.* Cambridge: Polity.

Halsall, A., & Roebben, B. (2006). Intercultural and Interfaith Dialogue Through Education. *Religious Education, 101*(4), 443–452.

Igwe, L. (2021). Dialogue and Inter-Faith Belief Communication in Nigeria. *The Guardian*, November 23. Retrieved January 19, 2023, from https://guardian.ng/opinion/dialogue-and-interfaith-belief-communications-in-nigeria/

Igwe, L. (2022). A Humanist Perspective on Interfaith Dialogue in Nigeria. *The Nigerian Tribune*, December 7. Retrieved January 17, 2023, from https://tribuneonlineng.com/a-humanist-perspective-on-interfaith-dialogue-in-nigeria/

Igwe, O. C., & Ugorie, U. M. (2013). Christian-Muslim Conflicts in Nigeria: An Assessment of the Role of the Nigeria Inter-religious Council (NIREC). *ABSU Journal of Arts, Management, Education, Law and Social Sciences, 3*(2013), 1–20.

Jeong, H. (2005). *Peacebuilding in Postconflict Societies: Strategy and Process.* L. Rienner.

Kadayifci-Orellana, S. A. (2013). Inter-religious Dialogue and Peacebuilding. In C. Cornille (Ed.), *The Wiley-Blackwell Companion to Inter-Religious Dialogue* (pp. 149–167). John Wiley & Sons Ltd.

KAICIID (2019). *Dialogue and Partnerships: Keys to Achieve the SDGs*. KAICIID Dialogue Centre, December 13. Retrieved December 22, 2022, from https://www.kaiciid.org/news-events/news/dialogue-and-partnerships-keys-achieve-sdgs

Karam, A. (2014). *Religion and Development Post 2015*. Retrieved January 17, 2023, from https://www.unfpa.org/sites/default/files/pub-pdf/DONOR-UN-FBO%20May%202014.pdf

Karam, A. (2016). *Realizing the Faith Dividend: Religion, Gender, Peace and Security in Agenda 2030*. Retrieved January 17, 2023, from https://www.unfpa.org/sites/default/files/pub-pdf/50426_UNFPA_Donor-UN-FBO-Consultations_Web.pdf

Kung, H. (1999). Inter-Cultural Dialogue Versus Confrontation. In H. Schmiegleow (Ed.), *Preventing the Clash of Civilizations: A Peace Strategy for the Twenty-First Century* (pp. 88–103). St. Martin's Press.

Lewis, P., & Bratton, M. (2000). *Attitudes Towards Democracy and Markets in Nigeria: Report of a National Opinion Survey, January–February 2000*. International Foundation for Election Systems, and Management Systems International.

Marbaniang, D. (2018). *Karmic and Abrahamic Faiths: Comparative Themes for Interreligious Dialogue*. Retrieved December 4, 2022, from https://www.academia.edu/38229382/Interreligious_Dialogue_and_Peacebuilding

McGarvey, K. (2022). Women of Faith Working Together as Mothers of a Culture of Peace: The Women's Interfaith Council in Northern Nigeria. In E. Chitando & I. S. Gusha (Eds.), *Interfaith Networks and Development* (Sustainable Development Goals Series) (pp. 99–116). Palgrave Macmillan.

Nnamdi, U. (2015). CAN Tackles Islamic Council Over NIREC Leadership. *National Accord*, July 16. Retrieved January 19, 2023, from https://www.nationalaccord-newspaper.com/can-tackles-islamic-council-over-nirec-leadership/

NIREC Website. (2020). https://www.nirec.org.ng

Office of the High Commissioner for Human Rights (OHCHR). (2020). *Call for Input: Report on Eliminating Intolerance and Discrimination Based on Religion or Belief and the Achievement of Sustainable Development Goal 16 (SDG 16)*. Issued by the Special Rapporteur on Freedom of Religion or Belief October 30. Retrieved December 5, 2022, from https://www.ohchr.org/en/calls-for-input/call-input-report-eliminating-intolerance-and-discrimination-based-religion-or

Olorunnisola, T. S. (2019). Beyond Interreligious Dialogue: Dialogue of Life as a Means to Peaceful Co-Existence in Nigeria. *European Scientific Journal*, 15(17), 28–45.

Oloyede, I. O. (2015). *NIREC and Conflict Management in Nigeria*. Public Lecture, Religion for Peace Consultation on Reflection on Best Practices Sealing Up Multi Religious Action, Sarajevo, Bosnia-Herzegovina (BIH), 24–26 July.

Onaiyekan, J. (2011). *Dividends of Religion in Nigeria*. Department of Religions, University of Ilorin.

Osaghae, E. E., & Suberu, R. T. (2005). *A History of Identities, Violence and Stability in Nigeria*. Centre for Research on Inequality, Human Security and Ethnicity (CRISE) Working Paper No. 6 January 2005. Queen Elizabeth House, University of Oxford, UK.

Philpott, G. & G. Powers (2010). (eds.) *Strategies of Peace: Transforming Conflict in a Violent World*. Oxford University Press.

Paneer, S., Subudhi, C., & Pushparaj, R. (Eds.). (2022). *Interfaith Dialogue and Communal Harmony for Sustainable Development*. Hauz Khas Enclave.

Patrick, G. (2022). Interfaith Dialogues: New Horizons and Pathways. In S. Paneer et al. (Eds.), *Interfaith Dialogue and Communal Harmony for Sustainable Development* (pp. 20–32). New Delhi, India.

Paul, J. O. (2019). Implications of Religious Conflicts on Peace, National Security and Development in Nigeria. *Ilorin Journal of Religious Studies (IJOURELS), 9*(1), 53–70.

Salawu, B. (2010). Ethno-Religious Conflicts in Nigeria: Causal Analysis and Proposals for New Management Strategies. *European Journal of Social Sciences, 13*(3), 345–353.

Scheffler, T. (2007). Interreligious Dialogue and Peacebuilding. *Die Friedens-Warte 82*(2/3), 173–187.

Sirin, C. V., Valentino, N. A., & Villalobos, J. D. (2021). *Seeing Us in Them Social Divisions and the Politics of Group Empathy*. Cambridge University Press.

Smock, D. (2002). *Interfaith Dialogue and Peacebuilding*. United States Institute of Peace Press.

Tomalin, E., Haustein, J., & Kidy, S. (2019). Religion and the Sustainable Development Goals. *Review of Faith and International Affairs, 17*(2), 102–118.

Ugorie, U. M. (2017). *Peaceful Co-Existence in Nigeria: The Role of the Nigeria Inter-Religious Council (NIREC)*. LAMBERT Academic Publishing (LAP).

United Nations (UN). (2022). The Sustainable Development Goals Report 2022. Retrieved December 5, 2022, from https://unstats.un.org/sdgs/report/2022/

Uysal, N. (2016). Peacebuilding Through Interfaith Dialogue: The Role of Faith-Based NGOs. In S. Roy & I. S. Shaw (Eds.), *Communicating Differences* (pp. 265–278). Palgrave Macmillan.

Wang, M. Y. (2011). *How can Religion Contribute to Peace in the Holy Land?: A Study of Religious Peacework in Jerusalem*. University of Oslo. https://www.duo.uio.no/bitstream/handle/10852/37783/dravhandlingwang.pdf?sequence=1&isAllowed=y

CHAPTER 32

# Xenophobia, Interfaith Networks, Peace Building and Development in Botswana

*Tshenolo J. Madigele and Elizabeth P. Motswapong*

## Introduction

This chapter establishes the link between xenophobia and interfaith-based peace building in Botswana. It argues that there is an urgent need for interfaith presence in the context of xenophobia. The situation of xenophobia in Botswana forces religious leaders to look beyond their religious differences and work together in promoting "peaceful and inclusive societies for sustainable development, provide access to justice for all and build effective, accountable and inclusive institutions at all levels" (SDG 16). Interfaith networks across the globe are playing a critical role in integrating United Nations (UN) Sustainable Development Goals (SDGs) Agenda 2030 in their institutional agendas. This chapter in particular deliberates on interfaith networks and development in Botswana paying attention to SDG 16. It explores how interfaith networks had responded to tensions in their local communities. The chapter further explores the relevance of methods and strategies used by interfaith networks in an attempt to address the problem of xenophobia in Botswana.

A certain kind of identity or religious expression that is aligned with interfaith networks could be adopted in Botswana in an attempt to curb xenophobic tendencies. Botswana is duly regarded as a Christian state because of its Christian majority population. However, there are other faiths such as Islam, Hinduism, Sikhism and the Baha'i Faith. People from these faiths worship

---

T. J. Madigele (✉) • E. P. Motswapong
Department of Theology and Religious Studies, University of Botswana, Gaborone, Botswana

© The Author(s), under exclusive license to Springer Nature Switzerland AG 2023
S. M. Kilonzo et al. (eds.), *The Palgrave Handbook of Religion, Peacebuilding, and Development in Africa*,
https://doi.org/10.1007/978-3-031-36829-5_32

freely without any hindrance (Amanze, 1994). To date, the country has no history of religious violence among people of different faiths. That makes the country a very fertile ground of peace, tolerance and compassion towards non-Batswana citizens. There is only one interfaith network organization in Botswana that was formed in the year 2011. This organization is called Botswana Faith-based Organization Network on HIV and AIDS (BOFABONETHA). Its main mandate is on responding to HIV and AIDS to the year 2023 and beyond. BOFABONETHA had evidently made a progressive difference in responding to HIV and AIDS in the country. Through BOFABONETHA, most of the religions in the country had been fully capacitated to provide HIV and AIDS counselling to all age groups, as well as children, youths and women in abusive relationships (Madigele, 2022).

Botswana and South Africa had always been hosting non-documented immigrants from different countries, especially from Africa. There had been a huge influx of non-documented immigrants from Zimbabwe in the past years due to economic and political instabilities. If caught, such immigrants would be apprehended and deported to their respective countries. Authorities seem to be playing a losing battle because mostly those who are deported would be soon back in the country. About $100,000 which is equivalent to one million Pula (P1,000,000) is used by the Botswana government to deport Zimbabwean illegal immigrants (Dube, 2014). To control these illegal movements, security and immigration officers had been deployed to patrol along the Botswana fence. Those who managed to find their way through to Botswana are mainly the ones at the receiving end of discrimination and sometimes violence. Their activities would not, in any way, be enhanced either economically, politically or socially by the host (Campbell, 2003b). This means that undocumented immigrants with potential would not be empowered to exercise their capabilities and creative energies. Akinola (2018b) argues that instead of portraying the negative attitude of exclusion to them, it is better for the country to harness skills that foreigners have for the benefit of the masses. Their labour would not only benefit the people and economic development of Batswana; it would also be of benefit to their families back home. That is basically a practice of regional interdependency. This form of interdependency, however, could be condemned because it reinforces dependency syndrome on neighbouring countries.

The illegal status of non-documented citizens is the one that render them as targets of exploitation, discrimination and violence. They are identified with different sorts of crimes by the local media and the government. When local authorities identify them as the problem and threat to the society, it places them outside any form of protection (Maphosa & Ntau, 2021). Zimbabweans had been blamed for the increasing rates of crime and other social ills in the country. As a result, poor services would be extended to them (Akinola, 2018b). The government of Botswana has been blamed for its reluctance in introducing less restrictive immigration policies and for being complacent over the subject of illegal migrants (Campbell, 2003).

This is despite the fact that in history, Botswana has been identified as the most accommodative country in Africa because of its relaxed policies towards Zimbabweans. Undocumented citizens would be entered into asylum and those in asylum would receive assistance in the form of food, accommodation, protection services and so on. The ones outside the asylum system would consequently be deported. The former were regarded as refugees, while the latter were regarded as economic migrants. The number of economic migrants increased to 160,644.00 in 2015, a 32.86% increase from 2010 in 2 million population of Botswana. The entire United Nations (UN) system thence refrained from protecting and assisting Zimbabweans in Botswana because they were too many (Betts, 2013). Refugee camps in Botswana also failed to provide for the large number of Zimbabweans who ultimately saw it fit to leave the asylum system, knowing very well that by so doing, they would be exposed to poverty and exploitation and be denied basic health care and access to education (Betts, 2013).

Most of the people in Botswana were raising concerns about Zimbabweans. The concerns were that Zimbabweans were competing for the same economic resources with them—jobs, in a community that has high unemployment rates. They blamed Zimbabweans for the rising rates of crime. As such, illegal immigrants found themselves in such unsafe environment. There was no protection from the civil society, the UN system and the government of Botswana (Betts, 2013). In a way, illegal immigrants found themselves in the mercy of local citizens.

This chapter maintains that the services of BOFABONETHA should be directed towards curbing xenophobia in Botswana from individual to national level. Strategies and positive religious values that had been found useful by different interfaith networks internationally which include acceptance, peace, hospitality, shared responsibility and compromise (Madigele, 2022) could be used alongside Setswana cultural values of democracy, cooperation, unity, love and compassion to curb xenophobic tendencies in Botswana.

The chapter adopts a thematic approach. Relevant literature from books, journals and newspapers is analysed. The chapter also makes use of theories from different fields such as migration studies, sociology and peace and conflict to examine the nature of xenophobia as well as its possible influence on causing conflicts among nations. The following discussion provides an overview of xenophobia and makes use of different perspectives from scholars to examine xenophobic tendencies across the globe. Thenceforth is the exploration of xenophobia in Botswana and how xenophobic tendencies cause further disintegration and conflict with African member countries especially Zimbabwe. In what follows, we examine how different strategies and values that other interfaith networks across the globe have been using to attain peace can be adopted in Botswana to curb intolerance and xenophobic attacks in the country. The conclusion affirms that deadly xenophobic tendencies are very much prevalent in Botswana. BOFABONETHA as the only interfaith network is duly positioned to curb xenophobic tendencies from individual to national levels. The organization's history and involvement in the community render it as a potential organ to bring social healing and interracial reconciliation. It also has a potential to provide justice for all.

## Understanding Xenophobia

Xenophobia has been defined as a deep fear and dislike for the unknown. It has also been defined as the deep dislike of non-nationals based on fear of the unknown or anything perceived as different. Xenophobia involves attitudes, prejudices and behaviour that reject and exclude people on the perceptions that those people are outsiders or foreign to the community, society or national identity (Agnes, 2000: 1589). In a nutshell, xenophobia could be defined as fear or hatred of strangers or foreigners or anything foreign or strange.

In many cases, people migrate due to corruption and oppression of the political system in their country of origin. People move from depressed economies to economically stronger regions with the hope of finding employment and better living conditions. Royce says that people undoubtedly leave home and country because they believe their opportunities will be greater elsewhere. In the United States newcomers, especially Chinese immigrants, are owners of businesses, commercial entrepreneurs, skilled labourers and traders. The Chinese immigrants prosper due to high profits and because of their low-priced goods (Royce, 2007: 80).

On the history of xenophobia, Wright says that xenophobia is as old as the origin of population itself. When a population decided to form a community of people with territory, economic life, distinctive culture and language in common, that community gave birth to xenophobia. He emphasizes that people from other nationalities should shed their cultural identity, assimilate themselves into the state's culture or leave its territory (Akinola, 2018a). Bordeau (2010) also sheds light on the issue of diversity. He argues that as far as this formation of community with its unique life and culture unites people in that particular locality, it has a tendency of alienating those who do not belong to that community. In such an environment, therefore, productivity and settlement of migrants would be affected. Hostile interactions are also result of politics of diversity.

Xenophobia is generally related to the context and time (Landau et al., 2005). For instance, when the economy of Botswana was booming, the mine, tourism, education and administrative sectors of Botswana needed more human power. Skilled and non-skilled non-citizens were welcomed to offer services that would help grow the economy. Recession affected the economy of the country. The mining industry, which the economy of Botswana heavily depended on, also got affected because gold and diamond became luxurious commodities. HIV and AIDS also affected the economy of Botswana. Botswana remains among one of the highest affected nations in Africa. In a nutshell, different life situations came and left the economy of Botswana deeply damaged.

Meanwhile, unemployment, especially among the young, became the country's biggest challenge. These are the 15–18-year-olds who are seeking employment. In fact, it is reported that in the year 2013 more than 42% of the youth were unemployed in the country. Youth unemployment declined slightly to 41.2 in 2022 (World Bank, 2021). This is a very significant number of youth and the situation is even more worrisome because most of them are tertiary-level graduates. Youth unemployment is normally aligned with social instability, violent street protests and political instability (Mogomotsi & Madigele, 2017). Youth unemployment rates further translate to increasing poverty. The majority of the people in Botswana are between the range of 12 and 35 years. This age range constitutes 46.5% of the total population. About 66% of the youth population are those who had dropped out of school and those who had never attended school. This renders the youth in Botswana unemployable due to a shortage of skills (Mogomotsi & Madigele, 2017). The context and times of HIV and AIDS, recession and high unemployment rate could therefore be possible triggers of xenophobic tendencies towards non-citizens in Botswana.

Scholars, especially those who have researched xenophobia in South Africa, came up with various hypotheses to explain the origins of xenophobia. These are scapegoating theory, the isolation theory and the bio-cultural theory. The scapegoating theory originates from limited resources such as education, employment, health care and housing. When there is competition for scarce resources, foreigners are blamed for unemployment, poverty and depreciation (Dassah, 2015: 130–140, Hewitt, et al. 2020: 9–11). These resonate with the claims above where Zimbabweans are being blamed for competing for resources and taking up jobs for locals.

The isolation hypothesis traces the case of xenophobia to long-term isolation between nationals of one country and foreigners. Batswana lived in isolation for quite a long time because it was seen as a country with less value. Investors could not be attracted, firstly because of the low population and secondly because the country was thought to be poor until gold and minerals were discovered at a later stage. Living in isolation for a long time could also be a possible trigger of xenophobic tendencies towards people from neighbouring countries, especially Zimbabwe.

There was a similar situation in the United States where Blacks from the Southern states and Slavs from northeast moved into coal mining towns in Pennsylvania, West Virginia and Kentucky. The resident population resented or disliked both groups. This issue here was that the local communities' interest is to reinforce ethnic boundaries. The locals do not want their culture to be diluted by other cultures; they are not ready to adopt a new life and culture because they do not want to lose their culture. The incoming foreigners were therefore a threat and that is the reason the locals resorted to violence and hate towards the foreigners.

The bio-cultural hypothesis locates the origins of xenophobia to different physical, biological and cultural traits between nationals and foreigners. History teaches that by the late 1930s German medical science had constructed elaborate worldviews equating mental infirmity, mental depravity and criminality to racial impurity. This complex of identifications was then used to justify the destruction of the Jews on medical, moral, criminological and anthropological grounds. The battle against the unfit and deviant began to reach its culmination in medicalized mass murder in 1939. This was reflected in an accelerated interest in criminal biology throughout the Nazi period, which contributed to the belief that Jews were racially disposed to commit certain forms of crime. Therefore, Jews were hunted, relocated, captured or killed (Royce, 2007: 39).

Similarly, in Botswana people from other countries, especially Zimbabweans and Nigerians, are mostly looked up with suspicion. Nigerians at most are never trusted because they are collectively accused of committing all sorts of crimes, including faking to be traditional doctors and church priests. This means that in some people's minds, to be Nigerian is to be a criminal. Non-citizen hate is further expressed towards people because of differences in terms of appearance, culture, experiences and language. People from majority ethnic groups marginalize others on those grounds. Therefore, national identity is identified as another determinant of xenophobia. Nigerians could be arrested for no apparent reason, beaten and detained by security agents in Botswana (Edike, 2013).

## Xenophobia in Botswana

History teaches that people from Botswana used to flock to South Africa for job opportunities, especially in the mining sector. Upon the discovery of diamonds in the 1970s, Botswana automatically became a host to migrants. Some of the migrants were South Africans fleeing from the apartheid regime, while some were Zimbabweans fleeing political turmoil and economic meltdown (Ntseane & Mupedziswa, 2018). This notwithstanding, there had been an evident rise of xenophobia in Botswana, especially towards Zimbabwean migrants in the cities of Gaborone and Francistown. This is despite the fact that Botswana is considered Africa's most economically and politically stable country (Campbell & Crush, 2015). The xenophobic nature of Batswana is mainly based on nationalistic and economic factors. There is a strong move to preserve economic success to citizens only (Campbell, 2003). There are concerns that non-citizens are acquiring prime land that has to be reserved for local citizens (Manatsha, 2020).

Moreover, foreigners, especially Zimbabweans, have been blamed for the rise in crime, the decline of economic opportunities and many other social ills in Botswana (Akinola, 2018a). Another common factor that leads to xenophobic attitudes towards the people from Zimbabwe is the issue of illegal immigration. Botswana had since adopted a policy of openness and acceptance towards non-Batswana, but there had been an informal reaction towards Zimbabweans who reside in Botswana without proper travel documents. Those with no proper documents are normally arrested and associated with rising criminal activities. In fact, the police had been doing door-to-door search operations holding weapons in an attempt to deport all undocumented Zimbabweans back to their country of origin (Morapedi, 2007). Border patrols have been intensified; police, military and immigration officers have been deployed to patrol along border fences. All these are attempts to keep foreign nationals away. The policy of inclusion therefore had consistently been challenged and disregarded by politics of entitlements to the benefits of economic growth in Botswana.

Botswana has been receiving many migrants because of its better economic status. The country's economic success is owed to the discovery of gold and diamonds, as well as the aggressive expansion of mines across the country. Migrants flocked to Botswana offering skilled and unskilled labour. There have been concerns of exploitation of workers as many non-citizens complain of getting low wages; skilled workers being forced to take up low-paying jobs that would otherwise be retained for unskilled workers and non-Batswana workers being asked not to bring their families along with them to stay in Botswana (Kopiński & Polus, 2012). At this point, Botswana desperately needed manpower to grow the economy, but trying to avoid the influx of other nationals who may benefit from the fruits of success that otherwise belong to citizens of Botswana. Batswana rather prefer non-citizens who would invest in the country and employ or create employment for locals instead of those who take money from Botswana to develop their own countries (Campbell & Oucho, 2003). These anti-immigrant attitudes expressed through denial to grant foreign workers rights are very pronounced in Botswana.

There has been more abuse in the area of employment in Botswana. The *East African Magazine* (2014) titled "Botswana being taken over by creeping xenophobia despite govt 'compassionate' policy" reports an incident where Zimbabwean maids would work for the whole month, but employers would instead call the police reporting them as illegal immigrants. In other instances, some would be made to work for months or long hours on farms but would face abuse upon enquiring about their payments.

Attitudes of xenophobia to non-Batswana are also expressed in the area of health. For instance, antiretroviral therapy (ART) is provided free to all citizens of the country. Non-citizens who are either documented or non-documented are denied access to ART. Refugees are to access ART only within the confines of the camp. These stringent measures render the country more vulnerable to the spread of HIV. Non-Batswana citizens in prisons are also denied access to ART. Immigrants face stigma at different health care centres in the country as they are being blamed for the spread of HIV in the country. Undocumented migrants fear seeking medical attention when sick as they are most likely to be referred to the police or immigration officers by health care professionals. They would rather stay away from health care facilities to avoid the risk of deportation (Escudero et al., 2019). Poor service delivery and disregard for the right to health therefore are attitudes that render Batswana xenophobic. Some

Batswana citizens, however, argue that the rights of illegal immigrants should be curtailed (Campbell & Oucho, 2003).

Some Zimbabweans come to Botswana because of historical, cultural, linguistic and blood links. Although undocumented, some may see themselves as having the same rights and privileges as people who have the same linguistic and cultural ties with them. One of the famous reasons for migration, therefore, is that some people would travel to neighbouring countries to visit their relatives, to go for medical care and to work. For instance, people from a country like Lesotho have relatives in Zimbabwe and in Botswana. Botswana and Zimbabwe have borders that divide similar ethnic groups. Earlier, Zimbabweans and Batswana have been visiting their relatives without necessarily going through the gazetted points or carrying valid travel documents. This hostility towards Zimbabweans, which is expressed by Batswana and the police, could possibly cause disintegration between the two nations.

Mostly people who are from unfortunate nations are desperate. They can do any job and receive any amount of money they are offered for their services. Although many people are unemployed, for instance, in Botswana, they are not prepared to work the minimal work that Zimbabweans are working. In a situation like this, who is to blame? Do the foreigners deserve to receive the blow? We are all victims of the new capitalist system. Globalization as a new capitalistic system deprives people and nations economically.

## GLOBALIZATION AND XENOPHOBIA IN BOTSWANA

Globalization is a process of making the world small by linking people, companies and nations through media, travel, investments and trade. This means that the process of globalization may be economic, political, socio-cultural or a mixture of the listed reasons (Dwyer, 2015). From the perspective of business, therefore, globalization has to do with people, companies or different nations owning companies together, depending on each other in terms of labour, knowledge or trading of goods. From the look of things, there are different means that drive globalization—the first one is money and power. Individuals or nations with money power could invest heavily in different companies and nations, thereby depriving local businesses an opportunity to make profit and impoverishing the locals. For instance, in Botswana, goods from China are relatively cheap and convenient for the low to middle class (Zi, 2015). This means that the majority of consumers would rather prefer buying from Chinese shops. Locals in the same industries such as the clothing industry would consequently suffer losses while Chinese shops gain a lot of profit.

The second one is media and ICT that makes it possible for information fluidity, hence a tendency to transform local traditional cultures and languages of the people. Technology has replaced the labour force (Khoapa, 2016) and is possibly the reason for the high unemployment rates in Botswana. The decline in human development is therefore the main cause of poverty. The third means entails easy transport that makes it easy for migration and transportation of goods and services. Although it may be cheap and easy to get goods and services from other nations, the receivers could easily adopt the spirit of consumerism and dependency syndrome, hence the lack of innovation and participation in means of production. Botswana's manufacturing sector is already small (Zi, 2015) and should be encouraged instead of depending heavily on other countries such as South Africa and China.

China and Botswana have inter-governmental cooperation and through this cooperation Botswana had been receiving financial support from China. There has been an influx of thousands of migrants from China to Botswana who participate in the construction and distribution of goods and different services. Even though the local market is being heavily threatened by the Chinese people, there has never been an alarming bash from locals or security agents towards Chinese people. China is literally competing with itself on the larger scale or level of the economy while Batswana are fighting for survival on the lower scale with other nationalities, especially Zimbabweans. The anger, bashings and beatings are rather directed to Zimbabweans because they compete with locals on the lower scale of the economy. This is to demonstrate how globalization is a potential catalyst of xenophobia in Botswana. Locals are deprived economically, develop anger and consequently employ violent means of dealing with those competing with them on a lower scale. Those enjoying economic benefits on a higher scale remain untouched because they have developed strategies of total control.

Under the globalization system, nationalization of companies, resources and services is discouraged, and hence societies would cease being self-sufficient. Little focus is directed towards developing areas of health, education and unemployment. Local communities become so consumed by foreign investment and neglect critical sectors of human development such as education and health care (Khoapa, 2016). Apart from creating an unhealthy nation, globalization consequently creates an uneducated nation that could possibly only participate on the lower economic scale while non-citizens are playing on the high economic scale. Some of the people who cross to other nations are vulnerable and in need of better socio-economic lives. They are most likely to be beneficial to the economic aspect of the community although they are perceived as a threat to public safety, national identity and the domestic job market.

Based on the above discussion, both Batswana locals and undocumented immigrants are striving for economic inclusion. In the year 2015, 17.5% of the population were unemployed. The percentage increased to 22.2% in the year 2020 and further to 26% in 2021. Although unemployment declined slightly to 25.4% in 2023, the unemployment rate remains a national concern more so that the majority of the unemployed in Botswana are the youths who had either dropped out of school or never attended school (Mogomotsi & Madigele, 2017). Unskilled and uneducated people in Botswana lose their jobs to the new worldwide technological reality. They are not able to compete with cheap products from countries such as China. Instead of dealing with this issue,

Botswana chooses to close borders to those who may potentially and sustainably participate meaningfully in the development of the country.

BOFABONETHA is therefore challenged to look closely at the root causes of xenophobia in order to make it possible for migrants to make positive contributions to inclusive societies. If social and economic inclusion is availed, xenophobic tendencies would be tackled. That would translate to sustainable development and access to justice for all. Interfaith networks across the globe had been doing a commendable work as heralds of peace building and development. BOFABONETHA is challenged to explore some of the possible ways of dealing with xenophobia in Botswana through exploring methods and strategies used by interfaith networks in a global society.

## Interfaith Networks, Peace Building and Development

This section explores interfaith networks and their contribution to peace building in diverse contexts and how tactics and strategies used could be used to curb xenophobic tendencies in Botswana. Interfaith networks normally bring together people of different faiths and cultural backgrounds in an attempt to harness from the spiritual values in order to bring sustainable development to all lives and promote harmonious coexistence for the common good. Different methods and peace building strategies include dialogues, mutual problem solving, practical actions borne out of mutual respect and understanding, and social equity. Through dialogues or respectful conversations, people from different faiths and cultures identify their common values, beliefs and experiences. Upon having clarity on their commonalities, they identify and modify misconceptions for the common good. Another method and way that interfaith networks had adopted to promote a harmonious coexistence is through acceptance of differences (CRC, 2019).

One of the methods adopted by interfaith networks which could sustainably bring peaceful coexistence among different people is the act which involves striving for individual transformation and healing. Using tools designed for progressive dialogues, facilitators enhance inward peace which would subsequently translate to social cohesion. United faith group would then speak with the same voice advocating for peace and justice in local communities (CRC, 2019).

Interfaith organizations have played a major role in international and transnational relations (Lynch, 2009, 2014) making policy recommendations that were later implemented. They have also contributed in the reduction of disputes and conflicts through usage of "Binding, Bonding, and Bridging" activities which are normally regarded as 3B's (Leguro, 2017). Binding has to do with intra-personal change process which we described above as endogenous. This approach deals with internalized hate of the other and dealing with conceptions and misconceptions about the other. From the intra-personal level, we move to bonding on the intragroup level. A level of trust, respect and regard is built among different faith groups for change to happen. Change here involves transforming hate into friendship, cooperation and love. People are empowered to be aware of conflict and come up with ways of addressing conflict. The groups would then work together for the common good through "bridging activities." These intragroup activities further cultivate trust and relationships that are necessary for social cohesion (Omer, 2021). This framework and mentioned strategies and tactics could be adopted by BOFABONETHA. It is essential for BOFABONETHA to have a peace-connect project which aims at peace and development in the context of xenophobia. The targeted audience should include religious, cultural and traditional leaders who had shown interest in dealing with xenophobia. As a united front, they should engage with secular groups in a community. Upon success on the national level, they should engage policy makers and the related government entities. In the case of Botswana, desired outcomes include personal transformation and the ability to engage in the process of peace and social cohesion. It also includes building stronger relationships between different faiths and cultural groups for the purpose of outreach. The whole idea of strong bonds between different faiths and cultures entails unified advocacy for socio-economic equity and inclusion of all regardless of gender, class, religion, cultural background or race. In the process, people would be empowered by using religious and cultural values on the sustainability of gains in intergroup relationships. Furthermore, the interfaith networks' focus on prophetic roles without political influence is encouraged. Religion should play a part in promoting peace and non-violence resiliency in the face of unfavourable circumstances brought by external influences. External policies should be monitored and evaluated in order to promote peace and communal survival (Omer, 2021). This strategy entails policy and social service provision change as demonstrated above.

Apparently, there are ad hoc interreligious committees across the continent of Africa which are affiliated to the United Nations (UN). They have been formed by the African Council for Religious Leaders to mainly grapple with problems faced by Africa today, such as food security, climate change, violence and conflict. They have programmes running that attempt to curb conflicts and restore peace in Africa. In their approach, they target regional governments because they believe that there are structural conflicts and violence in Africa. They further make use of religio-cultural and ethical values to guide intra and interpersonal relations as well as to bind different individuals for the common good. They call for harmonious relationships between immigrants and host communities. These networks are further aimed at spreading a resilient culture of peace in Africa. Their vision is to popularize the concept of "welcoming the other" as a process of building peace in Africa. Their advocacy is actualized in the form of education and empowerment. They also facilitate dialogues and mediate conflict situations (Bisung & Dickin, 2019). The whole idea behind these ad hoc committees is for them to advance effective multi-religious cooperation for peace on global, regional, national and local levels. Empowerment is identified as a crucial activity to the solutions of problems of conflict and violence. Empowerment mainly aims at systemic change and for social and economic justice for all.

The value of humility, which is found in different interfaith networks, has been identified as an important component in bringing peace among polarized people. Humility in this sense has to do with acknowledging and appreciating co-dependence and interrelations of humanity and all that is around us (Admirand, 2019). By this virtue, people are made aware that they are fully dependent on each other. Interfaith dialogues could be used to initiate and foster conversations of that realization at individual and national levels. This concept of humility is coupled with values of hospitality, compassion, love, accountability, responsibility and cooperation. It is expressed in Botswana as *Botho* under the Setswana maxim, *motho ke motho ka batho*, literally translated as a person is a person through and because of other persons (Gaie, 2007).

Humility is normally expressed during interfaith dialogues where meaningful and respectful conversations are held. These conversations are normally aimed at understanding holistic causes of conflict and violence (Adogame et al., 2020). They have to do with action. They are also to initiate a call for cooperation between different religious communities striving for peace, equality, justice and good towards the poor or other marginalized groups of people. Under the value of humility, all stakeholders such as experts in the area and academicians should partake in enlightening people on the importance of realizing and acknowledging coexistence (Admirand, 2019).

In the context of Botswana, the poor are the most affected because they are not enabled to participate on the higher economic scale. Xenophobic tendencies are mainly prevalent among those in the lower economic scale in the country and mainly reinforced by government security agents such as the police, army and at immigration offices. As an interfaith organization, therefore, BOFABONETHA should, through its diverse members, strive for social justice advocacy. Advocacy is a process of influencing all relevant stakeholders into taking action that leads to a desired goal (The Network for Religious and Traditional Peace Makers, 2022). In an attempt to achieve the desired goal Sustainable Development Goal 16 related to peace, justice and strong institutions, BOFABONETHA could collaborate with relevant stakeholders and with a united voice, channel all their grievances to policy makers.

The organization should further challenge government, societal and security laws for instigating violence against non-citizens through unfavourable policies. The power of interfaith engagements could further facilitate attention on the development of the most neglected areas of health and education in Botswana. There is no way uneducated and unhealthy people could meaningfully participate in economic development. Local economic activities, therefore, could be challenged to treat locals with dignity by attending to mentioned neglected areas of human development. Availing access to adequate health and education fosters the ability and opportunity for locals to be productive economically (Farris, 2017).

The other important factor to consider during interfaith dialogues and action is to facilitate the mitigation of the exogenous and endogenous factors on conflicts and violence (Adogame et al., 2020). This means that internal (endogenous) factors, which are primarily psychological in nature and external (exogenous) factors which are mainly sociological controls, are major drivers of xenophobic attacks. Internal factors could be influenced by socio-cultural factors that are against integration. Internal factors make people fail to see integration as a possibility of socio-economic mobility despite the fact that both countries share common history and culture. Other forms of disintegration which are internal include things such as personality, physical differences and attitude. Perceptual differences also have the potential to cause institutional discrimination where rules and policies of the country have unintentional discriminatory effects. In that case, non-Batswana citizens receive different treatment that is discriminatory. This means that if most of security officers are of Botswana origin, they are more likely to be influenced by socio-cultural prejudice. In cases as such this, there is a need for interpersonal maturity and moral development from an individual level.

BOFABONETHA would be challenged to educate individuals at the personal level. They are also to educate service providers especially social security system and policy makers on possible influence of endogenous and exogenous forces on individual behaviour and service provision. BOFABONETHA could also be challenged to design training materials that show appropriate behaviours in contrast with inappropriate behaviours that are directed to non-citizens. Documentaries should be produced to demonstrate narratives on the consequences of discrimination so that immediate perpetrators would be aware of the consequence of their actions.

Interfaith organizations encourage communities of practice to develop inclusive capacity building and training. Capacity building and training has been emphasized as a good approach towards effective collaboration. Collaboration would be demonstrated through inclusivity, where a trainer and trainee share their experiences and expertise (The Network for Religious and Traditional Peace Makers, 2022). Facilitators are therefore challenged to make use of strategic learning exchanges and methods. A deliberate intention to recognize power of everyone would ultimately enhance a more sustainable equitable peace that stems from within. Though change and transformation start with individuals, change is envisioned to consequently take place in the institutional and governance.

External factors are aligned with governance or forces which indirectly contribute to unequal share on national resources in a case of Botswana and elsewhere. They subsequently cause neglect of human development in favour of foreign investment. Under this system, human beings are not transformed in all spheres. Human beings are only valued in terms of economic growth. This exclusivistic approach would most likely cause a hierarchy of discontent, resentment, violence and conflict among people. Those at the lowest point of the hierarchy may consequently resort to criminal activities either as revenge on the immediate perpetrator or in order to serve their basic needs. This is the area to address as an interfaith organization. The most fruitful approach therefore is on addressing effects of exogenous forces.

BOFABONETHA as the only interfaith organization in Botswana is being identified as the appropriate organization to facilitate peace between concerned nations and neutralize the present polarized public sphere. As an interfaith organization, BOFABONETHA has never been involved in acts of violence and it has always been identified as a moral power that has the capacity to call people to the right action. Therefore, the organization could play a critical role in peace building, human development and policy work in Botswana. The value of interdependence which is upheld by BOFABONETHA makes the organization so exceptional. It makes the organization very much open to collaborate as an intergroup with other relevant sectors for socio-economic cohesion during these difficult times of xenophobia. The organization also has the potential to bring individual, social and interregional healing for sustainable communal flourishing. BOFABONETHA's contributions on HIV and AIDS and advocating for gender equality and equity project elements of a shared positive vision of peace. The organization is guided by shared values, which transcend differing doctrines.

Above discussions on the role of the interfaith network relate to the 2030 United Nations Agenda, Sustainable Development Goal 16 (SDG 16) which calls for all regions to "[p]romote peaceful and inclusive societies for sustainable development, provide access to justice for all and build effective, accountable and inclusive institutions at all levels." There is an undeniable link between religion, peace and development. Religious communities are challenged to be change setters in the area of peace and development, particularly in the context of xenophobia in Botswana. Such action should be directed at transforming structures (Freire, 2017). Interfaith organizations should be in solidarity with the majority poor and facilitate the challenging of oppressive structures. Socio-cultural ideologies that instigate violence should also be interrogated at intrapersonal, interpersonal and communal levels.

## Conclusion

Reflecting on the above discussion, therefore, the majority of locals are unemployed, hence poor. Human development areas such as education and health are neglected in favour of foreign investment and economic resources, which are largely controlled by economically powerful nations, companies and individuals. Non-Batswana citizens competing for the small remaining portion of resources face discrimination, abuse and deportation. This means that skilled or unskilled immigrants are competing for the remaining small portion of economic opportunities in Botswana. That may be a possible cause of resentment and xenophobic tendencies towards immigrants. Globalization remains a trigger of socio-economic inequalities and xenophobic attacks in Botswana. There is therefore a need for conflict resolution or discourse adopted from different interfaith networks across the globe for xenophobic attacks to stop. As long as there is economic inequality, there can never be social cohesion. Equality in this sense entails a fair distribution of resources among Batswana. This means that policies that are intended on bringing about equality in Botswana should be implemented. Key approaches that could be used by BOFABONETHA should be driven by the context, needs and conditions. Personal change has been identified as the essential aspect to build inclusive social cohesion in a more sustainable manner. It also fosters unity and intragroup zeal for advocacy. That is a pre-requisite step towards engagement with policy makers and relevant governing offices. Xenophobia tendencies and violence towards Zimbabwean neighbours cause further interregional disintegrations, which may possibly erase future attempts at unity and interregional cohesions. Therefore, BOFABONETHA should see an urgency in providing leadership in the area of integration, social cohesion and peace building in Botswana.

### References

Admirand, P. (2019). Humbling the Discourse: Why Interfaith Dialogue, Religious Pluralism, Liberation Theology, and Secular Humanism Are Needed for a Robust Public Square. *Religion, 10*, 450. https://doi.org/10.3390/rel10080450

Adogame, A., Adeboye, O., & Williams, C. L. (Eds.). (2020). *Fighting in God's Name: Religion and Conflict in Local-Global Perspectives*. Lexington Books.

Agnes, M. (2000). *Webster's New World Dictionary*. Wiley Publishing, Inc.

Akinola, A. O. (2018a). Introduction: Understanding Xenophobia in Africa. In A. O. Akinola (Ed.), *The Political Economy of Xenophobia in Africa* (pp. 1–8). Springer International Publishing.

Akinola, A. O. (2018b). The Scourge of Xenophobia: From Botswana to Zambia. In A. O. Akinola (Ed.), *The Political Economy of Xenophobia in Africa* (pp. 23–36). Springer International Publishing.

Amanze, J. (1994). *Botswana Handbook of Churches: A Handbook of Churches, Ecumenical Organisations, Theological Institutions & Other World Religions in Botswana*. Pula Press.

Betts, A. (2013). 4. Botswana: The Division of Zimbabweans into Refugees and Migrants. In *Survival Migration: Failed Governance and the Crisis of Displacement* (pp. 78–89). Cornell University Press. https://doi.org/10.7591/9780801468964-007

Bisung, E., & Dickin, S. (2019). Concept Mapping: Engaging Stakeholders to Identify Factors that Contribute to Empowerment in the Water and Sanitation Sector in West Africa. *SSM-Population Health, 9*, 100490.

Bordeau, J. (2010). *Xenophobia: The Violence of Fear and Hate*. Rosen Publishing Group.

Campbell, E., & Crush, J. (2015). 'They don't want foreigners': Zimbabwean Migration and Xenophobia in Botswana. *Crossings: Journal of Migration and Culture, 6*, 159–180.

Campbell, E., & Oucho, J. (2003). *Changing Attitudes to Immigration and Refugee Policy in Botswana*. Southern African Migration Project.

Campbell, E. K. (2003). Attitudes of Botswana Citizens Toward Immigrants: Signs of Xenophobia? *International Migration, 41*, 71–111.

CRC. (2019). https://www.crs.org/sites/default/files/tools-research/aip_learning_brief_1_feb2019.pdf

Dassah, M. O. (2015). Naming and exploring the causes of collective violence against African migrants in postapartheid South Africa: Whither Ubuntu?. *TD: The Journal for Transdisciplinary Research in Southern Africa, 11*(4), 127–142.

Dube, M. (2014, November 14). Botswana Being Taken Over by Creeping Xenophobia Despite Govt 'Compassionate' Policy. http://www.theeastafrican.co.ke/magazine/Xenophobia-in-Botswana-despite-policy-/434746-2522696-fy83bp/index.html

Dwyer, L. (2015). Globalization of Tourism: Drivers and Outcomes. *Tourism Recreation Research, 40*(3), 326–339.

Edike, T. (2013). Bostwana to Deport 7 Nigerians, Detains 16. https://www.vanguardngr.com/2013/08/bostwana-to-deport-7-nigerians-detains-16/

Escudero, D. J., Marukutira, T., McCormick, A., Makhema, J., & Seage, G. R. (2019). Botswana Should Consider Expansion of Free Antiretroviral Therapy to Immigrants. *Journal of the International AIDS Society, 22*(6), e25328.

Farris, S. (2017). *In the Name of Women's Rights: The Rise of Femonationalism*. Duke University Press.

Freire, P. (2017). *Pedagogy of the Oppressed* (4th ed.). Bloomsbury.

Gaie, J. (2007). *The Concept of Botho and HIV/AIDS in Botswana*. Zapf Chancery.

Hewitt, M. L., Masikane, C. M., & Toendepi, J. (2020). Dynamics informing xenophobia and leadership response in South Africa. *Acta Commercii, 20*(1), 1–11.

Khoapa, S. (2016). Xenophobia in Southern Africa: A Pan-Africanist Perspective for Modern Times. *Open Access Library Journal, 3*, 1–9. https://doi.org/10.4236/oalib.1102415

Kopiński, D., & Polus, A. (2012). *Is Botswana Creating A New Gaza Strip? An Analysis of the 'Fence Discourse' Crossing African Borders: Migration and Mobility*. Center of African Studies (CEA)/ISCTE-IUL, University Institute of Lisbon.

Landau, L. B., Ramjathan-Keogh K., & Singh, G. (2005). Xenophobia in South Africa and problems related to it. *Forced Migration Working Paper Series, No. 13*. Johannesburg: University of the Witwatersrand.

Leguro, M., & A3Bs Project Team. 2017. Mindanao: Binding, Bonding and Bridging. In T. Bamat, M. Leguro, N. Bolton, & A. Omer (Eds.), *Interreligious Action for Peace: Studies in Muslim-Christian Cooperation* (pp. 71–82).

Lynch, C. (2009). A Neo-Weberian Approach to Religion in International Politics. *International Theory, 1*, 381–408.

Lynch, C. (2014). A Neo-Weberian Approach to Studying Religion and Violence. *Millennium: Journal of International Studies, 43*, 273–290.

Madigele, T. J. (2022). Interfaith Collaboration, Sexual Diversity and Development in Botswana. In E. Chitando & I. S. Gusha (Eds.), *Interfaith Networks and Development: Case Studies from Africa* (Sustainable Development Goals Series). Palgrave Macmillan. https://doi.org/10.1007/978-3-030-89807-6_9

Manatsha, B. T. (2020). Reflections on the Acquisition of Land by Non-Citizens in Botswana. *Journal of Land and Rural Studies, 8*(2), 185–204.

Maphosa, F., & Ntau, C. (2021). Undocumented Migrants as Homo Sacer: Cases From Botswana and South Africa. *Journal of Asian and African Studies, 56*(4), 872–888. https://doi.org/10.1177/0021909620946349

Mogomotsi, G. E., & Madigele, P. K. (2017). A Cursory Discussion of Policy Alternatives for Addressing Youth Unemployment in Botswana. *Cogent Social Sciences*, *3*, 1–9.

Morapedi, W. (2007). Post-Liberation Xenophobia in Southern Africa: The Case of the Influx of Undocumented Zimbabwean Immigrants into Botswana, c. 1995–2004. *Journal of Contemporary African Studies*, *25*(2), 229–250.

Ntseane, D., & Mupedziswa, R. (2018). Fifty Years of Democracy: Botswana's Experience in Caring for Refugees and Displaced Persons. *International Journal of Development and Sustainability*, *7*(4), 1408–1427.

Omer, A. (2021). Religion and the Study of Peace: Practice Without Reflection. *Religion*, *12*(12), 1069. https://doi.org/10.3390/rel12121069

Royce, A. (2007). *Identity and Culture*. Free Press.

The Network for Religious and Traditional Peace Makers. (2022). https://www.peacemakersnetwork.org/wp-content/uploads/2022/03/theory-of-change-strengthening-leadership.pdf

World Bank. (2021). https://data.worldbank.org/indicator/SL.UEM.1524.ZS?locations=BW

Zi, Y. (2015). The 'Fong Kong' Phenomenon in Botswana: A Perspective on Globalisation from Below. *African East-Asian Affairs*. https://doi.org/10.7552/0-1-2-151

CHAPTER 33

# Role of Islamic Networks in Peacebuilding and Development in Kenya, and the War on Terror

*Newton Kahumbi*

## INTRODUCTION

The main objective of this chapter is to discuss the role of Islamic networks in peacebuilding and development in Kenya. The chapter focuses on Islamic faith whose followers are Muslims. The rationale being that the Muslim community represents a significant minority in Kenya where Christians predominate. Muslim (Islamic) networks refer to the various organizations operating under the ambit of Islam in peacebuilding and development in Kenya. These organizations are variously referred to as Islamic networks and are centered around three levels: local, national and international. The term "development" as adopted from the Sustainable Development Goals (SDGs) is defined as activities that contribute to reduction of poverty and other deprivations to improve health and education, reduce inequality and spur economic growth (https://sdgs.un.org›goals). As noted by Weiss (2020, p. 2), Muslim NGOs could be key partners in achieving the SDGs. Peacebuilding comprises various activities and efforts toward building social relations (Chepkorir, 2019, p. xi) for sustainable peace and development as per SDG 16. Religion refers to the system of religious beliefs of faith communities such as Muslims and Christians. The "war on terror (terrorism)" is the global campaign against terrorism, involving security operations, legislations and mitigations of terror attacks.

---

N. Kahumbi (✉)
Department of Philosophy & Religious Studies, Kenyatta University, Nairobi, Kenya

Through the use of secondary data and literature, the chapter interrogates Islamic networks which are subsumed under the Muslim community. Within that context, there is paucity of knowledge on the role of Islamic networks in peacebuilding and development. This chapter therefore intends to bring to the fore this contribution and add to the extant knowledge on Muslims in Kenya. In addition, as discussed later in the chapter, the war against terrorism has inadvertently sucked in Islamic networks and put them in the eye of the storm in the Kenya government's crackdown on the Muslim organizations perceived of abetting terrorism. It is therefore important to document the role of Islamic networks, as the voice of Muslims, in national political and religious discourses on peacebuilding and development efforts, in the backdrop of government's "war on terror."

## Theoretical Perspectives

The role of Islamic networks on peacebuilding and development in Kenya could be gleaned from available sources. The role of the mosque as an institution of peace, education and political development is expressed by Maina (1992), Ali (2012) and Nadwa (2016). Maina (1992) and Nadwa (2016) underline the historical role of the mosque in socialization, religious edification, promulgation of state policy and dispensing of justice. Ali (2012) underscores the role of the mosque in various activities of peacebuilding. The three authors' discussion shows the mosque as an important aspect of the Islamic networks. However, the scope of this chapter extends beyond the mosque by bringing in other Islamic networks. Literature on Muslim NGOs and their role in community development is offered by Mwakimako (1995). This treatise highlights the activities of the Muslim NGOs in Kenya and takes cognizance of the challenges that they experienced in unfavorable and skewed political environment of the eighties. Lynch's (2011) seminal article on Islamic NGOS in Kenya underlines the important role of the NGOs in peacebuilding and development by categorizing them as local, national and transnational. The article informs and greatly benefits this chapter. Her treatment of the Islamic networks forms part of the discourse which includes interfaith peacebuilding, post-election violence and constitutional debates, all of which are outside the scope of this chapter. Lynch (2011) further highlights how the "war on terror" affected the operationalization of Islamic networks. On the same train of thought, Chembea (2020) underpins the effects of the "war on terror" on Muslim charitable organizations. These include bearing the brunt of security agencies for allegedly abetting terror, contempt and profiling of the organizations and 'Relative Deprivation' which pushes beneficiaries to radicalization. While the works of Lynch (2011) and Chembea (2020) are germane to our discussion in this chapter, they fall short of underpinning their discourses within the context of SDG 16, hence the need to fill this gap. Faith and Development in Focus: Kenya (2017) provides an overview of Kenya's religious landscape in relation to major issues of development. Within that context, the study highlights some of the Muslim NGOs, both community-based and those with international links, that are involved in peacebuilding and development. Undoubtedly, this chapter has enormously benefitted from Faith and Development in Focus: Kenya (2017) study. However, the chapter has notably widened the scope to include the dimension of Muslim networks and the "war on terror." Omari's (2014) thesis on Islamic leadership zeroed in on Supreme Council of Kenya Muslims (SUPKEM). This dissertation offers probably one of latest and elaborate exposition of an Islamic organization in Kenya, which richly informed this chapter. From the foregoing, it is evident that much has been done on Islamic networks in Kenya, but there are still knowledge gaps that need to be filled as this brief review on extant works has shown. Hence the need for this chapter.

Over the years, the Muslim community in Kenya has operated under local, national and international organizations (networks). These networks emphasize the promotion of the socio-cultural and economic welfare of the community, and hence they are largely considered apolitical (Mwakimako, 1995, p. 226). The 1998 terrorist bomb blast at the American Embassy in Nairobi and the September 11, 2001, terror attacks in USA brought about global "war on terror," an American-led military global counterterrorism campaign which involved military operations and new security legislations (Global Policy Forum, 2005). Within the Kenyan context, the "war on terror" had some ramifications in the operations of Muslim organizations in the country. The subsequent banning of some Muslim NGOs and their repression by state agencies on suspicions of complicity in terrorism impeded the work of these groups in peace and development.

This chapter discusses the role of Islamic networks in peacebuilding and development in Kenya amidst the "war on terror." The chapter starts by situating Muslims and Islam within Kenya's religious demography; this follows the discussion on the Islamic networks which are divided into three categories: the local mosque-based networks, national organizations and the international-based networks. The chapter analyzes the Islamic network in the face of the "war on terror" followed by the way forward for Islamic networks. The chapter concludes that though the "war on terror" constrains their efforts, Islamic networks have endured, playing their role in peacebuilding and development in Kenya.

## Religious Demography in Kenya

The current population of Kenya according to some latest data from United Nations is approximately 57 million people (https://www.worldometers). There are no reliable figures on Kenya's religious demography, as data largely depends on sources, with some skewed in favor of some religious groups while others are skewed against those groups (Lynch, 2011, p. 23; Maina, 2019, p. 68). Certainly, Kenya is a Christian majority country, with a significant Muslim minority. The Christian population is estimated at 81 percent, Muslim

8.1 percent; adherents of African traditional religions 9.0 percent; Baha'is, 1.1 percent; Hindus, 0.5 percent; Buddhists, Sikhs, Jains, Zoroastrians and Jews 0.3 percent; Atheists and Agnostics about 0.1 percent (Maina, 2019, p. 68; Murimi, 2016, p. 605). For Muslims, more than 70 percent are Sunni of the Shafi'i school of jurisprudence, while the Shi'a Muslims, together with the Ahmadiyya, a Muslim missionary group, constitute less than 20 percent of the Muslim population (Maina, 2019, p. 68).

Regarding their geographical distribution, Muslims are predominant in the Coast and North Eastern counties of the country. There are also some pockets of Muslims in the rural country side and in the main urban areas where the majority of the Asian Muslim communities reside. The predominant Muslim areas suffered some economic neglect during the colonial and post-colonial eras. This has contributed to a feeling of socio-economic and political marginalization by Muslims (Maina, 2017, p. 26). Over the years, this perception has been reinforced by the Christian domination in political and socio-economic spheres of development in the country, a situation that Muslim networks attempt to address.

## Islamic (Muslim) Networks

Islamic networks in Kenya are classified as NGOs, and they operate under the NGO Co-ordination Board. The Board is a state corporation established by the NGO Co-ordination Act (Cap 19) of 1990 (https://ngobureau.go.ke). There are many Muslim networks in Kenya. Uncorroborated data by Omari (2014, p. 76) gives a figure of 300 Muslim organizations. These networks could be categorized as local (mosque-based), national and international. All these networks, like other religious institutions—churches, mosques and temples—are registered under the Societies Act, Chapter 108.

## Local (Mosque)-Based Networks

Religious sanctuaries symbolize the existence or presence of faith communities that use those sanctuaries for worship. By corollary, the presence of a mosque symbolizes the presence of Muslims within a given locality. In the history of Islam, the mosque played important roles in the life of the community: religious, educational and socialization, political and judicial. The mosque was an assembly and gathering of Muslims; it was a place of worship and the first place where Muslims received new teaching and guidance for their life (Nadwa, 2016, p. 55). The mosque was equally a hub of all Muslim communal activities and therefore a channel of socialization. Religious edification and state policy were proclaimed in the mosque. Justice was also dispensed within the confines of a mosque (Maina, 1992, pp. 49–50).

To date, the mosque has not dispensed with the historical invaluable roles of serving the Muslim community. The mosque is central to the entire life of the community since as a place of worship, it brings together Muslims from all walks of life. Hence, the mosque offers an avenue and opportunity for exchanging ideas which enhance Muslim solidarity, unity of purpose and action. Local mosques act as neighborhood NGOs through which *zakat* (poor due) is collected and distributed to the poor (Weiss, 2020, p. 21). Mosques dispense *waqf*—a religious endowment of money or property which is used for building mosques, schools, orphanages and health clinics. The mosque networks therefore provide the much need aid at the local level. They also liaise with national NGOs for purposes of humanitarian and social welfare programs in many parts of the country inhabited by Muslims.

Thus, the mosque plays an important role in peacebuilding in Kenya which is consistent with SDG 16. There is documented evidence showing how the mosque undertakes various peace activities to curb cattle rustling and banditry—which are forms of violence—in North Eastern Kenya. These activities according to Ali (2012) include peace caravans, religious roadside preaching, dialogue with the youth, positive behavior change, dialogue with chiefs, dialogue with the police, inter-*madrassa* (religious school) competition, rapid response initiatives and monitoring the implementation of peace agreements and trauma healing, among others.

The mosque networks through committees that manage their affairs offer guidance to Muslims through articulating the issues that affect the community. This role is exemplified by the Jamia Mosque Committee in Nairobi. According to Nadwa (2016, p. 64), the Committee "has fairly participated in articulating Muslim concerns and protecting their rights" such as issuing political statements and declarations in the aftermath of terrorist attacks. Therefore, it could be argued that through the committees, the mosque networks have been responsive in ensuring inclusive, participatory and representative decision-making of Muslims, which is a concern of SDG 16.7. The next section of the chapter examines some of the national Islamic networks.

## National-Based Networks

Besides mosque networks, there are several national organizations which provide services that promote peacebuilding and development. Since national Islamic networks are registered under the Societies Act, the Act requires them to deal singularly with matters of religion, peacebuilding and humanitarian activities such as improving the living standards, health and education of the Muslim community. These activities are replicated and cut across the networks. The networks are specifically identified as religious entities, and as discussed later in the chapter, within the context of "war on terror," some of the networks have been viewed with suspicion by the government.

The national Islamic networks include but are not limited to the following: Building Resilience Against Violent Extremism (BRAVE), Council of Imams and Preachers of Kenya (CIPK), Kenya Muslim Youth Alliance (KMYA), Muslim Education and Welfare Association (MEWA), National Muslim Leaders Forum (NAMLEF), SUPKEM and the Young Muslim Association (YMA).

The author selected some of these networks for explication based on their unique role vis-à-vis others whose activities do not fall within the purview of peacebuilding and development per se. Drawing from this argument, the following networks were selected: SUPKEM, CIPK, KMYA and BRAVE.

### Supreme Council of Kenya Muslims (SUPKEM)

SUPKEM is one of the largest Muslim umbrella organizations. It was founded in May 1973 as the umbrella body of all Muslim organizations, societies, mosque committees and groups in Kenya (Omari, 2014, p. 79; Lynch, 2011, p. 24). The following are some of the objectives of SUPKEM: to promote the growth and unity of member organizations; to facilitate cooperation and collaboration between member organizations, as an agent for reconciliation; to coordinate, advice and speak for all Muslim organizations in Kenya; and to set up and establish Islamic projects such as education institutions (Omari, 2014, p. 80).

SUPKEM has collaborated with other faith networks on issues surrounding the constitutional reforms in Kenya that brought the new constitution that was promulgated in 2010. SUPKEM joined the Ufungamano Initiative in 1999 and Peoples Commission of Kenya in 2000. These two were interfaith coalitions of religious groups that brought together Muslims, the Catholic church, leaders of National Council of Churches of Kenya (NCCK) and the Hindu Council of Kenya, among other faith groups. On the eve of the 2007 general elections, together with other Muslim organizations, SUPKEM appealed for Muslims to unite as they forged their political destiny.

Suffice it to say that as the umbrella body of Muslims in Kenya, SUPKEM is supposed to oversee and coordinate the operations of other Muslim networks in the country. Therefore, the activities of SUPKEM in achieving the various targets of SDG 16 on peacebuilding should be subsumed under the networks discussed below. Invariably, SUPKEM is the voice of the Muslims and therefore its role in peacebuilding and development should be seen as such. For example, following the Garissa University attack in April 2015 in which 147, mainly Christian, students were killed, Muslim scholars and clerics were accused of not doing enough to condemn the attack or counter radicalization. SUPKEM responded with a statement that urged the government to address radicalization. The SUPKEM leadership also issued a statement that assured the public that "contrary to the impression that has been created, we as Muslim scholars have been tirelessly working through various religious institutions and forums to address radicalization, the threat of terrorism and other crimes" (*Faith and Development in Focus*, 2017, p. 50). SUPKEM's stance was apparently fruitful because some months later on December 22, 2015, some Muslim passengers aboard a bus traveling from Nairobi city to Mandera in Northern Kenya were attacked by Al-Shabaab militants. The gunmen's attempts to separate Muslims from non-Muslims as was the practice in such attacks failed. The Muslims gave the non-Muslim headscarves (*hijab*) to disguise themselves and also helped others to hide behind bags in the bus (Ramos, 2015).

Earlier, on July 1, 2012, SUPKEM was involved in a peace initiative when its officials led by Secretary General together with government officials and other international organizations visited Garissa in North Eastern Kenya which was the scene of twin terror attacks (Omari, 2014, p. 75). More examples of SUPKEM as the voice of the Muslims in peacebuilding is accentuated under the section on "war on terror."

## Council of Imams and Preachers of Kenya (CIPK)

Council of Imams and Preachers of Kenya (CIPK) was registered in 1997 as a faith-based nonprofit and charitable organization. It brings together respected Islamic scholars, imams and Muslim preachers in Kenya. Generally, CIPK fosters the agenda of SDG 16.7: "ensure responsive, inclusive, participatory and representative decision-making at all levels." In this regard, CIPK was founded due to the realization of the urgent need by Muslim leaders to unite and find avenues to provide a voice of relief and reason for marginalized communities through building the community's capacity at the national level (Lynch, 2011; https://www.cipkmombasa.or.ke).

In line with SDG 16.11 to "strengthen national institutions to prevent violence and combat terrorism and crime," CIPK has two notable projects: Prison Religious Rehabilitation (PRR) Project and Strengthening Resilience to Violence and Extremism (STRIVE) Project. The PRR is a two-year project funded by United Nations Office on Drugs and Crime (UNODC). The aim of PRR Project is to prevent and respond to radicalism and violent extremism in prisons. This project has targeted two main maximum prisons in the country: Shimo la Tewa in Mombasa and Kamiti in Nairobi. To this end, CIPK enhances the capacity of prison imams and officers on how to prevent or counter the spread of extremist ideology within prisons by promoting alternative narratives. This is in addition to developing an attitudinal change in the inmates through building resilience that helps them to adopt anti-extremism actions. In the STRIVE Project, CIPK partners with the Royal United Services Institute for Defense and Security Studies (RUSI). STRIVE has a two-year program which is under implementation in Mombasa and Kwale counties of the Coast Province. The program aims at promoting alternative voices in coastal Kenya by enhancing the capacity of imams and management committees of mosques on importance of early prevention of extremism and enhancing the capacity of management committees of mosques on early warning of extremism; this is done through developing a guide on modalities that encourage better and more responsive engagement with youth (https://www.cipkmombasa.or.ke).

## Kenya Muslim Youth Alliance (KMYA)

Kenya Muslim Youth Alliance (KMYA) was founded in 2002 to fill the gap left by SUPKEM in addressing specific programs targeting the Muslim youth. These programs address the need for acquisition of knowledge, skills and attitudes to enable the Muslim youth cope with demands of the changing world without compromising Islamic values (Omari, 2014, p. 16). KMYA is the main umbrella organization for the Muslim youth population with 153 member organizations. It facilitates and promotes access to resources through knowledge creation and dissemination, and nurturing progressive and value-driven leadership among marginalized Muslim youth. As an organization targeting the needs of the Muslim youth, some of the objectives of the KMYA meet SDG 16.7 which is achieved through two main objectives. Firstly, the KMYA is positioned to effect change in peacebuilding and gender equality through involving women in peacebuilding programs, which is crucial in preventing the radicalization of Muslim youth. In this regard, KMYA strives to engage women to counter extremism, by teaching mothers how to detect signs when their children are being recruited into extremist groups. Secondly, KMYA brings Muslim women together at the community and national levels to learn about peacebuilding and sharing their experiences through dialogues that allow women to establish a support network and to learn from each other in order to develop effective peace programs (Faith to Action Network, 2022; *Faith and Development in Focus*, 2017, p. 73). Arguably, KMYA's activities in preventing radicalization and extremism go a long way in achieving SDG 16.11.

To actualize some of its objectives in peacebuilding and development, KMYA held an Interfaith Youth Camp in Kilifi County, Coast Province in the last week of December 2022. The week-long camp brought together youth from various religious, cultural and social backgrounds from across the county. The objective of the camp was to enhance the social understanding of young people from diverse faiths and beliefs to promote their involvement in peace building and human rights protection. One of the reasons why KMYA holds such youth learning events is to build the capacity of young people for leadership in the community (https://twitter.com›KMYA254).

## Building Resilience Against Violent Extremism (BRAVE)

Building Resilience Against Violent Extremism (BRAVE) was founded in 2015. It is a systematic strategy to counter the rising radicalization and extremism. BRAVE is the flagship program of Centre for Sustainable Conflict Resolution (CSCR). The program expects to trigger, initiate and sustain a momentum for actions on counter-violent extremism, counter-radicalization and de-radicalization in Kenya (CSCR, 2019). BRAVE focuses on the violent and non-violent manifestations of radicalization and extremism in Kenya. It seeks to mobilize stakeholders and counter the narratives of the extremists' groups by addressing the misuse of religion for violent extremist ends. A

BRAVE manual and resource guide provides guidance on early warning signs of possible radicalization so that parents, teachers, religious leaders and communities can identify the youth that may be vulnerable. BRAVE offers narratives to counter messages used by extremists, describing misinterpretations of the Qur'an and *Hadith* (sayings of Prophet Muhammad) by extremist groups (*Faith and Development in Focus*, 2017, p. 69; CSCR, 2019). Evidently, BRAVE's programs largely align with Target 16:11, as earlier mentioned. In addition, the programs address SDG 16.1: "reduce violence everywhere." This is in view of the programs' activities meant to mitigate violence and death wrought by terrorism resulting from radicalism and extremism.

An example of how BRAVE is involved in activities of peacebuilding to counter radicalization and extremism is evident through the work of the CSCR. Through BRAVE, the CSCR launched *Lenga Ugaidi Na Talanta* (Kiswahili for "Avoid Extremism with Talent") Competition in 2018. The competition is an initiative that seeks to channel youth creativity toward countering violent extremists' narratives. The competition targets Kenyan youth under 35 years to create messages to counter radicalization and violent extremism. The contest involves development of short films and art—songs and poems—to counter violent extremist narrative in specific thematic areas (CSCR, 2019). Having looked at some of the national-based Islamic networks, I now turn to the international networks.

## International Muslim Networks

The international-based networks incorporated in Kenya tend to replicate or reconstruct the situations in their countries of origin (Mwakimako, 1995, p. 226). These networks include Islamic Relief Worldwide (IRW), Aga Khan Development Network (AKDN), World Assembly of Muslim Youth (WAMY), and Bilal Muslim Mission, among others. It is worthwhile to discuss two of these networks, namely IRW and AKDN. The two networks tend to have ties with Western donors and emphasize their ostensible 'secular' orientations (Lynch, 2011) as opposed to their "religious" leaning counterparts who are largely viewed with suspicions by the government in the "war on terror."

## Islamic Relief Worldwide (IRW)

Islamic Relief Worldwide (IRW) is a transnational relief and development charity organization founded in the UK in 1984, with branches in 35 countries (Ndzovu, 2020, 126). It began its work in Kenya in 1992 with a small one-to-one orphan sponsorship program in the Mandera district. Its programs expanded during the drought in the Horn of Africa, to include larger scale humanitarian relief and development assistance in that area. Currently, IRW is one of the main international Muslim organizations which is active in Dadaab refugee center and surrounding community in Garissa County. Islamic Relief works in four main sectors: emergency relief, development, orphans, and poverty alleviation endowments. IRW undertakes programs through grassroots networks that include poverty alleviation endowments, orphan sponsorship, education, micro-credit, emergency relief and medical service (Ndzovu, 2020, p. 132; https://islamic-relief.org).

The IRW programs align with SDG 16.1 which is meant to promote peaceful and inclusive societies and particularly reducing violence and related death rates among refugees. Working among refugee communities, IRW humanitarian programs mitigate the debilitating effects of violence by providing access to justice for all and building effective, accountable and inclusive institutions. For example, IRW staff design programs of integrating formal education components into the Qur'anic (*duksi*) preschools in Dadaab refugee camp. Another IRW hallmark program is a Sharia compliant micro-finance program, where religious leaders explain and assure community members of the program's validity and compliance with Islamic law (Lynch, 2011, p. 25; https://islamic-relief.org).

## AGA KHAN DEVELOPMENT NETWORK

The Kenyan Ismaili community has played important roles in Kenya's economic development, notably through the Aga Khan Development Network (AKDN). AKDN is a group of private, international, non-denominational agencies working to improve living conditions and opportunities for people in the developing world. AKDN is dedicated to improving the quality of life of those in need, mainly in Asia and Africa, irrespective of their origin, faith or gender (AKDN). AKDN works through several independent entities, which include the Aga Khan Academies (AKA), Aga Khan Agency for Habitat (AKAH), Aga Khan Agency for Microfinance (AKAM), Aga Khan Education Services (AKES), Aga Khan Foundation (AKF), Aga Khan Health Services (AKHS), Aga Khan Trust for Culture (AKTC), and Aga Khan University (AKU). His Highness, Prince Karim Aga Khan, IV, the 49th Imam of the Shia Imami Ismaili Muslims is the leader of AKDN, which is spread out in over 30 countries Kenya included and employs about 80,000 people worldwide. AKDN emphasizes on pluralism, non-denominational engagement to create a shared concept of the common good and a common humanity (https://the.akdn; *Faith and Development in Focus*, 2017, p. 44; Walji, 1995, pp. 13–15).

Through the leadership of the Aga Khan IV, the Ismaili community has managed to establish major social welfare and economic development institutions. The Diamond Trust Bank and the Jubilee Insurance Company which are part of the Aga Khan Fund for Economic Development (AKFED) play major roles in national development. Profits from these companies are put into projects that support employment and agricultural development (https://the.akdn; *Faith and Development in Focus*, 2017, p. 44).

AKF and AKES make education a core activity of the AKDN. Through these organizations, the Ismaili community founded and have run schools and education programs in Kenya for many years. These schools offer the

International Baccalaureate (IB) curriculum, 8-4-4 curriculum and the newly introduced Competence Based Curriculum (CBC). Through the School Improvement Program, AKF works closely with the government, offering workshops and training. AKF offers resource centers for public primary school teachers and management that helps in improving the quality of education in the public school system (Maina, 2011a, p. 239; *Faith and Development in Focus*, 2017, p. 66). One of the most acclaimed program of AKF is the Madrasa Early Childhood Education which begun in Mombasa in the eighties under the Madrasa Resource Centre (MRC) in collaboration with the National Centre for Early Childhood Education (NACECE). The program trained teachers for schools that offered integrated curriculum (Maina, 2011a, p. 239). The program has supported over 960 preschools and has benefitted 75,000 young children in Kenya since 1986 (https://the.akdn).

To a greater extent, AKDN programs advance SDG 16. Indeed, in his keynote speech at the Conference on Culture and Development in Amsterdam on September 9, 2002, His Highness the Aga Khan, exhorted governments, civil societies and peoples of the world to enhance pluralism as a critical component for "the welfare and progress of human society as are poverty alleviation and conflict prevention" (Aga Khan stresses pluralism, 2008). Elsewhere, in Lamu County in coastal Kenya, AKF which is an agency of AKDN partners with the Ministry of Education "to integrate values-based education across curriculums, promoting tolerance, peace, and pluralism, to unite disparate groups and build a buttress against extremist ideology" (Creating hope in Kenya—AKDN, 2020).

## Islamic Networks and the "War on Terror"

This section of the chapter shows that some Muslim networks were caught up in the government's "war on terror" and subsequently banned. However, the "war on terror" has raised the profiles of some of these networks. The latter underlines the important role of the networks in peacebuilding and development among Muslims.

The August 7, 1998, simultaneous bombing of the USA embassies in Nairobi (Kenya) and Dar es Salaam (Tanzania) which killed thousands brought the reality of homegrown terrorism. These terror attacks were allegedly committed by Al-Qaeda terrorists. But the September 11, 2001, (9/11) terrorist attacks in the USA was a turning point in the operations of Islamic networks in Kenya, as tensions between them and the Kenyan government heightened under the "war on terror."

Currently, any discourse on terrorism invariably puts Islam and Muslims on the receiving end. The reason being majority of the terror attacks have been blamed on Muslim extremist groups such as Al-Qaeda, Al-Shabaab, ISIS (Islamic State in Iraq and Syria) and Boko Haram. Invariably, in the Western prism, the "global war on terror" has become "war against Islam and Muslims." While Islam has been accused of condoning terrorism through its teachings, Muslims have been accused of perpetrating the act. Nwaigbo (2006, p. 65) argues that Islamic texts are interpreted to fight and kill infidels in holy war as an act that will lead the perpetrators to paradise. According to Gullen (2010, p. 179), contemporary terrorism is almost limited to and synonymous with Islam and Muslims. It is within this context that this section discusses the role of Islamic networks in the backdrop of the "war on terror."

Terrorism and the "war on terror" have drastically affected the operations of the Muslim networks in peacebuilding, humanitarian and development work. Allegedly, some Muslim organizations are suspected of having links with extremist groups such as Al-Shabaab and Al-Qaeda; some of the organizations have been accused of spreading extremism, providing financial and logistical support to militants and terror groups and recruiting Muslim youth into the terror groups (Chembea, 2020; Duh, 2014). This scenario has therefore put the government security agencies on a collision course with the Muslim organizations.

After the 1998 terrorist attack, the Kenya government banned five Muslim NGOs which operated in North Eastern Kenya but with headquarters in Nairobi. These were Mercy Relief International Agency, Al-Haramain Foundation, Help African People, the International Relief Organization and Ibrahim Abd al-Aziz al-Ibrahim Foundation (Chembea, 2020, p. 151; Ndzovu, 2020, p. 134; Maina, 2017, p. 26; Oded, 2000, p. 84). The government through the NGO Co-ordination Board purported the NGOs were involved in clandestine activities and "matters that are not in the interest of state security," with some officials accused of aiding the terrorists and funding terror activities (Ndzovu, 2020, p. 134; Lynch, 2011, p. 26).

The ban on the Muslim NGOs disrupted the social welfare programs (Chembea, 2020, p. 151) and created antagonism between the NGOs and the government because of the humanitarian role that the latter were playing in the Muslim communities. The Muslim community reacted strongly against targeting only Muslim NGOs, making claims that this fed into the narrative of Islam as a global threat. Muslim leaders and SUPKEM united in defending the Muslim NGOs for their valuable charitable work and some mass demonstrations were staged in October 1998 (Maina, 2017, p. 27). In defense of the banned Muslim NGOs, Muslim leaders and SUPKEM rooted the case of Al-Haramain Foundation arguing that it operated orphanages, healthcare services, education and income-generating projects for poor families in North Eastern Kenya. A further argument was that the ban meant cutting of the bloodline of most of the inhabitants of the area who were relying on the humanitarian assistance from Al-Haramain and other organizations. Indeed, SUPKEM leadership condemned the raids accompanying some of the closures of the Islamic NGOs, with accusations that "Kenyan Muslims have been subjected to provocative, discriminatory, vindictive, anti-Muslim and anti-Islam" rhetoric (Lynch, 2011, p. 26). Following the ban of the Muslim NGOs, with the accompanied profiling of Muslims, the community largely felt the freedom of worship guaranteed in the constitution had been impinged on. This situation exacerbated frustration among members of the Muslim community to extent that some would perceive violence and recruitment to terror groups as a just cause to achieve what they were denied by the government (Chembea, 2020, p. 153).

After 1998 terror attacks, there was another major terrorist attack in Kenya on November 28, 2002, with the suicide bombing of the Israel owned Paradise Hotel in Kilifi, Coast Province. Thirteen people died and 80 were injured. Coming to terms with terrorism as a homegrown phenomenon, the government founded the Anti-terrorism Police Unit (ATPU) to mitigate and investigate all terrorism related cases in the country (Directorate of Criminal Investigations, 2020). The consequences of the operations of ATPU were immediate and dire for the Muslim community, with claims that the unit was responsible for illegal arrests of hundreds of Muslim youth, torture, extrajudicial killings and the forced disappearance of perceived Muslim militants and activists (Chembea, 2020; Maina, 2017). Muslims for Human Rights (MUHURI) supported by Coast Interfaith Council of Clerics (CICC) condemned these incidents (Lynch, 2011, p. 26).

Besides the security agencies, the "war on terror" has also involved the NGOs Co-ordination Board which in 2014 announced that 15 unnamed NGOs were under investigation for links with Al-Shabaab. In 2015, the Board deregistered 959 NGOs following its audit. Consequently, two Musim NGOs: Haki Africa and MUHURI, were listed as "entities suspected to be associated with Al-Shabaab," by the police; they unsuccessfully challenged the allegation in court (*Faith and Development in Focus*, 2017, p. 22). Accusations linking Muslim NGOs with terror groups damages their reputation and credibility in the eyes of the government, the international community and donors (Weiss, 2020). This affects the organizations' operations in humanitarian work and other aspects of development as they engage in litigations in courts of law to clear their names instead of concentrating on their core mandate. Ultimately, this may also affect the funding as some donors are wary of being associated with terrorism for fear of ostracism and profiling.

From the outset, Christians feared that some of the Muslim NGOs would interfere with the freedom of religion as they "had as their main goal making Kenya an Islamic country within the next two or three decades" (Oded, 2000, p. 84). Many Christians and the government in particular were concerned about the growth of Islamic radicalism in the country. Consequently, in 2003, the government floated the Anti-terrorism Bill. It was however withdrawn due to widespread criticism from Muslim leaders who saw the Bill as draconian, arguing that it was targeting Muslims. Muslims feared that the police would arbitrarily arrest them based on attire. A CIPK leader spoke out against targeting and detaining over 30 Muslims on allegations of terrorism (*Faith and Development in Focus*, 2017, p. 49).

Some Muslim networks like SUPKEM have acted and shown the directions regarding terrorism. Following the Garissa University terrorist attack, the government froze the bank accounts of three Muslim NGOs—among them Haki Africa and MUHURI—and imposed a dusk-to-dawn curfew in the counties of

Garissa, Wajir, Mandera and Tana River. In addition, 80 businesses dealing with informal money transfers (*hawala*) and foreign exchange bureaus were closed after the Mandera bus attacks. Muslims considered all these as attempts to strangle the economy of the Somalis in the pretext of fighting terrorism by a "Christian government." Notably, the Muslim perception of the Kenyan government as "Christian" is borne of many years of Christian domination of the social, political and economic sectors of Kenya since independence. Muslims in Coast and North Eastern counties have historically felt marginalized in the predominantly "Christian state, where socio-political and economic culture is infused with Christian language and imagery" (Nyagah et al., n.d., p. 10).

Islamic networks have continued to be the voice of the Muslim community in the war against terror. This was evident in the year 2021 when two prominent Muslim scholars: Abdulwahab Sheikh Abdiswamad and Hassan Nandwa were abducted. Muslim leaders led by SUPKEM and NAMLEF, with support from civil society groups, came out to strongly condemn the abductions. They called out what they termed a "war on terror"—turned—"war on Islam" and the treatment of Muslims as second-class citizens. Consequent to the outcry, the two scholars were released (Noor, 2022).

The response of Muslims to terrorism between 2013 and 2015 witnessed the emergence of two groups of Muslims: moderate Muslims and radical Muslims. While the former supported government crackdown on radicalism, the latter were sympathetic to terror groups. Consequently, this created discord in Muslim leadership. This partly occasioned supremacy battles between the moderates and radicals for the control of mosques (Maina, 2017, p. 27). In Mombasa, for example, several mosques were seized by youths who blamed the imams of lack of legitimacy to serve because of failing to resolve the myriad of problems affecting Muslims. With the government support for the moderates, some mosques were flagged for radicalization and extremism. Security forces were accused of abetting the killing of radical Muslim clerics, while radical clerics were accused of killing the pro-government imams in retaliatory attacks. Security agents stormed into Masjid Musa, and Swafaa and Mina mosques on February 2, 2014, and November 24, 2014, respectively (Maina, 2017; Akwiri, 2014). The two incidents which led to violence and loss of life exemplify the confrontation between moderates and radicals in the control of mosques in Mombasa. Arguably, the "war on terror" has affected the role of the mosque as a neighborhood NGO for peacebuilding and development, especially in situations where the mosque committees have been accused of working in cahoots with individuals sympathetic to terror groups such as Al-Shabaab. This part of the chapter shows that the "war on terror" is a challenge to the operations of Islamic networks in Kenya. This is coupled with leadership challenges of these networks to which the next section of the chapter now turns.

## Way Forward for Islamic Networks in Peacebuilding and Development

Going forward, besides the challenge posed by the "war on terror," Islamic networks face the challenges of leadership and professionalism in managing their affairs in peacebuilding and development. The sentiments of Mwakimako (1995) of lack of professionalism in the leadership and management skills of local Islamic NGOs in the 90s still obtains to date regarding these organizations. Omari (2014, p. 65) argues that the leadership of many Islamic organizations lack the requisite skills to articulate their issues. This is occasioned by low academic achievement in secular education where majority of Muslims lag behind other communities (Maina, 2011a). This situation may not be said of the organizations under the AKDN, which are run by highly educated and trained professionals.

Lack of unity among Muslim leaders is reflected in the local Islamic networks which cannot forge a common agenda in their programs and activities. Research by Omari (2014) shows that Muslim organizations have witnessed disunity over the years and efforts to unite them always come to naught. Disunity is apparent during elections when Muslims are divided along ethnic, region and race affiliations. Lack of unity is compounded by power struggles among the organizations due to a perception of the lackluster performance of SUPKEM in agitating for the rights of Muslims. Consequently, other local networks hardly recognize SUPKEM as the voice of Kenyan Muslims (Mwakimako, 1995; Omari, 2014). Regarding the "war on terror," CIPK accused SUPKEM of complicity in abetting government's anti-terror policies which targeted Muslims (Lynch, 2011). Such a perception gave rise to CIPK filling the leadership vacuum left by SUPKEM. Indeed, the differences between SUPKEM and CIPK are evident through war of words between the two. While SUPKEM accuses CIPK of lack of inclusivity in its leadership, CIPK accuses SUPKEM of not recognizing other Muslim networks (Omari, 2014, pp. 67, 71). Ultimately, leadership wrangles derail the work of local Islamic networks as they hardly speak in one voice which is crucial in negotiating for donor funding and spatial recognition in a competitive environment.

In view of the foregoing, the future operations of the Islamic networks in peacebuilding and development will depend on the way they will surmount the above challenges either individually or corporately.

## Conclusion

The Islamic networks are dynamic and ubiquitous and play an important role in peacebuilding and development of the Muslim community in Kenya. They express the voice of the Muslims, and their activities are deeply rooted and anchored on local communities. There is, however, a lot of duplication of the activities of Islamic networks in peace and development to the extent that the organizations apparently compete against each other in offering the same services to the community. For example, BRAVE and CIPK seems to be at cross-purposes in rendering the same services targeting radicalism and extremism. The author opines this as a weakness owing to lack of harmonization of programs offered by Islamic networks. Duplication of programs and the proliferation of Islamic networks performing the same activities point to the weakness of the NGOs Co-ordination Board which is supposed to regulate their activities.

The Islamic networks in Kenya face challenges occasioned by the "war on terror" which has undoubtedly affected their work in peacebuilding and development. Nevertheless, the networks continue to operate. On a positive note, the "war on terror" has been a blessing in disguise for the networks since they have managed to strategize for survival in a hostile environment. Survival tactics in the onslaught of "war on terror" have prompted the networks to collaborate and partner with one another while engaging other faith networks on issues of peacebuilding and development. The fact these networks have weathered the storms occasioned by the "war on terror" testifies to their enduring role in peacebuilding and development. A case in point was during the "*Kadhi Courts Debate*" during the constitutional reform process which birthed the 2010 Constitution. Largely, the unity of Muslim networks contributed to the inclusion of the courts in the new constitution (Maina, 2011b, pp. 49–55).

Notably, the Muslim community has taken up the gauntlet in challenging radicalism and extremism. This perhaps explains why new networks such as BRAVE and KMYA were founded to tackle radicalism and extremism while others such as CIPK have made tackling radicalism and extremism their *modus operandi*. This points to the realization by the Islamic networks that to operate and survive in the contemporary period of "war on terror," they have to tailor their programs to the fight against terrorism.

## Recommendations

In view of discussion in this chapter, the Kenyan government is duty bound to achieve SDG 16 and its various targets through reducing violence that has been wrought by contemporary spate of terrorism. In this case, Islamic networks have a moral duty and obligation to join the government in its efforts in stemming occurrences of terrorism-related violence.

The Islamic networks play an important role in peacebuilding and development in Kenya. They represent a significant proportion of the population, which has over the years felt politically and economically marginalized. The voice of Islamic networks should be incorporated as critical players in the government policy frameworks and decision-making processes. Inclusivity, participatory and fair representation of Muslims are critical as the country forges ahead to consolidate peace and in finding solutions to the myriad of socio-economic and political problems bedeviling the populace.

The ban on some Islamic organizations and arbitrary arrests and detentions of Muslims without recourse to judicial process is contrary to rule of law. It is therefore incumbent upon the government of Kenya to promote the rule of law and to ensure that equal justice applies to Muslims and other citizens of different faiths in the country. This is crucial for sustainable social and economic development of the country.

## References

https://the.akdn. Aga Khan Development Network (AKDN): Improving the Quality of Life.

Aga Khan Stresses Pluralism for Peace and Development. (2008). Retrieved June 16, 2008, from https://the.akdn/en/resources-media/whats-new/press-release/aga-khan-stresses-pluralism-peace-and-development

Akwiri, J. (2014). Mosque Raids Provoke Clashes in Kenya's Mombasa Port. https://www.reuters.com/article/cnews-us-kenya-attacks-idCAKCN0J50VH20141121

Ali, M. S. (2012). *The Role of the Mosque Institution in the Prevention of Cattle Rustling and Banditry in Mandera East, Mandera County, Kenya*. Unpublished Master's thesis, Kenyatta University.

Chembea, S. A. (2020). Between Charity and Financing 'Terror': The Dilemma of Muslim Charitable Organizations in Kenya. In H. Weiss (Ed.), *Muslim Faith-Based Organizations and Social Welfare in Africa* (pp. 143–168). Palgrave Macmillan. https://doi.org/10.1007/978-3-030-38308-4

Chepkorir, B. (2019). *Religious Approaches to Peacebuilding and Reconciliation in Areas Affected by Ethnic Conflicts Within Kuresoi North—Nakuru County, Kenya (1992–2008)*. Unpublished Master's thesis, Kenyatta University.

https://www.cipkmombasa.or.ke. Council of Imams and Preachers of Kenya (CIPK) Mombasa.

Creating Hope in Kenya—AKDN. (2020). https://the.akdn/en/resources-media/whats-new/spotlights

CSCR [Centre for Sustainable Conflict Resolution]. (2019). BRAVE (Building Resilience Against Violent Extremism). https://cscrcenter.org/building-resilience-against-violent-extremism-brave/

Directorate of Criminal Investigations. (2020). https://www.cid.go.ke/index.php/sections/formations/atpu.html

Duh, A. A. (2014). Muslim Faith-Based Organizations in Somalia and Kenya. *Afrikas Horn of Africa Journal*. https://afrikansarvi.fi/72-artikkeli/208-muslim-faith-based-organizations-in-somalia-and-kenya

*Faith and Development in Focus: Kenya*. (2017). Berkley Center for Religion, Peace & World Affairs at Georgetown University, World Faiths Development Dialogue (WFDD). https://s3.amazonaws.com/berkley-center/170328BCWFDDFaithDevelopmentFocusKenya.pdf

Faith to Action Network. (2022). Kenya Muslim Youth Alliance. https://www.faithtoactionnetwork.org/kenya-muslim-youth-alliance/

Global Policy Forum. (2005). War on Terrorism. https://archive.globalpolicy.org/war-on-terrorism.html

Gullen, M. F. (2010). *Toward a Global Civilization of Love and Tolerance*. Tughra Books. https://doi.org/10.1080/15423166.2011.993456741127

https://www.worldometers.info/world-population/

https://islamic-relief.org. Islamic Relief Worldwide—Faith Inspired Action.

https://twitter.com/kmya254. Kenya Muslim Youth Alliance (@KMYA254) /Twitter.
Lynch, C. (2011). Local and Global Influences on Islamic NGOS in Kenya. *Journal of Peacebuilding & Development, 6*(1), 21–34.
Maina, N. K. (1992). *Muslim Education in Kenya with Special Reference to Madrasa System in Nairobi.* Unpublished Master's thesis, Kenyatta University.
Maina, N. K. (2011a). *Islamic Influence on Education in Africa: Sampling Islamic Influence of Interpretations on Girls' Access to Secondary School Education in Mombasa and Kwale Districts, Kenya.* Lambert Academic Publishing.
Maina, N. K. (2011b). Islamophobia Among Christians and Its Challenge in Entrenchment of Kadhi Courts in Kenya. In A. Tayob & J. Wandera (Eds.), *Constitutional Review in Kenya and Kadhi Courts* (pp. 49–55). University of Cape Town.
Maina, N. K. (2017). A History of Christian—Muslim Relations in Kenya, 1963–2015. In L. H. Gordon & D. K. Tarus (Eds.), *Christian Responses to Terrorism: The Kenyan Experience* (pp. 12–32). Pickwick Publications.
Maina, N. K. (2019). Freedom of Religion—Individual and Collective as Perceived by the Kenyan State. In D. A. Forster, E. Gerle, & G. Gunner (Eds.), *Freedom of Religion at Stake* (pp. 65–87). Pickwick Publications.
Murimi, S. (2016). Christianity in Kenya. In I. A. Phiri & D. Werner (Eds.), *Anthology of African Christianity* (pp. 604–613). Regnum Books International.
Mwakimako, H. (1995). Muslim NGOs and Community Development: The Kenyan Experience. In M. Bakari & S. S. Yahya (Eds.), *Islam in Kenya: Proceedings of the National Seminar on Contemporary Islam in Kenya* (pp. 224–233). MEWA Publications.
Nadwa, H. (2016). The Role of a Mosque in Politics: Muslim Perspectives on Jamia Mosque in Nairobi. *Journal of Law, Policy and Globalization, 50.* https://iiste.org/Journals/index.php/JLPG/article/view/31291
Ndzovu, H. J. (2020). Sacralization of the Humanitarian Space: Faith Based Organizations, Mission-Aid and Development in Africa. In E. Chitando, M. R. Gunda, & L. Togarasei (Eds.), *Religion and Development in Africa* (pp. 125–138). University of Bamberg Press. https://doi.org/10.20378/irb-47759
Noor, M. H. (2022). Al-Shabaab Mobilization and Muslim Leadership in Kenya. https://www.theelephant.info/features/2022/03/28/al-shabaab-mobilization-and-muslim-leadership-in-kenya/
Nwaigbo, F. (2006). The American War on Terrorism in the 21st Century. *African Ecclesia Review (AFER), 48*(2), 31–73.
Nyagah, T., Mwangi, J., & Attree, L. (n.d.). Inside Kenya's War on Terror: The Case of Lamu. https://saferworld-indepth.squarespace.com/inside-kenyas-war-on-terror-the-case-of-lamu
Oded, A. (2000). *Islam and Politics in Kenya.* Lynne Rienner.
Omari, H. K. (2014). *Islamic Leadership in Kenya: A Case Study of the Supreme Council of Kenya Muslims (SUPKEM).* Unpublished Doctoral dissertation, University of Nairobi. http://erepository.uonbi.ac.ke/handle/11295/78259
Ramos, A. (2015). Muslims Hailed for Protecting Christians During Terror Attack. https://www.theguardian.com/world/2015/dec/22/kenya-al-shabaab-attack-muslims-protect-christians-mandera
https://ngobureau.go.ke. The Non-Governmental Organizations Co-ordination (NGO) Board.

https://sdgs.un.org/goals. United Nations, Department of Economic and Social Affairs: Sustainable Development Goals.

Walji, S. R. (1995). Ismailis in Kenya: Some Perspectives on Continuity and Change. In M. Bakari & S. S. Yahya (Eds.), *Islam in Kenya: Proceedings of the National Seminar on Contemporary Islam in Kenya* (pp. 1–18). MEWA Publications.

Weiss, H. (2020). Muslim NGOs, *zakat* and the Provision of Social Welfare in Sub-Saharan Africa: An Introduction. In H. Weiss (Ed.), *Muslim Faith-Based Organizations and Social Welfare in Africa* (pp. 1–38). Palgrave Macmillan. https://doi.org/10.1007/978-3-030-38308-4

CHAPTER 34

# Re-building Muslim-Christian Relations and Everyday Peace in West Nile, Uganda

*Patrick Karanja Mbugua*

## INTRODUCTION

After a trio of suicide bombers detonated bombs in Kampala City on 16 November 2021, killing 4 people and injuring 37 more, the government of Uganda blamed the attacks on the Allied Democratic Forces (ADF), an Islamist group that emerged in Uganda in the early 1990s and now operates from the eastern Democratic Republic of Congo (DRC). Since the ADF claims links with the Islamic State (IS), an international jihadist group, the government's position exposed the fragile relations between the Ugandan State and Muslims at the macro-level and between Christians and Muslims at the lower levels. One of the regions with a latent conflict between Christians and Muslims is the Yumbe district in the West Nile region. Located on the far north-west corner of Uganda, bordering the Republic of South Sudan and the Democratic Republic of the Congo (DRC), the district has the highest

---

The CRID consortium published a simplified general readers' version of this study using some of the evidence cited in this chapter as Case Study Series No. 5 in April 2022, which is available here: https://www.faithtoactionnetwork.org

---

P. K. Mbugua (✉)
Peace & Conflict Studies Academic and Consultant, Peacebuilding, Conflict Transformation, and Preventive Diplomacy, Nairobi, Kenya

© The Author(s), under exclusive license to Springer Nature Switzerland AG 2023
S. M. Kilonzo et al. (eds.), *The Palgrave Handbook of Religion, Peacebuilding, and Development in Africa*,
https://doi.org/10.1007/978-3-031-36829-5_34

concentration of Muslims in the country because 76% of its population follows Islam.[1]

A few years ago, hostilities between the majority Muslims and the minority Christians in the district almost exploded into communal violence, after the Christians complained that the Muslims were using their numerical advantage to persecute them; the Muslims, in turn, claimed the Christians were covertly converting Muslim youth to Christianity. The prevailing structural violence exacerbated the latent conflict, as Muslims and Christians competed for local government jobs and contracts, management of schools, land and water resources, and political positions. Concerned by the increasing incidents of violence between adherents of the two religions, the Uganda Joint Christian Council (UJCC)[2] partnered with the Muslim Centre for Justice and Law (MCJL)[3] in 2018 to de-escalate the rising tensions, promote tolerance, and improve relations between Muslims and Christians.

This chapter analyses the impact of the peacebuilding interventions that the two partners implemented from September 2018 to June 2020 in two sub-counties, Kululu and Yumbe Town Council, in the district. The chapter broadly applies the bottom-up peacebuilding approach but uses the concept of everyday peace as the principal analytical construct. Peacebuilding literature conceptualises everyday peace as social practices that ordinary people perform as they navigate their daily lives in conflict contexts or locations emerging from protracted conflicts to minimise the effects of direct, structural, and cultural violence and strengthen peaceful relations (Ware and Ware, 2021; Ware et al., 2022; Mac Ginty, 2014, 2015, 2017, 2021; Mac Ginty & Firchow, 2016; Richmond & Mac Ginty, 2019). Although the two partners do not mention the UN

---

[1] Yumbe District was initially named Aringa County in the larger Arua district before its elevation to a district in November 2000 because 89% of the population is Aringa, a subgroup of the Lugbara ethnic group, which comprises the majority of the population in the West Nile region and crosses into the Democratic Republic of the Congo (DRC) and South Sudan. The Aringa people speak the Aringa dialect of the Lugbara language. The other Lugbara subgroups are Ayivu, Maracha, Terego, and Vurra. Each of these groups speaks a dialect of Lugbara, but all are mutually intelligible. The Lugbara ethnic group is close to the Madi ethnic group of the West Nile and South Sudan. For anthropological studies of the Lugbara people, see Middleton, J. (1960). *Lugbara Religion: Ritual and Authority Among an East African People*. Oxford: Oxford University Press; Storer, E. (2020). *Lugbara Religion Revisited: A Study of Social Repair in the West Nile, North-West Uganda*. London: London School of Economics, PhD thesis.

[2] Uganda Joint Christian Council (UJCC) is a faith-based ecumenical organisation founded in 1963 by the Anglican, the Catholic, and Orthodox Churches as a forum for resolving religious conflicts that affected Uganda. The Council aims to promote peaceful coexistence in Uganda and implements programs on conflict resolution, peaceful coexistence, and economic and social justice through various programs and its member churches. Over the years, it has emerged as a critical voice in the country because the Government of Uganda pays attention to the opinions of UJCC's Chairperson and Executive Secretary on national issues.

[3] The Muslim Centre for Justice and Law (MCJL) is a human rights civil society organisation (CSO) that promotes human rights, justice, and tolerance for the Muslim community in Uganda. Its programs target the poor and vulnerable grassroots communities and empower local Muslim communities to advocate for their rights

Sustainable Development Goals (SDGs) in their documents, the empirical review will implicitly show that their impact relates to SDG 16, specifically target 16.1, which calls for the reduction of all forms of violence, and indicators 16.1.2 and 16.1.3, which encourage the reduction of conflict-related deaths and physical violence. A second aim is to contribute to the expanding body of literature on everyday peace by adding empirical data from Uganda to the list of documented theoretical arguments (Mac Ginty, 2013; Firchow, 2018) and country studies, such as India (Williams, 2015), Bosnia and Herzegovina (Marijan, 2017), Northern Ireland (Marijan, 2017), Colombia (Berents, 2018), Iraq (O'Driscoll, 2021), Cambodia (Lee, 2021), and Myanmar (Ware et al., 2022).

Research for the chapter scrutinised 46 primary documents from the field, including monthly, quarterly, and annual reports and baseline and endline surveys, which collected empirical data from 250 participants on different dates between October 2018 and February 2020.[4] In addition, the researcher listened to the audio and video recordings of the UJCC and MCJL team, local Muslim Sheikhs and Christian priests, the Yumbe District Police Commander, and the participants' and beneficiaries' lived experiences. The following sections will explain everyday peace as an analytical tool, highlight the change strategy the two organisations adopted in light of West Nile realities, relate their selection of indicators to that context, and then evaluate the empirical data and conclude the chapter.

## Everyday Peace in a Post-Conflict Context

Peacebuilding theory and practice have, in the last ten years, seen a debate between top-bottom liberal peacebuilding and bottom-up peacebuilding. Liberal peacebuilding, also referred to as liberal peace, liberal interventionism, or liberal internationalism, has been the dominant form of international peacebuilding practices (Paris, 2002, 2007, 2010; Richmond, 2006, 2007; Richmond & Franks, 2009). Associated with the liberal peace debate, one of the lines of argument in the democratic peace theory in International Relations (IR), the liberal peacebuilding approach involves building liberal democracy and market economies in countries emerging from protracted armed conflicts. As Paris (2010) observes, post-war liberal peacebuilding seeks to align the domestic governance of war-shattered states with the prevailing standards of the international system. However, critics have pointed to some limitations of the liberal peace approach, including interweaving peacebuilding interventions with liberal state-building, privileging global norms, and emphasising structural and institutional aspects of state-building. Accordingly, they have developed an alternative approach known as bottom-up peacebuilding.

---

[4] The author of this chapter served as Knowledge Management Advisor for the CRID project. His responsibilities included leading research and supervising field data collection. Permission to use the data has been granted by the Council of Anglican Provinces of Africa (CAPA).

Bottom-up peacebuilding, also known as peacebuilding from below, grassroots peacebuilding, community peacebuilding, local peacebuilding, citizen-to-citizen peacebuilding, or Track II diplomacy, contends that, attaining sustainable peace after a protracted civil war, especially in deeply divided societies, requires the involvement of all levels of society (Montville, 1990, 1993, 2009; Gopin, 2009; Mac Ginty, 2010, 2011, 2017, 2021; Mac Ginty & Richmond, 2013; Paffenholz, 2015; Randazzo, 2017, 2021; Richmond, 2001, 2009a, 2009b, 2011). A central component of bottom-up peacebuilding is the notion of everyday peace. As defined in the introduction, everyday peace implies privileging the daily experiences and perspectives of ordinary people in a conflict or post-conflict context. Accordingly, peacebuilding literature asserts that everyday peace has no universal indicators due to its contingent, contextual, and temporal nature. As Mac Ginty (2014, p. 550) explains, everyday within that understanding refers to "the normal habitus for individuals and groups even if what passes as normal in a conflict-affected society would be abnormal elsewhere." In other words, individuals and groups in a particular context and at a specific time determine their indicators of everyday peace. This chapter argues that, although MCJL and UJCC did not acknowledge it, the idea of everyday peace at the lower levels was the foundation of their peacebuilding interventions in the Yumbe district.

Since UJCC was a Christian organisation and MCJL was a Muslim organisation, and the conflict in the district involved Muslims and Christians, the two partners opted to integrate bottom-up peacebuilding with a religion-based approach to restore everyday peace in the villages. This approach agrees with the arguments in the peacebuilding literature that religious peacebuilding integrates secular activities with religious values, rituals, traditions, texts, narratives, and vocabulary to resolve conflicts and promote peace, reconciliation, and peaceful coexistence (Bercovitch & Kadayifci-Orellana, 2009; Dubois, 2008; Powers, 2010). Dubois (2008) maintains that the employment of the spiritual elements of culture makes religious peacebuilding community-oriented, relationship-centred, and broadly participatory. According to this literature, faith actors implement the same activities as secular interlocutors; however, they add unique religious tools, including spiritual guidance, prayers, meditation, empathy, and imagination in envisioning new possibilities. Peacebuilding literature also recognises the religious origin of concepts, such as healing, forgiveness, and restorative justice, and asserts that all religions have language that describes ways of healing broken human relationships and acceptance that enables humans to pursue peaceful relations (Hamber, 2007; Peterson, 2001). Due to the complexity of the situation in the Yumbe district, UJCC and MCJL believed that their approach of integrating bottom-up peacebuilding activities with religious values, rituals, traditions, texts, narratives, and vocabulary would be the most effective way of resolving the conflict between Muslims and Christians and restoring everyday peace at the grassroots level.

When UJCC and MCJL planned their interventions in 2018, Yumbe district and the entire West Nile region were still recovering from devastating armed rebellions, which ended in December 2002 when the last armed group from the region, Uganda National Rescue Front II (UNRF-II), and the Government of Uganda signed the Yumbe Peace Agreement (UN, 2002; Baaré, 2004; Mischnick & Bauer, 2009). UNRF-II was among the armed groups which operated in different parts of Uganda at different times between 1980 and 2006 (Ofcansky, 1999; Leopold, 2005; Christopher, 2011). A few of these groups emerged in the West Nile region after the collapse of the Idi Amin regime in 1979, but the majority of the groups emerged in the northern regions following the triumph of President Yoweri Museveni's National Resistance Movement (NRM) over the Milton Obote II regime in February 1986. Among these were the Holy Spirit Movement (HSM) (1986–1988) (Mamdani, 1988; Behrend, 2000); Uganda People's Democratic Army (UPDA) (1986–1988) (Lamwaka, 1998; Bell, 2016; Lindemann, 2011); Uganda Christian Army/Movement (UCA/M) which later became the Lord's Resistance Army (LRA) (1988–2006) (Acker, 2004; Apuuli, 2006; Tim & Vlassenroot, 2010); the Former Uganda National Army (FUNA) (1980–1997) (Ofcansky, 1996, 1999; RLP, 2004); and the West Nile Bank Front (WNBF) (1995–1998) (Ofcansky, 1999; Leopold, 1999; Christopher, 2011; Kaiser, 2000). Additionally, civil wars in the countries bordering the West Nile region, the DRC and South Sudan, adversely affected Yumbe district and the entire West Nile region in many ways, including the influx of 500,000 South Sudanese refugees to four districts in the region, Yumbe, Koboko, Moyo, and Adjumani, with Yumbe alone hosting more than 250,000 refugees in the sprawling Bidibidi refugee settlement.

Therefore, the district faced many challenges which affected post-war recovery. Among these problems were pending reparations for non-combatant survivors of the war (Bogner & Neubert, 2013), thousands of aggrieved ex-combatants due to the stalled disarmament, demobilisation, and reintegration (DDR) process (Finnegan & Flew, 2008), and conflicts between the local population and the nomadic pastoralists, locally known as *Balaalo*, over grazing lands (Monitor, 2018a; Independent, 2021). Other problems were tensions between the host community and South Sudanese refugees and economic grievances by the youth, represented by the *boda boda* operators, over benefits and employment by the international organisations which provide humanitarian support to the South Sudanese (NV Reporter, 2018; Kapo, 2018; Monitor, 2018b; Okema, 2018; Okiror, 2020). Exacerbating these problems was structural violence as the West Nile region remains one of the most underdeveloped regions of Uganda. For example, the 2017 household survey by the Uganda Bureau of Statistics (UBS) found that the literacy rate in the Yumbe district is 55.5% while the national average is 69%. Further, only 22.8% of the population had attained secondary education and only 4.1% had attained tertiary level education. The survey also found that 16.4% of young people were not in school or college and 64.8% of youth aged 18 to 30 years were unemployed. Since Yumbe is a rural district based on a subsistence economy and without infrastructure, and the only place that offers opportunities in the informal sector is Yumbe town, the district has one of the highest poverty rates in Uganda.

Because of the magnitude of the challenges, and since there was already a national peace agreement and an amnesty law providing a legal framework for the disarming of all combatants, and a DDR monitoring commission (Finnegan & Flew, 2008), the UJCC and MCJL chose bottom-up peacebuilding as the most effective approach to prevent violence, improve Muslim-Christian relations, and promote everyday peace. Indicators of everyday peace in this strategy were the transformation of individual perceptions towards the religious "other" and the improvement of relations between Muslims and Christians. UJCC documents explain that the two partners adopted a pathway for change that targeted the youth as change agents because young men led the recent episodes of riots in Yumbe Town in 2017 and 2018, violent clashes between Christians and Muslims, and fights between the host community and South Sudanese refugees in 2017. In particular, MCJL and UJCC designed activities that appealed to the youth, including sports, radio programs, and music, dance, and drama (MDD) performances. These interventions were consistent with the baseline survey which found that 44.4% of the Yumbe population relied on radio as the main source of information, 10.1% relied on the community megaphone, and less than 2% on television. Because of widespread poverty and low literacy rates, there was less usage of mobile phones (46.5%) and the internet (11%).

The approach began with empowering a selected group of youth, known as Community Own Resource Persons (CORPs), with basic conflict resolution and peacebuilding skills covering aspects such as conflict mitigation, justice in Islam and Christianity, resilience, confidence-building, community dialogues, and communication across religions. The training sessions took place from September to November 2018. After that, the trained youth were deployed to promote dialogue in their localities using religious spaces, institutions, texts, tools, and values and peer-to-peer outreach. They also organised sports for peace tournaments and music, dance, and drama (MDD) performances starting at the village level up to the district level. MDDs' attractions were their simple but effective way of highlighting suppressed religious issues, taboos, and prejudices. These activities occurred from December 2018 to September 2019. Then between May and September 2019, the CORPs also used popular programs on *Radio Pacis*, which broadcasts from Arua town and has the highest listenership in the district, to support and reinforce messages of Muslim-Christian unity and everyday peace. Also, the radio has listeners in the neighbouring Koboko, Arua, Marachi, and Moyo districts. The power of the radio lay not just in informing, educating, and entertaining, but also in framing public discussions and ordering and privileging narratives of peace in the popular imagination.

From the initial 30 CORPs, the number of participants increased upwards, as 712 people participated in dialogue forums, 10,337 participated in peer-to-peer outreach, sports, and MDD activities, and 71,850 people listened to *Radio Pacis*. The two partners reached an additional 5000 people through IEC materials. Although the UJCC and MCJL documents do not mention any of the UN Strategic Development Goals (SDGs), a global reading of their strategy indicates that it tacitly aligned with SDG 16, specifically target 16.1 which aims to reduce all forms of violence and deaths associated with them, as well as indicators 16.1.2 and 16.1.3 which aim to reduce conflict-related violence in both macro and micro environments. Importantly, attaining everyday peace in the district would create an environment for the implementation of development activities stipulated in the Yumbe Peace Agreement.

## Transforming Individual Perceptions and Improving Muslim-Christian Relations

Considering that the population of Yumbe is overwhelmingly Aringa (89%), who speak the Aringa dialect of the Lugbara language and understand the other Lugbara dialects, UJCC and MCJL aimed to change individual perceptions towards the religious "other" because religion was the only exclusion boundary. This approach concurred with the findings of the baseline survey that 97% of the respondents knew someone from the other religion and 87% had a neighbour from another religion; however, only 24% engaged with a neighbour from another religion and only 29% always engaged with a friend or someone from a different religion. Additionally, the baseline found that only 2% of the survey respondents knew a lot about the other religion, 47.4% knew very little, and 34.5% knew nothing at all. Thus, the UJCC and MCJL team believed that changing individual perceptions towards the religious "other" would lead to an understanding that all residents of Yumbe shared the same cultural heritage and historical narrative, occupied the same socio-cultural space, and shared a common humanity.

Empirical data suggests that the MCJL/EASS interventions, that is, training, dialogue forums, peer-to-peer outreaches, MDD, sports for peace, and radio programs, had considerable impacts and transformed the perceptions of the youth towards the religious 'other'. For instance, the endline survey found that the respondents had increased their engagement with neighbours from the other religion to 58%. While those who knew nothing about another religion dropped from 34.5% to 0%, those who had a little knowledge dropped from 47% to 2%, while those who knew a lot about the other religion increased from 2% to 73%. The immense improvement implies that the UJCC and MCJL's goal of changing the individual perception by imparting knowledge about each religion through training, peer-to-peer outreach, and community engagements had achieved the intended impact.

Additional evidence corroborates the above findings. An Anglican priest from Yumbe explained that they trained young men and women and helped them implement MDD and sports for peace. He added that young Anglicans, Catholics, and Muslims appreciated their shared cultural heritage, civic identity, and humanity after participating in those activities. "The situation now is calm; there is no violence between Muslims and Christians, and all government departments, including the police, can confirm that we have achieved peace in Yumbe," he asserted. Similarly, a Catholic priest from Yumbe admitted that

Christians are very few in the Yumbe district, about 22%. However, he added, "all participants started understanding the other religion after the dialogue meetings that we facilitated. The District Kadhi has been inviting me to speak to Muslim youth at the mosque since then. I know they are happy." This evidence highlights that UJCC and MCJL interventions provided opportunities for the youth to understand each religion, interact with the religious "other", and perform collective actions. In turn, inter-religious group activities helped them realise that they shared the same cultural heritage, civic identity, and a common humanity and, thus, started viewing each other positively.

Some youth who participated in the training, MDD, and sports for peace activities shared their transformation. A male Muslim from the Kululu sub-county, who dropped out of school and had no gainful employment when MCJL recruited him, explained his experience: "I was one of the peers that MCJL and UJCC trained at Moyo on how to relate to Christians. I learned how to solve conflicts in my village and how to advise my fellow youth on drug abuse. Now I understand Christians." Like other young Muslims, this young man probably shared the prevailing stereotypes and prejudices against Christians. While his involvement with the MCJL activities was his first serious engagement in life, it provided him with an opportunity to interact and engage with young Christians; these engagements exposed him to the many ways that he could use to change his social and physical environments and earn an income. His transformation affirmed the UJCC/MCJL approach that inter-religious interactions provided opportunities for individuals to reduce their prejudice and hostilities and encouraged them to form social networks and perform collective actions. As he admits, participating in MCJL/UJCC activities changed his views towards religious "others", changed his perception of them as enemies, and encouraged him to partner with young Christians in social networks.

Another male Muslim from Kululu shared similar evidence. As he explained, "it is difficult to get employment in Yumbe. When I heard about the UJCC/MCJL project on youth, I decided to join because, like most of the youth in Kululu, I was idle and spent my time causing trouble in the community." After the first training, he enthusiastically reached out to other youth through peer-to-peer outreach. Subsequent engagements motivated him to acquire gainful skills to enable him to earn an income. "During the training, most of the participants were more educated and skilled than me," he conceded. "I decided to acquire gainful skills by enrolling in a short training program on building and construction provided by Finn Church Aid (FCA)." Then he and his peers formed a youth association that applied for a government of Uganda registration and started constructing houses for people. Their breakthrough came when they received funding from Peace Wind Japan to advance their construction work. Clearly, his decision to obtain gainful skills and his efforts to reach out to his peers indicate that UJCC/MCJL interventions transformed his perceptions towards the religious "other". As a Catholic priest from Yumbe town observed, "we have seen a lot of positive changes. Drug abuse in Yumbe and Kululu has reduced and some youths in Kululu have started savings associations." Admitting that he knew some of the young men who changed, the priest added,

> I know some young men from Kululu who joined training courses and a technical school. I know one young man who attended training provided by the Finn Church Aid (FCA) on building and construction and then started a building association. I know another one who went to a technical school. I am very happy about these young men because they have changed their lives, homes, and communities.

The priest's evidence affirms the postulates of the UJCC/MCJL's strategy that integrating a bottom-up peacebuilding approach with religious symbols, texts, tools, narratives, and values would resonate with individuals, reduce prejudice and hostilities, and encourage them to form social networks. As a young Catholic woman from Yumbe town revealed,

> I was one of the trainees from Yumbe Town Council. When we started the activities, the Muslims and Christians were fighting; they did not want to understand each other. The Muslims were not listening to the Catholics while the Catholics did not want to hear the views of the Muslims.

Explaining how they beseeched them to join dialogue forums, she added,

> I led the team that brought youth to dialogue forums, and we explained to them why they ought to live together. Then we involved them in different activities, including MDD, football, and netball matches, and they accepted our message and started interacting with each other. They became friends and that is how we build peace in the villages around Yumbe Town.

Initially, the young woman was probably disregarded because of her age and gender in an area where a tradition of militarism, the legacies of armed conflicts, and patriarchal norms have normalised combat heroism, which is associated with young men. However, the strategy of combining activities that appealed to the youth with religious texts, narratives, vocabulary, spiritual guidance, and empathy built confidence, transformed perceptions, and enhanced the abilities of Muslim and Christian youth to form networks. Overall, changing individual perceptions towards the religious "other" became the foundation for breaking mutual hostility and improving Muslim-Christian relations. Since mutual hostility and occasional direct violence characterised relations between Muslims and Christians, UJCC/MCJL interventions aimed to end the hostilities and maintain everyday peace in the villages despite the prevailing structural violence. According to the Yumbe District Community Development Officer (CDO), "most of the young people here are not in school and are not working. Most of them play games all day at the taxi park. This is too much idleness; unemployment is a big problem in the district. Consequently, anyone can use them for any price."

Thus, whereas UJCC and MCJL lacked resources to address structural violence, they believed that attaining many islands of everyday peace in the villages would improve relations between Christians and Muslims and, thus, create the necessary conditions for the implementation of development activities documented in the Yumbe Peace Agreement. Supporting this approach, a female Christian from Yumbe town revealed that she no longer feared Muslim youth because UJCC/MCJL interventions had reduced hostilities and improved relations between Christians and Muslims. This was confirmed by the District Kadhi. As he revealed: "the project gave us the platform to engage young people and speak to them on issues of peace and living together as brothers and sisters. I can assure you that young people have transformed." Emphasising the role of leaders, he added, "we religious leaders live as examples. We have teamed up as Imams, Anglican, and Catholic priests to teach our youth about peaceful relations between Muslims and Christians." The argument here rests on two points. First, participants and beneficiaries of the UJCC/MCJL interventions embraced tolerance, re-humanised the religious "other", accepted that they shared the same cultural heritage, and appreciated their common civic identity and humanity. Second, religious leaders, that is, Anglican and Catholic priests and Imams, played a central role in the transformation of perspectives. Additional evidence from the District Police Commander further illuminated the changes:

> UJCC and MCJL have brought a significant impact to the district. Before they started their project, the youth used to be violent; they never listened to us as security officers, and they could not listen to their parents, priests, and Imams. The UJCC and MCJL have trained them; they no longer fight and they abide by the laws.

Similarly, an Anglican priest, who lived in Yumbe town, affirmed the improvement of Muslim-Christian relations after they brought them together in joint public performances. His revelation confirms that UJCC and MCJL's strategy effectively encouraged Muslim and Christian youth to embrace each other. As a male Muslim from Yumbe town revealed, his most memorable experiences during training sessions were realising the similarities between Muslims and Christians, including worshipping the same God of Abraham, Moses, and Isaac, a similar understanding of fairness, a belief in Jesus' virgin birth, reverence for Mary, and common verses, for example, John 17:21 and Quran 49:13 ("they may be one"). Lastly, a male Muslim, who participated in sports for peace, admitted that he used to idle around Yumbe town before UJCC/MCJL interventions. "We would chew *mairungi* (khat) the whole day and sometimes engage in crime. I participated in violence against Christians; we could not stay together because of hostilities. I thank UJCC and MCJL because football united us; we formed football teams, played as a team, shared meals, and used similar jerseys. I realised we are one people."

The essence of evidence in the preceding sections is the admission that MCJL and UJCC interventions changed their perceptions, reduced hostilities and violence, promoted tolerance, improved Christian-Muslim relations, and revealed their shared humanity, moral framework, and civic identity. In other words, the interventions demolished the hard religious boundary by demystifying pre-existing stereotypes and prejudices and improving communication between Muslims and Christians. Moreover, the interventions had unintended benefits because they motivated participants to acquire life skills that would enable them to earn an income. As noted earlier, UJCC and MCJL documents do not acknowledge the UN Sustainable Development Goal (SDG) 16 or other international instruments such as the African Union (AU) peacebuilding or Transitional Justice Policy. However, this chapter suggests that their goal of attaining everyday peace in the villages in the Yumbe district and the entire West Nile region was consistent with these international instruments, especially requirements of SDG 16, specifically target 16.1 that calls for reducing all forms of violence, as well as indicators 16.1.2 and 16.1.3 that call for reducing conflict-related violence at both local and national levels.

In summary, UJCC and MCJL understood that, since 89% of Yumbe residents are from the same ethnic group and speak the same language, a lack of understanding of Christian practices, beliefs, and doctrines by the majority Muslims and vice-versa contributed to hostilities. To end these hostile relations and attain everyday peace, the two parties adopted an intervention strategy that integrated bottom-up peacebuilding techniques with religious texts, values, narratives, and vocabulary. The pillars of the approach were training forums that empowered a selected group of youth with basic conflict resolution skills, peer-to-peer outreach, community dialogues, and edutainment activities that appealed to youth. Considering the magnitude of the challenges in the region, especially structural violence, the interventions preferred modest aims of transforming individuals' worldview towards the religious "other" and improving relations between Christians and Muslims as indicators of everyday peace. According to the analysed evidence, the training sessions imparted the foundational skills of resolving conflicts at the village level and provided opportunities for Muslim and Christian youth to interact with each other, gain knowledge about each religion, and change their worldview towards the religious "other". The main innovation in the model was the use of religious and cultural leaders and religious spaces, texts, and values. Overall, the UJCC/MCJL interventions contributed to changing individual perceptions towards the religious "other", improving relations between Muslims and Christians, and promoting everyday peace in the villages.

Finally, although everyday peace indicators are contextually specific, bottom-up interventions such as training and community dialogues by religious leaders are common in Africa. For example, the Acholi Religious Leaders Peace Initiative (ARLPI) employed the bottom-up strategy in its interventions in the Acholi sub-region in northern Uganda (Khadiagala, 2001). In Cameroon, the Catholic Church has in the past used training, peace education, and community dialogues to resolve ethnic conflicts in the north-west region (Lang, 2019). Similarly, Alfani (2019) has analysed the use of bottom-up peacebuilding interventions by churches to resolve the conflicts in the eastern regions of the DRC. Thus, the MCJL and UJCC model has universal utility on the African continent since its variants have already been implemented in different countries.

## Challenges and Lessons

The UJCC and MCJL interventions aimed to end violence and hostile relations between Muslims and Christians and maintain everyday peace in the villages in a context of enormous challenges of post-war recovery, including structural violence, a large number of aggrieved ex-combatants because of the stalled DDR process, and grievances over the presence of more than 250,000 South Sudanese refugees in the district. Ideally, peacebuilding interventions in such a context should be interwoven with long-term development objectives, which is the responsibility of national and local governments. Therefore, sustaining everyday peace as UJCC and MCJL intended required corresponding development interventions from the Government of Uganda to address structural violence as specified in the Yumbe Peace Agreement. Since UJCC and MCJL did not control the development plans of the national government for the region, they hoped that attaining many islands of peace would influence peace formation in the region, which would attract and inform the government's development plans for the entire West Nile region.

A slightly different challenge related to selecting agents of change. While these young men and women were versatile and easily reached out to their peers, UJCC and MCJL did not have a mechanism for sustaining them after the end of external funding. Also, as some of the young men and women advanced their skills, there was a possibility that they would move out of Yumbe to other towns in the West Nile, such as Arua, or other locations in Uganda, such as Kampala. Thus, the two partners could not guarantee that the trained young men and women would continue their peacebuilding work in the region after they pulled out. Lastly, UJCC and MCJL peacebuilding interventions in the West Nile region were dependent on external funding. By December 2021, they had not established a mechanism for raising local resources to sustain those interventions.

Nonetheless, peacebuilding interventions by UJCC and MCJL in the Yumbe district and the West Nile region and their goals of ending violence, improving relations between Muslims and Christians, and attaining everyday peace at the lower levels provide some valuable lessons. First, integrating techniques of bottom-up peacebuilding with religious texts, values, narratives, tools, and vocabulary resonated with grassroots communities and gained wide acceptance in the district. Ultimately, this strategy led to the end of violence and hostility between Christians and Muslims and promoted tolerance, mutual respect, peaceful relations, and everyday peace in the villages. It can therefore be universalised and applied in other contexts that experience similar hostilities. Second, UJCC/MCJL premised their pathway for change, and their logic of tolerance and everyday peace at the micro-level, on horizontal linkages. However, national and local government agencies, such as the Town Council, security officers, and the Resident District Commissioner's office, provided crucial support. The lesson here is that attaining everyday peace at the micro-levels in a context like Yumbe and West Nile requires engagement between grassroots actors and state agencies, particularly middle and lower-level state officers.

Third, the logic of building islands of peace at the micro-level in a post-war context, which contributes to ending cycles of violence, is powerful and widely applicable. Fourth, the use of the district Kadhi, Anglican priests, Catholic priests, and the Aringa cultural institution and elders demonstrates the crucial role of local agency in sustaining everyday peace in a post-war context. This approach agrees with Lederach's (1997, 2003, 2005) observation that grassroots agency plays a critical role in the transformation of a conflict and the attainment of long-term peace because such agents witness the hostilities and animosities at the local levels. As evidence has demonstrated, religious leaders had first-hand knowledge of the issues and animosities at the lower levels in the district, they were well acquainted with the effects of structural violence on the population, they had interacted with all the expressions of cultural violence, and they knew most of the young people that were involved in direct violence. Therefore, their involvement as advocates of everyday peace contributed to the achievement of the intended goal. In other words, involving religious leaders, who invoked religious symbols, language, and values, as well as cultural elders and government agents, proved effective in changing individuals' worldviews towards the religious "other", ending violence and hostilities, improving Muslim-Christian relations, and attaining everyday peace in micro-spaces. Finally, it is pertinent to remember that everyday peace indicators are contingent, contextual, and temporal, according to the everyday peace framework. Therefore, the indicators and achievements discussed in the chapter were specific to the Yumbe district in Uganda; they would be very different in another context in Uganda or anywhere else. Nevertheless, the model builds on the variations of bottom-up peacebuilding that religious leaders have already implemented in African countries.

## Conclusion

This chapter has examined peacebuilding activities that UJCC and MCJL implemented from September 2018 to June 2020 in the Yumbe district in the West Nile region of Uganda. As the two partners planned their interventions, the district and, to some extent, the West Nile region faced complex, intertwined post-civil war challenges. Among these challenges were a large number of aggrieved ex-combatants due to an incomplete DDR process, a traumatised population, unimplemented reparations for non-combatant survivors of the war, conflicts over natural resources and other aspects of structural violence, and tensions between the host community and thousands of South Sudanese refugees inhabiting the sprawling Bidibidi refugee settlement. Due to the enormity of the challenges, the two partners aimed to achieve the modest goals of ending

Muslim-Christian hostilities and violence, improving relations between followers of the two religions, and promoting tolerance and everyday peace in the villages. Their indicators of everyday peace were transformation of individual perceptions towards the religious 'other' and improvement in relations between Muslims and Christians. To achieve their goal, the two partners adopted an intervention strategy that integrated techniques of bottom-up peacebuilding with religious tools, values, texts, and narratives, which appealed to the Islamic and Christian sensibilities of the population.

Their bottom-up peacebuilding activities started with training sessions that empowered a select group of young men and women with basic conflict resolution skills and other life skills. Supported by religious and cultural leaders, who brought their legitimacy, moral power, and religious values, spaces, tools, texts, and narratives into the interventions, this select group of youth organised subsequent activities, which aimed to demystify the prevailing stereotypes, reduce prejudices and hostilities, break the religious boundary, and promote tolerance. These activities include peer-to-peer outreach, community dialogues, sports for peace, radio programs, and music, dance and drama (MDD) performances. An analysis of the adduced empirical evidence has shown that these activities transformed individuals' worldview towards the religious "other", ended violence and hostilities between Muslims and Christians, and improved relations between followers of Islam and Christianity in the district. The activities encouraged tolerance, conciliation, healing, forgiveness, and empathy as the foundations of everyday peace in the villages. From a global perspective, MCJL and UJCC did not acknowledge the UN Sustainable Development Goal (SDG) 16. Nonetheless, their aim of ending hostility and violence between Christians and Muslims and promoting everyday peace in the Yumbe District tacitly aligns with the requirements of SDG 16, specifically target 16.1, which stipulates reduction of all forms of violence, and indicators 16.1.2 and 16.1.3, which advocate reduction of armed conflicts.

However, attaining everyday peace was not an end in itself although it was a strong objective for moral and practical reasons. Overall, the two partners hoped that sufficient islands of everyday peace would create an enabling environment for the resolution of the root causes of Muslim-Christian hostilities and the direct violence in the Yumbe district. While interventions by the two partners targeted cultural violence, such as pre-existing stereotypes and prejudices, and proximate causes, including ignorance about each other's religion, structural violence aspects, such as land and property ownership, competition for political and administrative positions, economic marginalisation, and underdevelopment issues are connected to state institutions and political-economic power structures in Uganda. Therefore, these issues were beyond the control of the two partners. Some of the persistent grievances, especially economic and underdevelopment concerns, were negotiated in the 2002 Yumbe peace process and incorporated into the Yumbe Peace Agreement. In conclusion, the chapter suggests that the achieved impacts of ending micro-level violence and improving Muslim-Christian relations are impressive. However, their sustainability would ultimately depend on the ability of the two partners and other local agencies and grassroots actors in Yumbe and the entire West Nile region to liaise with the government of Uganda to resolve the structural issues as documented in the Yumbe Peace Agreement.

## References

Acker, F. V. (2004). Uganda and the Lord's Resistance Army: The New Order No One Ordered. *African Affairs, 103*(412), 335–357.

Alfani, R. (2019). *Religious Peacebuilding in the Democratic Republic of Congo*. Peter Lang Inc.

Apuuli, K. P. (2006). The ICC Arrest Warrants for the Lord's Resistance Army Leaders and Peace Prospects for Northern Uganda. *Journal of International Criminal Justice, 4*(1), 179–187.

Baaré, A. (2004). Development aid as Third-Party Intervention: A Case Study of the Uganda National Rescue Front II Peace Process. *Journal of Peacebuilding & Development, 2*(1), 21–36.

Behrend, H. (2000). *Alice Lakwena and the Holy Spirits: War in Northern Uganda 1986–97*. James Currey Ltd and Kampala: Fountain Publishers.

Bell, A. M. (2016). Military Culture and Restraint Toward Civilians in War: Examining the Ugandan Civil Wars. *Security Studies, 25*(3), 488–518.

Bercovitch, J., & Kadayifci-Orellana, S. A. (2009). Religion and Mediation: The Role of Faith-Based Actors in International Conflict Resolution. *International Negotiation, 14*(1), 175–204.

Berents, H. (2018). *Young People and Everyday Peace: Exclusion, Insecurity and Peacebuilding in Colombia*. Taylor & Francis.

Bogner, A., & Neubert, D. (2013). Negotiated Peace, Denied Justice? The Case of West Nile (Northern Uganda). *Africa Spectrum, 48*(3), 55–84.

Christopher, D. R. (2011). The Fates of Rebels: Insurgencies in Uganda. *Comparative Politics, 43*(4), 439–458.

Dubois, H. (2008). Religion and Peacebuilding: An Ambivalent Yet Vital Relationship. *Journal of Religion, Conflict and Peace, 1*(2), 1–21.

Finnegan, L., & Flew, C. (2008). *Disarmament, Demobilisation, and Reintegration in Uganda*. Saferworld and University of Bradford Report.

Firchow, P. (2018). *Reclaiming Everyday Peace: Local Voices in Measurement and Evaluation After War*. Cambridge University Press.

Gopin, M. (2009). *To Make the Earth Whole: The Art of Citizen Diplomacy in an Age of Religious Militancy*. Rowman & Littlefield Publishers.

Hamber, B. (2007). Forgiveness and Reconciliation: Paradise Lost or Pragmatism? *Peace and Conflict: Journal of Peace Psychology, 13*(1), 115–125.

Kaiser, T. (2000). The Experience and Consequences of Insecurity in a Refugee Populated Area in Northern Uganda 1996–97. *Refugee Survey Quarterly, 19*(1), 38–53.

Kapo, N. B. (2018, March 28). 2 Reported Dead in Yumbe Clashes, Several Cars Burnt. *Nile Post*. https://nilepost.co.ug/2018/03/28/2-reported-dead-in-yumbe-clashes-several-cars-burnt/

Khadiagala, G. M. (2001). *The role of the Acholi Religious Leaders Peace Initiative (ARLPI) in peace building in northern Uganda*. MSI Research Report.

Lamwaka, C. (1998). Civil War and the Peace Process in Uganda, 1986–1997. *East African Journal of Peace and Human Rights, 4*(2), 139–169.

Lang, M. K. (2019). Inter-Ethnic Conflict Management and Prevention in Cameroon's Northwest: Assessing the Role of the Justice and Peace Commission of the Catholic Archdiocese of Bamenda. *Asian Journal of Peacebuilding, 7*(1), 125–142.

Lederach, J. P. (1997). *Building Peace: Sustainable Reconciliation in Divided Societies.* United States Institute of Peace Press.

Lederach, J. P. (2003). *The Little Book of Conflict Transformation.* Good Books.

Lederach, J. P. (2005). *The Moral Imagination: The Art and Soul of Building Peace.* Oxford University Press.

Lee, S. (2021). Understanding Everyday Peace in Cambodia: Plurality, Subtlety, and Connectivity. *Journal of Peacebuilding & Development, 16*(1), 24–38.

Leopold, M. (1999). The War in the North: Ethnicity in Ugandan Press Explanations of Conflict 1996–97. In T. Allen & J. Seaton (Eds.), *The Media of Conflict: War Reporting and Representations of Ethnic Violence* (pp. 219–243). Zed Books.

Leopold, M. (2005). Why are We Cursed?: Writing History and Making Peace in North West Uganda. *Journal of the Royal Anthropological Institute, 1*(2), 211–229.

Lindemann, S. (2011). Just Another Change of Guard? Broad-Based Politics and Civil War in Museveni's Uganda. *African Affairs, 110*(440), 387–416.

Mac Ginty, R. (2010). Hybrid Peace: Interaction Between Top-Down and Bottom-Up Peace. *Security Dialogue, 41*(4), 391–412.

Mac Ginty, R. (2011). *International Peacebuilding and Local Resistance: Hybrid Forms of Peace.* Palgrave MacMillan.

Mac Ginty, R. (2013). Indicators+: A Proposal for Everyday Peace Indicators. *Evaluation and Program Planning, 36*(1), 56–63.

Mac Ginty, R. (2014). Everyday Peace: Bottom-up and Local Agency in Conflict-Affected Societies. *Security Dialogue, 45*(6), 548–564.

Mac Ginty, R. (2015). Where Is the Local? Critical Localism and Peacebuilding. *Third World Quarterly, 36*(5), 840–856.

Mac Ginty, R. (2021). *Everyday Peace: How So-Called Ordinary People Can Disrupt Violent Conflict.* Oxford University Press.

Mac Ginty, R., & Firchow, F. (2016). Top-Down and Bottom-Up Narratives of Peace and Conflict. *Politics, 36*(3), 308–323.

Mac Ginty, R., & Richmond, O. (2013). The Local Turn in Peace Building: A Critical Agenda for Peace. *Third World Quarterly, 34*(5), 763–783.

Mac Ginty, R. (2017). Everyday Social Practices and Boundary-Making in Deeply Divided Societies. *Civil Wars, 19*(1), 4–25.

Mamdani, M. (1988). Uganda in Transition: Two Years of the NRA/NRM. *Third World Quarterly, 10*(3), 1155–1181.

Marijan, B. (2017). The politics of everyday peace in Bosnia and Herzegovina and Northern Ireland. *Peacebuilding, 5*(1), 67–81.

Mischnick, R., & Bauer, I. (2009). *Yumbe Peace Process.* Fountain Publishers.

Monitor. (2018a, January 23). Museveni Orders Eviction of Balaalo from West Nile. *Monitor.* https://www.monitor.co.ug/uganda/news/national/museveni-orders-eviction-of-balaalo-from-west-nile-1737266

Monitor. (2018b, March 28). Two Shot as URA Officers Clash with Yumbe Boda-Boda Cyclists. *Monitor.* https://www.monitor.co.ug/uganda/news/national/two-shot-as-ura-officers-clash-with-yumbe-boda-boda-cyclists-1747680

Montville, J. (1990). The Arrow and the Olive Branch: A Case For Track Two Diplomacy. In D. V. Vamik et al. (Eds.), *The Psychodynamics of International Relationships* (pp. 161–175). Lexington Books.

Montville, J. (1993). The Healing Function in Political Conflict Resolution. In D Sandole and H. van der Merwe (Eds.). Conflict Resolution Theory and Practice: Integration and Application (pp.112-128). Manchester University Press.

Montville, J. (2009). Track Two Diplomacy: The Work of Healing History. *Journal of Diplomacy and International Relations, 7*(2), 15–25.

New Vision Reporter. (2018, March 28). Uganda Revenue Authority Press Release on Clarification on Yumbe Riots. *The New Vision*.

O'Driscoll, D. (2021). Everyday Peace and Conflict: (un)Privileged Interactions in Kirkuk, Iraq. *Third World Quarterly, 42*(10), 2227 2246.

Ofcansky, T. P. (1996). *Uganda: Tarnished Pearl of Africa*. Routledge.

Ofcansky, T. P. (1999). Museveni's War and the Ugandan Conflict. *Journal of Conflict Studies, 19*(1), 144–147.

Okema, D. (2018, March 28). Angry Rioters Burn NGO Vehicles, Smash Yumbe District Buildings. *PML Daily*. https://www.pmldaily.com/news/2018/03/angry-rioters-burn-ngo-vehicles-smash-yumbe-district-buildings.html

Okiror, S. (2020, September 15). Uganda Calls in Troops as Violence Flares Between Refugees and Locals. *The Guardian*. https://www.theguardian.com/global-development/2020/sep/15/uganda-calls-in-troops-as-violence-flares-between-refugees-and-locals

Paffenholz, T. (2015). Unpacking the Local Turn In Peacebuilding: A Critical Assessment Towards an Agenda for Future Research. *Third World Quarterly, 36*(5), 857–874.

Paris, R. (2002). International Peacebuilding and the 'Mission Civilisatrice'. *Review of International Studies, 28*(4), 637–657.

Paris, R. (2007). *At War's End: Building Peace After Civil Conflict*. Cambridge University Press.

Paris, R. (2010). Saving Liberal Peacebuilding. *Review of International Studies, 36*(2), 337–365.

Peterson, R. (2001). A Theology of Forgiveness. In R. Helmick & R. Petersen (Eds.), *Forgiveness and Reconciliation: Religion, Public Policy, and Conflict Transformation* (pp. 3–26). Templeton Foundation Press.

Powers, G. F. (2010). Religion and Peacebuilding. In D. Philpot & G. F. Powers (Eds.), *Strategies for Peace: Transforming Conflict in a Violent World* (pp. 317–352). Oxford University Press.

Randazzo, E. (2017). *Beyond Liberal Peacebuilding: A Critical Exploration of the Local Turn*. Routledge.

Randazzo, E. (2021). The Local, the 'Indigenous' and the Limits of Rethinking Peacebuilding. *Journal of Intervention and Statebuilding, 15*(2), 141–160.

Refugee Law Project (RLP). (2004). *Negotiating Peace: Resolution of Conflicts In Uganda's West Nile Region*. Refugee Law Project Working Paper No. 12.

Richmond, O. (2001). Rethinking Conflict Resolution: The Linkage Problematic Between "Track I" and "Track II". *Journal of Conflict Studies, 21*(2), 109–132.

Richmond, O. (2006). The Problem of Peace: Understanding the 'Liberal Peace'. *Conflict, Security & Development, 3*, 291–314.

Richmond, O. (2007). Emancipatory Forms of Human Security and Liberal Peacebuilding. *International Journal, 62*(3), 459–477.

Richmond, O. (2009a). A Post-Liberal Peace: Eirenism and the Everyday. *Review of International Studies, 35*(3), 557–580.

Richmond, O. (2009b). Becoming Liberal, Unbecoming Liberalism: Liberal-Local Hybridity Via the Everyday as a Response to the Paradoxes of Liberal Peacebuilding. *Journal of Intervention and Statebuilding, 3*(3), 324–344.

Richmond, O. (2011). De-Romanticising the Local, De-mystifying the International: Hybridity in Timor Leste and the Solomon Islands. *The Pacific Review, 24*(1), 115–136.

Richmond, O., & Franks, J. (2009). *Liberal Peace Transitions: Between Statebuilding and Peacebuilding.* Edinburgh University Press.

Richmond, O., & Mac Ginty, R. (2019). Mobilities and Peace. *Globalizations, 16)5)*, 606–624.

The Independent Reporter. (2021, March 12). Security Forces Start forceful Eviction of Balaalo from West Nile. *The Independent.* https://www.independent.co.ug/security-forces-start-forceful-eviction-of-balaalo-from-west-nile/

Tim, A., & Vlassenroot, K. (2010). *The Lord's Resistance Army: Myth and Reality.* Zed Books.

UN Peacemaker. (2002). *Peace Agreement Between the Government of the Republic of Uganda and the National Rescue Front II (Yumbe Peace Agreement).* https://peacemaker.un.org/uganda-yumbe-agreement2002

Ware, A., & Ware, V. (2021). Everyday Peace: Rethinking Typologies of Social Practice and Local Agency. *Peacebuilding, 10*(3), 222–241.

Ware, A., Ware, V. A., & Kelly, L. M. (2022). Strengthening Everyday Peace Formation After Ethnic Cleansing: Operationalising a Framework in Myanmar's Rohingya Conflict. *Third World Quarterly, 43*(2), 289–308.

Williams, P. (2015). *Everyday Peace? Politics, Citizenship and Muslim Lives in India.* Wiley Blackwell.

PART VI

# Gender, Religion, Peacebuilding and Development in Africa

CHAPTER 35

# Gender, Religion, Peacebuilding, and Development in Zimbabwe

*Lindiwe Princess Maseko and Sophia Chirongoma*

## INTRODUCTION

In an endeavour to articulate the interface of gender, religion, SGBV, and peacebuilding in Zimbabwe, our chapter uses the Zimbabwe Council of Churches (ZCC) as a case study of an ecumenical organization which has programmes addressing these components. Methodologically, we adopt two theoretical frameworks, the conflict transformation theory by Paul Lederach (2003) and the human needs theory by Burton (1990). John Paul Lederach (2003) is one of the main protagonists of the conflict transformation framework. He defines peace as a comprehensive term that surrounds the full array of stages and approaches needed to transform conflict towards sustainable peaceful relationships and outcomes (Lederach, 2003). His approach to peacebuilding focuses on practice more than theory. The proponents of this theory support the concepts and mechanisms for conflict transformation that are grounded in the local cultures and society involved in conflict (Obiekwe, 2009). By employing Lederach's framework, this chapter acknowledges context as a critical point

L. P. Maseko
College of Humanities, University of KwaZulu Natal, Pietermaritzburg, South Africa

S. Chirongoma (✉)
Religious Studies and Ethics Department, Midlands State University, Zvishavane, Zimbabwe

Research Institute of Theology and Religion, University of South Africa, Pretoria, South Africa of departure in pursuing transformation. By adopting a two-pronged theoretical framework, our chapter draws insights from both the conflict transformation theory and the human needs theory. Firstly, the study locates Zimbabwean women within and outside the church context. Secondly, it takes cognisance of cultural factors within the Zimbabwean society, particularly how culture shapes women's experiences of SGBV. Lastly, the chapter echoes some tenets of African Women's Theology to illustrate how the local ecumenical church bodies such as the ZCC can serve as vehicles for promoting practical transformational concepts, impart skills for addressing and healing the wounds caused by the past conflict and trauma endured by Zimbabwean women. Below, we turn to briefly unpack these two theories, illustrating their relevance to our study.

## Conflict Transformation Theory

The conflict transformation theory is defined in various ways. Conflict transformation requires multiple perspectives to see different aspects of a complex reality (Lederach, 2003). Three such perspectives to employ towards conflict transformation include, firstly: seeing the immediate situation; secondly: seeing beyond the presenting problems towards the deeper patterns of the relationship, including the context in which the conflict finds expression; and thirdly: is the need for a conceptual framework that holds the perspectives together, one that permits us to connect the presenting problems with deeper relational patterns. It is also important to note that this theory is beyond a set of techniques; hence it is employed here as a way of "looking" and "seeing." As noted by Lederach (2003), looking entails drawing attention to something. The conflict transformation theory will provide a basis for proposing that the faith community in Zimbabwe, for instance, ecumenical bodies like the ZCC, should be proactive in finding ways to enlighten society about the negative impact of Sexual and Gender Based Violence (SGBV) on women who form the bulk of those who are on the receiving end of SGBV in Zimbabwe. Furthermore, Lederach (2003) unpacks the term "see" as an act of seeking insight and understanding to create meaning and bringing reality into a sharper focus. In sync with the conflict transformation theory, our study argues that while faith communities in Zimbabwe have been focusing on addressing violence in the broad sense, there is an urgent need to shift the focus so as to understand and create meaning on the reality of SGBV and integrate that in peacebuilding processes in Zimbabwe. Conflict transformation therefore proposes the use of progressive perspectives when addressing social conflict. This framework provides an overall understanding of the conflict, while creating a platform for presenting issues and the changes needed at the level of deeper relational patterns. Using this framework is befitting as it awakens the faith community to realize the struggles endured by women exposed to SGBV induced by pre- and post-conflict contexts, as well as taking cognisance of how such traumas will negatively affect their mental health in future.

Paul Lederach's conflict transformation framework also focuses on inculcating a positive orientation towards conflict resolution in an endeavour to produce constructive change. This theory is also defined by its nature of looking at isolated conflict episodes seeking to understand how these episodes are embedded in the greater pattern of human relationships. In adopting this framework, our chapter seeks to highlight the fact that SGBV has not received enough attention when it comes to addressing the causes of social conflict not only in Zimbabwe, but globally. Hence, we argue that SGBV is often overlooked in a context like Zimbabwe whereby much focus is put on public and political conflict. Our chapter therefore draws from the conflict transformation theory to reveal the importance of addressing isolated intrapersonal conflicts emerging from Sexual and Gender Based Violence endured by women who are either survivors of SGBV or living in a context riddled with incidences of SGBV. We also highlight the fact that mental health and the deterioration of sexual reproductive health are some of the negative effects of SGBV which need attention within the context of isolated social conflict resolution. Resonating with the conflict transformation theory, our chapter reiterates the fact that conflict should not be perceived as a threat but a valuable opportunity to grow and to increase our understanding of ourselves and others.

By paying attention to isolated conflict in peacebuilding processes, the conflict transformation framework reduces violence and fosters peace, unity, and emotional healing by virtue of focusing on responding to the challenges, needs, and realities on the ground. The conflict transformation framework is therefore relevant to this study as it helps to answer the question on how best can the church in Zimbabwe, particularly the ZCC, promote sustainable peace within a context where a considerable number of women have endured SGBV not only as a result of politically motivated violence but also within their social circles. The overarching question raised in our chapter is: "Is SGBV seen as a conflicting reality that needs transformation in the Zimbabwean society?" A related question to this is: "How can one address conflict in a nonviolent manner which promotes peace and unity in human relationships?" Concurring with the conflict transformation theory, we reiterate the fact that for peacebuilding to become a reality, all people must be given an opportunity to influence and shape political procedures and they must have a voice in the decisions that affect their lives. In this context, we restate the importance of a strong political will to effectively reduce or eradicate incidences of SGBV in Zimbabwe through enacting stiffer punitive laws for sex offenders as well as offering medical and emotional care for the survivors of SGBV. The conflict transformation framework views peace as rooted in the quality of relationships; hence our study also emphasizes the importance of inculcating peaceful and harmonious relationships within the Zimbabwean populace in the hope that such amicable relationships will deter sexual offenders from inflicting SGBV.

Since our chapter draws insights from both the conflict transformation framework and the human need theory, below, we turn to briefly discuss the main tenets of the human needs theory and its relevance to our study.

## The Human Needs Theory

The human needs theory revolves around the idea that there are certain essentials that are needed for survival, which includes both physical and nonphysical elements (Walsh, 2015, p. 3). Burton (1990) identifies a set of needs which he considers to be universal in their occurrence but with no hierarchal significance. His list of human needs include distributive justice, safety and security, belongingness, self-esteem, personal fulfilment, identity, cultural security, and freedom. Additionally, the list includes Maslow's hierarchy of human needs, namely, food, water, shelter, love, personal fulfilment, and self-actualization. Danesh (2011) and Walsh (2015) buttress the fact that the lack of such human needs is the root cause of conflict. In concurrence with the human needs theory, our chapter proposes that sexual reproductive health and rights, as well as mental health and well-being, should be integrated in peacebuilding processes in Zimbabwe as part of addressing human (women's) essential needs. Leaning on the human needs framework, our study emphasizes the fact that faith communities such as the ZCC in Zimbabwe must invest more time and resources towards promoting better sexual reproductive health and rights and the mental health of women and girls impacted by SGBV, which occurred because of past and unresolved conflicts of both politically related violence and non-political violence (Maseko 2020).

In line with the human needs framework, it is our contention that sustainable peace begins with an individual from his or her inner self. Thus, we highlight the fact that it is practically impossible to work towards meaningful peacebuilding with women who are still wounded by traumatic past experiences involving incidences of Sexual and Gender-Based Violence. It is therefore apparent that if Zimbabwe is to be a peaceful and progressive community, then women's health and well-being should be critically integrated as core human needs in peacebuilding processes. Likewise, mental health, particularly for women, should be prioritized as an essential pillar towards the establishment of peaceful and progressive communities (Maseko 2020). This resonates with Burton (1990) who argues that people are not capable of living peacefully without their needs being fully fulfilled. Furthermore, Burton (1990) reiterates the fact that appropriate institutions within a society can fulfil these needs for all parties and this would create a conducive environment for fostering sustainable peace. It is against this backdrop that our chapter calls upon the church to serve as a channel through which sustainable peace can be fomented through paying particular attention to healing the wounds inflicted by SGBV mainly targeted towards women. Our vantage point is that by addressing this often-neglected challenge, the women's needs for healing and restoration will have been addressed, consequently contributing towards transforming their past violated narrative which is an important ingredient for establishing sustainable peace in Zimbabwe.

## Why Involving Women in Peacebuilding: A Broad Contextual Reality

Although the outbreak of conflict impacts on the nation and the majority of the population, there should be an understanding that any kind of conflict affects the vulnerable and the marginalized the most. The recurring question in peacebuilding "when two elephants fight, who suffers the most?" should guide the trajectory to critically involve and engage with women and their contextual realities in the peacebuilding process. In response to this question, one can note that whenever there's an outbreak of conflict, women and children are more vulnerable, but mostly women remain wounded the most as they try to protect themselves, children, and the elderly during a particular conflict. Women carry the bulk of the burden, particularly because, arguably, they are naturally more emotionally inclined. Sexually, they are vulnerable because of their anatomy and what they represent, given a patriarchal-conflicted society.

At a global level, women are tortured, imprisoned, raped, trafficked, enslaved, including sexual slavery, dislocated, impoverished, and countless numbers of them have succumbed to death during conflicts and post-conflicts (Mujinga, 2022; Aroussi, 2017, p. 1, Klot, 2007, Chirongoma, 2020a, 2022). As noted by Cohen and Nordas (2014), during such conflicts, the number of people vulnerable to sexual violence committed is connected to all types of violence in the world. Lee H. Hamilton (the director of the Woodrow Wilson Centre) describes women and girls as "victims"[1] of deadly conflicts as they are usually the target of abuse, refugee inhabitants of shattered communities and states. Despite their susceptibility to violence and various forms of abuse during times of conflict, women have not despaired; rather, they have continued to be resolute in exploring opportunities for peacebuilding (Pampell, 2002, p. 5). As noted by Bradley (2018, p. 123), "victimised" women from domestic and family violence, for instance, face stigma from the authorities when they need help, and this happens through the police who delay response and sometimes the law which fails to protect them from violence. Speaking of women, peace, and security at the UN Security Council Resolutions 1325, Carolyn Hannah, the director of the United Nations Divisions for the Advancement of Women, notes that gender views are not methodologically included in peace and security activities; hence, a systematic attention to gender must be integrated in all peacebuilding initiatives (Pampell, 2002, p. 9).

In Klot (2007)'s words, women's role has been confirmed by the World Summit and leaders from the year 2005 as a focus theme and commission that ensures that adequate attention has been paid towards advancing gender equality within peacebuilding work. The reason behind this is that research on

---

[1] We have put this in quotation marks because the term "victim" negatively connotes the lived experience of those who go through violence. Instead, we will subsequently use the term "survivors" throughout the discussion in this chapter.

women in peacebuilding has remained undiscovered and unindicated as Shulika (2016) puts it across. Furthermore, women's security has often been privately handled; it is usually referred to as a "women's issue" which is regarded as unimportant when it comes to discussing national, regional, or global security matters (Klot, 2007). Thus, systematically in the context of peace, particularly peacebuilding initiatives, gender competency has been absent, for example, in the UN's position on women's rights that entails quotas and emergency reproductive health care and under-representation of women in decision-making (Klot, 2007, p. 2). Further, at family, community, and national level, the peacebuilding process, particularly when it comes to addressing the incidences of Sexual and Gender Based Violence (SGBV), has received inadequate attention. This is often the case in under-resourced communities which lack consistent peacebuilding frameworks and priority plans (Klot, 2007, p. 7).

Worth noting but sad, although domestic and family violence have been criminalized, the reality on the ground is that in post-conflict societies, women with unpleasant past situations have less protection and less access to services like justice, economic security, and citizenship (Klugman, 2017, Klot, 2007, p. 1). Instead, the peacebuilding process at a large scale has put more emphasis on other national issues related to peace and security. For instance, street crimes, homicides, political corruption, gangs and arms control, demobilization, and re-integration initiatives receive more attention more than women's protection (Klot, 2007, p. 1). It is against this background that scholars like Bradley (2018) query why the protection of the vulnerable has been deprioritized in favour of state-building initiatives preferred by the officials who are usually men, who dictate peace agreements and state-building agendas. In a similar light, Krause et al. (2018) concur with Bradley (2018) who restate the fact that peace deals and state-building agenda are largely formulated and written by men to the exclusion of women. Clearly, the invisibility of women in peacebuilding processes, particularly gender and sexual-related issues, has a critical effect on peacebuilding work, and it also affects how women are perceived and treated in post-conflict decision-making (Klot, 2007).

Since sexual violence is harmful to the survivors' physical, economic, and social well-being, it will inadvertently have far-reaching consequences for the survivors, their families, and future communities (Aroussi, 2017). Furthermore, Klot (2007) avers that the psychological damage on the survivors and perpetrators is the most prevalent threat to social unity. Similarly, Aroussi (2017) restates that gender inequality remains the root cause and result of sexual violence during war and peace time. Hence, addressing sexual violence should be on the priority list of the security issues. It is therefore essential to pay attention to women's experiences of Sexual and Gender Based Violence in conflict and post-conflict resolution as a resource for promoting the survivors' mental health (Maseko 2020). As noted by Bradley (2018), in the context of women, ending a conflict does not only mean ending violence. Instead, peacebuilding processes must involve women by looking into the details of each scenario which affected them and their mental health, particularly sensitive issues like

SGBV. This will go a long way towards preserving mental health, which is an essential and holistic life course approach to health, access to justice and human rights, and sustainable economic development (Votruba et al., 2014). Preserving and enhancing mental health is a vital step in addressing key development issues like social inclusion and equality of universal health coverage (Votruba et al., 2014). More so, Bradley (2018) argues that protecting women and children should be a public policy priority aim since survivors of violence suffer from sexual traumas that affect their reproductive health as well as making them susceptible to sexually transmitted infections (STIs) and HIV infection. As such, prioritizing mental health can be a helpful concept in peacebuilding processes; this will particularly help to rehabilitate the survivors of SGBV, the bulk of whom are women. This is particularly important because rape is associated with stigma in peace times, which affects women's reproductive and mental health (Aroussi, 2017, p. 4).

Acknowledging women's experiences of violence, particularly when tackling issues to do with SGBV and other forms of violence against women (VAW) is also one of the key themes addressed by African women's theology. For instance, Mercy Amba Oduyoye (2001) foregrounds the fact that at the core of African Women's Theology is the study of people's daily experiences, particularly women's experiences. Hence, African Women Theologians regard people's experiences as an invaluable source for doing theology. Similarly, Christina Landman (1994) coheres that a holistic comprehension of African women's actual experiences is only feasible if researchers provide a platform for the community being researched on to re-tell their stories and inviting them to propose homegrown solutions. In the same light, Kasomo and Maseno (2011) aver that African Women's Theology pays special attention to the community, especially women, since women have often been pushed to the peripheries of society. Our chapter therefore resonates with the same views raised by African Women Theologians. Taking note of how there's still need for more African Women Theologians to research and write about women, conflict management, and peacebuilding, our chapter adopts the tenets of African Women's Theology to propound for the importance of embracing women's experiences when tackling issues to do with conflict management and peacebuilding not only in Zimbabwe, but other parts of Africa as well.

## WOMEN AND PEACEBUILDING IN ZIMBABWE

As has been articulated in the foregoing section, paying attention to the plight of women in peace and conflict studies, as well as the inclusion of women in peacebuilding processes, has gradually become a significant resource in conflict management and a topical research area. Cognisant of the various phases that Zimbabwe as a nation state has gone through, socially, politically, and economically, these various phases have become a seedbed of numerous unresolved conflicts. It is therefore important to acknowledge what women go through during and after conflicts be it political, social, and economic. Hence, the following overarching questions are pivotal: how much has been done so far to restore peace and security, especially for women in the post-conflict zones? What is the contribution of the nation, in particular, the faith- and church-based communities, towards involving women in peacebuilding programmes and to what extent have the complex realities of women, particularly incidences of SGBV in the post-conflict contexts, been addressed in peacebuilding processes in Zimbabwe?

Prior to responding to the questions raised above, it is also important to retrace the history of women's inclusion in conflict management and peacebuilding in Zimbabwe, and what it means to build and integrate gender into peacebuilding. Zimbabwean women were involved in the peacebuilding processes and conflict transformation since the time of the war of liberation (UN Women, 2014, p. 7). Although women were responsible for shouldering the bulk of the household chores, they were also involved in fighting the liberation struggle alongside their male counterparts. The United Nations women's report (2014) in a conference which was hosted by the Ministry of Women Affairs, Gender and Community Development (MWAGCD), in collaboration with the Organ for National Healing, Reconciliation and Integration (ONHRI), assesses women's experiences through various political transitions in Zimbabwean history till the present moment. In shaping peacebuilding processes to address gender inequalities and social injustice, Zimbabwean women actively participated in the liberation struggle, which ensued between 1966 and 1979. For example, some of them were part of the liberation fighters; they joined the war front. Others stayed behind but they offered material, logistical, and emotional support to the liberation fighters (Gaidzanwa, 2004).

Similarly, in our contemporary times, several women, particularly women's organizations, in Zimbabwe have exhibited their determination to contribute towards peacebuilding. For instance, they played a leading role in the process of formulating legal and constitutional reforms in the 1980–1990s. Furthermore, female politicians played a pivotal role in averting the humanitarian crisis which had been precipitated by the political turbulence in the aftermath of the 2008 parliamentary and presidential elections. They actively participated in the deliberations which led to the signing of the Global Political Agreement (GPA) in 2008. Such interventions not only resulted in the signing of the GPA, but they also subsequently led to the formation of an inclusive government in 2009. Furthermore, the UN Women (2014) report applauds how Zimbabwean female politicians played a formative role in 2010, in the aftermath of the signing of the GPA, where the leaders of the women's wings of three main political parties came together to signal their resolve to work across their political divides to accelerate the implementation of the GPA and to build the common agenda for women's empowerment.

Global ecumenical bodies led by women have also been recorded as having played a formative role in Zimbabwe's peacebuilding processes. For instance, UN Women (2014) reports that in 2011, several leaders of the Global Young Women's Christian Association visited Zimbabwe and the main purpose of the trip was to discuss ways for fostering national solidarity and peacebuilding. The delegates comprised renowned women leaders, including Mary Robinson. This contributed towards augmenting a sense of solidarity among women who engaged in peacebuilding. Also, in 2012, the embassy of the Kingdom of Netherlands joined with Zimbabwe to support the "Women and Peace Conference" organized by Musasa Project, a local NGO whose mandate is to protest against all forms of violence against women as part of a worldwide campaign: "16 days of Activism against Gender Based Violence." Another example is the Ecumenical Church Leaders Forum (ECLF), which has made some inroads in establishing a positive partnership between women's groups and the church. This has been achieved through women clergy and church leaders bringing the church and the community together for peace and sustainable development, based on peace and reconciliation sessions involving traditional leaders, local councils, and the security sector.

Furthermore, according to the UN Women (2014) report, efforts towards ensuring sustainable peace and security in Zimbabwe have so far identified that there is need to understand women's positionality in contrast to men, further looking into structural and political dynamics that influence women's participation. This method can be helpful in applying gender-sensitive intervention programmes for a more liberative society. Be that as it may, there are several overarching questions which still need to be answered, for instance: "What have the peace building processes contributed towards positively transforming women's experiences?" "In what ways has the healing process focused on addressing complex issues such as the effects of pandemics, particularly HIV&AIDS; COVID-19 and SGBV, which has been codenamed, 'the pandemic within a pandemic'?" These questions propel one to reflect on key issues to do with the holistic liberation of women. They also highlight the pertinent need for reflecting on what the faith-based organizations in Zimbabwe have contributed towards peacebuilding; this includes ecumenical bodies such as the ZCC. Hence, the forthcoming section focuses on responding to the following question: "To what extent has the ZCC contributed towards turning the tide of SGBV through its peace and nation building processes and programs?" It is to this question that we turn to below.

## THE ZIMBABWE COUNCIL OF CHURCHES AND PEACEBUILDING

The Zimbabwe Council of Churches (ZCC) is an interdenominational group of churches which was formed in 1964 to confess the triune nature of God (ZCC report, 2020). The objectives of the ZCC were to "increase mutual understanding, to develop more effective ecumenical witnesses in action on the local, national and international levels, to promote close unity through joint action service and by ecumenical studies in faith and order, life and work to encourage the cementing of unity and solidarity of denominations, to stimulate and facilitate the development of evangelistic and sustainable development programs" (Tarusarira, 2020, p. 66). According to Murwira and Manyeruke

(2020), the ZCC considers the intersectionality between building peace, democracy, stability, and the development of a nation. Hence, the ZCC focuses on justice, peace, reconciliation, church and development, leadership development and ecumenical unity, and university chaplaincy as vital thematic areas (Hallencreutz, 1988). The ZCC is a communion of thirty member churches, and through this communion, it brings churches and organizations for joint action, witness, and co-ordination to adapt united and common responses to social-related challenges in Zimbabwe (ZCC 2020 Report). The ZCC is ecumenical in nature and it collaborates with leadership development programmes, nation building, good governance programmes, humanitarian, and livelihood development programmes, as well as organizational and sustainability and management. As one of the oldest and well-established church-based organizations in Zimbabwe, the ZCC uses national dialogue as a strategy to address the challenges that have been historically and currently affecting Zimbabwe at all societal levels (ZCC report, 2020).

The ZCC has been involved in peace-making processes to reconcile issues affecting conflicting parties through facilitating political dialogue and negotiation. Its interventions can be traced back from the 2002 ZANU PF and MDC political violence, moving on to the 2008 election violence as well as proceeding to the formation of the GNU in Zimbabwe (Tarusarira, 2020). It was because of the denouncement of political violence through the ZCC that Zimbabwe as a country gave birth to the Ministry of National Healing and Reconciliation (Tarusarira, 2020, p. 103). The ZCC has also collaborated with another ecumenical board, the Zimbabwe Heads of Christian Denominations (ZHOCD), in promoting and advancing the programmes. For instance, the ZCC and the ZHOCD were capacitated to participate in public engagement and defending constitutional democracy (ZCC report, 2020). This journey has been navigated through corporate governance, devolution, nation building, and advocacy trainings for the ZHOCD and faith leaders in provinces like Masvingo, Midlands, Manicaland, and Mashonaland East Province involving both men and women in the process. Secondly, local peace council's trainings have been initiated on legal protection mechanisms and parish dialogue meetings which were intentional about gender inclusivity as well as paying particular attention to the needs of people living with disabilities. These dialogues were done through provincial leaders' forum meetings (ZCC report, 2020, p. 8) so as to strengthen the skills and knowledge of the ZHOCD membership. Multi-sectoral citizen duty-bearer engagements and campaigns were also conducted at district level (ZCC report, 2020).

In its endeavour to enhance nation building and to increase capacity knowledge and practice, the ZCC report (2020) records how the ZHOCD women and youth forum platforms initiated and revived a sense of priority for women and youths so that they will have the opportunity to engage with duty bearers over issues affecting them. This has subsequently opened opportunities for them to influence reforms of laws so that the legal system effectively responds to their existential needs. Furthermore, such forums enlighten women and the youth on the importance of participating in various national processes such as elections and budgeting. Consequently, this created an opportunity for women to be part of marriage, property rights, family, and inheritance law bill discussions. Through the local ecumenical fellowships undertaken in places like Gwanda, Bindura, Manicaland, Chivi, Gutu, Epworth, Gweru, and Harare South, the ZCC has managed to initiate dialogue and critical discussions on complex lived realities including the challenges posed by the COVID-19 pandemic, as well as the upsurge of gender-based violence incidences (ZCC report, 2020).

Another achievement that has been accomplished by the ZCC, which has a huge bearing on the welfare of women and the youth, is the establishment and co-ordination of the National Economic Justice desk to campaign for an inclusive National Economic Vision (ZCC report, 2020). It was through the initiatives emerging from the programmes being mainstreamed by this desk that women were capacitated to start sewing and tailoring projects. The income earned from these projects has considerably improved their household income-earning opportunities, progressing towards economic justice in those parts of the country. Additionally, the ZCC national building initiatives have immensely contributed towards the development of critical cross-sectoral basic services. This also entailed the provision of sanitary wear for the vulnerable and needy children and women in areas such as Bubi, Gwanda, Chipinge, Mberengwa, and Bindura district. Some of the beneficiaries included those residing at the children's homes, those who are incarcerated, and those who are living with disabilities to ensure that all women and girls will get to experience their sexual reproductive health rights with dignity. Such interventions also helped to maintain these women and girls' hygienic conditions and to restore their humanity and dignity especially during the economic constraints exacerbated by the COVID-19 pandemic. Such a holistic approach to the women and girls' needs made a whole world of difference in terms of reducing their vulnerabilities in various facets of life (ZCC report, 2020).

The ZCC also established a helpline and a psychosocial support management system which according to the 2020 report managed to handle over a 100 Psychosocial Support (PSS) and Gender Based Violence (GBV) cases in one year (ZCC report, 2020). During the peak of the COVID-19 lockdown, virtual communication with the "victims" was initiated, thereby providing legal advice, counselling, medical and psychosocial support, and food. Under the auspices of the ZCC, the pastors have been partaking in counselling services at their congregations, with their member churches as well as their constituencies (ZCC report, 2020). The ZCC has also engaged the church through public campaigns, promoting peace and tolerance through producing and circulating pastoral letters addressing these key issues (Tarusarira, 2020).

Contributing to health and the vulnerable in the society, the ZCC has worked with the Zimbabwe Association of Church Related Hospitals (ZACH). As noted by Chirongoma (2020b), ZACH is identified as a pivotal medical arm of the Christian churches in Zimbabwe, with a board of trustees constituted by the Heads of Christian Denominations and their representatives. Being responsive to contextual realities, particularly addressing health and well-being, supporting member institutions have made some inroads in the provision of quality health care and service delivery especially to the most vulnerable groups residing in the rural areas (Chirongoma, 2020b). Furthermore, collaborating with the Ministry of Health and Child Welfare (MOHCW) to further the mission mandate of rebuilding Zimbabwe's health system, ZACH has so far covered 126 hospitals and clinics in the country. This has also been achieved through the contribution of the parliamentary portfolio committee on health through its petition for improved service and resources for mission hospitals. Such interventions have positively contributed towards addressing the health and well-being for the vulnerable groups such as women and children as well as people living with disabilities (Chirongoma, 2020b).

## REFLECTIONS ON THE NEXUS OF GENDER, RELIGION, PEACEBUILDING, AND DEVELOPMENT IN AFRICA

As has been noted above, lasting peace and sustainable development in Zimbabwe will remain a pipedream in the absence of addressing gender justice and gender inclusion issues. Resonating with Sustainable Development Goal 16, which emphasizes the need for promoting peace, justice, and strong institutions, our study has illustrated that peacebuilding can be implemented as a tool for healing the inner wounds for the survivors of SGBV in Zimbabwe. It is apparent that people who are healthy physically and mentally are more progressive, innovative, and likely to uphold peace, justice, and unity. Conversely, communities that are riddled with poverty, food insecurity, and gender-based inequalities have a higher propensity for crime and violence, mainly exhibited through SGBV, corruption, and misappropriation of resources. All these vices are a threat to building peace and they hinder any initiatives for sustainable development.

As has been reiterated by the Circle of Concerned African Women Theologians, women are the pillars of development and they are the harbingers of peace, unity, and solidarity (Oduyoye, 1990, 2001; Dube, 2001; Mupangwa & Chirongoma, 2020; Chirongoma and Mupangwa 2021a, 2021b). Drawing insights from African Women's Theology, which falls under the category of liberation theologies, they articulate the importance of acknowledging women's pivotal role in building and transforming societies in partnership with their male counterparts. Mupangwa and Chirongoma (2021) articulate this point as follows:

> African women's theology addresses the injustices that African women encounter both in the religious and cultural milieu. This theology focuses on promoting equality in all things including power sharing. In African women's theology, men and women are recognised as equal because they are both created in the same image of God. African women theologians, therefore, challenge patriarchal hier-

archical structures and the subjugation of women. (Mupangwa & Chirongoma, 2021, p. 44)

African Women Theologians concur that women need to be empowered so that they can become their own liberators. Hence, in responding to SGBV as a major stumbling block in peacebuilding and sustainable development, African women must awaken to the fact that without enjoying equitable access to economic resources, they will remain straddling behind and they will not have a voice. Oduyoye (1995) fittingly puts it across as follows:

> Over time, African women had to learn to know their oppressors but had held their peace, because "when your hand is in someone's mouth, you do not hit that person on the head." (Oduyoye, 1995, p. 3)

In essence, the intertwined connection between gender, religion, peacebuilding, and development comes out clearly when reflecting on the views raised by African Women Theologians regarding gender equity. For instance, Oduyoye's (1995) analogy of the "two-winged theology" aptly demonstrates the inseparability of the quartet (gender, religion, peacebuilding, and development). Utilizing the imagery of a flying bird, Oduyoye (1995) poignantly illustrates that if the church and the community in general make decisions and policies whilst excluding women's experiences, hopes, and aspirations, then such an undertaking is akin to a bird flying with only one wing. She adopts this imagery to highlight the fact that for a community to be well-balanced and progressive, it necessitates adhering to gender justice and upholding gender empowerment and gender-inclusive policies. Hence, Oduyoye argues for the use of both wings, that is incorporating both men and women's views, experiences, and needs. This would propel the bird (church and society) to optimize its potential and soar above the skies. In resonance with Oduyoye's "two-winged theology," Chirongoma and Mupangwa (2021b) foreground the pertinent need for African women of faith to consistently critique religio-cultural traditions which are bent towards muting and marginalizing women amidst glaring patriarchal injustices. They put it across succinctly:

> The church still has people who trivialise gender issues and see women as subjects who need to be studied about and talked for. … In most cases, women have condoned oppression in the name of culture and church traditions. What has been normalised as how things should be done sometimes is what denies women their full humanity. In order to avoid gender blindness sometimes as women, we need to problematise what is logically seen as normal by society. (Chirongoma and Mupangwa 2021b, p. 205)

Echoing the views raised by fellow African Women Theologians above, our chapter proffers that the church, through the ZCC peacebuilding programmes, should provide a safe space for women to actively participate in rebuilding the broken minds and hearts affected by SGBV. Drawing insights from the Zimbabwean case study discussed herein, it is our contention that holistic development and peacebuilding in Africa can only be fully realized if our churches and communities embrace a two-winged theology, whereby men and women sit around the table as equals, mutually dialoguing and coming up with peacebuilding and development agendas which speak to the needs, struggles, hopes, and aspirations for all human beings created in *imago dei*. This elicits the vision of shalom where there is peace, justice, unity, and solidarity.

## Conclusion

Anchored on Lederach's conflict transformation framework and Burton's human needs theory, our chapter has highlighted the pertinent need for addressing people's holistic needs as portent for building sustainable peace and development. Reflecting on the preponderance of SGBV in Zimbabwe, the chapter used the work of the Zimbabwe Council of Churches in addressing the wounds of trauma as a vantage point for arguing that adherence to gender equality, gender empowerment, as well as peacefully and fairly addressing conflict, are pivotal pillars for attaining SDG 16. In sync with the key targets of SDG 16, "promoting peace, justice and strong institutions," the last segment of the chapter reflected on the two-winged theology proffered by African Women Theologians. The two-winged theology emphasizes partnership, mutuality, collaboration, fairness, and justice for all humans created in *imago dei*. As our chapter draws to a close, it seems befitting to reiterate that there can be no lasting peace in Africa if political and religious leaders ignore multifaceted factors negatively impacting on women's humanity and dignity, and one of these key factors is the cancerous worm of SGBV which has become indelibly etched in our African homes and communities.

## References

Aroussi, S. (2017). Women, Peace, and Security and the DRC: Time to Rethink Wartime Sexual Violence as Gender-Based Violence? *Politics & Gender, 13*(3), 488–515.

Bradley, S. (2018). Domestic and Family Violence in Post-Conflict Communities: International Human Rights Law and the State's Obligation to Protect Women and Children. *Health and Human Rights, 20*(2), 123–136.

Burton, J. (1990). *Conflict: Resolution and Prevention*. St. Martin's Press.

Chirongoma, S. (2020a). Women as Agents of Peace in the Midlands Province, Zimbabwe: Towards Sustainable Peace and Development. In A. Chitando (Ed.), *Women and Peacebuilding in Africa* (pp. 108–123). Routledge.

Chirongoma, S. (2020b). Church-Related Hospitals and Health-Care Provision in Zimbabwe. In E. Chitando (Ed.), *The Zimbabwe Council of Churches and Development in Zimbabwe* (pp. 125–147). Palgrave Macmillan.

Chirongoma, S. (2022). Young Christian Women As Agents of Sustainable Development in Zimbabwe: A Case Study of Murinye District, Masvingo. In E. Chitando,

S. Chirongoma, & K. Biri (Eds.), *Women and Religion in Zimbabwe Strides and Struggles* (pp. 266–286). Rowman and Littlefield.
Chirongoma, S., & Mupangwa, T. (2021a). Gender Disparity as a Colonial Matrix of Power: Demystifying Pastors' Call Narratives in the Apostolic Faith Mission in Zimbabwe. In L. Siwila & F. Kobo (Eds.), *Religion, Patriarchy and Empire: Festschrift in Honour of Mercy Amba Oduyoye* (pp. 211–260). Cluster Publications.
Chirongoma, S., & Mupangwa, T. (2021b). The quest for good governance and gender justice in the postcolonial church: A case study of the Apostolic Faith Mission in Zimbabwe. In B. Dube (Ed.), *Postcolonial Religio-political and Religious Education in Crisis: The Case of Zimbabwe, South Africa and Tanzania* (pp. 313–352). Cluster Publications: Pietermaritzburg, South Africa.
Cohen, D. K., & Nordas, R. (2014). Sexual Violence in Armed Conflict: Introducing the SVAC Dataset, 1989–2009. *Journal of Peace Research, 51*(3), 418–428.
Danesh, H. B. (2011). Human Needs Theory, Conflict, and Peace: In Search of an Integrated Model. In D. J. Christie (Ed.), *Encyclopaedia of Peace Psychology*. Hoboken, New Jersey: Wiley-Blackwell.
Dube, M. W. (Ed.). (2001). *Other Ways of Reading: African Women and the Bible*. Society of Biblical Literature.
Gaidzanwa, R. (2004). *Gender, Women and Electoral Politics in Zimbabwe*. EISA Research Report 8. Electoral Institute for Sustainable Democracy in Africa. http://www.eisa.org.za/WEP/zimwomen
Hallencreutz, Carl F. (1988). Policy of Religion: The New Framework. In C. Hallencreutz and A. Moyo, (Eds.), *Church and State in Zimbabwe*, 1–25. Gweru: Mambo Press.
Kasomo, D., & Maseno, L. M. (2011). A Critical Appraisal of African Feminist Theology. *International Journal of Current Research, 2*(1), 154–162.
Klot, J. F. (2007). Women and Peacebuilding. *Social Science Research Council, 29*, 1–12.
Klugman, J. (2017). *Gender Based Violence and the Law. World Development Report Background Paper*. World Bank. License: CC BY 3.0 IGO. https://openknowledge.worldbank.org/handle/10986/26198
Krause, J., Krause, W., & Bränfors, P. (2018). Women's Participation in Peace Negotiations and the Durability of Peace. *International Interactions, 44*(6), 985–1016.
Landman, C. (1994). Ten Years of Feminist Theology in South Africa. *Journal of Feminist Studies Religion, 11*(1), 143–148.
Lederach, J. P. (2003). *The Little Book of Conflict Transformation*. Good Books.
Maseko, L. P. (2020). Sustainable Peace and Development: Peace Building by the Ecumenical Church Leaders Forum. In E. Chitando, M. R. Gunda, & L. Togarasei (Eds.), *Religion and Development in Africa* (pp. 335–352). University of Bamberg Press.
Mujinga, M. (2022). The Triple Suffering of Zimbabwean Women Trafficked to the Middle East. In Chitando, E., Manyonganise, M., Chirongoma, S. (Eds.), *Gendered Spaces, Religion and Migration in Zimbabwe: Implications for Economic Development*, (p. 7). Palgrave and MacMillan.
Mupangwa, T., & Chirongoma, S. (2020). The Challenges of Being a Female Pastor: A Case of the Apostolic Faith Mission in Zimbabwe. *HTS Teologiese Studies/ Theological Studies, 76*(2), 1–10. https://doi.org/10.4102/hts.v76i2.5838
Mupangwa, T., & Chirongoma, S. (2021). Single Women and Church Leadership: A Case Study of the Apostolic Faith Mission in Zimbabwe. *Journal of Theology for Southern Africa, 171*, 42–64.

Murwira, A., & Manyeruke, C. (2020). Church-Politics Nexus: An Analysis of the Zimbabwe Council of Churches (ZCC) and Political Engagement. In E. Chitando (Ed.), *The Zimbabwe Council of Churches and Development in Zimbabwe* (pp. 95–108). Palgrave Macmillan.

Obiekwe K. (2009). In Search of Appropriate Peace-making/Peacebuilding Paradigm in dealing With Africa's Intrastate Violent Conflicts: Considering Lederach's Faith Based Conflict, Transformation and Peacebuilding Approach. *Journal of Peace, Conflict and Development*, (13) http://www.peacestudiesjournal.org.uk/

Oduyoye, M. A. (1990). *Who Will Roll the Stone Away? The Decade of the Churches in Solidarity with Women.* WCC Publications.

Oduyoye, M. A. (1995). *Daughters of Anowa: African Women and Patriarchy.* Orbis Books.

Oduyoye, M. A. (2001). *Introducing African Women's Theology.* The Pilgrim Press.

Pampell, C. (2002). More Than Victims: The Role of Women in Conflict Prevention. In *A Conference Report* (pp. 1–56).

Shulika, L. S. (2016). Women and Peace Building: From Historical to Contemporary African Perspectives. *Ubuntu: Journal of Conflict and Social Transformation*, 5(1), 7–31.

Tarusarira, J. (2020). The Zimbabwe Council of Churches and 'Crisis' Ecumenical Groups. In E. Chitando (Ed.), *The Zimbabwe Council of Churches and Development in Zimbabwe* (pp. 65–78). Palgrave Macmillan.

UN Women. (2014). *Zimbabwean Women in Conflict: Transformation and Peace Building, Past Experience and Future Opportunities.* UN Women.

Votruba, N., Eaton, J., Prince, M., & Thornicroft, G. (2014). The Importance of Global Mental Health for the Sustainable Development Goals. *Journal of Mental Health*, 23(6), 283–286.

Walsh, D. (2015). How a Human Needs Theory Understanding of Conflict Enhances the Use of Consociationalism as a Conflict Resolution Mechanism: The Good Friday Agreement in Northern Ireland. *Ethnopolitics* https://doi.org/10.1080/17449057.2015.1024012

Zimbabwe Council of Churches Annual Report. (2020). https://www.zcc-eco.org/images/documents/ZCC%202020%20Annual%20Report.pdf

CHAPTER 36

# Religion, Feminist Peace, and Security in Nigeria and Uganda

*Helen Kezie-Nwoha*

## INTRODUCTION

Defining religion remains a contested terrain. Scholars have failed on a common understanding and definition of religion (Horton, 1960). However, Bergunder (2014) suggests that debates around religion should be framed differently and suggests a theoretical framework that establishes 'religion' as the historical subject matter of religious studies. Martin (2009) agrees that religion should be defined and described based on the context and further suggested that religion could be defined as a belief system; something that specifically concerns supernatural matters; matters of faith; the meaning of life; spirituality or spiritual well-being; and a communal institution oriented around a set of beliefs, rituals, practices, and ethical or social norms. He proposed that the last aspect of the definition is more comprehensive and seems to capture the various components of what is generally believed to be religion.

However, it is important to note that the meaning of religion changes with time and is based on the context. For example, what the term religion meant in the sixteenth century is not the same as in the twenty-first century (Martin, 2009). Martin (2009) challenges the notion that history should be used to describe religion by tracing how and why a culture allows certain experiences to count as religion, as this has the potential to exclude other experiences. This chapter will adopt the definition of religion as spirituality or spiritual well-being and a communal institution oriented around a set of beliefs, rituals, practices,

H. Kezie-Nwoha (✉)
Women's International Peace Centre, Kampala, Uganda

© The Author(s), under exclusive license to Springer Nature Switzerland AG 2023
S. M. Kilonzo et al. (eds.), *The Palgrave Handbook of Religion, Peacebuilding, and Development in Africa*,
https://doi.org/10.1007/978-3-031-36829-5_36

and ethical or social norms. This allows me to situate two main religions that will form the basis of this write-up: Christianity and Islam. The reason for using these two religions is because they seem to interface a lot in African conflicts and both religions have done tremendous peacebuilding work; it will therefore be important to evaluate the extent to which they adopt feminist approaches to respond to SDG16. I therefore used literature review to identify case studies in Nigeria and Uganda to understand the current practice of interfaith religious institutions' contribution to SDG16 using a feminist lens. The choice of both countries is based on some similarities in conflicts and their different geographic locations; Nigeria in the west Africa region and Uganda in the east Africa region highlight the similarities in Africa conflicts. Nigeria and Uganda have had histories of religious conflicts; conflicts in both countries are influenced by ethnic and political ideologies. In addition, both countries have been fighting fundamentalist groups; ADF in Uganda (currently operating in the Democratic Republic of Congo) has been associated with the Islamic group al-Shabaab, while Boko Haram has been operating in northern Nigeria and has also been linked to al-Shabaab and al-Qaida. Al-Shabaab is operational in Uganda and conducted suicide bombings in 2010 and a failed attempt in 2014 (Eelco et al., 2016).

The impact of these conflicts have had an/or adverse effects on the development of these countries and has drawn a wide range of actors to respond in not only resolving the conflict but also providing development interventions as it is widely acknowledged that peace and development are closely linked. Development can help address the root causes of conflict such as incorporating usually marginalized groups or communities in development programs to address inequalities and unequal access to resources. One of the key actors in development is religious institutions, mostly through community-based initiatives. They have also been involved in developing and implementing frameworks such as the Millennium Development Goals (MDGs) and the Sustainable Development Goals (SDGs).

Many faith actors were involved in the development of the Sustainable Development Goals (SDGs). The SDGs comprise 17 goals with 169 targets that were signed by the 193 UN member states in 2015. They replaced the Millennium Development Goals (MDGs), which were implemented from 2000 to 2015, and are part of a broader Agenda 2030 that reflects the objectives that should be achieved by 2030. The MDGs had been unilaterally set within the United Nations (UN) with little to no consultation with civil society, compared to the SDGs development which was inclusive and was following a wide-reaching negotiation process within the UN as well as the largest civil society consultation ever held in its history (Tomalin et al., 2019).

The SDGs apply equally to all countries and contain goals and targets for countries of the Global North and South. The SDGs ensured a grassroots and locally owned type of development based on the recognition that 'local people' are better placed to understand and respond to development challenges. Since local societies in development-aid recipient countries are often centered around faith communities, the engagement and role played by them become even more critical to the discussion on sustainable development (Tomalin et al., 2019). The UN has made an/or efforts to ensure faith-based institutions are involved at all levels of development and implementation of the SDGs. This process is led by the UN inter-agency task force on engaging faith-based actors (Karam, 2014). One of the principles of the SDGs is the principle of 'leave no one behind' as inclusive approach to development that safeguards the poorest and most marginalized.

SDG16 aims to promote peaceful and inclusive societies for sustainable development; provide access to justice for all; and build effective, accountable, and inclusive institutions at all levels. SDG16's aspiration is to reduce conflict through justice and building strong institutions, uphold the rule of law and strengthen the presence of developing countries in global governance institutions. In situations of conflict, institutions are weak, justice is jeopardized, crime rates are high, and there is an increase in violation of human rights, exploitation, and corruption. In today's globalized world, conflict and instability in one region affect other parts of the world, as we have witnessed in the ongoing war between Russia and Ukraine. The importance of SDG16 in the achievement of all the SDGs cannot be overemphasized. The UN defines 12 targets to achieve SDG16. Goal 16.1 focuses on reducing all forms of violence and related death rates everywhere; Goal 16.2 aims to end abuse, exploitation, trafficking, and all forms of violence against children; Goal 16.3 is the promotion of the rule of law at the national and international levels and to ensure access to justice; Goal 16.4 aims to significantly reduce illicit financial and arms flow, strengthen the recovery and return of stolen assets, and combat all forms of organized crimes by 2030; Goal 16.5 focuses on reduction of corruption and bribery; Goal 16.6 focuses on developing effective, accountable, and transparent institutions; Goal 16.7 aims to ensure responsive, inclusive, participatory, and representative decision-making; Goal 16.8 focuses on broadening and strengthening the participation of developing countries in the institutions of global governance; Goal 16.9 aims to provide legal identity, including birth registration by 2030; while Goal 16.10 aims to ensure public access to information and the protection of fundamental freedoms, in accordance with national legislation and international agreements. Two additional targets 16a and 16b aim to strengthen relevant national institutions, including through international cooperation, for building capacity in developing countries, to prevent violence and combat terrorism and crime and to promote and enforce non-discriminatory laws and policies for sustainable development. From the description of the SDGs, it is evident that the goal is to build peace that is inclusive and will benefit everyone everywhere.

## Feminism and Peacebuilding

Peace is understood not simply as the absence of war, but rather as a complex multifaceted reality that requires long-term commitment and at least for some of the activists and theorists as a process rather than an end state (Muer, 2021). Muer (2021) argues that there is no simple binary between situations of war and situations of peace. Galtung (1964) in his editorial to the maiden edition of the *Journal of Peace Research* in 1964 distinguishes between two types of peace—negative peace as the absence of direct violence or absence of war and positive peace as the absence of indirect and structural violence. Different perspectives and conceptualizations of peace are very particular and subjective. Even the practices of peacebuilding are different and are informed by our subjectivities (Abu-Assab et al., 2022). The understanding of peace is based on the realities and context of a particular setting. Accepting peace as not the absence of war enables an understanding of peace in a broader term of conditions that make humans comfortable and safe always. Many writers view the term peace from a perspective of elitist political science, which is hegemonic and dominant, and serve the oppressive systems we all live within (Abu-Assab et al., 2022).

Feminist peace and conflict theory provide an alternative definition of peace beyond the absence of war. Writings on feminist peace and conflict theories have been shaped by critical writings on women's liberation movements in Latin America, Africa, and Asia, and critique of Western feminism by working-class, black, and lesbian scholars. They called for an analysis of war and conflict from the historical account of women in war to ensure the visibility of women in conflict and broaden the understanding of security from a human security angle (Weber, 2006). The debate also introduced the interconnectedness of all forms of violence both in conflict and in so-called peacetime and questioned the notion that women are inherently peaceful. The questioning of the normative standard is grounded in women's epistemologies. This is informed by the silencing of women's experiences and knowledge. The solution to silencing women's experiences is divided into the understanding of essentialist female nature and construction based on the understanding of gender as an expansive practice (Weber, 2006).

Just like feminism, feminist peace and conflict theory have diverse perspectives all arguing within their own terrain of understanding feminism. Essentialist feminists argue that peace is an innate characteristic in women that is predestined by motherhood and caring, and that war affects women disproportionally and is an ultimate attack on 'feminine' non-violent standards. They stress that feminine undertaking has the prospective to create a peaceful world. Liberal and equality feminists are concerned about the restriction of public space by war. They argue that the legitimization of violence and war is based on the conditioning of men toward aggression and women to submission as the patriarchal contract (Reardon, 1985; Pateman, 1988). Some feminists like Daly and

Shiva attributed war to male aggression boosted by patriarchy (Daly, 1978; Shiva, 1993).

Structuralist feminists believe that militarized masculinity extoled as the founding myth of nations perpetuates the construction of a gender clash. Sara Ruddick (1989) invented the concept of maternal thinking by arguing that care and "relation-based THINKING" (Gilligan, 1982; Chodorow, 1978) is the main prerequisite for a more peaceful society. Caretakers, they argue, do not have value in our societies and if men would take active roles in caretaking, fewer imagined, violence-based decisions would be made (Weber, 2006, p. 5).

In the late 1990s, post-modernist or deconstructivism feminists such as Judith Butler (1990) argued that gender and any other identity is created through conversational tradition. Since then, a broad variety of liberal, post-structural, and anti-essentialist feminists (Nicholson, 1985) argued on the assumption that, if gender is constructed, it can be deconstructed and has no prior relation to the sex of a person. By acknowledging women's experiences in war, both as active fighters and as victims, the question of inherent peacefulness and maternal thinking was crushed. Aggression and submission as gendered adjectives conditioning women and men have been mirrored afresh.

For this chapter, feminist peace will adopt the definition related to three perspectives on peace: peace as the absence of all types of structural violence; peace and security for all; and peace premised on the integration of a gender perspective and equal participation of women and men at all levels and in all peacebuilding processes. Equal participation would entail addressing gender power relations within households, the community, and institutions; interrogating the use of power and masculinities that perpetuate inequalities; and normalizing the abuse of women. It is important to acknowledge that all these different forms of inequalities exist in situations of conflict and post-conflict settings. Feminist peace as the absence of structural violence is a long-time goal that takes time to achieve in conflict and post-conflict settings. Feminist peace also pays attention to gender justice, demands more prevention, and challenges the practice of militarism and how military practices impact peacebuilding. It advances that peace cannot be achieved by allowing a militarized type of power, which nurtures environments where women suffer violence at home or in society. It calls for justice to be embedded in all attempts to seek peace and address impunity through various mechanisms, including tapping into traditional mechanisms that uphold fairness (Kezie-Nwoha, 2019).

## Literature Review

Literature indicates the increased attention to religious institutions as key players in peacebuilding and recognizes that religion is detrimental to peace as it has been a major reason for some of the worst conflicts witnessed in Africa and elsewhere. At the same time, religion has played a key role in reducing tension and in participating in mediation and negotiations; this has been reflected in the role of religion in responding to violent extremism (Ulrich &

Osman, 2006; Scharffs, 2018; Bercovitch & Kadayifci-Orellana, 2009; Saleh, 2022; Douglas, 2022). The various interpretations of different religions are often viewed as a source of tension and as part of the problem. General views about religious fundamentalism have guided the widening gap between different religious communities and an increasing awareness among (secular) policy-makers that religion can play an instrumental, potentially problematic role in local, national, and international conflicts. There is also a growing appreciation among practitioners that religious actors have the potential to resolve conflict and decrease tensions. This holds true particularly in post-conflict settings, where religion can contribute to peacebuilding activities. The combination of moral authority and the ability to create a candid commitment to peace among large parts of the population makes many international policy-makers regard religious communities as important 'drivers of change' in peacebuilding, as they have the right platform to preach and instruct on peaceful coexistence (Flanigan, 2013; Scharffs, 2018). Faith-Based Organizations (FBOs) have been instrumental to peace efforts globally. In Israel, the Interreligious Coordinating Council, which brings 60 religious institutions to enable dialogue between the different religions, has played a critical role in peacebuilding (Flanigan, 2013).

There is a recognition of the role of religion in development and in achieving the Sustainable Development Goals (SDGs) in literature (Litalien, 2019; Tomalin et al., 2019). One of the objectives of the SGDs is to address local needs by working with communities to ensure local ownership to fulfill its principle of leaving no one behind. Religious institutions have been key to ensure that the needs of local communities are met. As a result, a significant portion of development aid is channeled through faith-based institutions. The history of the role of religion in development has been structured around colonialism, where Christianity provided the pathway for colonialism as a civilizing mission and provided the Christian religion as an ideological justification by casting colonial efforts as a service in development. Christian mission was then seen as the root of modern ideas of global development, and other religions were judged on their compatibility with this civilizing project. The civilizing project gave birth to two movements: the modernization movement that complied with European social and economic visions and the other movement that used the process of reform to resist and critique colonization (Jörg & Tomalin, 2017). The modernization movement propelled this agenda as most religious institutions provided welfare services which were used as indicators of the civilization project providing health care, education, vocational training, as well as local information and advocacy (Tomalin et al., 2019). Many religious institutions including indigenous African Christian institutions have adopted the welfare approach providing services that should be the responsibility of the state; some have also turned such provisions into businesses and made/have come to make money in the name of providing services, particularly in education and health care.

Literature on the role of religious institutions in peacebuilding, particularly interfaith religious institutions in Africa, is growing; there are writings on the role of interfaith institutions in contributing to development generally and SDGs in particular (Chitando & Gusha, 2022; Litalien, 2019; McGarvey, 2022; Omona, 2022; Saleh, 2022), but not very specific to SDG16. Literature on gender and religion and feminism and peace is available (Abu-Assab et al., 2022; Seedet, 2016; Tickner, 1997; Verges, 2021; Weber, 2006). However, there are no indicators in the Global Gender Gap Index and Gender Development Index that account for a religious variable to determine the progress in gender equality in the religious sphere (Litalien, 2019). Litalien (2019) argues that SDGs are confronted with centuries-old institutionalized and systemic gender hierarchies; and as long as the SDGs neglect religion, which is a site of gender inequality, it is going to be difficult to achieve gender equality. There is a need for the SDGs to recognize and address the problems connected to gender equality and women's empowerment in the religious sphere (Litalien, 2019). Literature on the intersection between religion and feminist peace and security in Africa in relation to SDG16 is limited. This chapter aims to close this gap by examining feminist peace and security understanding and practice within interfaith religious institutions in Nigeria and Uganda using SDG16 as a benchmark.

I now turn to address the research objective which seeks to understand how the practice of feminist peace and security contributes to achieving SDG16 targets and sustainable peace and development. The research will use two case studies from Nigeria and Uganda to interrogate how interfaith religious institutions apply feminist peace in achieving SDG16.

## The Case Studies

Two case studies were selected in Nigeria and Uganda for this study: the Women's Interfaith Council in northern Nigeria and the Inter-Religious Council of Uganda (IRCU). Both are interfaith religious networks. Interfaith networks have been defined to represent initiatives that bring together actors from more than one faith institution or community to implement joint action that seeks to address a felt human need in a specific context (Chitando, 2022). The act of having different faiths come together to work on areas of interest and concern shows that they have put aside their differences and worked for the common good of their communities to provide the needed hope in a world that is increasingly becoming more complex. I choose the Women's Interfaith Council (WIC) in northern Nigeria in West Africa and the IRCU in East Africa. The reason for the choice is to draw lessons from two interfaith networks: one made up of different religious women's groups, WIC, and the other made up of different religious institutions, the IRCU. Clearly both institutions focus on peacebuilding and conflict transformation as well as provide a platform for networking among different religious groups. However, while the IRCU is led by men who head most of the religious institutions, WIC is led by women of the different faiths. Another distinct characteristic of the two groups is that the IRCU stands as an interfaith institution whose leadership is patriarchal in nature, while WIC is a subset of the main religious institutions and works within the guidelines of the main institution that limits the extent to which its feminist ideologies are applied in peacebuilding. The different characteristics of the interfaith groups enabled me to draw comparisons in the way they apply feminism in peacebuilding and development in the context of SDG16.

Since most religions are dominated by men in formal structures, many interfaith networks usually have more men in leadership positions. This has led to the marginalization of women and youth (Chitando, 2022). I, therefore, decided to use a women's interfaith network to address this marginalization and see how the mainstream network and the women's interfaith network compare in their peacebuilding work. Looking at the two cases enabled a better understanding of the different dynamics at play with the activities of the groups to provide a deeper understanding of different types of interfaith religious groups. Nigeria has a history of religious conflict, as religion has persistently been deployed to achieve political and ideological goals and represents a context where interfaith networks have sought to promote peace (Chitando, 2022; Omotosho, 2014). Uganda, since independence, has had several conflicts; however, the most intense and longest was the two decades of conflict between the Government of Uganda and the Lord's Resistant Army. The interfaith networks are making a critical contribution to development by striving to create a conducive environment in which development can take place (Chitando, 2022), although religious extremism remains a threat to peace (Adogame et al., 2020).

## WOMEN'S INTERFAITH COUNCIL IN NORTHERN NIGERIA

Due to the interreligious nature of conflicts in northern Nigeria, the women's religious leaders with the support of Sisters of Our Lady of the Apostle formed the Women's Interfaith Council (WIC) in 2010 in Kaduna state. However, most of the conflicts are a result of the political manipulation of religion for political and economic gain (McGarvey, 2022). WIC was formed to address the lack of peace, security, justice, poverty, and women's voices in religious communities in the region. The group also aimed to strengthen women's voices, by enabling them to speak as one. The executive council of WIC is made up of the state or diocesan leaders of each major women's faith group including Catholic Women's Organization (CWO), Federation of Muslim Women's Associations in Nigeria (FOMWAN), Anglican Mothers' Union, Muslim Sisters Organization, Baptist Missionary Union, Women's fellowship of the Association of Evangelical Churches (ECWA and TEKAN), Women's fellowships of the Pentecostal churches and of the Organization of African Instituted Churches, Women in Da'wah, NASFAT women's wing, Ansar ud deen, and Unique Muslim Sisters Association, among others. All major faith groups in the state are represented by their leaders (McGarvey, 2022, p.102).

The vision of WIC is "a society where Muslims and Christians live together in peace, where the rights of women are respected and where women and youth are protagonists of peaceful coexistence and development". Its mission is "to enable women of faith associations to work together to build peace and stability in Nigeria, Kaduna in particular, by addressing conflict issues and issues of concern to women with the primary focus on conflict, poverty, insecurity, and vulnerability" (WIC, 2013). The main goal of WIC is to provide a forum for leaders of women's faith organizations, and eventually its members, to come together in sincere and concrete dialogue from the perspective of their respective faiths, identify and address conflict and women's common and specific poverty-related concerns (WIC, 2013).

The effort of WIC is relevant in the context of northern Nigeria as women share common concerns in the social, political, cultural, and economic spheres, which in turn affect the entire population. WIC also addresses issues that are specific to women such as abuses within marriages, disinheritance, lack of access to resources, lack of participation in decision-making, and greater responsibility for sexual morality in society. These issues are intensified due to diverse forms of cultural and religious discrimination which women of both faiths experience (McGarvey, 2022).

## WIC Contribution to SDG16

Most of the activities carried out by WIC aim at building peace in Kaduna state. Since its inception, WIC conducts various activities such as interfaith prayers to build peace and they use United Nations international days such as International Women's Day and International Peace Day to preach peace and highlight that women and men experience violence and peace differently. They advocate that these different experiences must be brought to the table where the consequences of violence and the path to peace are discussed (McGarvey, 2022). The promotion of peaceful coexistence contributes to SDG16:1, which calls for a significant reduction of all forms of violence and related deaths. The recognition by WIC that violence is endemic in households and the focus of members on promoting peace at household and community levels contribute to the SDG16.1.4 target that promotes the ability of people to walk alone safely around the area they live.

WIC participated in the Bring Back our Girls Campaign, which called for the release of the Chibok girls who were abducted by Boko Haram. This campaign contributes to SDG16.2 target that calls for an end to abuse, exploitation, trafficking, and all forms of violence against the torture of children. In total, 276 Chibok girls were abducted from their school dormitory in the middle of the night on 14 April 2014. Within hours of their kidnapping, 57 managed to escape mostly by jumping off the lorries and running off into the bushes. Some have managed to escape over the years. Between 2016 and 2018, 103 of the victims were freed following negotiations between the

Nigerian government and the militants. However, the Campaign group Bring Back Our Girls says around 100 are still missing (BBC, 2022).

In addition to promoting peaceful coexistence, WIC also addresses gender-based violence issues such as abuses in marriages, disinheritance, lack of access to resources, and lack of participation of women in decision-making. The focus on these issues aims to ensure justice for victims by having laws in place to address them, as such contributes to SDG16.3 target on the promotion of rule of law at the national and international level and ensures equal access to justice for all.

WIC members received training on the role of women in building security infrastructure in their communities and society, and radicalization. WIC members believe they have a role to play as mothers in the eradication of extremism and the promotion of interfaith relations and social development. With the training received, women use soft power to provide psychosocial support of friendship and listening to individuals who are treading the path of violent extremism, being negotiators in communities, especially with women and youth where violent extremism has torn relationships apart. They also use storytelling to narrate the negative effects of violent extremism (McGarvey, 2022). This contributes to the SDG16a target that aims to strengthen relevant national institutions, including through international cooperation for building capacity at all levels, in particular in developing countries to prevent violence and combat terrorism and crimes.

## INTER-RELIGIOUS COUNCIL OF UGANDA—IRCU

The Inter-Religious Council of Uganda is an indigenous, national faith-based organization uniting efforts of religious institutions to jointly address issues of common concern. Established in 2001, IRCU's vision is "a divinely peaceful, united, prosperous Uganda where all people enjoy full health and freedoms for the common good", while its mission is "to promote peace, reconciliation, good governance, and holistic human development through interfaith action and collaboration, advocating for the empowerment of member bodies for common good" (IRCU, 2001). Its membership comprises the Roman Catholic Church (RCC), the Church of the Province of Uganda (COU), the Uganda Orthodox Church (UOC), and the Uganda Muslim Supreme Council (UMSC). It also includes the Seventh-Day Adventist Uganda Union (SDAUU), the Born-Again Faith in Uganda (BAF), and the National Alliance of Pentecostal and Evangelical Churches in Uganda (NAPECU). Besides, IRCU works in partnership with the Spiritual Assembly of the Baha'i, the Methodist Church, and the Lutheran Church.

The IRCU was established to respond to human suffering during the HIV and AIDS pandemic. At that time, the Secretary General of Religions for Peace (RfP) International, Dr. William F. Vendley, held private meetings with senior-most religious leaders from four religious communities in Uganda, namely the Roman Catholic Church, the Anglican Church (Church of Uganda), the

Orthodox Church of Uganda, and the Muslim Community. During the meeting, Dr. Vendley introduced the mission and vision of RfP, then known as the World's Council of Religions for Peace (WCRP), and the emerging initiative and unique opportunity for religious communities to address the plight of orphans affected by HIV/AIDS, and he also offered to facilitate the formation of a national interreligious structure (IRCU, 2001). Religious leaders unanimously held a view that the time was ripe for a national interreligious council to be co-built by both Christians and Muslims (IRCU, 2001).

IRCU works to promote peaceful coexistence in a multiethnic and multireligious context; it also promotes peace and conflict transformation, sustainable human development, and networking among religious leaders, communities, and women and youth. The IRCU works through religious leaders, structures, and infrastructure that cascade from national to grassroots levels. It also works with various institutions such as health facilities, educational institutions, and regional and district local governments (Omona, 2022). IRCU works through regional aims located in all the regions of Uganda.

## IRCU Contribution to SDG16

The IRCU as mentioned earlier works through its regional aims to build peace, through its member, the Acholi Religious Leaders Peace Initiatives (ARLPI); the IRCU worked in northern Uganda during and after the over 20 years of conflict between the Government of Uganda and the Lord Resistant Army. IRCU initiated peace talks between the warring parties and participated in the Juba Peace Process (Latigo & Ochola, 2015). The IRCU continues to support post-conflict reconstruction in northern Uganda by addressing land issues (Omona, 2022). Similar work is also being carried out in other parts of Uganda. Most recently, the IRCU visited relatives and family members who lost loved ones following the gruesome attack on the palace of the King of Bakonzo and held reconciliation meetings. They also provided food relief to victims of the conflict in Kasese and Bundibugyo (IRCU, 2017). These efforts contribute to SDG16.1 on reduction of violence of all forms, the initiation of peace talks, the participation in the Juba Peace Process, and the reconciliation meetings in western Uganda, all contribute to the reduction of violence. The Juba Peace Process brought an end to the conflict in northern Uganda.

The IRCU launched the Inter-Religious Institute for Peace (IRIP) in 2012 which pushed the agenda for peaceful coexistence by nurturing integrity, peace, justice, and good governance. IRCU took a stand against the change of the Uganda Constitution to lift the presidential age cap and extend the presidential tenure of office from five to seven years. Leaders of IRCU appealed to the government to allow the people of Uganda to take a decision through a referendum. Despite the efforts, the government made a decision based on its interest (Omona, 2022). The call for people to participate in taking decisions on changes in the Constitution is the promotion of rule of law as indicated in SDG16.3 target and inclusion in decision-making at all levels of SDG16.7 target.

To create and strengthen impartiality and provide independent space for dialogue and reconciliation, the IRCU and the Elders Forum of Uganda (TEFU) initiated the national dialogue process to address historical injustices that the country has experienced over the years. The Uganda National Dialogue (UND) was set to address eight agenda items, including national political consensus, national consensus on constitutionalism and the rule of law, values diversity, land justice, access to natural resources and the environment, an economy that works for everybody, minimum standards for quality public service delivery, and implementation mechanism for the outcomes of the national dialogue and the establishment of Working Committees (IRCU, 2019). Deliberating on these agenda items of the UND was necessary because it could have helped to clear historical misinformation and injustices perpetrated over the years, as well as address half a century of political instability and violence. The process was however marred by a lot of animosities, as it never materialized. If the process took place, it would have achieved the most yearned state in the lives of Ugandans, namely that of sustainable peace (Omona, 2022). This aspect of IRCU work contributes to SDG16.3 and SDG16.7.

## Feminism, Peacebuilding, and SDG16

The case studies reveal that religious practices and beliefs see men as actors in peacebuilding and leaders of influence while women are viewed within their domestic roles as mothers and caregivers; it is this role that determines the way religious institutions and women themselves view their role within faith institutions. In Nigeria, WIC places emphasis on women's important role in peacebuilding as mothers and sees this as a primary way women could be instrumental in promoting a culture of peace and development. This perspective is reflected in the WIC's motto, which is "Women of Faith Working Together as Mothers of a Culture of Peace". This essentialist feminist perspective sees potential for change by stressing the non-violent nature of 'feminine values' to create a peaceful world. The 'maternal thinking' notion as a pre-condition for a peaceful society and the feminine value of peacefulness hold the assumption that women are only victims, but experience has shown that women are active fighters and victims of violence. These perspectives silence women's experiences and knowledge and have been challenged by feminists who argue that without the collaboration of the mother character, the legitimization of violence enacted by men could not function (Kaplan, 1994; Scheper-Hughes, 1996). To ensure that the experiences of women inform peacebuilding their experience as perpetrators of violence and victims is required to build sustainable peace and development.

Similarly, one of the programs of the IRCU in Uganda focuses on business livelihood and environmental governance; according to the IRCU women were selected for this project as 'mothers of the nation' and bear the responsibility of ensuring the well-being of their families, empowering women means empowering the household (Omona, 2022, p.191). This perspective adopts the maternal thinking notion, evoking the motherhood of women to ensure the well-being of families. Here, the role of women is seen within the household; thus, the private-public divide comes into question. By situating women in the private sphere, bringing them as decision-makers in public institutions is problematic. Women's ability to influence public debates and contribute to peace and development must be moved beyond the household to ensure they influence institutions for sustainable peace and development.

To buttress the challenge of using the maternal thinking notion for peacebuilding, WIC members expressed the limitations they experience living their roles as mothers; they share their pains of motherhood and as wives in patriarchal cultures and in insecure environments (McGarvey, 2022). These experiences need to be at the peace table and in decision-making processes; they acknowledge that women and men experience violence and peace differently and that these differences should inform peacebuilding. Peace and feminism suffer from a mainstream understanding that women are usually the ones who suffer from conflict. This perspective reinforces an image of women as victims of patriarchy, undermines their agency, and recreates the historical trauma of violence women experience daily (Abu-Assab et al., 2022). Jodi York (1996) warns that using maternal thinking argument cannot be used as a justification to intervene in policy-making by moral appeal.

Based on the experience of the WIC in Nigeria and the women in Uganda, there is a need to promote the agency of women in peacebuilding and development, because women bring to the table issues ignored by men such as difficulties they experience as breadwinners and when men are killed in conflicts; the increased self-doubt faced by women due to lack of education and skills; vulnerabilities of women in the homes when villages are attacked; and difficulties of living in displaced people's camps and refugee settings. These new roles performed by women improve their leadership skills which need to be explored in peacebuilding. However, women are rarely admitted to the leadership of religious bodies as we see in IRCU Uganda. In most religions, women did not until recently have access to theological studies. In the Nigerian Anglican Church, for example, women are not ordained as priest, thus when interreligious encounters are held at official levels, women are absent (McGarvey, 2022). Even in Uganda, where women are now ordained, they have not been able to get to the top leadership of the Church of Uganda.

Little thought has been given to the way religions have treated women as the 'other' (McGarvey, 2022). In Nigeria, women are excluded from mediation processes and decision-making in religious bodies by both Christian and Muslim as well as in interfaith councils and state-sponsored religious bureaus. There are few instances when women are invited but usually as an afterthought or as a symbolic gesture of gender awareness (McGarvey, 2022). In the case of Uganda, Omona writes that the IRCU Christian Mother's Union, Catholic Action members at local levels engage actively in ensuring peace at family levels. Through giving strength to the believers to bear the unbearable, have hope even when all seems hopeless, and encourage forgiveness even to the unforgivable, such advocacy yields fruit at the community level. From a feminist perspective, such an approach puts so much burden on the woman and reinforces violence and subjugation building on existing unequal power relations between women and men. Locating the role of women within the family follows the essentialist approach that recognizes the traditional role of women this converges with religion to produce overlapping structures of subordination. This is what Crenshaw (1991) warned of when she coined the term intersectionality, which is clearly expressed in the way the Catholic Mother's Union have been portrayed and the nature of the work they are doing among their members. These women are experiencing different forms of violence and are being encouraged to bear the unbearable, so the identity of being a Christian woman in such a context determines the way violence is expressed, received, and addressed. It seems such violence is being silenced and made acceptable by women and thus will continue to be perpetuated by men within the household and community at large. From the foregoing, certain groups of women experience and will continue to experience everyday violence due to the interplay of their gender and religion (Borges, 2022). This approach has the potential to reduce the capacity to ensure violence against women is addressed as called by SDG16.1.3 which measures the proportion of population subjected to (a) physical violence, (b) psychological violence, and (c) sexual violence in the previous 12 months.

## Conclusion

The debate about feminism, religion, and peacebuilding is growing. Feminist peacebuilding calls for the interrogation of power and the recognition of the unique value that women bring to peacebuilding. However, this perspective conflicts with religious beliefs about the role women should play in peacebuilding. Since most religions do not have women in leadership positions, it remains a difficult task to infuse feminism without adopting the essentialist feminist approach. This approach seems to interact with existing gender social norms that maintain the status quo. For religious institutions such as those discussed in this chapter, the role of women remains in the private sphere compared to those of men which is more at the formal peace table, while women themselves know that they possess the capacity to influence decisions in public institutions they seem to conform to the belief that their contribution to the family contributes to nation building. While this is true, it does not enable their voices to be heard in the public sphere. Both case studies contribute to peacebuilding at two different levels; the peacebuilding efforts by IRCU focus on the formal table such as their participation in the Juba Peace Process and their ability to initiate peace talks and reconciliation meetings using their positions as religious leaders. On the other hand, women faith leaders do not have the political clout to initiate or participate in such processes. However, their efforts are concentrated on promoting peace at household level such as addressing gender-based violence which is usually not quantified as a peacebuilding initiative. Women's peace activists are currently calling for the recognition of the informal peacebuilding efforts by women, particularly at the family and community levels. To ensure that religious institutions such as interfaith bodies contribute effectively to the achievement of SDG16, it is important that they adopt an approach to peacebuilding that enables the voices and experiences of women to be heard at the peace table to ensure sustainable peace. Secondly, religious institutions must open the space for women to lead so that they can also engage at the highest level of peacebuilding and negotiations. Lastly, the implementers of SDGs must find a way to infuse religious institutions and religion as key players in the achievement of the SDGs if the 2030 target is to be achieved.

## References

Abu-Assab, N., Azarmandi, M., & Shroff, S. (2022). Feminist Peace Interrupted: A Critical Conversation on Conflict, Violence and Accountability. In S. Smith & K. Yoshida (Eds.), *Feminist Conversations on Peace*. Bristol University Press. https://bristoluniversitypressdigital.com/view/book/9781529222074/ch002.xml

Adogame, A., Olufunke, A., & Williams, C. L. (Eds.). (2020). *Fighting in God's Name: Religion and Conflict in Local-Global Perspectives*. Lexington Books.

Alexander, J. (2006). *Pedagogies of Crossing: Meditations on Feminism, Sexual Politics, Memory, and the Sacred*. Duke University Press.

Arya, S., & Singh, A. (2019). *Dalit Feminist Theory: A Reader*. Routledge.

Bercovitch, J., & Kadayifci-Orellana, A. S. (2009). Religion and Mediation: The Role of Faith-Based Actors in International Conflict Resolution. *International Negotiation, 14*(1), 175–204.

Bergunder, M. (2014). What is Religion? *Method & Theory in the Study of Religion, 26*(3), 246–286. https://doi.org/10.1163/15700682-12341320

Borges, A. M. (2022). Misogyny and Intersectionality. In J. Gillard (Ed.), *Ten Years on from the Misogyny Speech: Not Now, Note Ever*. Vintage Books.

Butler, J. (1990). *Gender Trouble: Feminism and the Subversion of Identity*. Routledge.

Chitando, E. (2022). Interfaith Networks and Development. In E. Chitando & S. I. Gusha (Eds.), *Interfaith Networks and Development, Sustainable Development Goals Series*. Palgrave Macmillan, https://doi.org/10.1007/978-3-030-89807-6_6

Chitando, E., & Gusha, I. S. (2022). Interfaith Networks and Development: Case Studies from Africa. Sustainable Development Goal Series in I. Chitando & S. Gusha (Eds.), *Interfaith Networks and Development, Sustainable Development Goals Series*. Palgrave Macmillan. https://doi.org/10.1007/978-3-030-89807-6_10

Chodorow, N. (1978). *The Reproduction of Mothering: Psychoanalysis and the Sociology of Gender*. University of California Press.

Crenshaw, K. (1991). Mapping the Margins: Intersectionality, Identity Politics and Violence Against Women of Color. *Stanford Law review, 43*(6), 1241–1299.

Daly, M. (1978). *Gyn/Ecology. The Metaethics of Radical Feminism*. Beacon Press.

Douglas, A. (2022). Issues of War and Peace: Is Religion More of the Problem and What Are Mahatma Gandhi's Insights? *Religions, 13*, 1088. https://doi.org/10.3390/rel13111088

Eelco, K., Durner, T., & Schwartz, M. (2016). UGANDA. *Violent Extremism and Instability in the Greater Horn of Africa: An Examination of Drivers and Responses*. Global Center on Cooperative Security. http://www.jstor.org/stable/resrep20264.14

Flanigan, S. T. (2013). Religion, Conflict, and Peacebuilding in the Development. In M. Clarke (Ed.), *Handbook of Research on Development And religion* (pp. 252–267). Edward Elgar Publishing.

Galtung, J. (1964). An Editorial. *Journal of Peace Research*, 1(1), 1–4. https://journals.sagepub.com/doi/abs/10.1177/002234336400100101

Gilligan, C. (1982). *In a Different Voice: Psychological Theory and Women's Development*. Harvard University Press.

Horton, R. (1960). A Definition of Religion, and its Uses. *The Journal of the Royal Anthropological Institute of Great Britain and Ireland*, 90(2), 201–226. https://doi.org/10.2307/2844344

IRCU. (2001, March 31 and April 3). IRCU History. https://www.ircu.or.ug/ircu-history/

IRCU. (2017, April 16). IRCU-TEFU, Pay Solidarity Visit to Kasese and Bundibugyo. https://ircu.or.ug/ircu-tefu-pay-solidarity-visitto-kasese-and-bundibugyo

IRCU. (2019, May 10). Press Statement Second Meeting of the UNaDiCoT. https://ircu.or.ug/press-statement-second-meeting-of-theuganda-national-dialogue-coordinating-team

Jörg, H., & Tomalin, E. (2017). Religion and Development in Africa and Asia. In P. Amakasu Raposo, D. Arase, & S. Cornelissen (Eds.), *Routledge Handbook of Africa–Asia Relations*. Routledge.

Kaplan, L. (1994). Women as Nurturer: An Archetype That Supports Patriarchal Militarism. *Hypatia*, 9(2), 123–133.

Karam, A. (2014). Religion and Development Post 2015. https://www.unfpa.org/sites/default/files/pub-pdf/DONOR-UN-FBO%20May%202014.pdf

Kezie-Nwoha, H. (2019). *What Feminist Peace means in Changing Context of Conflict*. African Feminism. https://africanfeminism.com/what-feminist-peace-means-in-changing-contexts-ofconflicts/#:~:text=Feminist%20peace%20calls%20for%20women's,conflict%20and%20post%20conflict%20settings

Khalid, J., & FitzGerald, J. (2022, July 27). Nigeria's Chibok Girls: Two Victims Found Eight Years On. *BBC News*. https://www.bbc.com/news/world-africa-62324294

Latigo, O. A., & Ochola, M. B. (2015). Northern Uganda—The Acholi Religious Leaders' Peace Initiative: Local mediation with the Lord's Resistance Army. In S. Haspeslagh & Z. Yuusuf (Eds.), *Local Engagement with Armed Groups in the Midst of Violence, Accord Insight 2* (pp. 15–20). Conciliation Resources.

Litalien, M. (2019). Gender, Religions and the SDGs: a Reflection on Empowering Buddhist Nuns. In *The Future of Humanity: Revisioning the Human in the Posthuman Age*. Rowman & Littlefield International.

Martin, C. (2009). Delimiting Religion. Method & Theory in the Study of Religion, 21(2), 157–176. http://www.jstor.org/stable/23555824

McGarvey, K. (2022). Women of Faith Working Together as Mothers of a Culture of Peace: The Women's Interfaith Council in Northern Nigeria. In E. Chitando & I. S. Gusha (Eds.), *Interfaith Networks and Development, Sustainable Development Goals Series*. https://doi.org/10.1007/978-3-030-89807-6_6

Muer, R. (2021). Claiming blessings: Theological Reflections with Quaker Peacebuilders on Overcoming Evil with Good. In C. Dahlgrün, C. Rehrmann, & A. Zempelburg

(Eds.), *Overcome Evil with Good: Interdisciplinary Reflections from Theology, Conflict Science, and the Military* (pp. 237–248). wbg Academic.

Nicholson, L. (Ed.). (1985). *Feminist Contentions: A Philosophical Exchange* (L. Nicholson, Ed.). Thinking Gender. Routledge, 1995.

Omotosho, M. (2014). Managing Religious Conflicts in Nigeria: The InterReligious Mediation Peace Strategy. *Africa Development, 39*(2), 133–151.

Pateman, C. (1988). *The Sexual Contract.* Stanford University Press.

Reardon, B. (1985). *Sexism and the War System.* Teachers College; Columbia University.

Ruddick, S. (1989). *Maternal Thinking: Toward a Politics of Peace.* Beacon Press.

Saleh, M. (2022). Role of Interfaith Mediation Centre in Managing Conflict Between Farmers and Herdsmen in Bauchi State, Nigeria. *Journal of African History, Culture and Arts, 2*(2), 110–123. https://doi.org/10.57040/jahca.v2i2.203

Scharffs, B. G. (2018). The Role of Religion and Religious Freedom in Responding to Violent Extremism. In M. C. Green, T. J. Gunn, & M. Hill (Eds.), *Religion, Law and Security in Africa* (Vol. 5, pp. 31–46). https://doi.org/10.2307/j.ctv21ptz2w.7

Scheper-Hughes, N. (1996). Small Wars and Invisible Genocides. *Social Science & Medicine, 43*(5), 889–900. https://doi.org/10.1016/0277-9536(96)00152-9

Shiva, V. (1993). *Ecofeminism, Kali for Women.* Zed Books.

Tickner, J. A. (1997). "You Just Don't Understand": Troubled Engagements Between Feminist and IR Theorists. *International Studies Quarterly, 41*, 611–632.

Tlostanova, M. (2010). *Gender Epistemologies and Eurasian Borderlands.* Palgrave Macmillan.

Tomalin, E., Haustein, J., & Kidy, S. (2019). Religion and the Sustainable Development Goals. *Review of Faith & International Affairs, 17*(2), 102–118. https://doi.org/10.1080/15570274.2019.1608664

Ulrich, M., & Osman, M. O. (2006). Faith-Based Peace-Building in Sudan's Transition. In O. Ali (Ed.), *Stuck in Change: Faith-based Peace-building in Sudan's Transition.* Netherlands Institute of International Relations 'Clingendael'.

Verges, F. (2021). *A Decolonial Feminism.* Pluto Press.

Weber, A. (2006). Feminist Peace Theory. *Routledge Encyclopaedia, 28*(07), 2006.

WIC. (2013, August). *WIC Newsletter. Volume 1, No. 1. A Publication of Interfaith Forum of Muslim and Christian Women's Association.* Women's Interfaith Council. http://www.womeninterfaithcouncil.org/doc/newsletter/newsLetter%20-%20August4.pdf

York, J. (1996). The Truth About Women and Peace. *Peace Review, 8*(3), 323–330.

CHAPTER 37

# Gender, Religion, Peacebuilding, and Development in Zambia: Doreen Mazuba Malambo's Trajectory in Peacekeeping Missions

*Nelly Mwale, Joseph Chita, and Habeenzu Mulunda*

## Introduction

This chapter explores the intersection of gender, religion, peacebuilding, and development through the narrative of Doreen Mazuba Malambo (the 2020 UN woman police officer of the year award winner) in peacekeeping missions. This is done by addressing the following research question, 'How does the trajectory of Doreen Mazuba Malambo in peacekeeping missions reflect the intersection of gender, religion, peacebuilding, and development?' This is with the view to shifting the dominant focus of discourses on peacebuilding in Zambia from the country's contributions to the liberation struggles, hosting of refugees, and engagement in peacekeeping missions to the narratives of individuals who have contributed to the country's record of peacebuilding. This is deemed significant, as observed by Marshall et al. (2011), that women in religious peacebuilding have largely been ignored whereby religion's role in driving conflict and its potential to open up avenues for peace and reconciliation is often viewed through a male prism, limiting comprehension of both the causes

N. Mwale (✉) • J. Chita
Department of Religious Studies, University of Zambia, Lusaka, Zambia
e-mail: nelly.mwale@unza.zm; joseph.chita@unza.zm

H. Mulunda
Communications Department, University of Zambia, Lusaka, Zambia
e-mail: habeenzu.mulunda@unza.zm

© The Author(s), under exclusive license to Springer Nature Switzerland AG 2023
S. M. Kilonzo et al. (eds.), *The Palgrave Handbook of Religion, Peacebuilding, and Development in Africa*,
https://doi.org/10.1007/978-3-031-36829-5_37

of and the solutions to the conflict. Marshall et al. (2011) view this oversight as counterintuitive since the role of women and of religion in peacebuilding has increasingly garnered interest among scholars and policy makers.

Given the complexity of the concepts of religion, peacebuilding, and development, the chapter carefully employs these concepts. Thus, of the two common approaches used to make meaning of religion, substantive approaches (which focus on the different elements that constitute religion—what religion *is) and* functionalist approaches (which emphasise the social and cultural consequences of religion—what religion *does* for a social group or an individual (Hamilton, 1995, pp 1–20; McGuire, 2002, pp. 5–12)), this chapter takes a functionalist approach to religion. In this regard, the focus is on what religion potentially does as opposed to how religion is carried out (Rakodi, 2012, p. 638). Given the religious pluralistic nature of Zambian society (as is the case in other parts of Africa), the chapter focuses on Christianity as a religious tradition, to which Doreen Malambo adheres to.

The understanding of 'peacebuilding' is informed by a conceptual framework for peace engagements in the paper 'An Agenda for Peace,' prepared in 1992 by the UN under the leadership of then Secretary General Boutros Boutros-Ghali (Boutros-Ghali, 1992, p. 11). This understanding is tied to the feminist stance which is curious about meanings attributed to peacebuilding, especially as it relates to women. As noted by Mazurana and McKay (1999, p. 9), peacebuilding includes gender-awareness and woman-empowerment politically, socially, economically, and in terms of human rights. It involves personal and group accountability and reconciliation processes that contribute to the reduction or prevention of violence. At the same time, it fosters the ability of women, men, girls, and boys in their own culture(s) to promote conditions of nonviolence, equality, justice, and human rights of all people, to build democratic institutions, and to sustain the environment. Given the multidimensional nature of peacebuilding, the chapter pays attention to religious peacebuilding, which Dubois (2008, p. 399) refers to as simply peacebuilding done by religious actors. It is motivated and strengthened by religious and spiritual resources. There are several religious actors in peacebuilding, including religious leaders, religious institutions, and religiously motivated lay figures.

In the context of conflict, religion is often viewed as a motivator for conflict but also as an integral factor in the peacebuilding and reconciliation process. Thus, our understanding and application of peacebuilding processes is informed by the USAID conceptual framework of religion, conflict, and peacebuilding summarised as follows:

> Understanding of the dynamics of conflict—both the sources of discord and the forces of resilience—require an awareness of the connections between conflict, religion and peace building ... a lack of understanding of the religious context may adversely affect interventions or provoke active resistance, even when large scale violence is not a significant risk. Where the risk of instability is higher, inattention to religious identities or to the views and aspirations of religious leaders

may result in mischaracterisation about what the conflict is actually about or how likely it is to become violent. And where violence is a reality, discounting the religious dimension or resisting engagement with religious actors may result in overlooking the many opportunity to tap into religion as a force for compassion and promoting peace. (USAID, 2009, p. 3)

The role of religion in peacebuilding as conceptualised by the USAID is in tandem with van den Berg's description of religion as a "motivator and mobiliser of masses in conflict areas. It is labelled as the negative contributor to conflict instead of a potential positive influence on conflict transformation" (van den Berg, 2016, p. 7). A critical consideration of religion in conflict situation is key, especially when viewed as a resource for peacebuilding.

Gender, religion, and peacebuilding are also linked to development in this chapter. This idea of development is closely linked to sustainable development as informed by the Brundtland (1987) definition of 'sustainable development' as development that meets the needs of the present without compromising the ability of future generations to meet their own needs (World Commission on Environment and Development (WCED) 1987). It is often understood in relation to the global goals that have seemingly become acceptable indicators for development for 2030.

The chapter particularly anchors the discussion on *Sustainable Development Goal Number 16* which focuses on peace, justice, and strong institutions. It is centred on significantly reducing all forms of violence and related death rates everywhere. It further focuses on ending abuse, exploitation, trafficking, and all forms of violence against and torture of children; promoting the rule of law at the national and international levels; and ensuring equal access to justice for all. It also seeks to significantly reduce illicit financial and arms flows, strengthen the recovery and return of stolen assets, and combat all forms of organised crime. Furthermore, it substantially aims to reduce corruption, and bribery in all their forms; develop effective, accountable, and transparent institutions at all levels; and ensure responsive, inclusive, participatory, and representative decision-making at all levels, including broadening and strengthening the participation of developing countries in the institutions of global governance. Over and above that, it aims to provide legal identity for all, including birth registration; ensure public access to information and protect fundamental freedoms in accordance with national legislation and international agreements; strengthen relevant national institutions through international cooperation, for building capacity at all levels, in particular in developing countries; prevent violence and combat terrorism and crime; and promote and enforce non-discriminatory laws and policies for sustainable development (UN, 2020). Of these indicators, the chapter focuses the trajectory of Doreen Malambo in peacekeeping missions on reducing all forms of violence and related death rates everywhere, ending abuse, exploitation, trafficking, and all forms of violence against and torture of children and promoting the rule of law at the national and international levels and ensuring equal access to justice for all.

Theoretically, the chapter approaches the interconnectedness of gender, religion, peacebuilding, and development from a 'feminist theoretical perspective.' This is because the feminist framework seeks to promote the notion that both women and men are individuals within society and should be treated equally, thereby overcoming all forms of gendered discrimination in society. Given the three major strands of feminism as postulated by Collins (2006), the chapter engages more with the *liberal feminist framework*, which wishes to see complete equality of opportunity between men and women in peacebuilding. This is because liberal feminists wish to see an ending to the exclusion of women in public life and are keen to see equal representation of women in the high offices of state and advocate the right of women to participate in activities, such as combat, that have traditionally been ascribed to men by society. The chapter takes the perspective that some women have attempted to minimise the effects of violence, if not actively to try to end the violence themselves, by acting as peacemakers (Ferris, 1995).

In terms of methodology, the chapter draws on a qualitative narrative research design (Clandinin & Connelly, 2000) in which data were collected through interviews and document analysis. Doreen Mazuba Malambo was purposively chosen based on the possession of the characteristics being sought. These included being a female person who was involved in peacebuilding underpinned by a religious worldview. The interviews were conducted in September 2021 at her home. Documents in the form of newspapers, photographs, and other media features were also consulted based on availability and recommendation by Malambo. The collected data and individual stories were situated within the participant's personal spaces and experiences (her job, home, culture, and her historical contexts [time and space]) and was then analysed through the process of restorying (Ollerenshaw & Creswell, 2000). The chapter unfolds by providing a brief review of related literature and Malambo's biography before exploring the intersection of gender, religion, peacebuilding, and development in her account underpinned by the liberal feminist lens.

## Literature Review

The chapter is located in both local and international studies. To start with, it is generally agreed that peacebuilding is gendered (Pankhurst, 2000; Munro, 2000; Strickland & Duvvury, 2003; Nakaya, 2004; De la Rey & McKay, 2006; Adeogun & Muthuki, 2018; Hudson, 2021). To this end, studies have dwelt not only on the gendered impacts of conflicts but also on the shifts in the role of women in peacebuilding. For example, it has been observed that women participation in peacebuilding was increasing steadily, partly due to the efforts of organisations and institutions in peacebuilding (Onsati, 2014, p. 66). Examples of scholars who have taken this approach include Klot (2007) who writes from the context of Sierra Leone. Klot shows that the United Nations Development Fund for Women (UNIFEM) and the Peacebuilding Support Office (PBSO) were engaged in the dissemination of knowledge among the women leaders and civil society organisations and helped in the establishment of a national peacebuilding agenda for women. These two initiatives effectively encouraged the participation of women in peacebuilding activities in Sierra Leone. The foregoing studies point to the role of institutionalised support for women and individual women initiatives in peacebuilding.

Other studies have focused on the formation of women's organisations and statutes which carry out an oversight role into the plight of women. For example, Porter (2007) highlighted some of the work of organisations such as the Convention on the Status of Women (CSW) and the Convention on the Elimination of All Forms of Discrimination Against Women (CEDAW). The CSW is concerned with monitoring the situation of women at a global level and fights for their rights. Adopted in 1979, and later enforced in 1981, the CEDAW seeks to establish universal standards of equality for both men and women. Other organisations incorporated in the UN include UNIFEM which works in close collaboration with UNDP to monitor and promote gender mainstreaming, women's empowerment strategies, and engendering governance to increase women's participation in decision-making, promoting women's human rights and making women's perspectives central to peace. Studies which take these perspectives are related to the current study as they lay grounds for the exploration of what individual women were/are doing to foster peacebuilding.

Additionally, some studies on gender, religion, and peacebuilding have often been situated in religious organisations. For example, Hampson (1996) concluded that religious institutions could play a positive role in maintaining sustainable peace as they are a critical space where diversity and pluralism can be cherished and fostered. This could be providing emotional and spiritual support to war-affected communities and mobilising their communities towards peace, mediation between conflict parties, and reconciliation. Steele (2011, p. 53) also observed that there were four types of roles that faith-based actors could play in peacebuilding, namely observation and witness, education and formation, advocacy and empowerment, and conciliation and mediation. The role of religious organisations was facilitated by their religious principles and values which motivates them to have the mandate to carry out peacebuilding activities. These values also provide motivation and inspiration to reach out to victims, preach peace, and maintain a longer lifespan of commitment to peace where political and other secular actors give up. Such perspectives not only show the potential of religious ideas and beliefs to promote peacebuilding but also became a background for understanding how persons affiliated to a religious tradition could tap into their religiosity for fostering a gendered peacebuilding narrative. For example, in the case of Liberia, the country witnessed the role of faith-based actors in peacebuilding processes in the 1990s. This was through the Inter-Faith Mediation Committee (IFMC), an amalgamation of the Liberian Council of Churches (LCC) and the National Muslim Council of Liberia (NMCL) who mediated a peaceful end to the crisis. To achieve its mandate, the IFMC held consultative talks with actors key to the conflicts and developed a proposal that was later adopted as a peace plan for Liberia. As part of its on-going activities, the consortium continued to organise and hold consultative meetings and conferences. It remained critical to flaws in numerous peace accords, protested against peace agreements that rewarded the armed factions with positions in government. IFMC further championed the disarmament of Liberia's fighters through the Campaign for Disarmament (CDC) and fostered the stay-home action (Toure, 2002.p. 10). Significant to this religious alliance to end war was "the cooperation between Liberian Muslims and Christian clerics through the IFMC in forestalling the emergence of religious disharmony as a component of the Liberian civil war" (Woods cited in Armon & Carl, 1990, p. 32).

The social role of religion in Liberia as highlighted in the case of the IFMC gave impetus to the formation of human rights organisations and women's groups like the Catholic Justice and Peace Commission (JPC) and the Liberian Women Initiative (LWI). The JPC and other human rights communities contributed to the upsurge of human rights and pro-democracy groups after the end of the civil war in 1997. The LWI attention was dedicated to advocating for responding to the plight of women and children during war, focusing on atrocities committed against women, and criticised the mass recruitment of child soldiers. The LWI is reported to have succeeded in placing women and children's issues on the agenda of Liberian peace process (African Watch, 1991; Human Rights Watch Report, 1994).

Consequently, the focus of scholarship on religion and peacebuilding has also tended to give attention to religious institutions or organisations who operate in the field, including the World Vision, Path finder, Bread for the World, Catholic Relief Services, among others. Additionally, attention has been given to religious persons who have contributed to peacebuilding. However, this perspective is often male-centred. For example, prominence is given to religious leaders who have carried out peacebuilding activities. An example is Archbishop Desmond Tutu of South Africa who was instrumental in the truth-seeking missions that were formed to address abuse inflicted on the masses through the apartheid policy. Through his capacity as a respected religious leader in the country, Tutu is said to have encouraged people to forgive their perpetrators in order to heal and unite as a country (Philpot, 2007). Despite this, some scholars have attempted to focus on the work of women in peacebuilding. Scholars who have trailed the work of women in peacebuilding include Manyonganise (2017) who has provided an overview on the often-excluded voices and experiences of women, not only in contexts of political conflict and violence, but also in contexts of peace and reconciliation. Using the case study of a platform called Churches in Manicaland (CiM), in Zimbabwe, Manyonganise concluded that women suffered significantly due to political conflict and violence and that they were afforded a minimal role in building peace and transforming the conflict. Ogega (2022) has also provided an analysis of peacebuilding efforts of the Maasai and Gusii women of faith in Kenya through the different chapters in an edited volume.

Country studies with a focus on Zambia have accounted for the principles which govern peacebuilding in the country. For example, it has been recognised that the 'Vision 2030' (National Long-Term Vision 2030) which summarises the long-term development for Zambia up to 2030 spells out six key basic principles. These include peaceful coexistence which reflects Zambia's commitment to peaceful diplomacy and domestic politics and positive stance towards peacebuilding (JICA, 2016). Accordingly, Zambia has laws and policies which relate to peace and security (such as Defence Act (1994), Zambia Police Act (1994), Prisons Act (Correctional Service Act No. 37 of 2016), to mention but a few). The JICA has also taken note of the protocols which Zambia has signed. These include the Protocol to the African Charter on Human and People's Rights on the Rights of Women in Africa, which stresses the need to uphold commitment to the rights of people to access to the courts, equal protection and peace.

At the international level, as a member of the African Union (AU), Zambia consents to the AU Post-conflict Reconstruction and Development (PCRD) policy framework of 2006. The PCRD supports and offers a perfect opportunity for AU member countries to reflect on the institutions' stance on women's participation in peace process, which has in the past been male dominated, thus posing a threat to gender dynamics and relationships (PSC Report, 2021).

Other structures that complement this call for women involvement in peace processes on the continent includes The Zambian government agreed with the United Nations Security Council Resolution 1325 (UNSCR 1325) which requests member countries of the UN to promote women's equal involvement in peace and security, to protect women in conflicts, and to prevent sexual violence as well as GBV (JICA, 2016). Another agreement worth highlighting is the African Charter on Human and People's Rights and Rights of Women in Africa, also known as the Maputo Protocol. Suffice to mention that women's involvement in peacebuilding processes is key to the AU and member states. Recently the AU reiterated its position on women's inclusion in conflict prevention, peace-making, negotiation, agreements, and peace support operations at its Peace and Security Council (PSC) 987th meeting of 22 March 2021 (PSC Report, 2021).

The contributions of the country to peacebuilding since independence in 1964 are also acknowledged. For example, Zambia has dispatched Peace Keeping Operation (PKO) personnel to politically unstable neighbouring countries in the past (JICA, 2016, p. 26) and has made positive efforts to achieve gender equality, including the introduction of a 30% quota system for women to encourage their participation in peacekeeping and the national defence force and the establishment of the Gender Desk to promote gender mainstreaming at the Ministry of Defence. Although happening before 2016, these efforts demonstrate that efforts to mainstream gender in peacebuilding as envisioned in SDG 16 have been on going in the country. These insights were significant for understanding the context in which Malambo worked from and for making meaning of her contributions to sustainable development through peacebuilding.

Given that the foregoing studies have not given much attention to individual women in peacebuilding and development as informed by their religiosity, the chapter seeks to shift the focus from religious organisations and their contributions to peacebuilding to individuals in secular work spaces, who carry out peacebuilding activities while informed by their religious worldviews. This will complement the emerging studies on the subject in the Zambian context. For example, Mofya (2022) explored the contributions of women to peacebuilding in Zambia since 1964 and reaffirmed the importance of women participation in peacebuilding and politics and at the same time brought to light the challenges hindering women participation in peacebuilding. Similarly, Mwale (2020) explored the contributions of Susan Sikaneta without any links to the religious dimension.

## A Brief Biography of Doreen Malambo

The biography of Malambo was gathered through an interview with her in 2021. Doreen Mazuba Malambo was born in (in 1976) Lusaka[1]—the capital city of Zambia. She is the first born in a family of seven. Her father was a police officer, so she grew up in a police camp in Lilayi [2](Lilayi Police Camp, Lusaka) before her father was moved to Namalundu, Kafue Gorge, a place 100 km south of Lusaka (off the Chirundu Road and nearby the Kafue Gorge Training Centre).

Malambo enjoyed being in a good family. She remarked thus:

> I enjoyed being in a good family. My parents were Christians (Adventists). I never saw dad lay his hand on mom; yes, they had some misunderstanding and would resolve them in no time, and we would be there and laugh. Dad was a jovial man, but he was not all that dedicated to the church activities compared to mom, who was a staunch one. We even nick named mum as "Dorcas" for she was dedicated to activities of the Dorcas women's group.

Malambo's religious worldview was also shaped by her Adventist faith. Besides the Adventist influence on Malambo, we cannot take away the role of her indigenous cultural (*baTonga* of Zambia) background in shaping her

---

[1] Lusaka is located close to the center of the country. All major routes to the east, west, north, and south flow through the city. The capital covers an area of 70 km² and is at an altitude of 1300 metres above sea level. (https://www.zambiatourism.com/towns/lusaka/)

[2] Lilayi Police Training College is located in the Southern part of Lusaka off the Kafue Road (Southern route). It is about 15 kms the Central Business District (CBD) of Lusaka. The college was opened in 1955 with objective of training police officers and judiciary officers in drill and law according to the British enacted laws, but over time (1965) the mandate has changed to providing training and development to the Police Service officers to meet the highest national and international policing standards (http://www.zambiapolice.gov.zm/index.php/advanced-stuff/docs-and-support).

positionalities along the way. The *baTonga* are a Bantu-speaking people who inhabit the southern part of Zambia and neighbouring areas of Northern Zimbabwe and Botswana occupying the Zambezi Escarpment (Colson, 2006).

Coming from a homestead where the parents had keen interest in their children's education, Malambo was able to complete her secondary education. It was not her intention to follow in the footsteps of her father (a police officer); she dreamt of doing radiography, as she explains:

> My intention was not to be in the police service and my dad wanted me to be a nurse but I never liked nursing. What was in me was radiography but when dad insisted, I went to apply for nursing at the University Teaching Hospital. I do not know, I think it was God's intervention … on a Friday, I went to Lilayi [police training college] to visit my uncle and on my way I met a friend of my dad who encouraged me to join the Zambia Police Service. During our chat, I showed him my school results and he was impressed. His advice was in form of a remark that "your friends are here (referring to the people I grew up with in Lilayi Police Camp who had joined the police as recruits), you can still be a nurse and police officer at the same time." (Interview with Malambo, 21 September 2021)

After this counselling, Malambo joined the Police Training College at Lilayi, and while in training, she was introduced to sign language course since the courts were having challenges dealing with convicts with hearing impairments. "I was one of the nine students who performed well in the sign language course and all of us went to Zambia Institute of Special Education (ZAMISE) for specialised sign language training" (Malambo, interview, 21 September 2021).

Upon graduating from Lilayi Police Training College, Malambo was deployed to Mazabuka[3] police station in Zambia's Southern Province where she was assigned to general duties and later oriented under traffic, prosecution, and the Victim Support Unit-VSU for a period of two years before finally settling for the VSU. The Victim Support Unit of the Zambia Police falls under the Community Service Directorate (CSD), which was created as a vehicle through which police could service the communities. This was intended to bridge the gap that existed in past years between the institution and members of the public. Through this directorate, the police wanted to develop a close relationship and full involvement of the public in community policing. The VSU was created with the mandate to investigate, arrest, and prosecute all cases (crime) committed against 'spouses,' women, children, and the aged. Through the VSU, counselling services to both victims and perpetrators of gender-based violence (GBV) and other crimes are offered. The Unit in partnership with other stakeholder does undertake community awareness on the

---

[3] Mazabuka is a town in the Southern Province of Zambia, lying about 75 miles South West of Lusaka, on the Lusaka—Livingstone road (Highway T1) and the railway to Livingstone (https://www.zambia-info.org/country/town/1332/mazabuka; https://www.latlong.net/place/mazabuka-southern-province-zambia-24445.html).

prevention of GBV offences (http://www.zambiapolice.gov.zm/index.php/services/community?showall=1).

Whilst serving as a police officer in Mazabuka, Malambo enrolled for a Diploma in Social Work at Mulungushi University and completed her studies in 2006. In 2007, while on tour of duty in the Southern Province, the Inspector General of Police (IG) and his entourage visited Mazabuka Police Station. According to Malambo, it was during this interaction that she came to learn about the UN peacekeeping missions:

> In 2007, the IG by then was touring Southern province and they toured Mazabuka. Among his team was Madam Joyce Kapampa Kasosa,[4] who at the time was working under the UN Directorate who talked to us on the importance of participation in peace operations. She encouraged officers to apply for UN peacekeeping. Four of us expressed interest and after the screening process, only 3 of us were picked for interviews, and I was the only female candidate. It was not easy to pull through the process of screening, male colleagues discouraged me through such sentiments as "peacekeeping was not for females," suggesting that I was not going to manage. I told myself that I will pass, if I fail, I will try next time. I attempted and passed! We underwent a lot of stressful interviews and I pulled through and was deployed to Liberia. And for sure, it was God. At times I tend to say that where there is always a will, there is a way. (Interview with Malambo, 21 September 2021)

The UN peacekeeping mission for Malambo started in 2008 when she was deployed in Liberia. In an interview, she is quoted saying, "She was only 32-year-old at the time and fiercely driven to prove herself as a capable gender advisor among international counterparts" (https://peacekeeping.un.org/en/beacon-of-hope-doreen-malambo-2020-un-woman-police-officer-of-year).

After her mission in Liberia had come to an end, Malambo was again seconded to another mission in South Sudan as the United Nations Police (UNPOL) gender adviser for the mission. The 'UN Police's mission is to enhance international peace and security by supporting Member-States in conflict, post-conflict and other crisis situations' (https://police.un.org/en). In an effort to meet the mandate of the UNPOL, Malambo took up various roles such as raising "awareness among national interlocutors such as the South Sudan National Police Service and the National Prisons Service about integrating gender perspectives into their daily functions" (https://peacekeeping.un.org/en/beacon-of-hope-doreen-malambo-2020-un-woman-police-officer-of-year).

After her return from the missions, Malambo assumed her new role as Deputy National Coordinator of the Gender Office under the Zambia Police Service. The aim of the gender unit in the service is to ensure that there is equality between men and women in terms of promotion, recruitment, and

---

[4] She was the Zambian High Commissioner to Kenya in 2021.

training. The unit also safeguards the needs of female police officers, especially in areas of deployment and operations.

In 2014, she enrolled for a Bachelor of Social Work at Cavendish University in Lusaka, Zambia, where she graduated with a distinction. Apart from emerging as the overall best student in her programme of study, Malambo was also honoured as a best student in research. At the time of the interview in 2021, she was pursuing a Master of Science, Peace, Leadership and Conflict Resolution at the University of Zambia in Lusaka.

In terms of her career, Malambo describes herself as one who had risen in the ranks through hard work. She has served the Zambia Police Service for about 27 years when "I have had an opportunity to explore my career both at the National and International levels. My studies in Social Work opened many doors for me. I am currently Assistant Superintendent, the rank that I received due to my hard work and for putting Zambia on the map when I won the United Nations woman police officer of the year 2020. I have five years of peacekeeping experience" (Facebook posting, Cavendish University 11 November 2020).

## Peacebuilding and Development Through the Work of Doreen Malambo

Malambo's contribution to peacebuilding and Sustainable Development Goal 16 is seen through the themes centred on her advisory and mentoring roles, mainstreaming gender and physical (mental) impairment in the police service, engendering peacebuilding and cultural awareness. These roles are explained below.

### *Advisory and Mentorship Roles*

Malambo's contribution as an adviser and mentor to the Liberia National Police from 2008 to 2009 is evidenced by her roles in the Women and Child Protection Section in Liberia. Malambo was until August 2010 the UN police gender adviser and an inspector for the Victim Support Unit for the UN Mission in Liberia. Through this role, she assisted the Liberia National Police to investigate and prevent sexual and gender-based violence and domestic violence. She was also adviser and mentor for the Liberia National Police, attached to the Women and Children Protection Section. She was also a UNPOL Gender Advisor at the UN Mission in South Sudan (UNMISS) where she was supporting vulnerable groups such as women, girls, children, and people with disabilities:

> Malambo was first deployed to UNMISS in 2016 as a joint integrated police trainer. She returned to UNMISS for the second time in 2019 and later served as a Gender Adviser in Juba, South Sudan. Her previous UN experience includes

deployment with the UN Mission in Liberia (UNMIL) from 2008 to 2009. (Africa Renewal News, 3 November 2020)

She was also instrumental in addressing the rights of girls and women. Malambo was influential in uplifting the plight of girls and women by contributing to the creation of initiatives for addressing sexual and gender-based violence (MBBA Global News, 8 November 2020). Working in partnership with the UN Population Fund (UNFPA), she helped to establish the Stand Up for Rights of Women and Girls initiative which assisted to reduce and prevent sexual and gender-based crime in South Sudan. Through this project, Malambo created a network of groups led by male local police officers to engage other men in the community to disseminate information and promote the protection and advancement of the rights of women and girls (MBBA Global News, 8 November 2020).

Her roles as an advisor and mentor are closely linked to the SDG Number 16, target 1, on reducing all forms of violence. It is no wonder that these efforts culminated in her nomination as the United Nations Woman Police Officer of the year 2020, as explained by the United Nations Police:

> Ms. Malambo was awarded the 2020 United Nations Woman Police Officer of the Year award for her work in partnership with the UN Population Fund (UNFPA), where she has helped establish the Stand Up for Rights of Women and Girls initiative that has helped to reduce and prevent sexual and gender-based crime in South Sudan. Her previous UN experience includes a deployment with the UN Mission in Liberia (UNMIL) from 2008 to 2009, where she assisted the Liberia National Police to prevent and investigate sexual and gender-based violence and domestic violence. Her national experience spans 24 years with the Zambia Police Service. (United Nations Police, 2 November 2020, n.d.)

As part of this project, Chief Inspector Malambo created a network of groups led by male local police officers to engage other men in the community to disseminate information and promote the protection and advancement of the rights of women and girls. Chief Inspector Malambo also contributed to UNMISS' efforts to disseminate information on COVID-19 prevention to vulnerable communities, including those with disabilities. Dr Simbyakula stated that the Government of the Republic of Zambia valued the contribution by women in peacekeeping operations and would therefore continue to champion the involvement of the female gender in peacekeeping (Lusaka Times, 11 November 2020, n.d.).

Her passion for working to end violence and in turn foster development through her advisory and mentorship roles are linked to her background. For example, Malambo recalled:

> I had an experience when growing up where one of our neighbours (head of the house) died, his relatives grabbed property from the surviving family members, again, the Police came in to help the vulnerable widow and orphans. These

experiences forced me to vow to myself that such things should not happen to me. Fortunately, when Dad died, I was already a police officer working under the Victim Support Unit (VSU). Dad's relatives attempted to grab properties from my family, but using my experience from the service I contained the situation by stopping them from getting anything, not even police uniforms. I challenged all those who that wanted to pick the properties to get the children (my siblings) as they were the only properties which my father left because the rest of the stuff was shared and owned by the entire nuclear family. (Interview, September 2021)

Her Christian teachings on being of service to others and embracing all people were at the centre of her actions to end violence. These were centred on the dignity of human life as she stated: "I am just an open person who loves everyone, I have no standards. People tell me that I am unique; I interact with everyone despite their career status, including a cleaner" (Interviewer, September 2021). This suggests that her personality tended to mirror her openness as shaped by her religious worldview on loving all humanity, regardless of status as all beings were created in the image of God. Thus, the religious values of love, truth, justice, and respect among others were positively tapped into to promote inclusive and just societies at both local and international levels. Her involvement to end violence by tapping into her religious teachings is also in line with the observation by Gopin (2000) that women tend to be successfully involved in peace efforts, as they seem to have a capacity to make connections and to use many means to achieve that connection.

### *Mainstreaming Gender and Physically (and Mentally) Challenged Persons in the Police Service*

Mainstreaming gender was understood as the process of assessing the implications for women and men of any planned action, including legislation, policies, or programmes, in all areas and at all levels and a strategy for making the concerns and experiences of women and men an integral dimension of the design, implementation, monitoring, and evaluation of policies and programmes in all political, economic, and societal spheres so that women and men benefit equally and inequality is not perpetuated (United Nations, 2002, p. 1). In relation to this, Malambo was also instrumental in making strides to mainstream gender in the police service in her peacekeeping mission. According to the UN News (2010), Ms. Malambo, 34, also noted that the presence of female police officers in Liberia has helped to increase the reporting of cases of sexual and gender-based violence. Previously, many believed "it was a family issue to be settled outside the police," but due to UNMIL's efforts, the increased presence of female LNP officers and mentoring by the UN has helped more women come forward, she said. "It is not very easy for a woman to [discuss] sexual violence issues with a male officer," she pointed out, but they "feel free to bring out their cases" with female police officers. She said that the percentage of women in the LNP has increased in recent years, currently standing at nearly

17%. When Liberian women see female UN police officers carrying out tasks, such as guarding Government sites, "which they feel are supposed to be performed by males, it has changed the public image of the Police Service as an organization," she noted. "They now know that policing is not for males alone, but for everybody," added Ms. Malambo, a mother of three, serving to encourage more women to join the LNP's ranks. In schools where she conducts awareness-raising sessions, "when they see a female peacekeeper standing in the front talking about these policing issues, they feel very good and they want to emulate you."

Malambo's view was that female UN police officers not only set the image of police as role models, but also helped to increase the reporting of cases of sexual and gender-based violence. While this resonated with the liberal feminist stance to seek equal representation of women in the high offices of state and advocate the right of women to participate in activities, such as combat, that have traditionally been ascribed to men by society, it was also closely aligned to fostering a just and inclusive society. These efforts point to the aspirations in SDG 16, specifically target number 3 which seeks to promote the rule of law at an international level and ensure equal justice and representation for all.

Additionally, Malambo showcased an inclusive service delivery by working with the hearing impaired as recounted by the UN News Centre (2010):

> A police officer serving with the United Nations peacekeeping mission in Liberia is giving a voice not only to women who have suffered from sexual violence, but also to the West African country's deaf people, thanks to her sign language skills. Doreen Malambo, the police gender adviser for the UN Mission in Liberia (UNMIL), happened to be "at the right place at the right time" at a police station when a deaf woman who had been assaulted came forward to report the crime. It was a situation "where no police officer could understand the language to take a statement from this person," she told the UN News Centre. Ms. Malambo, who was trained in sign language in her native Zambia, was able to help interpret the statement of the woman, who had been accompanied to the police station by several deaf friends. "They were so happy and they went and they broke the news to their counterparts," she said. The experience, the police officer added, "felt so good" because she was able to assist a marginalized group within Liberia, which was torn apart by civil war from 1989 until 2003. It also gave her the chance to repeat the success she had in Zambia to bridge the gap between the police and the deaf community. (18 June 2010, https://news.un.org/en/story/2010/06/342212)

In some cases, Malambo said, people would commit crimes in front of people with hearing impairment because "they know that they won't go anywhere, they won't say anything," (Interview, 2021) stressing the importance of having police officers who can communicate in sign language to document criminal evidence.

Malambo also assisted to incorporate sign language skills in the training of the Liberian police as explained by the United Nations Peacekeeping Missions

(2020) that Malambo utilised her skills to sensitise students in schools for the deaf upon her arrival in Liberia in 2008 by helping to incorporate sign language skills into the training of the Liberian National Police (LNP). Malambo noted that people with hearing impairment had a lot of problems just like any other person, but sometimes they could just keep quiet, dying with their own problems because they could not communicate with police (United Nations Peacekeeping Missions, 2020).

Mainstreaming gender and physically challenged persons in peacebuilding was therefore not only in line with the SDG agenda of promoting just and peaceful societies, but also the AU agenda of leaving no one behind. By this, marginalised groups such as women and those with physical or mental impairment were not to be left behind in the quest for justice. These strides to incorporate sign language could also be directly related to contributing towards SDG 16's target number 3 on ensuring equal access to justice to all. Her efforts to mainstream gender resonate with the conclusion by Ochieng (2019) that there needs to be more women in the formal processes as part of building a greater gender balanced and more inclusive peace in peacebuilding processes. This quest for equal justice for all also closely resonates with her religious teaching on caring and loving one's neighbours. As observed by Naber and Watson (2006), teachings and religious practices of major world religions such as Christianity reveal spiritual and moral resources that support peace, social justice, reconciliation, and harmony. Malambo's use of religion for development in essence demonstrated that women can be involved in shaping religious interpretations and responses to the conflict in their communities in their own ways.

### *Engendering Peacebuilding*

The numerous contexts where Malambo had been deployed have been characterised with their own gender dynamics. Starting with her initial deployment in Mazabuka, where she served in the VSU, women constituted the vulnerable category. Similarly, the war-tone contexts of Liberia and South Sudan not only impacted on women negatively but also had unequal women participation in peacebuilding. For example, Malambo recalled:

> In 2008, (first mission in Liberia), we had few women but Zambia was among the top 10. Currently we have high representation in mission in Zambia like in South Sudan. This has changed because I was the motivator. Before I was awarded in Liberia as gender advisor, I was engaged in a lot of activities such as gender awareness. We had a strategic plan and I came up with projects on women help the government. We called it deliberate actions to employ more women in the police—we did a campaign where women in Liberia came forth to join in what was previously seen as a man's job. (Interview with Malambo, September 2021)

At national level, Malambo spearheaded gender awareness within and beyond the police service as reported by Esther Freud:

> It was a young woman, Doreen Mazuba Malambo, who brought the campaign on gender awareness. She has spent her working life in police gender relations, is the daughter of a policeman, and the wife of one too—until she divorced him for beating her. (21 February 2014, https://www.ft.com/content/f3f94cbc-99bc-11e3-91cd-00144feab7de)

These efforts reflect her contributions towards improving women's participation in peacebuilding activities. Her own life experiences enabled her to work towards engendering peace. For example, she recounted:

> I was married to the father of my kids and he became abusive. The Bible says marriage should be enjoyed. Dad used to say, if you want to be happy be educated, do not depend on human beings. My great grandmother inspired me a lot on how to deal with gender issues. She only had two kids, why 2 kids? She never wanted a man to mistreat her so she divorced my great grandfather years ago. Grandma died in 2013 at the age of 110 years old. Her stance on abusive marriage gave me courage to move on from mistreatment. I say accepting to be abused is becoming a volunteer to abuse and not a victim especially if abuse repeats itself several times. I am a person who does things in my own way and I do not like to pretend as this is against my Christian conviction, God does not want a plastic (fake) smile. (Interview, September 2021)

Being an Adventist, she acknowledged that religion had a role to play in peacebuilding and development. She recalled:

> Wherever I have been, even in fights, religion is always there. In Liberia, it was Muslim and Christians, peacekeepers from Pakistan are Muslim were on standby for routine duties. Two people were fighting because of differences on Bible and Quran. In South Sudan, when teaching, you need to be neutral. When they pose questions, they use their own lens, like me I would take it that I would want to learn from the Quran, they would give me the Quran, I read and find areas where the Bible and Quran are at par. ... My experience showed the need for standardised training. My experience in Liberia showed that we had mixed Muslims and Christians so you would find that one religion would allow a certain practice and the other would not. So, I recommended universal training and I went to New York where I developed a standardised gender tool kit (copy is online) called gender focal persons and each gave scenarios where they were coming from, plus other policies. (Interview, September 2021)

This enabled her to work towards preventing violence and combating crime and promoting and enforcing non-discriminatory laws and policies for sustainable development. Consequently, the President's Insignia of Meritorious Achievement was awarded to Doreen Mazuba Malambo by the seventh Republican President of Zambia, Hakainde Hichilema (News Diggers 25 May

2022). As observed by Hampson (1996), religion has the ability to mobilise people to work towards peace based on its values. Malambo's efforts to engender peacebuilding are directly related to SDG 16's target 3 and 7 on developing effective, accountable, and transparent institutions at all levels and ensuring responsive, inclusive, participatory, and representative decision-making at all levels. Malambo's efforts are also in line with the principles of the feminist theory which call for complete equality of opportunity between men and women in peacebuilding (Collins, 2006).

### *Cultural Awareness*

Malambo's contribution to sustainable development was also through attempts to address cultural issues which negatively impacted on girls and women. Her family background and experiences gave her the passion to serve the vulnerable. In recounting what motivated her to serve the poor and needy, she remarked:

> When I was young and still at school, one of my colleagues was defiled. As she was going through the trauma, she started withdrawing from school. The way the police acted on this case was helpful and my dad explained to me the role of the police service in helping the vulnerable based on this incidence. I also had an experience when one of our neighbour—the father—died and relatives grabbed property. Again, the police came in. But I also said to myself that I don't want this to happen to me. Fortunately, when Dad died, I was under Victim Support Unit in the police service and no relative grabbed property. Right in the family during the funeral. I said the police will pick the uniforms. If you want to pick property, the property which my father left are these children. Go ahead and pick any of them. (Interview, September 2021)

Malambo tapped into her cultural awareness to foster peacebuilding. For example, Malambo advocated for inclusive participation of both men and women and worked with women to make a difference. She recalled that while in South Sudan:

> I went to community policing and began to engage women through gender, child, vulnerable people protection. I worked with them. I influenced women, most of them were supporting fights as they were married to generals. Even in the area of marriage, there was a culture which saw marriage as the only avenue for success for girls, resulting in marriage of young girls aged about 10 years, being married to men who could be 60 or 70 years of age. (Interview with Malambo, September 2021)

Similarly, discussions with women were held on peacebuilding and gender-based violence:

Through these talks, we were discouraging fellow women on certain practices such as those who play the role *nachimbusa*[5] (tutors of the transcendent) and began to educate them on genital mutilation by quoting the Bible that Jesus said circumcision, that this circumcision was not meant for girls. It goes beyond circumcision as we know. So, they began to understand the dangers of genital mutilation. We would work with medical personnel and they could see the danger. (Interview with Malambo, September 2021)

While child marriage could be directly linked to gender-based violence, her efforts to influence women who were supporting the men involved in war could amount to her strides to end all forms of violence (target 1) and discrimination against children (target 2). The cultural influence on women could be seen through using the cultural resource of working with women custodians of culture who were in charge of genital mutilation. Her efforts to raise cultural awareness also reflect her tapping into her religious capital in the form of biblical teachings which enabled the women to rethink their practices of genital mutilation and supporting the men in war. Malambo noted:

I used the Bible to help address marriage. Gender is constructed by culture. For example, the culture of marriage, a man is the head of the house, that's what the Bible says. Through a gender lens, we define a man and women as an individual who should have good opportunities. So, you find that there is a misunderstanding here as people think that a woman should be giving opportunities to man instead of giving each other giving each other opportunities. So here, I focused on showing them that a man and woman should be together. In the same way, gender-based violence has no place among Christians because a woman is like a rib of a man, it's like you are beating yourself. (Interview, September 2021)

Anderlini (2000, 2003) also agrees that engendering peacebuilding as the case was in Liberia through the members of the Liberian Women Initiatives which was open to all women regardless of ethnic, social, or religious background contributed to making women become resourceful during the regional peace talks and acted as monitors of the commitments made during the negotiations. It also affirmed the conclusion that women have attempted to minimise the effects of violence, if not actively to try to end the violence themselves, by acting as peacemakers (Ferris, 1995). Most importantly, Malambo's work in peacebuilding from a cultural perspective is also in line with the observation by Marshall et al. (2011) that women often seem better able and more willing to reach across religious and cultural divides to find common ground.

On the whole, Malambo's work in peacebuilding and in attaining Sustainable Development Goal Number 16 shows that despite the apparent invisibility of the women in religious peacebuilding, women have successfully carried out peacebuilding activities both as lay members in religious institutions and using

---

[5] In the Zambian context, these are elderly women who induct young women during marriage rites.

their respective platforms in leadership and even as individuals. This is affirmed by Africa Revival News (3 November 2020) that, like many peacekeepers during challenging times, Chief Inspector Malambo continued to go above and beyond the call of duty to serve communities. She not only tapped into her professional call to duty, but also weaved her religious beliefs, values, and practices as informed by her Adventist Christian background into her contributions towards the creation of a just, inclusive, and peaceful societies. This shows that the place of religion in peacebuilding is not just anchored in religious institutions but also individuals who are carriers of their religiosity in the secular spaces where they work from.

## Conclusion

This chapter trailed the narrative of Doreen Mazuba Malambo in peacebuilding in order to show the interconnectedness of religion, gender, peacebuilding, and development. It sought to show how Malambo's account mirrored a woman's contribution towards the creation of just, inclusive, and peaceful society. Given the involvement in peacebuilding through her service to the Zambia Police Service and deployment with the United Nations Missions, the chapter concludes that Malambo has contributed to the sustainable development at local and international levels. The chapter also showed that Malambo contributed to peacebuilding in ways which closely resonated with the aspirations of the SDG Number 16 through her roles as a gender advisor, where she helped to establish the Stand Up for Rights of Women and Girls initiative thereby promoting gender mainstreaming, peacebuilding, and development in different fronts. The chapter concludes that the contributions of Malambo were shaped by her personal experiences as a woman, an officer of the law, gender activist, and her religious worldview. This chapter argues that although the interaction of gender, religion, peacebuilding, and development is often centred on institutionalised religion, religion at a personal level also remained a resource for contributing towards the attainment of Sustainable Development Goal Number 16. Malambo's work in peacebuilding mirrors the ways in which the attainment of SDG 16 could be facilitated by non-informal efforts which intersect gender, religion, and peacebuilding from individual actors. Malambo's work has implications for peacebuilding frameworks and policies and points to the need to encompass such religious-oriented efforts in peacebuilding discourses. The chapter recommends more recognition of women like Malambo who intersect gender, religion, peacebuilding, and development not only for the lessons they bring to the fore, but also for documenting their success for posterity.

# REFERENCES

Adeogun, T. J., & Muthuki, J. M. (2018). Feminist Perspectives on Peacebuilding: The Case of Women's Organisations in South Sudan. *Agenda, 32*(2), 83–92.

Africa Renewal News. (2020). UN Woman Police Officer of the Year Award 2020 Winner: Chief Inspector Doreen Malambo of Zambia.

African Watch Report. (1991). *Liberia: The Cycle of Abuse*. African Watch.

Anderlini, S. (2003). The Untapped Resource: Women in Peace Negotiation, Conflict Trends, Women, Peace and Security. *Conflict Trends, 3*(3), 18–22.

Anderlini, S. B. N. (2000). *Women at the Peace Table: Making a Difference*. UNIFEM.

Armon, J., & Carl, A. (Eds.). (1990). *Accord, The Liberian Peace Process 1990–1996*. Concilian Resources.

Brundtland, G. H. (1987). What is sustainable development. *Our Common Future, 8*(9), 1–40.

Boutros-Ghali, B. (1992). An Agenda for Peace: Preventive Diplomacy, Peacemaking and Peace-keeping. *International Relations, 11*(3), 201–218.

Clandinin, D. J., & Connelly, F. M. (2000). *Narrative Inquiry: Experience and Story in Qualitative Research*. Jossey-Bass.

Collins, P. H. (2006). *From Black Power to Hip Hop: Racism, Nationalism, and Feminism*. Temple University Press.

Colson, E. (2006). *Tonga Religious Life in the Twentieth Century*. Bookworld.

De la Rey, C., & McKay, S. (2006). Peacebuilding as a Gendered Process. *Journal of Social Issues, 62*(1), 141–153.

Dubois, H. (2008). Religion and Peacebuilding. *Journal of Religion, Conflict and Peace, 1*(2), 393–405.

Ferris, E. (1995). Women, war and peace, life and peace research report 14, Uppsala International Alert.

Freud, E. (2014, February 21). Zambia's Campaign Against Male Violence. *Financial Times*.

Gopin, M. (2000). *Between Eden and Armageddon: The Future of World religions, Violence, and Peacemaking*. Oxford University Press, Inc.

Hamilton, M. B. (1995). *The Sociology of Religion: Theoretical and Comparative Perspectives*. Routledge.

Hampson, F. O. (1996). *Nurturing Peace: Why Peace Processes Succeed or Fail* (p. 4). USIP.

http://www.zambiapolice.gov.zm/index.php/advanced-stuff/docs-and-support.

http://www.zambiapolice.gov.zm/index.php/services/community?showall=1

https://news.un.org/en/story/2010/06/342212

https://peacekeeping.un.org/en/beacon-of-hope-doreen-malambo-2020-un-woman-police-officer-of-year

https://scholar.google.com/scholar?hl=en&as_sdt=0,5&q=Peacebuilding+is+gendered

https://www.britannica.com/topic/Tonga-African-people

https://www.ft.com/content/f3f94cbc-99bc-11e3-91cd-00144feab7de

https://www.latlong.net/place/mazabuka-southern-province-zambia-24445.html

https://www.lusakatimes.com/2020/11/11/women-effectively-contributing-to-peacekeeping-operations-amb-simbyakula/

https://www.zambia-info.org/country/town/1332/mazabuka

https://www.zambiatourism.com/towns/lusaka/

Hudson, H. (2021). It Matters How You 'Do' Gender in Peacebuilding: African Approaches and Challenges. *Insight on Africa, 13*(2), 142–159.

Human Rights Watch Report. (1994). *Child Soldiers in Liberia*. Human Rights Watch.

Japan International Cooperation Agency & Japan Development Services. (2016). Country Gender Profile: Zambia Final Report. JICA & JDS, Lusaka.

Klot, J. F. (2007). Women and Peacebuilding. *Social Science Research Council, 29*, 1–12.

Manyonganise, M. (2017). Invisibilising the Victimised: Churches in Manicaland and Women's Experiences of Political Violence in National Healing and Reconciliation in Zimbabwe. *Journal for the Study of Religion, 30*(1), 110–136.

Marshall, K., Hayward, S., Zambra, C., Breger, E., & Jackson, S. (2011). *Women in Religious Peacebuilding*. US Institute of Peace.

Mazurana, D. E., & McKay, S. R. (1999). *Women & Peacebuilding* (No. 8). International Centre for Human Rights and Democratic Development.

McGuire, M. (2002). *Religion: The Social Context*. Wadsworth.

Mofya, T. N. (2022). Role of Women in Peace Building in Zambia: Case of Northern Province. *International Journal of Conflict Management, 3*(1), 61–95.

Munro, J. (2000). *Gender and Peace Building*. International Development Research Centre.

Mwale, N. (2020). "Not all heroes wear caps": Women and Peacebuilding in the Public Sphere in Zambia through a Narrative of Susan Sikaneta. In A. Chitando (Ed.), *Women and Peacebuilding in Africa* (pp. 186–198). Routledge.

Naber, J. M. M., & Watson, R. (2006). *African Faith-Based Communities: Advancing Justice and Reconciliation in Relation to the ICC*. World Conference of Religions for Peace.

Nakaya, S. (2004). Women and Gender Equality in Peacebuilding: Somalia and Mozambique. In T. Keating & W. A. Knight (Eds.), *Building Sustainable Peace* (pp. 143–166). Alberta Press.

Ochieng, M. (2019). Role of Women in Peacebuilding and Post-Conflict Transformation Africa. *International Journal of Arts Humanities and Social Sciences, 1*(2), 1–12.

Ogega, J. (2022). *Women, Religion, and Peace-Building: Gusii and Maasai Women of Faith in Kenya*. Springer Nature.

Ollerenshaw, J. A., & Creswell, J. W. (2000). Data Analysis in Narrative Research: A Comparison of Two "restorying" Approaches. In *Annual Meeting of the American Educational Research Association, New Orleans, LA*.

Onsati, C. K. (2014). *Religion, Gender and Peace Building in Africa; A Case Study of Kenya 2007/8* (Doctoral dissertation, University of Nairobi).

Pankhurst, D. T. (2000). *Women, Gender and Peacebuilding*. Bradford: Centre for Conflict Resolution, Department of Peace Studies, University of Bradford, CCR Working Papers, No. 5.

Peace and Security Council (PSC) 987th Meeting of 2021, March 22nd (PSC Report, 2021).

Philpot D. (2007). Religion, Reconciliation and Transitional Justice: The State of the Field, New York: SSRC Working Papers, 1

Porter, E. (2007). *Peacebuilding: Women in International Perspective*. Routledge.

Rakodi, C. (2012). A Framework for Analysing the Links between Religion and Development. *Development in Practice, 22*(5–6), 634–650.

Steele, D. (2011). *A Manual to Facilitate Conversations on Religious Peacebuilding and Reconciliation*. US Institute of Peace.

Strickland, R., & Duvvury, N. (2003). Gender Equity and Peacebuilding: From Rhetoric to Reality; Finding the Way, a Discussion Paper.

Toure, A. (2002). *The Role of Civil Society in National Reconciliation and Peacebuilding in Liberia*. International Peace Institute.

UN News Centre. (2010). Liberia: In Liberia, UN Police Officer Deploys her Language Skills to Help Those in Need, June 18.

United Nations. (2002). *Gender Mainstreaming: An Overview*. UN.

United Nations Peacekeeping Missions News. (2020). A Beacon of Hope: Doreen Malambo, 2020 UN Woman Police Officer of the Year

USAID. (2009). Religion, Conflict and Peacebuilding: An Introductory Programming Guide. Office of Conflict Management and Mitigation.

van den Berg, H. (2016). *The Role of Religion in Peacebuilding*. Leiden University.

CHAPTER 38

# Disability and Migration: Religious and Traditional Disability Beliefs as Causes of Migration of Zimbabwean Mothers of Children with Disabilities to South Africa

*Willson Tarusarira and Joram Tarusarira*

## Introduction

Migration is a major issue of our time. The migration of Zimbabweans to South Africa has been attributed to the economic and political challenges in Zimbabwe. Disability and its attendant causal factors, especially religious and traditional beliefs about disability, have not been considered factors behind some Zimbabweans in South Africa. However, both African tradition and Christian beliefs have some influence on the migration of Zimbabwean refugee mothers of disabled children to South Africa. Cognisant of this reality, the chapter recommends a creative notion of peacebuilding involving addressing this dimension to ensure that the mothers of disabled children and their

W. Tarusarira (✉)
Centre for Disability & Rehabilitation Studies, Stellenbosch University, Stellenbosch, South Africa

J. Tarusarira
Department of Comparative Study of Religion, University of Groningen, Groningen, The Netherlands

Alliance of Bioversity International and CIAT, Rome, Italy
e-mail: j.tarusarira@rug.nl

mothers enjoy peace of mind and inclusion, as envisaged in the Sustainable Development Goal (SDG) 16. This SDG seeks to "[P]romote peaceful and inclusive societies for sustainable development, provide access to justice for all and build effective, accountable and inclusive institutions at all levels."[1]

Most migrants in South Africa, whether disabled or not, are reported to be coming from the African continent, with the majority coming from the fragile and conflict-ridden Zimbabwe. Among those migrating to South Africa are mothers of children living with disabilities. Recent information from the data base of a non-profit organization fighting for the rights of refugees, asylum seekers, and migrants shows an increase in Zimbabwean refugee mothers of disabled children in South Africa (PASSOP, 2017, 2020, 2022). However, the literature on Zimbabweans migrating to South Africa is silent on this significant migration by these mothers and children, despite them suffering psychological violence due to the circumstances driving them out of their country of origin and the stigma associated with giving birth to children with disabilities and who are impaired. The literature is also silent on factors forcing these mothers to leave Zimbabwe for South Africa. The assumption is that all Zimbabweans migrating to any country, especially South Africa, are pushed by politics and the country's economy. Disability has rarely been seen as a factor behind migration. As a result, Zimbabwean refugee mothers of disabled children remain on the margins of migration debates and policies and are seen in a way that disempowers them and denies their agency. Such marginalization compromises SDG 16's call for promoting peaceful and inclusive societies for sustainable development, providing access to justice for all, and building effective, accountable, and inclusive institutions at all levels. This chapter seeks to critically explore the religious and traditional beliefs behind the migration of Zimbabwean refugee mothers of children living with disabilities in South Africa towards this SDG.

## BACKGROUND TO THE STUDY

It is estimated that worldwide 270 million migrants live as refugees in various countries and cannot return to their countries (Amnesty International, 2019; Batalova et al., 2020). Of the 270 million migrants, 30 million are protected by international refugee laws, which oblige host countries to protect these refugees (Amnesty International, 2019). Factors such as conflict, war, and other forms of violence, which are of concern to SDG 16, have contributed to the movement of these refugees to neighbouring countries, and women and children are the most affected (Silove et al., 2017). In Africa, migration is not directed only to European countries but also to other African countries. Africa has a long history of people migrating from one country to another, and this has been an essential feature in the African continent's economy, politics, and culture. As of February 2019, the African continent had 6.3 million refugees

[1] https://sdgs.un.org/goals/goal16.

and 14.5 million internally displaced people, more than a third of all forcibly displaced people (African Union, 2020). This migration is attributed to socio-economic, political, and health-related factors (Africa Check, 2017).

As from the beginning of the twenty-first century, an increased number of Zimbabweans crossing borders to neighbouring countries have been witnessed, and the majority have been, and are, moving into South Africa (CoRMSA, 2011; Mathekga, 2022). Zimbabwe's ongoing economic and political disaster has contributed to the departure of many Zimbabweans, owing partly to the economic policies of Zimbabwe's ruling party (ZANU PF) and its use of violence to suppress political dissent (Africa Check, 2017; Chifamba, 2020). Although the total number of refugees living in South Africa is unknown, Zimbabwe is believed to be the main contributor to these numbers.

Besides Zimbabwe's political and economic challenges, which forced some Zimbabwean citizens to leave their country, unemployment, lack of essential commodities, and widespread poverty, which SDG 1—"End poverty in all its forms everywhere"—seeks to address, have contributed to the migration of Zimbabweans to neighbouring countries looking for goods and livelihood prospects (Chifamba, 2020; Mathekga, 2022). On the other hand, persecution for political reasons, that is, political torture and forced disappearances, have forced numerous Zimbabweans to seek refuge in South Africa, where they also face challenges of how to provide for their dependents and on the other hand fulfilling the difficult conditions of their refugee status (CoRMSA, 2011).

So, Zimbabweans' humanitarian problems and the probability of more Zimbabweans moving to South Africa remain high. In this chapter, we will show that beyond the most rehearsed economic and political factors, religious and traditional beliefs contributed to the migration of mothers with children with disabilities from Zimbabwe to South Africa. Religion and spirituality have some positive and negative influences on the perception and treatment of disabled people. They can be philosophies for coping with disability (Claasens et al., 2018), just as they can be a basis for the condemnation of both the mother and the disabled child. Jelinek-Menke (2022) calls such religion dis/abling religion to capture this ambivalence. While religious and traditional beliefs are rarely foregrounded, when raised, they are not a surprise considering that most African communities follow indigenous religions and other religions such as Christianity. At every moment, they prefer to live under a sacred canopy. Religious and traditional beliefs permeate all aspects of society and provide cognitive, emotional, and moral meaning. Providing effective responses to the challenges posed by some of these beliefs will make a profound and creative contribution to peacebuilding in Africa. This is because for the most part, peacebuilding has tended to concentrate on violent conflict, while overlooking the trauma and anguish borne by mothers of children with disabilities and the children themselves.

## Disability and Migration

People with disabilities are often socially excluded in conflict-affected communities (Pearce, 2014). Accessing humanitarian assistance programmes is a huge challenge for them, and they are at greater risk of violence than their nondisabled peers (Pearce, 2014). This social exclusion is worse for refugee women and girls with disabilities, who are seen as societal outcasts (Women's Refugee Commission (WRC), 2016). Religious and traditional beliefs play a big part in this exclusion. Refugee women and girls face discrimination and cultural violence, including gender-based violence (Women's Refugee Commission (WRC), 2016). According to the Women's Refugee Commission (2016), due to displacement, refugee women and girls with disabilities in refugee camps and host communities may experience discrimination, unsafe shelters, and a lack of access to services. Refugee women and girls with disabilities may lack access to water and health care during displacement (Pearce, 2014). For refugee mothers of disabled children, the situation may be dire. They face discrimination as foreign nationals for having a disabled child and being women. The lack of access to health facilities violates SDG 3, which focuses on ensuring healthy lives and promoting well-being for all ages. Discriminating against these women because of their gender violates SDG 5, which aims to achieve gender equality and empower all women and girls. Thus, their suffering has multiple layers; an intersectional analysis is strategically positioned to capture their experiences. According to the UNHCR (2020), 12 million people of forcibly displaced people in 2020 were people living with disabilities. Globally, the rights of refugees and people living with disabilities are violated almost daily, leaving these two groups exposed to trauma, including physical, sexual, and mental abuse (UNHCR, 2020). Recent literature and reports show that attention is focused on refugee rights (UNHCR, 2020), including how humanitarian organizations perceive refugee mothers. Some organizations with a keen interest in issues related to refugees with disabilities have looked at the challenges women with disabilities experience during their migration phases (UNHCR, 2020; Women's Refugee Commission, 2016).

Attention has been given to refugees with disabilities, including refugee mothers with disabilities (Women's Refugee Commission, 2016), but there is limited literature on Zimbabwean refugee mothers of disabled children. Several researchers have made calls to find ways to protect the most vulnerable refugees, including children, and for more studies to be done on the health care of refugees, their experiences with discrimination, and social stigmas about disabled people (Pearce, 2014; Women's Refugee Commission, 2016).

Migrant families have to deal with adopting a new culture and how they can rebuild new social networks (UNHCR, 2020; Women's Refugee Commission, 2016). Literature addressing disability and migration shows how migration causes a migrant family of a disabled child's social networks to contract and how these families depend solely on formal support services (Pisoni, 2021). Furthermore, access to support can be made difficult by the introduction of a new culture or language or because of a lack of available services (UNHCR, 2020; Women's Refugee Commission, 2016).

In many cases, migrant families are more concerned with the needs of their disabled child/ren and not their own needs (Arfa et al., 2020). However, concentrating on the child's needs alone may cause exhaustion on the parent, depletion of resources, and affect how the child develops. According to Owens et al. (2016), the request and use of support by migrant parents of disabled children are dependent on their migration pathway. These families may encounter challenges in adapting to a foreign country, while a decrease in sociocultural assistance obstructs these families' coping strategies (Owens et al., 2016). According to Marceca et al. (2019), migrant families favour certain types of interventions, such as visits to their houses by a practitioner and that the services be delivered to them by a professional from their background, as their cultural background will be considered. Approaches of this nature may build a positive relationship between these families and the service providers. Migrant parents of children with disabilities fail to mobilize some support fully because of the difference in languages and because they do not have enough knowledge of the welfare system of the country hosting them (Muenstermann, 2017). We also argue that their need for private visits from practitioners will heighten the chances of their cultures being considered and help with the religious and traditional stigma that may still be attached to them.

The lived experiences and the estimates of how many Zimbabweans live in South Africa have been explored comprehensively (Africa Check, 2017). However, less is known about Zimbabwean refugee mothers of children with disability in South Africa. The 2011 census in South Africa reported that at least 672,308 Zimbabweans are living in South Africa (Africa Check, 2017). Recently, the Zimbabwe National Statistics Agency (2022) reported that 773,246 Zimbabweans are living in South Africa, of which 461,293 are men and 311,593 are women. With these numbers, Zimbabwe is believed to be one of the highest contributors to immigrant populations in South Africa (Africa Check, 2017).

In general, refugee women and girls with disabilities face three layers of discrimination. First, they face discrimination because of their gender, disability, and nationality. Second, they experience stigmatization and discrimination in refugee camps and host countries (Women's Refugee Commission, 2016). Third, they lack safe shelter and access to basic services (Pearce, 2014), which are all aims of the SDGs. Finally, they face sexual and gender-based violence, mainly those with mental disabilities (Women's Refugee Commission, 2016). Given these challenges that refugee women face, refugee children with disabilities are likely most disadvantaged compared to other vulnerable groups. Considering this, we decided to carry out a study that would increase knowledge about these Zimbabwean refugee mothers who have migrated with children who are disabled.

## The South African Context

In 2019, South Africa had an estimate 90,000 refugees (UNHCR, 2020). Most refugees in South Africa are believed to be women and children and come from Zimbabwe (Africa Check, 2017; UNHCR, 2020). Among these refugees are Zimbabwean mothers living with disabled children (PASSOP Data Base, 2017, 2020, 2022). Although refugees are more vulnerable in South Africa due to issues related to xenophobia and restricted access to services, there are laws in South Africa that are meant to protect them (Refugee Acts No. 130, 1998). However, even though these laws are in place and prioritize the protection of refugees, it remains unclear as to what other barriers keep refugees, especially those with disabilities, from accessing services (Women's Refugee Commission, 2016).

For the past three decades, news media have reported on Zimbabweans fleeing their country to neighbouring countries, especially South Africa. At least 3.4 million Zimbabweans are estimated to be residing in South Africa, making Zimbabwe one of the top countries in Africa to contribute to migrants to South Africa (Misago et al., 2009). Recent unpublished data from the database of People Against Suffering, Suppression, Oppression and Poverty (PASSOP) shows the increasing numbers of both (1) refugee and (2) asylum-seeking mothers of disabled children in the Western Cape Province of South Africa.

As indicated in Table 38.1, there are more refugee mothers of children with disability from Zimbabwe in South Africa than from any other country, and they are increasing. However, the literature is silent about the factors forcing

**Table 38.1** Refugee and asylum-seeking mothers of disabled children in the Western Cape Province (PASSOP database per country; accessed February 2017, February 2020, & February 2022)

| Country of origin | (1) Refugee mothers of children who are disabled/year | | | (2) Asylum-seeking mothers of children who are disabled/year | | |
|---|---|---|---|---|---|---|
| | Feb 2017 | Feb 2020 | Feb 2022 | Feb 2017 | Feb 2020 | Feb 2022 |
| Angola | 8 | 8 | 9 | 5 | 6 | 6 |
| Bangladesh | 4 | 6 | 6 | 9 | 12 | 12 |
| Burundi | 5 | 5 | 6 | 8 | 10 | 10 |
| Cameroon | 1 | 2 | 2 | 5 | 5 | 5 |
| DRC | 9 | 10 | 10 | 11 | 13 | 13 |
| Ethiopia | 3 | 5 | 9 | 4 | 7 | 3 |
| Kenya | 3 | 3 | 4 | 2 | 3 | 4 |
| Lesotho | 1 | 1 | 2 | 6 | 8 | 8 |
| Libya | 1 | 1 | 1 | 2 | 2 | 2 |
| Malawi | 4 | 4 | 5 | 9 | 10 | 10 |
| Nigeria | 8 | 8 | 8 | 6 | 8 | 8 |
| Pakistan | 2 | 2 | 2 | 2 | 2 | 3 |

*(continued)*

Table 38.1 (continued)

| Country of origin | (1) Refugee mothers of children who are disabled/year | | | (2) Asylum-seeking mothers of children who are disabled/year | | |
|---|---|---|---|---|---|---|
| | Feb 2017 | Feb 2020 | Feb 2022 | Feb 2017 | Feb 2020 | Feb 2022 |
| Somalia | 11 | 13 | 13 | 11 | 13 | 13 |
| South Sudan | 1 | 3 | 3 | 3 | 3 | 4 |
| Syria | 2 | 2 | 2 | 0 | 0 | 0 |
| **Zimbabwe** | **17** | **21** | **31** | **25** | **27** | **37** |
| Grand total/year | 80 | 94 | 113 | 108 | 129 | 138 |

these mothers from Zimbabwe to move to South Africa with their disabled children and leave as refugees. This oversight raises concerns, given the increasing global migrations and the increasing numbers of people forced to leave their countries by situations beyond their control (UNHCR, 2020). More so at a time when the SDGs, especially SDG 16, call for promoting peaceful and inclusive societies for sustainable development, providing access to justice for all, and building effective, accountable, and inclusive institutions at all levels.

## Pre-migration Experiences: The Lived Experiences of Mothers of Children with Disability in Zimbabwe—Fleeing Rejection and Isolation

The pre-migration phase involves experiences encountered by refugees in their own countries, including planning and deciding to relocate to another country for refuge (Chen et al., 2017). During this period, refugees leave all their possessions behind. They cut ties with their previous way of living (Meda, 2017). Further, they may leave behind their beloved ones, becoming vulnerable and grief-stricken and being subjected to impairment.

In this chapter, pre-migration experiences refer to the experiences of Zimbabwean refugee mothers of children living with disabilities during their time in Zimbabwe. For the longest time, the political and economic stability in Zimbabwe has been cited as the main contributor to the migration of some Zimbabweans to other countries, especially to South Africa (Misago et al., 2009; Mathekga, 2022). However, as we have already intimated, there is a dearth of information surrounding the reasons for the migration of mothers of disabled children from Zimbabwe to South Africa. Research is needed to explore what influences the decisions and planning processes of these to critically understand their lived experiences before leaving Zimbabwe. This may help to understand their post-migration needs. Although no literature directly reports on the pre-migration experiences of refugee mothers of disabled children from Zimbabwe, sources available on the treatment of these mothers and of people living with disabilities in Zimbabwe may help us understand why these mothers are fleeing their country to South Africa. The data from the interviews with the mothers complement these sources.

Surveys done by the organization, People Against Suffering, Suppression, Oppression and Poverty (PASSOP), in 2017, 2020, and 2022 in the Western Cape Province suggest that hostile religious and traditional beliefs influenced the migration of Zimbabwean refugee mothers of disabled children to South Africa (PASSOP, 2017, 2020, 2022). These Zimbabwean refugee mothers of children living with disabilities were rejected by those close to them, including husbands and families, for giving birth to a child with a disability. In many instances, when a woman gives birth to a child with a disability in Zimbabwe, the blame is on the mother; hence, in many cases, the woman is rejected by her people (Choruma, 2007). A man divorcing such a woman will not be unusual (Nyakanyanga, 2017). Those born with albinism suffer discrimination in some African communities. In dealing with such a situation after birthing a child with albinism, some parents name their children with names that express their disappointment or disillusionment. Thus, names such as "Ndomupeyi," a Shona name meaning "what will I give the child," and "Try again," meaning to re-do, are commonly given to children with albinism (Kadenge et al., 2014).

As in some African countries, some Shona and Ndebele communities in Zimbabwe view disability as a punishment to the mother by ancestors or God who are believed to be unhappy with their family or bewitchment by enemies (Rugoho & Maphosa, 2016). In many cases, the mother is deemed responsible and punished when the child is born disabled (Rugoho & Maphosa, 2016). As a result, the whole family and the community often withdraw their support to these mothers and their disabled children. Because of the belief that religious and traditional factors are behind the birth of a child with disabilities, upon the birth of a disabled child in a family, the family will be preoccupied with curing the disability of the child in a traditional way; hence, rituals to cleanse the disability of the child are in many cases done as seen in this example: *"I was taken up a mountain and left overnight on the mountain on my own. They were to collect me the following morning; traditional rituals were performed. It was expected that was the way of really helping me out. It was terrible"* (Chimedza & Peters, 2001, p. 157).

A survey done by PASSOP in 2020 on refugee mothers of disabled children in the Western Cape also shows that the above-cited ritual is one typical example among many other rituals of how disabled people, especially children with disabilities in Zimbabwe, are treated by their families and their communities in trying to eliminate disability (PASSOP, 2017, 2020, 2022). During these rituals, mothers may also face ill-treatment from their family members and community members, sometimes resulting in being beaten or abused. Mothers are often forced to be "cleansed" with their children (PASSOP, 2017, 2022). In addition, the survey found that several children did not survive these rituals, dying in the "ritual process" (PASSOP, 2017, 2020, 2022). The above scenario illustrates how in many instances a disabled child from a young age in Zimbabwe is cultured to believe they are inferior, unworthy, unclean, and need cleaning to be like others. When these disabilities are inevitably not eliminated by rituals, the child is often faced with further discrimination, thereby reducing the child's ability to reach their goals, as they face enormous challenges in accessing basic services, thus, challenges in accessing education and accessing of healthcare services (Muderedzi & Ingstad, 2011; UNICEF, 2013). Peace and the idea of inclusive societies, as desired by SDG16, are thus compromised.

The above situation as reported by Chimedza and Peters (2001) is also confirmed by a study commissioned by UNICEF, where those close to a mother of a disabled child see the birth of a disabled child as a punishment on the family (UNICEF, 2013). Parents of disabled children revealed that family members would have an interest came to support them during rituals to cleanse children with disabilities. This means that family members were not interested in the disabled child but in eliminating the impairment or misfortune from the family. Unfortunately, such attitudes and religious traditional beliefs are still prevalent towards disability, even though people do not publicly show that they still exist (Avoke, 2002; Choruma, 2007; Rugoho & Maphosa, 2017).

There is a general expectation in Zimbabwe that children "bring happiness to marriage and that being a real woman is measured by giving birth to a 'normal' child" (Choruma, 2007). However, when a child has a disability, the mother's happiness in the Zimbabwean context may be short-lived. The whole family and community marginalize the mother once a child's disability is announced (Rugoho & Maphosa, 2017). This affects the mother's well-being and extends to the child's well-being (Rugoho & Maphosa, 2017). The birth of a disabled child often tears families apart (Choruma, 2007). Divorce among parents of disabled children is common in Zimbabwe (Rugoho & Maphosa, 2017). It is considered acceptable for relatives on the father's side to stop supporting the mother and child after the birth of a disabled child (Choruma, 2007; Rugoho & Maphosa, 2017).

The experience shared by Tatenda with Charowa (2005), whose child is disabled, explains how Zimbabwean fathers can easily divorce their wives on the grounds of a child born with a disability: *"I separated from my husband, who could not come to terms with the disability of our child and was under pressure from his relatives"* (Charowa, 2005, p. 2).

The Shona and the Ndebele traditions from Zimbabwe hide children with disabilities away from people to cope with the child's condition and maintain social status in the community (Rugoho & Maphosa, 2017). UNESCO (2001, p. 10) found out that:

> [o]ften, these children are excluded from society. For example, they might be hidden away at home if they look different because of fear and superstition. ... Often, their needs are not recognized, and they are thought to have little to contribute to their community. However, this exclusion reduces children's opportunities to learn, grow, and develop.

For Zimbabwean refugee mothers of children living with disabilities in the Western Cape Town Province of South Africa, their experiences before the migration included isolation and rejection by the family where they were married and the community at large because of having given birth to a disabled child. Such awful experiences of isolation by their people in their own country may contribute to psychological problems for these refugee mothers and their children and may have led to them fleeing (Rugoho & Maphosa, 2017).

In general, many persons with disabilities in Zimbabwe are poor and always excluded from their communities (Rugoho & Siziba, 2014; UNESCO, 2020). In addition, the existing hostile beliefs towards those living with disabilities, poverty, and HIV/AIDS worsen their situation (Ngazi et al., 2004)

The Zimbabwean culture and traditional beliefs shape how these mothers of disabled children are treated and interact with their community (Rugoho & Maphosa, 2017). Choruma (2006, 2007) and Rugoho (2017) report on the connection between perceptions of impairment and a non-human "liminal" status. This is the case in many developing countries but seems widespread in Zimbabwe, where people's perception of impairment is often reported as the reason for excluding persons in their communities (Chimedza & Peters, 2001; Rugoho & Siziba, 2014).

This exclusion of the disabled community in Zimbabwe pre-dates colonization, as disabled people have historically been side-lined and seen as less important than others. The terms "*Isilima*" (Ndebele) and "*chirema*" (an animal referent in the Shona language "*chi*" begins the word "*rema*") are common negative phrases used in Zimbabwe to refer to a disabled person, meaning unable or stupid. Disabled people are perceived to be physically present but without social value. Consequently, a person with a disability is seen as "like" a human but also "like" an animal, an incomplete human (Devlieger, 1998).

For Tilstone (2003) and Koszela (2013), traditional beliefs are difficult to eliminate as all community beliefs are centred on them. For example, a strong cultural belief exists in Zimbabwe that a pregnant woman is not allowed to stare or socialize with a disabled person to avoid giving birth to a disabled child. Our experience working with migrants living with disabilities shows that this belief is common among some Zimbabweans. For example, at a workshop that was to address documentation challenges faced by Zimbabwean migrants in Cape Town on 17 August 2018, at least one pregnant refugee mother and volunteer at PASSOP wondered what the possibilities were of her giving birth to a disabled child since there were disabled people in the same workshop and since this would not be the last workshop she would attend before giving birth.

The mother was only asserting the existence of the belief among some Zimbabweans that a pregnant woman must spit on her tummy whenever she meets a disabled person for her child not to be born disabled. This pregnant mother could not anticipate spitting at her tummy whenever she met a disabled person in the workshop. The mother was fully aware that our organization was going to have these workshops for the following two months, and she was going to meet people with disabilities. Such a belief is widespread in Zimbabwe, and it is a very dangerous belief as it leads to the isolation of disabled people. What society believes to be the cause of disability is usually adopted by families.

For some Christian believers in Zimbabwe, a child can only be disabled because the mother disobeyed God's commandments (Mukushi et al., 2019b; United Nation Education, Scientific and Cultural Organization (UNESCO),

2020). A study found that in Mayamba village in the Mashonaland West Province of Zimbabwe, disability is regarded as a punishment from God, and family members do not want to make it public and, as a result, lock up their disabled relatives (Moyo, 2019). According to UNESCO (2020), the reason why those who are disabled are locked up in the house is that they feel embarrassed by this punishment of a disabled family member by God. The UNESCO (2020) findings concur with Mabvurira, Makhubele, and Mukushi (2019a), who, in their study entitled "Cultural and Religious Beliefs and Practices Abusive to Children with Disabilities in Zimbabwe," found out that disability in Zimbabwe is believed to be a punishment from God for sins that one committed. The Bible in Exodus presents children with disabilities as suffering because of the wrong deeds of their parents (Miles, 2006). Some members in some churches, such as the Apostolic Faith Mission in Zimbabwe, believe prayer can cure disability, hence, preaches the gospel of healing (Sande, 2019). In his study entitled "Pastoral Ministry and Persons with Disabilities: The Case of the Apostolic Faith Mission in Zimbabwe," Sande (2019) reported that when he attended an AFM conference in Zimbabwe in August 2016, he heard the preacher calling persons with disabilities to come for a healing prayer (Sande, 2019). This shows that some churches believe disability can be cured by prayer.

## Discussion

Literature on the perception and treatment of a mother of a disabled child in Zimbabwe points to why these mothers end up living in neighbouring countries as refugees, especially in South Africa. Some cultures in Zimbabwe are very hostile towards a mother of a disabled child or those living with disabilities (Choruma, 2007; Rugoho & Maphosa, 2017). Deducing from all these factors, Zimbabwean mothers of disabled children may find themselves under difficult conditions to live with disabled children in Zimbabwe, hence, the reason for their migration to South Africa.

## Supernatural Causes

The belief that child disability or any form of disability is naturally caused is widespread in Zimbabwe. The causes of child disability or disability in Zimbabwe are connected to gods, ancestors, God, or evil spirits (Makamure, 2018; Rugoho & Maphosa, 2016). The mother is believed to have done something wrong to God or the ancestors, hence punished with a disabled child (Rugoho & Maphosa, 2017). Chimedza and Peters (2001) reported on the belief among some communities in Zimbabwe that the disability of the child is associated with the ancestors or God. Therefore, the disabled child is given as a form of punishment to the mother for having disobeyed God or the ancestors (Charowa, 2005). This finding by Chimedza and Peters (2001) and Charowa (2005) is further confirmed by the UNESCO's (2020) report entitled

"Interface of Disability, Gender and Culture in Zimbabwe Perspectives of Communities." *This report revealed that* some communities in Zimbabwe view a mother of a disabled child as being punished by the ancestors. This lack of understanding of the causes of child disability in Zimbabwe adds to the stigma experienced by mothers of disabled children in some Zimbabwean societies (Choruma, 2007; Rugoho & Maphosa, 2016). Because of such religious beliefs (Christian or African) in the family and community, mothers are mistreated and rejected by those who are supposed to support them. When there is a lack of support for a mother of a disabled child from those close to them, mothers may only be left with one option: to relocate to a place where they feel safe and welcome with their disabled children.

Because of the shame associated with the birth of a disabled child in Zimbabwe, families' focus is no longer on the child but on how to cure the disability traditionally (Chimedza & Peters, 2001). In other words, the families' focus is on curing the disability of the child. This, in many cases, is done using harmful untested traditional methods. Kajawu et al. (2016) reported on herbal formulas that are given in different ways to cure living with disabilities, especially those suffering from mental disorders. Besides formulas given to those who are disabled in a bid to cure them, Chimedza and Peters (2001) reported on how one late Zimbabwean activist, who was born with a disability, was taken to the mountain and left at the mountain for a night in order to cure the disability. Such treatment to a disabled person and the parents, in this case, the mother, may be harmful. Certain types of disability in Zimbabwe, for example, mental illness (*chipengo*) among the Karanga tribe, are best treated by the diviner—herbalist (Soko & Kubik, 2008). The patient is made to inhale steam from boiling water mixed with herbs, some seeds, and some medicinal plants placed on burning coal (Soko & Kubik, 2008). Such unscientifically tested methods are not only harmful to disabled people but can even lead to the death of the person.

Studies done in Zimbabwe on traditional methods used to cure disability resonate with some studies in some African countries. For example, in Kenya, like in Zimbabwe, some traditional methods of curing disability are very abusive and, at times, involve beating or lashing (Werner, 2011). In Malawi, mental illness in the Tumbuka tribe is believed to be cured by preparing and administering "more powerful" medicine to neutralize and exorcize the evil spirits and spells that had caused the mental illness (Soko & Kubik, 2008). In their study, The World Health Organization & Mental Health and Poverty Project, Mental Health and Development (2010) found out that a traditional method known as the "hyena cure" is practised in Somalia—where a person with a mental health condition is thrown into a pit with one or more hyenas that have been starved of food on the basis that the hyenas will scare away the djinns, or evil spirits, that inhabit the person.

Further to some of the harmful methods used to cure child disability in Zimbabwe, literature on the lived experiences of mothers of children with disability in Zimbabwe shows that these mothers are continuously subjected to various consequences. These consequences include mothers being abused, being denied participation, losing support, being rejected, and being divorced (Choruma, 2007). In their study entitled "Ostracised: Experiences of Mothers of Children with Disabilities in Zimbabwe," Rugoho and Maphosa (2017) found out that mothers of disabled children are beaten or humiliated for birthing a disabled child. According to Choruma (2007), mothers of disabled children in Zimbabwe are physically abused for giving birth to a disabled child. Such forms of abuse may have led mothers of disabled children to migrate to South Africa.

Besides mothers facing various forms of abuse, literature shows that, because of birthing a disabled child, mothers of disabled children in Zimbabwe face discrimination (Chimedza & Peters, 2001; Choruma, 2007). This finding is similar to what was established by Rugoho and Maphosa (2017), where some stigma in some communities in Zimbabwe leads to discrimination against a disabled person and their families.

The available literature also shows that discrimination against people with disabilities is common in some other African countries. According to McConkey, Kahonde, and McKenzie, (2016) disabled children in most developing countries face discrimination as they are hiden away or not allowed to participate in some activities because of the shame attached to the disability of the child. In some instances, due to misguided beliefs, children who have epilepsy have been denied education (Barauchi, 2011). In Ghana, people who are deaf are considered not suitable for attaining education (Ogoko, 2013).

As if abuse and discrimination based on giving birth are not enough, mothers of disabled children are divorced when their partners realize their children are disabled (Choruma, 2007; Rugoho & Maphosa, 2017). Dube et al. (2021) also found that some women are divorced by their partners for birthing a disabled child.

## Expanding the Scope of Peacebuilding in Africa for Sustainable Development

The preceding sections confirm the exclusion, marginalization, trauma, and stigmatization that mothers of children with disability (and their children) face in Zimbabwe, as well in South Africa upon completing their migrant journeys. We recognize that without inclusion and acceptance, the mothers of children with disability and their children feature prominently among those "left behind." This is contrary to the vision of the SDGs that seek to ensure that there is no one left behind. In particular, their situation is contrary to the vision of SDG 16, which aspires for "peaceful and inclusive societies for sustainable development." We contend that the experiences of Zimbabwean mothers of children with disability in South Africa call for an expansion of the notion of peacebuilding. While some scholars have reflected on the contribution of women with disability to peacebuilding (see e.g., Ortoleva, 2010 and

Fubara-Manuel & Ngwobia, 2021), there is currently very limited material on what peacebuilding means to mothers of children with disability, as well as to children with disability themselves.

We are of the view that peacebuilding for migrant mothers of children with disability and the children with disability implies responding to the stigma and discrimination that they experience. In order for them to regain peace of mind, there is a need for trauma counselling, as well as for their practical needs to be addressed. Peace can be achieved through the healing of memories, a profound shift from the prevailing societal attitude, and the emergence of a culture of embrace. There are adequate resources in the religions of Zimbabwe and South Africa (and globally) that can contribute towards the emergence of more liberating and inclusive attitudes towards mothers of children with disability in South Africa and Zimbabwe. Insights from African women scholars in theology and religious studies on disability (see, e.g., Chisale, 2018) would be valuable, since the mothers, by giving birth to children with disability, become themselves "disabled." The overall thrust would be to ensure that religions become sources of acceptance, inclusion, liberation, and development for mothers of children with disability and the children themselves. Further, religion would be deployed to revamp the context of migration from exclusion and stigma to that of inclusion and embrace.

## Conclusion

This chapter's main conclusions are drawn from when these mothers were in Zimbabwe. During this period in Zimbabwe, these refugee mothers faced numerous challenges as they were socially excluded and rejected by their families and communities for birthing disabled children. Due to the social and cultural beliefs found in many communities in Zimbabwe, disability is taboo, leaving mothers of disabled children marginalized. Literature on the lived experiences of mothers of disabled children in Zimbabwe shows that social exclusion and rejection are the main challenges faced by mothers of disabled children in most communities of Zimbabwe. Therefore, this chapter demonstrates that the interest in migrating these mothers was not only political or economic. Migration also resulted from traditional beliefs hostile towards mothers of disabled children in Zimbabwe. The chapter thus contributes to how to further SDGs 16's call for promoting peaceful and inclusive societies for sustainable development, providing access to justice for all, and building effective, accountable, and inclusive institutions at all levels. Mothers of children with disabilities and the children with disabilities themselves are often excluded from the mainstream societal process, thus, subjected to structural, cultural, and symbolic violence. In pursuit of this SDG, a comprehensive analysis of the factors that undermine peace and inclusion should go beyond economic and political factors to consider rarely foregrounded ones such as religion and traditional beliefs. The chapter proceeds to propose an expanded model of peacebuilding where the psychosocial and practical needs of the mothers and the children are met, thereby securing their peace of mind and enabling them to flourish.

**Acknowledgment** This work was carried out with support from the CGIAR Initiative on Climate Resilience, ClimBeR, and the CGIAR Initiative on Fragility, Conflict, and Migration. We would like to thank all funders who supported this research through their contributions to the CGIAR Trust Fund: https://www.cgiar.org/funders/.

## References

Africa Check. (2017). How Many Zimbabweans Live in South Africa? The Numbers are Unreliable: [Online]. https://africacheck.org/reports/how many-Zimbabweans-live in-south-Africa-the-numbers are unreliable/ (2022, the 20th of November).

African Union. (2020). Africa Migration Report. [Online]. https://au.int/en/documents/20201015/africa-migration-report (2022, the 10th of December).

Amnesty International. (2019). *South Africa: Living in Limbo: Rights of Asylum Seekers Denied*. Johannesburg: Amnesty International. [Online]. https://www.amnesty.org/en/documents/afr53/0983/2019/en/ (2022, the 20th of November).

Arfa, S., Solvang, P. K., Berg, B., et al. (2020). Disabled and Immigrant, a Double Minority Challenge: A Qualitative Study about the Experiences of Immigrant Parents of Children with Disabilities Navigating Health and Rehabilitation Services in Norway. *BMC Health Services Research, 20*, 134. https://doi.org/10.1186/s12913-020-5004-2

Avoke, M. (2002). Models of Disability in the Labelling and Attitudinal Discourse in Ghana. *Disability and Society, 17*, 769–777. https://doi.org/10.1080/0968759022000039064

Batalova, J., Shymonyak, A., & Mittelstadt, M. (2020). *Immigration Data Matters*. Washington, DC: Migration Policy Institute. [Online]. https://www.migrationpolicy.org/sites/default/files/publications/data-matters-nov2020-update_final.pdf (2022, the 12th of July).

Charowa, G. (2005). Body Blows New International Magazine: Poverty and Gender NI 384 [Online]. www.newintlorg/issues384/bodyblows.htm (2022, the 15th of August).

Chen, W., Hall, B. J., Ling, L., & Renzaho, A. M. (2017). Pre-migration and Post-migration Factors Associated with Mental Health in Humanitarian Migrants in Australia and the Moderation Effect of Post-migration Stressors: Findings from the First Wave Data of the BNLA Cohort Study. *The Lancet Psychiatry, 4*(3), 218–229.

Chifamba, C. (2020). Africa Report. Zimbabwe's Economic Woes: Sanctions or Poor Governance? [Online]. https://www.theafricareport.com/128007/zimbabwes-economic-woes-sanctions-or-poor-governance/ (2022, the 24th of June).

Chimedza, T. M., & Poters, Z. (2001). Disability issues in inclusive schools. *A Zimbabwean Perspective*. Pretoria: Sage Publications.

Chisale, S. S. (2018). 'Disabled Motherhood in an African Community': Towards an African Women Theology of Disability. *In die Skriflig, 52*(1), a2375. https://doi.org/10.4102/ids.v52i1.2375

Choruma, T. R. (2007). *The forgotten tribe*. London: Progressio.

Claasens, L. J., Shaikh, S., & Swartz, L. (2018). Engaging Disability and Religion in the Global South. In B. Watermeyer, J. McKenzie, & L. Swartz (Eds.), *The Palgrave Handbook of Disability and Citizenship in the Global South* (pp. 147–164). Palgrave Macmillan.

Consortium for Refugees and Migrants in South Africa (CoRMSA). (2011). Protecting Refugees, Asylum Seekers, and Immigrants in South Africa during 2010. CoRMSA. [Online]. http://www.cormsa.org.za/wpcontent/uploads/2008/06/CoRMSA-Report-2011.pdf (2022, the 4th of March).

Devlieger, P. J. (1998). (In) Competence in America in Comparative Perspective. In R. Jenkins (Ed.), *Questions of Competence* (pp. 54–75). Cambridge University Press.

Dube, T., Ncube, S. B., Mapuvire, C. C., Ndlovu, S., Ncube, C., & Mlotshwa, S. (2021). Interventions to Reduce the Exclusion of Children with Disabilities from Education: A Zimbabwean Perspective from the Field. *Cogent Social Sciences, 7*(1), 1913848. https://doi.org/10.1080/23311886.2021.1913848

Fubara-Manuel, J., & Ngwobia, J. M. (2021). Women with Disabilities, Peacebuilding and Development in Adamawa State, Nigeria. In A. Chitando (Ed.), *Women and Peacebuilding in Africa* (pp. 124–135). Routledge.

Jelinek-Menke, R. (2022). Dis/abling Religion: Introducing Dis/ability as a Social-Analytical Concept for the Study of Religions. *Zeitschrift für Religionswissenschaft, 30*(2), 300–320. https://doi.org/10.1515/zfr-2022-0016

Kadenge, M., Mabugu, P., Chivero, E., & Chiwara, R. (2014). Anthroponyms of Albinos among the Shona People of Zimbabwe. *Mediterranean Journal of Social Sciences, 5*(27 P3), 1230. https://www.mcser.org/journal/index.php/mjss/article/view/5202

Kajawu, L., et al. (2016). What do African Traditional Medical Practitioners do in the Treatment of Mental Disorders in Zimbabwe? *International Journal of Culture and Mental Health, 9*, 44–55.

Koszela, K. (2013). The Stigmatization of Disabilities in Africa and the Developmental Effects. *Independent Study Project (ISP) Collection*. 1639. [Online]. https://digitalcollections.sit.edu/isp_collection/1639 (2022, the 10th of October).

Makamure, C. (2018). Religion and Disability: A Reflection on the Role of Pentecostal Churches in Curbing Marginalization of People with Disability in Zimbabwe. [Online]. https://www.academia.edu/37604229/ (2022, the 21st of September).

Marceca, M., et al. (2019). Migrants' Health Protection: Socio-health and Legal Situation of Asylum Seekers and Refugees in Italy. In A. Krämer & F. Fischer (Eds.), *Refugee Migration and Health. Migration, Minorities and Modernity* (Vol. 4). Springer. https://doi.org/10.1007/978-3-030-03155-8_11

Mathekga, R. (2022). Migration Crisis in Southern Africa: [Online]. https://www.gisreportsonline.com/r/zimbabwe-immigration/ (2022, the 10th of October).

McConkey, R., Kahonde, C., & McKenzie, J. (2016). Tackling Stigma in Developing Countries: The Key Role of Families. In K. Scior & S. Werner (eds.). Intellectual Disability and Stigma: Stepping Out from the Margins. Palgrave Macmillan.

Meda, L. (2017). A Journey Without Planned Destination: Traumatic Transmigration Experiences of Refugee Children. *Journal of International Migration and Integration, 18*(1), 131–142. Springer.

Miles, M. (2006). Martin Luther and Childhood Disability in 16th Century Germany. What did He Write? What did He Say? *Journal of Religion, Disability and Health, 5*(4), 5–36. [Online]. https://doi.org/10.1300/J095v05n04_02 (2022, the 19th of September).

Misago, J. P., Landau, L. B., & Manson, T. (2009). Towards Tolerance, Law, and Dignity: Addressing Violence against Foreign Nationals in South Africa. IOM Regional Office for Southern Africa and the Department for International Development. University of Witwatersrand.

Moyo, J. (2019). Out of sight, out of mind: Zimbabwe locks up its disabled. Available at https://www.reuters.com/article/us-zimbabwe-disabled-idUSKCN1T1027, accessed 20 July 2023.

Muderedzi, J., & Ingstad, B. (2011). Disability and Social Suffering in Zimbabwe. In A. H. Eide & B. Ingstad (Eds.), *Disability and Poverty: A Global Challenge* (pp. 171–188). Policy Press.

Muenstermann, I. (Ed.). (2017). People's Movements in the 21st Century—Risks, Challenges and Benefits. *InTech*. https://doi.org/10.5772/63665

Mukushi, A. T., Makhubele, J. C., & Mabvurira, V. (2019a). Cultural and Religious Beliefs and Practices Abusive to Children With Disabilities in Zimbabwe. *Global Journal of Health Science, 11*(7), https://EconPapers.repec.org/RePEc:ibn:gjhsjl:v:11:y:2019:i:7:p:103

Mukushi, A. T., Mabvurira, V., Makhubele, J. C., & Matlakala, F. (2019b). Psychosocial Challenges Faced by Children in Residential Care Facilities. *Southern African Journal of Social Work and Social Development, 31*(2), 18. https://doi.org/10.25159/2415-5829/2892

Ngazi, P., et al. (2004). Disability and HIV and AIDS: A Participatory Rapid Assessment of the Vulnerability, Impact and Coping Mechanisms of Parents of Disabled Children. Bulawayo. Zimbabwe Parents of Handicapped Children.

Nyakanyanga, S. (2017). The New Humanitarian. When Having Children with a Disability Means Raising Them Alone. [Online]. https://deeply.thenewhumanitarian.org/womensadvancement/articles/2017/10/24/when-having-a-child-with-a-disability-means-raising-them-alone (2022, the 16th of September).

Ogoko, S. (2013). Interview on Disability Rights in Gabon, Harvard Project on Disability (On File with HPOD). The 27th of June 2013.

Ortoleva, S. (2010). Women with Disabilities: The Forgotten Peace Builders. *Loyola of Los Angeles International and Comparative Law Review, 33*, 83–142.

Owens, C., Dandy, J., & Hancock, P. (2016). Perceptions of Pregnancy Experiences When Using a Community-based Antenatal Service: A Qualitative Study of Refugee and Migrant Women in Perth, Western Australia. *Women and Birth: Journal of the Australian College of Midwives, 29*(2), 128–137.

PASSOP. 2017. PASSOP data base: New arrivals. Country of origin and reason for coming to South Africa.

PASSOP. 2020. PASSOP data base: New arrivals. Country of origin and reason for coming to South Africa.

PASSOP. 2022. PASSOP data base: New arrivals. Country of origin and reason for coming to South Africa.

Pearce, E. (2014). *Disability Inclusion: Translating Policy into Practice in Humanitarian Action*. New York: Women's Refugee Commission.

Pisoni, W. (2021). Intersectionality between Migrants and People with Disabilities. [Online]. https://pathforeurope.eu/intersectionality-between-migrants-and-people-with-disabilities/ (2022, the 25th of August).

Refugees Act. 1998. Republic of South Africa Government Gazette. *Refugees Act, 130*(1), 1–7.

Rugoho, T., & Maphosa, F. (2016). Ostracised: Experiences of Mothers of Children with Disabilities in Zimbabwe. *Gender Questions, 4*(1), 18. [Online]. https://doi.org/10.25159/2412-8457/1053 (2022, the 10th of October).

Rugoho, T., & Maphosa, F. (2017). Challenges Faced by Women with Disabilities in Accessing Sexual and Reproductive Health in Zimbabwe: The Case of Chitungwiza Town. *African Journal of Disability, 6*(0), a252. [Online]. https://doi.org/10.4102/ajod.v6i0.252 (2022, the 19th of October).

Rugoho, T., & Siziba, B. (2014). 'Rejected people: Beggars with disabilities in the City of Harare, Zimbabwe'. *Developing Country Studies, 4*(26), 51–56s.

Sande, N. (2019). Pastoral Ministry and Persons with Disabilities: The Case of the Apostolic Faith Mission in Zimbabwe. *African Journal of Disability, 8*(0), a431. https://doi.org/10.4102/ajod.v8i0.431

Silove, D., Ventevogel, P., & Rees, S. (2017). The Contemporary Refugee Crisis: An Overview of Mental Health Challenges. *World Psychiatry, 16,* 130–139. [Online]. https://doi.org/10.1002/wps.20438 (2022, the 7th of July).

Soko, B., & Kubik, G. (2008). *Nchimi Chikanga: The Battle Against Witchcraft in Malawi.* Kachere Series, Malawi.

Tilstone, C. (2003). Professional Development for Staff: Steps towards Developing Policies. In C. Tilstone & R. Rose (Eds.), *Strategies to Promote Inclusive Practice.* RoutledgeFalmer.

UNESCO. (2001). Promoting the Rights of Children with Disabilities. Innocenti Digest NO. 13. Innocenti Research Centre.

UNESCO. (2020). "Hear us too!" How to Improve the Lives and Rights of Persons with Disabilities in Zimbabwe? [Online]. https://en.unesco.org/news/hear-us-too-how-improve-lives-and-rights-persons-disabilities-zimbabwe (2022, the 18th of August).

UNHCR. (2020). Persons with Disabilities in the Context of Internal Displacement. Report of the Special Rapporteur on the Human Rights of Internally Displaced Persons* (A/HRC/44/41) (EN/AR/RU/ZH).

UNICEF. (2013). The State of the World's Children 2013: Children with Disabilities [Online]. https://www.unicef.org/media/84886/file/SOWC-2013.pdf

Werner, D. (2011). Foreword. In S. Kabue, E. Mombo, J. Galgalo, & C. B. Peter (Eds.), *Disability, Society and Theology: Voices from Africa* (pp. v–vii). Zapf Chancery Publishers Africa Ltd. https://doi.org/10.2307/j.ctvgc606m.2

Women's Refugee Commission (WRC). (2016). "Working to Improve Our Own Futures": Inclusion of Women and Girls with Disabilities in Humanitarian Action.

World Health Organization & Mental Health and Poverty Project, Mental Health and Development. (2010). ISBN:1-58030-159-2.

Zimbabwe National Statistics Agency. (2022). [Online]. https://www.zimstat.co.zw/wp content/uploads/2022/09/Migration_2022_PHC_Report_Final.pdf (2022, the 27 October).

CHAPTER 39

# Gender, SDG 16, Peacebuilding and Development in Kenya

*Loreen Maseno*

## Introduction

Research has shown that broader inclusivity in formal peace processes of women oftentimes plays a role in increasing the credibility of the peacebuilding process. At the same time, the frequent under-representation and participation of women continue to have adverse effects on any prospects for reaching durable agreements (Krause et al., 2018). It follows that women's consistent representation and participation in peace processes go a long way in contributing towards the sustainability of the peacebuilding processes. Unlike peacekeeping, peacebuilding has a more ambitious goal. Peacebuilding aims to foster the political, legal, economic and social transformation of post-conflict states. According to Potter, the active involvement of women in peacebuilding and development processes has been found to be more sustainable compared to those with no women's involvement (Potter, 2008). Out of that global context, a similar involvement can be traced among Kenyan women.

Kenyan women have been very active in peacebuilding in recent decades when post-election violence became the norm in the country. Sampson (1997) identifies several reasons for this increased activity to include the fact that Kenyan women find themselves organized at national and international levels

---

L. Maseno (✉)
Department of Religion, Theology and Philosophy, Maseno University, Maseno, Kenya

Faculty of Theology, University of Pretoria, Pretoria, South Africa

© The Author(s), under exclusive license to Springer Nature Switzerland AG 2023
S. M. Kilonzo et al. (eds.), *The Palgrave Handbook of Religion, Peacebuilding, and Development in Africa*,
https://doi.org/10.1007/978-3-031-36829-5_39

and so offer existing channels for communication and organization. It is clear that in Kenya, women have not been passive in development and peacebuilding efforts, as they are actively involved in peace advocacy; by waging conflict non-violently in pursuit of democracy and human rights, they also take up the roles of relief workers, mediators, and trauma healing counsellors, among others, and participate in development and decision-making processes (Onsanti, 2014, p. 3). The aforementioned interventions by women highlight the United Nations Sustainable Development Goal (SDG) 16 whose focus is to promote peaceful and inclusive societies for sustainable development, provide access to justice for all and build effective, accountable and inclusive institutions at all levels. This SDG has targets which consider the terrain in which different nation states find themselves. A consideration of SDG 16 in the Kenyan context shall proceed by unpacking four SDG 16 targets, namely, targets one, three, seven and ten, as exemplified within the Kenyan context. A closer analysis of this SDG uncovers the essence of involving women and children in efforts of peace, justice and development. Many women in Kenya have been included in measures taken at the community level and have been able to reach many others to spur one another towards sustainable development in the face of peace and inclusion. This chapter therefore embarks on tying together these aspects of gender, SDG 16 for peacebuilding and development in Kenya.

## THE PEACEBUILDING AND DEVELOPMENT LANDSCAPE IN KENYA

Peacebuilding as a concept encompasses not only internationally led forms of intervention, but also bottom-up and locally led approaches. It is not only restricted to post-war processes, but its methods are relevant during all phases of conflict transformation, from preventive diplomacy to peace processes and recovery. In general, peacebuilding efforts can be employed before, during and after violent conflict occurs, by a wide range of actors in government and civil society and at various levels as enumerated by Duncanson (2016).

Peacebuilding strategies seek to address all three dimensions of violent conflict (behavioural, attitudinal and structural). These share a common focus on methods to mitigate tension and adversity even as they seek to de-escalate the level of violent conflict. According to Lederach, peacebuilding at the attitudinal level seeks to redefine violent relationships into constructive and cooperative patterns through formal or informal dialogue and reconciliation efforts (1997, p. 71). Further, he points out that transformation in any conflict must be integrated into a systemic approach with a predominant focus on relationship, which is described as "the basis of both the conflict and its long-term solution" (1997, p. 26). In general, Lederach proposes a conceptual framework which includes the structure concerned with the systematic elements in a protracted conflict. Lederach also emphasizes process, which includes the long-term nature of the conflict as progresses, reconciliation, which stresses on full range of psychological dimensions central to conflict transformation and resources. Lederach, therefore, focuses on transforming violent destructive conflict into constructive, peaceful relationships as exemplified by Sampson (1997, p. 277). On the African continent, scholars have aptly shown the place of religion in peacebuilding (Alfani, 2019; Maseno, 2020; Chitando & Tarusarira, 2019). They show that religious actors play a significant role in peacebuilding efforts. Many religious practitioners and leaders, whether Muslims, Christians or Traditionalists, often end up at the forefront in peace meetings and in arbitration. At the same time, peacebuilding has been shown to be an important ingredient for sustainable development.

The rights-based approach to development considers specific ways in which sustainable development is interlinked to human rights and how achieving these may transform human societies (Njoh, 2006). Over the years, the human rights approach was embraced by development actors to include an understanding of development and human rights as interwoven and to include the principles of accountability, empowerment, participation, equality and equity in development programmes (Tomalin, 2006, p. 93). The human rights approach is still relevant in Kenya as it offers a coherent and consistent framework that is grounded in a consensual global regime. According to Petersen (2015), it has the potential to make people actively aware of their rights, empower people as holders of rights, assign duties to the people and address structural inequalities. Instrumentally, this approach improves development outcomes which lead to more effective poverty reduction. One critique, however, is that the rights-based approach is deemed capable of marginalizing people from the South when it does not take into consideration the social, cultural and religious milieu which shapes social ethics, as described by Petersen (2015, pp. 361–362).

Just like development has been embraced from the bottom up, in Kenya, so is peacebuilding which includes and involves the often marginalized sections of the population, such as women and children (Agengo, 2009). The bottom-up perspective allows that participation, equality and equity are entrenched in the processes of peacebuilding, gender and development. Adam Curle is known to have pioneered the idea of peacebuilding from below, currently recognized as a leading mode of peace-making amongst practitioners and academics. Curle developed a peace-making framework that emphasized the importance of a balance of power between conflicting parties. Primarily, Curle envisioned and explained how peacebuilding requires restructuring relationships between the two conflicting parties, thereby ensuring empowering of the weaker party and addressing structural sources of inequality (Woodhouse, 2010; Maseno, 2020).

For many women in the peace and development arena, the effectiveness and sustainability of peace and development cannot be achieved through the manipulation of peace agreements by those who have vested interests. Rather, communities of women, men and children are to be involved from the grassroots up. This school of thought advocates for bottom–top peacebuilding and development. The evolution of the thinking about the complex dynamics and processes of post-conflict peacebuilding and development has brought about the popularity of the concept of peacebuilding from below and what

Lederach calls indigenous empowerment. This form of peacebuilding seeks to empower people of goodwill in conflict-afflicted communities to rebuild democratic institutions as demonstrated by Ramsbotham (2007, p. 219).

In general, peacebuilding and development work over the long run and at all levels of society to establish and sustain relationships among people who are rooted locally and engage globally, which provides an environment for progress and development. Strategic peacebuilding and development connect people and groups of communities on the ground, at the very bottom, with policymakers and powerbrokers such as governments, corporations and banks, with the aim to build sustainable societies, institutions, policies and relationships that are better able to sustain development and peacebuilding (Ashworth & Ryan, 2013). All efforts towards peacebuilding and development, which are also captured in SDG 16, address issues of human rights, economic prosperity and environmental sustainability, stretching across generations. The Kenyan Nobel Laureate Prof. Wangari Maathai was able to embody a new vision of peace that connected peace-making with environmental stewardship. She was keen to convey the message of peace through sustainable development and the proper utilization of resources. As founder of the Green Belt Movement, she spearheaded a pathway to peace through the integration of tree planting and consciousness-raising. Her route to peacebuilding was through tree planting in order to bring together community-building efforts as well as environmental awareness (Anderson, 2014).

While it engages in immediate crises, peacebuilding is a long-term vocation that requires the building of cross-group networks and alliances that will survive intermittent conflicts and create a platform for sustainable human development and security. In what follows, SDG 16, which is closely linked with peace and sustainable development, shall be unpacked with reference to Kenya.

## SDG 16 in the Kenyan Context

In September 2015, world leaders adopted the 2030 Agenda for Sustainable Development and its 17 goals that cut across disciplines, sectors and institutional mandates, acknowledging the integrated nature of the many challenges that humanity faces—from gender inequality to inadequate infrastructure, from youth unemployment to environmental degradation. In the preamble to the 2030 Agenda, world leaders affirmed that they are determined to protect the planet from degradation, including through sustainable consumption and production, sustainably managing its natural resources and taking urgent action on climate change so that it can support the needs of the present and future generations.

The 2030 Agenda for Sustainable Development explicitly recognizes the strong impact violence and insecurity have on development and vice versa, stating that "there can be no sustainable development without peace and no peace without sustainable development". The Agenda 2030 includes peace as a cross-cutting focus area alongside four other critical areas—people, prosperity, planet and partnerships—and has its own "peace goal", SDG 16 of Peace, Justice and Strong Institutions. The principles of the rule of law—which include elements such as equality, equity, inclusion, rights, laws and institutions—are embedded throughout the 2030 Agenda for Sustainable Development and well-articulated in Sustainable Development Goal (SDG) 16. At the same time, the rule of law drives should anchor development and peacebuilding efforts at local and global levels.

Goal 16 is thus framed, "Promote peaceful and inclusive societies for sustainable development, provide access to justice for all and build effective, accountable and inclusive institutions at all levels". Sustainable Development Goal 16 requires all countries to promote peaceful and inclusive societies for sustainable development. Peace remains a very important element for any development to take place in a nation. That is why peace is given attention even in the future plans of the 2030 agenda together with other factors such as development. SDG 16 is fundamental because it frames the promotion of sustainable peace as a development issue with the involvement of women.

SDG 16 is about "peace, justice and strong institution". What is peace? A state or period in which there is no war or a war has ended (Retallic, 2019). The Kenya national anthem echoes the aspirations of many Kenyans, which include justice, peace, unity, liberty, plenty and the building of the nation jointly. As women and children sing this anthem, it is clear in their minds that, devoid of peace, many more women and children shall suffer and be displaced across nations and refugee camps.

A key peacebuilding legal framework is the Constitution of Kenya which clearly outlines a number of stakeholders, such as the judiciary, which has a crucial role in conflict management. The preamble to the Constitution underscores the aspiration for Kenyans to live peacefully and in harmony as one independent nation, irrespective of existing religious, ethnic and cultural diversity. The advancement of durable peace and security is embodied in the Constitution. Article 238 refers to national security as "the protection against internal and external threats to Kenya's territorial integrity and sovereignty, its people, their rights, freedoms, property, peace, stability and prosperity, and other national interests".

In Kenya, the Constitution provides a platform for addressing challenges that can generate conflict and weaken national cohesion. For example, it promotes the establishment of a devolved system of government which addresses the unequal distribution of economic and political resources that may cause conflicts. Also, it offers opportunities to strengthen platforms and mechanisms towards development and progress.

What is justice? The quality of being just, righteousness, equitableness or moral rightness. Chapter 10 of the Kenyan Constitution offers provisions for the judiciary, which plays a crucial role in the resolution of various disputes through official means. Another instrument available for women and others in Kenya is the National Policy on Peacebuilding and Conflict Management

(2015) to guarantee stability and create a long-lasting solution to violent conflicts. It provides a mechanism for coordination and synergy-building among key stakeholders involved in peacebuilding and conflict management. It also offers a regulatory framework for resource allocation to government-driven peace interventions that ensure real-time responses to conflict issues. Another instrument is the Truth, Justice and Reconciliation Act No. 6 of 2008 to advance peace, national unity, justice, healing and reconciliation among Kenyans through establishing complete and precise historical data of human rights abuses. Other instruments include the National Action Plan on Arms Control and Management (2006).

It is only in a democracy with strong institutions, which will be able to produce the essential elements of a fully democratic government through proper separation of powers, thereby enabling a system which allows for checks and balances of the various arms of government. In what follows, we proceed to consider SDG 16 with specific reference to women, development and peacebuilding in Kenya.

## Unpacking Some Targets of SDG 16[1] in Relation to Women, Peacebuilding and Development in Kenya

It is clear that when both women and men have access to justice and the rule of law, they are able to resolve conflicts, claim their rights, and seek and obtain remedies. The application and careful adherence to the rule of law in peacebuilding and development help to level the playing field between majorly vulnerable women and the powerful by addressing issues of impunity, corruption and discrimination. This angle and content of SDG make SDG 16 a critical driver for the achievement of all other SDGs.

Without respect for the rule of law, neither food security nor gender equality, neither poverty eradication nor economic development can be advanced for women and children in communities at the grassroots. Building institutions for peace and justice strengthens accountability, empowers women and girls and fights corruption, which is key to promoting inclusive economic growth, as noted by Agengo (2009).

Engaging in policy dialogue with governments, donors and policy thinkers at global and national levels highlights the significance of the rule of law for the achievement of Agenda 2030. Its advocacy was backed by robust research drawing on the lessons learned from programmatic experience. Goal 16 has ten "outcome targets". These targets include the following:

---

[1] Metadata-Millennium Development Goals-16.pdf visited on 22.10.22.

## Target 16.1 Significantly Reduces All Forms of Violence and Related Death Rates Everywhere

Researching violence against women to provide a suitable and practical guide for activists, Ellsberg and Heise (2005) show that 30 years ago, violence against women was not considered an issue worth international attention or concern. Victims of violence suffered in silence and shame. Gender-based violence (GBV) continued to happen when the victims and those who knew about it did not discuss it openly in our communities. However, Ellsberg and Heise show that in the 1980s, things began to change. For over three decades, women's advocacy groups around the world have been working to draw more attention to the physical, psychological and sexual abuse of women and to stimulate action. These groups decided to advocate for good health, justice and safety for women. Advocacy in this regard referred to a deliberate process, based on demonstrated evidence, to directly or indirectly influence decision-makers and stakeholders to support and implement actions that contribute to the well-being, mental, emotional and overall health of women.

Gender-based violence is associated with serious health problems affecting both women and children, including injuries, gynaecological disorders, mental health disorders, adverse pregnancy outcomes and sexually transmitted infections. For many women and girls, sexual coercion and abuse are defining features of their lives. It is also a violation of women's human rights. This violation against women has devastating effects on women's sexual and reproductive health. Ellsberg and Heise (2005) agree that violence against women is a serious health and development concern. There is a clear link between violence against women, health, peacebuilding and development in as far as women who are battered cannot engage in wholesome development owing to their health status, whether physical, mental or emotional. This target therefore brings a sharp focus to sensitize communities to uphold peacebuilding in homes and neighbourhoods. At the same time, it ensures that the most vulnerable in society are not victims of violence in any form.

The United Nations General Assembly defined gender-based violence as violence against women as any act that results in, or is likely to result in, physical, sexual or psychological harm or suffering to women, including threats of such acts, coercion or arbitrary deprivations of liberty, whether occurring in public or in private. In Kenya, violence against women is a manifestation of historically unequal power relations between men and women, which have led to the domination over and discrimination against women by men and by which women are forced into a subordinate position compared to men. According to Onditi and Odera (2021), there is an urgent need for scholars, practitioners and the community at large to not only have an in-depth understanding of the issues, policies and strategies surrounding violence against women but also comprehend the various strategies for addressing the symptoms and root causes of the same in sub-Saharan Africa.

It is noted in strongest terms that gender-based violence is a pandemic globally, regionally and nationally. The vice affects those outside the church and those in the church. According to Emily Onyango (2018), gender-based violence is a result of patriarchy, masculinity and social and economic factors. The pandemic stretches to workplace and institutions of learning. According to Jane Godia (2020), Western Kenya and Nyanza regions, as well as the capital city of Nairobi, report the highest level of physical and sexual abuse committed by spouses. At the 2020 national launching of the international campaign 16 Days of Activism Against Gender-Based Violence, Kenya's cabinet secretary for public service, youth and gender affairs noted the shocking state of gender-based violence in Kenya. Statistics indicate that five in every ten women in Kenya in the age bracket of 15–49 (about 47%) have suffered one or another form of violence. About 40% of women within that same bracket have also been victims of violence. There have been numerous reports of gender-based physical and gender-based sexual violence across Kenya. The Kenya Demographic and Health Survey of 2014 noted that 45% of women aged 15–49 had experienced physical violence since age 15 within the 12 months prior to the survey. Fourteen per cent of women aged 15–49 report having experienced sexual violence at least once in their lifetime (KDHS, 2014).

Busia and Vihiga counties in Western Kenya are reported to have exhibited the highest cases of gender-based violence. Many leaders in Western Kenya are worried about rising cases of gender-based violence in the area (Wanambisi, 2013). This high rate of violence against women in Kenya has had a negative impact on development and peacebuilding, as many women continue to be left out. Primarily, such women do not enjoy their basic freedoms, rights and liberties by which they can be able to contribute to sustainable development. Many of these women suffer psychosocial challenges, and their self-esteem is affected. In all, these women cannot contribute to development and peacebuilding programmes as their own rights are violated, and they are in a situation devoid of accountability, empowerment, participation and equality.

The link between this target of SDG 16 in relation to women, peacebuilding and development in Kenya is aptly demonstrated through a column by Henry Kahara in the monthly magazine of Peace Initiative Kenya (PIK), *Tusemezane* (2014). This magazine started in 2012 with the main purpose of supporting the prevention of gender-based violence and improving the current response frameworks at the national and local levels. This initiative seeks to discourage violence against women of any form and, in so doing, works on peace initiatives in the communities at large. The magazine articulates how gender-based violence is a common phenomenon in Kenya and that sexual and gender-based violence, including rape cases, has become so rampant in Kenya. In general, this magazine encourages peace initiatives geared at eliminating forms of violence and encouraging development from the grassroots.

## Target 16.3 Promote the Rule of Law at the National and International Levels and Ensure Equal Access to Justice for All

This target considers that both women and men in Kenya abide within the confines of the law, and in the event that one is aggrieved, one can be able to access justice in a timely manner. The Kenyan constitution provides channels in which aggrieved parties can seek justice. It values peace and justice, calling for stronger judicial systems that will enforce laws and work towards a more peaceful and just society.

All women need to be able to turn to a fair and effective institution to access justice and important services. There are policies and regulations in place by the government of Kenya to prevent and control various forms of violence against women and children, including in the Constitution of Kenya (2010), the Sexual Offences Act (2006), the Children's Act (2001), the Penal Code (2009) and the National Gender and Equality Commission Act (2011). However, the problem persists across the country. Peacebuilding in Kenya presupposes that there are available channels and institutions that can ensure restitution if the need arises so as to deter others from harming people. In this case, women of goodwill in Kenya have encouraged those who are taken advantage of, to institute legal proceedings against perpetrators through organizations such as the Federation of Women Lawyers (FIDA) and other pro bono agencies.

However, research has shown that many gender-based violence cases are not successful in court, where justice is supposed to be provided. This was due to a variety of factors, such as people not being willing to testify as witnesses in GBV cases, which had hindered the fight against gender-based violence. Findings also showed that for many victims, it was embarrassing to even report GBV cases. Another challenge in the fight against GBV was poverty, which served as a major obstacle to obtaining justice for the victims (Action Aid Kenya Annual Report 2019).

Emerging data on the impact of Covid-19 on women and girls highlighted that, once more, some women encountered additional challenges. Without access to private space, many women struggled to make emergency calls or to seek help online. To them, the impact of the Covid-19 pandemic was very devastating, and people continue to face the multifaceted effects. In order to curb and control the spread of the disease, the lockdown method was adopted in many parts of Africa (Labeodan et al., 2021). However, this partial lockdown affected many lives since home became everything: a resting place, workplace, worship place, school place and recreational place. Many women and girls also saw the burden of unpaid care work also quadruple during this period. During the Covid-19 pandemic, more challenges appeared to have cropped up regarding gender access to justice in the midst of gender-based violence (Decker et al., 2022). The curfews that were mandated and imposed in many regions of Kenya made it impossible to report sexual violence in a timely manner and receive the necessary samples and evidence that would allow for fair prosecution of the cases in court. Without evidence that could stand the test, many courts were forced to throw out many cases of women who have been violated.

This target of ensuring equal access to justice for all is a necessary angle for many women engaging in peacebuilding and development. Many women in Kenya seek to align themselves to promote peaceful and inclusive societies for sustainable development, providing access to justice for all. They are clear that individual and communal peace is a core integral part of society. Through their activities as parents, duty bearers and peacebuilders, they seem to discourage any forms of extremism and radicalization which have been witnessed over the years in Kenya. Many women view interfaith relations and tolerance as having a direct impact on peace, as elaborated by Maseno (2019).

### *Target 16.7 Ensure Responsive, Inclusive, Participatory and Representative Decision-making at All Levels*

As earlier indicated, a central focus of this chapter is the connection between peacebuilding and development from the grassroots or bottom up. This target encourages the participation and inclusion of women and youth from grassroots communities. The human rights-based approach to development proceeds in a similar vein so as to empower Kenyan women as holders of rights, assign duties to them and address structural inequalities. In Kenya, these are the development interventions targeting women for improved livelihoods. It has been noted over the years that many women and girls in Kenya continue to suffer inequalities. As many development actors continue to identify themselves as working in human rights, they seek to engage and include Kenyan women in decision-making at the local, county and national levels.

This SDG 16 target in Kenya attends to women, peacebuilding and development, seeing that it signals an important shift in practice where women's rights are considered in matters of development. Women's rights in gender and development provide an enabling tool for overcoming the social realities that violate those rights (Kerr, 2002, p. 10). Efforts towards women's participation and inclusion in Kenya are demonstrated in several ways. First, Kenya is a signatory to the Universal Declaration of Human Rights, the Beijing Declaration and Platform for Action (Beijing Declaration 1995), the African Union Protocol to the African Charter on Human and Peoples Rights on the Rights of Women in Africa (Maputo Protocol 2003) and others. Over the years, these instruments have placed a demand on Kenya to uphold these principles in order to attain equitable gender representation.

Recognizing these above-listed instruments, the Constitution of Kenya 2010 domesticates a number of these commitments to safeguard women's rights and fundamental freedoms and entrenches the concept in article 81 (b), which states, "Not more than two-thirds of the members of elective or appointive bodies shall be of the same gender". The intention, therefore, is to see to it that, owing to equitable gender representation, there is inclusive, participatory and representative decision-making at all levels. Although this intention is in the constitution, to date, the bone of contention since the promulgation of the Constitution is the matrix, logistics and formula in ensuring it is put into practice in all the houses and all elective public bodies.

In general, from this target and with the instruments listed, peacebuilding and development are to be participatory, and women should be included, making them actively aware of their rights. In Kenya, this target has the potential of bringing on board women and children and making them actively aware of their rights, even as they engage in peacebuilding and development. Many Kenyan women will find a stake in the processes that ensue within their communities as they serve in capacities such as duty bearers.

### Target 16.10 Ensure Public Access to Information and Protect Fundamental Freedoms in Accordance with National Legislation and International Agreements

Investing in databases with real-time information is important in the journey of peacebuilding and development. In many instances, much of the work of women in development and peacebuilding is often overlooked by scholars and other practitioners. Oftentimes, many of these women prefer anonymity and working away from the limelight, as noted by Marshall and Hayward (2011, pp. 11–12). Overall, the hard work and toil of these women are not appreciated nor documented and shared as they ought to be. Though there are women who consciously decide to keep a low profile and take pride in the quality of modesty, it is equally important to showcase their interventions within local communities even as we strive to have peacebuilding and development anchored from the bottom up in Kenya.

When viewed holistically, there are instruments that Kenya has appended its signature to uphold, as noted earlier. Kenyan women's engagement in peacebuilding and development finds a bearing within such policy instruments, and as such, this SDG target's emphasis on protecting fundamental freedoms is in light of such important national and international agreements. It is clear that SDG 16 and its targets, like the other SDGs, are formulated with an optimistic mindset, where better possibilities are envisioned for all across the world. Such hope and expectation are not always the case within the lived contexts of women and girls in some parts of Kenya. Therefore, there are pertinent critiques of the avenues by which peace and development are pursued in Kenya. This brings us to the next section, where feminist voices critique both peacebuilding and development.

## FEMINIST CRITIQUES OF PEACEBUILDING AND DEVELOPMENT USING RELEVANT EXAMPLES FROM KENYA

Feminist critiques of peacebuilding and development stem from analyses which tend to view how women are represented in the discourses that ensue. Within the peacebuilding and development landscape, feminist thinkers have pointed out the often one-dimensional and simplistic accounts equating women to victims in the context of peacebuilding and development. According to Wanyeki (2010), in Kenya, the narrated experiences of post-election violence tended to overlook the adjacent roles that many women played, as agents, collaborators, peacemakers and the like. When women are only viewed as victims, it is not possible to address the many other important roles that they play and enhance these additional roles for the betterment of society, as aptly demonstrated by Davaney (1997) and Eriksson (1995).

On the other hand, other than victims, some literature commonly misrepresents women as "natural" peacemakers. This has been largely discussed among feminist scholars such as Cockburn (1998). Such a posture has been critiqued as being an essentialization of all women, effectively lumping them into one category and which can be "a dangerous political force". This position works to sustain dominations, operating fixed and stereotyped dualism of "women victim, male warrior", as explained by Cockburn (1998, p. 13).

Feminist literature continues to raise several interesting points against one-dimensional and simplistic accounts equating women to victims. Firstly, it points out the need to understand the role of structural violence suffered by women during the conflict. In many cases, peacebuilding policies and conflict studies established the link between women and victimhood as their primary representation. In peacebuilding studies, women started to be visible as a monolithic and singular entity. They were depicted as sufferers of an evil and crazy violence that had no roots in any kind of structure. However, this violence has sexual underpinnings and was primarily sexual violence against women. On the other hand, it has also been claimed that, in working for peace, women challenge authorities (Sørensen, 1998). Women do not just take up positions for the sake of power, but they are agents who try to ensure that there be transformation, as enumerated by Nandera et al. (2018).

Further, feminist research has emphasized that women are not just victims but agents during and after the armed conflict. Some of these studies have focused on women's involvement in the military and in other movements that have used armed struggle. At the same time, studies on women and their opposition to violence have been numerous.

## CONCLUSION

Achieving SDG 16 requires grassroots' community partnerships, and integrated solutions, as women in Kenya and others take charge and lead in reshaping the institutional and social landscape that helps build sustainable peace. A recommendation for this SDG is that it is crucial to have women as agents in an inclusive and participatory approach to development and counteract the potentially destabilizing impact of marginalization in Kenya. In order to realize SDG 16 on peaceful, just and inclusive societies, there is a need for a power shift that re-centres work on equality, development and peace around women's voices, dignity and rights, including those of children and the vulnerable in society. Another recommendation for the success of this SDG and its targets is a deliberate structural, behavioural and attitudinal transformation that moves from institutionalizing any form of governance that enables domination and violence against women to forms of governance that enable equality and peace for women and all creation.

Across the world, when societies are ordered in peace, they often enjoy better business environments, higher per capita income, better health systems, higher educational attainment and stronger social cohesion. Better community relationships tend to encourage greater levels of peace by discouraging the formation of tensions and reducing the chances of tensions devolving into conflict. An additional recommendation is that many more women should venture into the arena of peacebuilding and development in Kenya. They should do so with the targets of SDG 16 in mind, done collaboratively at local, national and regional levels where women in communities, civil society organizations, governments, regional bodies and the private sector all play a role. It is clear that Kenya cannot achieve peaceful and inclusive societies through investing in security alone; it must address the various underlying factors such as poverty, marginalization, environmental degradation and corruption, among others. Promoting peaceful and inclusive societies for sustainable development in Kenya is a goal that is clearly attainable, in the fullness of time.

## References

Agengo, C. (2009). Kenya: Peace and Security Imperatives for Women. Nairobi: Pambazuka News. http://www.pambazuka.org/en/category/

Alfani, R. (2019). *Religious Peacebuilding in the Democratic Republic of Congo*. Peter Lang.

Anderson, V. (2014). Intersectional Activism: Wangari Maathai's Rhetorical Revolution for Peace, Democracy, and the Environment. Unpublished Master of Arts thesis, Colorado State University.

Ashworth, J., & Ryan, M. (2013). "One Nation from Every Tribe, Tongue, and People": The Church and Strategic Peacebuilding in South Sudan. *Journal of Catholic Social Thought, 10*(1), 47–67.

Chitando, E., & Tarusarira, J. (Eds.). (2019). *Religion and Human Security in Africa*. Routledge.

Cockburn, C. (1998). *The Space between Us: Negotiating Gender and National Identities in Conflict*. Zed Publishers.

Davaney, S. (1997). Continuing the Story, but Departing the Text: A Historicist Interpretation of Feminist Norms in Theology. In R. Chopp & S. Davaney (Eds.),

*Horizons in Feminist Theology: Identity, Tradition, and Norms* (pp. 193–210). Fortress Press.

Decker, M. R., Bevilacqua, K., Wood, S. N., et al. (2022). Gender-based Violence during COVID-19 among Adolescent Girls and Young Women in Nairobi, Kenya: A Mixed-Methods Prospective Study over 18 Months. *BMJ Global Health, 7*, e007807.

Duncanson, C. (2016). *Gender and Peacebuilding*. Polity Press.

Ellsberg, M., & Heise, L. (2005). Researching Violence Against Women: A Practical Guide for Researchers and Activists. World Health Organization.

Eriksson, A. (1995). *The Meaning of Gender in Theology: Problems and Possibilities*. A.L. Eriksson.

Godia, J. (2020). Violence Against Women Spikes during Heated Electioneering. Visited on November 11, 2022. https://www.un.org/africarenewal/news/violence-against-women-spikes-during-heated-electioneering

Kerr, J. (2002). From "WID" to "GAD" to Women's Rights: The First Twenty Years of AWID. *AWID's Occasional Paper No. 9*. Visited on November 12, 2022. https://www.awid.org/sites/default/files/atoms/files/the_first_twenty_years_of_awid.pdf

Krause, J., Krause, W., & Braenfors, P. (2018). Women's Participation in Peace Negotiations and the Durability of Peace. *International Interactions, 44*(6), 985–1016.

Labeodan, H., Amenga-Etego, R., Stiebert, J., & Aidoo, M. S. (Eds.). (2021). *Exploring Religion in Africa & Covid-19: African Women and the Will to Survive* (31 BiAS—Bible in African Studies). University of Bamberg Press.

Lederach, J. P. (1997). *Building Peace: Sustainable Reconciliation in Divided Societies*. United States Institute of Peace (USIP).

Marshall, K., & Hayward, S. (2011). Women in Religious Peacebuilding. *USIP Peaceworks Report No. 71*.

Maseno, L. (2019). Securitizing Places of Worship in Kenya. The Case of Faith Evangelistic Ministry (FEM). In E. Chitando & J. Tarusarira (Eds.), *Religion and Human Security in Africa* (pp. 102–113). Routledge.

Maseno, L. (2020). Women as Religious Citizens and Peacebuilding in Kenya. In A. Chitando (Ed.), *Women and Peacebuilding in Africa* (pp. 96–109). Routledge.

Nandera, M., Maseno, L., Mtata, K., & Senga, M. (2018). Modes of Legitimation by Female Pentecostal-Charismatic Preachers in East Africa: A Comparative Study in Kenya and Tanzania. *Journal of Contemporary African Studies*. https://doi.org/10.1080/02589001.2018.1504162

Njoh, A. J. (2006). *Tradition, Culture and Development in Africa: Historical Lessons for Modern Development Planning*. Ashgate.

Onditi, F., & Odera, J. (2021). *Understanding Violence Against Women in Africa: An Interdisciplinary Approach*. Springer International Publishing.

Onsanti, K. (2014). Religion, Gender and Peacebuilding in Africa: A Case Study of Kenya 2007/8. Unpublished Master Research Project submitted in International Conflict Management, University of Nairobi.

Onyango, E. (2018). *Gender and Development: A History of Women Education in Kenya*. Langham.

Petersen, M. (2015). Conflict or Compatibility? Reflections on the Nexus between Human Rights, Development and Religion in Muslim Organisations. In E. Tomalin (Ed.), *The Routledge Handbook of Religions and Global Development* (pp. 359–372). Routledge.

Potter, A. (2008). Gender Sensitivity, Nicety or Necessity in Peace Process Management? Geneva Centre for Humanitarian Dialogue.

Ramsbotham, O., Miall, H., & Woodhouse, T. (2007). *Contemporary Conflict Resolution: The Prevention, Management and Transformation of Deadly Conflict.* Polity Press.

Retallic, P. (2019). https://www.fortid.no/artikler/2019/defining-peace.html

Sampson, C. (1997). Religion and Peacebuilding. In I. William Zartman & J. Lewis Rasmussen (Eds.), *Peacemaking in International Conflict: Methods and Techniques* (pp. 273–316). United States Institute of Peace Press.

Sørensen, B. R. (1998). *Women and Post-conflict Reconstruction: Issues and Sources.* Diane Publishing.

The 2030 Agenda for Sustainable Development. Visited on November 13, 2022. https://sdgs.un.org › 2030agenda.

The Action Aid Kenya Annual Report. (2019). Action Aid Kenya.

The African Union Protocol to the African Charter on Human and Peoples Rights on the Rights of Women in Africa (Maputo Protocol). (2003). Visited on November 10, 2022. https://www.un.org/shestandsforpeace/content/protocol-african-charter-human-and-peoples-rights-rights-women-africa-maputo-protocol-2003

The Beijing Declaration and Platform for Action. (1995). Visited on November 11, 2022. https://www.un.org › daw › beijing › platform.

The Children's Act. (2001). Kenya Government Printers.

The Kenya Constitution. (2010). Kenya Government Printers.

The Kenya Demographic and Health Survey (KDHS). (2014). Kenya National Bureau of Statistics.

The National Action Plan on Arms Control and Management. (2006). Kenya Government Printers.

The National Gender and Equality Commission Act. (2011). Kenya Government Printers.

The National Policy on Peacebuilding and Conflict Management. (2015). Kenya Government Printers.

The Penal Code. (2009). Kenya Government Printers.

The Sexual Offences Act. (2006). Kenya Government Printers.

The Truth, Justice and Reconciliation Act No. 6. (2008). Kenya Government Printers.

The Universal Declaration of Human Rights. Visited on November 7, 2022. https://www.un.org/en/udhrbook/pdf/udhr_booklet_en_web.pdf

Tomalin, E. (2006). Religion and a Rights Based Approach to Development. *Progress in Development Studies, 6*(2), 93–108.

Wanambisi, L. (2013). *Report on looting after the Westgate Mall Attack.* Capital News.

Wanyeki, M. (2010). Lessons from Kenya: Women and the Post-Election Violence. *Standpoint—Feminist Africa, 10,* 91–97.

Woodhouse, T. (2010). Adam Curle: Radical Peacemaker and Pioneer of Peace Studies. *Journal of Conflictology, 1*(1), 1–8.

CHAPTER 40

# The Role of Women Church Leaders in Peacebuilding and Social Economic Transformation in Post-Conflict Uganda

*Alice Wabule*

## INTRODUCTION

Whereas women are mostly essentialized as victims in conflict situations and often times excluded from conflict resolution and transformation forums (Lubunga, 2016; Khodary, 2016; Angom, 2018; Mwenje, 2016; Chitando, 2019), women's efforts in harnessing socioeconomic transition and justice, which are a significant basis for sustainable peace, are also well documented. The focus on women in general and women church leaders in particular as spelt out by this study is informed by the United Nations Security Council Resolution 1325 (2000) and literature that emphasizes the agency and participation of women in peacebuilding (Chitando, 2019). Basing on field data generated from interviews with ten women with leadership positions in both the Catholic and Anglican churches and literature research, this chapter explores the role of women church leaders in social economic transition and peacebuilding in Uganda. It is concerned with targets 16.3.3 and 16.7.2 of Sustainable Development Goal (SDG) 16, of ensuring access to dispute resolution mechanism and inclusive and responsive decision making at all levels in the process securing peace and justice. The chapter responds to three major objectives, namely: (1) establishing the role played by women church leaders in harnessing sustainable peace and reconciliation at the grassroots communities;

A. Wabule (✉)
Faculty of Socioeconomic Sciences, Cavendish University, Kampala, Uganda

© The Author(s), under exclusive license to Springer Nature Switzerland AG 2023
S. M. Kilonzo et al. (eds.), *The Palgrave Handbook of Religion, Peacebuilding, and Development in Africa*,
https://doi.org/10.1007/978-3-031-36829-5_40

(2) strategies used by women church leaders in enhancing socioeconomic transition, peace and stability at the grassroots communities; and (3) challenges and prospects faced by women church leaders in their efforts at creating sustainable peace at the grassroots communities.

The United Nations recognizes the role of the church and broader civil society in fostering the culture of peace (United Nations, 2018). The link between churches, peacebuilding, gender equality and women's empowerment is also well appreciated by the UN. It is in this perspective that churches in Uganda have a role in forging genuine partnerships with all stakeholders to work for peace and justice. The challenge is, however, for the leadership of the church to include women at all levels in the peacebuilding initiatives. Notwithstanding the tension that sometimes arises between the different religious groups in Uganda as elsewhere, religious beliefs and prayer are invoked as useful tools for promoting peace and social justice (Angucia, 2010). Whereas predominantly Anglican and Catholic, other religions such as Islam, Orthodox, the Seventh-day Adventist and Pentecostals bring people together for harmonious co-existence. For instance, the Inter-Religious Council of Uganda (IRCU), a network organization, brings together the different religious sects on initiatives for achieving peace, harmony and social justice (see, e.g., Ntini & Omona, 2022).

Christianity was the central interest of this study because it encompasses 84% of the entire population of Uganda. Under the ecumenical organization that brings together the Catholics, the orthodox and the Anglican/Church of Uganda sects, the Uganda Joint Christian Council (UJCC), a range of activities is supported at the grassroots communities. Implemented either jointly, individually or with partners, components such as training in conflict prevention, negotiation and peace-making are conducted (Eliko, 2006). Educational materials and exchange visits are also conducted for sharing views, dialoguing and learning best practices.

Peacebuilding in study here and throughout will adopt Khodary's (2016, p. 497) definition, to mean a range of measures targeted to reduce the risk of lapsing or relapsing into conflict by strengthening national capacities at all levels for conflict management and to lay a foundation for sustainable peace. Thus, from the perspective of SDG 16, since high levels of violence and insecurity have a destructive impact on a country's development, working towards creating conditions and structures within the community that are life enhancing and that aim to eradicate all conditions that limit human flourishing is paramount. The peace process, which usually encompasses a range of institutional and socioeconomic transformations at the local and national levels, aims at ensuring social justice, equal opportunity, human security and, consequently, sustainable development (Datzberger & Le mat, 2018).

## LITERATURE REVIEW

### Overview

The UN Security Council Resolution (2000), as mentioned above, redefines the role of women in conflict and challenges the image of women as mere victims of violence. This draws the attention of this chapter to recognizing the achievements by women church leaders, but also the effectiveness of their interactions, especially in a male-dominated field (Chitando, 2019; Miller, 2016). The assumption of church leadership roles by an increasing number of women in contemporary experience is based on factors such as the biblical teaching that focuses on the role of the Holy Spirit among believers as uplifting, delighting, empowering and transforming (Miller, 2016, p. 53; Shooter, 2014), a belief that experiences of the Holy Spirit were open to all genders. Cremer (2019) indicates that the social and economic changes that take place within the church communities have presented opportunities for women to play a significant role in evangelical and other pastoral roles that were previously a preserve for the male. Moreover, increasing participation of women in church leadership is also attributed to the global trend which places gender equality at the core of any development agenda (United Nations, 2014). For instance, the world survey on the role of women in development (2014) points to the moral and ethical perspective of recognizing the human rights, dignity and capabilities of diverse groups of women. Thus, involving women in church leadership not only reduces the disproportionate impact of economic, social and environmental shocks that undermine participation in vital roles in their families and communities, but builds women's agency and capabilities to create better synergies between gender equality and sustainable development outcomes (United Nations, 2014, p. 12).

### *The Role of Women Church Leaders in Sustainable Peace and Socioeconomic Transition*

While literature produced by the church binds men and women together, most activities relating to women's church leadership are influenced by what Miller (2016) refers to as 'Conservative Fundamentalism', in reference to the seemingly separated roles and experiences of male and female within the church social boundaries. Embracing women in church leadership was and is attributed, firstly, to the growth of church congregations that led to a practical need for women's labour, especially in the early stages of their formation. Incidences of women exhibiting greater leadership abilities were based to a large measure on the traits and charisma of individuals (Miller, 2016, p. 53). Women in this case were called to servant leadership, which according to Newkirk and Cooper (2013, p. 4), focuses on meeting the needs of the followers and helping them become more knowledgeable, freer and autonomous. Secondly, positioning women as being more pragmatic and having better mobilization skills is said to have led to co-opting women in church leadership (Lubunga, 2016). However, my argument is that the women should not merely be accepted in church leadership but their roles be appreciated and recognized in ways that promote their visibility. A study on changing role of women in Pentecostal American Churches by Barfoot and Sheppards (1980) shows that prophetic female figures, guided by the philosophy of shepherding and caring oneness, have played a central role in most church movements through which they reach segments of congregations not reached by their male counterparts (Campbell, 1986 in Sekano & Masango, 2012). This particular study intended to establish the contributions made by women's religious movements to church philanthropic work in promoting peaceful and inclusive societies for sustainable development as spelt out by SDG 16.

### Strategies for Peacebuilding, Socioeconomic Transformation and Stability by Women Church Leaders

While country-specific measures have been undertaken in peacebuilding, cross-cutting initiatives in the literature reviewed include a range of community activities like lobbying for amnesty for the rebels, educating the population about peace and providing alternative forum for the articulation of local grievances (Khadiagala, 2001). A number of women have played significant role in peacebuilding (Lubunga, 2016; Chitando, 2019). As argued by Lubunga (2016), Christian women have been agents in transforming the warrior situation into non-violent society as one way of fulfilling God's mission of bringing peace in the community. Using different platforms, women have communicated and popularized their activities. For example, prominent African female theologians such as Mary-Anne Plaatjies van Huffel, Mercy Oduyoye, Isabel Phiri and Sarojini Nadar (Lubunga, 2016) are presented as advocates for transformation of society through church leadership. Through associations like the National Congress of Protestant Women in the Democratic Republic of Congo (DRC), women have spoken out on the need for demobilization and ending violence. Consequently, opportunities for state reconstruction and post-conflict peacebuilding through negotiations, peace agreements and political settlements have been provided (Lubunga, 2016). Additionally, seminars and international delegates, conferences and public gatherings are avenues to create awareness of the various sections of the law that govern the war-affected persons. By addressing underlying power dynamics, dialogue and debate with actors have been conducted to create a positive change in mindsets. Further, information concerning the people's right to fight against violence is disseminated through documentaries that share stories of their experiences. This has led to adaptations to both protectionist and precautionary measures that empower and improve the living conditions of war-affected persons.

In Zimbabwe, mediation and advocacy, education, self-help, music and the arts, spirituality, storytelling and bridge building are the common platforms used for dialoguing on peace (Chitando, 2019). Engaging in diverse peacebuilding activities, as pointed out by Chitando, young Christian women have solved family problems like wrangles on property ownership and marital problems. Moreover, church platforms for female church leaders have provided tremendous effort in caring for survivors of violence and other affected persons (Lubunga, 2016). In the DRC, just as it is with the community service centre in Cape Town, South Africa (Flaendorp, 2014), women church leaders have used their limited resources to provide basic needs such as clothing, shelter and food to vulnerable families (Lubunga, 2016). Additionally, the women church leaders through their associations organize fellowships and meetings where mechanisms for dealing with traumatic experiences of racism, war and violence are discussed. Ochen (2017) points to other efforts at peace, social justice and reconciliation as being dialogues between people of different ethnic groups to advance peace processes amongst them. By helping communities transcend the hatred and retaliation that divide the population, women serve as peace-markers in their own right.

Elsewhere in the world, religious-based pro-peace movements such as Mother's Front in Yugoslavia, Latin America and Russia, relatives of the detained and disappeared in Chile and Kashmir and association of widows in Guatemala and Rwanda are amongst women associations recognized for peace, justice and reconciliation (Khodary, 2016). Advocacy campaigns through security forums to discuss the plight of survivors after armed conflict help guard against extremism and terrorism. Moreover, addressing inequalities and structure barriers in the environments supports and promotes social cohesion, and builds trust, solidarity, a sense of collectivity and common purpose within the community.

## *Women Church Leaders, Peacebuilding and Contribution to Development in Uganda*

In Uganda, pro-peace movements were among the strategies that were adopted in response to the war that ravaged the country for decades (Ball, 2009; Khadiagala, 2001). Despite being victims of atrocities and brutality of the rebels, women were instrumental in bringing peace. By initiating peace talks and launching awareness campaigns, they facilitated the process of building trust, solidarity and common purpose among the people (Datzbeger & Le Mat, 2018). In his study on women's engagement with the post-conflict communities in Uganda, Ochen (2017) points to the resilience of women and the important role they play in social cohesion, and breaking structural barriers in the environment. This is evident in later years where the promotion of peace and security, poverty elimination, economic growth and employment creation have been at the core of post-conflict initiatives undertaken by women in Uganda. Using institutional networks, women have helped foster strong family units, parental care, harmony and reconciliation in homes and communities at large (Ochen, 2017).

Women church leaders in Uganda are specifically recognized for their role in peace and long-term transformation in their societies (Arostegui, 2013). Like elsewhere, either by rallying behind their own mobilization activities or by working in partnerships with women groups, core activities like research, advocacy and capacity building have been used for reshaping and rewriting societal rules and advancing human rights. As mentioned earlier, the inter-faith network provides a platform through which men and women of faith speak of the values inherent in building a culture of peace. At workshops, peace and reconciliation strategies are discussed, as well as dialoguing on accessibility to resources that address the social cultural and economic dimensions of conflict. In Gulu province of northern Uganda that endured 20 years of hostilities under the Lord's Resistance Army (LRA), several sisters (nuns) of the Catholic faith are recognized for their role in designing rehabilitation programmes for children and the youth to overcome the psychological trauma of their experiences. Skills of interpersonal communication, non-violent conflict resolution and life skills for personal development were among the key rehabilitation processes. Similar strategies have been applied in the Karamoja region where this study was conducted (Datzberger, 2017). In a nutshell, as stated by Ball (2009), women church leaders, working with other women groups, have frequently been at the forefront of grassroots peacebuilding initiatives. Informal peacebuilding activities such as community mobilization music, games and drama, creating opportunities for dialogue and non-violent conflict resolution mechanisms that aim at mending the ripped social fabric are conducted. These and other activities geared towards enhancing voice and economic empowerment, as required by SDG 16, pave the way and create an enabling environment for more formal or publicly recognized interventions.

### *Challenges Faced by the Women Church Leaders*

Far from being inclusive of difference and diversity, church leadership until today remains male dominated (Ball, 2009; Newkirk & Cooper, 2013). With fewer women taking up leadership, those who get into this servantship often undergo challenges and struggles rarely faced by their male counterparts, thus hindering them from performing to full capacity (Shooter, 2014). Influenced historically by the androcentric concept of religion and culture, negative perceptions and stereotypes about women church leadership continue to manifest (Sekano & Masango, 2012; Flaendorp, 2014). Miller (2016) points to the persistent feminine and masculine ideology that continues to subjugate women, thus putting them in positions in the ministries that are either creative or caring (Jennings, 2008 cited by Miller, 2016). In fact, as reported by most scholars, a significant number of males would resist any effort to be led by women. Largely normalized by patriarchal power, subjugation and dominance of women is justified by what would be considered misinterpretations of biblical verses such as 1 Corinthians 14:34–35, 1 Timothy 2:12–14 and the local cultural beliefs that promote patriarchy (Sekano & Masango, 2012).

Consequently, the image that women church leadership defies both the Bible and tradition is unjustly cemented (Flaendorp, 2014). Such cultural schemas and upbringing are also reproduced in most societal institutions such as schools, churches, homes and work places, even when society fully acknowledges the role of Christianity in cementing relationships. Thus, denying women agency to express their opinions remains high despite espoused values and the teaching of Christianity that tend towards a more non-sexist approach (Miller, 2016; Chitando, 2019; Yih, 2022).

Chitando (2019) points to other factors that deter women from taking an active role in peacebuilding as a weak political will, low levels of participation of women in politics and peace processes, limited awareness of policy resolutions at local levels, absence of a critical mass of female voices and a lack of effective networking among women. Such factors are not unique to the Zimbabwean context, but are also common to Uganda where the women more especially those involved in church leadership are not visible in the public sphere. As pointed out by Chitando and Miller, these biases and stereotypes reinforce patriarchy and male dominance, thus sanctioning women under deprived positions. Restrictions to accessing higher leadership positions is said to deter the women's access to resources and other life opportunities, thus cumulatively acting to diminish their audibility, visibility and social influence.

Yih (2022) in her study also found that women church leaders were mostly silenced and imposed both by the self and by external forces mentioned above. For instance, gendered cultural dynamics in the church institutions reinforce a stable gender binary distinguishing male and female. Ironically, women face obstacles not only from men but also from fellow women who do not support their upliftment. Besides the self-imposed silence that is nurtured into women in the socialization process and cultural limits, the jealousy and envy towards each other hinders women from working together and limits voice for women (Yih, 2022).

Other studies associate women's lack of effective participation in church leadership with insufficient preparation, training and the necessary support to empower them with authority to access and hold high-level leadership positions (Riesebrodt & Chong, 1999 in Miller, 2016; Newkirk and Cooper, 2013). In a context of unjust distribution of power in highly oppressive management structures, women continue to hold a lower profile in church leadership, just as it is with other leadership opportunities outside the home (Miller, 2016; Cremer, 2019). In Uganda, women's agency in political and social issues remains minimal and so is their participation in peacebuilding. Hindered mainly by the power dynamics that are culturally, socially, politically and economically perpetuated, I argue for a change in perception given the changing role of women in the new era. Perceiving women as less able in taking up church leadership would undermine the intention of promoting human rights, social justice and women empowerment as spelt out by the UN Women (2014) and would undermine the attainment of target 16.7.2 of SDG 16. Any prospects for improvement, as pointed out by Cremer (2019), rely in the power of prayer, persistence and consistencies. Adopting a strategic approach to mentoring, as suggested by Yih (2022), is as important as encouraging women to take courage in what they do, just as the women in the Bible do. Having looked at the literature, the next focus of the chapter is on the methods that were used for data collection.

## Methodology

This was a qualitative research in which data were collected from ten purposively selected female church leaders from both the Anglican and Catholic churches in the Karamoja region between May and August 2022. Situated in the north eastern region of Uganda, the people of Karamoja, the Karimojong, are an ethnic group known for their nomadic agropastoralism, cattle herding, cattle rustling and being in possession of unregistered firearms. Their love for cattle and strict adherence to tradition and culture has entangled the Karimojong in endless wars of cattle raiding with neighbouring ethnic groups both from within Uganda and across borders with Kenya and South Sudan (Datzberger, 2017). Whereas relative peace has been restored through the government disarmament programme, human rights abuses, violent conflicts and clashes within and along the boarders continue. Recently, issues of land rights and illegal exploitative mining have further threatened the peace processes. Thus, for many decades, Karamoja was and continues to be branded insecure, and her people isolated from the rest of the country, making it the poorest region despite the existence of precious mineral resources, fauna and flora. A non-government organization (NGO), Women for Peace, was used as a case study because, much as it was started by nuns from the Catholic Church, it works with women from the Anglican Church as well.

The study participants included women who are actively involved in church work. They ranged from the age of 25–85 years, many of whom having had experience working in different parts of Uganda. They were selected using the snowball sampling technique (Lune & Berg, 2017). This method was preferred because the first participant would lead me to the next one with similar attributes (Hennink et al., 2011). I approached a former workmate, a serving nun, who later introduced me to another person. Each person interviewed was asked to introduce another who they believed would provide useful information to the study.

Similarly, for the Anglicans, one female priest with whom I had informal contacts was identified, who also led me to another. I would seek informed consent before involvement. In-depth interviews were used (Creswell, 2012), to gain a deeper understanding of female church leaders who have a lived experience of addressing several challenges amongst the churchgoers. The aim was to allow voice to the participants to share their own experiences and also to ensure that the data reflect multiple perceptions and give maximum variation (Krueger, 1998; Cypress, 2017). The data generated were transcribed verbatim and then analysed with the aid of a computer software, AtlasTI. Transcripts are used to illustrate the voices of participants and pseudonyms are used to conceal their identities.

## Findings

Founded with the mission of improving livelihoods and enjoyment of economic, social and cultural freedom for women in Teso and Karamoja regions, several initiatives are undertaken by the Women for Peace organization in different parts of the country. What stood out in their activism mainly fell in the categories of economic empowerment, lobbying, advocacy, capacity building, information dissemination and networking. Cross-cutting was the identity with their roles as mobilizers, leaders, role models, initiators of programmes, trainers, advocates, educators, disseminators, formulators and conscientizers.

Thus, a range of activities were identified by women church leaders as a way of sustaining peace and development within grassroots communities. The initiatives undertaken were found to resonate well with targets 16.3.3 and 16.7.2 that stipulate for access to dispute resolution mechanisms and ensuring inclusive and responsive decision-making at all levels. Most of these, such as empowerment of previously disadvantaged communities and reconciliation forums, are core to building democratic structures that are key for development to be sustainable as stated by SDG 16. The initiatives were similar to those undertaken elsewhere (Lubunga, 2016; Flaendorp, 2014) and were not limited to leaders of a particular Christian faith. Important to note is their recognition of their role in peace and social transition as critical due to the growing peacelessness resulting from both the local and global crisis like wars, climate change, poverty, food insecurity, pandemics and family instability, among others. Just as the literature findings, their task involved working mainly with other women to bring about changes in the communities where they live and work.

In line with the biblical role of servant leadership, women church leaders were found to be engaged in evangelism, which links directly to the purpose of their vocation. The sisters mentioned that they visit the *Manyatta*s (homesteads), teaching about Jesus and his ways. As declared by Sister Cissy:

> Bible sharing is done and the emphasis is always on peace and the kindness of our Lord. In these meetings at the village meeting trees, the women and men are taught about working together and how to respect each other. Hygiene is normally taught. Parents are sensitised about sending their children to school to avoid becoming warriors who end up in acts of violence and thieving.

Teaching about Jesus and his ways, much as its application is contested as an empty signifier and ideological object (Fitch, 2006), could imply standing up for the poor, the marginalized and resisting injustices in the world. In the transcript above, values that promote peace such as respect, togetherness and kindness are highlighted. Through the fact that peace and reconciliation are emphasized in Jesus's teachings and Jesus's ways, a message of peace is re-echoed.

Raising awareness on the need for peace and social stability is another strategy for maintaining peace and stability, as explained by Sister Rebecca, who seems to have had substantial experience working with the local communities:

> The women were taught simple hygiene from using carbolic soap, washing their cloths, and keeping their compounds clean. They were taught how to feed their children. Later on, this programme developed further into a literacy programme. This is ongoing. The women for peace were taught to dialogue with their sons, husbands to dissuade them from raiding other villages for cows. They were sent as emissaries to the villages to discuss with their male family members how raiding and violence was futile and what they could do instead of fighting and dying to acquire a few more cows. Later on, this programme opened for men too. It is now a big project with funding for Karamoja Development Action and other donors.

Sister Rebecca's transcript contains a range of life skills which, if applied, promotes peaceful co-existence and socioeconomic transformation. For instance, life skilling in areas such as dialogue, good communication, decision-making, empathy and respect for other persons, which are instilled in the members, fosters good interpersonal relations, discipline and unity as advocated by SDG 16, target 16.3.3. In aiding the achievement of other SDGs, the simple hygiene taught to women rids them from conditions that could lead to ill health and subsequent loss of peace. The transcript also indicates that Women for Peace Organization works not only with the women but also with the children and their husbands. Working with men carries an aspect of gender inclusion, which is in line with target 16.7.2 of Sustainable Development Goal 16 on social sustainability, inclusion and responsive decision-making at all levels (Koch & Fritz, 2014). Inclusion, according to Koch and Fritz, empowers people and builds cohesion and resilience, which are key elements for peace, reconciliation and social justice.

Relatedly, is their contribution towards home-based care projects for home improvement. These range from social activities that promote family stability such as children, marital counselling and psychosocial support to individuals faced with life challenges. As revealed by the literature, their work was rooted in the belief that the church must act in the world for those in need (Flaendorp, 2014). Additionally, financial and technical support towards income-generating projects such as brick laying, handcrafts and commercial farming, which are key for achieving other SDGs such as SDG1 that aims to eradicate all forms of poverty, were offered. Subsequently, many women were actively engaged in poultry keeping, bee farming for honey, piggery projects and handcrafts for commercial purposes. Sister Linnet explained:

> This is a big project run by the Sacred Heart Sisters in Moroto, Naoi Parish. It is meant to support women and children mainly. These children and women are

HIV positive and they are given hope, treatment, food, and activities to earn a living. A big building was funded by Spanish donors and it has sections for many entrepreneurial groups working to train women in small trades like bead work, sewing ... seamstresses and cookery.

Additionally, it was reported that around 100 children are sponsored in the nearby primary schools and are supported in their medications and in their basic needs. The understanding is that if these children are supported, they will grow up loved and cared for, thus passing on the same values for creating peace in Karamoja and elsewhere. A sewing club in Naoi parish was set up by the sisters and has graduated many youth, as pointed out further:

> In this same Parish, another order, the Evangelizing Sisters of Mary, have a sewing club. Many young women and men have graduated with certificates and have begun small trades in sewing. These small employment opportunities help the men not to involve themselves in drunkenness, violence, and other vices. The women too are able to provide for their children and families.

As also revealed by the literature, a common practice was that women church leaders often worked with other women on issues of family discipline for the stability of the home. Reverend Harriet from the Anglican Church had this to say:

> Meetings are organized with married women, the Mothers' Union and married women learn about the importance of respect in the family, discipline for the children, forgiveness and other values that are important for peace in the home ... we also mediate to solve family conflicts ... unsolved family wrangles lead to broken families.

Reverend Harriet's submission confirms the role women church leaders have traditionally played. In line with literature findings (Shooter, 2014), it suggests that the women church leaders continue to pursue a feminist approach in the church ministry. Accordingly, women are mandated to institute family discipline, including disciplining their husbands as sanctioned by the church.

Meanwhile, Sister Vero recounts her experience working to bring about peace and reconciliation between the Iteso and Karamojong warriors in the transcript below:

> For three years, that is from 2001–2003, I was part of the Bishop's Justice and Peace Commission. We planned for demonstrations, educative ventures, meetings to bring peace between the Karamojong and the Atesot from Teso. This was a time when there was a real break down in peace and harmony between these two neighbouring tribes. We risked to visit the different areas working for reconciliation and helping people to forgive, move on, and to concentrate on their own development. I was also part of the diocesan Development Project.

Sister Vero's submission indicates that women church leaders are also co-opted on projects that are seemingly masculine and male dominated. This has a strong linkage to target 16: 7: 2 of ensuring inclusivity in decision-making. Risking to visit areas with total breakdown of peace implies the spirit of self-sacrifice, which is synonymous with servant leadership as pointed by the literature review.

In the area of education, it was revealed that Sisters from the different congregations teach in several schools in Moroto and they teach the message of peace all the time, as pointed out by Sarah:

> The former principal of the Teachers College in Moroto was a nun. She did a great job as she was Karimojong and knew how to address the most disturbing issues with the persistent violence in Moroto. I taught in this college for three years. Many schools have nuns. The best women's primary school in Moroto is run by the Comboni sisters … it is from here that the Minister for Ethics and Integrity, [Rose Akelo] Lilly went to school. We run Kangole Girls School from which came Minister Ester Anyakun and the Vice President.

Education is not only a major tool for empowerment and social justice, but education institutions are key avenues for mobilization and outreach. Pointing to some key persons in governments having been groomed by the nuns provides a form of self-approval and pride in what women church leaders have achieved in their service to humanity.

Not only do the sisters teach in schools, but the schools too are used as centres for mobilizing and meeting young women school drop-outs during the holiday recess. Sister Diana narrated as captured below:

> When children have holidays in our very good school … a group of young women-school drop-outs come in to use the facilities and follow school in courses like catering and sewing. It is a very good programme that helps the young ladies not to get into problems—early pregnancies and other forms of destructive situations. They learn bakery and they can begin life to be independent and not fall prey to violent and abusive husbands in the village situations.

Skilling young women school-drops, as clearly pointed out by Sister Diana, empowers them for economic independence but also with knowledge on reproductive health, which in the long run enhances better livelihoods and family stability for them.

The women church leaders were also working with prisoners on reforms and behavioural change programmes, as expressed further by Sister Vero:

> Our Sisters have worked with the prisoners in Moroto Prison for years. This helps the prisoners to reflect on their lives, and to reform. They prepare them for life after the prison. Sometimes they get sponsors for them for small needs such as soap. They help them communicate to their families so as to remain human and

to become better persons after this ordeal of imprisonment. Sr … and Sr … have done this for a number of years.

Given the fact that the majority of the prisoners might harbour destructive behaviours that cause social unrest and a destructive impact of a countries' development, helping them reform, become better persons and remain human, as mentioned above, is ideal for reducing on social violence and creating peace and social stability.

Besides, female church leaders revealed that they worked with refugees who come to Uganda from different countries within the region by providing psychosocial support and basic needs:

> Our sisters work with refugees from Congo. They get funding for them for their children's education and they begin small workshops and businesses for them or just talk to them when in distress. This helps them to cope with the new challenges and avoid them involving themselves in violence and in destructive behaviour such as prostitution and so much else.

Finally, working towards environmental protection was found to be among the roles played by the female church leaders in creating social harmony. Through a neighbourhood project called Green Faith Friends Action (GEFA), tree planting is done to educate village mates about environmental conservation. Educating communities on strategies for environmental conservation in a way helps guard against new threats brought about by climate hazards that pose a threat to food security and human flourishing, as explained by Sister Maggie:

> We have a neighborhood project GEFA … Green Earth Friend's Action. We plant trees, educate the village mates about the environment, we meet and talk about the steps to take and we study about the environment together at Njeru Primary School—when we can. There are always trees at our pick a tree station at the village main junction. People pick the trees we put there for free and plant them where they want in their homes and work places.

In my view, such neighbourhood projects promote tree planting for future economic gains but also help bring people together for a common cause. Working together on a similar project is one way of uniting members of a community. Moreover, bringing together various social demographic parts of the population on activities that impact society mirrors a sense of responsibility and belonging, thus leading to peace, social justice and levelling the ground for engaging in activities that bring about development. The tree planting project, as alluded earlier on, is an action towards combating the increasing ecological challenges of climate change and its devastating impact to humanity. From another angle (Flaendorp 2014), this could be an act of promoting environmental justice in fulfilment of the biblical understanding of humanity's responsibility to the earth.

## CHALLENGES

Several challenges were identified as limiting the work of women church leaders. First, the conservative stereotypes which perceive women's leadership as problematic continue to manifest. As also pointed out in the literature, male dominance and opposition from politicians was reported to be a major obstacle to creating effective and inclusive institutions. In Uganda, although gender equality and equity are high on the agenda, ideas of patriarchy are strongly entrenched in people's mindsets and beliefs. This, as pointed by Angom (2018), hinders tapping into their significant experiences and skills in peacebuilding efforts. Thus, while the work of women church leaders is commendable, the interviewed decried a lack of dialogue with government actors. It was reported that those in political circles, including fellow women, perceive their initiatives as a form of competition, which is counterproductive to their visibility. This lack of political will is not only limited to local initiatives undertaken by women, but is more of a cross-cutting issue. Second, was the theme of limited financial resources for sustaining their activities. As also revealed by the literature review, women are held back from engaging meaningfully in social life outside the home due to limited financial opportunities. Third, was the lack of motivation from the communities that are not always responsive to taking on certain responsibilities, and lastly, for Karamoja region specifically, the insecurity perpetuated by the guns supply to the warriors continue to pose a security threat and a great danger for the women leaders to streamline their innovations.

## CONCLUSION

This study has shown that female church leaders play a significant role in promoting peaceful co-existence and reconciliation among the grassroots communities in Uganda, just like their male counterparts. As also pointed out by literature, women possess significant experience and skills in building trust, communities, alleviating fear and making compromises (Angom, 2018). Thus, away from the previously held perceptions of women as docile objects in theological discourse, Christian women organizations are developed as sites of change (Flaendorp, 2014). Indeed, the interviewees described their roles as mobilizers, leaders, role models, initiators of programmes, trainers, advocates, educators, disseminators, formulators and conscientizers. They also categorized the strategies used for reaching out to the communities as lobbying, advocacy, capacity building, information dissemination and networking. Working with different categories of people implies that female church leaders are on the path to promoting inclusive societies for sustainable development.

As Pope Francis emphasizes the pastoral call for all to accept and care for the environment, refugees and immigrants across the planet (Cremer, 2019), acts of humility, justice and reconciliation were manifested in the narratives of the interviewed women. For instance, women church leaders were engaged in activities geared towards improving the spiritual, social and economic wellbeing of people at the grassroots communities. The study shows that female church leaders strive towards creating inclusive societies by working with different categories of people in the local communities. Engaging in activities such as evangelism and teaching, 'Jesus's way' is emphasized as a way of promoting peaceful and inclusive societies. More so, skilling them in income-generating activities, providing education, guidance and counselling, environmental protection initiatives and by providing their basic needs are avenues to building effective and inclusive societies at the grassroots level.

Of course, several obstacles like a lack of political will and lack of motivation from the communities also were cited. However, courage and resilience are the major coping strategies. For contemporary women leaders, access to 'spiritual power' is seen as a pinnacle of their leadership. Thus, traits of 'authenticity' and immediacy, accompanied by visible and overt femininity as pointed out by Yih (2022), clear all the fears about women holding key roles in church life. The bravery shown by the acts of women in this study, especially those working with warrior tribes, proves the concept of servant leadership in that they risk getting into danger in order to save or improve a life. Female bravery is also shown in the Bible when Esther went into the king's courtyard when she was not supposed because she could not stand seeing her people perish. Abigail in 1 Samuel 25:2–39 took the lead of interceding for the family to be spared. Other outstanding women in the Bible include Anna (Luke 2:36–38) and Deborah (Jude 4:4–9). Such biblical teachings serve to raise the women's self-esteem, courage and an understanding of the need for equal discipleship.

In a nutshell, both literature and the findings of this study show that the struggle for women in ministry is far from over (Flaendorp, 2014). A call for a complementary role of women and men and advocacy for social political and economic equality between the sexes rather than male dominance are re-echoed. Indeed, as indicated by Yih (2022) and SDG 16, male church leaders cannot build peace in isolation; they have to build the energy of the female counter parts and make their voice heard. Citing Ira Chalaff's concept of courageous fellowship (Yih, 2022), a professional call for assuming responsibility in the service of others requires dealing with hierarchical power structures that hinder effective participation of women. This study suggests adopting new models of participation and responsibility. For instance, building a strong sense of synergy among women could enhance support networks for engaging more in joint outreach activities by female church leaders, thus promoting their visibility. And to restore confidence in women's church leadership, the women need support and skills to perform their duties better, thus more training opportunities could serve as a means to strengthening female leadership. Finally, female church leaders could adopt a rights-based approach and perhaps demand for equal participation as enshrined both in the Constitution of the Republic of Uganda and spelt out by SDG 16. Equal participation not only promotes peaceful and inclusive societies for sustainable development but signals respect for difference, voice and visibility as a form of social justice for women. Thus, advocating for involvement of women at all levels of leadership is paramount for building effective institutions, including the church.

## REFERENCES

Angom, S. (2018). *Women in Peacemaking and Peacebuilding in Northern Uganda*. Springer.

Angucia, M. (2010). *Broken Citizenship. Formerly abducted Children and their social reintegration in northern Uganda*. Rozenberg Publishers.

Arostegui, J. (2013). Gender, Conflict, and Peace-building: How Conflict Can Catalyse Positive Change for Women. *Gender & Development, 21*(3), 533–549. https://doi.org/10.1080/13552074.2013.846624

Ball, J. (2009). *In Their Own Voices: Learning from Women Peacebuilders in Uganda*: Doctoral dissertation, University of Guelph. Library and Archives Canada. Published Heritage Branch.

Barfoot, C. H., & Sheppard, G. T. (1980). Prophetic vs. priestly religion: The changing role of women clergy in classical Pentecostal churches. *Review of Religious Research*, 2–17.

Chitando, A. (2019). From Victims to the Vaunted: Young Women and Peace Building in Mashonaland East, Zimbabwe. *African Security Review, 28*(2), 110–123. https://doi.org/10.1080/10246029.2019.1662462

Cremer, D. (2019). Mercy, Justice, and Reconciliation: Pope Francis, Inclusive Leadership, and the Roman Catholic Church. In *Peace, Reconciliation and Social Justice Leadership in the 21st Century*. Emerald Publishing Limited.

Creswell, J. W. (2012). *Education Research: Planning, Conducting and Evaluating Quantitative and Qualitative Research* (4th ed.). Pearson.

Cypress, B. S. (2017). Rigor or Reliability and Validity in Qualitative Research: Perspectives, Strategies, Reconceptualization, Recommendations. *Dimensions of Critical Core Nursing, 36*(4), 253–263. https://doi.org/10.1097/DCC.0000000000000253

Datzberger, S. (2017). Peace Building Through Non-formal Education Programmes: A Case Study from Karamoja, Uganda. *International Peace Keeping, 24*(2), 326–349.

Datzberger, S., & Le Mat, M. (2018). JUST ADD WOMEN AND STIR? Education, gender and peacebuilding in Uganda. *International Journal of Educational Development, 59*, 61–69.

Eliko, E. O. (2006). *A Study of the Contribution of the Uganda Joint Christian Council Toward Peace Building in Uganda*. A Masters Dissertation Submitted to Kampala International University. https://ir.kiu.ac.ug/bitstream/20.500.12306/10131/1/Mayende_Jackline-img-0105.pdf

Fitch, D. (2006). The Great Giveaway: Reclaiming the Mission of the Church from Big Business, Parachurch Organizations, Psychotherapy, Consumer Capitalism, and Other Modern Maladies. In *Theology, Ethics and Philosophy*. Baker Book. https://doi.org/10.1111/j.1467-9418.2006.00316_6.x.

Flaendorp, C. (2014). The Life and Times of Professor Mary-Anne Plaatjies van Huffel: A Transformative Church Leader in Sub-Saharan Africa. *Studia Historiae Ecclesiasticae, 40*, 53–63. http://www.scielo.org.za/scielo.php?script=sci_arttext&pid=S1017-04992014000200005

Hennink, M., Hutter, I., & Bailey, A. (2011). *Qualitative Research Methods*. Sage Publications.

Khadiagala G. M. (2001). The Role of Acholi Religious Leaders in Peace Initiatives and Peace Building in Northern Uganda. (USAID). The Full Report Can Be Found at: http://www.usaid.gov/regions/afr/conflictweb/pbp_report.pdf.

Khodary, Y. M. (2016). Women and Peace-Building in Iraq. *Peace Review, 28*(4), 499–507. https://doi.org/10.1080/10402659.2016.1237151

Koch, M., & Fritz, M. (2014, December). Potentials for Prosperity Without Growth: Ecological Sustainability, Social Inclusion and the Quality of Life in 38 Countries. *Ecological Economies, 108*, 191–199.

Krueger, R. A. (1998). *Analysing and Reporting Focus Group Results*. Sage Publications.

Lubunga, E. (2016). The Impact of Conflict in the Democratic Republic of Congo on Women and their Response to Peace-building. *Stellenbosch Theological Journal, 2*(2), 347–364.

Lune, H., & Berg, B. L. (2017). *Qualitative Research Methods in Social Sciences* (9th ed.). England. Pearson Education Ltd..

Miller, E. (2016). Women in Australian Pentecostalism: Leadership, Submission, and Feminism in Hillsong Church. *Journal of Academic Study of Religion (JASR), 29*(1), 52–76. https://doi.org/10.1558/jasr.v29i1.26869

Mwenje, J. (2016, February 14). An investigation of the leadership styles of Pentecostal church leaders in Zimbabwe. *African Journal of Business Management, 10*(3), 55–74. https://doi.org/10.5897/AJBM2015.7882

Newkirk, D., & Cooper, B. S. (2013). Preparing Women for Baptist Church Leadership: Mentoring Impact on Beliefs and Practices of Female Minister. *Journal of Research on Christian Education, 22*, 323–343.

Ntini, T., & Omona, J. (2022). Peacebuilding Through Early Childhood Care and Education in a Post-Conflict Society: The Roles of the Parents and the Early Childhood Development Centres in Gulu District, Northern Uganda. Published Online, March 1. https://hdl.handle.net/10520/ejc-socwork1-v34-n1-a4.

Ochen, E. A. (2017). Women and Liberal Peacebuilding in Post-Conflict Northern Uganda: community social work agenda revisited?. *African Sociological Review/Revue Africaine de Sociologie, 21*(2), 15–35.

Sekano, G. H., & Masango, M. J. (2012). In Support of Female Church Leadership: Grappling with the Setswana Male Perspective- Shepherding as Solution Offered. *Verbum et Ecclesia, 33*(1). https://doi.org/10.4102/ve.v33i1.433

Shooter, S. (2014). What a Feminine Participation in the Divine Might Renew the Church and Its Leadership. *Feminist Theology, 22*(2), 173–185. https://doi.org/10.1177/0966735013507854

United Nations. (2014). World Survey on the Role of Women in Development 2014. Gender Equity and Sustainable Development. Research and Data Sector of the UN Women A/69/156.

United Nations. (2018). United Nations and the Rule of Law. Sustainable Development Goal 16. Peace Justice and Strong Institutions. https://www.un.org/ruleoflaw/sdg-16/#.

Yih, C. (2022). Theological Reflection on Silencing and Gender Disenfranchisement. *Practical Theology*. https://doi.org/10.1080/1756073X.2022.2108822

PART VII

# Topical Issues in Religion, Peacebuilding and Development in Africa

CHAPTER 41

# Ubuntu, Peacebuilding, and Development in Africa: Reflections on the Promises and Challenges of a Popular Concept

*Ezra Chitando and Susan M. Kilonzo*

## INTRODUCTION

"Ubuntumania" might be appropriated as a concept that best captures the popularity of the concept of Ubuntu, particularly in (Southern) African Studies. Scholars, politicians, business people, motivation speakers, and others have recovered the concept of Ubuntu from African Indigenous Knowledge Systems (IKS) (see, e.g., Teleki & Kamga, 2021) to posit it as a powerful resource for peacebuilding and development in Africa and beyond. If the question has consistently been, "What can Africa possibly bring forth and share with the rest of the world?" the answer, for many, has been a resounding, "Ubuntu." Popularized by luminaries such as the late Archbishop Desmond Tutu, Ubuntu has enjoyed positive publicity by diverse social actors. Tutu considers Ubuntu to be central to what it means to be human. According to him, Ubuntu says that one's humanity is bound up with the humanity of others, and one becomes only fully human because she or he recognizes the humanity of others (Tutu, 1999. See also, Otieno, 2020 and Meiring, 2022). In peacebuilding, then the

E. Chitando (✉)
Department of Philosophy, Religion and Ethics, University of Zimbabwe, Harare, Zimbabwe

S. M. Kilonzo
Department of Religion, Theology & Philosophy, Maseno University, Maseno, Kenya

© The Author(s), under exclusive license to Springer Nature Switzerland AG 2023
S. M. Kilonzo et al. (eds.), *The Palgrave Handbook of Religion, Peacebuilding, and Development in Africa*,
https://doi.org/10.1007/978-3-031-36829-5_41

concept would be appreciated as it becomes a useful framework for uniting people and rallying calls on the need to mind one another.

Particularly due to its deployment in South Africa's Truth and Reconciliation Commission (December 1995–2002), where Tutu served as the Chair, Ubuntu has been widely embraced as Africa's most strategic concept for peacebuilding in the continent (e.g., Arthur et al., 2015) and beyond (see, e.g., Rampke, 2016; Aydin, 2022; Kurtz, 2022), as well as for the international social work profession (Mayaka & Truell, 2021). More critically, although the concept has greater currency in Southern Africa, its advocates contend that there are corresponding ideas across most parts of the continent and that it can be deployed as an indigenous concept for peacebuilding in Africa (see, e.g., Issifu, 2015). Ubuntu, therefore, enjoys pride of place in African Studies in Africa, particularly within the context of decolonization and decoloniality. These concepts speak to the desire to ensure that African ways of knowing are taken seriously, both in academia and in activism (see, e.g., Ndlovu-Gatsheni, 2018, and Masaka, 2022).

Recognizing the high rating that Ubuntu enjoys in African Studies in Africa and its popularity in indigenous approaches to peacebuilding in Africa, this chapter reviews the relevance and applicability of Ubuntu to peacebuilding and development in Africa. It undertakes this exercise within the context of the United Nations Sustainable Development Goal (SDG) 16, which seeks to "[p]romote peaceful and inclusive societies for sustainable development, provide access to justice for all and build effective, accountable and inclusive institutions at all levels." Given such a background, the chapter seeks to respond to the following related questions:

1. What is Ubuntu and how has it been regarded in terms of contributing towards securing peaceful and inclusive societies for sustainable development in contemporary Africa?
2. What are the strengths of Ubuntu in the context of ongoing violence and conflict in Africa?
3. In the context of the pursuit of SDG 16, how can an Appreciative Enquiry approach contribute towards a more effective Ubuntu in order to achieve peaceful and inclusive societies for sustainable development in contemporary Africa?

We shall strive to respond to these questions in an eclectic fashion, that is, we will not adopt a fundamentalist approach where only the specific sections dedicated to answering each one of these focus exclusively on the particular question. Instead, we shall strive to address them holistically in the sections below. In the section immediately following this introduction, we shall summarize the concept of Ubuntu, highlighting its major qualities with special reference to peacebuilding in Africa. This will be followed by a section that adopts an Appreciative Inquiry approach to identify areas of strength that could be enhanced in order to achieve the set targets. This includes where

Ubuntu has been found wanting in relation to the inclusion of groups and individuals on the margins in Africa. The penultimate section will review possible strategies for popularizing an inclusive Ubuntu for sustainable peace, security, and development in Africa. In conclusion, the chapter will underscore the relevance of Ubuntu, but with the proviso that it be amplified and reimagined to become radically inclusive. Overall, and as stated earlier, the chapter is informed by the urgency of reviewing a popular concept in the wake of a dominant development agenda. Thus:

> SDG 16 is about promoting peaceful and inclusive societies for sustainable development, providing access to justice, and accountable, inclusive institutions at all levels. The twelve targets of SDG 16 are to measure direct violence, drivers of violence, governance, and justice. This Goal is important because it speaks to the need by all human beings to be free from all forms of violence and discrimination, no matter their gender, ethnicity, religion and race. Conflicts and violence lead to weak institutions that are, therefore, a threat to sustainable development. (Nyakwaka & Chelang'a, 2021, p. 6)

## Ubuntu: A Few Letters, Weighty Expectations

Ubuntu: these are only six letters, yet it is a concept with massive expectations. It is also a concept with a rich history. Ubuntu has attracted generous acclaim and a few critical remarks. It will not be possible to do justice to the complexities of Ubuntu within the confines of this chapter, where the focus is solely on its applicability in relation to the peacebuilding and sustainable development agenda. However, in this section we shall endeavor to highlight some key dimensions of Ubuntu and peacebuilding in Africa.

The origins of Ubuntu can be traced back to the traditional African belief systems that existed before the arrival of colonialism that emphasized interconnectedness of all people and the importance of relationships and community. It is based on the idea that individuals cannot exist in isolation but are part of a larger whole, therefore there was a need for individuals to work together and support each other for the benefit of the entire community. This perspective is guided by values such as compassion, kindness, generosity, respect, and honesty. Compassion and kindness would require one to treat others with empathy and understanding. Respect and honesty are values that promote the importance of integrity and accountability. Subsequently, with roots among the Bantu speakers in Southern Africa, Ubuntu is one of the most popular concepts in this region (see Gade, 2017a) (with related concepts elsewhere in Africa) that has been widely deployed in academia. While there are numerous definitions of the term, the most popular ones include those by Desmond Tutu, namely "my humanity is bound to yours" (see, e.g., Nadar et al., 2021), "humanity towards others" (see Tutu, 1999), and John S. Mbiti's, "I am because you are; because you are therefore I am" (see, e.g., Gathogo, 2022). Mugumbate and Chereni define it as follows:

Ubuntu refers to a collection of values and practices that black people of Africa or of African origin view as making people authentic human beings. While the nuances of these values and practices vary across different ethnic groups, they all point to one thing—an authentic individual human being is part of a larger and more significant relational, communal, societal, environmental and spiritual world. (Mugumbate & Chereni, 2020, p. vi)

Although the values that it espouses are locatable in other cultures and settings, Ubuntu is presented as a quintessentially African concept (Bennett & Patrick, 2011, p. 223) that expresses the centrality of the community. It captures the idea that "we belong together" and that one's being is inextricably tied to the being of others. Ubuntu expresses the notion of community consciousness and collective belonging, accountability, and existence. The following citation summarizes the thrust of Ubuntu in this regard:

The philosophy of Ubuntu espouses a fundamental respect in the rights of others, as well as a deep allegiance to the collective identity. More importantly, Ubuntu regulates the exercise of individual rights by emphasising sharing and co-responsibility and the mutual enjoyment of rights by all. It also promotes good human relationships and enhances human value, trust and dignity. The most outstanding positive impact of Ubuntu on the community is the value it puts on life and human dignity, particularly its caring attitude towards the elderly, who played and continue to play an important communal role in consolidating Ubuntu values. (Mabovula, 2011, p. 40)

Various scholars, including Samkange and Samkange (1980), Ramose (1999), Shutte (2001), Villa-Vicencio (2009), Murove (2014), Mangena (2016), Gade (2017a and 2017b), Ogude (2018), and Chasi (2021), have explored the use of Ubuntu in ethical reflections, traced its linguistic derivation, reflected on its appeal in various disciplines, as well as synthesized its application to peacebuilding and reconciliation, in Africa and beyond. A longer study would be required to review these works than can be undertaken within the scope of this essay. There is unanimity in the literature, however, that Ubuntu is critical for appreciating some key values in the African worldview. Thus,

[a]n African is not a rugged individual, but a person living within a community. In a hostile environment, it is only through such community solidarity that hunger, isolation, deprivation, poverty and any emerging challenges can be survived, because of the community's brotherly and sisterly concern, cooperation, care, and sharing. (Khomba & Kangaude-Ulaya., 2013, p. 673)

Ubuntu has been put forward as a powerful resource for peacebuilding in Africa (see, e.g., Murithi, 2006). Murithi presents Ubuntu as an enabler and facilitator of peacebuilding in Africa due to its emphasis on dialogue, respect, and nonviolence, acknowledging and upholding the dignity of the other and other values. For him, recovering the fundamental tenets of Ubuntu is critical for reconciliation and development in Africa. Commenting on Tutu's rendering of Ubuntu as expressing the notion that a human being is a human being through others, Murithi makes the following submission:

> This notion of Ubuntu sheds light on the importance of peacemaking through the principles of reciprocity, inclusivity and a sense of shared destiny between peoples. It provides a value system for giving and receiving forgiveness. It provides a rationale for sacrificing or letting go off the desire to take revenge for past wrongs. It provides an inspiration and suggests guidelines for societies and their governments, on how to legislate and establish laws which will promote reconciliation. (Murithi, 2006, p. 29)

Murithi is in the company of many other African scholars (and others) who regard Ubuntu as a strategic resource for peacebuilding in Africa and beyond. Reflecting on the role of Ubuntu in peacebuilding in South Africa, where, as we have noted above, Tutu popularized it in the context of the TRC, Arthur et al. (2015) identify key issues relating to Ubuntu. They make reference to the importance given to story-telling where the participants were allowed to narrate their own experiences, the full participation of the parties, a joint problem-solving approach, and mutual respect. While recognizing some of the limitations of Ubuntu, particularly in contemporary pluralistic African settings, Akinola and Uzodike (2018) still reckon that it continues to be a relevant and valuable concept for effective peacebuilding. There is also an appreciation of Ubuntu for its inclusive approach. Ubuntu seeks to cover all members of the community in its purview. Thus,

> [w]henever conflicts arise, however, *Ubuntu* informs approaches to peacebuilding that focus on building better future relationships, tolerance between individuals and groups because we are by nature interdependent. In this view, no one is disposable, and everyone, young and old, women and men, the poor and affluent have a role to play. (Kurtz, 2022, p. 135)

Given the burning political question of Africa's search for recovering indigenous ways of knowing and doing, Ubuntu is enjoying increased popularity. For many, it provides hope that Africa can move forward while borrowing from its rich past. In particular, Ubuntu is presented as either replacing or complementing western peacebuilding strategies. When presented as an expression of an Alternative Dispute Resolution (ADR) strategy (see, e.g., Uwazie, 2014), Ubuntu is touted as replacing the dominant western strategies. In his critique of the "liberal peace" paradigm, Tom (2018) reflects on the potential of Ubuntu to provide a more sustainable approach to peacebuilding. On the other hand, de Coning (2021, p. 346) recognizes Ubuntu as contributing to Africa's resilience and as having preventing violence during the COVID-19 lockdowns. In this regard, Ubuntu is an effective resource that should be upheld, alongside other emerging (western) process systems such as Adaptive Peacebuilding. Ubuntu and other African indigenous knowledge systems equip individuals and communities with listening skills. Listening is a critical resource in conflict transformation (see, e.g., Beyene, 2020).

Alongside the quality of listening skills for effective peacebuilding, Ubuntu is also associated with empathy. Members of the community are enjoined to feel for and feel with those who are experiencing pain and exclusion. When one is cruel, violent, and without empathy, he or she is said to be lacking Ubuntu. To be fully human is to empathize and consistently act in solidarity with those who would be enduring the horrors of violence and war. Thus:

> [e]mpathy is an integral part of Ubuntu and, by parity of reasoning, peacebuilding. No one was left out of the effort to build peace. No one was ever too evil or guilty to learn through participation. The guilt of one was a shared responsibility of the collective. No one was too poor to give towards a peace outcome and the giver was not a donor. The act was extended to family, kinsfolk and strangers alike. (Kagoro, 2021, p. 11)

## UBUNTU AND PEACEBUILDING IN AFRICA: A REVIEW FROM AN APPRECIATIVE INQUIRY APPROACH

From the foregoing, it is clear that Ubuntu enjoys a special place in scholarship on peacebuilding in Africa. Indeed, as we indicated in the introduction to this chapter, Ubuntu is receiving positive reviews in other areas in African Studies in Africa. In this section, we adopt an Appreciative Inquiry approach to Ubuntu. At the core of Appreciative Inquiry is the conviction that evaluation must be understood in terms of building on existing strengths. Whereas the traditional approach to evaluation tends to project it as some form of fault-finding, Appreciative Inquiry recognizes the importance of identifying inner strengths, locating internal challenges, and strengthening systems in order to become more efficient and effective. Within Appreciative Inquiry is the belief that communities are inherently capable of generating positive change when they focus on what is working well and build upon those strengths (Cooperrider & Srivastva, 1987). Proponents of the approach argue that it offers a more positive and empowering approach to change than traditional problem-solving methods, and can help to create a sense of shared ownership and investment in the change process (Cooperrider & Whitney, 2005).

While analyzing how Appreciative Inquiry works, scholars have observed a structured process that involves several phases, including discovery, dream, design, and destiny (Cooperrider & Whitney, 2005). In the discovery phase, stakeholders are encouraged to share stories and experiences that highlight the positive aspects of the organization or community. This process helps to generate a sense of optimism and possibility, and lays the groundwork for future action. In the dream phase, stakeholders are invited to imagine a future in which the organization or community is thriving and achieving its goals. This process helps to create a shared vision for the future and identifies the values and principles that will guide future action. In the design phase, stakeholders work together to develop concrete action plans that will help to bring the vision to life. This may involve identifying specific goals and objectives, as well as developing strategies for achieving those goals. Finally, in the destiny phase, stakeholders reflect on their progress and evaluate the effectiveness of their efforts. This process helps to create a culture of continuous learning and improvement, and provides a foundation for ongoing positive change (Bushe & Kassam, 2005). We then could argue that Appreciative Inquiry carries the same motivation as Ubuntu! It seeks to bring together communities and build a common goal, a common destiny. Thus:

> [i]n its most practical construction, Appreciative Inquiry (also referred to as AI) is a form of transformational inquiry that selectively seeks to locate, highlight, and illuminate the life-giving forces of an organization's existence. It is based on the belief that human systems are made and imagined by those who live and work within them. AI leads these systems to move toward the creative images that reside in the positive core of an organization. This approach is based on solid, proven principles for enabling creativity, knowledge, and spirit in the workplace. These principles call people to work toward a common vision and a higher purpose. (Cooperrider et al., 2008, p. xi)

First, we acknowledge that Ubuntu is a grassroots/mountain top/community-based, traditional and indigenous African approach to peacebuilding (with global potential). It has contributed immensely to peacebuilding in Africa in the past, is doing so now, and can produce even more effective results in the future. Thus, we appreciate the capacity of Ubuntu to contribute towards the realization of SDG 16 in Africa. It offers a bottom-up approach to peacebuilding and sustainable development in Africa, as opposed to initiatives that are imposed from above. In this regard, Ubuntu is a pre-existing and ready-made peacebuilding and sustainable development resource.

However, we contend that there is a need to open up Ubuntu to the realities and tensions of contemporary Africa. While Ubuntu was quite effective in the past when African communities tended to be more closely bound up, its application in contemporary contexts of radical pluralism requires more strategic reflections. We, however, do not subscribe to the notion that the Ubuntu ethic is no longer applicable (see, e.g., Zimunya et al., 2015). Given the reality of xenophobia in some parts of the continent and the challenges this poses to Ubuntu (see, e.g., Murenje, 2020), we contend that there is a need to reactivate Ubuntu to respond to such unfortunate developments.

Second, although Ubuntu does accord space to African women and embraces their contribution to peacebuilding (see, e.g., Isike, 2017) and development, it continues to exude an overly patriarchal outlook (see Chitando, 2008; Mangena, 2009). While Manyonganise (2015) adopts an ambivalent position in relation to Ubuntu and women, we are persuaded that more needs to be done to expunge the patriarchal undertones that are found in Ubuntu. This will enable contemporary African women to contribute towards the achievement of SDG 16 in Africa. Whereas at the level of ideology, the current expression of Ubuntu is quite appealing, in practice we identify the persistence of male privilege. African men in particular will need to do more to appreciate the many sacrifices, talents, and gifts that African women bring to peacebuilding and development in Africa (see, e.g., Chitando, 2015). For Chisale (2018), however, Ubuntu promotes gender equality and communities have to live in "an unbroken circle." In this regard, the role of Ubuntu in enabling African women to articulate their voices and contribute toward peacebuilding and development in Africa is affirmed. If the emphasis of Ubuntu is relationships and the importance of mutual respect and understanding (Mbiti, 1990), then this should be a springboard for creating spaces for equality and shrinking the spaces that promote patriarchy. This will amplify the need to recognize and value the contributions of women in peacebuilding. Moreover, Ubuntu promotes the value of collective responsibility, meaning that society as a whole is responsible for ensuring the well-being of all its members, including women. This philosophy has been used to advocate for policies and programs that address gender-based violence, promote women's empowerment, and support women's participation in political and economic decision-making (Gyekye, 1996).

Third, Ubuntu is a powerful concept that is strategically placed to promote radical inclusion, the overarching focus of the SDGs. In its ideal form, Ubuntu strives to ensure that everyone (including the environment) is taken on board in relation to the journey to sustainable development. In terms of orientation, the SDGs were designed to cover people from the diverse class, social, religious, nationality, and ethnic, among other backgrounds. It is an ambitious undertaking which is motivated by the desire to achieve social and economic justice, peace, and prosperity. Using indices to try and measure progress, while helpful, will ultimately not capture the underlying conviction. This drive has been expressed as follows:

> The 2030 agenda is the people's agenda. It puts people first and its core principle is leaving no-one behind. The world cannot uphold to this principle unless the SDG progress assessment frameworks embrace it. In other words, no progress shall be counted, unless all progress together. (Bidarbakhtnia, 2020, p. 60)

While we appreciate Ubuntu's overall potential for radical inclusion, we are also aware of the different categories of persons who continue to be left behind. Where Ubuntu is supposed to ensure that no one is left behind, persons whose sexual orientation and gender identities are deemed non-conforming continue to experience exclusion. In different African contexts, the security and well-being of lesbian, gay, bisexual, transgender, intersex, and queer/questioning (LGBTIQ+) persons continue to be threatened. In fact, in most African countries, homosexuality is stigmatized and criminalized, and LGBTQI people face discrimination and violence. Some argue that this is due to cultural values that prioritize heterosexuality and traditional gender roles, which are seen as essential to the preservation of community and family structures (Amnesty International, 2013). Indeed, the African sense of community (Ubuntu) is sometimes deployed to deny the rights of LGBTIQ+ persons (see, e.g., Makamure, 2015). However, as Matolino (2017) argues, such an approach to communal solidarity is hardly convincing. It is, therefore, vital for the inclusive dimension of Ubuntu to be taken more seriously in order to ensure that no one is left behind, as expressed in the SDGs agenda. Ubuntu can be used to promote dialogue and understanding between LGBTQI people and their communities. By emphasizing the importance of relationships and mutual respect, Ubuntu provides a platform for challenging stereotypes and promoting acceptance of diversity (Mackay & Robinson, 2018).

Although there has been an improvement in the legislation, widows in many African countries continue to face sociocultural and economic challenges (see, e.g., Soussou, 2002). They are mostly prevented from contributing to peacebuilding and development in Africa, because they struggle to get a place at the table. While in its formulation Ubuntu prioritizes the role of older people for their wisdom and guidance, older people in general and older women in particular are often ostracized. This also true of younger and older female sex workers. While traditional African societies did not have prisoners, this is now a reality in contemporary Africa. Their potential to contribute toward the attainment of SDG 16 is mostly missed due to stigma and discrimination. Therefore, it will be critical for the concentric rings of Ubuntu, as well as its circle, to continue to spread out and embrace the marginalized and excluded in society.

Youth forms the largest chunk of Africa's population. Subsequently, a framework through which the youth can be engaged in peacebuilding can be sourced from the emphasis of Ubuntu on dialogue. Dialogue provides a platform for people to express their grievances and work toward a mutually beneficial solution. In the context of youth in Africa, Ubuntu may be used to create safe spaces for young people to engage in dialogue and express their views (Dessalegn, 2015). By providing opportunities for youth to communicate openly and honestly, through Ubuntu understanding and empathy, which are crucial for conflict resolution, are realized. Further, Ubuntu may be employed as a way of emphasizing the importance of youth leadership in peacebuilding. Young people are often disproportionately affected by conflict and violence, but they are also powerful agents of change (Chigudu, 2016). A framework that borrows on the principles of Ubuntu may empower young people and provide them with the tools they need to contribute to peacebuilding efforts in their communities. By promoting youth leadership and engagement, Ubuntu can help to build a more sustainable and peaceful future for Africa.

Finally, Ubuntu is built on an extremely positive interpretation of human nature. As Appreciative Inquiry dictates, it is vital to recognize the innate human capacity to do good. The human capacity to nurture peace and development is responsible for the emergence of successive civilizations. However, the reality of numerous and seemingly endless wars in Africa and other parts of the world suggests that humans also have the appetite and capacity to gravitate toward violence and destruction. It would seem that Ubuntu has not budgeted adequately for this dark, negative, destructive, and anti-development side of human nature.

## FOR SUCH A TIME AS THIS: SOME PROPOSALS FOR ENHANCING UBUNTU'S EFFICACY FOR PEACEBUILDING AND DEVELOPMENT IN CONTEMPORARY AFRICA

The preceding sections have outlined the key tenets and strengths of Ubuntu in the context of peacebuilding and sustainable development in Africa, with special focus on SDG 16. They have also identified some challenges associated with Ubuntu when reviewed in the context of the overall SDG agenda of leaving no one behind. In this section, we seek to suggest, still in the spirit of Appreciative Inquiry, some strategies that could be adopted and applied to enhance the efficacy of Ubuntu in contemporary Africa. This ensues from our observation that perhaps most proponents of Ubuntu for peacebuilding and development in Africa tend to adopt rather defensive standpoints. They are mostly not willing to entertain any suggestions on how Ubuntu could be recalibrated to respond more effectively to contemporary realities and challenges in Africa and beyond. To say this is not to suggest that Ubuntu and other African IKS are deficient or outdated. It is only to appreciate that every philosophy or ethical vantage point must be undergoing periodic and systematic review if it is going to remain relevant and effective.

First, it is highly strategic that the teaching and popularization of Ubuntu to be more deliberate, better coordinated, and intentional than is the case currently. The impact of processes such as globalization and urbanization on socialization in Africa needs to be appreciated more actively. As a result, many younger Africans only hear of Ubuntu sporadically and reckon it to be some fanciful concept from Africa's remote past. They do not readily regard it as a resource for peacebuilding and development in Africa. Therefore, an investment in mainstreaming and exploring key aspects of Ubuntu in the education curricula (all levels), as well as in the media (all forms), will equip more citizens with the relevant knowledge and skills to utilize it in conflict situations (in all their diversity). When elders decry the loss of Ubuntu (Gumbo, 2014), it is vital to come up with strategies to "reframe, rethink, capture and illustrate" (Ndhlovu, 2023) Ubuntu in innovative and more compelling ways for it to make effective contributions to peacebuilding and development in Africa.

Second, Ubuntu must be reconceptualized and synthesized with related concepts from Christianity, Islam, and other traditions. Granted that African Traditional Religions remain relevant (Aderibigbe & Falola, 2022), the reality of the matter is that a pluralistic ethos now pervades most African societies. Consequently, identifying synergies between Ubuntu and related concepts in Christianity, Islam, and other worldviews will enhance, not diminish, its role in meeting the objectives of SDG 16. For example, Ubuntu and the Christian concept of the dignity of all human beings and the idea of human flourishing can be deployed to promote the inclusion of all marginalized people. Marginalized groups, such as women, youth, persons living with disabilities, and LGBTQI+, among others, need to be included in decision-making processes, and policy structuring and restructuring tables (Dessalegn, 2015). This will ensure that Ubuntu promotes inclusivity through interconnectedness of all people as well as their opinion in conflict resolution and peacebuilding mechanisms. Although some tension is inevitable, when a creative approach is adopted, it is possible to reach a viable rapprochement (see, e.g., Banda, 2019 and, Magezi & Khlopa, 2021).

Third, and emerging from the realist reading of the human proclivity for violence and destruction, regional economic blocks and continental institutions must be more determined to marshal adequate resources to subdue threats to peace and security in Africa. We are fully aware that there is a very strong position that insists on puritanical approaches toward peacebuilding in Africa. Ubuntu itself is built on the idea of peaceful and exclusively non-violent approaches to peacebuilding. In an ideal world, we would readily and even happily endorse such an approach. However, as we conceded above, there are some individuals and groups who will go on a rampage, rape women and girls, and wantonly kill fellow human beings without any compunction. We propose that the African Union, for example, and the United Nations consider the responsibility to protect as an expression of Ubuntu. While space considerations do not allow us to elaborate on this theme, we are convinced that there are exceptional cases where threats to peace and security must be neutralized in order for Ubuntu to be exercised and for communities and individuals to enjoy opportunities for sustainable development.

Fourth, it is important to ensure that leadership training in Africa approaches Ubuntu in a decisive way. While the theme of Ubuntu and leadership in general has enjoyed considerable scholarly attention (see, e.g., Ncube, 2010), our specific focus is on Ubuntu and leadership for peacebuilding and development in Africa. The recurrence of violent conflict in Africa calls for the training of leaders who are imbued with the Ubuntu ethos and prioritize peacebuilding and sustainable development. They must be women, youth, and men who are passionate about the continent's progress and should be drawn from across the diverse sectors of society. A critical mass of empowered leaders will contribute toward the vision of a buoyant and successful continent.

## Conclusion

Ubuntu is one of the concepts that is enjoying a lot of scholarly attention. In this chapter, we adopted an Appreciative Inquiry approach and sought to understand Ubuntu's potential to contribute towards the achievement of SDG 16 in Africa. We highlighted the key features of Ubuntu, drawing attention to its valorization as a strategic resource in promoting peace, security, and development in Africa. In particular, we drew attention to how different scholars are united in presenting Ubuntu as enabling peaceful co-existence and recognizing the full rights of the other to exist and flourish. However, we also contended that Ubuntu is not fully inclusive and highlighted some of the categories of individuals and groups that are being left behind. We then presented some strategies that we deem valuable in enhancing Ubuntu's efficacy to meet the aspirations of SDG 16 in Africa. Ubuntu, like all human constructs, has some limitations. However, it remains a source of strength and, if approached with creativity and zeal, can have a positive impact on Africa's struggle for peace and sustainable development. Ubuntu calls for citizens to appreciate the full humanity of others. We envisage that even as it undergoes critique and refinement, Ubuntu can contribute towards the development of peace-loving and peace-promoting citizens who can affirm that their humanity is only complete when the humanity of the other is fully recognized. Such communities will be oases of peace and tranquility, providing the platform for sustainable development and human flourishing in Africa and beyond.

## References

Aderibigbe, I., & Falola, T. (Eds.). (2022). *The Palgrave Handbook of African Traditional Religion*. Palgrave Macmillan.

Akinola, A. O., & Uzodike, U. O. (2018). Ubuntu and the Quest for Conflict Resolution in Africa. *Journal of Black Studies, 49*(2), 91–113.

Amnesty International. (2013). Making love a Crime: Criminalization of Same-sex Conduct in Sub-Saharan Africa. Retrieved May 6, 2023, from https://www.amnesty.org/en/documents/afr01/001/2013/en/

Arthur, D., Issifu, A., & Marfo, S. (2015). An Analysis of the Influence of Ubuntu Principle on the South Africa Peace Building Process. *Journal of Global Peace and Conflict, 3*(2), 63–77.

Aydin, A. F. (2022). *Ubuntu: A New Approach to International Post-Conflict Peacebuilding*. A Thesis Submitted to the Graduate School of Social Sciences of the Middle East Technical University. Turkey.

Banda, C. (2019). *Ubuntu* as Human Flourishing? An African Traditional Religious Analysis of *Ubuntu* and its Challenge to Christian Anthropology. *Stellenbosch Theological Journal, 5*(3), 203–228.

Bennett, T., & Patrick, J. (2011). Ubuntu: The Ethics of Traditional Religion. In T. W. Bennett (Ed.), *Traditional African Religions in South African Law* (pp. 223–242). University of Cape Town Press.

Beyene, Z. (2020). Building Peace through Listening. In D. L. Worthington & G. D. Bodie (Eds.), *The Handbook of Listening* (pp. 419–426). John Wiley & Sons, Inc.

Bidarbakhtnia, A. (2020). Measuring Sustainable Development Goals (SDGs): An Inclusive Approach. *Global Policy, 11*(1), 56–67.

Bushe, G. R., & Kassam, A. F. (2005). When is Appreciative Inquiry Transformational? A Meta-Case Analysis. *Journal of Applied Behavioral Science, 41*(2), 161–181.

Chasi, C. T. (2021). *Ubuntu for Warriors*. Africa World Press.

Chigudu, O. (2016). Ubuntu as a Tool for Peacebuilding in Africa. *Journal of Peacebuilding and Development, 11*(1), 51–63.

Chisale, S. (2018). Ubuntu as Care: Deconstructing the Gendered Ubuntu. *Verbum et Ecclesia, 39*(1), a1790. https://doi.org/10.4102/ve.v39i1.1790

Chitando, E. (2008). Religious Ethics, HIV and AIDS and Masculinities in Southern Africa. In R. Nicolson (Ed.), *Persons in Community: African Ethics in a Global Culture* (pp. 45–63). University of KwaZulu-Natal Press.

Chitando, E. (2015). 'Do Not Tell the Person Carrying that s/he Stinks': Reflections on Ubuntu and Masculinities in the Context of Sexual and Gender-based Violence and HIV. In E. Mouton, G. Kapuma, L. Hansen, & T. Togom (Eds.), *Living with Dignity: African Perspectives on Gender Equality* (pp. 269–283). Sun Press.

Cooperrider, D. L., & Srivastva, S. (1987). Appreciative Inquiry in Organizational Life. *Research in Organizational Change and Development, 1*, 129–169.

Cooperrider, D. L., & Whitney, D. (2005). *Appreciative Inquiry: A Positive Revolution in Change*. Berrett-Koehler Publishers.

Cooperrider, L., Whitney, D., & Stavros, J. (2008). *Appreciative Inquiry Handbook: For Leaders of Change* (2nd ed.). Crown Custom Publishing, Inc; Berrett-Koehler Publishers, Inc.

de Coning, C. (2021). COVID-19 and the Resilience of Africa's Peace and Security Networks. *African Security, 14*(4), 341–369.

Dessalegn, A. (2015). Ubuntu as a Peacebuilding Philosophy in Africa. *International Journal of Peace and Conflict Studies, 2*(1), 1–9.

Gade, B. (2017a). *A Discourse on African Philosophy: A New Perspective on Transitional Justice in South Africa*. Lexington Books.

Gade, B. (2017b). Ubuntu and the Truth and Reconciliation Commission in South Africa. In C. M. Kelso & P. L. Harris (Eds.), *Truth and Reconciliation in South Africa: Miracle or Model?* (pp. 67–85). Routledge.

Gathogo, J. (2022). John Mbiti's Ubuntu Theology: Was it Rooted in his African Heritage? *Studia Historiae Ecclesiasticae, 48*(2), 22. https://doi.org/10.25159/2412-4265/10292

Gumbo, M. T. (2014). Elders Decry the Loss of Ubuntu. *Mediterranean Journal of Social Sciences, 5*(10), 67–77.

Gyekye, K. (1996). *African Cultural Values: An Introduction*. Sankofa Publishing.

Isike, C. (2017). Soft Power and a Feminist Ethics of Peacebuilding in Africa. *Peace Review, 29*(3), 350–357.

Issifu, K. (2015). Exploring Indigenous Approaches to Peacebuilding: The Case of Ubuntu in South Africa. *Peace Studies Journal, 8*(2), 59–72.

Kagoro, B. (2021). Afrocentric Conception of Conflict Transformation: Beyond Ubuntu Mythology and Romantic Traditionalism. Discussion Paper. Johannesburg: Centre for the Study of Violence and Reconciliation.

Khomba, K., & Kangaude-Ulaya. (2013). Indigenisation of Corporate Strategies in Africa: Lessons From the African Ubuntu Philosophy. *China-USA Business Review, 12*(7), 672–689.

Kurtz, M. (2022). Ubuntu as Peacebuilding. In L. R. Kurtz (Ed.), *Encyclopedia of Violence, Peace, and Conflict* (Vol. 4, pp. 145–152). Elsevier Academic Press.

Mabovula, N. M. (2011). The Erosion of African Communal Values: A Reappraisal of the African Ubuntu Philosophy. *Inkanyiso: Journal of Humanities & Social Science, 3*(1), 38–47.

Mackay, F., & Robinson, A. (2018). Ubuntu and LGBTIQ Rights: Challenging Stereotypes in African Societies. In C. Walker & M. Allen (Eds.), *Intersectionality in Practice* (pp. 1–17). Routledge.

Magezi, V., & Khlopa, C. (2021). The Tenet of Ubuntu in South (African) Ethics: Inclusive Hospitality and Christian Ethical Disposition of Effective Pastoral Care in Africa. *Stellenbosch Theological Journal, 7*(1), 1–32.

Makamure, C. (2015). Attitudes toward Homosexual Practices among the Karanga People: A Religious Perspective. *IOSR Journal of Humanities and Social Science (IOSR-JHSS), 20*(6), 50–56.

Mangena, F. (2009). The Search for an African Feminist Ethic: A Zimbabwean Perspective. *Journal of International Women's Studies, 11*(2), 18–30.

Mangena, F. (2016). African Ethics through Ubuntu: A Postmodern Exposition. *Africology: The Journal of Pan African Studies, 9*(2), 66–80.

Manyonganise, M. (2015). Oppressive and Liberative: A Zimbabwean Woman's Reflections on Ubuntu. *Verbum et Ecclesia, 36*(2), Art. #1438, 7. https://doi.org/10.4102/ve.v36i2.1438

Masaka, D. (Ed.). (2022). *Knowledge Production and the Search for Epistemic Liberation in Africa*. Palgrave Macmillan.

Matolino, B. (2017). Being Gay and African: A View from an African Philosopher. *Phronimon, 18*, 50–78.

Mayaka, B., & Truell, R. (2021). Ubuntu and its Potential impact on the International Social Work Profession. *International Social Work, 64*(5), 649–662.

Mbiti, J. S. (1990). *African Religions and Philosophy*. Heinemann.

Meiring, P. G. (2022). Forgiveness, Reconciliation and Justice á la Desmond Tutu. *Acta Theologica, 44*(2), 86–103.

Mugumbate, J. R., & Chereni, A. (2020). Now, the Theory of Ubuntu has its Space in Social Work. *African Journal of Social Work* (Special Issue on Ubuntu Social Work) 10(1): v–xiv.

Murenje, M. (2020). Ubuntu and Xenophobia in South Africa's International Migration. *African Journal of Social Work, 10*(1), 95–98.

Murithi, T. (2006). Practical Peacemaking Wisdom from Africa: Reflections on Ubuntu. *The Journal of Pan African Studies, 1*(4), 25–34.

Murove, M. F. (2014). Ubuntu. *Diogenes, 59*(3–4), 36–47.

Nadar, S., et al. (Eds.). (2021). *Ecumenical Encounters with Desmond Mpilo Tutu: Visions for Justice, Dignity and Peace*. Regnum Books International.

Ncube, L. B. (2010). Ubuntu: A Transformative Leadership Philosophy. *Journal of Leadership Studies, 4*(3), 77–82.

Ndhlovu, T. P. (2023). Food (in)security, the Moral Economy, and Ubuntu in South Africa: A Southern Perspective. *Review of International Political Economy*. https://doi.org/10.1080/09692290.2022.2161110.

Ndlovu-Gatsheni, S. J. (2018). *Epistemic Freedom in Africa: Deprovincialization and Decolonization*. Routledge.

Nyakwaka, D. A., & Chelang'a, J. (2021). Peace, Justice and Strong Institutions for Sustainable Development in Kenya. *Africa Habitat Review Journal* Special Issue: 3–12.

Ogude, J. (2018). *Ubuntu and Personhood*. Africa World Press.

Otieno, S. A. (2020). Ethical Thought of Archbishop Desmond Tutu: Ubuntu and Tutu's Moral Modeling as Transformation and Renewal. In N. Wariboko & T. Falola

(Eds.), *The Palgrave Handbook of African Social Ethics* (pp. 589–604). Palgrave Macmillan.

Ramose, M. B. (1999). *African Philosophy through Ubuntu*. Mond Books.

Rampke, B. (2016). Interconnectedness, Healing and Harmony: The Application of Ubuntu in Peace Research and in Namibia-German Postcolonial Disputes Emerging from the Return of Human Remains. Master's Thesis, Peace and Conflict Research, School of Social Sciences and Humanities, University of Tampere. Finland.

Samkange, S., & Samkange, T. M. (1980). *Hunhuism or Ubuntuism: A Zimbabwean Indigenous Political Philosophy*. Graham Publishing.

Shutte, A. (2001). *Ubuntu: An Ethic for the new South Africa*. Cluster Publications.

Soussou, M. (2002). Widowhood Practices in West Africa: The Silent Victims. *International Journal of Social Welfare, 11*(3), 201–209.

Teleki, M., & Kamga, S. (2021). The Ethics of Ubuntu and its Role in Fostering Justice for Development in South Africa. In V. Gumede, M. Muchie, & A. Shafi (Eds.), *Indigenous Systems and Africa's Development* (pp. 120–139). Africa Institute of South Africa.

Tom, P. (2018). A 'Post-liberal Peace' via *Ubuntu? Peacebuilding, 6*(1), 65–79.

Tutu, D. (1999). *No Future without Forgiveness*. Doubleday.

Uwazie, E. (Ed.). (2014). *Alternative Dispute Resolution and Peace-building in Africa*. Cambridge Scholars Publishing.

Villa-Vicencio, C. (2009). *Walk with Us and Listen: Political Reconciliation in Africa*. University of Cape Town Press.

Zimunya, C., Gwara, J., & Mlambo, O. (2015). The Feasibility of an Ubuntu Ethic in a Modernised World. *Journal of African Foreign Affairs, 2*(1/2), 5–26.

CHAPTER 42

# Shaping the Instruments of Peace: Religion in Digital Peacebuilding in Africa

*Sokfa F. John*

## INTRODUCTION

Religion and technology have both always been important sites of contestations and agency, and central to major defining moments in society's evolution. They are entangled in several ways. Religious visions and values shape the design and purpose of technology; technology shapes religious visions, values, and practices; technology has utility in proselytization, improving access to faith resources, facilitating religious experiences, bettering the lives of faith communities, and so on (Alexander, 2020; Hoover, 2012). Changes in digital media and digital cultures affect religion in terms of meaning, spirituality, and practice. One obvious realm of interaction between religion and technology is in conflicts and violence. Sophisticated technologies are deployed to fight religious wars or to pursue the goals of religious extremists. Online hate speech and disinformation targeting religious groups and identities or by religious actors; religious identity-based narratives of conflict; and the use of deep fakes and other advanced technologies for religion-related violent content are a few more of the many ways technology and religion intersect in violence. As Harari (2018) rightly argues, arguments about religious rituals and identities will continue to impact how new technologies are used, no matter how advanced such technologies become. The most sophisticated cyber and nuclear weapons may be used to settle religious disputes (Harari, 2018).

---

S. F. John (✉)
Centre for Mediation in Africa, University of Pretoria, Pretoria, South Africa

© The Author(s), under exclusive license to Springer Nature Switzerland AG 2023
S. M. Kilonzo et al. (eds.), *The Palgrave Handbook of Religion, Peacebuilding, and Development in Africa*,
https://doi.org/10.1007/978-3-031-36829-5_42

Such tendencies are not unique to religion. In fact, most violent uses of technology have nothing to do with religion. The intention here is to acknowledge that religion and technology are deeply interconnected, sometimes with violent outcomes. Understanding this relationship is also important for deepening our capacity to transform conflicts and build just, positive, and sustainable peace in an era where religion is implicated in major forms of violence and conflicts; and when religion's role in ending all kinds of violence and realizing peace is most pertinent.

Religious stakeholders and actors have always been instrumental in conflict transformation and peacebuilding in Africa and globally. Religious peacebuilders, like other peacebuilders, make use of the technology available to them in their work. However, religion rarely features in the current explosion of ideas and activities around technologies and peacebuilding. For nearly two decades, interests in using technology for peace have steadily increased, with the world's top institutions and organizations establishing technology labs and centres, and initiating relevant projects (Firchow et al., 2017). The COVID-19 pandemic accelerated these efforts due to restrictions on movements and physical interaction. Peacebuilding needed to continue and to further address emerging challenges to peace due to the pandemic. Thus, as with other sectors, technologies such as Zoom, social media, and the exploration of the possibilities of other advanced technologies became central to everyday peacebuilding work.

This chapter explores the field of digital peacebuilding, including projects in Africa, and reflects on possible ways that religions, in their many manifestations and embodiments, could further their requisite role in peacebuilding through full participation in digital peacebuilding. This is another avenue to deepen the contribution of religion to Sustainable Development Goal (SDG) 16, namely, the promotion of peaceful and inclusive societies for sustainable development, increasing access to justice and strengthening relevant institutions to be inclusive and accountable. I suggest that religious stakeholders and actors can contribute to digital peacebuilding through, among other things, critical religious participation in shaping technology ethics generally and in relation to peacebuilding; translating technology and deploying religious resources to understand digital society; designing religious technologies to be agents of peace; and creating opportunities for critical religious self-reflection on religion's role in all forms of violence.

## Religious Peacebuilding in Africa

Religions are intrinsically plural and ambivalent due to the diversity of human perception and interpretation of the sacred. This is the underlying idea in Appleby's (1999) explanation of religious violence and the potential of religions for peace. Thus, the same religious source and piety can inspire violence in one believer but selfless service for peace in another. Implied here, depending on one's interpretation, is the sense that religion is somehow neutral with regard to violence and can be deliberately deployed, politicized, or instrumentalized either for violence or for peace. This is a common perspective on the role of religion in violence. It is exemplified in the politicization of religion theory that dominates literature on religion and conflicts in Africa, arguing that religions and religious identities manifest in conflicts because they are politicized or exploited in the pursuits of political and other interests (Basedau et al., 2013; John, 2021a; Maiangwa, 2014; McCauley & Posner, 2019; Onapajo, 2012; Ottuh & Omosor, 2022). This thesis also underscores many efforts to combat public perceptions of religions, such as Islam, as essentially violent or as advocating violence in its theology, while highlighting peace as its defining ethos. Other perspectives include the discrimination and hierarchies embedded in the perception and social categorization of ethnicities and religions in some societies; the idea that religion is a platform for political pursuits rather than merely a tool in the hands of politicians; and that religion is a site for contesting identities and competing interests (John, 2021a; Kukah, 1993; Lergo, 2011).

These perspectives explain different ways that religions are involved in conflicts and possible opportunities or actions for peace, such as religious stakeholders refusing and actively working against the politicization of their faith. Yet, the precise way religion shapes or reinforces violence or peace is a complex matter that requires detailed engagement with contexts, situational factors, and the proximity of religious factors to other religious and non-religious factors (Basedau, 2017; Basedau & De Juan, 2008; Baumann et al., 2018; Slocum-Bradley, 2016). In many cases, actors in religious conflicts or peacebuilding are not necessarily or directly responding to any theological or spiritual motivation. Factors such as the trend in their religious community—for example, what Christians are doing in a given situation in a polarized religious environment, belonging to a religion in a nominal or cultural identification sense, among other factors—can inform participation of persons who by several criteria are not religious in 'religious' conflicts or peacebuilding. Also, religious belonging during interreligious conflicts can be a matter of exclusion by sections within one's own religion. For example, in Nigerian conflicts, Yoruba Muslims have been attacked by Hausa/Fulani Muslims who either saw them as inauthentic Muslims or still exclude them on the basis of ethnicity and see them as no different to Christians (Augustin, 2021). There have also been situations where Christians accommodate Yoruba Muslims during conflicts, viewing them as a different type of Muslims who are similar to Christians in character, or because for them the Muslim aggressor is inseparably Hausa/Fulani (Augustin, 2021).

With dynamics like this, religious digital peacebuilding needs to involve an evaluation of the traditional ways religions are involved in peacebuilding. It also cannot afford to limit itself to instrumental adoption or repurposing of existing technologies or excavating religious resources for digital peacebuilding. The religious foundations and practice of conflict transformation have demonstrated that religion can inspire and contribute to fundamental change beyond simply ending direct violence (Galtung, 2011; Martin, 2019). The different models of religious conflict transformation and peacebuilding are seen in African spaces. Themes identified by Omer (2015) in scholarly work on religious peacebuilding include interfaith dialogue, retrieval of religious ideas and resources that promote peace and nonviolence, and use of religious networks and faith diplomacy. Hundreds of local and international organizations are involved in religious or interfaith peacebuilding from the local community level to the highest diplomatic level, although with their work mostly concentrated at the community, and sometimes track two levels. Peacebuilding and diplomacy occur at levels that are often categorized as tracks. While some scholars model with up to six or nine tracks, the most commonly used is the three-track model. Track one involves formal negotiations at the national or highest levels, involving heads of states, organizations like the United Nations, and professional diplomats. Track two is conflict resolution involving actors such as international non-governmental organizations, religious leaders, academic institutions, government officials, and other stakeholders. It is sometimes less formal and includes more dialogue than formal negotiations. Track three is community and grassroots peacebuilding efforts. Several African states also have established institutions that specifically focus on interfaith relations and peacebuilding. Among other things, religious actors, resources, values, and entities have been instrumental in conflict prevention, early warning systems, peace mediation, post-conflict peacebuilding, humanitarian support, relationship building, demobilization, and de-escalation of conflicts (Dama, 2021; Ludovic, 2021; McNamee & Muyangwa, 2021).

The African religious peacebuilding environment is also challenged in many ways. Broadly, some of these challenges include the exclusion of religious communities due to a narrow understanding of religion and interfaith dialogue, which often only include established Christianity and Islam; the sometimes false line imposed on religion versus culture, which creates different types of conflicts and undermines the ability of intersecting cultural resources and African spiritualities to contribute to sustainable peace; persistent reliance on religious leaders who may not have appropriate training or genuine interest in peace; lack of resources; lack of appropriate models to comprehensively understand religion and their manifestations in conflicts; elitist understanding of interfaith dialogue that excludes people at the grassroots; inaccurate assumptions and poor understanding of Africa's religious demographics; legacies of colonialism and neocolonialism; and so on. Importantly, it is further limited by its failure to effectively explore and utilize appropriate current and emerging technologies for impactful peacebuilding.

Omer (2022) argues that religion, violence, and peacebuilding (RVP) as a field has continued to focus more on direct violence while overlooking other, often deeper forms of violence. Such neglected forms of violence include cultural, symbolic, structural, epistemic, and discursive violence. Additionally, that RVP must be decolonized and include integrative and intersectional analysis (Omer, 2022). This is an extremely crucial observation that cannot be stated enough. There are ongoing projects in Africa and other parts of the world which directly or indirectly address some of these forms of violence, such as religious work on social injustices, gender-based violence, gender equality, postcolonial/

decolonial theology and religion, and several efforts by religious entities to counter violent narratives. However, religious conflict transformation and peacebuilding work need to increasingly and more deliberately focus on addressing the deeper roots and causes of direct violence, such as the ones listed by Omer (2022) above. The digital turn in conflict and peacebuilding aims to address some of these and similar challenges in the broader peacebuilding environment. Religious peacebuilding can also explore opportunities in this space for addressing its own unique challenges and for contributing to the broader search for conflict transformation and permanent, sustainable, positive, and just peace beyond interfaith relations. To do so, a clear working understanding of digital peacebuilding is necessary; this is explained in the next section.

## Digital Peacebuilding

Digital peacebuilding includes the field, movement, trends, and practices that intersect peacebuilding with technologies, especially new and emerging digital technologies. According to Schirch (2020), PeaceTech describes technology which contributes to peacebuilding, while digital peacebuilding refers to the broader nexus of digital technologies and the field of peacebuilding. There are three interfaces in this nexus, according to Schirch (2020). The first is that peacebuilding work already makes use of regular technologies, including communication tools (Zoom, Skype, emails), word processors, websites, and databases. The second includes the development of specific technologies to be specifically used in various aspects of peacebuilding such as conflict analysis, facilitation of dialogue, protection of civilians, and so on. The third involves the field of peacebuilding addressing threats created by technologies, such as disinformation, hate speech, and other types of cyberwarfare strategies.

I would add another interface to this, which is mostly found in conversations about technology governance; critical algorithm studies; and ethics in technology, science, and innovation, such as AI ethics (John, 2021c). This is the infusion of peace-promoting, decolonial, and social justice and transformation values in innovation and technologies from their conceptualization and early development phases (see Fig. 42.1). It has great potential to create a digital culture of peace and transform society by addressing cultural, structural, and discursive aspects of conflicts, instead of only responding reactively to the harms of technology during the usage and application phases.

Figure 42.1 visualizes these four interfaces. Peacebuilding in the figure is represented as continuous, circular, and iterative rather than linear. At various stages, everyday technologies, such as Zoom, Facebook, or WhatsApp, are used by peacebuilders to advance their work. However, at various moments, new technologies emerge that are specifically designed for peacebuilding. Both regular and new technologies are also being used to fight violence and threats that are caused/created by or reproduced through digital technologies. The fourth interface recognizes current efforts and imagines a future where values such as decoloniality, social justice, conflict transformation, and other peace-promoting

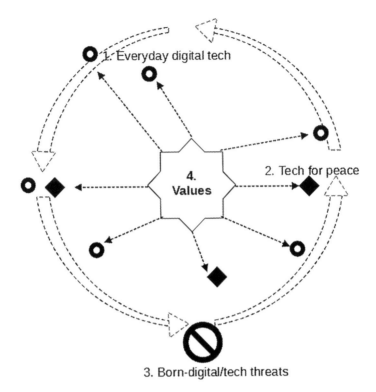

**Fig. 42.1** Four interfaces of peacebuilding and digital technologies. (Source: Author, with reference to Schirch, 2020)

values will not only be at the heart of digital peacebuilding but would infuse and shape the technologies that define this field from conception and innovation to utilization. Multidisciplinary and transdisciplinary collaboration is required to develop this nexus of technology and peacebuilding, which still requires significant attention.

Digital peacebuilding is also a major shift, an evolutionary stage of the multidisciplinary field of peacebuilding as a whole. Technology is continually integral to the field, such that speaking of digital peacebuilding as an 'intersection' of two different fields (digital technologies and peacebuilding) may soon become an under-representation. However, this is not an isolated evolution. Similar and parallel shifts are observed in fields that are traditionally the domains of peacebuilding. For example, Richmond and Tellidis (2020) make a distinction between peacebuilding in analogue and digital international relations. Analogue international relations are based on fixed notions of citizenship in sovereign territorial states and a multilateral system. It uses mediation, peacekeeping, and statebuilding, based on liberal and neoliberal ideals, to intervene in conflicts for the purpose of maintaining a twentieth-century invented homeostatic international order. Thus, it focused on international processes, institutions, and the state. It is characterized by face-to-face, elitist, and slow diplomacy and institutions, defined by western dominance, classism, capitalism, longstanding hierarchies, and inequalities. It produced liberal peace which prioritized the interests of global and regional powers and the post-conflict state at the expense of the people, communities, and networks that shaped both the conflict and the peace at the societal level. On the other hand, digital international relations and peacebuilding promises to address these limitations and to achieve fundamental changes at all levels because its affordances and tools disrupt the power dynamics and spatial structures of the old order (Richmond and Tellidis 2020).

Digital peacebuilding is extensive, with a broad range of activities and technologies. Schirch (2020) identified twenty-five spheres of work in this area, which demonstrate various aspects of the four interfaces discussed above. These are as follows: digital citizen journalism and cyber witnessing; digital conflict analysis and ceasefire monitoring; digital election monitoring; digital early warning of violence and dangerous speech; digital civilian protection; digital public opinion polling; digital coordinating and managing crisis information; digital governance; digital monitoring and evaluation; digital responses to violent extremism and terror; digital fact-checking to stop rumours; digital social marketing of peace narratives; modelling digital communication skills; facilitating intergroup digital dialogue; digital peace education through gaming; digital violence prevention; digital diplomacy, negotiation, and mediation; digital inclusion in peace processes; digital upstanding; digital social movements; digital hackathons and PeaceTech start-ups; peace engineering; The Hague Peace Data Standard; digital media literacy; and digital public safety. Due to space limitations, these spheres would not be discussed in any detail. They were listed to give a picture of the broad coverage of digital peacebuilding work.

Peace Direct's (2020) consultation with peacebuilders around the world on digital peacebuilding offers some insights on some digital peacebuilding practices. The report showed that, for example, peacebuilders use mobile and satellite technologies for crowdsourcing data and information that helped them comprehensively map on-the-ground conflict hotspots and trends. This has resulted in improved early warning and rapid response. Digital spaces like social media, podcasts, and other platforms are providing spaces for peace advocacy and awareness through storytelling and messaging. They have also increased access to the experiences of people who live in conflict situations. Online communities are used to create inclusive and safe spaces for open sharing, mobilization, collaboration, and other forms of exchanges for peace and social change. Artificial intelligence, Big Data, and blockchain are utilized to collect and analyse rich and dynamic data. Video games and virtual reality allow active interaction on peacebuilding efforts. These technologies are also used to reduce risks and improve delivery through hybrid programmes (Peace Direct, 2020).

Digital peacebuilding involves different levels of participation, from individuals and small PeaceTech start-ups, to institutions, civil society organizations, and large global tech companies. Some interventions are emerging on the platforms of engagements. Build Up's The Commons project, for example, seeks to address polarization around race and politics in the US through a system that reveals polarizing conversations on social media and allows moderators to depolarize them (Laurenson, 2019). Major global companies are constantly under scrutiny to implement policies and strategies that reduce harm, protect people's privacy, and do not exploit users. Google and other organizations have been deploying a strategy known as Redirect to address violent extremism by redirecting users who search the internet with keywords that expose them to extremist content to alternative content that provides counternarratives (Laurenson, 2019).

Given the mapping of the field presented in the preceding paragraphs and the focus of this chapter, the question that naturally follow, are: what is the state of digital peacebuilding in Africa? What are the impactful projects in this regard? Are they contextually and culturally responsive? What are the challenges of digital peacebuilding on the continent? The next section attempts to succinctly respond to some of these questions.

### *Digital Peacebuilding in Africa*

Various sources show that digital technologies are widely engaged in peacebuilding in Africa. One such source is Build Up's recent report, for the ECOWAS Commission, about technology in peacebuilding in Africa (Gichuhi, 2021). The report shows that in the past ten years, technologies have changed how peacebuilders operate in Africa. Social media is the most commonly used tool in West Africa, especially for youth engagement through training, campaigns, awareness, sensitization, responding to harmful narratives, storytelling, and more (Gichuhi, 2021). The Nigeria-based Youths for Peacebuilding & Development in Africa (YOUPEDA), for example, is reported to use Facebook to engage young people and deliberately engage Christian and Muslim religious identity in its choices of actors. Due to poor internet connectivity, radio is reported to be a widely used tool for peacebuilding. While young people are commonly engaged in peacebuilding, the scope of such engagement is narrow, often focusing on training and skills; and programmes do not involve the youth as collaboratively as they should (Gichuhi, 2021). Similar and other projects using different digital peacebuilding strategies can be found across Africa. Chitando (2019), for example, shows how young women in Zimbabwe use social media for peacebuilding.

Ushahidi, which means 'testimony' in Swahili, is one of the oldest and most successful digital peacebuilding projects in Africa. It was developed in 2007 in Kenya, following the post-electoral violence in the country. It is an open-source crowdsourcing platform that allows citizens, activists, civil society organizations, and others from anywhere, including places with low connectivity, to report on events, providing rich data for mapping and responding to conflict incidents (Rotich, 2017). Furthermore, it is a highly successful project deployed in a variety of over 90,000 conflicts and humanitarian crises situations around the world, and has collected millions of testimonies in over 160 countries (Rotich, 2017). The Community Initiative for Enhanced Peace and Development (CIEPD) in Nigeria utilizes Ushahidi in its projects. The CIEPD's Conflict Watch Centre crowdsources information on signs of conflict or violence through calls, SMS, WhatsApp, and online reporting, and uses Ushahidi to predict and track such events as part of its early warning system.

Early warning system is one of the longstanding investments in Africa. Most of Africa's Regional Economic Communities (RECs) have early warning and response systems to help tackle violence before they manifest (Gnanguenon, 2021). The Economic Community of West African States (ECOWAS) has the Early Warning and Response Network (ECOWARN), established to monitor security in its member countries. Its Consolidated Situation Room, located in Abuja, Nigeria, monitors, collects, and analyses relevant data and advises ECOWAS stakeholders. Dozens of field monitors in the region also collect relevant data weekly and send to ECOWARN. Similar projects by other RECs include the Central African Early Warning Mechanism (MARAC); the Inter-Governmental Authority on Development's (IGAD) Conflict Early Warning and Response Mechanism (CEWARN) in the Horn of Africa; the East African Warning Mechanism (EACWARN); the Regional Early Warning System of the Southern African Development Community (SADC); and the Conflict and Early Warning System (COMWARN) of the Common Market for Eastern and Southern Africa (COMESA). Several other projects and collaborations exist across Africa that use digital technologies and platforms to prevent conflicts and other crises, monitor elections, and enable rapid response to conflict incidents and humanitarian crisis situations.

Some projects aim to address online narratives and hate speech. For example, Bassiki Kalan Sô in Mali addresses revenge narratives and hate speech using videos and messages on Facebook and WhatsApp. Similar work is being done by organizations like the Center for Technology and Development in Nigeria (CITAD) and the West Africa Network for Peacebuilding (WANEP), amongst many others (Gichuhi, 2021). Another emerging use of digital technologies is in the mediation of conflicts and facilitation of dialogue. Examples can be seen in the work of the Centre for Humanitarian Dialogue (HD Centre) in Libya and its work which achieved a social media peace agreement in Nigeria (HD Centre, n.d.). HD Centre, the United Nations, and several other organizations have further developed various frameworks and toolkits for digital peacebuilding and mediation that are applied in various conflict situations in Africa.

An interesting digital peacebuilding project in Africa is the Maskani Commons, a collaboration between the Centre for Media, Democracy, Peace and Security at Rongo University and Build Up. It involves six universities in Western Kenya, comprising students, faculty, and other experts. The project uses social media and other tools to address security and other challenges, including ethnic politics and extremism. The conception and design of the project integrates key local and indigenous symbols and ideas of community and peace. The Centre for Ethno-Religious Mediation (ICERMediation) recently launched a mobile app to complement its online system that aims to create virtual indigenous kingdoms where traditional leaders can connect with their constituencies at home and abroad to engage in peacebuilding. The platform also offers avenues for ethnoreligious mediators and peacebuilders to connect and collaborate.

As noted previously, digital peacebuilding is a complex ecosystem, with many movements and grappling happening all at once. So much has been achieved, so much is still confusing, and so much still needs to be achieved. Digital peacebuilding faces a number of challenges that emerging technologies generally face, such as their potential for harm and to replicate pre-existing power dynamics and coloniality. Thus, as Hirblinger et al. (2022) argued, digital peacebuilding needs to take a critical-reflexive approach in research and practice, and engage in assumptions about both technology and peacebuilding. One of the most celebrated contributions of digital technologies to peacebuilding is the inclusion of more voices (Hirblinger, 2020) such as those of women, youth, and marginalized groups; their transnational reach; and their ability to circumvent barriers of analogue peacebuilding. However, important questions still remain about the new forms of exclusions that are produced by these technologies due to access, connectivity, ownership, control, location of projects, funding, and other issues. It is also not clear how digital technologies can, for example, address gaps such as the absence of women in high-level peace mediation as mediators. Several other access, regulatory, ethical, security, and privacy challenges further undermine digital peacebuilding efforts in Africa. Some of these include digital inequality, poverty, poor digital literacy, poor infrastructure, data, and device costs (Gichuhi, 2021; Peace Direct, 2020).

Longstanding conflicts and grievances tend to migrate to online spaces, creating multiple fronts and frontlines of conflicts and this can bring additional complex dynamics to conflicts. Surveillance, suppression, and blocking of internet and social media platforms by states have been a challenge in some African countries in the past few years. Twenty-five cases of partial or total internet shutdowns were recorded in 2019 alone (Giles & Mwai, 2021). States, political actors, and conflict entrepreneurs are also increasingly savvy at deploying the most sophisticated digital strategies to pursue their interests in Africa. Many digital peacebuilders are not equipped or do not have the resources to match such strategies in other to avoid conflicts. For example, it has been exposed that massive financial investment in deep fakes and digital influencing have been going on to tip the 2023 elections in Nigeria in some people's favour (Nwonwu et al., 2023).

These challenges offer a range of entry points and opportunities for religious stakeholders, actors, perspectives, and other resources to fully participate in digital peacebuilding and in shaping the trajectories of thinking and practice in the field. Religious actors and institutions need to see all aspects of peacebuilding and social transformation as a part of its core responsibility and domain of accountability. Many conflicts in Africa have a religious component or manifestation. The thousands of reported casualties of direct violence, which SDG 16.1 seeks to reduce, are members of religious constituencies. They were people who belonged to a religious group, openly identified as members of a religious community, held religious beliefs, and participated in religious life in other ways. Digital peacebuilding is, to some degree, about ensuring that these people—the everyday casualties of direct, structural, cultural, and other forms of violence—enjoy their right to live their lives to the full and to flourish, irrespective of their gender, location, culture, or religious beliefs. This is a noble cause that many sources of faith would support and encourage. Therefore, in the final section of this chapter, I reflect on some of the ways that religion can fully participate in digital peacebuilding.

## Opportunities for Increased Participation in Digital Peacebuilding

Confronting the ethical questions raised by the practical implications of new technologies in society demands revisiting and possibly expanding our ethical frameworks. Tough conversations are ongoing about the right way to build, deploy, and use technology to minimize or avoid harm while maximizing good and benefits to humans. These include conversations about bias in artificial intelligence and algorithmic processes, deceptive and addictive designs, privacy, the commodification of user data, issues around accountability, algorithmic manipulation and agency, and many more. Technologies designed for or adopted for peacebuilding work are not excluded from these questions. Platforms like Facebook, which have been implicated in some of the worst ethical failures, are also widely used for peacebuilding. While Facebook claims to fight disinformation and other sources of harm, it is a business whose goal is profit making, and which is designed to profit from the proliferation of the very things that peacebuilders are trying to use it to fight: hate speech, extremist content, bullying, disinformation, conspiracy theories, and discursive violence (Lauer, 2021; Tharoor, 2021).

This shows that for companies like Facebook, despite the good they do in other domains and their claims about user safety and combatting violence, the most important decisions are shaped by some values at the expense of others. As Goldberg (2021) explains, technologies are not value-neutral. They involve valuing some things at the expense of others. Using technology to more efficiently accomplish tasks or to achieve faster and more accurate identification of persons at a border crossing, for example, often involves valuing efficiency, security, and speed at the expense of privacy, inclusivity, and dignity (Goldberg, 2021). Also, the personal values of those who create and control technologies may shape these technologies as much as the values of the users who use and repurpose them for harm and violence or to do good and promote peace.

Thus, religious thinkers, institutions, and leaders can contribute to the ethical development, deployment, and usage of technologies generally and in peacebuilding in several ways. They could, for example, participate more actively in the conversation. Many creators, users, and people harmed by and through technologies hold a religious belief or identify with a religious or spiritual community. For many religious and spiritual people, their faith is a fundamental source of ethics. Religious actors could more actively participate in ensuring that the right values are translated into technological systems and outcomes. They could also bring the extensive experience and resources of religious traditions in addressing ethical questions to contribute to the broader ongoing conversations on issues like privacy, AI ethics, and technology ethics. While religions themselves have internal moral plurality and contradictions, they still have much to offer the debates to ensure that frameworks and codes that emerge and shape technologies are those that advance the highest human values and peace. Decisions about ethical choices around technology often also exclude many people affected by such decisions. Religious stakeholders can use their access to the grassroots to ensure that the values of those at the bottom of these decision pyramids receive consideration in the matrix of power that shape these decisions.

Religion can help us make sense of technologies and how they impact our lives. One of the noticeable trends in digital culture is the regular use of religious language and metaphors to describe technological phenomena. For example, algorithms have been variously theologized and conceptualized in theistic terms as Gods. Their social power, agency, ubiquity, and impact have been described using theistic attributes such as all-seeing, all-knowing, and ever-present in the most religious sense (Bogost, 2015; John, 2021b; Singler, 2020). While such theologizing is based on narrow understanding of, primarily, the Christian God, it also shows that religion, arguably, offers one of the most accessible languages for confronting and making sense of complex, powerful, and socio-culturally mysterious objects like algorithms. Theological and religious stakeholders and actors could, therefore, translate such technologies in ways that deepen our understanding of their values and potential harm, including in the context of peacebuilding. Religious language is accessible to religious persons. This also means that such religious actors need to develop a comprehensive understanding of technologies, or those with comprehensive understanding of technologies could be involved in such translations. The tendency to theologize technology is an opportunity for those who understand theologizing and religious language to help translate and improve participation in determining how complex technologies impact lives generally, and in the context of peacebuilding.

Digital peacebuilding is an opportunity for religious actors to engage in a critical self-examination on the role that their faith and its various entities have played in bringing society to its current violent reality. How do religions continue to contribute to these complex conflicts that necessitate peacebuilding interventions, including digital peacebuilding? Beyond criticizing agents who have drawn inspiration from their religion to mete violence and beyond excavating peace-promoting resources from religions, asking about the ways that good religion and good religious actors have been implicated in conflicts and violence should be a continuous practice. Digital peacebuilding and dialogue platforms, for example, could be established that specifically aim to deepen this reflective attitude. It is common in religious dialogue events in places like Nigeria, for example, for Christian and Muslim participants to focus on advancing the narrative that their religions promote peace and to draw on their scriptures to support this. This often involves implicit or explicit arguments that those who engage in violence in the name of religion are not true believers. Such conversations frequently ignore the self-critical conversation that needs to happen about everyone's complicity in enabling such violence within a broader cultural and structural context of religion. The flip side of this reflection is on how to participate in digital peacebuilding with greater consciousness, ensuring that aspects of religion and technology that reproduce violent socialities and cultures are critically addressed and edited out.

Religious peacebuilders could further invest in developing and using peacebuilding technologies. Since information and communication technologies are already an integral part of everyday life and work, religious actors naturally utilize these to promote peace and carry out their work as peacebuilders. However, my call here is to move beyond passive adoption and use of what is already the norm, but for a more creative and deliberate investment in technologies, akin to what was witnessed in the extensive appropriation of broadcasting technology by Pentecostal leaders in the 1990s and 2000s. Dedicated funds and budgets could seek to address barriers that limit the potential impact of digital peacebuilding in many parts of Africa. For example, religious institutions could invest in digital literacy and infrastructure in rural communities and poor communities affected by conflicts. They could develop digital centres in religious spaces that allow access to the internet for people who would otherwise not have access. Religious bodies and networks could establish their own early warning and rapid response systems or engage existing ones to help them respond to conflicts. Such approaches to peacebuilding have potentially highly transformative impact on peacebuilding generally and on religious institutions themselves. African religious spaces are dominated by young people who are equally technology adepts and digital natives. Thus, such initiatives would not only make religious spaces more homely, attractive, and interesting to young people, they would also offer opportunities for young people in Africa to become peacebuilders through their religious communities and spaces. Additionally, higher education institutions owned by religious bodies can become essential centres for digital peacebuilding innovations and for implementing relevant initiatives in communities which make possible the translation of insight or knowledge into solutions and peace.

Digital technologies have given rise to several concerns around social justice. Algorithmic bias and AI bias are emerging problems whereby AI or algorithmic systems produce outcomes that are socially biased and reinforce social inequalities. This includes unfair decisions based on certain categorization of people or groups. Many studies and content exist that demonstrate this to be a great concern. For example, search engines have been found to be racially or sexually biased, privileging whiteness over other races; facial recognition software have been shown to misidentify people of colour; financial service algorithms to charge Black people higher interests than White people; self-driving cars performing better at identifying white people than Black people; and other systems implicated in racial, gender, disability, and other biases (Knowlton, 2005; Leavy et al., 2020; Noble, 2018; PwC, 2022).

Religious actors have contributed in struggles against social injustices around the world. Social justice perpetuated through technology is also an area needing increased participation of religious actors as part of their broad commitment to social justice. From a conflict transformation perspective, building peace requires equal attention to the structures and cultures that create the environment for conflicts to thrive. These include digital spaces and questions of social justice. As discussed earlier, religion contributed to the emergence and practice of this transformative approach to conflict resolution. Religious actors should more actively engage questions of technology related to social justice from this perspective. This could be through theological reflections, religious activism and critique, collaboration in relevant research, and establishing unites that can apply religion's best intentions for humanity to assess social justice related harms in PeaceTech.

In the past few years, robot religious figures have been unveiled. BlessU-2 is a robot priest in Germany. Mindar is a Buddhist robot in Japan, which looks like the Buddhist deity of mercy. SanTO is a robot that services Catholics in Poland (Samuel, 2019; Webber, 2021). These robots are able to perform certain religious rituals and practices, including blessing faithfuls, giving sermons, offering comforting words, reciting scriptures, and more. While acceptance of such technology is still being negotiated by religious people, we have seen increased integration and use of technologies like mobile apps, avatars, virtual worlds, and others to support religious ritual, practice, and faith development (Campbell, 2013; Campbell & Evolvi, 2020). This shows that the technology avenues through which religion can promote peace and peacebuilding values and attitude are vast. Robot priests and monks can also be designed to be peacebuilders. Peace-promoting messages can be integrated into religious apps and software. In other words, these technologies designed and used by many for pious reasons can also be infused with faith-based resources that help promote a culture of peace and transformation in society.

Finally, it is crucial, for these proposals, to remember that Africa is highly receptive and adaptive to technology and itself is a continent with excellent and life-changing innovation and innovators at home abroad. This is important given the persistent colonial representations of African societies, in some quarters, as naturally conservative and resistant to technology, as highlighted by some contributions in Okyere-Manu (2021). Despite the governance, corruption, and many other challenges and innovation-stifling conditions that Africans live in, African societies are important sites for creation and adoption of technologies. As Banda (2021) demonstrates, while Africa is behind other regions in digital maturity and adoption, digital infrastructure buildout and adoption is currently happening faster in Africa than any other region of the world.

## Conclusion

For faith-based peacebuilders, many opportunities exist in the digital peacebuilding ecosystem for meaningful contribution. This chapter aimed to map out the field to make visible some of these potential channels for participation. It is a rapidly evolving field with many errors, challenges, and lessons. Religious stakeholders and actors could more actively be a part of this journey and contribute to the type of peace that emerges in conflict spaces through the use of digital technology. The suggestions made on how religion could contribute to shaping technology generally and in the peacebuilding are also areas that could be further explored through research to create better agendas for intervention in the light of SDG 16 and other religious aspirations for peace.

**Acknowledgement** The author wishes to acknowledge the funding and support of the National Institute for the Humanities and Social Sciences (NIHSS) through the Centre for Mediation in Africa (CMA), University of Pretoria.

## References

Alexander, J. K. (2020). Introduction: The Entanglement of Technology and Religion. *History and Technology, 36*(2), 165–186. https://doi.org/10.1080/07341512.2020.1814513

Appleby, S. R. (1999). *The Ambivalence of the Sacred: Religion, Violence, and Reconciliation*. Rowman & Littlefield Publishers.

Augustin, S. (2021). *'FEAR OF THE UNKNOWN'-Religion, Identity, and Conflict in Northern Nigeria*. https://www.mercycorps.org/sites/default/files/2021-07/FearoftheUnknown_Full_6-30-21.pdf

Banda, M. (2021, March 19). Digital Adoption in Africa Supersedes Other Regions Globally. *Intelligent CIO Africa*. https://www.intelligentcio.com/africa/2021/03/19/digital-adoption-in-africa-supersedes-other-regions-globally/

Basedau, M. (2017). *The Rise of Religious Armed Conflicts in Sub-Saharan Africa: No Simple Answers*. (GIGA Focus Afrika, 4). GIGA German Institute of Global and Area Studies—Leibniz-Institut für Globale und Regionale Studien, Institut für Afrika-Studien. https://nbn-resolving.org/urn:nbn:de:0168-ssoar-53174-4

Basedau, M., & De Juan, A. (2008). *The 'Ambivalence of the Sacred' in Africa: The Impact of Religion on Peace and Conflict in Sub-Saharan Africa*. German Institute of Global and Area Studies (GIGA), Working Papers.

Basedau, M., Vüllers, J., & Körner, P. (2013). What Drives Inter-Religious Violence? Lessons from Nigeria, Côte d'Ivoire, and Tanzania. *Studies in Conflict & Terrorism, 36*(10), 857–879.

Baumann, J., Finnbogason, D., & Svensson, I. (2018). Rethinking Mediation: Resolving Religious Conflicts. *CSS Policy Perspectives, 6*(1), 1–4.

Bogost, I. (2015, January 15). The Cathedral of Computation. *The Atlantic*. https://www.theatlantic.com/technology/archive/2015/01/the-cathedral-of-computation/384300/

Campbell, H. (2013). *Digital Religion: Understanding Religious Practice in New Media*. Routledge.

Campbell, H. A., & Evolvi, G. (2020). Contextualizing Current Digital Religion Research on Emerging Technologies. *Human Behavior and Emerging Technologies, 2*(1), 5–17.

Chitando, A. (2019). From Victims to the Vaunted: Young Women and Peace Building in Mashonaland East, Zimbabwe. *African Security Review, 28*(2), 110–123.

Dama, D. (2021). The African Epistemic Logic of Peacemaking: A Model for Reconciling the Sub-Saharan African Christians and Muslims. *Transformation, 38*(1), 46–62. https://doi.org/10.1177/0265378820940003

Firchow, P., Martin-Shields, C., Omer, A., & Ginty, R. M. (2017). PeaceTech: The Liminal Spaces of Digital Technology in Peacebuilding. *International Studies Perspectives, 18*(1), 4–42.

Galtung, J. (2011). TRANSCEND Method. In *The Encyclopedia of Peace Psychology*. John Wiley & Sons, Ltd.. https://doi.org/10.1002/9780470672532.wbepp280

Gichuhi, C. (2021). *Leveraging Technology for Peacebuilding in the Ecowas Region: Documentation of a Consultative Process*. ECOWAS Commission, Deutsche Gesellschaft für Internationale Zusammenarbeit (GIZ) GmbH. https://howtobuildup.medium.com/digital-tech-and-peacebuilding-in-west-africa-23b42ae03158

Giles, C., & Mwai, P. (2021, January 14). Africa Internet: Where and How Are Governments Blocking It? *BBC News*. https://www.bbc.com/news/world-africa-47734843

Gnanguenon, A. (2021). *Pivoting African Conflict Prevention?: An Analysis of Continental and Regional Early Warning Systems*. European Union Institute for Security Studies. Conflict Series.

Goldberg, Z. J. (2021, October 6). What Does the Ethics of Technology Mean? *Trilateral Research*. https://trilateralresearch.com/news/what-does-the-ethics-of-technology-mean

Harari, Y. N. (2018). *21 Lessons for the 21st Century*. Signal.

HD Centre. (n.d.). *Digital Conflict*. HD. Retrieved January 20, 2023, from https://hdcentre.org/area-work/digital-conflict/

Hirblinger, A. T. (2020). *Digital Inclusion in Mediated Peace Processes*. United States Institute of Peace.

Hirblinger, A. T., Hansen, J. M., Hoelscher, K., Kolås, Å., Lidén, K., & Martins, B. O. (2022). Digital Peacebuilding: A Framework for Critical–Reflexive Engagement. *International Studies Perspectives*. https://doi.org/10.1093/isp/ekac015

Hoover, S. M. (2012). Forward: Practice, Autonomy and Authenticity in the Digitally Religious and Digitally Spiritual. In P. H. Cheong, P. Fischer-Nielsen, S. Gelfgren, & C. Ess (Eds.), *Digital Religion, Social Media and Culture: Perspectives, Practices, and Futures* (Vol. 7800). Peter Lang.

John, S. F. (2021a). Identity, Masculinity, and Contested Domains in Africa's "Religious" Conflicts. In C. J. Kaunda (Ed.), *Religion, Gender, and Wellbeing in Africa* (pp. 115–128). Lexington Books.

John, S. F. (2021b). *If Algorithms Are Not Gods, What Are They? Religious Metaphors, Power and Agency in Digital Culture.* http://videolectures.net/dhasa2021_john_digital_culture/

John, S. F. (2021c). Technology Governance: Minding and Closing the Gaps in Africa. *African Journal of Governance & Development, 10*(2), Article 2. https://doi.org/10.36369/2616-9045/2021/v10i2a5

Knowlton, S. A. (2005). Three Decades since Prejudices and Antipathies: A Study of Changes in the Library of Congress Subject Headings. *Cataloging & Classification Quarterly, 40*(2), 123–145.

Kukah, M. H. (1993). *Religion, Politics and Power in Northern Nigeria.* Spectrum Books.

Lauer, D. (2021). Facebook's Ethical Failures Are Not Accidental; They Are Part of the Business Model. *AI and Ethics, 1*(4), 395–403. https://doi.org/10.1007/s43681-021-00068-x

Laurenson, L. (2019). *Polarisation and Peacebuilding Strategy on Digital Media Platforms: Current Strategies and Their Discontents.* Toda Peace Institute.

Leavy, S., O'Sullivan, B., & Siapera, E. (2020). *Data, Power and Bias in Artificial Intelligence.* ArXiv Preprint ArXiv:2008.07341.

Lergo, T. (2011). Deconstructing Ethnic Politics: The Emergence of a Fourth Force in Nigerian Political Discourse. *International Journal of Humanities and Social Science, 1*(15), 87–94.

Ludovic, S. J., Lado Tonlieu. (2021). Religion and Peacebuilding in Sub-Saharan Africa. In T. McNamee & M. Muyangwa (Eds.), *The State of Peacebuilding in Africa: Lessons Learned for Policymakers and Practitioners* (pp. 47–64). Springer International Publishing. https://doi.org/10.1007/978-3-030-46636-7_4

Maiangwa, B. (2014). 'Soldiers of God or Allah': Religious Politicization and the Boko Haram Crisis in Nigeria. *Contemporary Voices: St Andrews Journal of International Relations, 5*(1), 58–66.

Martin, M. S. (2019, December 29). What Is Conflict Transformation? *Brave Talk Project.* https://bravetalkproject.com/what-is-conflict-transformation/

McCauley, J. F., & Posner, D. N. (2019). The Political Sources of Religious Identification: Evidence from the Burkina Faso–Côte d'Ivoire Border. *British Journal of Political Science, 49*(2), 421–441.

McNamee, T., & Muyangwa, M. (Eds.). (2021). *The State of Peacebuilding in Africa: Lessons Learned for Policymakers and Practitioners.* Springer Nature. https://doi.org/10.1007/978-3-030-46636-7

Noble, S. U. (2018). *Algorithms of Oppression: How Search Engines Reinforce Racism.* New York University Press.

Nwonwu, C., Tukur, F., & Oyedepo, Y. (2023, January 18). Nigeria Elections 2023: How Influencers Are Secretly Paid by Political Parties. *BBC News.* https://www.bbc.com/news/world-africa-63719505

Okyere-Manu, B. D. (Ed.). (2021). *African Values, Ethics, and Technology: Questions, Issues, and Approaches.* Springer Nature.

Omer, A. (2015). Religious Peacebuilding: The Exotic, the Good, and the Theatrical. In A. Omer, R. S. Appleby, & D. Little (Eds.), *The Oxford Handbook of Religion, Conflict, and Peacebuilding.* Oxford University Press.

Omer, A. (2022). The Intersectional Turn. In *The Wiley Blackwell Companion to Religion and Peace* (pp. 49–62). John Wiley & Sons, Ltd.. https://doi.org/10.1002/9781119424420.ch4

Onapajo, H. (2012). Politics for God: Religion, Politics and Conflict in democratic Nigeria. *The Journal of Pan African Studies, 4*(9), 42–66.

Ottuh, P. O., & Omosor, F. O. (2022). Examination of Religiophobia and Politicization of Religious Conflicts in Postcolonial Nigeria. *Cogito, 14*(4), 37–54.

Peace Direct. (2020). *Digital Pathways for Peace: Insights and Lessons from a Global Online Consultation.* Peace Direct. https://www.peacedirect.org/publications/digital-pathways-for-peace/

PwC. (2022). *Understanding Algorithmic Bias and How to Build Trust in AI.* PwC. https://www.pwc.com/us/en/tech-effect/ai-analytics/algorithmic-bias-and-trust-in-ai.html

Richmond, O. P., & Tellidis, I. (2020). Analogue Crisis, Digital Renewal? Current Dilemmas of Peacebuilding. *Globalizations, 17*(6), 935–952.

Rotich, J. (2017). Ushahidi: Empowering Citizens through Crowdsourcing and Digital Data Collection. *Field Actions Science Reports. The Journal of Field Actions, Special Issue 16*, Article Special Issue 16.

Samuel, S. (2019, September 9). Robot Priests Can Bless You, Advise You, and Even Perform Your Funeral. *Vox.* https://www.vox.com/future-perfect/2019/9/9/20851753/ai-religion-robot-priest-mindar-buddhism-christianity

Schirch, L. (2020). *25 Spheres of Digital Peacebuilding and PeaceTech.* Toda Peace Institute and Alliance for Peacebuilding.

Singler, B. (2020). "Blessed by the Algorithm": Theistic Conceptions of Artificial Intelligence in Online Discourse. *AI & SOCIETY, 35*(4), 945–955. https://doi.org/10.1007/s00146-020-00968-2

Slocum-Bradley, N. R. (2016). *Promoting Conflict or Peace Through Identity.* Routledge.

Tharoor, I. (2021, October 26). Analysis | The Indisputable Harm Caused by Facebook. *Washington Post.* https://www.washingtonpost.com/world/2021/10/26/indisputable-harm-caused-by-facebook/

Webber, A. (2021). *Sermon-Giving 'Robotic Priest' Arrives in Poland to Support Faithful during Pandemic.* https://www.thefirstnews.com/article/sermon-giving-robotic-priest-arrives-in-poland-to-support-faithful-during-pandemic-25688

CHAPTER 43

# Religion and Agriculture for Peacebuilding in Rwanda: Analysing the Role of Christian Faith-Based Organisations in the Post-genocide Agrarian Change

*Fortunée Bayisenge*

## INTRODUCTION

In April 1994, Rwanda experienced a horrendous genocide against the Tutsi. The unprecedented political event brought in a total breakdown of the country and is believed to have claimed more than one million lives within three months between April and July 1994 (Izabiriza, 2005; Prunier, 1997). The post-genocide context has been fragile, engaging many efforts by the government and civil society organisations to accelerate the reconstruction of all aspects of the society that were shattered by the genocide. Rwanda's civil society includes faith-based actors, particularly Christian church-based organisations, as at the time of the genocide Rwanda was one of the African most Christian countries, more than 90% of the population were members of Christian faith communities (Schliesser, 2019). In this respect, different policy reforms were envisaged for boosting economic growth and building sustainable peace. The agriculture sector was one of the reforms envisaged by the post-genocide government, as the sector employs the majority of the workforce of the population (MINAGRI, 2009).

F. Bayisenge (✉)
Faculty of Development Studies, Protestant Institute of Arts and Social Sciences, Huye, Rwanda

© The Author(s), under exclusive license to Springer Nature Switzerland AG 2023
S. M. Kilonzo et al. (eds.), *The Palgrave Handbook of Religion, Peacebuilding, and Development in Africa*,
https://doi.org/10.1007/978-3-031-36829-5_43

Rwanda is an agrarian society; agriculture contributes about 40% of the GDP and employs more than 80% of the population, especially those who reside in rural areas (NISR, 2015). Around 80% of the population live in rural areas and depend on rain-fed agriculture. The average land holding at the household level dropped from 2 ha in 1960 to 1.2 ha in 1984, to just 0.7 ha in the early 1990s, and less than 0.7 ha in 2003. Consequently, more than 90% of households farm at least one plot of land, and because the land is becoming scarce, most farming is done on very small plots. Around 80% of farming households likely cultivate between 0.33 ha and 0.9 ha of land (Musahara & Huggins, 2005; NISR, 2015). The intensive pressure on land has led to widespread over-cultivation and consequently land degradation in the form of soil erosion and fragmentation, and conflict related to land was one of the factors which enriched the war and genocide between 1990 and 1994 (Musahara & Huggins, 2005; Ansoms, 2011; Randell & McCloskey, 2014; National Institute of Statistics of Rwanda, 2021).

Besides the explosion of the demographic pressure, other factors include the limited use of modern agricultural inputs and technologies and the use of traditional farming techniques, leading to subsistence farming system and low productivity by the sector. Hence, agricultural change has been adopted as a substantial strategy to overcome these constraints, enhance the agricultural development and sustainable peace (MINAGRI, 2013; Pritchard, 2012).

The aim of this chapter is to understand the role of Christian faith-based organisations in the post-genocide agrarian change and its impact of peacebuilding process. The chapter is composed by five sections. In the first section, the chapter presents briefly the background and context. This section provides the key factors that are relevant for understanding the role of Christian faith-based organisations (CFBOs) in agriculture development and peacebuilding in the post-genocide Rwanda and announces the research questions. In the second section, the chapter discusses agency and opportunity structure as the key concepts that are used to frame and discuss the research findings. The third section details the methods which guided the research process. This is followed by the presentation and discussion of findings. Here, the chapter narrates about different changes induced by the agriculture development programmes, the role of CFBOs, and its effects on the sustainable peacebuilding process. The fifth and last section is the conclusion which summarises the key argument of the chapter.

## The Background and Research Questions

The necessity for Rwanda's agrarian policy change coincided with the publication of the 2008 World Development Report which underlined green revolution policies as an effective strategy to foster agriculture development, economic growth, and poverty reduction in sub-Saharan Africa (World Bank, 2007). The assumption underlying this change is that transforming subsistence smallholdings into large-scale commercial farming will increase yields, ensure food security, and improve the living conditions of those involved in farming activities, where the poor constitute the majority (FAO, 2013; World Bank, 2007).

Emerging from this background, the government of Rwanda initiated the Crops Intensification Programme (CIP) since 2007, to transform agricultural production system to make it more productive and commercial-oriented (MINAGRI, 2009, 2013). Here, it is worth noting that in post-war and genocide context, agriculture development was regarded as an effective strategy to fasten the peacebuilding process. It is argued that the intensification of farming would increase the productivity, enhance food security and income and employments, thereby reducing the socio-economic frustrations which can feed tensions. Further, by increasing income particularly for the poor, disadvantaged, or those mostly affected by the war, agriculture development becomes a political strategy for boosting the democratisation and peacebuilding process (Addison, 2005).

The implementation of CIP involves four components or sub-programs, including, land use consolidation, the distribution of improved inputs, proximity extension services to farmers, and post-harvest handling and storage technologies (MINAGRI, 2009). Land Use Consolidation (LUC) is the main pillar or the driving component of CIP, as one of its objectives is to enhance the proper use of land, and among local communities, CIP is known as a government policy for land use consolidation (Mbonigaba & Dusengemungu, 2013).

The implementation process of CIP involves various actors: government entities, non-government institutions such as farmers' cooperatives, civil society organisations, and the market-related organisations. The faith-based organisations (FBOs) are part of civil society organisations and are regarded as the key actors in the post-conflict reconstruction process. In fact, more than 90% of the Rwanda's population are connected in some ways to the faith-based organisations, particularly the Christian churches. This is a factor justifying their position as actors in Rwanda's rural development since the pre-genocide era (Gatwa, 2005). In the views of some of these organisations, their involvement in development process constitutes a tool for converting local communities and adding new members. As such, they engage in different projects addressing different aspects, namely in the promotion of the health conditions, education, development infrastructure, and so forth (Schliesser, 2019).

Nevertheless, Christian faith-based organisations and other civil society organisations have been accused of having failed to effectively oppose the genocide, and that is one the factors, in the views of the government, which led the population into ethnic hatred, conflict, and genocide (Uvin, 1998; Gatwa 2005). Like other non-government organisations, the Christian faith-based organisations have to cope with or to fit into the corporatist model of civil society, a model that is preconized by the government from which the non-government actors act as compliant partners for the government. In other words, the non-government organisations are engaged in implementing policies and programmes rather than monitoring or criticising them. Henceforth, those organisations align programmes directly with the government's priorities. As a result of their engagement with government's policy, civil society actors involved in agriculture have enjoyed increased operating budgets (Huggins, 2017).

Since its implementation, different assessments claimed tremendous achievements by CIP in increasing yields of the selected food crops, such as maize, wheat, cassava, Irish potatoes, soybeans, and beans. Official reports highlight that between 2007 and 2012, the production of maize increased by five times; wheat and cassava by three times; Irish potato, soybean, and beans by about two times; and rice by around three times (Musahara et al., 2014; Mbonigaba & Dusengemungu, 2013). Furthermore, it is argued that the increased production have been contributing in fostering the national economic growth with an average of annual Gross Domestic Product (GDP) ranging from 7% to 8% between 2008 and 2019 (World Bank, 2020). Backing to this context, however, the concern for this research is, how such macro-level gains are benefiting smallholder farmers, and what are its effects on the peacebuilding process?

Studies on the post-genocide Rwandan agrarian development have mainly focused on the effectiveness of CIP in terms of agricultural productivity, food security, and poverty reduction (see, e.g., Ansoms, 2008, 2011; Mbonigaba & Dusengemungu, 2013, Huggins, 2013; Musahara et al., 2014, Bizoza & Havugimana 2016; Cioffo et al., 2016; Dawson et al., 2016; Ndushabandi 2017), but they did not explore the question about the implication of such an agrarian change for smallholder farmers and peacebuilding process as well as the contribution of religious actors. This chapter aims to bridge this research gap. More specifically, the chapter explores questions such as the following: What are the agricultural changes as per the implementation of CIP? How do agricultural changes under CIP benefit smallholder farmers? What is the contribution of Christian faith-based organisations to the implementation of CIP? How does the position of Christian faith-based organisations shape the benefits of CIP for smallholder farmers and the post-genocide peacebuilding process?

## Delineating Agency and Opportunity Structure: The Position of CFBOs in Agricultural Development for Peacebuilding

Agricultural intensification involves the process of transforming traditional farming into market-oriented agriculture. By doing this, it assumes a fundamental transformation of the modes of agricultural production. Such a change affects the relationship between different actors of the agrarian economy, such as the state, market, and the community-based organisations (De Janvry, 1981; Kusz, 2014). In countries where agriculture is less developed, modernising or intensifying agriculture has been regarded as a strategy for boosting the economy and development. Some countries have suggested the adoption of green revolution strategy is known as an ensemble of different techniques designed to increase yields per hectare, to increase cropping intensity per unit of land or other inputs, and to change land use from low-value crops or commodities to those that receive higher market prices (Pretty et al., 2011). However, Shivji (2009) argues that the process of modernising agriculture requires the state to engage in neoliberal policies, with a high risk of facilitating dispossession of different groups of small-scale farmers and causing capitalist accumulation. Herein the intensification of monoculture agriculture for export has been known to be the basis of such conditions, yet it is the most recommended and supported model of agricultural development in sub-Saharan Africa (Shivji, 2009, p. 172). More often than not, religion maintains a silent voice in contributions towards such debates of Rwanda's agrarian change. It is therefore imperative to scrutinise the structural factors underpinning agrarian change and identify how such factors shape the social relations between the actors involved in agricultural intensification, and their role in peacebuilding. Henceforth, the concepts of opportunity structure and agency are essential analytical tools that would explain those factors.

Anthony Giddens defined the concept of structures as a set of 'rules and resources', one presupposing the other. For him, structures involve 'both the medium and the outcome of the practices which constitute social systems' (Giddens, 1979, p. 27). Drawing from this definition, Sewell (1992) argued that agency is a constituent of structure, which means that structures shape people's practices, which in turn constitute or reproduce structures. In this sense, human agency and structure presuppose each other. In the same vein, Deepa Narayan discussed the concepts of agency and opportunity structure. For her 'opportunity structure evolves the broader institutional, social and political context of formal and informal rules and norms within which actors pursue their interests; whereas agency is the capacity of actors to take purposeful action, a function of both individual and collective assets and capabilities' (Narayan, 2005, p. 4). This author argues that, for an effective investment in poor people's development, there is a need to remove formal and informal institutional barriers that prevent the poor from taking effective action and which limit their choice. In other words, it implies the need for changes in social and political structures that perpetuate unequal power relations (ibid., p. 6).

Within the context of Rwanda's agrarian change, smallholder farmers need not only access and control over resources such as land and related property, but also capabilities to negotiate with other actors in agriculture such as the state and market or business companies involved in Crops Intensification Programme. In other words, they need the removal of structural barriers which hinder them from enjoying different opportunities offered by such agrarian change. This chapter draws from the concepts of agency and opportunity structure to understand structural factors underlying the implementation of

CIP, the position of CFBOs in this process, and how the latter shapes the benefits of CIP for smallholder farmers and the peacebuilding process.

## Methodology

The study drew from the lived experience of farmers involved in farmers' cooperatives under CIP in the Gisagara and Huye Districts of the Southern Province in Rwanda. The study used a qualitative approach characterised by an emerging and flexible ethnographic research design. To obtain relevant and complete information, multiple yet complementing data collection techniques were used, such as semi-structured interviews, participatory observation, and data extraction from documentation.

The study used purposive sampling technique to select four categories of participants: farmer (women and men) members of CIP cooperatives, the leaders of CIP cooperatives, district officials in charge of agriculture, and one agent of African Evangelistic Enterprise (AEE), a Christian faith-based organisation involved in promoting agricultural development. It was deemed appropriate to interview members of maize cooperatives, as maize is one of the selected crops under the CIP, and since the implementation of the latter, it is no longer regarded as a food crop but rather as a cash crop. Also, the two districts were selected to enable comparisons between rural and urban areas. As such, the study focused on the implementation of CIP in marshlands, and selected two cooperatives, one in each district: the KOABIDU (Cooperative of farmers of maize in Duwani marshland) in Gisagara District, and KOAGIMPA (Cooperative of farmers of maize in the Mpazi marshland) in Tumba Sector, Huye District. Concerning the selection of CFBOs, the study selected African Evangelistic Enterprise (AEE) Rwanda (an international Protestant church-based organisation involved in promoting rural and community development) as a case study, and interviewed one agent from this organisation. In total, 18 people participated in this study: 13 farmers (8 women and 5 men), 2 leaders of cooperatives (KOAGIMPA and KOABIDU), 2 officials in charge of agriculture in Gisagara and Huye Districts, and 1 agent from a Christian faith-based organisations. This is very well presented.

## The Role of CFBOs in the Implementation of CIP: Effects on Post-genocide Peacebuilding Process

Following the research questions presented in the first section, the findings are organised in three themes, which include the agricultural changes as per the implementation of CIP, the position/role of CFBOs in the implementation of CIP and its implication for peacebuilding.

## The Agricultural Changes from the CIP Policy

The implementation of CIP policy trigged different changes, namely in the agricultural production system and in the social relations between different actors or stakeholders of agriculture sector. More specifically, the changes involve the consolidation of the use of land, a shift from intercropping to monocropping, the use of modern farming techniques (such as planting in lines and the use of chemical fertilisers, pesticides, and improved seeds), the organisation of farmers into cooperatives, the use of performance contract system, as well as the marketing of inputs and outputs by the government.

### THE CONSOLIDATION OF THE USE OF LAND

As mentioned in the previous sections, the aim of CIP is to address the problem of land fragmentation and shift from small-scale to large-scale farming for increasing the national agricultural growth and enhancing the wellbeing of those involved in farming activities. To achieve this ambitious goal, farmers are required to consolidate the use of land. This means that farmers who have neighbouring plots have to grow the same priority crops in a synchronised manner to address land fragmentation and enhance large-scale production systems. By adhering to this condition, farmers obtain the usufruct of the land particularly in the marshes, as the latter are part of the public domain or the government's land. However, farmers can lose such usufruct in case of failure to comply with the farming conditions imposed by the CIP policy process. This means that the farming system under CIP gives power to the government over land use and management which affects the tenure security by farmers.,

### SHIFTING FROM INTERCROPPING TO MONOCROPPING

Before the implementation of the CIP, Rwanda's farmers were practicing the intercropping system, that is, to mixing diverse crops. Under this system, one could combine two or more crops in one farmland depending on local conditions. The most common combination is about mixing maize and beans, maize and sorghum, or in some cases, maize is intercropped with sorghum and cassava. With the implementation the CIP, however, this system has been banned. Farmers are required to practice monocropping, that is, to grow one among the six crops selected by the government. Those crops are, namely maize, wheat, rice, Irish potato, cassava, and different types of beans. In other words, in the area where the CIP is implemented, farmers are required to switch from intercropping to monocropping, and such regulation is a prerequisite for anyone to get land in the marshes, the land which belongs to the public domain owned by the government.

In the geographical location of the field research for this study, farmers are required to cultivate maize as one of the six selected crops under the CIP, especially for the first season (what the government calls season A) of each year because it is the rainy period (between October and February). In the agricultural seasons B and C, they can farm other crops, which do not require heavy rain or do not take a long time to grow, such as beans. At the beginning of each agricultural season, government officials inform farmers via the cooperative leaders about what crop to cultivate, when, and where. One-crop farming has been settled as a condition to access and farming in all marshlands, and the CIP is known as a programme which promotes monocropping or which facilitates land use consolidation for promoting large-scale commercial farming system.

However, when farmers were asked about their experience concerning this change, they provided diverging opinions. On one side, those who have possibilities to grow other food staples in their private lands appreciated the monocropping system for its contribution to increasing the productivity of selected crops. During the interview, one participant expressed that 'any change brings a challenge: at the beginning, it was not easy to change our mind-set about the programme, but, as the time went, I understood that, the good way to increase production and to get money is to grow one crop by the unit of land' (Interview with women farmers, November, 2022). This point was supported by the government official in charge of agriculture who also noted that, before the CIP programme, farmers were growing many crops in the same plot of land, but the production was very low, and they were facing difficulties to access the market once produced since the majority of those crops were traditional or locally consumed.

On the other side, some of the participants, especially those who depend upon government's land for food production, highlighted the loss or the gap in food production or the loss in food diversity as a result of practicing monocropping. For them, before the CIP programme, when they were mixing different crops on the same unit of land, they could easily produce diverse food staples at the same time. However, with the new model, they depend much more on food purchase, and the money they get out of one-crop production not only take a long to be paid by the business company, but also, it is not enough to cover all the needs in food provision.

## Farmers' Cooperatives

Another change as per the implementation of CIP is the organisation of farmers into cooperatives. The district official in charge of agriculture noted that farmers' cooperatives in CIP facilitate their organisation and their mobilisation and coordination of farming activities. According to this district official, it is via cooperatives that any authority can communicate with farmers or transmit any information concerning the farming process. Further, the committees coordinate interactions/relationships between different stakeholders of the CIP, such as government bodies, business companies, NGOs, or other community-based organisations. As such farmers' cooperatives are the tools through which the government can enhance the daily management of agricultural intensification programmes, and farmers can get access to agricultural extension services. The most mentioned services are the distribution of chemical fertilisers, pesticides, and improved seeds, which farmers can easily get on loan and at a low price due to the subsidies provided via cooperatives.

However, as expressed by participants in this research, some farmers criticised the approach that is being used by cooperatives, explaining that the latter have been using an overwhelming control that brings much pressure and limits individual freedom to the extent that farmers cannot even eat maize whenever they need it.

## THE USE OF MODERN FARMING TECHNIQUES

Another change in the farming system as per the implementation of the CIP programme is the shift from the use of traditional to modern farming techniques, that is, to plant in straight lines, to use improved seeds, mixing organic and chemical fertilisers while planting, and to use of pesticides. For the programme to be more efficient, the cooperative leaders and agronomists have to ensure that all farmers use these techniques throughout the farming process. In this respect, in collaboration with different partners in agriculture, they organise regular trainings for farmers to acquire knowledge about these techniques and skills to practice them. After being trained, farmers receive instructions regarding the whole farming process and the cooperative committee has to monitor the entire process.

Participants in this research revealed that what is challenging in the use of those techniques is that while planting maize, they have to mix chemical fertilisers with organic manure, and it is not easy to balance the quantity of both types of fertilisers. Hence, guidelines about the quality, quantity, and how to use chemical fertilisers and modern seeds are regularly provided to farmers by the ministry of agriculture and its partners. Trainings are basically organised for agriculture counsellors at the village level and the members of the cooperatives' committees, who are trained for training all members of cooperatives

When farmers were asked about their experience regarding their access and use of all required agricultural inputs such as fertilisers, pesticides, and seeds, all of them appreciated the contribution of these inputs in increasing productivity, and also highlighted the difficulties they have in accessing them given that their cost is quite high for a less resourceful farmer.

## DECISION-MAKING PROCESS UNDER CIP

*before joining the CIP, I owned land here and I was cultivating here (in this marshland) as I want, choosing for myself what to plant, including such crops as sorghum, beans, sweet potatoes, ... then, one day they (the government) came and told us to get organised into cooperatives and grow maize ... the government informs us about the price of maize every season, and then in collaboration with District authorities, the cooperative committee organise the marketing for our products.* (Interview with farmers involved in CIP, November 2022)

As expressed in the above quotation, before the implementation of the CIP programme, farmers had full autonomy regarding the management of land, agricultural inputs, as well as the production. In other words, they were concerned with all decisions regarding the agricultural production process, namely the selection of crops to grow, when and where, the seed and fertilisers, and the management of the harvest and post-harvest handling system.

However, with the implementation of the CIP, farmers receive decisions in the form of instructions, and the cooperative's committee coordinates the transmission of information between farmers and the government. Concerning the price, at the end of every agricultural season, the government via the Ministry of Trade and Industrial Development, publishes the price of one kilo for all selected crops under the CIP, including maize. This means that no one can change or negotiate this price, but rather all actors in agricultural market have to follow these decisions/instructions. Regarding the selection of the crops to grow for each agricultural season, farmers are informed at the beginning of every season about which crop to farm under the CIP, and in case there may be a need for change, farmers get information via their cooperative committee which organise regular meetings for general assembly.

In short, the programme does not give room for farmers to decide on how to use or manage their production, as it is upon the cooperative to determine how much quantity to sell and the quantity to take home for food consumption depending on the market's interest. In short, the marketing of inputs and outputs or the management of the whole production system under CIP are in the hands of the government.

### *Scaling the Benefits of CIP for Smallholder Farmers*

Drawing from the above-described changes in the farming system, participants to this study highlighted its benefits particularly in terms of increased productivity of the selected crops. With such an increase in the production, farmers state about its importance in improving their social welfare as they were able to pay for their health insurance, to buy clothes among other benefits. Furthermore, under CIP farmers receive regular trainings in modern farming techniques which improved their professional skills in modern farming system. For them, it helped to change their mind-set about the importance of market-oriented agriculture, and to a certain extent, their life is changing as they are shifting from subsistence to commercial agricultural farming system.

Beside the highlighted benefits, participants underlined challenges which are hindering them to cope with the CIP's implementation framework for effective benefits. Those challenges include namely, the management of cooperatives; access to resources such as land and fertilisers; climate change; government interventionism; and food (in) security.

As demonstrated above, the agricultural intensification program is a top-down government initiative. As such, the government regulates every stage of the policy process. Farmers who participated in this study described this intervention as an overly controlled process with many rules/regulations. These amount to oppressive agrarian model for farmers, limiting their opportunities.

Although, the CIP contributes to increased agricultural productivity, farmers highlighted its limitations in terms of food security: it does not allow them to manage their products or to decide about the use of the harvest, that is, the quantity for home consumption and the one for selling. For them, the programme does not help the poor to improve their living conditions, as they cannot consume what they produce. In other words, the programme does not improve their food provision despite the increase in productivity per unit of land. What they produce under CIP is not satisfying their needs in food provision as the CIP's priority is to supply the market.

Hence, despite being involved in the CIP, the smallholder farmers are still struggling to produce enough food for their families. They consider the government regulations about the management of the production as a constraint limiting them to enjoy the increased productivity under the CIP. The consequence of this situation is that many of the participants depend on *guca inshuro* or as wage labourers, meaning that, they need to work on somebody's farm for their daily survival. Their perspective is that they are producing for others, and it is not understandable how they can endure the costs/investment required for the operation of farming activities under CIP and end up not getting enough food. Lastly, participants highlighted climate change as another type of challenge from which they face unpredictable heavy rain or long period of dry season and as such this affects the farming process and productivity.

## THE ROLE/POSITION OF CFBOS IN THE IMPLEMENTATION OF CIP

As highlighted before, Rwanda is one of Africa's most Christian countries. More than 90% of the population adheres to Christian faith churches. Even though in the aftermath of the 1994 genocide some Christian churches have lost credibility due the complicity of some of their clergy and members in the genocide, the Christian faith is still deeply ingrained in Rwanda's sense of self-identity. As such, the Christian faith actors hold a paramount position as significant players in the Rwanda's post-conflict peacebuilding and development. The underlying idea for the implementation of the Rwanda's agrarian change was to accelerate the post-genocide reconstruction and sustainable peace through the intensification of agriculture. As described above, the Crops Intensification Programme involved different changes in the agricultural production system, which makes it highly demanding in terms of capital and labour. The interest of this research was to know to the extent to which

Christian faith actors get involved in the implementation of this agrarian model. Subsequently, the study selected African Evangelical Enterprise (AEE) Rwanda as the representative of Christian faith-based organisations that partner with the government in promoting rural and community development.

As a non-governmental and Christian organisation, one of the main development sectors which the AEE Rwanda is involved in is to enhance food security and livelihoods throughout the country. During an interview with one agent of AEE Rwanda who works for its agriculture promotion project in Huye and Gisagara districts in the southern Rwanda, he informed the study that the AEE provides technical support for farmers who are involved in commercial farming. The project also provides extension services and promotes value chain. It is also engaged in farmer capacity building and market linkages. In partnership with districts, the AEE Rwanda offers regular trainings to farmers involved in the CIP cooperatives to enable them increase their skills in modern farming techniques. The trainings cover different subjects such as the use of chemical and organic fertilisers, use of improved seeds and pesticides, planting in line, and use of soil erosion protection techniques. In addition, the project organises farmers into small self-help groups (between 20 and 30 members) enabling them to access saving and to credit services. According to the agent of AEE Rwanda, those approaches help farmers especially those who are involved in market-oriented agriculture to have the required knowledge in relation to modern farming techniques and enable those who have less resources to access affordable financial means. However, despite the important work this organisation has been doing, the interviewed agent recognised that the AEE has limitations compared to the existing needs especially because their work does not cover the entire country.

## IMPLICATION OF CFBOS IN THE IMPLEMENTATION OF CIP FOR PEACEBUILDING PROCESS

As already mentioned, in the aftermath of the 1994 genocide against the Tutsi, civil society organisations participated in the reconstruction and peace building process. Like other civil society organisations, CFBOs have been involved in that process. Rwanda's post-genocide peacebuilding process involved the agrarian reform as a strategy to transform agricultural production system. As such, the strategy aimed to boost agricultural growth and enhance the rehabilitation of the socio-economic fabric of the society, since majority of those involved in farming activities constitutes the most vulnerable group. Findings of this study articulated the benefits of CIP for farmers in terms of increasing agricultural productivity. Despite this contribution however, the program is criticised of not being inclusive, as the government controls almost the entire policy process.

As a Christian faith-based actor, the AEE Rwanda has been playing an important role in supporting smallholder farmers involved in the CIP, supplying them with various trainings on the use of modern farming techniques. This technical support increases their knowledge and skills regarding planting in row, the use of chemical fertilisers, improved seeds, pesticides, and post-harvest handling system. Furthermore, the AEE Rwanda organises those farmers in different groups of saving and credit, enabling them to access financial capital through self-help groups. This role is appreciated by farmers as it helps them access knowledge on how to use agricultural technologies and how to develop financial capacity, as both are the necessary resources for them to cope with the agrarian change.

However, the concern for this study was about how such contribution supported the program in the process of peacebuilding in the post-war context. As noted in the previous sections, for agricultural development policy to be effective in the post-war/genocide reconstruction, it needs to involve an inclusive governance system which allows different actors to get involved in decision-making process (Pritchard, 2012). In other words, as the main actors of CIP, farmers should not be treated as beneficiaries, but rather, as the active agents of the programme. In fact, like other civil society organisations, CFBOs are members of Joint Action Development Forum (JADF). The JADF constitutes all institutions/organisations (public, private, local and international NGOs, as well as faith-based organisations) operating at the district level. As such, CFBOs are important development partners of the government-Rwanda Governance Board (Transparency International Rwanda, 2015). This status of CFBOs including AEE Rwanda would put them in a position of power enabling them to interact with district authorities and other development actors, and hence advocate for smallholder farmers involved in the CIP. Nonetheless, the reality shows that, like a government development partner, AEE Rwanda cannot confront the state's policy framework. This was explained by the official of AEE Rwanda who participated in this study when he was asked if AEE Rwanda is aware of the situation of farmers involved in the CIP and its position in relation to this situation:

> *as actors in agriculture development and partner of the government we are aware of how the CIP is organised and the challenges that farmers are facing under that program. However, since the government coordinates the entire process, we believe that the concerned authorities are also aware of those problems and that they take care of them as the government mission is to protect the interest of the people ... we normally intervene in the area where the district shows up the need.* (Interview with an agent of AEE Rwanda, southern province, November 2022)

In the vies of the agent, although their organisation knows about the struggle of farmers under the CIP, it appears that they have not prioritised the issue of decision making within the programme, as the government did not show the need for intervention in this aspect. In other words, as far as the government does not call upon their intervention, they trust that the government is responsible and protects farmers' interests.

From this perspective, it is understood that although it is a CFBOs and would be much more concerned with the daily hardship of the members of Christian churches, as a partner of the government, AEE Rwanda is much more preoccupied with the interests of the government than those of farmers. Factors which may justify the position of AEE Rwanda as part of civil society organisations are grounded in the post-genocide political context. As mentioned above, the war and the genocide shattered all aspects of the social, economic, and political fabric of the society. Thereafter, the political legitimacy remains fragile as a result of human atrocities committed during the war and the genocide (between 1990 and 1994). Hence, the post-genocide state has had a great responsibility to rehabilitate the social and political issue of the society (Gatwa, 2005). In that process, like other civil society organisations, faith-based actors did not gain much trust by the government as some of them were accused of their failure to effectively oppose the genocide. With such model, non-government actors act as compliant partners for the government. This means that they are engaged in the implementing policies and programmes rather than monitoring or criticising them (Huggins, 2017). This implies that in front of the failure of the government, especially regarding the distribution of the political power or the provision of civil rights for a specific group of the population, the only option that is given to civil society organisations like AEE Rwanda is to be silent and/or to co-opt for the government's system.

## Conclusion

The objective of this chapter was to explain the role of CFBOs in the Rwanda's agrarian change and how that role contributes to the post-genocide peacebuilding process. The Rwanda's agrarian change is implemented via the Crops Intensification Programme (CIP), with the main goal of transforming the agriculture sector, enhancing the national economic growth, and improving the welfare of those involved in the sector whose majority were poor. As such, the programme was expected to contribute to the post-genocide peacebuilding and national recovery. The findings demonstrated that as an agricultural modernisation strategy, the initiation of the CIP engendered various changes in agricultural farming system. Those changes involved, but not limited to, the consolidation of the use of land; the use of improved seeds, organic and chemical fertilisers, and pesticides; shift from intercropping to monocropping; organisation of farmers into cooperatives; and the government control over the farming process. Those changes generated positive effects such as the increase of agricultural productivity by unit of land, especially for the crops selected under the CIP. Also, farmers gained much knowledge and skills in the use of modern farming techniques and professionalism in market-oriented agriculture. In this vein, as a Christian faith-based organisation, AEE Rwanda played an important role by providing capacity building regarding the practice of modern farming techniques, and in organising farmers' self-help groups for them to access the opportunities for saving and credit facilities, enabling them to cope with the required farming conditions as per the agricultural change.

Furthermore, findings revealed that the intervention of AEE Rwanda, like any other non-government organisation, is limited and therefore has less impact on the benefits of the CIP for smallholder farmers and on the peacebuilding process. This is because, as a development partner of the government, AEE Rwanda is not in good position to support farmers for them to overcome the government interventionism in CIP policy process, a factor that is threating their benefits for the agrarian change. The silence of AEE Rwanda on this issue has negative impact on the benefits of CIP as it favours farmers' proletarianisation and capitalist accumulation. In other words, the limited involvement of farmers in the decision-making process under CIP, the informal and formal rules regulating the selection of crops, the farming process and marketing of inputs and outputs limit their control over agricultural production process under the CIP. Hence, the position of CFBOs in the CIP policy process does not contribute to the peacebuilding as the growth generated through the agrarian change opens a room for business companies to generate profits to the detriment of farmers' interests. In other words, if farmers cannot exercise their agency or if they cannot make any choice, instead of contributing to the peacebuilding process, the program is oppressing.

Given that the post-genocide political context is still fragile for democratisation process, this study argues that CFBOs need to empower farmers to exercise their agency. Once empowered, farmers can be able to organise themselves for negotiating with the government regarding their rights as the main actors of CIP. However, as the scale of this debate is extensive and multifaceted, this study is not enough to explore effectively the subject. It henceforth suggests further researches to identify specific strategies that can be used by CFBOs to enhance their role in agriculture for peacebuilding in Rwanda.

## References

Addison, T. (2005). *Agriculture Development for Peace*. Research Paper No 2005/09. United Nations University.

Ansoms, A. (2008). *A Green Revolution for Rwanda? The Political Economy of Poverty and Agrarian Change*. Discussion Paper No. 6. Antwerp: Institute of Development Policy and Management. University of Antwerp.

Ansoms, A. (2011). Large-scale Land Deals and Local Livelihoods in Rwanda: The 'Bitter Fruit' of a New Agrarian Model. *Journal of Peasant Studies*, 56(3), 1–23.

Bizoza, A. R., & Havugimana, J. M. (2016). Land Use Consolidation in Rwanda: A Case Study of Nyanza District, Southern Province. *International Journal of Sustainable Land Use and Urban Planning*, 1(1), 64–75.

Cioffo, G. D., Ansoms, A., & Murison, J. (2016). Modernising Agriculture Through a 'New' Green Revolution: The Limits of the Crop Intensification Programme in Rwanda. *Review of African Political Economy*, 43(148), 277–293.

Dawson, N., Martin, A., & Skor, T. (2016). Green Revolution in Sub-Saharan Africa: Implications of Imposed Innovation for the Wellbeing of Rural Smallholders. *World Development, 78,* 204–218. https://doi.org/10.1016/j.worlddev.2015.10.008

De Janvry, A. (1981). The Role of Land Reform in Economic Development: Policies and Politics. *American Journal of Agricultural Economics, 63*(2), 384–392.

FAO. (2013). *Market-oriented Farming: An Overview.* Farm Management Extension Guide.

Gatwa, T. (2005). *The Churches and Ethnic Ideology in the Rwandan Crisis 1900–1994.* Regnum Books International, Oxford Centre for Mission Studies.

Giddens, A. (1979). *Central Problems in Social Theory: Action, Structure and Contradiction in Social Analysis.* University of California Press.

Huggins, C. (2013). *Consolidating Land, Consolidating Control: State-facilitated 'Agricultural Investment Through the "Green Revolution" in Rwanda'.* Land Deal Politics Initiative Working Paper 16.

Huggins, C. (2017). *Agricultural Reform in Rwanda: Authoritarianism, Markets and Zones of Governance.* Zed Books Ltd, The Foundry, 17 Oval Way, London, UK.

Izabiriza, J. (2005). *The Role of Women in Reconstruction: The Case of Rwanda.* Consultation on empowering women in the Great Lakes Region: Violence, Peace and Women's Leadership. Addis-Ababa, Ethiopia.

Kusz, D. (2014). *Modernisation of Agriculture Versus Sustainable Agriculture.* Rzeszów University of Technology.

Mbonigaba, M., & Dusengemungu, L. (2013). *Land Use Consolidation. A Home-Grown Solution for Food Security in Rwanda.* Rwanda Agricultural Board (RAB).

MINAGRI. (2009). *Strategic Plan for Transformation of Agriculture in Rwanda (Phase II).* Kigali.

MINAGRI. (2013). *Strategic Plan for the Transformation of Agriculture in Rwanda (PSTA III).* Kigali.

Musahara, H., & Huggins, C. (2005). Land Reform, Land Scarcity and Post-conflict Reconstruction: A Case Study of Rwanda. In *From the Ground Up: Land Rights, Conflict and Peace in Sub-Saharan Africa.* Institute for Security Studies.

Musahara, H., Nyamurinda, B., & Niyonzima, T. (2014). *Land Use Consolidation and Poverty Reduction in Rwanda.* A Paper presented at the World Bank Conference on Land and Poverty, Washington, DC, 24–27 March.

Narayan, D. (2005). *Measuring Empowerment, Cross-Disciplinary Perspectives.* The World Bank.

National Institute of Statistics of Rwanda (NISR) (2015). Rwanda Integrated Household Living Conditions Survey 2013/2014 - Thematic Report - Agriculture. Kigali.

National Institute of Statistics of Rwanda (2021). *Agricultural household survey 2020 report.* Kigali, Rwanda.

Ndushabandi, E. (2017). *Crop Intensification Program (CIP) Satisfaction Survey-2017.* Institute of Research and Dialogue for Peace.

Pretty, J., Toulmin, C., & Williams, S. (2011). Sustainable Intensification in African Agriculture. *International Journal of Agricultural Sustainability, 9*(1), 5–24. https://doi.org/10.3763/ijas.2010.0583

Pritchard, F. M. (2012). *Land, Power and Peace: Tenure Formalization, Agricultural Reform, and Livelihood Insecurity in Rural Rwanda.* Department of Geography, McGill University, 805 Sherbrooke Street West, Montreal, QC, Canada H3A 2K6

Prunier, G. (1997). The Rwanda crisis. *History of a genocide*. New York: Columbia University Press.
Randell, S., & McCloskey, M. (2014). Sustainable Rural Development in Rwanda: The Importance of a Focus on Women in Agricultural Extension. *International Journal of Agricultural Extension*, 107–119.
Schliesser, C. (2019). Contextualised Development in Post genocide Rwanda. University of Zurich. In A. Heuser & J. Kohrsen (Eds.), *Faith Based Organisations in Development Discourses and Practice*. Routledge. https://doi.org/10.4324/9780429351211-6
Sewell, W. H. (1992). A Theory of Structure: Duality, Agency, and Transformation. *American Journal of Sociology, 98*(1), 1–29.
Shivji, I. G. (2009). *Accumulation in African Periphery: A Theoretical Framework*. Nkukina Nyota Publisher.
Transparency International Rwanda. (2015). *Rwanda Civil Society Development Barometer*. Kigali, Rwanda.
Uvin, P. (1998). *Aiding Violence: The Development Enterprise in Rwanda*. Connecticut: Kumarian Press.
World Bank. (2007). *World Development Report 2008: Agriculture for Development*. The World Bank.
World Bank. (2020). *World Development Indicators. Data Set*. The World Bank. https://datacatalog.worldbank.org/dataset/world-development-indicators

CHAPTER 44

# Arts, Religion, Peacebuilding and Development in Post-conflict Northern Uganda

*Viola Karungi*

## INTRODUCTION

The overarching goal of this chapter is to examine how the arts, specifically drama, have articulated the influence of religion in view of peacebuilding and development in post-conflict Northern Uganda.[1] In the context of this chapter, the arts encompass performative 'cultural and individual dimensions of transitional processes' (de Greiff, 2014, pp. 11, 14) and include drama, theatre, poetry, folklore, music, dance, film, body art, museums, photography, and other kinds of artistic installations. The chapter focuses on a Ugandan play, *Silent Voices* (2019) by Adong Judith. The play is compelling in its intense portrayal of how Christianity was used as an instrument of violence during the conflict in Northern Uganda (1987–2006), and the implication of such instrumentalization on peace and development in the war's aftermath. This chapter is justified by two factors: the relative lack of scholarly attention to contemporary drama about the wr in northern Uganda; as well as the recent revival of a recent tradition of politically-engaged theatre in Uganda which existed from the 1960s to the 1980s.

---

[1] Uganda is an East African country. It shares its borders with South Sudan to the north, the Democratic Republic of Congo (DRC) to the west, Kenya to the east, and Tanzania and Rwanda to the south.

---

V. Karungi (✉)
College of Humanities and Social Sciences, Makerere University, Kampala, Uganda

© The Author(s), under exclusive license to Springer Nature Switzerland AG 2023
S. M. Kilonzo et al. (eds.), *The Palgrave Handbook of Religion, Peacebuilding, and Development in Africa*,
https://doi.org/10.1007/978-3-031-36829-5_44

The conflict in Northern Uganda began as an uprising by the Lord's Resistance Army (LRA), a rebel group commanded by Joseph Kony, against the Government of Uganda (GoU) led by President Museveni who assumed power in 1986 (Allen & Vlassenroot, 2010; Kassimeris, 2006; Lamwaka, 2016). Uganda's national army, the Uganda People's Defence Forces (UPDF), formerly, the National Resistance Army (NRA), played a significant role in countering the LRA. However, ultimately it ended up becoming a perpetrator of the same war (Lamwaka, 2016; Vinci, 2005). The LRA is popular for child abductions, child soldiers, mutilations, murder, rape of both men and women, looting of domestic animals and property (Acker, 2004; Soto, 2009).

The LRA was formed by remnants of crusades against the NRA led by the Uganda National Liberation Army (UNLA), which soon became obsolete and gave rise to the Uganda People's Democratic Army (UPDA). The UPDA quickly became defunct too, paving way for the Holy Spirit Movement (HSM) also known as the Holy Spirit Mobile Forces (HSMF) of Alice Lakwena (see Behrend, 1999, Lamwaka, 2016). The HSM was prominent until it lost a major battle in Jinja District in Eastern Uganda, prompting Lakwena to flee to exile in Kenya. Her flight gave room for Kony to emerge as her successor, and it was he who changed the group's name from HSM to LRA (Lamwaka, 2016; Titeca, 2010; Vinci, 2005). The change of name from HSM to LRA is testimony of the rebel group's attribution of the LRA's activities to divine instruction from God to fight President Museveni's government, an aspect highlighted in the play. Specifically, this attribution is embodied in the phrase 'the Lord's' within the rebel group's name.

Having claimed a divine instruction to fight the GoU, the LRA employed Christian religion ideologies in the form of Biblical allusions to indoctrinate abductees into terrorizing locals, under the guise of fulfilling the Lord's command to liberate Uganda from the government of President Museveni (Finnström, 2010; Titeca 2010; Vinci: 2005).[2] Religion here refers to the Christian faith-based actions of violence used by the LRA (Adam et al., 2007; Nkabala, 2017; Ward, 2001). *Silent Voices* bases on this history of the war to show that religion can be a tool for appropriating violence, which is an antithesis to the common view that religion should always be seen as a positive entity during conflicts.

Efforts to end the war finally culminated in the Juba Peace Talks conducted between the GoU and the LRA from 2006 to 2008.[3] The talks were mediated by Riek Machar, the vice president of South Sudan (Atkinson, 2010). Soto Carlos Rodriguez (2009), a Spanish Roman Catholic priest, who worked in the region, participated in the activities of the Acholi Religious Leaders Peace Initiative (ARLPI) during the conflict, and as part of the GoU's delegation known as the Presidential Peace Team (PPT). He notes that the talks had five

---

[2] The history about the beginning of the LRA has been addressed in detail (see Behrend, 1999; Titeca, 2010).

[3] Atkinson notes that the peace talks formally began on 14 July 2006 (2010, p. 214).

agendas that were to be deliberated on in five phases: 'Cessation of Hostilities; Comprehensive Solutions to the Problems of Northern Uganda; Accountability and Reconciliation; Official End of the War; and Disarmament and Reintegration of Combatants' (2009, p. 260). This history is highlighted in *Silent Voices* through flashbacks. Before these negotiations, there had been futile attempts at peace talks between the GoU and the LRA, spearheaded by the state minister for Northern Uganda, Betty Bigombe, from 1993 to 1994 (Atkinson, 2010, p. 205), and later in 2005 (Atkinson, 2010). As was the case in all these prior attempts, the victims were excluded from the Juba Peace Talks, and the exclusion had a negative impact on peacebuilding in view of religion.

The Juba Peace Talks were intermittent (Atkinson, 2010, p. 214), a situation that caused more suffering and diminished hope for peace, and the intermittency is reflected in *Silent Voices*. Following the abrupt end of the talks, the GoU adopted perpetrator-centred amnesty for transition from war to peace, and this involved excusing ex-LRA combatants who would have surrendered from retributive justice processes, as well as giving them resettlement packages. Survivors of violence were encouraged by the GoU to forgive the perpetrators, welcome them back into community, and reconcile for the sake of peace (Akello, 2019; Rose, 2008). *Silent Voices* portrays the amnesty to ex-LRA soldiers as a cause of inequity in justice between perpetrators and victims, especially because forgiveness was being enforced from a religious point of view. The same religion used by the LRA to torture locals was now the tool for forgiveness and reconciliation. Moreover, because the victims were not involved in the Juba peace talks, the play portrays that forgiveness was an executive decision since victims were not asked whether they wanted to forgive. The play makes a point that forgiveness is a personal matter, and the government should have refrained from extending its executive power into it. Here the play draws attention to the double standards of religion—religion being used to enforce both violence and peace, albeit by different authorities.[4] The playwright sets the play in a strong historical, religious, social, and cultural context, and this setting lays ground for a robust analytical framework in relation to religion, peacebuilding, and development.

The concept of peacebuilding in this chapter draws from the UN Secretary-General Boutros Boutros-Ghali's 1992 report, *An Agenda for Peace,* wherein it is viewed as 'action to identify and support structures which will tend to strengthen and solidify peace in order to prevent a relapse into conflict' (1992). The definition draws attention to not only ending violence but also creating a foundation for durable peace, hence, sustainable development. This chapter is not just interested in the idea 'development' but also in how it relates to the Sustainable Development Goals (SDGs), particularly Goal 16 on Peace, Justice, and Strong Institutions. The view on sustainable development as an integrated

---

[4] The play also features Mato Oput, a local peace-making ritual of the Acholi people, which this chapter does not address.

concept of three pillars: environmental, economic, and social growth by Giddings et al. (2002) is applicable.

In the context of this chapter, the discussion of the play leans more towards a contextual analysis than an in-depth interpretation. Attention is on the contextual dramaturgy of that play focusing on signals about how religion affects peacebuilding and sustainable development. Dramaturgy means 'the dramatic composition of a play or the typical way in which a playwright constructs a play' (Mangan, 2013, p. 166). It is appropriate to examine dramatized issues from the perspective of qualitative research, because, often, drama represents lived-experiences. In terms of structure, the chapter contains a brief literature review, an introduction of *Silent Voices,* and then a discussion of the play's portrayals of how religion was used as a tool of violence. I discuss insights from the play about peacebuilding and sustainable development and conclude with final thoughts about the subject.

## A Brief Overview About Arts, Conflict, and Religion in Uganda

The arts, specifically drama/theatre, have been historically produced about conflicts in Uganda. Attention has been given to drama about the various other episodes of war and/or violence that punctuated the country from the 1960s to the early 1980s, especially during the reigns of President Milton Obote (Obote I, 1966–1971), the rule of President Idi Amin Dada (1971–1979), and the second government of Obote (Obote II, 1980–1985) (see, e.g., Kaahwa, 2004; Kasule, 2013; Mbowa, 2003; Muhumuza, 2017; Mulekwa, 2011). The arts studied by these authors are about violent episodes prior to the war in Northern Uganda and are concerned with exposing, challenging, and in some instances resisting violent acts like brutal killings, unfair arrests, internal displacements, and exiling of political opponents by the respective governments. By contrast, the violence that punctuated the war in Northern Uganda was not characterized by unfair arrests, but rather by abductions of young children who were indoctrinated to use religion as a tool of violence.

Edmondson (2005) has studied how traumatizing stories of child returnees of the war in the north were told through theatre. She uses the insightful term 'marketing trauma' to show how experiences of former child soldiers of the LRA were commodified through theatre, for the purpose of humanitarianism. She draws on her experience as a participant-observer making theatre at the World Vision Children of War Rehabilitation Centre, for returnee children, in Gulu District in Northern Uganda. The circumstances of former child soldiers she refers to are very similar to those depicted in *Silent Voices.* Her focus is on sketch drama as opposed to a scripted play like *Silent Voices.*

This chapter fills a gap of the lack of scholarly attention to Uganda's contemporary drama's perspectives about religion concerning the war in the north. In fact, Yvette Hutchison and Amy Jephta, the editors of the book collection in which *Silent Voices* is published, note that the play was considered 'the spiritual rebirth of theatre in Uganda since the decline of critical theatre due to political persecution of artists during the Idi Amin Regime' (2019, p. 128, quotation marks in original). Playwrights faced death, exile, and jail during the 1960s and 1980s (Mulekwa, 2011; Mbowa, 2003; Kasule, 2013). Thus, *Silent Voices* deserves attention because it is one of the most recent politically-engaged Ugandan dramas that helps us to understand the actual and implied impact of religion in peacebuilding and development.[5]

## Contextualizing *Silent Voices* in Northern Uganda's Conflicts

Even though *Silent Voices* is deeply influenced by primary witness interviews by Adong as indicated in the 'Critical introduction' to the play by Hutchison and Jephta (2019, pp. 128–129), the play is not strictly a verbatim type as it does not explicitly use real people's words taken from recorded interviews. Instead, it employs a docudrama approach, combining fiction and real experiences, with emphasis on historical events of that conflict, and the Juba Peace Talks. Hence, the play is a docudrama with verbatim elements (see Crimmins, 2017; Wake, 2010 on verbatim drama; and Bignell, 2010; Terrone, 2020 on docudrama). By nature, a docudrama is well suited for giving voice to the views of excluded victims—views based on real-life experiences. *Silent Voices* was first staged at the National Theatre in Uganda's capital Kampala in 2012. It was staged again in 2015 at the same venue and was translated from English to Luo language of the Acholi for productions in the same year in the Northern Ugandan districts of Gulu, Kitgum, and Lira. It was also performed in South Africa in March 2019 as part of the Black Theatre Festival.

*Silent Voices* has been chosen as a case study because of the compelling way in which it facilitates a rethinking of religion in light of peacebuilding and development. It is a suitable case that allows focus on 'specificity and deep insights' while exploring the 'complex social situations' (Denscombe, 2004, pp. 30–35). As suggested by Schofield, 'studies in one situation can be used to speak or to help form a judgement about other situations' (1993, p. 207). Whereas the findings in this chapter are specific to Uganda, they are of broader relevance to other conflict-affected countries like Mali, Liberia, Nepal, South Sudan, Sierra Leone, Syria, and the Democratic Republic of Congo (DRC). The relevance is not meant to generalize, but rather to extrapolate the findings. As Alasuutari (1995, pp. 156–157) advises, generalizing means applying general concepts

---

[5] Other recent Ugandan unpublished plays about the same conflict include *Forgotten World* (2009) by Asiimwe Deborah Kawe, *Forged in Fire* (2010) by Sam Okello Kelo, and *MidNight Hour* (2009) by Charles Mulekwa. A radio play *River Yei Junction* (2007/2008) explored the questions of good governance and the rule of law during the war. A television drama series, *Yat Madit* (2017), addressed reconciliation and forgiveness among survivors in the war's aftermath. Theatre for Development (TfD) projects were also conducted (Edmondson, 2005).

obtained through inference from specific cases, while extrapolation is about extending known outcomes further than a known area.

*Silent Voices* is set in Atiak village in Northern Uganda. It features a main plot about MOTHER (Cecilia Achan), as well as two subplots: one about Mother's son OMONY and his girlfriend MARGARET, and the other about a couple, HUSBAND and WIFE. In the major plot, Mother is locked up in a fictional prison imagined by the playwright. She has just been arrested and imprisoned for killing Husband and Wife's child FIONA and is pending investigation and trial. Prior to killing Fiona, Mother kills four other children as vengeance for lack of justice given perpetrator-centred amnesty and the state-enforced forgiveness. All the five are grandchildren of MAN a character representing Joseph Kony the LRA rebel leader. Mother kills the five children to revenge for her five family members who were killed by the LRA: her father, Latigo; her mother, Amal; her brothers, Daniel Omoro and Richard Odokonyero; and her younger sister Flavia Aber. Of the five deaths, only Fiona's is dramatized in detail.

Mother's imprisonment sparks off her revisiting of the torturous past by the LRA through which we learn about how as an abductee at ten years, she along with her siblings Odokonyero and Aber, as well as other conscripted children, were tortured and forced to commit crimes in the name of religion. Particularly, when Mother was abducted, she ended up a child Mother (of Omony) whom she begot with one of the LRA commanders. She is represented in the play not only as a survivor, but an object of religious manipulation too. Currently, she is about fifty years of age and is tormented by the reality that the LRA were pardoned by the GoU and given resettlement packages while victims were only required to forgive them. Revisiting the past in the play is achieved through Mother's narratives, flashbacks, and dialogue.

The subplot about Omony and Margaret rotates around their inability to grow their love affair into a marriage in an environment where family members of former LRA rebels are unwelcome. Margaret is a granddaughter of Man, and for this reason, Mother objects to the romantic relationship between her son Omony and Margaret. Omony works in a small shop in Atiak village while Margaret is a teacher at Jua Kali Rehabilitation Centre. The centre is a rehabilitation home for child returnees. Her job is an irony considering that she must rehabilitate children subjected to suffering by the LRA commanded by her grandfather, Man.

In the second subplot, Husband (also Margaret's uncle) and Wife are trying to sustain their marriage in a turbulent environment caused by the disappearing children before it is discovered that Mother is killing them. Even before the death of Fiona, Wife cautions Husband that they should leave Atiak and start a life elsewhere, an idea he is opposed to because he just received a job transfer and is afraid to ask for another soon. This subplot, just like the one about Omony and Margaret, makes us aware that families of ex-combatants have difficulties co-existing with those of victims. The assumption that victims would forgive their tormentors (and perhaps their descendants) is portrayed in the play as false. In the play, Man is also known as BOY 1. The latter is used in bush scenes to depict the young version of Kony when he is commanding troupes of abductees to commit atrocities. The former is used in scenes that show the adult version of Kony during peace talks and after the war. The play has several other characters, and these will be revealed when necessary.

## SILENT VOICES AND RELIGION IN NORTHERN UGANDA

In this section, I discuss how *Silent Voices* portrays the LRA's use of Christian ideologies and the effect of this usage on peacebuilding and development. The LRA used Biblical allusions through direct quotes of verses and referencing of other Biblical events in both the Old and New Testaments. The allusions are meant to indoctrinate the child abductees into accepting to fight as child soldiers and to punish abductees who attempt to escape. Regarding in-text referencing of the play-text, whenever I quote or paraphrase from the play, I provide the year and page numbers in brackets as in (Hutchison & Jephta, 2019, p. 00). To enable easy flow for the reader, I avoid repeating names of the editors of the volume (Hutchison and Jephta) in which the play is published.

### BIBLICAL ALLUSIONS AND INDOCTRINATION INTO VIOLENCE

> We are your teachers, sent by God to teach you and together we will rescue our people from oppression. Am I clear?—Boy 1, *Silent Voices*.

The quote above is by Boy 1 when he is commanding his abductees to obey the LRA's divine authority. It immediately points our attention to the LRA's use of religion. In the play's opening scene when Mother has just been arrested and imprisoned pending trial, she revisits the past through a flash back when she (a young Cecilia Achan aged ten then) has just been abducted by LRA rebels along with other children including Odokonyero and Aber. Shortly before the abduction, the LRA raids Mother's parent's home during a marriage ceremony and accuses the gathered community of celebrating instead of joining the LRA's struggle to liberate Northern Uganda from President Museveni. After singling out children for abduction, Boy 1 instructs the soldiers to fire randomly at the villagers. This is when Mother's father, mother, and brother Omoro are killed (2019, pp. 207–208).

In the same flashback, the abductees, including Mother and her two siblings, walk a long way into the bush towards the base of the rebels. Aber is tired and is trickily asked by the commander whether she wants 'to go home' to which she agrees. Odokonyero innocently offers to take her home oblivious of the fact that going home means being killed by the LRA for no specific reason. Thus, he is instructed to kill her and he too is killed thereafter. The point here is Mother's witnessing of the unreasonable death of her two siblings. After the killings, Boy 1, who is the commander of the rebels, addresses the abductees, and it is from his address that the quote above is excerpted.

Boy 1:
>Good. I am Commander Man and I will be your commander until we make it to base. However, you will call me Teacher Man. And so will you call all the commanders you will meet at base. We are your teachers, sent by God to teach you and together we will rescue our people from oppression. Am I clear? (2019, pp. 141–142)

Here, Boy 1 or Teacher Man as he likes to be called, on behalf of himself and other LRA commanders, asserts divine authority. He uses the concept 'teacher,' which in the Bible can be seen in Matthew 4:12, Mark 6:34, Luke 5:3, and John 7:14, when Jesus is portrayed as a teacher in different places. By likening himself to Jesus, he presents his persona and personae of all the other commanders as knowledgeable, hence, eligible to impart knowledge about conflict. The use of that concept is a subtle way of applying religion to enforce obedience for the sake of conflict. When the abductees arrive at the base, Boy 1 states: 'I am Commander Man, the chosen messiah of our people' (2019, p. 152). In Matthew 16:15–16, Luke 2:11, and Acts 5:42, Jesus is referred to as a Messiah. Boy 1's reference of himself as a Messiah too, equates him to Jesus, thereby presenting himself as a saviour who should be revered. What this presentation does is allow him to perpetuate crimes without question, hence using religion to cause conflict than peace.

At the base, Boy 1 further convinces the abductees that they are the chosen ones to fight 'next to he who is chosen by the Lord Jesus himself to save the Acholi people' (2019, p. 152), thereby creating an impression of their abduction as a blessing if they collaborate with him. He further asserts: 'I am the word. The messenger of God to liberate and free our people! And that's why he has blessed me with supernatural powers. All we have to do is believe and we shall reign again! *(As he pounds his chest again)*' (2019, p. 152). He emphasizes the need to fight for 'Liberation, Freedom and Supremacy' and instructs the abductees to repeat those three words which they initially do '*timidly*', then '*fairly loud*', and eventually '*say it out loud with conviction*' according to the play's stage directions (2019, p. 152). The upward change in their energy is an indicator of acceptance of his teachings, out of fear of being sent home. His use of the exact words as those used by Jesus in the Bible when he says, 'I am the word' (John: 1:1) is blasphemous and positions him as right and unquestionable. The positioning serves the purposes of enforcing loyalty and diligence from the recruits, hence, a catalyst of conflict.

At the end of Boy 1's address, the captives break into a militant song led by Kadogo Action one of the LRA guards. In the song, they call on the saviour (Boy 1) to come and tell them the sweet words about Jesus. In between the choruses, Kadogo Action interjects: 'He changed water into wine', 'He even healed the blind', and 'He changed rocks into bombs' (2019, p. 154). Each of them pays allegiance by kissing the cross which Boy 1 wears. He then repeatedly pauses to them the question, 'So, do we believe?' They answer in the affirmative, and he shouts a prolonged 'Aleluyaaaaaa!' to which they reply a prolonged

'Ameeeeeeeeeeeen' (2019, p. 155). The song concludes the indoctrination or what Adam et al. relatedly explains as the ritual of 'purification' (2007, pp. 972–974). Whether the abductees believe as professed does not matter. What matters is that their proclamation frames their role as child soldiers. Indoctrination helps to reshape the identity of the children, encourages religious subjectivity, and reinforces group solidity to fight. This scene shows that leadership in conflict situations is revered, to an extent that the followers would imagine that the leader is some kind of a demigod. The play shows that in the quest for peace or good governance as the LRA claims to be doing, leaders use religious doctrines to brainwash the masses to join their course even when it hurts—children, women, and men who are not interested in this course.

## BIBLICAL ILLUSIONS AND PUNISHMENT

In another flashback scene, in the bush, four abductees are caught attempting to escape. Upon being captured, commander Boy 3 brands them traitors who do not want liberation and therefore, deserve death. Kadogo NoJoke and Kadogo Smiles (LRA guards) dully lay machetes which Boy 3 picks, hands over one to each of the child abductees, and then alludes to the Biblical verse 'Whosoever is not for us is against us' (Luke 9:10; Mark 9:40). This Biblical reference is based on Apostle John's account to Jesus that the apostles had attempted to stop a stranger (someone not considered an apostle) from driving out demons in Jesus' name. Jesus replied to John instead that there is no need to stop such a person because 'whosoever is not against you is for you.' Accordingly, the commander reversed the saying from 'not against you is for you' to 'not for us is against us.' The reversal is misuse of Biblical text to justify violence. The same reversal shows that leaders, however religious they claim to be, can actually misuse the very religion they claim to promote. The wrong interpretation of the verse falsely sways the abductees into believing the cause of the LRA.

In the same scene, after handing over the machetes, Kadogo NoJoke '*in an accustomed way*,' hands Boy 3 the Bible, a gesture that the LRA regularly uses the book (2019, p. 185). Then Boy 3 addresses the child soldiers:

Boy 3:
(*Raises the Bible up*) You see this great book of our Lord? It is a book full of the greatest wisdom ever from the Lord our God himself. It gives wisdom about everything from life to death.
*(He pauses and looks around).*
Kadogos, tell us what this great book tells us about traitors. (2019, p. 185)

The accustomed manner in which the Bible is used serves to show the abductees that the LRA has authority over Biblical issues. It is a way of mobilizing trust and support from the abductees. Following his instruction, the Kadogos, in turns, and out of memory, effortlessly quote different Biblical verses about traitors, betrayers, and the consequences of such behaviour. To demonstrate the point, I have reproduced here the entire excerpt of the quotations as portrayed in the play.

> Kadogo Nojoke:
> Isaiah 24:16. I waste away, I waste away! Woe to me! The treacherous betray! With treachery the treacherous betray!
> Kadogo Smiles:
> Isaiah 48:8. You have neither heard nor understood; from of old your ear has not been open. Well do I know how treacherous you are; you were called a rebel from birth.
> Kadogo Nojoke:
> 2 Timothy 3:4. Traitors, headstrong, conceited, lovers of pleasure rather than lovers of God.
> Kadogo Smiles:
> Mathew 7: 2. Woe to you, O traitor, you who have not been betrayed! When you stop destroying, you will be destroyed; when you stop betraying, you will be betrayed.
> Kadogo Nojoke:
> Revelation 21:8. But cowards, traitors, perverts, murderers, the immoral,
> those who practice magic, those who worship idols, and all liars—the place for them is the lake burning with fire and sulfur, which is the second death.
> Kadogo Smiles:
> Revelation 20:12. And I saw the dead, great and small, standing before the throne, and books were opened. Then another book was opened, which is the book of life. And the dead were judged by what was written in the books, according to what they had done. (2019, pp. 185–186)

It is interesting to note that the Kadogos easily quote the verses out of memory, an indication that they usually do it. All the verses singularly and collectively justify punishment by death as a consequence of betrayal—so the Bible says. The recitations demonstrate that the LRA knows the Bible by heart and is also a kind of a show-off about their mastery of religious views about dealing with traitors. The very recitations, however, inadvertently promote violence than peace.

After the lengthy exercise of reciting the verses, the commander emphasizes that the Bible gives endless wisdom about how to deal with traitors, and that in all, there is only one way. Before revealing that one way however, he creates tension by asking the abductees: 'Imagine if Jesus Christ our Lord had dealt with Judas Iscariot. Would he have been betrayed and killed?' (2019, p. 186). Judas Iscariot is the apostle who betrayed Jesus, and the LRA's concern was that Jesus knew it beforehand that Judas would betray him yet did not do anything to stop the betrayal as seen in gospels Matthew 26:24, Mark 14:21, John 6:70–71, and Luke 22:48. The guards are quick to answer with a firm 'no' while the four children and other abductees are unsure of the response. He asks a second time to which everybody answers 'no' (2019, p. 186). This is another instance of misappropriation of Biblical text. Whereas the Gospels John 6:64 and Matthew 26:25 indicate that Jesus foresaw Judas' betrayal, they also show that Jesus allowed the betrayal to happen (John 13:27–28). Accordingly, Judas' role in the life of Jesus was predetermined for God's will to be fulfilled through Jesus. Thus, Boy 3 errors by comparing the four abductees to Judas. Boy 3 then proceeds to make the final verdict:

> Boy 3:
> We must not make the mistake Jesus made. We must annihilate all our enemies and anything that stands in the way of our goal, our liberation, our freedom, our supremacy. We must annihilate these four. (2019, p. 186)[6]

After pronouncing his verdict, the children are sent home. The religious basis of violent acts like sending people home used by the LRA is similar to what Spivak refers to as 'religious terrorism' which is a 'cultural education/instruction' that 'coercively rearranges' minds of the coerced into acceptance (2004, pp. 91–94). Religious terrorists tend to dramatize their purpose to justify the 'ethic-ism' of religious wars by employing linguistic competence at a very sublime level (2004, p. 91). The LRA's actions are similar to those of the Ambonese Christian militias in the island of Ambon, Indonesia (1999–2002), and the National Liberation Front of Tripura, since 1989 in Northeast India, that have similarly utilized religion as a tool of conflict (Adam et al., 2007).

## Religion, Peacebuilding, and Development: Insights from *Silent Voices*

*Silent Voices* gives insight about religion in view of peacebuilding and development. Take an example of when religion is used, in futility to convince Mother to confess that she murdered Fiona. While in prison, the Criminal Investigation's Officer (CID) is frustrated when Mother seems unwilling to admit and confess that she murdered Fiona. In that moment, the Bishop who often comes in to counsel Mother and persuade her to confess for the sake of peace walks in. Mother scorns at Bishop saying: 'Bishop, you are here to purge my soul, are you? Hoping that I would pour my soul out to you and your God.' (2019, p. 167). Mother's question communicates her mistrust in God considering her abductee experiences, hence, her decision that God is only for some people and not for other implied in 'your God.' Bishop struggles to respond to Mother's question convincingly and the scene involves a physical attack by Mother when she grabs his leg. As opposed to child abductees who simply listen and obeyed the commanders' instructions during the war, here we see a firm survivor ready to confront a religious leader. One of Bishop's responses in the scene is direct reference to the Bible when he says:

---

[6] One girl out of the four children is not killed for a reason unrelated to this study. I do not delve into her story.

Bishop:

The holy book says thou shall not judge. Ours is a call to embrace heaven's paradise, far away from the fires of hell. *(Mother freezes)* But first we must redeem ourselves. Confess our sins. (2019, p. 168)

Mother's action of freezing is triggered by Bishop's mention of the holy book and what it says, and a reminder of how the LRA used the same book. Therein lies the contradiction in using religion to justify violence and peace. Mother objects to Bishop's religious advice and he exits the prison unceremoniously. Contextually, religion here is portrayed as an organizational structure that can face difficulty when promoting peace agendas to people who suffered its manipulation.

In another instance, at Margaret's workplace, the Jua kali Rehabilitation Centre, when children returnees are playing, Girl 2 and Girl 3 get into an argument about who should go first in a role-play storytelling session facilitated by Margaret. Girl 2 tells Girl 3, 'And yet considering what you did to us in captivity, we shouldn't even be playing with you' (2019, p. 143). This moment in the play demonstrates that even children are struggling to co-exist with fellow children who tormented them during the war. This incident is similar to Mother's rejection of Margaret in a scene wherein Omony introduces Margaret to Mother. The couple carries groceries for Mother which Omony points out are a gift from Margaret, but Mother turns them down and instead asks Margaret to leave. Mother cautions Omony to find another girl for marriage (2019, pp. 148–149). Omony thinks Mother is simply being 'bitter' and unreasonably holding Margaret accountable for the actions of her grandfather and other LRA rebels (2019, p. 150). Eventually, the lack of forgiveness further contributes to the destruction of Omony's love affair with Margaret. Omony tries to convince Mother to exercise patience saying that the 'leaders' [the GoU] only chose to compensate perpetrators first and that recompense for victims 'is coming soon' (2019, p. 150). She rejects his view and asks why the GoU started with abusers while the sufferers 'sprawl in poverty and more suffering' (2019, p. 150). She reminds Omony that he only sells 'little things in a village shop while they [former LRA rebels] cruise in luxuries' (2019, p. 150). The reminder makes nonsensical the demand that recompense for perpetrators is met with forgiveness from victims.[7]

The play depicts resistance to the sort of forgiveness that Jeffery (2011, p. 80) has termed 'political forgiveness' (2011, p. 80), a kind of pardon negotiated by political authorities on behalf of the offended people. The depiction draws attention to pertinent questions regarding who should forgive, who

---

[7] The chapter recognizes the GoU put in place recovery projects such as the Peace Recovery and Development Plan (PRDP) (2007–2010), whose overall goal was to consolidate peace and security and to lay the ground for recovery and development in Northern Uganda. Here https://www.brookings.edu/wp-content/uploads/2016/07/Uganda_PRDP-2007.pdf

should be forgiven, and who can mediate forgiveness. Moreover, she objects to state-enforced forgiveness based on Christian ideology yet the same ideology was used for violence. Jesson (2010) makes a compelling argument about forgiving which helps us to comprehend further the victims' refusal of state-enforced mercy. When discussing forgiveness and its reasons, he notes that the command to forgive is drawn from the gospel of Matthew[8] from the Lord's Prayer *Our Father*, in the expression 'and forgive us our trespasses, as we forgive those who trespass against us'[9] (2010, p. 1). Accordingly, forgiveness (pre) determines a harmonious relationship between God and a person, and God's forgiveness of man is conditional on man's. Mother objects the conditionality set by religious standards.

Considering that Mother refuses to co-exist with a family member of a former LRA rebel and also goes on to kill five children to revenge, her action is a direct implication that she does not embrace the idea of forgiveness. This portrayal in the play resonates with the actual history of the war wherein Catholic and Protestant churches actively took part in conflict resolution and peacebuilding, often in collaboration with NGOs (Ward, 2001). Bishop John Baptist Odama, a popular clergy of the Catholic church in Northern Uganda, for instance, advocated that Kony and the LRA rebels be treated as 'prodigal sons who can be forgiven and received back into the society' as reported in Uganda's national newspaper, *New Vision*, on 23 March 1999. The play, however, makes us aware that not all victims are opposed to forgiveness (and compensation for the LRA) as shown through Omony who states: 'It's forgiveness and compensation, Mother. The surest way to peace. Don't you want peace?' (2019, p. 150). Omony represents victims who are willing to forgive for the sake of peace. Nevertheless, it is important to note that the play's main character, Mother, advances an opposing view, and since she was abused in far more ways than her son, her view is given priority.

In regard to peacebuilding, the play portrays that Mother's action of revenge due to her rejection of forgiveness prompts another cycle of violence in Atiak village. The village members attempt to lynch her and her son Omony when they learn of the allegation that she is the one who murdered the children (2019, pp. 164–165, 175). At the end of the play during Mother's trial in court, the Judge asks the defense, 'So, for the case of five counts of murder, how does the defense plead?' and Mother's Lawyer responds, 'The defense pleads insanity' (2019, p. 202). However, Mother immediately '*jumps to her feet*' and states, firmly, 'I am not insane, Your Worship' (2019, p. 202). Mother insists that she wants to complete a burial ritual for Fiona as she did for the other four children. She insistently tells the Judge, 'I am half guilty, Your Honour! I must complete my ritual, Your Honour! I must gain my full guilt!' (2019, p. 203). Completing the ritual is her way of getting satisfaction from killing the five

[8] Matthew 5: 43–48.
[9] Matthew 6: 12, 15.

children in exchange for her five families killed by the LRA. Mother disrupts court proceedings prompting the Judge to adjourn court prematurely.

The Bishop and Lawyer are played by one actor and both characters, as portrayed in the play, struggle to understand Mother's dilemma. Just like Bishop fails to notice that religious ideology about confession cannot work under the circumstances, the Lawyer also fails to understand Mother's reason for killing the children but simply labels her as insane. By adjourning court hurriedly without a ruling on whether Mother is guilty or simply insane, and by ending the play when Mother is back in prison, the play suggests a possibility that judgement in her case is in jeopardy. Yet, if she goes unjudged and unpunished, it is likely that Man's family will in future protest the lack of justice and the cycle of counter-accusations and possibly counter-violence will go on.

## Final Reflections

The voice of the play suits well with SDG 16 on Peace, Justice, and Strong Institutions. In its attempt to address the aftermath of the conflict, the play, just like several conflict-related arts tend to do, frames an 'intentional proliferation of questions, multiple layers of meaning, doubt and uncertainty' (Breslin, 2017, p. 267) about the future in view of how religion was instrumentalized for both violence and peace in Northern Uganda. We observe that art is a space where real or fictious characters can have their unique voices elevated and as seen with the different characters in this docudrama. It magnifies lived-experiences such as those of religious manipulation in *Silent Voices*. Religion is used as a tool of oppression, to a point that the masses can read this weakness.

The decision of perpetrator-centred amnesty versus forgiveness on the part of victims is portrayed as causing Mother's action of vengeance which triggers another possible cycle of violence in the community. Relapsing into conflict means the aim of peacebuilding envisioned by the UN as mentioned in the introduction remains futile. A relapse hinders SDG 16 target 1 (16.1) which is about reducing violence everywhere and minimizing violence-related death. Consequently, sustainable development remains a myth as optimism and cohesion are lacking.

The play stimulates vital discourse about ecological existence of victims and survivors, all with multiple identities: women, men, former child soldiers, former sex slaves, child mothers, ex-LRA combatants and their relatives. Having been manipulated by religion, their participation in religious-based development activities is withheld. Here, the play reminds us of SDG 16 target 7 (16.7) which is concerned about inclusive and representative participation when making conflict-related decisions. Victims and survivors should be consulted about what works for peace and development to happen as opposed to simply using executive powers to decide for them. If the victims had been consulted in the case of this play, perhaps they would have chosen another approach other than forgiveness. In the play's epilogue, when Mother is returned to prison, after the aborted court hearing, just like in the prologue, she sits quietly in her jail cell with her '*legs heavily chained*' (2019, p. 210). What seems to be a heroic journey for her as she agitates for justice ends up making her powerless. The centrality of Mother, a complex vengeful victim turned into a propagator of the same violence she castigates, underlines the impact of religious-based violations.

Since the play addresses a recent conflict and the community is still dealing with psycho-social and development issues, it is still too early to make concrete conclusions about the course of development. Nevertheless, the insights about peacebuilding and development in relation to the complex social-political situation are not to be ignored. The play does not present Christianity or amnesty as the problem, but rather how they were conceived and employed by the respective actors. The play suggests further that state leaders should pay attention to the real and possible effects of religious manipulation when presiding over transition processes.

The chapter illuminates the plays' social and political commentaries aimed at causing social transformation. It also recognizes the expectation that 'art can and should play a social role' as Bystrom has noted (2014, p. 32). However, the chapter is also cognizant that writing about injustice through art has a limited capacity for changing society. Although art succeeds in showing religious manipulation, it certainly needs to be supplemented by practical social and political interventions for stronger impact. There is a need for researcher input on how art can be integrated within non-literary organizations and/or practices where concrete policies and political interventions on development are designed and implemented. This way, remarkably informative arts like *Silent Voices* can be used to realize more tangible post-war insights about development. More specifically, the role of art should be emphasized in the implementation of SDG 16, such that the arts are incorporated as part of formal mechanisms when addressing conflicts globally.

## References

Adam, J., Cordier, B., Titeca, K., & Vlassenroot, K. (2007). In the Name of the Father? Christian Militantism in Tripura, Northern Uganda, and Ambon. *Studies in Conflict & Terrorism, 30*(11), 963–983. https://doi.org/10.1080/10576100701611288

Adong, J. (2019). *Silent Voices*. In Y. Hutchison & A. Jephta (Eds.), *Contemporary Plays by African Women*. Methuen Drama.

Akello, G. (2019). Reintegration of Amnestied LRA Ex-Combatants and Survivors' Resistance Acts in Acholiland, Northern Uganda. *International Journal of Transitional Justice, 13*, 249–267. https://doi.org/10.1093/ijtj/ijz007

Alasuutari, P. (1995). *Researching Culture: Qualitative Method and Cultural Studies*. SAGE.

Allen, T. (2006). *Trial Justice: the International Criminal Court and the Lord's Resistance Army*. Zed Books/International African Institute.

Allen, T., & Vlassenroot, K. (eds.). (2010). *The Lord's Resistance Army: Myth and Reality*. London: Zed Books.

Atkinson, R. (2010). The Realists in Juba? An Analysis of the Juba Peace Talks. In T. Allen & K. Vlassenroot (Eds.), *The Lord's Resistance Army: Myth and Reality* (pp. 205–222). Zed Books Ltd.

Behrend, H. (1999). *Alice Lakwena & the Holy Spirits, War in Northern Uganda 1986-1997*. Oxford: James Currey. Kampala: Fountain Publishers; Nairobi: EAEP; Athens: Ohio University Press.

Bignell, J. (2010). Docudramatizing the Real: Developments in British TV docudrama since 1990. *Studies in Documentary Film*, (4), 195–208. https://doi.org/10.1386/sdf.4.3.195_1.

Boutros, B. (1992, January 31). *An Agenda for Peace: Preventative Diplomacy, Peacemaking and Peace-Keeping*, UN Doc A/47/277-S/2411.

Breslin, A. (2017). Art and Transitional Justice: The 'Infinite Incompleteness' of Transition. In C. Lawther, L. Moffett, & D. Jacobs (Eds.), *Research Handbook on Transitional Justice*. Edward Elgar Publishing.

Bystrom, K. (2014). Literature, Remediation, Remedy (The Case of Transitional Justice). *Comparative Literature*, 66(1), 25–34. http://www.jstor.com/stable/24694533

Crimmins, G. (2017). How a Verbatim Drama Based on the Lived Experience of Women Casual Academics in Australia Resonated with its Audience and Transformed a Narrative Inquiry into an Action Research Project. *Educational Action Research*, 25(3), 337–353. https://doi.org/10.1080/09650792.2016.1182042

de Greiff, P. (2014). On Making the Invisible Visible: The Role of Cultural Interventions in Transitional Justice Processes. In C. Ramírez-Barat (Ed.), *Transitional Justice, Culture and Society: Beyond Outreach* (pp. 11, 14). Social Science Research Council.

Denscombe, M. (2004). *The Good Research Guide: For Small-Scale Social Research Projects*. Berkshire: Open University Press.

Edmondson, L. (2005). Marketing Trauma and the Theatre of War in Northern Uganda. *Theatre Journal*, 57(3), 451–474.

Finnström, S. (2010). An African Hell of Colonial Imagination? The Lord's Resistance Army in Uganda, Another Story. In T. Allen & K. Vlassenroot (Eds.), *The Lord's Resistance Army: Myth and Reality* (pp. 74–89). Zed Books.

Giddings, B., Hopwood, B., & O'Brien, G. (2002). Environment, Economy and Society: Fitting Them Together into Sustainable Development. *Sustainable Development*, 10(4), 187–196. https://doi.org/10.1002/sd.199

Hutchison, Y., & Jephta, A. (Eds.). (2019). *Contemporary Plays by African Women*. Bloomsbury Publishing Plc.

Jeffery, R. (2011). Forgiveness, Amnesty, and Justice: The Case of the Lord's Resistance Army in Northern Uganda. *Cooperation and Conflict*, 46(1), 78–95.

Jesson, S. (2010). Forgiveness and its Reason. PhD Thesis. University of Nottingham.

Kaahwa, J. A. (2004). Ugandan Theatre: Paradigm Shifts. *South African Theatre Journal*, 18(1), 82–111.

Kassimeris, G. (Ed.). (2006). *Warrior's Dishonour: Barbarity, Morality and Torture in Modern Warfare*. Ashgate Publishing Limited.

Kasule, S. (2013). *Resistance and Politics in Contemporary East African Theatre: Trends in Ugandan Theatre since 1960*. Adonis and Abbey Publishers Ltd.

Lamwaka, C. (2016). *The Raging Storm: A Reporter's Inside Account of the Northern Uganda War 1986–2005*. Fountain Publishers.

Mangan, M. (2013). *The Drama, Theatre and Performance Companion* (Palgrave Student Companion Series). Palgrave Macmillan.

Mbowa, R. (2003). Artists Under Siege: Theater and the Dictatorial Regimes in Uganda. In *Theatre and Performance in Africa*. Bayreuth African Studies Series.

Muhumuza, M. (2017). *The Nature of Theatre in Uganda* (Uganda Theatre Series). Momo Centre for Talent Development Ltd.

Mulekwa, C. (2011). Theatre, War, and Peace in Uganda. In C. Cynthia et al. (Eds.), *Acting Together I: Performance and the Creative Transformation of Conflict: Resistance and Reconciliation in Regions of Violence* (pp. 45–71). NYU Press. https://www.jstor.org/stable/j.ctt21pxmd8.10

Nkabala, H. N. (2017). The Use of Violent Biblical Texts by the Lord's Resistance Army in Northern Uganda. *Transformation, 34*(2), 91–100.

Rose, C. (2008). Looking Beyond Amnesty and Traditional Justice and Reconciliation Mechanisms in Northern Uganda: Proposal for Truth-Telling and Reparations. *Boston College Third World Law Journal, 28*(2), 345–400.

Schofield, J. W. (1993). Increasing the Generalizability of Qualitative Research. In M. Hammersley (Ed.), *Social Research: Philosophy, Politics and Practice* (pp. 200–225). London: Sage.

Soto, C. R. (2009). *Tall Grass: Stories of Suffering and Peace in Northern Uganda*. Fountain Publishers.

Spivak, C. G. (2004). "Terror: A Speech After 9-11." Boundary 2. https://api.semanticscholar.org/CorpusID:161187420.

Terrone, E. (2020). Documentaries, Docudramas, and Perceptual Beliefs. *The Journal of Aesthetics and Art Criticism, 78*(1), 43–55.

Titeca, K. (2010). The Spiritual Order of the LRA. In A. Tim & K. Vlassenroot (Eds.), *The Lord's Resistance Army: Myth and Reality* (pp. 59–73). London.

van Acker, F. (2004). Uganda and the Lord's Resistance Army: The New Order No One Ordered. *African Affairs, 103*(412), 335–357.

Vinci, A. (2005). The Strategic Use of Fear by the Lord's Resistance Army. *Small Wars & Insurgencies*, (16), 360–38.

Wake, C. (2010). Verbatim Theatre Within a Spectrum of Practices. In P. Brown (Ed.), *Verbatim: Staging Memory and Community* (pp. 6–8). Currency Press.

Ward, K. (2001). 'The Armies of the Lord:' Christianity, Rebels and the State in Northern Uganda, 1986–1999. *Journal of Religion in Africa, 31*, 187–221.

# PART VIII

# Conclusion

CHAPTER 45

# Imagining the Future of Religion, Peacebuilding and Development in Africa

*Susan M. Kilonzo and Ezra Chitando*

### INTRODUCTION

The handbook has, through the various chapters herein, illustrated the central role of religion and religious institutions in peacebuilding and sustainable development in Africa. Paying particular attention to the interface between religion, peacebuilding and Sustainable Development Goal (SDG) 16 ("Promote peaceful and inclusive societies for sustainable development") and its various targets, the handbook has highlighted the strategic role of religion and religious institutions in contributing towards sustainable peacebuilding and development in Africa. As has become clear, the themes covered in this handbook are diverse. The introductory chapter by the editorial team lays a foundation on the need for institutional engagement in the wide range of conflicts that have characterized the continent, and whose causes are also as diverse as is the continent. From statistical evidence, the chapter shows that the trends of conflicts and magnitude vary across the continent, as do the resultant effects. Some countries remain hard hit, especially those that have had prolonged occurrences of ethnic, civil or political wars. At the time of writing these chapters, the Sudan and the Democratic Republic of Congo (DRC) were

S. M. Kilonzo (✉)
Department of Religion, Theology & Philosophy, Maseno University, Maseno, Kenya

E. Chitando
Department of Philosophy, Religion and Ethics, University of Zimbabwe, Harare, Zimbabwe

© The Author(s), under exclusive license to Springer Nature Switzerland AG 2023
S. M. Kilonzo et al. (eds.), *The Palgrave Handbook of Religion, Peacebuilding, and Development in Africa*,
https://doi.org/10.1007/978-3-031-36829-5_45

undergoing deadly ethno-political violence. Thus, the focus on religion and peacebuilding in Africa is not a luxury, but an existential necessity.

As promised in the introductory chapter, the different chapters in the handbook speak to diverse nature of conflicts and subsequently interrogate how religious tools and forms, including the very diverse religions, actors, religious institutions, interfaith networks, explore the place of religion in contributing towards achievement of the SDGs, with specific focus on Goal 16. This remains important because the goals have a timeframe (they have a 2030 target, but likely going beyond), and for any institution to claim stakeholdership in global development, the need to document their contributions is key. It is noteworthy indicating that each of the chapters allude to the perceived contributions, and although statistical measures may not be evidenced, there is a level of effort to explore how the contributions of religion and religious institutions or actors speak directly or indirectly to SDG 16, and its specific targets. On this, therefore, is the need for international actors, especially those building up architectures for peacebuilding, to interrogate the relevant ways of measuring contributions as well as achievements towards the targets set. As we shall see in this concluding chapter, although some of the contributions may not have a statistical measure, they are more important than the statistics that certain actors in the world desire to see.

## *Contextualizing Religion, Peacebuilding and Development in Africa*

The first part of the handbook which provides a general introduction that speaks to the broader agenda or religious peacebuilding is diversified to speak to, not just the theoretical understanding of religious peacebuilding, but how it has been applied in certain contexts with varied results. It draws attention to how it has been researched on within the continent, how it has been taught, and the intersectionalities that define our understanding of the same. Through historicization of the existing literature, Chitando explores the numerous publications that exist in the field of peacebuilding, which he notes that they are relevant albeit limited in scope of coverage. He appraises the contribution of African scholars of religion and theology to religion and peacebuilding and encourages an interrogation of diverse themes that still need further scholarly debates. As he notes, the concerns around what constitutes peacebuilding processes is still ongoing. In the context of the handbook, and with the focus on SDG 16, the argument would be that there is still a lot to be discovered on what exactly contributes to peacebuilding processes. The targets listed under SDG 16 mainly point towards statistical data. However, from the various accounts and cases presented in this handbook, qualitative contributions to the peacebuilding processes count as important "indicators." There is a place for narratives and lived experiences that help transform people's livelihoods in ways that cannot be quantified but which are valuable to their wellbeing. Such models of peacebuilding should be encouraged and documented, but also given a place in peacebuilding architecture. Future research should be dedicated to such models and funding made available for valuable contributions and documentation of the same.

On funding models, Chitando highlights the contributions of CODESRIA, OSSREA, APN, SSCR, the Harry Frank Guggenheim Foundation, whose focus is on peace research. Others, that fund a wide range of research with themes relating to peacebuilding include *inter alia*, Alexander von Humboldt Foundation, International Peace Research Network (IPRA) and the Mellon Foundation. A note on these funding agencies is that seemingly research and specifically peace research in Africa is more often funded from outside the continent. If the conflicts happen within the confines of the continent, would it not make sense for African leadership to have the obligation to look for solutions from within, and in the case of research, support their own? Besides, would research agenda conceived from within and funded from the continent not be much more meaningful? These are reflections that governments and academia need to engage. A further observation is that most of the outside funding agencies encourage a methodological approach that is fast spreading in the continent and which Chitando is quick to pick, namely a multi/trans/interdisciplinary approach. In fact, a number of the contributors to this handbook seem to already be oriented within the approach. With a wide range of understanding of the multiple faces of conflicts in the continent, this integrated approach is inevitable and would likely generate debates and potentially effective strategies far beyond religion, which then allows researchers to take interrogate the multiple-pronged solutions for dealing with conflicts in Africa. We, therefore, encourage more multidisciplinary research that contributes to a holistic understanding of conflicts in Africa, and the multiple roles of religion, religious institutions and religious actors. These, like some of the contributions in the handbook have already shown, will then integrate secular and religious approaches to peacebuilding processes, as peace cuts across secular and religious perspectives.

Central the multidisciplinary approach is the perspective on intersectionality, which Masiiwa touches on in his chapter. Although his piece is limited to the intersection between the colonial and evangelization legacies and contemporary conflicts in Africa, it remains key in showing the importance of cultural understanding of the African people, and the place of their religiosity in conflicts. More exposé on this area, especially with the current debates of decoloniality (see Zondi, 2017), remain important if Africans are to find their own solutions to the conflicts affecting them (Zeleza, 2008). The debates may start in the teaching-learning environment and, in the context, tertiary/higher institutions of learning where the current debates on conflicts and peacebuilding call for re-invigorated curricula. Strijdom's chapter highlights this and encourages the engagement of learners in critical analysis of the intersection between religion and conflicts. What we seem to lack is positioning of debates on practise. Seemingly, there is more and more theoretical and empirical data by researchers who are mainly in academia, while the voices of practitioners remain muted. Although we may argue that the researchers take the initiative to research, record and report from the practitioners, it would be a totally different perspective if those involved in religious peacebuilding reported and recorded their own experiences (Ayindo et al., 2001). This can be encouraged in diverse ways. For instance, how often do those in the academia think of inviting practitioners to conferences? How often do they work with practitioners in their research as co-research designers and implementers? How often do those in the academia take interest in the work they do as work that can contribute to practice? This interface is key in understanding the field of religious peacebuilding. The handbook highlights a few contributions from practitioners, such as Muyunga's chapter on the All Africa Conference of Churches (AACC). Muyunga works with the AACC and has written on the positioning of youth in the peacebuilding agenda within the organization. Opongo, an activist, a peacebuilder and community trainer has also contributed a chapter on some of the interactions he has had with the Fellowship of Christian Councils and Churches, and the peacebuilding work in the Horn of Africa.

## *A Spotlight on Religious Peacebuilding for Development in Specific African Countries*

The second part of the handbook, which provides country case studies on religion and peacebuilding efforts, is keen to show that religion is also double-edged. Consequently, it has played a contributory role in Africa's conflicts in diverse ways. In Rwanda, for instance, we get to see the engagement of Christian denominations in the country's conflicts, not just in the period leading to, and during the genocide, but also since the arrival of missionaries and colonial administrators. In fact, through the church, ethnic identity was strengthened because, as Ezechiel Sentama shows in his chapter on Rwanda, "ethnicity was a crucial factor in the Church's mission strategy to determine the elite and target them for conversion." Subsequently, the chapter gives an exposé of the long journey that various Christian denominations have had to walk to be recognized, and not be treated with suspicion, by the current government. Although the church in Rwanda is praised for the important efforts in peacebuilding before and after the genocide, a constant character that is devoid of blame and disrespect is key. Important to note here is the relevance of power and moral authority vested in religious leaders, and which once betrayed leads to scorning and disrepute of the leaders. It also leads to dissonance as well as general lack of confidence in the church as a whole. Co-working with the state or government leadership for peacebuilding then becomes a challenge. This calls for a rethinking and re-strategizing for the church leadership, and broadly, the repositioning of religious leadership in the continent. Although the handbook does well in highlighting exemplary actors who have steered peacebuilding within the echelons of religious circles, such accounts should further be documented and illustrations of their contribution the agenda clearly drawn, not just from numbers/statistics, but also narratives that evidence such contribution. There is also a *lacuna* that needs to be filled, on exemplifying the roles of religious leaders who hold political positions, in peacebuilding processes. Both positive and not so positive narratives of these religious political leaders in peacebuilding processes will amplify the need for interface of religion and secular approaches to peacebuilding. Investing in leadership for peace in the continent (see e.g. Mahmoud & Mbiatem, 2021) is, therefore, a critical enterprise.

This second part of the handbook provides specific evidence from several countries, including Rwanda, South Sudan, Nigeria, Burundi, Tanzania, the Democratic Republic of Congon (DRC), Uganda and Eswatini, on the diversity of contributions by different religions and religious actors in peacebuilding processes. This section is further strengthened by the subsequent parts that highlight cases of diverse religions, actors and interfaith networks. This second part is rich, with cases on how religious peacebuilding contributes to everyday peace, a term that is used and extensively applied by Mbugua and Nyuon while speaking to the efforts of religious actors in Uganda and South Sudan, respectively (see also Dery et al., 2022). The term speaks to continued activities from the community's grassroots and resonates with most of the chapters in the handbook since they speak to this form of religious peacebuilding. This approach borrows heavily from Lederach's models of grassroots approaches as seen in his works *Journey Toward Reconciliation* (1999) and *Building Peace: Sustainable Reconciliation in Divided Societies* (1997). Other terminologies that Mbugua uses in his chapter on Uganda are bottom-up peacebuilding, peacebuilding from below, grassroots peacebuilding, community peacebuilding, local peacebuilding, citizen-to-citizen peacebuilding, or Track II diplomacy. These terminologies remain relevant to the forms, and perspectives of grassroots peacebuilding and are strategic since religious peacebuilding can only be conceived from the communities. Religious leaders and the adherents of different religions and denominations are at communities' grassroots and through the relevant mechanisms are involved in everyday peace. While writing on grassroots peacebuilding, from a religious perspective, Kilonzo's chapter in the first part of the handbook speaks to a case study of *Amani Mashinani* (Swahili for peace at the grassroots), a model developed by a Catholic Bishop in response to recurrent ethnic violence in the North Rift region of Kenya (see her earlier publications on this, Kilonzo, 2022; Kilonzo & Onkware, 2022). All these are an indication of the important work going on in religious peacebuilding in the continent, which again in our opinion should find a place in the peacebuilding architectures, whether national, regional or international.

Reading from the above contributions, one realizes that there is more that researchers can dig out on various contributions to peacebuilding that engage a religious perspective. The topical issues discussed in the last part of the handbook illuminate this debate and encourage further engagement in fields that are still novel, yet show potential contributions towards peacebuilding processes. Of importance is for the scholarly world and practitioners as well as policy makers to understand that in the words of Mbugua in the Uganda case:

"everyday peacebuilding is privileging the daily experiences and perspectives of ordinary people in a conflict or post-conflict context." Subsequently, "...everyday peace has no universal indicators due to its contingent, contextual, and temporal nature," yet it contributes to harmonious co-existence of communities in the form of dialogue, reconciliation and on the overall, transitioning from conflicts to peace. The global peace architecture, and specifically the SDG 16 flagship, should be interrogated within these dimensions. If this happens, actors would be keen to structure models that take into account qualitative aspects that contribute to peace and conflict resolution, and demystify what is contained within indicators of peaceful and inclusive societies.

Closely tied to the country case studies is the third part of the handbook which focuses on diverse religions in the continent, and their roles in conflicts of peace processes. Mraja's for instance, demystifies the stereotype of Islam as a dangerous religion and provides a reflective framework for Islam's engagement in peacebuilding. Similarly, Chembea engages the question of the media, which he argues has moved towards an Islamophobic agenda through the information spread through the diverse media, most of which is propaganda, and the effects of which are destructive, especially to those practicing the religion. Sibanda the Rastafari Movement and provides an imagery of minority/neglected religions, which although ascribed to, and contribute in varied ways to peacebuilding processes, are never given the necessary limelight. All these arguments speak to the need for inclusion, dialogue and reconciliation—principles that are key in realizing the global development agenda. The handbook therefore sees a gap in the practical work that evidences the specific engagements of these religions and actors thereof in the peacebuilding processes.

## *Religious Actors and Interfaith Networks in Peacebuilding and Development*

Part IV and V, which are on actors and interfaith networks in religious peacebuilding, further strengthen the argument on the need for the relevance of qualitative research output, which might not have statistical evidence, but contribute to peaceful societies. From the chapters in this section, there is evidence that indigenous knowledge systems (IKS) in the continent are still useful, as seen in the role of traditional leaders. Ramadhan's focus on traditional leaders and their peacebuilding work in Kenya evidences that social governance system and traditional law improve legitimacy and ownership of local activities geared towards achieving sustainable peace. She documents the experiences from her work as a global coordinator of The Network for Religious and Traditional Peacemakers. As already pointed out, this kind of evidence from a practitioner is relevant. Under the actors, the case of South Africa by Dube and Chisale draws readers' attention to the voices of three traditional spiritual leaders on Ubuntu, peacebuilding and social cohesion. They draw from Lederach's peacebuilding pyramid (1997) to show how the last level, the grassroots leadership tier, is important to focus on, as conflicts are more often intense closer to the grassroots. In fact, most of those who suffer the effects are the population at this level. Traditional religious leaders and local leaders, who are always operating within this level, then become important actors as they are in touch not just with communities, but also with the realities of conflicts. This calls for further interrogation on how such grassroots model spread their output and find placement at the national and international peacebuilding outputs. The African Union Transitional Justice Policy (AU, 2019) gives a place to these non-formal contributions and encourages integration of the same with formal approaches. More research is therefore needed to show how the non-formal approaches are rated and indexed as useful influencers of peacebuilding efforts.

While focusing on Christianity, Omare and Kamaara historicize the role of Christian leaders in Kenya's elections and electoral violence. They lead the reader through a trajectory that shows the changing faces of churches and the leaders, while questioning the moral authority of such leadership especially in situations where they are unable to speak against abuse of human rights. They also show how religious leaders get "swallowed up" in political messes once they get into partisan politics, vie or get into politics. How then does the engagement of such leaders help in achieving SDG 16.5—reducing corruption and bribery, and 16.6—promoting effective accountable and transparent institutions? Research in this area in the context of religious peacebuilding and development is called for. This will contribute to debates around the need to institutionalize religious peacebuilding activities in ways that are not just recognizable, but also allow for national and international support, as Makulilo and Henry argue in their focus on Tanzania. This calls for creation and establishment of agencies that speak to the place of different actors. Muyunga, to this end, speaks to the role of youth as actors in peacebuilding process. He shows how, through the All Africa Conference of Churches (AACC), the youth have been vocal in ensuring that their voices, and their role in the peacebuilding agenda, is heard. Their several pre-general assembly meetings have been platforms to articulate their agenda and table it in the General Assembly. Such kind of positioning and repositioning helps create a strong agency, whose agenda and mandate cannot be ignored. This has led to establishment of a Youth Secretariat at the AACC. Research on these types of agencies historicize not just the factors leading to their formation but also the experiences and challenges of the groups agitating and working for peace and peacebuilding. The handbook may have missed out on numerous cases of the efforts to create such agencies on women, men, and vulnerable populations that are agitating to position themselves or their groups in the peacebuilding agenda. These case studies need to be documented.

While thinking about the future of research on this theme of actors in religious peacebuilding is the need to examine ways in which knowledge is transmitted, especially in the teaching and learning curricula in tertiary institutions, as noted earlier. The need to integrate the voices and experiences of these religious actors into existing theoretical arguments for the current generations to understand their place in peacebuilding and development is relevant. At policy research level, one would wish to understand how the activities of the religious actors speak to the broader agenda as well as architecture of peacebuilding. The need to come up with models that show how the outcome of the voices of religious leaders and their engagement in peacebuilding work contribute to the peace agenda would be highly strategic.

On interfaith networks, the handbook exemplifies, through five case studies, the diversity of networks of different faiths and their contribution to peacebuilding in Africa. Opongo exemplifies the role played by the Fellowship of Christian Councils and Churches in Eastern Africa, the Great Lakes and the Horn of Africa (FECCLAHA) in their activities related to social cohesion, gender rights and peacebuilding initiatives, youth engagement in conflict resolution, advocacy against the proliferation of small arms and light weapons, and advocacy for good governance and accountability. These are important activities in peacebuilding and development in the continent, which focus not only on individual African countries, but from lessons learned across these countries, experiences are used to contribute to peacebuilding in different contexts. From the activities of the Fellowship, our earlier argument that religious peacebuilding does not necessarily need to remain within religious tenets is evidenced. The need to solve secular contributions to conflicts, such as proliferation of small arms, abuse of huma rights, poor governance and lack of accountability, then call for a wider typology of peacebuilding mechanisms, and secular approaches, as a consequence become inevitable. This is exemplified in the cases of the Nigeria Interreligious Council and the efforts towards rebuilding Muslim-Christian relations for peace in Uganda in the chapters by Williams and Mbugua respectively. These move us beyond intrafaith engagements to interfaith platforms that call for a wider responsibility on the part of religious leaders and their role in uniting people of different faiths for peace and peacebuilding efforts. Complex relationships emerge from such approaches, and the building of trust amongst the religious leaders is important if these relationships are to be used for sustainable and just peace. Of importance here, and a major theme that emerges from most of the chapters in this section, and which should be pursued further, is the relevance of participatory peacebuilding approaches that are multi-layered in relation to stakeholders. On the latter, the position of civil society organizations, donors, decision-makers/legislators, and their role in interreligious dialogue for peacebuilding should be exemplified and/or encouraged if the models suggested are to be effective in the agenda for peace, and if we are to speak to inclusivity, as postulated in SDG 16.1.

On the issue of inclusivity, Africa's conflicts, like most conflicts in the world, have a devastating effect on women, children and the physically challenged. This lot carry the greatest burden of the effects of war and conflicts, yet more often than not, they are excluded in peacebuilding pacts. In Part VI, the handbook does well in engaging gender and vulnerability aspects in religious peacebuilding. The focus on challenging issues that are flagged by SDG 16, such as abuse of women and girls, have also been contributory factors to underdevelopment in the continent. An interrogation of the role of religion and religious actors in the response to all forms of violence, and specifically sexual and gender-based violence affecting women in the continent, is pertinent. Maseko and Chirongoma apply the conflict transformation theory to show how the Zimbabwe Council of Churches is influencing trajectories on sexual and gender-based violence. The safe spaces for women and girls that Maseko and Chirongoma advocate for speak to conflict transformation that in the end contributes to sustainable peace and psycho-social healing of the survivors of violence. Confidence-building and recovery of self-esteem among the survivors can be realized through not just enactment and implementation of laws, but also availing spaces where the survivors can freely express themselves and learn from each other's experiences as they go through the recovery processes. This exemplifies the role of the many other related approaches that deal with survivors of conflicts and which require documentation. Several chapters in this section also highlight the need to understand the challenges posed by pandemics such as HIV and AIDS, Covid-19, Ebola and others, in situations of conflicts, and gender implications for the same. The religious actors, therefore, need to borrow from experiences of such pandemics in the continent, experiences that will contribute towards more provision of justice and building strong institutions that advocate for viable approaches in the quest for peace and development in Africa. This requires models that speak directly to the experiences from such pandemics. The academy would then aim at developing training toolkits that explore these experiences, and which in turn empower trainers through realistic and hands-on knowledge transmission.

The theme on gender was also keen to highlight the direct involvement of women in situations of conflicts and peacebuilding activities in the aftermath of conflicts. Webule's chapter points to the role of women as "mobilizers, leaders, role models, initiators of programmes, trainers, advocates, educators, disseminators, formulators and conscientizers." The women, beyond community roles, are also keen to focus on their roles as homemakers, thus, the "social activities that promote family stability such as children, marital counselling and psychosocial support to individuals faced with life challenges." Subsequently, this echoes the need to focus more and more on documenting women's roles, experiences and contributions to peacebuilding. Contributions to this theme also speak to vulnerable populations, such as those forced to migrate, and subsequently the displaced, refugees or asylum seekers. Tarusarira and Tarusarira, in this case, provide the experiences of migrants from conflict-ridden areas in Zimbabwe, and the challenges they undergo as refugees and asylum seekers. The two in their chapter specifically single out women and girls with disabilities who face multiple layers of stigmatization and discrimination. In this section, we are keen to observe that discussions are almost silent on experiences of children. This is the case in wider literature that focus(es) on conflicts and peacebuilding. When children are mentioned, it is in passing, and in the context of their families, especially their mothers.

Their voices remain muted and there is hardly meaningful analysis on their spoken experiences, especially the trauma they go through, and how they perceive conflicts and challenges around them. The role of religion, religious actors and institutions in understanding these experiences is also lean. This opens an avenue for further research that speaks to the inclusion that SDG 16 speaks to.

A few more chapters in the last session of the handbook explore the interconnectedness of topical issues such as climate change, arts, culture, digitalization of world systems and agriculture. These are key aspects that shape Africa's development. In fact, all of these factors are enshrined within the broader discussions of the African Union and United Nations development agenda. In this handbook, these topical issues are therefore framed around how they influence, or are influenced by religion, for peacebuilding and development. Juxtaposing chapters in this final section of the handbook allows the reader to see the dichotomy of traditional and modern approaches to peacebuilding, but also ways in which these dichotomies should not be understood within a continuum of a typology, but iteratively as stakeholders try to marry the best practices for sustainable peace in the continent. For instance, a look at Tarusarira's chapter on religion and climate security research in Africa shows the need to understand the complex nature of climate crises and specifically the effects on cultural heritage and indigenous knowledge. Capitalizing on dominant positivist approaches, as Tarusarira shows, ignores the place of religion in climate change. He advocates for a complex theory approach that applies a multidisciplinary approach for holistic solutions to climate change risks. His argument for engaging African culture and traditions does not in any way negate modern approaches to peacebuilding, as the chapter on advocacy for digitalization of peacebuilding by Sokfa in the same section of the handbook espouses. The communication tools explained in Sokfa's chapter can be useful in engaging traditional mechanisms of peacebuilding. This then leaves a gap for future research on themes around this area—engaging both traditional and modern tools for religious peacebuilding. The insights from Sokfa's chapter on digital peacebuilding in relation to the role of religion further point out to a gap that has now existed for a while, which is religious peacebuilding in the digital era. Although seminal work exists on the use of social media in peacebuilding in general, under this theme, a lot of advancement, including the advent of Artificial Intelligence (AI), now requires serious attention.

Other topical issues discussed in the section are on religion, agriculture and development, as seen in Fortunée's argument. Although she shows that most of religious actors have the will to develop communities, especially through agriculture, the challenge is on the models set by the government. The models focus not on the farmer, but on cooperatives, and as such religious institutions may not do much within such models, but curve out spaces for themselves as peace is to be realized through agricultural development. Such strategies need to be explored further, especially in the contexts where they are already working, as a way of furthering the broader peacebuilding and development agenda as enshrined in SDG 16.

Overall, the handbook has a variety of chapters under the different themes. We observe that a number of chapters are theoretical and used already existing theories or literature to analyse the role of religion in peacebuilding in the context of SDG 16. A number used grand theory, in which case, some moved a notch higher to propose more suitable theories in understanding the place of religion in peacebuilding. A few chapters used grounded theories, drawing conclusions from observations made from empirical data, and proposed best practical approaches. This mix is useful, and we emphasize that the gaps we see is in the voices of practitioners: stakeholders/actors who are directly involved in peacebuilding work. A few contributions such as Muyunga's, Ramadhan's, Opongo's and a few others from the handbook suffice. Although the editorial team made an effort to invite a sizeable number, only few were realized. This calls for partnerships between academia and practitioners in a bid to articulate the voices and experiences of these important stakeholders in religious peacebuilding. These networks are relevant not just in publishing, but also in ensuring that the right knowledge base is transformed into practice.

## Religion, Peacebuilding and Sustainable Development in Africa: Insights into an Ongoing Discourse

The very rich and informative submissions that constitute this handbook do provide some valuable insights into the complex interplay between religion, peacebuilding and sustainable development, in Africa and beyond. For this concluding chapter, we raise only those dimensions that we have deemed central. First, we realize that the central concepts driving the discourse, namely "religion," "peacebuilding" and "sustainable development" (as represented by SDG 16), are loaded. As the chapters in this handbook confirm, they are unstable and have multiple meanings. What is clear, however, is that they are not as counterintuitive as much of the extant scholarship suggests. The chapters show how "religion" remains a helpful category, even as they confirm the wide range covered by the term. It speaks to individual religious actors (e.g. leaders, women, youth, faith-driven local groups in a specific context, national/continental institutions representing diverse faith groups, interfaith networks), and others. "Religion" is discernible in the motivation of representatives of different traditions, including those that are often overlooked, such as Rastafari (see the chapter by Sibanda in this volume). It remains a strategic concept in appreciating the "African maps of the universe," that is, the generally enchanted approach to reality (Kalu, 2002). Thus, the reality of religious people motivated by religion to engage in peacebuilding and development in Africa counters the idea of jettisoning the concept of religion because of the intractable difficulties in defining it (Smith, 1963).

Crucially, however, a number of chapters in this handbook confirm that scholars should not approach the religious-secular divide (at least in Africa) too strictly. There is ample evidence that perhaps the gap between "religious" and "secular" peacebuilding is actually not as wide in reality. Given the widespread nature of religion in Africa (see e.g. Afrobarometer, 2020), it follows with logical necessity that most secular peacebuilders in Africa are influenced by some religious tenets (especially Christian, Muslim or Traditional, but also others), while various religious peacebuilders address "secular" issues, using "secular" peacebuilding strategies. The later position has been confirmed by various case studies in this volume (see for instance Tarusarira, Karungi, Kilonzo, Opongo, and Ramadhan contributions). Religious peacebuilders (or, at least, the most effective ones) do not (overly) spiritualize issues. They have attained high levels of historical, political, economic and other forms of literacy. They are on high alert for non-religious factors in the brewing of religious and other conflicts in Africa. Thus, as much as technocrats, security architects and others are required to achieve religious literacy (see e.g. Seiple & Hoover, 2022), so too have religious actors had to achieve other literacies in order to become more effective peacebuilders.

The same dynamism accompanying "religion" also characterizes its companions in this volume, namely "peacebuilding" and "development." They remain sound heuristic devices that enable intelligible discussion of the key processes they seek to express. Contributors to this handbook have showcased multifarious expressions of peacebuilding as undertaken by religiously inspired actors in Africa (see the contributions by Chitando, Dube and Chisale, Omare and Kamaara, Agyeman, and Ramadhan). Unconstrained by reified definitions of peacebuilding (see e.g. Barnett et al., 2007; Zondi, 2017; Mahmoud & Mbiatem, 2021, pp. 18–23) diverse individuals, groups and institutions inspired by religion and often working in collaboration with other actors have sought to silence the guns, counter all forms of violence, as well as generate peace and tranquility for individuals, families, communities, nations and the continent of Africa. If the dominant model of peacebuilding is that it is an investment that seeks to prevent relapsing into war, chapters in this handbook confirm that there are in fact multiple approaches and understanding of peacebuilding. This confirms the standpoint that it is difficult to collapse these approaches and generate a unified theory for Peace and Conflict Studies, alongside the realization that "the causes, levels, manifestations, and management intervention strategies in conflict situations are so varied with different actors and factors" (Ndeche & Iroye, 2022, p. 31).

Finally (on this first point), the concept of "sustainable development," despite some trenchant critiques in relation to Africa (see e.g. Chitando, 2022), remains helpful. There is an overarching agreement by various actors that through different interventions, the everyday lives of everyday people in Africa can be improved considerably, including in economic and social terms (Gobo, 2020, p. 62). Chapters in this handbook confirm the conviction that religious actors have the social capital (Swart, 2006; Agbiji & Swart, 2015) required to contribute towards development. Although emerging from a different setting, various contributors have affirmed the following description of religious leaders in relation to peacebuilding and development:

> The religious leaders have a strong role in society because they are considered capable, highly knowledgeable, have noble character, and have expertise in the field of religion, both religious rituals and religious insights that can be used as role models by the surrounding community. The religious leaders contribute to invite, provide guidance, and motivate the community to support and participate in development through community empowerment activities. (Zuhri et al., 2021, pp. 39–40)

Second, there is no simple nor simplistic relationship between religion and peacebuilding, or between peacebuilding and development, or how religion relates to both peacebuilding and development. Across the handbook, contributors have demonstrated that having a peaceful and tranquil environment is a prerequisite for development. They show how in those contexts where peace has been shattered, de-development (conceptualized widely) has followed. Therefore, the standard expectation that peace is needed for development to be experienced has generally been confirmed. On the other hand, some essays have confirmed that sustainable development itself brings, and contributes towards securing, peace. Thus, if the popular activist slogan has been, "If You Want Peace, Work for Justice," there might be merit in also proclaiming, "If You Want Development, Work for Peace," and "If You Want Peace, Work for Development." However, the exact role of religion in both peace and development remains tenuous. Clearly, while religion has been actively deployed to promote peacebuilding in Africa as described in this volume, there have been many instances where it has contributed (working in tandem with other factors) towards violence and de-development in Africa (and beyond).

Third, the need to actively seek, recover and integrate indigenous approaches to peacebuilding in the quest for development remains. As chapters that refer to and draw from this rich resource have highlighted, the theory and practice of peacebuilding in general and religious peacebuilding in particular, benefits from acknowledging the contribution of African indigenous knowledge systems. This is critical, as the systematic exclusion of African ways of knowing and doing in relation to peacebuilding leaves the world poorer. Thus, the observation that "[T]he dominance of Western culture, institutions and frameworks has relegated the utility of African traditions to the back stage in peace and conflict resolution studies" (Osei-Hwedie & Abu-Nimer, 2009, p. 1) remains as valid as it was when it was initially made. However, a critical approach is required so that the "African traditions and institutions—in conflict resolution, and wider efforts to advance peace and human development" (ibid.) can be adjusted to remain relevant to the changing African and global contexts.

Fourth, there are limits to religious peacebuilding and development in Africa. Given the high prevalence of violent conflict in Africa, one would be forgiven for imagining that African peacebuilders seek more credit than is due to them. If they were/are so effective, why do vicious conflicts and wars continue to erupt across the continent? The answer might be in the form of an unfair response: "[F]or the same reason that the world is failing to stop the war between Russia and Ukraine, from early 2022 to the time of writing" (https://www.aljazeera.com/news/2023/5/1/russia-ukraine-war-list-of-key-events-day-432). Hans Kung provides a sobering commentary when writing as follows:

> Unfortunately, however many messages of peace and calls for peace are made by secular and religious quarters, however many preventive measures and bans are introduced, they will not be able to prevent wars completely and eliminate them once and for all. Thus when wars—which always signal an abject failure of human civilization—do occur, there is only one thing to do: even in that extreme situation, the minimum basic rules of humane conduct must be respected (Küng, 2005, p. 267).

Fifth, and finally, the existence of a critical mass of African scholars and activists in the field of religion, peacebuilding and development, as confirmed by the high number of contributors to this handbook and beyond, is a positive sign. Their creativity, commitment and astute awareness of the dynamics and complexity of their African context is a source of hope. It confirms that, indeed, African scholars and activists are taking up their rightful role in producing knowledge and investing in sustainable peacebuilding for the continent's development. We elaborate on this dimension in the closing section of this chapter below.

## Conclusion

In conclusion, we call for models that encourage a more vibrant approach to religious peacebuilding, which focus on not only the already existing data, but research that aims at encouraging the religious peacebuilders to speak their voices, provide their own lived experiences from the field. We also see a better understanding of the field if the practitioners were to be engaged in teaching-learning environment, in conferences and seminars to provide insights that can be used to build more sensible and practical theories and models in the field. Further, a challenge is posed to engage the policy environment. The academic scholar has for a long time been branded as one who sits in the ivory tower and speaks only to those of her/his ilk. With the challenges that the African continent is facing in relation to conflicts, solutions that speak to policy formulation, policy reformulation, revamping and rethinking, while directly engaging the policy makers/politicians in more strategic ways that speak directly to the existing national, African Union's and United Nation's peacebuilding architectures, are called for. If anything, some of these architectures such as the AU's Transitional Justice Policy (AU, 2019) encourage inclusivity, and a muti-dimensional approach to peacebuilding.

A more specific approach that the contributions in this handbook highlight is the peacebuilding-from-below/grassroots peacebuilding/community peacebuilding. Many chapters may not have spelt out these terminologies, but by and large, there seems to be consensus that most of the engagements by religious institutions and actors are geared towards this form of peacebuilding. In the case of Zambia, Mwale, Chita and Habeenzu focus on a policewoman who has been involved in peacekeeping missions, and through her experience influences peacebuilding at community, national and regional levels. This case is special, given the position of the actor. The need to interrogate the possibility of other actors and processes feeding into the broader national and regional frameworks is an area of scholarly lacuna that needs attention. Any peacebuilding effort, whether at the grassroots level or at national level, is a peacebuilding contribution. Ideally, if there is peace at the community's grassroots, there is calm and tranquility at the national level. The need to understand the role of citizens and communities in the broader peace agenda is therefore important. The challenge for us is to then explain and clearly show the wave and webs of the interconnections. In closing, since peace and development in Africa contributes towards global peace, security and development, we envision a situation where diverse actors from other contexts will do everything in their power to secure a peaceful, integrated and prosperous Africa.

## References

Afrobarometer. (2020). Religion in Africa: Tolerance and Trust in Leaders are High, But Many Would Allow Regulation of Religious Speech. Dispatch No. 339. Accra: Afrobarometer. Retrieved May 1, 2023, from https://www.afrobarometer.org/wp-content/uploads/migrated/files/publications/Policy%20papers/ab_r7_dispatchno339_pap12_religion_in_africa.pdf

Agbiji, O. M., & Swart, I. (2015). Religion and Social Transformation in Africa: A Critical and Appreciative Perspective. *Scriptura, 114*, 1–20.

AU. (2019). *African Union Transitional Justice Policy*. AU. Addis Ababa. Ethiopia.

Ayindo, B., Doe, S., & Jenner, J. (2001). *When You Are the Peacebuilder: Stories and Reflections on Peacebuilding from Africa*. Conflict Transformation Program: Eastern Mennonite University. Harrisonburg, VA. USA.

Barnett, M., et al. (2007). Peacebuilding: What Is In a Name? *Global Governance, 13*, 35–58.

Chitando, E. (2022). Africa and the Quest for Sustainable Development: A Critical Review. In E. Chitando & E. Kamaara (Eds.), *Values, Identity, and Sustainable Development in Africa* (pp. 69–84). Palgrave Macmillan.

Dery, I., Baataar, C., & Khan, A. R. (2022). Everyday Peacebuilding Among Ghanaian Men: Ambiguities, Resistances and Possibilities. *Journal of the British Academy, 10*(1), 35–53.

Gobo, P. (2020). Rethinking Religion and Sustainable Development in Africa. *East African Journal of Traditions, Culture and Religion, 2*(1), 60–71.

Kalu, O. U. (2002). Preserving a Worldview: Pentecostalism in African Maps of the Universe. *Pneuma, 24*(2), 110–137.

Kilonzo, S. (2022). Transitional Justice and the Mitigation of Electoral Violence through *Amani mashinani* Model in Uasin Gishu County, Kenya. In E. Opongo & T. Murithi (Eds.), *Elections, Violence and Transitional Justice in Africa* (pp. 136–159). Routledge.

Kilonzo, S., & Onkware, K. (2022). The Adaptability of Catholic Church's *Amani Mashinani* Model in Kenya's North Rift Conflicts. *International Bulletin of Mission Research (IBMR), 46*(2), 190–199.

Küng, H. (2005). Religion, Violence and "Holy Wars". *International Review of the Red Cross, 87*(858), 253–268.

Lederach, J. (1997). *Building Peace: Sustainable Reconciliation in Divided Societies*. USIP.

Lederach, J. (1999). *The Journey Toward Reconciliation*. Herald Press.

Mahmoud, Y., & Mbiatem, A. (2021). *Whose Peace Are We Building? Leadership for Peace in Africa*. I. B. Tauris.

Ndeche, O., & Iroye, S. O. (2022). Key Theories in Peace and Conflict Studies and their Impact on the Study and Practice. *NOUN International Journal of Peace Studies and Conflict Resolution [NIJPCR], 2*(2), 20–34.

Osei-Hwedie, B. Z., & Abu-Nimer, M. (2009). Enhancing the Positive Contributions of African Culture in Peacebuilding and Development. *Journal of Peacebuilding & Development, 4*(3), 1–5.

Seiple, C., & Hoover, D. R. (Eds.). (2022). *The Routledge Handbook of Religious Literacy, Pluralism, and Global Engagement*. Routledge.

Smith, W. C. (1963). *The Meaning and End of Religion: A New Approach to the Religious Traditions of Mankind*. Macmillan Co.

Swart, I. (2006). Churches as a Stock of Social Capital for Promoting Social Development in Western Cape Communities. *Journal of Religion in Africa, 36*(3/4), 346–378.

Zeleza, P. T. (2008). Introduction: The Causes & Costs of War in Africa: From Liberation Struggles to the 'War on Terror'. In A. Nhema & T. Zeleza (Eds.), *The Roots of African Conflicts* (pp. 1–70). Addis Ababa and Oxford.

Zondi, S. (2017). Africa Union Approaches to Peacebuilding: Efforts at Shifting the Continent Towards Decolonial Peace. *African Journal on Conflict Resolution, 17*(1), 105–131.

Zuhri, M. M., et al. (2021). Community Development: The Role of Religious Leaders in Community Empowerment. *IOSR Journal Of Humanities And Social Science (IOSR-JHSS), 26*(11), 37–41.

# Index[1]

**A**

Accountability, 9, 21, 22, 72, 186, 189, 320, 377, 391, 392, 395, 426, 477, 478, 532, 537, 545–547, 554, 580, 662, 703, 706, 708, 739, 740, 763, 816

Africa, 1–13, 19–36, 39–55, 63–76, 79–89, 93–103, 105–121, 125–139, 148, 183, 208, 236, 254, 287, 294–296, 308–312, 327, 348, 363–377, 401–414, 435, 439–441, 475, 494, 513–526, 531–547, 570, 595, 617, 633, 638–640, 644, 662, 684, 695–696, 709, 737–748, 753–767, 772, 809–823

African communitarian ethic, 289, 293–294, 299

African Religious Philosophy, 308

African religious studies, 39–55, 405

African scholars, 39–41, 43, 45, 53–55, 288, 402, 404–408, 741, 810, 822

African traditional spiritual leaders, 435–450

African traditions, 48, 51, 99, 255–257, 259, 401–414, 430, 506–508, 683, 821

African Women's Theology, 628, 633, 638

Agrarian change, 771–785

All Africa Conference of Churches (AACC), 9, 12, 155, 327, 513–526, 540, 812, 815

Anthropologic pauperization, 254

Appreciative Inquiry, 738, 742–746

Armed conflicts, 6, 80, 82, 129, 164, 166–168, 175, 176, 228, 229, 252, 365, 366, 368, 438, 495, 524, 525, 532, 544, 609, 615, 620, 712, 721

Arts, 13, 64, 266, 312, 456, 458, 461, 468–470, 595, 720, 789–803, 818

Arts for peacebuilding, 13, 789

**B**

Behaviour change, 457, 459, 468

Bible, 10, 45, 47, 79–89, 109, 115, 117, 121, 173, 190, 207, 391, 412, 516, 676, 678, 693, 723–725, 731, 796–799

Birth registration, 265, 266, 272, 645, 663

---

[1] Note: Page numbers followed by 'n' refer to notes.

© The Author(s), under exclusive license to Springer Nature Switzerland AG 2023
S. M. Kilonzo et al. (eds.), *The Palgrave Handbook of Religion, Peacebuilding, and Development in Africa*, https://doi.org/10.1007/978-3-031-36829-5

Botswana, 12, 54, 95, 100, 101, 569–583, 669
Burundi, 3, 11, 48, 51, 148, 154, 199–215, 217–231, 219n2, 365, 411, 438, 532, 533, 535, 536, 539, 541, 545–547, 813

## C

Children with disabilities, 12, 683–697
Christian faith-based organisation, 771–785
Christianity, 20, 47–49, 51, 54, 74, 88, 98, 102, 106–108, 110, 113–121, 147, 153, 154, 158, 159, 186–188, 194, 199, 200, 251–264, 266, 267, 273, 274, 283, 329, 330, 364, 368, 384, 408, 409, 446, 465, 476, 486, 516, 558–560, 563, 565, 608, 612, 620, 644, 648, 662, 675, 685, 718, 723, 746, 756, 789, 803, 815
Church leaders, 11, 12, 30, 47, 48, 153, 278, 390, 475–489, 518, 524, 535, 538, 539, 541, 635, 717–732
Climate security, 125–139, 818
Colonialism, 71, 82, 100, 113–115, 132, 255, 258, 261, 288, 402, 404, 437, 439, 445, 449, 648, 739, 756
Complexity, 46, 54, 110, 126, 134–138, 191, 223, 310, 406, 424, 532, 610, 662, 739, 822
Conflict resolution, 5, 7, 21–27, 52, 66, 68, 82, 84, 106–108, 111, 182–184, 187, 189, 190, 222, 228–229, 231, 238, 242–249, 280, 295, 308, 311, 312, 317, 320, 377, 423–425, 429, 431, 477, 495, 496, 500, 503, 504, 507–509, 531, 532, 536, 537, 539, 540, 542–543, 557, 559, 582, 608n2, 612, 617, 620, 629, 717, 722, 745, 747, 756, 766, 801, 814, 816, 821
Conflicts, 2–6, 19–36, 41–43, 66, 94, 95, 102, 105, 109–113, 125, 145–160, 164, 181–184, 199–215, 218, 228–229, 235, 241–242, 252, 271, 288, 294–296, 307, 309–312, 316–320, 327, 344, 377, 385, 420, 436, 460, 475, 493–509, 514, 531, 536–539, 542–543, 553, 571, 597, 607, 609–613, 627–629, 644, 661, 684, 702, 717, 738, 753, 772, 789, 792–795, 809
Conflict transformation, 42, 51, 106, 182–184, 190, 191, 310, 321, 493–509, 532, 536–540, 543, 561, 627–629, 634, 640, 649, 653, 663, 702, 742, 754, 755, 757, 766, 817
Crops Intensification Programme (CIP), 773–785

## D

Decolonising peacebuilding, 435–450
Democratic governance, 312, 320, 321
Deprived youth, 387
Development, 1–13, 19–36, 40, 63–76, 79–89, 93–103, 105–121, 126, 146, 164, 181, 206, 218, 271–283, 287–300, 307, 327–337, 345n7, 346, 363, 381, 401–414, 435–450, 456, 475, 493–509, 513–526, 531–547, 553–565, 569–583, 587–603, 613, 627–640, 644, 661–679, 684, 695–696, 701–713, 718, 721–722, 737–748, 754, 772, 774–776, 789–803, 809–823
Development agenda, 74, 94, 385, 521, 522, 553, 640, 719, 739, 814, 818, 819
Dialogues, 8, 9, 12, 25–27, 30, 31, 33, 34, 50, 70, 75, 84, 108, 155, 167, 168, 175, 183–191, 206, 222, 223, 225–227, 229, 231, 242–244, 247, 257, 261, 265, 279, 280, 373, 422, 423, 425, 448, 458, 461, 476, 485, 493, 498, 500, 502, 505–507, 515, 522, 523, 525, 533–535, 538, 539, 541, 542, 546, 553–565, 578–581, 591, 594, 612–615, 617, 620, 636, 637, 648, 651, 654, 702, 706, 720–722, 726, 730, 740, 745, 756, 757, 759, 761, 765, 794, 814, 816
Digital peacebuilding, 13, 753–767, 818
Digital society, 754
Disability beliefs, 12, 683–697
Drama, 13, 506, 722, 789, 792, 793, 793n5

**E**

Edutainment, 461, 464, 617
Elections, 4, 11, 24, 30, 72n1, 73, 83, 101, 184, 189, 203, 204, 220, 220n3, 223, 226, 247, 268, 278, 280, 307–310, 314–320, 336, 337, 365, 382, 389, 422, 425, 427, 475–479, 481–489, 504–506, 525, 533–535, 541, 545, 546, 563, 592, 601, 634, 636, 637, 759, 761, 762, 815
Electoral Commission, 319, 320, 482, 506
Electoral conflict, 11, 238, 309–312, 317, 319, 320, 478
Ethnicity, 4, 5, 82, 94, 95, 99, 103, 110, 111, 145, 150, 156, 158–160, 187, 204, 212, 215, 223, 224, 226, 231, 276, 309, 351, 357, 365, 368, 370, 387, 408, 411, 435, 439, 443, 444, 446, 482, 493, 494, 554, 558, 739, 755, 812
Evangelisation, 110, 113–118, 120, 150, 259, 811
Everyday peace, 10, 163–176, 187, 192, 217–231, 460, 467–471, 607–621, 813, 814

**F**

Female, 95–97, 102, 171, 173, 227–229, 336, 370, 388, 442, 456, 465, 467, 503, 560, 616, 634, 646, 664, 670–674, 719–721, 723, 724, 729–731, 745
Feminism, 646–647, 649, 650, 654–656, 664
Feminist peace, 643–657
Forgiveness, 9, 33, 51, 72, 115, 157, 167–169, 172, 173, 175, 189, 190, 208, 209, 222, 225, 231, 276, 279, 375, 376, 413, 443, 445, 485, 515, 516, 537, 610, 620, 655, 727, 741, 791, 793n5, 794, 800–802
Framing, 10, 126–129, 138, 139, 187, 221, 342, 343, 345, 346, 351, 353, 355, 356, 359, 612

**G**

Gender, 9, 12, 33, 35, 52, 53, 74, 94–96, 102, 103, 110, 132, 135, 206, 280, 281, 333, 334, 372, 402, 413, 422–424, 430, 435, 438, 443, 444, 509, 519, 521, 523, 525, 537, 539–542, 579, 582, 594, 596, 615, 627–640, 646, 647, 649, 655, 656, 661–679, 686, 687, 701–713, 718, 719, 723, 726, 730, 739, 744, 756, 763, 766, 816, 817
Gender rights, 539–542, 816
General Assemblies, 513, 514, 517, 520–526, 780, 815
Genocide, 5, 31, 41, 50, 52, 72n2, 82, 85, 111, 145–149, 153–160, 224, 366, 402, 408–410, 421, 535, 771–773, 781–784, 812
Ghana, 11, 44, 50, 54, 307–321, 365, 475, 489, 493–509, 525, 695
Good governance, 189, 204, 278, 307, 308, 320, 376, 487, 520, 537, 545, 546, 636, 652, 653, 793n5, 797, 816
Grassroots, 21, 24–26, 28, 30, 32, 65, 71, 108, 119, 163, 164, 168, 175, 182, 185, 187, 189, 191, 192, 218, 221, 223, 227–229, 299, 375, 406, 427, 441–447, 458, 461, 504, 506, 531, 532, 536, 538, 547, 553, 555, 556, 561, 596, 608n3, 610, 618, 619, 621, 644, 653, 703, 706, 708, 710, 712, 717, 718, 722, 725, 730, 731, 743, 756, 764, 813–815, 823

**H**

Harmony, 26, 49, 68, 89, 99, 183, 184, 193, 228, 264, 265, 267, 274, 278, 280, 292–294, 296, 299, 312–314, 327, 328, 331–337, 447, 448, 465, 505, 537, 558, 559, 563, 675, 705, 718, 721, 727, 729
Higher education, 44, 45, 94, 97, 765

## I

Identity politics, 435, 443
Inclusive societies, 2, 8, 12, 21, 40, 55, 79, 83, 87, 89, 94, 95, 99, 106, 107, 119, 121, 127, 133, 134, 138, 146, 160, 181, 199, 241–243, 248, 271, 281, 327, 334, 345n7, 346, 348, 354, 363, 375, 376, 420, 421, 426, 429, 435, 436, 443, 447, 466, 467, 470, 488, 494, 514, 532, 536, 537, 554, 564, 569, 578, 582, 596, 645, 673, 674, 679, 684, 689, 691, 695, 696, 702, 705, 710, 713, 720, 730, 731, 738, 739, 754, 809, 814
Inclusivity, 9, 22, 35, 117, 252, 348–359, 424, 436, 447, 542, 564, 581, 601, 602, 636, 701, 728, 741, 747, 763, 816, 823
*Incwala* ritual, 289, 292–299
(In-)security, 33, 106, 129, 131–133, 166, 186, 193, 278, 292, 298, 345, 346, 348–359, 363–369, 377, 409, 479, 494, 495, 495n1, 514, 524, 533, 534, 558–560, 638, 651, 704, 718, 725, 730
Institutionalization, 8, 151, 214, 235–249, 477
Interfaith, 9, 35, 49–50, 52, 69, 181, 182, 185–192, 194, 207, 227, 238, 241–242, 248, 272, 364, 521, 523, 557–560, 564, 569, 578, 580–582, 588, 592, 644, 649–652, 655, 657, 710, 756, 757, 816
Interfaith dialogue, 9, 50, 70, 184–186, 188, 189, 242, 243, 523, 534, 553–565, 580, 581, 756
Inter-faith network/interfaith networks, 12, 50, 531–547, 569–583, 649, 650, 722, 810, 813–819
Interfaith Peace Committee (IPC), 11, 235–249
Intersectionalities, 10, 105–121, 636, 656, 810, 811
Islam, 11, 20, 49–51, 54, 74, 75, 97, 101, 102, 111, 186–188, 194, 199, 200, 205–207, 209, 211, 212, 237, 253, 267, 273, 275, 329, 341, 342, 344–354, 356–358, 363–377, 384, 456, 458, 465, 486, 493, 498, 558–560, 563, 565, 569, 587, 589, 590, 597, 598, 608, 612, 620, 644, 718, 746, 755, 756, 814
Islamophobia, 11, 49, 342, 352, 354, 357, 359

## J

Justice, 2, 7, 8, 12, 21, 22, 28, 40, 42, 43, 47–49, 53–55, 66, 67, 69, 71, 72, 79, 83, 88, 94, 95, 99, 102, 106, 107, 118, 120, 121, 126, 138, 146, 149, 151, 156, 157, 159, 167, 174, 181, 183, 186, 191, 209, 222, 247, 251, 254, 266, 267, 271, 272, 278–281, 291, 307–321, 327, 334, 337, 345n7, 346, 363, 368, 369, 371–375, 377, 381, 384, 388, 394, 395, 401, 402, 406, 413, 419–421, 424, 426, 427, 430, 431, 436–438, 441, 444–445, 447–450, 475–489, 494, 507, 514, 517–521, 523, 525, 526, 532–534, 536–538, 540, 543–546, 554–557, 563–565, 569, 572, 578, 580, 582, 588, 590, 596, 603, 608n2, 608n3, 610, 612, 630, 632, 633, 636–640, 645, 647, 650, 652–654, 662, 663, 673–675, 684, 689, 696, 702, 705–707, 709–710, 717, 718, 721, 723, 726, 728–731, 738, 739, 744, 754, 757, 765, 766, 791, 794, 802, 803, 817

## K

Katongole, E., 11, 47, 48, 54, 150, 157, 158, 401–414
Kenya, 11, 12, 20, 23–28, 32, 34, 35, 44, 50, 52, 54, 127, 130, 132, 154, 155, 189, 219n2, 236, 238, 310, 311, 341–360, 364, 366, 367, 419, 475–489, 532, 535, 536, 539, 541–543, 545, 546, 587–603, 666, 670n4, 694, 701–713, 724, 760, 789n1, 790, 813–815

## L

Leadership, 3, 9, 23, 25, 29, 30, 34, 35, 41, 42, 49, 73, 74, 81, 108, 147, 149, 151, 152, 154, 163, 186, 213, 215, 241–243, 246, 263, 265, 273, 317, 334, 365, 366, 371, 375–377, 391, 392, 406, 413, 420, 425, 476–478, 483, 484, 487, 502, 503, 505, 521, 523, 525, 533, 535, 537, 542, 546, 562, 564, 583, 589, 592, 594, 596, 598, 600, 601, 636, 650, 655, 656, 662, 679, 717–720, 722, 723, 725, 728, 730–732, 745, 747, 797, 811–815

Legal identity, 251, 252, 265, 266, 268, 272, 645, 663

Local peacebuilding, 171, 218, 438, 610, 813

Lord's Resistance Army (LRA), 31–34, 279, 345, 365, 366, 611, 650, 653, 722, 790–792, 790n2, 794–802

Love, 31, 85, 87, 88, 109, 114, 190, 327, 328, 330–337, 373–375, 467, 516, 518, 520, 524, 525, 563, 571, 579, 580, 630, 673, 724, 794, 800

## M

Marginality, 259

Mental health, 114, 167, 172, 628–630, 632, 633, 694, 707

Micro-spaces, 163–165, 173, 176, 217–231, 619

Migration, 4, 128, 132, 228, 389, 445, 494, 524, 525, 532, 553, 571, 576, 683–697

Monarchy, 148, 149, 158, 201, 240, 296, 299, 476

Muslim community, 30, 190, 193, 347, 349, 350, 353, 354, 458, 459, 587–591, 598–602, 608n3, 653

Muslim (Islamic) networks, 587–603

Muslim organizations, 76, 588–590, 592, 595, 598, 601, 610

## N

National Peace Council (NPC), 11, 493–509

New Testament (NT), 80, 84–88, 117, 517, 795

Nigeria, 3, 5, 10, 12, 44, 46, 48, 50, 54, 81, 105, 129, 132, 181–194, 236, 253, 310, 367, 369, 372, 475, 495, 532, 544, 553–565, 643–657, 761, 762, 765, 813

Nigeria Inter-Religious Council (NIREC), 12, 186, 188, 553–565, 816

Northern Uganda, 13, 31–35, 48, 117, 279, 280, 366, 410, 617, 653, 722, 789–803

## P

Patriarchy, 647, 655, 708, 722, 723, 730, 744

Peace, 1, 19, 39, 66, 79, 94, 95, 99, 102, 105, 125, 146, 163–176, 181, 199, 217–231, 235, 252, 271, 288, 296–299, 308, 327, 334–337, 346, 363–377, 394, 401, 435, 456, 475–489, 494, 531, 553, 570, 587, 607–621, 627, 643–657, 661, 684, 701, 717, 739, 753–767, 771, 789, 811

Peacebuilding, 1–13, 19–36, 39–55, 63–76, 79–89, 93–103, 105–121, 135, 145–160, 164–167, 171, 173–176, 182, 184, 185, 187–190, 192, 193, 210, 212, 214, 217–219, 218n1, 221, 222, 228–230, 235–249, 251–268, 271–283, 287–300, 307–321, 327–337, 342, 345, 348, 368, 369, 374, 375, 390, 392, 401–414, 420–431, 435–450, 455–471, 493–509, 513–526, 531–547, 553–565, 569–583, 587–603, 608–610, 612, 615, 617–620, 627–640, 644, 646–650, 654–657, 661–679, 683, 685, 695–696, 701–713, 717–732, 737–748, 753–767, 771–785, 789–803, 809–823

Peacebuilding models, 424

Peaceful relations, 163, 165, 167, 169, 174, 176, 218, 222, 226, 228–231, 455, 456, 460, 461, 608, 610, 616, 618

Peace mediation, 181–194, 503, 665, 756, 762
Politics, 4, 6, 49, 75, 81, 82, 105, 145, 150, 152, 158, 160, 166, 186, 220n3, 236, 241, 259, 279, 283, 308, 314, 327, 330, 382, 385, 391, 410, 435, 440, 443, 444, 479, 482, 484, 487, 494, 496, 497, 506, 508, 509, 518, 533, 535, 558, 561, 564, 572, 575, 667, 668, 684, 723, 760, 761, 815
Post-genocide reconstruction, 781
Post-violence, 381–396

## R
Radicalization, 341–360, 368, 455–461, 470, 471, 523, 536, 543, 588, 592, 594, 595, 600, 652, 710
Rastafari, 11, 327–337, 814, 819
Reconciliation, 7–9, 27, 28, 30, 33, 42, 46–48, 51, 53, 67, 69, 72, 72n1, 88, 106, 120, 146, 149, 155–157, 159, 160, 167, 168, 171, 174, 175, 183, 184, 187, 188, 190, 202, 209, 219–223, 228–230, 271, 276, 277, 279, 310, 311, 317, 328, 374–375, 377, 406–408, 410, 412, 413, 420, 426, 428, 445, 448, 455, 483, 489, 502, 507, 514–518, 520, 521, 532, 534–538, 556, 557, 592, 610, 635, 636, 652–654, 656, 661, 662, 665, 666, 675, 702, 706, 717, 721, 722, 725–727, 730, 740, 741, 791, 793n5, 814
Religion(s), 1–13, 19–36, 39–55, 63–76, 82, 93–103, 105–121, 125–139, 145–160, 167, 181–194, 199–215, 222, 235–249, 251–268, 271–283, 287, 308, 328, 342, 363, 384, 401–414, 431, 436, 455, 475, 493–509, 513, 531, 553, 570, 587, 608, 627–640, 643–657, 661–679, 685, 703, 718, 739, 753–767, 771–785, 789–803, 809–823
Religious peacebuilding, 2, 6–9, 11–13, 20, 22–35, 46, 52, 55, 68, 70, 72, 75, 109, 121, 160, 167, 184, 187, 192, 222, 413, 436, 455–471, 556, 557, 610, 661, 662, 678, 754–757, 810, 812–816, 818, 819, 821, 822
Religious radicalisation, 455, 456, 458, 459, 470, 471, 523
Religious rituals, 8, 23, 282, 290, 355, 753, 766, 821
Religious studies, 10, 39–55, 65, 93–103, 135, 137, 404, 405, 643, 696
Resilience, 163–176, 219, 223, 276, 407, 465, 547, 593–595, 612, 662, 721, 726, 731, 741
Rwanda, 5, 10, 13, 41, 48, 50, 52, 54, 82, 88, 111, 145–160, 201, 202, 204, 214, 219n2, 366, 369, 375, 402, 406–410, 413, 421, 485, 522, 534, 535, 539, 541, 721, 771–785, 789n1, 812, 813

## S
Security, 2, 19, 42, 63, 79, 125–139, 169, 187, 218, 237, 273, 310, 342, 363–377, 385, 424, 436, 495, 556, 570, 587, 616, 630, 643–657, 667, 704, 718, 739, 761, 773, 800n7, 818
Servantship, 722
Sexual and gender based violence (SGBV), 46, 53, 429, 521, 523–525, 540–542, 627–630, 632–635, 638–640, 671–674, 687, 708, 817
Smallholder farmers, 774–776, 780–783, 785
Social challenges, 381–396
Social cohesion, 9, 28, 199, 204, 207–209, 211–215, 228, 420, 423, 426, 428, 430, 438, 450, 514, 531, 535, 537–539, 556, 578, 579, 583, 713, 721, 814, 816
Social economic transition, 717
South Africa, 4, 5, 11, 12, 39, 41, 48, 54, 69, 94, 95, 98, 100–102, 183, 365, 366, 369, 370, 375, 389, 435–450, 518, 519, 570, 573, 574, 577, 666, 683–697, 721, 738, 741, 793, 814

INDEX 831

Strong institutions, 28, 242, 307, 363, 394, 401, 402, 421, 475–489, 554, 557, 565, 580, 638, 640, 645, 663, 705, 706, 791, 802, 817

Sustainable development, 2, 8, 12, 13, 21, 22, 24, 35, 46, 55, 68, 71, 75, 76, 79–89, 94, 99, 106, 107, 126, 138, 149, 160, 182, 272–274, 281, 290, 299, 307, 308, 313, 327–337, 345n7, 363, 371, 385, 396, 409, 413, 420, 429, 436, 437, 475–479, 489, 514–517, 520–522, 525, 532, 536, 544, 553–565, 569, 578, 582, 635, 638, 639, 645, 663, 668, 676, 677, 679, 684, 689, 695–696, 702–705, 708, 710, 713, 718–720, 730, 731, 738, 739, 743, 744, 746–748, 754, 791, 792, 802, 809, 819–822

Sustainable Development Goal (SDGs), 1, 10, 21, 40, 71, 80, 94, 96, 102, 106, 107, 125–139, 169, 176, 223, 253, 268, 273, 291, 295, 299, 312, 320, 346, 354, 356, 363, 377, 384–385, 387, 394, 396, 401, 402, 413, 420, 436, 444, 517, 524, 553, 554, 564, 569, 587, 609, 644, 645, 648, 649, 657, 675, 684, 687, 689, 695, 696, 702, 706, 711, 713, 726, 744–746, 791, 810

Sustainable Development Goal (SDG) 16, 2, 6, 8–10, 12, 13, 21, 23, 28, 35, 36, 40, 53, 55, 79, 87, 89, 94, 95, 97, 99–102, 105–107, 109, 113, 116, 117, 119, 120, 126, 127, 133, 138, 146, 160, 165, 174–176, 181, 190, 193, 199, 219, 227, 229, 241, 252–254, 265–267, 272, 273, 275, 278, 281, 283, 288, 293, 307–309, 314, 321, 327, 334, 345, 354, 360, 363, 372, 375, 376, 381, 384–385, 388, 394, 401–403, 410, 413, 414, 420, 421, 423, 428, 431, 436–438, 443, 447, 449, 456, 461, 466, 467, 470, 471, 476, 479, 481, 483, 486, 488, 489, 494, 501, 506, 514, 522, 525, 532, 536–538, 542–547, 554, 558, 564–565, 569, 580, 582, 587, 588, 591, 592, 597, 602, 609, 612, 617, 620, 638, 640, 644, 645, 649–657, 663, 667, 671, 672, 674, 675, 677–679, 684, 689, 695, 696, 701–713, 717, 718, 720, 722, 723, 725, 726, 731, 738, 739, 743–748, 754, 767, 802, 803, 809, 810, 814, 816, 818, 819

Sustainable peace, 5, 8, 21, 25, 28, 34, 35, 53, 87, 118, 156, 165, 182, 183, 191, 192, 218, 291, 368, 377, 412, 419–431, 435, 444, 456, 460, 461, 478, 514, 532, 533, 543, 556, 559, 560, 587, 610, 629, 630, 635, 640, 649, 654, 655, 657, 665, 705, 712, 717–720, 739, 754, 756, 771, 772, 781, 814, 817, 818

T
Tanzania, 3, 11, 54, 154, 204, 219n2, 224, 225, 235–249, 311, 351n11, 355, 535, 543, 545, 597, 789n1, 813, 815

Technology for peace, 754

Techno-science, 137–138

Theology, 10, 39–55, 80, 145, 158, 159, 183, 209, 258, 262, 331, 349, 405–408, 412, 413, 518, 521, 633, 638, 640, 696, 755, 757, 810

Traditional customs, 421, 427, 499

Traditional leaders, 11, 185, 189, 295, 308, 309, 312, 317, 419–431, 554, 559, 579, 635, 762, 814

Transformative, 23, 28, 47, 55, 109, 116, 146, 182–184, 190, 191, 193, 384, 385, 431, 522, 765, 766

U
Ubuntu, 13, 51, 53, 54, 293, 420, 440, 445–450, 737–748, 814

Uganda, 4, 11, 12, 20, 24, 31–34, 54, 117, 149, 154, 172, 219n2, 271–283, 358, 365, 366, 406, 407, 475, 518, 521, 522, 532, 535, 536, 542, 543, 545, 546, 607–621, 643–657, 695, 717–732, 790, 792–793, 801, 813, 816

## V

Violent conflicts, 2, 11, 13, 21, 23, 28, 29, 41–43, 53, 54, 66, 119, 128, 129, 147, 159, 160, 189, 199, 239, 422, 425, 430, 495, 496, 501, 534, 537, 538, 544, 685, 702, 706, 724, 747, 822

Violent extremism, 2, 41, 189, 341–351, 355, 359, 368, 387, 455–471, 523, 553, 593–595, 647, 652, 759, 760

## W

War on terror, 12, 347, 352–354, 352n13, 357, 359, 587–603

Whiteness, 105–121, 766

Women, 12, 27, 41, 67, 85, 95–99, 102, 118, 132, 165, 186, 203, 223, 277, 294, 351, 367, 401, 422, 457, 502, 519, 535, 560, 570, 594, 613, 628, 646, 661, 684, 701, 717, 741, 760, 776, 790, 815

Women's experiences, 52, 628, 632–635, 639, 646, 647, 654

Women's Interfaith Council (WIC), 560, 649–652, 654, 655

Worldview, 127, 130, 132, 139, 168, 172, 184, 225, 227–229, 231, 251–254, 256, 259, 261, 267, 276, 277, 292, 294, 313, 328, 329, 468, 515, 516, 560, 574, 617, 619, 620, 664, 668, 673, 679, 740, 746

## X

Xenophobia, 12, 111, 116, 437, 439–441, 444–446, 449, 569–583, 688, 743

## Y

Youth, 11, 12, 19, 26, 27, 29, 35, 36, 151, 152, 175, 186, 190, 214, 219, 222, 226, 229, 230, 264, 268, 298, 332, 343, 349, 350, 353n16, 354, 381–396, 427, 428, 442, 455, 456, 456n1, 458–462, 465–470, 499, 499n2, 502, 505, 513–526, 536–538, 540–544, 547, 558, 560, 561, 565, 570, 573, 577, 591, 593–595, 598–600, 608, 611–617, 620, 636, 637, 650–653, 704, 708, 710, 722, 727, 745, 747, 760, 762, 812, 815, 816, 819

Youth violence, 386–387, 396

## Z

Zambia, 12, 519, 661–679, 695, 823

Zimbabwe, 11, 12, 44, 46, 48, 54, 69, 72–74, 72n2, 87, 105, 310, 328–330, 332–337, 381–396, 475, 520, 570–574, 576, 627–640, 666, 683–685, 687–696, 720, 760, 817

Zimbabwean mothers, 683–697